W9-BGE-369

NORTH AMERICAN INDUSTRY CLASSIFICATION SYSTEM

United States, 2017

EXECUTIVE OFFICE OF THE PRESIDENT
OFFICE OF MANAGEMENT AND BUDGET

Published and for sale by:
CLAITOR'S PUBLISHING DIVISION
P.O. Box 261333, Baton Rouge, LA 70826-1333
800-274-1403 (In LA 225-344-0476)
Fax: 225-344-0480
Internet address:
e mail: claitors@claitors.com
World Wide Web: http://www.claitors.com

*We acknowledge the input and assistance of the U.S. Census Bureau, since much of the following is extracted from their web site at http://www.census.gov

Foreword

The Instituto Nacional de Estadística y Geografía (INEGI) of Mexico, Statistics Canada, and the United States Office of Management and Budget, through its Economic Classification Policy Committee, have jointly updated the system of classification of economic activities that makes the industrial statistics produced in the three countries comparable. The North American Industry Classification System (NAICS) revision for 2017 is scheduled to go into effect for reference year 2017 in Canada and the United States, and 2018 in Mexico. NAICS was originally developed to provide a consistent framework for the collection, analysis, and dissemination of industrial statistics used by government policy analysts, by academics and researchers, by the business community, and by the public. Revisions for 2017 were made to account for our rapidly changing economies.

Classifications serve as a lens through which to view the data they classify. NAICS is the first industry classification system that was developed in accordance with a single principle of aggregation, the principle that producing units that use similar production processes should be grouped together. NAICS also reflects, in a much more explicit way, the enormous changes in technology and in the growth and diversification of services that have marked recent decades. Though NAICS differs from other industry classification systems, the three countries continue to strive to create industries that do not cross two-digit boundaries of the United Nations' International Standard Industrial Classification of All Economic Activities (ISIC).

The actual classification reveals only the tip of the work carried out by dedicated staff from INEGI, Statistics Canada, and U.S. statistical agencies. It is through their efforts, painstaking analysis, and spirit of accommodation that NAICS has emerged as a harmonized international classification of economic activities in North America.

Preface

The North American Industry Classification System (NAICS) represents a continuing cooperative effort among Statistics Canada, Mexico's Instituto Nacional de Estadística y Geografía (INEGI), and the Economic Classification Policy Committee (ECPC) of the United States, acting on behalf of the Office of Management and Budget, to create and maintain a common industry classification system. With its inception in 1997, NAICS replaced the existing classification of each country—the Standard Industrial Classification (1980) of Canada, the Mexican Classification of Activities and Products (1994), and the Standard Industrial Classification (1987) of the United States. Since 1997, the countries have collaborated in producing five-year revisions to NAICS in order to keep the classification system current with changes in economic activities.

The North American Industry Classification System is unique among industry classifications in that it is constructed within a single conceptual framework. Economic units that have similar production processes are classified in the same industry, and the lines drawn between industries demarcate, to the extent practicable, differences in production processes. This supply-based, or production-oriented, economic concept was adopted for NAICS because an industry classification system is a framework for collecting and publishing information on both inputs and outputs, for statistical uses that require that inputs and outputs be used together and be classified consistently. Examples of such uses include measuring productivity, unit labor costs, and the capital intensity of production, estimating employment-output relationships, constructing input-output tables, and other uses that imply the analysis of production relationships in the economy. The classification concept for NAICS leads to production of data that facilitate such analyses.

In the design of NAICS, attention was given to developing production-oriented classifications for (a) new and emerging industries, (b) service industries in general, and (c) industries engaged in the production of advanced technologies. These special emphases are embodied in the particular features of NAICS, discussed below. These same areas of special emphasis account for many of the differences between the structure of NAICS and the structures of industry classification systems in use elsewhere. NAICS provides enhanced industry comparability among the three North American Free Trade Agreement (NAFTA) trading partners, while also increasing compatibility with the two-digit level of the International Standard Industrial Classification (ISIC, Rev. 4) of the United Nations.

NAICS divides the economy into 20 sectors. Industries within these sectors are grouped according to the production criterion. A key feature of NAICS is the Information sector that groups industries that primarily create and disseminate a product subject to copyright. The NAICS Information sector brings together those activities that transform information into a commodity that is produced and distributed, and activities that provide the means for distributing those products, other than through traditional wholesale-retail distribution channels. Industries included in this sector are telecommunications; broadcasting; newspaper, book, and periodical publishing; motion picture and sound recording industries; libraries; and other information services.

Another feature of NAICS is a sector for Professional, Scientific, and Technical Services that comprises establishments engaged in activities where human capital is the major input. The industries within this sector are each defined by the expertise and training of the service provider. The sector includes such industries as offices of lawyers, engineering services, architectural services, advertising agencies, and interior design services.

A sector for Arts, Entertainment, and Recreation includes a wide range of establishments that operate facilities or provide services to meet varied cultural, entertainment, and recreational interests of their patrons.

Another key sector, Health Care and Social Assistance, recognizes the merging of the boundaries of health care and social assistance. The industries in this sector are arranged in an order that reflects the range and extent of health care and social assistance provided. Some important industries are family planning centers, outpatient mental health and substance abuse centers, and continuing care retirement communities.

In the Manufacturing sector, an important subsector, Computer and Electronic Product Manufacturing, brings together industries producing electronic products and their components. The manufacturers of computers, communications equipment, and semiconductors, for example, are grouped into the same subsector because of the inherent technological similarities of their production processes, and the likelihood that these technologies will continue to converge in the future. NAICS acknowledges the importance of these electronic industries, their rapid growth over the past several decades and the likelihood that these industries will, in the future, become even more important in the economies of the three North American countries.

This NAICS structure reflects the levels at which data comparability was agreed upon by the three countries' statistical agencies. The boundaries of all the sectors of NAICS are delineated. In most sectors, NAICS provides for comparability at the industry (five-digit) level. However, for one of the three subsectors in Mining, Quarrying, and Oil and Gas Extraction, one of the three industry groups in Utilities, one of the ten industry groups in Construction, two of the four subsectors in Finance and Insurance, one of the three industry groups in the Real Estate subsector, and two of the four subsectors in Other Services (except Public Administration), three-country comparability occurs either at the industry group (four-digit) or subsector (three-digit) level. For these sectors or subsectors, differences in the economies of the three countries prevent full comparability at the NAICS industry level. For Retail Trade, Wholesale Trade, and Public Administration, the three countries' statistical agencies have agreed, at this time, only on the boundaries of the sector (two-digit level). Below the agreed upon level of comparability, each country may add additional detailed industries, as necessary to meet national needs, provided that this additional detail aggregates to the NAICS level.

The United States has adopted the revised classification in their statistical programs for the reference year beginning in 2017.

Acknowledgments

This 2017 revision of the North American Industry Classification System (NAICS) was an immense undertaking requiring the time, energy, creativity, and cooperation of numerous people and organizations throughout the three countries. The work that has been accomplished is a testament to the individual and collective willingness of many persons and organizations both inside and outside the government to contribute to the development of NAICS. Within the United States, NAICS was revised under the guidance of the Office of Management and Budget by the Economic Classification Policy Committee (ECPC). Members of the ECPC were **Dennis Fixler** and **Edward T. Morgan**, Bureau of Economic Analysis, U.S. Department of Commerce; **William G. Bostic, Jr.** (retired) and **John B. Murphy** (Chair), Bureau of the Census, U.S. Department of Commerce; **David Talan**, Bureau of Labor Statistics, U.S. Department of Labor; and ex officio, **Paul Bugg** (retired), Office of Management and Budget.

In addition to the parties listed above, OMB would like to acknowledge the dedicated staff of the Classification Development Branch at the Bureau of the Census. This staff was responsible for researching, summarizing, and making preliminary recommendations to the ECPC for comments received from the public on 2017 NAICS revisions; for preparing documents summarizing the ECPC position for use in negotiations with Canada and Mexico; and for preparing all of the manuscript files for the published manual. It was their hard work and dedication that resulted in this complete documentation of 2017 NAICS United States.

Contents

Foreword 1

Preface 3

Acknowledgments 5

Explanation of Symbols 11

Introduction 13

NAICS United States Structure 25

Frequently Asked Questions About Economic Classifications 77

Part I. Titles and Descriptions of Industries 79

    Sector 11. Agriculture, Forestry, Fishing and Hunting 81

        Subsector 111. Crop Production 81

        Subsector 112. Animal Production and Aquaculture 92

        Subsector 113. Forestry and Logging 98

        Subsector 114. Fishing, Hunting and Trapping 99

        Subsector 115. Support Activities for Agriculture and Forestry 100

    Sector 21. Mining, Quarrying, and Oil and Gas Extraction 105

        Subsector 211. Oil and Gas Extraction 105

        Subsector 212. Mining (except Oil and Gas) 106

        Subsector 213. Support Activities for Mining 115

    Sector 22. Utilities 119

        Subsector 221. Utilities 119

    Sector 23. Construction 123

        Subsector 236. Construction of Buildings 123

        Subsector 237. Heavy and Civil Engineering Construction 127

        Subsector 238. Specialty Trade Contractors 131

    Sector 31-33. Manufacturing 143

        Subsector 311. Food Manufacturing 144

        Subsector 312. Beverage and Tobacco Product Manufacturing 164

        Subsector 313. Textile Mills 167

        Subsector 314. Textile Product Mills 169

        Subsector 315. Apparel Manufacturing 172

        Subsector 316. Leather and Allied Product Manufacturing 175

        Subsector 321. Wood Product Manufacturing 177

        Subsector 322. Paper Manufacturing 184

        Subsector 323. Printing and Related Support Activities 189

        Subsector 324. Petroleum and Coal Products Manufacturing 192

        Subsector 325. Chemical Manufacturing 195

        Subsector 326. Plastics and Rubber Products Manufacturing 207

        Subsector 327. Nonmetallic Mineral Product Manufacturing 214

        Subsector 331. Primary Metal Manufacturing 222

        Subsector 332. Fabricated Metal Product Manufacturing 230

        Subsector 333. Machinery Manufacturing 247

        Subsector 334. Computer and Electronic Product Manufacturing ... 266

Subsector 335. Electrical Equipment, Appliance, and Component
                       Manufacturing 276
Subsector 336. Transportation Equipment Manufacturing 286
Subsector 337. Furniture and Related Product Manufacturing 299
Subsector 339. Miscellaneous Manufacturing 304
Sector 42. Wholesale Trade 313
Subsector 423. Merchant Wholesalers, Durable Goods 313
Subsector 424. Merchant Wholesalers, Nondurable Goods 330
Subsector 425. Wholesale Electronic Markets and Agents and Brokers 342
Sector 44-45. Retail Trade 345
Subsector 441. Motor Vehicle and Parts Dealers 346
Subsector 442. Furniture and Home Furnishings Stores 349
Subsector 443. Electronics and Appliance Stores 352
Subsector 444. Building Material and Garden Equipment and Supplies
                       Dealers 353
Subsector 445. Food and Beverage Stores 356
Subsector 446. Health and Personal Care Stores 360
Subsector 447. Gasoline Stations 362
Subsector 448. Clothing and Clothing Accessories Stores 363
Subsector 451. Sporting Goods, Hobby, Musical Instrument, and Book
                       Stores 367
Subsector 452. General Merchandise Stores 370
Subsector 453. Miscellaneous Store Retailers 372
Subsector 454. Nonstore Retailers 377
Sector 48-49. Transportation and Warehousing 379
Subsector 481. Air Transportation 379
Subsector 482. Rail Transportation 383
Subsector 483. Water Transportation 384
Subsector 484. Truck Transportation 386
Subsector 485. Transit and Ground Passenger Transportation 389
Subsector 486. Pipeline Transportation 394
Subsector 487. Scenic and Sightseeing Transportation 395
Subsector 488. Support Activities for Transportation 397
Subsector 491. Postal Service 403
Subsector 492. Couriers and Messengers 404
Subsector 493. Warehousing and Storage 405
Sector 51. Information 409
Subsector 511. Publishing Industries (except Internet) 410
Subsector 512. Motion Picture and Sound Recording Industries 414
Subsector 515. Broadcasting (except Internet) 419
Subsector 517. Telecommunications 421
Subsector 518. Data Processing, Hosting, and Related Services 425
Subsector 519. Other Information Services 425
Sector 52. Finance and Insurance 429
Subsector 521. Monetary Authorities-Central Bank 430

Subsector 522. Credit Intermediation and Related Activities 430
Subsector 523. Securities, Commodity Contracts, and Other Financial
                Investments and Related Activities 435
Subsector 524. Insurance Carriers and Related Activities 440
Subsector 525. Funds, Trusts, and Other Financial Vehicles 445
Sector 53. Real Estate and Rental and Leasing 449
Subsector 531. Real Estate 449
Subsector 532. Rental and Leasing Services 453
Subsector 533. Lessors of Nonfinancial Intangible Assets (except
                Copyrighted Works) 459
Sector 54. Professional, Scientific, and Technical Services 461
Subsector 541. Professional, Scientific, and Technical Services 461
Sector 55. Management of Companies and Enterprises 485
Subsector 551. Management of Companies and Enterprises 485
Sector 56. Administrative and Support and Waste Management and Remediation
     Services 489
Subsector 561. Administrative and Support Services 489
Subsector 562. Waste Management and Remediation Services 505
Sector 61. Educational Services 513
Subsector 611. Educational Services 513
Sector 62. Health Care and Social Assistance 523
Subsector 621. Ambulatory Health Care Services 523
Subsector 622. Hospitals 533
Subsector 623. Nursing and Residential Care Facilities 534
Subsector 624. Social Assistance 538
Sector 71. Arts, Entertainment, and Recreation 543
Subsector 711. Performing Arts, Spectator Sports, and Related Industries 543
Subsector 712. Museums, Historical Sites, and Similar Institutions 549
Subsector 713. Amusement, Gambling, and Recreation Industries 551
Sector 72. Accommodation and Food Services 557
Subsector 721. Accommodation 557
Subsector 722. Food Services and Drinking Places 560
Sector 81. Other Services (except Public Administration) 567
Subsector 811. Repair and Maintenance 567
Subsector 812. Personal and Laundry Services 576
Subsector 813. Religious, Grantmaking, Civic, Professional, and Similar
                Organizations 583
Subsector 814. Private Households 590
Sector 92. Public Administration 591
Subsector 921. Executive, Legislative, and Other General Government
                Support 591
Subsector 922. Justice, Public Order, and Safety Activities 593
Subsector 923. Administration of Human Resource Programs 596
Subsector 924. Administration of Environmental Quality Programs 598

Subsector 925. Administration of Housing Programs, Urban Planning,
and Community Development 599
Subsector 926. Administration of Economic Programs 599
Subsector 927. Space Research and Technology 601
Subsector 928. National Security and International Affairs 602

Part II. List of Short Titles 605
Abbreviations and Acronyms 639

Part III. Appendixes 641
A. 2017 NAICS United States Matched to 2012 NAICS United States (Changes Only) 643
B. 2012 NAICS United States Matched to 2017 NAICS United States (Changes Only) 647

Part IV. Alphabetic Index 651

Explanation of Symbols

In NAICS United States Structure

Symbol	Explanation
T	Canadian, Mexican, and United States industries are comparable

In Part I, Titles and Descriptions of Industries

Symbol	Explanation
T	Canadian, Mexican, and United States industries are comparable

In Appendix A

Symbol	Explanation
N	New NAICS industry for 2017
*	Part of 2012 NAICS United States industry

In Appendix B

Symbol	Explanation
pt.	Part of 2017 NAICS United States industry

Introduction

Background

In 1937, the Central Statistical Board established an Interdepartmental Committee on Industrial Classification "to develop a plan of classification of various types of statistical data by industries and to promote the general adoption of such classification as the standard classification of the Federal Government."[1] The List of Industries for manufacturing was first available in 1938, with the List of Industries for nonmanufacturing following in 1939. These Lists of Industries became the first Standard Industrial Classification (SIC) for the United States.

The SIC was developed for use in the classification of establishments by type of activity in which they are primarily engaged; for purposes of facilitating the collection, tabulation, presentation, and analysis of data relating to establishments; and for promoting uniformity and comparability in the presentation of statistical data collected by various agencies of the United States Government, State agencies, trade associations, and private research organizations. The SIC covered the entire field of economic activities by defining industries in accordance with the composition and structure of the economy.

Since the inception of the SIC in the 1930's, the system was periodically revised to reflect the economy's changing industrial composition and organization. The last revision of the SIC was in 1987.

Rapid changes in both the U.S. and world economies brought the SIC under increasing criticism. In 1991, an International Conference on the Classification of Economic Activities was convened in Williamsburg, Virginia, to provide a forum for responding to such criticism and to explore new approaches to classifying economic activity. In July 1992, the Office of Management and Budget (OMB) established the Economic Classification Policy Committee (ECPC) and charged it with a "fresh slate" examination of economic classifications for statistical purposes. The ECPC prepared a number of issue papers regarding classification, consulted with outside users, and ultimately joined with Mexico's Instituto Nacional de Estadística, Geografía e Informática (now the Instituto Nacional de Estadística y Geografía) (INEGI) and Statistics Canada to develop the North American Industry Classification System (NAICS), which replaced the 1987 U.S. SIC and the classification systems of Canada (1980 SIC) and Mexico (1994 Mexican Classification of Activities and Products (CMAP)).

The dynamic nature of world economies continues to affect classification systems. The creators of NAICS agreed that the classification system should be reviewed every five years, and revised as appropriate to reflect the changing economies of the three countries. The U.S. statistical programs implemented NAICS for the first time in 1997. NAICS was revised in 2002, 2007, and 2012. This 2017 NAICS revision was undertaken to achieve one main goal—to modify or create industries to reflect new, emerging, or changing activities and technologies.

The impact of NAICS on various countries has brought about a renewed effort for additional convergence with the many industry classifications used throughout the world. Future revisions of NAICS will continue to strive for greater global comparability.

---

[1] Pearce, Esther, History of the Standard Industrial Classification, Executive Office of the President, Office of Statistical Standards, U.S. Bureau of the Budget, Washington, DC, July 1957 (mimeograph).

Purpose of NAICS

NAICS is an industry classification system that groups establishments into industries based on the similarity of their production processes. It is a comprehensive system covering all economic activities. There are 20 sectors and 1,057 industries in 2017 NAICS United States.

NAICS was initially developed and subsequently revised by Mexico's INEGI, Statistics Canada, and the U.S. ECPC (the latter acting on behalf of OMB) to provide common industry definitions for Canada, Mexico, and the United States that will facilitate economic analyses of the economies of the three North American countries. The statistical agencies in the three countries produce information on inputs and outputs, industrial performance, productivity, unit labor costs, and employment. NAICS, which is based on a production-oriented concept, ensures maximum usefulness of industrial statistics for these and similar purposes.

NAICS United States is used by U.S. statistical agencies to facilitate the collection, tabulation, presentation, and analysis of data relating to establishments; and to provide uniformity and comparability in the presentation of statistical data describing the U.S. economy. NAICS United States is designed for statistical purposes. Although the classification also may be used for various administrative, regulatory, and taxation purposes, the requirements of government agencies that use it for nonstatistical purposes played no role in its development or subsequent revision.

Development of NAICS as a Replacement for the U.S. SIC

The U.S. ECPC established by OMB in 1992 was chaired by the Bureau of Economic Analysis, U.S. Department of Commerce, with representatives from the Bureau of the Census, U.S. Department of Commerce, and the Bureau of Labor Statistics, U.S. Department of Labor. The ECPC was asked to examine economic classifications for statistical purposes and to determine the desirability of developing a new industry classification system for the United States based on a single economic concept. On March 31, 1993, OMB published a **Federal Register** notice (58 FR 16990-17004) announcing the intention to revise the SIC for 1997, the establishment of the ECPC, and the process for revising the SIC.

In July 1994, OMB announced plans to develop a new industry classification system in cooperation with Mexico's INEGI and Statistics Canada. The new system—NAICS—replaced the U.S. SIC. The concepts of the new system and the principles upon which NAICS was to be developed were announced in a July 26, 1994, **Federal Register** notice (59 FR 38092-38096) and were as follows:

1. NAICS will be erected on a production-oriented or supply-based conceptual framework. This means that producing units that use identical or similar production processes will be grouped together in NAICS.
2. The system will give special attention to developing production-oriented classifications for (a) new and emerging industries, (b) service industries in general, and (c) industries engaged in the production of advanced technologies.
3. Time series continuity will be maintained to the greatest extent possible. However, changes in the economy and proposals from data users must be considered. In addition, adjustments will be required for sectors where the United States, Canada, and Mexico have incompatible industry

classification definitions in order to produce a common industry system for all three North American countries.

4.   The system will strive for compatibility with the two-digit level of the International Standard Industrial Classification of All Economic Activities (ISIC, Rev. 3) of the United Nations.

The structure of NAICS was developed in a series of meetings among the three countries. Public proposals for individual industries from all three countries were considered for acceptance if the proposed industry was based on the production-oriented concept of the system. In the United States, public comments also were solicited as groups of subsectors of NAICS were completed and agreed upon by the three countries. The ECPC published the proposed industries for those subsectors in a series of five successive **Federal Register** notices, in 1995 and 1996, asking for comments from interested data users.

Revision of NAICS for 2017

OMB published a notification of potential revision to NAICS for 2017 in a May 22, 2014, **Federal Register** notice (79 FR 29626-29629). This notice solicited comments on: 1) new and emerging industries for consideration in potential revisions to NAICS for 2017; 2) the electronic dissemination of NAICS 2017; and 3) updating the structure of the oil and gas industries for NAICS 2017. This notice also provided an update on the treatment of manufacturing units that outsource all transformation activities. In addition, OMB published a notification regarding implementation of the Factoryless Goods Producer (FGP) classification in NAICS 2017 in an August 8, 2014, **Federal Register** notice (79 FR 46558-46559). This notice stated the directive of the August 17, 2011, **Federal Register** notice (76 FR 51240-51243) was no longer in force, to allow for additional research, testing, and evaluation of FGPs.

After considering all proposals from the public, consulting with a number of U.S. data users and industry groups, and undertaking extensive discussions with Statistics Canada and Mexico's Instituto Nacional de Estadística y Geografía (INEGI), the ECPC formulated a set of recommendations for revisions to NAICS for 2017. OMB published a solicitation of public comments on these recommendations in an August 4, 2015, **Federal Register** notice (80 FR 46480-46484). After reviewing comments to that notice and conducting further consultation with data users and industry groups, OMB decided to adopt the ECPC recommendations presented in the August 4, 2015, notice. OMB published a notice of final decisions regarding NAICS revisions for 2017 in an August 8, 2016, **Federal Register** notice (81 FR 52584).

Conceptual Framework

NAICS is erected on a production-oriented or supply-based conceptual framework that groups establishments into industries according to similarity in the processes used to produce goods or services. A production-oriented industry classification system ensures that statistical agencies in the three countries can produce information on inputs and outputs, industrial performance, productivity, unit labor costs, employment, and other statistics and structural changes occurring in each of the three economies.

When an industry is defined on a production-oriented concept, producing units within the industry's boundaries share a basic production process; they use closely similar technology. In the language of economics, producing units within an industry share the same production functions; producing units in different industries have different production functions. The boundaries between industries thus demarcate, in principle, differences in production processes and production technologies.

The reasoning behind the three countries' decision to base NAICS on a production-oriented concept is summarized as follows: An industry is a grouping of economic activities. Though it inevitably groups the products of the economic activities that are included in the industry definition, it is not solely a grouping of products; put another way, an industry groups producing units. Accordingly, an industry classification system provides a framework for collecting data on inputs and outputs together.

The uses of economic data that require that data on inputs and outputs be used together and be collected on the same basis include production analyses, productivity measurement, and studying input usage and input intensities. The North American statistical agencies developed NAICS using a production-oriented concept as the framework for two reasons: (1) an industry classification system groups producing units, not products or services; and (2) groupings of producing units permit the collection of data on inputs and outputs on a comparable basis, which is required for production-oriented analysis, but do not facilitate a comprehensive collection of data on the total output of any particular good or service, which is required for market-oriented analysis. Thus, the efficient organizing concept of an industry classification system is production-oriented rather than market-oriented.

Structure of NAICS

The structure of NAICS is hierarchical. The first two digits of the structure designate the NAICS sectors that represent general categories of economic activities.

NAICS classifies all economic activities into 20 sectors. The NAICS sectors, their two-digit codes, and the distinguishing activities of each are:

11 Agriculture, Forestry, Fishing and Hunting—Activities of this sector are growing crops, raising animals, harvesting timber, and harvesting fish and other animals from farms, ranches, or the animals' natural habitats.

21 Mining, Quarrying, and Oil and Gas Extraction—Activities of this sector are extracting naturally occurring mineral solids, such as coal and ore; liquid minerals, such as crude petroleum; and gases, such as natural gas; and beneficiating (e.g., crushing, screening, washing, and flotation) and other preparation at the mine site, or as part of mining activity.

22 Utilities—Activities of this sector are generating, transmitting, and/or distributing electricity, gas, steam, and water and removing sewage through a permanent infrastructure of lines, mains, and pipe.

23 Construction—Activities of this sector are erecting buildings and other structures (including additions); heavy construction other than buildings; and alterations, reconstruction, installation, and maintenance and repairs.

31-33 Manufacturing—Activities of this sector are the mechanical, physical, or chemical transformation of materials, substances, or components into new products.

42 Wholesale Trade—Activities of this sector are selling or arranging for the purchase or sale of goods for resale; capital or durable nonconsumer goods; and raw and intermediate materials and supplies used in production, and providing services incidental to the sale of the merchandise.

44-45 Retail Trade—Activities of this sector are retailing merchandise generally in small quantities to the general public and providing services incidental to the sale of the merchandise.

48-49 Transportation and Warehousing—Activities of this sector are providing transportation of passengers and cargo, warehousing and storing goods, scenic and sightseeing transportation, and supporting these activities.

51 Information—Activities of this sector are distributing information and cultural products, providing the means to transmit or distribute these products as data or communications, and processing data.

52 Finance and Insurance—Activities of this sector involve the creation, liquidation, or change in ownership of financial assets (financial transactions) and/or facilitating financial transactions.

53 Real Estate and Rental and Leasing—Activities of this sector are renting, leasing, or otherwise allowing the use of tangible or intangible assets (except copyrighted works), and providing related services.

54 Professional, Scientific, and Technical Services—Activities of this sector are performing professional, scientific, and technical services for the operations of other organizations.

55 Management of Companies and Enterprises—Activities of this sector are the holding of securities of companies and enterprises, for the purpose of owning controlling interest or influencing their management decisions, or administering, overseeing, and managing other establishments of the same company or enterprise and normally undertaking the strategic or organizational planning and decision-making role of the company or enterprise.

56 Administrative and Support and Waste Management and Remediation Services—Activities of this sector are performing routine support activities for the day-to-day operations of other organizations.

61 Educational Services—Activities of this sector are providing instruction and training in a wide variety of subjects.

62 Health Care and Social Assistance—Activities of this sector are providing health care and social assistance for individuals.

71 Arts, Entertainment, and Recreation—Activities of this sector are operating or providing services to meet varied cultural, entertainment, and recreational interests of their patrons.

72 Accommodation and Food Services—Activities of this sector are providing customers with lodging and/or preparing meals, snacks, and beverages for immediate consumption.

81 Other Services (except Public Administration)—Activities of this sector are providing services not elsewhere specified, including repairs, religious activities, grantmaking, advocacy, laundry, personal care, death care, and other personal services.

92 Public Administration—Activities of this sector are administration, management, and oversight of public programs by Federal, State, and local governments.

NAICS uses a six-digit coding system to identify particular industries and their placement in this hierarchical structure of the classification system. The first two digits of the code designate the sector, the third digit designates the subsector, the fourth digit designates the industry group, the fifth digit designates the NAICS industry, and the sixth digit designates the national industry. A zero as the sixth digit generally indicates that the NAICS industry and the U.S. industry are the same.

The subsectors, industry groups, and NAICS industries, in accord with the conceptual principle of NAICS, are production-oriented combinations of establishments. However, the production distinctions become more narrowly defined as one moves down the hierarchy.

NAICS agreements permit each country to designate detailed industries, below the level of a NAICS industry, to meet national needs. The United States has such industry detail in many places in the classification system to recognize large, important U.S. industries that cannot be recognized in the other countries because of size, specialization, or organization of the industry.

Typically the level at which comparable data will be available for Canada, Mexico, and the United States is the five-digit NAICS industry; for some sectors (or subsectors or industry groups) however, the three countries agreed upon the boundaries at a higher level of detail rather than the detailed industry structure (five-digit). There is agreement at the sector level for Wholesale Trade; Retail Trade; and Public Administration. There is agreement either at the industry group (four-digit) or subsector (three-digit) level for one of the three subsectors in the Mining, Quarrying, and Oil and Gas Extraction sector, one of the three industry groups in the Utilities sector, one of the ten industry groups in the Construction sector, two of the four subsectors in the Finance and Insurance sector, one of the three industry groups in the Real Estate subsector, and two of the four subsectors in the Other Services (except Public Administration) sector.

Differences in the economies of the three countries or time constraints necessitated establishing comparability at a higher level of detail for the sectors and subsectors noted above. For each of these sectors, except Wholesale Trade and Public Administration, Canada and the United States have agreed upon an industry structure and hierarchy to ensure comparability of statistics between those two countries. Canada and the United States also have established the same national detail (six-digit) industries where possible, adopting the same codes to describe comparable industries. For this reason, the numbers of the U.S. industries may not be consecutive. In a few cases, it was necessary for the United States to use all of the numbers available to establish its six-digit detail so that the same six-digit codes do not necessarily represent comparable industries in the U.S. and Canada.

NAICS with U.S. detail is known as NAICS United States, while Canada and Mexico produce six-digit detail and publish that detail as NAICS Canada and NAICS (SCIAN in Spanish) Mexico.

Definition of an Establishment

NAICS is a classification system for establishments. The establishment as a statistical unit is defined as the smallest operating entity for which records provide information on the cost of resources—materials, labor, and capital—employed to produce the units of output. The output may be sold to other establishments and receipts or sales recorded, or the output may be provided without explicit charge, that is, the good or service may be "sold" within the company itself.

The establishment, in NAICS United States, is generally a single physical location where business is conducted or where services or industrial operations are performed (for example, a factory, mill, store, hotel, movie theater, mine, farm, airline terminal, sales office, warehouse, or central administrative office). There are cases where records identify distinct and separate economic activities performed at a single physical location (e.g., shops in a hotel). These retailing activities, operated out of the same physical location as the hotel, are identified as separate establishments and classified in the Retail Trade sector, while the hotel is classified in the Accommodation subsector. In such cases, each activity is treated as a separate establishment provided: (1) no one industry description in the classification includes such combined activities; (2) separate reports can be prepared on the number of employees, their wages and salaries, sales or receipts, and expenses; and (3) employment and output are significant for both activities.

Exceptions to the single location exist for physically dispersed operations, such as construction, transportation, and telecommunications. For these activities the individual sites, projects, fields, networks, lines, or systems of such dispersed activities are not normally considered to be establishments. The establishment is represented by those relatively permanent main or branch offices, terminals, stations, and so forth, that are either (1) directly responsible for supervising such activities, or (2) the base from which personnel operate to carry out these activities.

Although an establishment may be identical with the enterprise (company), the two terms should not be confused. An enterprise (company) may consist of more than one establishment. Such multiunit enterprises may have establishments in more than one industry in NAICS. If such enterprises have a separate establishment primarily engaged in providing headquarters services, these establishments are classified in Sector 55, Management of Companies and Enterprises.

Although all establishments have output, they may or may not have receipts. In large enterprises, it is not unusual for establishments to exist to solely serve other establishments of the same enterprise (auxiliary, or enterprise support, establishments). In such cases, these units often do not collect receipts from the establishments they serve. This type of support (captive) activity is found throughout the economy and involves goods-producing activities as well as services. Units that carry out support activities for the enterprise to which they belong are classified, to the extent feasible, according to the NAICS code related to their own activity. This means that warehouses providing storage facilities for their own enterprise are classified as warehouses. For certain analytical purposes, an alternative code may be assigned corresponding to the activity of the enterprise that they support.

Determining an Establishment's Industry Classification

An establishment is classified in an industry when its primary activity meets the definition for that industry. Because establishments may perform more than one activity, it is necessary to determine procedures for identifying the primary activity of the establishment.

In most cases, if an establishment is engaged in more than one activity, the industry code is assigned based on the establishment's principal product or group of products produced or distributed, or services rendered. Ideally, the principal good or service should be determined by its relative share of current production costs and capital investment at the establishment. In practice, however, it is often necessary to use other variables such as revenue, shipments, or employment as proxies for measuring significance.

There are two types of combined activities that are given special attention in NAICS. They are vertical integration and joint production. These combined activities have an economic basis and occur in both goods-producing and services-producing sectors. In some cases, there are efficiencies to be gained from combining certain activities in the same establishment. Some of these combinations occur so commonly or frequently that their combination can be treated as a third activity in its own right and explicitly classified in a specific industry.

One approach to classifying these activities would be to use the primary activity rule, that is, whichever activity is largest. However, the fundamental principle of NAICS is that establishments that employ the same production process should be classified in the same industry. If the premise that the combined activities correspond to a distinct third activity is accepted, then using the primary activity rule would place establishments performing the same combination of activities in different industries, thereby violating the production principle of NAICS. A second reason for NAICS recognizing combined activities is to improve the stability of establishment classification, both over time and among the various agencies that implement the classification. An establishment should remain classified in the same industry unless its production process changes, and different agencies should code the same establishment or type of establishment in the same way. A consistent treatment of establishments with combined activities is more likely if they are classified to a single industry.

Vertical integration involves consecutive stages of fabrication or production processes in which the output of one step is the input of the next. In general, establishments are classified based on the final process in a vertically integrated production environment, unless specifically identified as classified in another industry. For example, paper may be produced either by establishments that first produce pulp and then consume that pulp to produce paper or by those establishments producing paper from purchased pulp. NAICS explicitly specifies that both of these types of paper-producing processes should be classified in NAICS 32212, Paper Mills, the final step in paper manufacturing, rather than in NAICS 32211, Pulp Mills. In other cases, NAICS specifies that vertically integrated establishments are classified in the industry representing the first stage of the manufacturing process. For example, steel mills that make steel and also perform other activities such as producing steel castings are classified in NAICS 33111,

Iron and Steel Mills and Ferroalloy Manufacturing, the first stage of the manufacturing process.

The joint production of goods or services represents the second type of combined activities. For example, automobile dealers both sell and repair autos; automotive parts dealers may both sell parts and repair automobiles; and musical instrument stores may both sell and rent instruments. In the Manufacturing sector, establishments may make two different products such as men's suits and women's suits, activities that are classified in two different NAICS United States detailed industries. In general, receipts/sales and revenue data are used as a proxy to determine primary activity for these establishments. The assumption is that the activity generating the most receipts is also the activity using the most resources and most indicative of the production process.

In some cases, however, these combined activities have been assigned to a specific NAICS industry. Most of these activities involve either the sale and repair of goods or the sale and rental of goods in the same establishment. For example, establishments that both sell automobile parts and repair automobiles are classified in NAICS 44131, Automotive Parts and Accessories Stores, and music stores that both sell and rent musical instruments are classified in NAICS 45114, Musical Instrument and Supplies Stores. In other cases, specific industries are identified for these combined activities, such as NAICS 44711, Gasoline Stations with Convenience Stores.

Classification rules related to the agreement to permit individual country detail at the six-digit level for NAICS sometimes result in less comparable NAICS industries at the five-digit level and above. For example in NAICS, the assignment of the industry code is at the most detailed level of the classification (the six-digit U.S. detail code), except for Agriculture. That is, if the value of an establishment's production consists of 30 percent from computers, 30 percent from computer storage devices, and 40 percent from semiconductors and related devices, it is classified in U.S. detail industry 334413, Semiconductor and Related Device Manufacturing, that is aggregated to NAICS 33441, Semiconductor and Other Electronic Component Manufacturing, the level that comparable information is shown for all three countries. If the classification for the above example were at the five-digit NAICS level, that establishment would be classified in NAICS 33411, Computer and Peripheral Equipment Manufacturing. There would then be more comparable information at the NAICS level, but it would be impossible to classify this establishment to a U.S. detail six-digit industry.

In Agriculture, however, NAICS coding begins at the top of the structure and continues down to the most detailed level (the six-digit U.S. detail code). The existence of a 50 percent rule in Agriculture and the presence of combination industries based on families of related agricultural products with none accounting for 50 percent or more of production require a top down coding procedure rather than coding at the most detailed level first as is done in the balance of the classification.

Use of Reporting Units Other than Establishments

NAICS is based on the economic principle that establishments should be grouped together based on their production processes. The NAICS definition of the establishment ensures that, at some level, "establishments": (1) identify the most refined (generally smallest) individual entity possible; (2) can provide the information needed when surveying economic activity; and (3) when aggregated, approximate the statistical universe of economic activity. Each economic survey program, in practice, determines whether the establishment is the most appropriate reporting unit to meet the three criteria listed above with respect to the program's objectives. If not, an alternative reporting unit is identified.

For example, an economic survey of employment or wage data may choose the establishment—generally a physical location—as the reporting unit. Physical locations generally have records for the number of employees and their wages readily available. Therefore, it is reasonable to expect that separate wage and employment data are available for each switching station in a multiunit telecommunications carrier enterprise and the physical location is a logical choice for the reporting unit.

If the economic survey collects output data, the individual switching stations would not have the total number of telephone calls or a complete accounting of inputs and outputs of the multiunit telecommunications carrier. If a telephone call is routed through three different switching stations and the price is determined at a fourth location, all of the related locations would need to be merged into an alternative reporting unit to measure the volume and value of the output. In this case, the physical location is not an appropriate reporting unit. The level of aggregation of physical units required to create reporting units will vary greatly depending on the business activity being studied. To efficiently define reporting units, statistical surveys need to evaluate the characteristics of the activities being studied and the organizational structure of the entities producing goods or services. In some cases, the physical location is appropriate, sometimes units will need to be grouped based on homogeneous production characteristics or geographical groupings, and in other cases, the enterprise (company) may form the most appropriate reporting unit.

The practical variation in reporting unit definitions affects comparability of data. A count of units defined as physical locations will be different from a count of units defined based on the need for complete input and output records in the telecommunications industries. It is critical that each data provider clearly identify the reporting unit definition used when presenting summary statistics. The analysis of statistical data from a variety of sources requires the transparency of clearly defined reporting units.

While the reporting unit definition can vary, NAICS is a classification system for establishments and is based on grouping establishments with similar production function characteristics.

Comparison of NAICS to the International Standard Industrial Classification of All Economic Activities (ISIC)

Recognizing the need for international comparability of economic statistics, the United Nations (UN) first adopted an International Standard Industrial Classification system in 1948. Revisions to the ISIC structure and codes were adopted by the UN's Statistical Commission in 1958, 1968, 1989, 2002, and 2007.[2]

Similar to NAICS, ISIC was designed primarily to provide classifications for grouping activities (rather than enterprises or firms), and the primary focus for the ISIC classification system is the kind of activity in which establishments or other statistical entities are engaged. The main criteria employed in delineating divisions and groups (the two- and three-digit categories, respectively) of ISIC are: (a) the character of the goods and services produced; (b) the uses to which the goods and services are put; and (c) the inputs, the process, and the technology of production.

---

[2] International Standard Industrial Classification of All Economic Activities, Statistical Papers, Series M, No. 4, Rev. 4, United Nations, New York, 2008.

The third classification criterion of the ISIC is the conceptual foundation of NAICS, and thus, NAICS is aligned more closely with ISIC than was the 1987 SIC system. However, there are differences between the NAICS and ISIC classification schemes. Most important, perhaps, is the single (production process) conceptual framework of NAICS. As noted elsewhere, this is unique among industry classifications.

ISIC, Rev. 4, groups economic activity into 21 broad Sections, 88 Divisions, 238 Groups, and 420 Classes. In the coding system, Sections are distinguished by the letters A through U, and the Divisions, Groups, and Classes are identified as the two-digit, three-digit, and four-digit groupings, respectively. As was the case with 2007 NAICS, the most recent revision of ISIC also focused on improvements to the detail in services sections.

In the development and subsequent revision of NAICS industries, the statistical agencies of the three countries strove to create industries that did not cross ISIC two-digit boundaries. The 2007 revisions of the NAICS and ISIC increased comparability beyond previous levels. Similar to the 2012 NAICS revision, this 2017 NAICS revision maintains a similar level of comparability with ISIC, Rev. 4.

2017 NAICS United States Structure

The following page contains a summary table of the 2017 NAICS United States structure. This table shows the counts of subsectors, industry groups, industries, and United States detail industries for each of the NAICS sectors.

Following the summary table is a complete listing of the 2017 NAICS United States structure. This list displays the codes and official full titles for the sectors, subsectors, industry groups, industries, and United States detail industries. A "T" superscript on the title indicates a level at which Canada, Mexico, and the United States formally agreed to maintain comparability. Detail below that level may or may not be comparable to detail for one or both of the other countries.

Part II of this manual contains a list of short titles that are recommended for use when space limitations preclude the use of the full titles for the dissemination of data classified using NAICS.

2017 NAICS United States Structure

Sector	Name	Subsectors (3-digit)	Industry Groups (4-digit)	NAICS Industries (5-digit)	6-digit Industries		
					U.S. Detail	Same as 5-digit	Total
11	Agriculture, Forestry, Fishing and Hunting	5	19	42	32	32	64
21	Mining, Quarrying, and Oil and Gas Extraction	3	5	11	24	4	28
22	Utilities	1	3	6	10	4	14
23	Construction	3	10	28	4	27	31
31-33	Manufacturing	21	86	180	265	95	360
42	Wholesale Trade	3	19	71	0	71	71
44-45	Retail Trade	12	27	57	17	49	66
48-49	Transportation and Warehousing	11	29	42	25	32	57
51	Information	6	11	25	12	19	31
52	Finance and Insurance	5	11	31	15	26	41
53	Real Estate and Rental and Leasing	3	8	17	11	13	24
54	Professional, Scientific, and Technical Services	1	9	35	20	29	49
55	Management of Companies and Enterprises	1	1	1	3	0	3
56	Administrative and Support and Waste Management and Remediation Services	2	11	29	25	19	44
61	Educational Services	1	7	12	7	10	17
62	Health Care and Social Assistance	4	18	30	16	23	39
71	Arts, Entertainment, and Recreation	3	9	23	3	22	25
72	Accommodation and Food Services	2	6	10	8	7	15
81	Other Services (except Public Administration)	4	14	30	30	19	49
92	Public Administration	8	8	29	0	29	29
	Total	99	311	709	527	530	1057

Sector 11--Agriculture, Forestry, Fishing and Hunting[T]

111 Crop Production[T]

1111 Oilseed and Grain Farming[T]
11111 Soybean Farming[T]
111110 Soybean Farming
11112 Oilseed (except Soybean) Farming[T]
111120 Oilseed (except Soybean) Farming
11113 Dry Pea and Bean Farming[T]
111130 Dry Pea and Bean Farming
11114 Wheat Farming[T]
111140 Wheat Farming
11115 Corn Farming[T]
111150 Corn Farming
11116 Rice Farming[T]
111160 Rice Farming
11119 Other Grain Farming[T]
111191 Oilseed and Grain Combination Farming
111199 All Other Grain Farming

1112 Vegetable and Melon Farming[T]
11121 Vegetable and Melon Farming[T]
111211 Potato Farming
111219 Other Vegetable (except Potato) and Melon Farming

1113 Fruit and Tree Nut Farming[T]
11131 Orange Groves[T]
111310 Orange Groves
11132 Citrus (except Orange) Groves[T]
111320 Citrus (except Orange) Groves
11133 Noncitrus Fruit and Tree Nut Farming[T]
111331 Apple Orchards
111332 Grape Vineyards
111333 Strawberry Farming
111334 Berry (except Strawberry) Farming
111335 Tree Nut Farming
111336 Fruit and Tree Nut Combination Farming
111339 Other Noncitrus Fruit Farming

1114 Greenhouse, Nursery, and Floriculture Production[T]
11141 Food Crops Grown Under Cover[T]
111411 Mushroom Production
111419 Other Food Crops Grown Under Cover
11142 Nursery and Floriculture Production[T]
111421 Nursery and Tree Production
111422 Floriculture Production

1119 Other Crop Farming[T]
11191 Tobacco Farming[T]
111910 Tobacco Farming
11192 Cotton Farming[T]
111920 Cotton Farming
11193 Sugarcane Farming[T]
111930 Sugarcane Farming

11194   Hay Farming[T]
111940 Hay Farming
11199   All Other Crop Farming[T]
111991 Sugar Beet Farming
111992 Peanut Farming
111998 All Other Miscellaneous Crop Farming

112   Animal Production and Aquaculture[T]

1121   Cattle Ranching and Farming[T]
11211   Beef Cattle Ranching and Farming, including Feedlots[T]
112111 Beef Cattle Ranching and Farming
112112 Cattle Feedlots
11212   Dairy Cattle and Milk Production[T]
112120 Dairy Cattle and Milk Production
11213   Dual-Purpose Cattle Ranching and Farming[T]
112130 Dual-Purpose Cattle Ranching and Farming

1122   Hog and Pig Farming[T]
11221   Hog and Pig Farming[T]
112210 Hog and Pig Farming

1123   Poultry and Egg Production[T]
11231   Chicken Egg Production[T]
112310 Chicken Egg Production
11232   Broilers and Other Meat Type Chicken Production[T]
112320 Broilers and Other Meat Type Chicken Production
11233   Turkey Production[T]
112330 Turkey Production
11234   Poultry Hatcheries[T]
112340 Poultry Hatcheries
11239   Other Poultry Production[T]
112390 Other Poultry Production

1124   Sheep and Goat Farming[T]
11241   Sheep Farming[T]
112410 Sheep Farming
11242   Goat Farming[T]
112420 Goat Farming

1125   Aquaculture[T]
11251   Aquaculture[T]
112511 Finfish Farming and Fish Hatcheries
112512 Shellfish Farming
112519 Other Aquaculture

1129   Other Animal Production[T]
11291   Apiculture[T]
112910 Apiculture
11292   Horses and Other Equine Production[T]
112920 Horses and Other Equine Production
11293   Fur-Bearing Animal and Rabbit Production[T]
112930 Fur-Bearing Animal and Rabbit Production
11299   All Other Animal Production[T]
112990 All Other Animal Production

113   Forestry and Logging[T]

1131   Timber Tract Operations[T]
11311   Timber Tract Operations[T]
113110 Timber Tract Operations

1132   Forest Nurseries and Gathering of Forest Products[T]
11321   Forest Nurseries and Gathering of Forest Products[T]
113210 Forest Nurseries and Gathering of Forest Products

1133   Logging[T]
11331   Logging[T]
113310 Logging

114   Fishing, Hunting and Trapping[T]

1141   Fishing[T]
11411   Fishing[T]
114111 Finfish Fishing
114112 Shellfish Fishing
114119 Other Marine Fishing

1142   Hunting and Trapping[T]
11421   Hunting and Trapping[T]
114210 Hunting and Trapping

115   Support Activities for Agriculture and Forestry[T]

1151   Support Activities for Crop Production[T]
11511   Support Activities for Crop Production[T]
115111 Cotton Ginning
115112 Soil Preparation, Planting, and Cultivating
115113 Crop Harvesting, Primarily by Machine
115114 Postharvest Crop Activities (except Cotton Ginning)
115115 Farm Labor Contractors and Crew Leaders
115116 Farm Management Services

1152   Support Activities for Animal Production[T]
11521   Support Activities for Animal Production[T]
115210 Support Activities for Animal Production

1153   Support Activities for Forestry[T]
11531   Support Activities for Forestry[T]
115310 Support Activities for Forestry

Sector 21--Mining, Quarrying, and Oil and Gas Extraction[T]

211   Oil and Gas Extraction[T]

2111   Oil and Gas Extraction[T]
21112   Crude Petroleum Extraction
211120 Crude Petroleum Extraction
21113   Natural Gas Extraction
211130 Natural Gas Extraction

212   Mining (except Oil and Gas)^T

2121   Coal Mining^T
 21211 Coal Mining^T
 212111 Bituminous Coal and Lignite Surface Mining
 212112 Bituminous Coal Underground Mining
 212113 Anthracite Mining

2122   Metal Ore Mining^T
 21221 Iron Ore Mining^T
 212210 Iron Ore Mining
 21222 Gold Ore and Silver Ore Mining^T
 212221 Gold Ore Mining
 212222 Silver Ore Mining
 21223 Copper, Nickel, Lead, and Zinc Mining^T
 212230 Copper, Nickel, Lead, and Zinc Mining
 21229 Other Metal Ore Mining^T
 212291 Uranium-Radium-Vanadium Ore Mining
 212299 All Other Metal Ore Mining

2123   Nonmetallic Mineral Mining and Quarrying^T
 21231 Stone Mining and Quarrying^T
 212311 Dimension Stone Mining and Quarrying
 212312 Crushed and Broken Limestone Mining and Quarrying
 212313 Crushed and Broken Granite Mining and Quarrying
 212319 Other Crushed and Broken Stone Mining and Quarrying
 21232 Sand, Gravel, Clay, and Ceramic and Refractory Minerals Mining and Quarrying^T
 212321 Construction Sand and Gravel Mining
 212322 Industrial Sand Mining
 212324 Kaolin and Ball Clay Mining
 212325 Clay and Ceramic and Refractory Minerals Mining
 21239 Other Nonmetallic Mineral Mining and Quarrying^T
 212391 Potash, Soda, and Borate Mineral Mining
 212392 Phosphate Rock Mining
 212393 Other Chemical and Fertilizer Mineral Mining
 212399 All Other Nonmetallic Mineral Mining

213   Support Activities for Mining^T

2131   Support Activities for Mining^T
 21311 Support Activities for Mining^T
 213111 Drilling Oil and Gas Wells
 213112 Support Activities for Oil and Gas Operations
 213113 Support Activities for Coal Mining
 213114 Support Activities for Metal Mining
 213115 Support Activities for Nonmetallic Minerals (except Fuels) Mining

Sector 22--Utilities^T

221   Utilities^T

2211   Electric Power Generation, Transmission and Distribution^T
 22111 Electric Power Generation^T

221111 Hydroelectric Power Generation
221112 Fossil Fuel Electric Power Generation
221113 Nuclear Electric Power Generation
221114 Solar Electric Power Generation
221115 Wind Electric Power Generation
221116 Geothermal Electric Power Generation
221117 Biomass Electric Power Generation
221118 Other Electric Power Generation
22112   Electric Power Transmission, Control, and Distribution[T]
221121 Electric Bulk Power Transmission and Control
221122 Electric Power Distribution

2212   Natural Gas Distribution[T]
22121   Natural Gas Distribution[T]
221210 Natural Gas Distribution

2213   Water, Sewage and Other Systems[T]
22131   Water Supply and Irrigation Systems
221310 Water Supply and Irrigation Systems
22132   Sewage Treatment Facilities
221320 Sewage Treatment Facilities
22133   Steam and Air-Conditioning Supply
221330 Steam and Air-Conditioning Supply

Sector 23--Construction[T]

236   Construction of Buildings[T]

2361   Residential Building Construction[T]
23611   Residential Building Construction[T]
236115 New Single-Family Housing Construction (except For-Sale Builders)
236116 New Multifamily Housing Construction (except For-Sale Builders)
236117 New Housing For-Sale Builders
236118 Residential Remodelers

2362   Nonresidential Building Construction[T]
23621   Industrial Building Construction[T]
236210 Industrial Building Construction
23622   Commercial and Institutional Building Construction[T]
236220 Commercial and Institutional Building Construction

237   Heavy and Civil Engineering Construction[T]

2371   Utility System Construction[T]
23711   Water and Sewer Line and Related Structures Construction[T]
237110 Water and Sewer Line and Related Structures Construction
23712   Oil and Gas Pipeline and Related Structures Construction[T]
237120 Oil and Gas Pipeline and Related Structures Construction
23713   Power and Communication Line and Related Structures Construction[T]
237130 Power and Communication Line and Related Structures Construction

2372   Land Subdivision[T]
23721   Land Subdivision[T]
237210 Land Subdivision

2373   Highway, Street, and Bridge Construction[T]
23731   Highway, Street, and Bridge Construction[T]
237310 Highway, Street, and Bridge Construction

2379   Other Heavy and Civil Engineering Construction[T]
23799   Other Heavy and Civil Engineering Construction[T]
237990 Other Heavy and Civil Engineering Construction

238   Specialty Trade Contractors[T]

2381   Foundation, Structure, and Building Exterior Contractors[T]
23811   Poured Concrete Foundation and Structure Contractors
238110 Poured Concrete Foundation and Structure Contractors
23812   Structural Steel and Precast Concrete Contractors
238120 Structural Steel and Precast Concrete Contractors
23813   Framing Contractors
238130 Framing Contractors
23814   Masonry Contractors
238140 Masonry Contractors
23815   Glass and Glazing Contractors
238150 Glass and Glazing Contractors
23816   Roofing Contractors
238160 Roofing Contractors
23817   Siding Contractors
238170 Siding Contractors
23819   Other Foundation, Structure, and Building Exterior Contractors
238190 Other Foundation, Structure, and Building Exterior Contractors

2382   Building Equipment Contractors[T]
23821   Electrical Contractors and Other Wiring Installation Contractors[T]
238210 Electrical Contractors and Other Wiring Installation Contractors
23822   Plumbing, Heating, and Air-Conditioning Contractors[T]
238220 Plumbing, Heating, and Air-Conditioning Contractors
23829   Other Building Equipment Contractors[T]
238290 Other Building Equipment Contractors

2383   Building Finishing Contractors[T]
23831   Drywall and Insulation Contractors[T]
238310 Drywall and Insulation Contractors
23832   Painting and Wall Covering Contractors[T]
238320 Painting and Wall Covering Contractors
23833   Flooring Contractors[T]
238330 Flooring Contractors
23834   Tile and Terrazzo Contractors[T]
238340 Tile and Terrazzo Contractors
23835   Finish Carpentry Contractors[T]
238350 Finish Carpentry Contractors
23839   Other Building Finishing Contractors[T]
238390 Other Building Finishing Contractors

2389   Other Specialty Trade Contractors[T]
23891   Site Preparation Contractors[T]
238910 Site Preparation Contractors
23899   All Other Specialty Trade Contractors[T]
238990 All Other Specialty Trade Contractors

Sector 31-33--Manufacturing[T]

311   Food Manufacturing[T]

3111   Animal Food Manufacturing[T]
31111   Animal Food Manufacturing[T]
311111   Dog and Cat Food Manufacturing
311119   Other Animal Food Manufacturing

3112   Grain and Oilseed Milling[T]
31121   Flour Milling and Malt Manufacturing[T]
311211   Flour Milling
311212   Rice Milling
311213   Malt Manufacturing
31122   Starch and Vegetable Fats and Oils Manufacturing[T]
311221   Wet Corn Milling
311224   Soybean and Other Oilseed Processing
311225   Fats and Oils Refining and Blending
31123   Breakfast Cereal Manufacturing[T]
311230   Breakfast Cereal Manufacturing

3113   Sugar and Confectionery Product Manufacturing[T]
31131   Sugar Manufacturing[T]
311313   Beet Sugar Manufacturing
311314   Cane Sugar Manufacturing
31134   Nonchocolate Confectionery Manufacturing[T]
311340   Nonchocolate Confectionery Manufacturing
31135   Chocolate and Confectionery Manufacturing[T]
311351   Chocolate and Confectionery Manufacturing from Cacao Beans
311352   Confectionery Manufacturing from Purchased Chocolate

3114   Fruit and Vegetable Preserving and Specialty Food Manufacturing[T]
31141   Frozen Food Manufacturing[T]
311411   Frozen Fruit, Juice, and Vegetable Manufacturing
311412   Frozen Specialty Food Manufacturing
31142   Fruit and Vegetable Canning, Pickling, and Drying[T]
311421   Fruit and Vegetable Canning
311422   Specialty Canning
311423   Dried and Dehydrated Food Manufacturing

3115   Dairy Product Manufacturing[T]
31151   Dairy Product (except Frozen) Manufacturing[T]
311511   Fluid Milk Manufacturing
311512   Creamery Butter Manufacturing
311513   Cheese Manufacturing
311514   Dry, Condensed, and Evaporated Dairy Product Manufacturing
31152   Ice Cream and Frozen Dessert Manufacturing[T]
311520   Ice Cream and Frozen Dessert Manufacturing

3116   Animal Slaughtering and Processing[T]
31161   Animal Slaughtering and Processing[T]
311611   Animal (except Poultry) Slaughtering
311612   Meat Processed from Carcasses
311613   Rendering and Meat Byproduct Processing
311615   Poultry Processing

3117 Seafood Product Preparation and Packaging[T]
31171 Seafood Product Preparation and Packaging[T]
311710 Seafood Product Preparation and Packaging

3118 Bakeries and Tortilla Manufacturing[T]
31181 Bread and Bakery Product Manufacturing[T]
311811 Retail Bakeries
311812 Commercial Bakeries
311813 Frozen Cakes, Pies, and Other Pastries Manufacturing
31182 Cookie, Cracker, and Pasta Manufacturing[T]
311821 Cookie and Cracker Manufacturing
311824 Dry Pasta, Dough, and Flour Mixes Manufacturing from Purchased Flour
31183 Tortilla Manufacturing[T]
311830 Tortilla Manufacturing

3119 Other Food Manufacturing[T]
31191 Snack Food Manufacturing[T]
311911 Roasted Nuts and Peanut Butter Manufacturing
311919 Other Snack Food Manufacturing
31192 Coffee and Tea Manufacturing[T]
311920 Coffee and Tea Manufacturing
31193 Flavoring Syrup and Concentrate Manufacturing[T]
311930 Flavoring Syrup and Concentrate Manufacturing
31194 Seasoning and Dressing Manufacturing[T]
311941 Mayonnaise, Dressing, and Other Prepared Sauce Manufacturing
311942 Spice and Extract Manufacturing
31199 All Other Food Manufacturing[T]
311991 Perishable Prepared Food Manufacturing
311999 All Other Miscellaneous Food Manufacturing

312 Beverage and Tobacco Product Manufacturing[T]

3121 Beverage Manufacturing[T]
31211 Soft Drink and Ice Manufacturing[T]
312111 Soft Drink Manufacturing
312112 Bottled Water Manufacturing
312113 Ice Manufacturing
31212 Breweries[T]
312120 Breweries
31213 Wineries[T]
312130 Wineries
31214 Distilleries[T]
312140 Distilleries

3122 Tobacco Manufacturing[T]
31223 Tobacco Manufacturing
312230 Tobacco Manufacturing

313 Textile Mills[T]

3131 Fiber, Yarn, and Thread Mills[T]
31311 Fiber, Yarn, and Thread Mills[T]
313110 Fiber, Yarn, and Thread Mills

3132   Fabric Mills[T]
    31321   Broadwoven Fabric Mills[T]
    313210 Broadwoven Fabric Mills
    31322   Narrow Fabric Mills and Schiffli Machine Embroidery[T]
    313220 Narrow Fabric Mills and Schiffli Machine Embroidery
    31323   Nonwoven Fabric Mills[T]
    313230 Nonwoven Fabric Mills
    31324   Knit Fabric Mills[T]
    313240 Knit Fabric Mills

3133   Textile and Fabric Finishing and Fabric Coating Mills[T]
    31331   Textile and Fabric Finishing Mills[T]
    313310 Textile and Fabric Finishing Mills
    31332   Fabric Coating Mills[T]
    313320 Fabric Coating Mills

314   Textile Product Mills[T]

3141   Textile Furnishings Mills[T]
    31411   Carpet and Rug Mills[T]
    314110 Carpet and Rug Mills
    31412   Curtain and Linen Mills[T]
    314120 Curtain and Linen Mills

3149   Other Textile Product Mills[T]
    31491   Textile Bag and Canvas Mills[T]
    314910 Textile Bag and Canvas Mills
    31499   All Other Textile Product Mills[T]
    314994 Rope, Cordage, Twine, Tire Cord, and Tire Fabric Mills
    314999 All Other Miscellaneous Textile Product Mills

315   Apparel Manufacturing[T]

3151   Apparel Knitting Mills[T]
    31511   Hosiery and Sock Mills[T]
    315110 Hosiery and Sock Mills
    31519   Other Apparel Knitting Mills[T]
    315190 Other Apparel Knitting Mills

3152   Cut and Sew Apparel Manufacturing[T]
    31521   Cut and Sew Apparel Contractors
    315210 Cut and Sew Apparel Contractors
    31522   Men's and Boys' Cut and Sew Apparel Manufacturing
    315220 Men's and Boys' Cut and Sew Apparel Manufacturing
    31524   Women's, Girls', and Infants' Cut and Sew Apparel Manufacturing
    315240 Women's, Girls', and Infants' Cut and Sew Apparel Manufacturing
    31528   Other Cut and Sew Apparel Manufacturing
    315280 Other Cut and Sew Apparel Manufacturing

3159   Apparel Accessories and Other Apparel Manufacturing[T]
    31599   Apparel Accessories and Other Apparel Manufacturing[T]
    315990 Apparel Accessories and Other Apparel Manufacturing

316   Leather and Allied Product Manufacturing[T]

3161   Leather and Hide Tanning and Finishing[T]
31611   Leather and Hide Tanning and Finishing[T]
316110 Leather and Hide Tanning and Finishing

3162   Footwear Manufacturing[T]
31621   Footwear Manufacturing[T]
316210 Footwear Manufacturing

3169   Other Leather and Allied Product Manufacturing[T]
31699   Other Leather and Allied Product Manufacturing[T]
316992 Women's Handbag and Purse Manufacturing
316998 All Other Leather Good and Allied Product Manufacturing

321   Wood Product Manufacturing[T]

3211   Sawmills and Wood Preservation[T]
32111   Sawmills and Wood Preservation[T]
321113 Sawmills
321114 Wood Preservation

3212   Veneer, Plywood, and Engineered Wood Product Manufacturing[T]
32121   Veneer, Plywood, and Engineered Wood Product Manufacturing[T]
321211 Hardwood Veneer and Plywood Manufacturing
321212 Softwood Veneer and Plywood Manufacturing
321213 Engineered Wood Member (except Truss) Manufacturing
321214 Truss Manufacturing
321219 Reconstituted Wood Product Manufacturing

3219   Other Wood Product Manufacturing[T]
32191   Millwork[T]
321911 Wood Window and Door Manufacturing
321912 Cut Stock, Resawing Lumber, and Planing
321918 Other Millwork (including Flooring)
32192   Wood Container and Pallet Manufacturing[T]
321920 Wood Container and Pallet Manufacturing
32199   All Other Wood Product Manufacturing[T]
321991 Manufactured Home (Mobile Home) Manufacturing
321992 Prefabricated Wood Building Manufacturing
321999 All Other Miscellaneous Wood Product Manufacturing

322   Paper Manufacturing[T]

3221   Pulp, Paper, and Paperboard Mills[T]
32211   Pulp Mills[T]
322110 Pulp Mills
32212   Paper Mills[T]
322121 Paper (except Newsprint) Mills
322122 Newsprint Mills
32213   Paperboard Mills[T]
322130 Paperboard Mills

3222   Converted Paper Product Manufacturing[T]
32221   Paperboard Container Manufacturing[T]

322211 Corrugated and Solid Fiber Box Manufacturing
322212 Folding Paperboard Box Manufacturing
322219 Other Paperboard Container Manufacturing
32222   Paper Bag and Coated and Treated Paper Manufacturing[T]
322220 Paper Bag and Coated and Treated Paper Manufacturing
32223   Stationery Product Manufacturing[T]
322230 Stationery Product Manufacturing
32229   Other Converted Paper Product Manufacturing[T]
322291 Sanitary Paper Product Manufacturing
322299 All Other Converted Paper Product Manufacturing

323   Printing and Related Support Activities[T]

3231   Printing and Related Support Activities[T]
32311   Printing[T]
323111 Commercial Printing (except Screen and Books)
323113 Commercial Screen Printing
323117 Books Printing
32312   Support Activities for Printing[T]
323120 Support Activities for Printing

324   Petroleum and Coal Products Manufacturing[T]

3241   Petroleum and Coal Products Manufacturing[T]
32411   Petroleum Refineries[T]
324110 Petroleum Refineries
32412   Asphalt Paving, Roofing, and Saturated Materials Manufacturing[T]
324121 Asphalt Paving Mixture and Block Manufacturing
324122 Asphalt Shingle and Coating Materials Manufacturing
32419   Other Petroleum and Coal Products Manufacturing[T]
324191 Petroleum Lubricating Oil and Grease Manufacturing
324199 All Other Petroleum and Coal Products Manufacturing

325   Chemical Manufacturing[T]

3251   Basic Chemical Manufacturing[T]
32511   Petrochemical Manufacturing[T]
325110 Petrochemical Manufacturing
32512   Industrial Gas Manufacturing[T]
325120 Industrial Gas Manufacturing
32513   Synthetic Dye and Pigment Manufacturing[T]
325130 Synthetic Dye and Pigment Manufacturing
32518   Other Basic Inorganic Chemical Manufacturing[T]
325180 Other Basic Inorganic Chemical Manufacturing
32519   Other Basic Organic Chemical Manufacturing[T]
325193 Ethyl Alcohol Manufacturing
325194 Cyclic Crude, Intermediate, and Gum and Wood Chemical Manufacturing
325199 All Other Basic Organic Chemical Manufacturing

3252   Resin, Synthetic Rubber, and Artificial and Synthetic Fibers and Filaments Manufacturing[T]
32521   Resin and Synthetic Rubber Manufacturing[T]
325211 Plastics Material and Resin Manufacturing
325212 Synthetic Rubber Manufacturing

32522   Artificial and Synthetic Fibers and Filaments Manufacturing[T]
325220 Artificial and Synthetic Fibers and Filaments Manufacturing

3253   Pesticide, Fertilizer, and Other Agricultural Chemical Manufacturing[T]
32531   Fertilizer Manufacturing[T]
325311 Nitrogenous Fertilizer Manufacturing
325312 Phosphatic Fertilizer Manufacturing
325314 Fertilizer (Mixing Only) Manufacturing
32532   Pesticide and Other Agricultural Chemical Manufacturing[T]
325320 Pesticide and Other Agricultural Chemical Manufacturing

3254   Pharmaceutical and Medicine Manufacturing[T]
32541   Pharmaceutical and Medicine Manufacturing[T]
325411 Medicinal and Botanical Manufacturing
325412 Pharmaceutical Preparation Manufacturing
325413 In-Vitro Diagnostic Substance Manufacturing
325414 Biological Product (except Diagnostic) Manufacturing

3255   Paint, Coating, and Adhesive Manufacturing[T]
32551   Paint and Coating Manufacturing[T]
325510 Paint and Coating Manufacturing
32552   Adhesive Manufacturing[T]
325520 Adhesive Manufacturing

3256   Soap, Cleaning Compound, and Toilet Preparation Manufacturing[T]
32561   Soap and Cleaning Compound Manufacturing[T]
325611 Soap and Other Detergent Manufacturing
325612 Polish and Other Sanitation Good Manufacturing
325613 Surface Active Agent Manufacturing
32562   Toilet Preparation Manufacturing[T]
325620 Toilet Preparation Manufacturing

3259   Other Chemical Product and Preparation Manufacturing[T]
32591   Printing Ink Manufacturing[T]
325910 Printing Ink Manufacturing
32592   Explosives Manufacturing[T]
325920 Explosives Manufacturing
32599   All Other Chemical Product and Preparation Manufacturing[T]
325991 Custom Compounding of Purchased Resins
325992 Photographic Film, Paper, Plate, and Chemical Manufacturing
325998 All Other Miscellaneous Chemical Product and Preparation Manufacturing

326   Plastics and Rubber Products Manufacturing[T]

3261   Plastics Product Manufacturing[T]
32611   Plastics Packaging Materials and Unlaminated Film and Sheet Manufacturing[T]
326111 Plastics Bag and Pouch Manufacturing
326112 Plastics Packaging Film and Sheet (including Laminated) Manufacturing
326113 Unlaminated Plastics Film and Sheet (except Packaging) Manufacturing
32612   Plastics Pipe, Pipe Fitting, and Unlaminated Profile Shape Manufacturing[T]
326121 Unlaminated Plastics Profile Shape Manufacturing
326122 Plastics Pipe and Pipe Fitting Manufacturing
32613   Laminated Plastics Plate, Sheet (except Packaging), and Shape
            Manufacturing[T]
326130 Laminated Plastics Plate, Sheet (except Packaging), and Shape
            Manufacturing

32614   Polystyrene Foam Product Manufacturing[T]
326140 Polystyrene Foam Product Manufacturing
32615   Urethane and Other Foam Product (except Polystyrene) Manufacturing[T]
326150 Urethane and Other Foam Product (except Polystyrene) Manufacturing
32616   Plastics Bottle Manufacturing[T]
326160 Plastics Bottle Manufacturing
32619   Other Plastics Product Manufacturing[T]
326191 Plastics Plumbing Fixture Manufacturing
326199 All Other Plastics Product Manufacturing

3262   Rubber Product Manufacturing[T]
32621   Tire Manufacturing[T]
326211 Tire Manufacturing (except Retreading)
326212 Tire Retreading
32622   Rubber and Plastics Hoses and Belting Manufacturing[T]
326220 Rubber and Plastics Hoses and Belting Manufacturing
32629   Other Rubber Product Manufacturing[T]
326291 Rubber Product Manufacturing for Mechanical Use
326299 All Other Rubber Product Manufacturing

327   Nonmetallic Mineral Product Manufacturing[T]

3271   Clay Product and Refractory Manufacturing[T]
32711   Pottery, Ceramics, and Plumbing Fixture Manufacturing[T]
327110 Pottery, Ceramics, and Plumbing Fixture Manufacturing
32712   Clay Building Material and Refractories Manufacturing[T]
327120 Clay Building Material and Refractories Manufacturing

3272   Glass and Glass Product Manufacturing[T]
32721   Glass and Glass Product Manufacturing[T]
327211 Flat Glass Manufacturing
327212 Other Pressed and Blown Glass and Glassware Manufacturing
327213 Glass Container Manufacturing
327215 Glass Product Manufacturing Made of Purchased Glass

3273   Cement and Concrete Product Manufacturing[T]
32731   Cement Manufacturing[T]
327310 Cement Manufacturing
32732   Ready-Mix Concrete Manufacturing[T]
327320 Ready-Mix Concrete Manufacturing
32733   Concrete Pipe, Brick, and Block Manufacturing[T]
327331 Concrete Block and Brick Manufacturing
327332 Concrete Pipe Manufacturing
32739   Other Concrete Product Manufacturing[T]
327390 Other Concrete Product Manufacturing

3274   Lime and Gypsum Product Manufacturing[T]
32741   Lime Manufacturing[T]
327410 Lime Manufacturing
32742   Gypsum Product Manufacturing[T]
327420 Gypsum Product Manufacturing

3279   Other Nonmetallic Mineral Product Manufacturing[T]
32791   Abrasive Product Manufacturing[T]
327910 Abrasive Product Manufacturing
32799   All Other Nonmetallic Mineral Product Manufacturing[T]

327991 Cut Stone and Stone Product Manufacturing
327992 Ground or Treated Mineral and Earth Manufacturing
327993 Mineral Wool Manufacturing
327999 All Other Miscellaneous Nonmetallic Mineral Product Manufacturing

331 Primary Metal Manufacturing[T]

3311 Iron and Steel Mills and Ferroalloy Manufacturing[T]
33111   Iron and Steel Mills and Ferroalloy Manufacturing[T]
331110 Iron and Steel Mills and Ferroalloy Manufacturing

3312 Steel Product Manufacturing from Purchased Steel[T]
33121   Iron and Steel Pipe and Tube Manufacturing from Purchased Steel[T]
331210 Iron and Steel Pipe and Tube Manufacturing from Purchased Steel
33122   Rolling and Drawing of Purchased Steel[T]
331221 Rolled Steel Shape Manufacturing
331222 Steel Wire Drawing

3313 Alumina and Aluminum Production and Processing[T]
33131   Alumina and Aluminum Production and Processing[T]
331313 Alumina Refining and Primary Aluminum Production
331314 Secondary Smelting and Alloying of Aluminum
331315 Aluminum Sheet, Plate, and Foil Manufacturing
331318 Other Aluminum Rolling, Drawing, and Extruding

3314 Nonferrous Metal (except Aluminum) Production and Processing[T]
33141   Nonferrous Metal (except Aluminum) Smelting and Refining[T]
331410 Nonferrous Metal (except Aluminum) Smelting and Refining
33142   Copper Rolling, Drawing, Extruding, and Alloying[T]
331420 Copper Rolling, Drawing, Extruding, and Alloying
33149   Nonferrous Metal (except Copper and Aluminum) Rolling, Drawing, Extruding, and Alloying[T]
331491 Nonferrous Metal (except Copper and Aluminum) Rolling, Drawing, and Extruding
331492 Secondary Smelting, Refining, and Alloying of Nonferrous Metal (except Copper and Aluminum)

3315 Foundries[T]
33151   Ferrous Metal Foundries[T]
331511 Iron Foundries
331512 Steel Investment Foundries
331513 Steel Foundries (except Investment)
33152   Nonferrous Metal Foundries[T]
331523 Nonferrous Metal Die-Casting Foundries
331524 Aluminum Foundries (except Die-Casting)
331529 Other Nonferrous Metal Foundries (except Die-Casting)

332 Fabricated Metal Product Manufacturing[T]

3321 Forging and Stamping[T]
33211   Forging and Stamping[T]
332111 Iron and Steel Forging
332112 Nonferrous Forging
332114 Custom Roll Forming
332117 Powder Metallurgy Part Manufacturing

332119 Metal Crown, Closure, and Other Metal Stamping (except
      Automotive)

3322   **Cutlery and Handtool Manufacturing[T]**
33221   Cutlery and Handtool Manufacturing[T]
332215 Metal Kitchen Cookware, Utensil, Cutlery, and Flatware (except Precious)
      Manufacturing
332216 Saw Blade and Handtool Manufacturing

3323   **Architectural and Structural Metals Manufacturing[T]**
33231   Plate Work and Fabricated Structural Product Manufacturing[T]
332311 Prefabricated Metal Building and Component Manufacturing
332312 Fabricated Structural Metal Manufacturing
332313 Plate Work Manufacturing
33232   Ornamental and Architectural Metal Products Manufacturing[T]
332321 Metal Window and Door Manufacturing
332322 Sheet Metal Work Manufacturing
332323 Ornamental and Architectural Metal Work Manufacturing

3324   **Boiler, Tank, and Shipping Container Manufacturing[T]**
33241   Power Boiler and Heat Exchanger Manufacturing[T]
332410 Power Boiler and Heat Exchanger Manufacturing
33242   Metal Tank (Heavy Gauge) Manufacturing[T]
332420 Metal Tank (Heavy Gauge) Manufacturing
33243   Metal Can, Box, and Other Metal Container (Light Gauge) Manufacturing[T]
332431 Metal Can Manufacturing
332439 Other Metal Container Manufacturing

3325   **Hardware Manufacturing[T]**
33251   Hardware Manufacturing[T]
332510 Hardware Manufacturing

3326   **Spring and Wire Product Manufacturing[T]**
33261   Spring and Wire Product Manufacturing[T]
332613 Spring Manufacturing
332618 Other Fabricated Wire Product Manufacturing

3327   **Machine Shops; Turned Product; and Screw, Nut, and Bolt Manufacturing[T]**
33271   Machine Shops[T]
332710 Machine Shops
33272   Turned Product and Screw, Nut, and Bolt Manufacturing[T]
332721 Precision Turned Product Manufacturing
332722 Bolt, Nut, Screw, Rivet, and Washer Manufacturing

3328   **Coating, Engraving, Heat Treating, and Allied Activities[T]**
33281   Coating, Engraving, Heat Treating, and Allied Activities[T]
332811 Metal Heat Treating
332812 Metal Coating, Engraving (except Jewelry and Silverware), and Allied
      Services to Manufacturers
332813 Electroplating, Plating, Polishing, Anodizing, and Coloring

3329   **Other Fabricated Metal Product Manufacturing[T]**
33291   Metal Valve Manufacturing[T]
332911 Industrial Valve Manufacturing
332912 Fluid Power Valve and Hose Fitting Manufacturing
332913 Plumbing Fixture Fitting and Trim Manufacturing

332919 Other Metal Valve and Pipe Fitting Manufacturing
33299   All Other Fabricated Metal Product Manufacturing[T]
332991 Ball and Roller Bearing Manufacturing
332992 Small Arms Ammunition Manufacturing
332993 Ammunition (except Small Arms) Manufacturing
332994 Small Arms, Ordnance, and Ordnance Accessories Manufacturing
332996 Fabricated Pipe and Pipe Fitting Manufacturing
332999 All Other Miscellaneous Fabricated Metal Product Manufacturing

333   Machinery Manufacturing[T]

3331   Agriculture, Construction, and Mining Machinery Manufacturing[T]
33311   Agricultural Implement Manufacturing[T]
333111 Farm Machinery and Equipment Manufacturing
333112 Lawn and Garden Tractor and Home Lawn and Garden Equipment
          Manufacturing
33312   Construction Machinery Manufacturing[T]
333120 Construction Machinery Manufacturing
33313   Mining and Oil and Gas Field Machinery Manufacturing[T]
333131 Mining Machinery and Equipment Manufacturing
333132 Oil and Gas Field Machinery and Equipment Manufacturing

3332   Industrial Machinery Manufacturing[T]
33324   Industrial Machinery Manufacturing[T]
333241 Food Product Machinery Manufacturing
333242 Semiconductor Machinery Manufacturing
333243 Sawmill, Woodworking, and Paper Machinery Manufacturing
333244 Printing Machinery and Equipment Manufacturing
333249 Other Industrial Machinery Manufacturing

3333   Commercial and Service Industry Machinery Manufacturing[T]
33331   Commercial and Service Industry Machinery Manufacturing[T]
333314 Optical Instrument and Lens Manufacturing
333316 Photographic and Photocopying Equipment Manufacturing
333318 Other Commercial and Service Industry Machinery Manufacturing

3334   Ventilation, Heating, Air-Conditioning, and Commercial Refrigeration Equipment Manufacturing[T]
33341   Ventilation, Heating, Air-Conditioning, and Commercial Refrigeration
          Equipment Manufacturing[T]
333413 Industrial and Commercial Fan and Blower and Air Purification Equipment
          Manufacturing
333414 Heating Equipment (except Warm Air Furnaces) Manufacturing
333415 Air-Conditioning and Warm Air Heating Equipment and Commercial and
          Industrial Refrigeration Equipment Manufacturing

3335   Metalworking Machinery Manufacturing[T]
33351   Metalworking Machinery Manufacturing[T]
333511 Industrial Mold Manufacturing
333514 Special Die and Tool, Die Set, Jig, and Fixture Manufacturing
333515 Cutting Tool and Machine Tool Accessory Manufacturing
333517 Machine Tool Manufacturing
333519 Rolling Mill and Other Metalworking Machinery Manufacturing

3336   Engine, Turbine, and Power Transmission Equipment Manufacturing[T]
33361   Engine, Turbine, and Power Transmission Equipment Manufacturing[T]

333611 Turbine and Turbine Generator Set Units Manufacturing
333612 Speed Changer, Industrial High-Speed Drive, and Gear Manufacturing
333613 Mechanical Power Transmission Equipment Manufacturing
333618 Other Engine Equipment Manufacturing

3339   Other General Purpose Machinery Manufacturing[T]
33391   Pump and Compressor Manufacturing[T]
333912 Air and Gas Compressor Manufacturing
333914 Measuring, Dispensing, and Other Pumping Equipment Manufacturing
33392   Material Handling Equipment Manufacturing[T]
333921 Elevator and Moving Stairway Manufacturing
333922 Conveyor and Conveying Equipment Manufacturing
333923 Overhead Traveling Crane, Hoist, and Monorail System Manufacturing
333924 Industrial Truck, Tractor, Trailer, and Stacker Machinery Manufacturing
33399   All Other General Purpose Machinery Manufacturing[T]
333991 Power-Driven Handtool Manufacturing
333992 Welding and Soldering Equipment Manufacturing
333993 Packaging Machinery Manufacturing
333994 Industrial Process Furnace and Oven Manufacturing
333995 Fluid Power Cylinder and Actuator Manufacturing
333996 Fluid Power Pump and Motor Manufacturing
333997 Scale and Balance Manufacturing
333999 All Other Miscellaneous General Purpose Machinery Manufacturing

334   Computer and Electronic Product Manufacturing[T]

3341   Computer and Peripheral Equipment Manufacturing[T]
33411   Computer and Peripheral Equipment Manufacturing[T]
334111 Electronic Computer Manufacturing
334112 Computer Storage Device Manufacturing
334118 Computer Terminal and Other Computer Peripheral Equipment Manufacturing

3342   Communications Equipment Manufacturing[T]
33421   Telephone Apparatus Manufacturing[T]
334210 Telephone Apparatus Manufacturing
33422   Radio and Television Broadcasting and Wireless Communications Equipment
            Manufacturing[T]
334220 Radio and Television Broadcasting and Wireless Communications Equipment
            Manufacturing
33429   Other Communications Equipment Manufacturing[T]
334290 Other Communications Equipment Manufacturing

3343   Audio and Video Equipment Manufacturing[T]
33431   Audio and Video Equipment Manufacturing[T]
334310 Audio and Video Equipment Manufacturing

3344   Semiconductor and Other Electronic Component Manufacturing[T]
33441   Semiconductor and Other Electronic Component Manufacturing[T]
334412 Bare Printed Circuit Board Manufacturing
334413 Semiconductor and Related Device Manufacturing
334416 Capacitor, Resistor, Coil, Transformer, and Other Inductor Manufacturing
334417 Electronic Connector Manufacturing
334418 Printed Circuit Assembly (Electronic Assembly) Manufacturing
334419 Other Electronic Component Manufacturing

3345   Navigational, Measuring, Electromedical, and Control Instruments Manufacturing[T]
   33451   Navigational, Measuring, Electromedical, and Control Instruments Manufacturing[T]
   334510   Electromedical and Electrotherapeutic Apparatus Manufacturing
   334511   Search, Detection, Navigation, Guidance, Aeronautical, and Nautical System and Instrument Manufacturing
   334512   Automatic Environmental Control Manufacturing for Residential, Commercial, and Appliance Use
   334513   Instruments and Related Products Manufacturing for Measuring, Displaying, and Controlling Industrial Process Variables
   334514   Totalizing Fluid Meter and Counting Device Manufacturing
   334515   Instrument Manufacturing for Measuring and Testing Electricity and Electrical Signals
   334516   Analytical Laboratory Instrument Manufacturing
   334517   Irradiation Apparatus Manufacturing
   334519   Other Measuring and Controlling Device Manufacturing

3346   Manufacturing and Reproducing Magnetic and Optical Media[T]
   33461   Manufacturing and Reproducing Magnetic and Optical Media[T]
   334613   Blank Magnetic and Optical Recording Media Manufacturing
   334614   Software and Other Prerecorded Compact Disc, Tape, and Record Reproducing

335   Electrical Equipment, Appliance, and Component Manufacturing[T]

3351   Electric Lighting Equipment Manufacturing[T]
   33511   Electric Lamp Bulb and Part Manufacturing[T]
   335110   Electric Lamp Bulb and Part Manufacturing
   33512   Lighting Fixture Manufacturing[T]
   335121   Residential Electric Lighting Fixture Manufacturing
   335122   Commercial, Industrial, and Institutional Electric Lighting Fixture Manufacturing
   335129   Other Lighting Equipment Manufacturing

3352   Household Appliance Manufacturing[T]
   33521   Small Electrical Appliance Manufacturing[T]
   335210   Small Electrical Appliance Manufacturing
   33522   Major Household Appliance Manufacturing[T]
   335220   Major Household Appliance Manufacturing

3353   Electrical Equipment Manufacturing[T]
   33531   Electrical Equipment Manufacturing[T]
   335311   Power, Distribution, and Specialty Transformer Manufacturing
   335312   Motor and Generator Manufacturing
   335313   Switchgear and Switchboard Apparatus Manufacturing
   335314   Relay and Industrial Control Manufacturing

3359   Other Electrical Equipment and Component Manufacturing[T]
   33591   Battery Manufacturing[T]
   335911   Storage Battery Manufacturing
   335912   Primary Battery Manufacturing
   33592   Communication and Energy Wire and Cable Manufacturing[T]
   335921   Fiber Optic Cable Manufacturing
   335929   Other Communication and Energy Wire Manufacturing
   33593   Wiring Device Manufacturing[T]

335931 Current-Carrying Wiring Device Manufacturing
335932 Noncurrent-Carrying Wiring Device Manufacturing
33599   All Other Electrical Equipment and Component Manufacturing[T]
335991 Carbon and Graphite Product Manufacturing
335999 All Other Miscellaneous Electrical Equipment and Component
            Manufacturing

336   Transportation Equipment Manufacturing[T]

3361   Motor Vehicle Manufacturing[T]
33611   Automobile and Light Duty Motor Vehicle Manufacturing[T]
336111 Automobile Manufacturing
336112 Light Truck and Utility Vehicle Manufacturing
33612   Heavy Duty Truck Manufacturing[T]
336120 Heavy Duty Truck Manufacturing

3362   Motor Vehicle Body and Trailer Manufacturing[T]
33621   Motor Vehicle Body and Trailer Manufacturing[T]
336211 Motor Vehicle Body Manufacturing
336212 Truck Trailer Manufacturing
336213 Motor Home Manufacturing
336214 Travel Trailer and Camper Manufacturing

3363   Motor Vehicle Parts Manufacturing[T]
33631   Motor Vehicle Gasoline Engine and Engine Parts Manufacturing[T]
336310 Motor Vehicle Gasoline Engine and Engine Parts Manufacturing
33632   Motor Vehicle Electrical and Electronic Equipment Manufacturing[T]
336320 Motor Vehicle Electrical and Electronic Equipment Manufacturing
33633   Motor Vehicle Steering and Suspension Components (except Spring)
            Manufacturing[T]
336330 Motor Vehicle Steering and Suspension Components (except Spring)
            Manufacturing
33634   Motor Vehicle Brake System Manufacturing[T]
336340 Motor Vehicle Brake System Manufacturing
33635   Motor Vehicle Transmission and Power Train Parts Manufacturing[T]
336350 Motor Vehicle Transmission and Power Train Parts Manufacturing
33636   Motor Vehicle Seating and Interior Trim Manufacturing[T]
336360 Motor Vehicle Seating and Interior Trim Manufacturing
33637   Motor Vehicle Metal Stamping[T]
336370 Motor Vehicle Metal Stamping
33639   Other Motor Vehicle Parts Manufacturing[T]
336390 Other Motor Vehicle Parts Manufacturing

3364   Aerospace Product and Parts Manufacturing[T]
33641   Aerospace Product and Parts Manufacturing[T]
336411 Aircraft Manufacturing
336412 Aircraft Engine and Engine Parts Manufacturing
336413 Other Aircraft Parts and Auxiliary Equipment Manufacturing
336414 Guided Missile and Space Vehicle Manufacturing
336415 Guided Missile and Space Vehicle Propulsion Unit and Propulsion Unit Parts
            Manufacturing
336419 Other Guided Missile and Space Vehicle Parts and Auxiliary Equipment
            Manufacturing

3365 Railroad Rolling Stock Manufacturing[T]
33651   Railroad Rolling Stock Manufacturing[T]
336510 Railroad Rolling Stock Manufacturing

3366 Ship and Boat Building[T]
33661   Ship and Boat Building[T]
336611 Ship Building and Repairing
336612 Boat Building

3369 Other Transportation Equipment Manufacturing[T]
33699   Other Transportation Equipment Manufacturing[T]
336991 Motorcycle, Bicycle, and Parts Manufacturing
336992 Military Armored Vehicle, Tank, and Tank Component Manufacturing
336999 All Other Transportation Equipment Manufacturing

337 Furniture and Related Product Manufacturing[T]

3371 Household and Institutional Furniture and Kitchen Cabinet Manufacturing[T]
33711   Wood Kitchen Cabinet and Countertop Manufacturing[T]
337110 Wood Kitchen Cabinet and Countertop Manufacturing
33712   Household and Institutional Furniture Manufacturing[T]
337121 Upholstered Household Furniture Manufacturing
337122 Nonupholstered Wood Household Furniture Manufacturing
337124 Metal Household Furniture Manufacturing
337125 Household Furniture (except Wood and Metal) Manufacturing
337127 Institutional Furniture Manufacturing

3372 Office Furniture (including Fixtures) Manufacturing[T]
33721   Office Furniture (including Fixtures) Manufacturing[T]
337211 Wood Office Furniture Manufacturing
337212 Custom Architectural Woodwork and Millwork Manufacturing
337214 Office Furniture (except Wood) Manufacturing
337215 Showcase, Partition, Shelving, and Locker Manufacturing

3379 Other Furniture Related Product Manufacturing[T]
33791   Mattress Manufacturing[T]
337910 Mattress Manufacturing
33792   Blind and Shade Manufacturing[T]
337920 Blind and Shade Manufacturing

339 Miscellaneous Manufacturing[T]

3391 Medical Equipment and Supplies Manufacturing[T]
33911   Medical Equipment and Supplies Manufacturing[T]
339112 Surgical and Medical Instrument Manufacturing
339113 Surgical Appliance and Supplies Manufacturing
339114 Dental Equipment and Supplies Manufacturing
339115 Ophthalmic Goods Manufacturing
339116 Dental Laboratories

3399 Other Miscellaneous Manufacturing[T]
33991   Jewelry and Silverware Manufacturing[T]
339910 Jewelry and Silverware Manufacturing
33992   Sporting and Athletic Goods Manufacturing[T]
339920 Sporting and Athletic Goods Manufacturing

33993   Doll, Toy, and Game Manufacturing[T]
339930 Doll, Toy, and Game Manufacturing
33994   Office Supplies (except Paper) Manufacturing[T]
339940 Office Supplies (except Paper) Manufacturing
33995   Sign Manufacturing[T]
339950 Sign Manufacturing
33999   All Other Miscellaneous Manufacturing[T]
339991 Gasket, Packing, and Sealing Device Manufacturing
339992 Musical Instrument Manufacturing
339993 Fastener, Button, Needle, and Pin Manufacturing
339994 Broom, Brush, and Mop Manufacturing
339995 Burial Casket Manufacturing
339999 All Other Miscellaneous Manufacturing

Sector 42--Wholesale Trade[T]

423   Merchant Wholesalers, Durable Goods

4231   Motor Vehicle and Motor Vehicle Parts and Supplies Merchant Wholesalers
42311   Automobile and Other Motor Vehicle Merchant Wholesalers
423110 Automobile and Other Motor Vehicle Merchant Wholesalers
42312   Motor Vehicle Supplies and New Parts Merchant Wholesalers
423120 Motor Vehicle Supplies and New Parts Merchant Wholesalers
42313   Tire and Tube Merchant Wholesalers
423130 Tire and Tube Merchant Wholesalers
42314   Motor Vehicle Parts (Used) Merchant Wholesalers
423140 Motor Vehicle Parts (Used) Merchant Wholesalers

4232   Furniture and Home Furnishing Merchant Wholesalers
42321   Furniture Merchant Wholesalers
423210 Furniture Merchant Wholesalers
42322   Home Furnishing Merchant Wholesalers
423220 Home Furnishing Merchant Wholesalers

4233   Lumber and Other Construction Materials Merchant Wholesalers
42331   Lumber, Plywood, Millwork, and Wood Panel Merchant Wholesalers
423310 Lumber, Plywood, Millwork, and Wood Panel Merchant Wholesalers
42332   Brick, Stone, and Related Construction Material Merchant Wholesalers
423320 Brick, Stone, and Related Construction Material Merchant Wholesalers
42333   Roofing, Siding, and Insulation Material Merchant Wholesalers
423330 Roofing, Siding, and Insulation Material Merchant Wholesalers
42339   Other Construction Material Merchant Wholesalers
423390 Other Construction Material Merchant Wholesalers

4234   Professional and Commercial Equipment and Supplies Merchant Wholesalers
42341   Photographic Equipment and Supplies Merchant Wholesalers
423410 Photographic Equipment and Supplies Merchant Wholesalers
42342   Office Equipment Merchant Wholesalers
423420 Office Equipment Merchant Wholesalers
42343   Computer and Computer Peripheral Equipment and Software Merchant
            Wholesalers
423430 Computer and Computer Peripheral Equipment and Software Merchant
            Wholesalers
42344   Other Commercial Equipment Merchant Wholesalers
423440 Other Commercial Equipment Merchant Wholesalers

      42345   Medical, Dental, and Hospital Equipment and Supplies Merchant
             Wholesalers
      423450 Medical, Dental, and Hospital Equipment and Supplies Merchant
             Wholesalers
      42346   Ophthalmic Goods Merchant Wholesalers
      423460 Ophthalmic Goods Merchant Wholesalers
      42349   Other Professional Equipment and Supplies Merchant Wholesalers
      423490 Other Professional Equipment and Supplies Merchant Wholesalers

4235   **Metal and Mineral (except Petroleum) Merchant Wholesalers**
      42351   Metal Service Centers and Other Metal Merchant Wholesalers
      423510 Metal Service Centers and Other Metal Merchant Wholesalers
      42352   Coal and Other Mineral and Ore Merchant Wholesalers
      423520 Coal and Other Mineral and Ore Merchant Wholesalers

4236   **Household Appliances and Electrical and Electronic Goods Merchant
        Wholesalers**
      42361   Electrical Apparatus and Equipment, Wiring Supplies, and Related Equipment
             Merchant Wholesalers
      423610 Electrical Apparatus and Equipment, Wiring Supplies, and Related Equipment
             Merchant Wholesalers
      42362   Household Appliances, Electric Housewares, and Consumer Electronics
             Merchant Wholesalers
      423620 Household Appliances, Electric Housewares, and Consumer Electronics
             Merchant Wholesalers
      42369   Other Electronic Parts and Equipment Merchant Wholesalers
      423690 Other Electronic Parts and Equipment Merchant Wholesalers

4237   **Hardware, and Plumbing and Heating Equipment and Supplies Merchant
        Wholesalers**
      42371   Hardware Merchant Wholesalers
      423710 Hardware Merchant Wholesalers
      42372   Plumbing and Heating Equipment and Supplies (Hydronics) Merchant
             Wholesalers
      423720 Plumbing and Heating Equipment and Supplies (Hydronics) Merchant
             Wholesalers
      42373   Warm Air Heating and Air-Conditioning Equipment and Supplies Merchant
             Wholesalers
      423730 Warm Air Heating and Air-Conditioning Equipment and Supplies Merchant
             Wholesalers
      42374   Refrigeration Equipment and Supplies Merchant Wholesalers
      423740 Refrigeration Equipment and Supplies Merchant Wholesalers

4238   **Machinery, Equipment, and Supplies Merchant Wholesalers**
      42381   Construction and Mining (except Oil Well) Machinery and Equipment
             Merchant Wholesalers
      423810 Construction and Mining (except Oil Well) Machinery and Equipment
             Merchant Wholesalers
      42382   Farm and Garden Machinery and Equipment Merchant Wholesalers
      423820 Farm and Garden Machinery and Equipment Merchant Wholesalers
      42383   Industrial Machinery and Equipment Merchant Wholesalers
      423830 Industrial Machinery and Equipment Merchant Wholesalers
      42384   Industrial Supplies Merchant Wholesalers
      423840 Industrial Supplies Merchant Wholesalers
      42385   Service Establishment Equipment and Supplies Merchant Wholesalers
      423850 Service Establishment Equipment and Supplies Merchant Wholesalers

      42386   Transportation Equipment and Supplies (except Motor Vehicle) Merchant
           Wholesalers
      423860 Transportation Equipment and Supplies (except Motor Vehicle) Merchant
           Wholesalers

4239   Miscellaneous Durable Goods Merchant Wholesalers
      42391   Sporting and Recreational Goods and Supplies Merchant Wholesalers
      423910 Sporting and Recreational Goods and Supplies Merchant Wholesalers
      42392   Toy and Hobby Goods and Supplies Merchant Wholesalers
      423920 Toy and Hobby Goods and Supplies Merchant Wholesalers
      42393   Recyclable Material Merchant Wholesalers
      423930 Recyclable Material Merchant Wholesalers
      42394   Jewelry, Watch, Precious Stone, and Precious Metal Merchant Wholesalers
      423940 Jewelry, Watch, Precious Stone, and Precious Metal Merchant Wholesalers
      42399   Other Miscellaneous Durable Goods Merchant Wholesalers
      423990 Other Miscellaneous Durable Goods Merchant Wholesalers

424   Merchant Wholesalers, Nondurable Goods

4241   Paper and Paper Product Merchant Wholesalers
      42411   Printing and Writing Paper Merchant Wholesalers
      424110 Printing and Writing Paper Merchant Wholesalers
      42412   Stationery and Office Supplies Merchant Wholesalers
      424120 Stationery and Office Supplies Merchant Wholesalers
      42413   Industrial and Personal Service Paper Merchant Wholesalers
      424130 Industrial and Personal Service Paper Merchant Wholesalers

4242   Drugs and Druggists' Sundries Merchant Wholesalers
      42421   Drugs and Druggists' Sundries Merchant Wholesalers
      424210 Drugs and Druggists' Sundries Merchant Wholesalers

4243   Apparel, Piece Goods, and Notions Merchant Wholesalers
      42431   Piece Goods, Notions, and Other Dry Goods Merchant Wholesalers
      424310 Piece Goods, Notions, and Other Dry Goods Merchant Wholesalers
      42432   Men's and Boys' Clothing and Furnishings Merchant Wholesalers
      424320 Men's and Boys' Clothing and Furnishings Merchant Wholesalers
      42433   Women's, Children's, and Infants' Clothing and Accessories Merchant
           Wholesalers
      424330 Women's, Children's, and Infants' Clothing and Accessories Merchant
           Wholesalers
      42434   Footwear Merchant Wholesalers
      424340 Footwear Merchant Wholesalers

4244   Grocery and Related Product Merchant Wholesalers
      42441   General Line Grocery Merchant Wholesalers
      424410 General Line Grocery Merchant Wholesalers
      42442   Packaged Frozen Food Merchant Wholesalers
      424420 Packaged Frozen Food Merchant Wholesalers
      42443   Dairy Product (except Dried or Canned) Merchant Wholesalers
      424430 Dairy Product (except Dried or Canned) Merchant Wholesalers
      42444   Poultry and Poultry Product Merchant Wholesalers
      424440 Poultry and Poultry Product Merchant Wholesalers
      42445   Confectionery Merchant Wholesalers
      424450 Confectionery Merchant Wholesalers
      42446   Fish and Seafood Merchant Wholesalers
      424460 Fish and Seafood Merchant Wholesalers

42447   Meat and Meat Product Merchant Wholesalers
424470   Meat and Meat Product Merchant Wholesalers
42448   Fresh Fruit and Vegetable Merchant Wholesalers
424480   Fresh Fruit and Vegetable Merchant Wholesalers
42449   Other Grocery and Related Products Merchant Wholesalers
424490   Other Grocery and Related Products Merchant Wholesalers

4245   **Farm Product Raw Material Merchant Wholesalers**
42451   Grain and Field Bean Merchant Wholesalers
424510   Grain and Field Bean Merchant Wholesalers
42452   Livestock Merchant Wholesalers
424520   Livestock Merchant Wholesalers
42459   Other Farm Product Raw Material Merchant Wholesalers
424590   Other Farm Product Raw Material Merchant Wholesalers

4246   **Chemical and Allied Products Merchant Wholesalers**
42461   Plastics Materials and Basic Forms and Shapes Merchant Wholesalers
424610   Plastics Materials and Basic Forms and Shapes Merchant Wholesalers
42469   Other Chemical and Allied Products Merchant Wholesalers
424690   Other Chemical and Allied Products Merchant Wholesalers

4247   **Petroleum and Petroleum Products Merchant Wholesalers**
42471   Petroleum Bulk Stations and Terminals
424710   Petroleum Bulk Stations and Terminals
42472   Petroleum and Petroleum Products Merchant Wholesalers (except Bulk
          Stations and Terminals)
424720   Petroleum and Petroleum Products Merchant Wholesalers (except Bulk
          Stations and Terminals)

4248   **Beer, Wine, and Distilled Alcoholic Beverage Merchant Wholesalers**
42481   Beer and Ale Merchant Wholesalers
424810   Beer and Ale Merchant Wholesalers
42482   Wine and Distilled Alcoholic Beverage Merchant Wholesalers
424820   Wine and Distilled Alcoholic Beverage Merchant Wholesalers

4249   **Miscellaneous Nondurable Goods Merchant Wholesalers**
42491   Farm Supplies Merchant Wholesalers
424910   Farm Supplies Merchant Wholesalers
42492   Book, Periodical, and Newspaper Merchant Wholesalers
424920   Book, Periodical, and Newspaper Merchant Wholesalers
42493   Flower, Nursery Stock, and Florists' Supplies Merchant Wholesalers
424930   Flower, Nursery Stock, and Florists' Supplies Merchant Wholesalers
42494   Tobacco and Tobacco Product Merchant Wholesalers
424940   Tobacco and Tobacco Product Merchant Wholesalers
42495   Paint, Varnish, and Supplies Merchant Wholesalers
424950   Paint, Varnish, and Supplies Merchant Wholesalers
42499   Other Miscellaneous Nondurable Goods Merchant Wholesalers
424990   Other Miscellaneous Nondurable Goods Merchant Wholesalers

425   Wholesale Electronic Markets and Agents and Brokers

4251   **Wholesale Electronic Markets and Agents and Brokers**
42511   Business to Business Electronic Markets
425110   Business to Business Electronic Markets
42512   Wholesale Trade Agents and Brokers
425120   Wholesale Trade Agents and Brokers

Sector 44-45--Retail Trade[T]

441   Motor Vehicle and Parts Dealers

4411   **Automobile Dealers**
44111   New Car Dealers
441110   New Car Dealers
44112   Used Car Dealers
441120   Used Car Dealers

4412   **Other Motor Vehicle Dealers**
44121   Recreational Vehicle Dealers
441210   Recreational Vehicle Dealers
44122   Motorcycle, Boat, and Other Motor Vehicle Dealers
441222   Boat Dealers
441228   Motorcycle, ATV, and All Other Motor Vehicle Dealers

4413   **Automotive Parts, Accessories, and Tire Stores**
44131   Automotive Parts and Accessories Stores
441310   Automotive Parts and Accessories Stores
44132   Tire Dealers
441320   Tire Dealers

442   Furniture and Home Furnishings Stores

4421   **Furniture Stores**
44211   Furniture Stores
442110   Furniture Stores

4422   **Home Furnishings Stores**
44221   Floor Covering Stores
442210   Floor Covering Stores
44229   Other Home Furnishings Stores
442291   Window Treatment Stores
442299   All Other Home Furnishings Stores

443   Electronics and Appliance Stores

4431   **Electronics and Appliance Stores**
44314   Electronics and Appliance Stores
443141   Household Appliance Stores
443142   Electronics Stores

444   Building Material and Garden Equipment and Supplies Dealers

4441   **Building Material and Supplies Dealers**
44411   Home Centers
444110   Home Centers
44412   Paint and Wallpaper Stores
444120   Paint and Wallpaper Stores
44413   Hardware Stores
444130   Hardware Stores
44419   Other Building Material Dealers
444190   Other Building Material Dealers

4442   Lawn and Garden Equipment and Supplies Stores
44421   Outdoor Power Equipment Stores
444210 Outdoor Power Equipment Stores
44422   Nursery, Garden Center, and Farm Supply Stores
444220 Nursery, Garden Center, and Farm Supply Stores

445   Food and Beverage Stores

4451   Grocery Stores
44511   Supermarkets and Other Grocery (except Convenience) Stores
445110 Supermarkets and Other Grocery (except Convenience) Stores
44512   Convenience Stores
445120 Convenience Stores

4452   Specialty Food Stores
44521   Meat Markets
445210 Meat Markets
44522   Fish and Seafood Markets
445220 Fish and Seafood Markets
44523   Fruit and Vegetable Markets
445230 Fruit and Vegetable Markets
44529   Other Specialty Food Stores
445291 Baked Goods Stores
445292 Confectionery and Nut Stores
445299 All Other Specialty Food Stores

4453   Beer, Wine, and Liquor Stores
44531   Beer, Wine, and Liquor Stores
445310 Beer, Wine, and Liquor Stores

446   Health and Personal Care Stores

4461   Health and Personal Care Stores
44611   Pharmacies and Drug Stores
446110 Pharmacies and Drug Stores
44612   Cosmetics, Beauty Supplies, and Perfume Stores
446120 Cosmetics, Beauty Supplies, and Perfume Stores
44613   Optical Goods Stores
446130 Optical Goods Stores
44619   Other Health and Personal Care Stores
446191 Food (Health) Supplement Stores
446199 All Other Health and Personal Care Stores

447   Gasoline Stations

4471   Gasoline Stations
44711   Gasoline Stations with Convenience Stores
447110 Gasoline Stations with Convenience Stores
44719   Other Gasoline Stations
447190 Other Gasoline Stations

448   Clothing and Clothing Accessories Stores

4481   Clothing Stores
44811   Men's Clothing Stores

448110 Men's Clothing Stores
44812   Women's Clothing Stores
448120 Women's Clothing Stores
44813   Children's and Infants' Clothing Stores
448130 Children's and Infants' Clothing Stores
44814   Family Clothing Stores
448140 Family Clothing Stores
44815   Clothing Accessories Stores
448150 Clothing Accessories Stores
44819   Other Clothing Stores
448190 Other Clothing Stores

4482   Shoe Stores
44821   Shoe Stores
448210 Shoe Stores

4483   Jewelry, Luggage, and Leather Goods Stores
44831   Jewelry Stores
448310 Jewelry Stores
44832   Luggage and Leather Goods Stores
448320 Luggage and Leather Goods Stores

451   Sporting Goods, Hobby, Musical Instrument, and Book Stores

4511   Sporting Goods, Hobby, and Musical Instrument Stores
45111   Sporting Goods Stores
451110 Sporting Goods Stores
45112   Hobby, Toy, and Game Stores
451120 Hobby, Toy, and Game Stores
45113   Sewing, Needlework, and Piece Goods Stores
451130 Sewing, Needlework, and Piece Goods Stores
45114   Musical Instrument and Supplies Stores
451140 Musical Instrument and Supplies Stores

4512   Book Stores and News Dealers
45121   Book Stores and News Dealers
451211 Book Stores
451212 News Dealers and Newsstands

452   General Merchandise Stores

4522   Department Stores
45221   Department Stores
452210 Department Stores

4523   General Merchandise Stores, including Warehouse Clubs and Supercenters
45231   General Merchandise Stores, including Warehouse Clubs and Supercenters
452311 Warehouse Clubs and Supercenters
452319 All Other General Merchandise Stores

453   Miscellaneous Store Retailers

4531   Florists
45311   Florists
453110 Florists

4532   Office Supplies, Stationery, and Gift Stores
   45321   Office Supplies and Stationery Stores
   453210 Office Supplies and Stationery Stores
   45322   Gift, Novelty, and Souvenir Stores
   453220 Gift, Novelty, and Souvenir Stores

4533   Used Merchandise Stores
   45331   Used Merchandise Stores
   453310 Used Merchandise Stores

4539   Other Miscellaneous Store Retailers
   45391   Pet and Pet Supplies Stores
   453910 Pet and Pet Supplies Stores
   45392   Art Dealers
   453920 Art Dealers
   45393   Manufactured (Mobile) Home Dealers
   453930 Manufactured (Mobile) Home Dealers
   45399   All Other Miscellaneous Store Retailers
   453991 Tobacco Stores
   453998 All Other Miscellaneous Store Retailers (except Tobacco Stores)

454   Nonstore Retailers

4541   Electronic Shopping and Mail-Order Houses
   45411   Electronic Shopping and Mail-Order Houses
   454110 Electronic Shopping and Mail-Order Houses

4542   Vending Machine Operators
   45421   Vending Machine Operators
   454210 Vending Machine Operators

4543   Direct Selling Establishments
   45431   Fuel Dealers
   454310 Fuel Dealers
   45439   Other Direct Selling Establishments
   454390 Other Direct Selling Establishments

Sector 48-49--Transportation and Warehousing[T]

481   Air Transportation[T]

4811   Scheduled Air Transportation[T]
   48111   Scheduled Air Transportation[T]
   481111 Scheduled Passenger Air Transportation
   481112 Scheduled Freight Air Transportation

4812   Nonscheduled Air Transportation[T]
   48121   Nonscheduled Air Transportation[T]
   481211 Nonscheduled Chartered Passenger Air Transportation
   481212 Nonscheduled Chartered Freight Air Transportation
   481219 Other Nonscheduled Air Transportation

482   Rail Transportation[T]

4821   **Rail Transportation[T]**
48211   Rail Transportation[T]
482111   Line-Haul Railroads
482112   Short Line Railroads

483   Water Transportation[T]

4831   **Deep Sea, Coastal, and Great Lakes Water Transportation[T]**
48311   Deep Sea, Coastal, and Great Lakes Water Transportation[T]
483111   Deep Sea Freight Transportation
483112   Deep Sea Passenger Transportation
483113   Coastal and Great Lakes Freight Transportation
483114   Coastal and Great Lakes Passenger Transportation

4832   **Inland Water Transportation[T]**
48321   Inland Water Transportation[T]
483211   Inland Water Freight Transportation
483212   Inland Water Passenger Transportation

484   Truck Transportation[T]

4841   **General Freight Trucking[T]**
48411   General Freight Trucking, Local[T]
484110   General Freight Trucking, Local
48412   General Freight Trucking, Long-Distance[T]
484121   General Freight Trucking, Long-Distance, Truckload
484122   General Freight Trucking, Long-Distance, Less Than Truckload

4842   **Specialized Freight Trucking[T]**
48421   Used Household and Office Goods Moving[T]
484210   Used Household and Office Goods Moving
48422   Specialized Freight (except Used Goods) Trucking, Local[T]
484220   Specialized Freight (except Used Goods) Trucking, Local
48423   Specialized Freight (except Used Goods) Trucking, Long-Distance[T]
484230   Specialized Freight (except Used Goods) Trucking, Long-Distance

485   Transit and Ground Passenger Transportation[T]

4851   **Urban Transit Systems[T]**
48511   Urban Transit Systems[T]
485111   Mixed Mode Transit Systems
485112   Commuter Rail Systems
485113   Bus and Other Motor Vehicle Transit Systems
485119   Other Urban Transit Systems

4852   **Interurban and Rural Bus Transportation[T]**
48521   Interurban and Rural Bus Transportation[T]
485210   Interurban and Rural Bus Transportation

4853   **Taxi and Limousine Service[T]**
48531   Taxi Service[T]
485310   Taxi Service

              48532 Limousine Service[T]
              485320 Limousine Service

4854   School and Employee Bus Transportation[T]
              48541 School and Employee Bus Transportation[T]
              485410 School and Employee Bus Transportation

4855   Charter Bus Industry[T]
              48551 Charter Bus Industry[T]
              485510 Charter Bus Industry

4859   Other Transit and Ground Passenger Transportation[T]
              48599 Other Transit and Ground Passenger Transportation[T]
              485991 Special Needs Transportation
              485999 All Other Transit and Ground Passenger Transportation

486   Pipeline Transportation[T]

4861   Pipeline Transportation of Crude Oil[T]
              48611 Pipeline Transportation of Crude Oil[T]
              486110 Pipeline Transportation of Crude Oil

4862   Pipeline Transportation of Natural Gas[T]
              48621 Pipeline Transportation of Natural Gas[T]
              486210 Pipeline Transportation of Natural Gas

4869   Other Pipeline Transportation[T]
              48691 Pipeline Transportation of Refined Petroleum Products[T]
              486910 Pipeline Transportation of Refined Petroleum Products
              48699 All Other Pipeline Transportation[T]
              486990 All Other Pipeline Transportation

487   Scenic and Sightseeing Transportation[T]

4871   Scenic and Sightseeing Transportation, Land[T]
              48711 Scenic and Sightseeing Transportation, Land[T]
              487110 Scenic and Sightseeing Transportation, Land

4872   Scenic and Sightseeing Transportation, Water[T]
              48721 Scenic and Sightseeing Transportation, Water[T]
              487210 Scenic and Sightseeing Transportation, Water

4879   Scenic and Sightseeing Transportation, Other[T]
              48799 Scenic and Sightseeing Transportation, Other[T]
              487990 Scenic and Sightseeing Transportation, Other

488   Support Activities for Transportation[T]

4881   Support Activities for Air Transportation[T]
              48811 Airport Operations[T]
              488111 Air Traffic Control
              488119 Other Airport Operations
              48819 Other Support Activities for Air Transportation[T]
              488190 Other Support Activities for Air Transportation

4882 **Support Activities for Rail Transportation**[T]
    48821   Support Activities for Rail Transportation[T]
    488210 Support Activities for Rail Transportation

4883 **Support Activities for Water Transportation**[T]
    48831   Port and Harbor Operations[T]
    488310 Port and Harbor Operations
    48832   Marine Cargo Handling[T]
    488320 Marine Cargo Handling
    48833   Navigational Services to Shipping[T]
    488330 Navigational Services to Shipping
    48839   Other Support Activities for Water Transportation[T]
    488390 Other Support Activities for Water Transportation

4884 **Support Activities for Road Transportation**[T]
    48841   Motor Vehicle Towing[T]
    488410 Motor Vehicle Towing
    48849   Other Support Activities for Road Transportation[T]
    488490 Other Support Activities for Road Transportation

4885 **Freight Transportation Arrangement**[T]
    48851   Freight Transportation Arrangement[T]
    488510 Freight Transportation Arrangement

4889 **Other Support Activities for Transportation**[T]
    48899   Other Support Activities for Transportation[T]
    488991 Packing and Crating
    488999 All Other Support Activities for Transportation

491   Postal Service[T]

4911 **Postal Service**[T]
    49111   Postal Service[T]
    491110 Postal Service

492   Couriers and Messengers[T]

4921 **Couriers and Express Delivery Services**[T]
    49211   Couriers and Express Delivery Services[T]
    492110 Couriers and Express Delivery Services

4922 **Local Messengers and Local Delivery**[T]
    49221   Local Messengers and Local Delivery[T]
    492210 Local Messengers and Local Delivery

493   Warehousing and Storage[T]

4931 **Warehousing and Storage**[T]
    49311   General Warehousing and Storage[T]
    493110 General Warehousing and Storage
    49312   Refrigerated Warehousing and Storage[T]
    493120 Refrigerated Warehousing and Storage
    49313   Farm Product Warehousing and Storage[T]
    493130 Farm Product Warehousing and Storage

49319   Other Warehousing and Storage[T]
493190   Other Warehousing and Storage

Sector 51--Information[T]

511   Publishing Industries (except Internet)[T]

5111   Newspaper, Periodical, Book, and Directory Publishers[T]
51111   Newspaper Publishers[T]
511110   Newspaper Publishers
51112   Periodical Publishers[T]
511120   Periodical Publishers
51113   Book Publishers[T]
511130   Book Publishers
51114   Directory and Mailing List Publishers[T]
511140   Directory and Mailing List Publishers
51119   Other Publishers[T]
511191   Greeting Card Publishers
511199   All Other Publishers

5112   Software Publishers[T]
51121   Software Publishers[T]
511210   Software Publishers

512   Motion Picture and Sound Recording Industries[T]

5121   Motion Picture and Video Industries[T]
51211   Motion Picture and Video Production[T]
512110   Motion Picture and Video Production
51212   Motion Picture and Video Distribution[T]
512120   Motion Picture and Video Distribution
51213   Motion Picture and Video Exhibition[T]
512131   Motion Picture Theaters (except Drive-Ins)
512132   Drive-In Motion Picture Theaters
51219   Postproduction Services and Other Motion Picture and Video Industries[T]
512191   Teleproduction and Other Postproduction Services
512199   Other Motion Picture and Video Industries

5122   Sound Recording Industries[T]
51223   Music Publishers[T]
512230   Music Publishers
51224   Sound Recording Studios[T]
512240   Sound Recording Studios
51225   Record Production and Distribution[T]
512250   Record Production and Distribution
51229   Other Sound Recording Industries[T]
512290   Other Sound Recording Industries

515   Broadcasting (except Internet)[T]

5151   Radio and Television Broadcasting[T]
51511   Radio Broadcasting[T]
515111   Radio Networks
515112   Radio Stations

51512 Television Broadcasting[T]
515120 Television Broadcasting

5152 Cable and Other Subscription Programming[T]
51521 Cable and Other Subscription Programming[T]
515210 Cable and Other Subscription Programming

517 Telecommunications[T]

5173 Wired and Wireless Telecommunications Carriers[T]
51731 Wired and Wireless Telecommunications Carriers[T]
517311 Wired Telecommunications Carriers
517312 Wireless Telecommunications Carriers (except Satellite)

5174 Satellite Telecommunications[T]
51741 Satellite Telecommunications[T]
517410 Satellite Telecommunications

5179 Other Telecommunications[T]
51791 Other Telecommunications[T]
517911 Telecommunications Resellers
517919 All Other Telecommunications

518 Data Processing, Hosting, and Related Services[T]

5182 Data Processing, Hosting, and Related Services[T]
51821 Data Processing, Hosting, and Related Services[T]
518210 Data Processing, Hosting, and Related Services

519 Other Information Services[T]

5191 Other Information Services[T]
51911 News Syndicates[T]
519110 News Syndicates
51912 Libraries and Archives[T]
519120 Libraries and Archives
51913 Internet Publishing and Broadcasting and Web Search Portals[T]
519130 Internet Publishing and Broadcasting and Web Search Portals
51919 All Other Information Services[T]
519190 All Other Information Services

Sector 52--Finance and Insurance[T]

521 Monetary Authorities-Central Bank[T]

5211 Monetary Authorities-Central Bank[T]
52111 Monetary Authorities-Central Bank[T]
521110 Monetary Authorities-Central Bank

522 Credit Intermediation and Related Activities[T]

5221 Depository Credit Intermediation
52211 Commercial Banking
522110 Commercial Banking

52212 Savings Institutions
522120 Savings Institutions
52213 Credit Unions
522130 Credit Unions
52219 Other Depository Credit Intermediation
522190 Other Depository Credit Intermediation

5222 Nondepository Credit Intermediation
52221 Credit Card Issuing
522210 Credit Card Issuing
52222 Sales Financing
522220 Sales Financing
52229 Other Nondepository Credit Intermediation
522291 Consumer Lending
522292 Real Estate Credit
522293 International Trade Financing
522294 Secondary Market Financing
522298 All Other Nondepository Credit Intermediation

5223 Activities Related to Credit Intermediation
52231 Mortgage and Nonmortgage Loan Brokers
522310 Mortgage and Nonmortgage Loan Brokers
52232 Financial Transactions Processing, Reserve, and Clearinghouse Activities
522320 Financial Transactions Processing, Reserve, and Clearinghouse Activities
52239 Other Activities Related to Credit Intermediation
522390 Other Activities Related to Credit Intermediation

523 Securities, Commodity Contracts, and Other Financial Investments and Related Activities[T]

5231 Securities and Commodity Contracts Intermediation and Brokerage[T]
52311 Investment Banking and Securities Dealing
523110 Investment Banking and Securities Dealing
52312 Securities Brokerage
523120 Securities Brokerage
52313 Commodity Contracts Dealing
523130 Commodity Contracts Dealing
52314 Commodity Contracts Brokerage
523140 Commodity Contracts Brokerage

5232 Securities and Commodity Exchanges[T]
52321 Securities and Commodity Exchanges[T]
523210 Securities and Commodity Exchanges

5239 Other Financial Investment Activities[T]
52391 Miscellaneous Intermediation
523910 Miscellaneous Intermediation
52392 Portfolio Management
523920 Portfolio Management
52393 Investment Advice
523930 Investment Advice
52399 All Other Financial Investment Activities
523991 Trust, Fiduciary, and Custody Activities
523999 Miscellaneous Financial Investment Activities

524   Insurance Carriers and Related Activities[T]

    5241   Insurance Carriers[T]
      52411   Direct Life, Health, and Medical Insurance Carriers
      524113 Direct Life Insurance Carriers
      524114 Direct Health and Medical Insurance Carriers
      52412   Direct Insurance (except Life, Health, and Medical) Carriers
      524126 Direct Property and Casualty Insurance Carriers
      524127 Direct Title Insurance Carriers
      524128 Other Direct Insurance (except Life, Health, and Medical) Carriers
      52413   Reinsurance Carriers
      524130 Reinsurance Carriers

    5242   Agencies, Brokerages, and Other Insurance Related Activities[T]
      52421   Insurance Agencies and Brokerages
      524210 Insurance Agencies and Brokerages
      52429   Other Insurance Related Activities
      524291 Claims Adjusting
      524292 Third Party Administration of Insurance and Pension Funds
      524298 All Other Insurance Related Activities

525   Funds, Trusts, and Other Financial Vehicles

    5251   Insurance and Employee Benefit Funds
      52511   Pension Funds
      525110 Pension Funds
      52512   Health and Welfare Funds
      525120 Health and Welfare Funds
      52519   Other Insurance Funds
      525190 Other Insurance Funds

    5259   Other Investment Pools and Funds
      52591   Open-End Investment Funds
      525910 Open-End Investment Funds
      52592   Trusts, Estates, and Agency Accounts
      525920 Trusts, Estates, and Agency Accounts
      52599   Other Financial Vehicles
      525990 Other Financial Vehicles

Sector 53--Real Estate and Rental and Leasing[T]

531   Real Estate[T]

    5311   Lessors of Real Estate[T]
      53111   Lessors of Residential Buildings and Dwellings
      531110 Lessors of Residential Buildings and Dwellings
      53112   Lessors of Nonresidential Buildings (except Miniwarehouses)
      531120 Lessors of Nonresidential Buildings (except Miniwarehouses)
      53113   Lessors of Miniwarehouses and Self-Storage Units
      531130 Lessors of Miniwarehouses and Self-Storage Units
      53119   Lessors of Other Real Estate Property
      531190 Lessors of Other Real Estate Property

5312   Offices of Real Estate Agents and Brokers[T]
   53121   Offices of Real Estate Agents and Brokers[T]
   531210 Offices of Real Estate Agents and Brokers

5313   Activities Related to Real Estate[T]
   53131   Real Estate Property Managers
   531311 Residential Property Managers
   531312 Nonresidential Property Managers
   53132   Offices of Real Estate Appraisers
   531320 Offices of Real Estate Appraisers
   53139   Other Activities Related to Real Estate
   531390 Other Activities Related to Real Estate

532   Rental and Leasing Services[T]

5321   Automotive Equipment Rental and Leasing[T]
   53211   Passenger Car Rental and Leasing[T]
   532111 Passenger Car Rental
   532112 Passenger Car Leasing
   53212   Truck, Utility Trailer, and RV (Recreational Vehicle) Rental and Leasing[T]
   532120 Truck, Utility Trailer, and RV (Recreational Vehicle) Rental and Leasing

5322   Consumer Goods Rental[T]
   53221   Consumer Electronics and Appliances Rental[T]
   532210 Consumer Electronics and Appliances Rental
   53228   Other Consumer Goods Rental[T]
   532281 Formal Wear and Costume Rental
   532282 Video Tape and Disc Rental
   532283 Home Health Equipment Rental
   532284 Recreational Goods Rental
   532289 All Other Consumer Goods Rental

5323   General Rental Centers[T]
   53231   General Rental Centers[T]
   532310 General Rental Centers

5324   Commercial and Industrial Machinery and Equipment Rental and Leasing[T]
   53241   Construction, Transportation, Mining, and Forestry Machinery and Equipment Rental and Leasing[T]
   532411 Commercial Air, Rail, and Water Transportation Equipment Rental and Leasing
   532412 Construction, Mining, and Forestry Machinery and Equipment Rental and Leasing
   53242   Office Machinery and Equipment Rental and Leasing[T]
   532420 Office Machinery and Equipment Rental and Leasing
   53249   Other Commercial and Industrial Machinery and Equipment Rental and Leasing[T]
   532490 Other Commercial and Industrial Machinery and Equipment Rental and Leasing

533   Lessors of Nonfinancial Intangible Assets (except Copyrighted Works)[T]

5331   Lessors of Nonfinancial Intangible Assets (except Copyrighted Works)[T]
   53311   Lessors of Nonfinancial Intangible Assets (except Copyrighted Works)[T]
   533110 Lessors of Nonfinancial Intangible Assets (except Copyrighted Works)

Sector 54--Professional, Scientific, and Technical Services[T]

541   Professional, Scientific, and Technical Services[T]

5411   Legal Services[T]
54111   Offices of Lawyers[T]
541110   Offices of Lawyers
54112   Offices of Notaries[T]
541120   Offices of Notaries
54119   Other Legal Services[T]
541191   Title Abstract and Settlement Offices
541199   All Other Legal Services

5412   Accounting, Tax Preparation, Bookkeeping, and Payroll Services[T]
54121   Accounting, Tax Preparation, Bookkeeping, and Payroll Services[T]
541211   Offices of Certified Public Accountants
541213   Tax Preparation Services
541214   Payroll Services
541219   Other Accounting Services

5413   Architectural, Engineering, and Related Services[T]
54131   Architectural Services[T]
541310   Architectural Services
54132   Landscape Architectural Services[T]
541320   Landscape Architectural Services
54133   Engineering Services[T]
541330   Engineering Services
54134   Drafting Services[T]
541340   Drafting Services
54135   Building Inspection Services[T]
541350   Building Inspection Services
54136   Geophysical Surveying and Mapping Services[T]
541360   Geophysical Surveying and Mapping Services
54137   Surveying and Mapping (except Geophysical) Services[T]
541370   Surveying and Mapping (except Geophysical) Services
54138   Testing Laboratories[T]
541380   Testing Laboratories

5414   Specialized Design Services[T]
54141   Interior Design Services[T]
541410   Interior Design Services
54142   Industrial Design Services[T]
541420   Industrial Design Services
54143   Graphic Design Services[T]
541430   Graphic Design Services
54149   Other Specialized Design Services[T]
541490   Other Specialized Design Services

5415   Computer Systems Design and Related Services[T]
54151   Computer Systems Design and Related Services[T]
541511   Custom Computer Programming Services
541512   Computer Systems Design Services
541513   Computer Facilities Management Services
541519   Other Computer Related Services

5416   Management, Scientific, and Technical Consulting Services[T]
   54161   Management Consulting Services[T]
   541611 Administrative Management and General Management Consulting
         Services
   541612 Human Resources Consulting Services
   541613 Marketing Consulting Services
   541614 Process, Physical Distribution, and Logistics Consulting Services
   541618 Other Management Consulting Services
   54162   Environmental Consulting Services[T]
   541620 Environmental Consulting Services
   54169   Other Scientific and Technical Consulting Services[T]
   541690 Other Scientific and Technical Consulting Services

5417   Scientific Research and Development Services[T]
   54171   Research and Development in the Physical, Engineering, and Life Sciences[T]
   541713 Research and Development in Nanotechnology
   541714 Research and Development in Biotechnology (except Nanobiotechnology)
   541715 Research and Development in the Physical, Engineering, and Life Sciences
         (except Nanotechnology and Biotechnology)
   54172   Research and Development in the Social Sciences and Humanities[T]
   541720 Research and Development in the Social Sciences and Humanities

5418   Advertising, Public Relations, and Related Services[T]
   54181   Advertising Agencies[T]
   541810 Advertising Agencies
   54182   Public Relations Agencies[T]
   541820 Public Relations Agencies
   54183   Media Buying Agencies[T]
   541830 Media Buying Agencies
   54184   Media Representatives[T]
   541840 Media Representatives
   54185   Outdoor Advertising[T]
   541850 Outdoor Advertising
   54186   Direct Mail Advertising[T]
   541860 Direct Mail Advertising
   54187   Advertising Material Distribution Services[T]
   541870 Advertising Material Distribution Services
   54189   Other Services Related to Advertising[T]
   541890 Other Services Related to Advertising

5419   Other Professional, Scientific, and Technical Services[T]
   54191   Marketing Research and Public Opinion Polling[T]
   541910 Marketing Research and Public Opinion Polling
   54192   Photographic Services[T]
   541921 Photography Studios, Portrait
   541922 Commercial Photography
   54193   Translation and Interpretation Services[T]
   541930 Translation and Interpretation Services
   54194   Veterinary Services[T]
   541940 Veterinary Services
   54199   All Other Professional, Scientific, and Technical Services[T]
   541990 All Other Professional, Scientific, and Technical Services

Sector 55--Management of Companies and Enterprises[T]

551   **Management of Companies and Enterprises[T]**

     5511   **Management of Companies and Enterprises[T]**
         55111   Management of Companies and Enterprises[T]
         551111 Offices of Bank Holding Companies
         551112 Offices of Other Holding Companies
         551114 Corporate, Subsidiary, and Regional Managing Offices

Sector 56--Administrative and Support and Waste Management and Remediation Services[T]

561   **Administrative and Support Services[T]**

     5611   **Office Administrative Services[T]**
         56111   Office Administrative Services[T]
         561110 Office Administrative Services

     5612   **Facilities Support Services[T]**
         56121   Facilities Support Services[T]
         561210 Facilities Support Services

     5613   **Employment Services[T]**
         56131   Employment Placement Agencies and Executive Search Services[T]
         561311 Employment Placement Agencies
         561312 Executive Search Services
         56132   Temporary Help Services[T]
         561320 Temporary Help Services
         56133   Professional Employer Organizations[T]
         561330 Professional Employer Organizations

     5614   **Business Support Services[T]**
         56141   Document Preparation Services[T]
         561410 Document Preparation Services
         56142   Telephone Call Centers[T]
         561421 Telephone Answering Services
         561422 Telemarketing Bureaus and Other Contact Centers
         56143   Business Service Centers[T]
         561431 Private Mail Centers
         561439 Other Business Service Centers (including Copy Shops)
         56144   Collection Agencies[T]
         561440 Collection Agencies
         56145   Credit Bureaus[T]
         561450 Credit Bureaus
         56149   Other Business Support Services[T]
         561491 Repossession Services
         561492 Court Reporting and Stenotype Services
         561499 All Other Business Support Services

     5615   **Travel Arrangement and Reservation Services[T]**
         56151   Travel Agencies[T]
         561510 Travel Agencies

56152 Tour Operators[T]
561520 Tour Operators
56159 Other Travel Arrangement and Reservation Services[T]
561591 Convention and Visitors Bureaus
561599 All Other Travel Arrangement and Reservation Services

5616   Investigation and Security Services[T]
56161   Investigation, Guard, and Armored Car Services[T]
561611 Investigation Services
561612 Security Guards and Patrol Services
561613 Armored Car Services
56162   Security Systems Services[T]
561621 Security Systems Services (except Locksmiths)
561622 Locksmiths

5617   Services to Buildings and Dwellings[T]
56171   Exterminating and Pest Control Services[T]
561710 Exterminating and Pest Control Services
56172   Janitorial Services[T]
561720 Janitorial Services
56173   Landscaping Services[T]
561730 Landscaping Services
56174   Carpet and Upholstery Cleaning Services[T]
561740 Carpet and Upholstery Cleaning Services
56179   Other Services to Buildings and Dwellings[T]
561790 Other Services to Buildings and Dwellings

5619   Other Support Services[T]
56191   Packaging and Labeling Services[T]
561910 Packaging and Labeling Services
56192   Convention and Trade Show Organizers[T]
561920 Convention and Trade Show Organizers
56199   All Other Support Services[T]
561990 All Other Support Services

562   Waste Management and Remediation Services[T]

5621   Waste Collection
56211   Waste Collection
562111 Solid Waste Collection
562112 Hazardous Waste Collection
562119 Other Waste Collection

5622   Waste Treatment and Disposal
56221   Waste Treatment and Disposal
562211 Hazardous Waste Treatment and Disposal
562212 Solid Waste Landfill
562213 Solid Waste Combustors and Incinerators
562219 Other Nonhazardous Waste Treatment and Disposal

5629   Remediation and Other Waste Management Services
56291   Remediation Services
562910 Remediation Services
56292   Materials Recovery Facilities
562920 Materials Recovery Facilities
56299   All Other Waste Management Services

562991 Septic Tank and Related Services
562998 All Other Miscellaneous Waste Management Services

Sector 61--Educational Services[T]

611 Educational Services[T]

6111 Elementary and Secondary Schools[T]
61111 Elementary and Secondary Schools
611110 Elementary and Secondary Schools

6112 Junior Colleges[T]
61121 Junior Colleges[T]
611210 Junior Colleges

6113 Colleges, Universities, and Professional Schools[T]
61131 Colleges, Universities, and Professional Schools[T]
611310 Colleges, Universities, and Professional Schools

6114 Business Schools and Computer and Management Training[T]
61141 Business and Secretarial Schools[T]
611410 Business and Secretarial Schools
61142 Computer Training[T]
611420 Computer Training
61143 Professional and Management Development Training[T]
611430 Professional and Management Development Training

6115 Technical and Trade Schools[T]
61151 Technical and Trade Schools[T]
611511 Cosmetology and Barber Schools
611512 Flight Training
611513 Apprenticeship Training
611519 Other Technical and Trade Schools

6116 Other Schools and Instruction[T]
61161 Fine Arts Schools[T]
611610 Fine Arts Schools
61162 Sports and Recreation Instruction[T]
611620 Sports and Recreation Instruction
61163 Language Schools[T]
611630 Language Schools
61169 All Other Schools and Instruction[T]
611691 Exam Preparation and Tutoring
611692 Automobile Driving Schools
611699 All Other Miscellaneous Schools and Instruction

6117 Educational Support Services[T]
61171 Educational Support Services[T]
611710 Educational Support Services

Sector 62--Health Care and Social Assistance[T]

621 Ambulatory Health Care Services[T]

6211   Offices of Physicians[T]
62111   Offices of Physicians[T]
621111   Offices of Physicians (except Mental Health Specialists)
621112   Offices of Physicians, Mental Health Specialists

6212   Offices of Dentists[T]
62121   Offices of Dentists[T]
621210   Offices of Dentists

6213   Offices of Other Health Practitioners[T]
62131   Offices of Chiropractors[T]
621310   Offices of Chiropractors
62132   Offices of Optometrists[T]
621320   Offices of Optometrists
62133   Offices of Mental Health Practitioners (except Physicians)[T]
621330   Offices of Mental Health Practitioners (except Physicians)
62134   Offices of Physical, Occupational and Speech Therapists, and Audiologists[T]
621340   Offices of Physical, Occupational and Speech Therapists, and Audiologists
62139   Offices of All Other Health Practitioners[T]
621391   Offices of Podiatrists
621399   Offices of All Other Miscellaneous Health Practitioners

6214   Outpatient Care Centers[T]
62141   Family Planning Centers[T]
621410   Family Planning Centers
62142   Outpatient Mental Health and Substance Abuse Centers[T]
621420   Outpatient Mental Health and Substance Abuse Centers
62149   Other Outpatient Care Centers[T]
621491   HMO Medical Centers
621492   Kidney Dialysis Centers
621493   Freestanding Ambulatory Surgical and Emergency Centers
621498   All Other Outpatient Care Centers

6215   Medical and Diagnostic Laboratories[T]
62151   Medical and Diagnostic Laboratories[T]
621511   Medical Laboratories
621512   Diagnostic Imaging Centers

6216   Home Health Care Services[T]
62161   Home Health Care Services[T]
621610   Home Health Care Services

6219   Other Ambulatory Health Care Services[T]
62191   Ambulance Services[T]
621910   Ambulance Services
62199   All Other Ambulatory Health Care Services[T]
621991   Blood and Organ Banks
621999   All Other Miscellaneous Ambulatory Health Care Services

622   Hospitals[T]

6221   General Medical and Surgical Hospitals[T]
62211   General Medical and Surgical Hospitals[T]
622110   General Medical and Surgical Hospitals

6222   Psychiatric and Substance Abuse Hospitals[T]
    62221   Psychiatric and Substance Abuse Hospitals[T]
    622210 Psychiatric and Substance Abuse Hospitals

6223   Specialty (except Psychiatric and Substance Abuse) Hospitals[T]
    62231   Specialty (except Psychiatric and Substance Abuse) Hospitals[T]
    622310 Specialty (except Psychiatric and Substance Abuse) Hospitals

623   Nursing and Residential Care Facilities[T]

6231   Nursing Care Facilities (Skilled Nursing Facilities)[T]
    62311   Nursing Care Facilities (Skilled Nursing Facilities)[T]
    623110 Nursing Care Facilities (Skilled Nursing Facilities)

6232   Residential Intellectual and Developmental Disability, Mental Health, and Substance Abuse Facilities[T]
    62321   Residential Intellectual and Developmental Disability Facilities[T]
    623210 Residential Intellectual and Developmental Disability Facilities
    62322   Residential Mental Health and Substance Abuse Facilities[T]
    623220 Residential Mental Health and Substance Abuse Facilities

6233   Continuing Care Retirement Communities and Assisted Living Facilities for the Elderly[T]
    62331   Continuing Care Retirement Communities and Assisted Living Facilities for the Elderly[T]
    623311 Continuing Care Retirement Communities
    623312 Assisted Living Facilities for the Elderly

6239   Other Residential Care Facilities[T]
    62399   Other Residential Care Facilities[T]
    623990 Other Residential Care Facilities

624   Social Assistance[T]

6241   Individual and Family Services[T]
    62411   Child and Youth Services[T]
    624110 Child and Youth Services
    62412   Services for the Elderly and Persons with Disabilities[T]
    624120 Services for the Elderly and Persons with Disabilities
    62419   Other Individual and Family Services[T]
    624190 Other Individual and Family Services

6242   Community Food and Housing, and Emergency and Other Relief Services[T]
    62421   Community Food Services[T]
    624210 Community Food Services
    62422   Community Housing Services[T]
    624221 Temporary Shelters
    624229 Other Community Housing Services
    62423   Emergency and Other Relief Services[T]
    624230 Emergency and Other Relief Services

6243   Vocational Rehabilitation Services[T]
    62431   Vocational Rehabilitation Services[T]
    624310 Vocational Rehabilitation Services

6244   Child Day Care Services[T]
    62441   Child Day Care Services[T]
    624410 Child Day Care Services

Sector 71--Arts, Entertainment, and Recreation[T]

711   Performing Arts, Spectator Sports, and Related Industries[T]

7111   Performing Arts Companies[T]
    71111   Theater Companies and Dinner Theaters[T]
    711110 Theater Companies and Dinner Theaters
    71112   Dance Companies[T]
    711120 Dance Companies
    71113   Musical Groups and Artists[T]
    711130 Musical Groups and Artists
    71119   Other Performing Arts Companies[T]
    711190 Other Performing Arts Companies

7112   Spectator Sports[T]
    71121   Spectator Sports[T]
    711211 Sports Teams and Clubs
    711212 Racetracks
    711219 Other Spectator Sports

7113   Promoters of Performing Arts, Sports, and Similar Events[T]
    71131   Promoters of Performing Arts, Sports, and Similar Events with Facilities[T]
    711310 Promoters of Performing Arts, Sports, and Similar Events with Facilities
    71132   Promoters of Performing Arts, Sports, and Similar Events without Facilities[T]
    711320 Promoters of Performing Arts, Sports, and Similar Events without Facilities

7114   Agents and Managers for Artists, Athletes, Entertainers, and Other Public Figures[T]
    71141   Agents and Managers for Artists, Athletes, Entertainers, and Other Public
              Figures[T]
    711410 Agents and Managers for Artists, Athletes, Entertainers, and Other Public
              Figures

7115   Independent Artists, Writers, and Performers[T]
    71151   Independent Artists, Writers, and Performers[T]
    711510 Independent Artists, Writers, and Performers

712   Museums, Historical Sites, and Similar Institutions[T]

7121   Museums, Historical Sites, and Similar Institutions[T]
    71211   Museums[T]
    712110 Museums
    71212   Historical Sites[T]
    712120 Historical Sites
    71213   Zoos and Botanical Gardens[T]
    712130 Zoos and Botanical Gardens
    71219   Nature Parks and Other Similar Institutions[T]
    712190 Nature Parks and Other Similar Institutions

713   Amusement, Gambling, and Recreation Industries[T]

7131   Amusement Parks and Arcades[T]
71311   Amusement and Theme Parks[T]
713110 Amusement and Theme Parks
71312   Amusement Arcades[T]
713120 Amusement Arcades

7132   Gambling Industries[T]
71321   Casinos (except Casino Hotels)[T]
713210 Casinos (except Casino Hotels)
71329   Other Gambling Industries[T]
713290 Other Gambling Industries

7139   Other Amusement and Recreation Industries[T]
71391   Golf Courses and Country Clubs[T]
713910 Golf Courses and Country Clubs
71392   Skiing Facilities[T]
713920 Skiing Facilities
71393   Marinas[T]
713930 Marinas
71394   Fitness and Recreational Sports Centers[T]
713940 Fitness and Recreational Sports Centers
71395   Bowling Centers[T]
713950 Bowling Centers
71399   All Other Amusement and Recreation Industries[T]
713990 All Other Amusement and Recreation Industries

Sector 72--Accommodation and Food Services[T]

721   Accommodation[T]

7211   Traveler Accommodation[T]
72111   Hotels (except Casino Hotels) and Motels[T]
721110 Hotels (except Casino Hotels) and Motels
72112   Casino Hotels[T]
721120 Casino Hotels
72119   Other Traveler Accommodation[T]
721191 Bed-and-Breakfast Inns
721199 All Other Traveler Accommodation

7212   RV (Recreational Vehicle) Parks and Recreational Camps[T]
72121   RV (Recreational Vehicle) Parks and Recreational Camps[T]
721211 RV (Recreational Vehicle) Parks and Campgrounds
721214 Recreational and Vacation Camps (except Campgrounds)

7213   Rooming and Boarding Houses, Dormitories, and Workers' Camps[T]
72131   Rooming and Boarding Houses, Dormitories, and Workers' Camps[T]
721310 Rooming and Boarding Houses, Dormitories, and Workers' Camps

722   Food Services and Drinking Places[T]

7223   Special Food Services[T]
72231   Food Service Contractors[T]
722310 Food Service Contractors

72232 Caterers[T]
722320 Caterers
72233 Mobile Food Services[T]
722330 Mobile Food Services

7224   Drinking Places (Alcoholic Beverages)[T]
72241   Drinking Places (Alcoholic Beverages)[T]
722410 Drinking Places (Alcoholic Beverages)

7225   Restaurants and Other Eating Places[T]
72251   Restaurants and Other Eating Places[T]
722511 Full-Service Restaurants
722513 Limited-Service Restaurants
722514 Cafeterias, Grill Buffets, and Buffets
722515 Snack and Nonalcoholic Beverage Bars

Sector 81--Other Services (except Public Administration)[T]

811   Repair and Maintenance[T]

8111   Automotive Repair and Maintenance[T]
81111   Automotive Mechanical and Electrical Repair and Maintenance[T]
811111 General Automotive Repair
811112 Automotive Exhaust System Repair
811113 Automotive Transmission Repair
811118 Other Automotive Mechanical and Electrical Repair and Maintenance
81112   Automotive Body, Paint, Interior, and Glass Repair[T]
811121 Automotive Body, Paint, and Interior Repair and Maintenance
811122 Automotive Glass Replacement Shops
81119   Other Automotive Repair and Maintenance[T]
811191 Automotive Oil Change and Lubrication Shops
811192 Car Washes
811198 All Other Automotive Repair and Maintenance

8112   Electronic and Precision Equipment Repair and Maintenance[T]
81121   Electronic and Precision Equipment Repair and Maintenance[T]
811211 Consumer Electronics Repair and Maintenance
811212 Computer and Office Machine Repair and Maintenance
811213 Communication Equipment Repair and Maintenance
811219 Other Electronic and Precision Equipment Repair and Maintenance

8113   Commercial and Industrial Machinery and Equipment (except Automotive and Electronic) Repair and Maintenance[T]
81131   Commercial and Industrial Machinery and Equipment (except Automotive and Electronic) Repair and Maintenance[T]
811310 Commercial and Industrial Machinery and Equipment (except Automotive and Electronic) Repair and Maintenance

8114   Personal and Household Goods Repair and Maintenance[T]
81141   Home and Garden Equipment and Appliance Repair and Maintenance[T]
811411 Home and Garden Equipment Repair and Maintenance
811412 Appliance Repair and Maintenance
81142   Reupholstery and Furniture Repair[T]
811420 Reupholstery and Furniture Repair

81143   Footwear and Leather Goods Repair[T]
811430 Footwear and Leather Goods Repair
81149   Other Personal and Household Goods Repair and Maintenance[T]
811490 Other Personal and Household Goods Repair and Maintenance

812   Personal and Laundry Services[T]

8121   Personal Care Services
81211   Hair, Nail, and Skin Care Services
812111 Barber Shops
812112 Beauty Salons
812113 Nail Salons
81219   Other Personal Care Services
812191 Diet and Weight Reducing Centers
812199 Other Personal Care Services

8122   Death Care Services
81221   Funeral Homes and Funeral Services
812210 Funeral Homes and Funeral Services
81222   Cemeteries and Crematories
812220 Cemeteries and Crematories

8123   Drycleaning and Laundry Services
81231   Coin-Operated Laundries and Drycleaners
812310 Coin-Operated Laundries and Drycleaners
81232   Drycleaning and Laundry Services (except Coin-Operated)
812320 Drycleaning and Laundry Services (except Coin-Operated)
81233   Linen and Uniform Supply
812331 Linen Supply
812332 Industrial Launderers

8129   Other Personal Services
81291   Pet Care (except Veterinary) Services
812910 Pet Care (except Veterinary) Services
81292   Photofinishing
812921 Photofinishing Laboratories (except One-Hour)
812922 One-Hour Photofinishing
81293   Parking Lots and Garages
812930 Parking Lots and Garages
81299   All Other Personal Services
812990 All Other Personal Services

813   Religious, Grantmaking, Civic, Professional, and Similar Organizations[T]

8131   Religious Organizations
81311   Religious Organizations
813110 Religious Organizations

8132   Grantmaking and Giving Services
81321   Grantmaking and Giving Services
813211 Grantmaking Foundations
813212 Voluntary Health Organizations
813219 Other Grantmaking and Giving Services

8133   Social Advocacy Organizations
    81331   Social Advocacy Organizations
    813311 Human Rights Organizations
    813312 Environment, Conservation and Wildlife Organizations
    813319 Other Social Advocacy Organizations

8134   Civic and Social Organizations
    81341   Civic and Social Organizations
    813410 Civic and Social Organizations

8139   Business, Professional, Labor, Political, and Similar Organizations
    81391   Business Associations
    813910 Business Associations
    81392   Professional Organizations
    813920 Professional Organizations
    81393   Labor Unions and Similar Labor Organizations
    813930 Labor Unions and Similar Labor Organizations
    81394   Political Organizations
    813940 Political Organizations
    81399   Other Similar Organizations (except Business, Professional, Labor, and Political Organizations)
    813990 Other Similar Organizations (except Business, Professional, Labor, and Political Organizations)

814   Private Households[T]

8141   Private Households[T]
    81411   Private Households[T]
    814110 Private Households

Sector 92--Public Administration[T]

921   Executive, Legislative, and Other General Government Support

9211   Executive, Legislative, and Other General Government Support
    92111   Executive Offices
    921110 Executive Offices
    92112   Legislative Bodies
    921120 Legislative Bodies
    92113   Public Finance Activities
    921130 Public Finance Activities
    92114   Executive and Legislative Offices, Combined
    921140 Executive and Legislative Offices, Combined
    92115   American Indian and Alaska Native Tribal Governments
    921150 American Indian and Alaska Native Tribal Governments
    92119   Other General Government Support
    921190 Other General Government Support

922   Justice, Public Order, and Safety Activities

9221   Justice, Public Order, and Safety Activities
    92211   Courts
    922110 Courts
    92212   Police Protection
    922120 Police Protection

92213	Legal Counsel and Prosecution
922130	Legal Counsel and Prosecution
92214	Correctional Institutions
922140	Correctional Institutions
92215	Parole Offices and Probation Offices
922150	Parole Offices and Probation Offices
92216	Fire Protection
922160	Fire Protection
92219	Other Justice, Public Order, and Safety Activities
922190	Other Justice, Public Order, and Safety Activities

923   Administration of Human Resource Programs

9231   Administration of Human Resource Programs

92311	Administration of Education Programs
923110	Administration of Education Programs
92312	Administration of Public Health Programs
923120	Administration of Public Health Programs
92313	Administration of Human Resource Programs (except Education, Public Health, and Veterans' Affairs Programs)
923130	Administration of Human Resource Programs (except Education, Public Health, and Veterans' Affairs Programs)
92314	Administration of Veterans' Affairs
923140	Administration of Veterans' Affairs

924   Administration of Environmental Quality Programs

9241   Administration of Environmental Quality Programs

92411	Administration of Air and Water Resource and Solid Waste Management Programs
924110	Administration of Air and Water Resource and Solid Waste Management Programs
92412	Administration of Conservation Programs
924120	Administration of Conservation Programs

925   Administration of Housing Programs, Urban Planning, and Community Development

9251   Administration of Housing Programs, Urban Planning, and Community Development

92511	Administration of Housing Programs
925110	Administration of Housing Programs
92512	Administration of Urban Planning and Community and Rural Development
925120	Administration of Urban Planning and Community and Rural Development

926   Administration of Economic Programs

9261   Administration of Economic Programs

92611	Administration of General Economic Programs
926110	Administration of General Economic Programs
92612	Regulation and Administration of Transportation Programs
926120	Regulation and Administration of Transportation Programs

92613 Regulation and Administration of Communications, Electric, Gas, and Other
      Utilities
926130 Regulation and Administration of Communications, Electric, Gas, and Other
      Utilities
92614 Regulation of Agricultural Marketing and Commodities
926140 Regulation of Agricultural Marketing and Commodities
92615 Regulation, Licensing, and Inspection of Miscellaneous Commercial
      Sectors
926150 Regulation, Licensing, and Inspection of Miscellaneous Commercial
      Sectors

927   Space Research and Technology

9271   Space Research and Technology
92711   Space Research and Technology
927110 Space Research and Technology

928   National Security and International Affairs

9281   National Security and International Affairs
92811   National Security
928110 National Security
92812   International Affairs
928120 International Affairs

Frequently Asked Questions About Economic Classifications

1. What is the purpose of an industry classification system?
   - An industry classification system facilitates the collection, tabulation, presentation, and analysis of data relating to establishments and ensures that data about the U.S. economy published by U.S. statistical agencies are uniform and comparable. NAICS ensures that such data are uniform and comparable among Canada, Mexico, and the United States.

2. What is an establishment?
   - An establishment is generally a single, physical location at which economic activity occurs (e.g., store, factory, farm, etc.). An enterprise consists of one or more locations that are more than 50 percent owned by the same entity performing the same or different types of economic activities. Each establishment of that enterprise is assigned a NAICS code, based on its own primary activity.

3. How can I determine the correct NAICS code for my business?
   - To determine the correct NAICS code for your establishment, first identify the primary business activity. Then refer either to: 1) the NAICS United States Structure near the beginning of the manual to search the titles from the 2-digit level down through the 6-digit, more detailed level, to find the appropriate code; or 2) the Alphabetic Index at the back of the book to search alphabetically for the primary activity and its corresponding code. Next, turn to the industry description of the specified code in Part I of the manual, read the full description of the industry (including the narrative, cross-references, and illustrative examples), and determine if that description fits the activities of your establishment. Electronic references are available at census.gov/naics.

4. Who assigns NAICS codes to businesses and how?
   - There is no central government agency with the role of assigning, monitoring, or approving NAICS codes for establishments. Different agencies maintain their own lists of business establishments to meet their own programmatic needs. These different agencies use their own methods for assigning NAICS codes to the establishments on their lists. Statistical agencies assign one NAICS code to each establishment based on its primary activity. For example, the Social Security Administration assigns a NAICS code to new businesses based on information provided on their application for an Employer Identification Number. The Census Bureau generally assigns NAICS codes to businesses on its list of establishments based on information provided by the business on a survey or census report form. The Bureau of Labor Statistics initially assigns NAICS codes based on business activity information provided on an application for unemployment insurance.

5. How do I apply for a NAICS code?
   - A business does not 'apply' for a NAICS code. As explained above, statistical agencies generally assign NAICS codes based on information provided by a business on an application form, an administrative report, or on a survey or census report form.

6. How can I get a new NAICS code created for my type of business?
- Every five years NAICS is reviewed for potential revisions, so that the classification system can keep pace with the changing economy. This is the only time that new NAICS codes can be considered. The Office of Management and Budget (OMB), through its Economic Classification Policy Committee (ECPC), will solicit public comments regarding changes to NAICS through a notice published in the **Federal Register**. The notice will provide details of the format in which comments should be submitted, how and to whom they should be submitted, and the deadline for submission. Generally, the comment period will close 90 days after publication of the notice. During that time, suggestions for new and emerging industries can be submitted to the ECPC. The next scheduled review of NAICS will be for a potential 2022 revision.

7. What is the relationship between NAICS and the Small Business Administration's (SBA) size standards?
- NAICS categories do not distinguish between small and large business, or between for-profit and non-profit. The Small Business Administration (SBA) develops size standards for each NAICS category. To find more information about the SBA size standards, or when the SBA will update their size standards to reflect 2017 NAICS revisions, visit the SBA Web site at www.sba.gov/size/indexsize.html. You may also contact SBA's Office of Size Standards on 202-205-6618 or via email to sizestandards@sba.gov.

8. How do the NAICS codes affect federal procurement and regulatory activities, such as those carried out by the Environmental Protection Agency, OSHA, the Department of Defense, and the General Services Administration?
- NAICS was developed specifically for the collection and publication of statistical data to foster the comparability of economic estimates for Canada, Mexico, and the United States. The NAICS categories and definitions were not developed to meet the needs of procurement and/or regulatory applications. However, other federal agencies and other organizations have adopted NAICS for procurement and regulatory purposes even though it does not entirely fit their specific needs. For questions regarding these agencies' use of the NAICS system, contact the specific agency.

For answers to other NAICS questions, you may visit the NAICS Web site at census.gov/naics.

Part I
Titles and Descriptions of Industries

Sector 11--Agriculture, Forestry, Fishing and Hunting[T]

The Sector as a Whole

The Agriculture, Forestry, Fishing and Hunting sector comprises establishments primarily engaged in growing crops, raising animals, harvesting timber, and harvesting fish and other animals from a farm, ranch, or their natural habitats.

The establishments in this sector are often described as farms, ranches, dairies, greenhouses, nurseries, orchards, or hatcheries. A farm may consist of a single tract of land or a number of separate tracts which may be held under different tenures. For example, one tract may be owned by the farm operator and another rented. It may be operated by the operator alone or with the assistance of members of the household or hired employees, or it may be operated by a partnership, corporation, or other type of organization. When a landowner has one or more tenants, renters, croppers, or managers, the land operated by each is considered a farm.

The sector distinguishes two basic activities: agricultural production and agricultural support activities. Agricultural production includes establishments performing the complete farm or ranch operation, such as farm owner-operators and tenant farm operators. Agricultural support activities include establishments that perform one or more activities associated with farm operation, such as soil preparation, planting, harvesting, and management, on a contract or fee basis.

Excluded from the Agriculture, Forestry, Fishing and Hunting sector are establishments primarily engaged in agricultural research and establishments primarily engaged in administering programs for regulating and conserving land, mineral, wildlife, and forest use. These establishments are classified in Industry 54171, Research and Development in the Physical, Engineering, and Life Sciences; and Industry 92412, Administration of Conservation Programs, respectively.

111   Crop Production[T]

Industries in the Crop Production subsector grow crops mainly for food and fiber. The subsector comprises establishments, such as farms, orchards, groves, greenhouses, and nurseries, primarily engaged in growing crops, plants, vines, or trees and their seeds.

The industries in this subsector are grouped by similarity of production activity, including biological and physiological characteristics and economic requirements, the length of growing season, degree of crop rotation, extent of input specialization, labor requirements, and capital demands. The production process is typically completed when the raw product or commodity grown reaches the "farm gate" for market, that is, at the point of first sale or price determination.

Establishments are classified in the Crop Production subsector when crop production (i.e., value of crops for market) accounts for one-half or more of the establishment's total agricultural production. Within the subsector, establishments are classified in a specific industry when a product or industry family of products (i.e., oilseed and grain farming, vegetable and melon farming, fruit and tree nut farming) account for one-half or more of the establishment's agricultural production. Establishments with one-half or more crop production with no one product or family of products of an industry accounting for one-half of the establishment's agricultural production are treated as general combination crop farming and are classified in Industry 11199, All Other Crop Farming.

Industries in the Crop Production subsector include establishments that own, operate, and manage and those that operate and manage. Those that manage only are classified in Subsector 115, Support Activities for Agriculture and Forestry. Establishments that raise aquatic plants in controlled or selected aquatic environments are classified in Subsector 112, Animal Production and Aquaculture.

1111   Oilseed and Grain Farming[T]

This industry group comprises establishments primarily engaged in (1) growing oilseed and/or grain crops and/or (2) producing oilseed and grain seeds. These crops have an annual life cycle and are typically grown in open fields.

11111   Soybean Farming[T]
See industry description for 111110.

T—Canadian, Mexican, and United States industries are comparable.

111110 Soybean Farming

This industry comprises establishments primarily engaged in growing soybeans and/or producing soybean seeds.

Cross-References.

Establishments engaged in growing soybeans in combination with grain(s) with the soybeans or grain(s) not accounting for one-half of the establishment's agricultural production (value of crops for market) are classified in U.S. Industry 111191, Oilseed and Grain Combination Farming.

11112 Oilseed (except Soybean) Farming[T]
See industry description for 111120.

111120 Oilseed (except Soybean) Farming

This industry comprises establishments primarily engaged in growing fibrous oilseed producing plants and/or producing oilseed seeds, such as sunflower, safflower, flax, rape, canola, and sesame.

Cross-References.   Establishments primarily engaged in--

- Growing soybeans--are classified in Industry 111110, Soybean Farming; and
- Growing oilseed(s) in combination with grain(s) with no one oilseed (or family of oilseeds) or grain(s) (or family of grains) accounting for one-half of the establishment's agricultural production (value of crops for market)--are classified in U.S. Industry 111191, Oilseed and Grain Combination Farming.

11113 Dry Pea and Bean Farming[T]
See industry description for 111130.

111130 Dry Pea and Bean Farming

This industry comprises establishments primarily engaged in growing dry peas, beans, and/or lentils.

Cross-References.

Establishments primarily engaged in growing fresh green beans and peas are classified in U.S. Industry 111219, Other Vegetable (except Potato) and Melon Farming.

11114 Wheat Farming[T]
See industry description for 111140.

111140 Wheat Farming

This industry comprises establishments primarily engaged in growing wheat and/or producing wheat seeds.

Cross-References.

Establishments growing wheat in combination with oilseed(s) with the wheat or oilseed(s) not accounting for one-half of the establishment's agricultural production (value of crops for market) are classified in U.S. Industry 111191, Oilseed and Grain Combination Farming.

11115 Corn Farming[T]
See industry description for 111150.

T—Canadian, Mexican, and United States industries are comparable.

111150 Corn Farming

This industry comprises establishments primarily engaged in growing corn (except sweet corn) and/or producing corn seeds.

Cross-References.   Establishments primarily engaged in--

- Growing sweet corn--are classified in U.S. Industry 111219, Other Vegetable (except Potato) and Melon Farming; and
- Growing corn in combination with oilseed(s) with the corn or oilseed(s) not accounting for one-half of the establishment's production (value of crops for market)--are classified in U.S. Industry 111191, Oilseed and Grain Combination Farming.

11116   Rice Farming^T
See industry description for 111160.

111160   Rice Farming

This industry comprises establishments primarily engaged in growing rice (except wild rice) and/or producing rice seeds.

Cross-References.   Establishments primarily engaged in--

- Growing wild rice--are classified in U.S. Industry 111199, All Other Grain Farming; and
- Growing rice in combination with oilseed(s) with the rice or oilseed(s) not accounting for one-half of the establishment's agricultural production (value of crops for market)--are classified in U.S. Industry 111191, Oilseed and Grain Combination Farming.

11119   Other Grain Farming^T

This industry comprises establishments primarily engaged in (1) growing grain(s) and/or producing grain seeds (except wheat, corn, and rice) or (2) growing a combination of grain(s) and oilseed(s) with no one grain (or family of grains) or oilseed (or family of oilseeds) accounting for one-half of the establishment's agricultural production (i.e., value of crops for market). Combination grain(s) and oilseed(s) establishments may produce oilseed(s) and grain(s) seeds and/or grow oilseed(s) and grain(s).

Illustrative Examples:

Barley farming	Oat farming
Rye farming	Wild rice farming
Milo farming	Oilseed and grain combination farming
Sorghum farming	

Cross-References.   Establishments primarily engaged in--

- Growing wheat--are classified in Industry 11114, Wheat Farming;
- Growing corn (except sweet corn)--are classified in Industry 11115, Corn Farming;
- Growing sweet corn--are classified in Industry 11121, Vegetable and Melon Farming; and
- Growing rice (except wild rice)--are classified in Industry 11116, Rice Farming.

111191   Oilseed and Grain Combination Farming

This U.S. industry comprises establishments engaged in growing a combination of oilseed(s) and grain(s) with no one oilseed (or family of oilseeds) or grain (or family of grains) accounting for one-half of the establishment's

---

T—Canadian, Mexican, and United States industries are comparable.

agricultural production (value of crops for market). These establishments may produce oilseed(s) and grain(s) seeds and/or grow oilseed(s) and grain(s).

Cross-References.

Establishments engaged in growing one grain (or family of grains) or oilseed (or family of oilseeds) accounting for one-half of the establishment's agricultural production (i.e., value of crops for market) are classified in Industry Group 1111, Oilseed and Grain Farming, accordingly by the prominent grain(s) or oilseed(s) grown.

111199 All Other Grain Farming

This U.S. industry comprises establishments primarily engaged in growing grains and/or producing grain(s) seeds (except wheat, corn, rice, and oilseed(s) and grain(s) combinations).

Illustrative Examples:

Barley farming	Wild rice farming
Sorghum farming	Rye farming
Oat farming	

Cross-References.   Establishments primarily engaged in--

- Growing wheat--are classified in Industry 111140, Wheat Farming;
- Growing corn (except sweet corn)--are classified in Industry 111150, Corn Farming;
- Growing rice (except wild rice)--are classified in Industry 111160, Rice Farming;
- Growing sweet corn--are classified in U.S. Industry 111219, Other Vegetable (except Potato) and Melon Farming; and
- Growing a combination of grain(s) and oilseed(s) with no one grain (or family of grains) or oilseed (or family of oilseeds) accounting for one-half of the establishment's agricultural production (value of crops for market)--are classified in U.S. Industry 111191, Oilseed and Grain Combination Farming.

1112 Vegetable and Melon Farming[T]

11121 Vegetable and Melon Farming[T]

This industry comprises establishments primarily engaged in one or more of the following: (1) growing vegetable and/or melon crops; (2) producing vegetable and/or melon seeds; and (3) growing vegetable and/or melon bedding plants. The crops included in this industry have an annual growth cycle and are grown in open fields. Climate and cultural practices limit producing areas but often permit the growing of a combination of crops in a year.

Cross-References.   Establishments primarily engaged in--

- Growing sugar beets--are classified in Industry 11199, All Other Crop Farming;
- Growing vegetables and melons under glass or protective cover--are classified in Industry 11141, Food Crops Grown Under Cover;
- Growing dry peas and beans--are classified in Industry 11113, Dry Pea and Bean Farming;
- Growing corn (except sweet corn)--are classified in Industry 11115, Corn Farming;
- Canning, pickling, and/or drying (artificially) vegetables--are classified in Industry 31142, Fruit and Vegetable Canning, Pickling, and Drying; and
- Growing fruit on trees and other fruit-bearing plants (except melons)--are classified in Industry Group 1113, Fruit and Tree Nut Farming.

T—Canadian, Mexican, and United States industries are comparable.

111211 Potato Farming

This U.S. industry comprises establishments primarily engaged in growing potatoes and/or producing seed potatoes.

Cross-References.

Establishments primarily engaged in canning or drying potatoes are classified in Industry 31142, Fruit and Vegetable Canning, Pickling, and Drying.

111219 Other Vegetable (except Potato) and Melon Farming

This U.S. industry comprises establishments primarily engaged in one or more of the following: (1) growing melons and/or vegetables (except potatoes; dry peas; dry beans; field, silage, or seed corn; and sugar beets); (2) producing vegetable and/or melon seeds; and (3) growing vegetable and/or melon bedding plants.

Illustrative Examples:

Carrot farming
Squash farming
Green bean farming
Tomato farming
Watermelon farming

Melon farming (e.g., cantaloupe, casaba, honeydew, watermelon)
Vegetable (except potato) farming
Pepper farming (e.g., bell, chili, green, red, sweet peppers)

Cross-References.   Establishments primarily engaged in--

- Growing potatoes, including sweet potatoes and yams--are classified in U.S. Industry 111211, Potato Farming;
- Growing sugar beets--are classified in U.S. Industry 111991, Sugar Beet Farming;
- Growing vegetables and melons under glass or protective cover--are classified in U.S. Industry 111419, Other Food Crops Grown Under Cover;
- Growing dry peas and beans--are classified in Industry 111130, Dry Pea and Bean Farming;
- Growing corn (except sweet corn)--are classified in Industry 111150, Corn Farming;
- Canning, pickling, and/or drying (artificially) vegetables--are classified in Industry 31142, Fruit and Vegetable Canning, Pickling, and Drying; and
- Growing fruit on trees and other fruit-bearing plants (except melons)--are classified in Industry Group 1113, Fruit and Tree Nut Farming.

1113   Fruit and Tree Nut Farming^T

This industry group comprises establishments primarily engaged in growing fruit and/or tree nut crops. The crops included in this industry group are generally not grown from seeds and have a perennial life cycle.

11131   Orange Groves^T
See industry description for 111310.

111310 Orange Groves

This industry comprises establishments primarily engaged in growing oranges.

11132   Citrus (except Orange) Groves^T
See industry description for 111320.

T—Canadian, Mexican, and United States industries are comparable.

111320 Citrus (except Orange) Groves

This industry comprises establishments primarily engaged in growing citrus fruits (except oranges).

Illustrative Examples:

Citrus groves (except oranges)	Tangelo groves
Mandarin groves	Lemon groves
Grapefruit groves	Tangerine groves

Cross-References.

Establishments primarily engaged in growing oranges are classified in Industry 111310, Orange Groves.

11133   Noncitrus Fruit and Tree Nut Farming[T]

This industry comprises establishments primarily engaged in one or more of the following: (1) growing noncitrus fruits (e.g., apples, grapes, berries, peaches); (2) growing tree nuts (e.g., pecans, almonds, pistachios); or (3) growing a combination of fruit(s) and tree nut(s) with no one fruit (or family of fruit) or family of tree nuts accounting for one-half of the establishment's agricultural production (i.e., value of crops for market).

Cross-References.   Establishments primarily engaged in--

- Harvesting berries or nuts from native and non-cultivated plants--are classified in Industry 11321, Forest Nurseries and Gathering of Forest Products; and
- Canning and/or drying (artificially) fruit--are classified in Industry 31142, Fruit and Vegetable Canning, Pickling, and Drying.

111331   Apple Orchards

This U.S. industry comprises establishments primarily engaged in growing apples.

Cross-References.

Establishments engaged in growing apples in combination with tree nut(s) with the apples or family of tree nuts not accounting for one-half of the establishment's agricultural production (i.e., value of crops for market) are classified in U.S. Industry 111336, Fruit and Tree Nut Combination Farming.

111332 Grape Vineyards

This U.S. industry comprises establishments primarily engaged in growing grapes and/or growing grapes to sun dry into raisins.

Cross-References.   Establishments primarily engaged in--

- Drying grapes artificially--are classified in U.S. Industry 311423, Dried and Dehydrated Food Manufacturing; and
- Growing grapes in combination with tree nut(s) with the grapes or family of tree nuts not accounting for one-half of the establishment's agricultural production (i.e., value of crops for market)--are classified in U.S. Industry 111336, Fruit and Tree Nut Combination Farming.

111333 Strawberry Farming

This U.S. industry comprises establishments primarily engaged in growing strawberries.

T—Canadian, Mexican, and United States industries are comparable.

Cross-References

Establishments engaged in growing strawberries in combination with tree nut(s) with the strawberries or family of tree nuts not accounting for one-half of the establishment's agricultural production (i.e., value of crops for market) are classified in U.S. Industry 111336, Fruit and Tree Nut Combination Farming.

111334 Berry (except Strawberry) Farming

This U.S. industry comprises establishments primarily engaged in growing berries.

Illustrative Examples:

Berry (except strawberries) farming	Currant farming
Cranberry farming	Blueberry farming
Blackberry farming	Raspberry farming

Cross-References.   Establishments primarily engaged in--

- Growing strawberries--are classified in U.S. Industry 111333, Strawberry Farming;
- Harvesting berries from native and non-cultivated bushes or vines--are classified in Industry 113210, Forest Nurseries and Gathering of Forest Products; and
- Growing berries in combination with tree nut(s) with the berries or family of tree nuts not accounting for one-half of the establishment's agricultural production (i.e., value of crops for market)--are classified in U.S. Industry 111336, Fruit and Tree Nut Combination Farming.

111335 Tree Nut Farming

This U.S. industry comprises establishments primarily engaged in growing tree nuts.

Illustrative Examples:

Almond farming	Macadamia farming
Pistachio farming	Walnut farming
Filbert farming	Pecan farming
Tree nut farming	

Cross-References.   Establishments primarily engaged in--

- Growing coconut and coffee--are classified in U.S. Industry 111339, Other Noncitrus Fruit Farming; and
- Growing tree nut(s) in combination with fruit(s) with no one fruit (or family of fruit or of tree nuts) accounting for one-half of the establishment's agricultural production (i.e., value of crops for market)--are classified in U.S. Industry 111336, Fruit and Tree Nut Combination Farming.

111336 Fruit and Tree Nut Combination Farming

This U.S. industry comprises establishments primarily engaged in growing a combination of fruit(s) and tree nut(s) with no one fruit (or family of fruit) or family of tree nuts accounting for one-half of the establishment's agricultural production (i.e., value of crops for market).

Cross-References.

Establishments engaged in growing fruit(s) or the family of tree nut(s) accounting for one-half of the establishment's agricultural production (i.e., value of crops for market) are classified in Industry Group 1113, Fruit and Tree Nut Farming, accordingly by the prominent fruit(s) or tree nut(s) grown.

T—Canadian, Mexican, and United States industries are comparable.

111339 Other Noncitrus Fruit Farming

This U.S. industry comprises establishments primarily engaged in growing noncitrus fruits (except apples, grapes, berries, and fruit(s) and tree nut(s) combinations).

Illustrative Examples:

Apricot farming	Peach farming
Fig farming	Coffee farming
Banana farming	Pineapple farming
Noncitrus fruit farming	Date farming
Cherry farming	Prune farming

Cross-References.   Establishments primarily engaged in--

- Growing apples--are classified in U.S. Industry 111331, Apple Orchards;
- Growing grapes including sun drying of grapes into raisins--are classified in U.S. Industry 111332, Grape Vineyards;
- Growing strawberries--are classified in U.S. Industry 111333, Strawberry Farming;
- Growing berries (except strawberries)--are classified in U.S. Industry 111334, Berry (except Strawberry) Farming;
- Drying fruit artificially--are classified in U.S. Industry 311423, Dried and Dehydrated Food Manufacturing; and
- Growing noncitrus fruit(s) in combination with tree nut(s) with no one fruit (or family of fruits) or family of tree nuts accounting for one-half of the establishment's agricultural production (i.e., value of crops for market)--are classified in U.S. Industry 111336, Fruit and Tree Nut Combination Farming.

1114 Greenhouse, Nursery, and Floriculture Production[T]

This industry group comprises establishments primarily engaged in growing crops of any kind under cover and/or growing nursery stock and flowers. "Under cover" is generally defined as greenhouses, cold frames, cloth houses, and lath houses. The crops grown are removed at various stages of maturity and have annual and perennial life cycles. The nursery stock includes short rotation woody crops that have growth cycles of 10 years or less.

11141 Food Crops Grown Under Cover[T]

This industry comprises establishments primarily engaged in growing food crops (e.g., fruits, melons, tomatoes) under glass or protective cover.

Cross-References.

Establishments primarily engaged in growing vegetable and melon bedding plants are classified in Industry 11121, Vegetable and Melon Farming.

111411 Mushroom Production

This U.S. industry comprises establishments primarily engaged in growing mushrooms under cover in mines underground, or in other controlled environments.

111419 Other Food Crops Grown Under Cover

This U.S. industry comprises establishments primarily engaged in growing food crops (except mushrooms) under glass or protective cover.

T—Canadian, Mexican, and United States industries are comparable.

Illustrative Examples:

Alfalfa sprout farming, grown under cover	Vegetable farming, grown under cover
Melon farming, grown under cover	Hydroponic crop farming
	Fruit farming, grown under cover

Cross-References.

Establishments primarily engaged in growing mushrooms under cover are classified in U.S. Industry 111411, Mushroom Production.

11142   Nursery and Floriculture Production[T]

This industry comprises establishments primarily engaged in (1) growing nursery and floriculture products (e.g., nursery stock, shrubbery, cut flowers, flower seeds, foliage plants) under cover or in open fields and/or (2) growing short rotation woody trees with a growing and harvesting cycle of 10 years or less for pulp or tree stock (e.g., cut Christmas trees, cottonwoods).

Cross-References.   Establishments primarily engaged in--

- Growing vegetable and melon bedding plants--are classified in Industry 11121, Vegetable and Melon Farming;
- Operating timber tracts (i.e., growing cycle greater than 10 years)--are classified in Industry 11311, Timber Tract Operations; and
- Retailing nursery, tree stock, and floriculture products primarily purchased from others--are classified in Industry 44422, Nursery, Garden Center, and Farm Supply Stores.

111421   Nursery and Tree Production

This U.S. industry comprises establishments primarily engaged in (1) growing nursery products, nursery stock, shrubbery, bulbs, fruit stock, sod, and so forth, under cover or in open fields and/or (2) growing short rotation woody trees with a growth and harvest cycle of 10 years or less for pulp or tree stock.

Cross-References.   Establishments primarily engaged in--

- Growing vegetable and melon bedding plants--are classified in Industry 11121, Vegetable and Melon Farming;
- Operating timber tracts (i.e., growing cycle greater than 10 years)--are classified in Industry 113110, Timber Tract Operations; and
- Retailing nursery, tree stock, and floriculture products primarily purchased from others--are classified in Industry 444220, Nursery, Garden Center, and Farm Supply Stores.

111422   Floriculture Production

This U.S. industry comprises establishments primarily engaged in growing and/or producing floriculture products (e.g., cut flowers and roses, cut cultivated greens, potted flowering and foliage plants, and flower seeds) under cover and in open fields.

Cross-References.

Establishments primarily engaged in retailing floriculture products primarily purchased from others are classified in Industry 444220, Nursery, Garden Center, and Farm Supply Stores.

T—Canadian, Mexican, and United States industries are comparable.

1119 Other Crop Farming[T]

This industry group comprises establishments primarily engaged in (1) growing crops (except oilseed and/or grain; vegetable and/or melon; fruit and tree nut; and greenhouse, nursery, and/or floriculture products), such as tobacco, cotton, sugarcane, hay, sugar beets, peanuts, agave, herbs and spices, and hay and grass seeds, or (2) growing a combination of crops (except a combination of oilseed(s) and grain(s) and a combination of fruit(s) and tree nut(s)).

11191 Tobacco Farming[T]
See industry description for 111910.

111910 Tobacco Farming

This industry comprises establishments primarily engaged in growing tobacco.

11192 Cotton Farming[T]
See industry description for 111920.

111920 Cotton Farming

This industry comprises establishments primarily engaged in growing cotton.

Cross-References.

Establishments primarily engaged in ginning cotton are classified in U.S. Industry 115111, Cotton Ginning.

11193 Sugarcane Farming[T]
See industry description for 111930.

111930 Sugarcane Farming

This industry comprises establishments primarily engaged in growing sugarcane.

11194 Hay Farming[T]
See industry description for 111940.

111940 Hay Farming

This industry comprises establishments primarily engaged in growing hay, alfalfa, clover, and/or mixed hay.

Cross-References.   Establishments primarily engaged in--

- Growing grain hay--are classified in Industry Group 1111, Oilseed and Grain Farming; and
- Growing grass and hay seeds--are classified in U.S. Industry 111998, All Other Miscellaneous Crop Farming.

11199 All Other Crop Farming[T]

This industry comprises establishments primarily engaged in (1) growing crops (except oilseeds and/or grains; vegetables and/or melons; fruits and/or tree nuts; greenhouse, nursery, and/or floriculture products; tobacco; cotton; sugarcane; or hay) or (2) growing a combination of crops (except a combination of oilseed(s) and grain(s); and a combination of fruit(s) and tree nut(s)) with no one crop or family of crops accounting for one-half of the establishment's agricultural production (i.e., value of crops for market).

T—Canadian, Mexican, and United States industries are comparable.

Illustrative Examples:

Agave farming
Spice farming
General combination crop farming (except oilseed
and grain; vegetables and melons; fruit and nut
combinations)
Tea farming

Hay seed farming
Maple sap gathering
Peanut farming
Sugar beet farming
Grass seed farming

Cross-References.   Establishments primarily engaged in--

- Growing oilseeds and/or wheat, corn, rice, or other grains--are classified in Industry Group 1111, Oilseed and Grain Farming;
- Growing vegetables and/or melons--are classified in Industry Group 1112, Vegetable and Melon Farming;
- Growing fruits and/or tree nuts--are classified in Industry Group 1113, Fruit and Tree Nut Farming;
- Growing greenhouse, nursery, and/or floriculture products--are classified in Industry Group 1114, Greenhouse, Nursery, and Floriculture Production;
- Growing tobacco--are classified in Industry 11191, Tobacco Farming;
- Growing cotton--are classified in Industry 11192, Cotton Farming;
- Growing sugarcane--are classified in Industry 11193, Sugarcane Farming;
- Growing hay--are classified in Industry 11194, Hay Farming; and
- Growing algae, seaweed, or other aquatic plants--are classified in Industry 11251, Aquaculture.

111991 Sugar Beet Farming

This U.S. industry comprises establishments primarily engaged in growing sugar beets.

Cross-References.

Establishments primarily engaged in growing beets (except sugar beets) are classified in U.S. Industry 111219, Other Vegetable (except Potato) and Melon Farming.

111992 Peanut Farming

This U.S. industry comprises establishments primarily engaged in growing peanuts.

111998 All Other Miscellaneous Crop Farming

This U.S. industry comprises establishments primarily engaged in one of the following: (1) growing crops (except oilseeds and/or grains; vegetables and/or melons; fruits and/or tree nuts; greenhouse, nursery, and/or floriculture products; tobacco; cotton; sugarcane; hay; sugar beets; or peanuts); (2) growing a combination of crops (except a combination of oilseed(s) and grain(s); and a combination of fruit(s) and tree nut(s)) with no one crop or family of crops accounting for one-half of the establishment's agricultural production (i.e., value of crops for market); or (3) gathering tea or maple sap.

Illustrative Examples:

Agave farming
Mint farming
General combination crop farming (except oilseed
and grain; vegetables and melons; fruit and tree nut
combinations)

Hay seed farming
Grass seed farming
Hop farming
Spice farming

T—Canadian, Mexican, and United States industries are comparable.

Cross-References.   Establishments primarily engaged in--

- Growing oilseeds and/or wheat, corn, rice, or other grains--are classified in Industry Group 1111, Oilseed and Grain Farming;
- Growing vegetables and/or melons--are classified in Industry Group 1112, Vegetable and Melon Farming;
- Growing fruits and/or tree nuts--are classified in Industry Group 1113, Fruit and Tree Nut Farming;
- Growing greenhouse, nursery, and/or floriculture products--are classified in Industry Group 1114, Greenhouse, Nursery, and Floriculture Production;
- Growing tobacco--are classified in Industry 111910, Tobacco Farming;
- Growing cotton--are classified in Industry 111920, Cotton Farming;
- Growing sugarcane--are classified in Industry 111930, Sugarcane Farming;
- Growing hay--are classified in Industry 111940, Hay Farming;
- Growing sugar beets--are classified in U.S. Industry 111991, Sugar Beet Farming;
- Growing peanuts--are classified in U.S. Industry 111992, Peanut Farming; and
- Growing algae, seaweed, or other aquatic plants--are classified in U.S. Industry 112519, Other Aquaculture.

112   Animal Production and Aquaculture[T]

Industries in the Animal Production and Aquaculture subsector raise or fatten animals for the sale of animals or animal products and/or raise aquatic plants and animals in controlled or selected aquatic environments for the sale of aquatic plants, animals, or their products. The subsector includes establishments, such as ranches, farms, and feedlots, primarily engaged in keeping, grazing, breeding, or feeding animals. These animals are kept for the products they produce or for eventual sale. The animals are generally raised in various environments, from total confinement or captivity to feeding on an open range pasture.

The industries in this subsector are grouped by important factors, such as suitable grazing or pasture land, specialized buildings, type of equipment, and the amount and types of labor required. Establishments are classified in the Animal Production and Aquaculture subsector when animal production (i.e., value of animals for market) accounts for one-half or more of the establishment's total agricultural production. Establishments with one-half or more animal production with no one animal product or family of animal products of an industry accounting for one-half of the establishment's agricultural production are treated as combination animal farming classified in Industry 11299, All Other Animal Production.

1121   Cattle Ranching and Farming[T]

This industry group comprises establishments primarily engaged in raising cattle, milking dairy cattle, or feeding cattle for fattening.

11211   Beef Cattle Ranching and Farming, including Feedlots[T]

This industry comprises establishments primarily engaged in raising cattle (including cattle for dairy herd replacements), or feeding cattle for fattening.

Cross-References.   Establishments primarily engaged in--

- Milking dairy cattle--are classified in Industry 11212, Dairy Cattle and Milk Production; and
- Operating stockyards for transportation and not buying, selling, or auctioning livestock--are classified in Industry 48899, Other Support Activities for Transportation.

112111 Beef Cattle Ranching and Farming

This U.S. industry comprises establishments primarily engaged in raising cattle (including cattle for dairy herd replacements).

T—Canadian, Mexican, and United States industries are comparable.

Cross-References.

Establishments primarily engaged in milking dairy cattle are classified in Industry 112120, Dairy Cattle and Milk Production.

112112 Cattle Feedlots

This U.S. industry comprises establishments primarily engaged in feeding cattle for fattening.

Cross-References.

Establishments primarily engaged in operating stockyards for transportation and not buying, selling, or auctioning livestock are classified in U.S. Industry 488999, All Other Support Activities for Transportation.

11212 Dairy Cattle and Milk Production[T]
See industry description for 112120.

112120 Dairy Cattle and Milk Production

This industry comprises establishments primarily engaged in milking dairy cattle.

Cross-References.   Establishments primarily engaged in--

- Raising dairy herd replacements--are classified in U.S. Industry 112111, Beef Cattle Ranching and Farming; and
- Milking goats--are classified in Industry 112420, Goat Farming.

11213 Dual-Purpose Cattle Ranching and Farming[T]
See industry description for 112130.

112130 Dual-Purpose Cattle Ranching and Farming

This industry comprises establishments primarily engaged in raising cattle for both milking and meat production.

Cross-References.   Establishments primarily engaged in--

- Milking dairy cattle--are classified in Industry 112120, Dairy Cattle and Milk Production;
- Raising cattle or feeding cattle for fattening--are classified in Industry 11211, Beef Cattle Ranching and Farming, including Feedlots; and
- Operating stockyards for transportation and not buying, selling, or auctioning livestock--are classified in U.S. Industry 488999, All Other Support Activities for Transportation.

1122 Hog and Pig Farming[T]

11221 Hog and Pig Farming[T]
See industry description for 112210.

112210 Hog and Pig Farming

This industry comprises establishments primarily engaged in raising hogs and pigs. These establishments may include farming activities, such as breeding, farrowing, and the raising of weanling pigs, feeder pigs, or market size hogs.

T—Canadian, Mexican, and United States industries are comparable.

Cross-References.

Establishments primarily engaged in operating stockyards for transportation and not buying, selling, or auctioning livestock are classified in U.S. Industry 488999, All Other Support Activities for Transportation.

1123   Poultry and Egg Production[T]

This industry group comprises establishments primarily engaged in breeding, hatching, and raising poultry for meat or egg production.

11231   Chicken Egg Production[T]
See industry description for 112310.

112310 Chicken Egg Production

This industry comprises establishments primarily engaged in raising chickens for egg production. The eggs produced may be for use as table eggs or hatching eggs.

Cross-References.

Establishments primarily engaged in raising chickens for the production of meat are classified in Industry 112320, Broilers and Other Meat Type Chicken Production.

11232   Broilers and Other Meat Type Chicken Production[T]
See industry description for 112320.

112320 Broilers and Other Meat Type Chicken Production

This industry comprises establishments primarily engaged in raising broilers, fryers, roasters, and other meat type chickens.

Cross-References.

Establishments primarily engaged in raising chickens for egg production are classified in Industry 112310, Chicken Egg Production.

11233   Turkey Production[T]
See industry description for 112330.

112330 Turkey Production

This industry comprises establishments primarily engaged in raising turkeys for meat or egg production.

11234   Poultry Hatcheries[T]
See industry description for 112340.

112340 Poultry Hatcheries

This industry comprises establishments primarily engaged in hatching poultry of any kind.

11239   Other Poultry Production[T]
See industry description for 112390.

T—Canadian, Mexican, and United States industries are comparable.

census.gov/naics

112390 Other Poultry Production

This industry comprises establishments primarily engaged in raising poultry (except chickens for meat or egg production and turkeys).

Illustrative Examples:

Duck production
Ostrich production
Emu production

Pheasant production
Geese production
Quail production

Cross-References. Establishments primarily engaged in--

- Raising aviary birds, such as parakeets, canaries, and love birds--are classified in Industry 112990, All Other Animal Production;
- Raising chickens for egg production--are classified in Industry 112310, Chicken Egg Production;
- Raising broilers and other meat type chickens--are classified in Industry 112320, Broilers and Other Meat Type Chicken Production;
- Raising turkeys--are classified in Industry 112330, Turkey Production; and
- Raising swans, peacocks, flamingos or other "adornment birds"--are classified in Industry 112990, All Other Animal Production.

1124 Sheep and Goat Farming[T]

This industry group comprises establishments primarily engaged in raising sheep, lambs, and goats, or feeding lambs for fattening.

11241 Sheep Farming[T]
See industry description for 112410.

112410 Sheep Farming

This industry comprises establishments primarily engaged in raising sheep and lambs, or feeding lambs for fattening. The sheep or lambs may be raised for sale or wool production.

Cross-References.

Establishments primarily engaged in operating stockyards for transportation and not buying, selling, or auctioning livestock are classified in U.S. Industry 488999, All Other Support Activities for Transportation.

11242 Goat Farming[T]
See industry description for 112420.

112420 Goat Farming

This industry comprises establishments primarily engaged in raising goats.

1125 Aquaculture[T]

11251 Aquaculture[T]

This industry comprises establishments primarily engaged in the farm raising and production of aquatic animals or plants in controlled or selected aquatic environments. These establishments use some form of intervention in the rearing process to enhance production, such as holding in captivity, regular stocking, feeding, and protecting from predators, pests, and disease.

T—Canadian, Mexican, and United States industries are comparable.

Cross-References.

Establishments primarily engaged in the catching or taking of fish and other aquatic animals from their natural habitat are classified in Industry 11411, Fishing.

112511 Finfish Farming and Fish Hatcheries

This U.S. industry comprises establishments primarily engaged in (1) farm raising finfish (e.g., catfish, trout, goldfish, tropical fish, minnows) and/or (2) hatching fish of any kind.

Cross-References.

Establishments primarily engaged in the catching or taking of finfish from their natural habitat are classified in U.S. Industry 114111, Finfish Fishing.

112512 Shellfish Farming

This U.S. industry comprises establishments primarily engaged in farm raising shellfish (e.g., crayfish, shrimp, oysters, clams, mollusks).

Cross-References.

Establishments primarily engaged in the catching or taking of shellfish from their natural habitat are classified in U.S. Industry 114112, Shellfish Fishing.

112519 Other Aquaculture

This U.S. industry comprises establishments primarily engaged in (1) farm raising of aquatic animals (except finfish and shellfish) and/or (2) farm raising of aquatic plants. Alligator, algae, frog, seaweed, or turtle production is included in this industry.

Cross-References.   Establishments primarily engaged in--

- Miscellaneous fishing activities, such as catching or taking of terrapins, turtles, and frogs from their natural habitat--are classified in U.S. Industry 114119, Other Marine Fishing;
- Farm raising finfish--are classified in U.S. Industry 112511, Finfish Farming and Fish Hatcheries;
- Farm raising shellfish--are classified in U.S. Industry 112512, Shellfish Farming; and
- Growing hydroponic crops--are classified in U.S. Industry 111419, Other Food Crops Grown Under Cover.

1129   Other Animal Production[T]

This industry group comprises establishments primarily engaged in raising animals and insects (except cattle, hogs and pigs, poultry, sheep and goats, and aquaculture) for sale or product production. These establishments are primarily engaged in raising one of the following: bees, horses and other equines, rabbits and other fur-bearing animals, and so forth, and producing products, such as honey and other bee products. Establishments primarily engaged in raising a combination of animals with no one animal or family of animals accounting for one-half of the establishment's agricultural production (i.e., value of animals for market) are included in this industry group.

11291   Apiculture[T]
See industry description for 112910.

T—Canadian, Mexican, and United States industries are comparable.

112910 Apiculture

This industry comprises establishments primarily engaged in raising bees. These establishments may collect and gather honey; and/or sell queen bees, packages of bees, royal jelly, bees' wax, propolis, venom, pollen, and/or other bee products.

11292   Horses and Other Equine Production[T]
      See industry description for 112920.

112920 Horses and Other Equine Production

This industry comprises establishments primarily engaged in raising horses, mules, donkeys, and other equines.

Cross-References.

- Establishments primarily engaged in equine boarding are classified in Industry 115210, Support Activities for Animal Production; and
- Equine owners entering horses in racing or other spectator sporting events are classified in U.S. Industry 711219, Other Spectator Sports.

11293   Fur-Bearing Animal and Rabbit Production[T]
      See industry description for 112930.

112930 Fur-Bearing Animal and Rabbit Production

This industry comprises establishments primarily engaged in raising fur-bearing animals including rabbits. These animals may be raised for sale or for their pelt production.

Cross-References.

Establishments primarily engaged in the trapping or hunting of wild fur-bearing animals are classified in Industry 114210, Hunting and Trapping.

11299   All Other Animal Production[T]
      See industry description for 112990.

112990 All Other Animal Production

This industry comprises establishments primarily engaged in (1) raising animals (except cattle, hogs and pigs, poultry, sheep and goats, aquaculture, apiculture, horses and other equines; and fur-bearing animals including rabbits) or (2) raising a combination of animals, with no one animal or family of animals accounting for one-half of the establishment's agricultural production (i.e., value of animals for market).

Illustrative Examples:

Bird production (e.g., canaries, parakeets, parrots)	Companion animals production (e.g., cats, dogs)
Laboratory animal production (e.g., rats, mice, guinea pigs)	Worm production
	Deer production
Combination animal farming (except dairy, poultry)	Llama production

Cross-References.   Establishments primarily engaged in--

- Raising cattle, dairy cattle, or feeding cattle for fattening--are classified in Industry Group 1121, Cattle Ranching and Farming;
- Raising hogs and pigs--are classified in Industry Group 1122, Hog and Pig Farming;

T—Canadian, Mexican, and United States industries are comparable.

- Raising poultry and raising poultry for egg production--are classified in Industry Group 1123, Poultry and Egg Production;
- Raising sheep and goats--are classified in Industry Group 1124, Sheep and Goat Farming;
- Animal aquaculture--are classified in Industry 11251, Aquaculture;
- Raising bees--are classified in Industry 112910, Apiculture;
- Raising horses and other equines--are classified in Industry 112920, Horses and Other Equine Production; and
- Raising fur-bearing animals including rabbits--are classified in Industry 112930, Fur-Bearing Animal and Rabbit Production.

113　　Forestry and Logging[T]

Industries in the Forestry and Logging subsector grow and harvest timber on a long production cycle (i.e., of 10 years or more). Long production cycles use different production processes than short production cycles, which require more horticultural interventions prior to harvest, resulting in processes more similar to those found in the Crop Production subsector. Consequently, Christmas tree production and other production involving production cycles of less than 10 years, are classified in the Crop Production subsector.

Industries in this subsector specialize in different stages of the production cycle. Reforestation requires production of seedlings in specialized nurseries. Timber production requires natural forest or suitable areas of land that are available for a long duration. The maturation time for timber depends upon the species of tree, the climatic conditions of the region, and the intended purpose of the timber. The harvesting of timber (except when done on an extremely small scale) requires specialized machinery unique to the industry. Establishments gathering forest products, such as gums, barks, balsam needles, rhizomes, fibers, Spanish moss, and ginseng and truffles, are also included in this subsector.

1131　　Timber Tract Operations[T]

11311　　Timber Tract Operations[T]
See industry description for 113110.

113110　Timber Tract Operations

This industry comprises establishments primarily engaged in the operation of timber tracts for the purpose of selling standing timber.

Cross-References.　　　　Establishments primarily engaged in--

- Acting as lessors of land with trees as real estate property--are classified in Industry 531190, Lessors of Other Real Estate Property;
- Growing short rotation woody trees (i.e., growing and harvesting cycle is 10 years or less)--are classified in U.S. Industry 111421, Nursery and Tree Production; and
- Cutting timber--are classified in Industry 113310, Logging.

1132　　Forest Nurseries and Gathering of Forest Products[T]

11321　　Forest Nurseries and Gathering of Forest Products[T]
See industry description for 113210.

113210　Forest Nurseries and Gathering of Forest Products

This industry comprises establishments primarily engaged in (1) growing trees for reforestation and/or (2) gathering forest products, such as gums, barks, balsam needles, rhizomes, fibers, Spanish moss, ginseng, and truffles.

T—Canadian, Mexican, and United States industries are comparable.

Cross-References.   Establishments primarily engaged in--

- Gathering tea and maple sap--are classified in U.S. Industry 111998, All Other Miscellaneous Crop Farming; and
- Processing maple syrup into other products--are classified in Industry 31199, All Other Food Manufacturing.

1133   Logging[T]

11331   Logging[T]
See industry description for 113310.

113310   Logging

This industry comprises establishments primarily engaged in one or more of the following: (1) cutting timber; (2) cutting and transporting timber; and (3) producing wood chips in the field.

Cross-References.   Establishments primarily engaged in--

- Trucking timber without cutting timber--are classified in Industry 484220, Specialized Freight (except Used Goods) Trucking, Local; and
- Producing wood chips in sawmills--are classified in U.S. Industry 321113, Sawmills.

114   Fishing, Hunting and Trapping[T]

Industries in the Fishing, Hunting and Trapping subsector harvest fish and other wild animals from their natural habitats and are dependent upon a continued supply of the natural resource. The harvesting of fish is the predominant economic activity of this subsector and it usually requires specialized vessels that, by the nature of their size, configuration and equipment, are not suitable for any other type of production, such as transportation.

Hunting and trapping activities utilize a wide variety of production processes and are classified in the same subsector as fishing because the availability of resources and the constraints imposed, such as conservation requirements and proper habitat maintenance, are similar.

1141   Fishing[T]

11411   Fishing[T]

This industry comprises establishments primarily engaged in the commercial catching or taking of finfish, shellfish, or miscellaneous marine products from a natural habitat, such as the catching of bluefish, eels, salmon, tuna, clams, crabs, lobsters, mussels, oysters, shrimp, frogs, sea urchins, and turtles.

Cross-References.   Establishments primarily engaged in--

- Farm raising finfish, shellfish or other marine animals and plants--are classified in Industry 11251, Aquaculture; and
- Gathering and processing seafood into canned seafood products--are classified in Industry 31171, Seafood Product Preparation and Packaging.

114111   Finfish Fishing

This U.S. industry comprises establishments primarily engaged in the commercial catching or taking of finfish (e.g., bluefish, salmon, trout, tuna) from their natural habitat.

T—Canadian, Mexican, and United States industries are comparable.

Cross-References.   Establishments primarily engaged in--

- Farm raising finfish--are classified in U.S. Industry 112511, Finfish Farming and Fish Hatcheries; and
- Gathering and processing (known as "floating factory ships") seafood into canned seafood products--are classified in Industry 311710, Seafood Product Preparation and Packaging.

114112 Shellfish Fishing

This U.S. industry comprises establishments primarily engaged in the commercial catching or taking of shellfish (e.g., clams, crabs, lobsters, mussels, oysters, sea urchins, shrimp) from their natural habitat.

Cross-References.

Establishments primarily engaged in farm raising shellfish are classified in U.S. Industry 112512, Shellfish Farming.

114119 Other Marine Fishing

This U.S. industry comprises establishments primarily engaged in the commercial catching or taking of marine animals (except finfish and shellfish).

Cross-References.   Establishments primarily engaged in--

- Animal or plant aquaculture (except finfish and shellfish)--are classified in U.S. Industry 112519, Other Aquaculture;
- The commercial catching or taking of finfish from their natural habitat--are classified in U.S. Industry 114111, Finfish Fishing; and
- The commercial catching or taking of shellfish from their natural habitat--are classified in U.S. Industry 114112, Shellfish Fishing.

1142   Hunting and Trapping[T]

11421   Hunting and Trapping[T]
See industry description for 114210.

114210 Hunting and Trapping

This industry comprises establishments primarily engaged in one or more of the following: (1) commercial hunting and trapping; (2) operating commercial game preserves, such as game retreats; and (3) operating hunting preserves.

Cross-References.   Establishments primarily engaged in--

- Operating nature preserves--are classified in Industry 712190, Nature Parks and Other Similar Institutions; and
- Farm raising rabbits and other fur-bearing animals--are classified in Industry 112930, Fur-Bearing Animal and Rabbit Production.

115   Support Activities for Agriculture and Forestry[T]

Industries in the Support Activities for Agriculture and Forestry subsector provide support services that are an essential part of agricultural and forestry production. These support activities may be performed by the agriculture or forestry producing establishment or conducted independently as an alternative source of inputs required for the production process for a given crop, animal, or forestry industry. Establishments that primarily perform these activities independent of the agriculture or forestry producing establishment are in this subsector.

T—Canadian, Mexican, and United States industries are comparable.

1151 Support Activities for Crop Production[T]

11511 Support Activities for Crop Production[T]

This industry comprises establishments primarily engaged in providing support activities for growing crops.

Illustrative Examples:

Aerial crop dusting or spraying (i.e., using specialized or dedicated aircraft)
Farm management services
Cotton ginning

Planting crops
Cultivating services
Vineyard cultivation services

Cross-References.　　Establishments primarily engaged in--

- Performing crop production that are generally known as farms, orchards, groves, or vineyards (including tenant farms)--are classified in the appropriate crop industry within Subsector 111, Crop Production;
- Providing support activities for forestry--are classified in Industry 11531, Support Activities for Forestry;
- Landscaping and horticultural services, such as lawn and maintenance care and ornamental shrub and tree services--are classified in Industry 56173, Landscaping Services;
- Land clearing, land leveling, and earth moving for terracing, ponds, and irrigation--are classified in Industry 23891, Site Preparation Contractors;
- Artificially drying and dehydrating fruits and vegetables--are classified in Industry 31142, Fruit and Vegetable Canning, Pickling, and Drying;
- Stemming and redrying tobacco--are classified in Industry 31223, Tobacco Manufacturing;
- Providing water for irrigation--are classified in Industry 22131, Water Supply and Irrigation Systems; and
- Buying farm products, such as fruits or vegetables, for resale to other wholesalers or retailers, and preparing them for market or further processing--are classified in Industry 42448, Fresh Fruit and Vegetable Merchant Wholesalers.

115111 Cotton Ginning

This U.S. industry comprises establishments primarily engaged in ginning cotton.

115112 Soil Preparation, Planting, and Cultivating

This U.S. industry comprises establishments primarily engaged in performing a soil preparation activity or crop production service, such as plowing, fertilizing, seed bed preparation, planting, cultivating, and crop protecting services.

Cross-References.　　Establishments primarily engaged in--

- Mulching and seeding burned forests from the air in support of reforestation or on an emergency basis--are classified in Industry 115310, Support Activities for Forestry;
- Land clearing, land leveling, and earth moving for terracing, ponds, and irrigation--are classified in Industry 238910, Site Preparation Contractors; and
- Providing water for irrigation--are classified in Industry 221310, Water Supply and Irrigation Systems.

115113 Crop Harvesting, Primarily by Machine

This U.S. industry comprises establishments primarily engaged in mechanical harvesting, picking, and combining of crops, and related activities. The machinery used is provided by the servicing establishment.

T—Canadian, Mexican, and United States industries are comparable.

Cross-References.   Establishments primarily engaged in--

- Providing personnel for manual harvesting--are classified in U.S. Industry 115115, Farm Labor Contractors and Crew Leaders; and
- Providing farm management services (i.e., on a contract or fee basis) and arranging or contracting crop mechanical or manual harvesting operations for the farm(s) they manage--are classified in U.S. Industry 115116, Farm Management Services.

115114 Postharvest Crop Activities (except Cotton Ginning)

This U.S. industry comprises establishments primarily engaged in performing services on crops, subsequent to their harvest, with the intent of preparing them for market or further processing. These establishments provide postharvest activities, such as crop cleaning, sun drying, shelling, fumigating, curing, sorting, grading, packing, and cooling.

Cross-References.   Establishments primarily engaged in--

- Ginning cotton--are classified in U.S. Industry 115111, Cotton Ginning;
- Custom grain grinding for animal feed--are classified in U.S. Industry 311119, Other Animal Food Manufacturing;
- Artificially drying and dehydrating fruits and vegetables--are classified in U.S. Industry 311423, Dried and Dehydrated Food Manufacturing;
- Stemming and redrying tobacco--are classified in Industry 312230, Tobacco Manufacturing;
- Buying farm products for resale to other wholesalers or retailers and preparing them for market or further processing--are classified in Industry 424480, Fresh Fruit and Vegetable Merchant Wholesalers; and
- Providing farm management services (i.e., on a contract or fee basis) and arranging or contracting postharvesting crop activities for the farm(s) they manage--are classified in U.S. Industry 115116, Farm Management Services.

115115 Farm Labor Contractors and Crew Leaders

This U.S. industry comprises establishments primarily engaged in supplying labor for agricultural production or harvesting.

Cross-References.   Establishments primarily engaged in--

- Providing machine harvesting--are classified in U.S. Industry 115113, Crop Harvesting, Primarily by Machine; and
- Providing farm management services (i.e., on a contract or fee basis) and arranging or contracting farm labor for the farm(s) they manage--are classified in U.S. Industry 115116, Farm Management Services.

115116 Farm Management Services

This U.S. industry comprises establishments primarily engaged in providing farm management services on a contract or fee basis usually to citrus groves, orchards, or vineyards. These establishments always provide management and may arrange or contract for the partial or the complete operations of the farm establishment(s) they manage. Operational activities may include cultivating, harvesting, and/or other specialized agricultural support activities.

Cross-References.

Establishments primarily engaged in crop production that are generally known as farms, orchards, groves, or vineyards (including tenant farms), are classified in the appropriate crop industry within Subsector 111, Crop Production.

T—Canadian, Mexican, and United States industries are comparable.

1152   Support Activities for Animal Production[T]

11521   Support Activities for Animal Production[T]
See industry description for 115210.

115210 Support Activities for Animal Production

This industry comprises establishments primarily engaged in performing support activities related to raising livestock (e.g., cattle, goats, hogs, horses, poultry, sheep). These establishments may perform one or more of the following: (1) breeding services for animals, including companion animals (e.g., cats, dogs, pet birds); (2) pedigree record services; (3) boarding horses; (4) dairy herd improvement activities; (5) livestock spraying; and (6) sheep dipping and shearing.

Cross-References.

Establishments primarily engaged in raising companion animals (e.g., cats, dogs, pet birds) for sale are classified in Industry 112990, All Other Animal Production.

1153   Support Activities for Forestry[T]

11531   Support Activities for Forestry[T]
See industry description for 115310.

115310 Support Activities for Forestry

This industry comprises establishments primarily engaged in performing particular support activities related to timber production, wood technology, forestry economics and marketing, and forest protection. These establishments may provide support activities for forestry, such as estimating timber, forest firefighting, forest pest control, treating burned forests from the air for reforestation or on an emergency basis, and consulting on wood attributes and reforestation.

Cross-References.   Establishments primarily engaged in--

- Public administration and conservation of forest lands--are classified in Industry 924120, Administration of Conservation Programs; and
- Individual activities as part of a restoration project--are classified according to the primary activity.

T—Canadian, Mexican, and United States industries are comparable.

Sector 21--Mining, Quarrying, and Oil and Gas Extraction[T]

The Sector as a Whole

The Mining, Quarrying, and Oil and Gas Extraction sector comprises establishments that extract naturally occurring mineral solids, such as coal and ores; liquid minerals, such as crude petroleum; and gases, such as natural gas. The term mining is used in the broad sense to include quarrying, well operations, beneficiating (e.g., crushing, screening, washing, and flotation), and other preparation customarily performed at the mine site, or as a part of mining activity.

The Mining, Quarrying, and Oil and Gas Extraction sector distinguishes two basic activities: mine operation and mining support activities. Mine operation includes establishments operating mines, quarries, or oil and gas wells on their own account or for others on a contract or fee basis. Mining support activities include establishments that perform exploration (except geophysical surveying) and/or other mining services on a contract or fee basis (except mine site preparation and construction of oil/gas pipelines).

Establishments in the Mining, Quarrying, and Oil and Gas Extraction sector are grouped and classified according to the natural resource mined or to be mined. Industries include establishments that develop the mine site, extract the natural resources, and/or those that beneficiate (i.e., prepare) the mineral mined. Beneficiation is the process whereby the extracted material is reduced to particles that can be separated into mineral and waste, the former suitable for further processing or direct use. The operations that take place in beneficiation are primarily mechanical, such as grinding, washing, magnetic separation, and centrifugal separation. In contrast, manufacturing operations primarily use chemical and electrochemical processes, such as electrolysis and distillation. However, some treatments, such as heat treatments, take place in both the beneficiation and the manufacturing (i.e., smelting/refining) stages. The range of preparation activities varies by mineral and the purity of any given ore deposit. While some minerals, such as petroleum and natural gas, require little or no preparation, others are washed and screened, while yet others, such as gold and silver, can be transformed into bullion before leaving the mine site.

Mining, beneficiating, and manufacturing activities often occur in a single location. Separate receipts will be collected for these activities whenever possible. When receipts cannot be broken out between mining and manufacturing, establishments that mine or quarry nonmetallic minerals, and then beneficiate the nonmetallic minerals into more finished manufactured products are classified based on the primary activity of the establishment. A mine that manufactures a small amount of finished products will be classified in Sector 21, Mining, Quarrying, and Oil and Gas Extraction. An establishment that mines whose primary output is a more finished manufactured product will be classified in Sector 31-33, Manufacturing.

211 Oil and Gas Extraction[T]

Industries in the Oil and Gas Extraction subsector operate and/or develop oil and gas field properties. Such activities may include exploration for crude petroleum and natural gas; drilling, completing, and equipping wells; operating separators, emulsion breakers, desilting equipment, and field gathering lines for crude petroleum and natural gas; and all other activities in the preparation of oil and gas up to the point of shipment from the producing property. This subsector includes the production of crude petroleum, the mining and extraction of oil from oil shale and oil sands, the production of natural gas, sulfur recovery from natural gas, and recovery of hydrocarbon liquids.

Establishments in this subsector include those that operate oil and gas wells on their own account or for others on a contract or fee basis. Establishments primarily engaged in providing support services, on a contract or fee basis, required for the drilling or operation of oil and gas wells (except geophysical surveying and mapping, mine site preparation, and construction of oil/gas pipelines) are classified in Subsector 213, Support Activities for Mining.

2111 Oil and Gas Extraction[T]

21112 Crude Petroleum Extraction
See industry description for 211120.

T—Canadian, Mexican, and United States industries are comparable.

211120 Crude Petroleum Extraction

This industry comprises establishments primarily engaged in (1) the exploration, development, and/or the production of petroleum from wells in which the hydrocarbons will initially flow or can be produced using normal or enhanced drilling and extraction techniques or (2) the production of crude petroleum from surface shales or tar sands or from reservoirs in which the hydrocarbons are semisolids. Establishments in this industry operate oil wells on their own account or for others on a contract or fee basis.

Cross-References.   Establishments primarily engaged in--

- Performing oil field services for operators on a contract or fee basis--are classified in Industry 21311, Support Activities for Mining; and
- Refining crude petroleum into refined petroleum and liquid hydrocarbons--are classified in Industry 324110, Petroleum Refineries.

21113   Natural Gas Extraction
See industry description for 211130.

211130 Natural Gas Extraction

This industry comprises establishments primarily engaged in (1) the exploration, development, and/or the production of natural gas from wells in which the hydrocarbons will initially flow or can be produced using normal or enhanced drilling and extraction techniques or (2) the recovery of liquid hydrocarbons from oil and gas field gases. Establishments primarily engaged in sulfur recovery from natural gas are included in this industry.

Cross-References.   Establishments primarily engaged in--

- Performing gas field services for operators on a contract or fee basis--are classified in Industry 21311, Support Activities for Mining;
- Manufacturing acyclic and cyclic hydrocarbons from refined petroleum or converting refined petroleum into liquid hydrocarbons (i.e., petrochemicals)--are classified in Industry 325110, Petrochemical Manufacturing;
- Refining crude petroleum into refined petroleum and liquid hydrocarbons--are classified in Industry 324110, Petroleum Refineries; and
- Recovering helium from natural gas--are classified in Industry 325120, Industrial Gas Manufacturing.

212   Mining (except Oil and Gas)[T]

Industries in the Mining (except Oil and Gas) subsector primarily engage in mining, mine site development, and beneficiating (i.e., preparing) metallic minerals and nonmetallic minerals, including coal. The term "mining" is used in the broad sense to include ore extraction, quarrying, and beneficiating (e.g., crushing, screening, washing, sizing, concentrating, and flotation), customarily done at the mine site.

Beneficiation is the process whereby the extracted material is reduced to particles which can be separated into mineral and waste, the former suitable for further processing or direct use. The operations that take place in beneficiation are primarily mechanical, such as grinding, washing, magnetic separation, centrifugal separation, and so on. In contrast, manufacturing operations primarily use chemical and electrochemical processes, such as electrolysis, distillation, and so on. However some treatments, such as heat treatments, take place in both stages: the beneficiation and the manufacturing (i.e., smelting/refining) stages. The range of preparation activities varies by mineral and the purity of any given ore deposit. While some minerals, such as petroleum and natural gas, require little or no preparation, others are washed and screened, while yet others, such as gold and silver, can be transformed into bullion before leaving the mine site.

Establishments in the Mining (except Oil and Gas) subsector include those that have complete responsibility for operating mines and quarries (except oil and gas wells) and those that operate mines and quarries (except oil and gas wells) for others on a contract or fee basis. Establishments primarily engaged in providing support services, on a

_____

T—Canadian, Mexican, and United States industries are comparable.

contract or fee basis, required for the mining and quarrying of minerals are classified in Subsector 213, Support Activities for Mining.

2121   Coal Mining[T]

21211   Coal Mining[T]

This industry comprises establishments primarily engaged in one or more of the following: (1) mining bituminous coal, anthracite, and lignite by underground mining, auger mining, strip mining, culm bank mining, and other surface mining; (2) developing coal mine sites; and (3) beneficiating (i.e., preparing) coal (e.g., cleaning, washing, screening, and sizing coal).

Cross-References.   Establishments primarily engaged in--

- Manufacturing coke oven products in coke oven establishments--are classified in Industry 32419, Other Petroleum and Coal Products Manufacturing; and
- Manufacturing coal products in steel mills--are classified in Industry 33111, Iron and Steel Mills and Ferroalloy Manufacturing.

212111   Bituminous Coal and Lignite Surface Mining

This U.S. industry comprises establishments primarily engaged in one or more of the following: (1) surface mining of bituminous coal and lignite; (2) developing bituminous coal and lignite surface mine sites; (3) surface mining and beneficiating (e.g., cleaning, washing, screening, and sizing) of bituminous coal; or (4) beneficiating (e.g., cleaning, washing, screening, and sizing coal), but not mining, bituminous coal.

Cross-References.   Establishments primarily engaged in--

- Manufacturing coke oven products in coke oven establishments--are classified in U.S. Industry 324199, All Other Petroleum and Coal Products Manufacturing;
- Underground mining of bituminous coal--are classified in U.S. Industry 212112, Bituminous Coal Underground Mining; and
- Mining and/or beneficiating anthracite coal--are classified in U.S. Industry 212113, Anthracite Mining.

212112   Bituminous Coal Underground Mining

This U.S. industry comprises establishments primarily engaged in one or more of the following: (1) underground mining of bituminous coal; (2) developing bituminous coal underground mine sites; and (3) underground mining and beneficiating of bituminous coal (e.g., cleaning, washing, screening, and sizing coal).

Cross-References.   Establishments primarily engaged in--

- Manufacturing coke oven products in coke oven establishments--are classified in U.S. Industry 324199, All Other Petroleum and Coal Products Manufacturing;
- Surface mining and/or beneficiating of bituminous coal or lignite--are classified in U.S. Industry 212111, Bituminous Coal and Lignite Surface Mining; and
- Mining and/or beneficiating anthracite coal--are classified in U.S. Industry 212113, Anthracite Mining.

212113   Anthracite Mining

This U.S. industry comprises establishments primarily engaged in one or more of the following: (1) mining anthracite coal; (2) developing anthracite coal mine sites; and (3) beneficiating anthracite coal (e.g., cleaning, washing, screening, and sizing coal).

T—Canadian, Mexican, and United States industries are comparable.

Cross-References.   Establishments primarily engaged in--

- Manufacturing coke oven products in coke oven establishments--are classified in U.S. Industry 324199, All Other Petroleum and Coal Products Manufacturing;
- Surface mining and/or beneficiating bituminous coal or lignite--are classified in U.S. Industry 212111, Bituminous Coal and Lignite Surface Mining; and
- Underground mining of bituminous coal--are classified in U.S. Industry 212112, Bituminous Coal Underground Mining.

2122   Metal Ore Mining[T]

This industry group comprises establishments primarily engaged in developing mine sites or mining metallic minerals, and establishments primarily engaged in ore dressing and beneficiating (i.e., preparing) operations, such as crushing, grinding, washing, drying, sintering, concentrating, calcining, and leaching. Beneficiating may be performed at mills operated in conjunction with the mines served or at mills, such as custom mills, operated separately.

21221   Iron Ore Mining[T]
See industry description for 212210.

212210 Iron Ore Mining

This industry comprises establishments primarily engaged in (1) developing mine sites, mining, and/or beneficiating (i.e., preparing) iron ores and manganiferous ores valued chiefly for their iron content and/or (2) producing sinter iron ore (except iron ore produced in iron and steel mills) and other iron ore agglomerates.

Cross-References.

Establishments primarily engaged in manufacturing pig iron ore are classified in Industry 331110, Iron and Steel Mills and Ferroalloy Manufacturing.

21222   Gold Ore and Silver Ore Mining[T]

This industry comprises establishments primarily engaged in developing the mine site, mining, and/or beneficiating (i.e., preparing) ores valued chiefly for their gold and/or silver content. Establishments primarily engaged in the transformation of the gold and silver into bullion or dore bar in combination with mining activities are included in this industry.

Cross-References.

Establishments primarily engaged in manufacturing gold or silver bullion or dore bar without mining are classified in Industry 33141, Nonferrous Metal (except Aluminum) Smelting and Refining.

212221 Gold Ore Mining

This U.S. industry comprises establishments primarily engaged in developing the mine site, mining, and/or beneficiating (i.e., preparing) ores valued chiefly for their gold content. Establishments primarily engaged in transformation of the gold into bullion or dore bar in combination with mining activities are included in this industry.

Cross-References.

Establishments primarily engaged in manufacturing gold bullion or dore bar without mining are classified in Industry 331410, Nonferrous Metal (except Aluminum) Smelting and Refining.

T—Canadian, Mexican, and United States industries are comparable.

212222   Silver Ore Mining

This U.S. industry comprises establishments primarily engaged in developing the mine site, mining, and/or beneficiating (i.e., preparing) ores valued chiefly for their silver content. Establishments primarily engaged in transformation of the silver into bullion or dore bar in combination with mining activities are included in this industry.

Cross-References.

Establishments primarily engaged in manufacturing silver bullion or dore bar without mining are classified in Industry 331410, Nonferrous Metal (except Aluminum) Smelting and Refining.

21223   Copper, Nickel, Lead, and Zinc Mining[T]
See industry description for 212230.

212230   Copper, Nickel, Lead, and Zinc Mining

This industry comprises establishments primarily engaged in developing the mine site, mining, and/or beneficiating (i.e., preparing) ores valued chiefly for their copper, nickel, lead, or zinc content. Beneficiating includes the transformation of ores into concentrates. Establishments primarily engaged in recovering copper concentrates by the precipitation, leaching, or electrowinning of copper ore are included in this industry.

Cross-References.   Establishments primarily engaged in--

- Refining copper concentrates--are classified in Industry 331410, Nonferrous Metal (except Aluminum) Smelting and Refining; and
- Developing the mine site, mining, and/or beneficiating iron and manganiferous ores valued for their iron content--are classified in Industry 212210, Iron Ore Mining.

21229   Other Metal Ore Mining[T]

This industry comprises establishments primarily engaged in developing the mine site, mining, and/or beneficiating (i.e., preparing) metal ores (except iron and manganiferous ores valued for their iron content, gold ore, silver ore, copper, nickel, lead, and zinc ore).

Illustrative Examples:

Antimony ores mining and/or beneficiating	Ilmenite ores mining and/or beneficiating
Tantalum ores mining and/or beneficiating	Uranium-radium-vanadium ores mining and/or
Columbite ores mining and/or beneficiating	beneficiating
Tungsten ores mining and/or beneficiating	Molybdenum ores mining and/or beneficiating

Cross-References.   Establishments primarily engaged in--

- Developing the mine site, mining, and/or beneficiating iron and manganiferous ores valued chiefly for their iron content--are classified in Industry 21221, Iron Ore Mining;
- Developing the mine site, mining, and/or beneficiating ores valued chiefly for their gold or silver content-- are classified in Industry 21222, Gold Ore and Silver Ore Mining;
- Developing the mine site, mining, and/or beneficiating ores valued chiefly for their copper, nickel, lead, or zinc content--are classified in Industry 21223, Copper, Nickel, Lead, and Zinc Mining; and
- Enriching uranium--are classified in Industry 32518, Other Basic Inorganic Chemical Manufacturing.

T—Canadian, Mexican, and United States industries are comparable.

212291 Uranium-Radium-Vanadium Ore Mining

This U.S. industry comprises establishments primarily engaged in developing the mine site, mining, and/or beneficiating (i.e., preparing) uranium-radium-vanadium ores.

Cross-References.

Establishments primarily engaged in enriching uranium are classified in Industry 325180, Other Basic Inorganic Chemical Manufacturing.

212299 All Other Metal Ore Mining

This U.S. industry comprises establishments primarily engaged in developing the mine site, mining, and/or beneficiating (i.e., preparing) metal ores (except iron and manganiferous ores valued for their iron content, gold ore, silver ore, copper, nickel, lead, zinc, and uranium-radium-vanadium ore).

Illustrative Examples:

Antimony ores mining and/or beneficiating
Rare earth metal ores mining and/or beneficiating
Columbite ores mining and/or beneficiating
Tantalum ores mining and/or beneficiating

Ilmenite ores mining and/or beneficiating
Tungsten ores mining and/or beneficiating
Molybdenum ores mining and/or beneficiating

Cross-References.   Establishments primarily engaged in--

- Developing the mine site, mining, and/or beneficiating iron and manganiferous ores valued for their iron content--are classified in Industry 212210, Iron Ore Mining;
- Developing the mine site, mining, and/or beneficiating ores valued chiefly for their gold or silver content-- are classified in Industry 21222, Gold Ore and Silver Ore Mining;
- Developing the mine site, mining, and/or beneficiating ores valued chiefly for their copper, nickel, lead, or zinc content--are classified in Industry 212230, Copper, Nickel, Lead, and Zinc Mining; and
- Developing the mine site, mining, and/or beneficiating uranium-radium-vanadium ores--are classified in U.S. Industry 212291, Uranium-Radium-Vanadium Ore Mining.

2123   Nonmetallic Mineral Mining and Quarrying[T]

This industry group comprises establishments primarily engaged in developing mine sites, or in mining or quarrying nonmetallic minerals (except fuels). Also included are certain well and brine operations, and preparation plants primarily engaged in beneficiating (e.g., crushing, grinding, washing, and concentrating) nonmetallic minerals.
Beneficiation is the process whereby the extracted material is reduced to particles which can be separated into mineral and waste, the former suitable for further processing or direct use. The operations that take place in beneficiation are primarily mechanical, such as grinding, washing, magnetic separation, and centrifugal separation. In contrast, manufacturing operations primarily use chemical and electrochemical processes, such as electrolysis and distillation. However, some treatments, such as heat treatments, take place in both the beneficiation and the manufacturing (i.e., smelting/refining) stages. The range of preparation activities varies by mineral and the purity of any given ore deposit. While some minerals, such as petroleum and natural gas, require little or no preparation, others are washed and screened, while yet others, such as gold and silver, can be transformed into bullion before leaving the mine site.

21231   Stone Mining and Quarrying[T]

This industry comprises (1) establishments primarily engaged in developing the mine site, mining or quarrying dimension stone (i.e., rough blocks and/or slabs of stone), or mining and quarrying crushed and broken stone and/or

---

T—Canadian, Mexican, and United States industries are comparable.

(2) preparation plants primarily engaged in beneficiating stone (e.g., crushing, grinding, washing, screening, pulverizing, and sizing).

Cross-References.   Establishments primarily engaged in--

- Producing lime--are classified in Industry 32741, Lime Manufacturing; and
- Quarrying and dressing dimension stone--are classified in Industry 32799, All Other Nonmetallic Mineral Product Manufacturing.

212311 Dimension Stone Mining and Quarrying

This U.S. industry comprises establishments primarily engaged in developing the mine site and/or mining or quarrying dimension stone (i.e., rough blocks and/or slabs of stone).

Cross-References.

Establishments primarily engaged in dressing dimension stone and manufacturing stone products are classified in U.S. Industry 327991, Cut Stone and Stone Product Manufacturing.

212312 Crushed and Broken Limestone Mining and Quarrying

This U.S. industry comprises (1) establishments primarily engaged in developing the mine site, mining or quarrying crushed and broken limestone (including related rocks, such as dolomite, cement rock, marl, travertine, and calcareous tufa) and (2) preparation plants primarily engaged in beneficiating limestone (e.g., grinding or pulverizing).

Cross-References.   Establishments primarily engaged in--

- Producing lime--are classified in Industry 327410, Lime Manufacturing; and
- Mining or quarrying bituminous limestone--are classified in U.S. Industry 212319, Other Crushed and Broken Stone Mining and Quarrying.

212313 Crushed and Broken Granite Mining and Quarrying

This U.S. industry comprises (1) establishments primarily engaged in developing the mine site, and/or mining or quarrying crushed and broken granite (including related rocks, such as gneiss, syenite (except nepheline), and diorite) and (2) preparation plants primarily engaged in beneficiating granite (e.g., grinding or pulverizing).

212319 Other Crushed and Broken Stone Mining and Quarrying

This U.S. industry comprises: (1) establishments primarily engaged in developing the mine site and/or mining or quarrying crushed and broken stone (except limestone and granite); (2) preparation plants primarily engaged in beneficiating (e.g., grinding and pulverizing) stone (except limestone and granite); and (3) establishments primarily engaged in mining or quarrying bituminous limestone and bituminous sandstone.

Illustrative Examples:

Bituminous limestone mining and/or beneficiating
Marble crushed and broken stone mining and/or beneficiating

Bituminous sandstone mining and/or beneficiating
Sandstone crushed and broken stone mining and/or beneficiating

Cross-References.   Establishments primarily engaged in--

- Mining or quarrying crushed and broken limestone--are classified in U.S. Industry 212312, Crushed and Broken Limestone Mining and Quarrying; and

---

T—Canadian, Mexican, and United States industries are comparable.

- Mining or quarrying crushed and broken granite--are classified in U.S. Industry 212313, Crushed and Broken Granite Mining and Quarrying.

21232   Sand, Gravel, Clay, and Ceramic and Refractory Minerals Mining and Quarrying[T]

This industry comprises (1) establishments primarily engaged in developing the mine site and/or mining, quarrying, dredging for sand and gravel, or mining clay (e.g., china clay, paper clay and slip clay) and (2) preparation plants primarily engaged in beneficiating (e.g., washing, screening, and grinding) sand and gravel, clay, and ceramic and refractory minerals.

Cross-References.   Establishments primarily engaged in--

- Calcining, dead burning, or otherwise processing (i.e., beyond basic preparation) clay or refractory minerals--are classified in Industry 32799, All Other Nonmetallic Mineral Product Manufacturing;
- Shaping, molding, baking, burning, or hardening nonclay ceramics, clay and nonclay refractories, and structural clay products--are classified in Industry 32712, Clay Building Material and Refractories Manufacturing; and
- Shaping, molding, glazing, and firing pottery, ceramics, and plumbing fixtures--are classified in Industry 32711, Pottery, Ceramics, and Plumbing Fixture Manufacturing.

212321 Construction Sand and Gravel Mining

This U.S. industry comprises establishments primarily engaged in one or more of the following: (1) operating commercial grade (i.e., construction) sand and gravel pits; (2) dredging for commercial grade sand and gravel; and (3) washing, screening, or otherwise preparing commercial grade sand and gravel.

Cross-References.

Establishments primarily engaged in mining industrial grade sand are classified in U.S. Industry 212322, Industrial Sand Mining.

212322 Industrial Sand Mining

This U.S. industry comprises establishments primarily engaged in one or more of the following: (1) operating industrial grade sand pits; (2) dredging for industrial grade sand; and (3) washing, screening, or otherwise preparing industrial grade sand.

Cross-References.

Establishments primarily engaged in mining commercial (i.e., construction) grade gravel are classified in U.S. Industry 212321, Construction Sand and Gravel Mining.

212324 Kaolin and Ball Clay Mining

This U.S. industry comprises (1) establishments primarily engaged in developing the mine site and/or mining kaolin or ball clay (e.g., china clay, paper clay, and slip clay) and (2) establishments primarily engaged in beneficiating (i.e., preparing) kaolin or ball clay.

Cross-References.

Establishments primarily engaged in calcining, dead burning, or otherwise processing (i.e., beyond basic preparation) kaolin and ball clay are classified in U.S. Industry 327992, Ground or Treated Mineral and Earth Manufacturing.

T—Canadian, Mexican, and United States industries are comparable.

212325 Clay and Ceramic and Refractory Minerals Mining

This U.S. industry comprises establishments primarily engaged in one or more of the following: (1) mining clay (except kaolin and ball), ceramic, or refractory minerals; (2) developing the mine site for clay, ceramic, or refractory minerals; and (3) beneficiating (i.e., preparing) clay (except kaolin and ball), ceramic, or refractory minerals.

Illustrative Examples:

Bentonite mining and/or beneficiating
Fuller's earth mining and/or beneficiating
Common clay mining and/or beneficiating
Magnesite mining and/or beneficiating

Feldspar mining and/or beneficiating
Nepheline syenite mining and/or beneficiating
Fire clay mining and/or beneficiating
Shale (except oil shale) mining and/or beneficiating

Cross-References.   Establishments primarily engaged in--

- Shaping, molding, baking, burning, or hardening clay and nonclay refractories, and structural clay products--are classified in Industry 327120, Clay Building Material and Refractories Manufacturing;
- Developing the mine site, mining, and/or beneficiating kaolin or ball clay--are classified in U.S. Industry 212324, Kaolin and Ball Clay Mining; and
- Shaping, molding, glazing, and firing pottery, ceramics, and plumbing fixtures--are classified in Industry 327110, Pottery, Ceramics, and Plumbing Fixture Manufacturing.

21239   Other Nonmetallic Mineral Mining and Quarrying[T]

This industry comprises establishments primarily engaged in developing the mine site, mining, and/or milling or otherwise beneficiating (i.e., preparing) nonmetallic minerals (except coal, stone, sand, gravel, clay, ceramic, and refractory minerals).

Illustrative Examples:

Barite mining and/or beneficiating
Phosphate rock mining and/or beneficiating
Borate, natural, mining and/or beneficiating

Potash mining and/or beneficiating
Peat mining and/or beneficiating
Rock salt mining and/or beneficiating

Cross-References.   Establishments primarily engaged in--

- Mining or quarrying dimension stone--are classified in Industry 21231, Stone Mining and Quarrying;
- Mining or quarrying sand, gravel, clay, and ceramic and refractory minerals--are classified in Industry 21232, Sand, Gravel, Clay, and Ceramic and Refractory Minerals Mining and Quarrying;
- Calcining, dead burning, or otherwise processing (i.e., beyond basic preparation) minerals, such as talc, mica, feldspar, barite, and soapstone--are classified in Industry 32799, All Other Nonmetallic Mineral Product Manufacturing;
- Manufacturing boron compounds and potassium salts--are classified in Industry 32518, Other Basic Inorganic Chemical Manufacturing;
- Manufacturing table salt--are classified in Industry 31194, Seasoning and Dressing Manufacturing;
- Manufacturing salt (except table salt)--are classified in Industry 32599, All Other Chemical Product and Preparation Manufacturing; and
- Manufacturing phosphoric acid, superphosphates, or other phosphatic fertilizer materials--are classified in Industry 32531, Fertilizer Manufacturing.

212391 Potash, Soda, and Borate Mineral Mining

This U.S. industry comprises establishments primarily engaged in developing the mine site, mining and/or milling, or otherwise beneficiating (i.e., preparing) natural potassium, sodium, or boron compounds. Drylake brine

---

T—Canadian, Mexican, and United States industries are comparable.

operations are included in this industry, as well as establishments engaged in producing the specified minerals from underground and open pit mines.

Cross-References.   Establishments primarily engaged in--

- Manufacturing sodium carbonate, boron compounds, and/or potassium salts--are classified in Industry 325180, Other Basic Inorganic Chemical Manufacturing; and
- Manufacturing table salt--are classified in U.S. Industry 311942, Spice and Extract Manufacturing.

212392 Phosphate Rock Mining

This U.S. industry comprises establishments primarily engaged in developing the mine site, mining, milling, and/or drying or otherwise beneficiating (i.e., preparing) phosphate rock.

Cross-References.

Establishments primarily engaged in manufacturing phosphoric acid, superphosphates, or other phosphatic fertilizer materials are classified in U.S. Industry 325312, Phosphatic Fertilizer Manufacturing.

212393 Other Chemical and Fertilizer Mineral Mining

This U.S. industry comprises establishments primarily engaged in developing the mine site, mining, milling, and/or drying or otherwise beneficiating (i.e., preparing) chemical or fertilizer mineral raw materials (except potash, soda, boron, and phosphate rock).

Illustrative Examples:

Barite mining and/or beneficiating
Rock salt mining and/or beneficiating
Celestite mining and/or beneficiating

Sulfur mining and/or beneficiating
Fluorspar mining and/or beneficiating

Cross-References.   Establishments primarily engaged in--

- Mining and/or milling or otherwise beneficiating natural potassium, sodium, or boron compounds--are classified in U.S. Industry 212391, Potash, Soda, and Borate Mineral Mining;
- Manufacturing industrial salt--are classified in U.S. Industry 325998, All Other Miscellaneous Chemical Product and Preparation Manufacturing;
- Mining, milling, drying, and/or sintering or otherwise beneficiating phosphate rock--are classified in U.S. Industry 212392, Phosphate Rock Mining; and
- Manufacturing table salt--are classified in U.S. Industry 311942, Spice and Extract Manufacturing.

212399 All Other Nonmetallic Mineral Mining

This U.S. industry comprises establishments primarily engaged in developing the mine site, mining and/or milling, or otherwise beneficiating (i.e., preparing) nonmetallic minerals (except stone, sand, gravel, clay, ceramic, refractory minerals, and chemical and fertilizer minerals).

Illustrative Examples:

Gypsum mining and/or beneficiating
Soapstone mining and/or beneficiating
Mica mining and/or beneficiating

Talc mining and/or beneficiating
Pyrophyllite mining and/or beneficiating

T—Canadian, Mexican, and United States industries are comparable.

Cross-References.   Establishments primarily engaged in--

- Mining or quarrying stone--are classified in Industry 21231, Stone Mining and Quarrying;
- Mining, quarrying, or beneficiating sand, gravel, clay, and ceramic and refractory minerals--are classified in Industry 21232, Sand, Gravel, Clay, and Ceramic and Refractory Minerals Mining and Quarrying;
- Mining, quarrying, or beneficiating natural potash, soda, and borate--are classified in U.S. Industry 212391, Potash, Soda, and Borate Mineral Mining; and
- Mining and/or milling or otherwise beneficiating phosphate rock--are classified in U.S. Industry 212392, Phosphate Rock Mining.

213   Support Activities for Mining[T]

Industries in the Support Activities for Mining subsector group establishments primarily providing support services, on a contract or fee basis, required for the mining and quarrying of minerals and for the extraction of oil and gas. Establishments performing exploration (except geophysical surveying and mapping) for minerals, on a contract or fee basis, are included in this subsector. Exploration includes traditional prospecting methods, such as taking core samples and making geological observations at prospective sites.

The activities performed on a contract or fee basis by establishments in the Support Activities for Mining subsector are also often performed in-house by mining operators. These activities include taking core samples, making geological observations at prospective sites, excavating slush pits and cellars, and such oil and gas operations as spudding in, drilling in, redrilling, directional drilling, and well surveying; running, cutting, and pulling casings, tubes, and rods; cementing and shooting wells; perforating well casings; acidizing and chemically treating wells; cleaning out, bailing, and swabbing wells; and operating oil and gas field gathering lines.

2131   Support Activities for Mining[T]

21311   Support Activities for Mining[T]

This industry comprises establishments primarily engaged in providing support services, on a contract or fee basis, required for the mining and quarrying of minerals and for the extraction of oil and gas. Drilling, taking core samples, and making geological observations at prospective sites (except geophysical surveying and mapping) for minerals, on a contract or fee basis, are included in this industry.

Cross-References.   Establishments primarily engaged in--

- Performing geophysical surveying and mapping services for minerals (i.e., coal, metal ores, oil and gas, and nonmetallic minerals) on a contract or fee basis--are classified in Industry 54136, Geophysical Surveying and Mapping Services;
- Mining, quarrying, and/or beneficiating on a contract or fee basis--are classified in Subsector 212, Mining (except Oil and Gas), based on the mineral mined;
- Operating oil and gas field properties on a contract or fee basis--are classified in Subsector 211, Oil and Gas Extraction, based on the activity;
- Oil and gas pipeline and related structures construction and repair--are classified in Industry 23712, Oil and Gas Pipeline and Related Structures Construction;
- Site preparation and related construction activities on a contract or fee basis--are classified in Industry 23891, Site Preparation Contractors; and
- Mining machinery and equipment repair and maintenance--are classified in Industry 81131, Commercial and Industrial Machinery and Equipment (except Automotive and Electronic) Repair and Maintenance.

213111   Drilling Oil and Gas Wells

This U.S. industry comprises establishments primarily engaged in drilling oil and gas wells for others on a contract or fee basis. This industry includes contractors that specialize in spudding in, drilling in, redrilling, and directional drilling.

T—Canadian, Mexican, and United States industries are comparable.

Cross-References.   Establishments primarily engaged in--

- Performing exploration (except geophysical surveying and mapping) services for oil and gas on a contract or fee basis--are classified in U.S. Industry 213112, Support Activities for Oil and Gas Operations; and
- Performing geophysical surveying and mapping services for oil and gas on a contract or fee basis--are classified in Industry 541360, Geophysical Surveying and Mapping Services.

213112 Support Activities for Oil and Gas Operations

This U.S. industry comprises establishments primarily engaged in performing support activities on a contract or fee basis for oil and gas operations (except site preparation and related construction activities). Services included are exploration (except geophysical surveying and mapping); excavating slush pits and cellars, well surveying; running, cutting, and pulling casings, tubes, and rods; cementing wells, shooting wells; perforating well casings; acidizing and chemically treating wells; and cleaning out, bailing, and swabbing wells.

Cross-References.   Establishments primarily engaged in--

- Contract drilling for oil and gas--are classified in U.S. Industry 213111, Drilling Oil and Gas Wells;
- Operating oil and gas field properties on a contract or fee basis--are classified in Industry Group 2111, Oil and Gas Extraction;
- Performing geophysical surveying and mapping services for oil and gas on a contract or fee basis--are classified in Industry 541360, Geophysical Surveying and Mapping Services;
- Oil and gas pipeline and related structures construction and repair--are classified in Industry 237120, Oil and Gas Pipeline and Related Structures Construction;
- Inspecting pipelines--are classified in Industry 541990, All Other Professional, Scientific, and Technical Services;
- Site preparation and related construction activities on a contract or fee basis--are classified in Industry 238910, Site Preparation Contractors; and
- Mining machinery and equipment repair and maintenance--are classified in Industry 811310, Commercial and Industrial Machinery and Equipment (except Automotive and Electronic) Repair and Maintenance.

213113 Support Activities for Coal Mining

This U.S. industry comprises establishments primarily engaged in providing support activities for coal mining (except site preparation and related construction activities) on a contract or fee basis. Exploration for coal is included in this industry. Exploration includes traditional prospecting methods, such as taking core samples and making geological observations at prospective sites.

Cross-References.   Establishments primarily engaged in--

- Performing geophysical surveying and mapping services for coal on a contract or fee basis--are classified in Industry 541360, Geophysical Surveying and Mapping Services;
- Operating coal mines or quarries on a contract or fee basis--are classified in Industry 21211, Coal Mining, based on the type of coal mined; and
- Site preparation and related construction activities on a contract or fee basis--are classified in Industry 238910, Site Preparation Contractors.

213114 Support Activities for Metal Mining

This U.S. industry comprises establishments primarily engaged in providing support activities (except site preparation and related construction activities) on a contract or fee basis for the mining and quarrying of metallic minerals and for the extraction of metal ores. Exploration for these minerals is included in this industry. Exploration (except geophysical surveying and mapping services) includes traditional prospecting methods, such as taking core samples and making geological observations at prospective sites.

T—Canadian, Mexican, and United States industries are comparable.

Cross-References.   Establishments primarily engaged in--

- Performing geophysical surveying and mapping services for metallic minerals on a contract or fee basis-- are classified in Industry 541360, Geophysical Surveying and Mapping Services;
- Operating metallic mineral mines or quarries on a contract or fee basis--are classified in Industry Group 2122, Metal Ore Mining, based on the type of ore mined; and
- Site preparation and related construction activities on a contract or fee basis--are classified in Industry 238910, Site Preparation Contractors.

213115 Support Activities for Nonmetallic Minerals (except Fuels) Mining

This U.S. industry comprises establishments primarily engaged in providing support activities, on a contract or fee basis, for the mining and quarrying of nonmetallic minerals (except fuel) and for the extraction of nonmetallic minerals (except site preparation and related construction activities). Exploration for these minerals is included in this industry. Exploration (except geophysical surveying and mapping services) includes traditional prospecting methods, such as taking core samples and making geological observations at prospective sites.

Cross-References.   Establishments primarily engaged in--

- Performing geophysical surveying and mapping services for nonmetallic minerals on a contract or fee basis--are classified in Industry 541360, Geophysical Surveying and Mapping Services;
- Operating nonmetallic mineral mines or quarries on a contract or fee basis--are classified in Industry Group 2123, Nonmetallic Mineral Mining and Quarrying, based on the type of mineral mined or quarried; and
- Site preparation and related construction activities on a contract or fee basis--are classified in Industry 238910, Site Preparation Contractors.

T—Canadian, Mexican, and United States industries are comparable.

Sector 22--Utilities[T]

The Sector as a Whole

The Utilities sector comprises establishments engaged in the provision of the following utility services: electric power, natural gas, steam supply, water supply, and sewage removal. Within this sector, the specific activities associated with the utility services provided vary by utility: electric power includes generation, transmission, and distribution; natural gas includes distribution; steam supply includes provision and/or distribution; water supply includes treatment and distribution; and sewage removal includes collection, treatment, and disposal of waste through sewer systems and sewage treatment facilities.

Excluded from this sector are establishments primarily engaged in waste management services classified in Subsector 562, Waste Management and Remediation Services. These establishments also collect, treat, and dispose of waste materials; however, they do not use sewer systems or sewage treatment facilities.

221 Utilities[T]

Industries in the Utilities subsector provide electric power, natural gas, steam supply, water supply, and sewage removal through a permanent infrastructure of lines, mains, and pipes. Establishments are grouped together based on the utility service provided and the particular system or facilities required to perform the service.

2211 Electric Power Generation, Transmission and Distribution[T]

This industry group comprises establishments primarily engaged in generating, transmitting, and/or distributing electric power. Establishments in this industry group may perform one or more of the following activities: (1) operate generation facilities that produce electric energy; (2) operate transmission systems that convey the electricity from the generation facility to the distribution system; and (3) operate distribution systems that convey electric power received from the generation facility or the transmission system to the final consumer.

22111 Electric Power Generation[T]

This industry comprises establishments primarily engaged in operating electric power generation facilities. These facilities convert other forms of energy, such as water power (i.e., hydroelectric), fossil fuels, nuclear power, and solar power, into electrical energy. The establishments in this industry produce electric energy and provide electricity to transmission systems or to electric power distribution systems.

Cross-References.

Establishments primarily engaged in operating trash incinerators that also generate electricity are classified in Industry 56221, Waste Treatment and Disposal.

221111 Hydroelectric Power Generation

This U.S. industry comprises establishments primarily engaged in operating hydroelectric power generation facilities. These facilities use water power to drive a turbine and produce electric energy. The electric energy produced in these establishments is provided to electric power transmission systems or to electric power distribution systems.

221112 Fossil Fuel Electric Power Generation

This U.S. industry comprises establishments primarily engaged in operating fossil fuel powered electric power generation facilities. These facilities use fossil fuels, such as coal, oil, or gas, in internal combustion or combustion turbine conventional steam process to produce electric energy. The electric energy produced in these establishments is provided to electric power transmission systems or to electric power distribution systems.

T—Canadian, Mexican, and United States industries are comparable.

221113　Nuclear Electric Power Generation

This U.S. industry comprises establishments primarily engaged in operating nuclear electric power generation facilities. These facilities use nuclear power to produce electric energy. The electric energy produced in these establishments is provided to electric power transmission systems or to electric power distribution systems.

221114　Solar Electric Power Generation

This U.S. industry comprises establishments primarily engaged in operating solar electric power generation facilities. These facilities use energy from the sun to produce electric energy. The electric energy produced in these establishments is provided to electric power transmission systems or to electric power distribution systems.

221115　Wind Electric Power Generation

This U.S. industry comprises establishments primarily engaged in operating wind electric power generation facilities. These facilities use wind power to drive a turbine and produce electric energy. The electric energy produced in these establishments is provided to electric power transmission systems or to electric power distribution systems.

221116　Geothermal Electric Power Generation

This U.S. industry comprises establishments primarily engaged in operating geothermal electric power generation facilities. These facilities use heat derived from the Earth to produce electric energy. The electric energy produced in these establishments is provided to electric power transmission systems or to electric power distribution systems.

221117　Biomass Electric Power Generation

This U.S. industry comprises establishments primarily engaged in operating biomass electric power generation facilities. These facilities use biomass (e.g., wood, waste, alcohol fuels) to produce electric energy. The electric energy produced in these establishments is provided to electric power transmission systems or to electric power distribution systems.

Cross-References.

Establishments primarily engaged in operating trash disposal incinerators that also generate electricity are classified in U.S. Industry 562213, Solid Waste Combustors and Incinerators.

221118　Other Electric Power Generation

This U.S. industry comprises establishments primarily engaged in operating electric power generation facilities (except hydroelectric, fossil fuel, nuclear, solar, wind, geothermal, biomass). These facilities convert other forms of energy, such as tidal power, into electric energy. The electric energy produced in these establishments is provided to electric power transmission systems or to electric power distribution systems.

Cross-References.　　　　Establishments primarily engaged in--

- Operating trash disposal incinerators that also generate electricity--are classified in U.S. Industry 562213, Solid Waste Combustors and Incinerators;
- Operating hydroelectric power generation facilities--are classified in U.S. Industry 221111, Hydroelectric Power Generation;
- Operating fossil fuel powered electric power generation facilities--are classified in U.S. Industry 221112, Fossil Fuel Electric Power Generation;
- Operating nuclear electric power generation facilities--are classified in U.S. Industry 221113, Nuclear Electric Power Generation;

T—Canadian, Mexican, and United States industries are comparable.

- Operating solar electric power generation facilities--are classified in U.S. Industry 221114, Solar Electric Power Generation;
- Operating wind electric power generation facilities--are classified in U.S. Industry 221115, Wind Electric Power Generation;
- Operating geothermal electric power generation facilities--are classified in U.S. Industry 221116, Geothermal Electric Power Generation; and
- Operating biomass electric power generation facilities--are classified in U.S. Industry 221117, Biomass Electric Power Generation.

22112   Electric Power Transmission, Control, and Distribution[T]

This industry comprises establishments primarily engaged in operating electric power transmission systems, controlling (i.e., regulating voltages) the transmission of electricity, and/or distributing electricity. The transmission system includes lines and transformer stations. These establishments arrange, facilitate, or coordinate the transmission of electricity from the generating source to the distribution centers, other electric utilities, or final consumers. The distribution system consists of lines, poles, meters, and wiring that deliver the electricity to final consumers.

Cross-References.

Establishments primarily engaged in generating electric energy are classified in Industry 22111, Electric Power Generation.

221121   Electric Bulk Power Transmission and Control

This U.S. industry comprises establishments primarily engaged in operating electric power transmission systems and/or controlling (i.e., regulating voltages) the transmission of electricity from the generating source to distribution centers or other electric utilities. The transmission system includes lines and transformer stations.

Cross-References.   Establishments primarily engaged in--

- Generating electric energy--are classified in Industry 22111, Electric Power Generation; and
- Distributing electricity to final consumers--are classified in U.S. Industry 221122, Electric Power Distribution.

221122   Electric Power Distribution

This U.S. industry comprises electric power establishments primarily engaged in either (1) operating electric power distribution systems (i.e., consisting of lines, poles, meters, and wiring) or (2) operating as electric power brokers or agents that arrange the sale of electricity via power distribution systems operated by others.

Cross-References.   Establishments primarily engaged in--

- Generating electric energy--are classified in Industry 22111, Electric Power Generation; and
- Transmitting electricity between generating sources or distribution centers--are classified in U.S. Industry 221121, Electric Bulk Power Transmission and Control.

2212   Natural Gas Distribution[T]

22121   Natural Gas Distribution[T]
See industry description for 221210.

T—Canadian, Mexican, and United States industries are comparable.

221210 Natural Gas Distribution

This industry comprises: (1) establishments primarily engaged in operating gas distribution systems (e.g., mains, meters); (2) establishments known as gas marketers that buy gas from the well and sell it to a distribution system; (3) establishments known as gas brokers or agents that arrange the sale of gas over gas distribution systems operated by others; and (4) establishments primarily engaged in transmitting and distributing gas to final consumers.

Cross-References.   Establishments primarily engaged in--

- Pipeline transportation of natural gas from process plants to local distribution systems--are classified in Industry 486210, Pipeline Transportation of Natural Gas; and
- Retailing liquefied petroleum (LP) gas via direct selling--are classified in Industry 454310, Fuel Dealers.

2213   Water, Sewage and Other Systems[T]

This industry group comprises establishments primarily engaged in: (1) operating water treatment plants and/or water supply systems; (2) operating sewer systems or sewage treatment facilities; or (3) providing steam, heated air, or cooled air.

22131   Water Supply and Irrigation Systems
See industry description for 221310.

221310 Water Supply and Irrigation Systems

This industry comprises establishments primarily engaged in operating water treatment plants and/or operating water supply systems. The water supply system may include pumping stations, aqueducts, and/or distribution mains. The water may be used for drinking, irrigation, or other uses.

22132   Sewage Treatment Facilities
See industry description for 221320.

221320 Sewage Treatment Facilities

This industry comprises establishments primarily engaged in operating sewer systems or sewage treatment facilities that collect, treat, and dispose of waste.

Cross-References.   Establishments primarily engaged in--

- Operating waste treatment or disposal facilities (except sewer systems or sewage treatment facilities)--are classified in Industry 56221, Waste Treatment and Disposal;
- Pumping (i.e., cleaning) septic tanks and cesspools--are classified in U.S. Industry 562991, Septic Tank and Related Services; and
- Cleaning and rodding sewers and catch basins--are classified in U.S. Industry 562998, All Other Miscellaneous Waste Management Services.

22133   Steam and Air-Conditioning Supply
See industry description for 221330.

221330 Steam and Air-Conditioning Supply

This industry comprises establishments primarily engaged in providing steam, heated air, or cooled air. The steam distribution may be through mains.

T—Canadian, Mexican, and United States industries are comparable.

Sector 23--Construction[T]

The Sector as a Whole

The Construction sector comprises establishments primarily engaged in the construction of buildings or engineering projects (e.g., highways and utility systems). Establishments primarily engaged in the preparation of sites for new construction and establishments primarily engaged in subdividing land for sale as building sites also are included in this sector.

Construction work done may include new work, additions, alterations, or maintenance and repairs. Activities of these establishments generally are managed at a fixed place of business, but they usually perform construction activities at multiple project sites. Production responsibilities for establishments in this sector are usually specified in (1) contracts with the owners of construction projects (prime contracts) or (2) contracts with other construction establishments (subcontracts).

Establishments primarily engaged in contracts that include responsibility for all aspects of individual construction projects are commonly known as general contractors, but also may be known as design-builders, construction managers, turnkey contractors, or (in cases where two or more establishments jointly secure a general contract) joint-venture contractors. Construction managers that provide oversight and scheduling only (i.e., agency) as well as construction managers that are responsible for the entire project (i.e., at risk) are included as general contractor type establishments. Establishments of the "general contractor type" frequently arrange construction of separate parts of their projects through subcontracts with other construction establishments.

Establishments primarily engaged in activities to produce a specific component (e.g., masonry, painting, and electrical work) of a construction project are commonly known as specialty trade contractors. Activities of specialty trade contractors are usually subcontracted from other construction establishments, but especially in remodeling and repair construction, the work may be done directly for the owner of the property.

Establishments primarily engaged in activities to construct buildings to be sold on sites that they own are known as for-sale builders, but also may be known as speculative builders or merchant builders. For-sale builders produce buildings in a manner similar to general contractors, but their production processes also include site acquisition and securing of financial backing. For-sale builders are most often associated with the construction of residential buildings. Like general contractors, they may subcontract all or part of the actual construction work on their buildings.

There are substantial differences in the types of equipment, work force skills, and other inputs required by establishments in this sector. To highlight these differences and variations in the underlying production functions, this sector is divided into three subsectors.

Subsector 236, Construction of Buildings, comprises establishments of the general contractor type and for-sale builders involved in the construction of buildings. Subsector 237, Heavy and Civil Engineering Construction, comprises establishments involved in the construction of engineering projects. Subsector 238, Specialty Trade Contractors, comprises establishments engaged in specialty trade activities generally needed in the construction of all types of buildings.

Force account construction is construction work performed by an enterprise primarily engaged in some business other than construction for its own account, using employees of the enterprise. This activity is not included in the construction sector unless the construction work performed is the primary activity of a separate establishment of the enterprise. The installation and the ongoing repair and maintenance of telecommunications and utility networks is excluded from construction when the establishments performing the work are not independent contractors. Although a growing proportion of this work is subcontracted to independent contractors in the Construction sector, the operating units of telecommunications and utility companies performing this work are included with the telecommunications or utility activities.

236   Construction of Buildings[T]

The Construction of Buildings subsector comprises establishments primarily responsible for the construction of buildings. The work performed may include new work, additions, alterations, or maintenance and repairs. The on-site assembly of precut, panelized, and prefabricated buildings and construction of temporary buildings are included in this subsector. Part or all of the production work for which the establishments in this subsector have responsibility may be subcontracted to other construction establishments--usually specialty trade contractors.

T—Canadian, Mexican, and United States industries are comparable.

Establishments in this subsector are classified based on the types of buildings they construct. This classification reflects variations in the requirements of the underlying production processes.

2361   Residential Building Construction[T]

23611   Residential Building Construction[T]

This industry comprises establishments primarily responsible for the construction or remodeling and renovation of single-family and multifamily residential buildings. Included in this industry are residential housing general contractors (i.e., new construction, remodeling, or renovating existing residential structures), for-sale builders and remodelers of residential structures, residential project construction management firms, and residential design-build firms.

Cross-References.   Establishments primarily engaged in--

- Performing specialized construction work on houses and other residential buildings, generally on a subcontract basis--are classified in Subsector 238, Specialty Trade Contractors;
- Performing manufactured (mobile) home set up and tie-down work--are classified in Industry 23899, All Other Specialty Trade Contractors; and
- Constructing and leasing residential buildings on their own account--are classified in Industry 53111, Lessors of Residential Buildings and Dwellings.

236115 New Single-Family Housing Construction (except For-Sale Builders)

This U.S. industry comprises general contractor establishments primarily responsible for the entire construction of new single-family housing, such as single-family detached houses and town houses or row houses where each housing unit (1) is separated from its neighbors by a ground-to-roof wall and (2) has no housing units constructed above or below. This industry includes general contractors responsible for the on-site assembly of modular and prefabricated houses. Single-family housing design-build firms and single-family construction management firms acting as general contractors are included in this industry.

Cross-References.   Establishments primarily engaged in--

- Building single-family houses on their own account for sale as speculative builders or merchant builders-- are classified in U.S. Industry 236117, New Housing For-Sale Builders;
- Remodeling or repairing existing houses and other residential buildings--are classified in U.S. Industry 236118, Residential Remodelers;
- Performing manufactured (mobile) home set up and tie-down work--are classified in Industry 238990, All Other Specialty Trade Contractors;
- Performing specialized construction work on houses and other residential buildings, generally on a subcontract basis--are classified in Subsector 238, Specialty Trade Contractors; and
- Constructing and leasing residential buildings on their own account--are classified in Industry 531110, Lessors of Residential Buildings and Dwellings.

236116 New Multifamily Housing Construction (except For-Sale Builders)

This U.S. industry comprises general contractor establishments primarily responsible for the construction of new multifamily residential housing units (e.g., high-rise, garden, town house apartments, and condominiums where each unit is not separated from its neighbors by a ground-to-roof wall). Multifamily design-build firms and multifamily housing construction management firms acting as general contractors are included in this industry.

Cross-References.   Establishments primarily engaged in--

- Building multifamily buildings on their own account for sale as speculative builders or merchant builders-- are classified in U.S. Industry 236117, New Housing For-Sale Builders;

T—Canadian, Mexican, and United States industries are comparable.

- Remodeling or repairing existing multifamily housing and other residential buildings--are classified in U.S. Industry 236118, Residential Remodelers;
- Performing specialized construction work on multifamily housing and other residential buildings, generally on a subcontract basis--are classified in Subsector 238, Specialty Trade Contractors; and
- Constructing and leasing residential buildings on their own account--are classified in Industry 531110, Lessors of Residential Buildings and Dwellings.

236117 New Housing For-Sale Builders

This U.S. industry comprises establishments primarily engaged in building new homes on land that is owned or controlled by the builder rather than the homebuyer or investor. The land is included with the sale of the home. Establishments in this industry build single-family and/or multifamily homes. These establishments are often referred to as merchant builders, but are also known as production or for-sale builders.

Cross-References.   Establishments primarily engaged in--

- Building single-family houses for others as general contractors--are classified in U.S. Industry 236115, New Single-Family Housing Construction (except For-Sale Builders);
- Building multifamily residential buildings for others as general contractors--are classified in U.S. Industry 236116, New Multifamily Housing Construction (except For-Sale Builders);
- Remodeling or repairing existing houses and other residential buildings, either for others or on own account for sale--are classified in U.S. Industry 236118, Residential Remodelers;
- Performing specialized construction work on houses or other residential buildings, generally on a subcontract basis--are classified in Subsector 238, Specialty Trade Contractors; and
- Constructing and leasing residential buildings on their own account--are classified in Industry 531110, Lessors of Residential Buildings and Dwellings.

236118 Residential Remodelers

This U.S. industry comprises establishments primarily responsible for the remodeling construction (including additions, alterations, reconstruction, maintenance, and repairs) of houses and other residential buildings, single-family and multifamily. Included in this industry are remodeling general contractors, for-sale remodelers, remodeling design-build firms, and remodeling project construction management firms.

Cross-References.   Establishments primarily engaged in--

- Building single-family houses for others as general contractors--are classified in U.S. Industry 236115, New Single-Family Housing Construction (except For-Sale Builders);
- Building multifamily buildings for others as general contractors--are classified in U.S. Industry 236116, New Multifamily Housing Construction (except For-Sale Builders);
- Building houses or other residential buildings, on their own account for sale as speculative builders or merchant builders--are classified in U.S. Industry 236117, New Housing For-Sale Builders;
- Remodeling nonresidential buildings--are classified in Industry Group 2362, Nonresidential Building Construction, based on the type of structure being remodeled;
- Performing specialized construction work on houses or other residential buildings, generally on a subcontract basis--are classified in Subsector 238, Specialty Trade Contractors; and
- Constructing and leasing residential buildings on their own account--are classified in Industry 531110, Lessors of Residential Buildings and Dwellings.

2362   Nonresidential Building Construction[T]

This industry group comprises establishments primarily responsible for the construction (including new work, additions, alterations, maintenance, and repairs) of nonresidential buildings. This industry group includes nonresidential general contractors, nonresidential for-sale builders, nonresidential design-build firms, and nonresidential project construction management firms.

T—Canadian, Mexican, and United States industries are comparable.

23621   Industrial Building Construction^T
See industry description for 236210.

236210 Industrial Building Construction

This industry comprises establishments primarily responsible for the construction (including new work, additions, alterations, maintenance, and repairs) of industrial buildings (except warehouses). The construction of selected additional structures, whose production processes are similar to those for industrial buildings (e.g., incinerators, cement plants, blast furnaces, and similar nonbuilding structures), is included in this industry. Included in this industry are industrial building general contractors, industrial building for-sale builders, industrial building design-build firms, and industrial building construction management firms.

Illustrative Examples:

Assembly plant construction	Pharmaceutical manufacturing plant construction
Furnace, industrial plant, construction	Factory construction
Cannery construction	Steel mill construction
Mine loading and discharging station construction	Food processing plant construction
Cement plant construction	Waste disposal plant (except sewage treatment)
Paper or pulp mill construction	construction
Chemical plant (except petrochemical) construction	

Cross-References.   Establishments primarily engaged in--

- Constructing oil refineries and petrochemical plants--are classified in Industry 237120, Oil and Gas Pipeline and Related Structures Construction;
- Constructing water treatment plants, sewage treatment plants, and pumping stations for water and sewer systems--are classified in Industry 237110, Water and Sewer Line and Related Structures Construction;
- Constructing power generation plants (except hydroelectric)--are classified in Industry 237130, Power and Communication Line and Related Structures Construction;
- Constructing industrial warehouses--are classified in Industry 236220, Commercial and Institutional Building Construction; and
- Performing specialized construction work on industrial buildings, generally on a subcontract basis--are classified in Subsector 238, Specialty Trade Contractors.

23622   Commercial and Institutional Building Construction^T
See industry description for 236220.

236220 Commercial and Institutional Building Construction

This industry comprises establishments primarily responsible for the construction (including new work, additions, alterations, maintenance, and repairs) of commercial and institutional buildings and related structures, such as stadiums, grain elevators, and indoor swimming facilities. This industry includes establishments responsible for the on-site assembly of modular or prefabricated commercial and institutional buildings. Included in this industry are commercial and institutional building general contractors, commercial and institutional building for-sale builders, commercial and institutional building design-build firms, and commercial and institutional building project construction management firms.

Illustrative Examples:

Airport building construction	Prison construction
Office building construction	Farm building construction
Arena construction	Radio and television broadcast studio construction
Parking garage construction	Fire station construction
Barrack construction	Grain elevator or bin construction

T—Canadian, Mexican, and United States industries are comparable.

Religious building (e.g., church, synagogue, mosque, temple) construction
Restaurant construction
Hospital construction
School building construction

Hotel construction
Shopping mall construction
Indoor swimming facility construction
Warehouse construction (e.g., commercial, industrial, manufacturing, private)

Cross-References.   Establishments primarily engaged in--

- Constructing structures that are integral parts of utility systems (e.g., storage tanks, pumping stations) or are used to produce products for these systems (e.g., power plants, refineries)--are classified in Industry Group 2371, Utility System Construction, based on the type of construction project;
- Performing specialized construction work on commercial and institutional buildings, generally on a subcontract basis--are classified in Subsector 238, Specialty Trade Contractors; and
- Constructing buildings on their own account for rent or lease--are classified in Industry Group 5311, Lessors of Real Estate.

237   Heavy and Civil Engineering Construction[T]

The Heavy and Civil Engineering Construction subsector comprises establishments whose primary activity is the construction of entire engineering projects (e.g., highways and dams), and specialty trade contractors, whose primary activity is the production of a specific component for such projects. Specialty trade contractors in the Heavy and Civil Engineering Construction subsector generally are performing activities that are specific to heavy and civil engineering construction projects and are not normally performed on buildings. The work performed may include new work, additions, alterations, or maintenance and repairs.

Specialty trade activities are classified in this subsector if the skills and equipment present are specific to heavy or civil engineering construction projects. For example, specialized equipment is needed to paint lines on highways. This equipment is not normally used in building applications so the activity is classified in this subsector. Traffic signal installation, while specific to highways, uses much of the same skills and equipment that are needed for electrical work in building projects and is therefore classified in Subsector 238, Specialty Trade Contractors.

Construction projects involving water resources (e.g., dredging and land drainage) and projects involving open space improvement (e.g., parks and trails) are included in this subsector. Establishments whose primary activity is the subdivision of land into individual building lots usually perform various additional site-improvement activities (e.g., road building and utility line installation) and are included in this subsector.

Establishments in this subsector are classified based on the types of structures that they construct. This classification reflects variations in the requirements of the underlying production processes.

2371   Utility System Construction[T]

This industry group comprises establishments primarily engaged in the construction of distribution lines and related buildings and structures for utilities (i.e., water, sewer, petroleum, gas, power, and communication). All structures (including buildings) that are integral parts of utility systems (e.g., storage tanks, pumping stations, power plants, and refineries) are included in this industry group.

23711   Water and Sewer Line and Related Structures Construction[T]
See industry description for 237110.

237110   Water and Sewer Line and Related Structures Construction

This industry comprises establishments primarily engaged in the construction of water and sewer lines, mains, pumping stations, treatment plants, and storage tanks. The work performed may include new work, reconstruction, rehabilitation, and repairs. Specialty trade contractors are included in this industry if they are engaged in activities primarily related to water, sewer line, and related structures construction. All structures (including buildings) that are integral parts of water and sewer networks (e.g., storage tanks, pumping stations, water treatment plants, and sewage treatment plants) are included in this industry.

T—Canadian, Mexican, and United States industries are comparable.

Illustrative Examples:

Distribution line, sewer and water, construction
Sewer main, pipe and connection, construction
Fire hydrant installation
Storm sewer construction
Irrigation systems construction
Water main and line construction
Sewage disposal plant construction

Pumping station, water and sewage system, construction
Water system storage tank and tower construction
Reservoir construction
Water treatment plant construction
Water well drilling, digging, boring, or sinking (except water intake wells in oil and gas fields)

Cross-References.

Establishments primarily engaged in constructing marine facilities (e.g., ports), flood control structures, dams, or hydroelectric power generation facilities are classified in Industry 237990, Other Heavy and Civil Engineering Construction.

23712   Oil and Gas Pipeline and Related Structures Construction[T]
See industry description for 237120.

237120 Oil and Gas Pipeline and Related Structures Construction

This industry comprises establishments primarily engaged in the construction of oil and gas lines, mains, refineries, and storage tanks. The work performed may include new work, reconstruction, rehabilitation, and repairs. Specialty trade contractors are included in this industry if they are engaged in activities primarily related to oil and gas pipeline and related structures construction. All structures (including buildings) that are integral parts of oil and gas networks (e.g., storage tanks, pumping stations, and refineries) are included in this industry.

Illustrative Examples:

Distribution line, gas and oil, construction
Oil refinery construction
Gas main construction
Petrochemical plant construction
Gathering line, gas and oil field, construction
Natural gas pipeline construction

Pumping station, gas and oil transmission, construction
Storage tank, natural gas or oil, tank farm or field, construction
Natural gas processing plant construction

Cross-References.   Establishments primarily engaged in--

- Building chemical plants (except petrochemical) and similar process or batch facilities--are classified in Industry 236210, Industrial Building Construction;
- Oil well rig building, repairing, and dismantling, on a contract basis--are classified in U.S. Industry 213112, Support Activities for Oil and Gas Operations;
- Inspecting pipelines--are classified in Industry 541990, All Other Professional, Scientific, and Technical Services; and
- Mining machinery and equipment repair and maintenance--are classified in Industry 811310, Commercial and Industrial Machinery and Equipment (except Automotive and Electronic) Repair and Maintenance.

23713   Power and Communication Line and Related Structures Construction[T]
See industry description for 237130.

237130 Power and Communication Line and Related Structures Construction

This industry comprises establishments primarily engaged in the construction of power lines and towers, power plants, and radio, television, and telecommunications transmitting/receiving towers. The work performed may include new work, reconstruction, rehabilitation, and repairs. Specialty trade contractors are included in this

---

T—Canadian, Mexican, and United States industries are comparable.

industry if they are engaged in activities primarily related to power and communication line and related structures construction. All structures (including buildings) that are integral parts of power and communication networks (e.g., transmitting towers, substations, and power plants) are included.

Illustrative Examples:

Alternative energy (e.g., geothermal, ocean wave, solar, wind) structure construction
Power line stringing
Cellular phone tower construction
Radio transmitting tower construction
Co-generation plant construction
Satellite receiving station construction
Communication tower construction
Nuclear power plant construction
Telephone line stringing
Electric light and power plant (except hydroelectric) construction
Transformer station and substation, electric power, construction
Electric power transmission line and tower construction
Underground cable (e.g., cable television, electricity, telephone) laying

Cross-References.   Establishments primarily engaged in--

- Constructing hydroelectric generating facilities--are classified in Industry 237990, Other Heavy and Civil Engineering Construction;
- Constructing broadcast studios and similar nonresidential buildings--are classified in Industry 236220, Commercial and Institutional Building Construction;
- Performing electrical work within buildings--are classified in Industry 238210, Electrical Contractors and Other Wiring Installation Contractors;
- Line slashing or cutting (except maintenance)--are classified in Industry 238910, Site Preparation Contractors;
- Installing and maintaining communication transmission lines performed by telecommunications companies--are classified in Subsector 517, Telecommunications;
- Locating underground utility lines prior to digging--are classified in Industry 561990, All Other Support Services; and
- Tree and brush trimming for overhead utility lines--are classified in Industry 561730, Landscaping Services.

2372   Land Subdivision[T]

23721   Land Subdivision[T]
See industry description for 237210.

237210 Land Subdivision

This industry comprises establishments primarily engaged in servicing land and subdividing real property into lots, for subsequent sale to builders. Servicing of land may include excavation work for the installation of roads and utility lines. The extent of work may vary from project to project. Land subdivision precedes building activity and the subsequent building is often residential, but may also be commercial tracts and industrial parks. These establishments may do all the work themselves or subcontract the work to others. Establishments that perform only the legal subdivision of land are not included in this industry.

Cross-References.   Establishments primarily engaged in--

- Constructing buildings, for sale, on lots they subdivide--are classified based on the type of construction project, in Industry Group 2361, Residential Building Construction, or Industry Group 2362, Nonresidential Building Construction;
- Installing roads on a subcontract basis for land subdividers--are classified in Industry 237310, Highway, Street, and Bridge Construction;

T—Canadian, Mexican, and United States industries are comparable.

- Installing utilities on a subcontract basis for land subdividers--are classified in Industry Group 2371, Utility System Construction;
- Preparing land owned by others for building construction--are classified in Industry 238910, Site Preparation Contractors;
- Constructing buildings, for rent or lease, on lots they subdivide--are classified in Industry Group 5311, Lessors of Real Estate;
- Subdividing and servicing land for cemetery development--are classified in Industry 812220, Cemeteries and Crematories; and
- Legal subdivision of land without land preparation--are classified elsewhere in the classification system based on the primary activity of the establishment.

2373   Highway, Street, and Bridge Construction[T]

23731   Highway, Street, and Bridge Construction[T]
See industry description for 237310.

237310 Highway, Street, and Bridge Construction

This industry comprises establishments primarily engaged in the construction of highways (including elevated), streets, roads, airport runways, public sidewalks, or bridges. The work performed may include new work, reconstruction, rehabilitation, and repairs. Specialty trade contractors are included in this industry if they are engaged in activities primarily related to highway, street, and bridge construction (e.g., installing guardrails on highways).

Illustrative Examples:

Airport runway construction	Pothole filling, highway, road, street, or bridge
Highway line painting	Elevated highway construction
Causeway construction	Resurfacing, highway, road, street, or bridge
Painting traffic lanes or parking lot lines	Guardrail construction
Culverts, highway, road, and street, construction	Sign erection, highway, road, street, or bridge

Cross-References.   Establishments primarily engaged in--

- Constructing tunnels--are classified in Industry 237990, Other Heavy and Civil Engineering Construction;
- Highway lighting and signal installation--are classified in Industry 238210, Electrical Contractors and Other Wiring Installation Contractors;
- Painting bridges--are classified in Industry 238320, Painting and Wall Covering Contractors;
- Road decommissioning or removing culverts or bridges--are classified in Industry 238910, Site Preparation Contractors; and
- Constructing parking lots, private driveways, sidewalks, or erecting billboards--are classified in Industry 238990, All Other Specialty Trade Contractors.

2379   Other Heavy and Civil Engineering Construction[T]

23799   Other Heavy and Civil Engineering Construction[T]
See industry description for 237990.

237990 Other Heavy and Civil Engineering Construction

This industry comprises establishments primarily engaged in heavy and civil engineering construction projects (excluding highway, street, bridge, and distribution line construction). The work performed may include new work, reconstruction, rehabilitation, and repairs. Specialty trade contractors are included in this industry if they are engaged in activities primarily related to heavy and civil engineering construction projects (excluding highway, street, bridge, distribution line, oil and gas structure, and utilities building and structure construction). Construction

---

T—Canadian, Mexican, and United States industries are comparable.

projects involving water resources (e.g., dredging and land drainage), development of marine facilities, and projects involving open space improvement (e.g., parks and trails) are included in this industry.

Illustrative Examples:

Channel construction
Land drainage contractors
Dam construction
Marine construction
Dock construction
Microtunneling contractors
Dredging (e.g., canal, channel, ditch, waterway)
Nuclear waste disposal site construction
Earth retention system construction
Flood control project construction

Park ground and recreational open space improvement construction
Railroad construction
Golf course construction
Subway construction
Horizontal drilling (e.g., cable, pipeline, sewer installation)
Trenching, underwater
Hydroelectric generating station construction
Tunnel construction

Cross-References.   Establishments primarily engaged in--

- Constructing water mains, sewers, and related structures--are classified in Industry 237110, Water and Sewer Line and Related Structures Construction;
- Constructing oil and gas pipelines and related structures--are classified in Industry 237120, Oil and Gas Pipeline and Related Structures Construction;
- Constructing power and communication transmission lines and related structures--are classified in Industry 237130, Power and Communication Line and Related Structures Construction;
- Constructing highways, streets, and bridges--are classified in Industry 237310, Highway, Street, and Bridge Construction;
- Trenching (except underwater) or removing dams, dikes, and other heavy and civil engineering constructions--are classified in Industry 238910, Site Preparation Contractors; and
- Inspecting pipelines--are classified in Industry 541990, All Other Professional, Scientific, and Technical Services.

238   Specialty Trade Contractors[T]

The Specialty Trade Contractors subsector comprises establishments whose primary activity is performing specific activities (e.g., pouring concrete, site preparation, plumbing, painting, and electrical work) involved in building construction or other activities that are similar for all types of construction, but that are not responsible for the entire project. The work performed may include new work, additions, alterations, maintenance, and repairs. The production work performed by establishments in this subsector is usually subcontracted from establishments of the general contractor type or for-sale builders, but especially in remodeling and repair construction, work also may be done directly for the owner of the property. Specialty trade contractors usually perform most of their work at the construction site, although they may have shops where they perform prefabrication and other work. Establishments primarily engaged in preparing sites for new construction are also included in this subsector.

There are substantial differences in types of equipment, work force skills, and other inputs required by specialty trade contractors. Establishments in this subsector are classified based on the underlying production function for the specialty trade in which they specialize. Throughout the Specialty Trade Contractors subsector, establishments commonly provide both the parts and labor required to complete work. For example, electrical contractors supply the current-carrying and noncurrent-carrying wiring devices that are required to install a circuit. Plumbing, heating, and air-conditioning contractors also supply the parts required to complete a contract.

Establishments that specialize in activities primarily related to heavy and civil engineering construction that are not normally performed on buildings, such as the painting of lines on highways, are classified in Subsector 237, Heavy and Civil Engineering Construction.

Establishments that are primarily engaged in selling construction materials are classified in Sector 42, Wholesale Trade, or Sector 44-45, Retail Trade, based on the characteristics of the selling unit.

T—Canadian, Mexican, and United States industries are comparable.

2381   Foundation, Structure, and Building Exterior Contractors[T]

This industry group comprises establishments primarily engaged in the specialty trades needed to complete the basic structure (i.e., foundation, frame, and shell) of buildings. The work performed may include new work, additions, alterations, maintenance, and repairs.

23811   Poured Concrete Foundation and Structure Contractors
See industry description for 238110.

238110 Poured Concrete Foundation and Structure Contractors

This industry comprises establishments primarily engaged in pouring and finishing concrete foundations and structural elements. This industry also includes establishments performing grout and shotcrete work. The work performed may include new work, additions, alterations, maintenance, and repairs.

Illustrative Examples:

Concrete pouring and finishing
Gunite contractors
Concrete pumping (i.e., placement)
Mud-jacking contractors

Concrete work (except paving)
Shotcrete contractors
Footing and foundation concrete contractors

Cross-References.   Establishments primarily engaged in--

- Constructing or paving streets, highways, and public sidewalks--are classified in Industry 237310, Highway, Street, and Bridge Construction;
- Concrete sealing, coating, waterproofing, or dampproofing--are classified in Industry 238390, Other Building Finishing Contractors; and
- Paving residential driveways, commercial parking lots, and other private parking areas--are classified in Industry 238990, All Other Specialty Trade Contractors.

23812   Structural Steel and Precast Concrete Contractors
See industry description for 238120.

238120 Structural Steel and Precast Concrete Contractors

This industry comprises establishments primarily engaged in (1) erecting and assembling structural parts made from steel or precast concrete (e.g., steel beams, structural steel components, and similar products of precast concrete) and/or (2) assembling and installing other steel construction products (e.g., steel rods, bars, rebar, mesh, and cages) to reinforce poured-in-place concrete. The work performed may include new work, additions, alterations, maintenance, and repairs.

Illustrative Examples:

Concrete product (e.g., structural precast, structural prestressed) installation
Rebar contractors
Erecting structural steel
Reinforcing steel contractors

Placing and tying reinforcing rod at a construction site
Structural steel contractors
Precast concrete panel, slab, or form installation

Cross-References.

Establishments primarily engaged in pouring concrete at the construction site for building foundations or structural elements are classified in Industry 238110, Poured Concrete Foundation and Structure Contractors.

T—Canadian, Mexican, and United States industries are comparable.

23813   Framing Contractors
See industry description for 238130.

238130   Framing Contractors

This industry comprises establishments primarily engaged in structural framing and sheathing using materials other than structural steel or concrete. The work performed may include new work, additions, alterations, maintenance, and repairs.

Illustrative Examples:

Building framing (except structural steel)
Post framing contractors
Foundation, building, wood, contractors
Steel framing contractors

Framing contractors
Wood frame component (e.g., truss) fabrication on site

Cross-References.   Establishments primarily engaged in--

- Finish carpentry--are classified in Industry 238350, Finish Carpentry Contractors; and
- Installing structural steel, precast concrete framing, or structural elements--are classified in Industry 238120, Structural Steel and Precast Concrete Contractors.

23814   Masonry Contractors
See industry description for 238140.

238140   Masonry Contractors

This industry comprises establishments primarily engaged in masonry work, stone setting, bricklaying, and other stone work. The work performed may include new work, additions, alterations, maintenance, and repairs.

Illustrative Examples:

Block laying
Marble, granite, and slate, exterior, contractors
Bricklaying
Masonry pointing, cleaning, or caulking

Concrete block laying
Stucco contractors
Foundation (e.g., brick, block, stone), building, contractors

Cross-References.   Establishments primarily engaged in--

- Erecting the basic structure of buildings by pouring concrete--are classified in Industry 238110, Poured Concrete Foundation and Structure Contractors;
- Interior marble, granite, and slate work--are classified in Industry 238340, Tile and Terrazzo Contractors; and
- Laying precast stones or bricks for patios, sidewalks, and driveways; or paving residential driveways, commercial parking lots and other private parking areas--are classified in Industry 238990, All Other Specialty Trade Contractors.

23815   Glass and Glazing Contractors
See industry description for 238150.

238150   Glass and Glazing Contractors

This industry comprises establishments primarily engaged in installing glass panes in prepared openings (i.e., glazing work) and other glass work for buildings. The work performed may include new work, additions, alterations, maintenance, and repairs.

T—Canadian, Mexican, and United States industries are comparable.

Illustrative Examples:

Decorative glass and mirror installation	Glass coating and tinting (except automotive)
Glazing contractors	contractors
Glass cladding installation	Window pane or sheet installation
Stained glass installation	Glass installation (except automotive) contractors

Cross-References.   Establishments primarily engaged in--

- Installing prefabricated window units--are classified in Industry 238350, Finish Carpentry Contractors; and
- The replacement, repair, and/or tinting of automotive glass--are classified in U.S. Industry 811122, Automotive Glass Replacement Shops.

23816   Roofing Contractors
See industry description for 238160.

238160 Roofing Contractors

   This industry comprises establishments primarily engaged in roofing. This industry also includes establishments treating roofs (i.e., spraying, painting, or coating) and installing skylights. The work performed may include new work, additions, alterations, maintenance, and repairs.

Illustrative Examples:

Painting, spraying, or coating, roof	Shake and shingle, roof, installation
Sheet metal roofing installation	Skylight installation

Cross-References.   Establishments primarily engaged in--

- Installing roof trusses and sheathing attached to trusses--are classified in Industry 238130, Framing Contractors; and
- Installing downspouts, gutters, fascia, and soffits--are classified in Industry 238170, Siding Contractors.

23817   Siding Contractors
See industry description for 238170.

238170 Siding Contractors

   This industry comprises establishments primarily engaged in installing siding of wood, aluminum, vinyl, or other exterior finish material (except brick, stone, stucco, or curtain wall). This industry also includes establishments installing gutters and downspouts. The work performed may include new work, additions, alterations, maintenance, and repairs.

Illustrative Examples:

Downspout, gutter, and gutter guard installation	Siding (e.g., vinyl, wood, aluminum) installation
Fascia and soffit installation	

Cross-References.   Establishments primarily engaged in--

- Installing brick, stone, or stucco building exterior finish materials--are classified in Industry 238140, Masonry Contractors;
- Installing curtain wall--are classified in Industry 238190, Other Foundation, Structure, and Building Exterior Contractors; and

---

T—Canadian, Mexican, and United States industries are comparable.

census.gov/naics

- Installing sheet metal duct work--are classified in Industry 238220, Plumbing, Heating, and Air-Conditioning Contractors.

23819 Other Foundation, Structure, and Building Exterior Contractors
See industry description for 238190.

238190 Other Foundation, Structure, and Building Exterior Contractors

This industry comprises establishments primarily engaged in building foundation and structure trades work (except poured concrete, structural steel, precast concrete, framing, masonry, glass and glazing, roofing, and siding). The work performed may include new work, additions, alterations, maintenance, and repairs.

Illustrative Examples:

Curtain wall, metal, installation	Ornamental metal work installation
Forms for poured concrete, erecting and dismantling	Fire escape installation
Welding, on-site, contractors	Decorative steel and wrought iron work installation

Cross-References.   Establishments primarily engaged in--

- Poured concrete foundation and structure work--are classified in Industry 238110, Poured Concrete Foundation and Structure Contractors;
- Installation of structural steel or precast concrete building components--are classified in Industry 238120, Structural Steel and Precast Concrete Contractors;
- Framing buildings--are classified in Industry 238130, Framing Contractors;
- Masonry work--are classified in Industry 238140, Masonry Contractors;
- Glass and glazing work--are classified in Industry 238150, Glass and Glazing Contractors;
- Installing or repairing roofs--are classified in Industry 238160, Roofing Contractors;
- Installing siding--are classified in Industry 238170, Siding Contractors; and
- Fireproofing buildings--are classified in Industry 238310, Drywall and Insulation Contractors.

2382 Building Equipment Contractors[T]

This industry group comprises establishments primarily engaged in installing or servicing equipment that forms part of a building mechanical system (e.g., electricity, water, heating, and cooling). The work performed may include new work, additions, alterations, maintenance, and repairs. Contractors installing specialized building equipment, such as elevators, escalators, service station equipment, and central vacuum cleaning systems, are also included.

23821 Electrical Contractors and Other Wiring Installation Contractors[T]
See industry description for 238210.

238210 Electrical Contractors and Other Wiring Installation Contractors

This industry comprises establishments primarily engaged in installing and servicing electrical wiring and equipment. Contractors included in this industry may include both the parts and labor when performing work. These contractors may perform new work, additions, alterations, maintenance, and repairs.

Illustrative Examples:

Airport runway lighting contractors	Highway, street, and bridge lighting and electrical signal installation
Fiber optic cable (except transmission line) contractors	Audio equipment (except automotive) installation contractors
Alarm system (e.g., fire, burglar), electric, installation only	Home automation system installation

---

T—Canadian, Mexican, and United States industries are comparable.

Lighting system installation
Cable television hookup contractors
Telecommunications equipment and wiring (except transmission line) installation contractors

Computer and network cable installation
Traffic signal installation
Environmental control system installation
Cable splicing, electrical or fiber optic

Cross-References.   Establishments primarily engaged in--

- Installing and maintaining telecommunications lines by telecommunications companies--are classified in Subsector 517, Telecommunications;
- Constructing power and communication transmission lines--are classified in Industry 237130, Power and Communication Line and Related Structures Construction; and
- Burglar and fire alarm installation combined with sales, maintenance, or monitoring services--are classified in U.S. Industry 561621, Security Systems Services (except Locksmiths).

23822   Plumbing, Heating, and Air-Conditioning Contractors[T]
See industry description for 238220.

238220 Plumbing, Heating, and Air-Conditioning Contractors

   This industry comprises establishments primarily engaged in installing and servicing plumbing, heating, and air-conditioning equipment. Contractors in this industry may provide both parts and labor when performing work. The work performed may include new work, additions, alterations, maintenance, and repairs.

Illustrative Examples:

Cooling tower installation
Heating, ventilation, and air-conditioning (HVAC) contractors
Duct work (e.g., cooling, dust collection, exhaust, heating, ventilation) installation
Lawn sprinkler system installation
Fire sprinkler system installation

Mechanical contractors
Fireplace, natural gas, installation
Refrigeration system (e.g., commercial, industrial, scientific) installation
Furnace installation
Sewer hookup and connection, building

Cross-References.   Establishments primarily engaged in--

- Installing electrical controls for HVAC systems--are classified in Industry 238210, Electrical Contractors and Other Wiring Installation Contractors;
- Duct cleaning--are classified in Industry 561790, Other Services to Buildings and Dwellings; and
- Installing septic tanks--are classified in Industry 238910, Site Preparation Contractors.

23829   Other Building Equipment Contractors[T]
See industry description for 238290.

238290 Other Building Equipment Contractors

   This industry comprises establishments primarily engaged in installing or servicing building equipment (except electrical, plumbing, heating, cooling, or ventilation equipment). The repair and maintenance of miscellaneous building equipment is included in this industry. The work performed may include new work, additions, alterations, maintenance, and repairs.

Illustrative Examples:

Automated and revolving door installation
Lightning protection equipment (e.g., lightning rod) installation

Boiler and pipe insulation installation
Machine rigging
Commercial-type door installation

T—Canadian, Mexican, and United States industries are comparable.

Millwrights
Conveyor system installation
Overhead door, commercial- or industrial-type, installation
Dismantling large-scale machinery and equipment
Revolving door installation

Elevator installation
Satellite dish, household-type, installation
Escalator installation
Vacuum cleaning system, built-in, installation
Gasoline pump, service station, installation

Cross-References. Establishments primarily engaged in--

- Manufacturing industrial equipment with incidental installation--are classified in Sector 31-33, Manufacturing; and
- Repair and maintenance of commercial refrigeration equipment or production equipment--are classified in Industry 811310, Commercial and Industrial Machinery and Equipment (except Automotive and Electronic) Repair and Maintenance.

2383 Building Finishing Contractors[T]

This industry group comprises establishments primarily engaged in the specialty trades needed to finish buildings. The work performed may include new work, additions, alterations, maintenance, and repairs.

23831 Drywall and Insulation Contractors[T]
See industry description for 238310.

238310 Drywall and Insulation Contractors

This industry comprises establishments primarily engaged in drywall, plaster work, and building insulation work. Plaster work includes applying plain or ornamental plaster, and installation of lath to receive plaster. The work performed may include new work, additions, alterations, maintenance, and repairs. Establishments primarily engaged in providing firestop services are included in this industry.

Illustrative Examples:

Acoustical ceiling tile and panel installation
Lathing contractors
Drop ceiling installation
Plastering (i.e., ornamental, plain) contractors
Drywall contractors
Soundproofing contractors

Firestop contractors
Fresco (i.e., decorative plaster finishing) contractors
Taping and finishing drywall
Gypsum board installation
Wall cavity and attic space insulation installation

Cross-References. Establishments primarily engaged in--

- Applying stucco--are classified in Industry 238140, Masonry Contractors; and
- Insulating pipes and boilers--are classified in Industry 238290, Other Building Equipment Contractors.

23832 Painting and Wall Covering Contractors[T]
See industry description for 238320.

238320 Painting and Wall Covering Contractors

This industry comprises establishments primarily engaged in interior or exterior painting or interior wall covering. The work performed may include new work, additions, alterations, maintenance, and repairs.

Illustrative Examples:

Bridge painting

Paperhanging or removal contractors

T—Canadian, Mexican, and United States industries are comparable.

House painting   Paint and wallpaper stripping
Ship painting contractors   Wallpaper hanging and removal contractors

Cross-References.   Establishments primarily engaged in--

- Painting lines on highways, streets, and parking lots--are classified in Industry 237310, Highway, Street, and Bridge Construction;
- Roof painting--are classified in Industry 238160, Roofing Contractors; and
- Installing wood paneling--are classified in Industry 238350, Finish Carpentry Contractors.

23833   Flooring Contractors[T]
See industry description for 238330.

238330   Flooring Contractors

This industry comprises establishments primarily engaged in the installation of resilient floor tile, carpeting, linoleum, and hardwood flooring. The work performed may include new work, additions, alterations, maintenance, and repairs.

Illustrative Examples:

Carpet, installation only   Resurfacing hardwood flooring
Resilient floor tile or sheet (e.g., linoleum, rubber,   Hardwood flooring, installation only
vinyl), installation only   Floor laying, scraping, finishing, and refinishing
Vinyl flooring contractors

Cross-References.   Establishments primarily engaged in--

- Laying concrete flooring--are classified in Industry 238110, Poured Concrete Foundation and Structure Contractors;
- Installing fireproof flooring--are classified in Industry 238310, Drywall and Insulation Contractors;
- Installing stone or ceramic floor tile--are classified in Industry 238340, Tile and Terrazzo Contractors; and
- Selling and installing carpet and other flooring products as retail establishments--are classified in Sector 44-45, Retail Trade.

23834   Tile and Terrazzo Contractors[T]
See industry description for 238340.

238340   Tile and Terrazzo Contractors

This industry comprises establishments primarily engaged in setting and installing ceramic tile, stone (interior only), and mosaic and/or mixing marble particles and cement to make terrazzo at the job site. The work performed may include new work, additions, alterations, maintenance, and repairs.

Illustrative Examples:

Ceramic tile installation   Stone flooring installation
Mosaic work   Marble, granite, and slate, interior installation
Mantel, marble or stone, installation   contractors
Tile (except resilient) laying and setting

Cross-References.   Establishments primarily engaged in--

- Exterior marble, granite, and slate work--are classified in Industry 238140, Masonry Contractors;

T—Canadian, Mexican, and United States industries are comparable.

- Manufacturing precast terrazzo products--are classified in Industry 327390, Other Concrete Product Manufacturing; and
- Installing, without selling resilient floor tile--are classified in Industry 238330, Flooring Contractors.

23835 Finish Carpentry Contractors[T]
See industry description for 238350.

238350 Finish Carpentry Contractors

This industry comprises establishments primarily engaged in finish carpentry work. The work performed may include new work, additions, alterations, maintenance, and repairs.

Illustrative Examples:

Built-in wood cabinets constructed on site
Molding or trim, wood or plastic, installation
Countertop, residential-type, installation
Paneling installation
Door and window frame construction
Garage door, residential-type, installation

Prefabricated kitchen and bath cabinet, residential-type, installation
Ship joinery contractors
Millwork installation
Window and door, residential-type, of any material, prefabricated, installation

Cross-References.   Establishments primarily engaged in--

- Installing skylights--are classified in Industry 238160, Roofing Contractors;
- Framing--are classified in Industry 238130, Framing Contractors; and
- Building custom kitchen and bath cabinets (except freestanding) in a shop--are classified in Industry 337110, Wood Kitchen Cabinet and Countertop Manufacturing.

23839 Other Building Finishing Contractors[T]
See industry description for 238390.

238390 Other Building Finishing Contractors

This industry comprises establishments primarily engaged in building finishing trade work (except drywall, plaster, and insulation work; painting and wall covering work; flooring work; tile and terrazzo work; and finish carpentry work). The work performed may include new work, additions, alterations, maintenance, and repairs.

Illustrative Examples:

Bathtub refinishing, on-site
Fabricating metal cabinets or countertops on site
Closet organizer system installation
Modular furniture system attachment and installation
Concrete coating, glazing, or sealing
Trade show exhibit installation and dismantling

Countertop and cabinet, metal (except residential-type), installation
Waterproofing contractors
Drapery fixture (e.g., hardware, rods, tracks) installation
Window shade and blind installation

Cross-References.   Establishments primarily engaged in--

- Installing drywall, plaster, or insulation--are classified in Industry 238310, Drywall and Insulation Contractors;
- Installing or removing paint or wall coverings--are classified in Industry 238320, Painting and Wall Covering Contractors;
- Installing or repairing wood floors, resilient flooring, and carpet--are classified in Industry 238330, Flooring Contractors;

T—Canadian, Mexican, and United States industries are comparable.

- Setting tile or performing terrazzo work--are classified in Industry 238340, Tile and Terrazzo Contractors; and
- Finish carpentry--are classified in Industry 238350, Finish Carpentry Contractors.

2389 Other Specialty Trade Contractors[T]

This industry group comprises establishments primarily engaged in site preparation activities and in specialized trades (except foundation, structure, and building exterior contractors; building equipment contractors; and building finishing contractors). The specialty trade work performed includes new work, additions, alterations, maintenance, and repairs.

23891 Site Preparation Contractors[T]
See industry description for 238910.

238910 Site Preparation Contractors

This industry comprises establishments primarily engaged in site preparation activities, such as excavating and grading, demolition of buildings and other structures, and septic system installation. Earthmoving and land clearing for all types of sites (e.g., building, nonbuilding, mining) is included in this industry. Establishments primarily engaged in construction equipment rental with operator (except cranes) are also included.

Illustrative Examples:

Blasting, building demolition
Foundation digging (i.e., excavation)
Concrete breaking and cutting for demolition
Foundation drilling contractors
Cutting new rights of way
Grading construction sites
Demolition, building and structure
Line slashing or cutting (except maintenance)
Dewatering contractors

Septic system contractors
Dirt moving for construction
Trenching (except underwater)
Equipment rental (except crane), construction, with operator
Underground tank (except hazardous) removal
Excavating, earthmoving, or land clearing contractors
Wrecking, building or other structure

Cross-References. Establishments primarily engaged in--

- Earth retention or underwater trenching--are classified in Industry 237990, Other Heavy and Civil Engineering Construction;
- Crane rental with operator--are classified in Industry 238990, All Other Specialty Trade Contractors;
- Overburden removal as an activity prior to mineral removal from quarries or open pit mines--are classified in Sector 21, Mining, Quarrying, and Oil and Gas Extraction;
- Drilling oil and gas field water intake wells--are classified in U.S. Industry 213111, Drilling Oil and Gas Wells;
- Dismantling tanks in oil fields--are classified in U.S. Industry 213112, Support Activities for Oil and Gas Operations;
- Construction equipment rental without an operator--are classified in U.S. Industry 532412, Construction, Mining, and Forestry Machinery and Equipment Rental and Leasing;
- Tree and brush trimming for overhead utility lines--are classified in Industry 561730, Landscaping Services; and
- Nuclear power plant decommissioning and environmental remediation work, such as the removal of underground steel tanks for hazardous materials--are classified in Industry 562910, Remediation Services.

23899 All Other Specialty Trade Contractors[T]
See industry description for 238990.

T—Canadian, Mexican, and United States industries are comparable.

238990 All Other Specialty Trade Contractors

This industry comprises establishments primarily engaged in specialized trades (except foundation, structure, and building exterior contractors; building equipment contractors; building finishing contractors; and site preparation contractors). The specialty trade work performed includes new work, additions, alterations, maintenance, and repairs.

Illustrative Examples:

Billboard erection
Outdoor swimming pool construction
Cleaning building interiors during and immediately
after construction
Paver, brick (e.g., driveway, patio, sidewalk),
installation
Crane rental with operator
Paving, residential and commercial driveway and
parking lot

Sandblasting building exteriors
Fence installation
Scaffold erecting and dismantling
Interlocking brick and block installation
Steeplejack work
Manufactured (mobile) home set up and tie-down
work
Driveway paving or sealing

Cross-References.   Establishments primarily engaged in--

- Foundation, structure, and building exterior work--are classified in Industry Group 2381, Foundation, Structure, and Building Exterior Contractors;
- Installing, repairing, or maintaining building mechanical systems--are classified in Industry Group 2382, Building Equipment Contractors;
- Finishing buildings--are classified in Industry Group 2383, Building Finishing Contractors;
- Paving public highways, streets, and roads--are classified in Industry 237310, Highway, Street, and Bridge Construction;
- Construction equipment rental with an operator (except cranes) or preparing land for building construction--are classified in Industry 238910, Site Preparation Contractors;
- Construction equipment rental without an operator--are classified in U.S. Industry 532412, Construction, Mining, and Forestry Machinery and Equipment Rental and Leasing;
- Radon testing--are classified in Industry 541380, Testing Laboratories;
- Power washing and other building exterior cleaning (except sandblasting)--are classified in Industry 561790, Other Services to Buildings and Dwellings; and
- Environmental remediation work, such as asbestos abatement--are classified in Industry 562910, Remediation Services.

T—Canadian, Mexican, and United States industries are comparable.

Sector 31-33--Manufacturing[T]

The Sector as a Whole

The Manufacturing sector comprises establishments engaged in the mechanical, physical, or chemical transformation of materials, substances, or components into new products. The assembling of component parts of manufactured products is considered manufacturing, except in cases where the activity is appropriately classified in Sector 23, Construction.

Establishments in the Manufacturing sector are often described as plants, factories, or mills and characteristically use power-driven machines and material handling equipment. However, establishments that transform materials or substances into new products by hand or in the worker's home and those engaged in selling to the general public products made on the same premises from which they are sold, such as bakeries, candy stores, and custom tailors, may also be included in this sector. Manufacturing establishments may process materials or may contract with other establishments to process their materials for them. Both types of establishments are included in manufacturing.

The materials, substances, or components transformed by manufacturing establishments are raw materials that are products of agriculture, forestry, fishing, mining, or quarrying as well as products of other manufacturing establishments. The materials used may be purchased directly from producers, obtained through customary trade channels, or secured without recourse to the market by transferring the product from one establishment to another, under the same ownership.

The new product of a manufacturing establishment may be finished in the sense that it is ready for utilization or consumption, or it may be semi-finished to become an input for an establishment engaged in further manufacturing. For example, the product of the alumina refinery is the input used in the primary production of aluminum; primary aluminum is the input to an aluminum wire drawing plant; and aluminum wire is the input for a fabricated wire product manufacturing establishment.

The subsectors in the Manufacturing sector generally reflect distinct production processes related to material inputs, production equipment, and employee skills. In the machinery area, where assembling is a key activity, parts and accessories for manufactured products are classified in the industry of the finished manufactured item when they are made for separate sale. For example, a replacement refrigerator door would be classified with refrigerators and an attachment for a piece of metalworking machinery would be classified with metalworking machinery. However, components, input from other manufacturing establishments, are classified based on the production function of the component manufacturer. For example, electronic components are classified in Subsector 334, Computer and Electronic Product Manufacturing, and stampings are classified in Subsector 332, Fabricated Metal Product Manufacturing.

Manufacturing establishments often perform one or more activities that are classified outside the Manufacturing sector of NAICS. For instance, almost all manufacturing has some captive research and development or administrative operations, such as accounting, payroll, or management. These captive services are treated the same as captive manufacturing activities. When the services are provided by separate establishments, they are classified in the NAICS sector where such services are primary, not in manufacturing.

The boundaries of manufacturing and the other sectors of the classification system can be somewhat blurry. The establishments in the Manufacturing sector are engaged in the transformation of materials into new products. Their output is a new product. However, the definition of what constitutes a new product can be somewhat subjective. As clarification, the following activities are considered manufacturing in NAICS:

Milk bottling and pasteurizing;
Water bottling and processing;
Fresh fish packaging (oyster shucking, fish filleting);
Apparel jobbing (assigning materials to contract factories or shops for fabrication or other contract operations) as well as contracting on materials owned by others;
Printing and related activities;
Ready-mix concrete production;
Leather converting;
Grinding lenses to prescription;

Wood preserving;
Electroplating, plating, metal heat treating, and polishing for the trade;
Lapidary work for the trade;
Fabricating signs and advertising displays;
Rebuilding or remanufacturing machinery (i.e., automotive parts);
Ship repair and renovation;
Machine shops; and
Tire retreading.

T—Canadian, Mexican, and United States industries are comparable.

Conversely, there are activities that are sometimes considered manufacturing, but which for NAICS are classified in another sector (i.e., not classified as manufacturing). They include:

1. Logging, classified in Sector 11, Agriculture, Forestry, Fishing and Hunting, is considered a harvesting operation;
2. Beneficiating ores and other minerals, classified in Sector 21, Mining, Quarrying, and Oil and Gas Extraction, is considered part of the activity of mining;
3. Constructing structures and fabricating at the construction site by contractors are classified in Sector 23, Construction;
4. Breaking bulk and redistributing in smaller lots, including packaging, repackaging, or bottling products, such as liquors or chemicals; assembling computers on a custom basis; sorting scrap; mixing paints to customer order; and cutting metals to customer order, classified in Sector 42, Wholesale Trade, or Sector 44-45, Retail Trade, produce a modified version of the same product, not a new product; and
5. Publishing and the combined activity of publishing and printing, classified in Sector 51, Information, transform information into a product for which the value to the consumer lies in the information content, not in the format in which it is distributed (i.e., the book or software compact disc).

311　　Food Manufacturing[T]

Industries in the Food Manufacturing subsector transform livestock and agricultural products into products for intermediate or final consumption. The industry groups are distinguished by the raw materials (generally of animal or vegetable origin) processed into food products.

The food products manufactured in these establishments are typically sold to wholesalers or retailers for distribution to consumers, but establishments primarily engaged in retailing bakery and candy products made on the premises not for immediate consumption are included.

Establishments primarily engaged in manufacturing beverages are classified in Subsector 312, Beverage and Tobacco Product Manufacturing.

3111　　Animal Food Manufacturing[T]

31111　　Animal Food Manufacturing[T]

This industry comprises establishments primarily engaged in manufacturing food and feed for animals from ingredients, such as grains, oilseed mill products, and meat products.

Cross-References.　　Establishments primarily engaged in--

- Slaughtering animals for feed--are classified in Industry 31161, Animal Slaughtering and Processing; and
- Manufacturing vitamins and minerals for animals--are classified in Industry 32541, Pharmaceutical and Medicine Manufacturing.

311111　Dog and Cat Food Manufacturing

This U.S. industry comprises establishments primarily engaged in manufacturing dog and cat food from ingredients, such as grains, oilseed mill products, and meat products.

Cross-References.　　Establishments primarily engaged in--

- Manufacturing food for animals (except dog and cat)--are classified in U.S. Industry 311119, Other Animal Food Manufacturing;
- Slaughtering animals for feed--are classified in Industry 31161, Animal Slaughtering and Processing; and
- Manufacturing vitamins and minerals for dogs and cats--are classified in Industry 32541, Pharmaceutical and Medicine Manufacturing.

T—Canadian, Mexican, and United States industries are comparable.

311119 Other Animal Food Manufacturing

This U.S. industry comprises establishments primarily engaged in manufacturing animal food (except dog and cat) from ingredients, such as grains, oilseed mill products, and meat products.

Cross-References.   Establishments primarily engaged in--

- Manufacturing dog and cat foods--are classified in U.S. Industry 311111, Dog and Cat Food Manufacturing;
- Slaughtering animals for feed--are classified in Industry 31161, Animal Slaughtering and Processing; and
- Manufacturing vitamins and minerals for animals--are classified in Industry 32541, Pharmaceutical and Medicine Manufacturing.

3112   Grain and Oilseed Milling[T]

This industry group comprises establishments primarily engaged in milling flour or meal from grains or vegetables, manufacturing malt, wet milling corn and other vegetables, crushing oilseeds and tree nuts, refining and/or blending vegetable oils, and manufacturing breakfast cereals.

31121   Flour Milling and Malt Manufacturing[T]

This industry comprises establishments primarily engaged in one or more of the following: (1) milling flour or meal from grains or vegetables; (2) preparing flour mixes or doughs from flour milled in the same establishment; (3) milling, cleaning, and polishing rice; and (4) manufacturing malt from barley, rye, or other grains.

Cross-References.   Establishments primarily engaged in--

- Preparing breakfast cereals from flour milled in the same establishment--are classified in Industry 31123, Breakfast Cereal Manufacturing;
- Crushing soybeans or wet milling corn and vegetables--are classified in Industry 31122, Starch and Vegetable Fats and Oils Manufacturing;
- Manufacturing prepared flour mixes or doughs from flour ground elsewhere--are classified in Industry 31182, Cookie, Cracker, and Pasta Manufacturing;
- Brewing malt beverages--are classified in Industry 31212, Breweries;
- Mixing purchased dried and dehydrated ingredients with purchased rice--are classified in Industry 31199, All Other Food Manufacturing;
- Drying and/or dehydrating ingredients and packaging them with purchased rice--are classified in Industry 31142, Fruit and Vegetable Canning, Pickling, and Drying; and
- Manufacturing malt extract and syrups--are classified in Industry 31194, Seasoning and Dressing Manufacturing.

311211 Flour Milling

This U.S. industry comprises establishments primarily engaged in (1) milling flour or meal from grains (except rice) or vegetables and/or (2) milling flour and preparing flour mixes or doughs.

Cross-References.   Establishments primarily engaged in--

- Preparing breakfast cereals from flour milled in the same establishment--are classified in Industry 311230, Breakfast Cereal Manufacturing;
- Manufacturing prepared flour mixes or doughs from flour ground elsewhere--are classified in U.S. Industry 311824, Dry Pasta, Dough, and Flour Mixes Manufacturing from Purchased Flour;
- Milling rice or cleaning and polishing rice--are classified in U.S. Industry 311212, Rice Milling;
- Wet milling corn and vegetables--are classified in U.S. Industry 311221, Wet Corn Milling; and

---

T—Canadian, Mexican, and United States industries are comparable.

- Crushing soybeans and extracting soybean oil--are classified in U.S. Industry 311224, Soybean and Other Oilseed Processing.

311212 Rice Milling

This U.S. industry comprises establishments primarily engaged in one of the following: (1) milling rice; (2) cleaning and polishing rice; or (3) milling, cleaning, and polishing rice. The establishments in this industry may package the rice they mill with other ingredients.

Cross-References.   Establishments primarily engaged in--

- Drying and/or dehydrating ingredients and packaging them with purchased rice--are classified in U.S. Industry 311423, Dried and Dehydrated Food Manufacturing; and
- Mixing purchased dried and/or dehydrated ingredients with purchased rice--are classified in U.S. Industry 311999, All Other Miscellaneous Food Manufacturing.

311213 Malt Manufacturing

This U.S. industry comprises establishments primarily engaged in manufacturing malt from barley, rye, or other grains.

Cross-References.   Establishments primarily engaged in--

- Brewing malt beverages--are classified in Industry 312120, Breweries; and
- Manufacturing malt extract and syrups--are classified in U.S. Industry 311942, Spice and Extract Manufacturing.

31122 Starch and Vegetable Fats and Oils Manufacturing[T]

This industry comprises establishments primarily engaged in one or more of the following: (1) wet milling corn and vegetables; (2) crushing oilseeds and tree nuts; (3) refining and/or blending vegetable oils; (4) manufacturing shortening and margarine; and (5) blending purchased animal fats with vegetable fats.

Cross-References.   Establishments primarily engaged in--

- Manufacturing table syrups from corn syrup and starch base dessert powders--are classified in Industry 31199, All Other Food Manufacturing;
- Reducing maple sap to maple syrup--are classified in Industry 11199, All Other Crop Farming;
- Milling flour or meal from grains and vegetables--are classified in Industry 31121, Flour Milling and Malt Manufacturing;
- Wet milling corn to produce nonpotable ethyl alcohol--are classified in Industry 32519, Other Basic Organic Chemical Manufacturing;
- Rendering or refining animal fats and oils--are classified in Industry 31161, Animal Slaughtering and Processing; and
- Manufacturing laundry starches--are classified in Industry 32561, Soap and Cleaning Compound Manufacturing.

311221 Wet Corn Milling

This U.S. industry comprises establishments primarily engaged in wet milling corn and other vegetables (except to make ethyl alcohol). Examples of products made in these establishments are corn sweeteners, such as glucose, dextrose, and fructose; corn oil; and starches (except laundry).

T—Canadian, Mexican, and United States industries are comparable.

Cross-References.   Establishments primarily engaged in--

- Refining and/or blending corn oil from purchased oils--are classified in U.S. Industry 311225, Fats and Oils Refining and Blending;
- Manufacturing sweetening syrups from corn syrup and starch base dessert powders--are classified in U.S. Industry 311999, All Other Miscellaneous Food Manufacturing;
- Reducing maple sap to maple syrup--are classified in U.S. Industry 111998, All Other Miscellaneous Crop Farming;
- Milling (except wet milling) corn--are classified in U.S. Industry 311211, Flour Milling;
- Wet milling corn to produce nonpotable ethyl alcohol--are classified in U.S. Industry 325193, Ethyl Alcohol Manufacturing; and
- Manufacturing laundry starches--are classified in U.S. Industry 325612, Polish and Other Sanitation Good Manufacturing.

311224 Soybean and Other Oilseed Processing

This U.S. industry comprises establishments primarily engaged in crushing oilseeds and tree nuts, such as soybeans, cottonseeds, linseeds, peanuts, and sunflower seeds. Examples of products produced in these establishments are oilseed oils, cakes, meals, and protein isolates and concentrates.

Cross-References.   Establishments primarily engaged in--

- Wet milling corn and other vegetables--are classified in U.S. Industry 311221, Wet Corn Milling; and
- Refining and/or blending vegetable, oilseed, and tree nut oils from purchased oils--are classified in U.S. Industry 311225, Fats and Oils Refining and Blending.

311225 Fats and Oils Refining and Blending

This U.S. industry comprises establishments primarily engaged in one or more of the following: (1) manufacturing shortening and margarine from purchased fats and oils; (2) refining and/or blending vegetable, oilseed, and tree nut oils from purchased oils; and (3) blending purchased animal fats with purchased vegetable fats.

Cross-References.   Establishments primarily engaged in--

- Refining and/or blending corn oil made by wet corn milling--are classified in U.S. Industry 311221, Wet Corn Milling;
- Refining and/or blending oilseed and tree nut oils in crushing mills--are classified in U.S. Industry 311224, Soybean and Other Oilseed Processing; and
- Rendering or refining animal fats and oils--are classified in Industry 31161, Animal Slaughtering and Processing.

31123 Breakfast Cereal Manufacturing[T]
See industry description for 311230.

311230 Breakfast Cereal Manufacturing

This industry comprises establishments primarily engaged in manufacturing breakfast cereal foods.

Cross-References.   Establishments primarily engaged in--

- Manufacturing nonchocolate-coated granola bars and other types of breakfast bars--are classified in Industry 311340, Nonchocolate Confectionery Manufacturing;
- Manufacturing chocolate-coated granola bars from purchased chocolate--are classified in U.S. Industry 311352, Confectionery Manufacturing from Purchased Chocolate;

T—Canadian, Mexican, and United States industries are comparable.

- Manufacturing chocolate-coated granola bars from cacao beans--are classified in U.S. Industry 311351, Chocolate and Confectionery Manufacturing from Cacao Beans; and
- Manufacturing coffee substitutes from grain--are classified in Industry 311920, Coffee and Tea Manufacturing.

3113   Sugar and Confectionery Product Manufacturing[T]

This industry group comprises (1) establishments that process agricultural inputs, such as sugarcane, beet, and cacao, to give rise to a new product (sugar or chocolate) and (2) those that begin with sugar and chocolate and process these further.

31131   Sugar Manufacturing[T]

This industry comprises establishments primarily engaged in manufacturing raw sugar, liquid sugar, and refined sugar from sugarcane, raw cane sugar and sugar beets.

Cross-References.   Establishments primarily engaged in--

- Manufacturing corn sweeteners by wet milling corn--are classified in Industry 31122, Starch and Vegetable Fats and Oils Manufacturing;
- Manufacturing table syrups from corn syrup and starch base dessert powders--are classified in Industry 31199, All Other Food Manufacturing;
- Reducing maple sap to maple syrup or maple sugar--are classified in Industry 11199, All Other Crop Farming; and
- Manufacturing synthetic sweeteners (i.e., sweetening agents), such as saccharin and sugar substitutes (i.e., synthetic sweetener blended with other ingredients)--are classified in Subsector 325, Chemical Manufacturing.

311313 Beet Sugar Manufacturing

This U.S. industry comprises establishments primarily engaged in manufacturing refined beet sugar from sugar beets.

Cross-References.   Establishments primarily engaged in--

- Manufacturing raw cane sugar and/or refined cane sugar--are classified in U.S. Industry 311314, Cane Sugar Manufacturing;
- Manufacturing corn sweeteners by wet milling corn--are classified in U.S. Industry 311221, Wet Corn Milling;
- Manufacturing table syrups from corn syrup--are classified in U.S. Industry 311999, All Other Miscellaneous Food Manufacturing;
- Reducing maple sap to maple syrup or maple sugar--are classified in U.S. Industry 111998, All Other Miscellaneous Crop Farming; and
- Manufacturing synthetic sweeteners (i.e., sweetening agents), such as saccharin and sugar substitutes (i.e., synthetic sweetener blended with other ingredients)--are classified in Subsector 325, Chemical Manufacturing.

311314 Cane Sugar Manufacturing

This U.S. industry comprises establishments primarily engaged in (1) processing sugarcane and/or (2) refining cane sugar from raw cane sugar.

Cross-References.   Establishments primarily engaged in--

- Manufacturing beet sugar--are classified in U.S. Industry 311313, Beet Sugar Manufacturing;

T—Canadian, Mexican, and United States industries are comparable.

- Manufacturing corn sweeteners by wet milling corn--are classified in U.S. Industry 311221, Wet Corn Milling;
- Reducing maple sap to maple syrup or maple sugar--are classified in U.S. Industry 111998, All Other Miscellaneous Crop Farming;
- Manufacturing table syrups from corn syrup--are classified in U.S. Industry 311999, All Other Miscellaneous Food Manufacturing; and
- Manufacturing synthetic sweeteners (i.e., sweetening agents), such as saccharin and sugar substitutes (i.e., synthetic sweetener blended with other ingredients)--are classified in Subsector 325, Chemical Manufacturing.

31134   Nonchocolate Confectionery Manufacturing[T]
See industry description for 311340.

311340 Nonchocolate Confectionery Manufacturing

This industry comprises establishments primarily engaged in manufacturing nonchocolate confectioneries. Included in this industry are establishments primarily engaged in retailing nonchocolate confectionery products not for immediate consumption made on the premises.

Cross-References.   Establishments primarily engaged in--

- Manufacturing chocolate confectioneries from cacao beans--are classified in U.S. Industry 311351, Chocolate and Confectionery Manufacturing from Cacao Beans;
- Manufacturing chocolate confectioneries from chocolate made elsewhere--are classified in U.S. Industry 311352, Confectionery Manufacturing from Purchased Chocolate;
- Retailing confectioneries not for immediate consumption made elsewhere--are classified in U.S. Industry 445292, Confectionery and Nut Stores;
- Preparing and selling confectioneries for immediate consumption--are classified in U.S. Industry 722515, Snack and Nonalcoholic Beverage Bars; and
- Roasting, salting, drying, cooking, or canning nuts and seeds--are classified in U.S. Industry 311911, Roasted Nuts and Peanut Butter Manufacturing.

31135   Chocolate and Confectionery Manufacturing[T]

This industry comprises establishments primarily engaged in (1) manufacturing chocolate and chocolate confectioneries from cacao beans or (2) manufacturing chocolate confectioneries from chocolate produced elsewhere. Included in this industry are establishments primarily engaged in retailing chocolate confectionery products not for immediate consumption made on the premises from chocolate made elsewhere.

Cross-References.   Establishments primarily engaged in--

- Manufacturing, not for immediate consumption, nonchocolate confectioneries--are classified in Industry 31134, Nonchocolate Confectionery Manufacturing;
- Retailing confectioneries not for immediate consumption made elsewhere--are classified in Industry 44529, Other Specialty Food Stores; and
- Preparing and selling confectioneries for immediate consumption--are classified in Industry 72251, Restaurants and Other Eating Places.

311351 Chocolate and Confectionery Manufacturing from Cacao Beans

This U.S. industry comprises establishments primarily engaged in shelling, roasting, and grinding cacao beans and making chocolate cacao products and chocolate confectioneries.

T—Canadian, Mexican, and United States industries are comparable.

Cross-References.   Establishments primarily engaged in--

- Manufacturing, not for immediate consumption, chocolate confectioneries from chocolate made elsewhere--are classified in U.S. Industry 311352, Confectionery Manufacturing from Purchased Chocolate;
- Manufacturing, not for immediate consumption, nonchocolate candies--are classified in Industry 311340, Nonchocolate Confectionery Manufacturing;
- Preparing and selling confectioneries for immediate consumption--are classified in U.S. Industry 722515, Snack and Nonalcoholic Beverage Bars; and
- Retailing confectioneries not for immediate consumption made elsewhere--are classified in U.S. Industry 445292, Confectionery and Nut Stores.

311352 Confectionery Manufacturing from Purchased Chocolate

This U.S. industry comprises establishments primarily engaged in manufacturing chocolate confectioneries from chocolate produced elsewhere. Included in this industry are establishments primarily engaged in retailing chocolate confectionery products not for immediate consumption made on the premises from chocolate made elsewhere.

Cross-References.   Establishments primarily engaged in--

- Manufacturing chocolate confectioneries from cacao beans--are classified in U.S. Industry 311351, Chocolate and Confectionery Manufacturing from Cacao Beans;
- Manufacturing, not for immediate consumption, nonchocolate confectioneries--are classified in Industry 311340, Nonchocolate Confectionery Manufacturing;
- Retailing confectioneries not for immediate consumption made elsewhere--are classified in U.S. Industry 445292, Confectionery and Nut Stores; and
- Preparing and selling confectioneries for immediate consumption--are classified in U.S. Industry 722515, Snack and Nonalcoholic Beverage Bars.

3114   Fruit and Vegetable Preserving and Specialty Food Manufacturing[T]

This industry group includes (1) establishments that freeze food and (2) those that use preservation processes, such as pickling, canning, and dehydrating. Both types begin their production process with inputs of vegetable or animal origin.

31141   Frozen Food Manufacturing[T]

This industry comprises establishments primarily engaged in manufacturing frozen fruit, frozen juices, frozen vegetables, and frozen specialty foods (except seafood), such as frozen dinners, entrees, and side dishes; frozen pizza; frozen whipped toppings; and frozen waffles, pancakes, and french toast.

Cross-References.   Establishments primarily engaged in--

- Manufacturing frozen dairy specialties--are classified in Industry 31152, Ice Cream and Frozen Dessert Manufacturing;
- Manufacturing frozen bakery products--are classified in Industry 31181, Bread and Bakery Product Manufacturing;
- Manufacturing frozen seafood products--are classified in Industry 31171, Seafood Product Preparation and Packaging; and
- Manufacturing frozen meat products--are classified in Industry 31161, Animal Slaughtering and Processing.

311411 Frozen Fruit, Juice, and Vegetable Manufacturing

This U.S. industry comprises establishments primarily engaged in manufacturing frozen fruits; frozen vegetables; and frozen fruit juices, ades, drinks, cocktail mixes and concentrates.

T—Canadian, Mexican, and United States industries are comparable.

Cross-References.

Establishments primarily engaged in manufacturing frozen specialty foods are classified in U.S. Industry 311412, Frozen Specialty Food Manufacturing.

311412 Frozen Specialty Food Manufacturing

This U.S. industry comprises establishments primarily engaged in manufacturing frozen specialty foods (except seafood), such as frozen dinners, entrees, and side dishes; frozen pizza; frozen whipped topping; and frozen waffles, pancakes, and french toast.

Cross-References.   Establishments primarily engaged in--

- Manufacturing frozen dairy specialties--are classified in Industry 311520, Ice Cream and Frozen Dessert Manufacturing;
- Manufacturing frozen bakery products--are classified in U.S. Industry 311813, Frozen Cakes, Pies, and Other Pastries Manufacturing;
- Manufacturing frozen fruits, frozen fruit juices, and frozen vegetables--are classified in U.S. Industry 311411, Frozen Fruit, Juice, and Vegetable Manufacturing;
- Manufacturing frozen meat products--are classified in Industry 31161, Animal Slaughtering and Processing; and
- Manufacturing frozen seafood products--are classified in Industry 311710, Seafood Product Preparation and Packaging.

31142 Fruit and Vegetable Canning, Pickling, and Drying[T]

This industry comprises establishments primarily engaged in manufacturing canned, pickled, and dried fruits, vegetables, and specialty foods. Establishments in this industry may package the dried or dehydrated ingredients they make with other purchased ingredients. Examples of products made by these establishments are canned juices; canned baby foods; canned soups (except seafood); canned dry beans; canned tomato-based sauces, such as catsup, salsa, chili sauce, spaghetti sauce, barbeque sauce, and tomato paste; pickles and relishes; jams and jellies; dried soup mixes and bouillon; and sauerkraut.

Cross-References.   Establishments primarily engaged in--

- Manufacturing canned dairy products--are classified in Industry 31151, Dairy Product (except Frozen) Manufacturing;
- Manufacturing canned seafood soups and seafood products--are classified in Industry 31171, Seafood Product Preparation and Packaging;
- Manufacturing canned meat products--are classified in Industry 31161, Animal Slaughtering and Processing;
- Milling rice and packaging it with other ingredients or manufacturing vegetable flours and meals--are classified in Industry 31121, Flour Milling and Malt Manufacturing;
- Manufacturing dry pasta and packaging it with other ingredients--are classified in Industry 31182, Cookie, Cracker, and Pasta Manufacturing;
- Mixing purchased dried and/or dehydrated potatoes, rice, and pasta and packaging them with other purchased ingredients; mixing purchased dried and/or dehydrated ingredients for soup mixes and bouillon; and manufacturing canned puddings--are classified in Industry 31199, All Other Food Manufacturing;
- Manufacturing dry salad dressing and dry sauce mixes--are classified in Industry 31194, Seasoning and Dressing Manufacturing; and
- Manufacturing canned fruit and vegetable drinks, cocktails, and ades--are classified in Industry 31211, Soft Drink and Ice Manufacturing.

T—Canadian, Mexican, and United States industries are comparable.

311421 Fruit and Vegetable Canning

This U.S. industry comprises establishments primarily engaged in manufacturing canned, pickled, and brined fruits and vegetables. Examples of products made in these establishments are canned juices; canned jams and jellies; canned tomato-based sauces, such as catsup, salsa, chili sauce, spaghetti sauce, barbeque sauce, and tomato paste; and pickles, relishes, and sauerkraut.

Cross-References.   Establishments primarily engaged in--

- Manufacturing canned baby foods, canned soups (except seafood), and canned specialty foods (except seafood)--are classified in U.S. Industry 311422, Specialty Canning;
- Manufacturing canned seafood soups and canned seafood products--are classified in Industry 311710, Seafood Product Preparation and Packaging;
- Manufacturing canned meat products--are classified in Industry 31161, Animal Slaughtering and Processing; and
- Manufacturing canned fruit and vegetable drinks, cocktails, and ades--are classified in U.S. Industry 312111, Soft Drink Manufacturing.

311422 Specialty Canning

This U.S. industry comprises establishments primarily engaged in manufacturing canned specialty foods. Examples of products made in these establishments are canned baby food, canned baked beans, canned soups (except seafood), canned spaghetti, and other canned nationality foods.

Cross-References.   Establishments primarily engaged in--

- Manufacturing canned dairy products--are classified in U.S. Industry 311514, Dry, Condensed, and Evaporated Dairy Product Manufacturing;
- Manufacturing canned fruits, canned vegetables, and canned juices--are classified in U.S. Industry 311421, Fruit and Vegetable Canning;
- Manufacturing canned seafood soups and canned seafood products--are classified in Industry 311710, Seafood Product Preparation and Packaging;
- Manufacturing canned meat products--are classified in Industry 31161, Animal Slaughtering and Processing; and
- Manufacturing canned puddings--are classified in U.S. Industry 311999, All Other Miscellaneous Food Manufacturing.

311423 Dried and Dehydrated Food Manufacturing

This U.S. industry comprises establishments primarily engaged in (1) drying (including freeze-dried) and/or dehydrating fruits, vegetables, and soup mixes and bouillon and/or (2) drying and/or dehydrating ingredients and packaging them with other purchased ingredients, such as rice and dry pasta.

Cross-References.   Establishments primarily engaged in--

- Milling rice and packaging it with other ingredients--are classified in U.S. Industry 311212, Rice Milling;
- Manufacturing dry pasta and packaging it with other ingredients--are classified in U.S. Industry 311824, Dry Pasta, Dough, and Flour Mixes Manufacturing from Purchased Flour;
- Manufacturing vegetable flours and meals--are classified in U.S. Industry 311211, Flour Milling;
- Mixing purchased dried and/or dehydrated potatoes, rice, and pasta, and packaging them with other purchased ingredients, and mixing purchased dried and/or dehydrated ingredients for soup mixes and bouillon--are classified in U.S. Industry 311999, All Other Miscellaneous Food Manufacturing; and
- Manufacturing dry salad dressing and dry sauce mixes--are classified in U.S. Industry 311942, Spice and Extract Manufacturing.

T—Canadian, Mexican, and United States industries are comparable.

3115   Dairy Product Manufacturing^T

This industry group comprises establishments that manufacture dairy products from raw milk, processed milk, and dairy substitutes.

31151   Dairy Product (except Frozen) Manufacturing^T

This industry comprises establishments primarily engaged in one or more of the following: (1) manufacturing dairy products (except frozen) from raw milk and/or processed milk products; (2) manufacturing dairy substitutes (except frozen) from soybeans and other nondairy substances; and (3) manufacturing dry, condensed, concentrated, and evaporated dairy and dairy substitute products.

Cross-References.   Establishments primarily engaged in--

- Manufacturing cheese-based salad dressings--are classified in Industry 31194, Seasoning and Dressing Manufacturing;
- Manufacturing margarine or margarine-butter blends--are classified in Industry 31122, Starch and Vegetable Fats and Oils Manufacturing;
- Manufacturing frozen whipped toppings--are classified in Industry 31141, Frozen Food Manufacturing; and
- Manufacturing ice cream, frozen yogurt, and other frozen dairy desserts--are classified in Industry 31152, Ice Cream and Frozen Dessert Manufacturing.

311511   Fluid Milk Manufacturing

This U.S. industry comprises establishments primarily engaged in (1) manufacturing processed milk products, such as pasteurized milk or cream and sour cream and/or (2) manufacturing fluid milk dairy substitutes from soybeans and other nondairy substances.

Cross-References.   Establishments primarily engaged in--

- Manufacturing dry mix whipped toppings, canned milk, and ultra high temperature milk--are classified in U.S. Industry 311514, Dry, Condensed, and Evaporated Dairy Product Manufacturing;
- Manufacturing frozen whipped toppings--are classified in U.S. Industry 311412, Frozen Specialty Food Manufacturing; and
- Manufacturing ice cream and frozen yogurt and other frozen desserts--are classified in Industry 311520, Ice Cream and Frozen Dessert Manufacturing.

311512   Creamery Butter Manufacturing

This U.S. industry comprises establishments primarily engaged in manufacturing creamery butter from milk and/or processed milk products.

Cross-References.

Establishments primarily engaged in manufacturing margarine or margarine-butter blends are classified in U.S. Industry 311225, Fats and Oils Refining and Blending.

311513   Cheese Manufacturing

This U.S. industry comprises establishments primarily engaged in (1) manufacturing cheese products (except cottage cheese) from raw milk and/or processed milk products and/or (2) manufacturing cheese substitutes from soybean and other nondairy substances.

T—Canadian, Mexican, and United States industries are comparable.

Cross-References.   Establishments primarily engaged in--

- Manufacturing cheese-based salad dressings--are classified in U.S. Industry 311941, Mayonnaise, Dressing, and Other Prepared Sauce Manufacturing; and
- Manufacturing cottage cheese--are classified in U.S. Industry 311511, Fluid Milk Manufacturing.

311514 Dry, Condensed, and Evaporated Dairy Product Manufacturing

This U.S. industry comprises establishments primarily engaged in manufacturing dry, condensed, and evaporated milk and dairy substitute products.

Cross-References.   Establishments primarily engaged in--

- Manufacturing fluid milk products--are classified in U.S. Industry 311511, Fluid Milk Manufacturing;
- Manufacturing creamery butter--are classified in U.S. Industry 311512, Creamery Butter Manufacturing; and
- Manufacturing cheese products--are classified in U.S. Industry 311513, Cheese Manufacturing.

31152   Ice Cream and Frozen Dessert Manufacturing[T]
See industry description for 311520.

311520 Ice Cream and Frozen Dessert Manufacturing

This industry comprises establishments primarily engaged in manufacturing ice cream, frozen yogurts, frozen ices, sherbets, frozen tofu, and other frozen desserts (except bakery products).

Cross-References.   Establishments primarily engaged in--

- Manufacturing frozen bakery products--are classified in U.S. Industry 311813, Frozen Cakes, Pies, and Other Pastries Manufacturing; and
- Manufacturing ice cream and ice milk mixes--are classified in U.S. Industry 311514, Dry, Condensed, and Evaporated Dairy Product Manufacturing.

3116   Animal Slaughtering and Processing[T]

31161   Animal Slaughtering and Processing[T]

This industry comprises establishments primarily engaged in one or more of the following: (1) slaughtering animals; (2) preparing processed meats and meat byproducts; and (3) rendering and/or refining animal fat, bones, and meat scraps. This industry includes establishments primarily engaged in assembly cutting and packing of meats (i.e., boxed meats) from purchased carcasses.

Cross-References.   Establishments primarily engaged in--

- Manufacturing canned meat for baby food--are classified in Industry 31142, Fruit and Vegetable Canning, Pickling, and Drying;
- Manufacturing meat-based animal feeds from carcasses--are classified in Industry 31111, Animal Food Manufacturing;
- Blending purchased animal fats with vegetable fats--are classified in Industry 31122, Starch and Vegetable Fats and Oils Manufacturing;
- Manufacturing canned and frozen specialty foods containing meat, such as nationality foods (e.g., enchiladas, pizza, egg rolls) and frozen dinners--are classified in Industry Group 3114, Fruit and Vegetable Preserving and Specialty Food Manufacturing;
- Drying, freezing, or breaking eggs--are classified in Industry 31199, All Other Food Manufacturing; and

---

T—Canadian, Mexican, and United States industries are comparable.

- Cutting meat (except boxed meat)--are classified in Industry 42447, Meat and Meat Product Merchant Wholesalers.

311611 Animal (except Poultry) Slaughtering

This U.S. industry comprises establishments primarily engaged in slaughtering animals (except poultry and small game). Establishments that slaughter and prepare meats are included in this industry.

Cross-References.　　　Establishments primarily engaged in--

- Processing meat and meat byproducts (except poultry and small game) from purchased meats--are classified in U.S. Industry 311612, Meat Processed from Carcasses;
- Slaughtering and/or processing poultry and small game--are classified in U.S. Industry 311615, Poultry Processing;
- Rendering lard and other animal fats and oils, bones, and meat scraps--are classified in U.S. Industry 311613, Rendering and Meat Byproduct Processing; and
- Manufacturing canned and frozen specialty foods containing meat, such as nationality foods (e.g., enchiladas, egg rolls, pizza) and frozen dinners--are classified in Industry Group 3114, Fruit and Vegetable Preserving and Specialty Food Manufacturing.

311612 Meat Processed from Carcasses

This U.S. industry comprises establishments primarily engaged in processing or preserving meat and meat byproducts (except poultry and small game) from purchased meats. This industry includes establishments primarily engaged in assembly cutting and packing of meats (i.e., boxed meats) from purchased meats.

Cross-References.　　　Establishments primarily engaged in--

- Slaughtering animals (except poultry and small game)--are classified in U.S. Industry 311611, Animal (except Poultry) Slaughtering;
- Slaughtering poultry and small game--are classified in U.S. Industry 311615, Poultry Processing;
- Rendering lard and other animal fats and oils, bones, and meat scraps--are classified in U.S. Industry 311613, Rendering and Meat Byproduct Processing;
- Manufacturing canned meats for baby food--are classified in U.S. Industry 311422, Specialty Canning;
- Manufacturing meat-based animal feeds from carcasses--are classified in Industry 31111, Animal Food Manufacturing;
- Manufacturing canned and frozen specialty foods containing meat, such as nationality foods (e.g., enchiladas, egg rolls, pizza) and frozen dinners--are classified in Industry Group 3114, Fruit and Vegetable Preserving and Specialty Food Manufacturing; and
- Cutting meat (except boxed meat)--are classified in Industry 424470, Meat and Meat Product Merchant Wholesalers.

311613 Rendering and Meat Byproduct Processing

This U.S. industry comprises establishments primarily engaged in rendering animal fat, bones, and meat scraps.

Cross-References.

Establishments primarily engaged in blending purchased animal fats with vegetable fats are classified in U.S. Industry 311225, Fats and Oils Refining and Blending.

311615 Poultry Processing

This U.S. industry comprises establishments primarily engaged in (1) slaughtering poultry and small game and/or (2) preparing processed poultry and small game meat and meat byproducts.

T—Canadian, Mexican, and United States industries are comparable.

Cross-References.   Establishments primarily engaged in--

- Slaughtering animals (except poultry and small game) and/or preparing meats--are classified in U.S. Industry 311611, Animal (except Poultry) Slaughtering;
- Preparing meat and meat byproducts (except poultry and small game) from purchased meats--are classified in U.S. Industry 311612, Meat Processed from Carcasses;
- Rendering animal fats and oils, bones, and meat scraps--are classified in U.S. Industry 311613, Rendering and Meat Byproduct Processing;
- Canning poultry and small game for baby food--are classified in U.S. Industry 311422, Specialty Canning;
- Producing poultry-based animal feeds from carcasses--are classified in Industry 31111, Animal Food Manufacturing;
- Manufacturing frozen meat and poultry products, such as nationality foods (e.g., enchiladas, egg rolls, pizza) and frozen dinners--are classified in U.S. Industry 311412, Frozen Specialty Food Manufacturing; and
- Drying, freezing, and breaking eggs--are classified in U.S. Industry 311999, All Other Miscellaneous Food Manufacturing.

3117   Seafood Product Preparation and Packaging[T]

31171   Seafood Product Preparation and Packaging[T]
See industry description for 311710.

311710 Seafood Product Preparation and Packaging

This industry comprises establishments primarily engaged in one or more of the following: (1) canning seafood (including soup); (2) smoking, salting, and drying seafood; (3) eviscerating fresh fish by removing heads, fins, scales, bones, and entrails; (4) shucking and packing fresh shellfish; (5) processing marine fats and oils; and (6) freezing seafood. Establishments known as "floating factory ships" that are engaged in the gathering and processing of seafood into canned seafood products are included in this industry.

3118   Bakeries and Tortilla Manufacturing[T]

This industry group comprises establishments primarily engaged in one of the following: (1) manufacturing fresh and frozen bread and other bakery products; (2) retailing bread and other bakery products not for immediate consumption made on the premises from flour, not from prepared dough; (3) manufacturing cookies, crackers, and dry pasta; (4) manufacturing prepared flour mixes or dough from flour ground elsewhere; or (5) manufacturing tortillas.

31181   Bread and Bakery Product Manufacturing[T]

This industry comprises establishments primarily engaged in manufacturing fresh and frozen bread and other bakery products.

Cross-References.   Establishments primarily engaged in--

- Manufacturing cookies and crackers--are classified in Industry 31182, Cookie, Cracker, and Pasta Manufacturing;
- Preparing and selling bakery products (e.g., cookies, pretzels) for immediate consumption--are classified in Industry 72251, Restaurants and Other Eating Places;
- Retailing bakery products not for immediate consumption made elsewhere--are classified in Industry 44529, Other Specialty Food Stores; and
- Manufacturing pretzels (except soft)--are classified in Industry 31191, Snack Food Manufacturing.

T—Canadian, Mexican, and United States industries are comparable.

311811 Retail Bakeries

This U.S. industry comprises establishments primarily engaged in retailing bread and other bakery products not for immediate consumption made on the premises from flour, not from prepared dough.

Cross-References.   Establishments primarily engaged in--

- Retailing bakery products not for immediate consumption made elsewhere--are classified in U.S. Industry 445291, Baked Goods Stores;
- Preparing and selling bakery products (e.g., cookies, pretzels) for immediate consumption--are classified in U.S. Industry 722515, Snack and Nonalcoholic Beverage Bars;
- Manufacturing fresh or frozen breads and other fresh bakery (except cookies and crackers) products--are classified in U.S. Industry 311812, Commercial Bakeries; and
- Manufacturing cookies and crackers--are classified in U.S. Industry 311821, Cookie and Cracker Manufacturing.

311812 Commercial Bakeries

This U.S. industry comprises establishments primarily engaged in manufacturing fresh and frozen bread and bread-type rolls and other fresh bakery (except cookies and crackers) products.

Cross-References.   Establishments primarily engaged in--

- Retailing bread and other bakery products not for immediate consumption made on the premises from flour, not from prepared dough--are classified in U.S. Industry 311811, Retail Bakeries;
- Manufacturing frozen bakery products (except bread)--are classified in U.S. Industry 311813, Frozen Cakes, Pies, and Other Pastries Manufacturing;
- Preparing and selling bakery products (e.g., cookies, pretzels) for immediate consumption--are classified in U.S. Industry 722515, Snack and Nonalcoholic Beverage Bars;
- Retailing bakery products not for immediate consumption made elsewhere--are classified in U.S. Industry 445291, Baked Goods Stores;
- Manufacturing cookies and crackers--are classified in U.S. Industry 311821, Cookie and Cracker Manufacturing; and
- Manufacturing pretzels (except soft)--are classified in U.S. Industry 311919, Other Snack Food Manufacturing.

311813 Frozen Cakes, Pies, and Other Pastries Manufacturing

This U.S. industry comprises establishments primarily engaged in manufacturing frozen bakery products (except bread), such as cakes, pies, and doughnuts.

Cross-References.   Establishments primarily engaged in--

- Manufacturing frozen breads--are classified in U.S. Industry 311812, Commercial Bakeries;
- Retailing bakery products not for immediate consumption made on the premises from flour, not from prepared dough--are classified in U.S. Industry 311811, Retail Bakeries;
- Preparing and selling bakery products (e.g., cookies, pretzels) for immediate consumption--are classified in U.S. Industry 722515, Snack and Nonalcoholic Beverage Bars;
- Manufacturing cookies and crackers--are classified in U.S. Industry 311821, Cookie and Cracker Manufacturing; and
- Retailing bakery products not for immediate consumption made elsewhere--are classified in U.S. Industry 445291, Baked Goods Stores.

T—Canadian, Mexican, and United States industries are comparable.

31182   Cookie, Cracker, and Pasta Manufacturing[T]

This industry comprises establishments primarily engaged in one of the following: (1) manufacturing cookies and crackers; (2) preparing flour and dough mixes and dough from flour ground elsewhere; and (3) manufacturing dry pasta. The establishments in this industry may package the dry pasta they manufacture with other ingredients.

Cross-References.   Establishments primarily engaged in--

- Preparing and selling bakery products (e.g., cookies, pretzels) for immediate consumption--are classified in Industry 72251, Restaurants and Other Eating Places;
- Retailing bakery products not for immediate consumption made elsewhere--are classified in Industry 44529, Other Specialty Food Stores;
- Manufacturing bakery products (e.g., bread, cookies, pies)--are classified in Industry 31181, Bread and Bakery Product Manufacturing;
- Milling flour and preparing flour mixes or doughs--are classified in Industry 31121, Flour Milling and Malt Manufacturing;
- Manufacturing canned pasta specialties--are classified in Industry 31142, Fruit and Vegetable Canning, Pickling, and Drying;
- Manufacturing fresh pasta--are classified in Industry 31199, All Other Food Manufacturing;
- Manufacturing pretzels (except soft)--are classified in Industry 31191, Snack Food Manufacturing;
- Mixing purchased dried and/or dehydrated ingredients with purchased dry pasta--are classified in Industry 31199, All Other Food Manufacturing; and
- Drying and/or dehydrating ingredients and packaging them with purchased dry pasta--are classified in Industry 31142, Fruit and Vegetable Canning, Pickling, and Drying.

311821 Cookie and Cracker Manufacturing

This U.S. industry comprises establishments primarily engaged in manufacturing cookies, crackers, and other products, such as ice cream cones.

Cross-References.   Establishments primarily engaged in--

- Preparing and selling bakery products (e.g., cookies, pretzels) for immediate consumption--are classified in U.S. Industry 722515, Snack and Nonalcoholic Beverage Bars;
- Retailing bakery products not for immediate consumption made elsewhere--are classified in U.S. Industry 445291, Baked Goods Stores;
- Manufacturing bakery products (e.g., breads, cookies, pies)--are classified in Industry 31181, Bread and Bakery Product Manufacturing; and
- Manufacturing pretzels (except soft)--are classified in U.S. Industry 311919, Other Snack Food Manufacturing.

311824 Dry Pasta, Dough, and Flour Mixes Manufacturing from Purchased Flour

This U.S. industry comprises establishments primarily engaged in (1) manufacturing dry pasta and/or (2) manufacturing prepared flour mixes or dough from flour ground elsewhere. The establishments in this industry may package the dry pasta they manufacture with other ingredients.

Cross-References.   Establishments primarily engaged in--

- Milling flour and preparing flour mixes or doughs--are classified in U.S. Industry 311211, Flour Milling;
- Manufacturing fresh pasta--are classified in U.S. Industry 311991, Perishable Prepared Food Manufacturing;
- Manufacturing pasta specialties--are classified in Industry Group 3114, Fruit and Vegetable Preserving and Specialty Food Manufacturing;

T—Canadian, Mexican, and United States industries are comparable.

- Mixing purchased dried and/or dehydrated ingredients with purchased dry pasta--are classified in U.S. Industry 311999, All Other Miscellaneous Food Manufacturing; and
- Drying and/or dehydrating ingredients packaged with purchased dry pasta--are classified in U.S. Industry 311423, Dried and Dehydrated Food Manufacturing.

31183   Tortilla Manufacturing[T]
See industry description for 311830.

311830   Tortilla Manufacturing

This industry comprises establishments primarily engaged in manufacturing tortillas.

Cross-References.   Establishments primarily engaged in--

- Manufacturing canned nationality foods using tortillas--are classified in U.S. Industry 311422, Specialty Canning;
- Manufacturing frozen nationality foods using tortillas--are classified in U.S. Industry 311412, Frozen Specialty Food Manufacturing; and
- Manufacturing tortilla chips--are classified in U.S. Industry 311919, Other Snack Food Manufacturing.

3119   Other Food Manufacturing[T]

This industry group comprises establishments primarily engaged in manufacturing food (except animal food; grain and oilseed milling; sugar and confectionery products; preserved fruits, vegetables, and specialty foods; dairy products; meat products; seafood products; and bakery products and tortillas). This industry group includes industries with different production processes, such as snack food manufacturing; coffee and tea manufacturing; concentrate, syrup, condiment, and spice manufacturing; and, in general, an entire range of other miscellaneous food product manufacturing.

31191   Snack Food Manufacturing[T]

This industry comprises establishments primarily engaged in one or more of the following: (1) salting, roasting, drying, cooking, or canning nuts; (2) processing grains or seeds into snacks; (3) manufacturing peanut butter; and (4) manufacturing potato chips, corn chips, popped popcorn, pretzels (except soft), pork rinds, and similar snacks.

Cross-References.   Establishments primarily engaged in--

- Manufacturing crackers--are classified in Industry 31182, Cookie, Cracker, and Pasta Manufacturing;
- Manufacturing unpopped popcorn--are classified in Industry 31199, All Other Food Manufacturing;
- Manufacturing chocolate or candy-coated nuts and candy-covered popcorn--are classified in Industry Group 3113, Sugar and Confectionery Product Manufacturing; and
- Manufacturing soft pretzels--are classified in Industry 31181, Bread and Bakery Product Manufacturing.

311911   Roasted Nuts and Peanut Butter Manufacturing

This U.S. industry comprises establishments primarily engaged in one or more of the following: (1) salting, roasting, drying, cooking, or canning nuts; (2) processing grains or seeds into snacks; and (3) manufacturing peanut butter.

Cross-References.

Establishments primarily engaged in manufacturing chocolate or candy-coated nuts and candy-covered popcorn are classified in Industry Group 3113, Sugar and Confectionery Product Manufacturing.

T—Canadian, Mexican, and United States industries are comparable.

311919 Other Snack Food Manufacturing

This U.S. industry comprises establishments primarily engaged in manufacturing snack foods (except roasted nuts and peanut butter).

Illustrative Examples:

Corn chips and related corn snacks manufacturing
Popped popcorn (except candy-covered) manufacturing
Pork rinds manufacturing

Potato chips manufacturing
Pretzels (except soft) manufacturing
Tortilla chips manufacturing

Cross-References.   Establishments primarily engaged in--

- Manufacturing cookies and crackers--are classified in U.S. Industry 311821, Cookie and Cracker Manufacturing;
- Manufacturing candy-covered popcorn and nonchocolate granola bars--are classified in Industry 311340, Nonchocolate Confectionery Manufacturing;
- Salting, roasting, drying, cooking, or canning nuts and seeds--are classified in U.S. Industry 311911, Roasted Nuts and Peanut Butter Manufacturing;
- Manufacturing unpopped popcorn--are classified in U.S. Industry 311999, All Other Miscellaneous Food Manufacturing; and
- Manufacturing soft pretzels--are classified in U.S. Industry 311812, Commercial Bakeries.

31192 Coffee and Tea Manufacturing[T]
See industry description for 311920.

311920 Coffee and Tea Manufacturing

This industry comprises establishments primarily engaged in one or more of the following: (1) roasting coffee; (2) manufacturing coffee and tea concentrates (including instant and freeze-dried); (3) blending tea; (4) manufacturing herbal tea; and (5) manufacturing coffee extracts, flavorings, and syrups.

Cross-References.

Establishments primarily engaged in bottling and canning iced tea are classified in U.S. Industry 312111, Soft Drink Manufacturing.

31193 Flavoring Syrup and Concentrate Manufacturing[T]
See industry description for 311930.

311930 Flavoring Syrup and Concentrate Manufacturing

This industry comprises establishments primarily engaged in manufacturing flavoring syrup drink concentrates and related products for soda fountain use or for the manufacture of soft drinks.

Cross-References.   Establishments primarily engaged in--

- Manufacturing chocolate syrup--are classified in Industry 31135, Chocolate and Confectionery Manufacturing;
- Manufacturing flavoring extracts (except coffee and meat) and natural food colorings--are classified in U.S. Industry 311942, Spice and Extract Manufacturing;
- Manufacturing coffee extracts and/or coffee-based syrups--are classified in Industry 311920, Coffee and Tea Manufacturing;

T—Canadian, Mexican, and United States industries are comparable.

- Manufacturing liquid meat extracts from slaughtered or purchased carcasses--are classified in Industry 31161, Animal Slaughtering and Processing;
- Manufacturing canned gravies by mixing liquid meat extracts with other ingredients--are classified in U.S. Industry 311422, Specialty Canning;
- Manufacturing powdered drink mixes (except coffee, tea, chocolate, or milk based), table syrup from corn syrup, or sweetening syrups (except pure maple)--are classified in U.S. Industry 311999, All Other Miscellaneous Food Manufacturing;
- Reducing maple sap to maple syrup--are classified in U.S. Industry 111998, All Other Miscellaneous Crop Farming; and
- Manufacturing natural nonfood colorings--are classified in U.S. Industry 325199, All Other Basic Organic Chemical Manufacturing.

31194 Seasoning and Dressing Manufacturing[T]

This industry comprises establishments primarily engaged in one or more of the following: (1) manufacturing dressings and sauces, such as mayonnaise, salad dressing, vinegar, mustard, horseradish, soy sauce, tarter sauce, Worcestershire sauce, and other prepared sauces (except tomato-based and gravies); (2) manufacturing spices, table salt, seasoning, and flavoring extracts (except coffee and meat), and natural food colorings; and (3) manufacturing dry mix food preparations, such as salad dressing mixes, gravy and sauce mixes, frosting mixes, and other dry mix preparations.

Cross-References.   Establishments primarily engaged in--

- Manufacturing catsup and other tomato-based sauces--are classified in Industry 31142, Fruit and Vegetable Canning, Pickling, and Drying;
- Mixing purchased dried and/or dehydrated potato, rice, and pasta and packaging them with other purchased ingredients, and manufacturing prepared frosting--are classified in Industry 31199, All Other Food Manufacturing;
- Drying and/or dehydrating ingredients for dry soup mixes and bouillon--are classified in Industry 31142, Fruit and Vegetable Canning, Pickling, and Drying;
- Mixing purchased dried and/or dehydrated ingredients for dry soup mixes and bouillon--are classified in Industry 31199, All Other Food Manufacturing;
- Manufacturing industrial salts--are classified in Industry 32599, All Other Chemical Product and Preparation Manufacturing;
- Manufacturing flavoring syrups (except chocolate and coffee-based syrups)--are classified in Industry 31193, Flavoring Syrup and Concentrate Manufacturing;
- Manufacturing synthetic food colorings--are classified in Industry 32513, Synthetic Dye and Pigment Manufacturing;
- Manufacturing natural organic colorings for nonfood uses--are classified in Industry 32519, Other Basic Organic Chemical Manufacturing;
- Manufacturing coffee extracts--are classified in Industry 31192, Coffee and Tea Manufacturing;
- Manufacturing liquid meat extracts from slaughtered or purchased carcasses--are classified in Industry 31161, Animal Slaughtering and Processing; and
- Manufacturing canned liquid gravies--are classified in Industry 31142, Fruit and Vegetable Canning, Pickling, and Drying.

311941 Mayonnaise, Dressing, and Other Prepared Sauce Manufacturing

This U.S. industry comprises establishments primarily engaged in manufacturing mayonnaise, salad dressing, vinegar, mustard, horseradish, soy sauce, tarter sauce, Worcestershire sauce, and other prepared sauces (except tomato-based and gravy).

T—Canadian, Mexican, and United States industries are comparable.

Cross-References.   Establishments primarily engaged in--

- Manufacturing catsup and other tomato-based sauces--are classified in U.S. Industry 311421, Fruit and Vegetable Canning;
- Manufacturing dry salad dressing and dry sauce mixes--are classified in U.S. Industry 311942, Spice and Extract Manufacturing; and
- Manufacturing canned liquid gravies--are classified in U.S. Industry 311422, Specialty Canning.

311942 Spice and Extract Manufacturing

This U.S. industry comprises establishments primarily engaged in (1) manufacturing spices, table salt, seasonings, flavoring extracts (except coffee and meat), and natural food colorings and/or (2) manufacturing dry mix food preparations, such as salad dressing mixes, gravy and sauce mixes, frosting mixes, and other dry mix preparations.

Cross-References.   Establishments primarily engaged in--

- Manufacturing catsup and other tomato-based sauces--are classified in U.S. Industry 311421, Fruit and Vegetable Canning;
- Manufacturing mayonnaise, dressings, and prepared sauces (except tomato-based and gravy)--are classified in U.S. Industry 311941, Mayonnaise, Dressing, and Other Prepared Sauce Manufacturing;
- Manufacturing canned liquid gravies--are classified in U.S. Industry 311422, Specialty Canning;
- Manufacturing industrial salts--are classified in U.S. Industry 325998, All Other Miscellaneous Chemical Product and Preparation Manufacturing;
- Drying and/or dehydrating ingredients for dry soup mixes and bouillon--are classified in U.S. Industry 311423, Dried and Dehydrated Food Manufacturing;
- Mixing purchased dried and/or dehydrated ingredients for dry soup mixes and bouillon--are classified in U.S. Industry 311999, All Other Miscellaneous Food Manufacturing;
- Manufacturing flavoring syrups (except chocolate and coffee-based syrups)--are classified in Industry 311930, Flavoring Syrup and Concentrate Manufacturing;
- Mixing purchased dried and/or dehydrated potato, rice, and pasta and packaging them with other purchased ingredients, and manufacturing prepared frosting--are classified in U.S. Industry 311999, All Other Miscellaneous Food Manufacturing;
- Manufacturing coffee extracts and/or coffee-based syrups--are classified in Industry 311920, Coffee and Tea Manufacturing;
- Manufacturing liquid meat extracts from slaughtered or purchased carcasses--are classified in Industry 31161, Animal Slaughtering and Processing;
- Manufacturing synthetic food colorings--are classified in Industry 325130, Synthetic Dye and Pigment Manufacturing; and
- Manufacturing natural organic colorings for nonfood uses--are classified in U.S. Industry 325199, All Other Basic Organic Chemical Manufacturing.

31199   All Other Food Manufacturing[T]

This industry comprises establishments primarily engaged in manufacturing food (except animal food; grain and oilseed milling; sugar and confectionery products; preserved fruits, vegetables, and specialty foods; dairy products; meat products; seafood products; baked goods and tortillas; snack foods; coffee and tea; flavoring syrups and concentrates; seasonings; and dressings). Included in this industry are establishments primarily engaged in mixing purchased dried and/or dehydrated ingredients, including those mixing purchased dried and/or dehydrated ingredients for soup mixes and bouillon.

Illustrative Examples:

Baking powder manufacturing
Cut or peeled fresh vegetables manufacturing
Dessert puddings manufacturing

Egg substitutes manufacturing
Sweetening syrups (except pure maple) manufacturing

T—Canadian, Mexican, and United States industries are comparable.

Fresh pasta manufacturing
Fresh pizza manufacturing
Honey processing

Popcorn (except popped) manufacturing
Powdered drink mixes (except chocolate, coffee, tea, or milk based) manufacturing

Cross-References. Establishments primarily engaged in--

- Manufacturing animal foods--are classified in Industry Group 3111, Animal Food Manufacturing;
- Milling grains and oilseeds--are classified in Industry Group 3112, Grain and Oilseed Milling;
- Manufacturing sugar and confectionery products--are classified in Industry Group 3113, Sugar and Confectionery Product Manufacturing;
- Preserving fruit, vegetables, and specialty foods--are classified in Industry Group 3114, Fruit and Vegetable Preserving and Specialty Food Manufacturing;
- Manufacturing dairy products--are classified in Industry Group 3115, Dairy Product Manufacturing;
- Manufacturing meat products--are classified in Industry Group 3116, Animal Slaughtering and Processing;
- Manufacturing seafood products--are classified in Industry Group 3117, Seafood Product Preparation and Packaging;
- Manufacturing bakery products and tortillas--are classified in Industry Group 3118, Bakeries and Tortilla Manufacturing;
- Manufacturing snack foods--are classified in Industry 31191, Snack Food Manufacturing;
- Manufacturing coffee and tea--are classified in Industry 31192, Coffee and Tea Manufacturing;
- Manufacturing flavoring syrups and concentrates (except chocolate and coffee-based)--are classified in Industry 31193, Flavoring Syrup and Concentrate Manufacturing;
- Manufacturing seasonings and dressings--are classified in Industry 31194, Seasoning and Dressing Manufacturing;
- Milling rice and packaging it with other ingredients--are classified in Industry 31121, Flour Milling and Malt Manufacturing;
- Manufacturing dry pasta and packaging it with other ingredients--are classified in Industry 31182, Cookie, Cracker, and Pasta Manufacturing; and
- Drying and/or dehydrating ingredients and packaging them with other purchased ingredients--are classified in Industry 31142, Fruit and Vegetable Canning, Pickling, and Drying.

311991 Perishable Prepared Food Manufacturing

This U.S. industry comprises establishments primarily engaged in manufacturing perishable prepared foods, such as salads, sandwiches, prepared meals, fresh pizza, fresh pasta, and peeled or cut vegetables.

311999 All Other Miscellaneous Food Manufacturing

This U.S. industry comprises establishments primarily engaged in manufacturing food (except animal food; grain and oilseed milling; sugar and confectionery products; preserved fruits, vegetables, and specialties; dairy products; meat products; seafood products; bakeries and tortillas; snack foods; coffee and tea; flavoring syrups and concentrates; seasonings and dressings; and perishable prepared food). Included in this industry are establishments primarily engaged in mixing purchased dried and/or dehydrated ingredients including those mixing purchased dried and/or dehydrated ingredients for soup mixes and bouillon.

Illustrative Examples:

Baking powder manufacturing
Cake frosting, prepared, manufacturing
Dessert puddings manufacturing
Sweetening syrups (except pure maple) manufacturing
Egg substitutes manufacturing

Gelatin dessert preparations manufacturing
Honey processing
Powdered drink mixes (except chocolate, coffee, tea, or milk based) manufacturing
Popcorn (except popped) manufacturing
Yeast manufacturing

T—Canadian, Mexican, and United States industries are comparable.

Cross-References.   Establishments primarily engaged in--

- Manufacturing animal foods--are classified in Industry Group 3111, Animal Food Manufacturing;
- Milling grains and oilseeds--are classified in Industry Group 3112, Grain and Oilseed Milling;
- Manufacturing sugar and confectionery products--are classified in Industry Group 3113, Sugar and Confectionery Product Manufacturing;
- Preserving fruit, vegetable, and specialty foods--are classified in Industry Group 3114, Fruit and Vegetable Preserving and Specialty Food Manufacturing;
- Manufacturing dairy products--are classified in Industry Group 3115, Dairy Product Manufacturing;
- Manufacturing meat products--are classified in Industry Group 3116, Animal Slaughtering and Processing;
- Manufacturing seafood products--are classified in Industry Group 3117, Seafood Product Preparation and Packaging;
- Manufacturing bakery products and tortillas--are classified in Industry Group 3118, Bakeries and Tortilla Manufacturing;
- Manufacturing snack foods--are classified in Industry 31191, Snack Food Manufacturing;
- Manufacturing coffee and tea--are classified in Industry 31192, Coffee and Tea Manufacturing;
- Manufacturing flavoring syrups and concentrates (except coffee-based)--are classified in Industry 31193, Flavoring Syrup and Concentrate Manufacturing;
- Manufacturing seasonings and dressings--are classified in Industry 31194, Seasoning and Dressing Manufacturing;
- Manufacturing perishable prepared foods--are classified in U.S. Industry 311991, Perishable Prepared Food Manufacturing;
- Milling rice and packaging it with other ingredients--are classified in U.S. Industry 311212, Rice Milling;
- Manufacturing dry pasta and packaging it with ingredients--are classified in U.S. Industry 311824, Dry Pasta, Dough, and Flour Mixes Manufacturing from Purchased Flour; and
- Drying and/or dehydrating ingredients and packaging them with other purchased ingredients--are classified in U.S. Industry 311423, Dried and Dehydrated Food Manufacturing.

312   Beverage and Tobacco Product Manufacturing[T]

Industries in the Beverage and Tobacco Product Manufacturing subsector manufacture beverages and tobacco products. The Beverage Manufacturing industry group includes three types of establishments: (1) those that manufacture nonalcoholic beverages; (2) those that manufacture alcoholic beverages through the fermentation process; and (3) those that produce distilled alcoholic beverages. Ice manufacturing, while not a beverage, is included with nonalcoholic beverage manufacturing because it uses the same production process as water purification.

In the case of activities related to the manufacture of beverages, the structure follows the defined production processes. Brandy, a distilled beverage, is not placed under distillery product manufacturing, but rather under winery product manufacturing since the production process used in the manufacturing of alcoholic grape-based beverages produces both wines (fermented beverage) and brandies (distilled beverage).

The Tobacco Manufacturing industry group includes two types of establishments: (1) those engaged in redrying and stemming tobacco and (2) those that manufacture tobacco products, such as cigarettes and cigars.

3121   Beverage Manufacturing[T]

This industry group comprises establishments primarily engaged in manufacturing soft drinks and ice; purifying and bottling water; and manufacturing brewery, winery, and distillery products.

31211   Soft Drink and Ice Manufacturing[T]

This industry comprises establishments primarily engaged in one or more of the following: (1) manufacturing soft drinks; (2) manufacturing ice; and (3) purifying and bottling water.

T—Canadian, Mexican, and United States industries are comparable.

Cross-References.   Establishments primarily engaged in--

- Canning fruit and vegetable juices--are classified in Industry 31142, Fruit and Vegetable Canning, Pickling, and Drying;
- Manufacturing soft drink bases--are classified in Industry 31193, Flavoring Syrup and Concentrate Manufacturing;
- Manufacturing nonalcoholic cider--are classified in Industry 31194, Seasoning and Dressing Manufacturing;
- Manufacturing dry ice--are classified in Industry 32512, Industrial Gas Manufacturing;
- Manufacturing milk based drinks--are classified in Industry 31151, Dairy Product (except Frozen) Manufacturing;
- Manufacturing nonalcoholic beers--are classified in Industry 31212, Breweries;
- Manufacturing nonalcoholic wines--are classified in Industry 31213, Wineries; and
- Bottling purchased purified water--are classified in Industry 42449, Other Grocery and Related Products Merchant Wholesalers.

312111 Soft Drink Manufacturing

This U.S. industry comprises establishments primarily engaged in manufacturing soft drinks and artificially carbonated waters.

Cross-References.   Establishments primarily engaged in--

- Canning fruit and vegetable juices--are classified in U.S. Industry 311421, Fruit and Vegetable Canning;
- Manufacturing fruit syrups for flavoring--are classified in Industry 311930, Flavoring Syrup and Concentrate Manufacturing;
- Manufacturing nonalcoholic cider--are classified in U.S. Industry 311941, Mayonnaise, Dressing, and Other Prepared Sauce Manufacturing;
- Purifying and bottling water (except artificially carbonated and flavored water)--are classified in U.S. Industry 312112, Bottled Water Manufacturing;
- Manufacturing milk based drinks--are classified in U.S. Industry 311511, Fluid Milk Manufacturing;
- Manufacturing nonalcoholic beers--are classified in Industry 312120, Breweries; and
- Manufacturing nonalcoholic wines--are classified in Industry 312130, Wineries.

312112 Bottled Water Manufacturing

This U.S. industry comprises establishments primarily engaged in purifying and bottling water (including naturally carbonated).

Cross-References.   Establishments primarily engaged in--

- Manufacturing artificially carbonated or flavored waters--are classified in U.S. Industry 312111, Soft Drink Manufacturing; and
- Bottling purchased purified water--are classified in Industry 424490, Other Grocery and Related Products Merchant Wholesalers.

312113 Ice Manufacturing

This U.S. industry comprises establishments primarily engaged in manufacturing ice.

Cross-References.

Establishments primarily engaged in manufacturing dry ice are classified in Industry 325120, Industrial Gas Manufacturing.

T—Canadian, Mexican, and United States industries are comparable.

31212 Breweries^T
See industry description for 312120.

312120 Breweries

This industry comprises establishments primarily engaged in brewing beer, ale, lager, malt liquors, and nonalcoholic beer.

Cross-References.   Establishments primarily engaged in--

- Bottling purchased malt beverages--are classified in Industry 424810, Beer and Ale Merchant Wholesalers; and
- Manufacturing malt--are classified in U.S. Industry 311213, Malt Manufacturing.

31213 Wineries^T
See industry description for 312130.

312130 Wineries

This industry comprises establishments primarily engaged in one or more of the following: (1) growing grapes and manufacturing wines and brandies; (2) manufacturing wines and brandies from grapes and other fruits grown elsewhere; and (3) blending wines and brandies.

Cross-References.

Establishments primarily engaged in bottling purchased wines are classified in Industry 424820, Wine and Distilled Alcoholic Beverage Merchant Wholesalers.

31214 Distilleries^T
See industry description for 312140.

312140 Distilleries

This industry comprises establishments primarily engaged in one or more of the following: (1) distilling potable liquors (except brandies); (2) distilling and blending liquors; and (3) blending and mixing liquors and other ingredients.

Cross-References.   Establishments primarily engaged in--

- Manufacturing nonpotable ethyl alcohol--are classified in U.S. Industry 325193, Ethyl Alcohol Manufacturing;
- Bottling liquors made elsewhere--are classified in Industry 424820, Wine and Distilled Alcoholic Beverage Merchant Wholesalers; and
- Manufacturing brandies--are classified in Industry 312130, Wineries.

3122 Tobacco Manufacturing^T

31223 Tobacco Manufacturing
See industry description for 312230.

312230 Tobacco Manufacturing

This industry comprises establishments primarily engaged in (1) stemming and redrying tobacco and/or (2) manufacturing cigarettes or other tobacco products.

T—Canadian, Mexican, and United States industries are comparable.

Illustrative Examples:

Chewing tobacco manufacturing	Snuff manufacturing
Cigar manufacturing	Prepared pipe tobacco manufacturing
Cigarettes manufacturing (except electronic)	Tobacco leaf processing and aging

Cross-References.   Establishments primarily engaged in--

- Manufacturing tobacco pipes or electronic cigarettes--are classified in U.S. Industry 339999, All Other Miscellaneous Manufacturing;
- Manufacturing electronic cigarette vapor refills--are classified in U.S. Industry 325998, All Other Miscellaneous Chemical Product and Preparation Manufacturing;
- Selling leaf tobacco as merchant wholesalers that also engage in stemming tobacco--are classified in Industry 424940, Tobacco and Tobacco Product Merchant Wholesalers; and
- Selling leaf tobacco as agents or brokers that also engage in stemming tobacco--are classified in Industry 425120, Wholesale Trade Agents and Brokers.

313   Textile Mills[T]

Industries in the Textile Mills subsector group establishments that transform a basic fiber (natural or synthetic) into a product, such as yarn or fabric that is further manufactured into usable items, such as apparel, sheets, towels, and textile bags for individual or industrial consumption. The further manufacturing may be performed in the same establishment and classified in this subsector, or it may be performed at a separate establishment and be classified elsewhere in manufacturing.

The main processes in this subsector include preparation and spinning of fiber, knitting or weaving of fabric, and the finishing of the textile. The NAICS structure follows and captures this process flow. Major industries in this flow, such as preparation of fibers, weaving of fabric, knitting of fabric, and fiber and fabric finishing, are uniquely identified. Texturizing, throwing, twisting, and winding of yarn contain aspects of both fiber preparation and fiber finishing and are classified with preparation of fibers rather than with finishing of fibers.

NAICS separates the manufacturing of primary textiles and the manufacturing of textile products (except apparel) produced from purchased primary textiles, such as fabric. The manufacturing of textile products (except apparel) from purchased fabric is classified in Subsector 314, Textile Product Mills, and apparel from purchased fabric is classified in Subsector 315, Apparel Manufacturing.

Excluded from this subsector are establishments that weave or knit fabric and make garments. These establishments are included in Subsector 315, Apparel Manufacturing.

3131   Fiber, Yarn, and Thread Mills[T]

31311   Fiber, Yarn, and Thread Mills[T]
See industry description for 313110.

313110 Fiber, Yarn, and Thread Mills

This industry comprises establishments primarily engaged in one or more of the following: (1) spinning yarn; (2) manufacturing thread of any fiber; (3) texturizing, throwing, twisting, and winding purchased yarn or manmade fiber filaments; and (4) producing hemp yarn and further processing into rope or bags.

Cross-References.

Establishments primarily engaged in manufacturing artificial and synthetic fibers and filaments and texturizing these filaments are classified in Industry 325220, Artificial and Synthetic Fibers and Filaments Manufacturing.

T—Canadian, Mexican, and United States industries are comparable.

3132   Fabric Mills[T]

This industry group comprises establishments primarily engaged in one of the following: (1) weaving broadwoven fabrics and felts (except tire fabrics and rugs); (2) weaving or braiding narrow fabrics; (3) making fabric-covered elastic yarn and thread; (4) manufacturing Schiffli machine embroideries; (5) manufacturing nonwoven fabrics and felts; (6) knitting weft (i.e., circular) and warp (i.e., flat) fabric; (7) knitting and finishing weft and warp fabric; (8) manufacturing lace; or (9) manufacturing, dyeing, and finishing lace and lace goods.

31321   Broadwoven Fabric Mills[T]
See industry description for 313210.

313210 Broadwoven Fabric Mills

This industry comprises establishments primarily engaged in weaving broadwoven fabrics and felts (except tire fabrics and rugs). Establishments in this industry may weave only, weave and finish, or weave, finish, and further fabricate fabric products.

Cross-References.   Establishments primarily engaged in--

- Weaving widths specifically constructed for cutting to narrow widths--are classified in Industry 313220, Narrow Fabric Mills and Schiffli Machine Embroidery;
- Weaving or tufting carpet and rugs--are classified in Industry 314110, Carpet and Rug Mills; and
- Making tire cord and tire fabrics--are classified in U.S. Industry 314994, Rope, Cordage, Twine, Tire Cord, and Tire Fabric Mills.

31322   Narrow Fabric Mills and Schiffli Machine Embroidery[T]
See industry description for 313220.

313220 Narrow Fabric Mills and Schiffli Machine Embroidery

This industry comprises establishments primarily engaged in one or more of the following: (1) weaving or braiding narrow fabrics in their final form or initially made in wider widths that are specially constructed for narrower widths; (2) making fabric-covered elastic yarn and thread; and (3) manufacturing Schiffli machine embroideries. Establishments in this industry may weave only; weave and finish; or weave, finish, and further fabricate fabric products.

31323   Nonwoven Fabric Mills[T]
See industry description for 313230.

313230 Nonwoven Fabric Mills

This industry comprises establishments primarily engaged in manufacturing nonwoven fabrics and felts. Processes used include bonding and/or interlocking fibers by mechanical, chemical, thermal, or solvent means, or by combinations thereof.

31324   Knit Fabric Mills[T]
See industry description for 313240.

313240 Knit Fabric Mills

This industry comprises establishments primarily engaged in one of the following: (1) knitting weft (i.e., circular) and warp (i.e., flat) fabric; (2) knitting and finishing weft and warp fabric; (3) manufacturing lace; or (4) manufacturing, dyeing, and finishing lace and lace goods. Establishments in this industry may knit only; knit and finish; or knit, finish, and further fabricate fabric products (except apparel).

T—Canadian, Mexican, and United States industries are comparable.

Cross-References.

Establishments primarily engaged in knitting apparel are classified in Industry Group 3151, Apparel Knitting Mills.

3133 Textile and Fabric Finishing and Fabric Coating Mills[T]

This industry group comprises establishments primarily engaged in one of the following: (1) finishing textiles, fabrics, and apparel; (2) converting fabrics and textiles by buying fabric goods in the grey, having them finished on contract, and selling them at wholesale; or (3) coating, laminating, varnishing, waxing, and rubberizing textiles and apparel.

31331 Textile and Fabric Finishing Mills[T]
See industry description for 313310.

313310 Textile and Fabric Finishing Mills

This industry comprises (1) establishments primarily engaged in finishing textiles, fabrics, and apparel and (2) establishments of converters who buy fabric goods in the grey, have them finished on contract, and sell at wholesale. Finishing operations include: bleaching, dyeing, printing (e.g., roller, screen, flock, plisse), stonewashing, and other mechanical finishing, such as preshrinking, shrinking, sponging, calendering, mercerizing, and napping; as well as cleaning, scouring, and the preparation of natural fibers and raw stock.

Cross-References.   Establishments primarily engaged in--

- Coating or impregnating fabrics--are classified in Industry 313320, Fabric Coating Mills;
- Knitting or knitting and finishing fabric--are classified in Industry 313240, Knit Fabric Mills;
- Manufacturing and finishing apparel--are classified in Subsector 315, Apparel Manufacturing;
- Weaving and finishing fabrics--are classified in Industry Group 3132, Fabric Mills;
- Manufacturing and finishing rugs and carpets--are classified in Industry 314110, Carpet and Rug Mills; and
- Printing on apparel--are classified in Industry 32311, Printing.

31332 Fabric Coating Mills[T]
See industry description for 313320.

313320 Fabric Coating Mills

This industry comprises establishments primarily engaged in coating, laminating, varnishing, waxing, and rubberizing textiles and apparel.

Cross-References.

Establishments primarily engaged in dyeing and finishing textiles are classified in Industry 313310, Textile and Fabric Finishing Mills.

314 Textile Product Mills[T]

Industries in the Textile Product Mills subsector group establishments that make textile products (except apparel). With a few exceptions, processes used by these establishments are generally cut and sew (i.e., purchasing fabric and cutting and sewing to make nonapparel textile products, such as sheets and towels).

T—Canadian, Mexican, and United States industries are comparable.

3141   Textile Furnishings Mills[T]

This industry group comprises establishments primarily engaged in (1) manufacturing woven, tufted, and other carpets and rugs and (2) manufacturing household textile products from purchased materials. The household textile products may be made on a stock or custom basis for sale to individual retail customers.

31411   Carpet and Rug Mills[T]
See industry description for 314110.

314110 Carpet and Rug Mills

This industry comprises establishments primarily engaged in (1) manufacturing woven, tufted, and other carpets and rugs, such as art squares, floor mattings, needlepunch carpeting, and door mats and mattings, from textile materials or from twisted paper, grasses, reeds, sisal, jute, or rags and/or (2) finishing carpets and rugs.

31412   Curtain and Linen Mills[T]
See industry description for 314120.

314120 Curtain and Linen Mills

This industry comprises establishments primarily engaged in manufacturing household textile products, such as curtains, draperies, linens, bedspreads, sheets, tablecloths, towels, and shower curtains, from purchased materials. The household textile products may be made on a stock or custom basis for sale to individual retail customers.

Cross-References.   Establishments primarily engaged in--

- Weaving broadwoven fabrics--are classified in Industry 313210, Broadwoven Fabric Mills;
- Manufacturing lace curtains on lace machines--are classified in Industry 313240, Knit Fabric Mills;
- Manufacturing textile blanket, wardrobe, and laundry bags--are classified in Industry 314910, Textile Bag and Canvas Mills; and
- Manufacturing mops--are classified in U.S. Industry 339994, Broom, Brush, and Mop Manufacturing.

3149   Other Textile Product Mills[T]

This industry group comprises establishments primarily engaged in making textile products (except carpets and rugs, curtains and draperies, and other household textile products) from purchased materials.

31491   Textile Bag and Canvas Mills[T]
See industry description for 314910.

314910 Textile Bag and Canvas Mills

This industry comprises establishments primarily engaged in manufacturing textile bags or other canvas and canvas-like products, such as awnings, sails, tarpaulins, and tents from purchased textile fabrics or yarns.

Illustrative Examples:

Covers (e.g., boat, swimming pool, truck) made from purchased fabrics
Laundry bags made from purchased woven or knitted materials

Seed bags made from purchased woven or knitted materials
Textile bags made from purchased woven or knitted materials

Cross-References.   Establishments primarily engaged in--

- Manufacturing plastic bags--are classified in U.S. Industry 326111, Plastics Bag and Pouch Manufacturing;

T—Canadian, Mexican, and United States industries are comparable.

- Manufacturing canvas blinds and shades--are classified in Industry 337920, Blind and Shade Manufacturing;
- Manufacturing women's handbags and purses of leather or other material (except precious metal)--are classified in U.S. Industry 316992, Women's Handbag and Purse Manufacturing; and
- Manufacturing luggage--are classified in U.S. Industry 316998, All Other Leather Good and Allied Product Manufacturing.

31499   All Other Textile Product Mills[T]

This industry comprises establishments primarily engaged in manufacturing nonapparel textile products (except carpet, rugs, curtains, linens, bags, and canvas products) from purchased materials. This industry includes establishments primarily engaged in decorative stitching such as embroidery or other art needlework on textile products, including apparel.

Illustrative Examples:

Batts and batting (except nonwoven fabrics) manufacturing
Carpet cutting and binding
Diapers (except disposable) made from purchased materials
Fishing nets made from purchased materials

Embroidering on textile products or apparel for the trade
Ropes (except wire rope) manufacturing
Sleeping bags manufacturing
Tire cord and fabric, all materials, manufacturing
Twines manufacturing

Cross-References.   Establishments primarily engaged in--

- Manufacturing yarns and thread--are classified in Industry 31311, Fiber, Yarn, and Thread Mills;
- Manufacturing carpets and rugs--are classified in Industry 31411, Carpet and Rug Mills;
- Manufacturing apparel--are classified in Subsector 315, Apparel Manufacturing;
- Manufacturing curtains and linens--are classified in Industry 31412, Curtain and Linen Mills; and
- Manufacturing textile bags and canvas products--are classified in Industry 31491, Textile Bag and Canvas Mills.

314994 Rope, Cordage, Twine, Tire Cord, and Tire Fabric Mills

This U.S. industry comprises establishments primarily engaged in (1) manufacturing rope, cable, cordage, twine, and related products from all materials (e.g., abaca, sisal, henequen, cotton, paper, jute, flax, manmade fibers including glass) and/or (2) manufacturing cord and fabric of polyester, rayon, cotton, glass, steel, or other materials for use in reinforcing rubber tires, industrial belting, and similar uses.

Cross-References.

Establishments primarily engaged in spinning yarns and filaments are classified in Industry 313110, Fiber, Yarn, and Thread Mills.

314999 All Other Miscellaneous Textile Product Mills

This U.S. industry comprises establishments primarily engaged in manufacturing textile products (except carpets and rugs; curtains and linens; textile bags and canvas products; rope, cordage, and twine; and tire cords and tire fabrics) from purchased materials. These establishments may further embellish the textile products they manufacture with decorative stitching. Establishments primarily engaged in adding decorative stitching such as embroidery or other art needlework on textile products, including apparel, on a contract or fee basis for the trade, are included in this industry.

T—Canadian, Mexican, and United States industries are comparable.

Illustrative Examples:

Batts and batting (except nonwoven fabrics) manufacturing
Embroidering on textile products or apparel for the trade
Fishing nets made from purchased materials
Carpet cutting and binding

Sleeping bags manufacturing
Diapers (except disposable) made from purchased materials
Textile fire hoses made from purchased materials
Dust cloths made from purchased fabric
Weatherstripping made from purchased textiles

Cross-References.   Establishments primarily engaged in--

- Manufacturing yarns and thread--are classified in Industry 313110, Fiber, Yarn, and Thread Mills;
- Manufacturing carpets and rugs--are classified in Industry 314110, Carpet and Rug Mills;
- Manufacturing curtains and linens--are classified in Industry 314120, Curtain and Linen Mills;
- Manufacturing textile bags and canvas products--are classified in Industry 314910, Textile Bag and Canvas Mills; and
- Manufacturing rope, cordage, twine, tire cord, and tire fabrics--are classified in U.S. Industry 314994, Rope, Cordage, Twine, Tire Cord, and Tire Fabric Mills.

315   Apparel Manufacturing[T]

Industries in the Apparel Manufacturing subsector group establishments with two distinct manufacturing processes: (1) cut and sew (i.e., purchasing fabric and cutting and sewing to make a garment) and (2) the manufacture of garments in establishments that first knit fabric and then cut and sew the fabric into a garment. The Apparel Manufacturing subsector includes a diverse range of establishments manufacturing full lines of ready-to-wear apparel and custom apparel: apparel contractors, performing cutting or sewing operations on materials owned by others; jobbers, performing entrepreneurial functions involved in apparel manufacturing; and tailors, manufacturing custom garments for individual clients. Knitting fabric, when done alone, is classified in the Textile Mills subsector, but when knitting is combined with the production of complete garments, the activity is classified in the Apparel Manufacturing subsector.

3151   Apparel Knitting Mills[T]

This industry group comprises establishments primarily engaged in knitting apparel or knitting fabric and then manufacturing apparel. This industry group includes jobbers performing entrepreneurial functions involved in knitting apparel and accessories. Knitting fabric, without manufacturing apparel, is classified in Subsector 313, Textile Mills.

31511   Hosiery and Sock Mills[T]
See industry description for 315110.

315110 Hosiery and Sock Mills

This industry comprises establishments primarily engaged in knitting or knitting and finishing hosiery and socks.

Cross-References.   Establishments primarily engaged in--

- Manufacturing orthopedic hosiery--are classified in U.S. Industry 339113, Surgical Appliance and Supplies Manufacturing;
- Manufacturing slipper socks from purchased socks--are classified in Industry 316210, Footwear Manufacturing; and
- Finishing apparel products only--are classified in Industry 313310, Textile and Fabric Finishing Mills.

31519   Other Apparel Knitting Mills[T]
See industry description for 315190.

T—Canadian, Mexican, and United States industries are comparable.

315190 Other Apparel Knitting Mills

This industry comprises establishments primarily engaged in one of the following: (1) knitting underwear, outerwear, and/or nightwear; (2) knitting fabric and manufacturing underwear, outerwear, and/or nightwear; or (3) knitting, manufacturing, and finishing knit underwear, outerwear, and/or nightwear.

Cross-References.   Establishments primarily engaged in--

- Manufacturing outerwear, underwear, and nightwear from purchased fabric--are classified in Industry Group 3152, Cut and Sew Apparel Manufacturing; and
- Finishing apparel products only--are classified in Industry 313310, Textile and Fabric Finishing Mills.

3152   Cut and Sew Apparel Manufacturing[T]

This industry group comprises establishments primarily engaged in manufacturing cut and sew apparel from woven fabric or purchased knit fabric. Included in this industry group is a diverse range of establishments manufacturing full lines of ready-to-wear apparel and custom apparel: apparel contractors, performing cutting or sewing operations on materials owned by others; jobbers, performing entrepreneurial functions involved in apparel manufacturing; and tailors, manufacturing custom garments for individual clients. Establishments weaving or knitting fabric, without manufacturing apparel, are classified in Subsector 313, Textile Mills.

31521   Cut and Sew Apparel Contractors
See industry description for 315210.

315210 Cut and Sew Apparel Contractors

This industry comprises establishments commonly referred to as contractors primarily engaged in (1) cutting materials owned by others for apparel and accessories and/or (2) sewing materials owned by others for apparel and accessories.

Cross-References.   Establishments primarily engaged in--

- Manufacturing men's and boys' apparel from purchased fabric--are classified in Industry 315220, Men's and Boys' Cut and Sew Apparel Manufacturing;
- Manufacturing women's, girls', and infants' apparel from purchased fabric--are classified in Industry 315240, Women's, Girls', and Infants' Cut and Sew Apparel Manufacturing;
- Manufacturing all other cut and sew apparel from purchased fabric--are classified in Industry 315280, Other Cut and Sew Apparel Manufacturing;
- Manufacturing apparel accessories from purchased fabric--are classified in Industry 315990, Apparel Accessories and Other Apparel Manufacturing; and
- Embroidering apparel on a contract or fee basis for the trade--are classified in U.S. Industry 314999, All Other Miscellaneous Textile Product Mills.

31522   Men's and Boys' Cut and Sew Apparel Manufacturing
See industry description for 315220.

315220 Men's and Boys' Cut and Sew Apparel Manufacturing

This industry comprises establishments primarily engaged in manufacturing men's and boys' cut and sew apparel from purchased fabric. Men's and boys' clothing jobbers, who perform entrepreneurial functions involved in apparel manufacture, including buying raw materials, designing and preparing samples, arranging for apparel to be made from their materials, and marketing finished apparel, are included.

T—Canadian, Mexican, and United States industries are comparable.

Cross-References.   Establishments primarily engaged in--

- Cutting and/or sewing materials owned by others for men's and boys' apparel--are classified in Industry 315210, Cut and Sew Apparel Contractors;
- Knitting men's and boys' apparel or knitting fabric and manufacturing men's and boys' apparel--are classified in Industry Group 3151, Apparel Knitting Mills; and
- Manufacturing fur or leather apparel and team athletic uniforms--are classified in Industry 315280, Other Cut and Sew Apparel Manufacturing.

31524 Women's, Girls', and Infants' Cut and Sew Apparel Manufacturing
See industry description for 315240.

315240 Women's, Girls', and Infants' Cut and Sew Apparel Manufacturing

This industry comprises establishments primarily engaged in manufacturing women's, girls', and infants' apparel from purchased fabric. Women's, girls', and infants' clothing jobbers, who perform entrepreneurial functions involved in apparel manufacture, including buying raw materials, designing and preparing samples, arranging for apparel to be made from their materials, and marketing finished apparel, are included.

Cross-References.   Establishments primarily engaged in--

- Knitting women's, girls', and infants' apparel or knitting fabric and manufacturing women's, girls', and infants' apparel--are classified in Industry Group 3151, Apparel Knitting Mills;
- Manufacturing unisex outerwear garments, such as T-shirts, sweatshirts, and sweat pants that are sized without reference to specific gender (i.e., adult S, M, L, XL)--are classified in Industry 315220, Men's and Boys' Cut and Sew Apparel Manufacturing;
- Cutting and/or sewing materials owned by others for women's, girls', and infants' apparel--are classified in Industry 315210, Cut and Sew Apparel Contractors;
- Manufacturing fur or leather apparel and team athletic uniforms--are classified in Industry 315280, Other Cut and Sew Apparel Manufacturing; and
- Manufacturing cloth diapers--are classified in U.S. Industry 314999, All Other Miscellaneous Textile Product Mills.

31528 Other Cut and Sew Apparel Manufacturing
See industry description for 315280.

315280 Other Cut and Sew Apparel Manufacturing

This industry comprises establishments primarily engaged in manufacturing cut and sew apparel from purchased fabric (except men's, boys', women's, girls', and infants' apparel). Clothing jobbers for these products, who perform entrepreneurial functions involved in apparel manufacture, including buying raw materials, designing and preparing samples, arranging for apparel to be made from their materials, and marketing finished apparel, are included. Examples of products made by these establishments are fur or leather apparel, sheep-lined clothing, team athletic uniforms, band uniforms, academic caps and gowns, clerical vestments, and costumes.

Cross-References.   Establishments primarily engaged in--

- Manufacturing men's and boys' apparel from purchased fabric--are classified in Industry 315220, Men's and Boys' Cut and Sew Apparel Manufacturing;
- Manufacturing women's, girls', and infants' apparel from purchased fabric--are classified in Industry 315240, Women's, Girls', and Infants' Cut and Sew Apparel Manufacturing;
- Knitting apparel or knitting fabric and manufacturing apparel--are classified in Industry Group 3151, Apparel Knitting Mills;
- Cutting and/or sewing materials owned by others for apparel--are classified in Industry 315210, Cut and Sew Apparel Contractors;

T—Canadian, Mexican, and United States industries are comparable.

- Manufacturing fur and leather mittens and gloves--are classified in Industry 315990, Apparel Accessories and Other Apparel Manufacturing; and
- Dyeing and dressing furs--are classified in Industry 316110, Leather and Hide Tanning and Finishing.

3159   Apparel Accessories and Other Apparel Manufacturing[T]

31599   Apparel Accessories and Other Apparel Manufacturing[T]
See industry description for 315990.

315990   Apparel Accessories and Other Apparel Manufacturing

This industry comprises establishments primarily engaged in manufacturing apparel and accessories (except apparel knitting mills, cut and sew apparel contractors, men's and boys' cut and sew apparel, women's, girls', and infants' cut and sew apparel, and other cut and sew apparel). Jobbers, who perform entrepreneurial functions involved in apparel accessories manufacture, including buying raw materials, designing and preparing samples, arranging for apparel accessories to be made from their materials, and marketing finished apparel accessories, are included. Examples of products made by these establishments are belts, caps, gloves (except medical, sporting, safety), hats, and neckties.

Cross-References.   Establishments primarily engaged in--

- Cutting and/or sewing materials owned by others for apparel accessories--are classified in Industry 315210, Cut and Sew Apparel Contractors;
- Manufacturing paper hats and caps--are classified in U.S. Industry 322299, All Other Converted Paper Product Manufacturing;
- Manufacturing plastics or rubber hats and caps (except bathing caps)--are classified in Subsector 326, Plastics and Rubber Products Manufacturing;
- Manufacturing athletic gloves, such as boxing gloves, baseball gloves, golf gloves, batting gloves, and racquetball gloves--are classified in Industry 339920, Sporting and Athletic Goods Manufacturing;
- Manufacturing metal fabric, metal mesh, or rubber gloves--are classified in U.S. Industry 339113, Surgical Appliance and Supplies Manufacturing;
- Knitting apparel, mittens, gloves, hats, and caps or knitting fabric and manufacturing apparel, mittens, gloves, hats, and caps--are classified in Industry Group 3151, Apparel Knitting Mills;
- Cutting and/or sewing materials owned by others for apparel--are classified in Industry 315210, Cut and Sew Apparel Contractors;
- Manufacturing men's and boys' underwear and outerwear from purchased fabric--are classified in Industry 315220, Men's and Boys' Cut and Sew Apparel Manufacturing;
- Manufacturing women's, girls', and infants' underwear and outerwear from purchased fabric--are classified in Industry 315240, Women's, Girls', and Infants' Cut and Sew Apparel Manufacturing; and
- Manufacturing other apparel from purchased fabric and manufacturing fur and leather apparel--are classified in Industry 315280, Other Cut and Sew Apparel Manufacturing.

316   Leather and Allied Product Manufacturing[T]

Establishments in the Leather and Allied Product Manufacturing subsector transform hides into leather by tanning or curing and fabricating the leather into products for final consumption. This subsector also includes the manufacture of similar products from other materials, including products (except apparel) made from "leather substitutes," such as rubber, plastics, or textiles. Rubber footwear, textile luggage, and plastics purses or wallets are examples of "leather substitute" products included in this subsector. The products made from leather substitutes are included in this subsector because they are made in similar ways leather products are made (e.g., luggage). They are made in the same establishments, so it is not practical to separate them.

The inclusion of leather and hide tanning and finishing in this subsector is partly because it is a relatively small industry that has few close neighbors as a production process, partly because leather is an input to some of the other products classified in this subsector, and partly for historical reasons.

T—Canadian, Mexican, and United States industries are comparable.

3161   Leather and Hide Tanning and Finishing[T]

31611   Leather and Hide Tanning and Finishing[T]
See industry description for 316110.

316110   Leather and Hide Tanning and Finishing

This industry comprises establishments primarily engaged in one or more of the following: (1) tanning, currying, and finishing hides and skins; (2) having others process hides and skins on a contract basis; and (3) dyeing or dressing furs.

3162   Footwear Manufacturing[T]

31621   Footwear Manufacturing[T]
See industry description for 316210.

316210   Footwear Manufacturing

This industry comprises establishments primarily engaged in manufacturing footwear (except orthopedic extension footwear).

Illustrative Examples:

Athletic shoes manufacturing
Ballet slippers manufacturing
Cleated athletic shoes manufacturing
Shoes, children's and infants' (except orthopedic extension), manufacturing

Shoes, men's (except orthopedic extension), manufacturing
Shoes, women's (except orthopedic extension), manufacturing

Cross-References.

Establishments primarily engaged in manufacturing orthopedic extension footwear are classified in U.S. Industry 339113, Surgical Appliance and Supplies Manufacturing.

3169   Other Leather and Allied Product Manufacturing[T]

31699   Other Leather and Allied Product Manufacturing[T]

This industry comprises establishments primarily engaged in manufacturing leather products (except footwear and apparel) from purchased leather or leather substitutes (e.g., fabric, plastics).

Illustrative Examples:

Billfolds, all materials, manufacturing
Boot and shoe cut stock and findings, leather, manufacturing
Dog furnishings (e.g., collars, leashes, harnesses, muzzles), manufacturing
Luggage, all materials, manufacturing
Shoe soles, leather, manufacturing

Purses, women's, all materials (except metal), manufacturing
Toilet kits and cases (except metal) manufacturing
Watch bands (except metal) manufacturing
Welders' jackets, leggings, and sleeves, leather, manufacturing

Cross-References.   Establishments primarily engaged in--

- Manufacturing leather apparel--are classified in Industry 31528, Other Cut and Sew Apparel Manufacturing;

T—Canadian, Mexican, and United States industries are comparable.

census.gov/naics

- Manufacturing leather gloves, mittens, belts, and apparel accessories--are classified in Industry 31599, Apparel Accessories and Other Apparel Manufacturing;
- Manufacturing footwear--are classified in Industry 31621, Footwear Manufacturing;
- Manufacturing nonleather soles--are classified elsewhere based on the primary input material;
- Manufacturing small articles made of metal carried on or about the person--are classified in Industry 33991, Jewelry and Silverware Manufacturing; and
- Manufacturing leather gaskets--are classified in Industry 33999, All Other Miscellaneous Manufacturing.

316992 Women's Handbag and Purse Manufacturing

This U.S. industry comprises establishments primarily engaged in manufacturing women's handbags and purses of any material (except precious metal).

Cross-References.

Establishments primarily engaged in manufacturing precious metal handbags and purses are classified in Industry 339910, Jewelry and Silverware Manufacturing.

316998 All Other Leather Good and Allied Product Manufacturing

This U.S. industry comprises establishments primarily engaged in manufacturing leather products (except footwear, handbags, purses, and apparel) from purchased leather or leather substitutes (e.g., fabric, plastics).

Illustrative Examples:

Billfolds, all materials, manufacturing
Boot and shoe cut stock and findings, leather, manufacturing
Coin purses (except metal) manufacturing
Dog furnishings (e.g., collars, leashes, harnesses, muzzles) manufacturing
Key cases (except metal) manufacturing
Luggage, all materials, manufacturing

Leather belting for machinery (e.g., flat, solid, twisted, built-up) manufacturing
Shoe soles, leather, manufacturing
Toilet kits and cases (except metal) manufacturing
Watch bands (except metal) manufacturing
Welders' jackets, leggings, and sleeves, leather, manufacturing

Cross-References.   Establishments primarily engaged in--

- Manufacturing handbags and purses--are classified in U.S. Industry 316992, Women's Handbag and Purse Manufacturing;
- Manufacturing leather apparel--are classified in Industry 315280, Other Cut and Sew Apparel Manufacturing;
- Manufacturing leather gloves, mittens, belts, and apparel accessories--are classified in Industry 315990, Apparel Accessories and Other Apparel Manufacturing;
- Manufacturing footwear--are classified in Industry 316210, Footwear Manufacturing;
- Manufacturing nonleather soles--are classified elsewhere based on the primary input material;
- Manufacturing small articles made of metal carried on or about the person--are classified in Industry 339910, Jewelry and Silverware Manufacturing; and
- Manufacturing leather gaskets--are classified in U.S. Industry 339991, Gasket, Packing, and Sealing Device Manufacturing.

321 Wood Product Manufacturing[T]

Establishments in the Wood Product Manufacturing subsector manufacture wood products, such as lumber, plywood, veneers, wood containers, wood flooring, wood trusses, manufactured homes (i.e., mobile homes), and prefabricated wood buildings. The production processes of the Wood Product Manufacturing subsector include sawing, planing, shaping, laminating, and assembling wood products starting from logs that are cut into bolts, or

---

T—Canadian, Mexican, and United States industries are comparable.

lumber that then may be further cut, or shaped by lathes or other shaping tools. The lumber or other transformed wood shapes may also be subsequently planed or smoothed, and assembled into finished products, such as wood containers. The Wood Product Manufacturing subsector includes establishments that make wood products from logs and bolts that are sawed and shaped, and establishments that purchase sawed lumber and make wood products. With the exception of sawmills and wood preservation establishments, the establishments are grouped into industries mainly based on the specific products manufactured.

3211   Sawmills and Wood Preservation[T]

32111   Sawmills and Wood Preservation[T]

This industry comprises establishments primarily engaged in one or more of the following: (1) sawing dimension lumber, boards, beams, timber, poles, ties, shingles, shakes, siding, and wood chips from logs or bolts; (2) sawing round wood poles, pilings, and posts and treating them with preservatives; and (3) treating wood sawed, planed, or shaped in other establishments with creosote or other preservatives to prevent decay and to protect against fire and insects. Sawmills may plane the rough lumber that they make with a planing machine to achieve smoothness and uniformity of size.

Cross-References.   Establishments primarily engaged in--

- Operating portable chipper mills in the field--are classified in Industry 11331, Logging;
- Manufacturing wood products (except round wood poles, pilings, and posts) and treating them with preservatives--are classified elsewhere in Subsector 321, Wood Product Manufacturing, based on the related production process;
- Manufacturing veneer from logs and bolts or manufacturing engineered lumber and structural members other than solid wood--are classified in Industry 32121, Veneer, Plywood, and Engineered Wood Product Manufacturing; and
- Planing purchased lumber or manufacturing cut stock or dimension stock (i.e., shapes) from logs or bolts-- are classified in Industry 32191, Millwork.

321113 Sawmills

This U.S. industry comprises establishments primarily engaged in sawing dimension lumber, boards, beams, timbers, poles, ties, shingles, shakes, siding, and wood chips from logs or bolts. Sawmills may plane the rough lumber that they make with a planing machine to achieve smoothness and uniformity of size.

Cross-References.   Establishments primarily engaged in--

- Planing purchased lumber or manufacturing cut stock or dimension stock (i.e., shapes) from logs or bolts-- are classified in Industry 32191, Millwork;
- Manufacturing veneer from logs or bolts--are classified in Industry 32121, Veneer, Plywood, and Engineered Wood Product Manufacturing; and
- Operating portable chipper mills in the field--are classified in Industry 113310, Logging.

321114 Wood Preservation

This U.S. industry comprises establishments primarily engaged in (1) treating wood sawed, planed, or shaped in other establishments with creosote or other preservatives, such as alkaline copper quat, copper azole, and sodium borates, to prevent decay and to protect against fire and insects and/or (2) sawing round wood poles, pilings, and posts and treating them with preservatives.

T—Canadian, Mexican, and United States industries are comparable.

Cross-References.

Establishments primarily engaged in manufacturing wood products (except round wood poles, pilings, and posts) and treating them with preservatives are classified elsewhere in Subsector 321, Wood Product Manufacturing, based on the related production process.

3212   Veneer, Plywood, and Engineered Wood Product Manufacturing[T]

32121   Veneer, Plywood, and Engineered Wood Product Manufacturing[T]

This industry comprises establishments primarily engaged in one or more of the following: (1) manufacturing veneer and/or plywood; (2) manufacturing engineered wood members; and (3) manufacturing reconstituted wood products. This industry includes manufacturing plywood from veneer made in the same establishment or from veneer made in other establishments, and manufacturing plywood faced with nonwood materials, such as plastics or metal.

Illustrative Examples:

Fabricated structural wood members manufacturing
Laminated structural wood members manufacturing
Medium density fiberboard (MDF) manufacturing
Oriented strandboard (OSB) manufacturing
Particleboard manufacturing

Plywood manufacturing
Reconstituted wood sheets and boards manufacturing
Roof trusses, wood, manufacturing
Veneer mills
Waferboard manufacturing

Cross-References.   Establishments primarily engaged in--

- Manufacturing veneer and further processing that veneer into wood containers or wood container parts in the same establishment--are classified in Industry 32192, Wood Container and Pallet Manufacturing;
- Manufacturing prefabricated wood buildings or wood sections and panels for buildings--are classified in Industry 32199, All Other Wood Product Manufacturing; and
- Manufacturing solid wood structural members, such as dimension lumber and timber from logs or bolts in sawmills--are classified in Industry 32111, Sawmills and Wood Preservation.

321211   Hardwood Veneer and Plywood Manufacturing

This U.S. industry comprises establishments primarily engaged in manufacturing hardwood veneer and/or hardwood plywood.

Cross-References.   Establishments primarily engaged in--

- Manufacturing veneer and further processing that veneer into wood containers or wood container parts--are classified in Industry 321920, Wood Container and Pallet Manufacturing;
- Manufacturing softwood veneer and softwood plywood--are classified in U.S. Industry 321212, Softwood Veneer and Plywood Manufacturing; and
- Manufacturing reconstituted wood sheets and boards--are classified in U.S. Industry 321219, Reconstituted Wood Product Manufacturing.

321212   Softwood Veneer and Plywood Manufacturing

This U.S. industry comprises establishments primarily engaged in manufacturing softwood veneer and/or softwood plywood.

T—Canadian, Mexican, and United States industries are comparable.

Cross-References.   Establishments primarily engaged in--

- Manufacturing veneer and further processing that veneer into wood containers or wood container parts--are classified in Industry 321920, Wood Container and Pallet Manufacturing;
- Manufacturing hardwood veneer and hardwood plywood--are classified in U.S. Industry 321211, Hardwood Veneer and Plywood Manufacturing; and
- Manufacturing reconstituted wood sheets and boards--are classified in U.S. Industry 321219, Reconstituted Wood Product Manufacturing.

321213 Engineered Wood Member (except Truss) Manufacturing

This U.S. industry comprises establishments primarily engaged in manufacturing fabricated or laminated wood arches and/or other fabricated or laminated wood structural members.

Illustrative Examples:

Finger joint lumber manufacturing	Parallel strand lumber manufacturing
I-joists, wood, fabricating	Timbers, structural, glue laminated or pre-engineered
Laminated veneer lumber (LVL) manufacturing	wood, manufacturing

Cross-References.   Establishments primarily engaged in--

- Manufacturing prefabricated wood buildings or wood sections and panels for buildings--are classified in U.S. Industry 321992, Prefabricated Wood Building Manufacturing;
- Manufacturing wood trusses--are classified in U.S. Industry 321214, Truss Manufacturing; and
- Manufacturing solid wood structural members, such as dimension lumber and timber from logs or bolts-- are classified in U.S. Industry 321113, Sawmills.

321214 Truss Manufacturing

This U.S. industry comprises establishments primarily engaged in manufacturing laminated or fabricated wood roof and floor trusses.

Cross-References.

Establishments primarily engaged in manufacturing wood I-joists are classified in U.S. Industry 321213, Engineered Wood Member (except Truss) Manufacturing.

321219 Reconstituted Wood Product Manufacturing

This U.S. industry comprises establishments primarily engaged in manufacturing reconstituted wood sheets and boards.

Illustrative Examples:

Medium density fiberboard (MDF) manufacturing	Reconstituted wood sheets and boards manufacturing
Oriented strandboard (OSB) manufacturing	Waferboard manufacturing
Particleboard manufacturing	

Cross-References.   Establishments primarily engaged in--

- Manufacturing softwood plywood--are classified in U.S. Industry 321212, Softwood Veneer and Plywood Manufacturing; and
- Manufacturing hardwood plywood--are classified in U.S. Industry 321211, Hardwood Veneer and Plywood Manufacturing.

T—Canadian, Mexican, and United States industries are comparable.

3219   Other Wood Product Manufacturing^T

This industry group comprises establishments primarily engaged in manufacturing wood products (except establishments operating sawmills and wood preservation facilities; and establishments manufacturing veneer, plywood, or engineered wood products).

32191   Millwork^T

This industry comprises establishments primarily engaged in manufacturing hardwood and softwood cut stock and dimension stock (i.e., shapes); wood windows and wood doors; and other millwork including wood flooring. Dimension stock or cut stock is defined as lumber and worked wood products cut or shaped to specialized sizes. These establishments generally use woodworking machinery, such as jointers, planers, lathes, and routers to shape wood.

Cross-References.   Establishments primarily engaged in--

- Manufacturing dimension lumber, boards, beams, timbers, poles, ties, shingles, shakes, siding, and wood chips from logs and bolts--are classified in Industry 32111, Sawmills and Wood Preservation;
- Fabricating millwork at the construction site--are classified in Industry 23835, Finish Carpentry Contractors; and
- Manufacturing wood furniture frames and finished wood furniture parts--are classified in Industry 33721, Office Furniture (including Fixtures) Manufacturing.

321911 Wood Window and Door Manufacturing

This U.S. industry comprises establishments primarily engaged in manufacturing window and door units, sash, window and door frames, and doors from wood or wood clad with metal or plastics.

Cross-References.

Establishments primarily engaged in fabricating wood windows or wood doors at the construction site are classified in Industry 238350, Finish Carpentry Contractors.

321912 Cut Stock, Resawing Lumber, and Planing

This U.S. industry comprises establishments primarily engaged in one or more of the following: (1) manufacturing dimension lumber from purchased lumber; (2) manufacturing dimension stock (i.e., shapes) or cut stock; (3) resawing the output of sawmills; and (4) planing purchased lumber. These establishments generally use woodworking machinery, such as jointers, planers, lathes, and routers to shape wood.

Cross-References.   Establishments primarily engaged in--

- Manufacturing dimension lumber, boards, beams, timbers, poles, ties, shingles, shakes, siding, and wood chips from logs or bolts--are classified in U.S. Industry 321113, Sawmills;
- Manufacturing wood stairwork, wood molding, wood trim, and other millwork--are classified in U.S. Industry 321918, Other Millwork (including Flooring); and
- Manufacturing wood furniture frames and finished wood furniture parts--are classified in U.S. Industry 337215, Showcase, Partition, Shelving, and Locker Manufacturing.

321918 Other Millwork (including Flooring)

This U.S. industry comprises establishments primarily engaged in manufacturing millwork (except wood windows, wood doors, and cut stock).

T—Canadian, Mexican, and United States industries are comparable.

Illustrative Examples:

Clear and finger joint wood moldings manufacturing
Decorative wood moldings (e.g., base, chair rail, crown, shoe) manufacturing
Ornamental woodwork (e.g., cornices, mantel) manufacturing

Planing mills, millwork
Stairwork (e.g., newel posts, railings, stairs, staircases), wood, manufacturing
Wood flooring manufacturing
Wood shutters manufacturing

Cross-References.   Establishments primarily engaged in--

- Manufacturing wood windows and doors--are classified in U.S. Industry 321911, Wood Window and Door Manufacturing; and
- Manufacturing cut stock, resawing lumber, and/or planing purchased lumber--are classified in U.S. Industry 321912, Cut Stock, Resawing Lumber, and Planing.

32192   Wood Container and Pallet Manufacturing[T]
See industry description for 321920.

321920 Wood Container and Pallet Manufacturing

This industry comprises establishments primarily engaged in manufacturing wood pallets, wood box shook, wood boxes, other wood containers, and wood parts for pallets and containers.

Cross-References.

Establishments primarily engaged in manufacturing wood burial caskets are classified in U.S. Industry 339995, Burial Casket Manufacturing.

32199   All Other Wood Product Manufacturing[T]

This industry comprises establishments primarily engaged in manufacturing wood products (except establishments operating sawmills and wood preservation facilities; and establishments manufacturing veneer, plywood, engineered wood products, millwork, wood containers, or pallets).

Illustrative Examples:

Mobile homes manufacturing
Panels, prefabricated wood building, manufacturing
Prefabricated wood buildings manufacturing
Sections, prefabricated wood building, manufacturing

Wood dowels manufacturing
Wood handles (e.g., broom, handtool, mop) manufacturing

Cross-References.   Establishments primarily engaged in--

- Operating sawmills or preserving wood--are classified in Industry 32111, Sawmills and Wood Preservation;
- Manufacturing veneer, plywood, and engineered wood products--are classified in Industry 32121, Veneer, Plywood, and Engineered Wood Product Manufacturing;
- Manufacturing millwork--are classified in Industry 32191, Millwork;
- Manufacturing wood containers, pallets, and wood container parts--are classified in Industry 32192, Wood Container and Pallet Manufacturing;
- Manufacturing travel trailers with self-contained facilities for storage of water and waste--are classified in Industry 33621, Motor Vehicle Body and Trailer Manufacturing; and
- Fabricating wood buildings or wood sections and panels for buildings at the construction site, or setting up manufactured homes (i.e., mobile homes) at the construction site--are classified in Sector 23, Construction.

T—Canadian, Mexican, and United States industries are comparable.

321991 Manufactured Home (Mobile Home) Manufacturing

This U.S. industry comprises establishments primarily engaged in making manufactured homes (i.e., mobile homes) and nonresidential mobile buildings. Manufactured homes are designed to accept permanent water, sewer, and utility connections and although equipped with wheels, they are not intended for regular highway movement.

Cross-References. Establishments primarily engaged in--

- Manufacturing prefabricated wood buildings not equipped with wheels--are classified in U.S. Industry 321992, Prefabricated Wood Building Manufacturing;
- Manufacturing travel trailers with self-contained facilities for storage of water and waste--are classified in U.S. Industry 336214, Travel Trailer and Camper Manufacturing; and
- Setting up manufactured homes (i.e., mobile homes) at the construction site--are classified in Industry 238990, All Other Specialty Trade Contractors.

321992 Prefabricated Wood Building Manufacturing

This U.S. industry comprises establishments primarily engaged in manufacturing prefabricated wood buildings and wood sections and panels for prefabricated wood buildings.

Cross-References. Establishments primarily engaged in--

- Fabricating wood buildings or wood sections and panels for buildings at the construction site--are classified in Sector 23, Construction;
- Making manufactured homes (i.e., mobile homes)--are classified in U.S. Industry 321991, Manufactured Home (Mobile Home) Manufacturing; and
- Setting up manufactured homes (i.e., mobile homes) at the construction site--are classified in Industry 238990, All Other Specialty Trade Contractors.

321999 All Other Miscellaneous Wood Product Manufacturing

This U.S. industry comprises establishments primarily engaged in manufacturing wood products (except establishments operating sawmills and preservation facilities; establishments manufacturing veneer, engineered wood products, millwork, wood containers, pallets, and wood container parts; and establishments making manufactured homes (i.e., mobile homes) and prefabricated buildings and components).

Illustrative Examples:

Cabinets (i.e., housings), wood (e.g., sewing machines, stereo, television), manufacturing
Cork products (except gaskets) manufacturing
Kiln drying lumber
Shoe trees manufacturing
Wood dowels manufacturing
Wood extension ladders manufacturing

Wood handles (e.g., broom, handtool, mop), manufacturing
Wood kitchenware manufacturing
Wood stepladders manufacturing
Wood toilet seats manufacturing
Wood toothpicks manufacturing

Cross-References. Establishments primarily engaged in--

- Operating sawmills and preserving wood--are classified in Industry 32111, Sawmills and Wood Preservation;
- Manufacturing veneer and engineered wood products--are classified in Industry 32121, Veneer, Plywood, and Engineered Wood Product Manufacturing;
- Manufacturing millwork--are classified in Industry 32191, Millwork;
- Manufacturing boxes, box shook, wood containers, pallets, and wood parts for containers--are classified in Industry 321920, Wood Container and Pallet Manufacturing;

T—Canadian, Mexican, and United States industries are comparable.

- Making manufactured homes (i.e., mobile homes)--are classified in U.S. Industry 321991, Manufactured Home (Mobile Home) Manufacturing; and
- Manufacturing prefabricated wood buildings or wood sections and panels for buildings--are classified in U.S. Industry 321992, Prefabricated Wood Building Manufacturing.

322   Paper Manufacturing[T]

Industries in the Paper Manufacturing subsector make pulp, paper, or converted paper products. The manufacturing of these products is grouped together because they constitute a series of vertically connected processes. More than one is often carried out in a single establishment. There are essentially three activities. The manufacturing of pulp involves separating the cellulose fibers from other impurities in wood or used paper. The manufacturing of paper involves matting these fibers into a sheet. The manufacturing of converted paper products involves converting paper and other materials by various cutting and shaping techniques and includes coating and laminating activities.

The Paper Manufacturing subsector is subdivided into two industry groups, the first for the manufacturing of pulp and paper and the second for the manufacturing of converted paper products. Paper making is treated as the core activity of the subsector. Therefore, any establishment that makes paper (including paperboard), either alone or in combination with pulp manufacturing or paper converting, is classified as a paper or paperboard mill. Establishments that make pulp without making paper are classified as pulp mills. Pulp mills, paper mills and paperboard mills comprise the first industry group.

Establishments that make products from purchased paper and other materials make up the second industry group, Converted Paper Product Manufacturing. This general activity is then subdivided based, for the most part, on process distinctions. Paperboard container manufacturing uses corrugating, cutting, and shaping machinery to form paperboard into containers. Paper bag and coated and treated paper manufacturing establishments cut and coat paper and foil. Stationery product manufacturing establishments make a variety of paper products used for writing, filing, and similar applications. Other converted paper product manufacturing includes, in particular, the conversion of sanitary paper stock into such things as tissue paper and disposable diapers.

An important process used in the Paper Bag and Coated and Treated Paper Manufacturing industry is lamination, often combined with coating. Lamination and coating make a composite material with improved properties of strength, impermeability, and so on. The laminated materials may be paper, metal foil, or plastics film. While paper is often one of the components, it is not always. Lamination of plastics film to plastics film is classified in Subsector 326, Plastics and Rubber Products Manufacturing, because establishments that do this often first make the film. The same situation holds with respect to bags. The manufacturing of bags from plastics only, whether or not laminated, is classified in Subsector 326, Plastics and Rubber Products Manufacturing, but all other bag manufacturing is classified in this subsector.

Excluded from this subsector are photosensitive papers. These papers are chemically treated and are classified in Industry 32599, All Other Chemical Product and Preparation Manufacturing.

3221   Pulp, Paper, and Paperboard Mills[T]

This industry group comprises establishments primarily engaged in manufacturing pulp, paper, or paperboard.

32211   Pulp Mills[T]
See industry description for 322110.

322110   Pulp Mills

This industry comprises establishments primarily engaged in manufacturing pulp without manufacturing paper or paperboard. The pulp is made by separating the cellulose fibers from the other impurities in wood or other materials, such as used or recycled rags, linters, scrap paper, and straw.

Cross-References.   Establishments primarily engaged in--

- Manufacturing both pulp and paper--are classified in Industry 32212, Paper Mills; and
- Manufacturing both pulp and paperboard--are classified in Industry 322130, Paperboard Mills.

T—Canadian, Mexican, and United States industries are comparable.

32212   Paper Mills[T]

This industry comprises establishments primarily engaged in manufacturing paper from pulp. These establishments may manufacture or purchase pulp. In addition, the establishments may convert the paper they make. The activity of making paper classifies an establishment into this industry regardless of the output.

Cross-References.   Establishments primarily engaged in--

- Manufacturing pulp without manufacturing paper--are classified in Industry 32211, Pulp Mills;
- Manufacturing paperboard--are classified in Industry 32213, Paperboard Mills;
- Converting paper without manufacturing paper--are classified in Industry Group 3222, Converted Paper Product Manufacturing; and
- Manufacturing photographic sensitized paper from purchased paper--are classified in Industry 32599, All Other Chemical Product and Preparation Manufacturing.

322121 Paper (except Newsprint) Mills

This U.S. industry comprises establishments primarily engaged in manufacturing paper (except newsprint and uncoated groundwood paper) from pulp. These establishments may manufacture or purchase pulp. In addition, the establishments may also convert the paper they make.

Cross-References.   Establishments primarily engaged in--

- Manufacturing newsprint and uncoated groundwood paper--are classified in U.S. Industry 322122, Newsprint Mills;
- Converting paper without manufacturing paper--are classified in Industry Group 3222, Converted Paper Product Manufacturing;
- Manufacturing paperboard--are classified in Industry 322130, Paperboard Mills;
- Manufacturing pulp without manufacturing paper--are classified in Industry 322110, Pulp Mills; and
- Manufacturing photographic sensitized paper from purchased paper--are classified in U.S. Industry 325992, Photographic Film, Paper, Plate, and Chemical Manufacturing.

322122 Newsprint Mills

This U.S. industry comprises establishments primarily engaged in manufacturing newsprint and uncoated groundwood paper from pulp. These establishments may manufacture or purchase pulp. In addition, the establishments may also convert the paper they make.

Cross-References.   Establishments primarily engaged in--

- Manufacturing paper (except newsprint and uncoated groundwood)--are classified in U.S. Industry 322121, Paper (except Newsprint) Mills;
- Converting paper without manufacturing paper--are classified in Industry Group 3222, Converted Paper Product Manufacturing;
- Manufacturing paperboard--are classified in Industry 322130, Paperboard Mills; and
- Manufacturing pulp without manufacturing paper--are classified in Industry 322110, Pulp Mills.

32213   Paperboard Mills[T]
See industry description for 322130.

322130 Paperboard Mills

This industry comprises establishments primarily engaged in manufacturing paperboard (e.g., can/drum stock, container board, corrugating medium, folding carton stock, linerboard, tube) from pulp. These establishments may manufacture or purchase pulp. In addition, the establishments may also convert the paperboard they make.

T—Canadian, Mexican, and United States industries are comparable.

Cross-References.   Establishments primarily engaged in--

- Manufacturing pulp without manufacturing paperboard--are classified in Industry 322110, Pulp Mills;
- Converting paperboard without manufacturing paperboard--are classified in Industry Group 3222, Converted Paper Product Manufacturing; and
- Manufacturing insulation board and other reconstituted wood fiberboard--are classified in U.S. Industry 321219, Reconstituted Wood Product Manufacturing.

3222   Converted Paper Product Manufacturing[T]

This industry group comprises establishments primarily engaged in converting paper or paperboard without manufacturing paper or paperboard.

32221   Paperboard Container Manufacturing[T]

This industry comprises establishments primarily engaged in converting paperboard into containers without manufacturing paperboard. These establishments use corrugating, cutting, and shaping machinery to form paperboard into containers. Products made by these establishments include boxes, corrugated sheets, pads, pallets, paper dishes, and fiber drums and reels.

Cross-References.   Establishments primarily engaged in--

- Manufacturing similar items of plastics materials--are classified in Industry Group 3261, Plastics Product Manufacturing;
- Manufacturing paperboard and converting paperboard into containers--are classified in Industry 32213, Paperboard Mills;
- Manufacturing egg cartons, food trays, and other food containers from molded pulp--are classified in Industry 32229, Other Converted Paper Product Manufacturing;
- Manufacturing paper and converting paper into containers--are classified in Industry 32212, Paper Mills; and
- Manufacturing paper bags without manufacturing paper--are classified in Industry 32222, Paper Bag and Coated and Treated Paper Manufacturing.

322211   Corrugated and Solid Fiber Box Manufacturing

This U.S. industry comprises establishments primarily engaged in laminating purchased paper or paperboard into corrugated or solid fiber boxes and related products, such as pads, partitions, pallets, and corrugated paper without manufacturing paperboard. These boxes are generally used for shipping.

Cross-References.   Establishments primarily engaged in--

- Manufacturing setup paperboard boxes (except corrugated or laminated solid fiber boxes)--are classified in U.S. Industry 322219, Other Paperboard Container Manufacturing;
- Manufacturing folding paperboard boxes (except corrugated or laminated solid fiber boxes)--are classified in U.S. Industry 322212, Folding Paperboard Box Manufacturing; and
- Manufacturing paperboard and converting paperboard into boxes--are classified in Industry 322130, Paperboard Mills.

322212   Folding Paperboard Box Manufacturing

This U.S. industry comprises establishments primarily engaged in converting paperboard (except corrugated) into folding paperboard boxes without manufacturing paper and paperboard.

T—Canadian, Mexican, and United States industries are comparable.

Cross-References.   Establishments primarily engaged in--

- Manufacturing setup paperboard boxes (except corrugated or laminated solid fiber boxes) or milk cartons-- are classified in U.S. Industry 322219, Other Paperboard Container Manufacturing;
- Manufacturing corrugated and solid fiber boxes--are classified in U.S. Industry 322211, Corrugated and Solid Fiber Box Manufacturing;
- Manufacturing paperboard and converting paperboard into containers--are classified in Industry 322130, Paperboard Mills;
- Manufacturing paper and converting paper into containers--are classified in Industry 32212, Paper Mills; and
- Manufacturing paper bags--are classified in Industry 322220, Paper Bag and Coated and Treated Paper Manufacturing.

322219 Other Paperboard Container Manufacturing

This U.S. industry comprises establishments primarily engaged in converting paperboard into paperboard containers (except corrugated, solid fiber, and folding paperboard boxes) without manufacturing paperboard.

Illustrative Examples:

Fiber cans and drums (i.e., all-fiber, nonfiber ends of any material) made from purchased paperboard
Milk cartons made from purchased paper or paperboard

Sanitary food containers (except folding) made from purchased paper or paperboard
Setup (i.e., not shipped flat) boxes made from purchased paperboard

Cross-References.   Establishments primarily engaged in--

- Manufacturing sanitary food containers of solely plastics materials--are classified in Industry Group 3261, Plastics Product Manufacturing;
- Manufacturing paperboard and converting paperboard into containers--are classified in Industry 322130, Paperboard Mills;
- Manufacturing corrugated and solid fiber boxes--are classified in U.S. Industry 322211, Corrugated and Solid Fiber Box Manufacturing;
- Manufacturing folding paperboard boxes (except corrugated or laminated solid fiber boxes)--are classified in U.S. Industry 322212, Folding Paperboard Box Manufacturing; and
- Manufacturing egg cartons, food trays, and other food containers from molded pulp--are classified in U.S. Industry 322299, All Other Converted Paper Product Manufacturing.

32222 Paper Bag and Coated and Treated Paper Manufacturing[T]
See industry description for 322220.

322220 Paper Bag and Coated and Treated Paper Manufacturing

This industry comprises establishments primarily engaged in one or more of the following: (1) cutting and coating paper and paperboard; (2) cutting and laminating paper, paperboard, and other flexible materials (except plastics film to plastics film); (3) manufacturing bags, multiwall bags, sacks of paper, metal foil, coated paper, laminates, or coated combinations of paper and foil with plastics film; (4) manufacturing laminated aluminum and other converted metal foils from purchased foils; and (5) surface coating paper or paperboard.

Cross-References.   Establishments primarily engaged in--

- Manufacturing paper from pulp--are classified in Industry 32212, Paper Mills;
- Manufacturing textile bags--are classified in Industry 314910, Textile Bag and Canvas Mills;
- Manufacturing single wall and multiwall plastics bags--are classified in U.S. Industry 326111, Plastics Bag and Pouch Manufacturing;

T—Canadian, Mexican, and United States industries are comparable.

- Manufacturing plastics to plastics packaging laminations--are classified in U.S. Industry 326112, Plastics Packaging Film and Sheet (including Laminated) Manufacturing;
- Manufacturing unsupported plastic film--are classified in U.S. Industry 326113, Unlaminated Plastics Film and Sheet (except Packaging) Manufacturing;
- Manufacturing photographic sensitized paper from purchased paper--are classified in U.S. Industry 325992, Photographic Film, Paper, Plate, and Chemical Manufacturing;
- Printing on purchased packaging materials--are classified in Industry 32311, Printing, based on the printing process used;
- Manufacturing foil cookware, dinnerware, and other semi-rigid metal containers--are classified in U.S. Industry 332999, All Other Miscellaneous Fabricated Metal Product Manufacturing;
- Making aluminum and aluminum foil--are classified in Industry 33131, Alumina and Aluminum Production and Processing; and
- Cutting purchased aluminum foil into smaller lengths and widths--are classified in U.S. Industry 332999, All Other Miscellaneous Fabricated Metal Product Manufacturing.

32223   Stationery Product Manufacturing[T]
See industry description for 322230.

322230   Stationery Product Manufacturing

This industry comprises establishments primarily engaged in converting paper or paperboard into products used for writing, filing, art work, and similar applications.

Illustrative Examples:

Computer paper, die-cut, made from purchased paper
Die-cut paper products for office use made from purchased paper or paperboard
Envelopes (i.e., mailing, stationery) made from any material

Stationery made from purchased paper
Tablets (e.g., memo, note, writing) made from purchased paper
Tapes (e.g., adding machine, calculator, cash register) made from purchased paper

Cross-References.

Establishments primarily engaged in manufacturing die-cut paper and paperboard products other than office supplies are classified in U.S. Industry 322299, All Other Converted Paper Product Manufacturing.

32229   Other Converted Paper Product Manufacturing[T]

This industry comprises establishments primarily engaged in (1) converting paper and paperboard into products (except containers, bags, coated and treated paper and paperboard, and stationery products) or (2) converting pulp into pulp products, such as disposable diapers, or molded pulp egg cartons, food trays, and dishes. Processes used include laminating or lining purchased paper or paperboard.

Illustrative Examples:

Crepe paper made from purchased paper
Die-cut paper products (except for office use) made from purchased paper or paperboard
Paper novelties made from purchased paper

Molded pulp products (e.g., egg cartons, food containers, food trays) manufacturing
Sanitary products made from purchased sanitary paper stock

Cross-References.   Establishments primarily engaged in--

- Manufacturing pulp from wood or from other materials--are classified in Industry 32211, Pulp Mills;
- Manufacturing paper from pulp or making pulp and manufacturing paper--are classified in Industry 32212, Paper Mills;

T—Canadian, Mexican, and United States industries are comparable.

- Manufacturing paperboard from pulp or making pulp and manufacturing paperboard--are classified in Industry 32213, Paperboard Mills;
- Manufacturing paperboard containers--are classified in Industry 32221, Paperboard Container Manufacturing;
- Manufacturing bags of coated, laminated, or uncoated paper, of metal foil, or combinations thereof--are classified in Industry 32222, Paper Bag and Coated and Treated Paper Manufacturing; and
- Manufacturing stationery and other related office supplies--are classified in Industry 32223, Stationery Product Manufacturing.

322291 Sanitary Paper Product Manufacturing

This U.S. industry comprises establishments primarily engaged in converting purchased sanitary paper stock or wadding into sanitary paper products, such as facial tissues, handkerchiefs, table napkins, toilet paper, towels, disposable diapers, sanitary napkins, and tampons.

322299 All Other Converted Paper Product Manufacturing

This U.S. industry comprises establishments primarily engaged in converting paper or paperboard into products (except containers, bags, coated and treated paper, stationery products, and sanitary paper products) or converting pulp into pulp products, such as egg cartons, food trays, and other food containers from molded pulp.

Illustrative Examples:

Crepe paper made from purchased paper
Die-cut paper products (except for office use) made
from purchased paper or paperboard

Molded pulp products (e.g., egg cartons, food
containers, food trays) manufacturing
Paper novelties made from purchased paper

Cross-References.   Establishments primarily engaged in--

- Manufacturing pulp from wood or from other materials--are classified in Industry 322110, Pulp Mills;
- Manufacturing paper from pulp or making pulp and manufacturing paper--are classified in Industry 32212, Paper Mills;
- Manufacturing paperboard from pulp or making pulp and manufacturing paperboard--are classified in Industry 322130, Paperboard Mills;
- Manufacturing paperboard containers--are classified in Industry 32221, Paperboard Container Manufacturing;
- Manufacturing bags of coated, laminated, or uncoated paper, of metal foil, or combinations thereof--are classified in Industry 322220, Paper Bag and Coated and Treated Paper Manufacturing; and
- Manufacturing stationery and other related office supplies--are classified in Industry 322230, Stationery Product Manufacturing.

323   Printing and Related Support Activities[T]

Industries in the Printing and Related Support Activities subsector print products, such as newspapers, books, labels, business cards, stationery, business forms, and other materials, and perform support activities, such as data imaging, platemaking services, and bookbinding. The support activities included here are an integral part of the printing industry, and a product (a printing plate, a bound book, or a computer disk or file) that is an integral part of the printing industry is almost always provided by these operations.

Processes used in printing include a variety of methods used to transfer an image from a plate, screen, film, or computer file to some medium, such as paper, plastics, metal, textile articles, or wood. The printing processes employed include, but are not limited to, lithographic, gravure, screen, flexographic, digital, and letterpress.

In contrast to many other classification systems that locate publishing of printed materials in manufacturing, NAICS classifies the publishing of printed products in Subsector 511, Publishing Industries (except Internet). Though printing and publishing are often carried out by the same enterprise (a newspaper, for example), it is less and less the case that these distinct activities are carried out in the same establishment. When publishing and

---

T—Canadian, Mexican, and United States industries are comparable.

printing are done in the same establishment, the establishment is classified in Sector 51, Information, in the appropriate NAICS industry even if the receipts for printing exceed those for publishing.

This subsector includes printing on clothing because the production process for that activity is printing, not clothing manufacturing. For instance, the printing of T-shirts is included in this subsector. In contrast, printing on fabric (or grey goods) is not included. This activity is part of the process of finishing the fabric and is included in the Textile Mills subsector in Industry 31331, Textile and Fabric Finishing Mills.

3231   Printing and Related Support Activities[T]

32311   Printing[T]

This industry comprises establishments primarily engaged in printing on apparel and textile products, paper, metal, glass, plastics, and other materials, except fabric (grey goods). The printing processes employed include, but are not limited to, lithographic, gravure, screen, flexographic, digital, and letterpress. Establishments in this industry do not manufacture the stock that they print, but may perform postprinting activities, such as folding, cutting, or laminating the materials they print, and mailing.

Cross-References.   Establishments primarily engaged in--

- Providing photocopying service on photocopy equipment without performing traditional printing activities--are classified in Industry 56143, Business Service Centers;
- Printing on grey goods--are classified in Industry 31331, Textile and Fabric Finishing Mills;
- Printing and publishing, known as publishers--are classified in Subsector 511, Publishing Industries (except Internet);
- Performing prepress or postpress services without performing traditional printing activities--are classified in Industry 32312, Support Activities for Printing; and
- Manufacturing and printing advertising specialties--are classified in the Manufacturing sector according to the products made.

323111 Commercial Printing (except Screen and Books)

This U.S. industry comprises establishments primarily engaged in commercial printing (except screen printing, books printing) without publishing (except grey goods printing). The printing processes used in this industry include, but are not limited to, lithographic, gravure, flexographic, letterpress, engraving, and various digital printing technologies. This industry includes establishments engaged in commercial printing on purchased stock materials, such as stationery, invitations, labels, and similar items, on a job-order basis. Establishments primarily engaged in traditional printing activities combined with document photocopying services (i.e., quick printers) or primarily engaged in printing graphical materials using digital printing equipment are included in this industry.

Cross-References.   Establishments primarily engaged in--

- Screen printing on purchased stock materials (except books, grey goods, and manifold business forms)--are classified in U.S. Industry 323113, Commercial Screen Printing;
- Printing on grey goods--are classified in Industry 313310, Textile and Fabric Finishing Mills;
- Printing books and pamphlets--are classified in U.S. Industry 323117, Books Printing;
- Manufacturing printed stationery, invitations, labels, and similar items--are classified in Subsector 322, Paper Manufacturing;
- Manufacturing and printing advertising specialties--are classified in the Manufacturing sector according to the products made;
- Providing photocopying service on photocopy equipment without performing traditional printing activities--are classified in U.S. Industry 561439, Other Business Service Centers (including Copy Shops); and
- Printing and publishing, known as publishers--are classified in Subsector 511, Publishing Industries (except Internet).

T—Canadian, Mexican, and United States industries are comparable.

323113 Commercial Screen Printing

This U.S. industry comprises establishments primarily engaged in screen printing without publishing (except books, grey goods, and manifold business forms). This industry includes establishments engaged in screen printing on purchased stock materials, such as stationery, invitations, labels, and similar items, on a job-order basis. Establishments primarily engaged in printing on apparel and textile products, such as T-shirts, caps, jackets, towels, and napkins, are included in this industry.

Cross-References. Establishments primarily engaged in--

- Printing on grey goods--are classified in Industry 313310, Textile and Fabric Finishing Mills;
- Printing books and pamphlets--are classified in U.S. Industry 323117, Books Printing;
- Printing manifold business forms including checkbooks--are classified in U.S. Industry 323111, Commercial Printing (except Screen and Books);
- Manufacturing printed stationery, invitations, labels, and similar items--are classified in Subsector 322, Paper Manufacturing;
- Manufacturing and printing advertising specialties--are classified in the Manufacturing sector according to the products made; and
- Printing and publishing, known as publishers--are classified in Subsector 511, Publishing Industries (except Internet).

323117 Books Printing

This U.S. industry comprises establishments primarily engaged in printing or printing and binding books and pamphlets without publishing.

Cross-References. Establishments primarily engaged in--

- Printing and publishing, known as publishers--are classified in Subsector 511, Publishing Industries (except Internet); and
- Binding books without printing in the same establishment--are classified in Industry 323120, Support Activities for Printing.

32312 Support Activities for Printing[T]
See industry description for 323120.

323120 Support Activities for Printing

This industry comprises establishments primarily engaged in performing prepress and postpress services in support of printing activities. Prepress services may include such things as platemaking, typesetting, trade binding, and sample mounting. Postpress services include such things as book or paper bronzing, die cutting, edging, embossing, folding, gilding, gluing, and indexing.

Cross-References. Establishments primarily engaged in--

- Engraving on metal--are classified in U.S. Industry 332812, Metal Coating, Engraving (except Jewelry and Silverware), and Allied Services to Manufacturers;
- Manufacturing photosensitive plates for printing--are classified in U.S. Industry 325992, Photographic Film, Paper, Plate, and Chemical Manufacturing;
- Manufacturing blank plates (except photosensitive plates) for printing--are classified in U.S. Industry 333244, Printing Machinery and Equipment Manufacturing; and
- Printing books or printing and binding books--are classified in U.S. Industry 323117, Books Printing.

T—Canadian, Mexican, and United States industries are comparable.

324   Petroleum and Coal Products Manufacturing[T]

The Petroleum and Coal Products Manufacturing subsector is based on the transformation of crude petroleum and coal into usable products. The dominant process is petroleum refining that involves the separation of crude petroleum into component products through such techniques as cracking and distillation.
In addition, this subsector includes establishments that primarily further process refined petroleum and coal products and produce products, such as asphalt coatings and petroleum lubricating oils. However, establishments that manufacture petrochemicals from refined petroleum are classified in Industry 32511, Petrochemical Manufacturing.

3241   Petroleum and Coal Products Manufacturing[T]

32411   Petroleum Refineries[T]
     See industry description for 324110.

324110 Petroleum Refineries

This industry comprises establishments primarily engaged in refining crude petroleum into refined petroleum. Petroleum refining involves one or more of the following activities: (1) fractionation; (2) straight distillation of crude oil; and (3) cracking.

Cross-References.   Establishments primarily engaged in--

- Manufacturing asphalt paving, roofing, and saturated materials from refined petroleum--are classified in Industry 32412, Asphalt Paving, Roofing, and Saturated Materials Manufacturing;
- Manufacturing paper mats and felts and saturating them with asphalt or tar into rolls and sheets--are classified in U.S. Industry 322121, Paper (except Newsprint) Mills;
- Blending or compounding refined petroleum to make lubricating oils and greases and/or re-refining used petroleum lubricating oils--are classified in U.S. Industry 324191, Petroleum Lubricating Oil and Grease Manufacturing;
- Blending purchased biodiesel fuels and purchased refined petroleum--are classified in U.S. Industry 324199, All Other Petroleum and Coal Products Manufacturing;
- Converting nonpetroleum materials into biodiesel fuels--are classified in U.S. Industry 325199, All Other Basic Organic Chemical Manufacturing;
- Manufacturing synthetic lubricating oils and greases--are classified in U.S. Industry 325998, All Other Miscellaneous Chemical Product and Preparation Manufacturing;
- Recovering natural gasoline and/or liquid hydrocarbons from oil and gas field gases--are classified in Industry 211130, Natural Gas Extraction;
- Manufacturing acyclic and cyclic aromatic hydrocarbons (i.e., petrochemicals) from refined petroleum or liquid hydrocarbons--are classified in Industry 325110, Petrochemical Manufacturing;
- Manufacturing cyclic and acyclic chemicals (except petrochemicals)--are classified in Industry 32519, Other Basic Organic Chemical Manufacturing;
- Manufacturing coke oven products in steel mills--are classified in Industry 331110, Iron and Steel Mills and Ferroalloy Manufacturing; and
- Manufacturing coke oven products in coke oven establishments--are classified in U.S. Industry 324199, All Other Petroleum and Coal Products Manufacturing.

32412   Asphalt Paving, Roofing, and Saturated Materials Manufacturing[T]

This industry comprises establishments primarily engaged in (1) manufacturing asphalt and tar paving mixtures and blocks and roofing cements and coatings from purchased asphaltic materials and/or (2) saturating purchased mats and felts with asphalt or tar from purchased asphaltic materials.

T—Canadian, Mexican, and United States industries are comparable.

Cross-References.   Establishments primarily engaged in--

- Refining crude petroleum and manufacturing asphalt and tar paving, roofing, and saturated materials--are classified in Industry 32411, Petroleum Refineries; and
- Manufacturing paper mats and felts and saturating them with asphalt or tar--are classified in Industry 32212, Paper Mills.

324121 Asphalt Paving Mixture and Block Manufacturing

This U.S. industry comprises establishments primarily engaged in manufacturing asphalt and tar paving mixtures and blocks from purchased asphaltic materials.

Cross-References.

Establishments primarily engaged in refining crude petroleum and manufacturing asphalt and tar paving mixtures and blocks are classified in Industry 324110, Petroleum Refineries.

324122 Asphalt Shingle and Coating Materials Manufacturing

This U.S. industry comprises establishments primarily engaged in (1) saturating purchased mats and felts with asphalt or tar from purchased asphaltic materials and (2) manufacturing asphalt and tar and roofing cements and coatings from purchased asphaltic materials.

Cross-References.   Establishments primarily engaged in--

- Refining crude petroleum and saturating purchased mats and felts with asphalt or tar into rolls and sheets and/or refining crude petroleum and manufacturing asphalt and tar roofing cements and coatings--are classified in Industry 324110, Petroleum Refineries; and
- Manufacturing paper mats and felts and saturating them with asphalt or tar into rolls and sheets--are classified in U.S. Industry 322121, Paper (except Newsprint) Mills.

32419 Other Petroleum and Coal Products Manufacturing[T]

This industry comprises establishments primarily engaged in manufacturing petroleum products (except asphalt paving, roofing, and saturated materials) from refined petroleum or coal products made in coke ovens not integrated with a steel mill.

Illustrative Examples:

Biodiesel fuels not made in petroleum refineries and blended with purchased refined petroleum
Coke oven products (e.g., coke, gases, tars) made in coke oven establishments
Petroleum brake fluids made from refined petroleum
Petroleum briquettes made from refined petroleum

Petroleum jelly made from refined petroleum
Petroleum lubricating oils and greases made from refined petroleum
Petroleum waxes made from refined petroleum
Re-refining used petroleum lubricating oils

Cross-References.   Establishments primarily engaged in--

- Manufacturing petroleum products by refining crude petroleum--are classified in Industry 32411, Petroleum Refineries;
- Converting nonpetroleum materials into biodiesel fuels--are classified in Industry 32519, Other Basic Organic Chemical Manufacturing;
- Manufacturing asphalt and tar paving, roofing, and saturated materials from refined petroleum--are classified in Industry 32412, Asphalt Paving, Roofing, and Saturated Materials Manufacturing;

T—Canadian, Mexican, and United States industries are comparable.

- Manufacturing coke oven products in steel mills--are classified in Industry 33111, Iron and Steel Mills and Ferroalloy Manufacturing;
- Manufacturing acyclic and cyclic aromatic hydrocarbons (i.e., petrochemicals) from refined petroleum or liquid hydrocarbons--are classified in Industry 32511, Petrochemical Manufacturing;
- Manufacturing cyclic and acyclic organic chemicals (except petrochemicals)--are classified in Industry 32519, Other Basic Organic Chemical Manufacturing; and
- Manufacturing synthetic lubricating oils and greases--are classified in Industry 32599, All Other Chemical Product and Preparation Manufacturing.

324191 Petroleum Lubricating Oil and Grease Manufacturing

This U.S. industry comprises establishments primarily engaged in blending or compounding refined petroleum to make lubricating oils and greases and/or re-refining used petroleum lubricating oils.

Cross-References. Establishments primarily engaged in--

- Refining crude petroleum and manufacturing lubricating oils and greases--are classified in Industry 324110, Petroleum Refineries; and
- Manufacturing synthetic lubricating oils and greases--are classified in U.S. Industry 325998, All Other Miscellaneous Chemical Product and Preparation Manufacturing.

324199 All Other Petroleum and Coal Products Manufacturing

This U.S. industry comprises establishments primarily engaged in manufacturing petroleum products (except asphalt paving, roofing, and saturated materials and lubricating oils and greases) from refined petroleum and coal products made in coke ovens not integrated with a steel mill.

Illustrative Examples:

Biodiesel fuels not made in petroleum refineries and blended with purchased refined petroleum
Coke oven products (e.g., coke, gases, tars) made in coke oven establishments

Petroleum briquettes made from refined petroleum
Petroleum jelly made from refined petroleum
Petroleum waxes made from refined petroleum

Cross-References. Establishments primarily engaged in--

- Manufacturing petroleum products by refining crude petroleum--are classified in Industry 324110, Petroleum Refineries;
- Converting nonpetroleum materials into biodiesel fuels--are classified in U.S. Industry 325199, All Other Basic Organic Chemical Manufacturing;
- Manufacturing asphalt paving and roofing materials from refined petroleum--are classified in Industry 32412, Asphalt Paving, Roofing, and Saturated Materials Manufacturing;
- Blending and compounding petroleum lubricating oils and greases and/or re-refining used petroleum lubrication oils and greases--are classified in U.S. Industry 324191, Petroleum Lubricating Oil and Grease Manufacturing;
- Manufacturing coke oven products in steel mills--are classified in Industry 331110, Iron and Steel Mills and Ferroalloy Manufacturing;
- Manufacturing acyclic and cyclic aromatic hydrocarbons (i.e., petrochemicals) from refined petroleum or liquid hydrocarbons--are classified in Industry 325110, Petrochemical Manufacturing; and
- Manufacturing cyclic and acyclic organic chemicals (except petrochemicals)--are classified in Industry 32519, Other Basic Organic Chemical Manufacturing.

T—Canadian, Mexican, and United States industries are comparable.

325 Chemical Manufacturing[T]

The Chemical Manufacturing subsector is based on the transformation of organic and inorganic raw materials by a chemical process and the formulation of products. This subsector distinguishes the production of basic chemicals that comprise the first industry group from the production of intermediate and end products produced by further processing of basic chemicals that make up the remaining industry groups.

This subsector does not include all industries transforming raw materials by a chemical process. It is common for some chemical processing to occur during mining operations. These beneficiating operations, such as copper concentrating, are classified in Sector 21, Mining, Quarrying, and Oil and Gas Extraction. Furthermore, the refining of crude petroleum is included in Subsector 324, Petroleum and Coal Products Manufacturing. In addition, the manufacturing of aluminum oxide is included in Subsector 331, Primary Metal Manufacturing; and beverage distilleries are classified in Subsector 312, Beverage and Tobacco Product Manufacturing. As is the case of these two activities, the grouping of industries into subsectors may take into account the association of the activities performed with other activities in the subsector.

3251 Basic Chemical Manufacturing[T]

This industry group comprises establishments primarily engaged in manufacturing chemicals using basic processes, such as thermal cracking and distillation. Chemicals manufactured in this industry group are usually separate chemical elements or separate chemically-defined compounds.

32511 Petrochemical Manufacturing[T]
See industry description for 325110.

325110 Petrochemical Manufacturing

This industry comprises establishments primarily engaged in (1) manufacturing acyclic (i.e., aliphatic) hydrocarbons such as ethylene, propylene, and butylene made from refined petroleum or liquid hydrocarbons and/or (2) manufacturing cyclic aromatic hydrocarbons such as benzene, toluene, styrene, xylene, ethyl benzene, and cumene made from refined petroleum or liquid hydrocarbons.

Cross-References. Establishments primarily engaged in--

- Manufacturing petrochemicals by refining crude petroleum--are classified in Industry 324110, Petroleum Refineries;
- Manufacturing acetylene--are classified in Industry 325120, Industrial Gas Manufacturing;
- Manufacturing basic organic chemicals (except petrochemicals)--are classified in Industry 32519, Other Basic Organic Chemical Manufacturing; and
- Recovering liquid hydrocarbons from oil and gas field gases--are classified in Industry 211130, Natural Gas Extraction.

32512 Industrial Gas Manufacturing[T]
See industry description for 325120.

325120 Industrial Gas Manufacturing

This industry comprises establishments primarily engaged in manufacturing industrial organic and inorganic gases in compressed, liquid, and solid forms.

Cross-References. Establishments primarily engaged in--

- Manufacturing chlorine gas--are classified in Industry 325180, Other Basic Inorganic Chemical Manufacturing; and
- Manufacturing ethane and butane gases made from refined petroleum or liquid hydrocarbons--are classified in Industry 325110, Petrochemical Manufacturing.

T—Canadian, Mexican, and United States industries are comparable.

32513   Synthetic Dye and Pigment Manufacturing[T]
See industry description for 325130.

325130 Synthetic Dye and Pigment Manufacturing

This industry comprises establishments primarily engaged in manufacturing synthetic organic and inorganic dyes and pigments, such as lakes and toners (except electrostatic and photographic).

Cross-References.   Establishments primarily engaged in--

- Manufacturing natural food colorings--are classified in U.S. Industry 311942, Spice and Extract Manufacturing;
- Manufacturing natural organic colorings for nonfood uses (except wood byproducts)--are classified in U.S. Industry 325199, All Other Basic Organic Chemical Manufacturing;
- Manufacturing electrostatic and photographic toners--are classified in U.S. Industry 325992, Photographic Film, Paper, Plate, and Chemical Manufacturing;
- Manufacturing wood byproducts used as dyeing materials--are classified in U.S. Industry 325194, Cyclic Crude, Intermediate, and Gum and Wood Chemical Manufacturing; and
- Manufacturing carbon, bone, and lamp black--are classified in Industry 325180, Other Basic Inorganic Chemical Manufacturing.

32518   Other Basic Inorganic Chemical Manufacturing[T]
See industry description for 325180.

325180 Other Basic Inorganic Chemical Manufacturing

This industry comprises establishments primarily engaged in manufacturing basic inorganic chemicals (except industrial gases and synthetic dyes and pigments).

Illustrative Examples:

Alkalies manufacturing
Aluminum compounds, not specified elsewhere by process, manufacturing
Carbides (e.g., baron, calcium, silicon, tungsten) manufacturing
Carbon black manufacturing
Chlorine manufacturing

Hydrochloric acid manufacturing
Potassium inorganic compounds, not specified elsewhere by process, manufacturing
Radioactive isotopes manufacturing
Sulfides and sulfites manufacturing
Sulfuric acid manufacturing

Cross-References.   Establishments primarily engaged in--

- Manufacturing industrial gases--are classified in Industry 325120, Industrial Gas Manufacturing;
- Manufacturing inorganic dyes and pigments--are classified in Industry 325130, Synthetic Dye and Pigment Manufacturing;
- Manufacturing household bleaches--are classified in U.S. Industry 325612, Polish and Other Sanitation Good Manufacturing;
- Mining and/or beneficiating alkalies--are classified in U.S. Industry 212391, Potash, Soda, and Borate Mineral Mining;
- Manufacturing chlorine preparations (e.g., for swimming pools)--are classified in U.S. Industry 325998, All Other Miscellaneous Chemical Product and Preparation Manufacturing;
- Manufacturing nitrogenous and phosphoric fertilizers and fertilizer materials--are classified in Industry 32531, Fertilizer Manufacturing;
- Manufacturing pharmaceuticals, medicines, and dietary supplements--are classified in Industry Group 3254, Pharmaceutical and Medicine Manufacturing;

T—Canadian, Mexican, and United States industries are comparable.

- Manufacturing aluminum oxide (alumina)--are classified in U.S. Industry 331313, Alumina Refining and Primary Aluminum Production;
- Manufacturing inorganic insecticidal, herbicidal, fungicidal and pesticidal preparations--are classified in Industry 325320, Pesticide and Other Agricultural Chemical Manufacturing; and
- Manufacturing photographic chemicals--are classified in U.S. Industry 325992, Photographic Film, Paper, Plate, and Chemical Manufacturing.

32519 Other Basic Organic Chemical Manufacturing[T]

This industry comprises establishments primarily engaged in manufacturing basic organic chemicals (except petrochemicals, industrial gases, and synthetic dyes and pigments).

Illustrative Examples:

Biodiesel fuels not made in petroleum refineries and not blended with petroleum
Carbon organic compounds, not specified elsewhere by process, manufacturing
Cyclic intermediates made from refined petroleum or natural gas (except aromatic petrochemicals)
Enzyme proteins (i.e., basic synthetic chemicals) (except pharmaceutical use) manufacturing
Gum and wood chemicals manufacturing

Fatty acids (e.g., margaric, oleic, stearic) manufacturing
Organo-inorganic compound manufacturing
Plasticizers (i.e., basic synthetic chemical) manufacturing
Silicone (except resins) manufacturing
Synthetic sweeteners (i.e., sweetening agents) manufacturing

Cross-References.   Establishments primarily engaged in--

- Manufacturing petrochemicals from refined petroleum or liquid hydrocarbons--are classified in Industry 32511, Petrochemical Manufacturing;
- Manufacturing petrochemicals by refining crude petroleum--are classified in Industry 32411, Petroleum Refineries;
- Blending purchased biodiesel fuels and purchased refined petroleum--are classified in Industry 32419, Other Petroleum and Coal Products Manufacturing;
- Manufacturing organic industrial gases--are classified in Industry 32512, Industrial Gas Manufacturing;
- Manufacturing synthetic organic dyes and pigments--are classified in Industry 32513, Synthetic Dye and Pigment Manufacturing;
- Manufacturing natural glycerin--are classified in Industry 32561, Soap and Cleaning Compound Manufacturing;
- Manufacturing activated charcoal--are classified in Industry 32599, All Other Chemical Product and Preparation Manufacturing;
- Manufacturing organic insecticidal, herbicidal, fungicidal, and pesticidal preparations--are classified in Industry 32532, Pesticide and Other Agricultural Chemical Manufacturing;
- Manufacturing elastomers--are classified in Industry 32521, Resin and Synthetic Rubber Manufacturing;
- Manufacturing urea--are classified in Industry 32531, Fertilizer Manufacturing;
- Manufacturing pharmaceuticals, medicines, and dietary supplements--are classified in Industry Group 3254, Pharmaceutical and Medicine Manufacturing;
- Manufacturing coal tar crudes in integrated steel mills with coke ovens--are classified in Industry 33111, Iron and Steel Mills and Ferroalloy Manufacturing;
- Manufacturing coal tar crudes in coke ovens not integrated with steel mills and fuel briquettes from refined petroleum--are classified in Industry 32419, Other Petroleum and Coal Products Manufacturing; and
- Manufacturing natural food colorings--are classified in Industry 31194, Seasoning and Dressing Manufacturing.

325193 Ethyl Alcohol Manufacturing

This U.S. industry comprises establishments primarily engaged in manufacturing nonpotable ethyl alcohol.

T—Canadian, Mexican, and United States industries are comparable.

Cross-References.   Establishments primarily engaged in--

- Distilling liquors (except brandy)--are classified in Industry 312140, Distilleries; and
- Manufacturing brandies--are classified in Industry 312130, Wineries.

325194 Cyclic Crude, Intermediate, and Gum and Wood Chemical Manufacturing

This U.S. industry comprises establishments primarily engaged in one or more of the following: (1) distilling wood or gum into products, such as tall oil and wood distillates; (2) distilling coal tars; (3) manufacturing wood or gum chemicals, such as naval stores, natural tanning materials, charcoal briquettes, and charcoal (except activated); and (4) manufacturing cyclic crudes or cyclic intermediates (i.e., hydrocarbons, except aromatic petrochemicals) from refined petroleum or natural gas.

Cross-references.   Establishments primarily engaged in--

- Manufacturing cyclic chemicals (except aromatic and intermediates)--are classified in U.S. Industry 325199, All Other Basic Organic Chemical Manufacturing;
- Manufacturing aromatic petrochemicals from refined petroleum or natural gas--are classified in Industry 325110, Petrochemical Manufacturing;
- Manufacturing aromatic petrochemicals by refining crude petroleum--are classified in Industry 324110, Petroleum Refineries;
- Manufacturing coal tar crudes in steel mills with coke ovens--are classified in Industry 331110, Iron and Steel Mills and Ferroalloy Manufacturing;
- Manufacturing fuel briquettes from refined petroleum--are classified in U.S. Industry 324199, All Other Petroleum and Coal Products Manufacturing; and
- Manufacturing activated charcoal--are classified in U.S. Industry 325998, All Other Miscellaneous Chemical Product and Preparation Manufacturing.

325199 All Other Basic Organic Chemical Manufacturing

This U.S. industry comprises establishments primarily engaged in manufacturing basic organic chemical products (except aromatic petrochemicals, industrial gases, synthetic organic dyes and pigments, gum and wood chemicals, cyclic crudes and intermediates, and ethyl alcohol).

Illustrative Examples:

Biodiesel fuels not made in petroleum refineries and not blended with petroleum
Calcium organic compounds, not specified elsewhere by process, manufacturing
Carbon organic compounds, not specified elsewhere by process, manufacturing
Enzyme proteins (i.e., basic synthetic chemicals) (except pharmaceutical use) manufacturing

Fatty acids (e.g., margaric, oleic, stearic) manufacturing
Organo-inorganic compound manufacturing
Plasticizers (i.e., basic synthetic chemicals) manufacturing
Silicone (except resins) manufacturing
Synthetic sweeteners (i.e., sweetening agents) manufacturing

Cross-References.   Establishments primarily engaged in--

- Manufacturing aromatic petrochemicals from refined petroleum or natural gas--are classified in Industry 325110, Petrochemical Manufacturing;
- Manufacturing aromatic petrochemicals or biodiesel fuels by refining crude petroleum--are classified in Industry 324110, Petroleum Refineries;
- Blending purchased biodiesel fuels and purchased refined petroleum--are classified in U.S. Industry 324199, All Other Petroleum and Coal Products Manufacturing;
- Manufacturing organic industrial gases--are classified in Industry 325120, Industrial Gas Manufacturing;

T—Canadian, Mexican, and United States industries are comparable.

- Manufacturing synthetic organic dyes and pigments--are classified in Industry 325130, Synthetic Dye and Pigment Manufacturing;
- Manufacturing ethyl alcohol--are classified in U.S. Industry 325193, Ethyl Alcohol Manufacturing;
- Manufacturing organic insecticidal, herbicidal, fungicidal, and pesticidal preparations--are classified in Industry 325320, Pesticide and Other Agricultural Chemical Manufacturing;
- Manufacturing elastomers--are classified in Industry 32521, Resin and Synthetic Rubber Manufacturing;
- Manufacturing urea--are classified in U.S. Industry 325311, Nitrogenous Fertilizer Manufacturing;
- Manufacturing pharmaceuticals, medicines, and dietary supplements--are classified in Industry Group 3254, Pharmaceutical and Medicine Manufacturing;
- Manufacturing natural glycerin--are classified in U.S. Industry 325611, Soap and Other Detergent Manufacturing; and
- Manufacturing natural food colorings--are classified in U.S. Industry 311942, Spice and Extract Manufacturing.

3252 Resin, Synthetic Rubber, and Artificial and Synthetic Fibers and Filaments Manufacturing[T]

This industry group comprises establishments primarily engaged in one of the following: (1) manufacturing synthetic resins, plastics materials, and nonvulcanizable elastomers and mixing and blending resins on a custom basis; (2) manufacturing noncustomized synthetic resins; (3) manufacturing synthetic rubber; (4) manufacturing cellulosic (e.g., rayon, acetate) and noncellulosic (e.g., nylon, polyolefin, polyester) fibers and filaments in the form of monofilament, filament yarn, staple, or tow; or (5) manufacturing and texturizing cellulosic and noncellulosic fibers and filaments.

32521 Resin and Synthetic Rubber Manufacturing[T]

This industry comprises establishments primarily engaged in one or more of the following: (1) manufacturing synthetic resins, plastics materials, and nonvulcanizable elastomers and mixing and blending resins on a custom basis; (2) manufacturing noncustomized synthetic resins; and (3) manufacturing synthetic rubber.

Cross-References.   Establishments primarily engaged in--

- Manufacturing plastics resins and converting resins into plastics products--are classified in Industry Group 3261, Plastics Product Manufacturing;
- Processing natural, synthetic, or reclaimed rubber into intermediate or final products--are classified in Industry Group 3262, Rubber Product Manufacturing;
- Custom compounding resins made elsewhere--are classified in Industry 32599, All Other Chemical Product and Preparation Manufacturing; and
- Manufacturing resin adhesives--are classified in Industry 32552, Adhesive Manufacturing.

325211 Plastics Material and Resin Manufacturing

This U.S. industry comprises establishments primarily engaged in (1) manufacturing resins, plastics materials, and nonvulcanizable thermoplastic elastomers and mixing and blending resins on a custom basis and/or (2) manufacturing noncustomized synthetic resins.

Cross-References.   Establishments primarily engaged in--

- Manufacturing plastics resins and converting resins into plastics products--are classified in Industry Group 3261, Plastics Product Manufacturing;
- Custom compounding resins made elsewhere--are classified in U.S. Industry 325991, Custom Compounding of Purchased Resins; and
- Manufacturing plastics adhesives--are classified in Industry 325520, Adhesive Manufacturing.

T—Canadian, Mexican, and United States industries are comparable.

325212 Synthetic Rubber Manufacturing

This U.S. industry comprises establishments primarily engaged in manufacturing synthetic rubber.

Cross-References.   Establishments primarily engaged in--

- Processing natural, synthetic, or reclaimed rubber into intermediate or final products (except adhesives)-- are classified in Industry Group 3262, Rubber Product Manufacturing; and
- Manufacturing rubber adhesives--are classified in Industry 325520, Adhesive Manufacturing.

32522   Artificial and Synthetic Fibers and Filaments Manufacturing[T]
See industry description for 325220.

325220 Artificial and Synthetic Fibers and Filaments Manufacturing

This industry comprises establishments primarily engaged in (1) manufacturing cellulosic (e.g., rayon, acetate) and noncellulosic (e.g., nylon, polyolefin, polyester) fibers and filaments in the form of monofilament, filament yarn, staple, or tow or (2) manufacturing and texturizing cellulosic and noncellulosic fibers and filaments.

Cross-References.   Establishments primarily engaged in--

- Texturizing cellulosic and noncellulosic fibers and filaments made elsewhere--are classified in Industry 313110, Fiber, Yarn, and Thread Mills; and
- Manufacturing textile glass fibers--are classified in U.S. Industry 327212, Other Pressed and Blown Glass and Glassware Manufacturing.

3253   Pesticide, Fertilizer, and Other Agricultural Chemical Manufacturing[T]

This industry group comprises establishments primarily engaged in one or more of the following: (1) manufacturing nitrogenous or phosphatic fertilizer materials; (2) manufacturing fertilizers from sewage or animal waste; (3) manufacturing nitrogenous or phosphatic materials and mixing with other ingredients into fertilizers; (4) mixing ingredients made elsewhere into fertilizers; and (5) formulating and preparing pesticides and other agricultural chemicals.

32531   Fertilizer Manufacturing[T]

This industry comprises establishments primarily engaged in one or more of the following: (1) manufacturing nitrogenous or phosphatic fertilizer materials; (2) manufacturing fertilizers from sewage or animal waste; (3) manufacturing nitrogenous or phosphatic materials and mixing with other ingredients into fertilizers; and (4) mixing ingredients made elsewhere into fertilizers.

325311 Nitrogenous Fertilizer Manufacturing

This U.S. industry comprises establishments primarily engaged in one or more of the following: (1) manufacturing nitrogenous fertilizer materials and mixing ingredients into fertilizers; (2) manufacturing fertilizers from sewage or animal waste; and (3) manufacturing nitrogenous materials and mixing them into fertilizers.

Cross-References.

Establishments primarily engaged in mixing ingredients made elsewhere into nitrogenous fertilizers are classified in U.S. Industry 325314, Fertilizer (Mixing Only) Manufacturing.

T—Canadian, Mexican, and United States industries are comparable.

325312 Phosphatic Fertilizer Manufacturing

This U.S. industry comprises establishments primarily engaged in (1) manufacturing phosphatic fertilizer materials or (2) manufacturing phosphatic materials and mixing them into fertilizers.

Cross-References.

Establishments primarily engaged in mixing ingredients made elsewhere into phosphatic fertilizers are classified in U.S. Industry 325314, Fertilizer (Mixing Only) Manufacturing.

325314 Fertilizer (Mixing Only) Manufacturing

This U.S. industry comprises establishments primarily engaged in mixing ingredients made elsewhere into fertilizers.

Cross-References. Establishments primarily engaged in--

- Manufacturing nitrogenous fertilizer materials or fertilizer materials from sewage or animal waste and mixing these ingredients into nitrogenous fertilizers--are classified in U.S. Industry 325311, Nitrogenous Fertilizer Manufacturing; and
- Manufacturing phosphatic fertilizer materials and mixing these ingredients into phosphatic fertilizers--are classified in U.S. Industry 325312, Phosphatic Fertilizer Manufacturing.

32532 Pesticide and Other Agricultural Chemical Manufacturing[T]
See industry description for 325320.

325320 Pesticide and Other Agricultural Chemical Manufacturing

This industry comprises establishments primarily engaged in the formulation and preparation of agricultural and household pest control chemicals (except fertilizers).

Cross-References. Establishments primarily engaged in--

- Manufacturing basic chemicals requiring further processing before use as agriculture chemicals--are classified in Industry Group 3251, Basic Chemical Manufacturing;
- Manufacturing fertilizers--are classified in Industry 32531, Fertilizer Manufacturing; and
- Manufacturing agricultural lime products--are classified in Industry 327410, Lime Manufacturing.

3254 Pharmaceutical and Medicine Manufacturing[T]

32541 Pharmaceutical and Medicine Manufacturing[T]

This industry comprises establishments primarily engaged in one or more of the following: (1) manufacturing biological and medicinal products; (2) processing (i.e., grading, grinding, and milling) botanical drugs and herbs; (3) isolating active medicinal principals from botanical drugs and herbs; and (4) manufacturing pharmaceutical products intended for internal and external consumption in such forms as ampoules, tablets, capsules, vials, ointments, powders, solutions, and suspensions.

325411 Medicinal and Botanical Manufacturing

This U.S. industry comprises establishments primarily engaged in (1) manufacturing uncompounded medicinal chemicals and their derivatives (i.e., generally for use by pharmaceutical preparation manufacturers) and/or (2) grading, grinding, and milling uncompounded botanicals.

T—Canadian, Mexican, and United States industries are comparable.

Cross-References.   Establishments primarily engaged in--

- Manufacturing packaged compounded medicinals and botanicals--are classified in U.S. Industry 325412, Pharmaceutical Preparation Manufacturing; and
- Manufacturing vaccines, toxoids, blood fractions, and culture media of plant or animal origin (except for diagnostic use)--are classified in U.S. Industry 325414, Biological Product (except Diagnostic) Manufacturing.

325412 Pharmaceutical Preparation Manufacturing

This U.S. industry comprises establishments primarily engaged in manufacturing in-vivo diagnostic substances and pharmaceutical preparations (except biological) intended for internal and external consumption in dose forms, such as ampoules, tablets, capsules, vials, ointments, powders, solutions, and suspensions.

Cross-References.   Establishments primarily engaged in--

- Manufacturing uncompounded medicinal chemicals and their derivatives--are classified in U.S. Industry 325411, Medicinal and Botanical Manufacturing;
- Manufacturing in-vitro diagnostic substances--are classified in U.S. Industry 325413, In-Vitro Diagnostic Substance Manufacturing; and
- Manufacturing vaccines, toxoids, blood fractions, and culture media of plant or animal origin (except for diagnostic use)--are classified in U.S. Industry 325414, Biological Product (except Diagnostic) Manufacturing.

325413 In-Vitro Diagnostic Substance Manufacturing

This U.S. industry comprises establishments primarily engaged in manufacturing in-vitro (i.e., not taken internally) diagnostic substances, such as chemical, biological, or radioactive substances. The substances are used for diagnostic tests that are performed in test tubes, petri dishes, machines, and other diagnostic test-type devices.

Cross-References.

Establishments primarily engaged in manufacturing in-vivo diagnostic substances are classified in U.S. Industry 325412, Pharmaceutical Preparation Manufacturing.

325414 Biological Product (except Diagnostic) Manufacturing

This U.S. industry comprises establishments primarily engaged in manufacturing vaccines, toxoids, blood fractions, and culture media of plant or animal origin (except diagnostic).

Cross-References.   Establishments primarily engaged in--

- Manufacturing in-vitro diagnostic substances--are classified in U.S. Industry 325413, In-Vitro Diagnostic Substance Manufacturing; and
- Manufacturing pharmaceutical preparations (except biological and in-vitro diagnostic substances)--are classified in U.S. Industry 325412, Pharmaceutical Preparation Manufacturing.

3255 Paint, Coating, and Adhesive Manufacturing[T]

This industry group comprises establishments primarily engaged in one or more of the following: (1) mixing pigments, solvents, and binders into paints and other coatings; (2) manufacturing allied paint products; and (3) manufacturing adhesives, glues, and caulking compounds.

32551 Paint and Coating Manufacturing[T]
See industry description for 325510.

T—Canadian, Mexican, and United States industries are comparable.

325510 Paint and Coating Manufacturing

This industry comprises establishments primarily engaged in (1) mixing pigments, solvents, and binders into paints and other coatings, such as stains, varnishes, lacquers, enamels, shellacs, and water-repellent coatings for concrete and masonry, and/or (2) manufacturing allied paint products, such as putties, paint and varnish removers, paint brush cleaners, and frit.

Cross-References.   Establishments primarily engaged in--

- Manufacturing creosote or turpentine--are classified in U.S. Industry 325194, Cyclic Crude, Intermediate, and Gum and Wood Chemical Manufacturing;
- Manufacturing caulking compounds and sealants--are classified in Industry 325520, Adhesive Manufacturing; and
- Manufacturing artists' paints--are classified in Industry 339940, Office Supplies (except Paper) Manufacturing.

32552 Adhesive Manufacturing[T]
See industry description for 325520.

325520 Adhesive Manufacturing

This industry comprises establishments primarily engaged in manufacturing adhesives, glues, and caulking compounds.

Cross-References.   Establishments primarily engaged in--

- Manufacturing asphalt and tar roofing cements from purchased asphaltic materials--are classified in U.S. Industry 324122, Asphalt Shingle and Coating Materials Manufacturing; and
- Manufacturing gypsum based caulking compounds--are classified in Industry 327420, Gypsum Product Manufacturing.

3256 Soap, Cleaning Compound, and Toilet Preparation Manufacturing[T]

This industry group comprises establishments primarily engaged in (1) manufacturing and packaging soaps, detergents, polishes, surface active agents, textile and leather finishing agents, and other sanitation goods or (2) preparing, blending, compounding, and packaging toilet preparations.

32561 Soap and Cleaning Compound Manufacturing[T]

This industry comprises establishments primarily engaged in manufacturing and packaging soaps and other cleaning compounds, surface active agents, and textile and leather finishing agents used to reduce tension or speed the drying process.

Cross-References.   Establishments primarily engaged in--

- Manufacturing synthetic glycerin--are classified in Industry 32519, Other Basic Organic Chemical Manufacturing;
- Manufacturing industrial bleaches--are classified in Industry 32518, Other Basic Inorganic Chemical Manufacturing; and
- Manufacturing shampoos and shaving preparations--are classified in Industry 32562, Toilet Preparation Manufacturing.

325611 Soap and Other Detergent Manufacturing

This U.S. industry comprises establishments primarily engaged in manufacturing and packaging soaps and other detergents, such as laundry and dishwashing detergents; toothpaste gels and tooth powders; and natural glycerin.

Cross-References.   Establishments primarily engaged in--

- Manufacturing synthetic glycerin--are classified in U.S. Industry 325199, All Other Basic Organic Chemical Manufacturing; and
- Manufacturing shampoos and shaving preparations--are classified in Industry 325620, Toilet Preparation Manufacturing.

325612 Polish and Other Sanitation Good Manufacturing

This U.S. industry comprises establishments primarily engaged in manufacturing and packaging polishes and specialty cleaning preparations.

Cross-References.

Establishments primarily engaged in manufacturing chlorine dioxide (i.e., industrial bleaching agent) are classified in Industry 325180, Other Basic Inorganic Chemical Manufacturing.

325613 Surface Active Agent Manufacturing

This U.S. industry comprises establishments primarily engaged in (1) manufacturing bulk surface active agents for use as wetting agents, emulsifiers, and penetrants and/or (2) manufacturing textile and leather finishing agents used to reduce tension or speed the drying process.

32562 Toilet Preparation Manufacturing[T]
See industry description for 325620.

325620 Toilet Preparation Manufacturing

This industry comprises establishments primarily engaged in preparing, blending, compounding, and packaging toilet preparations, such as perfumes, shaving preparations, hair preparations, face creams, lotions (including sunscreens), and other cosmetic preparations.

Cross-References.

Establishments primarily engaged in manufacturing toothpaste are classified in U.S. Industry 325611, Soap and Other Detergent Manufacturing.

3259 Other Chemical Product and Preparation Manufacturing[T]

This industry group comprises establishments primarily engaged in manufacturing chemical products (except basic chemicals; resins, synthetic rubber, cellulosic and noncellulosic fibers and filaments; pesticides, fertilizers, and other agricultural chemicals; pharmaceuticals and medicines; paints, coatings, and adhesives; soaps and cleaning compounds; and toilet preparations).

32591 Printing Ink Manufacturing[T]
See industry description for 325910.

T—Canadian, Mexican, and United States industries are comparable.

325910 Printing Ink Manufacturing

This industry comprises establishments primarily engaged in manufacturing printing and inkjet inks and inkjet cartridges.

Cross-References.   Establishments primarily engaged in--

- Recycling inkjet cartridges--are classified in U.S. Industry 811212, Computer and Office Machine Repair and Maintenance;
- Manufacturing writing, drawing, and stamping inks--are classified in U.S. Industry 325998, All Other Miscellaneous Chemical Product and Preparation Manufacturing; and
- Manufacturing toners and toner cartridges for photocopiers, fax machines, computer printers, and similar office machines--are classified in U.S. Industry 325992, Photographic Film, Paper, Plate, and Chemical Manufacturing.

32592 Explosives Manufacturing[T]
See industry description for 325920.

325920 Explosives Manufacturing

This industry comprises establishments primarily engaged in manufacturing explosives.

Cross-References.   Establishments primarily engaged in--

- Manufacturing ammunition, ammunition detonators, and percussion caps--are classified in U.S. Industry 332992, Small Arms Ammunition Manufacturing; and
- Manufacturing pyrotechnics--are classified in U.S. Industry 325998, All Other Miscellaneous Chemical Product and Preparation Manufacturing.

32599 All Other Chemical Product and Preparation Manufacturing[T]

This industry comprises establishments primarily engaged in manufacturing chemical products (except basic chemicals, resins, and synthetic rubber; cellulosic and noncellulosic fibers and filaments; pesticides, fertilizers, and other agricultural chemicals; pharmaceuticals and medicines; paints, coatings, and adhesives; soaps, cleaning compounds, and toilet preparations; printing inks; and explosives).

Illustrative Examples:

Activated carbon and charcoal manufacturing
Antifreeze preparations manufacturing
Custom compounding (i.e., blending and mixing) of purchased plastics resins
Electronic cigarette vapor refills manufacturing
Industrial salt manufacturing
Matches and matchbook manufacturing
Photographic chemicals manufacturing

Pyrotechnics (e.g., flares, flashlight bombs, signals) manufacturing
Sugar substitutes (i.e., synthetic sweeteners blended with other ingredients) made from purchased synthetic sweeteners
Swimming pool chemical preparations manufacturing
Writing inks manufacturing

Cross-References.   Establishments primarily engaged in--

- Manufacturing basic chemicals--are classified in Industry Group 3251, Basic Chemical Manufacturing;
- Manufacturing resins, synthetic rubber, and artificial and synthetic fibers and filaments--are classified in Industry Group 3252, Resin, Synthetic Rubber, and Artificial and Synthetic Fibers and Filaments Manufacturing;
- Manufacturing pesticides, fertilizers, and other agricultural chemicals--are classified in Industry Group 3253, Pesticide, Fertilizer, and Other Agricultural Chemical Manufacturing;

T—Canadian, Mexican, and United States industries are comparable.

- Manufacturing pharmaceuticals and medicines including medicinal vegetable gelatin (i.e., agar-agar)--are classified in Industry Group 3254, Pharmaceutical and Medicine Manufacturing;
- Manufacturing paints, coatings, and adhesives--are classified in Industry Group 3255, Paint, Coating, and Adhesive Manufacturing;
- Manufacturing soaps and cleaning compounds--are classified in Industry Group 3256, Soap, Cleaning Compound, and Toilet Preparation Manufacturing;
- Manufacturing printing and inkjet inks--are classified in Industry 32591, Printing Ink Manufacturing;
- Manufacturing explosives--are classified in Industry 32592, Explosives Manufacturing;
- Manufacturing photographic paper stock (i.e., unsensitized) and paper mats, mounts, easels, and folders for photographic use--are classified in Subsector 322, Paper Manufacturing;
- Manufacturing dessert gelatins--are classified in Industry 31199, All Other Food Manufacturing; and
- Manufacturing medicinal gelatins--are classified in Industry 32541, Pharmaceutical and Medicine Manufacturing.

325991 Custom Compounding of Purchased Resins

This U.S. industry comprises establishments primarily engaged in (1) custom mixing and blending plastics resins made elsewhere or (2) reformulating plastics resins from recycled plastics products.

Cross-References.

Establishments primarily engaged in manufacturing synthetic resins and custom mixing and blending resins are classified in U.S. Industry 325211, Plastics Material and Resin Manufacturing.

325992 Photographic Film, Paper, Plate, and Chemical Manufacturing

This U.S. industry comprises establishments primarily engaged in manufacturing sensitized film, sensitized paper, sensitized cloth, sensitized plates, toners (i.e., for photocopiers, laser printers, and similar electrostatic printing devices), toner cartridges, and photographic chemicals.

Cross-References.

Establishments primarily engaged in manufacturing photographic paper stock (i.e., unsensitized) and paper mats, mounts, easels, and folders for photographic use are classified in Subsector 322, Paper Manufacturing.

325998 All Other Miscellaneous Chemical Product and Preparation Manufacturing

This U.S. industry comprises establishments primarily engaged in manufacturing chemical products (except basic chemicals, resins, and synthetic rubber; cellulosic and noncellulosic fibers and filaments; pesticides, fertilizers, and other agricultural chemicals; pharmaceuticals and medicines; paints, coatings and adhesives; soaps, cleaning compounds, and toilet preparations; printing inks; explosives; custom compounding of purchased resins; and photographic films, papers, plates, and chemicals).

Illustrative Examples:

Activated carbon and charcoal manufacturing
Antifreeze preparations manufacturing
Electronic cigarette vapor refills manufacturing
Industrial salt manufacturing
Lighter fluids (e.g., charcoal, cigarette) manufacturing
Matches and matchbook manufacturing

Pyrotechnics (e.g., flares, flashlight bombs, signals) manufacturing
Sugar substitutes (i.e., synthetic sweeteners blended with other ingredients) made from purchased synthetic sweeteners
Swimming pool chemical preparations manufacturing
Writing inks manufacturing

Cross-References.   Establishments primarily engaged in--

- Manufacturing basic chemicals--are classified in Industry Group 3251, Basic Chemical Manufacturing;
- Manufacturing resins, synthetic rubber, and artificial and synthetic fibers and filaments--are classified in Industry Group 3252, Resin, Synthetic Rubber, and Artificial and Synthetic Fibers and Filaments Manufacturing;
- Manufacturing pesticides, fertilizers, and other agricultural chemicals--are classified in Industry Group 3253, Pesticide, Fertilizer, and Other Agricultural Chemical Manufacturing;
- Manufacturing pharmaceuticals and medicines including medicinal vegetable gelatin (i.e., agar-agar)--are classified in Industry Group 3254, Pharmaceutical and Medicine Manufacturing;
- Manufacturing paints, coatings, and adhesives--are classified in Industry Group 3255, Paint, Coating, and Adhesive Manufacturing;
- Manufacturing soaps and cleaning compounds--are classified in Industry 32561, Soap and-Cleaning Compound Manufacturing;
- Manufacturing printing and inkjet inks--are classified in Industry 325910, Printing Ink Manufacturing;
- Manufacturing explosives--are classified in Industry 325920, Explosives Manufacturing;
- Custom compounding purchased plastics resins--are classified in U.S. Industry 325991, Custom Compounding of Purchased Resins;
- Manufacturing photographic films, papers, plates, and chemicals--are classified in U.S. Industry 325992, Photographic Film, Paper, Plate, and Chemical Manufacturing; and
- Manufacturing dessert gelatin--are classified in U.S. Industry 311999, All Other Miscellaneous Food Manufacturing.

326   Plastics and Rubber Products Manufacturing[T]

Industries in the Plastics and Rubber Products Manufacturing subsector make goods by processing plastics materials and raw rubber. The core technology employed by establishments in this subsector is that of plastics or rubber product production. Plastics and rubber are combined in the same subsector because plastics are increasingly being used as a substitute for rubber; however the subsector is generally restricted to the production of products made of just one material, either solely plastics or rubber.

Many manufacturing activities use plastics or rubber, for example the manufacture of footwear or furniture. Typically, the production process of these products involves more than one material. In these cases, technologies that allow disparate materials to be formed and combined are of central importance in describing the manufacturing activity. In NAICS, such activities (footwear and furniture manufacturing) are not classified in the Plastics and Rubber Products Manufacturing subsector because the core technologies for these activities are diverse and involve multiple materials.

Within the Plastics and Rubber Products Manufacturing subsector, a distinction is made between plastics and rubber products at the industry group level, although it is not a rigid distinction, as can be seen from the definition of Industry 32622, Rubber and Plastics Hoses and Belting Manufacturing. As materials technology progresses, plastics are increasingly being used as a substitute for rubber; and eventually, the distinction may disappear as a basis for establishment classification.

In keeping with the core technology focus of plastics, lamination of plastics film to plastics film as well as the production of bags from plastics only is classified in this subsector. Lamination and bag production involving plastics and materials other than plastics are classified in Subsector 322, Paper Manufacturing.

3261   Plastics Product Manufacturing[T]

This industry group comprises establishments primarily engaged in processing new or spent (i.e., recycled) plastics resins into intermediate or final products, using such processes as compression molding; extrusion molding; injection molding; blow molding; and casting. Within most of these industries, the production process is such that a wide variety of products can be made.

T—Canadian, Mexican, and United States industries are comparable.

32611   Plastics Packaging Materials and Unlaminated Film and Sheet Manufacturing[T]

This industry comprises establishments primarily engaged in (1) converting plastics resins into unsupported plastics film and sheet and/or (2) forming, coating, or laminating plastics film and sheet into plastics bags.

Cross-References.   Establishments primarily engaged in--

- Laminating plastics sheet (except for packaging)--are classified in Industry 32613, Laminated Plastics Plate, Sheet (except Packaging), and Shape Manufacturing;
- Manufacturing plastics blister and bubble packaging--are classified in Industry 32619, Other Plastics Product Manufacturing; and
- Coating or laminating combinations of plastics, foils and paper (except plastics film to plastics film) into film, sheet or bags--are classified in Industry 32222, Paper Bag and Coated and Treated Paper Manufacturing.

326111   Plastics Bag and Pouch Manufacturing

This U.S. industry comprises establishments primarily engaged in (1) converting plastics resins into plastics bags or pouches and/or (2) forming, coating, or laminating plastics film or sheet into single-web or multiweb plastics bags or pouches. Establishments in this industry may print on the bags or pouches they manufacture.

Cross-References.   Establishments primarily engaged in--

- Manufacturing laminated or coated combinations of plastics, foils, and paper (except plastics film to plastics film) materials into single wall or multiwall bags--are classified in Industry 322220, Paper Bag and Coated and Treated Paper Manufacturing; and
- Printing on purchased packaging materials--are classified in Industry Group 3231, Printing and Related Support Activities, based on the printing process used.

326112   Plastics Packaging Film and Sheet (including Laminated) Manufacturing

This U.S. industry comprises establishments primarily engaged in converting plastics resins into plastics packaging (flexible) film and packaging sheet.

Cross-References.   Establishments primarily engaged in--

- Converting plastics resins into plastics film and unlaminated sheet (except packaging)--are classified in U.S. Industry 326113, Unlaminated Plastics Film and Sheet (except Packaging) Manufacturing;
- Laminating or coating combinations of plastics, foils, and paper (except plastics film to plastics film) film and sheet, packaging or nonpackaging--are classified in Industry 322220, Paper Bag and Coated and Treated Paper Manufacturing;
- Laminating plastics sheet (except for packaging)--are classified in Industry 326130, Laminated Plastics Plate, Sheet (except Packaging), and Shape Manufacturing; and
- Manufacturing plastics bags--are classified in U.S. Industry 326111, Plastics Bag and Pouch Manufacturing.

326113   Unlaminated Plastics Film and Sheet (except Packaging) Manufacturing

This U.S. industry comprises establishments primarily engaged in converting plastics resins into plastics film and unlaminated sheet (except packaging).

Cross-References.   Establishments primarily engaged in--

- Converting plastics resins into plastics packaging film and unlaminated packaging sheet--are classified in U.S. Industry 326112, Plastics Packaging Film and Sheet (including Laminated) Manufacturing;

T—Canadian, Mexican, and United States industries are comparable.

- Laminating plastics sheet (except for packaging)--are classified in Industry 326130, Laminated Plastics Plate, Sheet (except Packaging), and Shape Manufacturing;
- Laminating or coating combinations of plastics, foils, and paper (except plastics film to plastics film) film and sheet, packaging or nonpackaging--are classified in Industry 322220, Paper Bag and Coated and Treated Paper Manufacturing; and
- Manufacturing plastics bags--are classified in U.S. Industry 326111, Plastics Bag and Pouch Manufacturing.

32612 Plastics Pipe, Pipe Fitting, and Unlaminated Profile Shape Manufacturing[T]

This industry comprises establishments primarily engaged in manufacturing plastics pipes and pipe fittings, and plastics profile shapes such as rod, tube, and sausage casings.

Cross-References.   Establishments primarily engaged in--

- Manufacturing plastics hose--are classified in Industry 32622, Rubber and Plastics Hoses and Belting Manufacturing;
- Manufacturing noncurrent-carrying plastics conduit--are classified in Industry 33593, Wiring Device Manufacturing;
- Manufacturing plastics plumbing fixtures--are classified in Industry 32619, Other Plastics Product Manufacturing; and
- Manufacturing plastics film, plastics unlaminated sheet, and plastics bags--are classified in Industry 32611, Plastics Packaging Materials and Unlaminated Film and Sheet Manufacturing.

326121 Unlaminated Plastics Profile Shape Manufacturing

This U.S. industry comprises establishments primarily engaged in converting plastics resins into nonrigid plastics profile shapes (except film, sheet, and bags), such as rod, tube, and sausage casings.

Cross-References.   Establishments primarily engaged in--

- Manufacturing plastics film, plastics unlaminated sheet, and plastics bags--are classified in Industry 32611, Plastics Packaging Materials and Unlaminated Film and Sheet Manufacturing; and
- Manufacturing plastics hoses--are classified in Industry 326220, Rubber and Plastics Hoses and Belting Manufacturing.

326122 Plastics Pipe and Pipe Fitting Manufacturing

This U.S. industry comprises establishments primarily engaged in converting plastics resins into rigid plastics pipes and pipe fittings.

Cross-References.   Establishments primarily engaged in--

- Manufacturing plastics hose--are classified in Industry 326220, Rubber and Plastics Hoses and Belting Manufacturing;
- Manufacturing noncurrent-carrying plastics conduit--are classified in U.S. Industry 335932, Noncurrent-Carrying Wiring Device Manufacturing; and
- Manufacturing plastics plumbing fixtures--are classified in U.S. Industry 326191, Plastics Plumbing Fixture Manufacturing.

32613 Laminated Plastics Plate, Sheet (except Packaging), and Shape Manufacturing[T]
See industry description for 326130.

T—Canadian, Mexican, and United States industries are comparable.

326130 Laminated Plastics Plate, Sheet (except Packaging), and Shape Manufacturing

This industry comprises establishments primarily engaged in laminating plastics profile shapes such as plate, sheet (except packaging), and rod. The lamination process generally involves bonding or impregnating profiles with plastics resins and compressing them under heat.

Cross-References.   Establishments primarily engaged in--

- Manufacturing plastics film, plastics unlaminated sheet, and plastics bags--are classified in Industry 32611, Plastics Packaging Materials and Unlaminated Film and Sheet Manufacturing; and
- Coating or laminating nonplastics film, sheet, or bags with plastics--are classified in Industry 322220, Paper Bag and Coated and Treated Paper Manufacturing.

32614 Polystyrene Foam Product Manufacturing[T]
See industry description for 326140.

326140 Polystyrene Foam Product Manufacturing

This industry comprises establishments primarily engaged in manufacturing polystyrene foam products.

Cross-References.

Establishments primarily engaged in manufacturing plastics foam products (except polystyrene) are classified in Industry 326150, Urethane and Other Foam Product (except Polystyrene) Manufacturing.

32615 Urethane and Other Foam Product (except Polystyrene) Manufacturing[T]
See industry description for 326150.

326150 Urethane and Other Foam Product (except Polystyrene) Manufacturing

This industry comprises establishments primarily engaged in manufacturing plastics foam products (except polystyrene).

Cross-References.

Establishments primarily engaged in manufacturing polystyrene foam products are classified in Industry 326140, Polystyrene Foam Product Manufacturing.

32616 Plastics Bottle Manufacturing[T]
See industry description for 326160.

326160 Plastics Bottle Manufacturing

This industry comprises establishments primarily engaged in manufacturing plastics bottles.

Cross-References.

Establishments primarily engaged in manufacturing plastics containers (except bottles) and plastics bottle caps are classified in U.S. Industry 326199, All Other Plastics Product Manufacturing.

32619 Other Plastics Product Manufacturing[T]

This industry comprises establishments primarily engaged in manufacturing plastics plumbing fixtures and other plastics products (except film, sheet, bags, profile shapes, pipes, pipe fittings, laminates, foam products, and bottles).

T—Canadian, Mexican, and United States industries are comparable.

Illustrative Examples:

Inflatable plastics swimming pool rafts and similar
flotation devices manufacturing
Plastics air mattresses manufacturing
Plastics bottle caps and lids manufacturing
Plastics bowls and bowl covers manufacturing
Plastics clothes hangers manufacturing
Plastics cups (except foam) manufacturing
Plastics dinnerware (except foam) manufacturing
Plastics gloves manufacturing
Plastics hardware manufacturing

Plastics ice chests or coolers (except plastics foam)
manufacturing
Plastics or fiberglass plumbing fixtures (e.g., toilets,
shower stalls, urinals) manufacturing
Plastics prefabricated buildings manufacturing
Plastics siding manufacturing
Plastics trash containers manufacturing
Resilient floor coverings (e.g., sheet, tiles)
manufacturing

Cross-References.   Establishments primarily engaged in--

- Manufacturing plastics film, plastics unlaminated sheet, and plastics bags--are classified in Industry 32611, Plastics Packaging Materials and Unlaminated Film and Sheet Manufacturing;
- Manufacturing plastics pipes, pipe fittings, and plastics profile shapes (except film, sheet, bags)--are classified in Industry 32612, Plastics Pipe, Pipe Fitting, and Unlaminated Profile Shape Manufacturing;
- Laminating plastics profile shapes, such as plate, sheet, and rod--are classified in Industry 32613, Laminated Plastics Plate, Sheet (except Packaging), and Shape Manufacturing;
- Manufacturing polystyrene foam products--are classified in Industry 32614, Polystyrene Foam Product Manufacturing;
- Manufacturing foam products (except polystyrene)--are classified in Industry 32615, Urethane and Other Foam Product (except Polystyrene) Manufacturing;
- Manufacturing plastics bottles--are classified in Industry 32616, Plastics Bottle Manufacturing;
- Manufacturing plastics furniture parts--are classified in Industry 33721, Office Furniture (including Fixtures) Manufacturing;
- Assembling plastics components into plumbing fixture fittings, such as faucets--are classified in Industry 33291, Metal Valve Manufacturing; and
- Manufacturing rubber floor mats and rubber treads--are classified in Industry 32629, Other Rubber Product Manufacturing.

326191 Plastics Plumbing Fixture Manufacturing

This U.S. industry comprises establishments primarily engaged in manufacturing plastics or fiberglass plumbing fixtures. Examples of products made by these establishments are plastics or fiberglass bathtubs, hot tubs, portable toilets, and shower stalls.

Cross-References.   Establishments primarily engaged in--

- Assembling plastics components into plumbing fixture fittings, such as faucets--are classified in U.S. Industry 332913, Plumbing Fixture Fitting and Trim Manufacturing; and
- Manufacturing plastics pipe and pipe fittings--are classified in U.S. Industry 326122, Plastics Pipe and Pipe Fitting Manufacturing.

326199 All Other Plastics Product Manufacturing

This U.S. industry comprises establishments primarily engaged in manufacturing plastics products (except film, sheet, bags, profile shapes, pipes, pipe fittings, laminates, foam products, bottles, and plumbing fixtures).

Illustrative Examples:

Inflatable plastics swimming pool rafts and similar
flotation devices manufacturing

Plastics air mattresses manufacturing
Plastics bottle caps and lids manufacturing

T—Canadian, Mexican, and United States industries are comparable.

Plastics bowls and bowl covers manufacturing
Plastics clothes hangers manufacturing
Plastics cups (except foam) manufacturing
Plastics dinnerware (except foam) manufacturing
Plastics gloves manufacturing

Plastics hardware manufacturing
Plastics siding manufacturing
Plastics trash containers manufacturing
Resilient floor coverings (e.g., sheet, tiles)
manufacturing

Cross-References.   Establishments primarily engaged in--

- Manufacturing plastics film, plastics unlaminated sheet, and plastics bags--are classified in Industry 32611, Plastics Packaging Materials and Unlaminated Film and Sheet Manufacturing;
- Manufacturing plastics pipes, pipe fittings, and plastics profile shapes (except film, sheet, bags)--are classified in Industry 32612, Plastics Pipe, Pipe Fitting, and Unlaminated Profile Shape Manufacturing;
- Laminating plastics profile shapes, such as plate, sheet, and rod--are classified in Industry 326130, Laminated Plastics Plate, Sheet (except Packaging), and Shape Manufacturing;
- Manufacturing polystyrene foam products--are classified in Industry 326140, Polystyrene Foam Product Manufacturing;
- Manufacturing foam (except polystyrene) products--are classified in Industry 326150, Urethane and Other Foam Product (except Polystyrene) Manufacturing;
- Manufacturing plastics bottles--are classified in Industry 326160, Plastics Bottle Manufacturing;
- Manufacturing heavy-duty inflatable plastics boats--are classified in U.S. Industry 336612, Boat Building;
- Manufacturing plastics furniture parts and components--are classified in U.S. Industry 337215, Showcase, Partition, Shelving, and Locker Manufacturing;
- Manufacturing rubber floor mats and rubber treads--are classified in U.S. Industry 326299, All Other Rubber Product Manufacturing;
- Manufacturing plastics plumbing fixtures--are classified in U.S. Industry 326191, Plastics Plumbing Fixture Manufacturing; and
- Assembling plastics components into plumbing fixture fittings, such as faucets--are classified in U.S. Industry 332913, Plumbing Fixture Fitting and Trim Manufacturing.

3262   Rubber Product Manufacturing[T]

This industry group comprises establishments primarily engaged in processing natural, synthetic, or reclaimed rubber materials into intermediate or final products using processes, such as vulcanizing, cementing, molding, extruding, and lathe-cutting.

32621   Tire Manufacturing[T]

This industry comprises establishments primarily engaged in manufacturing tires and inner tubes from natural and synthetic rubber and retreading or rebuilding tires.

Cross-References.   Establishments primarily engaged in--

- Repairing tires, such as plugging--are classified in Industry 81119, Other Automotive Repair and Maintenance; and
- Retailing tires--are classified in Industry 44132, Tire Dealers.

326211 Tire Manufacturing (except Retreading)

This U.S. industry comprises establishments primarily engaged in manufacturing tires and inner tubes from natural and synthetic rubber.

Cross-References.

Establishments primarily engaged in retreading or rebuilding tires are classified in U.S. Industry 326212, Tire Retreading.

T—Canadian, Mexican, and United States industries are comparable.

326212 Tire Retreading

This U.S. industry comprises establishments primarily engaged in retreading or rebuilding tires.

Cross-References. Establishments primarily engaged in--

- Repairing tires, such as plugging--are classified in U.S. Industry 811198, All Other Automotive Repair and Maintenance;
- Retailing tires--are classified in Industry 441320, Tire Dealers; and
- Manufacturing tires and inner tubes from natural and synthetic rubber--are classified in U.S. Industry 326211, Tire Manufacturing (except Retreading).

32622 Rubber and Plastics Hoses and Belting Manufacturing[T]
See industry description for 326220.

326220 Rubber and Plastics Hoses and Belting Manufacturing

This industry comprises establishments primarily engaged in manufacturing rubber hose and/or plastics (reinforced) hose and belting from natural and synthetic rubber and/or plastics resins. Establishments manufacturing garden hoses from purchased hose are included in this industry.

Cross-References. Establishments primarily engaged in--

- Manufacturing rubber tubing--are classified in U.S. Industry 326299, All Other Rubber Product Manufacturing;
- Manufacturing plastics tubing--are classified in U.S. Industry 326121, Unlaminated Plastics Profile Shape Manufacturing;
- Manufacturing extruded, lathe-cut, or molded rubber goods (except tubing) for mechanical applications-- are classified in U.S. Industry 326291, Rubber Product Manufacturing for Mechanical Use; and
- Manufacturing fluid power hose assemblies--are classified in U.S. Industry 332912, Fluid Power Valve and Hose Fitting Manufacturing.

32629 Other Rubber Product Manufacturing[T]

This industry comprises establishments primarily engaged in manufacturing rubber products (except tires, hoses, and belting) from natural and synthetic rubber.

Illustrative Examples:

Birth control devices (e.g., diaphragms, prophylactics) manufacturing	Rubber balloons manufacturing
Latex foam rubber manufacturing	Rubber bands manufacturing
Mechanical rubber goods (i.e., molded, extruded, lathe-cut) manufacturing	Rubber floor mats (e.g., door, bath) manufacturing
Reclaiming rubber from waste and scrap	Rubber hair care products (e.g., combs, curlers) manufacturing
	Rubber tubing manufacturing

Cross-References. Establishments primarily engaged in--

- Manufacturing tires and inner tubes--are classified in Industry 32621, Tire Manufacturing;
- Manufacturing rubber hoses and belting--are classified in Industry 32622, Rubber and Plastics Hoses and Belting Manufacturing;
- Rubberizing fabric--are classified in Industry 31332, Fabric Coating Mills;
- Manufacturing rubber gaskets, packing, and sealing devices--are classified in Industry 33999, All Other Miscellaneous Manufacturing;

T—Canadian, Mexican, and United States industries are comparable.

- Manufacturing rubber gloves--are classified in Industry 33911, Medical Equipment and Supplies Manufacturing;
- Manufacturing rubber clothing accessories (e.g., bathing caps)--are classified in Industry 31599, Apparel Accessories and Other Apparel Manufacturing; and
- Manufacturing rubber toys--are classified in Industry 33993, Doll, Toy, and Game Manufacturing.

326291 Rubber Product Manufacturing for Mechanical Use

This U.S. industry comprises establishments primarily engaged in manufacturing rubber goods (except tubing) for mechanical applications, using the processes of molding, extruding or lathe-cutting. Products of this industry are generally parts for motor vehicles, machinery, and equipment.

Cross-References.

Establishments primarily engaged in manufacturing rubber tubing from natural and synthetic rubber or in manufacturing rubber products for mechanical applications using processes other than molding, extruding or lathe-cutting are classified in U.S. Industry 326299, All Other Rubber Product Manufacturing.

326299 All Other Rubber Product Manufacturing

This U.S. industry comprises establishments primarily engaged in manufacturing rubber products (except tires; hoses and belting; and molded, extruded, and lathe-cut rubber goods for mechanical applications (except rubber tubing)) from natural and synthetic rubber. Establishments manufacturing rubber tubing made from natural and synthetic rubber, regardless of process used, are included in this industry.

Illustrative Examples:

Birth control devices (i.e., diaphragms, prophylactics) manufacturing
Latex foam rubber manufacturing
Reclaiming rubber from waste and scrap
Rubber balloons manufacturing

Rubber bands manufacturing
Rubber floor mats (e.g., door, bath) manufacturing
Rubber hair care products (e.g., combs, curlers) manufacturing
Rubber tubing manufacturing

Cross-References.   Establishments primarily engaged in--

- Manufacturing tires and inner tubes and rebuilding tires--are classified in Industry 32621, Tire Manufacturing;
- Manufacturing rubber hoses and belting--are classified in Industry 326220, Rubber and Plastics Hoses and Belting Manufacturing;
- Manufacturing heavy-duty inflatable rubber boats--are classified in U.S. Industry 336612, Boat Building;
- Molding, extruding, and lathe-cutting rubber to manufacture rubber goods (except tubing) for mechanical applications--are classified in U.S. Industry 326291, Rubber Product Manufacturing for Mechanical Use;
- Rubberizing fabrics--are classified in Industry 313320, Fabric Coating Mills;
- Manufacturing rubber gasket, packing, and sealing devices--are classified in U.S. Industry 339991, Gasket, Packing, and Sealing Device Manufacturing;
- Manufacturing rubber toys--are classified in Industry 339930, Doll, Toy, and Game Manufacturing;
- Manufacturing rubber gloves--are classified in U.S. Industry 339113, Surgical Appliance and Supplies Manufacturing; and
- Manufacturing rubber clothing accessories (e.g., bathing caps)--are classified in Industry 315990, Apparel Accessories and Other Apparel Manufacturing.

327   Nonmetallic Mineral Product Manufacturing[T]

The Nonmetallic Mineral Product Manufacturing subsector transforms mined or quarried nonmetallic minerals, such as sand, gravel, stone, clay, and refractory materials, into products for intermediate or final consumption.

T—Canadian, Mexican, and United States industries are comparable.

Processes used include grinding, mixing, cutting, shaping, and honing. Heat often is used in the process and chemicals are frequently mixed to change the composition, purity, and chemical properties for the intended product. For example, glass is produced by heating silica sand to the melting point (sometimes combined with cullet or recycled glass) and then drawn, floated, or blow molded to the desired shape or thickness. Refractory materials are heated and then formed into bricks or other shapes for use in industrial applications.

The Nonmetallic Mineral Product Manufacturing subsector includes establishments that manufacture bricks, refractories, ceramic products, and glass and glass products, such as plate glass and containers. Also included are cement and concrete products, lime, gypsum and other nonmetallic mineral products including abrasive products, ceramic plumbing fixtures, statuary, cut stone products, and mineral wool. The products are used in a wide range of activities from construction and heavy and light manufacturing to articles for personal use.

Mining, beneficiating, and manufacturing activities often occur in a single location. Separate receipts will be collected for these activities whenever possible. When receipts cannot be broken out between mining and manufacturing, establishments that mine or quarry nonmetallic minerals, beneficiate the nonmetallic minerals, and further process the nonmetallic minerals into a more finished manufactured product are classified based on the primary activity of the establishment. A mine that manufactures a small amount of finished products is classified in Sector 21, Mining, Quarrying, and Oil and Gas Extraction. An establishment that mines whose primary output is a more finished manufactured product is classified in the Manufacturing sector.

Excluded from the Nonmetallic Mineral Product Manufacturing subsector are establishments that primarily beneficiate mined nonmetallic minerals. Beneficiation is the process whereby the extracted material is reduced to particles that can be separated into mineral and waste, the former suitable for further processing or direct use. Beneficiation establishments are included in Sector 21, Mining, Quarrying, and Oil and Gas Extraction.

3271 Clay Product and Refractory Manufacturing[T]

This industry group comprises establishments primarily engaged in (1) shaping, molding, glazing, and firing pottery, ceramics, and plumbing fixtures, and electrical supplies made entirely or partly of clay or other ceramic materials or (2) shaping, molding, baking, burning, or hardening clay refractories, nonclay refractories, ceramic tile, structural clay tile, brick, and other structural clay building materials.

32711 Pottery, Ceramics, and Plumbing Fixture Manufacturing[T]
See industry description for 327110.

327110 Pottery, Ceramics, and Plumbing Fixture Manufacturing

This industry comprises establishments primarily engaged in shaping, molding, glazing, and firing pottery, ceramics, plumbing fixtures, and electrical supplies made entirely or partly of clay or other ceramic materials.

Illustrative Examples:

Bathroom accessories, vitreous china and earthenware, manufacturing
Ceramic or ferrite permanent magnets manufacturing
Chemical stoneware (i.e., pottery products) manufacturing

Clay and ceramic statuary manufacturing
Earthenware table and kitchen articles, coarse, manufacturing
Porcelain electrical insulators manufacturing
Vitreous china plumbing fixtures manufacturing

Cross-References.   Establishments primarily engaged in--

- Manufacturing enameled iron and steel plumbing fixtures--are classified in U.S. Industry 332999, All Other Miscellaneous Fabricated Metal Product Manufacturing;
- Manufacturing metal bathroom accessories--are classified in Subsector 332, Fabricated Metal Product Manufacturing;
- Manufacturing cultured marble and other plastics plumbing fixtures--are classified in U.S. Industry 326191, Plastics Plumbing Fixture Manufacturing;
- Manufacturing clay building materials, such as ceramic tile, bricks, and clay roofing tiles, and refractories-- are classified in Industry 327120, Clay Building Material and Refractories Manufacturing;

T—Canadian, Mexican, and United States industries are comparable.

- Manufacturing ferrite microwave devices and electronic components--are classified in Subsector 334, Computer and Electronic Product Manufacturing; and
- Manufacturing plastics bathroom accessories--are classified in U.S. Industry 326199, All Other Plastics Product Manufacturing.

32712   Clay Building Material and Refractories Manufacturing[T]
See industry description for 327120.

327120   Clay Building Material and Refractories Manufacturing

This industry comprises establishments primarily engaged in shaping, molding, baking, burning, or hardening clay refractories, nonclay refractories, ceramic tile, structural clay tile, brick, and other structural clay building materials. A refractory is a material that will retain its shape and chemical identity when subjected to high temperatures and is used in applications that require extreme resistance to heat, such as furnace linings.

Cross-References.   Establishments primarily engaged in--

- Manufacturing resilient flooring and asphalt floor tiles--are classified in U.S. Industry 326199, All Other Plastics Product Manufacturing;
- Manufacturing concrete bricks--are classified in U.S. Industry 327331, Concrete Block and Brick Manufacturing; and
- Manufacturing glass bricks and blocks--are classified in Industry 32721, Glass and Glass Product Manufacturing.

3272   Glass and Glass Product Manufacturing[T]

32721   Glass and Glass Product Manufacturing[T]

This industry comprises establishments primarily engaged in manufacturing glass and/or glass products. Establishments in this industry may manufacture glass and/or glass products by melting silica sand or cullet, or from purchased glass.

Cross-References.   Establishments primarily engaged in--

- Manufacturing glass wool (i.e., fiberglass) insulation products--are classified in Industry 32799, All Other Nonmetallic Mineral Product Manufacturing;
- Manufacturing optical lenses (except ophthalmic), such as magnifying, photographic, and projection lenses--are classified in Industry 33331, Commercial and Service Industry Machinery Manufacturing;
- Grinding ophthalmic (i.e., eyeglass) lenses for the trade--are classified in Industry 33911, Medical Equipment and Supplies Manufacturing; and
- Manufacturing fiber optic cable from purchased fiber optic strand--are classified in Industry 33592, Communication and Energy Wire and Cable Manufacturing.

327211   Flat Glass Manufacturing

This U.S. industry comprises establishments primarily engaged in (1) manufacturing flat glass by melting silica sand or cullet or (2) manufacturing both flat glass and laminated glass by melting silica sand or cullet.

Cross-References.

Establishments primarily engaged in manufacturing laminated glass from purchased flat glass are classified in U.S. Industry 327215, Glass Product Manufacturing Made of Purchased Glass.

T—Canadian, Mexican, and United States industries are comparable.

327212 Other Pressed and Blown Glass and Glassware Manufacturing

This U.S. industry comprises establishments primarily engaged in manufacturing glass by melting silica sand or cullet and making pressed, blown, or shaped glass or glassware (except glass packaging containers).

Cross-References.   Establishments primarily engaged in--

- Manufacturing flat glass--are classified in U.S. Industry 327211, Flat Glass Manufacturing;
- Manufacturing glass packaging containers in glassmaking operations--are classified in U.S. Industry 327213, Glass Container Manufacturing;
- Manufacturing glass wool (i.e., fiberglass) insulation--are classified in U.S. Industry 327993, Mineral Wool Manufacturing;
- Manufacturing glassware from purchased glass--are classified in U.S. Industry 327215, Glass Product Manufacturing Made of Purchased Glass; and
- Manufacturing fiber optic cable from purchased fiber optic strand--are classified in U.S. Industry 335921, Fiber Optic Cable Manufacturing.

327213 Glass Container Manufacturing

This U.S. industry comprises establishments primarily engaged in manufacturing glass packaging containers.

327215 Glass Product Manufacturing Made of Purchased Glass

This U.S. industry comprises establishments primarily engaged in coating, laminating, tempering, or shaping purchased glass.

Cross-References.   Establishments primarily engaged in--

- Manufacturing optical lenses (except ophthalmic), such as magnifying, photographic, and projection lenses--are classified in U.S. Industry 333314, Optical Instrument and Lens Manufacturing;
- Manufacturing ophthalmic (i.e., eyeglass) lenses--are classified in U.S. Industry 339115, Ophthalmic Goods Manufacturing; and
- Manufacturing fiber optic cable from purchased fiber optic strand--are classified in U.S. Industry 335921, Fiber Optic Cable Manufacturing.

3273   Cement and Concrete Product Manufacturing[T]

This industry group comprises establishments primarily engaged in one of the following: (1) manufacturing portland, natural, masonry, pozzolanic, and other hydraulic cements; (2) acting as batch or mixing plants, manufacturing concrete delivered to a purchaser in a plastic and unhardened state; (3) manufacturing concrete pipe, brick, and block; or (4) manufacturing other concrete products (except block, brick, and pipe).

32731   Cement Manufacturing[T]
See industry description for 327310.

327310 Cement Manufacturing

This industry comprises establishments primarily engaged in manufacturing portland, natural, masonry, pozzolanic, and other hydraulic cements. Cement manufacturing establishments may calcine earths or mine, quarry, manufacture, or purchase lime.

Cross-References.   Establishments primarily engaged in--

- Mining or quarrying limestone--are classified in U.S. Industry 212312, Crushed and Broken Limestone Mining and Quarrying;

T—Canadian, Mexican, and United States industries are comparable.

- Manufacturing lime--are classified in Industry 327410, Lime Manufacturing;
- Manufacturing ready-mix concrete--are classified in Industry 327320, Ready-Mix Concrete Manufacturing; and
- Manufacturing dry mix concrete--are classified in U.S. Industry 327999, All Other Miscellaneous Nonmetallic Mineral Product Manufacturing.

32732 Ready-Mix Concrete Manufacturing[T]
See industry description for 327320.

327320 Ready-Mix Concrete Manufacturing

This industry comprises establishments, such as batch plants or mix plants, primarily engaged in manufacturing concrete delivered to a purchaser in a plastic and unhardened state. Ready-mix concrete manufacturing establishments may mine, quarry, or purchase sand and gravel.

Cross-References.   Establishments primarily engaged in--

- Operating sand or gravel pits--are classified in U.S. Industry 212321, Construction Sand and Gravel Mining; and
- Manufacturing dry mix concrete--are classified in U.S. Industry 327999, All Other Miscellaneous Nonmetallic Mineral Product Manufacturing.

32733 Concrete Pipe, Brick, and Block Manufacturing[T]

This industry comprises establishments primarily engaged in manufacturing concrete pipe, brick, and block.

Cross-References.

Establishments primarily engaged in manufacturing concrete products (except block, brick, and pipe) are classified in Industry 32739, Other Concrete Product Manufacturing.

327331 Concrete Block and Brick Manufacturing

This U.S. industry comprises establishments primarily engaged in manufacturing concrete block and brick.

327332 Concrete Pipe Manufacturing

This U.S. industry comprises establishments primarily engaged in manufacturing concrete pipe.

32739 Other Concrete Product Manufacturing[T]
See industry description for 327390.

327390 Other Concrete Product Manufacturing

This industry comprises establishments primarily engaged in manufacturing concrete products (except block, brick, and pipe).

Cross-References.   Establishments primarily engaged in--

- Manufacturing concrete block and brick--are classified in U.S. Industry 327331, Concrete Block and Brick Manufacturing; and
- Manufacturing concrete pipe--are classified in U.S. Industry 327332, Concrete Pipe Manufacturing.

T—Canadian, Mexican, and United States industries are comparable.

3274   Lime and Gypsum Product Manufacturing^T

This industry group comprises establishments primarily engaged in (1) manufacturing lime from calcitic limestone, dolomitic limestone, or other calcareous materials or (2) manufacturing gypsum products.

32741   Lime Manufacturing^T
See industry description for 327410.

327410 Lime Manufacturing

This industry comprises establishments primarily engaged in manufacturing lime from calcitic limestone, dolomitic limestone, or other calcareous materials, such as coral, chalk, and shells. Lime manufacturing establishments may mine, quarry, collect, or purchase the sources of calcium carbonate.

Cross-References.

Establishments primarily engaged in manufacturing dolomite refractories are classified in Industry 327120, Clay Building Material and Refractories Manufacturing.

32742   Gypsum Product Manufacturing^T
See industry description for 327420.

327420 Gypsum Product Manufacturing

This industry comprises establishments primarily engaged in manufacturing gypsum products, such as wallboard, plaster, plasterboard, molding, ornamental moldings, statuary, and architectural plaster work. Gypsum product manufacturing establishments may mine, quarry, or purchase gypsum.

Cross-References.

Establishments primarily engaged in operating gypsum mines or quarries are classified in U.S. Industry 212399, All Other Nonmetallic Mineral Mining.

3279   Other Nonmetallic Mineral Product Manufacturing^T

This industry group comprises establishments manufacturing nonmetallic mineral products (except clay products, refractory products, glass products, cement and concrete products, lime, and gypsum products).

32791   Abrasive Product Manufacturing^T
See industry description for 327910.

327910 Abrasive Product Manufacturing

This industry comprises establishments primarily engaged in manufacturing abrasive grinding wheels of natural or synthetic materials, abrasive-coated products, and other abrasive products.

Illustrative Examples:

Aluminum oxide (fused) abrasives manufacturing
Buffing and polishing wheels, abrasive and
nonabrasive, manufacturing
Diamond dressing wheels manufacturing

Sandpaper manufacturing
Silicon carbide abrasives manufacturing
Whetstones manufacturing

T—Canadian, Mexican, and United States industries are comparable.

Cross-References.   Establishments primarily engaged in--

- Mining and cutting grindstones, pulpstones, and whetstones--are classified in U.S. Industry 212399, All Other Nonmetallic Mineral Mining;
- Manufacturing plastic scouring pads--are classified in U.S. Industry 326199, All Other Plastics Product Manufacturing; and
- Manufacturing metallic scouring pads and steel wool--are classified in U.S. Industry 332999, All Other Miscellaneous Fabricated Metal Product Manufacturing.

32799   All Other Nonmetallic Mineral Product Manufacturing[T]

This industry comprises establishments primarily engaged in manufacturing nonmetallic mineral products (except pottery and plumbing fixtures; clay building materials and refractories; glass and glass products; cement; ready-mix concrete; concrete products; lime; gypsum products; and abrasive products).

Cross-References.   Establishments primarily engaged in--

- Manufacturing pottery, ceramics, and plumbing fixtures--are classified in Industry 32711, Pottery, Ceramics, and Plumbing Fixture Manufacturing;
- Mining or quarrying stone, earth, or other nonmetallic minerals--are classified in Industry Group 2123, Nonmetallic Mineral Mining and Quarrying;
- Buying and selling semi-finished monuments and tombstones with no work other than polishing, lettering, or shaping to custom order--are classified in Sector 42, Wholesale Trade, or Sector 44-45, Retail Trade;
- Manufacturing clay building materials and refractories--are classified in Industry 32712, Clay Building Material and Refractories Manufacturing;
- Manufacturing glass and glass products--are classified in Industry 32721, Glass and Glass Product Manufacturing;
- Manufacturing cement--are classified in Industry 32731, Cement Manufacturing;
- Mixing and delivering ready-mix concrete--are classified in Industry 32732, Ready-Mix Concrete Manufacturing;
- Manufacturing concrete pipe, brick, and block--are classified in Industry 32733, Concrete Pipe, Brick, and Block Manufacturing;
- Manufacturing concrete products (except pipe, brick, and block)--are classified in Industry 32739, Other Concrete Product Manufacturing;
- Manufacturing lime--are classified in Industry 32741, Lime Manufacturing;
- Manufacturing gypsum products--are classified in Industry 32742, Gypsum Product Manufacturing;
- Manufacturing abrasive products--are classified in Industry 32791, Abrasive Product Manufacturing; and
- Manufacturing metallic scouring pads and steel wool--are classified in Industry 33299, All Other Fabricated Metal Product Manufacturing.

327991 Cut Stone and Stone Product Manufacturing

This U.S. industry comprises establishments primarily engaged in cutting, shaping, and finishing granite, marble, limestone, slate, and other stone for building and miscellaneous uses. Stone product manufacturing establishments may mine, quarry, or purchase stone.

Cross-References.   Establishments primarily engaged in--

- Mining or quarrying stone--are classified in Industry Group 2123, Nonmetallic Mineral Mining and Quarrying; and
- Buying and selling semi-finished monuments and tombstones with no work other than polishing, lettering, or shaping to custom order--are classified in Sector 42, Wholesale Trade, or Sector 44-45, Retail Trade.

T—Canadian, Mexican, and United States industries are comparable.

327992 Ground or Treated Mineral and Earth Manufacturing

This U.S. industry comprises establishments primarily engaged in calcining, dead burning, or otherwise processing beyond beneficiation, clays, ceramic and refractory minerals, barite, and miscellaneous nonmetallic minerals.

Cross-References.

Establishments primarily engaged in crushing, grinding, pulverizing, washing, screening, sizing, or otherwise beneficiating mined clays, ceramics and refractory, and other miscellaneous nonmetallic minerals are classified in Industry Group 2123, Nonmetallic Mineral Mining and Quarrying.

327993 Mineral Wool Manufacturing

This U.S. industry comprises establishments primarily engaged in manufacturing mineral wool and mineral wool (i.e., fiberglass) insulation products made of such siliceous materials as rock, slag, and glass or combinations thereof.

Cross-References.

Establishments primarily engaged in manufacturing metallic scouring pads and steel wool are classified in U.S. Industry 332999, All Other Miscellaneous Fabricated Metal Product Manufacturing.

327999 All Other Miscellaneous Nonmetallic Mineral Product Manufacturing

This U.S. industry comprises establishments primarily engaged in manufacturing nonmetallic mineral products (except pottery, ceramics, and plumbing fixtures; clay building materials and refractories; glass and glass products; cement; ready-mix concrete; concrete products; lime; gypsum products; abrasive products; cut stone and stone products; ground and treated minerals and earth; and mineral wool).

Illustrative Examples:

Dry mix concrete manufacturing
Mica products manufacturing
Manmade and engineered proppants (e.g., resin-coated sand, ceramic materials) manufacturing

Stucco and stucco products manufacturing
Synthetic stones, for gem stones and industrial use, manufacturing

Cross-References.   Establishments primarily engaged in--

- Manufacturing pottery, ceramics, and plumbing fixtures--are classified in Industry 327110, Pottery, Ceramics, and Plumbing Fixture Manufacturing;
- Manufacturing clay building materials and refractories--are classified in Industry 327120, Clay Building Material and Refractories Manufacturing;
- Manufacturing glass and glass products--are classified in Industry 32721, Glass and Glass Product Manufacturing;
- Manufacturing cement--are classified in Industry 327310, Cement Manufacturing;
- Mixing and delivering ready-mix concrete--are classified in Industry 327320, Ready-Mix Concrete Manufacturing;
- Manufacturing concrete pipe, brick, and block--are classified in Industry 32733, Concrete Pipe, Brick, and Block Manufacturing;
- Manufacturing concrete products (except pipe, brick, and block)--are classified in Industry 327390, Other Concrete Product Manufacturing;
- Manufacturing lime--are classified in Industry 327410, Lime Manufacturing;
- Manufacturing gypsum products--are classified in Industry 327420, Gypsum Product Manufacturing;
- Manufacturing abrasives and abrasive products--are classified in Industry 327910, Abrasive Product Manufacturing;

T—Canadian, Mexican, and United States industries are comparable.

- Manufacturing cut stone and stone products--are classified in U.S. Industry 327991, Cut Stone and Stone Product Manufacturing;
- Manufacturing ground and treated minerals and earth (i.e., not at the mine site)--are classified in U.S. Industry 327992, Ground or Treated Mineral and Earth Manufacturing; and
- Manufacturing mineral wool and fiberglass insulation products--are classified in U.S. Industry 327993, Mineral Wool Manufacturing.

331 Primary Metal Manufacturing[T]

Industries in the Primary Metal Manufacturing subsector smelt and/or refine ferrous and nonferrous metals from ore, pig or scrap, using electrometallurgical and other process metallurgical techniques. Establishments in this subsector also manufacture metal alloys and superalloys by introducing other chemical elements to pure metals. The output of smelting and refining, usually in ingot form, is used in rolling, drawing, and extruding operations to make sheet, strip, bar, rod, or wire, and in molten form to make castings and other basic metal products.

Primary manufacturing of ferrous and nonferrous metals begins with ore or concentrate as the primary input. Establishments manufacturing primary metals from ore and/or concentrate remain classified in the primary smelting, primary refining, or iron and steel mill industries regardless of the form of their output. Establishments primarily engaged in secondary smelting and/or secondary refining recover ferrous and nonferrous metals from scrap and/or dross. The output of the secondary smelting and/or secondary refining industries is limited to shapes such as ingot or billet that will be further processed. Recovery of metals from scrap often occurs in establishments that are primarily engaged in activities, such as rolling, drawing, extruding, or similar processes.

Excluded from the Primary Metal Manufacturing subsector are establishments primarily engaged in manufacturing ferrous and nonferrous forgings (except ferrous forgings made in steel mills) and stampings. Although forging, stamping, and casting are all methods used to make metal shapes, forging and stamping do not use molten metals and are included in Subsector 332, Fabricated Metal Product Manufacturing. Establishments primarily engaged in operating coke ovens are classified in Industry 32419, Other Petroleum and Coal Products Manufacturing.

3311 Iron and Steel Mills and Ferroalloy Manufacturing[T]

33111 Iron and Steel Mills and Ferroalloy Manufacturing[T]
See industry description for 331110.

331110 Iron and Steel Mills and Ferroalloy Manufacturing

This industry comprises establishments primarily engaged in one or more of the following: (1) direct reduction of iron ore; (2) manufacturing pig iron in molten or solid form; (3) converting pig iron into steel; (4) making steel; (5) making steel and manufacturing shapes (e.g., bar, plate, rod, sheet, strip, wire); (6) making steel and forming pipe and tube; and (7) manufacturing electrometallurgical ferroalloys. Ferroalloys add critical elements, such as silicon and manganese for carbon steel and chromium, vanadium, tungsten, titanium, and molybdenum for low- and high-alloy metals. Ferroalloys include iron-rich alloys and more pure forms of elements added during the steel manufacturing process that alter or improve the characteristics of the metal.

Cross-References.		Establishments primarily engaged in--

- Operating coke ovens--are classified in U.S. Industry 324199, All Other Petroleum and Coal Products Manufacturing;
- Manufacturing nonferrous superalloys, such as cobalt or nickel-based superalloys--are classified in U.S. Industry 331492, Secondary Smelting, Refining, and Alloying of Nonferrous Metal (except Copper and Aluminum);
- Manufacturing concrete reinforcing bar by rolling and drawing steel from purchased steel--are classified in U.S. Industry 331221, Rolled Steel Shape Manufacturing; and
- Manufacturing fabricated structural metal products from concrete reinforcing bars and fabricated bar joists--are classified in U.S. Industry 332312, Fabricated Structural Metal Manufacturing.

T—Canadian, Mexican, and United States industries are comparable.

3312   Steel Product Manufacturing from Purchased Steel[T]

This industry group comprises establishments primarily engaged in manufacturing iron and steel tube and pipe, drawing steel wire, and rolling or drawing shapes from purchased iron or steel.

33121   Iron and Steel Pipe and Tube Manufacturing from Purchased Steel[T]
See industry description for 331210.

331210 Iron and Steel Pipe and Tube Manufacturing from Purchased Steel

This industry comprises establishments primarily engaged in manufacturing welded, riveted, or seamless pipe and tube from purchased iron or steel.

Cross-References.

Establishments primarily engaged in making steel and further processing the steel into steel pipe and tube are classified in Industry 331110, Iron and Steel Mills and Ferroalloy Manufacturing.

33122   Rolling and Drawing of Purchased Steel[T]

This industry comprises establishments primarily engaged in rolling and/or drawing steel shapes, such as plate, sheet, strip, rod, and bar, from purchased steel.

Cross-References.   Establishments primarily engaged in--

- Making steel and rolling and/or drawing steel--are classified in Industry 33111, Iron and Steel Mills and Ferroalloy Manufacturing; and
- Manufacturing wire products from purchased wire--are classified in Industry 33261, Spring and Wire Product Manufacturing.

331221 Rolled Steel Shape Manufacturing

This U.S. industry comprises establishments primarily engaged in rolling or drawing shapes (except wire), such as plate, sheet, strip, rod, and bar, from purchased steel.

Cross-References.   Establishments primarily engaged in--

- Making steel and rolling or drawing steel shapes, or manufacturing concrete reinforcing bars in an iron and steel mill--are classified in Industry 331110, Iron and Steel Mills and Ferroalloy Manufacturing;
- Drawing wire from purchased steel--are classified in U.S. Industry 331222, Steel Wire Drawing; and
- Manufacturing fabricated structural metal products from concrete reinforcing bars and fabricated bar joists--are classified in U.S. Industry 332312, Fabricated Structural Metal Manufacturing.

331222 Steel Wire Drawing

This U.S. industry comprises establishments primarily engaged in drawing wire from purchased steel.

Cross-References.   Establishments primarily engaged in--

- Making steel and drawing steel wire--are classified in Industry 331110, Iron and Steel Mills and Ferroalloy Manufacturing; and
- Manufacturing wire products, such as nails, spikes, and paper clips, from purchased steel wire--are classified in Industry 33261, Spring and Wire Product Manufacturing.

T—Canadian, Mexican, and United States industries are comparable.

3313   Alumina and Aluminum Production and Processing[T]

33131   Alumina and Aluminum Production and Processing[T]

This industry comprises establishments primarily engaged in one or more of the following: (1) refining alumina; (2) making (i.e., the primary production) aluminum from alumina; (3) recovering aluminum from scrap or dross; (4) alloying purchased aluminum; and (5) manufacturing aluminum primary forms (e.g., bar, foil, pipe, plate, rod, sheet, tube, wire).

Cross-References.   Establishments primarily engaged in--

- Manufacturing aluminum oxide abrasives and refractories--are classified in Subsector 327, Nonmetallic Mineral Product Manufacturing;
- Sorting, breaking up, and wholesaling scrap aluminum metal without also smelting or refining--are classified in Industry 42393, Recyclable Material Merchant Wholesalers; and
- Operating facilities where commingled recyclable materials, such as paper, plastics, used beverage cans, and metals, are sorted into distinct categories without also smelting or refining--are classified in Industry 56292, Materials Recovery Facilities.

331313 Alumina Refining and Primary Aluminum Production

This U.S. industry comprises establishments primarily engaged in one or more of the following: (1) refining alumina (i.e., aluminum oxide) generally from bauxite; (2) making aluminum from alumina; and/or (3) making aluminum from alumina and rolling, drawing, extruding, or casting the aluminum they make into primary forms. Establishments in this industry may make primary aluminum or aluminum-based alloys from alumina.

Cross-references.   Establishments primarily engaged in--

- Manufacturing aluminum oxide abrasives and refractories--are classified in Subsector 327, Nonmetallic Mineral Product Manufacturing; and
- Recovering aluminum from scrap or alloying purchased aluminum--are classified in U.S. Industry 331314, Secondary Smelting and Alloying of Aluminum.

331314 Secondary Smelting and Alloying of Aluminum

This U.S. industry comprises establishments primarily engaged in (1) recovering aluminum and aluminum alloys from scrap and/or dross (i.e., secondary smelting) and making billet or ingot (except by rolling) and/or (2) manufacturing alloys, powder, paste, or flake from purchased aluminum.

Cross-References.   Establishments primarily engaged in--

- Refining alumina or making aluminum and/or aluminum alloys from alumina--are classified in U.S. Industry 331313, Alumina Refining and Primary Aluminum Production;
- Manufacturing aluminum sheet, plate, and foil from purchased aluminum or by recovering aluminum from scrap and flat rolling or continuous casting--are classified in U.S. Industry 331315, Aluminum Sheet, Plate, and Foil Manufacturing;
- Manufacturing aluminum extruded products or rolled ingot or billet from purchased aluminum or by recovering aluminum from scrap and extruding, rolling, or drawing--are classified in U.S. Industry 331318, Other Aluminum Rolling, Drawing, and Extruding;
- Sorting, breaking up, and wholesaling scrap metal without also smelting or refining--are classified in Industry 423930, Recyclable Material Merchant Wholesalers; and
- Operating facilities where commingled recyclable materials, such as paper, plastics, used beverage cans, and metals, are sorted into distinct categories without also smelting or refining--are classified in Industry 562920, Materials Recovery Facilities.

T—Canadian, Mexican, and United States industries are comparable.

331315 Aluminum Sheet, Plate, and Foil Manufacturing

This U.S. industry comprises establishments primarily engaged in (1) flat rolling or continuous casting sheet, plate, foil and welded tube from purchased aluminum and/or (2) recovering aluminum from scrap and flat rolling or continuous casting sheet, plate, foil, and welded tube in integrated mills.

Cross-References.

Establishments primarily engaged in making aluminum from alumina and flat rolling or continuous casting aluminum sheet, plate, foil, and welded tube are classified in U.S. Industry 331313, Alumina Refining and Primary Aluminum Production.

331318 Other Aluminum Rolling, Drawing, and Extruding

This U.S. industry comprises establishments primarily engaged in (1) rolling, drawing, or extruding shapes (except flat rolled sheet, plate, foil, and welded tube) from purchased aluminum and/or (2) recovering aluminum from scrap and rolling, drawing, or extruding shapes (except flat rolled sheet, plate, foil, and welded tube) in integrated mills.

Illustrative Examples:

Aluminum bar made by extruding purchased aluminum
Nails, aluminum, made in wire drawing plants
Rod made by extruding purchased aluminum
Wire, bare, made in aluminum wire drawing plants

Structural shapes made by rolling purchased aluminum
Tube made by drawing or extruding purchased aluminum

Cross-References.   Establishments primarily engaged in--

- Flat rolling sheet, plate, foil, and welded tube from either purchased aluminum or by recovering aluminum from scrap and flat rolling or continuous casting--are classified in U.S. Industry 331315, Aluminum Sheet, Plate, and Foil Manufacturing; and
- Making aluminum from alumina and making aluminum shapes--are classified in U.S. Industry 331313, Alumina Refining and Primary Aluminum Production.

3314   Nonferrous Metal (except Aluminum) Production and Processing[T]

This industry group comprises establishments primarily engaged in nonferrous metal (except aluminum) smelting, refining, rolling, drawing, extruding, and alloying.

33141   Nonferrous Metal (except Aluminum) Smelting and Refining[T]
See industry description for 331410.

331410 Nonferrous Metal (except Aluminum) Smelting and Refining

This industry comprises establishments primarily engaged in (1) smelting ores into nonferrous metals and/or (2) the primary refining of nonferrous metals (except aluminum) by electrolytic methods or other processes.

Cross-References.   Establishments primarily engaged in--

- Mining and making copper and other nonferrous concentrates (including gold and silver bullion), by processes, such as solvent extraction or electrowinning--are classified in Industry Group 2122, Metal Ore Mining;
- Recovering copper or copper alloys from scrap or dross and/or alloying, rolling, drawing, and extruding purchased copper--are classified in Industry 331420, Copper Rolling, Drawing, Extruding, and Alloying;

T—Canadian, Mexican, and United States industries are comparable.

- Rolling, drawing, and/or extruding nonferrous metal shapes (except copper and aluminum) from purchased nonferrous metals (except copper and aluminum) or by recovering nonferrous metals (except copper and aluminum) and rolling, drawing, or extruding--are classified in U.S. Industry 331491, Nonferrous Metal (except Copper and Aluminum) Rolling, Drawing, and Extruding;
- Recovering nonferrous metals (except copper and aluminum) from scrap and making primary forms and/or alloying purchased nonferrous metals (except copper and aluminum)--are classified in U.S. Industry 331492, Secondary Smelting, Refining, and Alloying of Nonferrous Metal (except Copper and Aluminum);
- Making aluminum from alumina--are classified in U.S. Industry 331313, Alumina Refining and Primary Aluminum Production;
- Operating facilities where commingled recyclable materials, such as paper, plastics, used beverage cans, and metals, are sorted into distinct categories without also smelting or refining--are classified in Industry 562920, Materials Recovery Facilities; and
- Sorting, breaking up, and wholesaling scrap metal without also smelting or refining--are classified in Industry 423930, Recyclable Material Merchant Wholesalers.

33142   Copper Rolling, Drawing, Extruding, and Alloying[T]
See industry description for 331420.

331420 Copper Rolling, Drawing, Extruding, and Alloying

This industry comprises establishments primarily engaged in one or more of the following: (1) recovering copper or copper alloys from scraps; (2) alloying purchased copper; (3) rolling, drawing, or extruding shapes (e.g., bar, plate, sheet, strip, tube, wire) from purchased copper; and (4) recovering copper or copper alloys from scrap and rolling, drawing, or extruding shapes (e.g., bar, plate, sheet, strip, tube, wire).

Cross-References.   Establishments primarily engaged in--

- Smelting copper ore, primary copper refining, and/or rolling, drawing, or extruding primary copper made in the same establishment--are classified in Industry 331410, Nonferrous Metal (except Aluminum) Smelting and Refining;
- Manufacturing wire products from purchased copper wire--are classified in Industry 33261, Spring and Wire Product Manufacturing;
- Die-casting purchased copper--are classified in U.S. Industry 331523, Nonferrous Metal Die-Casting Foundries;
- Rolling, drawing, or extruding shapes from purchased nonferrous metals (except copper and aluminum) or recovering nonferrous metals (except copper and aluminum) from scrap and rolling, drawing, or extruding--are classified in U.S. Industry 331491, Nonferrous Metal (except Copper and Aluminum) Rolling, Drawing, and Extruding;
- Recovering nonferrous metals (except copper, aluminum) from scrap and making primary forms and/or alloying purchased nonferrous metals (except copper and aluminum)--are classified in U.S. Industry 331492, Secondary Smelting, Refining, and Alloying of Nonferrous Metal (except Copper and Aluminum);
- Insulating purchased copper wire--are classified in U.S. Industry 335929, Other Communication and Energy Wire Manufacturing;
- Operating facilities where commingled recyclable materials, such as paper, plastics, used beverage cans, and metals, are sorted into distinct categories without also smelting or refining--are classified in Industry 562920, Materials Recovery Facilities; and
- Sorting, breaking up, and wholesaling scrap metal without also smelting or refining--are classified in Industry 423930, Recyclable Material Merchant Wholesalers.

33149   Nonferrous Metal (except Copper and Aluminum) Rolling, Drawing, Extruding, and Alloying[T]

This industry comprises establishments primarily engaged in one or more of the following: (1) recovering nonferrous metals (except copper and aluminum) and nonferrous metal alloys from scrap; (2) alloying purchased nonferrous metals (except copper and aluminum); (3) rolling, drawing, and extruding shapes from purchased

---

T—Canadian, Mexican, and United States industries are comparable.

nonferrous metals (except copper and aluminum); and (4) recovering nonferrous metals from scrap (except copper and aluminum) and rolling, drawing, or extruding shapes in integrated facilities.

Cross-References.　　Establishments primarily engaged in--

- Rolling, drawing, and/or extruding aluminum or secondary smelting and alloying of aluminum--are classified in Industry 33131, Alumina and Aluminum Production and Processing;
- Recovering copper and copper alloys from scrap, alloying purchased copper, rolling, drawing, or extruding shapes from purchased copper, and recovering copper or copper alloys from scrap and rolling, drawing, or extruding shapes in integrated mills--are classified in Industry 33142, Copper Rolling, Drawing, Extruding, and Alloying;
- Insulating purchased nonferrous wire--are classified in Industry 33592, Communication and Energy Wire and Cable Manufacturing;
- Making primary nonferrous metals and rolling, drawing, or extruding nonferrous metal shapes--are classified in Industry 33141, Nonferrous Metal (except Aluminum) Smelting and Refining;
- Manufacturing products from purchased wire--are classified in Industry 33261, Spring and Wire Product Manufacturing;
- Sorting, breaking up, and wholesaling scrap metal without also smelting or refining--are classified in Industry 42393, Recyclable Material Merchant Wholesalers; and
- Operating facilities where commingled recyclable materials, such as paper, plastics, used beverage cans, and metals, are sorted into distinct categories without also smelting or refining--are classified in Industry 56292, Materials Recovery Facilities.

331491 Nonferrous Metal (except Copper and Aluminum) Rolling, Drawing, and Extruding

This U.S. industry comprises establishments primarily engaged in (1) rolling, drawing, or extruding shapes (e.g., bar, plate, sheet, strip, tube) from purchased nonferrous metals and/or (2) recovering nonferrous metals from scrap and rolling, drawing, and/or extruding shapes (e.g., bar, plate, sheet, strip, tube) in integrated mills.

Cross-References.　　Establishments primarily engaged in--

- Rolling, drawing, and/or extruding shapes from purchased copper or recovering copper from scrap and rolling, drawing, or extruding shapes--are classified in Industry 331420, Copper Rolling, Drawing, Extruding, and Alloying;
- Recovering nonferrous metals (except copper and aluminum) from scrap and making primary forms and/or alloying purchased nonferrous metals--are classified in U.S. Industry 331492, Secondary Smelting, Refining, and Alloying of Nonferrous Metal (except Copper and Aluminum);
- Rolling, drawing, and/or extruding aluminum--are classified in Industry 33131, Alumina and Aluminum Production and Processing;
- Making primary nonferrous metals and rolling, drawing, or extruding nonferrous metal shapes--are classified in Industry 331410, Nonferrous Metal (except Aluminum) Smelting and Refining; and
- Insulating purchased nonferrous wire--are classified in U.S. Industry 335929, Other Communication and Energy Wire Manufacturing.

331492 Secondary Smelting, Refining, and Alloying of Nonferrous Metal (except Copper and Aluminum)

This U.S. industry comprises establishments primarily engaged in (1) alloying purchased nonferrous metals and/or (2) recovering nonferrous metals from scrap. Establishments in this industry make primary forms (e.g., bar, billet, bloom, cake, ingot, slab, slug, wire) using smelting or refining processes.

Cross-References.　　Establishments primarily engaged in--

- Recovering aluminum and aluminum alloys from scrap and/or alloying purchased aluminum--are classified in U.S. Industry 331314, Secondary Smelting and Alloying of Aluminum;

T--Canadian, Mexican, and United States industries are comparable.

- Sorting, breaking up, and wholesaling scrap metal without also smelting or refining--are classified in Industry 423930, Recyclable Material Merchant Wholesalers;
- Recovering nonferrous metals from scrap and rolling, drawing, or extruding shapes in integrated facilities-- are classified in U.S. Industry 331491, Nonferrous Metal (except Copper and Aluminum) Rolling, Drawing, and Extruding;
- Operating facilities where commingled recyclable materials, such as paper, plastics, used beverage cans, and metals, are sorted into distinct categories without also smelting or refining--are classified in Industry 562920, Materials Recovery Facilities; and
- Recovering copper and copper alloys from scrap and making primary forms, and/or alloying purchased copper--are classified in Industry 331420, Copper Rolling, Drawing, Extruding, and Alloying.

3315   Foundries[T]

This industry group comprises establishments primarily engaged in pouring molten metal into molds or dies to form castings. Establishments making castings and further manufacturing, such as machining or assembling, a specific manufactured product are classified in the industry of the finished product. Foundries may perform operations, such as cleaning and deburring, on the castings they manufacture. More involved processes, such as tapping, threading, milling, or machining to tight tolerances, that transform castings into more finished products are classified elsewhere in the Manufacturing sector based on the product made.

Establishments in this industry group make castings from purchased metals or in integrated secondary smelting and casting facilities. When the production of primary metals is combined with making castings, the establishment is classified in Subsector 331, Primary Metal Manufacturing, with the primary metal made.

33151   Ferrous Metal Foundries[T]

This industry comprises establishments primarily engaged in pouring molten iron and steel into molds of a desired shape to make castings. Establishments in this industry purchase iron and steel made in other establishments.

Cross-References.

Establishments primarily engaged in manufacturing iron or steel castings and further manufacturing them into finished products are classified based on the specific finished product.

331511 Iron Foundries

This U.S. industry comprises establishments primarily engaged in pouring molten pig iron or iron alloys into molds to manufacture castings (e.g., cast iron manhole covers, cast iron pipe, cast iron skillets). Establishments in this industry purchase iron made in other establishments.

Cross-References.

Establishments primarily engaged in manufacturing iron castings and further manufacturing them into finished products are classified based on the specific finished product.

331512 Steel Investment Foundries

This U.S. industry comprises establishments primarily engaged in manufacturing steel investment castings. Investment molds are formed by covering a wax shape with a refractory slurry. After the refractory slurry hardens, the wax is melted, leaving a seamless mold. Investment molds provide highly detailed, consistent castings. Establishments in this industry purchase steel made in other establishments.

Cross-References.   Establishments primarily engaged in--

- Manufacturing steel castings (except steel investment castings)--are classified in U.S. Industry 331513, Steel Foundries (except Investment); and

---

T—Canadian, Mexican, and United States industries are comparable.

- Manufacturing steel investment castings and further manufacturing them into finished products--are classified based on the specific finished product.

331513 Steel Foundries (except Investment)

This U.S. industry comprises establishments primarily engaged in manufacturing steel castings (except steel investment castings). Establishments in this industry purchase steel made in other establishments.

Cross-References.   Establishments primarily engaged in--

- Manufacturing steel investment castings--are classified in U.S. Industry 331512, Steel Investment Foundries; and
- Manufacturing steel castings and further manufacturing them into finished products--are classified based on the specific finished product.

33152 Nonferrous Metal Foundries[T]

This industry comprises establishments primarily engaged in pouring and/or introducing molten nonferrous metal, under high pressure, into metal molds or dies to manufacture castings. Establishments in this industry purchase nonferrous metals made in other establishments.

Cross-References.   Establishments primarily engaged in--

- Manufacturing iron or steel castings--are classified in Industry 33151, Ferrous Metal Foundries; and
- Manufacturing nonferrous metal castings and further manufacturing them into finished products--are classified based on the specific finished product.

331523 Nonferrous Metal Die-Casting Foundries

This U.S. industry comprises establishments primarily engaged in introducing molten nonferrous metal, under high pressure, into molds or dies to make nonferrous metal die-castings. Establishments in this industry purchase nonferrous metals made in other establishments.

Cross-references.   Establishments primarily engaged in--

- Pouring molten aluminum into molds to manufacture aluminum castings--are classified in U.S. Industry 331524, Aluminum Foundries (except Die-Casting);
- Pouring molten nonferrous metal (except aluminum) into molds to manufacture nonferrous (except aluminum) castings--are classified in U.S. Industry 331529, Other Nonferrous Metal Foundries (except Die-Casting); and
- Manufacturing nonferrous die-castings and further manufacturing them into finished products--are classified based on the specific finished product.

331524 Aluminum Foundries (except Die-Casting)

This U.S. industry comprises establishments primarily engaged in pouring molten aluminum into molds to manufacture aluminum castings (except nonferrous die-castings). Establishments in this industry purchase aluminum made in other establishments.

Cross-References.   Establishments primarily engaged in--

- Manufacturing aluminum die-castings--are classified in U.S. Industry 331523, Nonferrous Metal Die-Casting Foundries; and
- Manufacturing aluminum or aluminum alloy castings and further manufacturing them into finished products--are classified based on the specific finished product.

T—Canadian, Mexican, and United States industries are comparable.

331529 Other Nonferrous Metal Foundries (except Die-Casting)

This U.S. industry comprises establishments primarily engaged in pouring molten nonferrous metals (except aluminum) into molds to manufacture nonferrous castings (except nonferrous die-castings and aluminum castings). Establishments in this industry purchase nonferrous metals, such as copper, nickel, lead, and zinc, made in other establishments.

Cross-references.   Establishments primarily engaged in--

- Manufacturing nonferrous die-castings--are classified in U.S. Industry 331523, Nonferrous Metal Die-Casting Foundries;
- Pouring molten aluminum into molds to manufacture aluminum castings--are classified in U.S. Industry 331524, Aluminum Foundries (except Die-Casting); and
- Manufacturing nonferrous castings and further manufacturing them into finished products--are classified based on the specific finished product.

332 Fabricated Metal Product Manufacturing[T]

Industries in the Fabricated Metal Product Manufacturing subsector transform metal into intermediate or end products, other than machinery, computers and electronics, and metal furniture, or treat metals and metal formed products fabricated elsewhere. Important fabricated metal processes are forging, stamping, bending, forming, and machining, used to shape individual pieces of metal; and other processes, such as welding and assembling, used to join separate parts together. Establishments in this subsector may use one of these processes or a combination of these processes.

The NAICS structure for this subsector distinguishes the forging and stamping processes in a single industry. The remaining industries in the subsector group establishments based on similar combinations of processes used to make products.

The manufacturing performed in the Fabricated Metal Product Manufacturing subsector begins with manufactured metal shapes. The establishments in this subsector further fabricate the purchased metal shapes into a product. For instance, the Spring and Wire Product Manufacturing industry starts with wire and fabricates such items.

Within manufacturing there are other establishments that make the same products made by this subsector; only these establishments begin production further back in the production process. These establishments have a more integrated operation. For instance, one establishment may manufacture steel, draw it into wire, and make wire products in the same establishment. Such operations are classified in the Primary Metal Manufacturing subsector.

3321 Forging and Stamping[T]

33211 Forging and Stamping[T]

This industry comprises establishments primarily engaged in one or more of the following: (1) manufacturing forgings from purchased metals; (2) manufacturing metal custom roll forming products; (3) manufacturing metal stamped and spun products (except automotive, cans, coins); and (4) manufacturing powder metallurgy products. Establishments making metal forgings, metal stampings, and metal spun products and further manufacturing (e.g., machining, assembling) a specific manufactured product are classified in the industry of the finished product. Metal forging, metal stamping, and metal spun products establishments may perform surface finishing operations, such as cleaning and deburring, on the products they manufacture.

Cross-References.   Establishments primarily engaged in--

- Manufacturing metal forgings in integrated primary metal establishments--are classified in Subsector 331, Primary Metal Manufacturing;
- Manufacturing automotive stampings--are classified in Industry 33637, Motor Vehicle Metal Stamping;
- Manufacturing and installing roll formed seamless gutters at construction sites--are classified in Industry 23817, Siding Contractors; and
- Stamping coins--are classified in Industry 33991, Jewelry and Silverware Manufacturing.

T—Canadian, Mexican, and United States industries are comparable.

332111 Iron and Steel Forging

This U.S. industry comprises establishments primarily engaged in manufacturing iron and steel forgings from purchased iron and steel by hammering mill shapes. Establishments making iron and steel forgings and further manufacturing (e.g., machining, assembling) a specific manufactured product are classified in the industry of the finished product. Iron and steel forging establishments may perform surface finishing operations, such as cleaning and deburring, on the forgings they manufacture.

Cross-References.   Establishments primarily engaged in--

- Manufacturing iron and steel forgings in integrated iron and steel mills--are classified in Industry 331110, Iron and Steel Mills and Ferroalloy Manufacturing; and
- Manufacturing nonferrous forgings--are classified in U.S. Industry 332112, Nonferrous Forging.

332112 Nonferrous Forging

This U.S. industry comprises establishments primarily engaged in manufacturing nonferrous forgings from purchased nonferrous metals by hammering mill shapes. Establishments making nonferrous forgings and further manufacturing (e.g., machining, assembling) a specific manufactured product are classified in the industry of the finished product. Nonferrous forging establishments may perform surface finishing operations, such as cleaning and deburring, on the forgings they manufacture.

Cross-References.   Establishments primarily engaged in--

- Manufacturing iron and steel forgings--are classified in U.S. Industry 332111, Iron and Steel Forging; and
- Manufacturing nonferrous forgings in integrated primary or secondary nonferrous metal production facilities--are classified in Subsector 331, Primary Metal Manufacturing.

332114 Custom Roll Forming

This U.S. industry comprises establishments primarily engaged in custom roll forming metal products by use of rotary motion of rolls with various contours to bend or shape the products.

Cross-References.

Establishments primarily engaged in manufacturing and installing roll formed seamless gutters at construction sites are classified in Industry 238170, Siding Contractors.

332117 Powder Metallurgy Part Manufacturing

This U.S. industry comprises establishments primarily engaged in manufacturing powder metallurgy products using any of the various powder metallurgy processing techniques, such as pressing and sintering or metal injection molding. Establishments in this industry generally make a wide range of parts on a job or order basis.

332119 Metal Crown, Closure, and Other Metal Stamping (except Automotive)

This U.S. industry comprises establishments primarily engaged in (1) stamping metal crowns and closures, such as bottle caps and home canning lids and rings, and/or (2) manufacturing other unfinished metal stampings and spinning unfinished metal products (except automotive, cans, and coins). Establishments making metal stampings and metal spun products and further manufacturing (e.g., machining, assembling) a specific product are classified in the industry of the finished product. Metal stamping and metal spun products establishments may perform surface finishing operations, such as cleaning and deburring, on the products they manufacture.

T—Canadian, Mexican, and United States industries are comparable.

Cross-References.   Establishments primarily engaged in--

- Manufacturing automotive stampings--are classified in Industry 336370, Motor Vehicle Metal Stamping;
- Manufacturing metal cans--are classified in U.S. Industry 332431, Metal Can Manufacturing; and
- Stamping coins--are classified in Industry 339910, Jewelry and Silverware Manufacturing.

3322   Cutlery and Handtool Manufacturing^T

33221   Cutlery and Handtool Manufacturing^T

This industry comprises establishments primarily engaged in one or more of the following: (1) manufacturing metal kitchen cookware (except by casting (e.g., cast iron skillets) or stamped without further fabrication), utensils, and/or nonprecious and precious plated metal cutlery and flatware; (2) manufacturing saw blades, all types (including those for power sawing machines); and (3) manufacturing nonpowered handtools and edge tools.

Cross-References.   Establishments primarily engaged in--

- Manufacturing precious (except precious plated) metal cutlery and flatware--are classified in Industry 33991, Jewelry and Silverware Manufacturing;
- Manufacturing electric razors and hair clippers for use on humans--are classified in Industry 33521, Small Electrical Appliance Manufacturing;
- Manufacturing power hedge shears and trimmers and electric hair clippers for use on animals--are classified in Industry 33311, Agricultural Implement Manufacturing;
- Manufacturing metal cutting dies, attachments, and accessories for machine tools--are classified in Industry 33351, Metalworking Machinery Manufacturing;
- Manufacturing power-driven handtools--are classified in Industry 33399, All Other General Purpose Machinery Manufacturing; and
- Manufacturing finished cast iron kitchen utensils and cookware (i.e., cast iron skillets) and castings for kitchen utensils and cookware--are classified in Industry Group 3315, Foundries.

332215 Metal Kitchen Cookware, Utensil, Cutlery, and Flatware (except Precious) Manufacturing

This U.S. industry comprises establishments primarily engaged in manufacturing metal kitchen cookware (except by casting (e.g., cast iron skillets) or stamped without further fabrication), utensils, and/or nonprecious and precious plated metal cutlery and flatware.

Cross-References.   Establishments primarily engaged in--

- Manufacturing precious (except precious plated) metal cutlery and flatware--are classified in Industry 339910, Jewelry and Silverware Manufacturing;
- Manufacturing electric razors and hair clippers for use on humans--are classified in Industry 335210, Small Electrical Appliance Manufacturing;
- Manufacturing power hedge shears and trimmers--are classified in U.S. Industry 333112, Lawn and Garden Tractor and Home Lawn and Garden Equipment Manufacturing;
- Manufacturing nonelectric hair clippers for use on animals--are classified in U.S. Industry 332216, Saw Blade and Handtool Manufacturing;
- Manufacturing finished cast iron kitchen utensils and cookware (i.e., cast iron skillets) and castings for kitchen utensils and cookware--are classified in Industry Group 3315, Foundries; and
- Manufacturing stampings for kitchen utensils, pots, and pans--are classified in U.S. Industry 332119, Metal Crown, Closure, and Other Metal Stamping (except Automotive).

332216 Saw Blade and Handtool Manufacturing

This U.S. industry comprises establishments primarily engaged in (1) manufacturing saw blades, all types (including those for power sawing machines) and/or (2) manufacturing nonpowered handtools and edge tools.

T—Canadian, Mexican, and United States industries are comparable.

Cross-References.   Establishments primarily engaged in--

- Manufacturing metal cutting dies, attachments, and accessories for machine tools--are classified in Industry 33351, Metalworking Machinery Manufacturing;
- Manufacturing power-driven handtools--are classified in U.S. Industry 333991, Power-Driven Handtool Manufacturing;
- Manufacturing electric razors and hair clippers for use on humans--are classified in Industry 335210, Small Electrical Appliance Manufacturing;
- Manufacturing electric hair clippers for use on animals--are classified in U.S. Industry 333111, Farm Machinery and Equipment Manufacturing; and
- Manufacturing nonelectric household-type scissors and shears--are classified in U.S. Industry 332215, Metal Kitchen Cookware, Utensil, Cutlery, and Flatware (except Precious) Manufacturing.

3323   Architectural and Structural Metals Manufacturing[T]

This industry group comprises establishments primarily engaged in manufacturing one or more of the following: (1) prefabricated metal buildings, panels and sections; (2) structural metal products; (3) metal plate work products; (4) metal framed windows (i.e., typically using purchased glass) and metal doors; (5) sheet metal work; and (6) ornamental and architectural metal products.

33231   Plate Work and Fabricated Structural Product Manufacturing[T]

This industry comprises establishments primarily engaged in manufacturing one or more of the following: (1) prefabricated metal buildings, panels and sections; (2) structural metal products; and (3) metal plate work products.

Cross-References.   Establishments primarily engaged in--

- Making manufactured homes (i.e., mobile homes) and prefabricated wood buildings--are classified in Industry 32199, All Other Wood Product Manufacturing;
- Constructing buildings, bridges, and other heavy construction projects on site--are classified in Sector 23, Construction;
- Building ships, boats, and barges--are classified in Industry 33661, Ship and Boat Building;
- Manufacturing power boilers and heat exchangers--are classified in Industry 33241, Power Boiler and Heat Exchanger Manufacturing;
- Manufacturing heavy gauge tanks--are classified in Industry 33242, Metal Tank (Heavy Gauge) Manufacturing;
- Manufacturing metal plate cooling towers--are classified in Industry 33341, Ventilation, Heating, Air-Conditioning, and Commercial Refrigeration Equipment Manufacturing; and
- Manufacturing metal windows, doors, and studs--are classified in Industry 33232, Ornamental and Architectural Metal Products Manufacturing.

332311 Prefabricated Metal Building and Component Manufacturing

This U.S. industry comprises establishments primarily engaged in manufacturing prefabricated metal buildings, panels, and sections.

Cross-References.   Establishments primarily engaged in--

- Making manufactured homes (i.e., mobile homes) and prefabricated wood buildings--are classified in Industry 32199, All Other Wood Product Manufacturing;
- Constructing prefabricated buildings on site--are classified in Subsector 236, Construction of Buildings; and
- Manufacturing metal windows and doors--are classified in U.S. Industry 332321, Metal Window and Door Manufacturing.

T—Canadian, Mexican, and United States industries are comparable.

332312 Fabricated Structural Metal Manufacturing

This U.S. industry comprises establishments primarily engaged in fabricating structural metal products, such as assemblies of concrete reinforcing bars and fabricated bar joists.

Cross-References.   Establishments primarily engaged in--

- Manufacturing concrete reinforcing bars in an iron and steel mill--are classified in Industry 331110, Iron and Steel Mills and Ferroalloy Manufacturing;
- Manufacturing metal windows and doors--are classified in U.S. Industry 332321, Metal Window and Door Manufacturing;
- Manufacturing metal studs--are classified in U.S. Industry 332322, Sheet Metal Work Manufacturing;
- Constructing buildings, bridges, and other heavy construction projects on site--are classified in Sector 23, Construction;
- Manufacturing concrete reinforcing bar by rolling and drawing steel from purchased steel--are classified in U.S. Industry 331221, Rolled Steel Shape Manufacturing;
- Building ships, boats, and barges--are classified in Industry 33661, Ship and Boat Building; and
- Prefabricating metal buildings, panels, and sections--are classified in U.S. Industry 332311, Prefabricated Metal Building and Component Manufacturing.

332313 Plate Work Manufacturing

This U.S. industry comprises establishments primarily engaged in manufacturing fabricated metal plate work by cutting, punching, bending, shaping, and welding purchased metal plate.

Cross-References.   Establishments primarily engaged in--

- Manufacturing power boilers and heat exchangers--are classified in Industry 332410, Power Boiler and Heat Exchanger Manufacturing;
- Manufacturing heavy gauge tanks--are classified in Industry 332420, Metal Tank (Heavy Gauge) Manufacturing; and
- Manufacturing metal plate cooling towers--are classified in U.S. Industry 333415, Air-Conditioning and Warm Air Heating Equipment and Commercial and Industrial Refrigeration Equipment Manufacturing.

33232 Ornamental and Architectural Metal Products Manufacturing[T]

This industry comprises establishments primarily engaged in manufacturing one or more of the following: (1) metal framed windows (i.e., typically using purchased glass) and metal doors; (2) sheet metal work; and (3) ornamental and architectural metal products.

Cross-References.   Establishments primarily engaged in--

- Manufacturing metal covered (i.e., clad) wood windows and doors--are classified in Industry 32191, Millwork;
- Manufacturing bins, cans, vats, and light tanks of sheet metal--are classified in Industry 33243, Metal Can, Box, and Other Metal Container (Light Gauge) Manufacturing;
- Manufacturing prefabricated metal buildings, panels, and sections--are classified in Industry 33231, Plate Work and Fabricated Structural Product Manufacturing;
- Fabricating sheet metal work on site--are classified in Subsector 238, Specialty Trade Contractors;
- Manufacturing metal stampings (except automotive, coins) and custom roll forming products--are classified in Industry 33211, Forging and Stamping;
- Manufacturing automotive stampings--are classified in Industry 33637, Motor Vehicle Metal Stamping; and
- Stamping coins--are classified in Industry 33991, Jewelry and Silverware Manufacturing.

T—Canadian, Mexican, and United States industries are comparable.

332321 Metal Window and Door Manufacturing

This U.S. industry comprises establishments primarily engaged in manufacturing metal framed windows (i.e., typically using purchased glass) and metal doors. Examples of products made by these establishments are metal door frames; metal framed window and door screens; and metal molding and trim (except automotive).

Cross-References.   Establishments primarily engaged in--

- Manufacturing wood or metal covered (i.e., clad) wood framed windows and doors--are classified in U.S. Industry 321911, Wood Window and Door Manufacturing; and
- Manufacturing metal automotive molding and trim--are classified in Industry 336370, Motor Vehicle Metal Stamping.

332322 Sheet Metal Work Manufacturing

This U.S. industry comprises establishments primarily engaged in manufacturing sheet metal work (except stampings).

Cross-References.   Establishments primarily engaged in--

- Manufacturing sheet metal bins, vats, and light tanks of sheet metal--are classified in U.S. Industry 332439, Other Metal Container Manufacturing;
- Manufacturing metal cans, lids, and ends--are classified in U.S. Industry 332431, Metal Can Manufacturing;
- Fabricating sheet metal work on site--are classified in Subsector 238, Specialty Trade Contractors;
- Manufacturing metal stampings (except automotive, coins) and custom roll forming products--are classified in Industry 33211, Forging and Stamping;
- Manufacturing automotive stampings--are classified in Industry 336370, Motor Vehicle Metal Stamping; and
- Stamping coins--are classified in Industry 339910, Jewelry and Silverware Manufacturing.

332323 Ornamental and Architectural Metal Work Manufacturing

This U.S. industry comprises establishments primarily engaged in manufacturing ornamental and architectural metal work, such as staircases, metal open steel flooring, fire escapes, railings, and scaffolding.

Cross-References.

Establishments primarily engaged in manufacturing prefabricated metal buildings, panels, and sections are classified in U.S. Industry 332311, Prefabricated Metal Building and Component Manufacturing.

3324   Boiler, Tank, and Shipping Container Manufacturing[T]

This industry group comprises establishments primarily engaged in one of the following: (1) manufacturing power boilers and heat exchangers; (2) cutting, forming, and joining heavy gauge metal to manufacture tanks, vessels, and other containers; or (3) forming light gauge metal containers.

33241   Power Boiler and Heat Exchanger Manufacturing[T]
See industry description for 332410.

332410 Power Boiler and Heat Exchanger Manufacturing

This industry comprises establishments primarily engaged in manufacturing power boilers and heat exchangers. Establishments in this industry may perform installation in addition to manufacturing power boilers and heat exchangers.

T—Canadian, Mexican, and United States industries are comparable.

Cross-References.	Establishments primarily engaged in--

- Manufacturing heavy gauge metal tanks--are classified in Industry 332420, Metal Tank (Heavy Gauge) Manufacturing;
- Manufacturing steam or hot water low pressure heating boilers--are classified in U.S. Industry 333414, Heating Equipment (except Warm Air Furnaces) Manufacturing; and
- Installing power boilers and heat exchangers without manufacturing--are classified in Industry 238220, Plumbing, Heating, and Air-Conditioning Contractors.

### 33242	Metal Tank (Heavy Gauge) Manufacturing[T]
See industry description for 332420.

### 332420	Metal Tank (Heavy Gauge) Manufacturing

This industry comprises establishments primarily engaged in cutting, forming, and joining heavy gauge metal to manufacture tanks, vessels, and other containers.

Cross-References.	Establishments primarily engaged in--

- Manufacturing power boilers--are classified in Industry 332410, Power Boiler and Heat Exchanger Manufacturing;
- Manufacturing light gauge metal containers--are classified in Industry 33243, Metal Can, Box, and Other Metal Container (Light Gauge) Manufacturing; and
- Installing heavy gauge metal tanks without manufacturing--are classified in Industry 238120, Structural Steel and Precast Concrete Contractors.

### 33243	Metal Can, Box, and Other Metal Container (Light Gauge) Manufacturing[T]

This industry comprises establishments primarily engaged in forming light gauge metal containers.

Cross-References.	Establishments primarily engaged in--

- Manufacturing foil containers--are classified in Industry 33299, All Other Fabricated Metal Product Manufacturing;
- Reconditioning barrels and drums--are classified in Industry 81131, Commercial and Industrial Machinery and Equipment (except Automotive and Electronic) Repair and Maintenance; and
- Manufacturing heavy gauge metal containers--are classified in Industry 33242, Metal Tank (Heavy Gauge) Manufacturing.

### 332431	Metal Can Manufacturing

This U.S. industry comprises establishments primarily engaged in manufacturing metal cans, lids, and ends.

Cross-References.	Establishments primarily engaged in--

- Manufacturing foil containers--are classified in U.S. Industry 332999, All Other Miscellaneous Fabricated Metal Product Manufacturing; and
- Manufacturing light gauge metal containers (except cans)--are classified in U.S. Industry 332439, Other Metal Container Manufacturing.

### 332439	Other Metal Container Manufacturing

This U.S. industry comprises establishments primarily engaged in manufacturing metal (light gauge) containers (except cans).

T—Canadian, Mexican, and United States industries are comparable.

Illustrative Examples:

Light gauge metal bins manufacturing	Light gauge metal tool boxes manufacturing
Light gauge metal drums manufacturing	Light gauge metal vats manufacturing
Light gauge metal garbage cans manufacturing	Metal air cargo containers manufacturing
Light gauge metal lunch boxes manufacturing	Metal barrels manufacturing
Light gauge metal mailboxes manufacturing	Vacuum bottles and jugs manufacturing

Cross-References.   Establishments primarily engaged in--

- Manufacturing foil containers--are classified in U.S. Industry 332999, All Other Miscellaneous Fabricated Metal Product Manufacturing;
- Manufacturing metal cans--are classified in U.S. Industry 332431, Metal Can Manufacturing;
- Reconditioning barrels and drums--are classified in Industry 811310, Commercial and Industrial Machinery and Equipment (except Automotive and Electronic) Repair and Maintenance; and
- Manufacturing heavy gauge metal containers--are classified in Industry 332420, Metal Tank (Heavy Gauge) Manufacturing.

3325   Hardware Manufacturing[T]

33251   Hardware Manufacturing[T]
See industry description for 332510.

332510 Hardware Manufacturing

This industry comprises establishments primarily engaged in manufacturing metal hardware, such as metal hinges, metal handles, keys, and locks (except coin-operated, time locks).

Cross-References.   Establishments primarily engaged in--

- Manufacturing bolts, nuts, screws, rivets, washers, hose clamps, and turnbuckles--are classified in U.S. Industry 332722, Bolt, Nut, Screw, Rivet, and Washer Manufacturing;
- Manufacturing nails and spikes from wire drawn elsewhere--are classified in U.S. Industry 332618, Other Fabricated Wire Product Manufacturing;
- Manufacturing metal furniture parts (except hardware)--are classified in U.S. Industry 337215, Showcase, Partition, Shelving, and Locker Manufacturing;
- Drawing wire and manufacturing nails and spikes--are classified in Subsector 331, Primary Metal Manufacturing;
- Manufacturing pole line and transmission hardware--are classified in U.S. Industry 335932, Noncurrent-Carrying Wiring Device Manufacturing;
- Manufacturing coin-operated locking mechanisms--are classified in U.S. Industry 333318, Other Commercial and Service Industry Machinery Manufacturing;
- Manufacturing time locks--are classified in U.S. Industry 334519, Other Measuring and Controlling Device Manufacturing;
- Manufacturing fireplace fixtures and equipment, traps, handcuffs and leg irons, ladder jacks, and other like metal products--are classified in U.S. Industry 332999, All Other Miscellaneous Fabricated Metal Product Manufacturing;
- Manufacturing fire hose nozzles and metal hose couplings (except fluid power)--are classified in U.S. Industry 332919, Other Metal Valve and Pipe Fitting Manufacturing; and
- Manufacturing luggage and utility racks--are classified in Industry 336390, Other Motor Vehicle Parts Manufacturing.

3326   Spring and Wire Product Manufacturing[T]

T--Canadian, Mexican, and United States industries are comparable.

33261 Spring and Wire Product Manufacturing[T]

This industry comprises establishments primarily engaged in (1) manufacturing steel springs by forming, such as cutting, bending, and heat winding, metal rod or strip stock and/or (2) manufacturing wire springs and fabricated wire products from wire drawn elsewhere (except watch and clock springs).

Cross-References.   Establishments primarily engaged in--

- Manufacturing watch and clock springs from purchased wire--are classified in Industry 33451, Navigational, Measuring, Electromedical, and Control Instruments Manufacturing;
- Drawing wire and manufacturing wire products--are classified in Subsector 331, Primary Metal Manufacturing; and
- Manufacturing nonferrous insulated wire from wire drawn elsewhere--are classified in Industry 33592, Communication and Energy Wire and Cable Manufacturing.

332613 Spring Manufacturing

This U.S. industry comprises establishments primarily engaged in manufacturing springs from purchased wire, strip, or rod.

Cross-References.   Establishments primarily engaged in--

- Manufacturing watch and clock springs--are classified in U.S. Industry 334519, Other Measuring and Controlling Device Manufacturing; and
- Producing wire, strip, or rod and further fabricating springs--are classified in Subsector 331, Primary Metal Manufacturing.

332618 Other Fabricated Wire Product Manufacturing

This U.S. industry comprises establishments primarily engaged in manufacturing fabricated wire products (except springs) made from purchased wire.

Illustrative Examples:

Barbed wire made from purchased wire
Chain link fencing and fence gates made from purchased wire
Metal baskets made from purchased wire

Nails, brads, and staples made from purchased wire
Noninsulated wire cable made from purchased wire
Paper clips made from purchased wire
Woven wire cloth made from purchased wire

Cross-References.   Establishments primarily engaged in--

- Drawing wire and manufacturing wire products--are classified in Subsector 331, Primary Metal Manufacturing;
- Manufacturing springs from purchased wire, strip, or rod--are classified in U.S. Industry 332613, Spring Manufacturing; and
- Insulating nonferrous wire from wire drawn elsewhere--are classified in U.S. Industry 335929, Other Communication and Energy Wire Manufacturing.

3327 Machine Shops; Turned Product; and Screw, Nut, and Bolt Manufacturing[T]

This industry group comprises establishments primarily engaged in one of the following: (1) operating machine shops primarily engaged in machining metal and plastic parts and parts of other composite materials on a job or order basis; (2) machining precision turned products; or (3) manufacturing metal bolts, nuts, screws, rivets, and other industrial fasteners.

T—Canadian, Mexican, and United States industries are comparable.

33271   Machine Shops[T]
See industry description for 332710.

332710   Machine Shops

This industry comprises establishments known as machine shops primarily engaged in machining metal and plastic parts and parts of other composite materials on a job or order basis. Generally machine shop jobs are low volume using machine tools, such as lathes (including computer numerically controlled); automatic screw machines; and machines for boring, grinding, milling, and additive manufacturing.

Cross-References.   Establishments primarily engaged in--

- Repairing industrial machinery and equipment--are classified in Industry 811310, Commercial and Industrial Machinery and Equipment (except Automotive and Electronic) Repair and Maintenance; and
- Manufacturing parts (except on a job or order basis) for machinery and equipment--are generally classified in the same manufacturing industry that makes complete machinery and equipment.

33272   Turned Product and Screw, Nut, and Bolt Manufacturing[T]

This industry comprises establishments primarily engaged in (1) machining precision turned products or (2) manufacturing metal bolts, nuts, screws, rivets, and other industrial fasteners. Included in this industry are establishments primarily engaged in manufacturing parts for machinery and equipment on a custom basis.

Cross-References.

Establishments primarily engaged in manufacturing plastics fasteners are classified in Industry 32619, Other Plastics Product Manufacturing.

332721   Precision Turned Product Manufacturing

This U.S. industry comprises establishments known as precision turned manufacturers primarily engaged in machining precision products of all materials on a job or order basis. Generally precision turned product jobs are large volume using machines, such as automatic screw machines, rotary transfer machines, computer numerically controlled (CNC) lathes, or turning centers.

Cross-References.

Establishments primarily engaged in manufacturing metal bolts, nuts, screws, rivets, washers, and other industrial fasteners using machines, such as headers, threaders, and nut forming machines, are classified in U.S. Industry 332722, Bolt, Nut, Screw, Rivet, and Washer Manufacturing.

332722   Bolt, Nut, Screw, Rivet, and Washer Manufacturing

This U.S. industry comprises establishments primarily engaged in manufacturing metal bolts, nuts, screws, rivets, washers, and other industrial fasteners using machines, such as headers, threaders, and nut forming machines.

Cross-References.   Establishments primarily engaged in--

- Manufacturing precision turned products--are classified in U.S. Industry 332721, Precision Turned Product Manufacturing; and
- Manufacturing plastics fasteners--are classified in U.S. Industry 326199, All Other Plastics Product Manufacturing.

T—Canadian, Mexican, and United States industries are comparable.

3328   Coating, Engraving, Heat Treating, and Allied Activities[T]

33281   Coating, Engraving, Heat Treating, and Allied Activities[T]

This industry comprises establishments primarily engaged in one or more of the following: (1) heat treating metals and metal products; (2) enameling, lacquering, and varnishing metals and metal products; (3) hot dip galvanizing metals and metal products; (4) engraving, chasing, or etching metals and metal products (except jewelry; personal goods carried on or about the person, such as compacts and cigarette cases; precious metal products (except precious plated flatware and other plated ware); and printing plates); (5) powder coating metals and metal products; (6) electroplating, plating, anodizing, coloring, and finishing metals and metal products; and (7) providing other metal surfacing services for the trade. Establishments in this industry coat, engrave, and heat treat metals and metal formed products fabricated elsewhere.

Cross-References.   Establishments primarily engaged in--

- Engraving, chasing, or etching jewelry, metal personal goods, or precious metal products (except precious plated flatware and other plated ware)--are classified in Industry 33991, Jewelry and Silverware Manufacturing;
- Engraving, chasing, or etching printing plates--are classified in Industry 32312, Support Activities for Printing; and
- Both fabricating and coating, engraving, and heat treating metals and metal products--are classified in the Manufacturing sector according to the product made.

332811 Metal Heat Treating

This U.S. industry comprises establishments primarily engaged in heat treating, such as annealing, tempering, and brazing, and cryogenically treating metals and metal products for the trade.

Cross-References.

Establishments primarily engaged in both fabricating and heat treating metal products are classified in the Manufacturing sector according to the product made.

332812 Metal Coating, Engraving (except Jewelry and Silverware), and Allied Services to Manufacturers

This U.S. industry comprises establishments primarily engaged in one or more of the following: (1) enameling, lacquering, and varnishing metals and metal products; (2) hot dip galvanizing metals and metal products; (3) engraving, chasing, or etching metals and metal products (except jewelry; personal goods carried on or about the person, such as compacts and cigarette cases; precious metal products (except precious plated flatware and other plated ware); and printing plates); (4) powder coating metals and metal products; and (5) providing other metal surfacing services for the trade. Included in this industry are establishments that perform these processes on other materials, such as plastics, in addition to metals.

Cross-References.   Establishments primarily engaged in--

- Both fabricating and coating and engraving products--are classified in the Manufacturing sector according to the product made;
- Engraving, chasing, or etching jewelry, metal personal goods, or precious metal products (except precious plated flatware and other plated ware)--are classified in Industry 339910, Jewelry and Silverware Manufacturing; and
- Engraving, chasing, or etching printing plates--are classified in Industry 323120, Support Activities for Printing.

T—Canadian, Mexican, and United States industries are comparable.

332813 Electroplating, Plating, Polishing, Anodizing, and Coloring

This U.S. industry comprises establishments primarily engaged in electroplating, plating, anodizing, coloring, buffing, polishing, cleaning, and sandblasting metals and metal products for the trade. Included in this industry are establishments that perform these processes on other materials, such as plastics, in addition to metals.

Cross-References.

Establishments primarily engaged in both fabricating and electroplating, plating, polishing, anodizing, and coloring products are classified in the Manufacturing sector according to the product made.

3329   Other Fabricated Metal Product Manufacturing[T]

This industry group comprises establishments primarily engaged in manufacturing fabricated metal products (except forgings and stampings, cutlery and handtools, architectural and structural metals, boilers, tanks, shipping containers, hardware, spring and wire products, machine shop products, turned products, screws, and nuts and bolts).

33291   Metal Valve Manufacturing[T]

This industry comprises establishments primarily engaged in manufacturing one or more of the following metal valves: (1) industrial valves; (2) fluid power valves and hose fittings; (3) plumbing fixture fittings and trim; and (4) other metal valves and pipe fittings.

Cross-References.   Establishments primarily engaged in--

- Manufacturing fluid power cylinders and pumps--are classified in Industry 33399, All Other General Purpose Machinery Manufacturing;
- Manufacturing intake and exhaust valves for internal combustion engines--are classified in Industry 33631, Motor Vehicle Gasoline Engine and Engine Parts Manufacturing;
- Manufacturing metal shower rods and metal couplings from purchased metal pipe--are classified in Industry 33299, All Other Fabricated Metal Product Manufacturing;
- Manufacturing plastics aerosol spray nozzles--are classified in Industry 32619, Other Plastics Product Manufacturing;
- Casting iron pipe fittings and couplings without machining--are classified in Industry 33151, Ferrous Metal Foundries; and
- Manufacturing plastics pipe fittings and couplings--are classified in Industry 32612, Plastics Pipe, Pipe Fitting, and Unlaminated Profile Shape Manufacturing.

332911 Industrial Valve Manufacturing

This U.S. industry comprises establishments primarily engaged in manufacturing industrial valves and valves for water works and municipal water systems.

Illustrative Examples:

Complete fire hydrants manufacturing
Industrial-type ball valves manufacturing
Industrial-type butterfly valves manufacturing
Industrial-type check valves manufacturing
Industrial-type gate valves manufacturing
Industrial-type globe valves manufacturing

Industrial-type plug valves manufacturing
Industrial-type solenoid valves (except fluid power) manufacturing
Industrial-type steam traps manufacturing
Valves for nuclear applications manufacturing

T—Canadian, Mexican, and United States industries are comparable.

Cross-References.   Establishments primarily engaged in--

- Manufacturing fluid power valves--are classified in U.S. Industry 332912, Fluid Power Valve and Hose Fitting Manufacturing; and
- Manufacturing plumbing and heating inline valves--are classified in U.S. Industry 332919, Other Metal Valve and Pipe Fitting Manufacturing.

332912 Fluid Power Valve and Hose Fitting Manufacturing

This U.S. industry comprises establishments primarily engaged in manufacturing fluid power valves and hose fittings.

Illustrative Examples:

Fluid power aircraft subassemblies manufacturing
Hose assemblies for fluid power systems manufacturing

Hydraulic and pneumatic hose and tube fittings manufacturing
Hydraulic and pneumatic valves manufacturing

Cross-References.   Establishments primarily engaged in--

- Manufacturing fluid power cylinders--are classified in U.S. Industry 333995, Fluid Power Cylinder and Actuator Manufacturing;
- Manufacturing fluid power pumps--are classified in U.S. Industry 333996, Fluid Power Pump and Motor Manufacturing;
- Manufacturing intake and exhaust valves for internal combustion engines--are classified in Industry 336310, Motor Vehicle Gasoline Engine and Engine Parts Manufacturing;
- Manufacturing industrial-type valves--are classified in U.S. Industry 332911, Industrial Valve Manufacturing; and
- Manufacturing plumbing and heating inline valves--are classified in U.S. Industry 332919, Other Metal Valve and Pipe Fitting Manufacturing.

332913 Plumbing Fixture Fitting and Trim Manufacturing

This U.S. industry comprises establishments primarily engaged in manufacturing metal and plastics plumbing fixture fittings and trim, such as faucets, flush valves, and shower heads.

Cross-References.   Establishments primarily engaged in--

- Manufacturing metal shower rods--are classified in U.S. Industry 332999, All Other Miscellaneous Fabricated Metal Product Manufacturing; and
- Manufacturing fire hose nozzles, lawn hose nozzles, water traps, metal hose couplings (except fluid power), and plumbing and heating inline valves--are classified in U.S. Industry 332919, Other Metal Valve and Pipe Fitting Manufacturing.

332919 Other Metal Valve and Pipe Fitting Manufacturing

This U.S. industry comprises establishments primarily engaged in manufacturing metal valves (except industrial valves, fluid power valves, fluid power hose fittings, and plumbing fixture fittings and trim).

Illustrative Examples:

Aerosol valves manufacturing
Firefighting nozzles manufacturing
Lawn hose nozzles manufacturing

Lawn sprinklers manufacturing
Metal hose couplings (except fluid power) manufacturing

T—Canadian, Mexican, and United States industries are comparable.

Metal pipe flanges and flange unions manufacturing
Water traps manufacturing

Plumbing and heating inline valves (e.g., check, cutoff, stop) manufacturing

Cross-References.   Establishments primarily engaged in--

- Manufacturing fluid power valves and hose fittings--are classified in U.S. Industry 332912, Fluid Power Valve and Hose Fitting Manufacturing;
- Manufacturing industrial valves--are classified in U.S. Industry 332911, Industrial Valve Manufacturing;
- Manufacturing plumbing fixture fittings and trim--are classified in U.S. Industry 332913, Plumbing Fixture Fitting and Trim Manufacturing;
- Manufacturing plastics aerosol spray nozzles--are classified in U.S. Industry 326199, All Other Plastics Product Manufacturing;
- Casting iron pipe fittings and couplings without machining--are classified in U.S. Industry 331511, Iron Foundries;
- Manufacturing metal couplings from purchased metal pipe--are classified in U.S. Industry 332996, Fabricated Pipe and Pipe Fitting Manufacturing; and
- Manufacturing plastics pipe fittings and couplings--are classified in U.S. Industry 326122, Plastics Pipe and Pipe Fitting Manufacturing.

33299   All Other Fabricated Metal Product Manufacturing[T]

This industry comprises establishments primarily engaged in manufacturing fabricated metal products (except forgings and stampings, cutlery and handtools, architectural and structural metal products, boilers, tanks, shipping containers, hardware, spring and wire products, machine shop products, turned products, screws, nuts and bolts, and metal valves).

Illustrative Examples:

Ammunition manufacturing
Ball and roller bearing manufacturing
Enameled iron and metal sanitary ware manufacturing
Fabricated pipe and pipe fittings made from purchased metal pipe

Foil containers (except bags) manufacturing
Industrial pattern manufacturing
Metal safes manufacturing
Portable metal ladders manufacturing
Small arms and other ordnance manufacturing
Steel wool manufacturing

Cross-References.   Establishments primarily engaged in--

- Manufacturing forgings, stampings, and powder metallurgy parts--are classified in Industry 33211, Forging and Stamping;
- Manufacturing cutlery and handtools--are classified in Industry 33221, Cutlery and Handtool Manufacturing;
- Manufacturing architectural and structural metals--are classified in Industry Group 3323, Architectural and Structural Metals Manufacturing;
- Manufacturing boilers, tanks, and shipping containers--are classified in Industry Group 3324, Boiler, Tank, and Shipping Container Manufacturing;
- Manufacturing hardware and safe and vault locks--are classified in Industry 33251, Hardware Manufacturing;
- Manufacturing spring and wire products--are classified in Industry 33261, Spring and Wire Product Manufacturing;
- Manufacturing machine shop products, turned products, screws, and nuts and bolts--are classified in Industry Group 3327, Machine Shops; Turned Product; and Screw, Nut, and Bolt Manufacturing;
- Coating, engraving, heat treating, and allied activities--are classified in Industry 33281, Coating, Engraving, Heat Treating, and Allied Activities;
- Manufacturing plain bearings--are classified in Industry 33361, Engine, Turbine, and Power Transmission Equipment Manufacturing;

T—Canadian, Mexican, and United States industries are comparable.

- Manufacturing military tanks--are classified in Industry 33699, Other Transportation Equipment Manufacturing;
- Manufacturing guided missiles--are classified in Industry 33641, Aerospace Product and Parts Manufacturing;
- Manufacturing cast iron pipe and fittings--are classified in Industry 33151, Ferrous Metal Foundries;
- Manufacturing pipe system fittings (except cast iron couplings and couplings made from purchased pipe) and metal aerosol spray nozzles--are classified in Industry 33291, Metal Valve Manufacturing;
- Manufacturing welded and seamless steel pipes from purchased steel--are classified in Industry 33121, Iron and Steel Pipe and Tube Manufacturing from Purchased Steel;
- Manufacturing plastics plumbing fixtures and plastics portable chemical toilets--are classified in Industry 32619, Other Plastics Product Manufacturing;
- Manufacturing vitreous and semivitreous pottery sanitary ware--are classified in Industry 32711, Pottery, Ceramics, and Plumbing Fixture Manufacturing;
- Manufacturing blasting caps, detonating caps, and safety fuses--are classified in Industry 32592, Explosives Manufacturing;
- Manufacturing fireworks--are classified in Industry 32599, All Other Chemical Product and Preparation Manufacturing;
- Manufacturing metal furniture frames--are classified in Industry 33721, Office Furniture (including Fixtures) Manufacturing;
- Manufacturing metal mechanically refrigerated drinking fountains--are classified in Industry 33341, Ventilation, Heating, Air-Conditioning, and Commercial Refrigeration Equipment Manufacturing;
- Manufacturing metal foil bags--are classified in Industry 32222, Paper Bag and Coated and Treated Paper Manufacturing;
- Manufacturing aluminum foil--are classified in Industry 33131, Alumina and Aluminum Production and Processing;
- Manufacturing metal foil (except aluminum)--are classified in Industry Group 3314, Nonferrous Metal (except Aluminum) Production and Processing; and
- Manufacturing metal burial vaults--are classified in Industry 33999, All Other Miscellaneous Manufacturing.

332991 Ball and Roller Bearing Manufacturing

This U.S. industry comprises establishments primarily engaged in manufacturing ball and roller bearings of all materials.

Cross-References.

Establishments primarily engaged in manufacturing plain bearings are classified in U.S. Industry 333613, Mechanical Power Transmission Equipment Manufacturing.

332992 Small Arms Ammunition Manufacturing

This U.S. industry comprises establishments primarily engaged in manufacturing small arms ammunition.

Cross-References.   Establishments primarily engaged in--

- Manufacturing ammunition (except small arms)--are classified in U.S. Industry 332993, Ammunition (except Small Arms) Manufacturing;
- Manufacturing blasting and detonating caps and safety fuses--are classified in Industry 325920, Explosives Manufacturing; and
- Manufacturing fireworks--are classified in U.S. Industry 325998, All Other Miscellaneous Chemical Product and Preparation Manufacturing.

T—Canadian, Mexican, and United States industries are comparable.

332993 Ammunition (except Small Arms) Manufacturing

This U.S. industry comprises establishments primarily engaged in manufacturing ammunition (except small arms). Examples of products made by these establishments are bombs, depth charges, rockets (except guided missiles), grenades, mines, and torpedoes.

Cross-References.   Establishments primarily engaged in--

- Manufacturing small arms ammunition--are classified in U.S. Industry 332992, Small Arms Ammunition Manufacturing;
- Manufacturing blasting and detonating caps and safety fuses--are classified in Industry 325920, Explosives Manufacturing;
- Manufacturing fireworks--are classified in U.S. Industry 325998, All Other Miscellaneous Chemical Product and Preparation Manufacturing; and
- Manufacturing guided missiles--are classified in U.S. Industry 336414, Guided Missile and Space Vehicle Manufacturing.

332994 Small Arms, Ordnance, and Ordnance Accessories Manufacturing

This U.S. industry comprises establishments primarily engaged in manufacturing small arms, other ordnance, and/or ordnance accessories.

Cross-References.   Establishments primarily engaged in--

- Manufacturing military tanks--are classified in U.S. Industry 336992, Military Armored Vehicle, Tank, and Tank Component Manufacturing; and
- Manufacturing guided missiles--are classified in U.S. Industry 336414, Guided Missile and Space Vehicle Manufacturing.

332996 Fabricated Pipe and Pipe Fitting Manufacturing

This U.S. industry comprises establishments primarily engaged in fabricating, such as cutting, threading, and bending, metal pipes and pipe fittings made from purchased metal pipe.

Cross-References.   Establishments primarily engaged in--

- Manufacturing cast iron pipe and fittings--are classified in U.S. Industry 331511, Iron Foundries;
- Manufacturing pipe system fittings (except cast iron couplings and couplings made from purchased pipe)-- are classified in U.S. Industry 332919, Other Metal Valve and Pipe Fitting Manufacturing; and
- Manufacturing welded and seamless steel pipes from purchased steel--are classified in Industry 331210, Iron and Steel Pipe and Tube Manufacturing from Purchased Steel.

332999 All Other Miscellaneous Fabricated Metal Product Manufacturing

This U.S. industry comprises establishments primarily engaged in manufacturing fabricated metal products (except forgings and stampings, cutlery and handtools, architectural and structural metals, boilers, tanks, shipping containers, hardware, spring and wire products, machine shop products, turned products, screws, nuts and bolts, metal valves, ball and roller bearings, ammunition, small arms and other ordnances and accessories, and fabricated pipes and pipe fittings).

Illustrative Examples:

Foil containers (except bags) manufacturing	Metal ironing boards manufacturing
Industrial pattern manufacturing	Metal pallets manufacturing
Metal hair curlers manufacturing	Metal pipe hangers and supports manufacturing

---

T—Canadian, Mexican, and United States industries are comparable.

Metal safes manufacturing
Metal vaults (except burial) manufacturing
Permanent metallic magnets manufacturing
Portable metal ladders manufacturing

Sanitary ware (e.g., bathtubs, lavatories, sinks), metal and enameled metal, manufacturing
Steel wool manufacturing

Cross-References.　　Establishments primarily engaged in--

- Manufacturing forgings and stampings--are classified in Industry 33211, Forging and Stamping;
- Manufacturing cutlery and handtools--are classified in Industry 33221, Cutlery and Handtool Manufacturing;
- Manufacturing architectural and structural metals--are classified in Industry Group 3323, Architectural and Structural Metals Manufacturing;
- Manufacturing boilers, tanks, and shipping containers--are classified in Industry Group 3324, Boiler, Tank, and Shipping Container Manufacturing;
- Manufacturing hardware and safe and vault locks--are classified in Industry 332510, Hardware Manufacturing;
- Manufacturing spring and wire products--are classified in Industry 33261, Spring and Wire Product Manufacturing;
- Manufacturing machine shop products, turned products, screws, and nuts and bolts--are classified in Industry Group 3327, Machine Shops; Turned Product; and Screw, Nut, and Bolt Manufacturing;
- Coating, engraving, heat treating, and allied activities--are classified in Industry 33281, Coating, Engraving, Heat Treating, and Allied Activities;
- Manufacturing ball and roller bearings--are classified in U.S. Industry 332991, Ball and Roller Bearing Manufacturing;
- Manufacturing small arms ammunition--are classified in U.S. Industry 332992, Small Arms Ammunition Manufacturing;
- Manufacturing ammunition (except small arms)--are classified in U.S. Industry 332993, Ammunition (except Small Arms) Manufacturing;
- Manufacturing small firearms that are carried and fired by the individual and/or other ordnance and accessories--are classified in U.S. Industry 332994, Small Arms, Ordnance, and Ordnance Accessories Manufacturing;
- Manufacturing metal pipes and pipe fittings from metal pipe produced elsewhere--are classified in U.S. Industry 332996, Fabricated Pipe and Pipe Fitting Manufacturing;
- Manufacturing cast iron pipe and fittings--are classified in U.S. Industry 331511, Iron Foundries;
- Manufacturing welded and seamless steel pipes from purchased steel--are classified in Industry 331210, Iron and Steel Pipe and Tube Manufacturing from Purchased Steel;
- Manufacturing metal furniture frames--are classified in U.S. Industry 337215, Showcase, Partition, Shelving, and Locker Manufacturing;
- Manufacturing powder metallurgy parts--are classified in U.S. Industry 332117, Powder Metallurgy Part Manufacturing;
- Manufacturing metal boxes--are classified in U.S. Industry 332439, Other Metal Container Manufacturing;
- Manufacturing metal nozzles, hose couplings, and aerosol valves--are classified in U.S. Industry 332919, Other Metal Valve and Pipe Fitting Manufacturing;
- Manufacturing metal foil bags--are classified in Industry 322220, Paper Bag and Coated and Treated Paper Manufacturing;
- Manufacturing aluminum foil--are classified in Industry 33131, Alumina and Aluminum Production and Processing;
- Manufacturing metal foil (except aluminum)--are classified in Industry Group 3314, Nonferrous Metal (except Aluminum) Production and Processing;
- Manufacturing metal burial vaults--are classified in U.S. Industry 339995, Burial Casket Manufacturing;
- Manufacturing plastics plumbing fixtures--are classified in U.S. Industry 326191, Plastics Plumbing Fixture Manufacturing;
- Manufacturing vitreous and semivitreous pottery sanitary ware--are classified in Industry 327110, Pottery, Ceramics, and Plumbing Fixture Manufacturing;

T—Canadian, Mexican, and United States industries are comparable.

- Manufacturing plastics portable chemical toilets--are classified in U.S. Industry 326199, All Other Plastics Product Manufacturing; and
- Manufacturing metal mechanically refrigerated drinking fountains--are classified in U.S. Industry 333415, Air-Conditioning and Warm Air Heating Equipment and Commercial and Industrial Refrigeration Equipment Manufacturing.

333 Machinery Manufacturing[T]

Industries in the Machinery Manufacturing subsector create end products that apply mechanical force, for example, the application of gears and levers, to perform work. Some important processes for the manufacture of machinery are forging, stamping, bending, forming, and machining that are used to shape individual pieces of metal. Processes, such as welding and assembling are used to join separate parts together. Although these processes are similar to those used in metal fabricating establishments, machinery manufacturing is different because it typically employs multiple metal forming processes in manufacturing the various parts of the machine. Moreover, complex assembly operations are an inherent part of the production process.

In general, design considerations are very important in machinery production. Establishments specialize in making machinery designed for particular applications. Thus, design is considered to be part of the production process for the purpose of implementing NAICS. The NAICS structure reflects this by defining industries and industry groups that make machinery for different applications. A broad distinction exists between machinery that is generally used in a variety of industrial applications (i.e., general purpose machinery) and machinery that is designed to be used in a particular industry (i.e., special purpose machinery). Three industry groups consist of special purpose machinery-- Agricultural, Construction, and Mining Machinery Manufacturing; Industrial Machinery Manufacturing; and Commercial and Service Industry Machinery Manufacturing. The other industry groups make general purpose machinery: Ventilation, Heating, Air-Conditioning, and Commercial Refrigeration Equipment Manufacturing; Metalworking Machinery Manufacturing; Engine, Turbine, and Power Transmission Equipment Manufacturing; and Other General Purpose Machinery Manufacturing.

3331 Agriculture, Construction, and Mining Machinery Manufacturing[T]

This industry group comprises establishments primarily engaged in manufacturing one or more of the following: (1) farm machinery and equipment, power mowing equipment, and other powered home lawn and garden equipment; (2) construction machinery, surface mining machinery, and logging equipment; and (3) oil and gas field and underground mining machinery and equipment.

33311 Agricultural Implement Manufacturing[T]

This industry comprises establishments primarily engaged in manufacturing farm machinery and equipment, powered mowing equipment, and other powered home lawn and garden equipment.

Illustrative Examples:

Combines (i.e., harvester-threshers) manufacturing
Cotton ginning machinery manufacturing
Fertilizing machinery, farm-type, manufacturing
Haying machines manufacturing
Milking machines manufacturing
Planting machines, farm-type, manufacturing
Plows, farm-type, manufacturing

Poultry brooders, feeders, and waterers manufacturing
Powered lawnmowers manufacturing
Snowblowers and throwers, residential-type, manufacturing
Tractors and attachments, lawn and garden-type and farm-type, manufacturing

Cross-References. Establishments primarily engaged in--

- Manufacturing agricultural handtools and nonpowered lawnmowers--are classified in Industry 33221, Cutlery and Handtool Manufacturing;
- Manufacturing farm conveyors--are classified in Industry 33392, Material Handling Equipment Manufacturing; and

T—Canadian, Mexican, and United States industries are comparable.

- Manufacturing forestry machinery and equipment, such as brush, limb, and log chippers; log splitters; and construction equipment--are classified in Industry 33312, Construction Machinery Manufacturing.

333111 Farm Machinery and Equipment Manufacturing

This U.S. industry comprises establishments primarily engaged in manufacturing agricultural and farm machinery and equipment, and other turf and grounds care equipment, including planting, harvesting, and grass mowing equipment (except lawn and garden-type).

Illustrative Examples:

Combines (i.e., harvester-threshers) manufacturing
Cotton ginning machinery manufacturing
Feed processing equipment, farm-type, manufacturing
Fertilizing machinery, farm-type, manufacturing
Grass mowing equipment (except lawn and garden) manufacturing

Haying machines manufacturing
Milking machines manufacturing
Planting machines, farm-type, manufacturing
Plows, farm-type, manufacturing
Poultry brooders, feeders, and waterers manufacturing
Tractors and attachments, farm-type, manufacturing

Cross-References.   Establishments primarily engaged in--

- Manufacturing farm conveyors--are classified in U.S. Industry 333922, Conveyor and Conveying Equipment Manufacturing;
- Manufacturing tractors and lawnmowers for home lawn and garden care--are classified in U.S. Industry 333112, Lawn and Garden Tractor and Home Lawn and Garden Equipment Manufacturing; and
- Manufacturing construction-type tractors--are classified in Industry 333120, Construction Machinery Manufacturing.

333112 Lawn and Garden Tractor and Home Lawn and Garden Equipment Manufacturing

This U.S. industry comprises establishments primarily engaged in manufacturing powered lawnmowers, lawn and garden tractors, and other home lawn and garden equipment, such as tillers, shredders, yard vacuums, and leaf blowers.

Cross-References.   Establishments primarily engaged in--

- Manufacturing commercial mowing and other turf and grounds care equipment--are classified in U.S. Industry 333111, Farm Machinery and Equipment Manufacturing; and
- Manufacturing nonpowered lawn and garden shears, edgers, pruners, and lawnmowers--are classified in U.S. Industry 332216, Saw Blade and Handtool Manufacturing.

33312 Construction Machinery Manufacturing[T]
See industry description for 333120.

333120 Construction Machinery Manufacturing

This industry comprises establishments primarily engaged in manufacturing construction machinery, surface mining machinery, and logging equipment.

Illustrative Examples:

Backhoes manufacturing
Bulldozers manufacturing
Construction and surface mining-type rock drill bits manufacturing

Construction-type tractors and attachments manufacturing
Off-highway trucks manufacturing
Pile-driving equipment manufacturing

T—Canadian, Mexican, and United States industries are comparable.

Portable crushing, pulverizing, and screening
machinery manufacturing
Powered post hole diggers manufacturing

Road graders manufacturing
Surface mining machinery (except drilling)
manufacturing

Cross-References.   Establishments primarily engaged in--

- Manufacturing drilling and underground mining machinery and equipment--are classified in Industry 33313, Mining and Oil and Gas Field Machinery Manufacturing;
- Manufacturing industrial plant overhead traveling cranes and hoists, truck-type cranes and hoists, winches, aerial work platforms, and automotive wrecker hoists--are classified in Industry 33392, Material Handling Equipment Manufacturing; and
- Manufacturing rail layers, ballast distributors and other railroad track-laying equipment--are classified in Industry 336510, Railroad Rolling Stock Manufacturing.

33313   Mining and Oil and Gas Field Machinery Manufacturing[T]

This industry comprises establishments primarily engaged in manufacturing oil and gas field and underground mining machinery and equipment.

Illustrative Examples:

Coal breakers, cutters, and pulverizers manufacturing
Core drills, underground mining-type, manufacturing
Mineral processing and beneficiating machinery
manufacturing
Mining cars manufacturing
Oil and gas field-type derricks manufacturing

Oil and gas field-type drilling machinery and
equipment (except offshore floating platforms)
manufacturing
Stationary rock crushing machinery manufacturing
Water well drilling machinery manufacturing

Cross-References.   Establishments primarily engaged in--

- Manufacturing offshore oil and gas well drilling and production floating platforms--are classified in Industry 33661, Ship and Boat Building;
- Manufacturing surface mining machinery and equipment--are classified in Industry 33312, Construction Machinery Manufacturing;
- Manufacturing coal and ore conveyors--are classified in Industry 33392, Material Handling Equipment Manufacturing;
- Manufacturing underground mining locomotives--are classified in Industry 33651, Railroad Rolling Stock Manufacturing; and
- Manufacturing pumps and pumping equipment--are classified in Industry 33391, Pump and Compressor Manufacturing.

333131   Mining Machinery and Equipment Manufacturing

This U.S. industry comprises establishments primarily engaged in (1) manufacturing underground mining machinery and equipment, such as coal breakers, mining cars, core drills, coal cutters, and rock drills, and (2) manufacturing mineral beneficiating machinery and equipment used in surface or underground mines.

Cross-References.   Establishments primarily engaged in--

- Manufacturing surface mining machinery and equipment--are classified in Industry 333120, Construction Machinery Manufacturing;
- Manufacturing well drilling machinery--are classified in U.S. Industry 333132, Oil and Gas Field Machinery and Equipment Manufacturing;
- Manufacturing coal and ore conveyors--are classified in U.S. Industry 333922, Conveyor and Conveying Equipment Manufacturing; and

---

T—Canadian, Mexican, and United States industries are comparable.

- Manufacturing underground mining locomotives--are classified in Industry 336510, Railroad Rolling Stock Manufacturing.

333132 Oil and Gas Field Machinery and Equipment Manufacturing

This U.S. industry comprises establishments primarily engaged in (1) manufacturing oil and gas field machinery and equipment, such as oil and gas field drilling machinery and equipment; oil and gas field production machinery and equipment; and oil and gas field derricks, and (2) manufacturing water well drilling machinery.

Cross-References.   Establishments primarily engaged in--

- Manufacturing offshore oil and gas well drilling and production floating platforms--are classified in U.S. Industry 336611, Ship Building and Repairing;
- Manufacturing underground mining drills--are classified in U.S. Industry 333131, Mining Machinery and Equipment Manufacturing; and
- Manufacturing pumps and pumping equipment--are classified in U.S. Industry 333914, Measuring, Dispensing, and Other Pumping Equipment Manufacturing.

3332   Industrial Machinery Manufacturing[T]

33324   Industrial Machinery Manufacturing[T]

This industry comprises establishments primarily engaged in manufacturing industrial machinery, such as food and beverage manufacturing machinery, semiconductor manufacturing machinery, sawmill and woodworking machinery (except handheld), machinery for making paper and paper products, printing and binding machinery and equipment, textile making machinery, and machinery for making plastics and rubber products.

Cross-References.   Establishments primarily engaged in--

- Manufacturing agricultural and farm-type, construction, and mining machinery--are classified in Industry Group 3331, Agriculture, Construction, and Mining Machinery Manufacturing;
- Manufacturing food and beverage packaging machinery or power-driven handtools--are classified in Industry 33399, All Other General Purpose Machinery Manufacturing;
- Manufacturing commercial and industrial refrigeration and freezer equipment--are classified in Industry 33341, Ventilation, Heating, Air-Conditioning, and Commercial Refrigeration Equipment Manufacturing;
- Manufacturing commercial-type cooking and food warming equipment, automotive maintenance equipment (except mechanics' handtools), or photocopiers--are classified in Industry 33331, Commercial and Service Industry Machinery Manufacturing; and
- Manufacturing mechanics' handtools and other nonpowered handtools--are classified in Industry 33221, Cutlery and Handtool Manufacturing.

333241 Food Product Machinery Manufacturing

This U.S. industry comprises establishments primarily engaged in manufacturing food and beverage manufacturing-type machinery and equipment, such as dairy product plant machinery and equipment (e.g., homogenizers, pasteurizers, ice cream freezers), bakery machinery and equipment (e.g., dough mixers, bake ovens, pastry rolling machines), meat and poultry processing and preparation machinery, and other commercial food products machinery (e.g., slicers, choppers, and mixers).

Cross-References.   Establishments primarily engaged in--

- Manufacturing food and beverage packaging machinery--are classified in U.S. Industry 333993, Packaging Machinery Manufacturing;

T--Canadian, Mexican, and United States industries are comparable.

- Manufacturing commercial and industrial refrigeration and freezer equipment--are classified in U.S. Industry 333415, Air-Conditioning and Warm Air Heating Equipment and Commercial and Industrial Refrigeration Equipment Manufacturing; and
- Manufacturing commercial-type cooking and food warming equipment--are classified in U.S. Industry 333318, Other Commercial and Service Industry Machinery Manufacturing.

333242 Semiconductor Machinery Manufacturing

This U.S. industry comprises establishments primarily engaged in manufacturing wafer processing equipment, semiconductor assembly and packaging equipment, and other semiconductor making machinery.

Cross-References.   Establishments primarily engaged in--

- Manufacturing printed circuit board manufacturing machinery--are classified in U.S. Industry 333249, Other Industrial Machinery Manufacturing; and
- Manufacturing semiconductor testing instruments--are classified in U.S. Industry 334515, Instrument Manufacturing for Measuring and Testing Electricity and Electrical Signals.

333243 Sawmill, Woodworking, and Paper Machinery Manufacturing

This U.S. industry comprises establishments primarily engaged in (1) manufacturing sawmill and woodworking machinery (except handheld), such as circular and band sawing equipment, planing machinery, and sanding machinery, and/or (2) manufacturing paper industry machinery for making paper and paper products, such as pulp making machinery, paper and paperboard making machinery, and paper and paperboard converting machinery.

Cross-References.   Establishments primarily engaged in--

- Manufacturing planes, axes, drawknives, and handsaws--are classified in U.S. Industry 332216, Saw Blade and Handtool Manufacturing;
- Manufacturing power-driven handtools--are classified in U.S. Industry 333991, Power-Driven Handtool Manufacturing; and
- Manufacturing printing machinery--are classified in U.S. Industry 333244, Printing Machinery and Equipment Manufacturing.

333244 Printing Machinery and Equipment Manufacturing

This U.S. industry comprises establishments primarily engaged in manufacturing printing and bookbinding machinery and equipment, such as printing presses, typesetting machinery, and bindery machinery.

Cross-References.   Establishments primarily engaged in--

- Manufacturing textile printing machinery--are classified in U.S. Industry 333249, Other Industrial Machinery Manufacturing; and
- Manufacturing photocopiers--are classified in U.S. Industry 333316, Photographic and Photocopying Equipment Manufacturing.

333249 Other Industrial Machinery Manufacturing

This U.S. industry comprises establishments primarily engaged in manufacturing industrial machinery (except agricultural and farm-type; construction and mining machinery; food manufacturing-type machinery; semiconductor making machinery; sawmill, woodworking, and paper making machinery; and printing machinery and equipment).

T—Canadian, Mexican, and United States industries are comparable.

Illustrative Examples:

Additive manufacturing machinery manufacturing
Chemical processing machinery and equipment
manufacturing
Cigarette making machinery manufacturing
Glass making machinery (e.g., blowing, forming,
molding) manufacturing
Petroleum refining machinery manufacturing

Plastics working machinery manufacturing
Rubber working machinery manufacturing
Sewing machines (including household-type)
manufacturing
Shoe making and repairing machinery manufacturing
Tannery machinery manufacturing
Textile making machinery manufacturing

Cross-References.   Establishments primarily engaged in--

- Manufacturing agricultural and farm-type, construction, and mining machinery--are classified in Industry Group 3331, Agriculture, Construction, and Mining Machinery Manufacturing;
- Manufacturing food and beverage manufacturing-type machinery--are classified in U.S. Industry 333241, Food Product Machinery Manufacturing;
- Manufacturing semiconductor making machinery--are classified in U.S. Industry 333242, Semiconductor Machinery Manufacturing;
- Manufacturing sawmill, woodworking, and paper and paperboard making machinery--are classified in U.S. Industry 333243, Sawmill, Woodworking, and Paper Machinery Manufacturing;
- Manufacturing printing and bookbinding machinery and equipment--are classified in U.S. Industry 333244, Printing Machinery and Equipment Manufacturing;
- Manufacturing automotive maintenance equipment (except mechanics' handtools)--are classified in U.S. Industry 333318, Other Commercial and Service Industry Machinery Manufacturing;
- Manufacturing mechanics' handtools--are classified in U.S. Industry 332216, Saw Blade and Handtool Manufacturing; and
- Manufacturing industrial metal molds for plastics and rubber products making machinery--are classified in U.S. Industry 333511, Industrial Mold Manufacturing.

3333   Commercial and Service Industry Machinery Manufacturing[T]

33331   Commercial and Service Industry Machinery Manufacturing[T]

This industry comprises establishments primarily engaged in manufacturing commercial and service industry machinery, such as optical instruments, photographic and photocopying equipment, automatic vending machinery, commercial laundry and drycleaning machinery, office machinery, automotive maintenance equipment (except mechanics' handtools), and commercial-type cooking equipment.

Cross-References.   Establishments primarily engaged in--

- Manufacturing household-type appliances--are classified in Industry Group 3352, Household Appliance Manufacturing;
- Manufacturing computer and peripheral equipment (including point-of-sale terminals and automatic teller machines (ATMs))--are classified in Industry 33411, Computer and Peripheral Equipment Manufacturing;
- Manufacturing facsimile equipment--are classified in Industry 33421, Telephone Apparatus Manufacturing;
- Manufacturing time clocks, time stamps, and electron and proton microscopes--are classified in Industry 33451, Navigational, Measuring, Electromedical, and Control Instruments Manufacturing;
- Manufacturing pencil sharpeners and staplers--are classified in Industry 33994, Office Supplies (except Paper) Manufacturing;
- Manufacturing sensitized film, paper, cloth, and plates, and prepared photographic chemicals--are classified in Industry 32599, All Other Chemical Product and Preparation Manufacturing;
- Manufacturing ophthalmic focus lenses--are classified in Industry 33911, Medical Equipment and Supplies Manufacturing;
- Manufacturing television and video cameras--are classified in Subsector 334, Computer and Electronic Product Manufacturing;

T—Canadian, Mexican, and United States industries are comparable.

- Manufacturing coin-operated arcade games--are classified in Industry 33999, All Other Miscellaneous Manufacturing;
- Manufacturing mechanics' handtools--are classified in Industry 33221, Cutlery and Handtool Manufacturing;
- Manufacturing molded plastics lens blanks--are classified in Industry 32619, Other Plastics Product Manufacturing; and
- Manufacturing molded glass lens blanks--are classified in Industry 32721, Glass and Glass Product Manufacturing.

333314 Optical Instrument and Lens Manufacturing

This U.S. industry comprises establishments primarily engaged in one or more of the following: (1) manufacturing optical instruments and lenses, such as binoculars, microscopes (except electron, proton), telescopes, prisms, and lenses (except ophthalmic); (2) coating or polishing lenses (except ophthalmic); and (3) mounting lenses (except ophthalmic).

Cross-References.   Establishments primarily engaged in--

- Manufacturing ophthalmic focus lenses--are classified in U.S. Industry 339115, Ophthalmic Goods Manufacturing;
- Manufacturing electron and proton microscopes--are classified in U.S. Industry 334516, Analytical Laboratory Instrument Manufacturing;
- Manufacturing molded plastics lens blanks--are classified in U.S. Industry 326199, All Other Plastics Product Manufacturing; and
- Manufacturing molded glass lens blanks--are classified in U.S. Industry 327212, Other Pressed and Blown Glass and Glassware Manufacturing.

333316 Photographic and Photocopying Equipment Manufacturing

This U.S. industry comprises establishments primarily engaged in manufacturing photographic and photocopying equipment, such as cameras (except television and video), projectors, film developing equipment, photocopying equipment, and microfilm equipment.

Cross-References.   Establishments primarily engaged in--

- Manufacturing sensitized film, paper, cloth, and plates, and prepared photographic chemicals--are classified in U.S. Industry 325992, Photographic Film, Paper, Plate, and Chemical Manufacturing;
- Manufacturing photographic lenses--are classified in U.S. Industry 333314, Optical Instrument and Lens Manufacturing; and
- Manufacturing television and video cameras--are classified in Subsector 334, Computer and Electronic Product Manufacturing.

333318 Other Commercial and Service Industry Machinery Manufacturing

This U.S. industry comprises establishments primarily engaged in manufacturing commercial and service industry equipment (except optical instruments and lenses, and photographic and photocopying equipment).

Illustrative Examples:

Calculators manufacturing
Carnival and amusement park rides manufacturing
Car washing machinery manufacturing
Commercial-type coffee makers and urns manufacturing
Mechanical carpet sweepers manufacturing

Commercial-type cooking equipment (i.e., fryers, microwave ovens, ovens, ranges) manufacturing
Industrial and commercial-type vacuum cleaners manufacturing
Laundry machinery and equipment (except household-type) manufacturing

T—Canadian, Mexican, and United States industries are comparable.

Motor vehicle alignment equipment manufacturing
Power washer cleaning equipment manufacturing
Vending machines manufacturing

Teaching machines (e.g., flight simulators) manufacturing
Water treatment equipment manufacturing

Cross-References.   Establishments primarily engaged in--

- Manufacturing optical instruments and lenses--are classified in U.S. Industry 333314, Optical Instrument and Lens Manufacturing;
- Manufacturing photographic and photocopying equipment--are classified in U.S. Industry 333316, Photographic and Photocopying Equipment Manufacturing;
- Manufacturing household-type appliances--are classified in Industry Group 3352, Household Appliance Manufacturing;
- Manufacturing mechanics' handtools--are classified in U.S. Industry 332216, Saw Blade and Handtool Manufacturing;
- Manufacturing coin-operated arcade games--are classified in U.S. Industry 339999, All Other Miscellaneous Manufacturing;
- Manufacturing computers and peripheral equipment (including point-of-sale terminals and automatic teller machines (ATMs))--are classified in Industry 33411, Computer and Peripheral Equipment Manufacturing;
- Manufacturing facsimile equipment--are classified in Industry 334210, Telephone Apparatus Manufacturing;
- Manufacturing time clocks and time stamps--are classified in U.S. Industry 334519, Other Measuring and Controlling Device Manufacturing; and
- Manufacturing pencil sharpeners, staplers, staple removers, hand paper punches, cutters, trimmers, and other hand office equipment--are classified in Industry 339940, Office Supplies (except Paper) Manufacturing.

3334   Ventilation, Heating, Air-Conditioning, and Commercial Refrigeration Equipment Manufacturing[T]

33341   Ventilation, Heating, Air-Conditioning, and Commercial Refrigeration Equipment Manufacturing[T]

This industry comprises establishments primarily engaged in manufacturing ventilating, heating, air-conditioning, and commercial and industrial refrigeration and freezer equipment.

Illustrative Examples:

Air-conditioner filters manufacturing
Air-conditioning and warm air heating combination units manufacturing
Attic fans manufacturing
Dust and fume collecting equipment manufacturing
Gas fireplaces manufacturing

Heating boilers manufacturing
Industrial and commercial-type fans manufacturing
Refrigerated counter and display cases manufacturing
Refrigerated drinking fountains manufacturing
Space heaters (except portable electric) manufacturing

Cross-References.   Establishments primarily engaged in--

- Manufacturing household-type fans (except attic), portable electric space heaters, humidifiers, dehumidifiers, and air purification equipment--are classified in Industry 33521, Small Electrical Appliance Manufacturing;
- Manufacturing household-type appliances, such as cooking stoves, ranges, refrigerators, and freezers--are classified in Industry 33522, Major Household Appliance Manufacturing;
- Manufacturing commercial-type cooking equipment--are classified in Industry 33331, Commercial and Service Industry Machinery Manufacturing;
- Manufacturing industrial, power, and marine boilers--are classified in Industry 33241, Power Boiler and Heat Exchanger Manufacturing;
- Manufacturing industrial process furnaces and ovens--are classified in Industry 33399, All Other General Purpose Machinery Manufacturing; and

---

T—Canadian, Mexican, and United States industries are comparable.

- Manufacturing motor vehicle air-conditioning systems and compressors--are classified in Industry 33639, Other Motor Vehicle Parts Manufacturing.

333413 Industrial and Commercial Fan and Blower and Air Purification Equipment Manufacturing

This U.S. industry comprises establishments primarily engaged in (1) manufacturing stationary air purification equipment, such as industrial dust and fume collection equipment, electrostatic precipitation equipment, warm air furnace filters, air washers, and other dust collection equipment, and/or (2) manufacturing attic fans and industrial and commercial fans and blowers, such as commercial exhaust fans and commercial ventilating fans.

Cross-References.   Establishments primarily engaged in--

- Manufacturing air-conditioning equipment (except motor vehicle)--are classified in U.S. Industry 333415, Air-Conditioning and Warm Air Heating Equipment and Commercial and Industrial Refrigeration Equipment Manufacturing;
- Manufacturing motor vehicle air-conditioning systems and compressors--are classified in Industry 336390, Other Motor Vehicle Parts Manufacturing; and
- Manufacturing household-type fans (except attic) and portable air purification equipment--are classified in Industry 335210, Small Electrical Appliance Manufacturing.

333414 Heating Equipment (except Warm Air Furnaces) Manufacturing

This U.S. industry comprises establishments primarily engaged in manufacturing heating equipment (except electric and warm air furnaces), such as heating boilers, heating stoves, floor and wall furnaces, and wall and baseboard heating units.

Cross-References.   Establishments primarily engaged in--

- Manufacturing warm air furnaces--are classified in U.S. Industry 333415, Air-Conditioning and Warm Air Heating Equipment and Commercial and Industrial Refrigeration Equipment Manufacturing;
- Manufacturing electric space heaters--are classified in Industry 335210, Small Electrical Appliance Manufacturing;
- Manufacturing household-type cooking stoves and ranges--are classified in Industry 335220, Major Household Appliance Manufacturing;
- Manufacturing industrial, power, and marine boilers--are classified in Industry 332410, Power Boiler and Heat Exchanger Manufacturing;
- Manufacturing industrial process furnaces and ovens--are classified in U.S. Industry 333994, Industrial Process Furnace and Oven Manufacturing; and
- Manufacturing commercial-type cooking equipment--are classified in U.S. Industry 333318, Other Commercial and Service Industry Machinery Manufacturing.

333415 Air-Conditioning and Warm Air Heating Equipment and Commercial and Industrial Refrigeration Equipment Manufacturing

This U.S. industry comprises establishments primarily engaged in (1) manufacturing air-conditioning (except motor vehicle) and warm air furnace equipment and/or (2) manufacturing commercial and industrial refrigeration and freezer equipment.

Illustrative Examples:

Air-conditioning and warm air heating combination units manufacturing
Air-conditioning compressors (except motor vehicle) manufacturing
Heat pumps manufacturing

Air-conditioning condensers and condensing units manufacturing
Dehumidifiers (except portable electric) manufacturing
Refrigerated counter and display cases manufacturing

T—Canadian, Mexican, and United States industries are comparable.

Humidifying equipment (except portable) manufacturing

Refrigerated drinking fountains manufacturing

Snow making machinery manufacturing

Soda fountain cooling and dispensing equipment manufacturing

Cross-References.   Establishments primarily engaged in--

- Manufacturing motor vehicle air-conditioning systems and compressors--are classified in Industry 336390, Other Motor Vehicle Parts Manufacturing;
- Manufacturing household-type refrigerators and freezers--are classified in Industry 335220, Major Household Appliance Manufacturing;
- Manufacturing portable electric space heaters, humidifiers, and dehumidifiers--are classified in Industry 335210, Small Electrical Appliance Manufacturing;
- Manufacturing heating boilers, heating stoves, floor and wall mount furnaces, and electric wall and baseboard heating units--are classified in U.S. Industry 333414, Heating Equipment (except Warm Air Furnaces) Manufacturing; and
- Manufacturing furnace air filters--are classified in U.S. Industry 333413, Industrial and Commercial Fan and Blower and Air Purification Equipment Manufacturing.

3335   Metalworking Machinery Manufacturing[T]

33351   Metalworking Machinery Manufacturing[T]

This industry comprises establishments primarily engaged in manufacturing metalworking machinery, such as metal cutting and metal forming machine tools; cutting tools; accessories for metalworking machinery; special dies, tools, jigs, and fixtures; industrial molds; rolling mill machinery; assembly machinery; coil handling, conversion, or straightening equipment; and wire drawing and fabricating machines.

Cross-References.   Establishments primarily engaged in--

- Manufacturing handtools (except power-driven), cutting dies (except metal cutting), saw blades, and handsaws--are classified in Industry 33221, Cutlery and Handtool Manufacturing;
- Manufacturing casting molds for heavy steel ingots--are classified in Industry 33151, Ferrous Metal Foundries; and
- Manufacturing power-driven handtools and welding and soldering equipment--are classified in Industry 33399, All Other General Purpose Machinery Manufacturing.

333511   Industrial Mold Manufacturing

This U.S. industry comprises establishments primarily engaged in manufacturing industrial molds for casting metals or forming other materials, such as plastics, glass, or rubber.

Cross-References.

Establishments primarily engaged in manufacturing casting molds for steel ingots are classified in U.S. Industry 331511, Iron Foundries.

333514   Special Die and Tool, Die Set, Jig, and Fixture Manufacturing

This U.S. industry comprises establishments, known as tool and die shops, primarily engaged in manufacturing special tools and fixtures, such as cutting dies and jigs.

T—Canadian, Mexican, and United States industries are comparable.

Cross-References.   Establishments primarily engaged in--

- Manufacturing molds for die-casting and foundry casting; and metal molds for plaster working, rubber working, plastics working, and glass working machinery--are classified in U.S. Industry 333511, Industrial Mold Manufacturing;
- Manufacturing molds for heavy steel ingots--are classified in U.S. Industry 331511, Iron Foundries; and
- Manufacturing cutting dies for materials other than metal--are classified in U.S. Industry 332216, Saw Blade and Handtool Manufacturing.

333515 Cutting Tool and Machine Tool Accessory Manufacturing

This U.S. industry comprises establishments primarily engaged in manufacturing accessories and attachments for metal cutting and metal forming machine tools.

Illustrative Examples:

Knives and bits for metalworking lathes, planers, and shapers manufacturing
Measuring attachments (e.g., sine bars) for machine tool manufacturing

Metalworking drill bits manufacturing
Taps and dies (i.e., machine tool accessories) manufacturing

Cross-References.

Establishments primarily engaged in manufacturing saw blades, handsaws, and accessories and attachments for saw blades and for nonpowered metal cutting and forming handtools are classified in U.S. Industry 332216, Saw Blade and Handtool Manufacturing.

333517 Machine Tool Manufacturing

This U.S. industry comprises establishments primarily engaged in (1) manufacturing metal cutting machine tools (except handtools) and/or (2) manufacturing metal forming machine tools (except handtools), such as punching, sheering, bending, forming, pressing, forging and die-casting machines.

Illustrative Examples:

Bending and forming machines, metalworking, manufacturing
Buffing and polishing machines, metalworking, manufacturing
Drilling machines, metalworking, manufacturing
Grinding machines, metalworking, manufacturing

Home workshop metal cutting machine tools (except handtools, welding equipment) manufacturing
Metalworking lathes manufacturing
Milling machines, metalworking, manufacturing
Stamping machines, metalworking, manufacturing

Cross-References.   Establishments primarily engaged in--

- Manufacturing welding and soldering equipment--are classified in U.S. Industry 333992, Welding and Soldering Equipment Manufacturing;
- Manufacturing power-driven handtools--are classified in U.S. Industry 333991, Power-Driven Handtool Manufacturing;
- Manufacturing rolling mill machinery and equipment--are classified in U.S. Industry 333519, Rolling Mill and Other Metalworking Machinery Manufacturing; and
- Manufacturing accessories and attachments for metal cutting and forming machine tools (except saw blades)--are classified in U.S. Industry 333515, Cutting Tool and Machine Tool Accessory Manufacturing.

T—Canadian, Mexican, and United States industries are comparable.

333519 Rolling Mill and Other Metalworking Machinery Manufacturing

This U.S. industry comprises establishments primarily engaged in manufacturing rolling mill machinery and equipment and/or other metalworking machinery (except industrial molds; special dies and tools, die sets, jigs, and fixtures; cutting tools and machine tool accessories; and machine tools).

Illustrative Examples:

Assembly machines manufacturing
Cradle assemblies machinery (i.e., wire making equipment) manufacturing
Metalworking coil winding and cutting machinery manufacturing

Rolling mill roll machines, metalworking, manufacturing
Wire drawing and fabricating machinery and equipment (except dies) manufacturing

Cross-References.   Establishments primarily engaged in--

- Manufacturing industrial molds--are classified in U.S. Industry 333511, Industrial Mold Manufacturing;
- Manufacturing metal cutting and metal forming machine tools--are classified in U.S. Industry 333517, Machine Tool Manufacturing;
- Manufacturing special dies and tools, die sets, jigs, and fixtures--are classified in U.S. Industry 333514, Special Die and Tool, Die Set, Jig, and Fixture Manufacturing; and
- Manufacturing accessories and attachments for metal cutting and forming machine tools (except saw blades)--are classified in U.S. Industry 333515, Cutting Tool and Machine Tool Accessory Manufacturing.

3336   Engine, Turbine, and Power Transmission Equipment Manufacturing[T]

33361   Engine, Turbine, and Power Transmission Equipment Manufacturing[T]

This industry comprises establishments primarily engaged in manufacturing turbines, power transmission equipment, and internal combustion engines (except automotive gasoline and aircraft).

Illustrative Examples:

Clutches and brakes (except electromagnetic industrial controls, motor vehicle) manufacturing
Diesel and semidiesel engines manufacturing
Electric outboard motors manufacturing
Internal combustion engines for hybrid drive systems (except automotive) manufacturing
Plain bearings (except internal combustion engine) manufacturing
Power transmission pulleys manufacturing

Plain bushings (except internal combustion engine) manufacturing
Speed changers (i.e., power transmission equipment) manufacturing
Speed reducers (i.e., power transmission equipment) manufacturing
Turbine generator set units manufacturing
Universal joints (except aircraft, motor vehicle) manufacturing

Cross-References.   Establishments primarily engaged in--

- Manufacturing motor vehicle power transmission equipment--are classified in Industry 33635, Motor Vehicle Transmission and Power Train Parts Manufacturing;
- Manufacturing aircraft engines and aircraft power transmission equipment--are classified in Industry 33641, Aerospace Product and Parts Manufacturing;
- Manufacturing ball and roller bearings--are classified in Industry 33299, All Other Fabricated Metal Product Manufacturing;
- Manufacturing gasoline automotive engines--are classified in Industry 33631, Motor Vehicle Gasoline Engine and Engine Parts Manufacturing; and

---

T—Canadian, Mexican, and United States industries are comparable.

- Manufacturing electric power transmission, electric power distribution equipment, generators, or prime mover generator sets (except turbines)--are classified in Industry 33531, Electrical Equipment Manufacturing.

333611 Turbine and Turbine Generator Set Units Manufacturing

This U.S. industry comprises establishments primarily engaged in manufacturing turbines (except aircraft); and complete turbine generator set units, such as steam, hydraulic, gas, and wind.

Cross-References.   Establishments primarily engaged in--

- Manufacturing aircraft turbines--are classified in U.S. Industry 336412, Aircraft Engine and Engine Parts Manufacturing; and
- Manufacturing generators or prime mover generator sets (except turbines)--are classified in U.S. Industry 335312, Motor and Generator Manufacturing.

333612 Speed Changer, Industrial High-Speed Drive, and Gear Manufacturing

This U.S. industry comprises establishments primarily engaged in manufacturing gears, speed changers, and industrial high-speed drives (except hydrostatic).

Cross-References.   Establishments primarily engaged in--

- Manufacturing motor vehicle power transmission equipment--are classified in Industry 336350, Motor Vehicle Transmission and Power Train Parts Manufacturing;
- Manufacturing aircraft power transmission equipment--are classified in U.S. Industry 336413, Other Aircraft Parts and Auxiliary Equipment Manufacturing; and
- Manufacturing industrial hydrostatic transmissions--are classified in U.S. Industry 333996, Fluid Power Pump and Motor Manufacturing.

333613 Mechanical Power Transmission Equipment Manufacturing

This U.S. industry comprises establishments primarily engaged in manufacturing mechanical power transmission equipment (except motor vehicle and aircraft), such as plain bearings, clutches (except motor vehicle and electromagnetic industrial control), couplings, joints, and drive chains.

Cross-References.   Establishments primarily engaged in--

- Manufacturing motor vehicle power transmission equipment--are classified in Industry 336350, Motor Vehicle Transmission and Power Train Parts Manufacturing;
- Manufacturing aircraft power transmission equipment--are classified in U.S. Industry 336413, Other Aircraft Parts and Auxiliary Equipment Manufacturing;
- Manufacturing ball and roller bearings--are classified in U.S. Industry 332991, Ball and Roller Bearing Manufacturing; and
- Manufacturing gears, speed changers, and industrial high-speed drives (except hydrostatic)--are classified in U.S. Industry 333612, Speed Changer, Industrial High-Speed Drive, and Gear Manufacturing.

333618 Other Engine Equipment Manufacturing

This U.S. industry comprises establishments primarily engaged in manufacturing internal combustion engines (except automotive gasoline and aircraft).

T—Canadian, Mexican, and United States industries are comparable.

Cross-References.   Establishments primarily engaged in--

- Manufacturing gasoline motor vehicle engines and motor vehicle transmissions--are classified in Industry Group 3363, Motor Vehicle Parts Manufacturing;
- Manufacturing gasoline aircraft engines and aircraft transmissions--are classified in Industry 33641, Aerospace Product and Parts Manufacturing;
- Manufacturing turbine and turbine generator set units--are classified in U.S. Industry 333611, Turbine and Turbine Generator Set Units Manufacturing;
- Manufacturing speed changers and industrial high-speed drives and gears--are classified in U.S. Industry 333612, Speed Changer, Industrial High-Speed Drive, and Gear Manufacturing; and
- Manufacturing mechanical power transmission equipment (except motor vehicle and aircraft)--are classified in U.S. Industry 333613, Mechanical Power Transmission Equipment Manufacturing.

3339   Other General Purpose Machinery Manufacturing[T]

This industry group comprises establishments primarily engaged in manufacturing pumps and compressors, material handling equipment, and all other general purpose machinery (except ventilation, heating, air-conditioning, and commercial refrigeration equipment; metalworking machinery; and engines, turbines, and power transmission equipment).

33391   Pump and Compressor Manufacturing[T]

This industry comprises establishments primarily engaged in manufacturing pumps and compressors, such as general purpose air and gas compressors, nonagricultural spraying and dusting equipment, general purpose pumps and pumping equipment (except fluid power pumps and motors), and measuring and dispensing pumps.

Cross-References.   Establishments primarily engaged in--

- Manufacturing fluid power pumps and motors and handheld pneumatic spray guns--are classified in Industry 33399, All Other General Purpose Machinery Manufacturing;
- Manufacturing agricultural spraying and dusting equipment--are classified in Industry 33311, Agricultural Implement Manufacturing;
- Manufacturing laboratory vacuum pumps--are classified in Industry 33911, Medical Equipment and Supplies Manufacturing;
- Manufacturing pumps and air-conditioning systems and compressors for motor vehicles--are classified in Industry Group 3363, Motor Vehicle Parts Manufacturing; and
- Manufacturing air-conditioning systems and compressors (except motor vehicle)--are classified in Industry 33341, Ventilation, Heating, Air-Conditioning, and Commercial Refrigeration Equipment Manufacturing.

333912 Air and Gas Compressor Manufacturing

This U.S. industry comprises establishments primarily engaged in manufacturing general purpose air and gas compressors, such as reciprocating compressors, centrifugal compressors, vacuum pumps (except laboratory), and nonagricultural spraying and dusting compressors and spray gun units.

Cross-References.   Establishments primarily engaged in--

- Manufacturing refrigeration and air-conditioning (except motor vehicle) systems and compressors--are classified in U.S. Industry 333415, Air-Conditioning and Warm Air Heating Equipment and Commercial and Industrial Refrigeration Equipment Manufacturing;
- Manufacturing motor vehicle air-conditioning systems and compressors--are classified in Industry 336390, Other Motor Vehicle Parts Manufacturing;
- Manufacturing fluid power pumps and motors--are classified in U.S. Industry 333996, Fluid Power Pump and Motor Manufacturing;

T—Canadian, Mexican, and United States industries are comparable.

- Manufacturing agricultural spraying and dusting equipment--are classified in U.S. Industry 333111, Farm Machinery and Equipment Manufacturing;
- Manufacturing laboratory vacuum pumps--are classified in U.S. Industry 339113, Surgical Appliance and Supplies Manufacturing; and
- Manufacturing handheld pneumatic spray guns--are classified in U.S. Industry 333991, Power-Driven Handtool Manufacturing.

333914 Measuring, Dispensing, and Other Pumping Equipment Manufacturing

This U.S. industry comprises establishments primarily engaged in (1) manufacturing measuring and dispensing pumps, such as gasoline pumps and lubricating oil measuring and dispensing pumps and/or (2) manufacturing general purpose pumps and pumping equipment (except fluid power pumps and motors), such as reciprocating pumps, turbine pumps, centrifugal pumps, rotary pumps, diaphragm pumps, domestic water system pumps, oil well and oil field pumps, and sump pumps.

Cross-References.   Establishments primarily engaged in--

- Manufacturing fluid power pumps and motors--are classified in U.S. Industry 333996, Fluid Power Pump and Motor Manufacturing;
- Manufacturing vacuum pumps (except laboratory)--are classified in U.S. Industry 333912, Air and Gas Compressor Manufacturing;
- Manufacturing laboratory vacuum pumps--are classified in U.S. Industry 339113, Surgical Appliance and Supplies Manufacturing; and
- Manufacturing fluid pumps for motor vehicles, such as oil pumps, water pumps, and power steering pumps--are classified in Industry Group 3363, Motor Vehicle Parts Manufacturing.

33392 Material Handling Equipment Manufacturing[T]

This industry comprises establishments primarily engaged in manufacturing material handling equipment, such as elevators and moving stairs; conveyors and conveying equipment; overhead traveling cranes, hoists, and monorail systems; and industrial trucks, tractors, trailers, and stacker machinery.

Cross-References.   Establishments primarily engaged in--

- Manufacturing motor vehicle-type trailers--are classified in Industry 33621, Motor Vehicle Body and Trailer Manufacturing;
- Manufacturing farm-type tractors--are classified in Industry 33311, Agricultural Implement Manufacturing;
- Manufacturing construction-type tractors and cranes--are classified in Industry 33312, Construction Machinery Manufacturing; and
- Manufacturing power transmission pulleys--are classified in Industry 33361, Engine, Turbine, and Power Transmission Equipment Manufacturing.

333921 Elevator and Moving Stairway Manufacturing

This U.S. industry comprises establishments primarily engaged in manufacturing elevators and moving stairways.

Illustrative Examples:

Automobile lifts (i.e., garage-type, service station) manufacturing
Escalators manufacturing

Moving walkways manufacturing
Passenger and freight elevators manufacturing

T—Canadian, Mexican, and United States industries are comparable.

Cross-References.

Establishments primarily engaged in manufacturing commercial conveyor systems and equipment are classified in U.S. Industry 333922, Conveyor and Conveying Equipment Manufacturing.

333922 Conveyor and Conveying Equipment Manufacturing

This U.S. industry comprises establishments primarily engaged in manufacturing conveyors and conveying equipment, such as gravity conveyors, trolley conveyors, tow conveyors, pneumatic tube conveyors, carousel conveyors, farm conveyors, and belt conveyors.

Cross-References.   Establishments primarily engaged in--

- Manufacturing passenger or freight elevators, dumbwaiters, and moving stairways--are classified in U.S. Industry 333921, Elevator and Moving Stairway Manufacturing; and
- Manufacturing overhead traveling cranes and monorail systems--are classified in U.S. Industry 333923, Overhead Traveling Crane, Hoist, and Monorail System Manufacturing.

333923 Overhead Traveling Crane, Hoist, and Monorail System Manufacturing

This U.S. industry comprises establishments primarily engaged in manufacturing overhead traveling cranes, hoists, and monorail systems.

Illustrative Examples:

Aerial work platforms manufacturing
Automobile wrecker (i.e., tow truck) hoists
manufacturing
Block and tackle manufacturing

Metal pulleys (except power transmission)
manufacturing
Winches manufacturing

Cross-References.   Establishments primarily engaged in--

- Manufacturing construction-type cranes--are classified in Industry 333120, Construction Machinery Manufacturing;
- Manufacturing aircraft loading hoists--are classified in U.S. Industry 333924, Industrial Truck, Tractor, Trailer, and Stacker Machinery Manufacturing; and
- Manufacturing power transmission pulleys--are classified in U.S. Industry 333613, Mechanical Power Transmission Equipment Manufacturing.

333924 Industrial Truck, Tractor, Trailer, and Stacker Machinery Manufacturing

This U.S. industry comprises establishments primarily engaged in manufacturing industrial trucks, tractors, trailers, and stackers (i.e., truck-type) such as forklifts, pallet loaders and unloaders, and portable loading docks.

Cross-References.   Establishments primarily engaged in--

- Manufacturing motor vehicle-type trailers--are classified in Industry 33621, Motor Vehicle Body and Trailer Manufacturing;
- Manufacturing farm-type tractors--are classified in U.S. Industry 333111, Farm Machinery and Equipment Manufacturing; and
- Manufacturing construction-type tractors--are classified in Industry 333120, Construction Machinery Manufacturing.

T—Canadian, Mexican, and United States industries are comparable.

33399   All Other General Purpose Machinery Manufacturing[T]

This industry comprises establishments primarily engaged in manufacturing general purpose machinery (except ventilation, heating, air-conditioning, and commercial refrigeration equipment; metalworking-machinery; engines, turbines, and power transmission equipment; pumps and compressors; and material handling equipment).

Illustrative Examples:

Automatic fire sprinkler systems manufacturing
Bridge and gate lifting machinery manufacturing
Fluid power cylinders manufacturing
Fluid power pumps manufacturing
Hydraulic and pneumatic jacks manufacturing

Industrial-type furnaces manufacturing
Packaging machinery manufacturing
Power-driven handtools manufacturing
Scales manufacturing
Welding equipment manufacturing

Cross-References.   Establishments primarily engaged in--

- Manufacturing ventilating, heating, air-conditioning (except motor vehicle), commercial refrigeration, and furnace filters--are classified in Industry 33341, Ventilation, Heating, Air-Conditioning, and Commercial Refrigeration Equipment Manufacturing;
- Manufacturing engine, turbine, and power transmission equipment--are classified in Industry Group 3336, Engine, Turbine, and Power Transmission Equipment Manufacturing;
- Manufacturing pumps and compressors--are classified in Industry 33391, Pump and Compressor Manufacturing;
- Manufacturing material handling equipment--are classified in Industry 33392, Material Handling Equipment Manufacturing;
- Manufacturing motor vehicle air-conditioning systems and compressors, engine filters, and pumps--are classified in Industry Group 3363, Motor Vehicle Parts Manufacturing;
- Manufacturing metal cutting, metal forming, and other metalworking machinery--are classified in Industry 33351, Metalworking Machinery Manufacturing;
- Manufacturing power-driven heavy construction or mining hand operated tools, such as tampers, jackhammers, and augers--are classified in Industry 33312, Construction Machinery Manufacturing, or Industry 33313, Mining and Oil and Gas Field Machinery Manufacturing;
- Manufacturing bakery ovens and industrial kilns, such as cement, wood, and chemical--are classified in Industry 33324, Industrial Machinery Manufacturing;
- Manufacturing mechanical jacks, handheld soldering irons, countersink bits, drill bits, router bits, milling cutters, and other machine tools for woodcutting--are classified in Industry 33221, Cutlery and Handtool Manufacturing;
- Manufacturing carnival and amusement park equipment, automotive maintenance equipment, and coin-operated vending machines--are classified in Industry 33331, Commercial and Service Industry Machinery Manufacturing; and
- Manufacturing arc-welding transformers--are classified in Industry 33531, Electrical Equipment Manufacturing.

333991 Power-Driven Handtool Manufacturing

This U.S. industry comprises establishments primarily engaged in manufacturing power-driven (e.g., battery, corded, pneumatic) handtools, such as drills, screwguns, circular saws, chain saws, staplers, and nailers.

Cross-References.   Establishments primarily engaged in--

- Manufacturing metal cutting and metal forming machines (including home workshop)--are classified in Industry 33351, Metalworking Machinery Manufacturing;
- Manufacturing countersink bits, drill bits, router bits, milling cutters, and other machine tools for woodcutting--are classified in U.S. Industry 332216, Saw Blade and Handtool Manufacturing;

T—Canadian, Mexican, and United States industries are comparable.

- Manufacturing power-driven heavy construction or mining hand operated tools, such as tampers, jackhammers, and augers--are classified in Industry 333120, Construction Machinery Manufacturing, or Industry 33313, Mining and Oil and Gas Field Machinery Manufacturing; and
- Manufacturing powered home lawn and garden equipment--are classified in U.S. Industry 333112, Lawn and Garden Tractor and Home Lawn and Garden Equipment Manufacturing.

333992 Welding and Soldering Equipment Manufacturing

This U.S. industry comprises establishments primarily engaged in manufacturing welding and soldering equipment and accessories (except transformers), such as arc, resistance, gas, plasma, laser, electron beam, and ultrasonic welding equipment; welding electrodes; coated or cored welding wire; and soldering equipment (except handheld).

Cross-References.   Establishments primarily engaged in--

- Manufacturing handheld soldering irons--are classified in U.S. Industry 332216, Saw Blade and Handtool Manufacturing; and
- Manufacturing arc-welding transformers--are classified in U.S. Industry 335311, Power, Distribution, and Specialty Transformer Manufacturing.

333993 Packaging Machinery Manufacturing

This U.S. industry comprises establishments primarily engaged in manufacturing packaging machinery, such as wrapping, bottling, canning, and labeling machinery.

333994 Industrial Process Furnace and Oven Manufacturing

This U.S. industry comprises establishments primarily engaged in manufacturing industrial process ovens, induction and dielectric heating equipment, and kilns (except cement, chemical, wood). Included in this industry are establishments manufacturing laboratory furnaces and ovens.

Cross-References.   Establishments primarily engaged in--

- Manufacturing bakery ovens--are classified in U.S. Industry 333241, Food Product Machinery Manufacturing;
- Manufacturing cement, wood, and chemical kilns--are classified in U.S. Industry 333249, Other Industrial Machinery Manufacturing; and
- Manufacturing cremating ovens--are classified in U.S. Industry 333999, All Other Miscellaneous General Purpose Machinery Manufacturing.

333995 Fluid Power Cylinder and Actuator Manufacturing

This U.S. industry comprises establishments primarily engaged in manufacturing fluid power (i.e., hydraulic and pneumatic) cylinders and actuators.

333996 Fluid Power Pump and Motor Manufacturing

This U.S. industry comprises establishments primarily engaged in manufacturing fluid power (i.e., hydraulic and pneumatic) pumps and motors.

Cross-References.   Establishments primarily engaged in--

- Manufacturing fluid pumps for motor vehicles, such as oil pumps, water pumps, and power steering pumps--are classified in Industry Group 3363, Motor Vehicle Parts Manufacturing;
- Manufacturing general purpose pumps (except fluid power)--are classified in U.S. Industry 333914, Measuring, Dispensing, and Other Pumping Equipment Manufacturing; and

---

T—Canadian, Mexican, and United States industries are comparable.

- Manufacturing air compressors--are classified in U.S. Industry 333912, Air and Gas Compressor Manufacturing.

333997 Scale and Balance Manufacturing

This U.S. industry comprises establishments primarily engaged in manufacturing scales and balances, including those used in laboratories.

333999 All Other Miscellaneous General Purpose Machinery Manufacturing

This U.S. industry comprises establishments primarily engaged in manufacturing general purpose machinery (except ventilating, heating, air-conditioning, and commercial refrigeration equipment; metalworking machinery; engines, turbines, and power transmission equipment; pumps and compressors; material handling equipment; power-driven handtools; welding and soldering equipment; packaging machinery; industrial process furnaces and ovens; fluid power cylinders and actuators; fluid power pumps and motors; and scales and balances).

Illustrative Examples:

Automatic fire sprinkler systems manufacturing
Baling machinery (e.g., paper, scrap metal) manufacturing
Bridge and gate lifting machinery manufacturing
Centrifuges, industrial and laboratory-type, manufacturing
Cremating ovens manufacturing

General purpose-type sieves and screening equipment manufacturing
Hydraulic and pneumatic jacks manufacturing
Industrial and general purpose-type filters (except internal combustion engine, warm air furnace) manufacturing

Cross-References.   Establishments primarily engaged in--

- Manufacturing ventilating, heating, air-conditioning (except motor vehicle), and commercial refrigeration--are classified in Industry 33341, Ventilation, Heating, Air-Conditioning, and Commercial Refrigeration Equipment Manufacturing;
- Manufacturing motor vehicle air-conditioning systems and compressors--are classified in Industry 336390, Other Motor Vehicle Parts Manufacturing;
- Manufacturing material handling equipment--are classified in Industry 33392, Material Handling Equipment Manufacturing;
- Manufacturing power-driven handtools--are classified in U.S. Industry 333991, Power-Driven Handtool Manufacturing;
- Manufacturing welding and soldering equipment (except handheld soldering irons)--are classified in U.S. Industry 333992, Welding and Soldering Equipment Manufacturing;
- Manufacturing packaging machinery--are classified in U.S. Industry 333993, Packaging Machinery Manufacturing;
- Manufacturing bakery ovens--are classified in U.S. Industry 333241, Food Product Machinery Manufacturing;
- Manufacturing cement, wood, and chemical kilns--are classified in U.S. Industry 333249, Other Industrial Machinery Manufacturing;
- Manufacturing industrial process furnaces and ovens (except bakery)--are classified in U.S. Industry 333994, Industrial Process Furnace and Oven Manufacturing;
- Manufacturing fluid power cylinders and actuators--are classified in U.S. Industry 333995, Fluid Power Cylinder and Actuator Manufacturing;
- Manufacturing fluid power pumps and motors--are classified in U.S. Industry 333996, Fluid Power Pump and Motor Manufacturing;
- Manufacturing scales and balances--are classified in U.S. Industry 333997, Scale and Balance Manufacturing;

T—Canadian, Mexican, and United States industries are comparable.

- Manufacturing carnival and amusement park equipment, automotive maintenance equipment, and coin-operated vending machines--are classified in Industry 33331, Commercial and Service Industry Machinery Manufacturing;
- Manufacturing motor vehicle engine filters and pumps--are classified in Industry Group 3363, Motor Vehicle Parts Manufacturing; and
- Manufacturing mechanical jacks--are classified in U.S. Industry 332216, Saw Blade and Handtool Manufacturing.

334   Computer and Electronic Product Manufacturing[T]

Industries in the Computer and Electronic Product Manufacturing subsector group establishments that manufacture computers, computer peripherals, communications equipment, and similar electronic products, and establishments that manufacture components for such products. The Computer and Electronic Product Manufacturing industries have been combined in the hierarchy of NAICS because of the economic significance they have attained. Their rapid growth suggests that they will become even more important to the economies of all three North American countries in the future, and in addition their manufacturing processes are fundamentally different from the manufacturing processes of other machinery and equipment. The design and use of integrated circuits and the application of highly specialized miniaturization technologies are common elements in the production technologies of the Computer and Electronic Product Manufacturing subsector. Convergence of technology motivates this NAICS subsector. Digitalization of sound recording, for example, causes both the medium (the compact disc) and the equipment to resemble the technologies for recording, storing, transmitting, and manipulating data. Communications technology and equipment have been converging with computer technology. When technologically-related components are in the same sector, it makes it easier to adjust the classification for future changes, without needing to redefine its basic structure. The creation of the Computer and Electronic Product Manufacturing subsector assists in delineating new and emerging industries because the activities that will serve as the probable sources of new industries, such as computer manufacturing and communications equipment manufacturing, or computers and audio equipment, are brought together. As new activities emerge, they are less likely to cross the subsector boundaries of the classification.

3341   Computer and Peripheral Equipment Manufacturing[T]

33411   Computer and Peripheral Equipment Manufacturing[T]

This industry comprises establishments primarily engaged in manufacturing and/or assembling electronic computers, such as mainframes, personal computers, workstations, laptops, and computer servers; and computer peripheral equipment, such as storage devices, printers, monitors, and input/output devices and terminals. Computers can be analog, digital, or hybrid. Digital computers, the most common type, are devices that do all of the following: (1) store the processing program or programs and the data immediately necessary for the execution of the program; (2) can be freely programmed in accordance with the requirements of the user; (3) perform arithmetical computations specified by the user; and (4) execute, without human intervention, a processing program that requires the computer to modify its execution by logical decision during the processing run. Analog computers are capable of simulating mathematical models and comprise at least analog, control, and programming elements.

Cross-References.   Establishments primarily engaged in--

- Manufacturing digital telecommunications switches, and local area network and wide area network communications equipment, such as bridges, routers, and gateways--are classified in Industry 33421, Telephone Apparatus Manufacturing;
- Manufacturing blank magnetic and optical recording media--are classified in Industry 33461, Manufacturing and Reproducing Magnetic and Optical Media;
- Manufacturing machinery or equipment that incorporates electronic computers for operation or control purposes and embedded control applications--are classified in the Manufacturing sector based on the classification of the complete machinery or equipment;
- Manufacturing external audio speakers for computer use--are classified in Industry 33431, Audio and Video Equipment Manufacturing;

T—Canadian, Mexican, and United States industries are comparable.

- Manufacturing internal loaded printed circuit board devices, such as sound, video, controller, and network interface cards; internal and external computer modems; and semiconductor storage devices--are classified in Industry 33441, Semiconductor and Other Electronic Component Manufacturing; and
- Manufacturing other parts, such as casings, stampings, cable sets, and switches, for computers, storage devices and other peripheral equipment--are classified in the Manufacturing sector based on their associated production processes.

334111 Electronic Computer Manufacturing

This U.S. industry comprises establishments primarily engaged in manufacturing and/or assembling electronic computers, such as mainframes, personal computers, workstations, laptops, and computer servers. Computers can be analog, digital, or hybrid. Digital computers, the most common type, are devices that do all of the following: (1) store the processing program or programs and the data immediately necessary for the execution of the program; (2) can be freely programmed in accordance with the requirements of the user; (3) perform arithmetical computations specified by the user; and (4) execute, without human intervention, a processing program that requires the computer to modify its execution by logical decision during the processing run. Analog computers are capable of simulating mathematical models and contain at least analog, control, and programming elements. The manufacture of computers includes the assembly or integration of processors, coprocessors, memory, storage, and input/output devices into a user-programmable final product.

Cross-References.   Establishments primarily engaged in--

- Manufacturing digital telecommunications switches, and local area network and wide area network communication equipment, such as bridges, routers, and gateways--are classified in Industry 334210, Telephone Apparatus Manufacturing;
- Manufacturing blank magnetic and optical recording media--are classified in U.S. Industry 334613, Blank Magnetic and Optical Recording Media Manufacturing;
- Manufacturing machinery or equipment that incorporates electronic computers for operation or control purposes and embedded control applications--are classified in the Manufacturing sector based on the classification of the complete machinery or equipment;
- Manufacturing internal, loaded, printed circuit board devices, such as sound, video, controller, and network interface cards; internal and external computer modems; and solid-state storage devices for computers--are classified in Industry 33441, Semiconductor and Other Electronic Component Manufacturing;
- Manufacturing other parts, such as casings, stampings, cable sets, and switches, for computers--are classified in the Manufacturing sector based on their associated production processes; and
- Retailing computers with on-site assembly--are classified in U.S. Industry 443142, Electronics Stores.

334112 Computer Storage Device Manufacturing

This U.S. industry comprises establishments primarily engaged in manufacturing computer storage devices that allow the storage and retrieval of data from a phase change, magnetic, optical, or magnetic/optical media. Examples of products made by these establishments are CD-ROM drives, floppy disk drives, hard disk drives, and tape storage and backup units.

Cross-References.   Establishments primarily engaged in--

- Manufacturing blank magnetic and optical recording media--are classified in U.S. Industry 334613, Blank Magnetic and Optical Recording Media Manufacturing;
- Manufacturing semiconductor storage devices, such as memory chips--are classified in U.S. Industry 334413, Semiconductor and Related Device Manufacturing;
- Manufacturing drive controller cards, internal or external to the storage device--are classified in U.S. Industry 334418, Printed Circuit Assembly (Electronic Assembly) Manufacturing; and
- Manufacturing other parts, such as casings, stampings, cable sets, and switches, for computer storage devices--are classified in the Manufacturing sector based on their associated production processes.

T—Canadian, Mexican, and United States industries are comparable.

334118 Computer Terminal and Other Computer Peripheral Equipment Manufacturing

This U.S. industry comprises establishments primarily engaged in manufacturing computer terminals and other computer peripheral equipment (except storage devices).

Illustrative Examples:

Automatic teller machines (ATM) manufacturing
Computer terminals manufacturing
Joystick devices manufacturing
Keyboards, computer peripheral equipment, manufacturing
Monitors, computer peripheral equipment, manufacturing

Mouse devices, computer peripheral equipment, manufacturing
Optical readers and scanners manufacturing
Plotters, computer, manufacturing
Point-of-sale terminals manufacturing
Printers, computer, manufacturing

Cross-References.   Establishments primarily engaged in--

- Manufacturing local area network and wide area network communications equipment, such as bridges, routers, and gateways--are classified in Industry 334210, Telephone Apparatus Manufacturing;
- Manufacturing computer storage devices--are classified in U.S. Industry 334112, Computer Storage Device Manufacturing;
- Manufacturing external audio speakers for computer use--are classified in Industry 334310, Audio and Video Equipment Manufacturing;
- Manufacturing internal, loaded, printed circuit board devices, such as sound, video, controller, and network interface cards; and internal and external computer modems used as computer peripherals--are classified in U.S. Industry 334418, Printed Circuit Assembly (Electronic Assembly) Manufacturing;
- Manufacturing digital cameras--are classified in U.S. Industry 333316, Photographic and Photocopying Equipment Manufacturing; and
- Manufacturing other parts, such as casings, stampings, cable sets, and switches, for computer peripheral equipment--are classified in the Manufacturing sector based on their associated production processes.

3342   Communications Equipment Manufacturing[T]

This industry group comprises establishments primarily engaged in manufacturing wire telephone and data communications equipment, radio and television broadcast and wireless communications equipment, and all other communications equipment.

33421   Telephone Apparatus Manufacturing[T]
See industry description for 334210.

334210 Telephone Apparatus Manufacturing

This industry comprises establishments primarily engaged in manufacturing wire telephone and data communications equipment. These products may be stand-alone or board-level components of a larger system. Examples of products made by these establishments are central office switching equipment, cordless and wire telephones (except cellular), PBX equipment, telephone answering machines, LAN modems, multi-user modems, and other data communications equipment, such as bridges, routers, and gateways.

Cross-References.   Establishments primarily engaged in--

- Manufacturing internal and external computer modems, single-user fax/modems and electronic components used in telephone apparatus--are classified in Industry 33441, Semiconductor and Other Electronic Component Manufacturing; and
- Manufacturing cellular telephones--are classified in Industry 334220, Radio and Television Broadcasting and Wireless Communications Equipment Manufacturing.

T—Canadian, Mexican, and United States industries are comparable.

33422   Radio and Television Broadcasting and Wireless Communications Equipment Manufacturing[T]
See industry description for 334220

334220 Radio and Television Broadcasting and Wireless Communications Equipment Manufacturing

This industry comprises establishments primarily engaged in manufacturing radio and television broadcast and wireless communications equipment. Examples of products made by these establishments are transmitting and receiving antennas, cable television equipment, GPS equipment, pagers, cellular phones, mobile communications equipment, and radio and television studio and broadcasting equipment.

Cross-References.   Establishments primarily engaged in--

- Manufacturing household-type audio and video equipment, such as televisions and radio sets--are classified in Industry 334310, Audio and Video Equipment Manufacturing;
- Manufacturing wired and wireless intercommunications equipment (i.e., intercoms)--are classified in Industry 334290, Other Communications Equipment Manufacturing; and
- Manufacturing equipment for measuring and testing communications signals--are classified in U.S. Industry 334515, Instrument Manufacturing for Measuring and Testing Electricity and Electrical Signals.

33429   Other Communications Equipment Manufacturing[T]
See industry description for 334290.

334290 Other Communications Equipment Manufacturing

This industry comprises establishments primarily engaged in manufacturing communications equipment (except telephone apparatus, radio and television broadcast equipment, and wireless communications equipment).

Illustrative Examples:

Fire detection and alarm systems manufacturing
Intercom systems and equipment manufacturing
Video-based stadium displays manufacturing

Signals (e.g., highway, pedestrian, railway, traffic) manufacturing

Cross-References.   Establishments primarily engaged in--

- Manufacturing telephone apparatus--are classified in Industry 334210, Telephone Apparatus Manufacturing;
- Manufacturing radio and television broadcast and wireless communications equipment (except wireless intercoms)--are classified in Industry 334220, Radio and Television Broadcasting and Wireless Communications Equipment Manufacturing; and
- Manufacturing automobile audio and related equipment--are classified in Industry 334310, Audio and Video Equipment Manufacturing.

3343   Audio and Video Equipment Manufacturing[T]

33431   Audio and Video Equipment Manufacturing[T]
See industry description for 334310.

334310 Audio and Video Equipment Manufacturing

This industry comprises establishments primarily engaged in manufacturing electronic audio and video equipment for home entertainment, motor vehicles, and public address and musical instrument amplification. Examples of products made by these establishments are digital video recorders, televisions, stereo equipment, speaker systems, household-type video cameras, jukeboxes, and amplifiers for musical instruments and public address systems.

T—Canadian, Mexican, and United States industries are comparable.

Cross-References.   Establishments primarily engaged in--

- Manufacturing photographic (i.e., still and motion picture) equipment--are classified in U.S. Industry 333316, Photographic and Photocopying Equipment Manufacturing;
- Manufacturing phonograph needles and cartridges--are classified in Industry 33441, Semiconductor and Other Electronic Component Manufacturing;
- Manufacturing auto theft alarms or video-based stadium displays--are classified in Industry 334290, Other Communications Equipment Manufacturing; and
- Manufacturing mobile radios, such as citizens band and FM transceivers for household or motor vehicle uses; studio and broadcast video cameras; and cable decoders and satellite television equipment--are classified in Industry 334220, Radio and Television Broadcasting and Wireless Communications Equipment Manufacturing.

3344   Semiconductor and Other Electronic Component Manufacturing[T]

33441   Semiconductor and Other Electronic Component Manufacturing[T]

This industry comprises establishments primarily engaged in manufacturing semiconductors and other components for electronic applications. Examples of products made by these establishments are capacitors, resistors, microprocessors, bare and loaded printed circuit boards, electron tubes, electronic connectors, and computer modems.

Cross-References.   Establishments primarily engaged in--

- Manufacturing X-ray tubes--are classified in Industry 33451, Navigational, Measuring, Electromedical, and Control Instruments Manufacturing;
- Manufacturing glass blanks for electron tubes--are classified in Industry 32721, Glass and Glass Product Manufacturing;
- Manufacturing telephone system components or modules--are classified in Industry 33421, Telephone Apparatus Manufacturing;
- Manufacturing finished products that incorporate loaded printed circuit boards--are classified in the Manufacturing sector based on the production process of making the final product;
- Manufacturing communications antennas--are classified in Industry 33422, Radio and Television Broadcasting and Wireless Communications Equipment Manufacturing; and
- Manufacturing coils, switches, transformers, connectors, capacitors, rheostats, and similar devices for electrical applications--are classified in Subsector 335, Electrical Equipment, Appliance, and Component Manufacturing.

334412 Bare Printed Circuit Board Manufacturing

This U.S. industry comprises establishments primarily engaged in manufacturing bare (i.e., rigid or flexible) printed circuit boards without mounted electronic components. These establishments print, perforate, plate, screen, etch, or photoprint interconnecting pathways for electric current on laminates.

Cross-References.   Establishments primarily engaged in--

- Loading components onto printed circuit boards or manufacturing loaded printed circuit boards--are classified in U.S. Industry 334418, Printed Circuit Assembly (Electronic Assembly) Manufacturing; and
- Manufacturing printed circuit laminates--are classified in U.S. Industry 334419, Other Electronic Component Manufacturing.

T—Canadian, Mexican, and United States industries are comparable.

334413 Semiconductor and Related Device Manufacturing

This U.S. industry comprises establishments primarily engaged in manufacturing semiconductors and related solid-state devices. Examples of products made by these establishments are integrated circuits, memory chips, microprocessors, diodes, transistors, solar cells and other optoelectronic devices.

334416 Capacitor, Resistor, Coil, Transformer, and Other Inductor Manufacturing

This U.S. industry comprises establishments primarily engaged in one or more of the following: (1) manufacturing electronic fixed and variable capacitors and condensers; (2) manufacturing electronic resistors, such as fixed and variable resistors, resistor networks, thermistors, and varistors; and (3) manufacturing electronic inductors, such as coils and transformers.

Cross-References.   Establishments primarily engaged in--

- Manufacturing electrical capacitors for power generation and distribution, heavy industrial equipment, induction heating and melting, and similar industrial applications--are classified in U.S. Industry 335999, All Other Miscellaneous Electrical Equipment and Component Manufacturing;
- Manufacturing electronic rheostats--are classified in U.S. Industry 334419, Other Electronic Component Manufacturing; and
- Manufacturing electrical transformers used in the generation, storage, transmission, transformation, distribution, and utilization of electrical energy--are classified in U.S. Industry 335311, Power, Distribution, and Specialty Transformer Manufacturing.

334417 Electronic Connector Manufacturing

This U.S. industry comprises establishments primarily engaged in manufacturing electronic connectors, such as coaxial, cylindrical, rack and panel, pin and sleeve, printed circuit and fiber optic.

Cross-References.

Establishments primarily engaged in manufacturing electrical connectors, such as plugs, bus bars, twist on wire connectors and terminals, are classified in U.S. Industry 335931, Current-Carrying Wiring Device Manufacturing.

334418 Printed Circuit Assembly (Electronic Assembly) Manufacturing

This U.S. industry comprises establishments primarily engaged in loading components onto printed circuit boards or who manufacture and ship loaded printed circuit boards. Also known as printed circuit assemblies, electronics assemblies, or modules, these products are printed circuit boards that have some or all of the semiconductor and electronic components inserted or mounted and are inputs to a wide variety of electronic systems and devices.

Cross-References.   Establishments primarily engaged in--

- Manufacturing printed circuit laminates--are classified in U.S. Industry 334419, Other Electronic Component Manufacturing;
- Manufacturing bare printed circuit boards--are classified in U.S. Industry 334412, Bare Printed Circuit Board Manufacturing;
- Manufacturing telephone system components or modules--are classified in Industry 334210, Telephone Apparatus Manufacturing; and
- Manufacturing finished products that incorporate loaded printed circuit boards--are classified in the Manufacturing sector based on the production process of making the final product.

T—Canadian, Mexican, and United States industries are comparable.

334419 Other Electronic Component Manufacturing

This U.S. industry comprises establishments primarily engaged in manufacturing electronic components (except bare printed circuit boards; semiconductors and related devices; electronic capacitors; electronic resistors; coils, transformers and other inductors; connectors; and loaded printed circuit boards).

Illustrative Examples:

Crystals and crystal assemblies, electronic, manufacturing
Electron tubes manufacturing
LCD (liquid crystal display) unit screens manufacturing

Microwave components manufacturing
Piezoelectric devices manufacturing
Printed circuit laminates manufacturing
Switches for electronic applications manufacturing
Transducers (except pressure) manufacturing

Cross-References.   Establishments primarily engaged in--

- Manufacturing bare printed circuit boards--are classified in U.S. Industry 334412, Bare Printed Circuit Board Manufacturing;
- Manufacturing semiconductors, photonic integrated circuits, and/or silicon wave guides--are classified in U.S. Industry 334413, Semiconductor and Related Device Manufacturing;
- Manufacturing electronic capacitors, electronic resistors, and electronic inductors--are classified in U.S. Industry 334416, Capacitor, Resistor, Coil, Transformer, and Other Inductor Manufacturing;
- Manufacturing electronic connectors--are classified in U.S. Industry 334417, Electronic Connector Manufacturing;
- Loading components onto printed circuit boards or manufacturing loaded printed circuit boards--are classified in U.S. Industry 334418, Printed Circuit Assembly (Electronic Assembly) Manufacturing;
- Manufacturing communications antennas--are classified in Industry 334220, Radio and Television Broadcasting and Wireless Communications Equipment Manufacturing;
- Manufacturing X-ray tubes--are classified in U.S. Industry 334517, Irradiation Apparatus Manufacturing; and
- Manufacturing glass blanks for electron tubes--are classified in Industry 32721, Glass and Glass Product Manufacturing.

3345   Navigational, Measuring, Electromedical, and Control Instruments Manufacturing[T]

33451 Navigational, Measuring, Electromedical, and Control Instruments Manufacturing[T]

This industry comprises establishments primarily engaged in manufacturing navigational, measuring, electromedical, and control instruments. Examples of products made by these establishments are aeronautical instruments, appliance regulators and controls (except switches), laboratory analytical instruments, navigation and guidance systems, and physical properties testing equipment.

Cross-References.   Establishments primarily engaged in--

- Manufacturing global positioning system (GPS) equipment--are classified in Industry 33422, Radio and Television Broadcasting and Wireless Communications Equipment Manufacturing;
- Manufacturing motor control switches and relays (including timing relays)--are classified in Industry 33531, Electrical Equipment Manufacturing;
- Manufacturing switches for appliances--are classified in Industry 33593, Wiring Device Manufacturing;
- Manufacturing optical instruments--are classified in Industry 33331, Commercial and Service Industry Machinery Manufacturing;
- Manufacturing glass watch and clock crystals--are classified in Industry 32721, Glass and Glass Product Manufacturing;
- Manufacturing plastics watch and clock crystals--are classified in Industry 32619, Other Plastics Product Manufacturing; and

---

T—Canadian, Mexican, and United States industries are comparable.

- Manufacturing medical thermometers and other nonelectrical medical apparatus--are classified in Industry 33911, Medical Equipment and Supplies Manufacturing.

334510 Electromedical and Electrotherapeutic Apparatus Manufacturing

This U.S. industry comprises establishments primarily engaged in manufacturing electromedical and electrotherapeutic apparatus, such as magnetic resonance imaging equipment, medical ultrasound equipment, pacemakers, hearing aids, electrocardiographs, and electromedical endoscopic equipment.

Cross-References.   Establishments primarily engaged in--

- Manufacturing medical irradiation apparatus--are classified in U.S. Industry 334517, Irradiation Apparatus Manufacturing; and
- Manufacturing nonelectrical medical and therapeutic apparatus--are classified in Industry 33911, Medical Equipment and Supplies Manufacturing.

334511 Search, Detection, Navigation, Guidance, Aeronautical, and Nautical System and Instrument Manufacturing

This U.S. industry comprises establishments primarily engaged in manufacturing search, detection, navigation, guidance, aeronautical, and nautical systems and instruments. Examples of products made by these establishments are aircraft instruments (except engine), flight recorders, navigational instruments and systems, radar systems and equipment, and sonar systems and equipment.

Cross-References.   Establishments primarily engaged in--

- Manufacturing global positioning system (GPS) equipment--are classified in Industry 334220, Radio and Television Broadcasting and Wireless Communications Equipment Manufacturing; and
- Manufacturing aircraft engine instruments and meteorological systems and equipment--are classified in U.S. Industry 334519, Other Measuring and Controlling Device Manufacturing.

334512 Automatic Environmental Control Manufacturing for Residential, Commercial, and Appliance Use

This U.S. industry comprises establishments primarily engaged in manufacturing automatic controls and regulators for applications, such as heating, air-conditioning, refrigeration and appliances.

Cross-References.   Establishments primarily engaged in--

- Manufacturing industrial process controls--are classified in U.S. Industry 334513, Instruments and Related Products Manufacturing for Measuring, Displaying, and Controlling Industrial Process Variables;
- Manufacturing motor control switches and relays--are classified in U.S. Industry 335314, Relay and Industrial Control Manufacturing;
- Manufacturing switches for appliances--are classified in U.S. Industry 335931, Current-Carrying Wiring Device Manufacturing; and
- Manufacturing appliance timers--are classified in U.S. Industry 334519, Other Measuring and Controlling Device Manufacturing.

334513 Instruments and Related Products Manufacturing for Measuring, Displaying, and Controlling Industrial Process Variables

This U.S. industry comprises establishments primarily engaged in manufacturing instruments and related devices for measuring, displaying, indicating, recording, transmitting, and controlling industrial process variables. These instruments measure, display or control (monitor, analyze, and so forth) industrial process variables, such as temperature, humidity, pressure, vacuum, combustion, flow, level, viscosity, density, acidity, concentration, and rotation.

T—Canadian, Mexican, and United States industries are comparable.

Cross-References.   Establishments primarily engaged in--

- Manufacturing instruments for measuring or testing electricity and electrical signals--are classified in U.S. Industry 334515, Instrument Manufacturing for Measuring and Testing Electricity and Electrical Signals;
- Manufacturing medical thermometers--are classified in U.S. Industry 339112, Surgical and Medical Instrument Manufacturing;
- Manufacturing glass hydrometers and thermometers for other non-medical uses--are classified in U.S. Industry 334519, Other Measuring and Controlling Device Manufacturing;
- Manufacturing instruments and instrumentation systems for laboratory analysis of samples--are classified in U.S. Industry 334516, Analytical Laboratory Instrument Manufacturing; and
- Manufacturing optical alignment and display instruments, optical comparators, and optical test and inspection equipment--are classified in U.S. Industry 333314, Optical Instrument and Lens Manufacturing.

334514 Totalizing Fluid Meter and Counting Device Manufacturing

This U.S. industry comprises establishments primarily engaged in manufacturing totalizing (i.e., registering) fluid meters and counting devices. Examples of products made by these establishments are gas consumption meters, water consumption meters, parking meters, taxi meters, motor vehicle gauges, and fare collection equipment.

Cross-References.   Establishments primarily engaged in--

- Manufacturing integrating meters and counters for measuring the characteristics of electricity and electrical signals--are classified in U.S. Industry 334515, Instrument Manufacturing for Measuring and Testing Electricity and Electrical Signals; and
- Manufacturing instruments and devices that measure, display, or control (i.e., monitor or analyze) related industrial process variables--are classified in U.S. Industry 334513, Instruments and Related Products Manufacturing for Measuring, Displaying, and Controlling Industrial Process Variables.

334515 Instrument Manufacturing for Measuring and Testing Electricity and Electrical Signals

This U.S. industry comprises establishments primarily engaged in manufacturing instruments for measuring and testing the characteristics of electricity and electrical signals. Examples of products made by these establishments are circuit and continuity testers, voltmeters, ohm meters, wattmeters, multimeters, and semiconductor test equipment.

Cross-References.

Establishments primarily engaged in manufacturing electronic monitoring, evaluating, and other electronic support equipment for navigational, radar, and sonar systems are classified in U.S. Industry 334511, Search, Detection, Navigation, Guidance, Aeronautical, and Nautical System and Instrument Manufacturing.

334516 Analytical Laboratory Instrument Manufacturing

This U.S. industry comprises establishments primarily engaged in manufacturing instruments and instrumentation systems for laboratory analysis of the chemical or physical composition or concentration of samples of solid, fluid, gaseous, or composite material.

Cross-References.   Establishments primarily engaged in--

- Manufacturing instruments for monitoring and analyzing continuous samples from medical patients--are classified in U.S. Industry 334510, Electromedical and Electrotherapeutic Apparatus Manufacturing; and
- Manufacturing instruments and related devices that measure, display, or control (i.e., monitor or analyze) industrial process variables--are classified in U.S. Industry 334513, Instruments and Related Products Manufacturing for Measuring, Displaying, and Controlling Industrial Process Variables.

T—Canadian, Mexican, and United States industries are comparable.

334517 Irradiation Apparatus Manufacturing

This U.S. industry comprises establishments primarily engaged in manufacturing irradiation apparatus and tubes for applications, such as medical diagnostic, medical therapeutic, industrial, research and scientific evaluation. Irradiation can take the form of beta-rays, gamma-rays, X-rays, or other ionizing radiation.

334519 Other Measuring and Controlling Device Manufacturing

This U.S. industry comprises establishments primarily engaged in manufacturing measuring and controlling devices (except search, detection, navigation, guidance, aeronautical, and nautical instruments and systems; automatic environmental controls for residential, commercial, and appliance use; instruments for measurement, display, and control of industrial process variables; totalizing fluid meters and counting devices; instruments for measuring and testing electricity and electrical signals; analytical laboratory instruments; irradiation equipment; and electromedical and electrotherapeutic apparatus).

Illustrative Examples:

Aircraft engine instruments manufacturing
Automotive emissions testing equipment manufacturing
Clocks assembling
Meteorological instruments manufacturing
Physical properties testing and inspection equipment manufacturing

Polygraph machines manufacturing
Radiation detection and monitoring instruments manufacturing
Surveying instruments manufacturing
Thermometers, liquid-in-glass and bimetal types (except medical), manufacturing
Watches and parts (except crystals) manufacturing

Cross-References.　　Establishments primarily engaged in--

- Manufacturing medical thermometers--are classified in U.S. Industry 339112, Surgical and Medical Instrument Manufacturing;
- Manufacturing search, detection, navigation, guidance, aeronautical, and nautical systems and instruments-- are classified in U.S. Industry 334511, Search, Detection, Navigation, Guidance, Aeronautical, and Nautical System and Instrument Manufacturing;
- Manufacturing automatic controls and regulators for applications, such as heating, air-conditioning, refrigeration and appliances--are classified in U.S. Industry 334512, Automatic Environmental Control Manufacturing for Residential, Commercial, and Appliance Use;
- Manufacturing instruments and related devices that measure, display, or control (i.e., monitor or analyze) industrial process variables--are classified in U.S. Industry 334513, Instruments and Related Products Manufacturing for Measuring, Displaying, and Controlling Industrial Process Variables;
- Manufacturing totalizing (i.e., registering) fluid meters and counting devices, including motor vehicle gauges--are classified in U.S. Industry 334514, Totalizing Fluid Meter and Counting Device Manufacturing;
- Manufacturing instruments for measuring and testing the characteristics of electricity and electrical signals- -are classified in U.S. Industry 334515, Instrument Manufacturing for Measuring and Testing Electricity and Electrical Signals;
- Manufacturing instruments for laboratory analysis of the physical composition or concentration of samples of solid, fluid, gaseous, or composite materials--are classified in U.S. Industry 334516, Analytical Laboratory Instrument Manufacturing;
- Manufacturing X-ray apparatus, tubes, or related irradiation apparatus--are classified in U.S. Industry 334517, Irradiation Apparatus Manufacturing;
- Manufacturing electromedical and electrotherapeutic apparatus--are classified in U.S. Industry 334510, Electromedical and Electrotherapeutic Apparatus Manufacturing;
- Manufacturing glass watch and clock crystals--are classified in Industry 32721, Glass and Glass Product Manufacturing;
- Manufacturing plastics watch and clock crystals--are classified in U.S. Industry 326199, All Other Plastics Product Manufacturing; and

T—Canadian, Mexican, and United States industries are comparable.

• Manufacturing timing relays--are classified in U.S. Industry 335314, Relay and Industrial Control Manufacturing.

3346   Manufacturing and Reproducing Magnetic and Optical Media[T]

33461   Manufacturing and Reproducing Magnetic and Optical Media[T]

This industry comprises establishments primarily engaged in (1) manufacturing optical and magnetic media, such as blank audio tapes, blank video tapes, and blank diskettes, and/or (2) mass duplicating (i.e., making copies) audio, video, software, and other data on magnetic, optical, and similar media.

Cross-References.   Establishments primarily engaged in--

• Designing, developing, and publishing prepackaged software--are classified in Industry 51121, Software Publishers; and
• Audio, motion picture, and/or video production and/or distribution--are classified in Subsector 512, Motion Picture and Sound Recording Industries.

334613 Blank Magnetic and Optical Recording Media Manufacturing

This U.S. industry comprises establishments primarily engaged in manufacturing blank magnetic and optical recording media, such as blank magnetic tape, blank diskettes, blank optical discs, hard drive media, and blank magnetic tape cassettes.

Cross-References.

Establishments primarily engaged in mass reproducing computer software and other audio and video material are classified in U.S. Industry 334614, Software and Other Prerecorded Compact Disc, Tape, and Record Reproducing.

334614 Software and Other Prerecorded Compact Disc, Tape, and Record Reproducing

This U.S. industry comprises establishments primarily engaged in mass reproducing computer software or other prerecorded audio and video material on magnetic or optical media, such as CD-ROMs, DVDs, tapes, or cartridges. These establishments do not generally develop any software or produce any audio or video content. This industry includes establishments that mass reproduce game CDs and cartridges.

Cross-References.   Establishments primarily engaged in--

• Designing, developing, and publishing prepackaged software--are classified in Industry 511210, Software Publishers;
• Audio, motion picture, and/or video production and/or distribution--are classified in Subsector 512, Motion Picture and Sound Recording Industries; and
• Manufacturing blank audio and video tapes, blank diskettes, and blank optical discs--are classified in U.S. Industry 334613, Blank Magnetic and Optical Recording Media Manufacturing.

335   Electrical Equipment, Appliance, and Component Manufacturing[T]

Industries in the Electrical Equipment, Appliance, and Component Manufacturing subsector manufacture products that generate, distribute and use electrical power. Electric Lighting Equipment Manufacturing establishments produce electric lamp bulbs, lighting fixtures, and parts. Household Appliance Manufacturing establishments make both small and major electrical appliances and parts. Electrical Equipment Manufacturing establishments make goods, such as electric motors, generators, transformers, and switchgear apparatus. Other Electrical Equipment and Component Manufacturing establishments make devices for storing electrical power (e.g., batteries), for transmitting electricity (e.g., insulated wire), and wiring devices (e.g., electrical outlets, fuse boxes, and light switches).

T—Canadian, Mexican, and United States industries are comparable.

3351   Electric Lighting Equipment Manufacturing[T]

This industry group comprises establishments primarily engaged in (1) manufacturing electric light bulbs and tubes, and parts and components (except glass blanks for electric light bulbs) or (2) manufacturing electric lighting fixtures (except vehicular), nonelectric lighting equipment, lamp shades (except glass and plastics), and lighting fixture components (except current-carrying wiring devices).

33511   Electric Lamp Bulb and Part Manufacturing[T]
See industry description for 335110.

335110   Electric Lamp Bulb and Part Manufacturing

This industry comprises establishments primarily engaged in manufacturing electric light bulbs and tubes, and parts and components (except glass blanks for electric light bulbs).

Cross-References.   Establishments primarily engaged in--

- Manufacturing glass blanks for electric light bulbs--are classified in U.S. Industry 327212, Other Pressed and Blown Glass and Glassware Manufacturing;
- Manufacturing vehicular lighting fixtures--are classified in Industry 336320, Motor Vehicle Electrical and Electronic Equipment Manufacturing;
- Manufacturing light emitting diodes (LEDs)--are classified in U.S. Industry 334413, Semiconductor and Related Device Manufacturing; and
- Manufacturing other lighting fixtures (except vehicular)--are classified in Industry 33512, Lighting Fixture Manufacturing.

33512   Lighting Fixture Manufacturing[T]

This industry comprises establishments primarily engaged in manufacturing electric lighting fixtures (except vehicular), nonelectric lighting equipment, lamp shades (except glass and plastics), and lighting fixture components (except current-carrying wiring devices).

Cross-References.   Establishments primarily engaged in--

- Manufacturing vehicular lighting fixtures--are classified in Industry 33632, Motor Vehicle Electrical and Electronic Equipment Manufacturing;
- Manufacturing electric light bulbs, tubes, and parts--are classified in Industry 33511, Electric Lamp Bulb and Part Manufacturing;
- Manufacturing current-carrying wiring devices for lighting fixtures--are classified in Industry 33593, Wiring Device Manufacturing;
- Manufacturing ceiling fans or bath fans with integrated lighting fixtures--are classified in Industry 33521, Small Electrical Appliance Manufacturing;
- Manufacturing plastics lamp shades--are classified in Industry 32619, Other Plastics Product Manufacturing;
- Manufacturing glassware and glass parts for lighting fixtures--are classified in Industry 32721, Glass and Glass Product Manufacturing; and
- Manufacturing signaling devices that incorporate electric light bulbs, such as traffic and railway signals--are classified in Industry 33429, Other Communications Equipment Manufacturing.

335121   Residential Electric Lighting Fixture Manufacturing

This U.S. industry comprises establishments primarily engaged in manufacturing fixed or portable residential electric lighting fixtures and lamp shades of metal, paper, or textiles. Residential electric lighting fixtures include those for use both inside and outside the residence.

T—Canadian, Mexican, and United States industries are comparable.

Illustrative Examples:

Ceiling lighting fixtures, residential, manufacturing   Table lamps (i.e., lighting fixtures) manufacturing
Chandeliers, residential, manufacturing

Cross-References.   Establishments primarily engaged in--

- Manufacturing glassware for residential lighting fixtures--are classified in Industry 32721, Glass and Glass Product Manufacturing;
- Manufacturing plastics lamp shades--are classified in U.S. Industry 326199, All Other Plastics Product Manufacturing;
- Manufacturing electric light bulbs, tubes, and parts--are classified in Industry 335110, Electric Lamp Bulb and Part Manufacturing;
- Manufacturing ceiling fans or bath fans with integrated lighting fixtures--are classified in Industry 335210, Small Electrical Appliance Manufacturing;
- Manufacturing current-carrying wiring devices for lighting fixtures--are classified in U.S. Industry 335931, Current-Carrying Wiring Device Manufacturing;
- Manufacturing commercial, industrial, and institutional electric lighting fixtures--are classified in U.S. Industry 335122, Commercial, Industrial, and Institutional Electric Lighting Fixture Manufacturing; and
- Manufacturing other lighting fixtures, such as street lights (except traffic signals), flashlights, and nonelectric lighting fixtures--are classified in U.S. Industry 335129, Other Lighting Equipment Manufacturing.

335122 Commercial, Industrial, and Institutional Electric Lighting Fixture Manufacturing

This U.S. industry comprises establishments primarily engaged in manufacturing commercial, industrial, and institutional electric lighting fixtures.

Cross-References.   Establishments primarily engaged in--

- Manufacturing glassware for commercial, industrial, and institutional electric lighting fixtures--are classified in Industry 32721, Glass and Glass Product Manufacturing;
- Manufacturing residential electric lighting fixtures--are classified in U.S. Industry 335121, Residential Electric Lighting Fixture Manufacturing;
- Manufacturing current-carrying wiring devices for lighting fixtures--are classified in U.S. Industry 335931, Current-Carrying Wiring Device Manufacturing;
- Manufacturing vehicular lighting fixtures--are classified in Industry 336320, Motor Vehicle Electrical and Electronic Equipment Manufacturing;
- Manufacturing electric light bulbs, tubes, and parts--are classified in Industry 335110, Electric Lamp Bulb and Part Manufacturing;
- Manufacturing other lighting fixtures, such as street lights (except traffic signals), flashlights, and nonelectric lighting equipment--are classified in U.S. Industry 335129, Other Lighting Equipment Manufacturing; and
- Manufacturing signaling devices that incorporate electric light bulbs, such as traffic and railway signals--are classified in Industry 334290, Other Communications Equipment Manufacturing.

335129 Other Lighting Equipment Manufacturing

This U.S. industry comprises establishments primarily engaged in manufacturing electric lighting fixtures (except residential, commercial, industrial, institutional, and vehicular electric lighting fixtures) and nonelectric lighting equipment.

Illustrative Examples:

Christmas tree lighting sets, electric, manufacturing   Fireplace logs, electric, manufacturing

---

T—Canadian, Mexican, and United States industries are comparable.

Flashlights manufacturing
Insect lamps, electric, manufacturing
Lanterns (e.g., carbide, electric, gas, gasoline, kerosene) manufacturing

Spotlights (except vehicular) manufacturing
Street lighting fixtures (except traffic signals) manufacturing

Cross-References.   Establishments primarily engaged in--

- Manufacturing glassware for lighting fixtures--are classified in Industry 32721, Glass and Glass Product Manufacturing;
- Manufacturing electric light bulbs, tubes, and parts--are classified in Industry 335110, Electric Lamp Bulb and Part Manufacturing;
- Manufacturing current-carrying wiring devices for lighting fixtures--are classified in U.S. Industry 335931, Current-Carrying Wiring Device Manufacturing;
- Manufacturing residential electric lighting fixtures--are classified in U.S. Industry 335121, Residential Electric Lighting Fixture Manufacturing;
- Manufacturing commercial, industrial, and institutional electric lighting fixtures--are classified in U.S. Industry 335122, Commercial, Industrial, and Institutional Electric Lighting Fixture Manufacturing;
- Manufacturing vehicular lighting fixtures--are classified in Industry 336320, Motor Vehicle Electrical and Electronic Equipment Manufacturing; and
- Manufacturing signaling devices that incorporate electric light bulbs, such as traffic and railway signals--are classified in Industry 334290, Other Communications Equipment Manufacturing.

3352   Household Appliance Manufacturing[T]

This industry group comprises establishments primarily engaged in manufacturing small electric appliances, electric housewares, and major household appliances.

33521   Small Electrical Appliance Manufacturing[T]
See industry description for 335210.

335210 Small Electrical Appliance Manufacturing

This industry comprises establishments primarily engaged in manufacturing small electric appliances and electric housewares, household-type fans (except attic fans), household-type vacuum cleaners, and other electric household-type floor care machines.

Illustrative Examples:

Bath fans, residential, manufacturing
Carpet and floor cleaning equipment, household-type electric, manufacturing
Ceiling fans, residential, manufacturing
Curling irons, household-type electric, manufacturing
Electric blankets manufacturing
Portable electric space heaters manufacturing
Portable hair dryers, electric, manufacturing

Portable cooking appliances (except microwave, convection ovens), household-type electric, manufacturing
Portable humidifiers and dehumidifiers manufacturing
Scissors, electric, manufacturing
Ventilating and exhaust fans (except attic fans), household-type, manufacturing

Cross-References.   Establishments primarily engaged in--

- Manufacturing attic fans--are classified in U.S. Industry 333413, Industrial and Commercial Fan and Blower and Air Purification Equipment Manufacturing;
- Manufacturing wall and baseboard heating units for permanent installation--are classified in U.S. Industry 333414, Heating Equipment (except Warm Air Furnaces) Manufacturing;
- Manufacturing room air-conditioners--are classified in U.S. Industry 333415, Air-Conditioning and Warm Air Heating Equipment and Commercial and Industrial Refrigeration Equipment Manufacturing;

T—Canadian, Mexican, and United States industries are comparable.

- Manufacturing microwave and convection ovens--are classified in Industry 335220, Major Household Appliance Manufacturing;
- Manufacturing electric vacuum cleaners for commercial, industrial, and institutional uses, and mechanical carpet sweepers--are classified in U.S. Industry 333318, Other Commercial and Service Industry Machinery Manufacturing; and
- Installing central vacuum cleaning systems--are classified in Industry 238290, Other Building Equipment Contractors.

33522   Major Household Appliance Manufacturing[T]
See industry description for 335220.

335220 Major Household Appliance Manufacturing

This industry comprises establishments primarily engaged in manufacturing household-type cooking appliances, household-type laundry equipment, household-type refrigerators, upright and chest freezers, and other electrical and nonelectrical major household-type appliances, such as dishwashers, water heaters, and garbage disposal units.

Cross-References.   Establishments primarily engaged in--

- Manufacturing small electric appliances and electric housewares, such as hot plates, griddles, toasters, and electric irons--are classified in Industry 335210, Small Electrical Appliance Manufacturing;
- Manufacturing commercial and industrial refrigerators and freezers--are classified in U.S. Industry 333415, Air-Conditioning and Warm Air Heating Equipment and Commercial and Industrial Refrigeration Equipment Manufacturing;
- Manufacturing commercial-type cooking equipment and commercial-type laundry, drycleaning, and pressing equipment--are classified in U.S. Industry 333318, Other Commercial and Service Industry Machinery Manufacturing; and
- Manufacturing household-type sewing machines--are classified in U.S. Industry 333249, Other Industrial Machinery Manufacturing.

3353   Electrical Equipment Manufacturing[T]

33531   Electrical Equipment Manufacturing[T]

This industry comprises establishments primarily engaged in manufacturing power, distribution, and specialty transformers; electric motors, generators, and motor generator sets; switchgear and switchboard apparatus; relays; and industrial controls.

Cross-References.   Establishments primarily engaged in--

- Manufacturing turbine generator set units and electric outboard motors--are classified in Industry 33361, Engine, Turbine, and Power Transmission Equipment Manufacturing;
- Manufacturing electronic component-type transformers and switches--are classified in Industry 33441, Semiconductor and Other Electronic Component Manufacturing;
- Manufacturing environmental controls and industrial process control instruments--are classified in Industry 33451, Navigational, Measuring, Electromedical, and Control Instruments Manufacturing;
- Manufacturing switches for electrical circuits, such as pushbutton and snap switches--are classified in Industry 33593, Wiring Device Manufacturing;
- Manufacturing welding and soldering equipment (except handheld soldering irons)--are classified in Industry 33399, All Other General Purpose Machinery Manufacturing; and
- Manufacturing starting motors and generators for internal combustion engines--are classified in Industry 33632, Motor Vehicle Electrical and Electronic Equipment Manufacturing.

T—Canadian, Mexican, and United States industries are comparable.

335311 Power, Distribution, and Specialty Transformer Manufacturing

This U.S. industry comprises establishments primarily engaged in manufacturing power, distribution, and specialty transformers (except electronic components). Industrial-type and consumer-type transformers in this industry vary (e.g., step up or step down) voltage but do not convert alternating to direct or direct to alternating current.

Illustrative Examples:

Fluorescent ballasts (i.e., transformers) manufacturing
Substation transformers, electric power distribution, manufacturing

Distribution transformers, electric, manufacturing
Transmission and distribution voltage regulators manufacturing

Cross-References.

Establishments primarily engaged in manufacturing electronic component-type transformers are classified in U.S. Industry 334416, Capacitor, Resistor, Coil, Transformer, and Other Inductor Manufacturing.

335312 Motor and Generator Manufacturing

This U.S. industry comprises establishments primarily engaged in manufacturing electric motors (except internal combustion engine starting motors), power generators (except battery charging alternators for internal combustion engines), and motor generator sets (except turbine generator set units). This industry includes establishments rewinding armatures on a factory basis.

Cross-References.   Establishments primarily engaged in--

- Manufacturing electric outboard motors--are classified in U.S. Industry 333618, Other Engine Equipment Manufacturing;
- Manufacturing gas, steam, or hydraulic turbine generator set units--are classified in U.S. Industry 333611, Turbine and Turbine Generator Set Units Manufacturing;
- Manufacturing starting motors and battery charging alternators for internal combustion engines--are classified in Industry 336320, Motor Vehicle Electrical and Electronic Equipment Manufacturing;
- Rewinding armatures, not on a factory basis--are classified in Industry 811310, Commercial and Industrial Machinery and Equipment (except Automotive and Electronic) Repair and Maintenance; and
- Manufacturing welding and soldering equipment (except handheld soldering irons)--are classified in U.S. Industry 333992, Welding and Soldering Equipment Manufacturing.

335313 Switchgear and Switchboard Apparatus Manufacturing

This U.S. industry comprises establishments primarily engaged in manufacturing switchgear and switchboard apparatus.

Illustrative Examples:

Circuit breakers, power, manufacturing
Control panels, electric power distribution, manufacturing
Ducts for electrical switchboard apparatus manufacturing

Fuses, electric, manufacturing
Power switching equipment manufacturing
Switches, electric power (except pushbutton, snap, solenoid, tumbler), manufacturing

Cross-References.   Establishments primarily engaged in--

- Manufacturing relays--are classified in U.S. Industry 335314, Relay and Industrial Control Manufacturing;

T—Canadian, Mexican, and United States industries are comparable.

- Manufacturing switches for electronic applications--are classified in U.S. Industry 334419, Other Electronic Component Manufacturing; and
- Manufacturing snap, pushbutton, and similar switches for electrical circuits--are classified in U.S. Industry 335931, Current-Carrying Wiring Device Manufacturing.

335314 Relay and Industrial Control Manufacturing

This U.S. industry comprises establishments primarily engaged in manufacturing relays, motor starters and controllers, and other industrial controls and control accessories.

Cross-References.   Establishments primarily engaged in--

- Manufacturing environmental and appliance control equipment--are classified in U.S. Industry 334512, Automatic Environmental Control Manufacturing for Residential, Commercial, and Appliance Use; and
- Manufacturing instruments for controlling industrial process variables--are classified in U.S. Industry 334513, Instruments and Related Products Manufacturing for Measuring, Displaying, and Controlling Industrial Process Variables.

3359   Other Electrical Equipment and Component Manufacturing[T]

This industry group comprises establishments manufacturing electrical equipment and components (except electric lighting equipment, household-type appliances, transformers, switchgear, relays, motors, and generators).

33591   Battery Manufacturing[T]

This industry comprises establishments primarily engaged in manufacturing primary and storage batteries.

335911 Storage Battery Manufacturing

This U.S. industry comprises establishments primarily engaged in manufacturing storage batteries.

Illustrative Examples:

Lead acid storage batteries manufacturing
Lithium storage batteries manufacturing

Rechargeable nickel-cadmium (NICAD) batteries manufacturing

Cross-References.

Establishments primarily engaged in manufacturing primary batteries are classified in U.S. Industry 335912, Primary Battery Manufacturing.

335912 Primary Battery Manufacturing

This U.S. industry comprises establishments primarily engaged in manufacturing wet or dry primary batteries.

Illustrative Examples:

Disposable flashlight batteries manufacturing
Dry cells, primary (e.g., AAA, AA, C, D, 9V), manufacturing

Lithium batteries, primary, manufacturing
Watch batteries manufacturing

Cross-References.

Establishments primarily engaged in manufacturing storage batteries are classified in U.S. Industry 335911, Storage Battery Manufacturing.

T—Canadian, Mexican, and United States industries are comparable.

33592   Communication and Energy Wire and Cable Manufacturing[T]

This industry comprises establishments insulating fiber optic cable, and manufacturing insulated nonferrous wire and cable from nonferrous wire drawn in other establishments.

Cross-References.   Establishments primarily engaged in--

- Drawing nonferrous wire--are classified in Subsector 331, Primary Metal Manufacturing;
- Manufacturing cable sets consisting of insulated wire and various connectors for electronic applications-- are classified in Industry 33441, Semiconductor and Other Electronic Component Manufacturing;
- Manufacturing extension cords, appliance cords, and similar electrical cord sets from purchased, insulated wire or cable--are classified in Industry 33599, All Other Electrical Equipment and Component Manufacturing; and
- Manufacturing unsheathed fiber optic materials--are classified in Industry 32721, Glass and Glass Product Manufacturing.

335921   Fiber Optic Cable Manufacturing

This U.S. industry comprises establishments primarily engaged in manufacturing insulated fiber optic cable from purchased fiber optic strand.

Cross-References.   Establishments primarily engaged in--

- Manufacturing unsheathed fiber optic materials--are classified in Industry 32721, Glass and Glass Product Manufacturing; and
- Manufacturing insulated nonferrous wire and cable from purchased wire--are classified in U.S. Industry 335929, Other Communication and Energy Wire Manufacturing.

335929   Other Communication and Energy Wire Manufacturing

This U.S. industry comprises establishments primarily engaged in manufacturing insulated wire and cable of nonferrous metals from purchased wire.

Cross-References.   Establishments primarily engaged in--

- Manufacturing cable sets consisting of insulated wire and various connectors for electronic applications-- are classified in U.S. Industry 334419, Other Electronic Component Manufacturing;
- Manufacturing extension cords, appliance cords, and similar electrical cord sets from purchased insulated wire--are classified in U.S. Industry 335999, All Other Miscellaneous Electrical Equipment and Component Manufacturing;
- Drawing and insulating copper wire in the same establishment--are classified in Industry 331420, Copper Rolling, Drawing, Extruding, and Alloying;
- Drawing and insulating aluminum wire in the same establishment--are classified in U.S. Industry 331318, Other Aluminum Rolling, Drawing, and Extruding; and
- Drawing nonferrous wire (except copper and aluminum)--are classified in U.S. Industry 331491, Nonferrous Metal (except Copper and Aluminum) Rolling, Drawing, and Extruding.

33593   Wiring Device Manufacturing[T]

This industry comprises establishments primarily engaged in manufacturing current-carrying wiring devices and noncurrent-carrying wiring devices for wiring electrical circuits.

T—Canadian, Mexican, and United States industries are comparable.

Cross-References.   Establishments primarily engaged in--

- Manufacturing ceramic and glass insulators--are classified in Subsector 327, Nonmetallic Mineral Product Manufacturing; and
- Manufacturing electronic component-type connectors, sockets, and switches--are classified in Industry 33441, Semiconductor and Other Electronic Component Manufacturing.

335931 Current-Carrying Wiring Device Manufacturing

This U.S. industry comprises establishments primarily engaged in manufacturing current-carrying wiring devices.

Illustrative Examples:

Bus bars, electrical conductors (except switchgear-type), manufacturing
GFCI (ground fault circuit interrupters) manufacturing
Lamp holders manufacturing

Lightning arrestors and coils manufacturing
Receptacles (i.e., outlets), electrical, manufacturing
Switches for electrical wiring (e.g., pressure, pushbutton, snap, tumbler) manufacturing

Cross-References.   Establishments primarily engaged in--

- Manufacturing electronic component-type connectors--are classified in U.S. Industry 334417, Electronic Connector Manufacturing;
- Manufacturing noncurrent-carrying wiring devices--are classified in U.S. Industry 335932, Noncurrent-Carrying Wiring Device Manufacturing; and
- Manufacturing electronic component-type sockets and switches--are classified in U.S. Industry 334419, Other Electronic Component Manufacturing.

335932 Noncurrent-Carrying Wiring Device Manufacturing

This U.S. industry comprises establishments primarily engaged in manufacturing noncurrent-carrying wiring devices.

Illustrative Examples:

Boxes, electrical wiring (e.g., junction, outlet, switch), manufacturing
Conduits and fittings, electrical, manufacturing

Face plates (i.e., outlet or switch covers) manufacturing
Transmission pole and line hardware manufacturing

Cross-References.   Establishments primarily engaged in--

- Manufacturing porcelain and ceramic insulators--are classified in Industry 327110, Pottery, Ceramics, and Plumbing Fixture Manufacturing;
- Manufacturing current-carrying wiring devices--are classified in U.S. Industry 335931, Current-Carrying Wiring Device Manufacturing; and
- Manufacturing glass insulators--are classified in Industry 32721, Glass and Glass Product Manufacturing.

33599 All Other Electrical Equipment and Component Manufacturing[T]

This industry comprises establishments primarily engaged in manufacturing electrical equipment (except electric lighting equipment, household-type appliances, transformers, motors, generators, switchgear, relays, industrial controls, batteries, communication and energy wire and cable, and wiring devices).

T—Canadian, Mexican, and United States industries are comparable.

Illustrative Examples:

Carbon and graphite electrodes and brushes manufacturing

Extension cords made from purchased insulated wire

Door opening and closing devices, electrical, manufacturing

Surge suppressors manufacturing

Cross-References.   Establishments primarily engaged in--

- Manufacturing lighting equipment--are classified in Industry Group 3351, Electric Lighting Equipment Manufacturing;
- Manufacturing household-type appliances--are classified in Industry Group 3352, Household Appliance Manufacturing;
- Manufacturing transformers, motors, generators, switchgear, relays, and industrial controls--are classified in Industry 33531, Electrical Equipment Manufacturing;
- Manufacturing batteries--are classified in Industry 33591, Battery Manufacturing;
- Manufacturing communication and energy wire--are classified in Industry 33592, Communication and Energy Wire and Cable Manufacturing;
- Manufacturing current-carrying and noncurrent-carrying wiring devices--are classified in Industry 33593, Wiring Device Manufacturing;
- Manufacturing carbon or graphite gaskets--are classified in Industry 33999, All Other Miscellaneous Manufacturing;
- Manufacturing electronic component-type rectifiers, voltage regulating integrated circuits, power converting integrated circuits, electronic capacitors, electronic resistors, and similar devices--are classified in Industry 33441, Semiconductor and Other Electronic Component Manufacturing; and
- Manufacturing equipment incorporating lasers--are classified in the Manufacturing sector based on the associated production process of the finished equipment.

335991 Carbon and Graphite Product Manufacturing

This U.S. industry comprises establishments primarily engaged in manufacturing carbon, graphite, and metal-graphite brushes and brush stock; carbon or graphite electrodes for thermal and electrolytic uses; carbon and graphite fibers; and other carbon, graphite, and metal-graphite products.

Cross-References.

Establishments primarily engaged in manufacturing carbon or graphite gaskets are classified in U.S. Industry 339991, Gasket, Packing, and Sealing Device Manufacturing.

335999 All Other Miscellaneous Electrical Equipment and Component Manufacturing

This U.S. industry comprises establishments primarily engaged in manufacturing industrial and commercial electric apparatus and other equipment (except lighting equipment, household appliances, transformers, motors, generators, switchgear, relays, industrial controls, batteries, communication and energy wire and cable, wiring devices, and carbon and graphite products). This industry includes power converters (i.e., AC to DC and DC to AC), power supplies, surge suppressors, and similar equipment for industrial-type and consumer-type equipment.

Illustrative Examples:

Appliance cords made from purchased insulated wire

Battery chargers, solid-state, manufacturing

Door opening and closing devices, electrical, manufacturing

Electric bells manufacturing

Extension cords made from purchased insulated wire

Inverters manufacturing

Surge suppressers manufacturing

Uninterruptible power supplies (UPS) manufacturing

T—Canadian, Mexican, and United States industries are comparable.

Cross-References.   Establishments primarily engaged in--

- Manufacturing lighting equipment--are classified in Industry Group 3351, Electric Lighting Equipment Manufacturing;
- Manufacturing household-type appliances--are classified in Industry Group 3352, Household Appliance Manufacturing;
- Manufacturing transformers, motors, generators, switchgear, relays, and industrial controls--are classified in Industry 33531, Electrical Equipment Manufacturing;
- Manufacturing primary and storage batteries--are classified in Industry 33591, Battery Manufacturing;
- Manufacturing communication and energy wire and cable from purchased wire or fiber optic strand--are classified in Industry 33592, Communication and Energy Wire and Cable Manufacturing;
- Manufacturing current-carrying and noncurrent-carrying wiring devices--are classified in Industry 33593, Wiring Device Manufacturing;
- Manufacturing electronic component-type rectifiers (except semiconductor)--are classified in U.S. Industry 334419, Other Electronic Component Manufacturing;
- Manufacturing semiconductor rectifiers, voltage regulating integrated circuits, power converting integrated circuits, and similar semiconductor devices--are classified in U.S. Industry 334413, Semiconductor and Related Device Manufacturing;
- Manufacturing electronic component-type capacitors and condensers--are classified in U.S. Industry 334416, Capacitor, Resistor, Coil, Transformer, and Other Inductor Manufacturing;
- Manufacturing carbon and graphite products--are classified in U.S. Industry 335991, Carbon and Graphite Product Manufacturing; and
- Manufacturing equipment incorporating lasers--are classified in the Manufacturing sector based on the associated production process of the finished equipment.

336   Transportation Equipment Manufacturing[T]

Industries in the Transportation Equipment Manufacturing subsector produce equipment for transporting people and goods. Transportation equipment is a type of machinery. An entire subsector is devoted to this activity because of the significance of its economic size in all three North American countries.

Establishments in this subsector utilize production processes similar to those of other machinery manufacturing establishments—bending, forming, welding, machining, and assembling metal or plastic parts into components and finished products. However, the assembly of components and subassemblies and their further assembly into finished vehicles tends to be a more common production process in this subsector than in the Machinery Manufacturing subsector.

NAICS has industry groups for the manufacture of equipment for each mode of transport—road, rail, air and water. Parts for motor vehicles warrant a separate industry group because of their importance and because they require less assembly than complete vehicles.

Land use motor vehicle equipment not designed for highway operation (e.g., agricultural equipment, construction equipment, and material handling equipment) is classified in the appropriate NAICS subsector based on the type and use of the equipment.

3361   Motor Vehicle Manufacturing[T]

This industry group comprises establishments primarily engaged in (1) manufacturing complete automobiles, light duty motor vehicles, and heavy duty trucks (i.e., body and chassis or unibody) or (2) manufacturing motor vehicle chassis only.

33611   Automobile and Light Duty Motor Vehicle Manufacturing[T]

This industry comprises establishments primarily engaged in (1) manufacturing complete automobile and light duty motor vehicles (i.e., body and chassis or unibody) or (2) manufacturing automobile and light duty motor vehicle chassis only.

T—Canadian, Mexican, and United States industries are comparable.

Cross-References.

Establishments primarily engaged in manufacturing car, truck, and bus bodies and assembling vehicles on purchased chassis and manufacturing kit cars for highway use are classified in Industry 33621, Motor Vehicle Body and Trailer Manufacturing.

336111 Automobile Manufacturing

This U.S. industry comprises establishments primarily engaged in (1) manufacturing complete automobiles (i.e., body and chassis or unibody) or (2) manufacturing automobile chassis only.

Cross-References.

Establishments primarily engaged in manufacturing car bodies and assembling vehicles on purchased chassis and manufacturing kit cars for highway use are classified in U.S. Industry 336211, Motor Vehicle Body Manufacturing.

336112 Light Truck and Utility Vehicle Manufacturing

This U.S. industry comprises establishments primarily engaged in (1) manufacturing complete light trucks and utility vehicles (i.e., body and chassis) or (2) manufacturing light truck and utility vehicle chassis only. Vehicles made include light duty vans, pick-up trucks, minivans, and sport utility vehicles.

Cross-References.

Establishments primarily engaged in manufacturing truck and bus bodies and assembling vehicles on purchased chassis are classified in U.S. Industry 336211, Motor Vehicle Body Manufacturing.

33612 Heavy Duty Truck Manufacturing[T]
See industry description for 336120.

336120 Heavy Duty Truck Manufacturing

This industry comprises establishments primarily engaged in (1) manufacturing heavy duty truck chassis and assembling complete heavy duty trucks, buses, heavy duty motor homes, and other special purpose heavy duty motor vehicles for highway use or (2) manufacturing heavy duty truck chassis only.

Cross-References.   Establishments primarily engaged in--

- Manufacturing truck and bus bodies and assembling vehicles on purchased chassis--are classified in U.S. Industry 336211, Motor Vehicle Body Manufacturing;
- Manufacturing motor homes on purchased chassis--are classified in U.S. Industry 336213, Motor Home Manufacturing;
- Manufacturing vans, minivans, and light trucks--are classified in U.S. Industry 336112, Light Truck and Utility Vehicle Manufacturing;
- Manufacturing military armored vehicles--are classified in U.S. Industry 336992, Military Armored Vehicle, Tank, and Tank Component Manufacturing; and
- Manufacturing off-highway construction equipment--are classified in Industry 333120, Construction Machinery Manufacturing.

3362 Motor Vehicle Body and Trailer Manufacturing[T]

33621 Motor Vehicle Body and Trailer Manufacturing[T]

This industry comprises establishments primarily engaged in (1) manufacturing motor vehicle bodies and cabs or (2) manufacturing truck, automobile and utility trailers, truck trailer chassis, detachable trailer bodies, and

---

T—Canadian, Mexican, and United States industries are comparable.

detachable trailer chassis. The products made may be sold separately or may be assembled on purchased chassis and sold as complete vehicles.

Motor homes are units where the motor and the living quarters are contained in the same integrated unit, while travel trailers are designed to be towed by a motor unit, such as an automobile or a light truck.

Illustrative Examples:

Bodies and cabs, truck, manufacturing
Camper units, slide-in, for pick-up trucks, manufacturing
Pick-up canopies, caps, or covers manufacturing

Motor homes, self-contained, assembling on purchased chassis
Semi-trailers manufacturing
Travel trailers, recreational, manufacturing

Cross-References.　　Establishments primarily engaged in--

- Making manufactured homes (i.e., mobile homes)--are classified in Industry 32199, All Other Wood Product Manufacturing;
- Customizing automotive vehicle and trailer interiors (i.e., van conversions) on an individual basis--are classified in Industry 81112, Automotive Body, Paint, Interior, and Glass Repair;
- Manufacturing light duty motor home chassis and assembling complete motor homes--are classified in Industry 33611, Automobile and Light Duty Motor Vehicle Manufacturing; and
- Manufacturing heavy duty truck chassis and assembling heavy duty trucks, buses, motor homes, and other special purpose heavy duty motor vehicles for highway use--are classified in Industry 33612, Heavy Duty Truck Manufacturing.

336211 Motor Vehicle Body Manufacturing

This U.S. industry comprises establishments primarily engaged in manufacturing truck and bus bodies and cabs and automobile bodies. The products made may be sold separately or may be assembled on purchased chassis and sold as complete vehicles.

Cross-References.

Establishments primarily engaged in manufacturing heavy duty chassis and assembling heavy duty trucks, buses, motor homes, and other special purpose heavy duty motor vehicles for highway use are classified in Industry 336120, Heavy Duty Truck Manufacturing.

336212 Truck Trailer Manufacturing

This U.S. industry comprises establishments primarily engaged in manufacturing truck trailers, truck trailer chassis, cargo container chassis, detachable trailer bodies, and detachable trailer chassis for sale separately.

Cross-References.

Establishments primarily engaged in manufacturing utility trailers, light-truck trailers, and travel trailers are classified in U.S. Industry 336214, Travel Trailer and Camper Manufacturing.

336213 Motor Home Manufacturing

This U.S. industry comprises establishments primarily engaged in (1) manufacturing motor homes on purchased chassis and/or (2) manufacturing conversion vans on an assembly line basis. Motor homes are units where the motor and the living quarters are integrated in the same unit.

T—Canadian, Mexican, and United States industries are comparable.

Cross-References.   Establishments primarily engaged in--

- Manufacturing light duty motor home chassis and assembling complete motor homes--are classified in U.S. Industry 336112, Light Truck and Utility Vehicle Manufacturing;
- Customizing automotive vehicle and trailer interiors (i.e., van conversions) on an individual basis--are classified in U.S. Industry 811121, Automotive Body, Paint, and Interior Repair and Maintenance; and
- Producing manufactured homes (i.e., mobile homes)--are classified in U.S. Industry 321991, Manufactured Home (Mobile Home) Manufacturing.

336214 Travel Trailer and Camper Manufacturing

This U.S. industry comprises establishments primarily engaged in one or more of the following: (1) manufacturing travel trailers and campers designed to attach to motor vehicles; (2) manufacturing pick-up coaches (i.e., campers) and caps (i.e., covers) for mounting on pick-up trucks; and (3) manufacturing automobile, utility and light-truck trailers. Travel trailers do not have their own motor but are designed to be towed by a motor unit, such as an automobile or a light truck.

Illustrative Examples:

Automobile transporter trailers, single car, manufacturing
Camper units, slide-in, for pick-up trucks, manufacturing
Camping trailers and chassis manufacturing

Horse trailers (except fifth-wheel-type) manufacturing
Pick-up canopies, caps, or covers manufacturing
Travel trailers, recreational, manufacturing
Utility trailers manufacturing

Cross-References.

Establishments primarily engaged in making manufactured homes (i.e., mobile homes) designed to accept permanent water, sewer, and utility connections and equipped with wheels, but not intended for regular highway use, are classified in U.S. Industry 321991, Manufactured Home (Mobile Home) Manufacturing.

3363   Motor Vehicle Parts Manufacturing[T]

This industry group comprises establishments primarily engaged in manufacturing motor vehicle gasoline engines and engine parts, motor vehicle electrical and electronic equipment, motor vehicle steering and suspension components (except springs), motor vehicle brake systems, motor vehicle transmission and power train parts, motor vehicle seating and interior trim, motor vehicle metal stampings, and other motor vehicle parts and accessories. This industry group includes establishments that rebuild motor vehicle parts.

33631   Motor Vehicle Gasoline Engine and Engine Parts Manufacturing[T]
See industry description for 336310.

336310 Motor Vehicle Gasoline Engine and Engine Parts Manufacturing

This industry comprises establishments primarily engaged in (1) manufacturing and/or rebuilding motor vehicle gasoline engines and engine parts and/or (2) manufacturing and/or rebuilding carburetors, pistons, piston rings, and engine valves, whether or not for vehicular use.

Illustrative Examples:

Carburetors, all types, manufacturing
Crankshaft assemblies, automotive and truck gasoline engine, manufacturing
Cylinder heads, automotive and truck gasoline engine, manufacturing

Fuel injection systems and parts, automotive and truck gasoline engine, manufacturing
Gasoline engines for hybrid automotive vehicles manufacturing
Pistons and piston rings manufacturing

T—Canadian, Mexican, and United States industries are comparable.

Manifolds (i.e., intake and exhaust), automotive and truck gasoline engine, manufacturing

Timing gears and chains, automotive and truck gasoline engine, manufacturing

Pumps (e.g., fuel, oil, water), mechanical, automotive and truck gasoline engine (except power steering), manufacturing

Valves, engine, intake and exhaust, manufacturing

Cross-References.   Establishments primarily engaged in--

- Manufacturing wiring harnesses and other vehicular electrical and electronic equipment--are classified in Industry 336320, Motor Vehicle Electrical and Electronic Equipment Manufacturing;
- Manufacturing transmission and power train equipment--are classified in Industry 336350, Motor Vehicle Transmission and Power Train Parts Manufacturing;
- Manufacturing radiators--are classified in Industry 336390, Other Motor Vehicle Parts Manufacturing;
- Manufacturing steering and suspension components--are classified in Industry 336330, Motor Vehicle Steering and Suspension Components (except Spring) Manufacturing;
- Manufacturing parts for machine repair and equipment parts (except electric) on a job or shop basis--are classified in Industry 332710, Machine Shops;
- Manufacturing rubber and plastic belts and hoses without fittings--are classified in Industry 326220, Rubber and Plastics Hoses and Belting Manufacturing; and
- Manufacturing stationary and diesel engines--are classified in U.S. Industry 333618, Other Engine Equipment Manufacturing.

33632   Motor Vehicle Electrical and Electronic Equipment Manufacturing[T]
See industry description for 336320.

336320 Motor Vehicle Electrical and Electronic Equipment Manufacturing

This industry comprises establishments primarily engaged in manufacturing and/or rebuilding electrical and electronic equipment for motor vehicles and internal combustion engines. The products made can be used for all types of transportation equipment (i.e., aircraft, automobiles, trucks, trains, ships) or stationary internal combustion engine applications.

Illustrative Examples:

Alternators and generators for internal combustion engines manufacturing

Automotive lighting fixtures manufacturing

Coils, ignition, internal combustion engines, manufacturing

Distributors for internal combustion engines manufacturing

Electrical control chips (modules), motor vehicle, manufacturing

Electrical ignition cable sets for internal combustion engines manufacturing

Generators for internal combustion engines manufacturing

Ignition wiring harness for internal combustion engines manufacturing

Instrument control panels (i.e., assembling purchased gauges), automotive, truck, and bus, manufacturing

Spark plugs for internal combustion engines manufacturing

Windshield washer pumps, automotive, truck, and bus, manufacturing

Cross-References.   Establishments primarily engaged in--

- Manufacturing automotive lamps (i.e., bulbs)--are classified in Industry 335110, Electric Lamp Bulb and Part Manufacturing;
- Manufacturing automotive batteries--are classified in U.S. Industry 335911, Storage Battery Manufacturing;
- Manufacturing electric motors for electric vehicles--are classified in U.S. Industry 335312, Motor and Generator Manufacturing;
- Manufacturing railway traffic control signals and passenger car alarms--are classified in Industry 334290, Other Communications Equipment Manufacturing; and

---

T—Canadian, Mexican, and United States industries are comparable.

- Manufacturing car stereos--are classified in Industry 334310, Audio and Video Equipment Manufacturing.

33633   Motor Vehicle Steering and Suspension Components (except Spring) Manufacturing[T]
See industry description for 336330.

336330 Motor Vehicle Steering and Suspension Components (except Spring) Manufacturing

This industry comprises establishments primarily engaged in manufacturing and/or rebuilding motor vehicle steering mechanisms and suspension components (except springs).

Illustrative Examples:

Power steering pumps manufacturing
Rack and pinion steering assemblies manufacturing
Shock absorbers, automotive, truck, and bus, manufacturing
Struts, automotive, truck, and bus, manufacturing

Steering columns, automotive, truck, and bus, manufacturing
Steering wheels, automotive, truck, and bus, manufacturing

Cross-References.

Establishments primarily engaged in manufacturing springs are classified in Industry 33261, Spring and Wire Product Manufacturing.

33634   Motor Vehicle Brake System Manufacturing[T]
See industry description for 336340.

336340 Motor Vehicle Brake System Manufacturing

This industry comprises establishments primarily engaged in manufacturing and/or rebuilding motor vehicle brake systems and related components.

Illustrative Examples:

Brake cylinders, master and wheel, automotive, truck, and bus, manufacturing
Brake drums, automotive, truck, and bus, manufacturing
Brake hose assemblies manufacturing

Brake pads and shoes, automotive, truck, and bus, manufacturing
Calipers, brake, automotive, truck, and bus, manufacturing

Cross-References.

Establishments primarily engaged in manufacturing rubber and plastics belts and hoses without fittings are classified in Industry 326220, Rubber and Plastics Hoses and Belting Manufacturing.

33635   Motor Vehicle Transmission and Power Train Parts Manufacturing[T]
See industry description for 336350.

336350 Motor Vehicle Transmission and Power Train Parts Manufacturing

This industry comprises establishments primarily engaged in manufacturing and/or rebuilding motor vehicle transmissions and power train parts.

T—Canadian, Mexican, and United States industries are comparable.

Illustrative Examples:

Automatic transmissions, automotive, truck, and bus, manufacturing

Axle bearings, automotive, truck, and bus, manufacturing

Constant velocity joints, automotive, truck, and bus, manufacturing

Differential and rear axle assemblies, automotive, truck, and bus, manufacturing

Torque converters, automotive, truck, and bus, manufacturing

Universal joints, automotive, truck, and bus, manufacturing

33636   Motor Vehicle Seating and Interior Trim Manufacturing[T]
See industry description for 336360.

336360 Motor Vehicle Seating and Interior Trim Manufacturing

This industry comprises establishments primarily engaged in manufacturing motor vehicle seating, seats, seat frames, seat belts, and interior trimmings.

Cross-References.

Establishments primarily engaged in manufacturing convertible tops for vehicles and those manufacturing air bags are classified in Industry 336390, Other Motor Vehicle Parts Manufacturing.

33637   Motor Vehicle Metal Stamping[T]
See industry description for 336370.

336370 Motor Vehicle Metal Stamping

This industry comprises establishments primarily engaged in manufacturing motor vehicle stampings, such as fenders, tops, body parts, trim, and molding.

Cross-References.   Establishments primarily engaged in--

- Manufacturing stampings and further processing the stampings--are classified according to the process of the specific product made; and
- Manufacturing stampings (except motor vehicle)--are classified in U.S. Industry 332119, Metal Crown, Closure, and Other Metal Stamping (except Automotive).

33639   Other Motor Vehicle Parts Manufacturing[T]
See industry description for 336390.

336390 Other Motor Vehicle Parts Manufacturing

This industry comprises establishments primarily engaged in manufacturing and/or rebuilding motor vehicle parts and accessories (except motor vehicle gasoline engines and engine parts, motor vehicle electrical and electronic equipment, motor vehicle steering and suspension components, motor vehicle brake systems, motor vehicle transmissions and power train parts, motor vehicle seating and interior trim, and motor vehicle stampings).

Illustrative Examples:

Air bag assemblies manufacturing

Air-conditioners, motor vehicle, manufacturing

Air filters, automotive, truck, and bus, manufacturing

Radiators and cores manufacturing

Catalytic converters, engine exhaust, automotive, truck, and bus, manufacturing

Compressors, motor vehicle air-conditioning, manufacturing

Mufflers and resonators, motor vehicle, manufacturing

Wheels (i.e., rims), automotive, truck, and bus, manufacturing

---

T—Canadian, Mexican, and United States industries are comparable.

Cross-References.   Establishments primarily engaged in--

- Manufacturing motor vehicle gasoline engines and engine parts--are classified in Industry 336310, Motor Vehicle Gasoline Engine and Engine Parts Manufacturing;
- Manufacturing motor vehicle electrical and electronic equipment--are classified in Industry 336320, Motor Vehicle Electrical and Electronic Equipment Manufacturing;
- Manufacturing motor vehicle steering and suspension components--are classified in Industry 336330, Motor Vehicle Steering and Suspension Components (except Spring) Manufacturing;
- Manufacturing motor vehicle brake systems--are classified in Industry 336340, Motor Vehicle Brake System Manufacturing;
- Manufacturing motor vehicle transmissions and power train parts--are classified in Industry 336350, Motor Vehicle Transmission and Power Train Parts Manufacturing;
- Manufacturing motor vehicle seating and interior trim--are classified in Industry 336360, Motor Vehicle Seating and Interior Trim Manufacturing;
- Manufacturing motor vehicle stampings--are classified in Industry 336370, Motor Vehicle Metal Stamping; and
- Manufacturing air-conditioning systems and compressors (except motor vehicle air-conditioning systems)-- are classified in U.S. Industry 333415, Air-Conditioning and Warm Air Heating Equipment and Commercial and Industrial Refrigeration Equipment Manufacturing.

3364   Aerospace Product and Parts Manufacturing[T]

33641   Aerospace Product and Parts Manufacturing[T]

This industry comprises establishments primarily engaged in one or more of the following: (1) manufacturing complete aircraft, missiles, or space vehicles; (2) manufacturing aerospace engines, propulsion units, auxiliary equipment or parts; (3) developing and making prototypes of aerospace products; (4) aircraft conversion (i.e., major modifications to systems); and (5) complete aircraft or propulsion systems overhaul and rebuilding (i.e., periodic restoration of aircraft to original design specifications).

Cross-References.

- Establishments primarily engaged in manufacturing space satellites are classified in Industry 33422, Radio and Television Broadcasting and Wireless Communications Equipment Manufacturing;
- Establishments primarily engaged in manufacturing flight simulators are classified in Industry 33331, Commercial and Service Industry Machinery Manufacturing;
- Establishments primarily engaged in the repair of aircraft or aircraft engines (except overhauling, conversion, and rebuilding) are classified in Industry 48819, Other Support Activities for Air Transportation;
- Research and development establishments primarily engaged in aerospace R&D (except prototype production) are classified in Industry 54171, Research and Development in the Physical, Engineering, and Life Sciences;
- Establishments primarily engaged in manufacturing aircraft engine intake and exhaust valves, pistons, or engine filters are classified in Industry 33631, Motor Vehicle Gasoline Engine and Engine Parts Manufacturing;
- Establishments primarily engaged in manufacturing aircraft seating are classified in Industry 33636, Motor Vehicle Seating and Interior Trim Manufacturing;
- Establishments primarily engaged in manufacturing aeronautical, navigational, and guidance systems and instruments are classified in Industry 33451, Navigational, Measuring, Electromedical, and Control Instruments Manufacturing;
- Establishment primarily engaged in manufacturing aircraft engine electrical (aeronautical electrical) equipment or aircraft lighting fixtures are classified in Industry 33632, Motor Vehicle Electrical and Electronic Equipment Manufacturing; and
- Establishments primarily engaged in manufacturing aircraft fluid power subassemblies are classified in Industry 33291, Metal Valve Manufacturing.

T—Canadian, Mexican, and United States industries are comparable.

336411 Aircraft Manufacturing

This U.S. industry comprises establishments primarily engaged in one or more of the following: (1) manufacturing or assembling complete aircraft; (2) developing and making aircraft prototypes; (3) aircraft conversion (i.e., major modifications to systems); and (4) complete aircraft overhaul and rebuilding (i.e., periodic restoration of aircraft to original design specifications).

Cross-References.

- Establishments primarily engaged in manufacturing guided missiles and space vehicles are classified in U.S. Industry 336414, Guided Missile and Space Vehicle Manufacturing;
- Establishments primarily engaged in manufacturing flight simulators are classified in U.S. Industry 333318, Other Commercial and Service Industry Machinery Manufacturing;
- Establishments primarily engaged in the repair of aircraft (except overhauling, conversion, and rebuilding) are classified in Industry 488190, Other Support Activities for Air Transportation; and
- Research and development establishments primarily engaged in aircraft R&D (except prototype production) are classified in U.S. Industry 541715, Research and Development in the Physical, Engineering, and Life Sciences (except Nanotechnology and Biotechnology).

336412 Aircraft Engine and Engine Parts Manufacturing

This U.S. industry comprises establishments primarily engaged in one or more of the following: (1) manufacturing aircraft engines and engine parts; (2) developing and making prototypes of aircraft engines and engine parts; (3) aircraft propulsion system conversion (i.e., major modifications to systems); and (4) aircraft propulsion systems overhaul and rebuilding (i.e., periodic restoration of aircraft propulsion system to original design specifications).

Cross-References.

- Establishments primarily engaged in manufacturing guided missile and space vehicle propulsion units and parts are classified in U.S. Industry 336415, Guided Missile and Space Vehicle Propulsion Unit and Propulsion Unit Parts Manufacturing;
- Establishments primarily engaged in manufacturing aircraft intake and exhaust valves and pistons and aircraft internal combustion engine filters are classified in Industry 336310, Motor Vehicle Gasoline Engine and Engine Parts Manufacturing;
- Establishments primarily engaged in the repair of aircraft engines (except overhauling, conversion, and rebuilding) are classified in Industry 488190, Other Support Activities for Air Transportation;
- Research and development establishments primarily engaged in aircraft engine and engine parts R&D (except prototype production) are classified in U.S. Industry 541715, Research and Development in the Physical, Engineering, and Life Sciences (except Nanotechnology and Biotechnology); and
- Establishments primarily engaged in manufacturing aeronautical instruments are classified in U.S. Industry 334511, Search, Detection, Navigation, Guidance, Aeronautical, and Nautical System and Instrument Manufacturing.

336413 Other Aircraft Parts and Auxiliary Equipment Manufacturing

This U.S. industry comprises establishments primarily engaged in (1) manufacturing aircraft parts or auxiliary equipment (except engines and aircraft fluid power subassemblies) and/or (2) developing and making prototypes of aircraft parts and auxiliary equipment. Auxiliary equipment includes such items as crop dusting apparatus, armament racks, inflight refueling equipment, and external fuel tanks.

Cross-References.

- Establishments primarily engaged in manufacturing aircraft engines and engine parts are classified in U.S. Industry 336412, Aircraft Engine and Engine Parts Manufacturing;

T—Canadian, Mexican, and United States industries are comparable.

- Establishments primarily engaged in manufacturing aeronautical instruments are classified in U.S. Industry 334511, Search, Detection, Navigation, Guidance, Aeronautical, and Nautical System and Instrument Manufacturing;
- Establishments primarily engaged in manufacturing aircraft lighting fixtures and aircraft engine electrical (aeronautical electrical) equipment are classified in Industry 336320, Motor Vehicle Electrical and Electronic Equipment Manufacturing;
- Establishments primarily engaged in manufacturing guided missile and space vehicle parts and auxiliary equipment are classified in U.S. Industry 336419, Other Guided Missile and Space Vehicle Parts and Auxiliary Equipment Manufacturing;
- Establishments primarily engaged in manufacturing of aircraft fluid power subassemblies are classified in U.S. Industry 332912, Fluid Power Valve and Hose Fitting Manufacturing;
- Establishments primarily engaged in manufacturing aircraft seating are classified in Industry 336360, Motor Vehicle Seating and Interior Trim Manufacturing; and
- Research and development establishments primarily engaged in aircraft parts and auxiliary equipment R&D (except prototype production) are classified in U.S. Industry 541715, Research and Development in the Physical, Engineering, and Life Sciences (except Nanotechnology and Biotechnology).

336414 Guided Missile and Space Vehicle Manufacturing

This U.S. industry comprises establishments primarily engaged in (1) manufacturing complete guided missiles and space vehicles and/or (2) developing and making prototypes of guided missiles or space vehicles.

Cross-References.

- Establishments primarily engaged in manufacturing space satellites are classified in Industry 334220, Radio and Television Broadcasting and Wireless Communications Equipment Manufacturing; and
- Research and development establishments primarily engaged in guided missile and space vehicle R&D (except prototype production) are classified in U.S. Industry 541715, Research and Development in the Physical, Engineering, and Life Sciences (except Nanotechnology and Biotechnology).

336415 Guided Missile and Space Vehicle Propulsion Unit and Propulsion Unit Parts Manufacturing

This U.S. industry comprises establishments primarily engaged in (1) manufacturing guided missile and/or space vehicle propulsion units and propulsion unit parts and/or (2) developing and making prototypes of guided missile and space vehicle propulsion units and propulsion unit parts.

Cross-References.

Research and development establishments primarily engaged in guided missile and space propulsion unit and propulsion unit parts R&D (except prototype production) are classified in U.S. Industry 541715, Research and Development in the Physical, Engineering, and Life Sciences (except Nanotechnology and Biotechnology).

336419 Other Guided Missile and Space Vehicle Parts and Auxiliary Equipment Manufacturing

This U.S. industry comprises establishments primarily engaged in (1) manufacturing guided missile and space vehicle parts and auxiliary equipment (except guided missile and space vehicle propulsion units and propulsion unit parts) and/or (2) developing and making prototypes of guided missile and space vehicle parts and auxiliary equipment.

Cross-References.

- Establishments primarily engaged in manufacturing navigational and guidance systems are classified in U.S. Industry 334511, Search, Detection, Navigation, Guidance, Aeronautical, and Nautical System and Instrument Manufacturing;

T—Canadian, Mexican, and United States industries are comparable.

- Establishments primarily engaged in manufacturing guided missile and space vehicle propulsion units and propulsion unit parts are classified in U.S. Industry 336415, Guided Missile and Space Vehicle Propulsion Unit and Propulsion Unit Parts Manufacturing; and
- Research and development establishments primarily engaged in guided missile and space vehicle parts and auxiliary equipment R&D (except prototype production) are classified in U.S. Industry 541715, Research and Development in the Physical, Engineering, and Life Sciences (except Nanotechnology and Biotechnology).

3365 Railroad Rolling Stock Manufacturing[T]

33651 Railroad Rolling Stock Manufacturing[T]
See industry description for 336510.

336510 Railroad Rolling Stock Manufacturing

This industry comprises establishments primarily engaged in one or more of the following: (1) manufacturing and/or rebuilding locomotives, locomotive frames and parts; (2) manufacturing railroad, street, and rapid transit cars and car equipment for operation on rails for freight and passenger service; and (3) manufacturing rail layers, ballast distributors, rail tamping equipment and other railway track maintenance equipment.

Cross-References.

- Establishments primarily engaged in manufacturing mining rail cars are classified in U.S. Industry 333131, Mining Machinery and Equipment Manufacturing;
- Establishments primarily engaged in manufacturing locomotive fuel lubricating or cooling medium pumps are classified in U.S. Industry 333914, Measuring, Dispensing, and Other Pumping Equipment Manufacturing;
- Repair establishments of railroad and local transit companies primarily engaged in repairing railroad and transit cars are classified in Industry 488210, Support Activities for Rail Transportation; and
- Establishments not owned by railroad or local transit companies engaged in repairing railroad cars and locomotive engines are classified in Industry 811310, Commercial and Industrial Machinery and Equipment (except Automotive and Electronic) Repair and Maintenance.

3366 Ship and Boat Building[T]

33661 Ship and Boat Building[T]

This industry comprises establishments primarily engaged in operating shipyards or boat yards (i.e., ship or boat manufacturing facilities). Shipyards are fixed facilities with drydocks and fabrication equipment capable of building a ship, defined as watercraft typically suitable or intended for other than personal or recreational use. Boats are defined as watercraft typically suitable or intended for personal use. Activities of shipyards include the construction of ships, their repair, conversion and alteration, production of prefabricated ship and barge sections, and specialized services, such as ship scaling.

Illustrative Examples:

Barge building
Boat yards (i.e., boat manufacturing facilities)
Cargo ship building
Drilling and production platforms, floating, oil and gas, building

Inflatable plastic boats, heavy-duty, manufacturing
Inflatable rubber boats, heavy-duty, manufacturing
Passenger ship building
Rigid inflatable boats (RIBs) manufacturing
Rowboats manufacturing

T—Canadian, Mexican, and United States industries are comparable.

Cross-References.   Establishments primarily engaged in--

- Manufacturing inflatable rubber swimming pool rafts and similar flotation devices--are classified in Industry 32629, Other Rubber Product Manufacturing;
- Manufacturing inflatable plastic swimming pool rafts and similar flotation devices--are classified in Industry 32619, Other Plastics Product Manufacturing;
- Fabricating structural assemblies or components for ships, or subcontractors engaged in ship painting, joinery, carpentry work, and electrical wiring installation--are classified based on the production process used; and
- Ship repairs performed in floating drydocks--are classified in Industry 48839, Other Support Activities for Water Transportation.

336611 Ship Building and Repairing

This U.S. industry comprises establishments primarily engaged in operating shipyards. Shipyards are fixed facilities with drydocks and fabrication equipment capable of building a ship, defined as watercraft typically suitable or intended for other than personal or recreational use. Activities of shipyards include the construction of ships, their repair, conversion and alteration, the production of prefabricated ship and barge sections, and specialized services, such as ship scaling.

Illustrative Examples:

Barge building
Cargo ship building
Passenger ship building

Drilling and production platforms, floating, oil and gas, building
Submarine building

Cross-References.   Establishments primarily engaged in--

- Fabricating structural assemblies or components for ships, or subcontractors engaged in ship painting, joinery, carpentry work, and electrical wiring installation--are classified based on the production process used; and
- Ship repairs performed in floating drydocks--are classified in Industry 488390, Other Support Activities for Water Transportation.

336612 Boat Building

This U.S. industry comprises establishments primarily engaged in building boats. Boats are defined as watercraft not built in shipyards and typically of the type suitable or intended for personal use. Included in this industry are establishments that manufacture heavy-duty inflatable rubber or inflatable plastic boats (RIBs).

Illustrative Examples:

Dinghy (except inflatable rubber) manufacturing
Inflatable plastic boats, heavy-duty, manufacturing
Inflatable rubber boats, heavy-duty, manufacturing
Motorboats, inboard or outboard, building

Rigid inflatable boats (RIBs) manufacturing
Rowboats manufacturing
Sailboat building, not done in shipyards
Yacht building, not done in shipyards

Cross-References.   Establishments primarily engaged in--

- Ship building or ship repairs performed in a shipyard--are classified in U.S. Industry 336611, Ship Building and Repairing;
- Manufacturing inflatable rubber swimming pool rafts and similar flotation devices--are classified in U.S. Industry 326299, All Other Rubber Product Manufacturing; and
- Manufacturing inflatable plastic swimming pool rafts and similar flotation devices--are classified in U.S. Industry 326199, All Other Plastics Product Manufacturing.

T—Canadian, Mexican, and United States industries are comparable.

3369   Other Transportation Equipment Manufacturing[T]

33699   Other Transportation Equipment Manufacturing[T]

This industry comprises establishments primarily engaged in manufacturing motorcycles, bicycles, metal tricycles, complete military armored vehicles, tanks, self-propelled weapons, vehicles pulled by draft animals, and other transportation equipment (except motor vehicles, boats, ships, railroad rolling stock, and aerospace products), including parts thereof.

Cross-References.   Establishments primarily engaged in--

- Manufacturing ships and boats--are classified in Industry 33661, Ship and Boat Building;
- Manufacturing aerospace products and parts--are classified in Industry 33641, Aerospace Product and Parts Manufacturing;
- Manufacturing motor vehicle parts--are classified in Industry Group 3363, Motor Vehicle Parts Manufacturing;
- Manufacturing children's vehicles (except bicycles and metal tricycles)--are classified in Industry 33993, Doll, Toy, and Game Manufacturing;
- Manufacturing railroad rolling stock--are classified in Industry 33651, Railroad Rolling Stock Manufacturing; and
- Manufacturing motor vehicles--are classified in Industry Group 3361, Motor Vehicle Manufacturing.

336991 Motorcycle, Bicycle, and Parts Manufacturing

This U.S. industry comprises establishments primarily engaged in manufacturing motorcycles, bicycles, tricycles and similar equipment, and parts.

Cross-References.   Establishments primarily engaged in--

- Manufacturing children's vehicles (except bicycles and metal tricycles)--are classified in Industry 339930, Doll, Toy, and Game Manufacturing; and
- Manufacturing powered golf carts and other similar motorized personnel carriers--are classified in U.S. Industry 336999, All Other Transportation Equipment Manufacturing.

336992 Military Armored Vehicle, Tank, and Tank Component Manufacturing

This U.S. industry comprises establishments primarily engaged in manufacturing complete military armored vehicles, combat tanks, specialized components for combat tanks, and self-propelled weapons.

Cross-References.

Establishments primarily engaged in manufacturing nonarmored military universal carriers are classified in U.S. Industry 336112, Light Truck and Utility Vehicle Manufacturing.

336999 All Other Transportation Equipment Manufacturing

This U.S. industry comprises establishments primarily engaged in manufacturing transportation equipment (except motor vehicles, motor vehicle parts, boats, ships, railroad rolling stock, aerospace products, motorcycles, bicycles, armored vehicles and tanks).

Illustrative Examples:

All-terrain vehicles (ATVs), wheeled or tracked, manufacturing

Golf carts and similar motorized passenger carriers manufacturing

---

T—Canadian, Mexican, and United States industries are comparable.

Animal-drawn vehicles and parts manufacturing	Race cars manufacturing
Gocarts (except children's) manufacturing	Snowmobiles and parts manufacturing

Cross-References.   Establishments primarily engaged in--

- Manufacturing motorcycles, bicycles, and parts--are classified in U.S. Industry 336991, Motorcycle, Bicycle, and Parts Manufacturing;
- Manufacturing military armored vehicles, tanks, and tank components--are classified in U.S. Industry 336992, Military Armored Vehicle, Tank, and Tank Component Manufacturing;
- Manufacturing ships and boats--are classified in Industry 33661, Ship and Boat Building;
- Manufacturing aerospace products and parts--are classified in Industry 33641, Aerospace Product and Parts Manufacturing;
- Manufacturing motor vehicle parts--are classified in Industry Group 3363, Motor Vehicle Parts Manufacturing;
- Manufacturing railroad rolling stock--are classified in Industry 336510, Railroad Rolling Stock Manufacturing; and
- Manufacturing motor vehicles--are classified in Industry Group 3361, Motor Vehicle Manufacturing.

337   Furniture and Related Product Manufacturing[T]

Industries in the Furniture and Related Product Manufacturing subsector make furniture and related articles, such as mattresses, window blinds, cabinets, and fixtures. The processes used in the manufacture of furniture include the cutting, bending, molding, laminating, and assembly of such materials as wood, metal, glass, plastics, and rattan. However, the production process for furniture is not solely bending metal, cutting and shaping wood, or extruding and molding plastics. Design and fashion trends play an important part in the production of furniture. The integrated design of the article for both esthetic and functional qualities is also a major part of the process of manufacturing furniture. Design services may be performed by the furniture establishment's work force or may be purchased from industrial designers.

Furniture may be made of any material, but the most common ones used in North America are metal and wood. Furniture manufacturing establishments may specialize in making articles primarily from one material. Some of the equipment required to make a wooden table, for example, is different from that used to make a metal one. However, furniture is usually made from several materials. A wooden table might have metal brackets, and a wooden chair a fabric or plastics seat. Therefore, in NAICS, furniture initially is classified based on the type of furniture (application for which it is designed) rather than the material used. For example, an upholstered sofa is treated as household furniture, although it may also be used in hotels or offices.

When classifying furniture according to the component material from which it is made, furniture made from more than one material is classified based on the material used in the frame, or if there is no frame, the predominant component material. Upholstered household furniture (excluding kitchen and dining room chairs with upholstered seats) is classified without regard to the frame material. Kitchen or dining room chairs with upholstered seats are classified according to the frame material.

Furniture may be made on a stock or custom basis and may be shipped assembled or unassembled (i.e., knockdown). The manufacture of furniture parts and frames is included in this subsector.

Some of the processes used in furniture manufacturing are similar to processes that are used in other segments of manufacturing. For example, cutting and assembly occurs in the production of wood trusses that are classified in Subsector 321, Wood Product Manufacturing. However, the multiple processes that distinguish wood furniture manufacturing from wood product manufacturing warrant inclusion of wooden furniture manufacturing in the Furniture and Related Product Manufacturing subsector. Metal furniture manufacturing uses techniques that are also employed in the manufacturing of roll formed products classified in Subsector 332, Fabricated Metal Product Manufacturing. The molding process for plastics furniture is similar to the molding of other plastics products. However, plastics furniture producing establishments tend to specialize in furniture.

NAICS attempts to keep furniture manufacturing together, but there are two notable exceptions: seating for transportation equipment and specialized hospital furniture (e.g., hospital beds and operating tables). These exceptions are related to the fact that some of the aspects of the production process for these products, primarily the design, are highly integrated with the other manufactured goods, namely motor vehicles and medical equipment.

T—Canadian, Mexican, and United States industries are comparable.

3371 Household and Institutional Furniture and Kitchen Cabinet Manufacturing[T]

This industry group comprises establishments manufacturing household-type furniture, such as living room, kitchen and bedroom furniture and institutional (i.e., public building) furniture, such as furniture for schools, theaters, and churches.

33711 Wood Kitchen Cabinet and Countertop Manufacturing[T]
See industry description for 337110.

337110 Wood Kitchen Cabinet and Countertop Manufacturing

This industry comprises establishments primarily engaged in manufacturing wood or plastics laminated on wood kitchen cabinets, bathroom vanities, and countertops (except freestanding). The cabinets and counters may be made on a stock or custom basis.

Cross-References.   Establishments primarily engaged in--

- Manufacturing metal kitchen and bathroom cabinets (except freestanding)--are classified in U.S. Industry 337124, Metal Household Furniture Manufacturing;
- Manufacturing plastics countertops--are classified in U.S. Industry 326199, All Other Plastics Product Manufacturing;
- Manufacturing stone countertops--are classified in U.S. Industry 327991, Cut Stone and Stone Product Manufacturing; and
- Manufacturing wood or plastics laminated on wood countertops (except kitchen and bathroom)--are classified in U.S. Industry 337215, Showcase, Partition, Shelving, and Locker Manufacturing.

33712 Household and Institutional Furniture Manufacturing[T]

This industry comprises establishments primarily engaged in manufacturing household-type and public building furniture (i.e., library, school, theater, and church furniture). This industry includes establishments that manufacture general purpose hospital, laboratory and/or dental furniture (e.g., stools, tables, benches). The furniture may be made on a stock or custom basis and may be assembled or unassembled (i.e., knockdown).

Cross-References.   Establishments primarily engaged in--

- Manufacturing specialized hospital and/or dental furniture (e.g., hospital beds, operating tables, dental chairs)--are classified in Industry 33911, Medical Equipment and Supplies Manufacturing;
- Manufacturing wood or plastics laminated on wood kitchen cabinets, bathroom vanities, and countertops (except freestanding)--are classified in Industry 33711, Wood Kitchen Cabinet and Countertop Manufacturing;
- Manufacturing office-type furniture and/or office or store fixtures--are classified in Industry 33721, Office Furniture (including Fixtures) Manufacturing; and
- Repairing or refinishing furniture--are classified in Industry 81142, Reupholstery and Furniture Repair.

337121 Upholstered Household Furniture Manufacturing

This U.S. industry comprises establishments primarily engaged in manufacturing upholstered household-type furniture. The furniture may be made on a stock or custom basis.

Cross-References.   Establishments primarily engaged in--

- Reupholstering furniture or upholstering frames to individual order--are classified in Industry 811420, Reupholstery and Furniture Repair;
- Manufacturing wood kitchen and dining room chairs with upholstered seats or backs--are classified in U.S. Industry 337122, Nonupholstered Wood Household Furniture Manufacturing;

T—Canadian, Mexican, and United States industries are comparable.

- Manufacturing metal kitchen and dining room chairs with upholstered seats or backs--are classified in U.S. Industry 337124, Metal Household Furniture Manufacturing; and
- Manufacturing kitchen and dining room chairs (except wood and metal) with upholstered seats or backs-- are classified in U.S. Industry 337125, Household Furniture (except Wood and Metal) Manufacturing.

337122 Nonupholstered Wood Household Furniture Manufacturing

This U.S. industry comprises establishments primarily engaged in manufacturing nonupholstered wood household-type furniture and freestanding cabinets (except television, stereo, and sewing machine cabinets). The furniture may be made on a stock or custom basis and may be assembled or unassembled (i.e., knockdown).

Cross-References.   Establishments primarily engaged in--

- Manufacturing reed, rattan, plastics and similar furniture--are classified in U.S. Industry 337125, Household Furniture (except Wood and Metal) Manufacturing;
- Manufacturing wood television, stereo, and sewing machine cabinets (i.e., housings)--are classified in U.S. Industry 321999, All Other Miscellaneous Wood Product Manufacturing;
- Manufacturing wood or plastics laminated on wood kitchen cabinets, bathroom vanities, and countertops (except freestanding)--are classified in Industry 337110, Wood Kitchen Cabinet and Countertop Manufacturing; and
- Repairing or refinishing furniture--are classified in Industry 811420, Reupholstery and Furniture Repair.

337124 Metal Household Furniture Manufacturing

This U.S. industry comprises establishments primarily engaged in manufacturing metal household-type furniture and freestanding cabinets. The furniture may be made on a stock or custom basis and may be assembled or unassembled (i.e., knockdown).

Cross-References.

Establishments primarily engaged in manufacturing specialized metal dental and hospital furniture (e.g., dental chairs, hospital beds, operating tables) are classified in Industry 33911, Medical Equipment and Supplies Manufacturing.

337125 Household Furniture (except Wood and Metal) Manufacturing

This U.S. industry comprises establishments primarily engaged in manufacturing household-type furniture of materials other than wood or metal, such as plastics, reed, rattan, wicker, and fiberglass. The furniture may be made on a stock or custom basis and may be assembled or unassembled (i.e., knockdown).

Cross-References.   Establishments primarily engaged in--

- Manufacturing concrete, ceramic, or stone furniture--are classified in Subsector 327, Nonmetallic Mineral Product Manufacturing, according to the materials used;
- Manufacturing upholstered household-type furniture--are classified in U.S. Industry 337121, Upholstered Household Furniture Manufacturing;
- Manufacturing metal household-type furniture--are classified in U.S. Industry 337124, Metal Household Furniture Manufacturing; and
- Manufacturing nonupholstered wood household-type furniture--are classified in U.S. Industry 337122, Nonupholstered Wood Household Furniture Manufacturing.

337127 Institutional Furniture Manufacturing

This U.S. industry comprises establishments primarily engaged in manufacturing institutional-type furniture (e.g., library, school, theater, and church furniture). Included in this industry are establishments primarily engaged in

---

T—Canadian, Mexican, and United States industries are comparable.

manufacturing general purpose hospital, laboratory, and dental furniture (e.g., tables, stools, and benches). The furniture may be made on a stock or custom basis and may be assembled or unassembled (i.e., knockdown).

Cross-References.   Establishments primarily engaged in--

- Manufacturing specialized hospital furniture (e.g., hospital beds, operating tables)--are classified in U.S. Industry 339113, Surgical Appliance and Supplies Manufacturing;
- Manufacturing specialized dental furniture (e.g., dental chairs)--are classified in U.S. Industry 339114, Dental Equipment and Supplies Manufacturing;
- Manufacturing wood or plastics laminated on wood kitchen cabinets, bathroom vanities, and countertops (except freestanding)--are classified in Industry 337110, Wood Kitchen Cabinet and Countertop Manufacturing;
- Manufacturing office-type furniture and/or office or store fixtures--are classified in Industry 33721, Office Furniture (including Fixtures) Manufacturing; and
- Repairing or refinishing furniture--are classified in Industry 811420, Reupholstery and Furniture Repair.

3372   Office Furniture (including Fixtures) Manufacturing[T]

33721   Office Furniture (including Fixtures) Manufacturing[T]

This industry comprises establishments primarily engaged in manufacturing office furniture and/or office and store fixtures. The furniture may be made on a stock or custom basis and may be assembled or unassembled (i.e., knockdown).

Cross-References.   Establishments primarily engaged in--

- Manufacturing millwork on a factory basis--are classified in Industry 32191, Millwork;
- Manufacturing household-type and institutional-type furniture--are classified in Industry 33712, Household and Institutional Furniture Manufacturing;
- Manufacturing refrigerated cabinets, showcases, and display cases--are classified in Industry 33341, Ventilation, Heating, Air-Conditioning, and Commercial Refrigeration Equipment Manufacturing; and
- Manufacturing metal safes and vaults--are classified in Industry 33299, All Other Fabricated Metal Product Manufacturing.

337211 Wood Office Furniture Manufacturing

This U.S. industry comprises establishments primarily engaged in manufacturing wood office-type furniture. The furniture may be made on a stock or custom basis and may be assembled or unassembled (i.e., knockdown).

337212 Custom Architectural Woodwork and Millwork Manufacturing

This U.S. industry comprises establishments primarily engaged in manufacturing custom designed interiors consisting of architectural woodwork and fixtures utilizing wood, wood products, and plastics laminates. All of the industry output is made to individual order on a job shop basis and requires skilled craftsmen as a labor input. A job might include custom manufacturing of display fixtures, gondolas, wall shelving units, entrance and window architectural detail, sales and reception counters, wall paneling, and matching furniture.

Cross-References.   Establishments primarily engaged in--

- Manufacturing millwork on a factory basis--are classified in U.S. Industry 321918, Other Millwork (including Flooring);
- Manufacturing wood office-type furniture on a stock or custom basis--are classified in U.S. Industry 337211, Wood Office Furniture Manufacturing; and
- Manufacturing wood office-type and store fixtures on a stock or custom basis--are classified in U.S. Industry 337215, Showcase, Partition, Shelving, and Locker Manufacturing.

T—Canadian, Mexican, and United States industries are comparable.

337214 Office Furniture (except Wood) Manufacturing

This U.S. industry comprises establishments primarily engaged in manufacturing nonwood office-type furniture. The furniture may be made on a stock or custom basis and may be assembled or unassembled (i.e., knockdown).

337215 Showcase, Partition, Shelving, and Locker Manufacturing

This U.S. industry comprises establishments primarily engaged in manufacturing wood and nonwood office and store fixtures, shelving, lockers, frames, partitions, and related fabricated products of wood and nonwood materials, including plastics laminated fixture tops. The products are made on a stock or custom basis and may be assembled or unassembled (i.e., knockdown). Establishments exclusively making furniture parts (e.g., frames) are included in this industry.

Cross-References.   Establishments primarily engaged in--

- Manufacturing refrigerated cabinets, showcases, and display cases--are classified in U.S. Industry 333415, Air-Conditioning and Warm Air Heating Equipment and Commercial and Industrial Refrigeration Equipment Manufacturing;
- Manufacturing metal safes and vaults--are classified in U.S. Industry 332999, All Other Miscellaneous Fabricated Metal Product Manufacturing; and
- Manufacturing wood or plastics laminated kitchen and bathroom countertops--are classified in Industry 337110, Wood Kitchen Cabinet and Countertop Manufacturing.

3379   Other Furniture Related Product Manufacturing[T]

This industry group comprises establishments manufacturing furniture related products, such as mattresses, blinds, and shades.

33791   Mattress Manufacturing[T]
See industry description for 337910.

337910 Mattress Manufacturing

This industry comprises establishments primarily engaged in manufacturing innerspring, box spring, and noninnerspring mattresses, including mattresses for waterbeds.

Cross-References.   Establishments primarily engaged in--

- Manufacturing individual wire springs--are classified in Industry 33261, Spring and Wire Product Manufacturing; and
- Manufacturing inflatable mattresses--are classified in Subsector 326, Plastics and Rubber Products Manufacturing.

33792   Blind and Shade Manufacturing[T]
See industry description for 337920.

337920 Blind and Shade Manufacturing

This industry comprises establishments primarily engaged in manufacturing one or more of the following: venetian blinds, other window blinds, and shades; curtain and drapery rods and poles; and/or curtain and drapery fixtures. The blinds and shades may be made on a stock or custom basis and may be made of any material.

Cross-References.   Establishments primarily engaged in--

- Manufacturing canvas awnings--are classified in Industry 314910, Textile Bag and Canvas Mills; and

---

T—Canadian, Mexican, and United States industries are comparable.

- Manufacturing curtains and draperies--are classified in Industry 314120, Curtain and Linen Mills.

339   Miscellaneous Manufacturing[T]

Industries in the Miscellaneous Manufacturing subsector make a wide range of products that cannot readily be classified in specific NAICS subsectors in manufacturing. Processes used by these establishments vary significantly, both among and within industries. For example, a variety of manufacturing processes are used in manufacturing sporting and athletic goods that include products such as tennis racquets and golf balls. The processes for these products differ from each other, and the processes differ significantly from the fabrication processes used in making dolls or toys, the melting and shaping of precious metals to make jewelry, and the bending, forming, and assembly used in making medical products.

The industries in this subsector are defined by what is made rather than how it is made. Although individual establishments might be appropriately classified elsewhere in the NAICS structure, for historical continuity, these product-based industries were maintained. In most cases, no one process or material predominates for an industry.

Establishments in this subsector manufacture products as diverse as medical equipment and supplies, jewelry, sporting goods, toys, and office supplies.

3391   Medical Equipment and Supplies Manufacturing[T]

33911   Medical Equipment and Supplies Manufacturing[T]

This industry comprises establishments primarily engaged in manufacturing medical equipment and supplies. Examples of products made by these establishments are surgical and medical instruments, surgical appliances and supplies, dental equipment and supplies, orthodontic goods, ophthalmic goods, dentures, and orthodontic appliances.

Cross-References.   Establishments primarily engaged in--

- Manufacturing laboratory instruments, X-ray apparatus, electromedical apparatus (including electronic hearing aids), and thermometers (except medical)--are classified in Industry 33451, Navigational, Measuring, Electromedical, and Control Instruments Manufacturing;
- Manufacturing molded glass lens blanks--are classified in Industry 32721, Glass and Glass Product Manufacturing;
- Manufacturing molded plastics lens blanks--are classified in Industry 32619, Other Plastics Product Manufacturing;
- Retailing and grinding prescription eyeglasses--are classified in Industry 44613, Optical Goods Stores;
- Manufacturing sporting goods helmets and protective equipment--are classified in Industry 33992, Sporting and Athletic Goods Manufacturing;
- Manufacturing general purpose hospital, laboratory, and/or dental furniture (e.g., stools, tables, benches)--are classified in Industry 33712, Household and Institutional Furniture Manufacturing;
- Manufacturing laboratory scales and balances, laboratory furnaces and ovens, and/or laboratory centrifuges--are classified in Industry 33399, All Other General Purpose Machinery Manufacturing;
- Manufacturing laboratory distilling equipment--are classified in Industry 33324, Industrial Machinery Manufacturing; and
- Manufacturing laboratory freezers--are classified in Industry 33341, Ventilation, Heating, Air-Conditioning, and Commercial Refrigeration Equipment Manufacturing.

339112 Surgical and Medical Instrument Manufacturing

This U.S. industry comprises establishments primarily engaged in manufacturing medical, surgical, ophthalmic, and veterinary instruments and apparatus (except electrotherapeutic, electromedical and irradiation apparatus). Examples of products made by these establishments are syringes, hypodermic needles, anesthesia apparatus, blood transfusion equipment, catheters, surgical clamps, and medical thermometers.

T—Canadian, Mexican, and United States industries are comparable.

Cross-References. Establishments primarily engaged in--

- Manufacturing electromedical and electrotherapeutic apparatus--are classified in U.S. Industry 334510, Electromedical and Electrotherapeutic Apparatus Manufacturing;
- Manufacturing irradiation apparatus--are classified in U.S. Industry 334517, Irradiation Apparatus Manufacturing;
- Manufacturing surgical (except dental) and orthopedic appliances or specialized hospital furniture (e.g., hospital beds, operating tables)--are classified in U.S. Industry 339113, Surgical Appliance and Supplies Manufacturing;
- Manufacturing dental equipment, dental supplies, dental laboratory apparatus, and dental laboratory furniture--are classified in U.S. Industry 339114, Dental Equipment and Supplies Manufacturing;
- Manufacturing general purpose hospital, laboratory, and/or dental furniture (e.g., stools, tables, benches)-- are classified in U.S. Industry 337127, Institutional Furniture Manufacturing;
- Manufacturing thermometers (except medical)--are classified in U.S. Industry 334519, Other Measuring and Controlling Device Manufacturing; and
- Manufacturing ophthalmic goods--are classified in U.S. Industry 339115, Ophthalmic Goods Manufacturing.

339113 Surgical Appliance and Supplies Manufacturing

This U.S. industry comprises establishments primarily engaged in manufacturing surgical appliances and supplies. Examples of products made by these establishments are orthopedic devices, prosthetic appliances, surgical dressings, crutches, surgical sutures, personal industrial safety devices (except protective eyewear), hospital beds, and operating room tables.

Cross-References. Establishments primarily engaged in--

- Manufacturing dental equipment, dental supplies, dental laboratory apparatus, and specialized dental laboratory furniture (e.g., dental chairs)--are classified in U.S. Industry 339114, Dental Equipment and Supplies Manufacturing;
- Manufacturing general purpose hospital, laboratory, and/or dental furniture (e.g., stools, tables, benches)-- are classified in U.S. Industry 337127, Institutional Furniture Manufacturing;
- Manufacturing electronic hearing aids--are classified in U.S. Industry 334510, Electromedical and Electrotherapeutic Apparatus Manufacturing;
- Manufacturing industrial protective eyewear--are classified in U.S. Industry 339115, Ophthalmic Goods Manufacturing; and
- Manufacturing sporting goods helmets and protective equipment--are classified in Industry 339920, Sporting and Athletic Goods Manufacturing.

339114 Dental Equipment and Supplies Manufacturing

This U.S. industry comprises establishments primarily engaged in manufacturing dental equipment and supplies used by dental laboratories and offices of dentists, such as dental chairs, dental instrument delivery systems, dental hand instruments, dental impression material, and dental cements.

Cross-References.

Establishments primarily engaged in manufacturing dentures, crowns, bridges, and orthodontic appliances customized for individual application are classified in U.S. Industry 339116, Dental Laboratories.

339115 Ophthalmic Goods Manufacturing

This U.S. industry comprises establishments primarily engaged in manufacturing ophthalmic goods. Examples of products made by these establishments are prescription eyeglasses (except manufactured in a retail setting), contact lenses, sunglasses, eyeglass frames, reading glasses made to standard powers, and protective eyewear.

T—Canadian, Mexican, and United States industries are comparable.

Cross-References. Establishments primarily engaged in--

- Manufacturing molded glass lens blanks--are classified in U.S. Industry 327212, Other Pressed and Blown Glass and Glassware Manufacturing;
- Manufacturing molded plastics lens blanks--are classified in U.S. Industry 326199, All Other Plastics Product Manufacturing; and
- Retailing and grinding prescription eyeglasses--are classified in Industry 446130, Optical Goods Stores.

339116 Dental Laboratories

This U.S. industry comprises establishments primarily engaged in manufacturing dentures, crowns, bridges, and orthodontic appliances customized for individual application.

Cross-References.

Establishments primarily engaged in manufacturing dental equipment and supplies are classified in U.S. Industry 339114, Dental Equipment and Supplies Manufacturing.

3399 Other Miscellaneous Manufacturing[T]

This industry group comprises establishments primarily engaged in miscellaneous manufacturing, such as jewelry and silverware manufacturing, sporting and athletic goods manufacturing, doll, toy, and game manufacturing, office supplies (except paper) manufacturing, sign manufacturing, and all other miscellaneous manufacturing.

33991 Jewelry and Silverware Manufacturing[T]
See industry description for 339910.

339910 Jewelry and Silverware Manufacturing

This industry comprises establishments primarily engaged in one or more of the following: (1) manufacturing, engraving, chasing, or etching jewelry; (2) manufacturing, engraving, chasing, or etching metal personal goods (i.e., small articles carried on or about the person, such as compacts or cigarette cases); (3) manufacturing, engraving, chasing, or etching precious metal solid, precious metal clad, or pewter flatware and other hollowware; (4) stamping coins; (5) manufacturing unassembled jewelry parts and stock shop products, such as sheet, wire, and tubing; (6) cutting, slabbing, tumbling, carving, engraving, polishing, or faceting precious or semiprecious stones and gems; (7) recutting, repolishing, and setting gem stones; and (8) drilling, sawing, and peeling cultured and costume pearls. This industry includes establishments primarily engaged in manufacturing precious solid, precious clad, and precious plated jewelry and personal goods.

Cross-References. Establishments primarily engaged in--

- Manufacturing nonprecious and precious plated metal cutlery and flatware--are classified in U.S. Industry 332215, Metal Kitchen Cookware, Utensil, Cutlery, and Flatware (except Precious) Manufacturing;
- Manufacturing nonprecious metal plated ware (except cutlery and flatware)--are classified in U.S. Industry 332999, All Other Miscellaneous Fabricated Metal Product Manufacturing;
- Engraving, chasing, or etching nonprecious and precious plated metal cutlery, flatware and other plated ware--are classified in U.S. Industry 332812, Metal Coating, Engraving (except Jewelry and Silverware), and Allied Services to Manufacturers;
- Plating jewelry--are classified in U.S. Industry 332813, Electroplating, Plating, Polishing, Anodizing, and Coloring;
- Manufacturing synthetic stones--are classified in U.S. Industry 327999, All Other Miscellaneous Nonmetallic Mineral Product Manufacturing; and
- Manufacturing personal goods (except metal) carried on or about the person, such as compacts and cigarette cases--are classified in U.S. Industry 316998, All Other Leather Good and Allied Product Manufacturing.

T—Canadian, Mexican, and United States industries are comparable.

33992   Sporting and Athletic Goods Manufacturing[T]
See industry description for 339920.

339920   Sporting and Athletic Goods Manufacturing

This industry comprises establishments primarily engaged in manufacturing sporting and athletic goods (except apparel and footwear).

Cross-References.   Establishments primarily engaged in--

- Manufacturing athletic apparel--are classified in Subsector 315, Apparel Manufacturing;
- Manufacturing athletic footwear--are classified in Industry 316210, Footwear Manufacturing; and
- Manufacturing small arms and small arms ammunition--are classified in Industry 33299, All Other Fabricated Metal Product Manufacturing.

33993   Doll, Toy, and Game Manufacturing[T]
See industry description for 339930.

339930   Doll, Toy, and Game Manufacturing

This industry comprises establishments primarily engaged in manufacturing complete dolls, doll parts, doll clothes, action figures, toys, games (including electronic), hobby kits, and children's vehicles (except metal bicycles and tricycles).

Cross-References.   Establishments primarily engaged in--

- Manufacturing metal tricycles and bicycles--are classified in U.S. Industry 336991, Motorcycle, Bicycle, and Parts Manufacturing;
- Manufacturing sporting and athletic goods--are classified in Industry 339920, Sporting and Athletic Goods Manufacturing;
- Manufacturing coin-operated game machines--are classified in U.S. Industry 339999, All Other Miscellaneous Manufacturing;
- Manufacturing electronic video game cartridges and reproducing video game software--are classified in U.S. Industry 334614, Software and Other Prerecorded Compact Disc, Tape, and Record Reproducing; and
- Publishing or publishing and reproducing game software--are classified in Industry 511210, Software Publishers.

33994   Office Supplies (except Paper) Manufacturing[T]
See industry description for 339940.

339940   Office Supplies (except Paper) Manufacturing

This industry comprises establishments primarily engaged in manufacturing office supplies. Examples of products made by these establishments are pens, pencils, felt tip markers, crayons, chalk, pencil sharpeners, staplers, modeling clay, hand operated stamps, stamp pads, stencils, carbon paper, and inked ribbons.

Cross-References.   Establishments primarily engaged in--

- Manufacturing writing, drawing, and india inks--are classified in U.S. Industry 325998, All Other Miscellaneous Chemical Product and Preparation Manufacturing;
- Manufacturing rubber erasers--are classified in U.S. Industry 326299, All Other Rubber Product Manufacturing;
- Manufacturing paper office supplies--are classified in Subsector 322, Paper Manufacturing;
- Printing manifold business forms and manufacturing blankbooks, looseleaf binders, and looseleaf devices-- are classified in U.S. Industry 323111, Commercial Printing (except Screen and Books);

T—Canadian, Mexican, and United States industries are comparable.

- Manufacturing drafting tables and boards--are classified in U.S. Industry 337127, Institutional Furniture Manufacturing; and
- Manufacturing inkjet and toner cartridges--are classified in Industry Group 3259, Other Chemical Product and Preparation Manufacturing.

33995 Sign Manufacturing[T]
See industry description for 339950.

339950 Sign Manufacturing

This industry comprises establishments primarily engaged in manufacturing signs and related displays of all materials (except printing paper and paperboard signs, notices, displays).

Cross-References.   Establishments primarily engaged in--

- Printing advertising specialties or printing paper and paperboard signs, notices, and displays--are classified in Industry 32311, Printing;
- Manufacturing and printing advertising specialties--are classified in the Manufacturing sector according to the products made;
- Manufacturing die-cut paperboard displays--are classified in U.S. Industry 322299, All Other Converted Paper Product Manufacturing; and
- Sign lettering and painting--are classified in Industry 541890, Other Services Related to Advertising.

33999 All Other Miscellaneous Manufacturing[T]

This industry comprises establishments primarily engaged in miscellaneous manufacturing (except medical equipment and supplies, jewelry and flatware, sporting and athletic goods, dolls, toys, games, office supplies (except paper), and signs).

Illustrative Examples:

Artificial Christmas trees manufacturing
Burial caskets and cases manufacturing
Candles manufacturing
Coin-operated amusement machines (except jukebox) manufacturing
Electronic cigarettes manufacturing
Floor and dust mops manufacturing

Fasteners, buttons, needles, and pins (except precious metals or precious and semiprecious stones and gems) manufacturing
Gasket, packing, and sealing devices manufacturing
Musical instruments (except toy) manufacturing
Portable fire extinguishers manufacturing
Umbrellas manufacturing

Cross-References.   Establishments primarily engaged in--

- Manufacturing medical equipment and supplies--are classified in Industry Group 3391, Medical Equipment and Supplies Manufacturing;
- Manufacturing jewelry and flatware--are classified in Industry 33991, Jewelry and Silverware Manufacturing;
- Manufacturing sporting and athletic goods--are classified in Industry 33992, Sporting and Athletic Goods Manufacturing;
- Manufacturing dolls, toys, and games--are classified in Industry 33993, Doll, Toy, and Game Manufacturing;
- Manufacturing office supplies (except paper)--are classified in Industry 33994, Office Supplies (except Paper) Manufacturing;
- Manufacturing signs--are classified in Industry 33995, Sign Manufacturing;
- Manufacturing concrete burial vaults--are classified in Industry 32739, Other Concrete Product Manufacturing;

T—Canadian, Mexican, and United States industries are comparable.

- Manufacturing Christmas tree glass ornaments and glass lamp shades--are classified in Industry 32721, Glass and Glass Product Manufacturing;
- Manufacturing Christmas tree lighting sets--are classified in Industry 33512, Lighting Fixture Manufacturing;
- Manufacturing beauty and barber chairs--are classified in Industry 33712, Household and Institutional Furniture Manufacturing;
- Manufacturing burnt wood articles--are classified in Industry 32199, All Other Wood Product Manufacturing;
- Dressing and bleaching furs--are classified in Industry 31611, Leather and Hide Tanning and Finishing;
- Manufacturing paper, textile, and metal lamp shades--are classified in Industry 33512, Lighting Fixture Manufacturing;
- Manufacturing plastics lamp shades--are classified in Industry 32619, Other Plastics Product Manufacturing;
- Manufacturing matches and electronic cigarette vapor refills--are classified in Industry 32599, All Other Chemical Product and Preparation Manufacturing;
- Manufacturing metal products, such as metal combs and hair curlers--are classified in Industry 33299, All Other Fabricated Metal Product Manufacturing;
- Manufacturing plastics products, such as plastics combs and hair curlers--are classified in Industry 32619, Other Plastics Product Manufacturing; and
- Manufacturing electric hair clippers for use on humans--are classified in Industry 33521, Small Electrical Appliance Manufacturing.

339991 Gasket, Packing, and Sealing Device Manufacturing

This U.S. industry comprises establishments primarily engaged in manufacturing gaskets, packing, and sealing devices of all materials.

339992 Musical Instrument Manufacturing

This U.S. industry comprises establishments primarily engaged in manufacturing musical instruments (except toys).

Cross-References.

Establishments primarily engaged in manufacturing toy musical instruments are classified in Industry 339930, Doll, Toy, and Game Manufacturing.

339993 Fastener, Button, Needle, and Pin Manufacturing

This U.S. industry comprises establishments primarily engaged in manufacturing fasteners, buttons, needles, pins, and buckles (except made of precious metals or precious and semiprecious stones and gems).

Cross-References.   Establishments primarily engaged in--

- Manufacturing buttons, pins, and buckles made of precious metals or precious and semiprecious stones and gems--are classified in Industry 339910, Jewelry and Silverware Manufacturing;
- Manufacturing hypodermic and suture needles--are classified in U.S. Industry 339112, Surgical and Medical Instrument Manufacturing; and
- Manufacturing phonograph and styli needles--are classified in U.S. Industry 334419, Other Electronic Component Manufacturing.

339994 Broom, Brush, and Mop Manufacturing

This U.S. industry comprises establishments primarily engaged in manufacturing brooms, mops, and brushes.

T—Canadian, Mexican, and United States industries are comparable.

339995 Burial Casket Manufacturing

This U.S. industry comprises establishments primarily engaged in manufacturing burial caskets, cases, and vaults (except concrete).

Cross-References.

Establishments primarily engaged in manufacturing concrete burial vaults are classified in Industry 327390, Other Concrete Product Manufacturing.

339999 All Other Miscellaneous Manufacturing

This U.S. industry comprises establishments primarily engaged in miscellaneous manufacturing (except medical equipment and supplies, jewelry and flatware, sporting and athletic goods, dolls, toys, games, office supplies (except paper), musical instruments, fasteners, buttons, needles, pins, brooms, brushes, mops, and burial caskets).

Illustrative Examples:

Artificial Christmas trees manufacturing
Candles manufacturing
Christmas tree ornaments (except glass and electric) manufacturing
Cigarette lighters (except precious metal) manufacturing
Coin-operated amusement machines (except jukebox) manufacturing

Electronic cigarettes manufacturing
Hairpieces (e.g., wigs, toupees, wiglets) manufacturing
Portable fire extinguishers manufacturing
Potpourri manufacturing
Tobacco pipes manufacturing
Umbrellas manufacturing

Cross-References.   Establishments primarily engaged in--

- Manufacturing medical equipment and supplies--are classified in Industry Group 3391, Medical Equipment and Supplies Manufacturing;
- Manufacturing jewelry and flatware--are classified in Industry 339910, Jewelry and Silverware Manufacturing;
- Manufacturing sporting and athletic goods--are classified in Industry 339920, Sporting and Athletic Goods Manufacturing;
- Manufacturing dolls, toys, and games--are classified in Industry 339930, Doll, Toy, and Game Manufacturing;
- Manufacturing office supplies (except paper)--are classified in Industry 339940, Office Supplies (except Paper) Manufacturing;
- Manufacturing signs--are classified in Industry 339950, Sign Manufacturing;
- Manufacturing gasket, packing, and sealing devices--are classified in U.S. Industry 339991, Gasket, Packing, and Sealing Device Manufacturing;
- Manufacturing musical instruments--are classified in U.S. Industry 339992, Musical Instrument Manufacturing;
- Manufacturing fasteners, buttons, needles, and pins--are classified in U.S. Industry 339993, Fastener, Button, Needle, and Pin Manufacturing;
- Manufacturing brooms, brushes, and mops--are classified in U.S. Industry 339994, Broom, Brush, and Mop Manufacturing;
- Manufacturing burial caskets--are classified in U.S. Industry 339995, Burial Casket Manufacturing;
- Manufacturing Christmas tree glass ornaments and glass lamp shades--are classified in U.S. Industry 327215, Glass Product Manufacturing Made of Purchased Glass;
- Manufacturing Christmas tree lighting sets--are classified in U.S. Industry 335129, Other Lighting Equipment Manufacturing;
- Manufacturing beauty and barber chairs--are classified in U.S. Industry 337127, Institutional Furniture Manufacturing;

T—Canadian, Mexican, and United States industries are comparable.

- Manufacturing burnt wood articles--are classified in U.S. Industry 321999, All Other Miscellaneous Wood Product Manufacturing;
- Dressing and bleaching furs--are classified in Industry 316110, Leather and Hide Tanning and Finishing;
- Manufacturing paper, textile, and metal lamp shades--are classified in U.S. Industry 335121, Residential Electric Lighting Fixture Manufacturing;
- Manufacturing plastics lamp shades--are classified in U.S. Industry 326199, All Other Plastics Product Manufacturing;
- Manufacturing matches and electronic cigarette vapor refills--are classified in U.S. Industry 325998, All Other Miscellaneous Chemical Product and Preparation Manufacturing;
- Manufacturing metal products, such as metal combs and hair curlers--are classified in U.S. Industry 332999, All Other Miscellaneous Fabricated Metal Product Manufacturing;
- Manufacturing plastics products, such as plastics combs and hair curlers--are classified in U.S. Industry 326199, All Other Plastics Product Manufacturing; and
- Manufacturing electric hair clippers for use on humans--are classified in Industry 335210, Small Electrical Appliance Manufacturing.

T—Canadian, Mexican, and United States industries are comparable.

Sector 42--Wholesale Trade[T]

The Sector as a Whole

The Wholesale Trade sector comprises establishments engaged in wholesaling merchandise, generally without transformation, and rendering services incidental to the sale of merchandise. The merchandise described in this sector includes the outputs of agriculture, mining, manufacturing, and certain information industries, such as publishing.

The wholesaling process is an intermediate step in the distribution of merchandise. Wholesalers are organized to sell or arrange the purchase or sale of (a) goods for resale (i.e., goods sold to other wholesalers or retailers), (b) capital or durable nonconsumer goods, and (c) raw and intermediate materials and supplies used in production.

Wholesalers sell merchandise to other businesses and normally operate from a warehouse or office. These warehouses and offices are characterized by having little or no display of merchandise. In addition, neither the design nor the location of the premises is intended to solicit walk-in traffic. Wholesalers do not normally use advertising directed to the general public. Customers are generally reached initially via telephone, in-person marketing, or by specialized advertising that may include Internet and other electronic means. Follow-up orders are either vendor-initiated or client-initiated, generally based on previous sales, and typically exhibit strong ties between sellers and buyers. In fact, transactions are often conducted between wholesalers and clients that have long-standing business relationships.

This sector comprises two main types of wholesalers: merchant wholesalers that sell goods on their own account and business-to-business electronic markets, agents, and brokers that arrange sales and purchases for others generally for a commission or fee.

(1) Establishments that sell goods on their own account are known as wholesale merchants, distributors, jobbers, drop shippers, and import/export merchants. Also included as wholesale merchants are sales offices and sales branches (but not retail stores) maintained by manufacturing, refining, or mining enterprises apart from their plants or mines for the purpose of marketing their products and group purchasing organizations (e.g., purchasing and selling goods on their own account). Merchant wholesale establishments typically maintain their own warehouse, where they receive and handle goods for their customers. Goods are generally sold without transformation, but may include integral functions, such as sorting, packaging, labeling, and other marketing services.

(2) Establishments arranging for the purchase or sale of goods owned by others or purchasing goods, generally on a commission basis are known as business-to-business electronic markets, agents and brokers, commission merchants, import/export agents and brokers, auction companies, group purchasing organizations (e.g., purchasing or arranging for the purchases of goods owned by others), and manufacturers' representatives. These establishments operate from offices and generally do not own or handle the goods they sell.

Some wholesale establishments may be connected with a single manufacturer and promote and sell the particular manufacturer's products to a wide range of other wholesalers or retailers. Other wholesalers may be connected to a retail chain, or limited number of retail chains, and only provide a variety of products needed by that particular retail operation(s). These wholesalers may obtain the products from a wide range of manufacturers. Still other wholesalers may not take title to the goods, but act as agents and brokers for a commission.

Although, in general, wholesaling normally denotes sales in large volumes, durable nonconsumer goods may be sold in single units. Sales of capital or durable nonconsumer goods used in the production of goods and services, such as farm machinery, medium- and heavy-duty trucks, and industrial machinery, are always included in wholesale trade.

423   Merchant Wholesalers, Durable Goods

Industries in the Merchant Wholesalers, Durable Goods subsector sell capital or durable goods to other businesses. Merchant wholesalers generally take title to the goods that they sell; in other words, they buy and sell goods on their own account. Durable goods are new or used items generally with a normal life expectancy of three years or more. Durable goods merchant wholesale trade establishments are engaged in wholesaling products, such as motor vehicles, furniture, construction materials, machinery and equipment (including household-type appliances), metals and minerals (except petroleum), sporting goods, toys and hobby goods, recyclable materials, and parts.

T—Canadian, Mexican, and United States industries are comparable.

Business-to-business electronic markets, agents, and brokers primarily engaged in wholesaling durable goods, generally on a commission or fee basis, are classified in Subsector 425, Wholesale Electronic Markets and Agents and Brokers.

4231   Motor Vehicle and Motor Vehicle Parts and Supplies Merchant Wholesalers

This industry group comprises establishments primarily engaged in the merchant wholesale distribution of automobiles and other motor vehicles, motor vehicle supplies, tires, and new and used parts.

42311   Automobile and Other Motor Vehicle Merchant Wholesalers
See industry description for 423110.

423110 Automobile and Other Motor Vehicle Merchant Wholesalers

This industry comprises establishments primarily engaged in the merchant wholesale distribution of new and used passenger automobiles, trucks, trailers, and other motor vehicles, such as motorcycles, motor homes, and snowmobiles.

42312   Motor Vehicle Supplies and New Parts Merchant Wholesalers
See industry description for 423120.

423120 Motor Vehicle Supplies and New Parts Merchant Wholesalers

This industry comprises establishments primarily engaged in the merchant wholesale distribution of motor vehicle supplies, accessories, tools, and equipment; and new motor vehicle parts (except new tires and tubes).

Cross-References.   Establishments primarily engaged in--

- Merchant wholesale distribution of new and/or used tires and tubes--are classified in Industry 423130, Tire and Tube Merchant Wholesalers;
- Merchant wholesale distribution of automotive chemicals (except lubricating oils and greases)--are classified in Industry 424690, Other Chemical and Allied Products Merchant Wholesalers;
- Merchant wholesale distribution of lubricating oils and greases--are classified in Industry 424720, Petroleum and Petroleum Products Merchant Wholesalers (except Bulk Stations and Terminals); and
- Merchant wholesale distribution of used motor vehicle parts--are classified in Industry 423140, Motor Vehicle Parts (Used) Merchant Wholesalers.

42313   Tire and Tube Merchant Wholesalers
See industry description for 423130.

423130 Tire and Tube Merchant Wholesalers

This industry comprises establishments primarily engaged in the merchant wholesale distribution of new and/or used tires and tubes for passenger and commercial vehicles.

Cross-References.   Establishments primarily engaged in--

- Merchant wholesale distribution of other new automobile parts and accessories--are classified in Industry 423120, Motor Vehicle Supplies and New Parts Merchant Wholesalers; and
- Merchant wholesale distribution of other used automobile parts and accessories--are classified in Industry 423140, Motor Vehicle Parts (Used) Merchant Wholesalers.

42314   Motor Vehicle Parts (Used) Merchant Wholesalers
See industry description for 423140.

T—Canadian, Mexican, and United States industries are comparable.

423140 Motor Vehicle Parts (Used) Merchant Wholesalers

This industry comprises establishments primarily engaged in the merchant wholesale distribution of used motor vehicle parts (except used tires and tubes) and establishments primarily engaged in dismantling motor vehicles for the purpose of selling the parts.

Cross-References.   Establishments primarily engaged in--

- Dismantling motor vehicles for the purpose of selling scrap--are classified in Industry 423930, Recyclable Material Merchant Wholesalers; and
- Merchant wholesale distribution of new and/or used tires and tubes--are classified in Industry 423130, Tire and Tube Merchant Wholesalers.

4232   Furniture and Home Furnishing Merchant Wholesalers

This industry group comprises establishments primarily engaged in the merchant wholesale distribution of furniture (except hospital beds, medical furniture, and drafting tables), home furnishings, and/or housewares.

42321   Furniture Merchant Wholesalers
See industry description for 423210.

423210 Furniture Merchant Wholesalers

This industry comprises establishments primarily engaged in the merchant wholesale distribution of furniture (except hospital beds, medical furniture, and drafting tables).

Illustrative Examples:

Household-type furniture merchant wholesalers
Outdoor furniture merchant wholesalers
Mattresses merchant wholesalers

Public building furniture merchant wholesalers
Office furniture merchant wholesalers
Religious furniture merchant wholesalers

Cross-References.   Establishments primarily engaged in--

- Merchant wholesale distribution of partitions, shelving, lockers, and store fixtures--are classified in Industry 423440, Other Commercial Equipment Merchant Wholesalers;
- Merchant wholesale distribution of hospital beds and medical furniture--are classified in Industry 423450, Medical, Dental, and Hospital Equipment and Supplies Merchant Wholesalers; and
- Merchant wholesale distribution of drafting tables--are classified in Industry 423490, Other Professional Equipment and Supplies Merchant Wholesalers.

42322   Home Furnishing Merchant Wholesalers
See industry description for 423220.

423220 Home Furnishing Merchant Wholesalers

This industry comprises establishments primarily engaged in the merchant wholesale distribution of home furnishings and/or housewares.

Illustrative Examples:

Carpet merchant wholesalers
Glassware, household-type, merchant wholesalers
Chinaware, household-type, merchant wholesalers
Curtains merchant wholesalers

Household-type cooking utensils merchant
wholesalers
Lamps (i.e., lighting fixtures) merchant wholesalers
Draperies merchant wholesalers

T—Canadian, Mexican, and United States industries are comparable.

Linens (e.g., bath, bed, table) merchant wholesalers   Window shades and blinds merchant wholesalers
Floor coverings merchant wholesalers

Cross-References.   Establishments primarily engaged in--

- Merchant wholesale distribution of household-type gas and electric appliances (except water heaters and heating stoves (i.e., noncooking))--are classified in Industry 423620, Household Appliances, Electric Housewares, and Consumer Electronics Merchant Wholesalers; and
- Merchant wholesale distribution of precious metal flatware--are classified in Industry 423940, Jewelry, Watch, Precious Stone, and Precious Metal Merchant Wholesalers.

4233   Lumber and Other Construction Materials Merchant Wholesalers

This industry group comprises establishments primarily engaged in the merchant wholesale distribution of lumber, plywood, millwork, and wood panels; brick, stone, and related construction materials; roofing, siding, and insulation materials; and other construction materials, including manufactured homes (i.e., mobile homes) and/or prefabricated buildings.

42331   Lumber, Plywood, Millwork, and Wood Panel Merchant Wholesalers
See industry description for 423310.

423310   Lumber, Plywood, Millwork, and Wood Panel Merchant Wholesalers

This industry comprises establishments primarily engaged in the merchant wholesale distribution of lumber; plywood; reconstituted wood fiber products; wood fencing; doors and windows and their frames (all materials); wood roofing and siding; and/or other wood or metal millwork.

Cross-References.   Establishments primarily engaged in--

- Merchant wholesale distribution of nonwood roofing and siding materials--are classified in Industry 423330, Roofing, Siding, and Insulation Material Merchant Wholesalers; and
- Merchant wholesale distribution of timber and timber products, such as railroad ties, logs, firewood, and pulpwood--are classified in Industry 423990, Other Miscellaneous Durable Goods Merchant Wholesalers.

42332   Brick, Stone, and Related Construction Material Merchant Wholesalers
See industry description for 423320.

423320   Brick, Stone, and Related Construction Material Merchant Wholesalers

This industry comprises establishments primarily engaged in the merchant wholesale distribution of stone, cement, lime, construction sand, and gravel; brick; asphalt and concrete mixtures; and/or concrete, stone, and structural clay products.

Cross-References.   Establishments primarily engaged in--

- Merchant wholesale distribution of refractory brick and other refractory products--are classified in Industry 423840, Industrial Supplies Merchant Wholesalers; and
- Selling ready-mix concrete--are classified in Industry 327320, Ready-Mix Concrete Manufacturing.

42333   Roofing, Siding, and Insulation Material Merchant Wholesalers
See industry description for 423330.

T—Canadian, Mexican, and United States industries are comparable.

423330 Roofing, Siding, and Insulation Material Merchant Wholesalers

This industry comprises establishments primarily engaged in the merchant wholesale distribution of nonwood roofing and nonwood siding and insulation materials.

Cross-References.

Establishments primarily engaged in the merchant wholesale distribution of wood roofing and wood siding are classified in Industry 423310, Lumber, Plywood, Millwork, and Wood Panel Merchant Wholesalers.

42339 Other Construction Material Merchant Wholesalers
See industry description for 423390.

423390 Other Construction Material Merchant Wholesalers

This industry comprises (1) establishments primarily engaged in the merchant wholesale distribution of manufactured homes (i.e., mobile homes) and/or prefabricated buildings and (2) establishments primarily engaged in the merchant wholesale distribution of construction materials (except lumber, plywood, millwork, wood panels, brick, stone, roofing, siding, electrical and wiring supplies, and insulation materials).

Illustrative Examples:

Flat glass merchant wholesalers
Prefabricated buildings (except wood) merchant wholesalers
Ornamental ironwork merchant wholesalers

Wire fencing and fencing accessories merchant wholesalers
Plate glass merchant wholesalers

Cross-References.   Establishments primarily engaged in--

- Merchant wholesale distribution of products of the primary metals industries--are classified in Industry 423510, Metal Service Centers and Other Metal Merchant Wholesalers;
- Merchant wholesale distribution of lumber; plywood; reconstituted wood fiber products; wood fencing; doors, windows, and their frames; wood roofing and wood siding; and other wood or metal millwork--are classified in Industry 423310, Lumber, Plywood, Millwork, and Wood Panel Merchant Wholesalers;
- Merchant wholesale distribution of stone, cement, lime, construction sand and gravel; brick; asphalt and concrete mixtures (except ready-mix concrete); and/or concrete, stone, and structural clay products--are classified in Industry 423320, Brick, Stone, and Related Construction Material Merchant Wholesalers;
- Merchant wholesale distribution of nonwood roofing and nonwood siding and insulation materials--are classified in Industry 423330, Roofing, Siding, and Insulation Material Merchant Wholesalers;
- Merchant wholesale distribution of electrical supplies and wiring supplies--are classified in Industry 423610, Electrical Apparatus and Equipment, Wiring Supplies, and Related Equipment Merchant Wholesalers; and
- Selling ready-mix concrete--are classified in Industry 327320, Ready-Mix Concrete Manufacturing.

4234 Professional and Commercial Equipment and Supplies Merchant Wholesalers

This industry group comprises establishments primarily engaged in the merchant wholesale distribution of photographic equipment and supplies; office, computer, and computer peripheral equipment; and medical, dental, hospital, ophthalmic, and other commercial and professional equipment and supplies.

42341 Photographic Equipment and Supplies Merchant Wholesalers
See industry description for 423410.

T—Canadian, Mexican, and United States industries are comparable.

423410 Photographic Equipment and Supplies Merchant Wholesalers

This industry comprises establishments primarily engaged in the merchant wholesale distribution of photographic equipment and supplies (except office equipment).

Illustrative Examples:

Photofinishing equipment merchant wholesalers
Television cameras merchant wholesalers
Photographic camera equipment and supplies merchant wholesalers

Video cameras (except household-type) merchant wholesalers
Photographic film and plates merchant wholesalers

Cross-References.   Establishments primarily engaged in--

- Merchant wholesale distribution of household-type video cameras--are classified in Industry 423620, Household Appliances, Electric Housewares, and Consumer Electronics Merchant Wholesalers; and
- Merchant wholesale distribution of office equipment, such as photocopy and microfilm equipment--are classified in Industry 423420, Office Equipment Merchant Wholesalers.

42342   Office Equipment Merchant Wholesalers
See industry description for 423420.

423420 Office Equipment Merchant Wholesalers

This industry comprises establishments primarily engaged in the merchant wholesale distribution of office machines and related equipment (except computers and computer peripheral equipment).

Illustrative Examples:

Accounting machines merchant wholesalers
Mailing machines merchant wholesalers
Calculators and calculating machines merchant wholesalers
Cash registers merchant wholesalers

Security safes merchant wholesalers
Copying machines merchant wholesalers
Microfilm equipment and supplies merchant wholesalers

Cross-References.   Establishments primarily engaged in--

- Merchant wholesale distribution of office furniture--are classified in Industry 423210, Furniture Merchant Wholesalers;
- Merchant wholesale distribution of computers and computer peripheral equipment--are classified in Industry 423430, Computer and Computer Peripheral Equipment and Software Merchant Wholesalers; and
- Merchant wholesale distribution of office supplies--are classified in Industry 424120, Stationery and Office Supplies Merchant Wholesalers.

42343   Computer and Computer Peripheral Equipment and Software Merchant Wholesalers
See industry description for 423430.

423430 Computer and Computer Peripheral Equipment and Software Merchant Wholesalers

This industry comprises establishments primarily engaged in the merchant wholesale distribution of computers, computer peripheral equipment, loaded computer boards, and/or computer software.

T—Canadian, Mexican, and United States industries are comparable.

Cross-References.   Establishments primarily engaged in--

- Merchant wholesale distribution of modems and other electronic communications equipment--are classified in Industry 423690, Other Electronic Parts and Equipment Merchant Wholesalers; and
- Selling, planning, and designing computer systems that integrate computer hardware, software, and communication technologies--are classified in U.S. Industry 541512, Computer Systems Design Services.

42344   Other Commercial Equipment Merchant Wholesalers
See industry description for 423440.

423440   Other Commercial Equipment Merchant Wholesalers

This industry comprises establishments primarily engaged in the merchant wholesale distribution of commercial and related machines and equipment (except photographic equipment and supplies; office equipment; and computers and computer peripheral equipment and software) generally used in restaurants and stores.

Illustrative Examples:

Balances and scales (except laboratory) merchant wholesalers
Commercial shelving merchant wholesalers
Coin-operated merchandising machine merchant wholesalers
Electrical signs merchant wholesalers

Commercial chinaware merchant wholesalers
Partitions merchant wholesalers
Commercial cooking equipment merchant wholesalers
Store fixtures (except refrigerated) merchant wholesalers

Cross-References.   Establishments primarily engaged in--

- Merchant wholesale distribution of photographic equipment and supplies--are classified in Industry 423410, Photographic Equipment and Supplies Merchant Wholesalers;
- Merchant wholesale distribution of office machines and related equipment--are classified in Industry 423420, Office Equipment Merchant Wholesalers;
- Merchant wholesale distribution of computers, computer peripheral equipment, and computer software--are classified in Industry 423430, Computer and Computer Peripheral Equipment and Software Merchant Wholesalers;
- Merchant wholesale distribution of laboratory scales and balances (except medical and dental)--are classified in Industry 423490, Other Professional Equipment and Supplies Merchant Wholesalers; and
- Merchant wholesale distribution of refrigerated store fixtures--are classified in Industry 423740, Refrigeration Equipment and Supplies Merchant Wholesalers.

42345   Medical, Dental, and Hospital Equipment and Supplies Merchant Wholesalers
See industry description for 423450.

423450   Medical, Dental, and Hospital Equipment and Supplies Merchant Wholesalers

This industry comprises establishments primarily engaged in the merchant wholesale distribution of professional medical equipment, instruments, and supplies (except ophthalmic equipment and instruments and goods used by ophthalmologists, optometrists, and opticians).

Illustrative Examples:

Dental equipment and supplies merchant wholesalers
Surgical dressings merchant wholesalers
Electromedical equipment merchant wholesalers
Patient monitoring equipment merchant wholesalers

Hospital beds merchant wholesalers
Prosthetic appliances and supplies merchant wholesalers
Hospital furniture merchant wholesalers

T—Canadian, Mexican, and United States industries are comparable.

Surgical instruments and apparatus merchant wholesalers

Medical and dental X-ray machines and parts merchant wholesalers

Cross-References.

Establishments primarily engaged in the merchant wholesale distribution of professional equipment, instruments, and/or goods sold, prescribed, or used by ophthalmologists, optometrists, and opticians are classified in Industry 423460, Ophthalmic Goods Merchant Wholesalers.

42346   Ophthalmic Goods Merchant Wholesalers
See industry description for 423460.

423460 Ophthalmic Goods Merchant Wholesalers

This industry comprises establishments primarily engaged in the merchant wholesale distribution of professional equipment, instruments, and/or goods sold, prescribed, or used by ophthalmologists, optometrists, and opticians.

Illustrative Examples:

Binoculars merchant wholesalers
Optometric equipment and supplies merchant wholesalers

Ophthalmic frames merchant wholesalers
Sunglasses merchant wholesalers
Ophthalmic lenses merchant wholesalers

42349   Other Professional Equipment and Supplies Merchant Wholesalers
See industry description for 423490.

423490 Other Professional Equipment and Supplies Merchant Wholesalers

This industry comprises establishments primarily engaged in the merchant wholesale distribution of professional equipment and supplies (except ophthalmic goods and medical, dental, and hospital equipment and supplies).

Illustrative Examples:

Church supplies (except silverware, plated ware) merchant wholesalers
School equipment and supplies (except books, furniture) merchant wholesalers
Drafting tables and instruments merchant wholesalers

Scientific instruments merchant wholesalers
Laboratory equipment (except medical, dental) merchant wholesalers
Surveying equipment and supplies merchant wholesalers

Cross-References.   Establishments primarily engaged in--

- Merchant wholesale distribution of professional equipment, instruments, and/or goods sold, prescribed, or used by ophthalmologists, optometrists, and opticians, such as ophthalmic frames and lenses, and sunglasses--are classified in Industry 423460, Ophthalmic Goods Merchant Wholesalers;
- Merchant wholesale distribution of professional medical equipment, instruments, and supplies used by medical and dental practitioners (except ophthalmic equipment, instruments, and goods used by ophthalmologists, optometrists, and opticians) and medical facilities--are classified in Industry 423450, Medical, Dental, and Hospital Equipment and Supplies Merchant Wholesalers;
- Merchant wholesale distribution of silverware and plated flatware--are classified in Industry 423940, Jewelry, Watch, Precious Stone, and Precious Metal Merchant Wholesalers;
- Merchant wholesale distribution of books--are classified in Industry 424920, Book, Periodical, and Newspaper Merchant Wholesalers; and
- Merchant wholesale distribution of school furniture--are classified in Industry 423210, Furniture Merchant Wholesalers.

T—Canadian, Mexican, and United States industries are comparable.

4235   Metal and Mineral (except Petroleum) Merchant Wholesalers

This industry group comprises establishments primarily engaged in the merchant wholesale distribution of products of the primary metals industries (including metal service centers) and coal, coke, metal ores, and/or nonmetallic minerals (except precious and semiprecious stones and minerals used in construction).

42351   Metal Service Centers and Other Metal Merchant Wholesalers
See industry description for 423510.

423510   Metal Service Centers and Other Metal Merchant Wholesalers

This industry comprises establishments primarily engaged in the merchant wholesale distribution of products of the primary metals industries. Service centers maintain inventory and may perform functions, such as sawing, shearing, bending, leveling, cleaning, or edging, on a custom basis as part of sales transactions.

Illustrative Examples:

Cast iron pipe merchant wholesalers
Metal rods merchant wholesalers
Metal bars (except precious) merchant wholesalers
Metal sheets merchant wholesalers
Metal ingots (except precious) merchant wholesalers

Metal spikes merchant wholesalers
Metal pipe merchant wholesalers
Nails merchant wholesalers
Metal plates merchant wholesalers
Noninsulated wire merchant wholesalers

Cross-References.   Establishments primarily engaged in--

- Merchant wholesale distribution of gold, silver, and platinum--are classified in Industry 423940, Jewelry, Watch, Precious Stone, and Precious Metal Merchant Wholesalers;
- Merchant wholesale distribution of automotive, industrial, and other recyclable metal scrap--are classified in Industry 423930, Recyclable Material Merchant Wholesalers; and
- Merchant wholesale distribution of insulated wire--are classified in Industry 423610, Electrical Apparatus and Equipment, Wiring Supplies, and Related Equipment Merchant Wholesalers.

42352   Coal and Other Mineral and Ore Merchant Wholesalers
See industry description for 423520.

423520   Coal and Other Mineral and Ore Merchant Wholesalers

This industry comprises establishments primarily engaged in the merchant wholesale distribution of coal, coke, metal ores, and/or nonmetallic minerals (except precious and semiprecious stones and minerals used in construction, such as sand and gravel).

Cross-References.   Establishments primarily engaged in--

- Merchant wholesale distribution of nonmetallic minerals used in construction, such as sand and gravel--are classified in Industry 423320, Brick, Stone, and Related Construction Material Merchant Wholesalers;
- Merchant wholesale distribution of crude petroleum--are classified in Industry Group 4247, Petroleum and Petroleum Products Merchant Wholesalers; and
- Merchant wholesale distribution of precious and semiprecious stones and metals--are classified in Industry 423940, Jewelry, Watch, Precious Stone, and Precious Metal Merchant Wholesalers.

4236   Household Appliances and Electrical and Electronic Goods Merchant Wholesalers

This industry group comprises establishments primarily engaged in the merchant wholesale distribution of electrical apparatus and equipment, wiring supplies, and related equipment; household appliances, electric housewares, and consumer electronics; and other electronic parts and equipment.

T—Canadian, Mexican, and United States industries are comparable.

42361   Electrical Apparatus and Equipment, Wiring Supplies, and Related Equipment Merchant Wholesalers
See industry description for 423610.

423610   Electrical Apparatus and Equipment, Wiring Supplies, and Related Equipment Merchant Wholesalers

This industry comprises establishments primarily engaged in the merchant wholesale distribution of electrical construction materials; wiring supplies; electric light fixtures; light bulbs; and/or electrical power equipment for the generation, transmission, distribution, or control of electric energy.

42362   Household Appliances, Electric Housewares, and Consumer Electronics Merchant Wholesalers
See industry description for 423620.

423620   Household Appliances, Electric Housewares, and Consumer Electronics Merchant Wholesalers

This industry comprises establishments primarily engaged in the merchant wholesale distribution of household-type gas and electric appliances (except water heaters and heating stoves (i.e., noncooking)), room air-conditioners, and/or household-type audio or video equipment.

Illustrative Examples:

Household-type sewing machines merchant wholesalers
Household-type radios (including automotive) merchant wholesalers
Household-type video cameras merchant wholesalers

Household-type refrigerators merchant wholesalers
Television sets merchant wholesalers
Toothbrushes, electric, merchant wholesalers
Curling irons, electric, merchant wholesalers

Cross-References.   Establishments primarily engaged in--

- Merchant wholesale distribution of gas and electric water heaters and heating stoves (i.e., noncooking)--are classified in Industry 423720, Plumbing and Heating Equipment and Supplies (Hydronics) Merchant Wholesalers; and
- Merchant wholesale distribution of nonhousehold-type video cameras--are classified in Industry 423410, Photographic Equipment and Supplies Merchant Wholesalers.

42369   Other Electronic Parts and Equipment Merchant Wholesalers
See industry description for 423690.

423690   Other Electronic Parts and Equipment Merchant Wholesalers

This industry comprises establishments primarily engaged in the merchant wholesale distribution of electronic parts and equipment (except electrical apparatus and equipment, wiring supplies, and construction materials; electrical and electronic appliances; and television sets and radios).

Illustrative Examples:

Blank audio and video tapes merchant wholesalers
Communications equipment merchant wholesalers
Blank compact discs (CDs) merchant wholesalers
Radar equipment merchant wholesalers
Blank digital video discs (DVDs) merchant wholesalers

Telegraph equipment merchant wholesalers
Blank diskettes merchant wholesalers
Telephone equipment merchant wholesalers
Broadcasting equipment merchant wholesalers
Unloaded computer boards merchant wholesalers

T—Canadian, Mexican, and United States industries are comparable.

Cross-References.   Establishments primarily engaged in--

- Merchant wholesale distribution of household-type gas and electric appliances (except water heaters and heating stoves (i.e., noncooking)), room air-conditioners, clothes dryers, and/or household-type audio or video equipment--are classified in Industry 423620, Household Appliances, Electric Housewares, and Consumer Electronics Merchant Wholesalers;
- Merchant wholesale distribution of computers, computer peripheral equipment, and loaded computer boards--are classified in Industry 423430, Computer and Computer Peripheral Equipment and Software Merchant Wholesalers; and
- Merchant wholesale distribution of electrical construction materials, wiring supplies, electric light fixtures, light bulbs, and/or electrical power equipment for generation, transmission, distribution, or control of electric energy--are classified in Industry 423610, Electrical Apparatus and Equipment, Wiring Supplies, and Related Equipment Merchant Wholesalers.

4237   Hardware, and Plumbing and Heating Equipment and Supplies Merchant Wholesalers

This industry group comprises establishments primarily engaged in the merchant wholesale distribution of hardware; plumbing and heating equipment and supplies (hydronics); warm air heating and air-conditioning equipment and supplies; and refrigeration equipment and supplies.

42371   Hardware Merchant Wholesalers
See industry description for 423710.

423710 Hardware Merchant Wholesalers

This industry comprises establishments primarily engaged in the merchant wholesale distribution of hardware, knives, or handtools.

Illustrative Examples:

Brads merchant wholesalers
Cutlery merchant wholesalers
Knives (except disposable plastics) merchant wholesalers
Power handtools (e.g., drills, saws, sanders) merchant wholesalers

Fasteners (e.g., bolts, nuts, rivets, screws) merchant wholesalers
Staples merchant wholesalers
Handtools (except motor vehicle, machinists' precision) merchant wholesalers
Tacks merchant wholesalers

Cross-References.   Establishments primarily engaged in--

- Merchant wholesale distribution of nails, noninsulated wire, and screening--are classified in Industry 423510, Metal Service Centers and Other Metal Merchant Wholesalers;
- Merchant wholesale distribution of motor vehicle handtools and equipment--are classified in Industry 423120, Motor Vehicle Supplies and New Parts Merchant Wholesalers;
- Merchant wholesale distribution of machinists' precision handtools--are classified in Industry 423830, Industrial Machinery and Equipment Merchant Wholesalers; and
- Merchant wholesale distribution of disposable plastics knives and eating utensils--are classified in Industry 424130, Industrial and Personal Service Paper Merchant Wholesalers.

42372   Plumbing and Heating Equipment and Supplies (Hydronics) Merchant Wholesalers
See industry description for 423720.

423720 Plumbing and Heating Equipment and Supplies (Hydronics) Merchant Wholesalers

This industry comprises establishments primarily engaged in the merchant wholesale distribution of plumbing equipment, hydronic heating equipment, household-type water heaters, and/or supplies.

T—Canadian, Mexican, and United States industries are comparable.

Cross-References.   Establishments primarily engaged in--

- Selling and installing plumbing, heating and air-conditioning equipment--are classified in Industry 238220, Plumbing, Heating, and Air-Conditioning Contractors;
- Merchant wholesale distribution of warm air heating and air-conditioning equipment--are classified in Industry 423730, Warm Air Heating and Air-Conditioning Equipment and Supplies Merchant Wholesalers; and
- Merchant wholesale distribution of household-type gas and electric appliances (except water heaters and heating stoves (i.e., noncooking)), room air-conditioners, clothes dryers, and/or household-type audio or video equipment--are classified in Industry 423620, Household Appliances, Electric Housewares, and Consumer Electronics Merchant Wholesalers.

42373   Warm Air Heating and Air-Conditioning Equipment and Supplies Merchant Wholesalers
See industry description for 423730.

423730   Warm Air Heating and Air-Conditioning Equipment and Supplies Merchant Wholesalers

This industry comprises establishments primarily engaged in the merchant wholesale distribution of warm air heating and air-conditioning equipment and supplies.

Illustrative Examples:

Air pollution control equipment and supplies
merchant wholesalers
Automotive air-conditioners merchant wholesalers
Non-portable electric baseboard heaters merchant
wholesalers

Air-conditioning equipment (except room units)
merchant wholesalers
Warm air central heating equipment merchant
wholesalers

Cross-References.   Establishments primarily engaged in--

- Merchant wholesale distribution of household-type gas and electric appliances (except water heaters and heating stoves (i.e., noncooking)) and room air-conditioners--are classified in Industry 423620, Household Appliances, Electric Housewares, and Consumer Electronics Merchant Wholesalers;
- Merchant wholesale distribution of hydronic heating equipment--are classified in Industry 423720, Plumbing and Heating Equipment and Supplies (Hydronics) Merchant Wholesalers; and
- Selling and installing warm air heating and air-conditioning equipment--are classified in Industry 238220, Plumbing, Heating, and Air-Conditioning Contractors.

42374   Refrigeration Equipment and Supplies Merchant Wholesalers
See industry description for 423740.

423740   Refrigeration Equipment and Supplies Merchant Wholesalers

This industry comprises establishments primarily engaged in the merchant wholesale distribution of refrigeration equipment (except household-type refrigerators, freezers, and air-conditioners).

Illustrative Examples:

Cold storage machinery merchant wholesalers
Refrigerated display cases merchant wholesalers

Commercial refrigerators merchant wholesalers
Water coolers merchant wholesalers

T—Canadian, Mexican, and United States industries are comparable.

Cross-References.   Establishments primarily engaged in--

- Merchant wholesale distribution of household-type refrigerators, freezers, and room air-conditioners--are classified in Industry 423620, Household Appliances, Electric Housewares, and Consumer Electronics Merchant Wholesalers; and
- Merchant wholesale distribution of air-conditioning equipment (except room units)--are classified in Industry 423730, Warm Air Heating and Air-Conditioning Equipment and Supplies Merchant Wholesalers.

4238   Machinery, Equipment, and Supplies Merchant Wholesalers

This industry group comprises establishments primarily engaged in the merchant wholesale distribution of construction, mining, farm, garden, industrial, service establishment, and transportation machinery, equipment, and supplies.

42381   Construction and Mining (except Oil Well) Machinery and Equipment Merchant Wholesalers
See industry description for 423810.

423810   Construction and Mining (except Oil Well) Machinery and Equipment Merchant Wholesalers

This industry comprises establishments primarily engaged in the merchant wholesale distribution of specialized machinery, equipment, and related parts generally used in construction, mining (except oil well), and logging activities.

Illustrative Examples:

Excavating machinery and equipment merchant wholesalers
Road construction and maintenance machinery merchant wholesalers

Forestry machinery and equipment merchant wholesalers
Scaffolding merchant wholesalers
Mining cranes merchant wholesalers

Cross-References.

Establishments primarily engaged in the merchant wholesale distribution of oil well machinery and equipment are classified in Industry 423830, Industrial Machinery and Equipment Merchant Wholesalers.

42382   Farm and Garden Machinery and Equipment Merchant Wholesalers
See industry description for 423820.

423820   Farm and Garden Machinery and Equipment Merchant Wholesalers

This industry comprises establishments primarily engaged in the merchant wholesale distribution of specialized machinery, equipment, and related parts generally used in agricultural, farm, and lawn and garden activities.

Illustrative Examples:

Animal feeders merchant wholesalers
Milking machinery and equipment merchant wholesalers
Lawnmowers merchant wholesalers

Harvesting machinery and equipment merchant wholesalers
Planting machinery and equipment merchant wholesalers

42383   Industrial Machinery and Equipment Merchant Wholesalers
See industry description for 423830.

T—Canadian, Mexican, and United States industries are comparable.

423830 Industrial Machinery and Equipment Merchant Wholesalers

This industry comprises establishments primarily engaged in the merchant wholesale distribution of specialized machinery, equipment, and related parts generally used in manufacturing, oil well, and warehousing activities.

Illustrative Examples:

Fluid power transmission equipment merchant wholesalers
Metalworking machinery and equipment merchant wholesalers
Food processing machinery and equipment merchant wholesalers

Oil well machinery and equipment merchant wholesalers
Material handling machinery and equipment merchant wholesalers

Cross-References.   Establishments primarily engaged in--

- Merchant wholesale distribution of specialized machinery, equipment, and related parts generally used in construction, mining (except oil well), and logging activities--are classified in Industry 423810, Construction and Mining (except Oil Well) Machinery and Equipment Merchant Wholesalers; and
- Merchant wholesale distribution of supplies used in machinery and equipment generally used in manufacturing, oil well, and warehousing activities--are classified in Industry 423840, Industrial Supplies Merchant Wholesalers.

42384   Industrial Supplies Merchant Wholesalers
See industry description for 423840.

423840 Industrial Supplies Merchant Wholesalers

This industry comprises establishments primarily engaged in the merchant wholesale distribution of supplies for machinery and equipment generally used in manufacturing, oil well, and warehousing activities.

Illustrative Examples:

Industrial containers merchant wholesalers
Refractory materials (e.g., brick, blocks, shapes) merchant wholesalers
Industrial diamonds merchant wholesalers

Welding supplies (except welding gases) merchant wholesalers
Printing inks merchant wholesalers

Cross-References.   Establishments primarily engaged in--

- Merchant wholesale distribution of hydraulic and pneumatic (fluid power) pumps, motors, pistons, and valves--are classified in Industry 423830, Industrial Machinery and Equipment Merchant Wholesalers; and
- Merchant wholesale distribution of welding gases--are classified in Industry 424690, Other Chemical and Allied Products Merchant Wholesalers.

42385   Service Establishment Equipment and Supplies Merchant Wholesalers
See industry description for 423850.

423850 Service Establishment Equipment and Supplies Merchant Wholesalers

This industry comprises establishments primarily engaged in the merchant wholesale distribution of specialized equipment and supplies of the type used by service establishments (except specialized equipment and supplies used in offices, stores, hotels, restaurants, schools, health and medical facilities, photographic facilities, and specialized equipment used in transportation and construction activities).

T—Canadian, Mexican, and United States industries are comparable.

Illustrative Examples:

Amusement park equipment merchant wholesalers
Janitorial equipment and supplies merchant
wholesalers
Beauty parlor equipment and supplies merchant
wholesalers
Undertakers' equipment and supplies merchant
wholesalers

Car wash equipment and supplies merchant
wholesalers
Upholsterers' equipment and supplies (except fabrics)
merchant wholesalers
Drycleaning equipment and supplies merchant
wholesalers

Cross-References.   Establishments primarily engaged in--

- Merchant wholesale distribution of janitorial and automotive chemicals--are classified in Industry 424690, Other Chemical and Allied Products Merchant Wholesalers;
- Merchant wholesale distribution of piece goods, fabrics, knitting yarns (except industrial), thread and other notions--are classified in Industry 424310, Piece Goods, Notions, and Other Dry Goods Merchant Wholesalers; and
- Merchant wholesale distribution of industrial yarns--are classified in Industry 424990, Other Miscellaneous Nondurable Goods Merchant Wholesalers.

42386   Transportation Equipment and Supplies (except Motor Vehicle) Merchant Wholesalers
See industry description for 423860.

423860   Transportation Equipment and Supplies (except Motor Vehicle) Merchant Wholesalers

This industry comprises establishments primarily engaged in the merchant wholesale distribution of transportation equipment and supplies (except marine pleasure craft and motor vehicles).

Illustrative Examples:

Aircraft merchant wholesalers
Railroad cars merchant wholesalers

Motorized passenger golf carts merchant wholesalers
Ships merchant wholesalers

Cross-References.   Establishments primarily engaged in--

- Merchant wholesale distribution of motor vehicles and motor vehicle parts--are classified in Industry Group 4231, Motor Vehicle and Motor Vehicle Parts and Supplies Merchant Wholesalers; and
- Merchant wholesale distribution of marine pleasure craft--are classified in Industry 423910, Sporting and Recreational Goods and Supplies Merchant Wholesalers.

4239   Miscellaneous Durable Goods Merchant Wholesalers

This industry group comprises establishments primarily engaged in the merchant wholesale distribution of sporting, recreational, toy, hobby, and jewelry goods and supplies, and precious stones and metals.

42391   Sporting and Recreational Goods and Supplies Merchant Wholesalers
See industry description for 423910.

423910   Sporting and Recreational Goods and Supplies Merchant Wholesalers

This industry comprises establishments primarily engaged in the merchant wholesale distribution of sporting goods and accessories; billiard and pool supplies; sporting firearms and ammunition; and/or marine pleasure craft, equipment, and supplies.

T—Canadian, Mexican, and United States industries are comparable.

Cross-References.   Establishments primarily engaged in--

- Merchant wholesale distribution of motor vehicles and trailers--are classified in Industry 423110, Automobile and Other Motor Vehicle Merchant Wholesalers;
- Merchant wholesale distribution of motorized passenger golf carts--are classified in Industry 423860, Transportation Equipment and Supplies (except Motor Vehicle) Merchant Wholesalers; and
- Merchant wholesale distribution of athletic apparel and athletic footwear--are classified in Industry Group 4243, Apparel, Piece Goods, and Notions Merchant Wholesalers.

42392   Toy and Hobby Goods and Supplies Merchant Wholesalers
See industry description for 423920.

423920 Toy and Hobby Goods and Supplies Merchant Wholesalers

This industry comprises establishments primarily engaged in the merchant wholesale distribution of games, toys, fireworks, playing cards, hobby goods and supplies, and/or related goods.

42393   Recyclable Material Merchant Wholesalers
See industry description for 423930.

423930 Recyclable Material Merchant Wholesalers

This industry comprises establishments primarily engaged in the merchant wholesale distribution of automotive scrap, industrial scrap, and other recyclable materials. Included in this industry are auto wreckers primarily engaged in dismantling motor vehicles for the purpose of wholesaling scrap.

Cross-References.   Establishments primarily engaged in--

- Dismantling motor vehicles for the purpose of selling used parts--are classified in Industry 423140, Motor Vehicle Parts (Used) Merchant Wholesalers; and
- Operating facilities where commingled recyclable materials, such as paper, plastics, used beverage cans, and metals, are sorted into distinct categories--are classified in Industry 562920, Materials Recovery Facilities.

42394   Jewelry, Watch, Precious Stone, and Precious Metal Merchant Wholesalers
See industry description for 423940.

423940 Jewelry, Watch, Precious Stone, and Precious Metal Merchant Wholesalers

This industry comprises establishments primarily engaged in the merchant wholesale distribution of jewelry, precious and semiprecious stones, precious metals and metal flatware, costume jewelry, watches, clocks, silverware, and/or jewelers' findings.

Cross-References.   Establishments primarily engaged in--

- Merchant wholesale distribution of precious metal ores or concentrates--are classified in Industry 423520, Coal and Other Mineral and Ore Merchant Wholesalers; and
- Merchant wholesale distribution of nonprecious flatware--are classified in Industry 423220, Home Furnishing Merchant Wholesalers.

42399   Other Miscellaneous Durable Goods Merchant Wholesalers
See industry description for 423990.

T—Canadian, Mexican, and United States industries are comparable.

423990 Other Miscellaneous Durable Goods Merchant Wholesalers

This industry comprises establishments primarily engaged in the merchant wholesale distribution of durable goods (except motor vehicles and motor vehicle parts and supplies; furniture and home furnishings; lumber and other construction materials; professional and commercial equipment and supplies; metals and minerals (except petroleum); electrical goods; hardware, and plumbing and heating equipment and supplies; machinery, equipment and supplies; sporting and recreational goods and supplies; toy and hobby goods and supplies; recyclable materials; and jewelry, watches, precious stones and precious metals).

Illustrative Examples:

Firearms (except sporting) merchant wholesalers
Musical instruments merchant wholesalers
Prerecorded audio and video tapes and discs merchant wholesalers
Phonograph records merchant wholesalers

Prerecorded compact discs (CDs) and digital video discs (DVDs) merchant wholesalers
Timber and timber products (except lumber) merchant wholesalers

Cross-References.   Establishments primarily engaged in--

- Merchant wholesale distribution of automobiles and other motor vehicles, motor vehicle supplies, tires, and new and used parts--are classified in Industry Group 4231, Motor Vehicle and Motor Vehicle Parts and Supplies Merchant Wholesalers;
- Merchant wholesale distribution of furniture and home furnishings--are classified in Industry Group 4232, Furniture and Home Furnishing Merchant Wholesalers;
- Merchant wholesale distribution of lumber, plywood, millwork, wood panels, brick, stone, roofing, siding, and other nonelectrical construction materials--are classified in Industry Group 4233, Lumber and Other Construction Materials Merchant Wholesalers;
- Merchant wholesale distribution of photographic, office, computer and computer peripheral, medical, dental, hospital, ophthalmic, and other commercial and professional equipment and supplies--are classified in Industry Group 4234, Professional and Commercial Equipment and Supplies Merchant Wholesalers;
- Merchant wholesale distribution of coal and other minerals and ores and semi-finished metal products--are classified in Industry Group 4235, Metal and Mineral (except Petroleum) Merchant Wholesalers;
- Merchant wholesale distribution of household appliances and electrical goods--are classified in Industry Group 4236, Household Appliances and Electrical and Electronic Goods Merchant Wholesalers;
- Merchant wholesale distribution of hardware; and plumbing, heating, air-conditioning, and refrigeration equipment and supplies--are classified in Industry Group 4237, Hardware, and Plumbing and Heating Equipment and Supplies Merchant Wholesalers;
- Merchant wholesale distribution of construction, mining, farm, garden, industrial, service establishment, and transportation machinery, equipment and supplies--are classified in Industry Group 4238, Machinery, Equipment, and Supplies Merchant Wholesalers;
- Merchant wholesale distribution of sporting goods and accessories; billiard and pool supplies; sporting firearms and ammunition; and/or marine pleasure craft, equipment, and supplies--are classified in Industry 423910, Sporting and Recreational Goods and Supplies Merchant Wholesalers;
- Merchant wholesale distribution of toys, fireworks, playing cards, hobby goods and supplies and/or related goods--are classified in Industry 423920, Toy and Hobby Goods and Supplies Merchant Wholesalers;
- Merchant wholesale distribution of automotive, industrial, and other recyclable materials--are classified in Industry 423930, Recyclable Material Merchant Wholesalers;
- Merchant wholesale distribution of jewelry, precious and semiprecious stones, precious metals and metal flatware, costume jewelry, watches, clocks, silverware, and/or jewelers' findings--are classified in Industry 423940, Jewelry, Watch, Precious Stone, and Precious Metal Merchant Wholesalers; and
- Selling and installing fire suppression systems and fire extinguishers--are classified in Industry 238220, Plumbing, Heating, and Air-Conditioning Contractors.

T—Canadian, Mexican, and United States industries are comparable.

424   Merchant Wholesalers, Nondurable Goods

Industries in the Merchant Wholesalers, Nondurable Goods subsector sell nondurable goods to other businesses. Nondurable goods are items generally with a normal life expectancy of less than three years. Nondurable goods merchant wholesale trade establishments are engaged in wholesaling products, such as paper and paper products, chemicals and chemical products, drugs, textiles and textile products, apparel, footwear, groceries, farm products, petroleum and petroleum products, alcoholic beverages, books, magazines, newspapers, flowers and nursery stock, and tobacco products.
The detailed industries within the subsector are organized in the classification structure based on the products sold.
Business-to-business electronic markets, agents, and brokers primarily engaged in wholesaling nondurable goods, generally on a commission or fee basis, are classified in Subsector 425, Wholesale Electronic Markets and Agents and Brokers.

4241   Paper and Paper Product Merchant Wholesalers

This industry group comprises establishments primarily engaged in the merchant wholesale distribution of bulk printing and writing paper; stationery and office supplies; and industrial and personal service paper.

42411   Printing and Writing Paper Merchant Wholesalers
          See industry description for 424110.

424110 Printing and Writing Paper Merchant Wholesalers

This industry comprises establishments primarily engaged in the merchant wholesale distribution of bulk printing and/or writing paper generally on rolls for further processing.

Illustrative Examples:

Bulk envelope paper merchant wholesalers
Bulk paper (e.g., fine, printing, writing) merchant wholesalers

Bulk groundwood paper merchant wholesalers
Newsprint merchant wholesalers

Cross-References.

Establishments primarily engaged in the merchant wholesale distribution of stationery and office paper (e.g., carbon, computer, copier, typewriter) are classified in Industry 424120, Stationery and Office Supplies Merchant Wholesalers.

42412   Stationery and Office Supplies Merchant Wholesalers
          See industry description for 424120.

424120 Stationery and Office Supplies Merchant Wholesalers

This industry comprises establishments primarily engaged in the merchant wholesale distribution of stationery, office supplies, and/or gift wrap.

Illustrative Examples:

Photocopy supplies merchant wholesalers
Envelope merchant wholesalers
Social stationery merchant wholesalers
File cards and folders merchant wholesalers
Greeting cards merchant wholesalers

Office paper (e.g., carbon, computer, copier, typewriter) merchant wholesalers
Writing pens merchant wholesalers
Pencils merchant wholesalers

T—Canadian, Mexican, and United States industries are comparable.

Cross-References.

Establishments primarily engaged in the merchant wholesale distribution of bulk printing and/or writing paper are classified in Industry 424110, Printing and Writing Paper Merchant Wholesalers.

42413   Industrial and Personal Service Paper Merchant Wholesalers
See industry description for 424130.

424130 Industrial and Personal Service Paper Merchant Wholesalers

This industry comprises establishments primarily engaged in the merchant wholesale distribution of kraft wrapping and other coarse paper, paperboard, converted paper (except stationery and office supplies), and/or related disposable plastics products.

Illustrative Examples:

Corrugated paper merchant wholesalers
Disposable plastics eating utensils merchant wholesalers
Paper napkins merchant wholesalers
Paper and disposable plastics dishes merchant wholesalers
Paperboard and disposable plastics boxes merchant wholesalers
Paper towels merchant wholesalers

Paper and disposable plastics shipping supplies merchant wholesalers
Plastics bags merchant wholesalers
Paper bags merchant wholesalers
Sanitary paper products merchant wholesalers
Wrapping paper (except gift wrap) merchant wholesalers
Waxed paper merchant wholesalers

Cross-References.

Establishments primarily engaged in the merchant wholesale distribution of stationery, office supplies, and/or gift wrap are classified in Industry 424120, Stationery and Office Supplies Merchant Wholesalers.

4242   Drugs and Druggists' Sundries Merchant Wholesalers

42421   Drugs and Druggists' Sundries Merchant Wholesalers
See industry description for 424210.

424210 Drugs and Druggists' Sundries Merchant Wholesalers

This industry comprises establishments primarily engaged in the merchant wholesale distribution of biological and medical products; botanical drugs and herbs; and pharmaceutical products intended for internal and/or external consumption in such forms as ampoules, tablets, capsules, vials, ointments, powders, solutions, and suspensions.

Illustrative Examples:

Antibiotics merchant wholesalers
Endocrine substances merchant wholesalers
Blood derivatives merchant wholesalers
In-vitro and in-vivo diagnostics merchant wholesalers

Botanicals merchant wholesalers
Vaccines merchant wholesalers
Cosmetics merchant wholesalers
Vitamins merchant wholesalers

Cross-References.

Establishments primarily engaged in the merchant wholesale distribution of surgical, dental, and hospital equipment are classified in Industry 423450, Medical, Dental, and Hospital Equipment and Supplies Merchant Wholesalers.

T—Canadian, Mexican, and United States industries are comparable.

4243   Apparel, Piece Goods, and Notions Merchant Wholesalers

This industry group comprises establishments primarily engaged in the merchant wholesale distribution of piece goods, notions, and other dry goods; men's and boys' clothing and furnishings; women's, children's, and infants' clothing and accessories; and footwear.

42431   Piece Goods, Notions, and Other Dry Goods Merchant Wholesalers
      See industry description for 424310.

424310 Piece Goods, Notions, and Other Dry Goods Merchant Wholesalers

This industry comprises establishments primarily engaged in the merchant wholesale distribution of piece goods, fabrics, knitting yarns (except industrial), thread and other notions, and/or hair accessories.

Cross-References.

- Establishments primarily engaged as converters who buy fabric goods in the grey, have them finished on a contract basis, and sell at wholesale are classified in Industry 313310, Textile and Fabric Finishing Mills; and
- Establishments primarily engaged in merchant wholesale distribution of industrial yarns are classified in Industry 424990, Other Miscellaneous Nondurable Goods Merchant Wholesalers.

42432   Men's and Boys' Clothing and Furnishings Merchant Wholesalers
      See industry description for 424320.

424320 Men's and Boys' Clothing and Furnishings Merchant Wholesalers

This industry comprises establishments primarily engaged in the merchant wholesale distribution of men's and/or boys' clothing and furnishings.

Illustrative Examples:

Men's and boys' hosiery merchant wholesalers	Men's and boys' underwear merchant wholesalers
Men's and boys' suits merchant wholesalers	Men's and boys' sportswear merchant wholesalers
Men's and boys' nightwear merchant wholesalers	Men's and boys' work clothing merchant wholesalers

Cross-References.

Establishments primarily engaged in the merchant wholesale distribution of unisex clothing and men's fur clothing are classified in Industry 424330, Women's, Children's, and Infants' Clothing and Accessories Merchant Wholesalers.

42433   Women's, Children's, and Infants' Clothing and Accessories Merchant Wholesalers
      See industry description for 424330.

424330 Women's, Children's, and Infants' Clothing and Accessories Merchant Wholesalers

This industry comprises establishments primarily engaged in the merchant wholesale distribution of (1) women's, children's, infants', and/or unisex clothing and accessories and/or (2) fur clothing.

Illustrative Examples:

Dresses merchant wholesalers	Women's, children's, and infants' hosiery merchant
Millinery merchant wholesalers	wholesalers
Fur clothing merchant wholesalers	Lingerie merchant wholesalers

---

T—Canadian, Mexican, and United States industries are comparable.

census.gov/naics

42434 Footwear Merchant Wholesalers
See industry description for 424340.

424340 Footwear Merchant Wholesalers

This industry comprises establishments primarily engaged in the merchant wholesale distribution of footwear (including athletic) of leather, rubber, and other materials.

4244 Grocery and Related Product Merchant Wholesalers

This industry group comprises establishments primarily engaged in the merchant wholesale distribution of (1) a general line of groceries; (2) packaged frozen food; (3) dairy products; (4) poultry and poultry products; (5) confectioneries; (6) fish and seafood; (7) meats and meat products; (8) fresh fruits and vegetables; and (9) other grocery and related products.

42441 General Line Grocery Merchant Wholesalers
See industry description for 424410.

424410 General Line Grocery Merchant Wholesalers

This industry comprises establishments primarily engaged in the merchant wholesale distribution of a general line (wide range) of groceries.

Cross-References.

Establishments primarily engaged in the merchant wholesale distribution of a specialized line of groceries are classified elsewhere in Sector 42, Wholesale Trade, according to the product sold.

42442 Packaged Frozen Food Merchant Wholesalers
See industry description for 424420.

424420 Packaged Frozen Food Merchant Wholesalers

This industry comprises establishments primarily engaged in the merchant wholesale distribution of packaged frozen foods (except dairy products).

Illustrative Examples:

Frozen bakery products merchant wholesalers
Packaged frozen fish merchant wholesalers
Frozen juices merchant wholesalers

Packaged frozen meats merchant wholesalers
Frozen vegetables merchant wholesalers
Packaged frozen poultry merchant wholesalers

Cross-References.

Establishments primarily engaged in the merchant wholesale distribution of frozen dairy products are classified in Industry 424430, Dairy Product (except Dried or Canned) Merchant Wholesalers.

42443 Dairy Product (except Dried or Canned) Merchant Wholesalers
See industry description for 424430.

424430 Dairy Product (except Dried or Canned) Merchant Wholesalers

This industry comprises establishments primarily engaged in the merchant wholesale distribution of dairy products (except dried or canned).

T—Canadian, Mexican, and United States industries are comparable.

Illustrative Examples:

Butter merchant wholesalers	Ice cream and ices merchant wholesalers
Fluid milk (except canned) merchant wholesalers	Cream merchant wholesalers
Cheese merchant wholesalers	Yogurt merchant wholesalers

Cross-References.   Establishments primarily engaged in--

- Merchant wholesale distribution of dried or canned dairy products and dairy substitutes--are classified in Industry 424490, Other Grocery and Related Products Merchant Wholesalers; and
- Pasteurizing and bottling milk--are classified in U.S. Industry 311511, Fluid Milk Manufacturing.

42444   Poultry and Poultry Product Merchant Wholesalers
See industry description for 424440.

424440   Poultry and Poultry Product Merchant Wholesalers

This industry comprises establishments primarily engaged in the merchant wholesale distribution of poultry and/or poultry products (except canned and packaged frozen).

Cross-References.   Establishments primarily engaged in--

- Merchant wholesale distribution of packaged frozen poultry--are classified in Industry 424420, Packaged Frozen Food Merchant Wholesalers;
- Merchant wholesale distribution of canned poultry--are classified in Industry 424490, Other Grocery and Related Products Merchant Wholesalers; and
- Slaughtering and dressing poultry--are classified in U.S. Industry 311615, Poultry Processing.

42445   Confectionery Merchant Wholesalers
See industry description for 424450.

424450   Confectionery Merchant Wholesalers

This industry comprises establishments primarily engaged in the merchant wholesale distribution of confectioneries; salted or roasted nuts; popcorn; potato, corn, and similar chips; and/or fountain fruits and syrups.

Cross-References.   Establishments primarily engaged in--

- Merchant wholesale distribution of frozen pretzels--are classified in Industry 424420, Packaged Frozen Food Merchant Wholesalers; and
- Merchant wholesale distribution of pretzels (except frozen)--are classified in Industry 424490, Other Grocery and Related Products Merchant Wholesalers.

42446   Fish and Seafood Merchant Wholesalers
See industry description for 424460.

424460   Fish and Seafood Merchant Wholesalers

This industry comprises establishments primarily engaged in the merchant wholesale distribution of fish and seafood (except canned or packaged frozen).

Cross-References.   Establishments primarily engaged in--

- Merchant wholesale distribution of packaged frozen fish and seafood--are classified in Industry 424420, Packaged Frozen Food Merchant Wholesalers;

T—Canadian, Mexican, and United States industries are comparable.

- Merchant wholesale distribution of canned fish and seafood--are classified in Industry 424490, Other Grocery and Related Products Merchant Wholesalers; and
- Canning, smoking, salting, drying, or freezing seafood and shucking and packing fresh shellfish--are classified in Industry 311710, Seafood Product Preparation and Packaging.

42447   Meat and Meat Product Merchant Wholesalers
See industry description for 424470.

424470   Meat and Meat Product Merchant Wholesalers

This industry comprises establishments primarily engaged in the merchant wholesale distribution of meats and meat products (except canned and packaged frozen) and/or lard.

Cross-References.   Establishments primarily engaged in--

- Merchant wholesale distribution of packaged frozen meats--are classified in Industry 424420, Packaged Frozen Food Merchant Wholesalers;
- Merchant wholesale distribution of canned meats--are classified in Industry 424490, Other Grocery and Related Products Merchant Wholesalers; and
- Preparing boxed beef from purchased carcasses--are classified in U.S. Industry 311612, Meat Processed from Carcasses.

42448   Fresh Fruit and Vegetable Merchant Wholesalers
See industry description for 424480.

424480   Fresh Fruit and Vegetable Merchant Wholesalers

This industry comprises establishments primarily engaged in the merchant wholesale distribution of fresh fruits and vegetables.

42449   Other Grocery and Related Products Merchant Wholesalers
See industry description for 424490.

424490   Other Grocery and Related Products Merchant Wholesalers

This industry comprises establishments primarily engaged in the merchant wholesale distribution of groceries and related products (except a general line of groceries; packaged frozen food; dairy products (except dried and canned); poultry products (except canned); confectioneries; fish and seafood (except canned); meat products (except canned); and fresh fruits and vegetables). Included in this industry are establishments primarily engaged in the bottling and merchant wholesale distribution of spring and mineral waters processed by others.

Illustrative Examples:

Bakery products (except frozen) merchant wholesalers
Canned seafood merchant wholesalers
Canned fish merchant wholesalers
Canned vegetables merchant wholesalers

Canned fruits merchant wholesalers
Dried milk merchant wholesalers
Canned meats merchant wholesalers
Soft drinks merchant wholesalers
Canned milk merchant wholesalers

Cross-References.   Establishments primarily engaged in--

- Merchant wholesale distribution of grains, field beans, livestock, and other farm product raw materials--are classified in Industry Group 4245, Farm Product Raw Material Merchant Wholesalers;
- Merchant wholesale distribution of beer, wine, and distilled alcoholic beverages--are classified in Industry Group 4248, Beer, Wine, and Distilled Alcoholic Beverage Merchant Wholesalers;

T--Canadian, Mexican, and United States industries are comparable.

- Bottling soft drinks--are classified in Industry 31211, Soft Drink and Ice Manufacturing;
- Merchant wholesale distribution of a general line of groceries--are classified in Industry 424410, General Line Grocery Merchant Wholesalers;
- Merchant wholesale distribution of packaged frozen foods (except dairy)--are classified in Industry 424420, Packaged Frozen Food Merchant Wholesalers;
- Merchant wholesale distribution of dairy products--are classified in Industry 424430, Dairy Product (except Dried or Canned) Merchant Wholesalers;
- Merchant wholesale distribution of poultry and poultry products (except canned and packaged frozen)--are classified in Industry 424440, Poultry and Poultry Product Merchant Wholesalers;
- Merchant wholesale distribution of confectioneries; salted or roasted nuts; popcorn; potato, corn, and similar chips; and/or fountain fruits and syrups--are classified in Industry 424450, Confectionery Merchant Wholesalers;
- Merchant wholesale distribution of fish and seafood (except canned and packaged frozen)--are classified in Industry 424460, Fish and Seafood Merchant Wholesalers;
- Merchant wholesale distribution of meats (except canned and packaged frozen)--are classified in Industry 424470, Meat and Meat Product Merchant Wholesalers;
- Merchant wholesale distribution of fresh fruits and vegetables--are classified in Industry 424480, Fresh Fruit and Vegetable Merchant Wholesalers;
- Purifying and bottling water--are classified in U.S. Industry 312112, Bottled Water Manufacturing; and
- Roasting coffee--are classified in Industry 311920, Coffee and Tea Manufacturing.

4245   Farm Product Raw Material Merchant Wholesalers

This industry group comprises establishments primarily engaged in the merchant wholesale distribution of agricultural products (except raw milk, live poultry, and fresh fruits and vegetables), such as grains, field beans, livestock, and other farm product raw materials (excluding seeds).

42451   Grain and Field Bean Merchant Wholesalers
See industry description for 424510.

424510 Grain and Field Bean Merchant Wholesalers

This industry comprises establishments primarily engaged in the merchant wholesale distribution of grains, such as corn, wheat, oats, barley, and unpolished rice; dry beans; and soybeans and other inedible beans. Included in this industry are establishments primarily engaged in operating country or terminal grain elevators primarily for the purpose of wholesaling.

Cross-References.   Establishments primarily engaged in--

- Merchant wholesale distribution of field and garden seeds--are classified in Industry 424910, Farm Supplies Merchant Wholesalers; and
- Operating grain elevators for storage only--are classified in Industry 493130, Farm Product Warehousing and Storage.

42452   Livestock Merchant Wholesalers
See industry description for 424520.

424520 Livestock Merchant Wholesalers

This industry comprises establishments primarily engaged in the merchant wholesale distribution of livestock (except horses and mules).

T—Canadian, Mexican, and United States industries are comparable.

Illustrative Examples:

Cattle merchant wholesalers
Hogs merchant wholesalers

Goats merchant wholesalers
Sheep merchant wholesalers

Cross-References.

Establishments primarily engaged in the merchant wholesale distribution of horses and mules are classified in Industry 424590, Other Farm Product Raw Material Merchant Wholesalers.

42459 Other Farm Product Raw Material Merchant Wholesalers
See industry description for 424590.

424590 Other Farm Product Raw Material Merchant Wholesalers

This industry comprises establishments primarily engaged in the merchant wholesale distribution of farm products (except grain and field beans, livestock, raw milk, live poultry, and fresh fruits and vegetables).

Illustrative Examples:

Chicks, live, merchant wholesalers
Mules merchant wholesalers
Hides merchant wholesalers
Raw cotton merchant wholesalers

Horses merchant wholesalers
Raw pelts merchant wholesalers
Leaf tobacco merchant wholesalers
Sod merchant wholesalers

Cross-References.   Establishments primarily engaged in--

- Merchant wholesale distribution of raw milk--are classified in Industry 424430, Dairy Product (except Dried or Canned) Merchant Wholesalers;
- Merchant wholesale distribution of live poultry (except chicks)--are classified in Industry 424440, Poultry and Poultry Product Merchant Wholesalers;
- Merchant wholesale distribution of grain, dry beans, and soybeans and other inedible beans--are classified in Industry 424510, Grain and Field Bean Merchant Wholesalers;
- Merchant wholesale distribution of livestock (except horses and mules), such as cattle, hogs, sheep, and goats--are classified in Industry 424520, Livestock Merchant Wholesalers; and
- Merchant wholesale distribution of fresh fruits and vegetables--are classified in Industry 424480, Fresh Fruit and Vegetable Merchant Wholesalers.

4246 Chemical and Allied Products Merchant Wholesalers

This industry group comprises establishments primarily engaged in the merchant wholesale distribution of chemicals, plastics materials and basic forms and shapes, and allied products.

42461 Plastics Materials and Basic Forms and Shapes Merchant Wholesalers
See industry description for 424610.

424610 Plastics Materials and Basic Forms and Shapes Merchant Wholesalers

This industry comprises establishments primarily engaged in the merchant wholesale distribution of plastics materials and resins, and unsupported plastics film, sheet, sheeting, rod, tube, and other basic forms and shapes.

42469 Other Chemical and Allied Products Merchant Wholesalers
See industry description for 424690.

T—Canadian, Mexican, and United States industries are comparable.

424690 Other Chemical and Allied Products Merchant Wholesalers

This industry comprises establishments primarily engaged in the merchant wholesale distribution of chemicals and allied products (except agricultural and medicinal chemicals, paints and varnishes, fireworks, and plastics materials and basic forms and shapes).

Illustrative Examples:

Acids merchant wholesalers
Industrial chemicals merchant wholesalers
Automotive chemicals (except lubricating oils and greases) merchant wholesalers
Industrial salts merchant wholesalers

Dyestuffs merchant wholesalers
Rosins merchant wholesalers
Explosives (except ammunition and fireworks) merchant wholesalers
Turpentine merchant wholesalers

Cross-References.   Establishments primarily engaged in--

- Merchant wholesale distribution of ammunition--are classified in Industry Group 4239, Miscellaneous Durable Goods Merchant Wholesalers;
- Merchant wholesale distribution of biological and medical products; botanical drugs and herbs; and pharmaceutical products intended for internal and external consumption in such forms as ampoules, tablets, capsules, vials, ointments, powders, solutions, and suspensions--are classified in Industry 424210, Drugs and Druggists' Sundries Merchant Wholesalers;
- Merchant wholesale distribution of farm supplies, such as animal feeds, fertilizers, agricultural chemicals, pesticides, seeds, and plant bulbs--are classified in Industry 424910, Farm Supplies Merchant Wholesalers;
- Merchant wholesale distribution of paints, varnishes, and similar coatings, pigments, wallpaper, and supplies, such as paintbrushes and rollers--are classified in Industry 424950, Paint, Varnish, and Supplies Merchant Wholesalers;
- Merchant wholesale distribution of lubricating oils and greases--are classified in Industry 424720, Petroleum and Petroleum Products Merchant Wholesalers (except Bulk Stations and Terminals);
- Merchant wholesale distribution of fireworks--are classified in Industry 423920, Toy and Hobby Goods and Supplies Merchant Wholesalers; and
- Merchant wholesale distribution of plastics materials and resins, and unsupported plastics film, sheet, sheeting, rod, tube, and other basic forms and shapes--are classified in Industry 424610, Plastics Materials and Basic Forms and Shapes Merchant Wholesalers.

4247   Petroleum and Petroleum Products Merchant Wholesalers

This industry group comprises establishments primarily engaged in the merchant wholesale distribution of petroleum and petroleum products, including liquefied petroleum gas.

42471   Petroleum Bulk Stations and Terminals
See industry description for 424710.

424710 Petroleum Bulk Stations and Terminals

This industry comprises establishments with bulk liquid storage facilities primarily engaged in the merchant wholesale distribution of crude petroleum and petroleum products, including liquefied petroleum gas.

Cross-References.

Establishments primarily engaged in bulk storage of petroleum are classified in Industry 493190, Other Warehousing and Storage.

42472   Petroleum and Petroleum Products Merchant Wholesalers (except Bulk Stations and Terminals)
See industry description for 424720.

T—Canadian, Mexican, and United States industries are comparable.

424720 Petroleum and Petroleum Products Merchant Wholesalers (except Bulk Stations and Terminals)

This industry comprises establishments primarily engaged in the merchant wholesale distribution of petroleum and petroleum products (except from bulk liquid storage facilities).

Illustrative Examples:

Gasoline merchant wholesalers (except bulk stations, terminals)
Lubricating oil and grease merchant wholesalers (except bulk stations, terminals)

Bottled liquid petroleum gas merchant wholesalers
Fuel oil merchant wholesalers (except bulk stations, terminals)

Cross-References.

Establishments primarily engaged in the merchant wholesale distribution of crude petroleum and petroleum products from bulk liquid storage facilities are classified in Industry 424710, Petroleum Bulk Stations and Terminals.

4248 Beer, Wine, and Distilled Alcoholic Beverage Merchant Wholesalers

This industry group comprises establishments primarily engaged in the merchant wholesale distribution of beer, ale, wine, and/or distilled alcoholic beverages.

42481 Beer and Ale Merchant Wholesalers
See industry description for 424810.

424810 Beer and Ale Merchant Wholesalers

This industry comprises establishments primarily engaged in the merchant wholesale distribution of beer, ale, porter, and other fermented malt beverages.

42482 Wine and Distilled Alcoholic Beverage Merchant Wholesalers
See industry description for 424820.

424820 Wine and Distilled Alcoholic Beverage Merchant Wholesalers

This industry comprises establishments primarily engaged in the merchant wholesale distribution of wine, distilled alcoholic beverages, and/or neutral spirits and ethyl alcohol used in blended wines and distilled liquors.

4249 Miscellaneous Nondurable Goods Merchant Wholesalers

This industry group comprises establishments primarily engaged in the merchant wholesale distribution of nondurable goods, such as farm supplies; books, periodicals and newspapers; flowers; nursery stock; paints; varnishes; tobacco and tobacco products; and other miscellaneous nondurable goods, such as cut Christmas trees and pet supplies.

42491 Farm Supplies Merchant Wholesalers
See industry description for 424910.

424910 Farm Supplies Merchant Wholesalers

This industry comprises establishments primarily engaged in the merchant wholesale distribution of farm supplies, such as animal feeds, fertilizers, agricultural chemicals, pesticides, plant seeds, and plant bulbs.

T—Canadian, Mexican, and United States industries are comparable.

Cross-References.   Establishments primarily engaged in--

- Merchant wholesale distribution of pet food--are classified in Industry 424490, Other Grocery and Related Products Merchant Wholesalers;
- Merchant wholesale distribution of grains--are classified in Industry 424510, Grain and Field Bean Merchant Wholesalers;
- Merchant wholesale distribution of pet supplies--are classified in Industry 424990, Other Miscellaneous Nondurable Goods Merchant Wholesalers; and
- Merchant wholesale distribution of nursery stock (except seeds and plant bulbs)--are classified in Industry 424930, Flower, Nursery Stock, and Florists' Supplies Merchant Wholesalers.

42492   Book, Periodical, and Newspaper Merchant Wholesalers
See industry description for 424920.

424920   Book, Periodical, and Newspaper Merchant Wholesalers

This industry comprises establishments primarily engaged in the merchant wholesale distribution of books, periodicals, and newspapers.

42493   Flower, Nursery Stock, and Florists' Supplies Merchant Wholesalers
See industry description for 424930.

424930   Flower, Nursery Stock, and Florists' Supplies Merchant Wholesalers

This industry comprises establishments primarily engaged in the merchant wholesale distribution of flowers, florists' supplies, and/or nursery stock (except plant seeds and plant bulbs).

Cross-References.   Establishments primarily engaged in--

- Merchant wholesale distribution of cut Christmas trees--are classified in Industry 424990, Other Miscellaneous Nondurable Goods Merchant Wholesalers; and
- Merchant wholesale distribution of plant seeds and plant bulbs--are classified in Industry 424910, Farm Supplies Merchant Wholesalers.

42494   Tobacco and Tobacco Product Merchant Wholesalers
See industry description for 424940.

424940   Tobacco and Tobacco Product Merchant Wholesalers

This industry comprises establishments primarily engaged in the merchant wholesale distribution of tobacco products, such as cigarettes, snuff, cigars, and pipe tobacco.

Cross-References.

Establishments primarily engaged in the merchant wholesale distribution of leaf tobacco are classified in Industry 424590, Other Farm Product Raw Material Merchant Wholesalers.

42495   Paint, Varnish, and Supplies Merchant Wholesalers
See industry description for 424950.

424950   Paint, Varnish, and Supplies Merchant Wholesalers

This industry comprises establishments primarily engaged in the merchant wholesale distribution of paints, varnishes, and similar coatings; pigments; wallpaper; and supplies, such as paintbrushes and rollers.

T—Canadian, Mexican, and United States industries are comparable.

Cross-References.

Establishments primarily engaged in the merchant wholesale distribution of artists' paints are classified in Industry 424990, Other Miscellaneous Nondurable Goods Merchant Wholesalers.

42499   Other Miscellaneous Nondurable Goods Merchant Wholesalers
See industry description for 424990.

424990   Other Miscellaneous Nondurable Goods Merchant Wholesalers

This industry comprises establishments primarily engaged in the merchant wholesale distribution of nondurable goods (except printing and writing paper; stationery and office supplies; industrial and personal service paper; drugs and druggists' sundries; apparel, piece goods, and notions; grocery and related products; farm product raw materials; chemical and allied products; petroleum and petroleum products; beer, wine, and distilled alcoholic beverages; farm supplies; books, periodicals, and newspapers; flowers, nursery stock, and florists' supplies; tobacco and tobacco products; and paint, varnishes, wallpaper, and supplies).

Illustrative Examples:

Artists' supplies merchant wholesalers
Pet supplies (except pet food) merchant wholesalers
Burlap merchant wholesalers
Statuary (except religious) merchant wholesalers

Christmas trees (e.g., artificial, cut) merchant wholesalers
Textile bags merchant wholesalers
Industrial yarns merchant wholesalers

Cross-References.   Establishments primarily engaged in--

- Distribution of advertising specialties--are classified in Industry 541890, Other Services Related to Advertising;
- Merchant wholesale distribution of farm supplies--are classified in Industry 424910, Farm Supplies Merchant Wholesalers;
- Merchant wholesale distribution of books, periodicals, and newspapers--are classified in Industry 424920, Book, Periodical, and Newspaper Merchant Wholesalers;
- Merchant wholesale distribution of flowers, nursery stock, and florists' supplies--are classified in Industry 424930, Flower, Nursery Stock, and Florists' Supplies Merchant Wholesalers;
- Merchant wholesale distribution of tobacco and its products--are classified in Industry 424940, Tobacco and Tobacco Product Merchant Wholesalers;
- Merchant wholesale distribution of paints, varnishes, and similar coatings; pigments; wallpaper; and supplies--are classified in Industry 424950, Paint, Varnish, and Supplies Merchant Wholesalers;
- Merchant wholesale distribution of bulk printing and/or writing paper--are classified in Industry 424110, Printing and Writing Paper Merchant Wholesalers;
- Merchant wholesale distribution of stationery, office supplies, and/or gift wrap--are classified in Industry 424120, Stationery and Office Supplies Merchant Wholesalers;
- Merchant wholesale distribution of kraft wrapping and other coarse paper, paperboard, converted paper (except stationery and office supplies), and related disposable plastics products--are classified in Industry 424130, Industrial and Personal Service Paper Merchant Wholesalers;
- Merchant wholesale distribution of biological and medical products; botanical drugs and herbs; and pharmaceutical products intended for internal and external consumption--are classified in Industry 424210, Drugs and Druggists' Sundries Merchant Wholesalers;
- Merchant wholesale distribution of clothing and accessories, footwear, piece goods, yard goods, notions, and/or hair accessories--are classified in Industry Group 4243, Apparel, Piece Goods, and Notions Merchant Wholesalers;
- Merchant wholesale distribution of meat, poultry, seafood, confectioneries, fruits and vegetables; and other groceries and related products--are classified in Industry Group 4244, Grocery and Related Product Merchant Wholesalers;

T—Canadian, Mexican, and United States industries are comparable.

- Merchant wholesale distribution of grains, field beans, livestock, and other farm product raw materials--are classified in Industry Group 4245, Farm Product Raw Material Merchant Wholesalers;
- Merchant wholesale distribution of chemicals; plastics materials and basic forms and shapes; and allied products--are classified in Industry Group 4246, Chemical and Allied Products Merchant Wholesalers;
- Merchant wholesale distribution of petroleum and petroleum products--are classified in Industry Group 4247, Petroleum and Petroleum Products Merchant Wholesalers;
- Merchant wholesale distribution of beer, ale, wine, and distilled alcoholic beverages--are classified in Industry Group 4248, Beer, Wine, and Distilled Alcoholic Beverage Merchant Wholesalers;
- Merchant wholesale distribution of pet foods--are classified in Industry 424490, Other Grocery and Related Products Merchant Wholesalers;
- Merchant wholesale distribution of religious statuary--are classified in Industry 423490, Other Professional Equipment and Supplies Merchant Wholesalers; and
- Merchant wholesale distribution of knitting yarns (except industrial)--are classified in Industry 424310, Piece Goods, Notions, and Other Dry Goods Merchant Wholesalers.

425   Wholesale Electronic Markets and Agents and Brokers

Industries in the Wholesale Electronic Markets and Agents and Brokers subsector arrange for the sale of goods owned by others, generally on a fee or commission basis. They act on behalf of the buyers and sellers of goods. This subsector contains agents and brokers as well as business-to-business electronic markets that facilitate wholesale trade.

4251   Wholesale Electronic Markets and Agents and Brokers

42511   Business to Business Electronic Markets
See industry description for 425110.

425110   Business to Business Electronic Markets

This industry comprises business-to-business electronic markets bringing together buyers and sellers of goods using the Internet or other electronic means and generally receiving a commission or fee for the service. Business-to-business electronic markets for durable and nondurable goods are included in this industry.

Cross-References.

Establishments primarily engaged in bringing together buyers and sellers of goods using the Internet in a business-to-consumer or consumer-to-consumer environment are classified in Industry 454110, Electronic Shopping and Mail-Order Houses.

42512   Wholesale Trade Agents and Brokers
See industry description for 425120.

425120   Wholesale Trade Agents and Brokers

This industry comprises wholesale trade agents and brokers acting on behalf of buyers or sellers in the wholesale distribution of goods. Agents and brokers do not take title to the goods being sold but rather receive a commission or fee for their service. Agents and brokers for all durable and nondurable goods are included in this industry.

Illustrative Examples:

Independent sales representatives   Manufacturers' sales representatives

---

T—Canadian, Mexican, and United States industries are comparable.

Cross-References.

Establishments acting in the capacity of agents or brokers that operate using the Internet or other electronic means instead of a sales force are classified in Industry 425110, Business to Business Electronic Markets.

T—Canadian, Mexican, and United States industries are comparable.

Sector 44-45--Retail Trade[T]

The Sector as a Whole

The Retail Trade sector comprises establishments engaged in retailing merchandise, generally without transformation, and rendering services incidental to the sale of merchandise.

The retailing process is the final step in the distribution of merchandise; retailers are, therefore, organized to sell merchandise in small quantities to the general public. This sector comprises two main types of retailers: store and nonstore retailers.

1. Store retailers operate fixed point-of-sale locations, located and designed to attract a high volume of walk-in customers. In general, retail stores have extensive displays of merchandise and use mass-media advertising to attract customers. They typically sell merchandise to the general public for personal or household consumption, but some also serve business and institutional clients. These include office supply stores, computer and software stores, building materials dealers, plumbing supply stores, and electrical supply stores. Catalog showrooms, gasoline stations, automotive dealers, and mobile home dealers are treated as store retailers.

In addition to retailing merchandise, some types of store retailers are also engaged in the provision of after-sales services, such as repair and installation. For example, new automobile dealers, electronics and appliance stores, and musical instrument and supplies stores often provide repair services. As a general rule, establishments engaged in retailing merchandise and providing after-sales services are classified in this sector.

The first eleven subsectors of retail trade are store retailers. The establishments are grouped into industries and industry groups typically based on one or more of the following criteria:

(a) The merchandise line or lines carried by the store; for example, specialty stores are distinguished from general-line stores.

(b) The usual trade designation of the establishments. This criterion applies in cases where a store type is well recognized by the industry and the public, but difficult to define strictly in terms of merchandise lines carried; for example, pharmacies, hardware stores, and department stores.

(c) Capital requirements in terms of display equipment; for example, food stores have equipment requirements not found in other retail industries.

(d) Human resource requirements in terms of expertise; for example, the staff of an automobile dealer requires knowledge in financing, registering, and licensing issues that are not necessary in other retail industries.

2. Nonstore retailers, like store retailers, are organized to serve the general public, but their retailing methods differ. The establishments of this subsector reach customers and market merchandise with methods, such as the broadcasting of "infomercials," the broadcasting and publishing of direct-response advertising, the publishing of paper and electronic catalogs, door-to-door solicitation, in-home demonstration, selling from portable stalls (street vendors, except food), and distribution through vending machines. Establishments engaged in the direct sale (nonstore) of products, such as home heating oil dealers and home delivery newspaper routes, are included here.

The buying of goods for resale is a characteristic of retail trade establishments that particularly distinguishes them from establishments in the agriculture, manufacturing, and construction industries. For example, farms that sell their products at or from the point of production are not classified in retail, but rather in agriculture. Similarly, establishments that both manufacture and sell their products to the general public are not classified in retail, but rather in manufacturing. However, establishments that engage in processing activities incidental to retailing are classified in retail. This includes optical goods stores that do in-store grinding of lenses, and meat and seafood markets.

Wholesalers also engage in the buying of goods for resale, but they are not usually organized to serve the general public. They typically operate from a warehouse or office, and neither the design nor the location of these premises is intended to solicit a high volume of walk-in traffic. Wholesalers supply institutional, industrial, wholesale, and retail clients; their operations are, therefore, generally organized to purchase, sell, and deliver merchandise in larger

---

T—Canadian, Mexican, and United States industries are comparable.

quantities. However, dealers of durable nonconsumer goods, such as farm machinery and heavy-duty trucks, are included in wholesale trade even if they often sell these products in single units.

441 Motor Vehicle and Parts Dealers

Industries in the Motor Vehicle and Parts Dealers subsector retail motor vehicles and parts from fixed point-of-sale locations. Establishments in this subsector typically operate from a showroom and/or an open lot where the vehicles are on display. The display of vehicles and the related parts require little by way of display equipment. The personnel generally include both the sales and sales support staff familiar with the requirements for registering and financing a vehicle as well as a staff of parts experts and mechanics trained to provide repair and maintenance services for the vehicles. Specific industries included in this subsector identify the type of vehicle being retailed.

Sales of capital or durable nonconsumer goods, such as medium- and heavy-duty trucks, are always included in wholesale trade. These goods are virtually never sold through retail methods.

4411 Automobile Dealers

This industry group comprises establishments primarily engaged in retailing new and used automobiles and light trucks, such as sport utility vehicles, and passenger and cargo vans.

44111 New Car Dealers
See industry description for 441110.

441110 New Car Dealers

This industry comprises establishments primarily engaged in retailing new automobiles and light trucks, such as sport utility vehicles, and passenger and cargo vans, or retailing these new vehicles in combination with activities, such as repair services, retailing used cars, and selling replacement parts and accessories.

Illustrative Examples:

Automobile dealers, new only, or new and used   Light utility truck dealers, new only, or new and used

Cross-References.   Establishments primarily engaged in--

- Retailing used automobiles and light trucks without retailing new automobiles and light trucks--are classified in Industry 441120, Used Car Dealers;
- Providing automotive repair services without retailing new automotive vehicles--are classified in Industry Group 8111, Automotive Repair and Maintenance; and
- Merchant wholesale distribution of new medium- and heavy-duty trucks, buses, and other motor vehicles-- are classified in Industry 423110, Automobile and Other Motor Vehicle Merchant Wholesalers.

44112 Used Car Dealers
See industry description for 441120.

441120 Used Car Dealers

This industry comprises establishments primarily engaged in retailing used automobiles and light trucks, such as sport utility vehicles, and passenger and cargo vans.

Illustrative Examples:

Antique auto dealers   Automobile dealers, used only
Light truck dealers, used only

T—Canadian, Mexican, and United States industries are comparable.

Cross-References.   Establishments primarily engaged in--

- Retailing new automobiles and light trucks--are classified in Industry 441110, New Car Dealers; and
- Merchant wholesale distribution of used medium- and heavy-duty trucks, buses, and other motor vehicles-- are classified in Industry 423110, Automobile and Other Motor Vehicle Merchant Wholesalers.

4412   Other Motor Vehicle Dealers

This industry group comprises establishments primarily engaged in retailing new and used vehicles (except automobiles, light trucks, such as sport utility vehicles, and passenger and cargo vans).

44121   Recreational Vehicle Dealers
See industry description for 441210.

441210 Recreational Vehicle Dealers

This industry comprises establishments primarily engaged in retailing new and/or used recreational vehicles commonly referred to as RVs or retailing these new vehicles in combination with activities, such as repair services and selling replacement parts and accessories.

Illustrative Examples:

Motor home dealers	Recreational vehicle (RV) dealers
Recreational vehicle (RV) parts and accessories stores	Travel trailer dealers

Cross-References.   Establishments primarily engaged in--

- Retailing new or used boat trailers and utility trailers--are classified in Industry 44122, Motorcycle, Boat, and Other Motor Vehicle Dealers; and
- Retailing manufactured homes (i.e., mobile homes), parts, and equipment--are classified in Industry 453930, Manufactured (Mobile) Home Dealers.

44122   Motorcycle, Boat, and Other Motor Vehicle Dealers

This industry comprises establishments primarily engaged in retailing new and used motorcycles, boats, and other vehicles (except automobiles, light trucks, and recreational vehicles), or retailing these new vehicles in combination with activities, such as repair services and selling replacement parts and accessories.

Illustrative Examples:

Aircraft dealers	Utility trailer dealers
Motorcycle dealers	Boat dealers, new and used
All-terrain vehicle (ATV) dealers	

Cross-References.   Establishments primarily engaged in--

- Retailing new nonmotorized bicycles, surfboards, or wind sailboards--are classified in Industry 45111, Sporting Goods Stores;
- Retailing used nonmotorized bicycles, surfboards, or wind sailboards--are classified in Industry 45331, Used Merchandise Stores;
- Retailing new or used automobiles and light trucks--are classified in Industry Group 4411, Automobile Dealers;
- Retailing new or used recreational vehicles, such as travel trailers--are classified in Industry 44121, Recreational Vehicle Dealers;

T—Canadian, Mexican, and United States industries are comparable.

- Providing repair services for vehicles without retailing new vehicles--are classified in the appropriate industry for the repair services; and
- Retailing fuel and marine supplies at a marina--are classified in Industry 71393, Marinas.

441222 Boat Dealers

This U.S. industry comprises establishments primarily engaged in (1) retailing new and/or used boats or retailing new boats in combination with activities, such as repair services and selling replacement parts and accessories, and/or (2) retailing new and/or used outboard motors, boat trailers, marine supplies, parts, and accessories.

Illustrative Examples:

Boat dealers (e.g., power boats, rowboats, sailboats)   Marine supply dealers
Outboard motor dealers

Cross-References.   Establishments primarily engaged in--

- Retailing new surfboards or wind sailboards--are classified in Industry 451110, Sporting Goods Stores;
- Retailing used surfboards or wind sailboards--are classified in Industry 453310, Used Merchandise Stores;
- Providing boat repair services without retailing new boats--are classified in Industry 811490, Other Personal and Household Goods Repair and Maintenance;
- Retailing new or used personal watercraft--are classified in U.S. Industry 441228, Motorcycle, ATV, and All Other Motor Vehicle Dealers; and
- Operating docking and/or storage facilities for pleasure craft owners--are classified in Industry 713930, Marinas.

441228 Motorcycle, ATV, and All Other Motor Vehicle Dealers

This U.S. industry comprises establishments primarily engaged in retailing new and/or used motorcycles, motor scooters, motorbikes, mopeds, off-road all-terrain vehicles (ATV), personal watercraft, utility trailers, and other motor vehicles (except automobiles, light trucks, recreational vehicles, and boats) or retailing these new vehicles in combination with activities, such as repair services and selling replacement parts and accessories.

Illustrative Examples:

All-terrain vehicle (ATV) dealers   Aircraft dealers
Motorcycle dealers   Snowmobile dealers
Moped dealers   Powered golf cart dealers
Motorcycle parts and accessories dealers   Utility trailer dealers
Personal watercraft dealers

Cross-References.   Establishments primarily engaged in--

- Retailing new automobiles and light trucks--are classified in Industry 441110, New Car Dealers;
- Retailing used automobiles and light trucks--are classified in Industry 441120, Used Car Dealers;
- Retailing new or used recreational vehicles, such as travel trailers--are classified in Industry 441210, Recreational Vehicle Dealers;
- Retailing new or used boats, outboard motors, boat trailers, and marine supplies--are classified in U.S. Industry 441222, Boat Dealers;
- Retailing new nonmotorized bicycles--are classified in Industry 451110, Sporting Goods Stores;
- Retailing used nonmotorized bicycles--are classified in Industry 453310, Used Merchandise Stores; and
- Providing vehicle repair services without retailing new vehicles--are classified in the appropriate industry for the repair services.

T—Canadian, Mexican, and United States industries are comparable.

4413 Automotive Parts, Accessories, and Tire Stores

This industry group comprises establishments primarily engaged in retailing new, used, and/or rebuilt automotive parts and accessories, including tires and tubes. Included in this industry group are establishments primarily engaged in retailing automotive parts and accessories in combination with automotive repair services.

44131 Automotive Parts and Accessories Stores
See industry description for 441310.

441310 Automotive Parts and Accessories Stores

This industry comprises one or more of the following: (1) establishments known as automotive supply stores primarily engaged in retailing new, used, and/or rebuilt automotive parts and accessories; (2) automotive supply stores that are primarily engaged in both retailing automotive parts and accessories and repairing automobiles; and (3) establishments primarily engaged in retailing and installing automotive accessories.

Illustrative Examples:

Automotive parts and supply stores
Truck cap stores
Automotive stereo stores

Used automotive parts stores
Speed shops

Cross-References.   Establishments primarily engaged in--

- Retailing automotive parts and accessories via electronic home shopping, mail-order, or direct sale--are classified in Subsector 454, Nonstore Retailers;
- Retailing new or used tires--are classified in Industry 441320, Tire Dealers; and
- Repairing and replacing automotive parts, such as transmissions, mufflers, and brake linings (except establishments known as automotive supply stores)--are classified in Industry 81111, Automotive Mechanical and Electrical Repair and Maintenance.

44132 Tire Dealers
See industry description for 441320.

441320 Tire Dealers

This industry comprises establishments primarily engaged in retailing new and/or used tires and tubes or retailing new tires in combination with automotive repair services.

Cross-References.   Establishments primarily engaged in--

- Retailing tires via electronic home shopping, mail-order, or direct sale--are classified in Subsector 454, Nonstore Retailers;
- Tire retreading or recapping--are classified in U.S. Industry 326212, Tire Retreading; and
- Merchant wholesale distribution of new/used tires for medium- and heavy-duty trucks, buses, and other motor vehicles--are classified in Industry 423130, Tire and Tube Merchant Wholesalers.

442 Furniture and Home Furnishings Stores

Industries in the Furniture and Home Furnishings Stores subsector retail new furniture and home furnishings from fixed point-of-sale locations. Establishments in this subsector usually operate from showrooms and have substantial areas for the presentation of their products. Many offer interior decorating services in addition to the sale of products.

T—Canadian, Mexican, and United States industries are comparable.

4421   Furniture Stores

44211   Furniture Stores
See industry description for 442110.

442110 Furniture Stores

This industry comprises establishments primarily engaged in retailing new furniture, such as household furniture (e.g., baby furniture, box springs, and mattresses) and outdoor furniture; office furniture (except sold in combination with office supplies and equipment); and/or furniture sold in combination with major appliances, home electronics, home furnishings, or floor coverings.

Cross-References.   Establishments primarily engaged in--

- Retailing furniture via electronic home shopping, mail-order, or direct sale--are classified in Subsector 454, Nonstore Retailers;
- Retailing used furniture--are classified in Industry 453310, Used Merchandise Stores;
- Retailing custom furniture made on the premises--are classified in Subsector 337, Furniture and Related Product Manufacturing; and
- Retailing new office furniture and a range of new office equipment and supplies--are classified in Industry 453210, Office Supplies and Stationery Stores.

4422   Home Furnishings Stores

This industry group comprises establishments primarily engaged in retailing new home furnishings (except furniture).

44221   Floor Covering Stores
See industry description for 442210.

442210 Floor Covering Stores

This industry comprises establishments primarily engaged in retailing new floor coverings, such as rugs and carpets, vinyl floor coverings, and floor tile (except ceramic or wood only); or retailing new floor coverings in combination with installation and repair services.

Cross-References.   Establishments primarily engaged in--

- Retailing floor coverings via electronic home shopping, mail-order, or direct sale--are classified in Subsector 454, Nonstore Retailers;
- Installing floor coverings without retailing new floor coverings--are classified in Industry 238330, Flooring Contractors;
- Retailing ceramic floor tile or wood floor coverings only--are classified in Industry 444190, Other Building Material Dealers; and
- Retailing used rugs and carpets--are classified in Industry 453310, Used Merchandise Stores.

44229   Other Home Furnishings Stores

This industry comprises establishments primarily engaged in retailing new home furnishings (except furniture and floor coverings).

Illustrative Examples:

Bath shops   Kitchenware stores

T—Canadian, Mexican, and United States industries are comparable.

census.gov/naics

Chinaware stores   Glassware stores
Window treatment stores

Cross-References.   Establishments primarily engaged in--

- Retailing home furnishings via electronic home shopping, mail-order, or direct sale--are classified in Subsector 454, Nonstore Retailers;
- Retailing custom curtains and draperies made on the premises--are classified in Industry 31412, Curtain and Linen Mills;
- Retailing new mirrored glass, lighting fixtures, and new ceramic floor tile or wood floor coverings only--are classified in Industry 44419, Other Building Material Dealers;
- Retailing new furniture--are classified in Industry 44211, Furniture Stores;
- Retailing new floor coverings (except ceramic or wood only)--are classified in Industry 44221, Floor Covering Stores; and
- Retailing used home furnishings--are classified in Industry 45331, Used Merchandise Stores.

442291 Window Treatment Stores

This U.S. industry comprises establishments primarily engaged in retailing new window treatments, such as curtains, drapes, blinds, and shades.

Cross-References.   Establishments primarily engaged in--

- Retailing window treatments via electronic home shopping, mail-order, or direct sale--are classified in Subsector 454, Nonstore Retailers; and
- Retailing custom curtains and draperies made on the premises--are classified in Industry 314120, Curtain and Linen Mills.

442299 All Other Home Furnishings Stores

This U.S. industry comprises establishments primarily engaged in retailing new home furnishings (except floor coverings, furniture, and window treatments).

Illustrative Examples:

Bath shops   Picture frame shops, custom
Kitchenware stores   Glassware stores
Chinaware stores   Wood-burning stove stores
Linen stores   Housewares stores
Electric lamp shops

Cross-References.   Establishments primarily engaged in--

- Retailing home furnishings via electronic home shopping, mail-order, or direct sale--are classified in Subsector 454, Nonstore Retailers;
- Retailing new mirrored glass or lighting fixtures--are classified in Industry 444190, Other Building Material Dealers;
- Retailing new furniture--are classified in Industry 442110, Furniture Stores;
- Retailing new floor coverings--are classified in Industry 442210, Floor Covering Stores;
- Retailing new window treatments--are classified in U.S. Industry 442291, Window Treatment Stores; and
- Retailing used home furnishings--are classified in Industry 453310, Used Merchandise Stores.

T—Canadian, Mexican, and United States industries are comparable.

443　　Electronics and Appliance Stores

Industries in the Electronics and Appliance Stores subsector retail new electronics and appliances from point-of-sale locations. Establishments in this subsector often operate from locations that have special provisions for floor displays requiring special electrical capacity to accommodate the proper demonstration of the products. The staff includes sales personnel knowledgeable in the characteristics and warranties of the line of goods retailed and may also include trained repair persons to handle the maintenance and repair of the electronic equipment and appliances. The classifications within this subsector are made principally on the type of product and knowledge required to operate each type of store.

4431　　Electronics and Appliance Stores

44314　　Electronics and Appliance Stores

This industry comprises establishments primarily engaged in one of the following: (1) retailing an array of new household-type appliances and consumer-type electronic products, such as televisions, computers, and cameras; (2) specializing in retailing a single line of new consumer-type electronic products; (3) retailing these new products in combination with repair and support services; (4) retailing new prepackaged computer software; and/or (5) retailing prerecorded audio and video media, such as CDs, DVDs, and tapes.

Illustrative Examples:

Appliance stores, household-type
Cellular telephone accessories stores

Consumer-type electronic stores (e.g., televisions, computers, cameras)

Cross-References.　　　Establishments primarily engaged in--

- Retailing new appliance and electronic products via electronic home shopping, mail-order, or direct sale--are classified in Subsector 454, Nonstore Retailers;
- Retailing new computers, computer peripherals, and prepackaged software in combination with retailing new office equipment, office furniture, and office supplies--are classified in Industry 45321, Office Supplies and Stationery Stores;
- Retailing new sewing machines in combination with selling new sewing supplies, fabrics, patterns, yarns, and other needlework accessories--are classified in Industry 45113, Sewing, Needlework, and Piece Goods Stores;
- Retailing new electronic toys, such as dedicated game consoles and handheld electronic games--are classified in Industry 45112, Hobby, Toy, and Game Stores;
- Providing television or other electronic equipment repair services without retailing new televisions or electronic equipment--are classified in Industry 81121, Electronic and Precision Equipment Repair and Maintenance;
- Providing household-type appliance repair services without retailing new appliances--are classified in Industry 81141, Home and Garden Equipment and Appliance Repair and Maintenance;
- Developing film and/or making photographic slides, prints, and enlargements without retailing a range of new photographic equipment and supplies--are classified in Industry 81292, Photofinishing;
- Retailing used appliance and electronic products--are classified in Industry 45331, Used Merchandise Stores; and
- Retailing automotive electronic sound systems--are classified in Industry 44131, Automotive Parts and Accessories Stores.

443141　Household Appliance Stores

This U.S. industry comprises establishments known as appliance stores primarily engaged in retailing an array of new household appliances, such as refrigerators, dishwashers, ovens, irons, coffee makers, hair dryers, electric razors, room air-conditioners, microwave ovens, sewing machines, and vacuum cleaners, or retailing new appliances in combination with appliance repair services.

T—Canadian, Mexican, and United States industries are comparable.

Cross-References.   Establishments primarily engaged in--

- Retailing household appliances via electronic home shopping, mail-order, or direct sale--are classified in Subsector 454, Nonstore Retailers;
- Retailing new sewing machines in combination with selling new sewing supplies, fabrics, patterns, yarns, and other needlework accessories--are classified in Industry 451130, Sewing, Needlework, and Piece Goods Stores;
- Providing household-type appliance repair services without retailing new appliances--are classified in U.S. Industry 811412, Appliance Repair and Maintenance; and
- Retailing used appliances--are classified in Industry 453310, Used Merchandise Stores.

443142 Electronics Stores

This U.S. industry comprises: (1) establishments known as consumer electronics stores primarily engaged in retailing a general line of new consumer-type electronic products such as televisions, computers, and cameras; (2) establishments specializing in retailing a single line of consumer-type electronic products; (3) establishments primarily engaged in retailing these new electronic products in combination with repair and support services; (4) establishments primarily engaged in retailing new prepackaged computer software; and/or (5) establishments primarily engaged in retailing prerecorded audio and video media, such as CDs, DVDs, and tapes.

Illustrative Examples:

Cellular telephone accessories stores
Consumer-type electronic stores (e.g., televisions, computers, cameras)

Stereo stores (except automotive)
Radio and television stores
Computer stores

Cross-References.   Establishments primarily engaged in--

- Retailing electronic goods via electronic home shopping, mail-order, or direct sale--are classified in Subsector 454, Nonstore Retailers;
- Retailing automotive electronic sound systems--are classified in Industry 441310, Automotive Parts and Accessories Stores;
- Retailing new computers, computer peripherals, and prepackaged software in combination with retailing new office equipment, office furniture, and office supplies--are classified in Industry 453210, Office Supplies and Stationery Stores;
- Retailing new cellular telephones and communication service plans--are classified in U.S. Industry 517312, Wireless Telecommunications Carriers (except Satellite);
- Providing television or other electronic equipment repair services without retailing new televisions or electronic products--are classified in Industry 81121, Electronic and Precision Equipment Repair and Maintenance;
- Developing film and/or making photographic slides, prints, and enlargements without retailing a range of new photographic equipment and supplies--are classified in Industry 81292, Photofinishing;
- Retailing new electronic toys, such as dedicated video game consoles and handheld electronic games--are classified in Industry 451120, Hobby, Toy, and Game Stores; and
- Retailing used electronics--are classified in Industry 453310, Used Merchandise Stores.

444   Building Material and Garden Equipment and Supplies Dealers

Industries in the Building Material and Garden Equipment and Supplies Dealers subsector retail new building material and garden equipment and supplies from fixed point-of-sale locations. Establishments in this subsector have display equipment designed to handle lumber and related products and garden equipment and supplies that may be kept either indoors or outdoors under covered areas. The staff is usually knowledgeable in the use of the specific products being retailed in the construction, repair, and maintenance of the home and associated grounds.

T—Canadian, Mexican, and United States industries are comparable.

4441   Building Material and Supplies Dealers

This industry group comprises establishments primarily engaged in retailing new building materials and supplies.

44411   Home Centers
     See industry description for 444110.

444110   Home Centers

This industry comprises establishments known as home centers primarily engaged in retailing a general line of new home repair and improvement materials and supplies, such as lumber, plumbing goods, electrical goods, tools, housewares, hardware, and lawn and garden supplies, with no one merchandise line predominating. The merchandise lines are normally arranged in separate departments.

Cross-References.

Establishments primarily engaged in retailing a general line of new hardware items, such as tools and builders' hardware, are classified in Industry 444130, Hardware Stores.

44412   Paint and Wallpaper Stores
     See industry description for 444120.

444120   Paint and Wallpaper Stores

This industry comprises establishments known as paint and wallpaper stores primarily engaged in retailing paint, wallpaper, and related supplies.

Cross-References.

Establishments primarily engaged in retailing automotive paints are classified in Industry 441310, Automotive Parts and Accessories Stores.

44413   Hardware Stores
     See industry description for 444130.

444130   Hardware Stores

This industry comprises establishments known as hardware stores primarily engaged in retailing a general line of new hardware items, such as tools and builders' hardware.

Cross-References.   Establishments primarily engaged in--

- Retailing hardware items via electronic home shopping, mail-order, or direct sale--are classified in Subsector 454, Nonstore Retailers;
- Retailing a general line of home repair and improvement materials and supplies, known as home centers-- are classified in Industry 444110, Home Centers; and
- Retailing used hardware items--are classified in Industry 453310, Used Merchandise Stores.

44419   Other Building Material Dealers
     See industry description for 444190.

444190   Other Building Material Dealers

This industry comprises establishments (except those known as home centers, paint and wallpaper stores, and hardware stores) primarily engaged in retailing specialized lines of new building materials, such as lumber, fencing,

---

T—Canadian, Mexican, and United States industries are comparable.

glass, doors, plumbing fixtures and supplies, electrical supplies, prefabricated buildings and kits, and kitchen and bath cabinets and countertops to be installed.

Illustrative Examples:

Electrical supply stores
Kitchen cabinet (except custom) stores
Fencing dealers
Lumber yards, retail
Floor covering stores, wood or ceramic tile only

Plumbing supply stores
Garage door dealers
Prefabricated building dealers
Glass stores

Cross-References.   Establishments primarily engaged in--

- Retailing building materials via electronic home shopping, mail-order, or direct sale--are classified in Subsector 454, Nonstore Retailers;
- Retailing used building materials--are classified in Industry 453310, Used Merchandise Stores;
- Providing carpentry/installation services for products--are classified in Industry 238350, Finish Carpentry Contractors;
- Installing plumbing fixtures and supplies--are classified in Industry 238220, Plumbing, Heating, and Air-Conditioning Contractors;
- Installing electrical supplies, such as lighting fixtures and ceiling fans--are classified in Industry 238210, Electrical Contractors and Other Wiring Installation Contractors;
- Making custom furniture (e.g., kitchen cabinets)--are classified in Subsector 337, Furniture and Related Product Manufacturing;
- Retailing a general line of new hardware items, known as hardware stores--are classified in Industry 444130, Hardware Stores;
- Retailing paint and wallpaper, known as paint and wallpaper stores--are classified in Industry 444120, Paint and Wallpaper Stores; and
- Retailing a general line of home repair and improvement materials and supplies, known as home centers--are classified in Industry 444110, Home Centers.

4442   Lawn and Garden Equipment and Supplies Stores

This industry group comprises establishments primarily engaged in retailing new lawn and garden equipment and supplies.

44421   Outdoor Power Equipment Stores
See industry description for 444210.

444210 Outdoor Power Equipment Stores

This industry comprises establishments primarily engaged in retailing new outdoor power equipment or retailing new outdoor power equipment in combination with activities, such as repair services and selling replacement parts.

Cross-References.   Establishments primarily engaged in--

- Retailing outdoor power equipment via electronic home shopping, mail-order, or direct sale--are classified in Subsector 454, Nonstore Retailers;
- Providing outdoor power equipment repair services without retailing new outdoor power equipment--are classified in U.S. Industry 811411, Home and Garden Equipment Repair and Maintenance; and
- Retailing used outdoor power equipment--are classified in Industry 453310, Used Merchandise Stores.

44422   Nursery, Garden Center, and Farm Supply Stores
See industry description for 444220.

T—Canadian, Mexican, and United States industries are comparable.

444220 Nursery, Garden Center, and Farm Supply Stores

This industry comprises establishments primarily engaged in retailing nursery and garden products, such as trees, shrubs, plants, seeds, bulbs, and sod, that are predominantly grown elsewhere. These establishments may sell a limited amount of a product they grow themselves. Also included in this industry are establishments primarily engaged in retailing farm supplies, such as animal (except pet) feed.

Cross-References.   Establishments primarily engaged in--

- Retailing nursery and garden products via electronic home shopping, mail-order, or direct sale--are classified in Subsector 454, Nonstore Retailers;
- Providing landscaping services--are classified in Industry 561730, Landscaping Services; and
- Growing and retailing nursery stock--are classified in U.S. Industry 111421, Nursery and Tree Production.

445   Food and Beverage Stores

Industries in the Food and Beverage Stores subsector usually retail food and beverage merchandise from fixed point-of-sale locations. Establishments in this subsector have special equipment (e.g., freezers, refrigerated display cases, refrigerators) for displaying food and beverage goods. They have staff trained in the processing of food products to guarantee the proper storage and sanitary conditions required by regulatory authority.

4451   Grocery Stores

This industry group comprises establishments primarily engaged in retailing a general line of food products.

44511   Supermarkets and Other Grocery (except Convenience) Stores
See industry description for 445110.

445110 Supermarkets and Other Grocery (except Convenience) Stores

This industry comprises establishments generally known as supermarkets and grocery stores primarily engaged in retailing a general line of food, such as canned and frozen foods; fresh fruits and vegetables; and fresh and prepared meats, fish, and poultry. Included in this industry are delicatessen-type establishments primarily engaged in retailing a general line of food.

Cross-References.   Establishments primarily engaged in--

- Retailing automotive fuels in combination with a convenience store or food mart--are classified in Industry 447110, Gasoline Stations with Convenience Stores;
- Retailing a limited line of goods, known as convenience stores or food marts (except those with fuel pumps)--are classified in Industry 445120, Convenience Stores;
- Retailing frozen food and freezer meal plans via direct sales to residential customers--are classified in Industry 454390, Other Direct Selling Establishments;
- Providing food services in delicatessen-type establishments--are classified in U.S. Industry 722513, Limited-Service Restaurants; and
- Retailing fresh meat in delicatessen-type establishments--are classified in Industry 445210, Meat Markets.

44512   Convenience Stores
See industry description for 445120.

445120 Convenience Stores

This industry comprises establishments known as convenience stores or food marts (except those with fuel pumps) primarily engaged in retailing a limited line of goods that generally includes milk, bread, soda, and snacks.

T—Canadian, Mexican, and United States industries are comparable.

Cross-References.   Establishments primarily engaged in--

- Retailing a general line of food, known as supermarkets and grocery stores--are classified in Industry 445110, Supermarkets and Other Grocery (except Convenience) Stores; and
- Retailing automotive fuels in combination with a convenience store or food mart--are classified in Industry 447110, Gasoline Stations with Convenience Stores.

4452   Specialty Food Stores

This industry group comprises establishments primarily engaged in retailing specialized lines of food.

44521   Meat Markets
See industry description for 445210.

445210 Meat Markets

This industry comprises establishments primarily engaged in retailing fresh, frozen, or cured meats and poultry. Delicatessen-type establishments primarily engaged in retailing fresh meat are included in this industry.

Illustrative Examples:

Baked ham stores	Poultry dealers
Meat markets	Frozen meat shops
Butcher shops	

Cross-References.   Establishments primarily engaged in--

- Retailing meat and poultry via electronic home shopping, mail-order, or direct sale--are classified in Subsector 454, Nonstore Retailers;
- Retailing a general line of food, known as supermarkets and grocery stores--are classified in Industry 445110, Supermarkets and Other Grocery (except Convenience) Stores; and
- Providing food services in delicatessen-type establishments--are classified in U.S. Industry 722513, Limited-Service Restaurants.

44522   Fish and Seafood Markets
See industry description for 445220.

445220 Fish and Seafood Markets

This industry comprises establishments primarily engaged in retailing fresh, frozen, or cured fish and seafood products.

Cross-References.

Establishments primarily engaged in retailing fish and seafood products via electronic home shopping, mail-order, or direct sale are classified in Subsector 454, Nonstore Retailers.

44523   Fruit and Vegetable Markets
See industry description for 445230.

445230 Fruit and Vegetable Markets

This industry comprises establishments primarily engaged in retailing fresh fruits and vegetables.

T—Canadian, Mexican, and United States industries are comparable.

Cross-References.   Establishments primarily engaged in--

- Retailing fruits and vegetables via electronic home shopping, mail-order, or direct sale--are classified in Subsector 454, Nonstore Retailers; and
- Growing and selling vegetables and/or fruits at roadside stands--are classified in Subsector 111, Crop Production.

44529   Other Specialty Food Stores

This industry comprises establishments primarily engaged in retailing specialty foods (except meat, fish, seafood, and fruits and vegetables) not for immediate consumption and not made on the premises.

Illustrative Examples:

Baked goods stores (except immediate consumption)   Gourmet food stores
Dairy product stores   Confectionery (i.e., packaged) stores
Coffee and tea (i.e., packaged) stores   Nut (i.e., packaged) stores

Cross-References.   Establishments primarily engaged in--

- Retailing specialty foods via electronic home shopping, mail-order, or direct sale--are classified in Subsector 454, Nonstore Retailers;
- Retailing baked goods made on the premises but not for immediate consumption--are classified in Industry 31181, Bread and Bakery Product Manufacturing;
- Retailing fresh, frozen, or cured meats and poultry--are classified in Industry 44521, Meat Markets;
- Retailing fresh, frozen, or cured fish and seafood products--are classified in Industry 44522, Fish and Seafood Markets;
- Retailing fresh fruits and vegetables--are classified in Industry 44523, Fruit and Vegetable Markets;
- Retailing candy and confectionery products not for immediate consumption and made on the premises--are classified in Industry Group 3113, Sugar and Confectionery Product Manufacturing; and
- Selling snack foods (e.g., doughnuts, bagels, ice cream, popcorn) for immediate consumption--are classified in Industry 72251, Restaurants and Other Eating Places.

445291   Baked Goods Stores

This U.S. industry comprises establishments primarily engaged in retailing baked goods not for immediate consumption and not made on the premises.

Cross-References.   Establishments primarily engaged in--

- Retailing baked goods via electronic home shopping, mail-order, or direct sale--are classified in Subsector 454, Nonstore Retailers;
- Selling snack foods (e.g., doughnuts, bagels, ice cream, popcorn) for immediate consumption--are classified in U.S. Industry 722515, Snack and Nonalcoholic Beverage Bars; and
- Retailing baked goods made on the premises but not for immediate consumption--are classified in U.S. Industry 311811, Retail Bakeries.

445292   Confectionery and Nut Stores

This U.S. industry comprises establishments primarily engaged in retailing candy and other confections, nuts, and popcorn not for immediate consumption and not made on the premises.

T—Canadian, Mexican, and United States industries are comparable.

Cross-References.   Establishments primarily engaged in--

- Retailing confectionery goods and nuts via electronic home shopping, mail-order, or direct sale--are classified in Subsector 454, Nonstore Retailers;
- Retailing confectionery goods and nuts made on the premises and not packaged for immediate consumption--are classified in Industry Group 3113, Sugar and Confectionery Product Manufacturing;
- Selling snack foods (e.g., doughnuts, bagels, ice cream, popcorn) for immediate consumption--are classified in U.S. Industry 722515, Snack and Nonalcoholic Beverage Bars; and
- Retailing baked goods made on the premises but not for immediate consumption--are classified in U.S. Industry 311811, Retail Bakeries.

445299 All Other Specialty Food Stores

This U.S. industry comprises establishments primarily engaged in retailing miscellaneous specialty foods (except meat, fish, seafood, fruit and vegetables, confections, nuts, popcorn, and baked goods) not for immediate consumption and not made on the premises.

Illustrative Examples:

Coffee and tea (i.e., packaged) stores
Soft drink (i.e., bottled) stores
Dairy product stores

Spice stores
Gourmet food stores
Water (i.e., bottled) stores

Cross-References.   Establishments primarily engaged in--

- Retailing specialty foods via electronic home shopping, mail-order, or direct sale--are classified in Subsector 454, Nonstore Retailers;
- Selling snack foods (e.g., doughnuts, bagels, ice cream, popcorn) for immediate consumption--are classified in U.S. Industry 722515, Snack and Nonalcoholic Beverage Bars;
- Retailing fresh, frozen, or cured meats and poultry--are classified in Industry 445210, Meat Markets;
- Retailing fresh, frozen, or cured fish and seafood products--are classified in Industry 445220, Fish and Seafood Markets;
- Retailing fresh fruits and vegetables--are classified in Industry 445230, Fruit and Vegetable Markets;
- Retailing candy and other confections, nuts, and popcorn not for immediate consumption and not made on the premises--are classified in U.S. Industry 445292, Confectionery and Nut Stores; and
- Retailing baked goods not for immediate consumption and not made on the premises--are classified in U.S. Industry 445291, Baked Goods Stores.

4453   Beer, Wine, and Liquor Stores

44531   Beer, Wine, and Liquor Stores
See industry description for 445310.

445310 Beer, Wine, and Liquor Stores

This industry comprises establishments primarily engaged in retailing packaged alcoholic beverages, such as ale, beer, wine, and liquor.

Cross-References.

Establishments primarily engaged in retailing packaged liquor in combination with providing prepared drinks for immediate consumption on the premises are classified in Industry 722410, Drinking Places (Alcoholic Beverages).

T—Canadian, Mexican, and United States industries are comparable.

446   Health and Personal Care Stores

Industries in the Health and Personal Care Stores subsector retail health and personal care merchandise from fixed point-of-sale locations. Establishments in this subsector are characterized principally by the products they retail, and some health and personal care stores may have specialized staff trained in dealing with the products. Staff may include pharmacists, opticians, and other professionals engaged in retailing, advising customers, and/or fitting the product sold to the customer's needs.

4461   Health and Personal Care Stores

44611   Pharmacies and Drug Stores
See industry description for 446110.

446110   Pharmacies and Drug Stores

This industry comprises establishments known as pharmacies and drug stores engaged in retailing prescription or nonprescription drugs and medicines.

Cross-References.   Establishments primarily engaged in--

- Retailing food supplement products, such as vitamins, nutrition supplements, and body enhancing supplements--are classified in U.S. Industry 446191, Food (Health) Supplement Stores; and
- Retailing prescription and nonprescription drugs via electronic home shopping, mail-order, or direct sale-- are classified in Subsector 454, Nonstore Retailers.

44612   Cosmetics, Beauty Supplies, and Perfume Stores
See industry description for 446120.

446120   Cosmetics, Beauty Supplies, and Perfume Stores

This industry comprises establishments known as cosmetic or perfume stores or beauty supply shops primarily engaged in retailing cosmetics, perfumes, toiletries, and personal grooming products.

Cross-References.   Establishments primarily engaged in--

- Providing beauty salon services--are classified in U.S. Industry 812112, Beauty Salons; and
- Retailing perfumes, cosmetics, and beauty supplies via electronic home shopping, mail-order, or direct sale--are classified in Subsector 454, Nonstore Retailers.

44613   Optical Goods Stores
See industry description for 446130.

446130   Optical Goods Stores

This industry comprises establishments primarily engaged in one or more of the following: (1) retailing and fitting prescription eyeglasses and contact lenses; (2) retailing prescription eyeglasses in combination with the grinding of lenses to order on the premises; and (3) selling nonprescription eyeglasses.

Cross-References.   Establishments primarily engaged in--

- Grinding ophthalmic lenses without retailing lenses--are classified in U.S. Industry 339115, Ophthalmic Goods Manufacturing;
- The private or group practice of optometry, even though glasses and contact lenses are sold at these establishments--are classified in Industry 621320, Offices of Optometrists; and

---

T—Canadian, Mexican, and United States industries are comparable.

- Retailing eyeglasses and contact lenses via electronic home shopping or mail-order--are classified in Industry 454110, Electronic Shopping and Mail-Order Houses.

44619   Other Health and Personal Care Stores

This industry comprises establishments primarily engaged in retailing health and personal care items (except drugs, medicines, optical goods, perfumes, cosmetics, and beauty supplies).

Illustrative Examples:

Convalescent supply stores   Sick room supply stores
Prosthetic stores   Hearing aid stores
Food (i.e., health) supplement stores

Cross-References.   Establishments primarily engaged in--

- Retailing health and personal care items via electronic home shopping, mail-order, or direct sale--are classified in Subsector 454, Nonstore Retailers;
- Retailing orthopedic shoes--are classified in Industry 44821, Shoe Stores;
- Retailing orthopedic and prosthetic appliances that are made on the premises--are classified in Industry 33911, Medical Equipment and Supplies Manufacturing;
- Retailing prescription and nonprescription drugs and medicines--are classified in Industry 44611, Pharmacies and Drug Stores;
- Retailing eyeglasses and contact lenses--are classified in Industry 44613, Optical Goods Stores;
- Retailing perfumes, cosmetics, and beauty supplies--are classified in Industry 44612, Cosmetics, Beauty Supplies, and Perfume Stores; and
- Retailing naturally organic foods, such as fruits and vegetables, dairy products, and cereals and grains--are classified in Subsector 445, Food and Beverage Stores.

446191   Food (Health) Supplement Stores

This U.S. industry comprises establishments primarily engaged in retailing food supplement products, such as vitamins, nutrition supplements, and body enhancing supplements.

Cross-References.   Establishments primarily engaged in--

- Retailing food supplement products via electronic home shopping, mail-order, or direct sale--are classified in Subsector 454, Nonstore Retailers;
- Retailing prescription and nonprescription drugs and medicines--are classified in Industry 446110, Pharmacies and Drug Stores; and
- Retailing naturally organic foods, such as fruits and vegetables, dairy products, and cereals and grains--are classified in Subsector 445, Food and Beverage Stores.

446199   All Other Health and Personal Care Stores

This U.S. industry comprises establishments primarily engaged in retailing specialized lines of health and personal care merchandise (except drugs, medicines, optical goods, cosmetics, beauty supplies, perfume, and food supplement products).

Illustrative Examples:

Convalescent supply stores   Hearing aid stores
Prosthetic stores   Sick room supply stores

T—Canadian, Mexican, and United States industries are comparable.

Cross-References.   Establishments primarily engaged in--

- Retailing specialized health and personal care merchandise via electronic home shopping, mail-order, or direct sale--are classified in Subsector 454, Nonstore Retailers;
- Retailing food supplement products--are classified in U.S. Industry 446191, Food (Health) Supplement Stores;
- Retailing prescription or nonprescription drugs and medicines--are classified in Industry 446110, Pharmacies and Drug Stores;
- Retailing eyeglasses and contact lenses--are classified in Industry 446130, Optical Goods Stores;
- Retailing perfumes, cosmetics, and beauty supplies--are classified in Industry 446120, Cosmetics, Beauty Supplies, and Perfume Stores;
- Retailing orthopedic shoes--are classified in Industry 448210, Shoe Stores; and
- Retailing orthopedic and prosthetic appliances that are made on the premises--are classified in U.S. Industry 339113, Surgical Appliance and Supplies Manufacturing.

447   Gasoline Stations

Industries in the Gasoline Stations subsector retail automotive fuels (e.g., gasoline, diesel fuel, gasohol, alternative fuels) and automotive oils or retail these products in combination with convenience store items. These establishments have specialized equipment for storing and dispensing automotive fuels.

4471   Gasoline Stations

44711   Gasoline Stations with Convenience Stores
See industry description for 447110.

447110   Gasoline Stations with Convenience Stores

This industry comprises establishments engaged in retailing automotive fuels (e.g., diesel fuel, gasohol, gasoline) in combination with convenience store or food mart items. These establishments can either be in a convenience store (i.e., food mart) setting or a gasoline station setting. These establishments may also provide automotive repair services.

Cross-References.   Establishments primarily engaged in--

- Retailing automotive fuels without a convenience store--are classified in Industry 447190, Other Gasoline Stations; and
- Retailing a limited line of goods, known as convenience stores or food marts (except those with fuel pumps)--are classified in Industry 445120, Convenience Stores.

44719   Other Gasoline Stations
See industry description for 447190.

447190   Other Gasoline Stations

This industry comprises establishments known as gasoline stations (except those with convenience stores) primarily engaged in (1) retailing automotive fuels (e.g., diesel fuel, gasohol, gasoline, alternative fuels) or (2) retailing these fuels in combination with activities, such as providing repair services; selling automotive oils, replacement parts, and accessories; and/or providing food services.

Illustrative Examples:

Gasoline stations without convenience stores   Marine service stations
Truck stops

T—Canadian, Mexican, and United States industries are comparable.

Cross-References.   Establishments primarily engaged in--

- Repairing motor vehicles without retailing automotive fuels--are classified in Industry Group 8111, Automotive Repair and Maintenance; and
- Retailing automotive fuels in combination with a convenience store or food mart--are classified in Industry 447110, Gasoline Stations with Convenience Stores.

448   Clothing and Clothing Accessories Stores

Industries in the Clothing and Clothing Accessories Stores subsector retail new clothing and clothing accessories from fixed point-of-sale locations. Establishments in this subsector have similar display equipment and staff that is knowledgeable regarding fashion trends and the proper match of styles, colors, and combinations of clothing and accessories to the characteristics and tastes of the customer.

4481   Clothing Stores

This industry group comprises establishments primarily engaged in retailing new clothing.

44811   Men's Clothing Stores
See industry description for 448110.

448110 Men's Clothing Stores

This industry comprises establishments primarily engaged in retailing a general line of new men's and boys' clothing. These establishments may provide basic alterations, such as hemming, taking in or letting out seams, or lengthening or shortening sleeves.

Cross-References.   Establishments primarily engaged in--

- Retailing men's and boys' clothing via electronic home shopping, mail-order, or direct sale--are classified in Subsector 454, Nonstore Retailers;
- Retailing custom men's clothing made on the premises--are classified in Industry Group 3152, Cut and Sew Apparel Manufacturing;
- Retailing new men's and boys' accessories--are classified in Industry 448150, Clothing Accessories Stores;
- Retailing specialized new apparel, such as raincoats, leather coats, fur apparel, and swimwear--are classified in Industry 448190, Other Clothing Stores;
- Retailing new clothing for all genders and age groups--are classified in Industry 448140, Family Clothing Stores;
- Retailing secondhand clothes--are classified in Industry 453310, Used Merchandise Stores; and
- Providing clothing alterations and repair--are classified in Industry 811490, Other Personal and Household Goods Repair and Maintenance.

44812   Women's Clothing Stores
See industry description for 448120.

448120 Women's Clothing Stores

This industry comprises establishments primarily engaged in retailing a general line of new women's, misses', and juniors' clothing, including maternity wear. These establishments may provide basic alterations, such as hemming, taking in or letting out seams, or lengthening or shortening sleeves.

Cross-References.   Establishments primarily engaged in--

- Retailing women's clothing via electronic home shopping, mail-order, or direct sale--are classified in Subsector 454, Nonstore Retailers;

T—Canadian, Mexican, and United States industries are comparable.

- Retailing custom women's clothing made on the premises--are classified in Industry Group 3152, Cut and Sew Apparel Manufacturing;
- Retailing new women's accessories--are classified in Industry 448150, Clothing Accessories Stores;
- Retailing new clothing for all genders and age groups--are classified in Industry 448140, Family Clothing Stores;
- Retailing specialized new apparel, such as bridal gowns, raincoats, leather coats, fur apparel, and swimwear--are classified in Industry 448190, Other Clothing Stores;
- Retailing secondhand clothes--are classified in Industry 453310, Used Merchandise Stores; and
- Providing clothing alterations and repair--are classified in Industry 811490, Other Personal and Household Goods Repair and Maintenance.

44813   Children's and Infants' Clothing Stores
See industry description for 448130.

448130 Children's and Infants' Clothing Stores

This industry comprises establishments primarily engaged in retailing a general line of new children's and infants' clothing. These establishments may provide basic alterations, such as hemming, taking in or letting out seams, or lengthening or shortening sleeves.

Cross-References.   Establishments primarily engaged in--

- Retailing children's and infants' clothing via electronic home shopping, mail-order, or direct sale--are classified in Subsector 454, Nonstore Retailers;
- Retailing new children's and infants' accessories--are classified in Industry 448150, Clothing Accessories Stores;
- Retailing new clothing for all genders or age groups--are classified in Industry 448140, Family Clothing Stores;
- Retailing secondhand clothes--are classified in Industry 453310, Used Merchandise Stores; and
- Providing clothing alterations and repair--are classified in Industry 811490, Other Personal and Household Goods Repair and Maintenance.

44814   Family Clothing Stores
See industry description for 448140.

448140 Family Clothing Stores

This industry comprises establishments primarily engaged in retailing a general line of new clothing for men, women, and children, without specializing in sales for an individual gender or age group. These establishments may provide basic alterations, such as hemming, taking in or letting out seams, or lengthening or shortening sleeves.

Cross-References.   Establishments primarily engaged in--

- Retailing clothing for all genders via electronic home shopping, mail-order, or direct sale--are classified in Subsector 454, Nonstore Retailers;
- Retailing new men's and boys' clothing--are classified in Industry 448110, Men's Clothing Stores;
- Retailing new women's, misses', and juniors' clothing--are classified in Industry 448120, Women's Clothing Stores;
- Retailing new children's and infants' clothing--are classified in Industry 448130, Children's and Infants' Clothing Stores;
- Retailing specialized new apparel, such as raincoats, bridal gowns, leather coats, fur apparel, and swimwear--are classified in Industry 448190, Other Clothing Stores;
- Providing clothing alterations and repair--are classified in Industry 811490, Other Personal and Household Goods Repair and Maintenance; and
- Retailing secondhand clothes--are classified in Industry 453310, Used Merchandise Stores.

T—Canadian, Mexican, and United States industries are comparable.

44815 Clothing Accessories Stores
See industry description for 448150.

448150 Clothing Accessories Stores

This industry comprises establishments primarily engaged in retailing single or combination lines of new clothing accessories, such as hats and caps, costume jewelry, gloves, handbags, ties, wigs, toupees, and belts.

Illustrative Examples:

Costume jewelry stores   Neckwear stores
Wig and hairpiece stores

Cross-References.   Establishments primarily engaged in--

- Retailing specialized lines of clothing via electronic home shopping, mail-order, or direct sale--are classified in Subsector 454, Nonstore Retailers;
- Retailing precious jewelry and watches--are classified in Industry 448310, Jewelry Stores;
- Retailing used clothing accessories--are classified in Industry 453310, Used Merchandise Stores;
- Retailing luggage, briefcases, trunks, or these products in combination with a general line of leather items (except leather apparel), known as luggage and leather goods stores--are classified in Industry 448320, Luggage and Leather Goods Stores; and
- Retailing leather apparel--are classified in Industry 448190, Other Clothing Stores.

44819 Other Clothing Stores
See industry description for 448190.

448190 Other Clothing Stores

This industry comprises establishments primarily engaged in retailing specialized lines of new clothing (except general lines of men's, women's, children's, infants', and family clothing). These establishments may provide basic alterations, such as hemming, taking in or letting out seams, or lengthening or shortening sleeves.

Illustrative Examples:

Bridal gown (except custom) shops   Fur apparel stores
Leather coat stores   Swimwear stores
Costume shops   Hosiery stores
Lingerie stores   Uniform (except athletic) stores

Cross-References.   Establishments primarily engaged in--

- Retailing specialized apparel via electronic home shopping, mail-order, or direct sale--are classified in Subsector 454, Nonstore Retailers;
- Retailing custom apparel and accessories made on the premises--are classified in Subsector 315, Apparel Manufacturing;
- Retailing new men's and boys' clothing--are classified in Industry 448110, Men's Clothing Stores;
- Retailing new women's, misses', and juniors' clothing, including maternity wear--are classified in Industry 448120, Women's Clothing Stores;
- Retailing new children's and infants' clothing--are classified in Industry 448130, Children's and Infants' Clothing Stores;
- Retailing new clothing for all genders or age groups--are classified in Industry 448140, Family Clothing Stores;
- Retailing athletic uniforms--are classified in Industry 451110, Sporting Goods Stores;
- Retailing secondhand clothes--are classified in Industry 453310, Used Merchandise Stores;

T—Canadian, Mexican, and United States industries are comparable.

- Retailing luggage, briefcases, trunks, or these products in combination with a general line of leather items (except leather apparel), known as luggage and leather goods stores--are classified in Industry 448320, Luggage and Leather Goods Stores; and
- Providing clothing alterations and repair--are classified in Industry 811490, Other Personal and Household Goods Repair and Maintenance.

4482   Shoe Stores

44821   Shoe Stores
See industry description for 448210.

448210   Shoe Stores

This industry comprises establishments primarily engaged in retailing all types of new footwear (except hosiery and specialty sports footwear, such as golf shoes, bowling shoes, and spiked shoes). Establishments primarily engaged in retailing new tennis shoes or sneakers are included in this industry.

Cross-References.   Establishments primarily engaged in--

- Retailing footwear via electronic home shopping, mail-order, or direct sale--are classified in Subsector 454, Nonstore Retailers;
- Retailing hosiery--are classified in Industry 448190, Other Clothing Stores;
- Retailing new specialty sports footwear (e.g., bowling shoes, golf shoes, spiked shoes)--are classified in Industry 451110, Sporting Goods Stores; and
- Retailing used footwear--are classified in Industry 453310, Used Merchandise Stores.

4483   Jewelry, Luggage, and Leather Goods Stores

This industry group comprises establishments primarily engaged in retailing new jewelry (except costume jewelry); new sterling and plated silverware; new watches and clocks; and new luggage with or without a general line of new leather goods and accessories, such as hats, gloves, handbags, ties, and belts.

44831   Jewelry Stores
See industry description for 448310.

448310   Jewelry Stores

This industry comprises establishments primarily engaged in retailing one or more of the following items: (1) new jewelry (except costume jewelry); (2) new sterling and plated silverware; and (3) new watches and clocks. Also included are establishments retailing these new products in combination with lapidary work and/or repair services.

Cross-References.   Establishments primarily engaged in--

- Retailing new costume jewelry--are classified in Industry 448150, Clothing Accessories Stores;
- Retailing jewelry via electronic home shopping, mail-order, or direct sale--are classified in Subsector 454, Nonstore Retailers;
- Retailing antique or used jewelry, silverware, and watches and clocks--are classified in Industry 453310, Used Merchandise Stores;
- Providing jewelry or watch and clock repair without retailing new jewelry or watches and clocks--are classified in Industry 811490, Other Personal and Household Goods Repair and Maintenance; and
- Cutting and setting gem stones--are classified in Industry 339910, Jewelry and Silverware Manufacturing.

44832   Luggage and Leather Goods Stores
See industry description for 448320.

T—Canadian, Mexican, and United States industries are comparable.

448320 Luggage and Leather Goods Stores

This industry comprises establishments known as luggage and leather goods stores primarily engaged in retailing new luggage, briefcases, and trunks, or retailing these new products in combination with a general line of leather items (except leather apparel), such as belts, gloves, and handbags.

Cross-References.   Establishments primarily engaged in--

- Retailing luggage and leather goods via electronic home shopping, mail-order, or direct sale--are classified in Subsector 454, Nonstore Retailers;
- Retailing used luggage and leather goods--are classified in Industry 453310, Used Merchandise Stores;
- Retailing single or combination lines of new clothing accessories (e.g., gloves, handbags, or leather belts)--are classified in Industry 448150, Clothing Accessories Stores; and
- Retailing new leather coats--are classified in Industry 448190, Other Clothing Stores.

451   Sporting Goods, Hobby, Musical Instrument, and Book Stores

Industries in the Sporting Goods, Hobby, Musical Instrument, and Book Stores subsector are engaged in retailing and providing expertise on the use of sporting equipment or supplies for other specific leisure activities, such as needlework and musical instruments. Book stores are also included in this subsector.

4511   Sporting Goods, Hobby, and Musical Instrument Stores

This industry group comprises establishments primarily engaged in retailing new sporting goods, games and toys, and musical instruments.

45111   Sporting Goods Stores
See industry description for 451110.

451110 Sporting Goods Stores

This industry comprises establishments primarily engaged in retailing new sporting goods, such as bicycles and bicycle parts; camping equipment; exercise and fitness equipment; athletic uniforms; specialty sports footwear; and other sporting goods, equipment, and accessories.

Illustrative Examples:

Athletic uniform supply stores
Fishing supply stores
Bicycle (except motorized) shops
Golf pro shops
Bowling equipment and supply stores

Saddlery stores
Diving equipment stores
Sporting goods (e.g., scuba, skiing, outdoor) stores
Exercise equipment stores
Sporting gun shops

Cross-References.   Establishments primarily engaged in--

- Retailing sporting goods via electronic home shopping, mail-order, or direct sale--are classified in Subsector 454, Nonstore Retailers;
- Retailing new or used campers (pick-up coaches) and camping trailers--are classified in Industry 441210, Recreational Vehicle Dealers;
- Retailing new or used snowmobiles, motorized bicycles, and motorized golf carts--are classified in U.S. Industry 441228, Motorcycle, ATV, and All Other Motor Vehicle Dealers;
- Retailing new shoes (except specialty sports footwear, such as golf shoes, bowling shoes, and spiked shoes)--are classified in Industry 448210, Shoe Stores;
- Repairing or servicing sporting goods, without retailing new sporting goods--are classified in Industry 811490, Other Personal and Household Goods Repair and Maintenance; and

T—Canadian, Mexican, and United States industries are comparable.

- Retailing used sporting goods and used bicycles--are classified in Industry 453310, Used Merchandise Stores.

45112 Hobby, Toy, and Game Stores
See industry description for 451120.

451120 Hobby, Toy, and Game Stores

This industry comprises establishments primarily engaged in retailing new toys, games, and hobby and craft supplies (except needlecraft).

Cross-References.   Establishments primarily engaged in--

- Retailing toys, games, and hobby and craft supplies via electronic home shopping, mail-order, or direct sale--are classified in Subsector 454, Nonstore Retailers;
- Retailing artists' supplies or collectors' items, such as coins, stamps, autographs, and cards--are classified in U.S. Industry 453998, All Other Miscellaneous Store Retailers (except Tobacco Stores);
- Retailing new computer software (e.g., game software)--are classified in U.S. Industry 443142, Electronics Stores;
- Retailing used toys, games, and hobby supplies--are classified in Industry 453310, Used Merchandise Stores; and
- Retailing new sewing supplies, fabrics, and needlework accessories--are classified in Industry 451130, Sewing, Needlework, and Piece Goods Stores.

45113 Sewing, Needlework, and Piece Goods Stores
See industry description for 451130.

451130 Sewing, Needlework, and Piece Goods Stores

This industry comprises establishments primarily engaged in retailing new sewing supplies, fabrics, patterns, yarns, and other needlework accessories or retailing these products in combination with selling new sewing machines.

Illustrative Examples:

Fabric shops	Needlecraft sewing supply stores
Sewing supply stores	Upholstery materials stores

Cross-References.   Establishments primarily engaged in--

- Retailing sewing supplies via electronic home shopping, mail-order, or direct sale--are classified in Subsector 454, Nonstore Retailers;
- Retailing new sewing machines only and in combination with retailing other new appliances--are classified in U.S. Industry 443141, Household Appliance Stores; and
- Retailing used sewing, needlework, and piece goods--are classified in Industry 453310, Used Merchandise Stores.

45114 Musical Instrument and Supplies Stores
See industry description for 451140.

451140 Musical Instrument and Supplies Stores

This industry comprises establishments primarily engaged in retailing new musical instruments, sheet music, and related supplies; or retailing these new products in combination with musical instrument repair, rental, or music instruction.

T—Canadian, Mexican, and United States industries are comparable.

Illustrative Examples:

Musical instrument stores
Sheet music stores

Piano stores

Cross-References.   Establishments primarily engaged in--

- Retailing musical instruments, sheet music, and related supplies via electronic home shopping, mail-order, or direct sale--are classified in Subsector 454, Nonstore Retailers;
- Retailing new musical recordings--are classified in U.S. Industry 443142, Electronics Stores; and
- Retailing used musical instruments (including used rare musical instruments), sheet music, and related supplies--are classified in Industry 453310, Used Merchandise Stores.

4512   Book Stores and News Dealers

45121   Book Stores and News Dealers

This industry comprises establishments primarily engaged in retailing new books, newspapers, magazines, and other periodicals.

Cross-References.   Establishments primarily engaged in--

- Retailing newspapers, magazines, and other periodicals via electronic home shopping, mail-order, or direct sale--are classified in Subsector 454, Nonstore Retailers;
- Home delivery of newspapers--are classified in Industry 45439, Other Direct Selling Establishments; and
- Retailing used books, newspapers, magazines, and other periodicals--are classified in Industry 45331, Used Merchandise Stores.

451211   Book Stores

This U.S. industry comprises establishments primarily engaged in retailing new books.

Cross-References.   Establishments primarily engaged in--

- Retailing books via electronic home shopping, mail-order, or direct sale--are classified in Subsector 454, Nonstore Retailers; and
- Retailing used books (including used rare books)--are classified in Industry 453310, Used Merchandise Stores.

451212   News Dealers and Newsstands

This U.S. industry comprises establishments primarily engaged in retailing current newspapers, magazines, and other periodicals.

Cross-References.   Establishments primarily engaged in--

- Home delivery of newspapers--are classified in Industry 454390, Other Direct Selling Establishments;
- Retailing newspapers and periodicals by mail-order--are classified in Industry 454110, Electronic Shopping and Mail-Order Houses; and
- Retailing used newspapers, magazines, and other periodicals--are classified in Industry 453310, Used Merchandise Stores.

T—Canadian, Mexican, and United States industries are comparable.

452   General Merchandise Stores

Industries in the General Merchandise Stores subsector retail new general merchandise from fixed point-of-sale locations. Establishments in this subsector are unique in that they have the equipment and staff capable of retailing a large variety of goods from a single location. This includes a variety of display equipment and staff trained to provide information on many lines of products.

4522   Department Stores

45221   Department Stores
See industry description for 452210.

452210   Department Stores

This industry comprises establishments known as department stores that have separate departments for general lines of new merchandise, such as apparel, jewelry, home furnishings, and toys, with no one merchandise line predominating. Department stores may sell perishable groceries, such as fresh fruits, vegetables, and dairy products, but such sales are insignificant. Department stores may have separate customer checkout areas in each department, central customer checkout areas, or both.

Cross-References.   Establishments primarily engaged in--

- Retailing a general line of merchandise via electronic home shopping, mail-order, or direct sale--are classified in Subsector 454, Nonstore Retailers;
- Retailing apparel without a significant amount of housewares or general merchandise--are classified in Subsector 448, Clothing and Clothing Accessories Stores;
- Retailing a general line of merchandise in combination with a general line of perishable groceries, known as warehouse clubs, superstores, or supercenters--are classified in U.S. Industry 452311, Warehouse Clubs and Supercenters; and
- Retailing used merchandise--are classified in Industry 453310, Used Merchandise Stores.

4523   General Merchandise Stores, including Warehouse Clubs and Supercenters

45231   General Merchandise Stores, including Warehouse Clubs and Supercenters

This industry comprises establishments primarily engaged in retailing new goods in general merchandise stores (except department stores). These establishments retail a general line of new merchandise, such as apparel, automotive parts, dry goods, hardware, groceries, housewares, and home furnishings, with no one merchandise line predominating. Establishments known as warehouse clubs, superstores, or supercenters are included in this industry.

Illustrative Examples:

Dollar stores
General merchandise catalog showrooms (except catalog mail-order)
General merchandise trading posts
General stores

Home and auto supply stores
Superstores (i.e., food and general merchandise)
Variety stores
Warehouse clubs (i.e., food and general merchandise)

Cross-References.   Establishments primarily engaged in--

- Retailing a general line of merchandise via electronic home shopping, mail-order, or direct sale--are classified in Subsector 454, Nonstore Retailers;
- Retailing a general line of food, known as supermarkets and grocery stores--are classified in Industry 44511, Supermarkets and Other Grocery (except Convenience) Stores;

T—Canadian, Mexican, and United States industries are comparable.

- Retailing automotive parts--are classified in Industry 44131, Automotive Parts and Accessories Stores;
- Retailing a general line of new merchandise, known as department stores--are classified in Industry 45221, Department Stores;
- Retailing merchandise in catalog showrooms of mail-order houses--are classified in Industry 45411, Electronic Shopping and Mail-Order Houses;
- Retailing a general line of new hardware items, known as hardware stores--are classified in Industry 44413, Hardware Stores;
- Retailing a general line of new home repair and improvement materials and supplies, known as home centers--are classified in Industry 44411, Home Centers; and
- Retailing used merchandise--are classified in Industry 45331, Used Merchandise Stores.

452311 Warehouse Clubs and Supercenters

This U.S. industry comprises establishments known as warehouse clubs, superstores, or supercenters, primarily engaged in retailing a general line of groceries, including a significant amount and variety of fresh fruits, vegetables, dairy products, meats, and other perishable groceries, in combination with a general line of new merchandise, such as apparel, furniture, and appliances.

Cross-References.   Establishments primarily engaged in--

- Retailing a general line of merchandise via electronic home shopping, mail-order, or direct sale--are classified in Subsector 454, Nonstore Retailers;
- Retailing a general line of food, known as supermarkets and grocery stores--are classified in Industry 445110, Supermarkets and Other Grocery (except Convenience) Stores;
- Retailing a general line of new merchandise, known as department stores--are classified in Industry 452210, Department Stores;
- Retailing a general line of new merchandise, except department stores, warehouse clubs, superstores, and supercenters--are classified in U.S. Industry 452319, All Other General Merchandise Stores; and
- Retailing used merchandise--are classified in Industry 453310, Used Merchandise Stores.

452319 All Other General Merchandise Stores

This U.S. industry comprises establishments primarily engaged in retailing new goods in general merchandise stores (except department stores, warehouse clubs, superstores, and supercenters). These establishments retail a general line of new merchandise, such as apparel, automotive parts, dry goods, hardware, housewares or home furnishings, and other lines in limited amounts, with none of the lines predominating.

Illustrative Examples:

Dollar stores
General merchandise catalog showrooms (except
catalog mail-order)
General merchandise trading posts

General stores
Home and auto supply stores
Variety stores

Cross-References.   Establishments primarily engaged in--

- Retailing a general line of merchandise via electronic home shopping, mail-order, or direct sale--are classified in Subsector 454, Nonstore Retailers;
- Retailing automotive parts--are classified in Industry 441310, Automotive Parts and Accessories Stores;
- Retailing a general line of new merchandise, known as department stores--are classified in Industry 452210, Department Stores;
- Retailing a general line of merchandise in combination with a general line of perishable groceries, known as warehouse clubs, superstores, or supercenters--are classified in U.S. Industry 452311, Warehouse Clubs and Supercenters;

T—Canadian, Mexican, and United States industries are comparable.

- Retailing merchandise in catalog showrooms of mail-order houses--are classified in Industry 454110, Electronic Shopping and Mail-Order Houses;
- Retailing a general line of new hardware items, known as hardware stores--are classified in Industry 444130, Hardware Stores;
- Retailing a general line of new home repair and improvement materials and supplies, known as home centers--are classified in Industry 444110, Home Centers; and
- Retailing used merchandise--are classified in Industry 453310, Used Merchandise Stores.

453   Miscellaneous Store Retailers

Industries in the Miscellaneous Store Retailers subsector retail merchandise from fixed point-of-sale locations (except new or used motor vehicles and parts; new furniture and home furnishings; new appliances and electronic products; new building materials and garden equipment and supplies; food and beverages; health and personal care goods; gasoline; new clothing and accessories; and new sporting goods, hobby goods, books, and music). Establishments in this subsector include stores with unique characteristics, such as florists, used merchandise stores, and pet and pet supply stores.

4531   Florists

45311   Florists
See industry description for 453110.

453110   Florists

This industry comprises establishments known as florists primarily engaged in retailing cut flowers, floral arrangements, and potted plants purchased from others. These establishments usually prepare the arrangements they sell.

Cross-References.   Establishments primarily engaged in--

- Retailing flowers or nursery stock grown on premises--are classified in Industry 11142, Nursery and Floriculture Production;
- Retailing trees, shrubs, plants, seeds, bulbs, and sod grown elsewhere--are classified in Industry 444220, Nursery, Garden Center, and Farm Supply Stores; and
- Retailing flowers via electronic home shopping, mail-order, or direct sale--are classified in Subsector 454, Nonstore Retailers.

4532   Office Supplies, Stationery, and Gift Stores

This industry group comprises establishments primarily engaged in retailing new office supplies, stationery, gifts, novelty merchandise, and souvenirs.

45321   Office Supplies and Stationery Stores
See industry description for 453210.

453210   Office Supplies and Stationery Stores

This industry comprises establishments primarily engaged in one or more of the following: (1) retailing new stationery, school supplies, and office supplies; (2) retailing a combination of new office equipment, furniture, and supplies; and (3) retailing new office equipment, furniture, and supplies in combination with selling new computers.

Cross-References.   Establishments primarily engaged in--

- Retailing stationery, school supplies, and office supplies via electronic shopping, mail-order, or direct sale-- are classified in Subsector 454, Nonstore Retailers;

T—Canadian, Mexican, and United States industries are comparable.

- Retailing greeting cards--are classified in Industry 453220, Gift, Novelty, and Souvenir Stores;
- Retailing new computers without retailing other consumer-type electronic products or office equipment, furniture, and supplies--are classified in U.S. Industry 443142, Electronics Stores;
- Printing business forms--are classified in Industry 32311, Printing;
- Retailing new office furniture--are classified in Industry 442110, Furniture Stores; and
- Retailing used office supplies--are classified in Industry 453310, Used Merchandise Stores.

45322   Gift, Novelty, and Souvenir Stores
See industry description for 453220.

453220 Gift, Novelty, and Souvenir Stores

This industry comprises establishments primarily engaged in retailing new gifts, novelty merchandise, souvenirs, greeting cards, seasonal and holiday decorations, and curios.

Illustrative Examples:

Balloon shops	Curio shops
Greeting card shops	Souvenir shops
Christmas stores	Gift shops
Novelty shops	Fruit basket or fruit bouquet stores

Cross-References.   Establishments primarily engaged in--

- Retailing gifts and novelties via electronic home shopping, mail-order, or direct sale--are classified in Subsector 454, Nonstore Retailers;
- Retailing stationery--are classified in Industry 453210, Office Supplies and Stationery Stores; and
- Retailing used curios and novelties--are classified in Industry 453310, Used Merchandise Stores.

4533   Used Merchandise Stores

45331   Used Merchandise Stores
See industry description for 453310.

453310 Used Merchandise Stores

This industry comprises establishments primarily engaged in retailing used merchandise, antiques, and secondhand goods (except motor vehicles, such as automobiles, RVs, motorcycles, and boats; motor vehicle parts; tires; and mobile homes).

Illustrative Examples:

Antique shops	Used merchandise thrift shops
Used household-type appliance stores	Used clothing stores
Used book stores	Used sporting goods stores

Cross-References.   Establishments primarily engaged in--

- Retailing used merchandise via electronic home shopping, mail-order, or direct sale--are classified in Subsector 454, Nonstore Retailers;
- Operating pawnshops--are classified in U.S. Industry 522298, All Other Nondepository Credit Intermediation;
- Retailing used automobiles--are classified in Industry 441120, Used Car Dealers;
- Retailing used automobile parts (except tires and tubes)--are classified in Industry 441310, Automotive Parts and Accessories Stores;

T—Canadian, Mexican, and United States industries are comparable.

- Retailing used tires--are classified in Industry 441320, Tire Dealers;
- Retailing used mobile homes--are classified in Industry 453930, Manufactured (Mobile) Home Dealers;
- Retailing used recreational vehicles--are classified in Industry 441210, Recreational Vehicle Dealers;
- Retailing used boats--are classified in U.S. Industry 441222, Boat Dealers;
- Retailing used motorcycles, aircraft, snowmobiles, and utility trailers--are classified in U.S. Industry 441228, Motorcycle, ATV, and All Other Motor Vehicle Dealers; and
- Retailing a general line of used merchandise on an auction basis (except electronic auctions)--are classified in U.S. Industry 453998, All Other Miscellaneous Store Retailers (except Tobacco Stores).

4539   Other Miscellaneous Store Retailers

This industry group comprises establishments primarily engaged in retailing new miscellaneous specialty store merchandise (except motor vehicle and parts dealers; furniture and home furnishings stores; consumer-type electronics and appliance stores; building material and garden equipment and supplies dealers; food and beverage stores; health and personal care stores; gasoline stations; clothing and clothing accessories stores; sporting goods, hobby, book, and music stores; general merchandise stores; florists; office supplies, stationery, and gift stores; and used merchandise stores). This industry group also includes establishments primarily engaged in retailing a general line of new and used merchandise on an auction basis (except electronic auctions).

45391   Pet and Pet Supplies Stores
See industry description for 453910.

453910   Pet and Pet Supplies Stores

This industry comprises establishments primarily engaged in retailing pets, pet foods, and pet supplies.

Cross-References.   Establishments primarily engaged in--

- Retailing pets, pet foods, and pet supplies via electronic home shopping, mail-order, or direct sale--are classified in Subsector 454, Nonstore Retailers;
- Providing pet grooming and boarding services--are classified in Industry 812910, Pet Care (except Veterinary) Services; and
- Providing veterinary services--are classified in Industry 541940, Veterinary Services.

45392   Art Dealers
See industry description for 453920.

453920   Art Dealers

This industry comprises establishments primarily engaged in retailing original and limited edition art works. Included in this industry are establishments primarily engaged in displaying works of art for retail sale in art galleries.

Cross-References.   Establishments primarily engaged in--

- Retailing original and limited edition art works via electronic home shopping, mail-order, or direct sale--are classified in Subsector 454, Nonstore Retailers;
- Retailing art reproductions (except limited editions)--are classified in U.S. Industry 442299, All Other Home Furnishings Stores;
- Retailing artists' supplies--are classified in U.S. Industry 453998, All Other Miscellaneous Store Retailers (except Tobacco Stores); and
- Displaying works of art not for retail sale in art galleries--are classified in Industry 712110, Museums.

45393   Manufactured (Mobile) Home Dealers
See industry description for 453930.

T—Canadian, Mexican, and United States industries are comparable.

453930 Manufactured (Mobile) Home Dealers

This industry comprises establishments primarily engaged in retailing new and/or used manufactured homes (i.e., mobile homes), parts, and equipment.

Cross-References.   Establishments primarily engaged in--

- Retailing new or used motor homes, campers, and travel trailers--are classified in Industry 441210, Recreational Vehicle Dealers; and
- Retailing prefabricated buildings and kits without construction--are classified in Industry 444190, Other Building Material Dealers.

45399   All Other Miscellaneous Store Retailers

This industry comprises establishments primarily engaged in retailing specialized lines of merchandise (except motor vehicle and parts dealers; furniture and home furnishings stores; electronics and appliance stores; building material and garden equipment and supplies dealers; food and beverage stores; health and personal care stores; gasoline stations; clothing and clothing accessories stores; sporting goods, hobby, book, and music stores; general merchandise stores; florists; office supplies, stationery, and gift stores; used merchandise stores; pet and pet supplies stores; art dealers; and manufactured home (i.e., mobile home) dealers). This industry also includes establishments primarily engaged in retailing a general line of new and used merchandise on an auction basis (except electronic auctions).

Illustrative Examples:

Art supply stores	Cemetery memorial (e.g., markers, headstones,
Swimming pool supply stores, new	vaults) dealers
Tobacco stores	Cigar stores

Cross-References.   Establishments primarily engaged in--

- Retailing merchandise via electronic home shopping, mail-order, or direct sale--are classified in Subsector 454, Nonstore Retailers;
- Retailing merchandise via electronic auctions--are classified in Industry 45411, Electronic Shopping and Mail-Order Houses;
- Auctioning on the location of others as independent auctioneers--are classified in Industry 56199, All Other Support Services;
- Retailing pets and pet supplies--are classified in Industry 45391, Pet and Pet Supplies Stores;
- Retailing original and limited edition art works--are classified in Industry 45392, Art Dealers;
- Retailing manufactured homes (i.e., mobile homes)--are classified in Industry 45393, Manufactured (Mobile) Home Dealers;
- Retailing new books--are classified in Industry 45121, Book Stores and News Dealers;
- Retailing new jewelry (except costume jewelry)--are classified in Industry 44831, Jewelry Stores;
- Retailing new costume jewelry--are classified in Industry 44815, Clothing Accessories Stores;
- Operating pawnshops--are classified in Industry 52229, Other Nondepository Credit Intermediation; and
- Retailing used merchandise (except automobiles, RVs, mobile homes, motorcycles, boats, motor vehicle parts, tires, aircraft, snowmobiles, and utility trailers)--are classified in Industry 45331, Used Merchandise Stores.

453991 Tobacco Stores

This U.S. industry comprises establishments primarily engaged in retailing cigarettes, cigars, tobacco, pipes, and other smokers' supplies.

T—Canadian, Mexican, and United States industries are comparable.

Illustrative Examples:

Cigar stores	Cigarette stands (i.e., permanent)
Smokers' supply stores	Tobacco stores

Cross-References.   Establishments primarily engaged in--

- Retailing tobacco products and smokers' supplies via electronic home shopping, mail-order, or direct sale--are classified in Subsector 454, Nonstore Retailers; and
- Retailing electronic cigarettes--are classified in U.S. Industry 453998, All Other Miscellaneous Store Retailers (except Tobacco Stores).

453998 All Other Miscellaneous Store Retailers (except Tobacco Stores)

This U.S. industry comprises establishments primarily engaged in retailing specialized lines of merchandise (except motor vehicle and parts dealers; furniture and home furnishings stores; electronics and appliance stores; building material and garden equipment and supplies dealers; food and beverage stores; health and personal care stores; gasoline stations; clothing and clothing accessories stores; sporting goods, hobby, book and music stores; general merchandise stores; florists; office supplies, stationery, and gift stores; used merchandise stores; pet and pet supplies stores; art dealers; manufactured home (i.e., mobile home) dealers; and tobacco stores). This industry also includes establishments primarily engaged in retailing a general line of new and used merchandise on an auction basis (except electronic auctions).

Illustrative Examples:

Art supply stores	Collectors' items (e.g., autograph, coin, card, stamp)
General merchandise auction houses	shops (except used rare items)
Candle shops	Swimming pool supply stores
Home security equipment stores	Fireworks shops (permanent location)
Cemetery memorial (e.g., headstones, markers,	Trophy (e.g., awards and plaques) shops
vaults) dealers	Flower shops, artificial or dried
Hot tub stores	

Cross-References.   Establishments primarily engaged in--

- Retailing specialized lines of merchandise via electronic home shopping, mail-order, or direct sale--are classified in Subsector 454, Nonstore Retailers;
- Retailing merchandise via electronic auctions--are classified in Industry 454110, Electronic Shopping and Mail-Order Houses;
- Auctioning on the location of others as independent auctioneers--are classified in Industry 561990, All Other Support Services;
- Retailing pets and pet supplies--are classified in Industry 453910, Pet and Pet Supplies Stores;
- Retailing original and limited edition art works--are classified in Industry 453920, Art Dealers;
- Retailing manufactured homes (i.e., mobile homes)--are classified in Industry 453930, Manufactured (Mobile) Home Dealers;
- Retailing cigarettes, cigars, tobacco, pipes, and other smokers' supplies--are classified in U.S. Industry 453991, Tobacco Stores;
- Retailing antiques--are classified in Industry 453310, Used Merchandise Stores;
- Retailing new books--are classified in U.S. Industry 451211, Book Stores;
- Retailing new jewelry (except costume jewelry)--are classified in Industry 448310, Jewelry Stores; and
- Retailing new costume jewelry--are classified in Industry 448150, Clothing Accessories Stores.

T—Canadian, Mexican, and United States industries are comparable.

454   Nonstore Retailers

Industries in the Nonstore Retailers subsector retail merchandise using methods, such as the broadcasting of infomercials, the broadcasting and publishing of direct-response advertising, the publishing of paper and electronic catalogs, door-to-door solicitation, in-home demonstration, selling from portable stalls, and distribution through vending machines. Establishments in this subsector include mail-order houses, vending machine operators, home delivery sales, door-to-door sales, party plan sales, electronic shopping, and sales through portable stalls (e.g., street vendors, except food). Establishments engaged in the direct sale (i.e., nonstore) of products, such as home heating oil dealers and newspaper delivery service providers, are included in this subsector.

4541   Electronic Shopping and Mail-Order Houses

45411   Electronic Shopping and Mail-Order Houses
See industry description for 454110.

454110   Electronic Shopping and Mail-Order Houses

This industry comprises establishments primarily engaged in retailing all types of merchandise using nonstore means, such as catalogs, toll free telephone numbers, or electronic media, such as interactive television or the Internet. Included in this industry are establishments primarily engaged in retailing from catalog showrooms of mail-order houses.

Illustrative Examples:

Catalog (i.e., order-taking) offices of mail-order houses
Collectors' items, mail-order houses
Computer software, mail-order houses
Home shopping television orders

Internet auction sites, retail
Mail-order book clubs (not publishing)
Mail-order houses
Web retailers

Cross-References.   Establishments primarily engaged in--

- Store retailing or a combination of store retailing and nonstore retailing in the same establishment--are classified in Sector 44-45, Retail Trade, based on the classification of the store portion of the activity;
- Retailing a general line of new and used merchandise on an auction basis from physical auction sites--are classified in U.S. Industry 453998, All Other Miscellaneous Store Retailers (except Tobacco Stores);
- Facilitating business-to-business electronic sales of new and used merchandise on an auction basis using the Internet--are classified in Industry 425110, Business to Business Electronic Markets;
- Providing telemarketing (e.g., telephone marketing) services for others--are classified in U.S. Industry 561422, Telemarketing Bureaus and Other Contact Centers;
- Providing Internet publishing of classified ads--are classified in Industry 519130, Internet Publishing and Broadcasting and Web Search Portals; and
- Hosting Internet retail sites without performing associated activities such as payment processing or fulfillment--are classified in Industry 518210, Data Processing, Hosting, and Related Services.

4542   Vending Machine Operators

45421   Vending Machine Operators
See industry description for 454210.

454210   Vending Machine Operators

This industry comprises establishments primarily engaged in retailing merchandise through vending machines that they service.

T—Canadian, Mexican, and United States industries are comparable.

Cross-References.   Establishments primarily engaged in--

- Supplying and servicing coin-operated photobooths, rest rooms, and lockers--are classified in Industry 812990, All Other Personal Services; and
- Supplying and servicing coin-operated amusement and gambling devices in places of business operated by others--are classified in Subsector 713, Amusement, Gambling, and Recreation Industries.

4543   Direct Selling Establishments

This industry group comprises establishments primarily engaged in nonstore retailing (except electronic, mail-order, or vending machine sales). These establishments typically go to the customers' location rather than the customer coming to them (e.g., door-to-door sales, home parties). Examples of establishments in this industry are home delivery newspaper routes; home delivery of heating oil, liquefied petroleum (LP) gas, and other fuels; locker meat provisioners; frozen food and freezer meal plan providers; coffee-break supplies providers; and bottled water or water softener services.

45431   Fuel Dealers
     See industry description for 454310.

454310 Fuel Dealers

This industry comprises establishments primarily engaged in retailing heating oil, liquefied petroleum (LP) gas, and other fuels via direct selling.

Cross-References.   Establishments primarily engaged in--

- Providing oil burner repair services--are classified in U.S. Industry 811411, Home and Garden Equipment Repair and Maintenance; and
- Installing oil burners--are classified in Industry 238220, Plumbing, Heating, and Air-Conditioning Contractors.

45439   Other Direct Selling Establishments
     See industry description for 454390.

454390 Other Direct Selling Establishments

This industry comprises establishments primarily engaged in retailing merchandise (except food for immediate consumption and fuel) via direct sale to the customer by means, such as in-house sales (i.e., party plan merchandising), truck or wagon sales, and portable stalls (i.e., street vendors).

Illustrative Examples:

Direct selling bottled water providers
Direct selling home delivery newspaper routes
Direct selling coffee-break supplies providers
Direct selling locker meat provisioners

Direct selling frozen food and freezer meal plan providers
Direct selling party plan merchandisers

Cross-References.   Establishments primarily engaged in--

- Preparing and selling meals and snacks for immediate consumption from motorized vehicles or nonmotorized carts, catering a route--are classified in Industry 722330, Mobile Food Services; and
- Retailing heating oil, liquefied petroleum (LP) gas, and other fuels via direct sale--are classified in Industry 454310, Fuel Dealers.

T—Canadian, Mexican, and United States industries are comparable.

Sector 48-49--Transportation and Warehousing[T]

The Sector as a Whole

The Transportation and Warehousing sector includes industries providing transportation of passengers and cargo, warehousing and storage for goods, scenic and sightseeing transportation, and support activities related to modes of transportation. Establishments in these industries use transportation equipment or transportation related facilities as a productive asset. The type of equipment depends on the mode of transportation. The modes of transportation are air, rail, water, road, and pipeline.

The Transportation and Warehousing sector distinguishes three basic types of activities: subsectors for each mode of transportation, a subsector for warehousing and storage, and a subsector for establishments providing support activities for transportation. In addition, there are subsectors for establishments that provide passenger transportation for scenic and sightseeing purposes, postal services, and courier services.

A separate subsector for support activities is established in the sector because, first, support activities for transportation are inherently multimodal, such as freight transportation arrangement, or have multimodal aspects. Secondly, there are production process similarities among the support activity industries.

One of the support activities identified in the Support Activities for Transportation subsector is the routine repair and maintenance of transportation equipment (e.g., aircraft at an airport, railroad rolling stock at a railroad terminal, or ships at a harbor or port facility). Such establishments do not perform complete overhauling or rebuilding of transportation equipment (i.e., periodic restoration of transportation equipment to original design specifications) or transportation equipment conversion (i.e., major modification to systems). An establishment that primarily performs factory (or shipyard) overhauls, rebuilding, or conversions of aircraft, railroad rolling stock, or ships is classified in Subsector 336, Transportation Equipment Manufacturing, according to the type of equipment.

Many of the establishments in this sector often operate on networks, with physical facilities, labor forces, and equipment spread over an extensive geographic area.

Warehousing establishments in this sector are distinguished from merchant wholesaling in that the warehouse establishments do not sell the goods.

Excluded from this sector are establishments primarily engaged in providing travel agent services that support transportation and other establishments, such as hotels, businesses, and government agencies. These establishments are classified in Sector 56, Administrative and Support and Waste Management and Remediation Services. Also, establishments primarily engaged in providing rental and leasing of transportation equipment without operator are classified in Subsector 532, Rental and Leasing Services.

481   Air Transportation[T]

Industries in the Air Transportation subsector provide air transportation of passengers and/or cargo using aircraft, such as airplanes and helicopters. The subsector distinguishes scheduled from nonscheduled air transportation. Scheduled air carriers fly regular routes on regular schedules and operate even if flights are only partially loaded. Nonscheduled carriers often operate during nonpeak time slots at busy airports. These establishments have more flexibility with respect to choice of airport, hours of operation, load factors, and similar operational characteristics. Nonscheduled carriers provide chartered air transportation of passengers, cargo, or specialty flying services. Specialty flying services establishments use general purpose aircraft to provide a variety of specialized flying services.

Scenic and sightseeing air transportation and air courier services are not included in this subsector but are included in Subsector 487, Scenic and Sightseeing Transportation, and in Subsector 492, Couriers and Messengers, respectively. Although these activities may use aircraft, they are different from the activities included in air transportation. Air sightseeing does not usually involve place-to-place transportation; the passenger's flight (e.g., balloon ride, aerial sightseeing) typically starts and ends at the same location. Courier services (individual package or cargo delivery) include more than air transportation; road transportation is usually required to deliver the cargo to the intended recipient.

T—Canadian, Mexican, and United States industries are comparable.

4811　Scheduled Air Transportation[T]

48111　Scheduled Air Transportation[T]

This industry comprises establishments primarily engaged in providing air transportation of passengers and/or cargo over regular routes and on regular schedules. Establishments in this industry operate flights even if partially loaded. Establishments primarily engaged in providing scheduled air transportation of mail on a contract basis are included in this industry.

Illustrative Examples:

Air commuter carriers, scheduled

Scheduled air passenger carriers

Scheduled air cargo carriers (except air couriers)

Scheduled helicopter passenger carriers

Cross-References.　　　Establishments primarily engaged in--

- Providing air courier services--are classified in Industry 49211, Couriers and Express Delivery Services;
- Providing air transportation of passengers, cargo, or specialty flying services with no regular routes and regular schedules--are classified in Industry 48121, Nonscheduled Air Transportation; and
- Providing helicopter rides for scenic and sightseeing transportation--are classified in Industry 48799, Scenic and Sightseeing Transportation, Other.

481111　Scheduled Passenger Air Transportation

This U.S. industry comprises establishments primarily engaged in providing air transportation of passengers or passengers and freight over regular routes and on regular schedules. Establishments in this industry operate flights even if partially loaded. Scheduled air passenger carriers including commuter and helicopter carriers (except scenic and sightseeing) are included in this industry.

Cross-References.　　　Establishments primarily engaged in--

- Providing air transportation of passengers or passengers and cargo with no regular routes and regular schedules--are classified in U.S. Industry 481211, Nonscheduled Chartered Passenger Air Transportation;
- Providing helicopter rides for scenic and sightseeing transportation--are classified in Industry 487990, Scenic and Sightseeing Transportation, Other; and
- Providing air transportation of cargo (without transporting passengers) over regular routes and on regular schedules--are classified in U.S. Industry 481112, Scheduled Freight Air Transportation.

481112　Scheduled Freight Air Transportation

This U.S. industry comprises establishments primarily engaged in providing air transportation of cargo without transporting passengers over regular routes and on regular schedules. Establishments in this industry operate flights even if partially loaded. Establishments primarily engaged in providing scheduled air transportation of mail on a contract basis are included in this industry.

Cross-References.　　　Establishments primarily engaged in--

- Providing air courier services--are classified in Industry 492110, Couriers and Express Delivery Services;
- Providing air transportation of cargo with no regular routes and regular schedules--are classified in U.S. Industry 481212, Nonscheduled Chartered Freight Air Transportation; and
- Providing air transportation of passengers or passengers and cargo over regular routes and on regular schedules--are classified in U.S. Industry 481111, Scheduled Passenger Air Transportation.

T—Canadian, Mexican, and United States industries are comparable.

4812   Nonscheduled Air Transportation[T]

48121   Nonscheduled Air Transportation[T]

This industry comprises establishments primarily engaged in (1) providing air transportation of passengers and/or cargo with no regular routes and regular schedules or (2) providing specialty flying services with no regular routes and regular schedules using general purpose aircraft. These establishments have more flexibility with respect to choice of airports, hours of operation, load factors, and similar operational characteristics.

Illustrative Examples:

Air taxi services
Nonscheduled air freight transportation services

Aircraft charter services
Nonscheduled air passenger transportation services

Cross-References.   Establishments primarily engaged in--

- Crop dusting using specialized aircraft--are classified in Industry 11511, Support Activities for Crop Production;
- Fighting forest fires using specialized water bombers--are classified in Industry 11531, Support Activities for Forestry;
- Providing air transportation of passengers and/or cargo over regular routes and on regular schedules--are classified in Industry 48111, Scheduled Air Transportation;
- Providing specialized air sightseeing services--are classified in Industry 48799, Scenic and Sightseeing Transportation, Other;
- Aerial gathering of geophysical data--are classified in Industry 54136, Geophysical Surveying and Mapping Services;
- Providing aerial and/or other surveying and mapping services--are classified in Industry 54137, Surveying and Mapping (except Geophysical) Services;
- Providing air ambulance services using specialized equipment--are classified in Industry 62191, Ambulance Services;
- Operating specialized flying schools, including all training for commercial pilots--are classified in Industry 61151, Technical and Trade Schools;
- Operating recreation aviation clubs--are classified in Industry 71399, All Other Amusement and Recreation Industries;
- Operating advocacy aviation clubs--are classified in Industry 81331, Social Advocacy Organizations; and
- Providing air courier services--are classified in Industry 49211, Couriers and Express Delivery Services.

481211   Nonscheduled Chartered Passenger Air Transportation

This U.S. industry comprises establishments primarily engaged in providing air transportation of passengers or passengers and cargo with no regular routes and regular schedules.

Cross-References.   Establishments primarily engaged in--

- Providing specialty air transportation or flying services with no regular routes and regular schedules using general purpose aircraft--are classified in U.S. Industry 481219, Other Nonscheduled Air Transportation;
- Providing specialized air sightseeing services--are classified in Industry 487990, Scenic and Sightseeing Transportation, Other;
- Providing air transportation of passengers or passengers and cargo over regular routes and on regular schedules--are classified in U.S. Industry 481111, Scheduled Passenger Air Transportation; and
- Providing air transportation of cargo (without transporting passengers) with no regular routes and schedules--are classified in U.S. Industry 481212, Nonscheduled Chartered Freight Air Transportation.

T—Canadian, Mexican, and United States industries are comparable.

481212 Nonscheduled Chartered Freight Air Transportation

This U.S. industry comprises establishments primarily engaged in providing air transportation of cargo without transporting passengers with no regular routes and regular schedules.

Cross-References.   Establishments primarily engaged in--

- Providing specialty air transportation or flying services with no regular routes and regular schedules using general purpose aircraft--are classified in U.S. Industry 481219, Other Nonscheduled Air Transportation;
- Providing air courier services--are classified in Industry 492110, Couriers and Express Delivery Services;
- Providing air transportation of cargo without transporting passengers over regular routes and on regular schedules--are classified in U.S. Industry 481112, Scheduled Freight Air Transportation; and
- Providing air transportation of cargo and passengers with no regular routes and schedules--are classified in U.S. Industry 481211, Nonscheduled Chartered Passenger Air Transportation.

481219 Other Nonscheduled Air Transportation

This U.S. industry comprises establishments primarily engaged in providing air transportation with no regular routes and regular schedules (except nonscheduled chartered passenger and/or cargo air transportation). These establishments provide a variety of specialty air transportation or flying services based on individual customer needs using general purpose aircraft.

Illustrative Examples:

Aircraft charter services (i.e., general purpose aircraft used for a variety of specialty air and flying services)

Aviation clubs providing a variety of air transportation activities to the general public

Cross-References.   Establishments primarily engaged in--

- Providing air transportation of passengers or passengers and cargo with no regular routes and regular schedules--are classified in U.S. Industry 481211, Nonscheduled Chartered Passenger Air Transportation;
- Providing air transportation of cargo without transporting passengers with no regular routes and regular schedules--are classified in U.S. Industry 481212, Nonscheduled Chartered Freight Air Transportation;
- Crop dusting using specialized aircraft--are classified in U.S. Industry 115112, Soil Preparation, Planting, and Cultivating;
- Fighting forest fires using specialized water bombers--are classified in Industry 115310, Support Activities for Forestry;
- Providing specialized air sightseeing services--are classified in Industry 487990, Scenic and Sightseeing Transportation, Other;
- Operating specialized flying schools, including all training for commercial pilots--are classified in U.S. Industry 611512, Flight Training;
- Providing specialized air ambulance services using specialized equipment--are classified in Industry 621910, Ambulance Services;
- Operating recreation aviation clubs--are classified in Industry 713990, All Other Amusement and Recreation Industries;
- Operating advocacy aviation clubs--are classified in U.S. Industry 813319, Other Social Advocacy Organizations;
- Aerial gathering of geophysical data for surveying and mapping--are classified in Industry 541360, Geophysical Surveying and Mapping Services; and
- Providing aerial and/or other surveying and mapping services--are classified in Industry 541370, Surveying and Mapping (except Geophysical) Services.

T—Canadian, Mexican, and United States industries are comparable.

482   Rail Transportation[T]

Industries in the Rail Transportation subsector provide rail transportation of passengers and/or cargo using railroad rolling stock. The railroads in this subsector primarily either operate on networks, with physical facilities, labor force, and equipment spread over an extensive geographic area, or operate over a short distance on a local rail line.

Scenic and sightseeing rail transportation and street railroads, commuter rail, and rapid transit are not included in this subsector but are included in Subsector 487, Scenic and Sightseeing Transportation, and Subsector 485, Transit and Ground Passenger Transportation, respectively. Although these activities use railroad rolling stock, they are different from the activities included in rail transportation. Sightseeing and scenic railroads do not usually involve place-to-place transportation; the passenger's trip typically starts and ends at the same location. Commuter railroads operate in a manner more consistent with local and urban transit and are often part of integrated transit systems.

4821   Rail Transportation[T]

48211   Rail Transportation[T]

This industry comprises establishments primarily engaged in operating railroads (except street railroads, commuter rail, urban rapid transit, and scenic and sightseeing trains). Line-haul railroads and short-line railroads are included in this industry.

Cross-References.   Establishments primarily engaged in--

- Operating street railroads, commuter rail, and urban rapid transit systems--are classified in Industry Group 4851, Urban Transit Systems;
- Operating scenic and sightseeing trains--are classified in Industry 48711, Scenic and Sightseeing Transportation, Land; and
- Operating switching and terminal facilities as separate establishments--are classified in Industry 48821, Support Activities for Rail Transportation.

482111 Line-Haul Railroads

This U.S. industry comprises establishments known as line-haul railroads primarily engaged in operating railroads for the transport of passengers and/or cargo over a long distance within a rail network. These establishments provide for the intercity movement of trains between the terminals and stations on main and branch lines of a line-haul rail network (except for local switching services).

Cross-References.   Establishments primarily engaged in--

- Operating switching and terminal facilities as separate establishments--are classified in Industry 488210, Support Activities for Rail Transportation;
- Operating railroads over a short distance on local rail lines--are classified in U.S. Industry 482112, Short Line Railroads; and
- Operating commuter rail systems--are classified in U.S. Industry 485112, Commuter Rail Systems.

482112 Short Line Railroads

This U.S. industry comprises establishments known as short-line railroads primarily engaged in operating railroads for the transport of cargo over a short distance on local rail lines not part of a rail network.

Cross-References.   Establishments primarily engaged in--

- Operating street railroads, commuter rail, and urban rapid transit systems--are classified in Industry Group 4851, Urban Transit Systems;
- Operating scenic and sightseeing trains--are classified in Industry 487110, Scenic and Sightseeing Transportation, Land;

T—Canadian, Mexican, and United States industries are comparable.

- Operating switching and terminal facilities as separate establishments--are classified in Industry 488210, Support Activities for Rail Transportation; and
- Operating railroads for the transport of passengers and/or cargo over a long distance--are classified in U.S. Industry 482111, Line-Haul Railroads.

483   Water Transportation[T]

Industries in the Water Transportation subsector provide water transportation of passengers and cargo using watercraft, such as ships, barges, and boats.

The subsector is composed of two industry groups: (1) one for deep sea, coastal, and Great Lakes; and (2) one for inland water transportation. This split typically reflects the difference in equipment used.

Scenic and sightseeing water transportation services are not included in this subsector but are included in Subsector 487, Scenic and Sightseeing Transportation. Although these activities use watercraft, they are different from the activities included in water transportation. Water sightseeing does not usually involve place-to-place transportation; the passenger's trip starts and ends at the same location.

4831   Deep Sea, Coastal, and Great Lakes Water Transportation[T]

48311   Deep Sea, Coastal, and Great Lakes Water Transportation[T]

This industry comprises establishments primarily engaged in providing deep sea, coastal, Great Lakes, and St. Lawrence Seaway water transportation. Marine transportation establishments using the facilities of the St. Lawrence Seaway Authority Commission are considered to be using the Great Lakes Water Transportation System.

Cross-References.   Establishments primarily engaged in--

- Providing inland water transportation on lakes, rivers, or intracoastal waterways (except on the Great Lakes System)--are classified in Industry 48321, Inland Water Transportation;
- Providing scenic and sightseeing water transportation, such as harbor cruises--are classified in Industry 48721, Scenic and Sightseeing Transportation, Water; and
- Operating floating casinos (i.e., gambling cruises, riverboat gambling casinos)--are classified in Industry 71321, Casinos (except Casino Hotels).

483111 Deep Sea Freight Transportation

This U.S. industry comprises establishments primarily engaged in providing deep sea transportation of cargo to or from foreign ports.

Cross-References.

Establishments primarily engaged in providing deep sea transportation of cargo to and from domestic ports are classified in U.S. Industry 483113, Coastal and Great Lakes Freight Transportation.

483112 Deep Sea Passenger Transportation

This U.S. industry comprises establishments primarily engaged in providing deep sea transportation of passengers to or from foreign ports.

Cross-References.   Establishments primarily engaged in--

- Providing deep sea transportation of passengers to and from domestic ports--are classified in U.S. Industry 483114, Coastal and Great Lakes Passenger Transportation; and
- Operating floating casinos (i.e., gambling cruises)--are classified in Industry 713210, Casinos (except Casino Hotels).

T—Canadian, Mexican, and United States industries are comparable.

483113 Coastal and Great Lakes Freight Transportation

This U.S. industry comprises establishments primarily engaged in providing water transportation of cargo in coastal waters, on the Great Lakes System, or deep seas between ports of the United States, Puerto Rico, and United States island possessions or protectorates. Marine transportation establishments using the facilities of the St. Lawrence Seaway Authority Commission are considered to be using the Great Lakes Water Transportation System. Establishments primarily engaged in providing coastal and/or Great Lakes barge transportation services are included in this industry.

Cross-References.   Establishments primarily engaged in--

- Providing deep sea transportation of cargo to or from foreign ports--are classified in U.S. Industry 483111, Deep Sea Freight Transportation; and
- Providing inland water transportation of cargo on lakes, rivers, or intracoastal waterways (except on the Great Lakes System)--are classified in U.S. Industry 483211, Inland Water Freight Transportation.

483114 Coastal and Great Lakes Passenger Transportation

This U.S. industry comprises establishments primarily engaged in providing water transportation of passengers in coastal waters, the Great Lakes System, or deep seas between ports of the United States, Puerto Rico, and United States island possessions and protectorates. Marine transportation establishments using the facilities of the St. Lawrence Seaway Authority Commission are considered to be using the Great Lakes Water Transportation System.

Cross-References.   Establishments primarily engaged in--

- Providing inland water transportation of passengers on lakes, rivers, or intracoastal waterways (except on the Great Lakes System)--are classified in U.S. Industry 483212, Inland Water Passenger Transportation;
- Providing scenic and sightseeing water transportation, such as harbor cruises--are classified in Industry 487210, Scenic and Sightseeing Transportation, Water; and
- Operating floating casinos (i.e., gambling cruises)--are classified in Industry 713210, Casinos (except Casino Hotels).

4832   Inland Water Transportation[T]

48321   Inland Water Transportation[T]

This industry comprises establishments primarily engaged in providing inland water transportation of passengers and/or cargo on lakes, rivers, or intracoastal waterways (except on the Great Lakes System).

Cross-References.   Establishments primarily engaged in--

- Providing water transportation in deep sea, coastal, or on the Great Lakes System--are classified in Industry Group 4831, Deep Sea, Coastal, and Great Lakes Water Transportation;
- Providing scenic and sightseeing water transportation, such as harbor cruises--are classified in Industry 48721, Scenic and Sightseeing Transportation, Water; and
- Operating floating casinos (i.e., gambling cruises, riverboat gambling casinos)--are classified in Industry 71321, Casinos (except Casino Hotels).

483211 Inland Water Freight Transportation

This U.S. industry comprises establishments primarily engaged in providing inland water transportation of cargo on lakes, rivers, or intracoastal waterways (except on the Great Lakes System).

T—Canadian, Mexican, and United States industries are comparable.

Cross-References.   Establishments primarily engaged in--

- Providing deep sea transportation of cargo to and from foreign ports--are classified in U.S. Industry 483111, Deep Sea Freight Transportation; and
- Providing water transportation of cargo in coastal waters or on the Great Lakes System--are classified in U.S. Industry 483113, Coastal and Great Lakes Freight Transportation.

483212 Inland Water Passenger Transportation

This U.S. industry comprises establishments primarily engaged in providing inland water transportation of passengers on lakes, rivers, or intracoastal waterways (except on the Great Lakes System).

Cross-References.   Establishments primarily engaged in--

- Providing deep sea transportation of passengers to and from foreign ports--are classified in U.S. Industry 483112, Deep Sea Passenger Transportation;
- Operating floating casinos (i.e., gambling cruises, riverboat gambling casinos)--are classified in Industry 713210, Casinos (except Casino Hotels);
- Operating cruise ships or ferries in coastal waters or on the Great Lakes System--are classified in U.S. Industry 483114, Coastal and Great Lakes Passenger Transportation; and
- Providing scenic and sightseeing water transportation, such as harbor cruises--are classified in Industry 487210, Scenic and Sightseeing Transportation, Water.

484   Truck Transportation[T]

Industries in the Truck Transportation subsector provide over-the-road transportation of cargo using motor vehicles, such as trucks and tractor trailers. The subsector is subdivided into general freight trucking and specialized freight trucking. This distinction reflects differences in equipment used, type of load carried, scheduling, terminal, and other networking services. General freight transportation establishments handle a wide variety of general commodities, generally palletized, and transported in a container or van trailer. Specialized freight transportation is the transportation of cargo that, because of size, weight, shape, or other inherent characteristics, requires specialized equipment for transportation.

Each of these industry groups is further subdivided based on distance traveled. Local trucking establishments primarily carry goods within a single metropolitan area and its adjacent nonurban areas. Long-distance trucking establishments carry goods between metropolitan areas.

The Specialized Freight Trucking industry group includes a separate industry for Used Household and Office Goods Moving. The household and office goods movers are separated because of the substantial network of establishments that has developed to deal with local and long-distance moving and the associated storage. In this area, the same establishment provides both local and long-distance services, while other specialized freight establishments generally limit their services to either local or long-distance hauling.

4841   General Freight Trucking[T]

This industry group comprises establishments primarily engaged in providing general freight trucking. General freight trucking establishments handle a wide variety of commodities, generally palletized, and transported in a container or van trailer. The establishments of this industry group provide a combination of the following network activities: local pick-up, local sorting and terminal operations, line-haul, destination sorting and terminal operations, and local delivery.

48411   General Freight Trucking, Local[T]
See industry description for 484110.

T—Canadian, Mexican, and United States industries are comparable.

484110   General Freight Trucking, Local

This industry comprises establishments primarily engaged in providing local general freight trucking. General freight trucking establishments handle a wide variety of commodities, generally palletized and transported in a container or van trailer. Local general freight trucking establishments usually provide trucking within a metropolitan area which may cross state lines. Generally the trips are same-day return.

Cross-References.   Establishments primarily engaged in--

- Operating independent trucking terminals--are classified in Industry 488490, Other Support Activities for Road Transportation; and
- Providing general freight long-distance trucking including all North American international travel--are classified in Industry 48412, General Freight Trucking, Long-Distance.

48412   General Freight Trucking, Long-Distance[T]

This industry comprises establishments primarily engaged in providing long-distance general freight trucking. General freight trucking establishments handle a wide variety of commodities, generally palletized and transported in a container or van trailer. Long-distance general freight trucking establishments usually provide trucking between metropolitan areas which may cross North American country borders. Included in this industry are establishments operating as truckload (TL) or less than truckload (LTL) carriers.

Cross-References.   Establishments primarily engaged in--

- Providing courier services--are classified in Industry 49211, Couriers and Express Delivery Services;
- Providing warehousing services of general freight--are classified in Industry 49311, General Warehousing and Storage;
- Providing specialized freight trucking--are classified in Industry Group 4842, Specialized Freight Trucking;
- Operating independent trucking terminals--are classified in Industry 48849, Other Support Activities for Road Transportation; and
- Providing local general freight trucking services--are classified in Industry 48411, General Freight Trucking, Local.

484121   General Freight Trucking, Long-Distance, Truckload

This U.S. industry comprises establishments primarily engaged in providing long-distance general freight truckload (TL) trucking. These long-distance general freight truckload carrier establishments provide full truck movement of freight from origin to destination. The shipment of freight on a truck is characterized as a full single load not combined with other shipments.

Cross-References.   Establishments primarily engaged in--

- Providing general freight long-distance, less than truckload trucking--are classified in U.S. Industry 484122, General Freight Trucking, Long-Distance, Less Than Truckload;
- Providing specialized freight trucking--are classified in Industry Group 4842, Specialized Freight Trucking;
- Operating independent trucking terminals--are classified in Industry 488490, Other Support Activities for Road Transportation; and
- Providing local general freight trucking services--are classified in Industry 484110, General Freight Trucking, Local.

484122   General Freight Trucking, Long-Distance, Less Than Truckload

This U.S. industry comprises establishments primarily engaged in providing long-distance, general freight, less than truckload (LTL) trucking. LTL carriage is characterized as multiple shipments combined onto a single truck for multiple deliveries within a network. These establishments are generally characterized by the following network

---

T—Canadian, Mexican, and United States industries are comparable.

activities: local pick-up, local sorting and terminal operations, line-haul, destination sorting and terminal operations, and local delivery.

Cross-References.   Establishments primarily engaged in--

- Providing courier services--are classified in Industry 492110, Couriers and Express Delivery Services;
- Providing warehousing services of general freight--are classified in Industry 493110, General Warehousing and Storage;
- Providing specialized freight trucking--are classified in Industry Group 4842, Specialized Freight Trucking;
- Operating independent trucking terminals--are classified in Industry 488490, Other Support Activities for Road Transportation;
- Providing general freight long-distance truckload trucking--are classified in U.S. Industry 484121, General Freight Trucking, Long-Distance, Truckload; and
- Providing local general freight trucking services--are classified in Industry 484110, General Freight Trucking, Local.

4842   Specialized Freight Trucking[T]

This industry group comprises establishments primarily engaged in providing local or long-distance specialized freight trucking. The establishments of this industry are primarily engaged in the transportation of freight which, because of size, weight, shape, or other inherent characteristics, requires specialized equipment, such as flatbeds, tankers, or refrigerated trailers. This industry includes the transportation of used household, institutional, and commercial furniture and equipment.

48421   Used Household and Office Goods Moving[T]
See industry description for 484210.

484210   Used Household and Office Goods Moving

This industry comprises establishments primarily engaged in providing local or long-distance trucking of used household, used institutional, or used commercial furniture and equipment. Incidental packing and storage activities are often provided by these establishments.

48422   Specialized Freight (except Used Goods) Trucking, Local[T]
See industry description for 484220.

484220   Specialized Freight (except Used Goods) Trucking, Local

This industry comprises establishments primarily engaged in providing local, specialized trucking. Local trucking establishments provide trucking within a metropolitan area that may cross state lines. Generally the trips are same-day return.

Illustrative Examples:

Local agricultural products trucking
Local dump trucking (e.g., gravel, sand, top-soil)
Local boat hauling

Local livestock trucking
Local bulk liquids trucking

Cross-References.   Establishments primarily engaged in--

- Providing long-distance specialized freight (except used goods) trucking including all North American international travel--are classified in Industry 484230, Specialized Freight (except Used Goods) Trucking, Long-Distance;
- Providing local general freight trucking--are classified in Industry 484110, General Freight Trucking, Local;

T—Canadian, Mexican, and United States industries are comparable.

- Providing trucking of used household and office goods--are classified in Industry 484210, Used Household and Office Goods Moving; and
- Providing waste collection--are classified in Industry Group 5621, Waste Collection.

48423   Specialized Freight (except Used Goods) Trucking, Long-Distance[T]
See industry description for 484230.

484230 Specialized Freight (except Used Goods) Trucking, Long-Distance

This industry comprises establishments primarily engaged in providing long-distance specialized trucking. These establishments provide trucking between metropolitan areas that may cross North American country borders.

Illustrative Examples:

Long-distance automobile carrier trucking   Long-distance trucking of waste
Long-distance refrigerated product trucking   Long-distance hazardous material trucking
Long-distance bulk liquid trucking

Cross-References.   Establishments primarily engaged in--

- Providing local specialized freight trucking (except used goods)--are classified in Industry 484220, Specialized Freight (except Used Goods) Trucking, Local;
- Providing long-distance general freight trucking including all North American international travel--are classified in Industry 48412, General Freight Trucking, Long-Distance;
- Providing trucking of used household and office goods--are classified in Industry 484210, Used Household and Office Goods Moving; and
- Collecting and/or hauling hazardous waste, nonhazardous waste, and/or recyclable materials within a local area--are classified in Industry 56211, Waste Collection.

485   Transit and Ground Passenger Transportation[T]

Industries in the Transit and Ground Passenger Transportation subsector include a variety of passenger transportation activities, such as urban transit systems; chartered bus, school bus, and interurban bus transportation; and taxis. These activities are distinguished based primarily on such production process factors as vehicle types, routes, and schedules.

In this subsector, the principal splits identify scheduled transportation as separate from nonscheduled transportation. The scheduled transportation industry groups are Urban Transit Systems, Interurban and Rural Bus Transportation, and School and Employee Bus Transportation. The nonscheduled industry groups are the Charter Bus Industry and Taxi and Limousine Service. The Other Transit and Ground Passenger Transportation industry group includes both scheduled and nonscheduled transportation.

Scenic and sightseeing ground transportation services are not included in this subsector but are included in Subsector 487, Scenic and Sightseeing Transportation. Sightseeing does not usually involve place-to-place transportation; the passenger's trip starts and ends at the same location.

4851   Urban Transit Systems[T]

48511   Urban Transit Systems[T]

This industry comprises establishments primarily engaged in operating local and suburban passenger transit systems over regular routes and on regular schedules within a metropolitan area and its adjacent nonurban areas. Such transportation systems involve the use of one or more modes of transport including light rail, commuter rail, subways, and streetcars, as well as buses and other motor vehicles.

T—Canadian, Mexican, and United States industries are comparable.

Cross-References. Establishments primarily engaged in--

- Providing scenic and sightseeing transportation on land--are classified in Industry 48711, Scenic and Sightseeing Transportation, Land;
- Providing support services to transit and ground transportation--are classified in Industry Group 4884, Support Activities for Road Transportation; and
- Providing interurban and rural bus transportation--are classified in Industry 48521, Interurban and Rural Bus Transportation.

485111 Mixed Mode Transit Systems

This U.S. industry comprises establishments primarily engaged in operating local and suburban ground passenger transit systems using more than one mode of transport over regular routes and on regular schedules within a metropolitan area and its adjacent nonurban areas.

Cross-References. Establishments primarily engaged in--

- Operating local and suburban passenger transit systems using only one mode of transportation--are classified according to the mode of transport; and
- Providing support services to transit and ground passenger transportation--are classified in Industry Group 4884, Support Activities for Road Transportation.

485112 Commuter Rail Systems

This U.S. industry comprises establishments primarily engaged in operating local and suburban commuter rail systems over regular routes and on a regular schedule within a metropolitan area and its adjacent nonurban areas. Commuter rail is usually characterized by reduced fares, multiple ride and commutation tickets, and mostly used by passengers during the morning and evening peak periods.

Cross-References. Establishments primarily engaged in--

- Operating local and suburban mass passenger transit systems using both commuter rail and another mode of transport--are classified in U.S. Industry 485111, Mixed Mode Transit Systems;
- Operating a subway system--are classified in U.S. Industry 485119, Other Urban Transit Systems; and
- Providing scenic and sightseeing transportation on land--are classified in Industry 487110, Scenic and Sightseeing Transportation, Land.

485113 Bus and Other Motor Vehicle Transit Systems

This U.S. industry comprises establishments primarily engaged in operating local and suburban passenger transportation systems using buses or other motor vehicles over regular routes and on regular schedules within a metropolitan area and its adjacent nonurban areas.

Cross-References. Establishments primarily engaged in--

- Operating local and suburban passenger transportation systems using both a bus or other motor vehicle and another mode of transport--are classified in U.S. Industry 485111, Mixed Mode Transit Systems;
- Providing interurban and rural bus transportation--are classified in Industry 485210, Interurban and Rural Bus Transportation; and
- Providing scenic and sightseeing transportation using buses or other motor vehicles--are classified in Industry 487110, Scenic and Sightseeing Transportation, Land.

T—Canadian, Mexican, and United States industries are comparable.

485119 Other Urban Transit Systems

This U.S. industry comprises establishments primarily engaged in operating local and suburban ground passenger transit systems (except mixed mode transit systems, commuter rail systems, and buses and other motor vehicles) over regular routes and on regular schedules within a metropolitan area and its adjacent nonurban areas.

Illustrative Examples:

Commuter cable car systems (i.e., stand-alone)
Light rail systems (i.e., stand-alone)
Commuter tramway systems (i.e., stand-alone)

Monorail transit systems (i.e., stand-alone)
Commuter trolley systems (i.e., stand-alone)

Cross-References.   Establishments primarily engaged in--

- Operating local and suburban ground passenger transit systems using more than one mode of transport--are classified in U.S. Industry 485111, Mixed Mode Transit Systems;
- Providing local and suburban passenger transportation using commuter rail systems--are classified in U.S. Industry 485112, Commuter Rail Systems; and
- Operating local and suburban bus transit systems--are classified in U.S. Industry 485113, Bus and Other Motor Vehicle Transit Systems.

4852   Interurban and Rural Bus Transportation[T]

48521   Interurban and Rural Bus Transportation[T]
See industry description for 485210.

485210 Interurban and Rural Bus Transportation

This industry comprises establishments primarily engaged in providing bus passenger transportation over regular routes and on regular schedules, principally outside a single metropolitan area and its adjacent nonurban areas.

Cross-References.   Establishments primarily engaged in--

- Providing scenic and sightseeing transportation using buses--are classified in Industry 487110, Scenic and Sightseeing Transportation, Land;
- Providing buses for charter--are classified in Industry 485510, Charter Bus Industry;
- Operating local and suburban bus transit systems--are classified in U.S. Industry 485113, Bus and Other Motor Vehicle Transit Systems; and
- Operating independent bus terminals--are classified in Industry 488490, Other Support Activities for Road Transportation.

4853   Taxi and Limousine Service[T]

This industry group comprises establishments primarily engaged in providing passenger transportation by automobile or van or providing an array of specialty and luxury passenger transportation services via limousine or luxury sedan generally on a reserved basis. These establishments do not operate over regular routes and on regular schedules.

48531   Taxi Service[T]
See industry description for 485310.

T—Canadian, Mexican, and United States industries are comparable.

485310 Taxi Service

This industry comprises establishments primarily engaged in providing passenger transportation by automobile or van, not operated over regular routes and on regular schedules. Establishments of taxicab owner/operators, taxicab fleet operators, or taxicab organizations are included in this industry.

Cross-References. Establishments primarily engaged in--

- Providing special needs transportation services (except to and from school or work) for the infirm, elderly, or handicapped--are classified in U.S. Industry 485991, Special Needs Transportation;
- Providing limousine services--are classified in Industry 485320, Limousine Service; and
- Providing scheduled shuttle services between hotels, airports, or other destination points--are classified in U.S. Industry 485999, All Other Transit and Ground Passenger Transportation.

48532 Limousine Service[T]
See industry description for 485320.

485320 Limousine Service

This industry comprises establishments primarily engaged in providing an array of specialty and luxury passenger transportation services via limousine or luxury sedan generally on a reserved basis. These establishments do not operate over regular routes and on regular schedules.

Cross-References. Establishments primarily engaged in--

- Providing taxi services--are classified in Industry 485310, Taxi Service; and
- Providing scheduled shuttle services between hotels, airports, or other destination points--are classified in U.S. Industry 485999, All Other Transit and Ground Passenger Transportation.

4854 School and Employee Bus Transportation[T]

48541 School and Employee Bus Transportation[T]
See industry description for 485410.

485410 School and Employee Bus Transportation

This industry comprises establishments primarily engaged in providing buses and other motor vehicles to transport pupils to and from school or employees to and from work.

Cross-References. Establishments primarily engaged in--

- Operating local and suburban bus transit systems--are classified in U.S. Industry 485113, Bus and Other Motor Vehicle Transit Systems;
- Providing interurban and rural bus transportation--are classified in Industry 485210, Interurban and Rural Bus Transportation; and
- Providing buses for charter--are classified in Industry 485510, Charter Bus Industry.

4855 Charter Bus Industry[T]

48551 Charter Bus Industry[T]
See industry description for 485510.

T--Canadian, Mexican, and United States industries are comparable.

485510 Charter Bus Industry

This industry comprises establishments primarily engaged in providing buses for charter. These establishments provide bus services to meet customers' road transportation needs and generally do not operate over fixed routes and on regular schedules.

Cross-References.   Establishments primarily engaged in--

- Providing scenic and local sightseeing transportation using buses--are classified in Industry 487110, Scenic and Sightseeing Transportation, Land; and
- Providing interurban and rural bus transportation--are classified in Industry 485210, Interurban and Rural Bus Transportation.

4859   Other Transit and Ground Passenger Transportation[T]

48599   Other Transit and Ground Passenger Transportation[T]

This industry comprises establishments primarily engaged in providing other transit and ground passenger transportation (except urban transit systems, interurban and rural bus transportation, taxi services, school and employee bus transportation, charter bus services, and limousine services (except shuttle services)). Shuttle services (except employee bus) and special needs transportation services are included in this industry. Shuttle services establishments generally travel within a metropolitan area and its adjacent nonurban areas on regular routes, on regular schedules and provide services between hotels, airports, or other destination points. Establishments in the Special Needs Transportation industry provide passenger transportation to the infirm, elderly, or handicapped. These establishments may use specially equipped vehicles to provide passenger transportation.

Cross-References.   Establishments primarily engaged in--

- Providing school or employee bus transportation for the infirm, elderly, or handicapped--are classified in Industry 48541, School and Employee Bus Transportation;
- Providing ambulance services for emergency and medical purposes--are classified in Industry 62191, Ambulance Services;
- Operating urban transit systems--are classified in Industry Group 4851, Urban Transit Systems;
- Providing interurban and rural bus transportation--are classified in Industry 48521, Interurban and Rural Bus Transportation;
- Providing taxi services and/or limousine services (except shuttle services)--are classified in Industry Group 4853, Taxi and Limousine Service; and
- Providing buses for charter--are classified in Industry 48551, Charter Bus Industry.

485991 Special Needs Transportation

This U.S. industry comprises establishments primarily engaged in providing special needs transportation (except to and from school or work) to the infirm, elderly, or handicapped. These establishments may use specially equipped vehicles to provide passenger transportation.

Cross-References.   Establishments primarily engaged in--

- Providing school or employee bus transportation for the infirm, elderly, or handicapped--are classified in Industry 485410, School and Employee Bus Transportation; and
- Providing ambulance services for emergency and medical purposes--are classified in Industry 621910, Ambulance Services.

T—Canadian, Mexican, and United States industries are comparable.

485999 All Other Transit and Ground Passenger Transportation

This U.S. industry comprises establishments primarily engaged in providing ground passenger transportation (except urban transit systems; interurban and rural bus transportation, taxi and/or limousine services (except shuttle services), school and employee bus transportation, charter bus services, and special needs transportation). Establishments primarily engaged in operating shuttle services and vanpools are included in this industry. Shuttle services establishments generally provide travel on regular routes and on regular schedules between hotels, airports, or other destination points.

Cross-References. Establishments primarily engaged in--

- Operating urban transit systems--are classified in Industry Group 4851, Urban Transit Systems;
- Providing interurban and rural bus transportation--are classified in Industry 485210, Interurban and Rural Bus Transportation;
- Providing taxi and/or limousine services (except shuttle services)--are classified in Industry Group 4853, Taxi and Limousine Service;
- Providing school and employee bus transportation (including for the infirm, elderly, or handicapped)--are classified in Industry 485410, School and Employee Bus Transportation;
- Providing buses for charter--are classified in Industry 485510, Charter Bus Industry;
- Providing special needs transportation (except to and from school or work) for the infirm, elderly, or handicapped--are classified in U.S. Industry 485991, Special Needs Transportation; and
- Providing ambulance services for emergency and medical purposes--are classified in Industry 621910, Ambulance Services.

486 Pipeline Transportation[T]

Industries in the Pipeline Transportation subsector use transmission pipelines to transport products, such as crude oil, natural gas, refined petroleum products, and slurry. Industries are identified based on the products transported (i.e., pipeline transportation of crude oil, natural gas, refined petroleum products, and other products).

The Pipeline Transportation of Natural Gas industry includes the storage of natural gas because the storage is usually done by the pipeline establishment and because a pipeline is inherently a network in which all the nodes are interdependent.

4861 Pipeline Transportation of Crude Oil[T]

48611 Pipeline Transportation of Crude Oil[T]
See industry description for 486110.

486110 Pipeline Transportation of Crude Oil

This industry comprises establishments primarily engaged in the pipeline transportation of crude oil.

Cross-References. Establishments primarily engaged in--

- Providing the pipeline transportation of natural gas--are classified in Industry 486210, Pipeline Transportation of Natural Gas;
- Providing the pipeline transportation of refined petroleum products--are classified in Industry 486910, Pipeline Transportation of Refined Petroleum Products; and
- Operating oil and gas field gathering lines--are classified in Sector 21, Mining, Quarrying, and Oil and Gas Extraction.

4862 Pipeline Transportation of Natural Gas[T]

48621 Pipeline Transportation of Natural Gas[T]
See industry description for 486210.

T—Canadian, Mexican, and United States industries are comparable.

486210 Pipeline Transportation of Natural Gas

This industry comprises establishments primarily engaged in the pipeline transportation of natural gas from processing plants to local distribution systems. This industry includes the storage of natural gas because the storage is usually done by the pipeline establishment and because a pipeline is inherently a network in which all the nodes are interdependent.

Cross-References.　　Establishments primarily engaged in--

- Operating oil and gas field gathering lines--are classified in Sector 21, Mining, Quarrying, and Oil and Gas Extraction; and
- Providing natural gas to the end consumer--are classified in Industry 221210, Natural Gas Distribution.

4869　Other Pipeline Transportation[T]

This industry group comprises establishments primarily engaged in the pipeline transportation of products (except crude oil and natural gas).

48691　Pipeline Transportation of Refined Petroleum Products[T]
See industry description for 486910.

486910 Pipeline Transportation of Refined Petroleum Products

This industry comprises establishments primarily engaged in the pipeline transportation of refined petroleum products.

48699　All Other Pipeline Transportation[T]
See industry description for 486990.

486990 All Other Pipeline Transportation

This industry comprises establishments primarily engaged in the pipeline transportation of products (except crude oil, natural gas, and refined petroleum products).

Cross-References.　　Establishments primarily engaged in--

- Providing pipeline transportation of crude oil--are classified in Industry 486110, Pipeline Transportation of Crude Oil;
- Providing pipeline transportation of natural gas--are classified in Industry 486210, Pipeline Transportation of Natural Gas;
- Providing pipeline transportation of refined petroleum products--are classified in Industry 486910, Pipeline Transportation of Refined Petroleum Products; and
- Operating water distribution systems--are classified in Industry 221310, Water Supply and Irrigation Systems.

487　Scenic and Sightseeing Transportation[T]

Industries in the Scenic and Sightseeing Transportation subsector utilize transportation equipment to provide recreation and entertainment. These activities have a production process distinct from passenger transportation carried out for the purpose of other types of for-hire transportation. This process does not emphasize efficient transportation; in fact, such activities often use obsolete vehicles, such as steam trains, to provide some extra ambience. The activity is local in nature, usually involving a same-day return to the point of departure.
The Scenic and Sightseeing Transportation subsector is separated into three industries based on the mode: land, water, and other.

T—Canadian, Mexican, and United States industries are comparable.

Activities that are recreational in nature and involve participation by the customer, such as white water rafting, are generally excluded from this subsector, unless they impose an impact on part of the transportation system. Charter boat fishing, for example, is included in the Scenic and Sightseeing Transportation, Water industry.

4871   Scenic and Sightseeing Transportation, Land[T]

48711   Scenic and Sightseeing Transportation, Land[T]
See industry description for 487110.

487110   Scenic and Sightseeing Transportation, Land

This industry comprises establishments primarily engaged in providing scenic and sightseeing transportation on land, such as sightseeing buses and trolleys, steam train excursions, and horse-drawn sightseeing rides. The services provided are usually local and involve same-day return to place of origin.

Cross-References.   Establishments primarily engaged in--

- Operating aerial trams or aerial cable cars--are classified in Industry 487990, Scenic and Sightseeing Transportation, Other;
- Providing sporting services, such as pack trains--are classified in Industry 713990, All Other Amusement and Recreation Industries;
- Providing intercity and rural bus transportation--are classified in Industry 485210, Interurban and Rural Bus Transportation;
- Providing buses for charter--are classified in Industry 485510, Charter Bus Industry;
- Operating local and suburban passenger transit systems--are classified in Industry 48511, Urban Transit Systems; and
- Providing passenger travel arrangements and tours--are classified in Industry Group 5615, Travel Arrangement and Reservation Services.

4872   Scenic and Sightseeing Transportation, Water[T]

48721   Scenic and Sightseeing Transportation, Water[T]
See industry description for 487210.

487210   Scenic and Sightseeing Transportation, Water

This industry comprises establishments primarily engaged in providing scenic and sightseeing transportation on water. The services provided are usually local and involve same-day return to place of origin.

Illustrative Examples:

Airboat (i.e., swamp buggy) operation   Harbor sightseeing tours
Excursion boat operation   Dinner cruises
Charter fishing boat services

Cross-References.   Establishments primarily engaged in--

- Providing recreation services, such as fishing guides, white water rafting, parasailing, and water skiing--are classified in Industry 713990, All Other Amusement and Recreation Industries;
- Providing water taxi services--are classified in Industry 48321, Inland Water Transportation;
- Providing water transportation of passengers--are classified in Subsector 483, Water Transportation;
- Operating floating casinos (i.e., gambling cruises or riverboat casinos)--are classified in Industry 713210, Casinos (except Casino Hotels); and
- Providing boat rental without operators--are classified in U.S. Industry 532284, Recreational Goods Rental.

T—Canadian, Mexican, and United States industries are comparable.

4879 Scenic and Sightseeing Transportation, Other[T]

48799 Scenic and Sightseeing Transportation, Other[T]
See industry description for 487990.

487990 Scenic and Sightseeing Transportation, Other

This industry comprises establishments primarily engaged in providing scenic and sightseeing transportation (except on land and water). The services provided are usually local and involve same-day return to place of departure.

Illustrative Examples:

Aerial cable cars, scenic and sightseeing operation
Helicopter rides, scenic and sightseeing operation
Aerial tramways, scenic and sightseeing operation

Hot air balloon rides, scenic and sightseeing operation
Glider excursions

Cross-References. Establishments primarily engaged in--

- Providing recreational activities, such as hang gliding--are classified in Industry 713990, All Other Amusement and Recreation Industries; and
- Providing scheduled or nonscheduled air transportation of passengers or specialty flying services--are classified in Subsector 481, Air Transportation.

488 Support Activities for Transportation[T]

Industries in the Support Activities for Transportation subsector provide services which support transportation. These services may be provided to transportation carrier establishments or to the general public. This subsector includes a wide array of establishments, including air traffic control services, marine cargo handling, and motor vehicle towing.

The Support Activities for Transportation subsector includes services to transportation but is separated by type of mode serviced. The Support Activities for Rail Transportation industry includes services to the rail industry (e.g., railroad switching and terminal establishments).

Ship repair and maintenance not done in a shipyard are included in the Other Support Activities for Water Transportation industry. An example would be floating drydock services in a harbor.

Excluded from this subsector are establishments primarily engaged in providing factory conversion and overhaul of transportation equipment, which are classified in Subsector 336, Transportation Equipment Manufacturing. Also, establishments primarily engaged in providing rental and leasing of transportation equipment without operator are classified in Subsector 532, Rental and Leasing Services.

4881 Support Activities for Air Transportation[T]

This industry group comprises establishments primarily engaged in providing services to the air transportation industry. These services include airport operation, servicing, repairing (except factory conversion and overhaul of aircraft), maintaining and storing aircraft, and ferrying aircraft.

48811 Airport Operations[T]

This industry comprises establishments primarily engaged in (1) operating international, national, or civil airports or public flying fields or (2) supporting airport operations (except special food services contractors), such as rental of hangar space, air traffic control services, baggage handling services, and cargo handling services.

T—Canadian, Mexican, and United States industries are comparable.

Cross-References.　　　Establishments primarily engaged in--

- Providing factory conversion, overhaul, and rebuilding of aircraft--are classified in Industry 33641, Aerospace Product and Parts Manufacturing;
- Wholesaling fuel at airports--are classified in Industry 42472, Petroleum and Petroleum Products Merchant Wholesalers (except Bulk Stations and Terminals);
- Providing airport janitorial services--are classified in Industry 56172, Janitorial Services; and
- Providing food services at airports on a contractual arrangement (i.e., food service contractors)--are classified in Industry 72231, Food Service Contractors.

488111 Air Traffic Control

This U.S. industry comprises establishments primarily engaged in providing air traffic control services to regulate the flow of air traffic.

488119 Other Airport Operations

This U.S. industry comprises establishments primarily engaged in (1) operating international, national, or civil airports, or public flying fields or (2) supporting airport operations, such as rental of hangar space, and providing baggage handling and/or cargo handling services.

Cross-References.　　　Establishments primarily engaged in--

- Providing air traffic control services--are classified in U.S. Industry 488111, Air Traffic Control;
- Providing factory conversion, overhaul, and rebuilding of aircraft--are classified in Industry 33641, Aerospace Product and Parts Manufacturing;
- Wholesaling fuel at airports--are classified in Industry 424720, Petroleum and Petroleum Products Merchant Wholesalers (except Bulk Stations and Terminals);
- Providing airport janitorial services--are classified in Industry 561720, Janitorial Services; and
- Providing food services at airports on a contractual arrangement (i.e., food service contractors)--are classified in Industry 722310, Food Service Contractors.

48819 Other Support Activities for Air Transportation[T]
See industry description for 488190.

488190 Other Support Activities for Air Transportation

This industry comprises establishments primarily engaged in providing specialized services for air transportation (except air traffic control and other airport operations).

Illustrative Examples:

Aircraft maintenance and repair services (except factory conversions, overhauls, rebuilding)

Aircraft passenger screening security services
Aircraft testing services

Cross-References.　　　Establishments primarily engaged in--

- Wholesaling fuel at airports--are classified in Industry 424720, Petroleum and Petroleum Products Merchant Wholesalers (except Bulk Stations and Terminals);
- Providing aircraft janitorial services--are classified in Industry 561720, Janitorial Services;
- Providing air traffic control services--are classified in U.S. Industry 488111, Air Traffic Control;
- Providing airport operations (except air traffic control)--are classified in U.S. Industry 488119, Other Airport Operations;
- Providing factory conversion, overhaul, and rebuilding of aircraft--are classified in Industry 33641, Aerospace Product and Parts Manufacturing; and

---

T—Canadian, Mexican, and United States industries are comparable.

- Providing food services to airlines on a contractual arrangement (i.e., food service contractors)--are classified in Industry 722310, Food Service Contractors.

4882 Support Activities for Rail Transportation[T]

48821 Support Activities for Rail Transportation[T]
See industry description for 488210.

488210 Support Activities for Rail Transportation

This industry comprises establishments primarily engaged in providing specialized services for railroad transportation including servicing, routine repairing (except factory conversion, overhaul, or rebuilding of rolling stock), and maintaining rail cars; loading and unloading rail cars; and operating independent terminals.

Cross-References. Establishments primarily engaged in--

- Providing railroad car rental--are classified in U.S. Industry 532411, Commercial Air, Rail, and Water Transportation Equipment Rental and Leasing;
- Factory conversion, overhaul, or rebuilding of railroad rolling stock--are classified in Industry 336510, Railroad Rolling Stock Manufacturing; and
- Providing rail car janitorial services--are classified in Industry 561720, Janitorial Services.

4883 Support Activities for Water Transportation[T]

This industry group comprises establishments primarily engaged in one of the following: (1) operating ports, harbors (including docking and pier facilities), or canals; (2) providing stevedoring and other marine cargo handling services (except warehousing); (3) providing navigational services to shipping; or (4) providing other services to water transportation.

48831 Port and Harbor Operations[T]
See industry description for 488310.

488310 Port and Harbor Operations

This industry comprises establishments primarily engaged in operating ports, harbors (including docking and pier facilities), or canals.

Cross-References. Establishments primarily engaged in--

- Providing stevedoring and other marine cargo handling services--are classified in Industry 488320, Marine Cargo Handling;
- Providing navigational services to shipping--are classified in Industry 488330, Navigational Services to Shipping; and
- Operating docking and/or storage facilities, known as marinas--are classified in Industry 713930, Marinas.

48832 Marine Cargo Handling[T]
See industry description for 488320.

488320 Marine Cargo Handling

This industry comprises establishments primarily engaged in providing stevedoring and other marine cargo handling services (except warehousing).

T—Canadian, Mexican, and United States industries are comparable.

Cross-References.   Establishments primarily engaged in--

- Preparing freight for transportation--are classified in U.S. Industry 488991, Packing and Crating;
- Operating general merchandise, refrigerated, or other warehousing and storage facilities--are classified in Subsector 493, Warehousing and Storage; and
- Operating docking and pier facilities--are classified in Industry 488310, Port and Harbor Operations.

48833   Navigational Services to Shipping[T]
See industry description for 488330.

488330 Navigational Services to Shipping

This industry comprises establishments primarily engaged in providing navigational services to shipping. Marine salvage establishments are included in this industry.

Illustrative Examples:

Docking and undocking marine vessel services
Piloting services, water transportation

Marine vessel traffic reporting services
Tugboat services, harbor operation

Cross-References.   Establishments primarily engaged in--

- Providing water transportation of barges (except coastal or Great Lakes barge transportation services)--are classified in U.S. Industry 483211, Inland Water Freight Transportation; and
- Providing coastal and/or Great Lakes barge transportation services--are classified in U.S. Industry 483113, Coastal and Great Lakes Freight Transportation.

48839   Other Support Activities for Water Transportation[T]
See industry description for 488390.

488390 Other Support Activities for Water Transportation

This industry comprises establishments primarily engaged in providing services to water transportation (except port and harbor operations; marine cargo handling services; and navigational services to shipping).

Illustrative Examples:

Floating drydocks (i.e., routine repair and
maintenance of ships)

Ship scaling services
Marine cargo checkers and surveyors

Cross-References.   Establishments primarily engaged in--

- Ship painting--are classified in Industry 238320, Painting and Wall Covering Contractors;
- Providing ship janitorial services--are classified in Industry 561720, Janitorial Services;
- Operating port, harbor, or canal facilities--are classified in Industry 488310, Port and Harbor Operations;
- Providing dredging services--are classified in Industry 237990, Other Heavy and Civil Engineering Construction;
- Providing stevedoring and other marine cargo handling services--are classified in Industry 488320, Marine Cargo Handling;
- Providing navigational services to shipping--are classified in Industry 488330, Navigational Services to Shipping; and
- Providing ship overhauling or repairs in a shipyard--are classified in U.S. Industry 336611, Ship Building and Repairing.

T—Canadian, Mexican, and United States industries are comparable.

4884 Support Activities for Road Transportation[T]

This industry group comprises establishments primarily engaged in (1) towing light or heavy motor vehicles, both local and long-distance, or (2) providing other services to road network users.

48841 Motor Vehicle Towing[T]
See industry description for 488410.

488410 Motor Vehicle Towing

This industry comprises establishments primarily engaged in towing light or heavy motor vehicles, both local and long-distance. These establishments may provide incidental services, such as storage and emergency road repair services.

Cross-References. Establishments primarily engaged in--

- Operating gasoline stations--are classified in Industry Group 4471, Gasoline Stations;
- Providing automotive repair and maintenance--are classified in Industry Group 8111, Automotive Repair and Maintenance; and
- Both retailing automotive parts and accessories, and repairing automobiles, known as automotive supply stores--are classified in Industry 441310, Automotive Parts and Accessories Stores.

48849 Other Support Activities for Road Transportation[T]
See industry description for 488490.

488490 Other Support Activities for Road Transportation

This industry comprises establishments primarily engaged in providing services (except motor vehicle towing) to road network users.

Illustrative Examples:

Bridge, tunnel, and highway operations
Pilot car services (i.e., wide load warning services)

Driving services (e.g., automobile, truck delivery)
Truck or weighing station operations

Cross-References. Establishments primarily engaged in--

- Providing automotive repair and maintenance--are classified in Industry Group 8111, Automotive Repair and Maintenance;
- Providing towing services to motor vehicles--are classified in Industry 488410, Motor Vehicle Towing;
- Providing a network for busing in combination with providing terminal services--are classified in Industry 485210, Interurban and Rural Bus Transportation; and
- Providing a network for trucking in combination with providing terminal services--are classified in Subsector 484, Truck Transportation.

4885 Freight Transportation Arrangement[T]

48851 Freight Transportation Arrangement[T]
See industry description for 488510.

488510 Freight Transportation Arrangement

This industry comprises establishments primarily engaged in arranging transportation of freight between shippers and carriers. These establishments are usually known as freight forwarders, marine shipping agents, or customs brokers and offer a combination of services spanning transportation modes.

T—Canadian, Mexican, and United States industries are comparable.

Cross-References.

Establishments primarily engaged in tariff and freight rate consulting services are classified in U.S. Industry 541614, Process, Physical Distribution, and Logistics Consulting Services.

4889   Other Support Activities for Transportation[T]

48899   Other Support Activities for Transportation[T]

This industry comprises establishments primarily engaged in providing support activities to transportation (except for air transportation; rail transportation; water transportation; road transportation; and freight transportation arrangement).

Illustrative Examples:

Arrangement of vanpools or carpools   Independent pipeline terminal facilities
Stockyards (i.e., not for fattening or selling livestock)

Cross-References.   Establishments primarily engaged in--

- Providing support activities for air transportation--are classified in Industry Group 4881, Support Activities for Air Transportation;
- Providing support activities for rail transportation--are classified in Industry Group 4882, Support Activities for Rail Transportation;
- Providing support activities for water transportation--are classified in Industry Group 4883, Support Activities for Water Transportation;
- Providing support activities for road transportation--are classified in Industry Group 4884, Support Activities for Road Transportation;
- Arranging transportation of freight between shippers and carriers--are classified in Industry 48851, Freight Transportation Arrangement;
- Providing tariff and freight rate consulting services--are classified in Industry 54161, Management Consulting Services;
- Operating stockyards for fattening livestock--are classified in Subsector 112, Animal Production and Aquaculture; and
- Providing packaging and labeling services--are classified in Industry 56191, Packaging and Labeling Services.

488991   Packing and Crating

This U.S. industry comprises establishments primarily engaged in packing, crating, and otherwise preparing goods for transportation.

Cross-References.

Establishments primarily engaged in providing packaging and labeling services are classified in Industry 561910, Packaging and Labeling Services.

488999   All Other Support Activities for Transportation

This U.S. industry comprises establishments primarily engaged in providing support activities to transportation (except for air transportation; rail transportation; water transportation; road transportation; freight transportation arrangement; and packing and crating).

T—Canadian, Mexican, and United States industries are comparable.

Illustrative Examples:

Arrangement of vanpools or carpools
Stockyards (i.e., not for fattening or selling livestock)

Independent pipeline terminal facilities

Cross-References.   Establishments primarily engaged in--

- Operating stockyards for fattening livestock--are classified in Subsector 112, Animal Production and Aquaculture;
- Providing tariff and freight rate consulting services--are classified in U.S. Industry 541614, Process, Physical Distribution, and Logistics Consulting Services;
- Providing packing and crating services for transportation--are classified in U.S. Industry 488991, Packing and Crating;
- Providing support activities for air transportation--are classified in Industry Group 4881, Support Activities for Air Transportation;
- Providing support activities for rail transportation--are classified in Industry 488210, Support Activities for Rail Transportation;
- Providing support activities for water transportation--are classified in Industry Group 4883, Support Activities for Water Transportation;
- Providing support activities for road transportation--are classified in Industry Group 4884, Support Activities for Road Transportation; and
- Arranging transportation of freight between shippers and carriers--are classified in Industry 488510, Freight Transportation Arrangement.

491   Postal Service[T]

The Postal Service subsector includes the activities of the National Post Office and its subcontractors operating under a universal service obligation to provide mail services, and using the infrastructure required to fulfill that obligation. These services include delivering letters and small parcels. These articles can be described as those that can be handled by one person without using special equipment. This allows the collection, pick-up, and delivery operations to be done with limited labor costs and minimal equipment. Sorting and transportation activities, where necessary, are generally mechanized. The restriction to small parcels distinguishes these establishments from those in the transportation industries. These establishments may also provide express delivery services using the infrastructure established for provision of basic mail services.

The traditional activity of the National Postal Service is described in this subsector. Subcontractors include rural post offices on contract to the Postal Service.

Bulk transportation of mail on contract to the Postal Service is not included here, because it is usually done by transportation establishments that carry other customers' cargo as well. Establishments that provide courier and express delivery services without operating under a universal service obligation are classified in Subsector 492, Couriers and Messengers.

4911   Postal Service[T]

49111   Postal Service[T]
See industry description for 491110.

491110   Postal Service

This industry comprises establishments primarily engaged in providing mail services under a universal service obligation. Mail services include the carriage of letters, printed matter, or mailable packages, including acceptance, collection, processing, and delivery. Due to the infrastructure requirements of providing mail service under a universal service obligation, postal service establishments often provide parcel and express delivery services in addition to the mail service. Establishments primarily engaged in performing one or more parts of the basic mail service, such as sorting, routing and/or delivery (except bulk transportation of mail) are included in this industry.

T—Canadian, Mexican, and United States industries are comparable.

Cross-References.   Establishments primarily engaged in--

- Providing bulk transportation of mail on a contract basis to and from postal service establishments--are classified in Industry Group 4841, General Freight Trucking;
- Providing services outside of the basic mail service, such as mail presort, mail consolidation, or address bar coding services, on a contract or fee basis--are classified in U.S. Industry 561499, All Other Business Support Services;
- Providing courier services--are classified in Industry 492110, Couriers and Express Delivery Services;
- Providing mailbox services along with other business services--are classified in U.S. Industry 561431, Private Mail Centers; and
- Providing local messenger and delivery services--are classified in Industry 492210, Local Messengers and Local Delivery.

492   Couriers and Messengers[T]

Industries in the Couriers and Messengers subsector provide intercity, local, and/or international delivery of parcels and documents (including express delivery services) without operating under a universal service obligation. These articles may originate in the U.S. but be delivered to another country and can be described as those that may be handled by one person without using special equipment. This allows the collection, pick-up, and delivery operations to be done with limited labor costs and minimal equipment. Sorting and transportation activities, where necessary, are generally mechanized. The restriction to small parcels partly distinguishes these establishments from those in the transportation industries. The complete network of courier services establishments also distinguishes these transportation services from local messenger and delivery establishments in this subsector. This includes the establishments that perform intercity transportation as well as establishments that, under contract to them, perform local pick-up and delivery. Messengers, which usually deliver within a metropolitan or single urban area, may use bicycle, foot, small truck, or van.

4921   Couriers and Express Delivery Services[T]

49211   Couriers and Express Delivery Services[T]
See industry description for 492110.

492110   Couriers and Express Delivery Services

This industry comprises establishments primarily engaged in providing air, surface, or combined mode courier and express delivery services of parcels, but not operating under a universal service obligation. These parcels can include goods and documents, but the express delivery services are not part of the normal mail service. These services are generally between metropolitan areas, urban centers, or international, but the establishments of this industry form a network that includes local pick-up and delivery to serve their customers' needs.

Illustrative Examples:

Air courier services, except establishments operating under a universal service obligation
Express delivery services, except establishments operating under a universal service obligation

Courier services (i.e., intercity network), except establishments operating under a universal service obligation

Cross-References.   Establishments primarily engaged in--

- Providing parcel and express delivery services in addition to mail services under a universal service obligation--are classified in Industry 491110, Postal Service;
- Providing messenger and delivery services within a metropolitan area or within an urban center--are classified in Industry 492210, Local Messengers and Local Delivery; and
- Providing the truck transportation of palletized general freight--are classified in Industry Group 4841, General Freight Trucking.

T--Canadian, Mexican, and United States industries are comparable.

4922   Local Messengers and Local Delivery^T

49221   Local Messengers and Local Delivery^T
See industry description for 492210.

492210 Local Messengers and Local Delivery

This industry comprises establishments primarily engaged in providing local messenger and delivery services of small items within a single metropolitan area or within an urban center. These establishments generally provide point-to-point pick-up and delivery and do not operate as part of an intercity courier network.

Illustrative Examples:

Letters, documents, or small parcels local delivery services
Grocery delivery services (i.e., independent service from grocery store)

Alcoholic beverages delivery services
Restaurant meals delivery services (i.e., independent service from restaurant)

Cross-References.   Establishments primarily engaged in--

- Providing local letter and parcel delivery services as part of an intercity courier network--are classified in Industry 492110, Couriers and Express Delivery Services;
- Operating the National Postal Service or providing postal services on a contract basis (except the bulk transportation of mail)--are classified in Industry 491110, Postal Service; and
- Providing the bulk transportation of mail on a contract basis to and from Postal Service establishments--are classified in Industry Group 4841, General Freight Trucking.

493   Warehousing and Storage^T

Industries in the Warehousing and Storage subsector are primarily engaged in operating warehousing and storage facilities for general merchandise, refrigerated goods, and other warehouse products. These establishments provide facilities to store goods. They do not sell the goods they handle. These establishments take responsibility for storing the goods and keeping them secure. They may also provide a range of services, often referred to as logistics services, related to the distribution of goods. Logistics services can include labeling, breaking bulk, inventory control and management, light assembly, order entry and fulfillment, packaging, pick and pack, price marking and ticketing, and transportation arrangement. However, establishments in this industry group always provide warehousing or storage services in addition to any logistic services. Furthermore, the warehousing or storage of goods must be more than incidental to the performance of services, such as price marking.
Bonded warehousing and storage services and warehouses located in free trade zones are included in the industries of this subsector.

4931   Warehousing and Storage^T

49311   General Warehousing and Storage^T
See industry description for 493110.

493110 General Warehousing and Storage

This industry comprises establishments primarily engaged in operating merchandise warehousing and storage facilities. These establishments generally handle goods in containers, such as boxes, barrels, and/or drums, using equipment, such as forklifts, pallets, and racks. They are not specialized in handling bulk products of any particular type, size, or quantity of goods or products.

T—Canadian, Mexican, and United States industries are comparable.

Cross-References.   Establishments primarily engaged in--

- Renting or leasing space for self-storage--are classified in Industry 531130, Lessors of Miniwarehouses and Self-Storage Units; and
- Selling in combination with handling and/or distributing goods to other wholesale or retail establishments-- are classified in Sector 42, Wholesale Trade.

49312   Refrigerated Warehousing and Storage[T]
See industry description for 493120.

493120 Refrigerated Warehousing and Storage

This industry comprises establishments primarily engaged in operating refrigerated warehousing and storage facilities. Establishments primarily engaged in the storage of furs for the trade are included in this industry. The services provided by these establishments include blast freezing, tempering, and modified atmosphere storage services.

Cross-References.

Establishments primarily engaged in storing furs (except for the trade) and garments are classified in Industry 812320, Drycleaning and Laundry Services (except Coin-Operated).

49313   Farm Product Warehousing and Storage[T]
See industry description for 493130.

493130 Farm Product Warehousing and Storage

This industry comprises establishments primarily engaged in operating bulk farm product warehousing and storage facilities (except refrigerated). Grain elevators primarily engaged in storage are included in this industry.

Cross-References.   Establishments primarily engaged in--

- Operating refrigerated warehousing and storage facilities--are classified in Industry 493120, Refrigerated Warehousing and Storage; and
- Storing grains and field beans (i.e., grain elevators) as an incidental activity to sales--are classified in Industry 424510, Grain and Field Bean Merchant Wholesalers.

49319   Other Warehousing and Storage[T]
See industry description for 493190.

493190 Other Warehousing and Storage

This industry comprises establishments primarily engaged in operating warehousing and storage facilities (except general merchandise, refrigerated, and farm product warehousing and storage).

Illustrative Examples:

Bulk petroleum storage   Document storage and warehousing
Lumber storage terminals   Whiskey warehousing

Cross-References.   Establishments primarily engaged in--

- Renting or leasing space for self-storage--are classified in Industry 531130, Lessors of Miniwarehouses and Self-Storage Units;

T—Canadian, Mexican, and United States industries are comparable.

- Storing hazardous materials for treatment and disposal--are classified in U.S. Industry 562211, Hazardous Waste Treatment and Disposal;
- Operating general warehousing and storage facilities--are classified in Industry 493110, General Warehousing and Storage;
- Wholesaling crude petroleum and petroleum products from bulk liquid storage facilities--are classified in Industry 424710, Petroleum Bulk Stations and Terminals;
- Operating refrigerated warehousing and storage facilities--are classified in Industry 493120, Refrigerated Warehousing and Storage; and
- Operating farm product warehousing and storage facilities--are classified in Industry 493130, Farm Product Warehousing and Storage.

T—Canadian, Mexican, and United States industries are comparable.

Sector 51--Information[T]

The Sector as a Whole

The Information sector comprises establishments engaged in the following processes: (a) producing and distributing information and cultural products, (b) providing the means to transmit or distribute these products as well as data or communications, and (c) processing data.

The main components of this sector are the publishing industries, including software publishing, and both traditional publishing and publishing exclusively on the Internet; the motion picture and sound recording industries; the broadcasting industries, including traditional broadcasting and broadcasting exclusively over the Internet; the telecommunications industries; and Web search portals, data processing industries, and the information services industries.

The expressions "information age" and "global information economy" are used with considerable frequency today. The general idea of an "information economy" includes both the notion of industries primarily producing, processing, and distributing information, as well as the idea that every industry is using available information and information technology to reorganize and make themselves more productive. For the purposes of NAICS, it is the transformation of information into a commodity that is produced and distributed by a number of growing industries that is at issue.

Cultural products are those that directly express attitudes, opinions, ideas, values, and artistic creativity; provide entertainment; or offer information and analysis concerning the past and present. Included in this definition are popular, mass-produced products as well as cultural products that normally have a more limited audience, such as poetry books, literary magazines, or classical records.

The unique characteristics of information and cultural products, and of the processes involved in their production and distribution, distinguish the Information sector from the goods-producing and service-producing sectors. Some of these characteristics are:

1. Unlike traditional goods, an "information or cultural product," such as an on-line newspaper or a television program, does not necessarily have tangible qualities, nor is it necessarily associated with a particular form. A movie can be shown at a movie theater, on a television broadcast, through video-on-demand or rented at a local video store. A sound recording can be aired on radio, embedded in multimedia products, or sold at a record store.

2. Unlike traditional services, the delivery of these products does not require direct contact between the supplier and the consumer.

3. The value of these products to the consumer lies in their informational, educational, cultural, or entertainment content, not in the format in which they are distributed. Most of these products are protected from unlawful reproduction by copyright laws.

4. The intangible property aspect of information and cultural products makes the processes involved in their production and distribution very different from goods and services. Only those possessing the rights to these works are authorized to reproduce, alter, improve, and distribute them. Acquiring and using these rights often involves significant costs. In addition, technology is revolutionizing the distribution of these products. It is possible to distribute them in a physical form, via broadcast, or on-line.

5. Distributors of information and cultural products can easily add value to the products they distribute. For instance, broadcasters add advertising not contained in the original product. This capacity means that unlike traditional distributors, they derive revenue not from sale of the distributed product to the final consumer, but from those who pay for the privilege of adding information to the original product. Similarly, a directory and mailing list publisher can acquire the rights to thousands of previously published newspaper and periodical articles and add new value by providing search and software and organizing the information in a way that facilitates research and retrieval. These products often command a much higher price than the original information.

The distribution modes for information commodities may either eliminate the necessity for traditional manufacture, or reverse the conventional order of manufacture-distribute: A newspaper distributed on-line, for

---

T—Canadian, Mexican, and United States industries are comparable.

example, can be printed locally or by the final consumer. Similarly, packaged software is available mainly on-line. The NAICS Information sector is designed to make such economic changes transparent as they occur, or to facilitate designing surveys that will monitor the new phenomena and provide data to analyze the changes.

Many of the industries in the NAICS Information sector are engaged in producing products protected by copyright law, or in distributing them (other than distribution by traditional wholesale and retail methods). Examples are traditional publishing industries, software and directory and mailing list publishing industries, and film and sound industries. Broadcasting and telecommunications industries and information providers and processors are also included in the Information sector, because their technologies are so closely linked to other industries in the Information sector.

511   Publishing Industries (except Internet)[T]

Industries in the Publishing Industries (except Internet) subsector group establishments engaged in the publishing of newspapers, magazines, other periodicals, and books, as well as directory and mailing list and software publishing. In general, these establishments, which are known as publishers, issue copies of works for which they usually possess copyright. Works may be in one or more formats including traditional print form, CD-ROM, or proprietary electronic networks. Publishers may publish works originally created by others for which they have obtained the rights and/or works that they have created in-house. Software publishing is included here because the activity, creation of a copyrighted product and bringing it to market, is equivalent to the creation process for other types of intellectual products.

In NAICS, publishing--the reporting, writing, editing, and other processes that are required to create an edition of a newspaper--is treated as a major economic activity in its own right, rather than as a subsidiary activity to a manufacturing activity, printing. Thus, publishing is classified in the Information sector; whereas, printing remains in the Manufacturing sector. In part, the NAICS classification reflects the fact that publishing increasingly takes place in establishments that are physically separate from the associated printing establishments. More crucially, the NAICS classification of book and newspaper publishing is intended to portray their roles in a modern economy, in which they do not resemble manufacturing activities.

Music publishers are not included in the Publishing Industries (except Internet) subsector, but are included in the Motion Picture and Sound Recording Industries subsector. Reproduction of prepackaged software is treated in NAICS as a manufacturing activity; on-line distribution of software products is in the Information sector; and custom design of software to client specifications is included in the Professional, Scientific, and Technical Services sector. These distinctions arise because of the different ways that software is created, reproduced, and distributed.

The Publishing Industries (except Internet) subsector includes establishments that publish software exclusively on the Internet but excludes establishments that publish other content exclusively on the Internet. Establishments publishing content other than software exclusively on the Internet are included in Subsector 519, Other Information Services. The Publishing Industries (except Internet) subsector also excludes products, such as manifold business forms and appointment books. Information is not the essential component of these items. Establishments producing these items are included in Subsector 323, Printing and Related Support Activities.

5111   Newspaper, Periodical, Book, and Directory Publishers[T]

This industry group comprises establishments primarily engaged in publishing newspapers, magazines, other periodicals, books, directories and mailing lists, and other works, such as calendars, greeting cards, and maps. These works are characterized by the intellectual creativity required in their development and are usually protected by copyright. Publishers distribute or arrange for the distribution of these works.

Publishing establishments may create the works in-house, or contract for, purchase, or compile works that were originally created by others. These works may be published in one or more formats, such as print and/or electronic form, including proprietary electronic networks. Establishments in this industry may print, reproduce, or offer direct access to the works themselves or may arrange with others to carry out such functions.

Establishments that both print and publish may fill excess capacity with commercial or job printing. However, the publishing activity is still considered to be the primary activity of these establishments.

51111   Newspaper Publishers[T]
See industry description for 511110.

T—Canadian, Mexican, and United States industries are comparable.

511110 Newspaper Publishers

This industry comprises establishments known as newspaper publishers. Establishments in this industry carry out operations necessary for producing and distributing newspapers, including gathering news; writing news columns, feature stories, and editorials; and selling and preparing advertisements. These establishments may publish newspapers in print or electronic form.

Cross-References.

- Establishments publishing newspapers exclusively on the Internet are classified in Industry 519130, Internet Publishing and Broadcasting and Web Search Portals;
- Establishments primarily engaged in printing newspapers without publishing are classified in Industry 32311, Printing;
- Establishments, such as trade associations, schools and universities, and social welfare organizations, that publish newsletters for distribution to their membership, but that are not commonly known as newspaper publishers, are classified according to their primary activity designation;
- Establishments primarily engaged in supplying the news media with information, such as news, reports, and pictures, are classified in Industry 519110, News Syndicates; and
- Establishments of independent representatives primarily engaged in selling advertising space are classified in Industry 541840, Media Representatives.

51112 Periodical Publishers[T]
See industry description for 511120.

511120 Periodical Publishers

This industry comprises establishments known either as magazine publishers or periodical publishers. These establishments carry out the operations necessary for producing and distributing magazines and other periodicals, such as gathering, writing, and editing articles, and selling and preparing advertisements. These establishments may publish magazines and other periodicals in print or electronic form.

Illustrative Examples:

Comic book publishers (except exclusive Internet publishing)
Radio and television guide publishers (except exclusive Internet publishing)
Magazine publishers (except exclusive Internet publishing)

Scholarly journal publishers (except exclusive Internet publishing)
Newsletter publishers (except exclusive Internet publishing)
Trade journal publishers (except exclusive Internet publishing)

Cross-References.

- Establishments publishing periodicals exclusively on the Internet are classified in Industry 519130, Internet Publishing and Broadcasting and Web Search Portals;
- Establishments primarily engaged in printing periodicals without publishing are classified in Industry 32311, Printing;
- Establishments, such as trade associations, schools and universities, and social welfare organizations, that publish magazines and periodicals for distribution to their membership, but that are not commonly known as periodical publishers, are classified according to their primary activity designation;
- Establishments primarily engaged in publishing directories and mailing lists are classified in Industry 511140, Directory and Mailing List Publishers; and
- Establishments of independent representatives primarily engaged in selling advertising space are classified in Industry 541840, Media Representatives.

T—Canadian, Mexican, and United States industries are comparable.

51113 Book Publishers[T]
See industry description for 511130.

511130 Book Publishers

This industry comprises establishments known as book publishers. Establishments in this industry carry out design, editing, and marketing activities necessary for producing and distributing books. These establishments may publish books in print, electronic, or audio form.

Illustrative Examples:

Atlas publishers (except exclusive Internet publishing)
Religious book publishers (except exclusive Internet publishing)
Book publishers (except exclusive Internet publishing)
School textbook publishers (except exclusive Internet publishing)

Encyclopedia publishers (except exclusive Internet publishing)
Technical manual publishers (except exclusive Internet publishing)
Map publishers (except exclusive Internet publishing)
Travel guide book publishers (except exclusive Internet publishing)

Cross-References.

- Establishments publishing books on the Internet exclusively are classified in Industry 519130, Internet Publishing and Broadcasting and Web Search Portals;
- Establishments primarily engaged in printing books without publishing are classified in U.S. Industry 323117, Books Printing;
- Establishments known as music publishers are classified in Industry 512230, Music Publishers;
- Establishments, such as trade associations, schools and universities, and social welfare organizations, that publish books for distribution to their membership, that are not commonly known as book publishers, are classified according to their primary activity designation; and
- Book clubs primarily engaged in direct sales activities without publishing are classified in Industry 454390, Other Direct Selling Establishments.

51114 Directory and Mailing List Publishers[T]
See industry description for 511140.

511140 Directory and Mailing List Publishers

This industry comprises establishments primarily engaged in publishing directories, mailing lists, and collections or compilations of fact. The products are typically protected in their selection, arrangement and/or presentation. Examples are lists of mailing addresses, telephone directories, directories of businesses, collections or compilations of proprietary drugs or legal case results, compilations of public records, etc. These establishments may publish directories and mailing lists in print or electronic form.

Illustrative Examples:

Business directory publishers (except exclusive Internet publishing)
Mailing list publishers (except exclusive Internet publishing)

Directory publishers (except exclusive Internet publishing)
Telephone directory publishers (except exclusive Internet publishing)

T—Canadian, Mexican, and United States industries are comparable.

census.gov/naics

Cross-References. Establishments primarily engaged in--

- Operating Web search portals or developing and publishing, exclusively on the Internet, collections or compilations of creative works or facts--are classified in Industry 519130, Internet Publishing and Broadcasting and Web Search Portals;
- Compiling mailing lists in conjunction with providing direct mail advertising services--are classified in Industry 541860, Direct Mail Advertising;
- Printing without publishing directories and mailing lists--are classified in Industry 32311, Printing;
- Publishing computer software--are classified in Industry 511210, Software Publishers;
- Creating and publishing encyclopedias and similar collections of creative works in print and/or electronic media--are classified in Industry 511130, Book Publishers; and
- Creating and publishing collections of creative works that are periodically updated--are classified in Industry 511120, Periodical Publishers.

51119 Other Publishers[T]

This industry comprises establishments known as publishers (except newspaper, magazine, book, directory, mailing list, and music publishers). These establishments may publish works in print or electronic form.

Illustrative Examples:

Art print publishers (except exclusive Internet publishing)
Greeting card publishers (except exclusive Internet publishing)

Calendar publishers (except exclusive Internet publishing)

Cross-References.

- Establishments publishing exclusively on the Internet are classified in Industry 51913, Internet Publishing and Broadcasting and Web Search Portals;
- Establishments known as newspaper publishers are classified in Industry 51111, Newspaper Publishers;
- Establishments known as magazine and other periodical publishers are classified in Industry 51112, Periodical Publishers;
- Establishments known as book publishers are classified in Industry 51113, Book Publishers;
- Establishments primarily engaged in publishing directories and mailing lists are classified in Industry 51114, Directory and Mailing List Publishers;
- Establishments known as music publishers are classified in Industry 51223, Music Publishers; and
- Establishments primarily engaged in manufacturing appointment books and/or manifold business forms are classified in Industry 32311, Printing.

511191 Greeting Card Publishers

This U.S. industry comprises establishments primarily engaged in publishing greeting cards.

Cross-References. Establishments primarily engaged in--

- Publishing greeting cards exclusively on the Internet--are classified in Industry 519130, Internet Publishing and Broadcasting and Web Search Portals; and
- Printing greeting cards without publishing--are classified in Industry 32311, Printing.

511199 All Other Publishers

This U.S. industry comprises establishments generally known as publishers (except newspaper, magazine, book, directory, database, music, and greeting card publishers). These establishments may publish works in print or electronic form.

T—Canadian, Mexican, and United States industries are comparable.

Illustrative Examples:

Art print publishers (except exclusive Internet publishing)

Calendar publishers (except exclusive Internet publishing)

Cross-References.

- Establishments publishing exclusively on the Internet are classified in Industry 519130, Internet Publishing and Broadcasting and Web Search Portals;
- Establishments known as newspaper publishers are classified in Industry 511110, Newspaper Publishers;
- Establishments known as magazine or other periodical publishers are classified in Industry 511120, Periodical Publishers;
- Establishments known as book publishers are classified in Industry 511130, Book Publishers;
- Establishments primarily engaged in publishing directories and mailing lists are classified in Industry 511140, Directory and Mailing List Publishers;
- Establishments primarily engaged in greeting card publishing are classified in U.S. Industry 511191, Greeting Card Publishers;
- Establishments known as music publishers are classified in Industry 512230, Music Publishers; and
- Establishments primarily engaged in manufacturing appointment books and/or manifold business forms are classified in U.S. Industry 323111, Commercial Printing (except Screen and Books).

5112   Software Publishers[T]

51121   Software Publishers[T]
See industry description for 511210.

511210 Software Publishers

This industry comprises establishments primarily engaged in computer software publishing or publishing and reproduction. Establishments in this industry carry out operations necessary for producing and distributing computer software, such as designing, providing documentation, assisting in installation, and providing support services to software purchasers. These establishments may design, develop, and publish, or publish only. These establishments may publish and distribute software remotely through subscriptions and downloads.

Cross-References.   Establishments primarily engaged in--

- Reselling packaged software--are classified in Sector 42, Wholesale Trade, or Sector 44-45, Retail Trade;
- Providing access for clients to software published by others from a central host site--are classified in Industry 518210, Data Processing, Hosting, and Related Services;
- Designing software to meet the needs of specific users--are classified in U.S. Industry 541511, Custom Computer Programming Services; and
- Mass duplication of software--are classified in U.S. Industry 334614, Software and Other Prerecorded Compact Disc, Tape, and Record Reproducing.

512   Motion Picture and Sound Recording Industries[T]

Industries in the Motion Picture and Sound Recording Industries subsector group establishments involved in the production and distribution of motion pictures and sound recordings. While producers and distributors of motion pictures and sound recordings issue works for sale as traditional publishers do, the processes are sufficiently different to warrant placing establishments engaged in these activities in a separate subsector. Production is typically a complex process that involves several distinct types of establishments that are engaged in activities, such as contracting with performers, creating the film or sound content, and providing technical postproduction services. Film distribution is often to exhibitors, such as theaters and broadcasters, rather than through the wholesale and retail distribution chain. When the product is in a mass-produced form, NAICS treats production and distribution as

---

T—Canadian, Mexican, and United States industries are comparable.

the major economic activity as it does in the Publishing Industries (except Internet) subsector, rather than as a subsidiary activity to the manufacture of such products.

This subsector does not include establishments primarily engaged in the wholesale distribution of video and sound recordings, such as compact discs and audio tapes; these establishments are included in the Wholesale Trade sector. Reproduction of video and sound recordings that is carried out separately from establishments engaged in production and distribution is treated in NAICS as a manufacturing activity.

5121 Motion Picture and Video Industries[T]

This industry group comprises establishments primarily engaged in the production and/or distribution of motion pictures, videos, television programs, or commercials; in the exhibition of motion pictures; or in the provision of postproduction and related services.

51211 Motion Picture and Video Production[T]
See industry description for 512110.

512110 Motion Picture and Video Production

This industry comprises establishments primarily engaged in producing, or producing and distributing motion pictures, videos, television programs, or television commercials.

Cross-References.   Establishments primarily engaged in--

- Producing motion pictures and videos on contract as independent producers--are classified in Industry 711510, Independent Artists, Writers, and Performers;
- Providing teleproduction and other postproduction services--are classified in U.S. Industry 512191, Teleproduction and Other Postproduction Services;
- Providing video taping of weddings, special events, and/or business inventories--are classified in Industry 54192, Photographic Services;
- Providing motion picture laboratory services--are classified in U.S. Industry 512199, Other Motion Picture and Video Industries;
- Providing mass duplication and packaging of video discs, tapes, and film--are classified in U.S. Industry 334614, Software and Other Prerecorded Compact Disc, Tape, and Record Reproducing; and
- Acquiring distribution rights and distributing motion pictures and videos--are classified in Industry 512120, Motion Picture and Video Distribution.

51212 Motion Picture and Video Distribution[T]
See industry description for 512120.

512120 Motion Picture and Video Distribution

This industry comprises establishments primarily engaged in acquiring distribution rights and distributing film and video productions to motion picture theaters, television networks and stations, and exhibitors.

Cross-References.   Establishments primarily engaged in--

- Producing and distributing motion pictures and videos--are classified in Industry 512110, Motion Picture and Video Production;
- Merchant wholesale distribution of blank video cassette tapes and discs--are classified in Industry 423690, Other Electronic Parts and Equipment Merchant Wholesalers;
- Merchant wholesale distribution of prerecorded video cassette tapes and discs--are classified in Industry 423990, Other Miscellaneous Durable Goods Merchant Wholesalers;
- Providing mass duplication and packaging of video tapes and discs--are classified in U.S. Industry 334614, Software and Other Prerecorded Compact Disc, Tape, and Record Reproducing;

T—Canadian, Mexican, and United States industries are comparable.

- Providing motion picture footage (via film libraries) to producers--are classified in U.S. Industry 512199, Other Motion Picture and Video Industries;
- Renting video tapes and discs to the general public--are classified in U.S. Industry 532282, Video Tape and Disc Rental; and
- Selling video cassettes and discs to the general public--are classified in U.S. Industry 443142, Electronics Stores.

51213 Motion Picture and Video Exhibition[T]

This industry comprises establishments primarily engaged in operating motion picture theaters and/or exhibiting motion pictures or videos at film festivals, and so forth.

512131 Motion Picture Theaters (except Drive-Ins)

This U.S. industry comprises establishments primarily engaged in operating motion picture theaters (except drive-ins) and/or exhibiting motion pictures or videos at film festivals, and so forth.

512132 Drive-In Motion Picture Theaters

This U.S. industry comprises establishments primarily engaged in operating drive-in motion picture theaters.

51219 Postproduction Services and Other Motion Picture and Video Industries[T]

This industry comprises establishments primarily engaged in providing postproduction services and other services to the motion picture industry, including specialized motion picture or video postproduction services, such as editing, film/tape transfers, titling, subtitling, credits, closed captioning, and computer-produced graphics, animation and special effects, as well as developing and processing motion picture film.

Illustrative Examples:

Motion picture film laboratories   Postproduction facilities
Stock footage film libraries   Teleproduction services

Cross-References.   Establishments primarily engaged in--

- Mass duplicating video discs, tapes, and film--are classified in Industry 33461, Manufacturing and Reproducing Magnetic and Optical Media;
- Providing audio services for film, television, and video productions--are classified in Industry 51224, Sound Recording Studios;
- Renting wardrobes and costumes for motion picture production--are classified in Industry 53228, Other Consumer Goods Rental;
- Renting studio equipment--are classified in Industry 53249, Other Commercial and Industrial Machinery and Equipment Rental and Leasing; and
- Casting actors and actresses with production companies--are classified in Industry 56131, Employment Placement Agencies and Executive Search Services.

512191 Teleproduction and Other Postproduction Services

This U.S. industry comprises establishments primarily engaged in providing specialized motion picture or video postproduction services, such as editing, film/tape transfers, subtitling, credits, closed captioning, and animation and special effects.

T—Canadian, Mexican, and United States industries are comparable.

Cross-References.   Establishments primarily engaged in--

- Mass duplicating video discs, tapes, and film--are classified in U.S. Industry 334614, Software and Other Prerecorded Compact Disc, Tape, and Record Reproducing;
- Developing and processing motion picture film--are classified in U.S. Industry 512199, Other Motion Picture and Video Industries;
- Providing audio services for film, television, and video productions--are classified in Industry 512240, Sound Recording Studios; and
- Acquiring distribution rights and distributing film and video productions to motion picture theaters, television networks and stations, and exhibitors--are classified in Industry 512120, Motion Picture and Video Distribution.

512199   Other Motion Picture and Video Industries

This U.S. industry comprises establishments primarily engaged in providing motion picture and video services (except motion picture and video production, distribution, exhibition, and teleproduction and other postproduction services).

Illustrative Examples:

Motion picture film laboratories   Film preservation services
Stock footage film libraries

Cross-References.   Establishments primarily engaged in--

- Renting wardrobes and costumes for motion picture production--are classified in U.S. Industry 532281, Formal Wear and Costume Rental;
- Renting studio equipment--are classified in Industry 532490, Other Commercial and Industrial Machinery and Equipment Rental and Leasing;
- Casting actors and actresses with production companies--are classified in U.S. Industry 561311, Employment Placement Agencies;
- Motion picture and video production--are classified in Industry 512110, Motion Picture and Video Production;
- Motion picture and video distribution--are classified in Industry 512120, Motion Picture and Video Distribution;
- Teleproduction and other postproduction services--are classified in U.S. Industry 512191, Teleproduction and Other Postproduction Services; and
- Motion picture and video exhibition--are classified in Industry 51213, Motion Picture and Video Exhibition.

5122   Sound Recording Industries[T]

This industry group comprises establishments primarily engaged in producing and distributing musical recordings, publishing music, or providing sound recording and related services.

51223   Music Publishers[T]
See industry description for 512230.

512230   Music Publishers

This industry comprises establishments primarily engaged in acquiring and registering copyrights for musical compositions in accordance with law and promoting and authorizing the use of these compositions in recordings, radio, television, motion pictures, live performances, print, or other media. Establishments in this industry represent the interests of the songwriter or other owners of musical compositions to produce revenues from the use of such works, generally through licensing agreements. These establishments may own the copyright or act as administrator

---

T—Canadian, Mexican, and United States industries are comparable.

of the music copyrights on behalf of copyright owners. Publishers of music books and sheet music are included in this industry.

Cross-References.

Establishments primarily engaged as independent songwriters who act as their own publishers are classified in Industry 711510, Independent Artists, Writers, and Performers.

51224   Sound Recording Studios[T]
    See industry description for 512240.

512240 Sound Recording Studios

This industry comprises establishments primarily engaged in providing the facilities and technical expertise for sound recording in a studio. This industry includes establishments that provide audio production and postproduction services to produce master recordings. These establishments may provide audio services for film, television, and video productions.

Cross-References.   Establishments primarily engaged in--

- Record production and/or releasing, promoting, and distributing sound recordings--are classified in Industry 512250, Record Production and Distribution; and
- Providing mass duplication of recorded products--are classified in U.S. Industry 334614, Software and Other Prerecorded Compact Disc, Tape, and Record Reproducing.

51225   Record Production and Distribution[T]
    See industry description for 512250.

512250 Record Production and Distribution

This industry comprises establishments primarily engaged in record production (e.g., tapes, CDs) and/or releasing, promoting, and distributing sound recordings to wholesalers, retailers, or directly to the public. These establishments contract with artists, arrange and finance the production of original master recordings, and/or produce master recordings themselves, such as audio tapes/cassettes and compact discs. Establishments in this industry hold the copyright to the master recording, or obtain reproduction and distribution rights to master recordings produced by others, and derive most of their revenues from the sales, leasing, licensing, or distribution of master recordings.

Cross-References.   Establishments primarily engaged in--

- Promoting and authorizing the use of musical works in various media--are classified in Industry 512230, Music Publishers;
- Providing facilities and technical expertise for recording musical performances--are classified in Industry 512240, Sound Recording Studios;
- Mass duplication of recorded products--are classified in U.S. Industry 334614, Software and Other Prerecorded Compact Disc, Tape, and Record Reproducing;
- Merchant wholesale distribution of blank audio cassettes, tapes, and discs--are classified in Industry 423690, Other Electronic Parts and Equipment Merchant Wholesalers;
- Merchant wholesale distribution of prerecorded audio cassettes, tapes, and discs--are classified in Industry 423990, Other Miscellaneous Durable Goods Merchant Wholesalers;
- Retailing records, tapes, and compact discs without producing recordings--are classified in Sector 44-45, Retail Trade;
- Managing the careers of artists--are classified in Industry 711410, Agents and Managers for Artists, Athletes, Entertainers, and Other Public Figures; and

---

T—Canadian, Mexican, and United States industries are comparable.

- Producing albums on contract as independent producers--are classified in Industry 711510, Independent Artists, Writers, and Performers.

51229 Other Sound Recording Industries^T
See industry description for 512290.

512290 Other Sound Recording Industries

This industry comprises establishments primarily engaged in providing sound recording services (except record production, distribution, music publishing, and sound recording in a studio). Establishments in this industry provide services, such as the audio recording of meetings and conferences.

Cross-References.   Establishments primarily engaged in--

- Promoting and authorizing the use of musical works in various media--are classified in Industry 512230, Music Publishers;
- Providing facilities and expertise for recording musical performances--are classified in Industry 512240, Sound Recording Studios;
- Record production and/or releasing, promoting, and distributing sound recordings--are classified in Industry 512250, Record Production and Distribution;
- Providing mass duplication of recorded products--are classified in U.S. Industry 334614, Software and Other Prerecorded Compact Disc, Tape, and Record Reproducing; and
- Organizing and promoting the presentation of performing arts productions--are classified in Industry Group 7113, Promoters of Performing Arts, Sports, and Similar Events.

515   Broadcasting (except Internet)^T

Industries in the Broadcasting (except Internet) subsector include establishments that create content or acquire the right to distribute content and subsequently broadcast the content. The industry groups (Radio and Television Broadcasting and Cable and Other Subscription Programming) are based on differences in the methods of communication and the nature of services provided. The Radio and Television Broadcasting industry group includes establishments that operate broadcasting studios and facilities for over-the-air or satellite delivery of radio and television programs of entertainment, news, talk, and the like. These establishments are often engaged in the production and purchase of programs and generating revenues from the sale of air time to advertisers and from donations, subsidies, and/or the sale of programs. The Cable and Other Subscription Programming industry group includes establishments operating studios and facilities for the broadcasting of programs that are typically narrowcast in nature (limited format, such as news, sports, education, and youth-oriented programming) on a subscription or fee basis.
The distribution of cable and other subscription programming is included in Subsector 517, Telecommunications. Establishments that broadcast exclusively on the Internet are included in Subsector 519, Other Information Services.

5151   Radio and Television Broadcasting^T

This industry group comprises establishments primarily engaged in operating broadcast studios and facilities for over-the-air or satellite delivery of radio and television programs. These establishments are often engaged in the production or purchase of programs or generate revenues from the sale of air time to advertisers, from donations and subsidies, or from the sale of programs.

51511   Radio Broadcasting^T

This industry comprises establishments primarily engaged in broadcasting audio signals. These establishments operate radio broadcasting studios and facilities for the transmission of aural programming to the public, to affiliates, or to subscribers. The radio programs may include entertainment, news, talk shows, business data, or religious services.

T—Canadian, Mexican, and United States industries are comparable.

Cross-References.　　　Establishments primarily engaged in--

- Broadcasting exclusively on the Internet--are classified in Industry 51913, Internet Publishing and Broadcasting and Web Search Portals; and
- Producing taped radio programming--are classified in Industry 51229, Other Sound Recording Industries.

515111　Radio Networks

This U.S. industry comprises establishments primarily engaged in assembling and transmitting aural programming to their affiliates or subscribers via over-the-air broadcasts, cable, or satellite. The programming covers a wide variety of material, such as news services, religious programming, weather, sports, or music.

Cross-References.　　　Establishments primarily engaged in--

- Broadcasting exclusively on the Internet--are classified in Industry 519130, Internet Publishing and Broadcasting and Web Search Portals; and
- Producing taped radio programming--are classified in Industry 512290, Other Sound Recording Industries.

515112　Radio Stations

This U.S. industry comprises establishments primarily engaged in broadcasting aural programs by radio to the public. Programming may originate in their own studio, from an affiliated network, or from external sources.

51512　Television Broadcasting[T]
See industry description for 515120.

515120　Television Broadcasting

This industry comprises establishments primarily engaged in broadcasting images together with sound. These establishments operate television broadcasting studios and facilities for the programming and transmission of programs to the public. These establishments also produce or transmit visual programming to affiliated broadcast television stations, which in turn broadcast the programs to the public on a predetermined schedule. Programming may originate in their own studio, from an affiliated network, or from external sources.

Cross-References.　　　Establishments primarily engaged in--

- Broadcasting exclusively on the Internet--are classified in Industry 519130, Internet Publishing and Broadcasting and Web Search Portals;
- Producing taped television program materials--are classified in Industry 512110, Motion Picture and Video Production;
- Furnishing cable and other pay television services--are classified in U.S. Industry 517311, Wired Telecommunications Carriers; and
- Producing and broadcasting television programs for cable and satellite television systems--are classified in Industry 515210, Cable and Other Subscription Programming.

5152　Cable and Other Subscription Programming[T]

51521　Cable and Other Subscription Programming[T]
See industry description for 515210.

515210　Cable and Other Subscription Programming

This industry comprises establishments primarily engaged in operating studios and facilities for the broadcasting of programs on a subscription or fee basis. The broadcast programming is typically narrowcast in nature (e.g., limited format, such as news, sports, education, or youth-oriented). These establishments produce programming in

---

T—Canadian, Mexican, and United States industries are comparable.

their own facilities or acquire programming from external sources. The programming material is usually delivered to a third party, such as cable systems or direct-to-home satellite systems, for transmission to viewers.

Cross-References.   Establishments primarily engaged in--

- Producing taped television program materials--are classified in Industry 512110, Motion Picture and Video Production;
- Producing and transmitting television programs to affiliated stations--are classified in Industry 515120, Television Broadcasting;
- Furnishing cable and other pay television services--are classified in U.S. Industry 517311, Wired Telecommunications Carriers; and
- Retailing merchandise by electronic media, such as television--are classified in Industry 454110, Electronic Shopping and Mail-Order Houses.

517   Telecommunications[T]

Industries in the Telecommunications subsector group establishments that provide telecommunications and the services related to that activity (e.g., telephony, including Voice over Internet Protocol (VoIP); cable and satellite television distribution services; Internet access; telecommunications reselling services). The Telecommunications subsector is primarily engaged in operating and/or providing access to facilities for the transmission of voice, data, text, sound, and video. Transmission facilities may be based on a single technology or a combination of technologies. Establishments in the Telecommunications subsector are grouped into three industry groups. The first two are comprised of establishments that operate transmission facilities and infrastructure that they own and/or lease, and provide telecommunications services using those facilities. The distinction between the first two industry groups is the type of infrastructure operated (i.e., wired and/or wireless or satellite). The third industry group is comprised of establishments that provide support activities, telecommunications reselling services, or many of the same services provided by establishments in the first two industry groups, but do not operate as telecommunications carriers. Establishments primarily engaged as independent contractors in the installation and maintenance of broadcasting and telecommunications systems are classified in Sector 23, Construction. Establishments known as Internet cafes, primarily engaged in offering limited Internet connectivity in combination with other services such as facsimile services, training, rental of on-site personal computers, game rooms, or food services are classified in Subsector 561, Administrative and Support Services, or Subsector 722, Food Services and Drinking Places, depending on the primary activity.

5173   Wired and Wireless Telecommunications Carriers[T]

51731   Wired and Wireless Telecommunications Carriers[T]

This industry comprises establishments primarily engaged in operating, maintaining, and/or providing access to switching and transmission facilities and infrastructure that they own and/or lease for the transmission of voice, data, text, sound, and video using wired and wireless telecommunications networks. Transmission facilities may be based on a single technology or a combination of technologies. By exception, establishments providing satellite television distribution services using facilities and infrastructure that they operate are included in this industry.

Illustrative Examples:

Broadband Internet service providers, wired (e.g., cable, DSL)
Cable television distribution services
Cellular telephone services
Direct-to-home satellite system (DTH) services
Satellite television distribution systems
Telecommunications carriers, wired

VoIP service providers, using own operated wired telecommunications infrastructure
Wireless Internet service providers, except satellite
Wireless telecommunications carriers, except satellite
Wireless telephone communications carriers, except satellite

T—Canadian, Mexican, and United States industries are comparable.

Cross-References.   Establishments primarily engaged in--

- Producing and distributing a channel of television programming for cable or satellite television systems-- are classified in Industry 51521, Cable and Other Subscription Programming;
- Producing and distributing radio programs for cable or satellite radio systems--are classified in Industry 51511, Radio Broadcasting;
- Reselling telecommunications services (except satellite telecommunications), without operating a network, and/or operating as mobile virtual network operations (MVNO)--are classified in Industry 51791, Other Telecommunications;
- Operating and maintaining satellite networks and/or reselling satellite telecommunications services--are classified in Industry 51741, Satellite Telecommunications;
- Providing Internet access services via client-supplied telecommunications connections (e.g., dial-up ISPs)-- are classified in Industry 51791, Other Telecommunications;
- Providing voice over Internet protocol (VoIP) services via client-supplied telecommunications connections- -are classified in Industry 51791, Other Telecommunications;
- Providing limited Internet connectivity at locations known as Internet cafes, in combination with other services such as facsimile services, training, rental of on-site personal computers, game rooms, or food services--are classified in Industry 56143, Business Service Centers, or Subsector 722, Food Services and Drinking Places, depending on the primary activity; and
- Operating coin-operated pay telephones--are classified in Industry 81299, All Other Personal Services.

517311 Wired Telecommunications Carriers

This U.S. industry comprises establishments primarily engaged in operating and/or providing access to transmission facilities and infrastructure that they own and/or lease for the transmission of voice, data, text, sound, and video using wired telecommunications networks. Transmission facilities may be based on a single technology or a combination of technologies. Establishments in this industry use the wired telecommunications network facilities that they operate to provide a variety of services, such as wired telephony services, including VoIP services; wired (cable) audio and video programming distribution; and wired broadband Internet services. By exception, establishments providing satellite television distribution services using facilities and infrastructure that they operate are included in this industry.

Illustrative Examples:

Broadband Internet service providers, wired (e.g., cable, DSL)
Cable television distribution services
Closed-circuit television (CCTV) services
Direct-to-home satellite system (DTH) services
Local telephone carriers, wired
Long-distance telephone carriers, wired

Multichannel multipoint distribution services (MMDS)
Satellite television distribution systems
Telecommunications carriers, wired
VoIP service providers, using own operated wired telecommunications infrastructure

Cross-References.   Establishments primarily engaged in--

- Producing and distributing a channel of television programming for cable or satellite television systems-- are classified in Industry 515210, Cable and Other Subscription Programming;
- Operating and maintaining wireless telecommunications networks--are classified in U.S. Industry 517312, Wireless Telecommunications Carriers (except Satellite);
- Producing and distributing radio programs for cable or satellite radio systems--are classified in U.S. Industry 515111, Radio Networks;
- Reselling telecommunications services (except satellite telecommunications), without operating a network- -are classified in U.S. Industry 517911, Telecommunications Resellers;
- Reselling satellite telecommunications services--are classified in Industry 517410, Satellite Telecommunications;

T—Canadian, Mexican, and United States industries are comparable.

- Providing Internet access services via client-supplied telecommunications connections (e.g., dial-up ISPs)--are classified in U.S. Industry 517919, All Other Telecommunications;
- Providing voice over Internet protocol (VoIP) services via client-supplied telecommunications connections--are classified in U.S. Industry 517919, All Other Telecommunications;
- Providing limited Internet connectivity at locations known as Internet cafes, in combination with other services such as facsimile services, training, rental of on-site personal computers, game rooms, or food services--are classified in U.S. Industry 561439, Other Business Service Centers (including Copy Shops), or Subsector 722, Food Services and Drinking Places, depending on the primary activity; and
- Operating coin-operated pay telephones--are classified in Industry 812990, All Other Personal Services.

517312 Wireless Telecommunications Carriers (except Satellite)

This U.S. industry comprises establishments primarily engaged in operating and maintaining switching and transmission facilities to provide communications via the airwaves. Establishments in this industry have spectrum licenses and provide services using that spectrum, such as cellular phone services, paging services, wireless Internet access, and wireless video services.

Illustrative Examples:

Cellular telephone services
Paging services, except satellite
Wireless Internet service providers, except satellite

Wireless telephone communications carriers, except satellite

Cross-References. Establishments primarily engaged in--

- Operating and maintaining wired telecommunications networks--are classified in U.S. Industry 517311, Wired Telecommunications Carriers;
- Operating and maintaining satellite networks--are classified in Industry 517410, Satellite Telecommunications;
- Providing satellite television distribution services--are classified in U.S. Industry 517311, Wired Telecommunications Carriers; and
- Operating as mobile virtual network operations (MVNO)--are classified in U.S. Industry 517911, Telecommunications Resellers.

5174 Satellite Telecommunications[T]

51741 Satellite Telecommunications[T]
See industry description for 517410.

517410 Satellite Telecommunications

This industry comprises establishments primarily engaged in providing telecommunications services to other establishments in the telecommunications and broadcasting industries by forwarding and receiving communications signals via a system of satellites or reselling satellite telecommunications.

Cross-References.

Establishments primarily engaged in providing direct-to-home satellite television services to individual households or consumers are classified in U.S. Industry 517311, Wired Telecommunications Carriers.

T—Canadian, Mexican, and United States industries are comparable.

5179   Other Telecommunications^T

51791   Other Telecommunications^T

This industry comprises establishments primarily engaged in (1) purchasing access and network capacity from owners and operators of telecommunications networks and reselling wired and wireless telecommunications services (except satellite) to businesses and households; (2) providing specialized telecommunications services, such as satellite tracking, communications telemetry, and radar station operation; (3) providing satellite terminal stations and associated facilities connected with one or more terrestrial systems and capable of transmitting telecommunications to, and receiving telecommunications from, satellite systems; or (4) providing Internet access services or Voice over Internet protocol (VoIP) services via client-supplied telecommunications connections. Establishments in this industry do not operate as telecommunications carriers. Mobile virtual network operators (MVNOs) are included in this industry.

517911   Telecommunications Resellers

This U.S. industry comprises establishments engaged in purchasing access and network capacity from owners and operators of telecommunications networks and reselling wired and wireless telecommunications services (except satellite) to businesses and households. Establishments in this industry resell telecommunications; they do not operate transmission facilities and infrastructure. Mobile virtual network operators (MVNOs) are included in this industry.

Cross-References.   Establishments primarily engaged in--

- Operating and maintaining wired telecommunications networks--are classified in U.S. Industry 517311, Wired Telecommunications Carriers;
- Operating and maintaining wireless telecommunications networks--are classified in U.S. Industry 517312, Wireless Telecommunications Carriers (except Satellite); and
- Reselling satellite telecommunications services--are classified in Industry 517410, Satellite Telecommunications.

517919   All Other Telecommunications

This U.S. industry comprises establishments primarily engaged in providing specialized telecommunications services, such as satellite tracking, communications telemetry, and radar station operation. This industry also includes establishments primarily engaged in providing satellite terminal stations and associated facilities connected with one or more terrestrial systems and capable of transmitting telecommunications to, and receiving telecommunications from, satellite systems. Establishments providing Internet services or Voice over Internet protocol (VoIP) services via client-supplied telecommunications connections are also included in this industry.

Illustrative Examples:

Dial-up Internet service providers
VoIP service providers, using client-supplied
telecommunications connections

Internet service providers using client-supplied
telecommunications connections (e.g., dial-up ISPs)
Satellite tracking stations

Cross-References.   Establishments primarily engaged in--

- Providing wired broadband Internet services or wired VoIP services via own operated telecommunications infrastructure--are classified in U.S. Industry 517311, Wired Telecommunications Carriers;
- Providing expert advice in the field of information technology or in integrating communication and computer systems--are classified in Industry 54151, Computer Systems Design and Related Services; and
- Providing satellite telecommunications services--are classified in Industry 517410, Satellite Telecommunications.

T—Canadian, Mexican, and United States industries are comparable.

518 Data Processing, Hosting, and Related Services^T

Industries in the Data Processing, Hosting, and Related Services subsector group establishments that provide the infrastructure for hosting and/or data processing services.

5182 Data Processing, Hosting, and Related Services^T

51821 Data Processing, Hosting, and Related Services^T
See industry description for 518210.

518210 Data Processing, Hosting, and Related Services

This industry comprises establishments primarily engaged in providing infrastructure for hosting or data processing services. These establishments may provide specialized hosting activities, such as Web hosting, streaming services, or application hosting (except software publishing), or they may provide general time-share mainframe facilities to clients. Data processing establishments provide complete processing and specialized reports from data supplied by clients or provide automated data processing and data entry services.

Illustrative Examples:

Application hosting
Optical scanning services
Web hosting
Computer data storage services

Video and audio streaming services
Computer input preparation services
Microfilm imaging services
Computer time rental

Cross-References.   Establishments primarily engaged in--

- Providing text processing and related document preparation activities--are classified in Industry 561410, Document Preparation Services;
- Providing on-site management and operation of a client's data processing facilities--are classified in U.S. Industry 541513, Computer Facilities Management Services;
- Software design, development, and publishing, or software publishing only--are classified in Industry 511210, Software Publishers;
- Providing wired broadband Internet access services using own operated telecommunications infrastructure, in combination with Web hosting--are classified in U.S. Industry 517311, Wired Telecommunications Carriers;
- Providing Internet access via client-supplied telecommunications connections in combination with Web hosting--are classified in U.S. Industry 517919, All Other Telecommunications;
- Operating Web search portals--are classified in Industry 519130, Internet Publishing and Broadcasting and Web Search Portals;
- Providing access to computers and office equipment, as well as other office support services--are classified in Industry 56143, Business Service Centers;
- Processing financial transactions, such as credit card transactions--are classified in Industry 522320, Financial Transactions Processing, Reserve, and Clearinghouse Activities; and
- Providing payroll processing services--are classified in U.S. Industry 541214, Payroll Services.

519 Other Information Services^T

Industries in the Other Information Services subsector group establishments supplying information, storing and providing access to information, searching and retrieving information, operating Web sites that use search engines to allow for searching information on the Internet, or publishing and/or broadcasting content exclusively on the Internet. The main components of the subsector are news syndicates, libraries, archives, exclusive Internet publishing and/or broadcasting, and Web search portals.

T—Canadian, Mexican, and United States industries are comparable.

5191   Other Information Services[T]

51911   News Syndicates[T]
See industry description for 519110.

519110   News Syndicates

This industry comprises establishments primarily engaged in supplying information, such as news reports, articles, pictures, and features, to the news media.

Cross-References.

Independent writers and journalists (including photojournalists) are classified in Industry 711510, Independent Artists, Writers, and Performers.

51912   Libraries and Archives[T]
See industry description for 519120.

519120 Libraries and Archives

This industry comprises establishments primarily engaged in providing library or archive services. These establishments are engaged in maintaining collections of documents (e.g., books, journals, newspapers, and music) and facilitating the use of such documents (recorded information regardless of its physical form and characteristics) as required to meet the informational, research, educational, or recreational needs of their user. These establishments may also acquire, research, store, preserve, and generally make accessible to the public historical documents, photographs, maps, audio material, audiovisual material, and other archival material of historical interest. All or portions of these collections may be accessible electronically.

Cross-References.   Establishments primarily engaged in--

- Providing stock footage (via motion picture and video tape libraries) to the media, multimedia, and advertising industries--are classified in U.S. Industry 512199, Other Motion Picture and Video Industries;
- Providing stock music to the media, multimedia, and advertising industries--are classified in Industry 512290, Other Sound Recording Industries;
- Providing stock photos to the media, multimedia, and advertising industries--are classified in Industry 519190, All Other Information Services; and
- Distributing film and video productions to motion picture theaters, television networks and stations, and exhibitors--are classified in Industry 512120, Motion Picture and Video Distribution.

51913   Internet Publishing and Broadcasting and Web Search Portals[T]
See industry description for 519130.

519130 Internet Publishing and Broadcasting and Web Search Portals

This industry comprises establishments primarily engaged in (1) publishing and/or broadcasting content on the Internet exclusively or (2) operating Web sites that use a search engine to generate and maintain extensive databases of Internet addresses and content in an easily searchable format (and known as Web search portals). The publishing and broadcasting establishments in this industry do not provide traditional (non-Internet) versions of the content that they publish or broadcast. They provide textual, audio, and/or video content of general or specific interest on the Internet exclusively. Establishments known as Web search portals often provide additional Internet services, such as email, connections to other Web sites, auctions, news, and other limited content, and serve as a home base for Internet users.

T—Canadian, Mexican, and United States industries are comparable.

Illustrative Examples:

Internet book publishers
Internet sports sites
Internet entertainment sites
Internet video broadcast sites
Internet news publishers
Internet periodical publishers

Internet radio stations
Internet search portals
Web search portals
Internet search Web sites
Internet social networking sites

Cross-References.   Establishments primarily engaged in--

- Providing wired broadband Internet access using own operated telecommunications infrastructure--are classified in U.S. Industry 517311, Wired Telecommunications Carriers;
- Providing both Internet publishing and other print or electronic (e.g., CD-ROM, diskette) editions in the same establishment or using proprietary networks to distribute content--are classified in Subsector 511, Publishing Industries (except Internet), based on the materials produced;
- Providing Internet access via client-supplied telecommunications connections--are classified in U.S. Industry 517919, All Other Telecommunications;
- Providing streaming services on content owned by others--are classified in Industry 518210, Data Processing, Hosting, and Related Services;
- Wholesaling goods on the Internet--are classified in Sector 42, Wholesale Trade;
- Retailing goods on the Internet--are classified in Sector 44-45, Retail Trade; and
- Operating stock brokerages, travel reservation systems, purchasing services, and similar activities using the Internet rather than traditional methods--are classified with the more traditional establishments providing these services.

51919   All Other Information Services[T]
See industry description for 519190.

519190   All Other Information Services

This industry comprises establishments primarily engaged in providing other information services (except news syndicates, libraries, archives, Internet publishing and broadcasting, and Web search portals).

Illustrative Examples:

News clipping services
Telephone-based recorded information services

Stock photo agencies

Cross-References.   Establishments primarily engaged in--

- Providing wired broadband Internet access services using own operated telecommunications infrastructure--are classified in U.S. Industry 517311, Wired Telecommunications Carriers;
- Providing Internet access via client-supplied telecommunications connections--are classified in U.S. Industry 517919, All Other Telecommunications;
- Publishing (except exclusively on the Internet)--are classified in Subsector 511, Publishing Industries (except Internet);
- Publishing or broadcasting exclusively on the Internet--are classified in Industry 519130, Internet Publishing and Broadcasting and Web Search Portals;
- Operating Web search portals--are classified in Industry 519130, Internet Publishing and Broadcasting and Web Search Portals;
- Operating news syndicates--are classified in Industry 519110, News Syndicates; and
- Operating libraries and archives--are classified in Industry 519120, Libraries and Archives.

T—Canadian, Mexican, and United States industries are comparable.

Sector 52--Finance and Insurance[T]

The Sector as a Whole

The Finance and Insurance sector comprises establishments primarily engaged in financial transactions (transactions involving the creation, liquidation, or change in ownership of financial assets) and/or in facilitating financial transactions. Three principal types of activities are identified:

1. Raising funds by taking deposits and/or issuing securities and, in the process, incurring liabilities. Establishments engaged in this activity use raised funds to acquire financial assets by making loans and/or purchasing securities. Putting themselves at risk, they channel funds from lenders to borrowers and transform or repackage the funds with respect to maturity, scale, and risk. This activity is known as financial intermediation.

2. Pooling of risk by underwriting insurance and annuities. Establishments engaged in this activity collect fees, insurance premiums, or annuity considerations; build up reserves; invest those reserves; and make contractual payments. Fees are based on the expected incidence of the insured risk and the expected return on investment.

3. Providing specialized services facilitating or supporting financial intermediation, insurance, and employee benefit programs.

In addition, monetary authorities charged with monetary control are included in this sector.

The subsectors, industry groups, and industries within the Finance and Insurance sector are defined on the basis of their unique production processes. As with all industries, the production processes are distinguished by their use of specialized human resources and specialized physical capital. In addition, the way in which these establishments acquire and allocate financial capital, their source of funds, and the use of those funds provides a third basis for distinguishing characteristics of the production process. For instance, the production process in raising funds through deposit-taking is different from the process of raising funds in bond or money markets. The process of making loans to individuals also requires different production processes than does the creation of investment pools or the underwriting of securities.

Most of the Finance and Insurance subsectors contain one or more industry groups of (1) intermediaries with similar patterns of raising and using funds and (2) establishments engaged in activities that facilitate, or are otherwise related to, that type of financial or insurance intermediation. Industries within this sector are defined in terms of activities for which a production process can be specified, and many of these activities are not exclusive to a particular type of financial institution. To deal with the varied activities taking place within existing financial institutions, the approach is to split these institutions into components performing specialized services. This requires defining the units engaged in providing those services and developing procedures that allow for their delineation. These units are the equivalents for finance and insurance of the establishments defined for other industries.

The output of many financial services, as well as the inputs and the processes by which they are combined, cannot be observed at a single location and can only be defined at a higher level of the organizational structure of the enterprise. Additionally, a number of independent activities that represent separate and distinct production processes may take place at a single location belonging to a multilocation financial firm. Activities are more likely to be homogeneous with respect to production characteristics than are locations, at least in financial services. The classification defines activities broadly enough that it can be used both by those classifying by location and by those employing a more top-down approach to the delineation of the establishment.

Establishments engaged in activities that facilitate, or are otherwise related to, the various types of intermediation are included in multiple subsectors, rather than in a separate subsector dedicated to services alone, because these services are performed by intermediaries, as well as by specialist establishments, and the extent to which the activity of the intermediaries can be separately identified is not clear.

Financial industries are extensive users of electronic means for facilitating the verification of financial balances, authorizing transactions, transferring funds to and from transactors' accounts, notifying banks (or credit card issuers) of the individual transactions, and providing daily summaries. Since these transaction processing activities are integral to the production of finance and insurance services, establishments that principally provide a financial transaction processing service are classified in this sector, rather than in the data processing industry in the Information sector.

T—Canadian, Mexican, and United States industries are comparable.

Legal entities that hold portfolios of assets on behalf of others are significant and data on them are required for a variety of purposes. Thus for NAICS, these funds, trusts, and other financial vehicles are the fifth subsector of the Finance and Insurance sector. These entities earn interest, dividends, and other property income, but have little or no employment and no revenue from the sale of services. Separate establishments and employees devoted to the management of funds are classified in Industry Group 5239, Other Financial Investment Activities.

521   Monetary Authorities-Central Bank[T]

The Monetary Authorities-Central Bank subsector groups establishments that engage in performing central banking functions, such as issuing currency, managing the Nation's money supply and international reserves, holding deposits that represent the reserves of other banks and other central banks, and acting as a fiscal agent for the central government.

5211   Monetary Authorities-Central Bank[T]

52111   Monetary Authorities-Central Bank[T]
See industry description for 521110.

521110 Monetary Authorities-Central Bank

This industry comprises establishments primarily engaged in performing central banking functions, such as issuing currency, managing the Nation's money supply and international reserves, holding deposits that represent the reserves of other banks and other central banks, and acting as a fiscal agent for the central government.

Cross-References.

Establishments of the Board of Governors of the Federal Reserve System are classified in Industry 921130, Public Finance Activities.

522   Credit Intermediation and Related Activities[T]

Industries in the Credit Intermediation and Related Activities subsector group establishments that (1) lend funds raised from depositors; (2) lend funds raised from credit market borrowing; or (3) facilitate the lending of funds or issuance of credit by engaging in such activities as mortgage and loan brokerage, clearinghouse and reserve services, and check cashing services.

5221   Depository Credit Intermediation

This industry group comprises establishments primarily engaged in accepting deposits (or share deposits) and in lending funds from these deposits. Within this group, industries are defined on the basis of differences in the types of deposit liabilities assumed and in the nature of the credit extended.

52211   Commercial Banking
See industry description for 522110.

522110 Commercial Banking

This industry comprises establishments primarily engaged in accepting demand and other deposits and making commercial, industrial, and consumer loans. Commercial banks and branches of foreign banks are included in this industry.

Cross-References.

- Establishments primarily engaged in credit card banking are classified in Industry 522210, Credit Card Issuing;

T—Canadian, Mexican, and United States industries are comparable.

- Establishments known as industrial banks and primarily engaged in accepting deposits are classified in Industry 522190, Other Depository Credit Intermediation; and
- Establishments of depository institutions primarily engaged in trust activities are classified in U.S. Industry 523991, Trust, Fiduciary, and Custody Activities.

52212 Savings Institutions
See industry description for 522120.

522120 Savings Institutions

This industry comprises establishments primarily engaged in accepting time deposits, making mortgage and real estate loans, and investing in high-grade securities. Savings and loan associations and savings banks are included in this industry.

Cross-References.

Establishments primarily engaged in accepting demand and other deposits and making all types of loans are classified in Industry 522110, Commercial Banking.

52213 Credit Unions
See industry description for 522130.

522130 Credit Unions

This industry comprises establishments primarily engaged in accepting members' share deposits in cooperatives that are organized to offer consumer loans to their members.

52219 Other Depository Credit Intermediation
See industry description for 522190.

522190 Other Depository Credit Intermediation

This industry comprises establishments primarily engaged in accepting deposits and lending funds (except commercial banking, savings institutions, and credit unions). Establishments known as industrial banks or Morris Plans and primarily engaged in accepting deposits, and private banks (i.e., unincorporated banks) are included in this industry.

Cross-References.

- Establishments primarily engaged in accepting demand and other deposits and making all types of loans are classified in Industry 522110, Commercial Banking;
- Establishments primarily engaged in accepting time deposits are classified in Industry 522120, Savings Institutions;
- Establishments primarily engaged in accepting members' share deposits in cooperatives are classified in Industry 522130, Credit Unions; and
- Establishments known as industrial banks and Morris Plans and primarily engaged in providing nondepository credit are classified in U.S. Industry 522298, All Other Nondepository Credit Intermediation.

5222 Nondepository Credit Intermediation

This industry group comprises establishments, both public (government-sponsored enterprises) and private, primarily engaged in extending credit or lending funds raised by credit market borrowing, such as issuing commercial paper or other debt instruments or by borrowing from other financial intermediaries. Within this group, industries are defined on the basis of the type of credit being extended.

T—Canadian, Mexican, and United States industries are comparable.

52221   Credit Card Issuing
See industry description for 522210.

522210 Credit Card Issuing

This industry comprises establishments primarily engaged in providing credit by issuing credit cards. Credit card issuance provides the funds required to purchase goods and services in return for payment of the full balance or payments on an installment basis. Credit card banks are included in this industry.

Cross-References.

Establishments primarily engaged in issuing cards that contain a stored pre-paid value are classified with the industry providing the service represented by the cards, such as transit fare cards in Subsector 482, Rail Transportation, and long-distance telephone cards in Subsector 517, Telecommunications.

52222   Sales Financing
See industry description for 522220.

522220 Sales Financing

This industry comprises establishments primarily engaged in sales financing or sales financing in combination with leasing. Sales financing establishments are primarily engaged in lending money for the purpose of providing collateralized goods through a contractual installment sales agreement, either directly from or through arrangements with dealers.

Cross-References.

Establishments not engaged in sales financing, but primarily engaged in providing leases for equipment and other assets are classified in Subsector 532, Rental and Leasing Services.

52229   Other Nondepository Credit Intermediation

This industry comprises establishments primarily engaged in making cash loans or extending credit through credit instruments (except credit cards and sales finance agreements).

Illustrative Examples:

Consumer finance companies (i.e., unsecured cash loans)
Mortgage companies

International trade financing
Secondary market financing

Cross-References.   Establishments primarily engaged in--

- Providing credit sales by issuing credit cards--are classified in Industry 52221, Credit Card Issuing;
- Providing leases for equipment and other assets without sales financing--are classified in Subsector 532, Rental and Leasing Services;
- Accepting deposits and lending funds from these deposits--are classified in Industry Group 5221, Depository Credit Intermediation;
- Arranging loans for others on a commission or fee basis--are classified in Industry 52231, Mortgage and Nonmortgage Loan Brokers; and
- Guaranteeing international trade loans--are classified in Industry 52412, Direct Insurance (except Life, Health, and Medical) Carriers.

T—Canadian, Mexican, and United States industries are comparable.

522291 Consumer Lending

This U.S. industry comprises establishments primarily engaged in making unsecured cash loans to consumers.

Illustrative Examples:

Finance companies (i.e., unsecured cash loans)
Personal credit institutions (i.e., unsecured cash loans)

Loan companies (i.e., consumer, personal, student, small)
Student loan companies

Cross-References. Establishments primarily engaged in--

- Accepting deposits and lending funds from these deposits--are classified in Industry Group 5221, Depository Credit Intermediation; and
- Arranging loans for others on a commission or fee basis--are classified in Industry 522310, Mortgage and Nonmortgage Loan Brokers.

522292 Real Estate Credit

This U.S. industry comprises establishments primarily engaged in lending funds with real estate as collateral.

Illustrative Examples:

Home equity credit lending
Mortgage companies

Mortgage banking (i.e., nondepository mortgage lending)

Cross-References. Establishments primarily engaged in--

- Servicing loans--are classified in Industry 522390, Other Activities Related to Credit Intermediation;
- Arranging loans for others on a commission or fee basis--are classified in Industry 522310, Mortgage and Nonmortgage Loan Brokers; and
- Accepting deposits and lending funds secured by real estate--are classified in Industry Group 5221, Depository Credit Intermediation.

522293 International Trade Financing

This U.S. industry comprises establishments primarily engaged in providing one or more of the following: (1) working capital funds to U.S. exporters; (2) lending funds to foreign buyers of U.S. goods; and/or (3) lending funds to domestic buyers of imported goods.

Illustrative Examples:

Agreement corporations (i.e., international trade financing)
Export-Import banks

Edge Act corporations (i.e., international trade financing)
Trade banks (i.e., international trade financing)

Cross-References. Establishments primarily engaged in--

- Guaranteeing international trade loans--are classified in U.S. Industry 524126, Direct Property and Casualty Insurance Carriers;
- Brokering international trade loans--are classified in Industry 522310, Mortgage and Nonmortgage Loan Brokers; and
- Accepting deposits and lending funds from these deposits--are classified in Industry Group 5221, Depository Credit Intermediation.

T—Canadian, Mexican, and United States industries are comparable.

522294 Secondary Market Financing

This U.S. industry comprises establishments primarily engaged in buying, pooling, and repackaging loans for sale to others on the secondary market.

Illustrative Examples:

Federal Home Loan Mortgage
Corporation (FHLMC)
Government National Mortgage
Association (GNMA)

Federal National Mortgage
Association (FNMA)
Student Loan Marketing
Association (SLMA)

522298 All Other Nondepository Credit Intermediation

This U.S. industry comprises establishments primarily engaged in providing nondepository credit (except credit card issuing, sales financing, consumer lending, real estate credit, international trade financing, and secondary market financing). Examples of types of lending in this industry are short-term inventory credit, agricultural lending (except real estate and sales financing), and consumer cash lending secured by personal property.

Illustrative Examples:

Commodity Credit Corporation
Morris Plans (i.e., known as), nondepository
Factoring accounts receivable

Pawnshops
Industrial banks (i.e., known as), nondepository

Cross-References.

- Establishments primarily engaged in providing credit sales funding are classified in Industry 522210, Credit Card Issuing;
- Establishments primarily engaged in sales financing or sales financing in combination with leasing are classified in Industry 522220, Sales Financing;
- Establishments primarily engaged in making unsecured cash loans to consumers are classified in U.S. Industry 522291, Consumer Lending;
- Establishments primarily engaged in lending funds with real estate as collateral are classified in U.S. Industry 522292, Real Estate Credit;
- Establishments primarily engaged in international trade financing are classified in U.S. Industry 522293, International Trade Financing;
- Establishments primarily engaged in buying, pooling, and repackaging loans for sale to others on the secondary market are classified in U.S. Industry 522294, Secondary Market Financing; and
- Establishments known as industrial banks or Morris Plans and primarily engaged in accepting deposits are classified in Industry 522190, Other Depository Credit Intermediation.

5223   Activities Related to Credit Intermediation

This industry group comprises establishments primarily engaged in facilitating credit intermediation by performing activities, such as arranging loans by bringing borrowers and lenders together and clearing checks and credit card transactions.

52231   Mortgage and Nonmortgage Loan Brokers
     See industry description for 522310.

522310 Mortgage and Nonmortgage Loan Brokers

This industry comprises establishments primarily engaged in arranging loans by bringing borrowers and lenders together on a commission or fee basis.

T—Canadian, Mexican, and United States industries are comparable.

Cross-References.   Establishments primarily engaged in--

- Lending funds with real estate as collateral--are classified in U.S. Industry 522292, Real Estate Credit; and
- Servicing loans--are classified in Industry 522390, Other Activities Related to Credit Intermediation.

52232   Financial Transactions Processing, Reserve, and Clearinghouse Activities
See industry description for 522320.

522320   Financial Transactions Processing, Reserve, and Clearinghouse Activities

This industry comprises establishments primarily engaged in providing one or more of the following: (1) financial transaction processing (except central bank); (2) reserve and liquidity services (except central bank); and/or (3) check or other financial instrument clearinghouse services (except central bank).

Illustrative Examples:

Automated clearinghouses, bank or check (except central bank)
Credit card processing services

Check clearing services (except central bank)
Electronic funds transfer services

Cross-References.

- Establishments primarily engaged in nonfinancial data and electronic transaction processing are classified in Industry 518210, Data Processing, Hosting, and Related Services; and
- Establishments of the central bank primarily engaged in check clearing and other financial transaction processing are classified in Industry 521110, Monetary Authorities-Central Bank.

52239   Other Activities Related to Credit Intermediation
See industry description for 522390.

522390   Other Activities Related to Credit Intermediation

This industry comprises establishments primarily engaged in facilitating credit intermediation (except mortgage and loan brokerage; and financial transactions processing, reserve, and clearinghouse activities).

Illustrative Examples:

Check cashing services
Money order issuance services
Loan servicing

Travelers' check issuance services
Money transmission services
Payday lending services

Cross-References.   Establishments primarily engaged in--

- Arranging loans for others on a commission or fee basis--are classified in Industry 522310, Mortgage and Nonmortgage Loan Brokers;
- Providing financial transactions processing, reserve, and clearinghouse activities--are classified in Industry 522320, Financial Transactions Processing, Reserve, and Clearinghouse Activities;
- Foreign currency exchange dealing--are classified in Industry 523130, Commodity Contracts Dealing; and
- Providing escrow services (except real estate)--are classified in U.S. Industry 523991, Trust, Fiduciary, and Custody Activities.

523   Securities, Commodity Contracts, and Other Financial Investments and Related Activities[T]

Industries in the Securities, Commodity Contracts, and Other Financial Investments and Related Activities subsector group establishments that are primarily engaged in one of the following: (1) underwriting securities issues

---

T—Canadian, Mexican, and United States industries are comparable.

and/or making markets for securities and commodities; (2) acting as agents (i.e., brokers) between buyers and sellers of securities and commodities; (3) providing securities and commodity exchange services; and (4) providing other services, such as managing portfolios of assets; providing investment advice; and trust, fiduciary, and custody services.

5231   Securities and Commodity Contracts Intermediation and Brokerage[T]

This industry group comprises establishments primarily engaged in putting capital at risk in the process of underwriting securities issues or in making markets for securities and commodities; and those acting as agents and/or brokers between buyers and sellers of securities and commodities, usually charging a commission.

52311   Investment Banking and Securities Dealing
See industry description for 523110.

523110   Investment Banking and Securities Dealing

This industry comprises establishments primarily engaged in underwriting, originating, and/or maintaining markets for issues of securities. Investment bankers act as principals (i.e., investors who buy or sell on their own account) in firm commitment transactions or act as agents in best effort and standby commitments. This industry also includes establishments acting as principals in buying or selling securities generally on a spread basis, such as securities dealers or stock option dealers.

Illustrative Examples:

Bond dealing (i.e., acting as a principal in dealing securities to investors)

Stock options dealing
Securities underwriting

Cross-References.

- Establishments primarily engaged in acting as agents (i.e., brokers) in buying or selling securities on a commission or transaction fee basis are classified in Industry 523120, Securities Brokerage; and
- Investment clubs or individual investors primarily engaged in buying or selling financial contracts (e.g., securities) on their own account are classified in Industry 523910, Miscellaneous Intermediation.

52312   Securities Brokerage
See industry description for 523120.

523120   Securities Brokerage

This industry comprises establishments primarily engaged in acting as agents (i.e., brokers) between buyers and sellers in buying or selling securities on a commission or transaction fee basis.

Illustrative Examples:

Mutual fund agencies (i.e., brokerages)
Stock brokerages

Securities brokerages

Cross-References.

Establishments primarily engaged in investment banking and securities dealing (i.e., buying or selling securities on their own account) are classified in Industry 523110, Investment Banking and Securities Dealing.

52313   Commodity Contracts Dealing
See industry description for 523130.

T—Canadian, Mexican, and United States industries are comparable.

census.gov/naics

523130 Commodity Contracts Dealing

This industry comprises establishments primarily engaged in acting as principals (i.e., investors who buy or sell for their own account) in buying or selling spot or futures commodity contracts or options, such as precious metals, foreign currency, oil, or agricultural products, generally on a spread basis.

Cross-References.   Establishments primarily engaged in--

- Acting as agents (i.e., brokers) in buying or selling spot or futures commodity contracts on a commission or transaction fee basis--are classified in Industry 523140, Commodity Contracts Brokerage; and
- Buying and selling physical commodities for resale to other than the general public--are classified in Sector 42, Wholesale Trade.

52314 Commodity Contracts Brokerage
See industry description for 523140.

523140 Commodity Contracts Brokerage

This industry comprises establishments primarily engaged in acting as agents (i.e., brokers) in buying or selling spot or futures commodity contracts or options on a commission or transaction fee basis.

Illustrative Examples:

Commodity contracts brokerages   Commodity futures brokerages
Financial futures brokerages

Cross-References.   Establishments primarily engaged in--

- Acting as principals in buying or selling spot or futures commodity contracts generally on a spread basis-- are classified in Industry 523130, Commodity Contracts Dealing; and
- Buying and selling physical commodities for resale to other than the general public--are classified in Sector 42, Wholesale Trade.

5232 Securities and Commodity Exchanges[T]

52321 Securities and Commodity Exchanges[T]
See industry description for 523210.

523210 Securities and Commodity Exchanges

This industry comprises establishments primarily engaged in furnishing physical or electronic marketplaces for the purpose of facilitating the buying and selling of stocks, stock options, bonds, or commodity contracts.

Cross-References.

Establishments primarily engaged in investment banking, securities dealing, securities brokering, commodity contracts dealing, or commodity contracts brokering are classified in Industry Group 5231, Securities and Commodity Contracts Intermediation and Brokerage.

5239 Other Financial Investment Activities[T]

This industry group comprises establishments primarily engaged in one of the following: (1) acting as principals in buying or selling financial contracts (except investment bankers, securities dealers, and commodity contracts dealers); (2) acting as agents (i.e., brokers) (except securities brokerages and commodity contracts brokerages) in

---

T—Canadian, Mexican, and United States industries are comparable.

buying or selling financial contracts; or (3) providing other investment services (except securities and commodity exchanges), such as portfolio management; investment advice; and trust, fiduciary, and custody services.

52391   Miscellaneous Intermediation
See industry description for 523910.

523910 Miscellaneous Intermediation

This industry comprises establishments primarily engaged in acting as principals (except investment bankers, securities dealers, and commodity contracts dealers) in buying or selling financial contracts generally on a spread basis. Principals are investors that buy or sell for their own account.

Illustrative Examples:

Investment clubs
Tax liens dealing (i.e., acting as a principal in dealing tax liens to investors)

Mineral royalties or leases dealing (i.e., acting as a principal in dealing royalties or leases to investors)
Venture capital companies

Cross-References.

Establishments primarily engaged in investment banking, securities dealing, securities brokering, commodity contracts dealing, or commodity contracts brokering are classified in Industry Group 5231, Securities and Commodity Contracts Intermediation and Brokerage.

52392   Portfolio Management
See industry description for 523920.

523920 Portfolio Management

This industry comprises establishments primarily engaged in managing the portfolio assets (i.e., funds) of others on a fee or commission basis. Establishments in this industry have the authority to make investment decisions, and they derive fees based on the size and/or overall performance of the portfolio.

Illustrative Examples:

Managing trusts
Pension fund managing

Mutual fund managing
Portfolio fund managing

Cross-References.

Establishments primarily engaged in investment banking, securities dealing, securities brokering, commodity contracts dealing, or commodity contracts brokering are classified in Industry Group 5231, Securities and Commodity Contracts Intermediation and Brokerage.

52393   Investment Advice
See industry description for 523930.

523930 Investment Advice

This industry comprises establishments primarily engaged in providing customized investment advice to clients on a fee basis, but do not have the authority to execute trades. Primary activities performed by establishments in this industry are providing financial planning advice and investment counseling to meet the goals and needs of specific clients.

T—Canadian, Mexican, and United States industries are comparable.

Illustrative Examples:

Financial investment advice services, customized, fees paid by client

Investment advisory services, customized, fees paid by client

Financial planning services, customized, fees paid by client

Cross-References.

- Establishments providing investment advice in conjunction with their primary activity, such as portfolio management, or the sale of stocks, bonds, annuities, and real estate, are classified according to their primary activity; and
- Establishments known as publishers providing generalized investment information to subscribers are classified in Subsector 511, Publishing Industries (except Internet), or Industry 519130, Internet Publishing and Broadcasting and Web Search Portals.

52399   All Other Financial Investment Activities

This industry comprises establishments primarily engaged in acting as agents or brokers (except securities brokerages and commodity contracts brokerages) in buying and selling financial contracts and those providing financial investment services (except securities and commodity exchanges, portfolio management, and investment advice).

Illustrative Examples:

Bank trust offices
Fiduciary agencies (except real estate)

Escrow agencies (except real estate)
Stock quotation services

Cross-References.   Establishments primarily engaged in--

- Investment banking, securities dealing, securities brokerage, commodity contracts dealing, or commodity contracts brokering--are classified in Industry Group 5231, Securities and Commodity Contracts Intermediation and Brokerage;
- Acting as principals (except investment bankers, securities dealers, and commodity contracts dealers) in buying or selling financial contracts (except securities or commodity contracts)--are classified in Industry 52391, Miscellaneous Intermediation;
- Furnishing physical or electronic marketplaces for the purpose of facilitating the buying and selling of securities and commodities--are classified in Industry 52321, Securities and Commodity Exchanges;
- Managing the portfolio assets (i.e., funds) of others--are classified in Industry 52392, Portfolio Management;
- Providing customized investment advice--are classified in Industry 52393, Investment Advice;
- Awarding grants from trust funds--are classified in Industry 81321, Grantmaking and Giving Services;
- Performing real estate escrow or real estate fiduciary activities--are classified in Industry 53139, Other Activities Related to Real Estate; and
- Financial transactions processing, reserve, and clearinghouse activities--are classified in Industry 52232, Financial Transactions Processing, Reserve, and Clearinghouse Activities.

523991 Trust, Fiduciary, and Custody Activities

This U.S. industry comprises establishments primarily engaged in providing trust, fiduciary, and custody services to others, as instructed, on a fee or contract basis, such as bank trust offices and escrow agencies (except real estate).

T—Canadian, Mexican, and United States industries are comparable.

Cross-References. Establishments primarily engaged in--

- Managing the portfolio assets (i.e., funds) of others--are classified in Industry 523920, Portfolio Management;
- Performing real estate escrow or real estate fiduciary activities--are classified in Industry 531390, Other Activities Related to Real Estate; and
- Awarding grants from trust funds--are classified in Industry 81321, Grantmaking and Giving Services.

523999 Miscellaneous Financial Investment Activities

This U.S. industry comprises establishments primarily engaged in acting as agents and/or brokers (except securities brokerages and commodity contracts brokerages) in buying or selling financial contracts and those providing financial investment services (except securities and commodity exchanges; portfolio management; investment advice; and trust, fiduciary, and custody services) on a fee or commission basis.

Illustrative Examples:

Exchange clearinghouses, commodities or securities   Gas lease brokers' offices
Stock quotation services

Cross-References. Establishments primarily engaged in--

- Investment banking, securities dealing, securities brokering, commodity contracts dealing, or commodity contracts brokering--are classified in Industry Group 5231, Securities and Commodity Contracts Intermediation and Brokerage;
- Acting as principals (except investment bankers, securities dealers, and commodity contracts dealers) in buying or selling financial contracts--are classified in Industry 523910, Miscellaneous Intermediation;
- Furnishing physical or electronic marketplaces for the purpose of facilitating the buying and selling of securities and commodities--are classified in Industry 523210, Securities and Commodity Exchanges;
- Managing the portfolio assets (i.e., funds) of others--are classified in Industry 523920, Portfolio Management;
- Providing customized investment advice--are classified in Industry 523930, Investment Advice;
- Providing trust, fiduciary, and custody services to others--are classified in U.S. Industry 523991, Trust, Fiduciary, and Custody Activities; and
- Financial transactions processing, reserve, and clearinghouse activities--are classified in Industry 522320, Financial Transactions Processing, Reserve, and Clearinghouse Activities.

524 Insurance Carriers and Related Activities[T]

Industries in the Insurance Carriers and Related Activities subsector group establishments that are primarily engaged in one of the following: (1) underwriting (assuming the risk, assigning premiums, and so forth) annuities and insurance policies or (2) facilitating such underwriting by selling insurance policies and by providing other insurance and employee benefit related services.

5241 Insurance Carriers[T]

This industry group comprises establishments primarily engaged in underwriting (assuming the risk, assigning premiums, and so forth) annuities and insurance policies and investing premiums to build up a portfolio of financial assets to be used against future claims. Direct insurance carriers are establishments that are primarily engaged in initially underwriting and assuming the risk of annuities and insurance policies. Reinsurance carriers are establishments that are primarily engaged in assuming all or part of the risk associated with an existing insurance policy (or set of policies) originally underwritten by another insurance carrier.

Industries are defined in terms of the type of risk being insured against, such as death, loss of employment because of age or disability, and/or property damage. Contributions and premiums are set on the basis of actuarial

---

T—Canadian, Mexican, and United States industries are comparable.

calculations of probable payouts based on risk factors from experience tables and expected investment returns on reserves.

52411 Direct Life, Health, and Medical Insurance Carriers

This industry comprises establishments primarily engaged in initially underwriting (i.e., assuming the risk and assigning premiums) annuities and life insurance policies, disability income insurance policies, accidental death and dismemberment insurance policies, and health and medical insurance policies.

Cross-References.

- Establishments primarily engaged in reinsuring insurance policies are classified in Industry 52413, Reinsurance Carriers;
- Legal entities (i.e., funds, plans, and/or programs) organized to provide insurance and employee benefits exclusively for the sponsor, firm, or its employees or members are classified in Industry Group 5251, Insurance and Employee Benefit Funds; and
- HMO establishments providing health care services are classified in Industry 62149, Other Outpatient Care Centers.

524113 Direct Life Insurance Carriers

This U.S. industry comprises establishments primarily engaged in initially underwriting (i.e., assuming the risk and assigning premiums) annuities and life insurance policies, disability income insurance policies, and accidental death and dismemberment insurance policies.

Cross-References.

- Establishments primarily engaged in reinsuring life insurance policies, disability income insurance policies, and accidental death and dismemberment insurance policies are classified in Industry 524130, Reinsurance Carriers; and
- Legal entities (i.e., funds, plans, and/or programs) organized to provide insurance and employee benefits exclusively for the sponsor, firm, or its employees or members are classified in Industry Group 5251, Insurance and Employee Benefit Funds.

524114 Direct Health and Medical Insurance Carriers

This U.S. industry comprises establishments primarily engaged in initially underwriting (i.e., assuming the risk and assigning premiums) health and medical insurance policies. Group hospitalization plans and HMO establishments that provide health and medical insurance policies without providing health care services are included in this industry.

Cross-References.

- HMO establishments that provide both health care services and underwrite health and medical insurance are classified in U.S. Industry 621491, HMO Medical Centers;
- Establishments primarily engaged in reinsuring health insurance policies are classified in Industry 524130, Reinsurance Carriers; and
- Legal entities (i.e., funds, plans, and/or programs) organized to provide health- and welfare-related employee benefits exclusively for the sponsor's employees or members are classified in Industry 525120, Health and Welfare Funds.

T—Canadian, Mexican, and United States industries are comparable.

52412 Direct Insurance (except Life, Health, and Medical) Carriers

This industry comprises establishments primarily engaged in initially underwriting (i.e., assuming the risk and assigning premiums) various types of insurance policies (except life, disability income, accidental death and dismemberment, and health and medical insurance policies).

Illustrative Examples:

Automobile insurance carriers, direct
Property and casualty insurance carriers, direct
Bank deposit insurance carriers, direct
Title insurance carriers, real estate, direct

Mortgage guaranty insurance carriers, direct
Warranty insurance carriers (e.g., appliance, automobile, homeowners', product), direct

Cross-References.

- Establishments primarily engaged in reinsuring insurance policies are classified in Industry 52413, Reinsurance Carriers;
- Legal entities (i.e., funds, plans, and/or programs) organized to provide insurance and employee benefits exclusively for the sponsor, firm, or its employees or members are classified in Industry Group 5251, Insurance and Employee Benefit Funds; and
- Establishments primarily engaged in initially underwriting annuities and life insurance policies, disability income insurance policies, accidental death and dismemberment insurance policies, and health and medical insurance policies are classified in Industry 52411, Direct Life, Health, and Medical Insurance Carriers.

524126 Direct Property and Casualty Insurance Carriers

This U.S. industry comprises establishments primarily engaged in initially underwriting (i.e., assuming the risk and assigning premiums) insurance policies that protect policyholders against losses that may occur as a result of property damage or liability.

Illustrative Examples:

Automobile insurance carriers, direct
Malpractice insurance carriers, direct
Fidelity insurance carriers, direct
Mortgage guaranty insurance carriers, direct

Homeowners' insurance carriers, direct
Surety insurance carriers, direct
Liability insurance carriers, direct

Cross-References.

Establishments primarily engaged in reinsuring property and casualty insurance policies are classified in Industry 524130, Reinsurance Carriers.

524127 Direct Title Insurance Carriers

This U.S. industry comprises establishments primarily engaged in initially underwriting (i.e., assuming the risk and assigning premiums) insurance policies to protect the owners of real estate or real estate creditors against loss sustained by reason of any title defect to real property.

Cross-References.

Establishments primarily engaged in reinsuring title insurance policies are classified in Industry 524130, Reinsurance Carriers.

T—Canadian, Mexican, and United States industries are comparable.

524128   Other Direct Insurance (except Life, Health, and Medical) Carriers

This U.S. industry comprises establishments primarily engaged in initially underwriting (e.g., assuming the risk, assigning premiums) insurance policies (except life, disability income, accidental death and dismemberment, health and medical, property and casualty, and title insurance policies).

Illustrative Examples:

Bank deposit insurance carriers, direct
Product warranty insurance carriers, direct
Deposit or share insurance carriers, direct

Warranty insurance carriers (e.g., appliance,
automobile, homeowners', product), direct

Cross-References.   Establishments primarily engaged in--

- Reinsuring insurance policies--are classified in Industry 524130, Reinsurance Carriers;
- Initially underwriting annuities and life insurance policies, disability income insurance policies, and accidental death and dismemberment insurance policies--are classified in U.S. Industry 524113, Direct Life Insurance Carriers;
- Initially underwriting health and medical insurance policies--are classified in U.S. Industry 524114, Direct Health and Medical Insurance Carriers;
- Initially underwriting property and casualty insurance policies--are classified in U.S. Industry 524126, Direct Property and Casualty Insurance Carriers; and
- Initially underwriting title insurance policies--are classified in U.S. Industry 524127, Direct Title Insurance Carriers.

52413   Reinsurance Carriers
See industry description for 524130.

524130   Reinsurance Carriers

This industry comprises establishments primarily engaged in assuming all or part of the risk associated with existing insurance policies originally underwritten by other insurance carriers.

Cross-References.   Establishments primarily engaged in--

- Initially underwriting annuities and life insurance policies, disability income insurance policies, accidental death and dismemberment insurance policies, and health and medical insurance policies--are classified in Industry 52411, Direct Life, Health, and Medical Insurance Carriers; and
- Initially underwriting various types of insurance policies (except life, disability income, accidental death and dismemberment, and health and medical insurance policies)--are classified in Industry 52412, Direct Insurance (except Life, Health, and Medical) Carriers.

5242   Agencies, Brokerages, and Other Insurance Related Activities[T]

This industry group comprises establishments primarily engaged in (1) acting as agents (i.e., brokers) in selling annuities and insurance policies or (2) providing other employee benefits and insurance related services, such as claims adjustment and third party administration.

52421   Insurance Agencies and Brokerages
See industry description for 524210.

524210   Insurance Agencies and Brokerages

This industry comprises establishments primarily engaged in acting as agents (i.e., brokers) in selling annuities and insurance policies.

T—Canadian, Mexican, and United States industries are comparable.

Cross-References.

Establishments primarily engaged in underwriting annuities and insurance policies are classified in Industry Group 5241, Insurance Carriers.

52429   Other Insurance Related Activities

This industry comprises establishments primarily engaged in providing services related to insurance (except insurance agencies and brokerages).

Illustrative Examples:

Claims adjusting, insurance   Insurance actuarial services
Insurance plan administrative services, third party   Insurance claims adjusting

Cross-References.   Establishments primarily engaged in--

- Managing the portfolio assets (i.e., funds) of others--are classified in Industry 52392, Portfolio Management;
- Acting as agents (i.e., brokers) in selling annuities and insurance policies--are classified in Industry 52421, Insurance Agencies and Brokerages; and
- Providing actuarial consulting services--are classified in Industry 54161, Management Consulting Services.

524291 Claims Adjusting

This U.S. industry comprises establishments primarily engaged in investigating, appraising, and settling insurance claims.

524292 Third Party Administration of Insurance and Pension Funds

This U.S. industry comprises establishments primarily engaged in providing third party administration services of insurance and pension funds, such as claims processing and other administrative services to insurance carriers, employee benefit plans, and self-insurance funds.

Cross-References.   Establishments primarily engaged in--

- Managing the portfolio assets (i.e., funds) of others--are classified in Industry 523920, Portfolio Management; and
- Providing actuarial consulting services--are classified in U.S. Industry 541612, Human Resources Consulting Services.

524298 All Other Insurance Related Activities

This U.S. industry comprises establishments primarily engaged in providing insurance services on a contract or fee basis (except insurance agencies and brokerages, claims adjusting, and third party administration). Insurance advisory services, insurance actuarial services, and insurance ratemaking services are included in this industry.

Cross-References.   Establishments primarily engaged in--

- Providing actuarial consulting services--are classified in U.S. Industry 541612, Human Resources Consulting Services;
- Acting as agents (i.e., brokers) in selling annuities and insurance policies--are classified in Industry 524210, Insurance Agencies and Brokerages;
- Insurance claims adjusting--are classified in U.S. Industry 524291, Claims Adjusting; and

---

T—Canadian, Mexican, and United States industries are comparable.

- Third party administration services of insurance and pension funds--are classified in U.S. Industry 524292, Third Party Administration of Insurance and Pension Funds.

525   Funds, Trusts, and Other Financial Vehicles

Industries in the Funds, Trusts, and Other Financial Vehicles subsector group legal entities (i.e., funds, plans, and/or programs) organized to pool securities or other assets on behalf of shareholders or beneficiaries of employee benefit or other trust funds. The portfolios are customized to achieve specific investment characteristics, such as diversification, risk, rate of return, and price volatility. These entities earn interest, dividends, and other investment income, but have little or no employment and no revenue from the sale of services. Establishments with employees devoted to the management of funds are classified in Industry Group 5239, Other Financial Investment Activities.

Establishments primarily engaged in holding the securities of (or other equity interests in) other firms are classified in Sector 55, Management of Companies and Enterprises. Equity real estate investment trusts (REITs) that are primarily engaged in leasing buildings, dwellings, or other real estate property to others are classified in Subsector 531, Real Estate.

5251   Insurance and Employee Benefit Funds

This industry group comprises legal entities (i.e., funds, plans, and/or programs) organized to provide insurance and employee benefits exclusively for the sponsor, firm, or its employees or members.

52511   Pension Funds
See industry description for 525110.

525110 Pension Funds

This industry comprises legal entities (i.e., funds, plans, and/or programs) organized to provide retirement income benefits exclusively for the sponsor's employees or members.

Illustrative Examples:

Employee benefit plans   Pension funds and plans
Retirement plans

Cross-References.   Establishments primarily engaged in--

- Managing portfolios of pension funds--are classified in Industry 523920, Portfolio Management; and
- Initially underwriting annuities--are classified in U.S. Industry 524113, Direct Life Insurance Carriers.

52512   Health and Welfare Funds
See industry description for 525120.

525120 Health and Welfare Funds

This industry comprises legal entities (i.e., funds, plans, and/or programs) organized to provide medical, surgical, hospital, vacation, training, and other health- and welfare-related employee benefits exclusively for the sponsor's employees or members.

Cross-References.   Establishments primarily engaged in--

- Managing portfolios of health and welfare funds--are classified in Industry 523920, Portfolio Management; and
- Third party claims administration of health and welfare plans--are classified in U.S. Industry 524292, Third Party Administration of Insurance and Pension Funds.

T—Canadian, Mexican, and United States industries are comparable.

52519   Other Insurance Funds
See industry description for 525190.

525190   Other Insurance Funds

This industry comprises legal entities (i.e., funds (except pension, and health- and welfare-related employee benefit funds)) organized to provide insurance exclusively for the sponsor, firm, or its employees or members. Self-insurance funds (except employee benefit funds) and workers' compensation insurance funds are included in this industry.

Cross-References.

- Legal entities (i.e., funds, plans, and/or programs) organized to provide retirement income benefits exclusively for the sponsor's employees or members are classified in Industry 525110, Pension Funds;
- Legal entities (i.e., funds, plans, and/or programs) organized to provide health- and welfare-related employee benefits exclusively for the sponsor's employees or members are classified in Industry 525120, Health and Welfare Funds;
- Establishments primarily engaged in managing portfolios of insurance funds are classified in Industry 523920, Portfolio Management;
- Establishments primarily engaged in third party claims administration of insurance and other employee benefit funds are classified in U.S. Industry 524292, Third Party Administration of Insurance and Pension Funds; and
- Establishments primarily engaged in providing insurance on a fee or contract basis are classified in Industry Group 5241, Insurance Carriers.

5259   Other Investment Pools and Funds

This industry group comprises legal entities (i.e., investment pools and/or funds) organized to pool securities or other assets (except insurance and employee benefit funds) on behalf of shareholders, unitholders, or beneficiaries.

52591   Open-End Investment Funds
See industry description for 525910.

525910   Open-End Investment Funds

This industry comprises legal entities (i.e., open-end investment funds) organized to pool assets that consist of securities or other financial instruments. Shares in these pools are offered to the public in an initial offering with additional shares offered continuously and perpetually and redeemed at a specific price determined by the net asset value.

Illustrative Examples:

Investment funds, open-ended   Money market mutual funds, open-ended

52592   Trusts, Estates, and Agency Accounts
See industry description for 525920.

525920   Trusts, Estates, and Agency Accounts

This industry comprises legal entities, trusts, estates, or agency accounts, administered on behalf of the beneficiaries under the terms of a trust agreement, will, or agency agreement.

T—Canadian, Mexican, and United States industries are comparable.

Illustrative Examples:

Bankruptcy estates
Private estates (i.e., administering on behalf of
beneficiaries)

Personal investment trusts
Testamentary trusts

Cross-References.   Establishments primarily engaged in--

- Managing portfolios of trusts--are classified in Industry 523920, Portfolio Management;
- Administering personal estates--are classified in U.S. Industry 523991, Trust, Fiduciary, and Custody Activities; and
- Operating businesses of trusts and bankruptcy estates--are classified according to the kind of business operated.

52599   Other Financial Vehicles
See industry description for 525990.

525990 Other Financial Vehicles

This industry comprises legal entities (i.e., funds (except insurance and employee benefit funds; open-end investment funds; trusts, estates, and agency accounts)). Included in this industry are mortgage real estate investment trusts (REITs).

Illustrative Examples:

Closed-end investment funds
Special purpose financial vehicles
Collateralized mortgage obligations (CMOs)
Unit investment trust funds

Face-amount certificate funds
Mortgage real estate investment trusts (REITs)
Real estate mortgage investment conduits (REMICs)

Cross-References.

- Legal entities (i.e., funds, plans, and programs) that provide insurance and employee benefits exclusively for the sponsor, firm, or its employees or members are classified in Industry Group 5251, Insurance and Employee Benefit Funds;
- Legal entities (i.e., open-end investment funds) organized to pool assets that consist of securities or other financial instruments, where the pools are offered to the public in an initial offering with additional shares offered continuously and perpetually at a specific price determined by the net asset value, are classified in Industry 525910, Open-End Investment Funds;
- Legal entities (i.e., trusts, estates, or agency accounts) administered on behalf of the beneficiaries under the terms of a trust agreement, will, or agency agreement are classified in Industry 525920, Trusts, Estates, and Agency Accounts; and
- Equity real estate investment trusts (REITs) that are primarily engaged in leasing buildings, dwellings, or other real estate property to others are classified in Industry Group 5311, Lessors of Real Estate, based on primary type of real estate property leased.

T—Canadian, Mexican, and United States industries are comparable.

Sector 53--Real Estate and Rental and Leasing[T]

The Sector as a Whole

The Real Estate and Rental and Leasing sector comprises establishments primarily engaged in renting, leasing, or otherwise allowing the use of tangible or intangible assets, and establishments providing related services. The major portion of this sector comprises establishments that rent, lease, or otherwise allow the use of their own assets by others. The assets may be tangible, as is the case of real estate and equipment, or intangible, as is the case with patents and trademarks.

This sector also includes establishments primarily engaged in managing real estate for others, selling, renting and/or buying real estate for others, and appraising real estate. These activities are closely related to this sector's main activity, and from a production basis they are included here. In addition, a substantial proportion of property management is self-performed by lessors.

The main components of this sector are the real estate lessors industries (including equity real estate investment trusts (REITs)); equipment lessors industries (including motor vehicles, computers, and consumer goods); and lessors of nonfinancial intangible assets (except copyrighted works).

Excluded from this sector are establishments primarily engaged in renting or leasing equipment with operators. Establishments renting or leasing equipment with operators are classified in various subsectors of NAICS depending on the nature of the services provided (e.g., transportation, construction, agriculture). These activities are excluded from this sector because the client is paying for the expertise and knowledge of the equipment operator, in addition to the rental of the equipment. In many cases, such as the rental of heavy construction equipment, the operator is essential to operate the equipment.

531 Real Estate[T]

Industries in the Real Estate subsector group establishments primarily engaged in renting or leasing real estate to others; managing real estate for others; selling, buying, or renting real estate for others; and providing other real estate related services, such as appraisal services.

This subsector includes equity real estate investment trusts (REITs) primarily engaged in leasing buildings, dwellings, or other real estate property to others. Mortgage REITs are classified in Subsector 525, Funds, Trusts, and Other Financial Vehicles.

Establishments primarily engaged in subdividing and developing unimproved real estate and constructing buildings for sale are classified in Subsector 236, Construction of Buildings. Establishments primarily engaged in subdividing and improving raw land for subsequent sale to builders are classified in Subsector 237, Heavy and Civil Engineering Construction.

5311 Lessors of Real Estate[T]

This industry group comprises establishments primarily engaged in acting as lessors of (1) residential buildings and dwellings; (2) nonresidential buildings (except miniwarehouses); (3) miniwarehouses and self-storage units; and (4) other real estate property.

53111 Lessors of Residential Buildings and Dwellings
See industry description for 531110.

531110 Lessors of Residential Buildings and Dwellings

This industry comprises establishments primarily engaged in acting as lessors of buildings used as residences or dwellings, such as single-family homes, apartment buildings, and town homes. Included in this industry are owner-lessors and establishments renting real estate and then acting as lessors in subleasing it to others. The establishments in this industry may manage the property themselves or have another establishment manage it for them.

T—Canadian, Mexican, and United States industries are comparable.

Cross-References.

Establishments primarily engaged in managing residential real estate for others are classified in U.S. Industry 531311, Residential Property Managers.

53112   Lessors of Nonresidential Buildings (except Miniwarehouses)
     See industry description for 531120.

531120 Lessors of Nonresidential Buildings (except Miniwarehouses)

This industry comprises establishments primarily engaged in acting as lessors of buildings (except miniwarehouses and self-storage units) that are not used as residences or dwellings. Included in this industry are: (1) owner-lessors of nonresidential buildings; (2) establishments renting real estate and then acting as lessors in subleasing it to others; and (3) establishments providing full service office space, whether on a lease or service contract basis. The establishments in this industry may manage the property themselves or have another establishment manage it for them.

Cross-References.   Establishments primarily engaged in--

- Acting as lessors of buildings used as residences or dwellings--are classified in Industry 531110, Lessors of Residential Buildings and Dwellings;
- Renting or leasing space for self-storage--are classified in Industry 531130, Lessors of Miniwarehouses and Self-Storage Units;
- Managing nonresidential real estate for others--are classified in U.S. Industry 531312, Nonresidential Property Managers;
- Providing a range of office support services, such as mailbox rental, other postal and mailing (except direct mail advertising) services, document copying services, facsimile services, word processing services or on-site personal computer rental, that are not providing office space--are classified in Industry 56143, Business Service Centers;
- Managing and operating arenas, stadiums, theaters, or other related facilities and promoting and organizing performing arts productions, sports events, and similar events at those facilities--are classified in Industry 711310, Promoters of Performing Arts, Sports, and Similar Events with Facilities; and
- Operating public and contract general merchandise warehousing and storage facilities--are classified in Industry 493110, General Warehousing and Storage.

53113   Lessors of Miniwarehouses and Self-Storage Units
     See industry description for 531130.

531130 Lessors of Miniwarehouses and Self-Storage Units

This industry comprises establishments primarily engaged in renting or leasing space for self-storage. These establishments provide secure space (i.e., rooms, compartments, lockers, containers, or outdoor space) where clients can store and retrieve their goods.

Cross-References.   Establishments primarily engaged in--

- Operating public and contract general merchandise warehousing and storage facilities--are classified in Industry 493110, General Warehousing and Storage; and
- Operating coin-operated lockers--are classified in Industry 812990, All Other Personal Services.

53119   Lessors of Other Real Estate Property
     See industry description for 531190.

T—Canadian, Mexican, and United States industries are comparable.

531190 Lessors of Other Real Estate Property

This industry comprises establishments primarily engaged in acting as lessors of real estate (except buildings), such as manufactured home (i.e., mobile home) sites, vacant lots, and grazing land.

Cross-References.   Establishments primarily engaged in--

- Acting as lessors of buildings used as residences or dwellings, including on-site manufactured (mobile) homes--are classified in Industry 531110, Lessors of Residential Buildings and Dwellings;
- Acting as lessors of buildings (except miniwarehouses and self-storage units) that are not used as residences or dwellings--are classified in Industry 531120, Lessors of Nonresidential Buildings (except Miniwarehouses); and
- Renting or leasing space for self-storage--are classified in Industry 531130, Lessors of Miniwarehouses and Self-Storage Units.

5312   Offices of Real Estate Agents and Brokers[T]

53121   Offices of Real Estate Agents and Brokers[T]
See industry description for 531210.

531210 Offices of Real Estate Agents and Brokers

This industry comprises establishments primarily engaged in acting as agents and/or brokers in one or more of the following: (1) selling real estate for others; (2) buying real estate for others; and (3) renting real estate for others.

5313   Activities Related to Real Estate[T]

This industry group comprises establishments primarily engaged in providing real estate services (except lessors of real estate and offices of real estate agents and brokers). Included in this industry group are establishments primarily engaged in managing real estate for others and appraising real estate.

53131   Real Estate Property Managers

This industry comprises establishments primarily engaged in managing real property for others. Management includes ensuring that various activities associated with the overall operation of the property are performed, such as collecting rents and overseeing other services (e.g., maintenance, security, trash removal.)

Cross-References.

- Establishments primarily engaged in acting as lessors of real estate are classified in Industry Group 5311, Lessors of Real Estate; and
- Establishments formed on behalf of individual condominium owners or homeowners are classified in Industry 81399, Other Similar Organizations (except Business, Professional, Labor, and Political Organizations).

531311 Residential Property Managers

This U.S. industry comprises establishments primarily engaged in managing residential real estate for others.

Cross-References.

- Establishments primarily engaged in managing nonresidential real estate for others are classified in U.S. Industry 531312, Nonresidential Property Managers;
- Establishments primarily engaged in acting as lessors of buildings used as residences or dwellings are classified in Industry 531110, Lessors of Residential Buildings and Dwellings; and

---

T—Canadian, Mexican, and United States industries are comparable.

- Establishments formed on behalf of individual residential condominium owners or homeowners are classified in Industry 813990, Other Similar Organizations (except Business, Professional, Labor, and Political Organizations).

531312 Nonresidential Property Managers

This U.S. industry comprises establishments primarily engaged in managing nonresidential real estate for others.

Cross-References.

- Establishments primarily engaged in managing residential real estate for others are classified in U.S. Industry 531311, Residential Property Managers;
- Establishments primarily engaged in acting as lessors of buildings (except miniwarehouses and self-storage units) that are not used as residences or dwellings are classified in Industry 531120, Lessors of Nonresidential Buildings (except Miniwarehouses);
- Establishments primarily engaged in renting or leasing space for self-storage are classified in Industry 531130, Lessors of Miniwarehouses and Self-Storage Units; and
- Establishments formed on behalf of individual nonresidential condominium owners are classified in Industry 813990, Other Similar Organizations (except Business, Professional, Labor, and Political Organizations).

53132   Offices of Real Estate Appraisers
See industry description for 531320.

531320 Offices of Real Estate Appraisers

This industry comprises establishments primarily engaged in estimating the fair market value of real estate.

53139   Other Activities Related to Real Estate
See industry description for 531390.

531390 Other Activities Related to Real Estate

This industry comprises establishments primarily engaged in performing real estate related services (except lessors of real estate, offices of real estate agents and brokers, real estate property managers, and offices of real estate appraisers).

Illustrative Examples:

Real estate escrow agencies   Real estate fiduciaries' offices
Real estate listing services

Cross-References.   Establishments primarily engaged in--

- Acting as lessors of real estate--are classified in Industry Group 5311, Lessors of Real Estate;
- Selling, buying, and/or renting real estate for others--are classified in Industry 531210, Offices of Real Estate Agents and Brokers;
- Managing real estate for others--are classified in Industry 53131, Real Estate Property Managers;
- Estimating fair market value of real estate--are classified in Industry 531320, Offices of Real Estate Appraisers; and
- Researching public land records for ownership of titles and/or conveying real estate titles--are classified in U.S. Industry 541191, Title Abstract and Settlement Offices.

T—Canadian, Mexican, and United States industries are comparable.

532   Rental and Leasing Services[T]

Industries in the Rental and Leasing Services subsector include establishments that provide a wide array of tangible goods, such as automobiles, computers, consumer goods, and industrial machinery and equipment, to customers in return for a periodic rental or lease payment.

The subsector includes two main types of establishments: (1) those that are engaged in renting consumer goods and equipment and (2) those that are engaged in leasing machinery and equipment often used for business operations. The first type typically operates from a retail-like or storefront facility and maintains inventories of goods that are rented for short periods of time. The latter type typically does not operate from retail-like locations or maintain inventories, and offers longer-term leases. These establishments work directly with clients to enable them to acquire the use of equipment on a lease basis, or they work with equipment vendors or dealers to support the marketing of equipment to their customers under lease arrangements. Equipment lessors generally structure lease contracts to meet the specialized needs of their clients and use their remarketing expertise to find other users for previously leased equipment. Establishments that provide operating and capital (i.e., finance) leases are included in this subsector.

Establishments primarily engaged in leasing in combination with providing loans are classified in Sector 52, Finance and Insurance. Establishments primarily engaged in leasing real property are classified in Subsector 531, Real Estate. Establishments primarily engaged in renting or leasing equipment with operators are classified in various subsectors of NAICS depending on the nature of the services provided (e.g., transportation, construction, agriculture). These activities are excluded from this subsector since the client is paying for the expertise and knowledge of the equipment operator, in addition to the rental of the equipment. In many cases, such as the rental of heavy construction equipment, the operator is essential to operate the equipment. Likewise, since the provision of crop harvesting services includes both the equipment and operator, it is included in Subsector 115, Support Activities for Agriculture and Forestry. The rental or leasing of copyrighted works is classified in Sector 51, Information, and the rental or leasing of assets, such as patents, trademarks, and/or licensing agreements, is classified in Subsector 533, Lessors of Nonfinancial Intangible Assets (except Copyrighted Works).

5321   Automotive Equipment Rental and Leasing[T]

This industry group comprises establishments primarily engaged in renting or leasing passenger cars and trucks without drivers and utility trailers. These establishments generally operate from a retail-like facility. Some establishments offer only short-term rental, others only longer-term leases, and some provide both types of services.

53211   Passenger Car Rental and Leasing[T]

This industry comprises establishments primarily engaged in renting or leasing passenger cars without drivers.

Cross-References.   Establishments primarily engaged in--

- Renting or leasing passenger cars with drivers (e.g., limousines, hearses, taxis)--are classified in Industry Group 4853, Taxi and Limousine Service;
- Retailing passenger cars through sales or lease arrangements--are classified in Industry Group 4411, Automobile Dealers; and
- Leasing passenger cars in combination with providing loans to buyers of such vehicles--are classified in Sector 52, Finance and Insurance.

532111   Passenger Car Rental

This U.S. industry comprises establishments primarily engaged in renting passenger cars without drivers, generally for short periods of time.

Cross-References.   Establishments primarily engaged in--

- Leasing passenger cars without drivers, generally for long periods of time--are classified in U.S. Industry 532112, Passenger Car Leasing; and

---

T—Canadian, Mexican, and United States industries are comparable.

- Renting or leasing passenger cars with drivers (e.g., limousines, hearses, taxis)--are classified in Industry Group 4853, Taxi and Limousine Service.

532112 Passenger Car Leasing

This U.S. industry comprises establishments primarily engaged in leasing passenger cars without drivers, generally for long periods of time.

Cross-References.   Establishments primarily engaged in--

- Renting passenger cars without drivers, generally for short periods of time--are classified in U.S. Industry 532111, Passenger Car Rental;
- Renting or leasing passenger cars with drivers (e.g., limousines, hearses, taxis)--are classified in Industry Group 4853, Taxi and Limousine Service;
- Retailing passenger cars through sales or lease arrangements--are classified in Industry Group 4411, Automobile Dealers; and
- Leasing passenger cars in combination with providing loans to buyers of such vehicles--are classified in Sector 52, Finance and Insurance.

53212   Truck, Utility Trailer, and RV (Recreational Vehicle) Rental and Leasing[T]
See industry description for 532120.

532120 Truck, Utility Trailer, and RV (Recreational Vehicle) Rental and Leasing

This industry comprises establishments primarily engaged in renting or leasing, without drivers, one or more of the following: trucks, truck tractors, buses, semi-trailers, utility trailers, or RVs (recreational vehicles).

Cross-References.   Establishments primarily engaged in--

- Renting recreational goods, such as pleasure boats, canoes, motorcycles, mopeds, or bicycles--are classified in U.S. Industry 532284, Recreational Goods Rental;
- Renting or leasing farm tractors, industrial equipment, and industrial trucks, such as forklifts and other material handling equipment--are classified in Industry 532490, Other Commercial and Industrial Machinery and Equipment Rental and Leasing;
- Renting or leasing mobile home sites--are classified in Industry 531190, Lessors of Other Real Estate Property;
- Retailing vehicles commonly referred to as RVs through sales or lease arrangements--are classified in Industry 441210, Recreational Vehicle Dealers; and
- Leasing trucks, utility trailers, and RVs in combination with providing loans to buyers of such vehicles--are classified in Sector 52, Finance and Insurance.

5322   Consumer Goods Rental[T]

This industry group comprises establishments primarily engaged in renting personal and household-type goods. Establishments classified in this industry group generally provide short-term rental although in some instances, the goods may be leased for longer periods of time. These establishments often operate from a retail-like or storefront facility.

53221   Consumer Electronics and Appliances Rental[T]
See industry description for 532210.

532210 Consumer Electronics and Appliances Rental

This industry comprises establishments primarily engaged in renting consumer electronics equipment and appliances, such as televisions, stereos, and refrigerators. Included in this industry are appliance rental centers.

T—Canadian, Mexican, and United States industries are comparable.

Cross-References.   Establishments primarily engaged in--

- Renting or leasing computers--are classified in Industry 532420, Office Machinery and Equipment Rental and Leasing; and
- Renting a range of consumer, commercial, and industrial equipment, such as lawn and garden equipment, home repair tools, and party and banquet equipment--are classified in Industry 532310, General Rental Centers.

53228   Other Consumer Goods Rental[T]

This industry comprises establishments primarily engaged in renting consumer goods (except consumer electronics and appliances).

Illustrative Examples:

Costume rental
Formal wear rental
Furniture (i.e., residential) rental centers
Hospital bed rental and leasing (i.e., home use)

Party rental supply centers
Sporting goods rental
Video disc rental for home electronic
equipment (e.g., DVD)

Cross-References.   Establishments primarily engaged in--

- Renting consumer electronics and appliances--are classified in Industry 53221, Consumer Electronics and Appliances Rental;
- Renting a general line of products, such as lawn and garden equipment, home repair tools, and party and banquet equipment--are classified in Industry 53231, General Rental Centers;
- Renting medical equipment (except home health equipment), such as electromedical and electrotherapeutic apparatus--are classified in Industry 53249, Other Commercial and Industrial Machinery and Equipment Rental and Leasing;
- Retailing and renting musical instruments--are classified in Industry 45114, Musical Instrument and Supplies Stores;
- Providing home health care services and home health equipment--are classified in Industry 62161, Home Health Care Services; and
- Laundering and supplying uniforms and other work apparel--are classified in Industry 81233, Linen and Uniform Supply.

532281   Formal Wear and Costume Rental

This U.S. industry comprises establishments primarily engaged in renting clothing, such as formal wear, costumes (e.g., theatrical), or other clothing (except laundered uniforms and work apparel).

Cross-References.

Establishments primarily engaged in laundering and supplying uniforms and other work apparel are classified in U.S. Industry 812332, Industrial Launderers.

532282   Video Tape and Disc Rental

This U.S. industry comprises establishments primarily engaged in renting prerecorded video tapes and discs for home electronic equipment.

Cross-References.   Establishments primarily engaged in--

- Renting video recorders and players--are classified in Industry 532210, Consumer Electronics and Appliances Rental;

T—Canadian, Mexican, and United States industries are comparable.

- Retailing prerecorded video tapes and discs--are classified in U.S. Industry 443142, Electronics Stores; and
- Theatrical distribution of motion pictures and videos--are classified in Subsector 512, Motion Picture and Sound Recording Industries.

532283 Home Health Equipment Rental

This U.S. industry comprises establishments primarily engaged in renting home-type health and invalid equipment, such as wheel chairs, hospital beds, oxygen tanks, walkers, and crutches.

Cross-References.   Establishments primarily engaged in--

- Renting medical equipment (except home health equipment), such as electromedical and electrotherapeutic apparatus--are classified in Industry 532490, Other Commercial and Industrial Machinery and Equipment Rental and Leasing; and
- Providing home health care services and home health equipment--are classified in Industry 621610, Home Health Care Services.

532284 Recreational Goods Rental

This U.S. industry comprises establishments primarily engaged in renting recreational goods, such as bicycles, canoes, motorcycles, skis, sailboats, beach chairs, and beach umbrellas.

532289 All Other Consumer Goods Rental

This U.S. industry comprises establishments primarily engaged in renting consumer goods and products (except consumer electronics and appliances; formal wear and costumes; prerecorded video tapes and discs for home electronic equipment; home health furniture and equipment; and recreational goods). Included in this industry are furniture rental centers and party rental supply centers.

Cross-References.   Establishments primarily engaged in--

- Renting consumer electronics and appliances--are classified in Industry 532210, Consumer Electronics and Appliances Rental;
- Renting formal wear and costumes--are classified in U.S. Industry 532281, Formal Wear and Costume Rental;
- Renting video tapes and discs--are classified in U.S. Industry 532282, Video Tape and Disc Rental;
- Renting home health furniture and equipment--are classified in U.S. Industry 532283, Home Health Equipment Rental;
- Renting recreational goods--are classified in U.S. Industry 532284, Recreational Goods Rental;
- Renting a range of consumer, commercial, and industrial equipment, such as lawn and garden equipment, home repair tools, and party and banquet equipment--are classified in Industry 532310, General Rental Centers; and
- Retailing and renting musical instruments--are classified in Industry 451140, Musical Instrument and Supplies Stores.

5323   General Rental Centers[T]

53231   General Rental Centers[T]
See industry description for 532310.

532310 General Rental Centers

This industry comprises establishments primarily engaged in renting a range of consumer, commercial, and industrial equipment. Establishments in this industry typically operate from conveniently located facilities where they maintain inventories of goods and equipment that they rent for short periods of time. The type of equipment

---

T—Canadian, Mexican, and United States industries are comparable.

that establishments in this industry provide often includes, but is not limited to: audio visual equipment, contractors' and builders' tools and equipment, home repair tools, lawn and garden equipment, moving equipment and supplies, and party and banquet equipment and supplies.

Cross-References. Establishments primarily engaged in--

- Renting trucks and trailers without drivers--are classified in Industry 532120, Truck, Utility Trailer, and RV (Recreational Vehicle) Rental and Leasing;
- Renting party and banquet equipment--are classified in U.S. Industry 532289, All Other Consumer Goods Rental;
- Renting heavy construction equipment without operators--are classified in U.S. Industry 532412, Construction, Mining, and Forestry Machinery and Equipment Rental and Leasing; and
- Renting specialized types of commercial and industrial equipment, such as garden tractors or public address systems--are classified in Industry 532490, Other Commercial and Industrial Machinery and Equipment Rental and Leasing.

5324 Commercial and Industrial Machinery and Equipment Rental and Leasing[T]

This industry group comprises establishments primarily engaged in renting or leasing commercial-type and industrial-type machinery and equipment. Establishments included in this industry group are generally involved in providing capital or investment-type equipment that clients use in their business operations. These establishments typically cater to a business clientele and do not generally operate a retail-like or storefront facility.

53241 Construction, Transportation, Mining, and Forestry Machinery and Equipment Rental and Leasing[T]

This industry comprises establishments primarily engaged in renting or leasing one or more of the following without operators: heavy construction, off-highway transportation, mining, and forestry machinery and equipment. Establishments in this industry may rent or lease products, such as aircraft, railroad cars, steamships, tugboats, bulldozers, earthmoving equipment, well drilling machinery and equipment, or cranes.

Cross-References. Establishments primarily engaged in--

- Renting or leasing automobiles or trucks without operators--are classified in Industry Group 5321, Automotive Equipment Rental and Leasing;
- Renting or leasing air, rail, highway, and water transportation equipment with operators--are classified in Sector 48-49, Transportation and Warehousing, based on their primary activity;
- Renting or leasing heavy construction equipment with operators--are classified in Industry Group 2389, Other Specialty Trade Contractors;
- Renting or leasing heavy equipment for mining with operators--are classified in Industry 21311, Support Activities for Mining;
- Renting or leasing heavy equipment for forestry with operators--are classified in Industry 11531, Support Activities for Forestry; and
- Leasing heavy equipment in combination with providing loans to buyers of such equipment--are classified in Sector 52, Finance and Insurance.

532411 Commercial Air, Rail, and Water Transportation Equipment Rental and Leasing

This U.S. industry comprises establishments primarily engaged in renting or leasing off-highway transportation equipment without operators, such as aircraft, railroad cars, steamships, or tugboats.

Cross-References. Establishments primarily engaged in--

- Renting or leasing air, rail, highway, and water transportation equipment with operators--are classified in Sector 48-49, Transportation and Warehousing, based on their primary activity;
- Renting pleasure boats--are classified in U.S. Industry 532284, Recreational Goods Rental; and

---

T—Canadian, Mexican, and United States industries are comparable.

- Renting or leasing automobiles or trucks without drivers--are classified in Industry Group 5321, Automotive Equipment Rental and Leasing.

532412 Construction, Mining, and Forestry Machinery and Equipment Rental and Leasing

This U.S. industry comprises establishments primarily engaged in renting or leasing heavy equipment without operators that may be used for construction, mining, or forestry, such as bulldozers, earthmoving equipment, well drilling machinery and equipment, or cranes.

Cross-References.   Establishments primarily engaged in--

- Renting or leasing cranes with operators--are classified in Industry 238990, All Other Specialty Trade Contractors;
- Renting or leasing construction equipment with operators (except cranes)--are classified in Industry 238910, Site Preparation Contractors;
- Renting or leasing heavy equipment for mining with operators--are classified in Industry 21311, Support Activities for Mining;
- Renting or leasing heavy equipment for forestry with operators--are classified in Industry 115310, Support Activities for Forestry; and
- Leasing heavy equipment in combination with providing loans to buyers of such equipment--are classified in Sector 52, Finance and Insurance.

53242   Office Machinery and Equipment Rental and Leasing[T]
See industry description for 532420.

532420 Office Machinery and Equipment Rental and Leasing

This industry comprises establishments primarily engaged in renting or leasing office machinery and equipment, such as computers, office furniture, duplicating machines (i.e., copiers), or facsimile machines.

Cross-References.   Establishments primarily engaged in--

- Renting or leasing residential furniture--are classified in U.S. Industry 532289, All Other Consumer Goods Rental; and
- Leasing office machinery and equipment in combination with providing loans to buyers of such equipment--are classified in Sector 52, Finance and Insurance.

53249   Other Commercial and Industrial Machinery and Equipment Rental and Leasing[T]
See industry description for 532490.

532490 Other Commercial and Industrial Machinery and Equipment Rental and Leasing

This industry comprises establishments primarily engaged in renting or leasing nonconsumer-type machinery and equipment (except heavy construction, transportation, mining, and forestry machinery and equipment without operators; and office machinery and equipment). Establishments in this industry rent or lease products, such as manufacturing equipment; metalworking, telecommunications, motion picture, theatrical machinery and equipment, or service industry machinery; institutional (i.e., public building) furniture, such as furniture for schools, theaters, or buildings; or agricultural equipment without operators.

Cross-References.   Establishments primarily engaged in--

- Renting or leasing heavy construction, off-highway transportation, mining, and forestry machinery and equipment without operators--are classified in Industry 53241, Construction, Transportation, Mining, and Forestry Machinery and Equipment Rental and Leasing;

T—Canadian, Mexican, and United States industries are comparable.

- Renting or leasing office machinery and equipment--are classified in Industry 532420, Office Machinery and Equipment Rental and Leasing;
- Renting or leasing agricultural machinery and equipment with operators--are classified in Subsector 115, Support Activities for Agriculture and Forestry;
- Renting or leasing dump trucks without operator--are classified in Industry 532120, Truck, Utility Trailer, and RV (Recreational Vehicle) Rental and Leasing;
- Renting home furniture or medical equipment for home use--are classified in Industry 53228, Other Consumer Goods Rental; and
- Leasing nonconsumer machinery and equipment in combination with providing loans to buyers of such equipment--are classified in Sector 52, Finance and Insurance.

533   Lessors of Nonfinancial Intangible Assets (except Copyrighted Works)[T]

Industries in the Lessors of Nonfinancial Intangible Assets (except Copyrighted Works) subsector include establishments primarily engaged in assigning rights to assets, such as patents, trademarks, brand names, and/or franchise agreements, for which a royalty payment or licensing fee is paid to the asset holder. Establishments in this subsector own the patents, trademarks, and/or franchise agreements that they allow others to use or reproduce for a fee and may or may not have created those assets.

Establishments that allow franchisees the use of the franchise name, contingent on the franchisee buying products or services from the franchisor, are classified elsewhere.

Excluded from this subsector are establishments primarily engaged in leasing real property and establishments primarily engaged in leasing tangible assets, such as automobiles, computers, consumer goods, and industrial machinery and equipment. These establishments are classified in Subsector 531, Real Estate, and Subsector 532, Rental and Leasing Services, respectively.

5331   Lessors of Nonfinancial Intangible Assets (except Copyrighted Works)[T]

53311   Lessors of Nonfinancial Intangible Assets (except Copyrighted Works)[T]
See industry description for 533110.

533110   Lessors of Nonfinancial Intangible Assets (except Copyrighted Works)

This industry comprises establishments primarily engaged in assigning rights to assets, such as patents, trademarks, brand names, and/or franchise agreements, for which a royalty payment or licensing fee is paid to the asset holder.

Cross-References.

- Establishments primarily engaged in producing, reproducing, and/or distributing copyrighted works are classified in Sector 51, Information;
- Independent artists, writers, and performers primarily engaged in creating copyrighted works are classified in Industry 711510, Independent Artists, Writers, and Performers;
- Establishments primarily engaged in leasing real property are classified in Subsector 531, Real Estate;
- Establishments primarily engaged in leasing tangible assets, such as automobiles, computers, consumer goods, and industrial machinery and equipment, are classified in Subsector 532, Rental and Leasing Services; and
- Establishments that allow franchisees the use of the franchise name, contingent on the franchisee buying products or services from the franchisor, are classified elsewhere.

T—Canadian, Mexican, and United States industries are comparable.

Sector 54--Professional, Scientific, and Technical Services^T

The Sector as a Whole

The Professional, Scientific, and Technical Services sector comprises establishments that specialize in performing professional, scientific, and technical activities for others. These activities require a high degree of expertise and training. The establishments in this sector specialize according to expertise and provide these services to clients in a variety of industries and, in some cases, to households. Activities performed include: legal advice and representation; accounting, bookkeeping, and payroll services; architectural, engineering, and specialized design services; computer services; consulting services; research services; advertising services; photographic services; translation and interpretation services; veterinary services; and other professional, scientific, and technical services.

This sector excludes establishments primarily engaged in providing a range of day-to-day office administrative services, such as financial planning, billing and recordkeeping, personnel supply, and physical distribution and logistics. These establishments are classified in Sector 56, Administrative and Support and Waste Management and Remediation Services.

541   Professional, Scientific, and Technical Services^T

Industries in the Professional, Scientific, and Technical Services subsector group establishments engaged in processes where human capital is the major input. These establishments make available the knowledge and skills of their employees, often on an assignment basis, where an individual or team is responsible for the delivery of services to the client. The individual industries of this subsector are defined on the basis of the particular expertise and training of the services provider.

The distinguishing feature of the Professional, Scientific, and Technical Services subsector is the fact that most of the industries grouped in it have production processes that are almost wholly dependent on worker skills. In most of these industries, equipment and materials are not of major importance, unlike health care, for example, where "high-tech" machines and materials are important collaborating inputs to labor skills in the production of health care. Thus, the establishments classified in this subsector sell expertise. Much of the expertise requires degrees, though not in every case.

5411   Legal Services^T

This industry group comprises establishments primarily engaged in offering legal services, such as those offered by offices of lawyers, offices of notaries, and title abstract and settlement offices, and paralegal services.

54111   Offices of Lawyers^T
See industry description for 541110.

541110 Offices of Lawyers

This industry comprises offices of legal practitioners known as lawyers or attorneys (i.e., counselors-at-law) primarily engaged in the practice of law. Establishments in this industry may provide expertise in a range or in specific areas of law, such as criminal law, corporate law, family and estate law, patent law, real estate law, or tax law.

Cross-References.

Establishments of legal practitioners (except lawyers or attorneys) primarily engaged in providing specialized legal or paralegal services are classified in Industry 54119, Other Legal Services.

54112   Offices of Notaries^T
See industry description for 541120.

T—Canadian, Mexican, and United States industries are comparable.

541120 Offices of Notaries

This industry comprises establishments (except offices of lawyers and attorneys) primarily engaged in drafting, approving, and executing legal documents, such as real estate transactions, wills, and contracts; and in receiving, indexing, and storing such documents.

Cross-References.

- Establishments of lawyers and attorneys primarily engaged in the practice of law are classified in Industry 541110, Offices of Lawyers; and
- Establishments of notaries public engaged in activities, such as administering oaths and taking affidavits and depositions, witnessing and certifying signatures on documents, but not empowered to draw and approve legal documents and contracts, are classified in U.S. Industry 541199, All Other Legal Services.

54119 Other Legal Services[T]

This industry comprises establishments of legal practitioners (except lawyers and attorneys) primarily engaged in providing specialized legal or paralegal services.

Illustrative Examples:

Notary public services
Process serving services
Paralegal services
Real estate settlement offices

Patent agent services (i.e., patent filing and searching services)
Real estate title abstract companies

Cross-References.

- Establishments of lawyers and attorneys primarily engaged in the practice of law are classified in Industry 54111, Offices of Lawyers; and
- Establishments (except offices of lawyers, attorneys, and paralegals) primarily engaged in providing arbitration and conciliation services are classified in Industry 54199, All Other Professional, Scientific, and Technical Services.

541191 Title Abstract and Settlement Offices

This U.S. industry comprises establishments (except offices of lawyers and attorneys) primarily engaged in one or more of the following activities: (1) researching public land records to gather information relating to real estate titles; (2) preparing documents necessary for the transfer of the title, financing, and settlement; (3) conducting final real estate settlements and closings; and (4) filing legal and other documents relating to the sale of real estate. Real estate settlement offices, title abstract companies, and title search companies are included in this industry.

Cross-References.

Establishments of lawyers and attorneys primarily engaged in the practice of law are classified in Industry 541110, Offices of Lawyers.

541199 All Other Legal Services

This U.S. industry comprises establishments of legal practitioners (except offices of lawyers and attorneys, settlement offices, and title abstract offices). These establishments are primarily engaged in providing specialized legal or paralegal services.

T—Canadian, Mexican, and United States industries are comparable.

Illustrative Examples:

Notary public services
Patent agent services (i.e., patent filing and searching services)

Paralegal services
Process serving services

Cross-References.

- Establishments of lawyers and attorneys primarily engaged in the practice of law are classified in Industry 541110, Offices of Lawyers;
- Establishments (except offices of lawyers and attorneys) primarily engaged in researching public land records for ownership or title; preparing documents necessary for the transfer of the title, financing, and settlement; conducting final real estate settlements and closings; and/or filing legal and other documents relating to the sale of real estate are classified in U.S. Industry 541191, Title Abstract and Settlement Offices; and
- Establishments (except offices of lawyers, attorneys, and paralegals) primarily engaged in providing arbitration and conciliation services are classified in Industry 541990, All Other Professional, Scientific, and Technical Services.

5412   Accounting, Tax Preparation, Bookkeeping, and Payroll Services[T]

54121   Accounting, Tax Preparation, Bookkeeping, and Payroll Services[T]

This industry comprises establishments primarily engaged in providing services, such as auditing of accounting records, designing accounting systems, preparing financial statements, developing budgets, preparing tax returns, processing payrolls, bookkeeping, and billing.

Illustrative Examples:

Accountants' offices
Payroll processing services

Bookkeeping services
Tax return preparation services

Cross-References.

Establishments providing computer data processing services at their own facility for others are classified in Industry 51821, Data Processing, Hosting, and Related Services.

541211 Offices of Certified Public Accountants

This U.S. industry comprises establishments of accountants that are certified to audit the accounting records of public and private organizations and to attest to compliance with generally accepted accounting practices. Offices of certified public accountants (CPAs) may provide one or more of the following accounting services: (1) auditing financial statements; (2) designing accounting systems; (3) preparing financial statements; (4) developing budgets; and (5) providing advice on matters related to accounting. These establishments may also provide related services, such as bookkeeping, tax return preparation, and payroll processing.

Cross-References.   Establishments primarily engaged in--

- Providing tax return preparation services only--are classified in U.S. Industry 541213, Tax Preparation Services;
- Providing payroll processing services only--are classified in U.S. Industry 541214, Payroll Services; and
- Providing accounting, bookkeeping, and billing services--are classified in U.S. Industry 541219, Other Accounting Services.

T—Canadian, Mexican, and United States industries are comparable.

541213 Tax Preparation Services

This U.S. industry comprises establishments (except offices of CPAs) engaged in providing tax return preparation services without also providing accounting, bookkeeping, billing, or payroll processing services. Basic knowledge of tax law and filing requirements is required.

Cross-References.

- Establishments of CPAs are classified in U.S. Industry 541211, Offices of Certified Public Accountants;
- Establishments of non-CPAs providing payroll services along with tax return preparation services are classified in U.S. Industry 541214, Payroll Services;
- Establishments of non-CPAs providing accounting, bookkeeping, or billing services along with tax return preparation services are classified in U.S. Industry 541219, Other Accounting Services; and
- Establishments providing computer data processing services at their own facility for others are classified in Industry 518210, Data Processing, Hosting, and Related Services.

541214 Payroll Services

This U.S. industry comprises establishments (except offices of CPAs) engaged in the following without also providing accounting, bookkeeping, or billing services: (1) collecting information on hours worked, pay rates, deductions, and other payroll-related data from their clients and (2) using that information to generate paychecks, payroll reports, and tax filings. These establishments may use data processing and tabulating techniques as part of providing their services.

Cross-References.

- Establishments of CPAs are classified in U.S. Industry 541211, Offices of Certified Public Accountants;
- Establishments of non-CPAs providing tax return preparation services only are classified in U.S. Industry 541213, Tax Preparation Services; and
- Establishments of non-CPAs providing accounting, bookkeeping, or billing services along with payroll services are classified in U.S. Industry 541219, Other Accounting Services.

541219 Other Accounting Services

This U.S. industry comprises establishments (except offices of CPAs) engaged in providing accounting services (except tax return preparation services only or payroll services only). These establishments may also provide tax return preparation or payroll services. Accountant (except CPA) offices, bookkeeper offices, and billing offices are included in this industry.

Cross-References.

- Establishments of CPAs are classified in U.S. Industry 541211, Offices of Certified Public Accountants;
- Establishments of non-CPAs engaged in providing tax return preparation services only are classified in U.S. Industry 541213, Tax Preparation Services; and
- Establishments of non-CPAs engaged in providing payroll services only are classified in U.S. Industry 541214, Payroll Services.

5413 Architectural, Engineering, and Related Services[T]

This industry group comprises establishments primarily engaged in architectural, engineering, and related services, such as drafting services, building inspection services, geophysical surveying and mapping services, surveying and mapping (except geophysical) services, and testing services.

54131 Architectural Services[T]
See industry description for 541310.

T—Canadian, Mexican, and United States industries are comparable.

541310 Architectural Services

This industry comprises establishments primarily engaged in planning and designing residential, institutional, leisure, commercial, and industrial buildings and structures by applying knowledge of design, construction procedures, zoning regulations, building codes, and building materials.

Cross-References. Establishments primarily engaged in--

- Planning and designing the development of land areas--are classified in Industry 541320, Landscape Architectural Services; and
- Both the design and construction of buildings, highways, or other structures or in managing construction projects--are classified in Sector 23, Construction, according to the type of project.

54132 Landscape Architectural Services[T]
See industry description for 541320.

541320 Landscape Architectural Services

This industry comprises establishments primarily engaged in planning and designing the development of land areas for projects, such as parks and other recreational areas; airports; highways; hospitals; schools; land subdivisions; and commercial, industrial, and residential areas, by applying knowledge of land characteristics, location of buildings and structures, use of land areas, and design of landscape projects.

Illustrative Examples:

Garden planning services
Landscape architects' offices
Golf course or ski area design services

Landscape consulting services
Industrial land use planning services
Landscape design services

Cross-References.

Establishments primarily engaged in providing landscape care and maintenance services and/or installing trees, shrubs, plants, lawns, or gardens along with the design of landscape plans are classified in Industry 561730, Landscaping Services.

54133 Engineering Services[T]
See industry description for 541330.

541330 Engineering Services

This industry comprises establishments primarily engaged in applying physical laws and principles of engineering in the design, development, and utilization of machines, materials, instruments, structures, processes, and systems. The assignments undertaken by these establishments may involve any of the following activities: provision of advice, preparation of feasibility studies, preparation of preliminary and final plans and designs, provision of technical services during the construction or installation phase, inspection and evaluation of engineering projects, and related services.

Illustrative Examples:

Civil engineering services
Environmental engineering services
Construction engineering services

Mechanical engineering services
Engineers' offices

T—Canadian, Mexican, and United States industries are comparable.

Cross-References.   Establishments primarily engaged in--

- Planning and designing computer systems that integrate computer hardware, software, and communication technologies--are classified in U.S. Industry 541512, Computer Systems Design Services;
- Performing surveying and mapping services of the surface of the earth, including the sea floor--are classified in Industry 541370, Surveying and Mapping (except Geophysical) Services;
- Gathering, interpreting, and mapping geophysical data--are classified in Industry 541360, Geophysical Surveying and Mapping Services;
- Creating and developing designs and specifications that optimize the use, value, and appearance of products--are classified in Industry 541420, Industrial Design Services;
- Providing advice and assistance to others on environmental issues, such as the control of environmental contamination from pollutants, toxic substances, and hazardous materials--are classified in Industry 541620, Environmental Consulting Services; and
- Both the design and construction of buildings, highways, and other structures or in managing construction projects--are classified in Sector 23, Construction, according to the type of project.

54134   Drafting Services[T]
See industry description for 541340.

541340 Drafting Services

  This industry comprises establishments primarily engaged in drawing detailed layouts, plans, and illustrations of buildings, structures, systems, or components from engineering and architectural specifications.

54135   Building Inspection Services[T]
See industry description for 541350.

541350 Building Inspection Services

  This industry comprises establishments primarily engaged in providing building inspection services. These establishments typically evaluate all aspects of the building structure and component systems and prepare a report on the physical condition of the property, generally for buyers or others involved in real estate transactions. Building inspection bureaus and establishments providing home inspection services are included in this industry.

Cross-References.   Establishments primarily engaged in--

- Inspecting buildings for termites and other pests--are classified in Industry 561710, Exterminating and Pest Control Services;
- Inspecting buildings for hazardous materials--are classified in Industry 541620, Environmental Consulting Services; and
- Conducting building inspections and enforcing building codes and standards--are classified in Industry 926150, Regulation, Licensing, and Inspection of Miscellaneous Commercial Sectors.

54136   Geophysical Surveying and Mapping Services[T]
See industry description for 541360.

541360 Geophysical Surveying and Mapping Services

  This industry comprises establishments primarily engaged in gathering, interpreting, and mapping geophysical data. Establishments in this industry often specialize in locating and measuring the extent of subsurface resources, such as oil, gas, and minerals, but they may also conduct surveys for engineering purposes. Establishments in this industry use a variety of surveying techniques depending on the purpose of the survey, including magnetic surveys, gravity surveys, seismic surveys, or electrical and electromagnetic surveys.

T—Canadian, Mexican, and United States industries are comparable.

Cross-References.

Establishments primarily engaged in taking core samples, drilling test wells, or other mine development activities (except geophysical surveying and mapping) on a contract basis for others are classified in Industry 21311, Support Activities for Mining.

54137   Surveying and Mapping (except Geophysical) Services[T]
See industry description for 541370.

541370   Surveying and Mapping (except Geophysical) Services

This industry comprises establishments primarily engaged in performing surveying and mapping services of the surface of the earth, including the sea floor. These services may include surveying and mapping of areas above or below the surface of the earth, such as the creation of view easements or segregating rights in parcels of land by creating underground utility easements.

Illustrative Examples:

Cadastral surveying services
Mapping (except geophysical) services
Cartographic surveying services

Topographic surveying services
Geodetic surveying services

Cross-References.   Establishments primarily engaged in--

- Providing geophysical surveying and mapping services--are classified in Industry 541360, Geophysical Surveying and Mapping Services;
- Publishing atlases and maps, except for exclusive Internet publishing--are classified in Industry 511130, Book Publishers; and
- Publishing atlases and maps exclusively on the Internet--are classified in Industry 519130, Internet Publishing and Broadcasting and Web Search Portals.

54138   Testing Laboratories[T]
See industry description for 541380.

541380   Testing Laboratories

This industry comprises establishments primarily engaged in performing physical, chemical, and other analytical testing services, such as acoustics or vibration testing, assaying, biological testing (except medical and veterinary), calibration testing, electrical and electronic testing, geotechnical testing, mechanical testing, nondestructive testing, or thermal testing. The testing may occur in a laboratory or on-site.

Cross-References.   Establishments primarily engaged in--

- Laboratory testing for the medical profession--are classified in Industry 62151, Medical and Diagnostic Laboratories;
- Veterinary testing services--are classified in Industry 541940, Veterinary Services; and
- Auto emissions testing--are classified in U.S. Industry 811198, All Other Automotive Repair and Maintenance.

5414   Specialized Design Services[T]

This industry group comprises establishments providing specialized design services (except architectural, engineering, and computer systems design).

T—Canadian, Mexican, and United States industries are comparable.

54141   Interior Design Services[T]
See industry description for 541410.

541410 Interior Design Services

This industry comprises establishments primarily engaged in planning, designing, and administering projects in interior spaces to meet the physical and aesthetic needs of people using them, taking into consideration building codes, health and safety regulations, traffic patterns and floor planning, mechanical and electrical needs, and interior fittings and furniture. Interior designers and interior design consultants work in areas, such as hospitality design, health care design, institutional design, commercial and corporate design, and residential design. This industry also includes interior decorating consultants engaged exclusively in providing aesthetic services associated with interior spaces.

54142   Industrial Design Services[T]
See industry description for 541420.

541420 Industrial Design Services

This industry comprises establishments primarily engaged in creating and developing designs and specifications that optimize the use, value, and appearance of their products. These services can include the determination of the materials, construction, mechanisms, shape, color, and surface finishes of the product, taking into consideration human characteristics and needs, safety, market appeal, and efficiency in production, distribution, use, and maintenance. Establishments providing automobile or furniture industrial design services or industrial design consulting services are included in this industry.

Cross-References.   Establishments primarily engaged in--

- Applying physical laws and principles of engineering in the design, development, and utilization of machines, materials, instruments, structures, processes, and systems--are classified in Industry 541330, Engineering Services; and
- Designing clothing, shoes, or jewelry--are classified in Industry 541490, Other Specialized Design Services.

54143   Graphic Design Services[T]
See industry description for 541430.

541430 Graphic Design Services

This industry comprises establishments primarily engaged in planning, designing, and managing the production of visual communication in order to convey specific messages or concepts, clarify complex information, or project visual identities. These services can include the design of printed materials, packaging, advertising, signage systems, and corporate identification (logos). This industry also includes commercial artists engaged exclusively in generating drawings and illustrations requiring technical accuracy or interpretative skills.

Illustrative Examples:

Commercial art studios   Medical art or illustration services
Independent commercial or graphic artists   Graphic design consulting services
Corporate identification (i.e., logo) design services

Cross-References.

- Establishments primarily engaged in creating and/or placing public display advertising material are classified in Industry 541850, Outdoor Advertising; and

---

T—Canadian, Mexican, and United States industries are comparable.

- Independent artists primarily engaged in creating and selling visual artwork for noncommercial use and independent cartoonists are classified in Industry 711510, Independent Artists, Writers, and Performers.

54149 Other Specialized Design Services[T]
See industry description for 541490.

541490 Other Specialized Design Services

This industry comprises establishments primarily engaged in providing professional design services (except architectural, landscape architecture, engineering, interior, industrial, graphic, and computer systems design).

Illustrative Examples:

Costume design services (except independent theatrical costume designers)
Jewelry design services
Fashion design services

Float design services
Shoe design services
Fur design services
Textile design services

Cross-References.   Establishments primarily engaged in--

- Providing architectural design services--are classified in Industry 541310, Architectural Services;
- Providing landscape architecture design services--are classified in Industry 541320, Landscape Architectural Services;
- Providing engineering design services--are classified in Industry 541330, Engineering Services;
- Providing interior design services--are classified in Industry 541410, Interior Design Services;
- Providing industrial design services--are classified in Industry 541420, Industrial Design Services;
- Providing graphic design services--are classified in Industry 541430, Graphic Design Services;
- Providing computer systems design services--are classified in U.S. Industry 541512, Computer Systems Design Services; and
- Operating as independent theatrical costume or set designers--are classified in Industry 711510, Independent Artists, Writers, and Performers.

5415 Computer Systems Design and Related Services[T]

54151 Computer Systems Design and Related Services[T]

This industry comprises establishments primarily engaged in providing expertise in the field of information technologies through one or more of the following activities: (1) writing, modifying, testing, and supporting software to meet the needs of a particular customer; (2) planning and designing computer systems that integrate computer hardware, software, and communication technologies; (3) on-site management and operation of clients' computer systems and/or data processing facilities; and (4) other professional and technical computer related advice and services.

Illustrative Examples:

Computer facilities management services
Custom computer programming services
Computer hardware or software consulting services

Software installation services
Computer systems integration design services

Cross-References.   Establishments primarily engaged in--

- Selling computer hardware or software products from retail-like locations and providing supporting services, such as customized assembly of personal computers--are classified in Industry 44314, Electronics and Appliance Stores;

T—Canadian, Mexican, and United States industries are comparable.

- Merchant wholesaling computer hardware or software products and providing supporting services, such as customized assembly of personal computers--are classified in Industry 42343, Computer and Computer Peripheral Equipment and Software Merchant Wholesalers;
- Software design, development, and publishing, or software publishing only--are classified in Industry 51121, Software Publishers; and
- Providing computer data processing services at their own facility for others--are classified in Industry 51821, Data Processing, Hosting, and Related Services.

541511   Custom Computer Programming Services

This U.S. industry comprises establishments primarily engaged in writing, modifying, testing, and supporting software to meet the needs of a particular customer.

Cross-References.   Establishments primarily engaged in--

- Software design, development, and publishing, or software publishing only--are classified in Industry 511210, Software Publishers; and
- Planning and designing computer systems that integrate computer hardware, software, and communication technologies, even though such establishments may provide custom software as an integral part of their services--are classified in U.S. Industry 541512, Computer Systems Design Services.

541512   Computer Systems Design Services

This U.S. industry comprises establishments primarily engaged in planning and designing computer systems that integrate computer hardware, software, and communication technologies. The hardware and software components of the system may be provided by this establishment or company as part of integrated services or may be provided by third parties or vendors. These establishments often install the system and train and support users of the system.

Illustrative Examples:

Computer systems integration design consulting services

Local area network (LAN) computer systems integration design services

Information management computer systems integration design services

Office automation computer systems integration design services

Cross-References.   Establishments primarily engaged in--

- Selling computer hardware or software products and systems from retail-like locations, and providing supporting services, such as customized assembly of personal computers--are classified in U.S. Industry 443142, Electronics Stores; and
- Merchant wholesaling computer hardware or software products and providing supporting services, such as customized assembly of personal computers--are classified in Industry 423430, Computer and Computer Peripheral Equipment and Software Merchant Wholesalers.

541513   Computer Facilities Management Services

This U.S. industry comprises establishments primarily engaged in providing on-site management and operation of clients' computer systems and/or data processing facilities. Establishments providing computer systems or data processing facilities support services are included in this industry.

Cross-References.

Establishments primarily engaged in providing computer data processing services at their own facility for others are classified in Industry 518210, Data Processing, Hosting, and Related Services.

T—Canadian, Mexican, and United States industries are comparable.

541519 Other Computer Related Services

This U.S. industry comprises establishments primarily engaged in providing computer related services (except custom programming, systems integration design, and facilities management services). Establishments providing computer disaster recovery services or software installation services are included in this industry.

Cross-References.   Establishments primarily engaged in--

- Providing custom computer programming services--are classified in U.S. Industry 541511, Custom Computer Programming Services;
- Providing computer systems integration design services--are classified in U.S. Industry 541512, Computer Systems Design Services; and
- Providing computer systems and/or data processing facilities management services--are classified in U.S. Industry 541513, Computer Facilities Management Services.

5416   Management, Scientific, and Technical Consulting Services[T]

This industry group comprises establishments primarily engaged in providing advice and assistance to businesses and other organizations on management, environmental, scientific, and technical issues.

54161   Management Consulting Services[T]

This industry comprises establishments primarily engaged in providing advice and assistance to businesses and other organizations on management issues, such as strategic and organizational planning; financial planning and budgeting; marketing objectives and policies; human resource policies, practices, and planning; production scheduling; and control planning.

Illustrative Examples:

Actuarial, benefit, and compensation consulting services
Marketing consulting services
Human resources consulting services

Administrative and general management consulting services
Process, physical distribution, and logistics consulting services

Cross-References.

- Establishments primarily engaged in providing a range of day-to-day office administrative services, such as financial planning, billing and recordkeeping, personnel, and physical distribution and logistics, are classified in Industry 56111, Office Administrative Services;
- Establishments primarily engaged in providing executive search, recruitment, and placement services are classified in Industry 56131, Employment Placement Agencies and Executive Search Services;
- Establishments primarily engaged in administering, overseeing, and managing other establishments of the company or enterprise (except government establishments) are classified in Industry 55111, Management of Companies and Enterprises;
- Government establishments primarily engaged in administering, overseeing, and managing governmental programs are classified in Sector 92, Public Administration;
- Establishments primarily engaged in professional and management development training are classified in Industry 61143, Professional and Management Development Training;
- Establishments primarily engaged in listing employment vacancies and in selecting, referring, and placing applicants in employment are classified in Industry 56131, Employment Placement Agencies and Executive Search Services;
- Establishments primarily engaged in developing and implementing public relations plans are classified in Industry 54182, Public Relations Agencies;
- Establishments primarily engaged in developing and conducting marketing research or public opinion polling are classified in Industry 54191, Marketing Research and Public Opinion Polling;

T—Canadian, Mexican, and United States industries are comparable.

- Establishments primarily engaged in planning and designing industrial processes and systems are classified in Industry 54133, Engineering Services;
- Establishments primarily engaged in planning and designing computer systems are classified in Industry 54151, Computer Systems Design and Related Services; and
- Establishments primarily engaged in providing financial investment advice services are classified in Industry 52393, Investment Advice.

541611   Administrative Management and General Management Consulting Services

This U.S. industry comprises establishments primarily engaged in providing operating advice and assistance to businesses and other organizations on administrative management issues, such as financial planning and budgeting, equity and asset management, records management, office planning, strategic and organizational planning, site selection, new business start-up, and business process improvement. This industry also includes establishments of general management consultants that provide a full range of administrative, human resource, marketing, process, physical distribution, logistics, or other management consulting services to clients.

Illustrative Examples:

Administrative management consulting services
Site selection consulting services
Strategic planning consulting services

Financial management (except investment advice) consulting services
General management consulting services

Cross-References.

- Establishments primarily engaged in providing a range of day-to-day office administrative services, such as financial planning, billing and recordkeeping, personnel, and physical distribution and logistics, are classified in Industry 561110, Office Administrative Services;
- Establishments providing operations consulting services are classified in U.S. Industry 541614, Process, Physical Distribution, and Logistics Consulting Services;
- Establishments primarily engaged in administering, overseeing, and managing other establishments of the company or enterprise (except government establishments) are classified in U.S. Industry 551114, Corporate, Subsidiary, and Regional Managing Offices;
- Government establishments primarily engaged in administering, overseeing, and managing governmental programs are classified in Sector 92, Public Administration;
- Establishments primarily engaged in providing investment advice are classified in Industry 523930, Investment Advice;
- Establishments primarily engaged in providing professional and management development training are classified in Industry 611430, Professional and Management Development Training; and
- Establishments primarily engaged in providing executive search, recruitment, and placement services are classified in U.S. Industry 561312, Executive Search Services.

541612   Human Resources Consulting Services

This U.S. industry comprises establishments primarily engaged in providing advice and assistance to businesses and other organizations in one or more of the following areas: (1) human resource and personnel policies, practices, and procedures; (2) employee benefits planning, communication, and administration; (3) compensation systems planning; and (4) wage and salary administration.

Illustrative Examples:

Benefit or compensation consulting services
Employee assessment consulting services

Personnel management consulting services
Human resources consulting services

T—Canadian, Mexican, and United States industries are comparable.

Cross-References.   Establishments primarily engaged in--

- Providing professional and management development training--are classified in Industry 611430, Professional and Management Development Training;
- Listing employment vacancies and selecting, referring, and placing applicants in employment--are classified in U.S. Industry 561311, Employment Placement Agencies; and
- Providing executive search, recruitment, and placement services--are classified in U.S. Industry 561312, Executive Search Services.

541613 Marketing Consulting Services

This U.S. industry comprises establishments primarily engaged in providing operating advice and assistance to businesses and other organizations on marketing issues, such as developing marketing objectives and policies, sales forecasting, new product developing and pricing, licensing and franchise planning, and marketing planning and strategy.

Illustrative Examples:

Customer services management consulting services   Marketing management consulting services
New product development consulting services   Sales management consulting services

Cross-References.   Establishments primarily engaged in--

- Developing and implementing public relations plans--are classified in Industry 541820, Public Relations Agencies; and
- Developing and conducting marketing research or public opinion polling--are classified in Industry 541910, Marketing Research and Public Opinion Polling.

541614 Process, Physical Distribution, and Logistics Consulting Services

This U.S. industry comprises establishments primarily engaged in providing operating advice and assistance to businesses and other organizations in: (1) manufacturing operations improvement; (2) productivity improvement; (3) production planning and control; (4) quality assurance and quality control; (5) inventory management; (6) distribution networks; (7) warehouse use, operations, and utilization; (8) transportation and shipment of goods and materials; and (9) materials management and handling.

Illustrative Examples:

Freight rate or tariff rate consulting services   Inventory planning and control management
Productivity improvement consulting services   consulting services
Transportation management consulting services   Manufacturing management consulting services

Cross-References.   Establishments primarily engaged in--

- Planning and designing industrial processes and systems--are classified in Industry 541330, Engineering Services; and
- Providing computer systems integration design services--are classified in U.S. Industry 541512, Computer Systems Design Services.

541618 Other Management Consulting Services

This U.S. industry comprises establishments primarily engaged in providing management consulting services (except administrative and general management consulting; human resources consulting; marketing consulting; or process, physical distribution, and logistics consulting). Establishments providing telecommunications or utilities management consulting services are included in this industry.

T—Canadian, Mexican, and United States industries are comparable.

Cross-References.   Establishments primarily engaged in--

- Providing administrative and general management consulting services--are classified in U.S. Industry 541611, Administrative Management and General Management Consulting Services;
- Providing human resources consulting services--are classified in U.S. Industry 541612, Human Resources Consulting Services;
- Providing marketing consulting services--are classified in U.S. Industry 541613, Marketing Consulting Services; and
- Providing process, physical distribution, and logistics consulting services--are classified in U.S. Industry 541614, Process, Physical Distribution, and Logistics Consulting Services.

54162   Environmental Consulting Services[T]
See industry description for 541620.

541620 Environmental Consulting Services

This industry comprises establishments primarily engaged in providing advice and assistance to businesses and other organizations on environmental issues, such as the control of environmental contamination from pollutants, toxic substances, and hazardous materials. These establishments identify problems (e.g., inspect buildings for hazardous materials), measure and evaluate risks, and recommend solutions. They employ a multidisciplined staff of scientists, engineers, and other technicians with expertise in areas, such as air and water quality, asbestos contamination, remediation, ecological restoration, and environmental law. Establishments providing sanitation or site remediation consulting services are included in this industry.

Cross-References.

- Establishments primarily engaged in environmental remediation are classified in Industry 562910, Remediation Services;
- Establishments primarily engaged in providing environmental engineering services are classified in Industry 541330, Engineering Services;
- Establishments primarily engaged in individual activities as part of an ecological restoration project are classified according to the primary activity; and
- Government establishments primarily engaged in administering, overseeing, and managing governmental ecological restoration programs are classified in Industry 924110, Administration of Air and Water Resource and Solid Waste Management Programs.

54169   Other Scientific and Technical Consulting Services[T]
See industry description for 541690.

541690 Other Scientific and Technical Consulting Services

This industry comprises establishments primarily engaged in providing advice and assistance to businesses and other organizations on scientific and technical issues (except environmental).

Illustrative Examples:

Agricultural consulting services	Radio consulting services
Motion picture consulting services	Economic consulting services
Biological consulting services	Safety consulting services
Physics consulting services	Energy consulting services
Chemical consulting services	Security consulting services

T—Canadian, Mexican, and United States industries are comparable.

Cross-References.

Establishments primarily engaged in environmental consulting are classified in Industry 541620, Environmental Consulting Services.

5417   Scientific Research and Development Services[T]

This industry group comprises establishments engaged in conducting original investigation undertaken on a systematic basis to gain new knowledge (research) and/or the application of research findings or other scientific knowledge for the creation of new or significantly improved products or processes (experimental development). Techniques may include modeling and simulation. The industries within this industry group are defined on the basis of the domain of research; that is, on the scientific expertise of the establishment.

54171   Research and Development in the Physical, Engineering, and Life Sciences[T]

This industry comprises establishments primarily engaged in conducting research and experimental development in the physical, engineering, and life sciences, such as agriculture, electronics, environmental, biology, botany, biotechnology, computers, chemistry, food, fisheries, forests, geology, health, mathematics, medicine, nanotechnology, oceanography, pharmacy, physics, veterinary, and other allied subjects.

Cross-References.   Establishments primarily engaged in--

- Providing veterinary testing services--are classified in Industry 54194, Veterinary Services;
- Providing medical laboratory testing for humans--are classified in Industry 62151, Medical and Diagnostic Laboratories;
- Providing physical, chemical, or other analytical testing services (except medical or veterinary), such as acoustics or vibration testing, calibration testing, electrical and electronic testing, geotechnical testing, mechanical testing, nondestructive testing, or thermal testing--are classified in Industry 54138, Testing Laboratories;
- Manufacturing products (e.g., apparel, electronic equipment, automotive equipment) using nanomaterials-- are classified in Sector 31-33, Manufacturing, according to the process of the specific product made; and
- Manufacturing vaccines, toxoids, blood fractions, and culture media of plant or animal origin (except diagnostic use) and/or uncompounded medicinal chemicals and their derivatives (i.e., enzyme proteins and antibiotics for pharmaceutical use)--are classified in Industry 32541, Pharmaceutical and Medicine Manufacturing.

541713 Research and Development in Nanotechnology

This U.S. industry comprises establishments primarily engaged in conducting nanotechnology research and experimental development. Nanotechnology research and experimental development involves the study of matter at the nanoscale (i.e., a scale of about 1 to 100 nanometers). This research and development in nanotechnology may result in development of new nanotechnology processes or in prototypes of new or altered materials and/or products that may be reproduced, utilized, or implemented by various industries.

Cross-References.   Establishments primarily engaged in--

- Conducting research and experimental development in biotechnology (except nanobiotechnology)--are classified in U.S. Industry 541714, Research and Development in Biotechnology (except Nanobiotechnology);
- Conducting research and experimental development in the physical, engineering, and life sciences (except nanotechnology and biotechnology)--are classified in U.S. Industry 541715, Research and Development in the Physical, Engineering, and Life Sciences (except Nanotechnology and Biotechnology);
- Providing veterinary testing services--are classified in Industry 541940, Veterinary Services;
- Providing physical, chemical, or other analytical testing services (except medical or veterinary), such as acoustics or vibration testing, calibration testing, electrical and electronic testing, geotechnical testing,

---

T—Canadian, Mexican, and United States industries are comparable.

mechanical testing, nondestructive testing, or thermal testing--are classified in Industry 541380, Testing Laboratories;
- Providing medical laboratory testing for humans--are classified in U.S. Industry 621511, Medical Laboratories; and
- Manufacturing products (e.g., apparel, electronic equipment, automotive equipment) using nanomaterials-- are classified in Sector 31-33, Manufacturing, according to the process of the specific product made.

541714 Research and Development in Biotechnology (except Nanobiotechnology)

This U.S. industry comprises establishments primarily engaged in conducting biotechnology (except nanobiotechnology) research and experimental development. Biotechnology (except nanobiotechnology) research and experimental development involves the study of the use of microorganisms and cellular and biomolecular processes to develop or alter living or non-living materials. This research and development in biotechnology (except nanobiotechnology) may result in development of new biotechnology (except nanobiotechnology) processes or in prototypes of new or genetically-altered products that may be reproduced, utilized, or implemented by various industries.

Illustrative Examples:

Cloning research and experimental development laboratories
DNA technologies (e.g., microarrays) research and experimental development laboratories
Nucleic acid chemistry research and experimental development laboratories

Protein engineering research and experimental development laboratories
Recombinant DNA research and experimental development laboratories

Cross-References.   Establishments primarily engaged in--

- Conducting research and experimental development in nanotechnology (e.g., nanobiotechnology)--are classified in U.S. Industry 541713, Research and Development in Nanotechnology;
- Conducting research and experimental development in the physical, engineering, and life sciences (except nanotechnology and biotechnology)--are classified in U.S. Industry 541715, Research and Development in the Physical, Engineering, and Life Sciences (except Nanotechnology and Biotechnology);
- Providing physical, chemical, or other analytical testing services (except medical or veterinary), such as acoustics or vibration testing, calibration testing, electrical and electronic testing, geotechnical testing, mechanical testing, nondestructive testing, or thermal testing--are classified in Industry 541380, Testing Laboratories;
- Providing veterinary testing services--are classified in Industry 541940, Veterinary Services;
- Providing medical laboratory testing for humans--are classified in U.S. Industry 621511, Medical Laboratories;
- Manufacturing vaccines, toxoids, blood fractions, and culture media of plant or animal origin (except diagnostic use)--are classified in U.S. Industry 325414, Biological Product (except Diagnostic) Manufacturing; and
- Manufacturing uncompounded medicinal chemicals and their derivatives (i.e., enzyme proteins and antibiotics for pharmaceutical use)--are classified in U.S. Industry 325411, Medicinal and Botanical Manufacturing.

541715 Research and Development in the Physical, Engineering, and Life Sciences (except Nanotechnology and Biotechnology)

This U.S. industry comprises establishments primarily engaged in conducting research and experimental development (except nanotechnology and biotechnology research and experimental development) in the physical, engineering, and life sciences, such as agriculture, electronics, environmental, biology, botany, computers, chemistry, food, fisheries, forests, geology, health, mathematics, medicine, oceanography, pharmacy, physics, veterinary and other allied subjects.

T—Canadian, Mexican, and United States industries are comparable.

Cross-References.   Establishments primarily engaged in--

- Conducting research and experimental development in nanotechnology--are classified in U.S. Industry 541713, Research and Development in Nanotechnology;
- Conducting research and experimental development in biotechnology (except nanobiotechnology)--are classified in U.S. Industry 541714, Research and Development in Biotechnology (except Nanobiotechnology);
- Providing physical, chemical, or other analytical testing services (except medical or veterinary), such as acoustics or vibration testing, calibration testing, electrical and electronic testing, geotechnical testing, mechanical testing, nondestructive testing, or thermal testing--are classified in Industry 541380, Testing Laboratories;
- Providing veterinary testing services--are classified in Industry 541940, Veterinary Services; and
- Providing medical laboratory testing for humans--are classified in U.S. Industry 621511, Medical Laboratories.

54172   Research and Development in the Social Sciences and Humanities[T]
See industry description for 541720.

541720 Research and Development in the Social Sciences and Humanities

This industry comprises establishments primarily engaged in conducting research and analyses in cognitive development, sociology, psychology, language, behavior, economic, and other social science and humanities research.

Cross-References.

Establishments primarily engaged in marketing research are classified in Industry 541910, Marketing Research and Public Opinion Polling.

5418   Advertising, Public Relations, and Related Services[T]

This industry group comprises establishments primarily engaged in advertising, public relations, and related services, such as media buying, independent media representation, outdoor advertising, direct mail advertising, advertising material distribution services, and other services related to advertising.

54181   Advertising Agencies[T]
See industry description for 541810.

541810 Advertising Agencies

This industry comprises establishments primarily engaged in creating advertising campaigns and placing such advertising in periodicals, newspapers, radio and television, or other media. These establishments are organized to provide a full range of services (i.e., through in-house capabilities or subcontracting), including advice, creative services, account management, production of advertising material, media planning, and buying (i.e., placing advertising).

Cross-References.   Establishments primarily engaged in--

- Purchasing advertising space from media outlets and reselling it directly to advertising agencies or individual companies--are classified in Industry 541830, Media Buying Agencies;
- Conceptualizing and producing artwork or graphic designs without providing other advertising agency services--are classified in Industry 541430, Graphic Design Services;
- Creating direct mail advertising campaigns--are classified in Industry 541860, Direct Mail Advertising;
- Providing marketing consulting services--are classified in U.S. Industry 541613, Marketing Consulting Services; and

---

T—Canadian, Mexican, and United States industries are comparable.

- Selling media time or space for media owners as independent representatives--are classified in Industry 541840, Media Representatives.

54182   Public Relations Agencies[T]
See industry description for 541820.

541820 Public Relations Agencies

This industry comprises establishments primarily engaged in designing and implementing public relations campaigns. These campaigns are designed to promote the interests and image of their clients. Establishments providing lobbying, political consulting, or public relations consulting are included in this industry.

54183   Media Buying Agencies[T]
See industry description for 541830.

541830 Media Buying Agencies

This industry comprises establishments primarily engaged in purchasing advertising time or space from media outlets and reselling it to advertising agencies or individual companies directly.

Cross-References.   Establishments primarily engaged in--

- Selling time and space to advertisers for media owners as independent representatives--are classified in Industry 541840, Media Representatives; and
- Creating advertising campaigns and placing such advertising in media--are classified in Industry 541810, Advertising Agencies.

54184   Media Representatives[T]
See industry description for 541840.

541840 Media Representatives

This industry comprises establishments of independent representatives primarily engaged in selling media time or space for media owners.

Illustrative Examples:

Newspaper advertising representatives (i.e., independent of media owners)
Radio advertising representatives (i.e., independent of media owners)

Publishers' advertising representatives (i.e., independent of media owners)
Television advertising representatives (i.e., independent of media owners)

Cross-References.   Establishments primarily engaged in--

- Purchasing advertising time or space from media outlets and reselling it directly to advertising agencies or individual companies--are classified in Industry 541830, Media Buying Agencies; and
- Creating advertising campaigns and placing such advertising in media--are classified in Industry 541810, Advertising Agencies.

54185   Outdoor Advertising[T]
See industry description for 541850.

T—Canadian, Mexican, and United States industries are comparable.

541850 Outdoor Advertising

This industry comprises establishments primarily engaged in creating and designing public display advertising campaign materials, such as printed, painted, or electronic displays; and/or placing such displays on indoor or outdoor billboards and panels, or on or within transit vehicles or facilities, shopping malls, retail (in-store) displays, and other display structures or sites.

Cross-References.   Establishments primarily engaged in--

- Providing sign lettering and painting services--are classified in Industry 541890, Other Services Related to Advertising;
- Printing paper or paperboard signs--are classified in Industry 32311, Printing;
- Erecting display boards--are classified in Industry 238990, All Other Specialty Trade Contractors; and
- Manufacturing electrical, mechanical, or plate signs and point-of-sale advertising displays--are classified in Industry 339950, Sign Manufacturing.

54186   Direct Mail Advertising[T]
See industry description for 541860.

541860 Direct Mail Advertising

This industry comprises establishments primarily engaged in (1) creating and designing advertising campaigns for the purpose of distributing advertising materials (e.g., coupons, flyers, samples) or specialties (e.g., keychains, magnets, pens with customized messages imprinted) by mail or other direct distribution and/or (2) preparing advertising materials or specialties for mailing or other direct distribution. These establishments may also compile, maintain, sell, and rent mailing lists.

Cross-References.   Establishments primarily engaged in--

- The direct distribution or delivery (e.g., door-to-door, windshield placement) of advertisements or samples--are classified in Industry 541870, Advertising Material Distribution Services;
- Distributing advertising specialties for clients who wish to use such materials for promotional purposes--are classified in Industry 541890, Other Services Related to Advertising;
- Creating advertising campaigns and placing such advertising in media--are classified in Industry 541810, Advertising Agencies;
- Compiling and selling mailing lists without providing direct mail advertising services--are classified in Industry 511140, Directory and Mailing List Publishers; and
- Publishing or broadcasting exclusively on the Internet--are classified in Industry 519130, Internet Publishing and Broadcasting and Web Search Portals.

54187   Advertising Material Distribution Services[T]
See industry description for 541870.

541870 Advertising Material Distribution Services

This industry comprises establishments primarily engaged in the direct distribution or delivery of advertisements (e.g., circulars, coupons, handbills) or samples. Establishments in this industry use methods, such as delivering advertisements or samples door-to-door, placing flyers or coupons on car windshields in parking lots, or handing out samples in retail stores.

Cross-References.   Establishments primarily engaged in--

- Creating and designing advertising campaigns for the purpose of distributing advertising materials or samples through the mail--are classified in Industry 541860, Direct Mail Advertising;

T—Canadian, Mexican, and United States industries are comparable.

- Publishing newspapers or operating television stations or on-line information services--are classified in Sector 51, Information; and
- Distributing advertising specialties (e.g., keychains, magnets, or pens with customized messages imprinted) to clients who wish to use such materials for promotional purposes--are classified in Industry 541890, Other Services Related to Advertising.

54189   Other Services Related to Advertising[T]
See industry description for 541890.

541890 Other Services Related to Advertising

This industry comprises establishments primarily engaged in providing advertising services (except advertising agency services, public relations agency services, media buying agency services, media representative services, display advertising services, direct mail advertising services, advertising material distribution services, and marketing consulting services).

Illustrative Examples:

Advertising specialties (e.g., keychains, magnets, pens) distribution services (except direct mail)
Sign lettering and painting services
Display lettering services

Store window dressing or trimming services
Mannequin decorating services
Welcoming services (i.e., advertising services)
Merchandise demonstration services

Cross-References.   Establishments primarily engaged in--

- Creating advertising campaigns and placing such advertising in newspapers, television, or other media--are classified in Industry 541810, Advertising Agencies;
- Designing and implementing public relations campaigns--are classified in Industry 541820, Public Relations Agencies;
- Purchasing advertising time or space from media outlets and reselling it directly to advertising agencies or individual companies--are classified in Industry 541830, Media Buying Agencies;
- Selling media time or space for media owners as independent representatives--are classified in Industry 541840, Media Representatives;
- Providing display advertising services (except aerial)--are classified in Industry 541850, Outdoor Advertising;
- Providing direct distribution or delivery (e.g., door-to-door, windshield placement) of advertisements or samples--are classified in Industry 541870, Advertising Material Distribution Services;
- Providing direct mail advertising services--are classified in Industry 541860, Direct Mail Advertising;
- Publishing newspapers or operating television stations or on-line information services--are classified in Sector 51, Information; and
- Providing marketing consulting services--are classified in U.S. Industry 541613, Marketing Consulting Services.

5419   Other Professional, Scientific, and Technical Services[T]

This industry group comprises establishments engaged in professional, scientific, and technical services (except legal services; accounting, tax preparation, bookkeeping, and related services; architectural, engineering, and related services; specialized design services; computer systems design and related services; management, scientific, and technical consulting services; scientific research and development services; and advertising, public relations, and related services).

54191   Marketing Research and Public Opinion Polling[T]
See industry description for 541910.

T—Canadian, Mexican, and United States industries are comparable.

541910   Marketing Research and Public Opinion Polling

This industry comprises establishments primarily engaged in systematically gathering, recording, tabulating, and presenting marketing and public opinion data.

Illustrative Examples:

Broadcast media rating services
Political opinion polling services
Marketing analysis or research services

Statistical sampling services
Opinion research services

Cross-References.   Establishments primarily engaged in--

- Providing research and analysis in economics, sociology, and related fields--are classified in Industry 541720, Research and Development in the Social Sciences and Humanities; and
- Providing advice and counsel on marketing strategies--are classified in U.S. Industry 541613, Marketing Consulting Services.

54192   Photographic Services[T]

This industry comprises establishments primarily engaged in providing still, video, or digital photography services. These establishments may specialize in a particular field of photography, such as commercial and industrial photography, portrait photography, and special events photography. Commercial or portrait photography studios are included in this industry.

Cross-References.   Establishments primarily engaged in--

- Producing film and videotape for commercial exhibition or sale--are classified in Industry 51211, Motion Picture and Video Production;
- Developing still photographs--are classified in Industry 81292, Photofinishing;
- Developing motion picture film--are classified in Industry 51219, Postproduction Services and Other Motion Picture and Video Industries;
- Taking, developing, and selling artistic, news, or other types of photographs on a freelance basis, such as photojournalists--are classified in Industry 71151, Independent Artists, Writers, and Performers; and
- Supplying and servicing automatic photography machines in places of business operated by others--are classified in Industry 81299, All Other Personal Services.

541921   Photography Studios, Portrait

This U.S. industry comprises establishments known as portrait studios primarily engaged in providing still, video, or digital portrait photography services.

Illustrative Examples:

Home photography services
School photography services
Passport photography services

Videotaping services for special events (e.g., weddings)

Cross-References.   Establishments primarily engaged in--

- Producing film and videotape for commercial exhibition or sale--are classified in Industry 512110, Motion Picture and Video Production;
- Developing still photographs--are classified in Industry 81292, Photofinishing;
- Developing motion picture film--are classified in U.S. Industry 512199, Other Motion Picture and Video Industries;

T—Canadian, Mexican, and United States industries are comparable.

- Taking, developing, and selling artistic, news, or other types of photographs on a freelance basis, such as photojournalists--are classified in Industry 711510, Independent Artists, Writers, and Performers; and
- Supplying and servicing automatic photography machines in places of business operated by others--are classified in Industry 812990, All Other Personal Services.

541922 Commercial Photography

This U.S. industry comprises establishments primarily engaged in providing commercial photography services, generally for advertising agencies, publishers, and other business and industrial users.

Cross-References.   Establishments primarily engaged in--

- Producing film and videotape for commercial exhibition or sale--are classified in Industry 512110, Motion Picture and Video Production;
- Developing still photographs--are classified in Industry 81292, Photofinishing;
- Developing motion picture film--are classified in U.S. Industry 512199, Other Motion Picture and Video Industries;
- Taking, developing, and selling artistic, news, or other types of photographs on a freelance basis, such as photojournalists--are classified in Industry 711510, Independent Artists, Writers, and Performers; and
- Supplying and servicing automatic photography machines in places of business operated by others--are classified in Industry 812990, All Other Personal Services.

54193   Translation and Interpretation Services[T]
See industry description for 541930.

541930 Translation and Interpretation Services

This industry comprises establishments primarily engaged in translating written material and interpreting speech from one language to another and establishments primarily engaged in providing sign language services.

Cross-References.   Establishments primarily engaged in--

- Providing transcription services--are classified in Industry 561410, Document Preparation Services;
- Providing real-time (i.e., simultaneous) closed captioning services for live television performances, at meetings and conferences--are classified in U.S. Industry 561492, Court Reporting and Stenotype Services;
- Providing film or tape closed captioning services--are classified in U.S. Industry 512191, Teleproduction and Other Postproduction Services; and
- Analyzing handwriting--are classified in Industry 541990, All Other Professional, Scientific, and Technical Services.

54194   Veterinary Services[T]
See industry description for 541940.

541940 Veterinary Services

This industry comprises establishments of licensed veterinary practitioners primarily engaged in the practice of veterinary medicine, dentistry, or surgery for animals; and establishments primarily engaged in providing testing services for licensed veterinary practitioners.

Illustrative Examples:

Animal hospitals
Veterinary clinics

Veterinarians' offices
Veterinary testing laboratories

T--Canadian, Mexican, and United States industries are comparable.

Cross-References.   Establishments primarily engaged in--

- Providing veterinary research and development services--are classified in Industry 54171, Research and Development in the Physical, Engineering, and Life Sciences;
- Providing nonveterinary pet care services, such as boarding or grooming pets--are classified in Industry 812910, Pet Care (except Veterinary) Services;
- Providing animal breeding services or boarding horses--are classified in Industry 115210, Support Activities for Animal Production; and
- Transporting pets--are classified in U.S. Industry 485991, Special Needs Transportation.

54199   All Other Professional, Scientific, and Technical Services[T]
See industry description for 541990.

541990 All Other Professional, Scientific, and Technical Services

This industry comprises establishments primarily engaged in the provision of professional, scientific, or technical services (except legal services; accounting, tax preparation, bookkeeping, and related services; architectural, engineering, and related services; specialized design services; computer systems design and related services; management, scientific, and technical consulting services; scientific research and development services; advertising, public relations, and related services; market research and public opinion polling; photographic services; translation and interpretation services; and veterinary services).

Illustrative Examples:

Appraisal (except real estate) services
Marine surveyor (i.e., appraiser) services
Arbitration and conciliation services (except by lawyer, attorney, or paralegal offices)
Patent broker services (i.e., patent marketing services)

Commodity inspector services
Pipeline or power line inspection (i.e., visual) services
Consumer credit counseling services
Weather forecasting services
Handwriting analysis services

Cross-References.   Establishments primarily engaged in--

- Providing legal services--are classified in Industry Group 5411, Legal Services;
- Providing accounting, tax preparation, bookkeeping, and payroll services--are classified in Industry Group 5412, Accounting, Tax Preparation, Bookkeeping, and Payroll Services;
- Providing architectural, engineering, and related services--are classified in Industry Group 5413, Architectural, Engineering, and Related Services;
- Providing specialized design services--are classified in Industry Group 5414, Specialized Design Services;
- Providing computer systems design and related services--are classified in Industry Group 5415, Computer Systems Design and Related Services;
- Providing management, scientific, and technical consulting services--are classified in Industry Group 5416, Management, Scientific, and Technical Consulting Services;
- Providing scientific research and development services--are classified in Industry Group 5417, Scientific Research and Development Services;
- Providing advertising and related services--are classified in Industry Group 5418, Advertising, Public Relations, and Related Services;
- Providing marketing research and public opinion polling--are classified in Industry 541910, Marketing Research and Public Opinion Polling;
- Providing photographic services--are classified in Industry 54192, Photographic Services;
- Providing translation and interpretation services--are classified in Industry 541930, Translation and Interpretation Services;
- Providing veterinary services--are classified in Industry 541940, Veterinary Services; and
- Providing real estate appraisal services--are classified in Industry 531320, Offices of Real Estate Appraisers.

T—Canadian, Mexican, and United States industries are comparable.

Sector 55--Management of Companies and Enterprises[T]

The Sector as a Whole

The Management of Companies and Enterprises sector comprises (1) establishments that hold the securities of (or other equity interests in) companies and enterprises for the purpose of owning a controlling interest or influencing management decisions or (2) establishments (except government establishments) that administer, oversee, and manage establishments of the company or enterprise and that normally undertake the strategic or organizational planning and decision-making role of the company or enterprise. Establishments that administer, oversee, and manage may hold the securities of the company or enterprise.

Establishments in this sector perform essential activities that are often undertaken in-house by establishments in many sectors of the economy. By consolidating the performance of these activities of the enterprise at one establishment, economies of scale are achieved.

Government establishments primarily engaged in administering, overseeing, and managing governmental programs are classified in Sector 92, Public Administration. Establishments primarily engaged in providing a range of day-to-day office administrative services, such as financial planning, billing and recordkeeping, personnel, and physical distribution and logistics, are classified in Industry 56111, Office Administrative Services.

551 Management of Companies and Enterprises[T]

Industries in the Management of Companies and Enterprises subsector include three main types of establishments: (1) those that hold the securities of (or other equity interests in) companies and enterprises; (2) those (except government establishments) that administer, oversee, and manage other establishments of the company or enterprise but do not hold the securities of these establishments; and (3) those that both administer, oversee, and manage other establishments of the company or enterprise and hold the securities of (or other equity interests in) these establishments. Those establishments that administer, oversee, and manage normally undertake the strategic or organizational planning and decision-making role of the company or enterprise.

5511 Management of Companies and Enterprises[T]

55111 Management of Companies and Enterprises[T]

This industry comprises (1) establishments primarily engaged in holding the securities of (or other equity interests in) companies and enterprises for the purpose of owning a controlling interest or influencing management decisions or (2) establishments (except government establishments) that administer, oversee, and manage other establishments of the company or enterprise and that normally undertake the strategic or organizational planning and decision-making role of the company or enterprise. Establishments that administer, oversee, and manage may hold the securities of the company or enterprise.

Cross-References.

- Establishments primarily engaged in holding the securities of companies or enterprises and operating these entities are classified according to the business operated;
- Establishments primarily engaged in holding the securities of depository banks and operating these entities are classified in Industry Group 5221, Depository Credit Intermediation;
- Establishments primarily engaged in providing a single service to other establishments of the company or enterprise, such as trucking, warehousing, research and development, and data processing, are classified according to the service provided; and
- Government establishments primarily engaged in administering, overseeing, and managing governmental programs are classified in Sector 92, Public Administration.

T—Canadian, Mexican, and United States industries are comparable.

551111 Offices of Bank Holding Companies

This U.S. industry comprises legal entities known as bank holding companies primarily engaged in holding the securities of (or other equity interests in) companies and enterprises for the purpose of owning a controlling interest or influencing the management decisions of these firms. The holding companies in this industry do not administer, oversee, and manage other establishments of the company or enterprise whose securities they hold.

Cross-References.   Establishments primarily engaged in--

- Holding the securities of (or other equity interests in) a company or enterprise and administering, overseeing, and managing establishments of the company or enterprise whose securities they hold--are classified in U.S. Industry 551114, Corporate, Subsidiary, and Regional Managing Offices; and
- Holding the securities of depository banks and operating these entities--are classified in Industry Group 5221, Depository Credit Intermediation.

551112 Offices of Other Holding Companies

This U.S. industry comprises legal entities known as holding companies (except bank holding) primarily engaged in holding the securities of (or other equity interests in) companies and enterprises for the purpose of owning a controlling interest or influencing the management decisions of these firms. The holding companies in this industry do not administer, oversee, and manage other establishments of the company or enterprise whose securities they hold.

Cross-References.   Establishments primarily engaged in--

- Holding the securities of (or other equity interests in) depository banks for the purpose of owning a controlling interest or influencing the management decisions of these firms--are classified in U.S. Industry 551111, Offices of Bank Holding Companies;
- Holding the securities of (or other equity interests in) a company or enterprise and administering, overseeing, and managing establishments of the company or enterprise whose securities they hold--are classified in U.S. Industry 551114, Corporate, Subsidiary, and Regional Managing Offices; and
- Holding the securities of companies or enterprises and operating these entities--are classified according to the business operated.

551114 Corporate, Subsidiary, and Regional Managing Offices

This U.S. industry comprises establishments (except government establishments) primarily engaged in administering, overseeing, and managing other establishments of the company or enterprise. These establishments normally undertake the strategic or organizational planning and decision-making role of the company or enterprise. Establishments in this industry may hold the securities of the company or enterprise.

Illustrative Examples:

Centralized administrative offices	Holding companies that manage
Head offices	District and regional offices
Corporate offices	Subsidiary management offices

Cross-References.

- Government establishments primarily engaged in administering, overseeing, and managing governmental programs are classified in Sector 92, Public Administration;
- Legal entities known as bank holding companies that do not administer, oversee, and manage other establishments of the companies or enterprises whose securities they hold are classified in U.S. Industry 551111, Offices of Bank Holding Companies; and

---

T—Canadian, Mexican, and United States industries are comparable.

- Legal entities known as holding companies (except bank holding) that do not administer, oversee, and manage other establishments of the companies or enterprises whose securities they hold are classified in U.S. Industry 551112, Offices of Other Holding Companies.

T—Canadian, Mexican, and United States industries are comparable.

Sector 56--Administrative and Support and Waste Management and Remediation Services[T]

The Sector as a Whole

The Administrative and Support and Waste Management and Remediation Services sector comprises establishments performing routine support activities for the day-to-day operations of other organizations. These essential activities are often undertaken in-house by establishments in many sectors of the economy. The establishments in this sector specialize in one or more of these support activities and provide these services to clients in a variety of industries and, in some cases, to households. Activities performed include: office administration, hiring and placing of personnel, document preparation and similar clerical services, solicitation, collection, security and surveillance services, cleaning, and waste disposal services.

The administrative and management activities performed by establishments in this sector are typically on a contract or fee basis. These activities may also be performed by establishments that are part of the company or enterprise. However, establishments involved in administering, overseeing, and managing other establishments of the company or enterprise are classified in Sector 55, Management of Companies and Enterprises. Establishments in Sector 55, Management of Companies and Enterprises, normally undertake the strategic and organizational planning and decision-making role of the company or enterprise. Government establishments engaged in administering, overseeing, and managing governmental programs are classified in Sector 92, Public Administration.

561 Administrative and Support Services[T]

Industries in the Administrative and Support Services subsector group establishments engaged in activities that support the day-to-day operations of other organizations. The processes employed in this sector (e.g., general management, personnel administration, clerical activities, cleaning activities) are often integral parts of the activities of establishments found in all sectors of the economy. The establishments classified in this subsector have specialization in one or more of these activities and can, therefore, provide services to clients in a variety of industries and, in some cases, to households. The individual industries of this subsector are defined on the basis of the particular process that they are engaged in and the particular services they provide.

Many of the activities performed in this subsector are ongoing routine support functions that all businesses and organizations must do and that they have traditionally done for themselves. Recent trends, however, are to contract or purchase such services from businesses that specialize in such activities and can, therefore, provide the services more efficiently.

The industries in this subsector cannot be viewed as strictly "support." The Travel Arrangement and Reservation Services industry group includes travel agents, tour operators, and providers of other travel arrangement services, such as hotel and restaurant reservations and arranging the purchase of tickets, serving many types of clients, including individual consumers. This group was placed in this subsector because the services are often of the "support" nature (e.g., travel arrangement), and businesses and other organizations increasingly purchase such services.

The administrative and management activities performed by establishments in this sector are typically on a contract or fee basis. These activities may also be performed by establishments that are part of the company or enterprise. However, establishments involved in administering, overseeing, and managing other establishments of the company or enterprise are classified in Sector 55, Management of Companies and Enterprises. Establishments in Sector 55, Management of Companies and Enterprises, normally undertake the strategic and organizational planning and decision-making role of the company or enterprise. Government establishments engaged in administering, overseeing, and managing governmental programs are classified in Sector 92, Public Administration.

5611 Office Administrative Services[T]

56111 Office Administrative Services[T]
See industry description for 561110.

T—Canadian, Mexican, and United States industries are comparable.

561110 Office Administrative Services

This industry comprises establishments primarily engaged in providing a range of day-to-day office administrative services, such as financial planning; billing and recordkeeping; personnel; and physical distribution and logistics, for others on a contract or fee basis. These establishments do not provide operating staff to carry out the complete operations of a business.

Cross-References.   Establishments primarily engaged in--

- Holding the securities or financial assets of companies and enterprises for the purpose of controlling them and influencing their management decisions--are classified in U.S. Industry 551111, Offices of Bank Holding Companies, or U.S. Industry 551112, Offices of Other Holding Companies;
- Administering, overseeing, and managing other establishments of the company or enterprise (except government establishments)--are classified in U.S. Industry 551114, Corporate, Subsidiary, and Regional Managing Offices;
- Providing computer facilities management--are classified in U.S. Industry 541513, Computer Facilities Management Services;
- Providing construction management--are classified in Sector 23, Construction, by type of construction project managed;
- Providing farm management--are classified in U.S. Industry 115116, Farm Management Services;
- Managing real property for others--are classified in Industry 53131, Real Estate Property Managers;
- Providing food services management at institutional, governmental, commercial, or industrial locations--are classified in Industry 722310, Food Service Contractors;
- Providing management advice without day-to-day management--are classified in Industry 54161, Management Consulting Services;
- Providing both management and operating staff for the complete operation of a client's business, such as a hotel, restaurant, mine site, or hospital--are classified according to the industry of the establishment operated; and
- Providing only one of the support services (e.g., accounting services) that establishments in this industry provide--are classified in the appropriate industry according to the service provided.

5612   Facilities Support Services[T]

56121   Facilities Support Services[T]
See industry description for 561210.

561210 Facilities Support Services

This industry comprises establishments primarily engaged in providing operating staff to perform a combination of support services within a client's facilities. Establishments in this industry typically provide a combination of services, such as janitorial, maintenance, trash disposal, guard and security, mail routing, reception, laundry, and related services to support operations within facilities. These establishments provide operating staff to carry out these support activities, but are not involved with or responsible for the core business or activities of the client. Establishments providing facilities (except computer and/or data processing) operation support services and establishments providing private jail services or operating correctional facilities (i.e., jails) on a contract or fee basis are included in this industry.

Cross-References.

- Establishments primarily engaged in providing only one of the support services (e.g., janitorial services) that establishments in this industry provide are classified in the appropriate industry according to the service provided;
- Establishments primarily engaged in providing management and operating staff for the complete operation of a client's establishment, such as a hotel, restaurant, mine, or hospital, are classified according to the industry of the establishment operated;

T—Canadian, Mexican, and United States industries are comparable.

- Establishments primarily engaged in providing on-site management and operation of a client's computer systems and/or data processing facilities are classified in U.S. Industry 541513, Computer Facilities Management Services; and
- Governmental correctional institutions are classified in Industry 922140, Correctional Institutions.

5613   Employment Services[T]

This industry group comprises establishments primarily engaged in one of the following: (1) listing employment vacancies and referring or placing applicants for employment; (2) providing executive search, recruitment, and placement services; (3) supplying workers to clients' businesses for limited periods of time to supplement the working force of the client; or (4) providing human resources and human resource management services to client businesses and households.

56131   Employment Placement Agencies and Executive Search Services[T]

This industry comprises establishments primarily engaged in one of the following: 1) listing employment vacancies and referring or placing applicants for employment; or 2) providing executive search, recruitment, and placement services.

Illustrative Examples:

Employment agencies   Executive search services
Executive placement agencies or services

Cross-References.   Establishments primarily engaged in--

- Supplying their own employees for limited periods of time to supplement the working force of a client's business--are classified in Industry 56132, Temporary Help Services;
- Providing human resources and human resource management services to client businesses and households-- are classified in Industry 56133, Professional Employer Organizations;
- Providing advice and assistance on human resource and personnel policies, practices, and procedures; and employee benefits and compensation systems--are classified in Industry 54161, Management Consulting Services; and
- Representing models, entertainers, athletes, and other public figures as their agent or manager--are classified in Industry 71141, Agents and Managers for Artists, Athletes, Entertainers, and Other Public Figures.

561311 Employment Placement Agencies

This U.S. industry comprises establishments primarily engaged in listing employment vacancies and in referring or placing applicants for employment. The individuals referred or placed are not employees of the employment agencies.

Illustrative Examples:

Babysitting bureaus (i.e., registries)   Casting agencies or bureaus (i.e., motion picture,
Employment registries   theatrical, video)
Model registries   Employment agencies

Cross-References.   Establishments primarily engaged in--

- Providing executive search, recruitment, and placement services--are classified in U.S. Industry 561312, Executive Search Services;
- Supplying their own employees for limited periods of time to supplement the working force of a client's business--are classified in Industry 561320, Temporary Help Services;

T—Canadian, Mexican, and United States industries are comparable.

- Providing human resources and human resource management services to client businesses and households--are classified in Industry 561330, Professional Employer Organizations; and
- Representing models, entertainers, athletes, and other public figures as their agent or manager--are classified in Industry 711410, Agents and Managers for Artists, Athletes, Entertainers, and Other Public Figures.

561312 Executive Search Services

This U.S. industry comprises establishments primarily engaged in providing executive search, recruitment, and placement services for clients with specific executive and senior management position requirements. The range of services provided by these establishments may include developing a search strategy and position specification based on the culture and needs of the client; researching, identifying, screening, and interviewing candidates; verifying candidate qualifications; and assisting in final offer negotiations and assimilation of the selected candidate. The individuals identified, recruited, or placed are not employees of the executive search services establishments.

Illustrative Examples:

Senior executive search services
Executive placement services

Executive search services

Cross-References.   Establishments primarily engaged in--

- Listing employment vacancies and in referring or placing applicants for employment--are classified in U.S. Industry 561311, Employment Placement Agencies;
- Supplying their own employees for limited periods of time to supplement the working force of a client's business--are classified in Industry 561320, Temporary Help Services;
- Providing human resources and human resource management services to client businesses and households--are classified in Industry 561330, Professional Employer Organizations;
- Providing administrative and general management consulting services--are classified in U.S. Industry 541611, Administrative Management and General Management Consulting Services;
- Providing advice and assistance on human resource and personnel policies, practices, and procedures; and employee benefits and compensation systems--are classified in U.S. Industry 541612, Human Resources Consulting Services;
- Providing professional and management development training--are classified in Industry 611430, Professional and Management Development Training; and
- Representing models, entertainers, athletes, and other public figures as their agent or manager--are classified in Industry 711410, Agents and Managers for Artists, Athletes, Entertainers, and Other Public Figures.

56132 Temporary Help Services[T]
See industry description for 561320.

561320 Temporary Help Services

This industry comprises establishments primarily engaged in supplying workers to clients' businesses for limited periods of time to supplement the working force of the client. The individuals provided are employees of the temporary help services establishment. However, these establishments do not provide direct supervision of their employees at the clients' work sites.

Illustrative Examples:

Help supply services
Model supply services
Labor (except farm) contractors (i.e., personnel suppliers)

Temporary employment or temporary staffing services
Manpower pools

T—Canadian, Mexican, and United States industries are comparable.

Cross-References. Establishments primarily engaged in--

- Providing human resources and human resource management services to client businesses and households--are classified in Industry 561330, Professional Employer Organizations;
- Supplying farm labor--are classified in U.S. Industry 115115, Farm Labor Contractors and Crew Leaders;
- Providing operating staff to perform a combination of services to support operations within a client's facilities--are classified in Industry 561210, Facilities Support Services;
- Providing executive search, recruitment, and placement services--are classified in U.S. Industry 561312, Executive Search Services;
- Listing employment vacancies and referring or placing applicants for employment--are classified in U.S. Industry 561311, Employment Placement Agencies; and
- Representing models, entertainers, athletes, and other public figures as their agent or manager--are classified in Industry 711410, Agents and Managers for Artists, Athletes, Entertainers, and Other Public Figures.

56133   Professional Employer Organizations^T
See industry description for 561330.

561330   Professional Employer Organizations

This industry comprises establishments primarily engaged in providing human resources and human resource management services to client businesses and households. Establishments in this industry operate in a co-employment relationship with client businesses or organizations and are specialized in performing a wide range of human resource and personnel management duties, such as payroll, payroll tax, benefits administration, workers' compensation, unemployment, and human resource administration. Professional employer organizations (PEOs) are responsible for payroll, including withholding and remitting employment-related taxes, for some or all of the employees of their clients, and also serve as the employer of those employees for benefits and related purposes.

Cross-References. Establishments primarily engaged in--

- Supplying their own employees for limited periods of time to supplement the working force of a client's business--are classified in Industry 561320, Temporary Help Services; and
- Listing employment vacancies and referring or placing applicants for employment--are classified in U.S. Industry 561311, Employment Placement Agencies.

5614   Business Support Services^T

This industry group comprises establishments engaged in performing activities that are ongoing routine business support functions that businesses and organizations traditionally do for themselves.

56141   Document Preparation Services^T
See industry description for 561410.

561410   Document Preparation Services

This industry comprises establishments primarily engaged in one or more of the following: (1) letter or resume writing; (2) document editing or proofreading; (3) typing, word processing, or desktop publishing; and (4) stenography (except court reporting or stenotype recording), transcription, and other secretarial services.

Cross-References. Establishments primarily engaged in--

- Providing verbatim reporting and stenotype recording of live legal proceedings and transcribing subsequent recorded materials--are classified in U.S. Industry 561492, Court Reporting and Stenotype Services;
- Performing prepress and postpress services in support of printing activities--are classified in Industry 323120, Support Activities for Printing;

T—Canadian, Mexican, and United States industries are comparable.

- Providing document translation services--are classified in Industry 541930, Translation and Interpretation Services;
- Photocopying, duplicating, and other document copying services, with or without a range of other office support services (except printing)--are classified in U.S. Industry 561439, Other Business Service Centers (including Copy Shops); and
- Providing document copying services in combination with printing services, with or without a range of other office support services, and establishments known as quick or digital printers--are classified in U.S. Industry 323111, Commercial Printing (except Screen and Books).

56142   Telephone Call Centers[T]

This industry comprises (1) establishments primarily engaged in answering telephone calls and relaying messages to clients and (2) establishments primarily engaged in providing telemarketing services on a contract or fee basis for others, such as promoting clients' products or services by telephone; taking orders for clients by telephone; and soliciting contributions or providing information for clients by telephone. Telemarketing establishments never own the product or provide the service that they are representing and generally originate and/or receive calls for others.

Cross-References.   Establishments primarily engaged in--

- Providing paging and beeper transmission services--are classified in Industry 51731, Wired and Wireless Telecommunications Carriers;
- Organizing and conducting fundraising campaigns on a contract or fee basis, that may include telephone solicitation services--are classified in Industry 56149, Other Business Support Services; and
- Gathering, recording, tabulating, and presenting marketing and public opinion data, that may include telephone canvassing services--are classified in Industry 54191, Marketing Research and Public Opinion Polling.

561421   Telephone Answering Services

This U.S. industry comprises establishments primarily engaged in answering telephone calls and relaying messages to clients.

Cross-References.

Establishments primarily engaged in providing paging or beeper transmission services are classified in U.S. Industry 517312, Wireless Telecommunications Carriers (except Satellite).

561422   Telemarketing Bureaus and Other Contact Centers

This U.S. industry comprises establishments primarily engaged in operating call centers that initiate or receive communications for others via telephone, facsimile, email, or other communication modes for purposes such as: (1) promoting clients' products or services, (2) taking orders for clients, (3) soliciting contributions for a client, and (4) providing information or assistance regarding a client's products or services. These establishments do not own the product or provide the services they are representing on behalf of clients.

Cross-References.   Establishments primarily engaged in--

- Answering telephone calls and relaying messages to clients--are classified in U.S. Industry 561421, Telephone Answering Services;
- Organizing and conducting fundraising campaigns on a contract or fee basis, that may include telephone solicitation services--are classified in U.S. Industry 561499, All Other Business Support Services; and
- Gathering, recording, tabulating, and presenting marketing and public opinion data, that may include telephone canvassing services--are classified in Industry 541910, Marketing Research and Public Opinion Polling.

T--Canadian, Mexican, and United States industries are comparable.

56143   Business Service Centers[T]

This industry comprises (1) establishments primarily engaged in providing mailbox rental and other postal and mailing services (except direct mail advertising); (2) establishments, generally known as copy centers or shops, primarily engaged in providing photocopying, duplicating, blueprinting, and other document copying services without also providing printing services (i.e., offset printing, quick printing, digital printing, prepress services); and (3) establishments that provide a range of office support services (except printing services), such as mailing services, document copying services, facsimile services, word processing services, on-site PC rental services, and office product sales.

Cross-References.   Establishments primarily engaged in--

- Operating contract post offices--are classified in Industry 49111, Postal Service;
- Delivering letters and parcels (except under a universal service obligation)--are classified in Subsector 492, Couriers and Messengers;
- Providing voice mailbox services--are classified in Industry 56142, Telephone Call Centers;
- Providing direct mail advertising services--are classified in Industry 54186, Direct Mail Advertising;
- Providing full service office space, whether on a lease or service contract basis--are classified in Industry 53112, Lessors of Nonresidential Buildings (except Miniwarehouses);
- Providing document copying services in combination with printing services, with or without a range of other office support services, and establishments known as quick or digital printers--are classified in Industry 32311, Printing; and
- Providing only one of the support services (e.g., word processing services) that establishments in this industry provide--are classified in the appropriate industry according to the service provided.

561431   Private Mail Centers

This U.S. industry comprises (1) establishments primarily engaged in providing mailbox rental and other postal and mailing (except direct mail advertising) services or (2) establishments engaged in providing these mailing services along with one or more other office support services, such as facsimile services, word processing services, on-site PC rental services, and office product sales.

Cross-References.   Establishments primarily engaged in--

- Operating contract post offices--are classified in Industry 491110, Postal Service;
- Delivering letters and parcels (except under a universal service obligation)--are classified in Subsector 492, Couriers and Messengers;
- Providing voice mailbox services--are classified in U.S. Industry 561421, Telephone Answering Services;
- Providing direct mail advertising services--are classified in Industry 541860, Direct Mail Advertising;
- Providing only one of the support services (e.g., word processing services) that establishments in this industry provide--are classified in the appropriate industry according to the service provided; and
- Providing full service office space, whether on a lease or service contract basis--are classified in Industry 531120, Lessors of Nonresidential Buildings (except Miniwarehouses).

561439   Other Business Service Centers (including Copy Shops)

This U.S. industry comprises (1) establishments generally known as copy centers or shops primarily engaged in providing photocopying, duplicating, blueprinting, and other document copying services, without also providing printing services (e.g., offset printing, quick printing, digital printing, prepress services) and (2) establishments (except private mail centers) engaged in providing a range of office support services (except printing services), such as document copying services, facsimile services, word processing services, on-site PC rental services, and office product sales.

T—Canadian, Mexican, and United States industries are comparable.

Cross-References.

- Establishments primarily engaged in providing document copying services in combination with printing services, with or without a range of other office support services, and establishments known as quick or digital printers are classified in U.S. Industry 323111, Commercial Printing (except Screen and Books);
- Establishments primarily engaged in providing mailbox rental and other postal and mailing services, with or without one or more other office support services (except printing), are classified in U.S. Industry 561431, Private Mail Centers;
- Establishments exclusively engaged in providing a single office support service (except document copying) to clients, but not the range of office support services that establishments in this industry may provide, are classified according to the service provided; and
- Establishments primarily engaged in providing full service office space, whether on a lease or service contract basis, are classified in Industry 531120, Lessors of Nonresidential Buildings (except Miniwarehouses).

56144   Collection Agencies[T]
See industry description for 561440.

561440   Collection Agencies

  This industry comprises establishments primarily engaged in collecting payments for claims and remitting payments collected to their clients.

Illustrative Examples:

Account or delinquent account collection services   Bill or debt collection services
Tax collection services on a contract or fee basis

Cross-References.   Establishments primarily engaged in--

- Repossessing tangible assets--are classified in U.S. Industry 561491, Repossession Services; and
- Providing financing to others by factoring accounts receivables (i.e., assuming the risk of collection and credit losses)--are classified in U.S. Industry 522298, All Other Nondepository Credit Intermediation.

56145   Credit Bureaus[T]
See industry description for 561450.

561450   Credit Bureaus

  This industry comprises establishments primarily engaged in compiling information, such as credit and employment histories, and providing the information to financial institutions, retailers, and others who have a need to evaluate the creditworthiness of individuals and businesses.

Illustrative Examples:

Credit agencies   Credit investigation services
Credit rating services   Credit reporting bureaus

56149   Other Business Support Services[T]

  This industry comprises establishments primarily engaged in providing business support services (except secretarial and other document preparation services; telephone answering or telemarketing services; private mail services or document copying services conducted as separate activities or in conjunction with other office support services; monetary debt collection services; and credit reporting services).

T—Canadian, Mexican, and United States industries are comparable.

Illustrative Examples:

Address bar coding services	Court reporting services
Mail presorting services	Repossession services
Bar code imprinting services	Fundraising organization services on a contract or fee
Real-time (i.e., simultaneous) closed captioning of	basis
live television performances, meetings, conferences	

Cross-References. Establishments primarily engaged in--

- Providing secretarial and other document preparation services--are classified in Industry 56141, Document Preparation Services;
- Providing telephone answering or telemarketing services--are classified in Industry 56142, Telephone Call Centers;
- Providing private mail services; document copying services (except printing services); and/or a range of office support services (except printing)--are classified in Industry 56143, Business Service Centers;
- Providing document copying services in combination with printing services, with or without a range of other office support services, and establishments known as quick or digital printers--are classified in Industry 32311, Printing;
- Providing monetary debt collection services--are classified in Industry 56144, Collection Agencies;
- Providing credit reporting services--are classified in Industry 56145, Credit Bureaus; and
- Providing film or tape captioning or subtitling services--are classified in Industry 51219, Postproduction Services and Other Motion Picture and Video Industries.

561491 Repossession Services

This U.S. industry comprises establishments primarily engaged in repossessing tangible assets (e.g., automobiles, boats, equipment, planes, furniture, appliances) for the creditor as a result of delinquent debts.

Cross-References.

Establishments primarily engaged in providing monetary debt collection services are classified in Industry 561440, Collection Agencies.

561492 Court Reporting and Stenotype Services

This U.S. industry comprises establishments primarily engaged in providing verbatim reporting and stenotype recording of live legal proceedings and transcribing subsequent recorded materials.

Illustrative Examples:

Real-time (i.e., simultaneous) closed captioning of	Court reporting or stenotype recording services
live television performances, meetings, conferences	Public stenography services

Cross-References. Establishments primarily engaged in--

- Providing stenotype recording of correspondence, reports, and other documents or in providing document transcription services--are classified in Industry 561410, Document Preparation Services; and
- Providing film or tape captioning or subtitling services--are classified in U.S. Industry 512191, Teleproduction and Other Postproduction Services.

561499 All Other Business Support Services

This U.S. industry comprises establishments primarily engaged in providing business support services (except secretarial and other document preparation services; telephone answering and telemarketing services; private mail

---

T—Canadian, Mexican, and United States industries are comparable.

services or document copying services conducted as separate activities or in conjunction with other office support services; monetary debt collection services; credit reporting services; repossession services; and court reporting and stenotype recording services).

Illustrative Examples:

Address bar coding services
Fundraising organization services on a contract or fee basis

Bar code imprinting services
Mail presorting services

Cross-References.   Establishments primarily engaged in--

- Providing secretarial and other document preparation services--are classified in Industry 561410, Document Preparation Services;
- Providing telephone answering or telemarketing services--are classified in Industry 56142, Telephone Call Centers;
- Providing private mail services, document copying services without printing services, and/or a range of office support services--are classified in Industry 56143, Business Service Centers;
- Providing document copying services in combination with printing services, with or without one or more other office support services, and establishments known as quick or digital printers--are classified in U.S. Industry 323111, Commercial Printing (except Screen and Books);
- Providing monetary debt collection services--are classified in Industry 561440, Collection Agencies;
- Providing credit reporting services--are classified in Industry 561450, Credit Bureaus;
- Providing repossession services--are classified in U.S. Industry 561491, Repossession Services; and
- Providing court reporting and stenotype services--are classified in U.S. Industry 561492, Court Reporting and Stenotype Services.

5615   Travel Arrangement and Reservation Services[T]

This industry group comprises establishments primarily engaged in one of the following: (1) travel agency services; (2) arranging and assembling tours; or (3) other travel arrangement and reservation services.

56151   Travel Agencies[T]
See industry description for 561510.

561510   Travel Agencies

This industry comprises establishments primarily engaged in acting as agents in selling travel, tour, and accommodation services to the general public and commercial clients.

Cross-References.   Establishments primarily engaged in--

- Arranging and assembling tours that they generally sell through travel agencies or on their own account--are classified in Industry 561520, Tour Operators;
- Providing guide services, such as archeological, museum, tourist, hunting, or fishing--are classified in Industry 713990, All Other Amusement and Recreation Industries; and
- Providing reservation services (e.g., accommodations, entertainment events, travel)--are classified in U.S. Industry 561599, All Other Travel Arrangement and Reservation Services.

56152   Tour Operators[T]
See industry description for 561520.

T—Canadian, Mexican, and United States industries are comparable.

561520 Tour Operators

This industry comprises establishments primarily engaged in arranging and assembling tours. The tours are sold through travel agencies or tour operators. Travel or wholesale tour operators are included in this industry.

Cross-References. Establishments primarily engaged in--

- Acting as agents in selling travel, tour, and accommodation services to the general public and commercial clients--are classified in Industry 561510, Travel Agencies;
- Conducting scenic and sightseeing tours--are classified in Subsector 487, Scenic and Sightseeing Transportation; and
- Providing guide services, such as archeological, museum, tourist, hunting, or fishing--are classified in Industry 713990, All Other Amusement and Recreation Industries.

56159 Other Travel Arrangement and Reservation Services[T]

This industry comprises establishments (except travel agencies and tour operators) primarily engaged in providing travel arrangement and reservation services.

Illustrative Examples:

Condominium time-share exchange services
Road and travel services automobile clubs
Convention or visitors bureaus
Ticket (e.g., amusement, sports, theatrical) agencies

Ticket (e.g., airline, bus, cruise ship, sports, theatrical) offices
Reservation (e.g., airline, car rental, hotel, restaurant) services

Cross-References.

- Establishments primarily engaged in arranging the rental of vacation properties are classified in Industry 53121, Offices of Real Estate Agents and Brokers;
- Travel agencies are classified in Industry 56151, Travel Agencies;
- Tour operators are classified in Industry 56152, Tour Operators;
- Automobile clubs (i.e., enthusiasts' clubs, except road and travel services) are classified in Industry 81341, Civic and Social Organizations; and
- Establishments primarily engaged in organizing, promoting, and/or managing events, such as business and trade shows, conventions, conferences, and meetings (whether or not they manage and provide the staff to operate the facilities in which these events take place), are classified in Industry 56192, Convention and Trade Show Organizers.

561591 Convention and Visitors Bureaus

This U.S. industry comprises establishments primarily engaged in marketing and promoting communities and facilities to businesses and leisure travelers through a range of activities, such as assisting organizations in locating meeting and convention sites; providing travel information on area attractions, lodging accommodations, restaurants; providing maps; and organizing group tours of local historical, recreational, and cultural attractions.

Cross-References.

Establishments primarily engaged in organizing, promoting, and/or managing events, such as business and trade shows, conventions, conferences, and meetings (whether or not they manage and provide the staff to operate the facilities in which these events take place), are classified in Industry 561920, Convention and Trade Show Organizers.

T—Canadian, Mexican, and United States industries are comparable.

561599 All Other Travel Arrangement and Reservation Services

This U.S. industry comprises establishments (except travel agencies, tour operators, and convention and visitors bureaus) primarily engaged in providing travel arrangement and reservation services.

Illustrative Examples:

Condominium time-share exchange services
Ticket (e.g., airline, bus, cruise ship, sports, theatrical) offices
Road and travel services automobile clubs

Reservation (e.g., airline, car rental, hotel, restaurant) services
Ticket (e.g., amusement, sports, theatrical) agencies

Cross-References.

- Establishments primarily engaged in arranging the rental of vacation properties are classified in Industry 531210, Offices of Real Estate Agents and Brokers;
- Travel agencies are classified in Industry 561510, Travel Agencies;
- Tour operators are classified in Industry 561520, Tour Operators;
- Convention and visitors bureaus are classified in U.S. Industry 561591, Convention and Visitors Bureaus;
- Establishments primarily engaged in organizing, promoting, and/or managing events, such as business and trade shows, conventions, conferences, and meetings (whether or not they manage and provide the staff to operate the facilities in which these events take place), are classified in Industry 561920, Convention and Trade Show Organizers; and
- Automobile clubs (i.e., enthusiasts' clubs, except road and travel services) are classified in Industry 813410, Civic and Social Organizations.

5616   Investigation and Security Services[T]

This industry group comprises establishments primarily engaged in one of the following: (1) investigation, guard, and armored car services; (2) selling security systems, such as burglar and fire alarms and locking devices, along with installation, repair, or monitoring services; or (3) remote monitoring of electronic security alarm systems.

56161   Investigation, Guard, and Armored Car Services[T]

This industry comprises establishments primarily engaged in providing one or more of the following: (1) investigation and detective services; (2) guard and patrol services; and (3) picking up and delivering money, receipts, or other valuable items with personnel and equipment to protect such properties while in transit.

Illustrative Examples:

Armored car services
Private detective services
Bodyguard services

Security guard services
Polygraph services

Cross-References.   Establishments primarily engaged in--

- Providing credit checks--are classified in Industry 56145, Credit Bureaus; and
- Selling, installing, monitoring, and maintaining security systems and devices (e.g., burglar and fire alarm systems)--are classified in Industry 56162, Security Systems Services.

561611 Investigation Services

This U.S. industry comprises establishments primarily engaged in providing investigation and detective services.

T—Canadian, Mexican, and United States industries are comparable.

Illustrative Examples:

Fingerprinting services	Polygraph services
Private detective services	Private investigative services

Cross-References.

Establishments primarily engaged in providing credit checks are classified in Industry 561450, Credit Bureaus.

561612 Security Guards and Patrol Services

This U.S. industry comprises establishments primarily engaged in providing guard and patrol services, such as bodyguard, guard dog, and parking security services.

Cross-References.

Establishments primarily engaged in selling, installing, monitoring, and maintaining security systems and devices, such as burglar and fire alarms and locking devices, are classified in Industry 56162, Security Systems Services.

561613 Armored Car Services

This U.S. industry comprises establishments primarily engaged in picking up and delivering money, receipts, or other valuable items. These establishments maintain personnel and equipment to protect such properties while in transit.

56162   Security Systems Services[T]

This industry comprises establishments engaged in (1) selling security systems, such as burglar and fire alarms and locking devices, along with installation, repair, or monitoring services or (2) remote monitoring of electronic security alarm systems.

Cross-References.   Establishments primarily engaged in--

- Selling security systems for buildings without installation, repair, or monitoring services--are classified in Sector 42, Wholesale Trade, or Sector 44-45, Retail Trade;
- Retailing motor vehicle security systems, with or without installation or repair services--are classified in Industry 44131, Automotive Parts and Accessories Stores; and
- Providing key duplication services--are classified in Industry 81149, Other Personal and Household Goods Repair and Maintenance.

561621 Security Systems Services (except Locksmiths)

This U.S. industry comprises establishments primarily engaged in (1) selling security alarm systems, such as burglar and fire alarms, along with installation, repair, or monitoring services or (2) remote monitoring of electronic security alarm systems.

Cross-References.   Establishments primarily engaged in--

- Selling security alarm systems for buildings, without installation, repair, or monitoring services--are classified in Sector 42, Wholesale Trade, or Sector 44-45, Retail Trade; and
- Retailing motor vehicle security systems, with or without installation or repair services--are classified in Industry 441310, Automotive Parts and Accessories Stores.

T—Canadian, Mexican, and United States industries are comparable.

561622 Locksmiths

This U.S. industry comprises establishments primarily engaged in (1) selling mechanical or electronic locking devices, safes, and security vaults, along with installation, repair, rebuilding, or adjusting services or (2) installing, repairing, rebuilding, and adjusting mechanical or electronic locking devices, safes, and security vaults.

Cross-References.   Establishments primarily engaged in--

- Selling security systems, such as locking devices, safes, and vaults, without installation or maintenance services--are classified in Sector 42, Wholesale Trade, or Sector 44-45, Retail Trade; and
- Providing key duplication services--are classified in Industry 811490, Other Personal and Household Goods Repair and Maintenance.

5617   Services to Buildings and Dwellings[T]

This industry group comprises establishments primarily engaged in one of the following: (1) exterminating and pest control services; (2) janitorial services; (3) landscaping services; (4) carpet and upholstery cleaning services; or (5) other services to buildings and dwellings.

56171   Exterminating and Pest Control Services[T]
See industry description for 561710.

561710 Exterminating and Pest Control Services

This industry comprises establishments primarily engaged in exterminating and controlling birds, mosquitoes, rodents, termites, and other insects and pests (except for crop production and forestry production). Establishments providing fumigation services are included in this industry.

Cross-References.

Establishments primarily engaged in providing pest control for crop or forestry production are classified in Subsector 115, Support Activities for Agriculture and Forestry.

56172   Janitorial Services[T]
See industry description for 561720.

561720 Janitorial Services

This industry comprises establishments primarily engaged in cleaning building interiors, interiors of transportation equipment (e.g., aircraft, rail cars, ships), and/or windows.

Illustrative Examples:

Custodial services
Service station cleaning and degreasing services
Housekeeping (i.e., cleaning) services

Washroom sanitation services
Maid (i.e., cleaning) services

Cross-References.   Establishments primarily engaged in--

- Cleaning building exteriors (except sandblasting and window cleaning) or chimneys--are classified in Industry 561790, Other Services to Buildings and Dwellings; and
- Sandblasting building exteriors--are classified in Industry 238990, All Other Specialty Trade Contractors.

56173   Landscaping Services[T]
See industry description for 561730.

T—Canadian, Mexican, and United States industries are comparable.

561730 Landscaping Services

This industry comprises (1) establishments primarily engaged in providing landscape care and maintenance services and/or installing trees, shrubs, plants, lawns, or gardens and (2) establishments primarily engaged in providing these services along with the design of landscape plans and/or the construction (i.e., installation) of walkways, retaining walls, decks, fences, ponds, and similar structures.

Cross-References.   Establishments primarily engaged in--

- Installing artificial turf or constructing (i.e., installing) walkways, retaining walls, decks, fences, ponds, or similar structures--are classified in Sector 23, Construction;
- Planning and designing the development of land areas for projects, such as parks and other recreational areas; airports; highways; hospitals; schools; land subdivisions; and commercial, industrial, and residential areas (without also installing trees, shrubs, plants, lawns/gardens, walkways, retaining walls, decks, and similar items or structures)--are classified in Industry 541320, Landscape Architectural Services; and
- Retailing landscaping materials and providing the installation and maintenance of these materials--are classified in Industry 444220, Nursery, Garden Center, and Farm Supply Stores.

56174 Carpet and Upholstery Cleaning Services[T]
See industry description for 561740.

561740 Carpet and Upholstery Cleaning Services

This industry comprises establishments primarily engaged in cleaning and dyeing used rugs, carpets, and upholstery.

Cross-References.   Establishments primarily engaged in--

- Rug repair not associated with rug cleaning--are classified in Industry 811490, Other Personal and Household Goods Repair and Maintenance; and
- Reupholstering and repairing furniture--are classified in Industry 811420, Reupholstery and Furniture Repair.

56179 Other Services to Buildings and Dwellings[T]
See industry description for 561790.

561790 Other Services to Buildings and Dwellings

This industry comprises establishments primarily engaged in providing services to buildings and dwellings (except exterminating and pest control; janitorial; landscaping care and maintenance; and carpet and upholstery cleaning).

Illustrative Examples:

Building exterior cleaning services (except sandblasting, window cleaning)
Swimming pool cleaning and maintenance services

Chimney cleaning services
Ventilation duct cleaning services
Drain or gutter cleaning services

Cross-References.   Establishments primarily engaged in--

- Providing exterminating and pest control services--are classified in Industry 561710, Exterminating and Pest Control Services;
- Providing janitorial services--are classified in Industry 561720, Janitorial Services;
- Providing landscaping care and maintenance--are classified in Industry 561730, Landscaping Services;
- Providing carpet and upholstery cleaning services--are classified in Industry 561740, Carpet and Upholstery Cleaning Services; and

---

T—Canadian, Mexican, and United States industries are comparable.

- Sandblasting building exteriors--are classified in Industry 238990, All Other Specialty Trade Contractors.

5619   Other Support Services[T]

This industry group comprises establishments primarily engaged in providing day-to-day business and other organizational support services (except office administrative services; facilities support services; employment services; business support services; travel arrangement and reservation services; security and investigation services; and services to buildings and dwellings).

56191   Packaging and Labeling Services[T]
See industry description for 561910.

561910   Packaging and Labeling Services

This industry comprises establishments primarily engaged in packaging client-owned materials. The services may include labeling and/or imprinting the package.

Illustrative Examples:

Apparel and textile folding and packaging services
Kit assembling and packaging services
Blister packaging services

Shrink wrapping services
Gift wrapping services

Cross-References.   Establishments primarily engaged in--

- Processing client-owned materials into a different product, such as mixing water and concentrate to produce soft drinks--are classified in Sector 31-33, Manufacturing;
- Providing aerosol packaging services--are classified in U.S. Industry 325998, All Other Miscellaneous Chemical Product and Preparation Manufacturing;
- Providing packing and crating services incidental to transportation--are classified in U.S. Industry 488991, Packing and Crating;
- Providing warehousing services, as well as packaging or other logistics services--are classified in Industry Group 4931, Warehousing and Storage; and
- Providing packing and crating services for agricultural products--are classified in U.S. Industry 115114, Postharvest Crop Activities (except Cotton Ginning).

56192   Convention and Trade Show Organizers[T]
See industry description for 561920.

561920   Convention and Trade Show Organizers

This industry comprises establishments primarily engaged in organizing, promoting, and/or managing events, such as business and trade shows, conventions, conferences, and meetings (whether or not they manage and provide the staff to operate the facilities in which these events take place).

Cross-References.

Establishments primarily engaged in organizing, promoting, and/or managing live performing arts productions, sports events, and similar events, such as festivals (whether or not they manage and provide the staff to operate the facilities in which these events take place), are classified in Industry Group 7113, Promoters of Performing Arts, Sports, and Similar Events.

56199   All Other Support Services[T]
See industry description for 561990.

T—Canadian, Mexican, and United States industries are comparable.

561990 All Other Support Services

This industry comprises establishments primarily engaged in providing day-to-day business and other organizational support services (except office administrative services, facilities support services, employment services, business support services, travel arrangement and reservation services, security and investigation services, services to buildings and other structures, packaging and labeling services, and convention and trade show organizing services).

Illustrative Examples:

Bartering services
Flagging (i.e., traffic control) services
Bottle exchanges
Float decorating services
Cloth cutting, bolting, or winding for the trade

Inventory taking services
Contract meter reading services
Lumber grading services
Diving services on a contract or fee basis

Cross-References.   Establishments primarily engaged in--

- Providing office administrative services--are classified in Industry 561110, Office Administrative Services;
- Providing facilities support services--are classified in Industry 561210, Facilities Support Services;
- Providing employment services--are classified in Industry Group 5613, Employment Services;
- Providing business support services--are classified in Industry Group 5614, Business Support Services;
- Providing travel arrangement and reservation services--are classified in Industry Group 5615, Travel Arrangement and Reservation Services;
- Providing security and investigation services--are classified in Industry Group 5616, Investigation and Security Services;
- Providing services to buildings and other structures--are classified in Industry Group 5617, Services to Buildings and Dwellings;
- Providing packaging and labeling services--are classified in Industry 561910, Packaging and Labeling Services; and
- Organizing, promoting, and/or managing conferences, conventions, and trade shows (whether or not they manage and provide the staff to operate the facilities in which these events take place)--are classified in Industry 561920, Convention and Trade Show Organizers.

562   Waste Management and Remediation Services[T]

Industries in the Waste Management and Remediation Services subsector group establishments engaged in the collection, treatment, and disposal of waste materials. This includes establishments engaged in local hauling of waste materials; operating materials recovery facilities (i.e., those that sort recyclable materials from the trash stream); providing remediation services (i.e., those that provide for the cleanup of contaminated buildings, mine sites, soil, or ground water); and providing septic pumping and other miscellaneous waste management services. There are three industry groups within the subsector that separate these activities into waste collection, waste treatment and disposal, and remediation and other waste management.

Excluded from this subsector are establishments primarily engaged in collecting, treating, and disposing waste through sewer systems or sewage treatment facilities that are classified in Industry 22132, Sewage Treatment Facilities, and establishments primarily engaged in long-distance hauling of waste materials that are classified in Industry 48423, Specialized Freight (except Used Goods) Trucking, Long-Distance. Also, there are some activities that appear to be related to waste management, but that are not included in this subsector. For example, establishments primarily engaged in providing waste management consulting services are classified in Industry 54162, Environmental Consulting Services.

T—Canadian, Mexican, and United States industries are comparable.

5621   Waste Collection

56211   Waste Collection

This industry comprises establishments primarily engaged in (1) collecting and/or hauling hazardous waste, nonhazardous waste, and/or recyclable materials within a local area and/or (2) operating hazardous or nonhazardous waste transfer stations. Hazardous waste collection establishments may be responsible for the identification, treatment, packaging, and labeling of waste for the purposes of transport.

Cross-References.   Establishments primarily engaged in--

- Long-distance trucking of waste--are classified in Industry 48423, Specialized Freight (except Used Goods) Trucking, Long-Distance;
- Operating facilities for separating and sorting recyclable materials from nonhazardous waste streams (i.e., garbage) and/or for sorting commingled recyclable materials, such as paper, plastics, and metal cans, into distinct categories--are classified in Industry 56292, Materials Recovery Facilities; and
- Collecting and/or hauling in combination with disposal of waste materials--are classified in Industry 56221, Waste Treatment and Disposal.

562111 Solid Waste Collection

This U.S. industry comprises establishments primarily engaged in one or more of the following: (1) collecting and/or hauling nonhazardous solid waste (i.e., garbage) within a local area; (2) operating nonhazardous solid waste transfer stations; and (3) collecting and/or hauling mixed recyclable materials within a local area.

Cross-References.   Establishments primarily engaged in--

- Long-distance trucking of waste--are classified in Industry 484230, Specialized Freight (except Used Goods) Trucking, Long-Distance;
- Collecting and/or hauling in combination with disposal of nonhazardous waste materials--are classified in Industry 56221, Waste Treatment and Disposal;
- Collecting and/or hauling hazardous waste within a local area and/or operating hazardous waste transfer stations--are classified in U.S. Industry 562112, Hazardous Waste Collection;
- Collecting and removing debris, such as brush or rubble, within a local area--are classified in U.S. Industry 562119, Other Waste Collection; and
- Operating facilities for separating and sorting recyclable materials from nonhazardous waste streams (i.e., garbage) and/or for sorting commingled recyclable materials, such as paper, plastics, and metal cans, into distinct categories--are classified in Industry 562920, Materials Recovery Facilities.

562112 Hazardous Waste Collection

This U.S. industry comprises establishments primarily engaged in collecting and/or hauling hazardous waste within a local area and/or operating hazardous waste transfer stations. Hazardous waste collection establishments may be responsible for the identification, treatment, packaging, and labeling of waste for the purposes of transport.

Cross-References.   Establishments primarily engaged in--

- Long-distance trucking of waste--are classified in Industry 484230, Specialized Freight (except Used Goods) Trucking, Long-Distance;
- Collecting and/or hauling in combination with disposal of hazardous waste materials--are classified in U.S. Industry 562211, Hazardous Waste Treatment and Disposal;
- Collecting and/or hauling nonhazardous solid waste (i.e., garbage) and/or recyclable materials within a local area and/or operating nonhazardous solid waste transfer stations--are classified in U.S. Industry 562111, Solid Waste Collection; and

---

T--Canadian, Mexican, and United States industries are comparable.

- Collecting and removing debris, such as brush or rubble, within a local area--are classified in U.S. Industry 562119, Other Waste Collection.

562119 Other Waste Collection

This U.S. industry comprises establishments primarily engaged in collecting and/or hauling waste (except nonhazardous solid waste and hazardous waste) within a local area. Establishments engaged in brush or rubble removal services are included in this industry.

Cross-References.   Establishments primarily engaged in--

- Long-distance trucking of waste--are classified in Industry 484230, Specialized Freight (except Used Goods) Trucking, Long-Distance;
- Collecting and/or hauling in combination with disposal of waste materials--are classified in Industry Group 5622, Waste Treatment and Disposal;
- Collecting and/or hauling nonhazardous solid waste (i.e., garbage) or mixed recyclable materials within a local area or operating nonhazardous solid waste transfer stations--are classified in U.S. Industry 562111, Solid Waste Collection;
- Collecting and/or hauling hazardous waste within a local area or operating hazardous waste transfer stations--are classified in U.S. Industry 562112, Hazardous Waste Collection; and
- Operating facilities for separating and sorting recyclable materials from nonhazardous waste streams (i.e., garbage) and/or for sorting commingled recyclable materials, such as paper, plastics, and metal cans, into distinct categories--are classified in Industry 562920, Materials Recovery Facilities.

5622   Waste Treatment and Disposal

56221   Waste Treatment and Disposal

This industry comprises establishments primarily engaged in (1) operating waste treatment or disposal facilities (except sewer systems or sewage treatment facilities) or (2) the combined activity of collecting and/or hauling of waste materials within a local area and operating waste treatment or disposal facilities. Waste combustors or incinerators (including those that may produce byproducts, such as electricity), solid waste landfills, and compost dumps are included in this industry.

Cross-References.   Establishments primarily engaged in--

- Collecting, treating, and disposing waste through sewer systems or sewage treatment facilities--are classified in Industry 22132, Sewage Treatment Facilities; and
- Manufacturing compost--are classified in Industry 32531, Fertilizer Manufacturing.

562211 Hazardous Waste Treatment and Disposal

This U.S. industry comprises establishments primarily engaged in (1) operating treatment and/or disposal facilities for hazardous waste or (2) the combined activity of collecting and/or hauling of hazardous waste materials within a local area and operating treatment or disposal facilities for hazardous waste.

Cross-References.   Establishments primarily engaged in--

- Operating landfills for the disposal of nonhazardous solid waste--are classified in U.S. Industry 562212, Solid Waste Landfill;
- Operating combustors and incinerators for the disposal of nonhazardous solid waste--are classified in U.S. Industry 562213, Solid Waste Combustors and Incinerators;
- Collecting, treating, and disposing waste through sewer systems or sewage treatment facilities--are classified in Industry 221320, Sewage Treatment Facilities; and

---

T—Canadian, Mexican, and United States industries are comparable.

- Operating nonhazardous waste treatment and disposal facilities (except landfills, combustors, incinerators, and sewer systems or sewage treatment facilities)--are classified in U.S. Industry 562219, Other Nonhazardous Waste Treatment and Disposal.

562212 Solid Waste Landfill

This U.S. industry comprises establishments primarily engaged in (1) operating landfills for the disposal of nonhazardous solid waste or (2) the combined activity of collecting and/or hauling nonhazardous waste materials within a local area and operating landfills for the disposal of nonhazardous solid waste. These establishments may produce byproducts, such as methane.

Cross-References.   Establishments primarily engaged in--

- Operating treatment and/or disposal facilities for hazardous waste--are classified in U.S. Industry 562211, Hazardous Waste Treatment and Disposal;
- Operating combustors and incinerators for the disposal of nonhazardous solid waste--are classified in U.S. Industry 562213, Solid Waste Combustors and Incinerators;
- Collecting, treating, and disposing waste through sewer systems or sewage treatment facilities--are classified in Industry 221320, Sewage Treatment Facilities;
- Operating nonhazardous waste treatment and disposal facilities (except landfills, combustors, incinerators, and sewer systems or sewage treatment facilities)--are classified in U.S. Industry 562219, Other Nonhazardous Waste Treatment and Disposal; and
- Manufacturing compost--are classified in U.S. Industry 325314, Fertilizer (Mixing Only) Manufacturing.

562213 Solid Waste Combustors and Incinerators

This U.S. industry comprises establishments primarily engaged in operating combustors and incinerators for the disposal of nonhazardous solid waste. These establishments may produce byproducts, such as electricity and steam.

Cross-References.   Establishments primarily engaged in--

- Operating treatment and/or disposal facilities for hazardous waste--are classified in U.S. Industry 562211, Hazardous Waste Treatment and Disposal;
- Operating landfills for the disposal of nonhazardous solid waste--are classified in U.S. Industry 562212, Solid Waste Landfill;
- Collecting, treating, and disposing waste through sewer systems or sewage treatment facilities--are classified in Industry 221320, Sewage Treatment Facilities; and
- Operating nonhazardous waste treatment and disposal facilities (except landfills, combustors, incinerators, and sewer systems or sewage treatment facilities)--are classified in U.S. Industry 562219, Other Nonhazardous Waste Treatment and Disposal.

562219 Other Nonhazardous Waste Treatment and Disposal

This U.S. industry comprises establishments primarily engaged in (1) operating nonhazardous waste treatment and disposal facilities (except landfills, combustors, incinerators and sewer systems or sewage treatment facilities) or (2) the combined activity of collecting and/or hauling of nonhazardous waste materials within a local area and operating waste treatment or disposal facilities (except landfills, combustors, incinerators and sewer systems, or sewage treatment facilities). Compost dumps are included in this industry.

Cross-References.   Establishments primarily engaged in--

- Operating landfills for the disposal of nonhazardous solid waste--are classified in U.S. Industry 562212, Solid Waste Landfill;
- Operating combustors and incinerators for the disposal of nonhazardous solid waste--are classified in U.S. Industry 562213, Solid Waste Combustors and Incinerators;

T—Canadian, Mexican, and United States industries are comparable.

- Collecting, treating, and disposing waste through sewer systems or sewage treatment facilities--are classified in Industry 221320, Sewage Treatment Facilities; and
- Manufacturing compost--are classified in U.S. Industry 325314, Fertilizer (Mixing Only) Manufacturing.

5629   Remediation and Other Waste Management Services

This industry group comprises establishments primarily engaged in remediation and other waste management services (except waste collection, waste treatment and disposal, and waste management consulting services).

56291   Remediation Services
See industry description for 562910.

562910   Remediation Services

This industry comprises establishments primarily engaged in one or more of the following: (1) remediation and cleanup of contaminated buildings, mine sites, soil, or ground water; (2) integrated mine reclamation activities, including demolition, soil remediation, waste water treatment, hazardous material removal, contouring land, and revegetation; and (3) asbestos, lead paint, and other toxic material abatement.

Cross-References.   Establishments primarily engaged in--

- Environmental engineering services--are classified in Industry 541330, Engineering Services;
- Developing remedial action plans--are classified in Industry 541620, Environmental Consulting Services;
- Excavating soil--are classified in Industry 238910, Site Preparation Contractors;
- Individual activities as part of a reclamation, remediation, or restoration project--are classified according to the primary activity;
- Building modifications to alleviate radon gas--are classified in Industry 238990, All Other Specialty Trade Contractors; and
- Collecting, treating, and disposing waste water through sewer systems or sewage treatment facilities--are classified in Industry 221320, Sewage Treatment Facilities.

56292   Materials Recovery Facilities
See industry description for 562920.

562920   Materials Recovery Facilities

This industry comprises establishments primarily engaged in (1) operating facilities for separating and sorting recyclable materials from nonhazardous waste streams (i.e., garbage) and/or (2) operating facilities where commingled recyclable materials, such as paper, plastics, used beverage cans, and metals, are sorted into distinct categories.

Cross-References.

Establishments primarily engaged in merchant wholesaling automotive, industrial, and other recyclable materials are classified in Industry 423930, Recyclable Material Merchant Wholesalers.

56299   All Other Waste Management Services

This industry comprises establishments primarily engaged in waste management services (except waste collection, waste treatment and disposal, remediation, operation of materials recovery facilities, and waste management consulting services).

T—Canadian, Mexican, and United States industries are comparable.

Illustrative Examples:

Beach cleaning and maintenance services
Pumping (i.e., cleaning) cesspools, portable toilets, or
septic tanks
Cesspool cleaning services

Sewer cleaning and rodding services
Portable toilet renting and/or servicing
Sewer or storm basin cleanout services

Cross-References.   Establishments primarily engaged in--

- Collecting and/or hauling waste within a local area--are classified in Industry 56211, Waste Collection;
- Long-distance trucking of waste--are classified in Industry 48423, Specialized Freight (except Used Goods) Trucking, Long-Distance;
- Operating treatment or disposal facilities (except sewer systems or sewage treatment facilities) for waste-- are classified in Industry 56221, Waste Treatment and Disposal;
- Collecting, treating, and disposing waste through sewer systems or sewage treatment facilities--are classified in Industry 22132, Sewage Treatment Facilities;
- Remediation and cleanup of contaminated buildings, mine sites, soil, or ground water--are classified in Industry 56291, Remediation Services;
- Operating facilities for separating and sorting recyclable materials from nonhazardous waste streams (i.e., garbage) or where commingled recyclable materials, such as paper, plastics, and metal cans, are sorted into distinct categories--are classified in Industry 56292, Materials Recovery Facilities;
- Installing septic tanks--are classified in Industry 23891, Site Preparation Contractors; and
- Providing waste management consulting services, such as developing remedial action plans--are classified in Industry 54162, Environmental Consulting Services.

562991 Septic Tank and Related Services

This U.S. industry comprises establishments primarily engaged in (1) pumping (i.e., cleaning) septic tanks and cesspools and/or (2) renting and/or servicing portable toilets.

Cross-References.   Establishments primarily engaged in--

- Installing septic tanks--are classified in Industry 238910, Site Preparation Contractors; and
- Cleaning and rodding sewers and catch basins--are classified in U.S. Industry 562998, All Other Miscellaneous Waste Management Services.

562998 All Other Miscellaneous Waste Management Services

This U.S. industry comprises establishments primarily engaged in providing waste management services (except waste collection, waste treatment and disposal, remediation, operation of materials recovery facilities, septic tank pumping and related services, and waste management consulting services).

Illustrative Examples:

Beach cleaning and maintenance services
Sewer or storm basin cleanout services
Catch basin cleaning services

Tank cleaning and disposal services, commercial or
industrial
Sewer cleaning and rodding services

Cross-References.   Establishments primarily engaged in--

- Collecting and/or hauling waste within a local area--are classified in Industry 56211, Waste Collection;
- Long-distance trucking of waste--are classified in Industry 484230, Specialized Freight (except Used Goods) Trucking, Long-Distance;
- Operating treatment or disposal facilities (except sewer systems or sewage treatment facilities) for waste-- are classified in Industry 56221, Waste Treatment and Disposal;

T—Canadian, Mexican, and United States industries are comparable.

- Collecting, treating, and disposing waste through sewer systems or sewage treatment facilities--are classified in Industry 221320, Sewage Treatment Facilities;
- Remediation and cleanup of contaminated buildings, mine sites, soil, or ground water--are classified in Industry 562910, Remediation Services;
- Operating facilities for separating and sorting recyclable materials from nonhazardous waste streams (i.e., garbage) or for sorting commingled recyclable materials, such as paper, plastics, and metal cans, into distinct categories--are classified in Industry 562920, Materials Recovery Facilities;
- Pumping (i.e., cleaning) cesspools, portable toilets, and septic tanks or renting portable toilets--are classified in U.S. Industry 562991, Septic Tank and Related Services; and
- Providing waste management consulting services, such as developing remedial action plans--are classified in Industry 541620, Environmental Consulting Services.

T—Canadian, Mexican, and United States industries are comparable.

Sector 61--Educational Services[T]

The Sector as a Whole

The Educational Services sector comprises establishments that provide instruction and training in a wide variety of subjects. This instruction and training is provided by specialized establishments, such as schools, colleges, universities, and training centers. These establishments may be privately owned and operated for profit or not for profit, or they may be publicly owned and operated. They may also offer food and/or accommodation services to their students.

Educational services are usually delivered by teachers or instructors that explain, tell, demonstrate, supervise, and direct learning. Instruction is imparted in diverse settings, such as educational institutions, the workplace, or the home, and through diverse means, such as correspondence, television, the Internet, or other electronic and distance-learning methods. The training provided by these establishments may include the use of simulators and simulation methods. It can be adapted to the particular needs of the students, for example sign language can replace verbal language for teaching students with hearing impairments. All industries in the sector share this commonality of process, namely, labor inputs of instructors with the requisite subject matter expertise and teaching ability.

611   Educational Services[T]

Industries in the Educational Services subsector provide instruction and training in a wide variety of subjects. The instruction and training is provided by specialized establishments, such as schools, colleges, universities, and training centers.

The subsector is structured according to level and type of educational services. Elementary and secondary schools, junior colleges and colleges, universities, and professional schools correspond to a recognized series of formal levels of education designated by diplomas, associate degrees (including equivalent certificates), and degrees. The remaining industry groups are based more on the type of instruction or training offered, and the levels are not always as formally defined. The establishments are often highly specialized, many offering instruction in a very limited subject matter, for example ski lessons or one specific computer software package. Within the subsector, the level and types of training that are required of the instructors and teachers vary depending on the industry.

Establishments that manage schools and other educational establishments on a contractual basis are classified in this subsector if they both manage the operation and provide the operating staff. Such establishments are classified in the Educational Services subsector based on the type of facility managed and operated.

6111   Elementary and Secondary Schools[T]

61111   Elementary and Secondary Schools
See industry description for 611110.

611110 Elementary and Secondary Schools

This industry comprises establishments primarily engaged in furnishing academic courses and associated course work that comprise a basic preparatory education. A basic preparatory education ordinarily constitutes kindergarten through 12th grade. This industry includes school boards and school districts.

Illustrative Examples:

Elementary schools
Parochial schools, elementary or secondary
High schools
Primary schools

Kindergartens
Schools for the physically disabled, elementary or secondary
Military academies, elementary or secondary

T—Canadian, Mexican, and United States industries are comparable.

Cross-References.

- Establishments primarily engaged in providing preschool or pre-kindergarten education are classified in Industry 624410, Child Day Care Services; and
- College level military academies are classified in Industry 611310, Colleges, Universities, and Professional Schools.

6112   Junior Colleges[T]

61121   Junior Colleges[T]
See industry description for 611210.

611210 Junior Colleges

This industry comprises establishments primarily engaged in furnishing academic, or academic and technical, courses and granting associate degrees, certificates, or diplomas below the baccalaureate level. The requirement for admission to an associate or equivalent degree program is at least a high school diploma or equivalent general academic training. Instruction may be provided in diverse settings, such as the establishment's or client's training facilities, educational institutions, the workplace, or the home, and through diverse means, such as correspondence, television, the Internet, or other electronic and distance-learning methods. The training provided by these establishments may include the use of simulators and simulation methods.

6113   Colleges, Universities, and Professional Schools[T]

61131   Colleges, Universities, and Professional Schools[T]
See industry description for 611310.

611310 Colleges, Universities, and Professional Schools

This industry comprises establishments primarily engaged in furnishing academic courses and granting degrees at baccalaureate or graduate levels. The requirement for admission is at least a high school diploma or equivalent general academic training. Instruction may be provided in diverse settings, such as the establishment's or client's training facilities, educational institutions, the workplace, or the home, and through diverse means, such as correspondence, television, the Internet, or other electronic and distance-learning methods. The training provided by these establishments may include the use of simulators and simulation methods.

Illustrative Examples:

Colleges (except junior colleges)	Universities
Theological seminaries offering baccalaureate or graduate degrees	Professional schools (e.g., business administration, dental, law, medical)
Military academies, college level	

Cross-References.

Establishments primarily engaged in furnishing academic, or academic and technical, courses and granting associate degrees, certificates, or diplomas below the baccalaureate level are classified in Industry 611210, Junior Colleges.

6114   Business Schools and Computer and Management Training[T]

This industry group comprises establishments primarily engaged in one of the following: (1) offering courses in office procedures and secretarial and stenographic skills and may offer courses in basic office skills, such as word processing; (2) conducting computer training (except computer repair); or (3) offering an array of short duration courses and seminars for management and professional development. Instruction may be provided in diverse

---

T—Canadian, Mexican, and United States industries are comparable.

settings, such as the establishment's or client's training facilities, educational institutions, the workplace, or the home, and through diverse means, such as correspondence, television, the Internet, or other electronic and distance-learning methods. The training provided by these establishments may include the use of simulators and simulation methods.

61141   Business and Secretarial Schools[T]
See industry description for 611410.

611410 Business and Secretarial Schools

This industry comprises establishments primarily engaged in offering courses in office procedures and secretarial and stenographic skills and may offer courses in basic office skills, such as word processing. In addition, these establishments may offer such classes as office machine operation, reception, communications, and other skills designed for individuals pursuing a clerical or secretarial career. Instruction may be provided in diverse settings, such as the establishment's or client's training facilities, educational institutions, the workplace, or the home, and through diverse means, such as correspondence, television, the Internet, or other electronic and distance-learning methods. The training provided by these establishments may include the use of simulators and simulation methods.

Cross-References.   Establishments primarily engaged in--

- Offering computer training (except computer repair)--are classified in Industry 611420, Computer Training;
- Offering academic degrees (e.g., baccalaureate, graduate level) in business education--are classified in Industry 611310, Colleges, Universities, and Professional Schools; and
- Offering training in the maintenance and repair of computers--are classified in U.S. Industry 611519, Other Technical and Trade Schools.

61142   Computer Training[T]
See industry description for 611420.

611420 Computer Training

This industry comprises establishments primarily engaged in conducting computer training (except computer repair), such as computer programming, software packages, computerized business systems, computer electronics technology, computer operations, and local area network management. Instruction may be provided in diverse settings, such as the establishment's or client's training facilities, educational institutions, the workplace, or the home, and through diverse means, such as correspondence, television, the Internet, or other electronic and distance-learning methods. The training provided by these establishments may include the use of simulators and simulation methods.

Cross-References.   Establishments primarily engaged in--

- Offering training in the maintenance and repair of computers--are classified in U.S. Industry 611519, Other Technical and Trade Schools; and
- Computer retailing, wholesaling, or computer system designing that may also provide computer training-- are classified in their appropriate industries.

61143   Professional and Management Development Training[T]
See industry description for 611430.

611430 Professional and Management Development Training

This industry comprises establishments primarily engaged in offering an array of short duration courses and seminars for management and professional development. Training for career development may be provided directly to individuals or through employers' training programs, and courses may be customized or modified to meet the

T—Canadian, Mexican, and United States industries are comparable.

special needs of customers. Instruction may be provided in diverse settings, such as the establishment's or client's training facilities, educational institutions, the workplace, or the home, and through diverse means, such as correspondence, television, the Internet, or other electronic and distance-learning methods. The training provided by these establishments may include the use of simulators and simulation methods.

Cross-References.   Establishments primarily engaged in--

- Advising clients on human resource and training issues without providing the training--are classified in U.S. Industry 541612, Human Resources Consulting Services; and
- Offering academic degrees (e.g., baccalaureate, graduate level)--are classified in Industry 611310, Colleges, Universities, and Professional Schools.

6115   Technical and Trade Schools^T

61151   Technical and Trade Schools^T

This industry comprises establishments primarily engaged in offering vocational and technical training in a variety of technical subjects and trades. The training often leads to job-specific certification. Instruction may be provided in diverse settings, such as the establishment's or client's training facilities, educational institutions, the workplace, or the home, and through diverse means, such as correspondence, television, the Internet, or other electronic and distance-learning methods. The training provided by these establishments may include the use of simulators and simulation methods.

Illustrative Examples:

Apprenticeship training programs
Graphic arts schools
Aviation and flight training schools
Modeling schools
Computer repair training

Nursing schools (except academic)
Cosmetology schools
Real estate schools
Electronic equipment repair training
Truck driving schools

Cross-References.   Establishments primarily engaged in--

- Offering courses in office procedures and secretarial and stenographic skills--are classified in Industry 61141, Business and Secretarial Schools;
- Offering computer training (except computer repair)--are classified in Industry 61142, Computer Training;
- Offering professional and management development training--are classified in Industry 61143, Professional and Management Development Training;
- Offering academic courses that may also offer technical and trade courses--are classified according to the type of school;
- Specialty air transportation services that may also provide flight training--are classified in Industry 48121, Nonscheduled Air Transportation; and
- Offering registered nursing training with academic degrees (e.g., associate, baccalaureate)--are classified in Industry 61121, Junior Colleges, or Industry 61131, Colleges, Universities, and Professional Schools.

611511 Cosmetology and Barber Schools

This U.S. industry comprises establishments primarily engaged in offering training in barbering, hair styling, or the cosmetic arts, such as makeup or skin care. These schools provide job-specific certification.

611512 Flight Training

This U.S. industry comprises establishments primarily engaged in offering aviation and flight training. These establishments may offer vocational training, recreational training, or both.

T—Canadian, Mexican, and United States industries are comparable.

Cross-References.   Establishments primarily engaged in--

- Offering specialized military training (except flight instruction, academies, and basic training)--are classified in U.S. Industry 611519, Other Technical and Trade Schools;
- Operating college level military academies--are classified in Industry 611310, Colleges, Universities, and Professional Schools;
- National security and military basic training (except academies)--are classified in Industry 928110, National Security; and
- Providing specialty air transportation services that may also provide flight training--are classified in U.S. Industry 481219, Other Nonscheduled Air Transportation.

611513 Apprenticeship Training

This U.S. industry comprises establishments primarily engaged in offering apprenticeship training programs. These programs involve applied training as well as course work.

611519 Other Technical and Trade Schools

This U.S. industry comprises establishments primarily engaged in offering job or career vocational or technical courses (except cosmetology and barber training, aviation and flight training, and apprenticeship training). The curriculums offered by these schools are highly structured and specialized and lead to job-specific certification.

Illustrative Examples:

Bartending schools
Modeling schools
Broadcasting schools
Real estate schools
Computer repair training

Truck driving schools
Graphic arts schools
Specialized military training (except flight instruction, academies, and basic training)

Cross-References.   Establishments primarily engaged in--

- Offering courses in office procedures and secretarial and stenographic skills--are classified in Industry 611410, Business and Secretarial Schools;
- Offering computer training (except computer repair)--are classified in Industry 611420, Computer Training;
- Offering professional and management development training--are classified in Industry 611430, Professional and Management Development Training;
- Offering registered nursing training with academic degrees (e.g., associate, baccalaureate)--are classified in Industry 611210, Junior Colleges, or Industry 611310, College, Universities, and Professional Schools;
- Offering aviation and flight training, including military flight instruction--are classified in U.S. Industry 611512, Flight Training;
- Operating college level military academies--are classified in Industry 611310, Colleges, Universities, and Professional Schools;
- National security and military basic training (except academies)--are classified in Industry 928110, National Security;
- Offering cosmetology and barber training--are classified in U.S. Industry 611511, Cosmetology and Barber Schools;
- Offering academic courses that may also offer technical and trade courses--are classified according to the type of school; and
- Offering apprenticeship training programs--are classified in U.S. Industry 611513, Apprenticeship Training.

T—Canadian, Mexican, and United States industries are comparable.

6116   Other Schools and Instruction[T]

This industry group comprises establishments primarily engaged in offering or providing instruction (except academic schools, colleges, and universities; and business, computer, management, technical, or trade instruction). Instruction may be provided in diverse settings, such as the establishment's or client's training facilities, educational institutions, the workplace, or the home, and through diverse means, such as correspondence, television, the Internet, or other electronic and distance-learning methods. The training provided by these establishments may include the use of simulators and simulation methods.

61161   Fine Arts Schools[T]
      See industry description for 611610.

611610 Fine Arts Schools

This industry comprises establishments primarily engaged in offering instruction in the arts, including dance, art, drama, and music.

Illustrative Examples:

Art (except commercial and graphic) instruction
Music instruction (e.g., piano, guitar)
Dance instruction
Music schools (except academic)
Dance studios

Performing arts schools (except academic)
Drama schools (except academic)
Photography schools (except commercial photography)
Fine arts schools (except academic)

Cross-References.

- Establishments offering high school diplomas or academic degrees (i.e., even if they specialize in fine arts) are classified elsewhere in this subsector according to the type of school; and
- Establishments primarily engaged in offering courses in commercial and graphic arts and commercial photography are classified in U.S. Industry 611519, Other Technical and Trade Schools.

61162   Sports and Recreation Instruction[T]
      See industry description for 611620.

611620 Sports and Recreation Instruction

This industry comprises establishments, such as camps and schools, primarily engaged in offering instruction in athletic activities to groups of individuals. Overnight and day sports instruction camps are included in this industry.

Illustrative Examples:

Camps, sports instruction
Professional sports instructors (i.e., not participating in sporting events)
Cheerleading instruction
Riding instruction academies or schools

Gymnastics instruction
Sports (e.g., baseball, basketball, football, golf) instruction
Martial arts instruction, camps or schools
Swimming instruction

Cross-References.

- Establishments primarily engaged in operating overnight recreational camps that may offer some athletic instruction in addition to other activities are classified in U.S. Industry 721214, Recreational and Vacation Camps (except Campgrounds);
- Establishments primarily engaged in operating sports and recreation establishments that also offer athletic instruction are classified in Sector 71, Arts, Entertainment, and Recreation;

T—Canadian, Mexican, and United States industries are comparable.

- Independent (i.e., freelance) athletes engaged in providing sports instruction and participating in spectator sporting events are classified in U.S. Industry 711219, Other Spectator Sports; and
- Establishments primarily engaged in offering academic courses that may also offer athletic instruction are classified according to the type of school.

61163   Language Schools[T]
See industry description for 611630.

611630   Language Schools

This industry comprises establishments primarily engaged in offering foreign language instruction (including sign language). These establishments are designed to offer language instruction ranging from conversational skills for personal enrichment to intensive training courses for career or educational opportunities.

Cross-References.   Establishments primarily engaged in--

- Offering academic courses that may also offer language instruction--are classified according to type of school; and
- Providing translation and interpretation services--are classified in Industry 541930, Translation and Interpretation Services.

61169   All Other Schools and Instruction[T]

This industry comprises establishments primarily engaged in offering instruction (except business, computer, management, technical, trade, fine arts, athletic, and language instruction). Also excluded from this industry are academic schools, colleges, and universities.

Illustrative Examples:

Academic tutoring services	Speed reading instruction
Public speaking training	Exam preparation services
Automobile driving schools	

Cross-References.   Establishments primarily engaged in--

- Offering elementary and secondary school instruction--are classified in Industry 61111, Elementary and Secondary Schools;
- Offering junior college instruction--are classified in Industry 61121, Junior Colleges;
- Offering college, university, and professional school instruction with academic degrees (e.g., baccalaureate, graduate)--are classified in Industry 61131, Colleges, Universities, and Professional Schools;
- Offering business, computer (except computer repair), and management training--are classified in Industry Group 6114, Business Schools and Computer and Management Training;
- Offering vocational and technical instruction (e.g., computer repair and maintenance)--are classified in Industry 61151, Technical and Trade Schools;
- Offering fine arts instruction--are classified in Industry 61161, Fine Arts Schools;
- Offering sports and recreation instruction--are classified in Industry 61162, Sports and Recreation Instruction; and
- Offering language instruction--are classified in Industry 61163, Language Schools.

611691   Exam Preparation and Tutoring

This U.S. industry comprises establishments primarily engaged in offering preparation for standardized examinations and/or academic tutoring services.

T—Canadian, Mexican, and United States industries are comparable.

Illustrative Examples:

Academic tutoring services	College board preparation centers
Learning centers offering remedial courses	Professional examination review instruction

611692   Automobile Driving Schools

This U.S. industry comprises establishments primarily engaged in offering automobile driving instruction.

Cross-References.

Establishments primarily engaged in offering truck and bus driving instruction are classified in U.S. Industry 611519, Other Technical and Trade Schools.

611699   All Other Miscellaneous Schools and Instruction

This U.S. industry comprises establishments primarily engaged in offering instruction (except business, computer, management, technical, trade, fine arts, athletic, language instruction, tutoring, and automobile driving instruction). Also excluded from this industry are academic schools, colleges, and universities.

Illustrative Examples:

Public speaking training	Speed reading instruction
Survival training	Yoga instruction, camps, or schools

Cross-References.   Establishments primarily engaged in--

- Offering elementary and secondary school instruction--are classified in Industry 611110, Elementary and Secondary Schools;
- Offering junior college instruction--are classified in Industry 611210, Junior Colleges;
- Offering college, university, and professional school instruction with academic degrees (e.g., baccalaureate, graduate)--are classified in Industry 611310, Colleges, Universities, and Professional Schools;
- Offering business, computer (except computer repair), and management training--are classified in Industry Group 6114, Business Schools and Computer and Management Training;
- Offering vocational and technical instruction (e.g., computer repair and maintenance)--are classified in Industry 61151, Technical and Trade Schools;
- Offering fine arts instruction--are classified in Industry 611610, Fine Arts Schools;
- Offering sports and recreation instruction--are classified in Industry 611620, Sports and Recreation Instruction;
- Offering language instruction--are classified in Industry 611630, Language Schools;
- Offering exam preparation and tutoring services--are classified in U.S. Industry 611691, Exam Preparation and Tutoring; and
- Offering automobile driving instruction--are classified in U.S. Industry 611692, Automobile Driving Schools.

6117   Educational Support Services[T]

61171   Educational Support Services[T]
See industry description for 611710.

611710   Educational Support Services

This industry comprises establishments primarily engaged in providing non-instructional services that support educational processes or systems.

T—Canadian, Mexican, and United States industries are comparable.

Illustrative Examples:

Educational consultants	Student exchange programs
Educational testing services	Educational testing evaluation services
Educational guidance counseling services	

Cross-References.   Establishments primarily engaged in--

- Providing job training for the unemployed, underemployed, physically disabled, and persons who have a job market disadvantage because of lack of education or job skills--are classified in Industry 624310, Vocational Rehabilitation Services; and
- Conducting research and analyses in cognitive development--are classified in Industry 541720, Research and Development in the Social Sciences and Humanities.

T—Canadian, Mexican, and United States industries are comparable.

Sector 62--Health Care and Social Assistance[T]

The Sector as a Whole

The Health Care and Social Assistance sector comprises establishments providing health care and social assistance for individuals. The sector includes both health care and social assistance because it is sometimes difficult to distinguish between the boundaries of these two activities. The industries in this sector are arranged on a continuum starting with establishments providing medical care exclusively, continuing with those providing health care and social assistance, and finally finishing with those providing only social assistance. Establishments in this sector deliver services by trained professionals. All industries in the sector share this commonality of process, namely, labor inputs of health practitioners or social workers with the requisite expertise. Many of the industries in the sector are defined based on the educational degree held by the practitioners included in the industry.

Excluded from this sector are aerobic classes in Subsector 713, Amusement, Gambling, and Recreation Industries, and non-medical diet and weight reducing centers in Subsector 812, Personal and Laundry Services. Although these can be viewed as health services, these services are not typically delivered by health practitioners.

621 Ambulatory Health Care Services[T]

Industries in the Ambulatory Health Care Services subsector provide health care services directly or indirectly to ambulatory patients and do not usually provide inpatient services. Health practitioners in this subsector provide outpatient services, with the facilities and equipment not usually being the most significant part of the production process.

6211 Offices of Physicians[T]

62111 Offices of Physicians[T]

This industry comprises establishments of health practitioners having the degree of M.D. (Doctor of Medicine) or D.O. (Doctor of Osteopathy) primarily engaged in the independent practice of general or specialized medicine (e.g., anesthesiology, oncology, ophthalmology, psychiatry) or surgery. These practitioners operate private or group practices in their own offices (e.g., centers, clinics) or in the facilities of others, such as hospitals or HMO medical centers.

Cross-References.

- Medical centers primarily engaged in providing emergency medical care for accident or trauma victims and ambulatory surgical centers primarily engaged in providing surgery on an outpatient basis are classified in Industry 62149, Other Outpatient Care Centers;
- Establishments of oral pathologists are classified in Industry 62121, Offices of Dentists; and
- Establishments of speech or voice pathologists are classified in Industry 62134, Offices of Physical, Occupational and Speech Therapists, and Audiologists.

621111 Offices of Physicians (except Mental Health Specialists)

This U.S. industry comprises establishments of health practitioners having the degree of M.D. (Doctor of Medicine) or D.O. (Doctor of Osteopathy) primarily engaged in the independent practice of general or specialized medicine (except psychiatry or psychoanalysis) or surgery. These practitioners operate private or group practices in their own offices (e.g., centers, clinics) or in the facilities of others, such as hospitals or HMO medical centers.

Cross-References.

- Establishments of physicians primarily engaged in the independent practice of psychiatry or psychoanalysis are classified in U.S. Industry 621112, Offices of Physicians, Mental Health Specialists;

T—Canadian, Mexican, and United States industries are comparable.

- Freestanding medical centers primarily engaged in providing emergency medical care for accident or catastrophe victims and freestanding ambulatory surgical centers primarily engaged in providing surgery on an outpatient basis are classified in U.S. Industry 621493, Freestanding Ambulatory Surgical and Emergency Centers;
- Establishments of oral pathologists are classified in Industry 621210, Offices of Dentists; and
- Establishments of speech or voice pathologists are classified in Industry 621340, Offices of Physical, Occupational and Speech Therapists, and Audiologists.

621112 Offices of Physicians, Mental Health Specialists

This U.S. industry comprises establishments of health practitioners having the degree of M.D. (Doctor of Medicine) or D.O. (Doctor of Osteopathy) primarily engaged in the independent practice of psychiatry or psychoanalysis. These practitioners operate private or group practices in their own offices (e.g., centers, clinics) or in the facilities of others, such as hospitals or HMO medical centers.

6212   Offices of Dentists[T]

62121   Offices of Dentists[T]
See industry description for 621210.

621210 Offices of Dentists

This industry comprises establishments of health practitioners having the degree of D.M.D. (Doctor of Dental Medicine), D.D.S. (Doctor of Dental Surgery), or D.D.Sc. (Doctor of Dental Science) primarily engaged in the independent practice of general or specialized dentistry or dental surgery. These practitioners operate private or group practices in their own offices (e.g., centers, clinics) or in the facilities of others, such as hospitals or HMO medical centers. They can provide either comprehensive preventive, cosmetic, or emergency care, or specialize in a single field of dentistry.

Cross-References.

- Establishments known as dental laboratories primarily engaged in making dentures, artificial teeth, and orthodontic appliances to order for dentists are classified in U.S. Industry 339116, Dental Laboratories; and
- Establishments of dental hygienists primarily engaged in cleaning teeth and gums or establishments of denturists primarily engaged in taking impressions for and fitting dentures are classified in U.S. Industry 621399, Offices of All Other Miscellaneous Health Practitioners.

6213   Offices of Other Health Practitioners[T]

This industry group comprises establishments of independent health practitioners (except physicians and dentists).

62131   Offices of Chiropractors[T]
See industry description for 621310.

621310 Offices of Chiropractors

This industry comprises establishments of health practitioners having the degree of D.C. (Doctor of Chiropractic) primarily engaged in the independent practice of chiropractic. These practitioners provide diagnostic and therapeutic treatment of neuromusculoskeletal and related disorders through the manipulation and adjustment of the spinal column and extremities, and operate private or group practices in their own offices (e.g., centers, clinics) or in the facilities of others, such as hospitals or HMO medical centers.

62132   Offices of Optometrists[T]
See industry description for 621320.

T—Canadian, Mexican, and United States industries are comparable.

621320 Offices of Optometrists

This industry comprises establishments of health practitioners having the degree of O.D. (Doctor of Optometry) primarily engaged in the independent practice of optometry. These practitioners examine, diagnose, treat, and manage diseases and disorders of the visual system, the eye, and associated structures as well as diagnose related systemic conditions. Offices of optometrists prescribe and/or provide eyeglasses, contact lenses, low vision aids, and vision therapy. They operate private or group practices in their own offices (e.g., centers, clinics) or in the facilities of others, such as hospitals or HMO medical centers, and may also provide the same services as opticians, such as selling and fitting prescription eyeglasses and contact lenses.

Cross-References.

- Offices of opticians primarily engaged in selling and fitting prescription eyeglasses and contact lenses are classified in Industry 446130, Optical Goods Stores; and
- Offices of physicians primarily engaged in the independent practice of ophthalmology are classified in U.S. Industry 621111, Offices of Physicians (except Mental Health Specialists).

62133 Offices of Mental Health Practitioners (except Physicians)[T]
See industry description for 621330.

621330 Offices of Mental Health Practitioners (except Physicians)

This industry comprises establishments of independent mental health practitioners (except physicians) primarily engaged in (1) the diagnosis and treatment of mental, emotional, and behavioral disorders and/or (2) the diagnosis and treatment of individual or group social dysfunction brought about by such causes as mental illness, alcohol and substance abuse, physical and emotional trauma, or stress. These practitioners operate private or group practices in their own offices (e.g., centers, clinics) or in the facilities of others, such as hospitals or HMO medical centers.

Cross-References.

Establishments of psychiatrists, psychoanalysts, and psychotherapists having the degree of M.D. (Doctor of Medicine) or D.O. (Doctor of Osteopathy) are classified in U.S. Industry 621112, Offices of Physicians, Mental Health Specialists.

62134 Offices of Physical, Occupational and Speech Therapists, and Audiologists[T]
See industry description for 621340.

621340 Offices of Physical, Occupational and Speech Therapists, and Audiologists

This industry comprises establishments of independent health practitioners primarily engaged in one of the following: (1) providing physical therapy services to patients who have impairments, functional limitations, disabilities, or changes in physical functions and health status resulting from injury, disease or other causes, or who require prevention, wellness or fitness services; (2) planning and administering educational, recreational, and social activities designed to help patients or individuals with disabilities regain physical or mental functioning or adapt to their disabilities; and (3) diagnosing and treating speech, language, or hearing problems. These practitioners operate private or group practices in their own offices (e.g., centers, clinics) or in the facilities of others, such as hospitals or HMO medical centers.

Illustrative Examples:

Audiologists' offices
Recreational (e.g., art, dance, music) therapists' offices
Industrial therapists' offices

Speech pathologists' offices
Occupational therapists' offices
Physical therapists' offices

T—Canadian, Mexican, and United States industries are comparable.

62139   Offices of All Other Health Practitioners[T]

This industry comprises establishments of independent health practitioners (except physicians; dentists; chiropractors; optometrists; mental health specialists; physical, occupational, and speech therapists; and audiologists). These practitioners operate private or group practices in their own offices (e.g., centers, clinics) or in the facilities of others, such as hospitals or HMO medical centers.

Illustrative Examples:

Acupuncturists' (except MDs or DOs) offices	Naturopaths' offices
Inhalation or respiratory therapists' offices	Dietitians' offices
Dental hygienists' offices	Podiatrists' offices
Midwives' offices	Homeopaths' offices
Denturists' offices	Registered or licensed practical nurses' offices

Cross-References.   Establishments primarily engaged in--

- The independent practice of medicine (i.e., physicians)--are classified in Industry 62111, Offices of Physicians;
- The independent practice of dentistry--are classified in Industry 62121, Offices of Dentists;
- The independent practice of chiropractic--are classified in Industry 62131, Offices of Chiropractors;
- The independent practice of optometry--are classified in Industry 62132, Offices of Optometrists;
- The independent practice of mental health (except physicians)--are classified in Industry 62133, Offices of Mental Health Practitioners (except Physicians); and
- The independent practice of physical, occupational, and speech therapy, and audiology--are classified in Industry 62134, Offices of Physical, Occupational and Speech Therapists, and Audiologists.

621391   Offices of Podiatrists

This U.S. industry comprises establishments of health practitioners having the degree of D.P.M. (Doctor of Podiatric Medicine) primarily engaged in the independent practice of podiatry. These practitioners diagnose and treat diseases and deformities of the foot and operate private or group practices in their own offices (e.g., centers, clinics) or in the facilities of others, such as hospitals or HMO medical centers.

621399   Offices of All Other Miscellaneous Health Practitioners

This U.S. industry comprises establishments of independent health practitioners (except physicians; dentists; chiropractors; optometrists; mental health specialists; physical, occupational, and speech therapists; audiologists; and podiatrists). These practitioners operate private or group practices in their own offices (e.g., centers, clinics) or in the facilities of others, such as hospitals or HMO medical centers.

Illustrative Examples:

Acupuncturists' (except MDs or DOs) offices	Midwives' offices
Hypnotherapists' offices	Dietitians' offices
Dental hygienists' offices	Naturopaths' offices
Inhalation or respiratory therapists' offices	Homeopaths' offices
Denturists' offices	Registered or licensed practical nurses' offices

Cross-References.   Establishments primarily engaged in--

- The independent practice of medicine (i.e., physicians)--are classified in Industry 62111, Offices of Physicians;
- The independent practice of dentistry--are classified in Industry 621210, Offices of Dentists;
- The independent practice of chiropractic--are classified in Industry 621310, Offices of Chiropractors;

T—Canadian, Mexican, and United States industries are comparable.

- The independent practice of optometry--are classified in Industry 621320, Offices of Optometrists;
- The independent practice of mental health (except physicians)--are classified in Industry 621330, Offices of Mental Health Practitioners (except Physicians);
- The independent practice of physical, occupational, and speech therapy, and audiology--are classified in Industry 621340, Offices of Physical, Occupational and Speech Therapists, and Audiologists; and
- The independent practice of podiatry--are classified in U.S. Industry 621391, Offices of Podiatrists.

6214 Outpatient Care Centers[T]

This industry group comprises establishments with medical staff primarily engaged in providing a range of outpatient services, such as family planning, diagnosis and treatment of mental health disorders and alcohol and other substance abuse, and other general or specialized outpatient care.

62141 Family Planning Centers[T]
See industry description for 621410.

621410 Family Planning Centers

This industry comprises establishments with medical staff primarily engaged in providing a range of family planning services on an outpatient basis, such as contraceptive services, genetic and prenatal counseling, voluntary sterilization, and therapeutic and medically induced termination of pregnancy.

Illustrative Examples:

Birth control clinics
Fertility clinics

Childbirth preparation classes
Pregnancy counseling centers

62142 Outpatient Mental Health and Substance Abuse Centers[T]
See industry description for 621420.

621420 Outpatient Mental Health and Substance Abuse Centers

This industry comprises establishments with medical staff primarily engaged in providing outpatient services related to the diagnosis and treatment of mental health disorders and alcohol and other substance abuse. These establishments generally treat patients who do not require inpatient treatment. They may provide a counseling staff and information regarding a wide range of mental health and substance abuse issues and/or refer patients to more extensive treatment programs, if necessary.

Illustrative Examples:

Outpatient alcoholism treatment centers and clinics (except hospitals)
Outpatient mental health centers and clinics (except hospitals)
Outpatient detoxification centers and clinics (except hospitals)

Outpatient substance abuse treatment centers and clinics (except hospitals)
Outpatient drug addiction treatment centers and clinics (except hospitals)

Cross-References.

- Establishments known and licensed as hospitals primarily engaged in the inpatient treatment of mental health and substance abuse illnesses with an emphasis on medical treatment and monitoring are classified in Industry 622210, Psychiatric and Substance Abuse Hospitals; and
- Establishments primarily engaged in the inpatient treatment of mental health and substance abuse illnesses with an emphasis on residential care and counseling rather than medical treatment are classified in Industry 623220, Residential Mental Health and Substance Abuse Facilities.

T—Canadian, Mexican, and United States industries are comparable.

62149   Other Outpatient Care Centers[T]

This industry comprises establishments with medical staff primarily engaged in providing general or specialized outpatient care (except family planning centers and outpatient mental health and substance abuse centers). Centers or clinics of health practitioners with different degrees from more than one industry practicing within the same establishment (i.e., Doctor of Medicine and Doctor of Dental Medicine) are included in this industry.

Illustrative Examples:

Dialysis centers and clinics
Outpatient biofeedback centers and clinics
Freestanding ambulatory surgical centers and clinics
Outpatient community health centers and clinics

Freestanding emergency medical centers and clinics
Outpatient sleep disorder centers and clinics
Health maintenance organization (HMO) medical centers and clinics

Cross-References.

- Physician walk-in centers are classified in Industry 62111, Offices of Physicians;
- Centers and clinics of health practitioners from the same industry primarily engaged in the independent practice of their profession are classified in Industry 62111, Offices of Physicians; Industry 62121, Offices of Dentists; and Industry Group 6213, Offices of Other Health Practitioners;
- Family planning centers are classified in Industry 62141, Family Planning Centers;
- Outpatient mental health and substance abuse centers are classified in Industry 62142, Outpatient Mental Health and Substance Abuse Centers;
- HMO establishments (except those providing health care services) primarily engaged in underwriting health and medical insurance policies are classified in Industry 52411, Direct Life, Health, and Medical Insurance Carriers; and
- Establishments known and licensed as hospitals that also perform ambulatory surgery and emergency room services are classified in Subsector 622, Hospitals.

621491   HMO Medical Centers

This U.S. industry comprises establishments with physicians and other medical staff primarily engaged in providing a range of outpatient medical services to the health maintenance organization (HMO) subscribers with a focus generally on primary health care. These establishments are owned by the HMO. Included in this industry are HMO establishments that both provide health care services and underwrite health and medical insurance policies.

Cross-References.

- Health practitioners or health practitioner groups contracting to provide their services to subscribers of pre-paid health plans are classified in Industry 62111, Offices of Physicians; Industry 621210, Offices of Dentists; and Industry Group 6213, Offices of Other Health Practitioners; and
- HMO establishments (except those providing health care services) primarily engaged in underwriting and administering health and medical insurance policies are classified in U.S. Industry 524114, Direct Health and Medical Insurance Carriers.

621492   Kidney Dialysis Centers

This U.S. industry comprises establishments with medical staff primarily engaged in providing outpatient kidney or renal dialysis services.

621493   Freestanding Ambulatory Surgical and Emergency Centers

This U.S. industry comprises establishments with physicians and other medical staff primarily engaged in (1) providing surgical services (e.g., orthoscopic and cataract surgery) on an outpatient basis or (2) providing emergency care services (e.g., setting broken bones, treating lacerations, or tending to patients suffering injuries as a

---

T—Canadian, Mexican, and United States industries are comparable.

result of accidents, trauma, or medical conditions necessitating immediate medical care) on an outpatient basis. Outpatient surgical establishments have specialized facilities, such as operating and recovery rooms, and specialized equipment, such as anesthetic or X-ray equipment.

Illustrative Examples:

Freestanding ambulatory surgical centers and clinics
Freestanding trauma centers (except hospitals)
Freestanding emergency medical centers and clinics

Urgent medical care centers and clinics (except hospitals)

Cross-References.

- Physician walk-in centers are classified in U.S. Industry 621111, Offices of Physicians (except Mental Health Specialists); and
- Establishments known and licensed as hospitals that also perform ambulatory surgery and emergency room services are classified in Subsector 622, Hospitals.

621498 All Other Outpatient Care Centers

This U.S. industry comprises establishments with medical staff primarily engaged in providing general or specialized outpatient care (except family planning centers, outpatient mental health and substance abuse centers, HMO medical centers, kidney dialysis centers, and freestanding ambulatory surgical and emergency centers). Centers or clinics of health practitioners with different degrees from more than one industry practicing within the same establishment (i.e., Doctor of Medicine and Doctor of Dental Medicine) are included in this industry.

Illustrative Examples:

Outpatient biofeedback centers and clinics
Outpatient pain therapy centers and clinics

Outpatient community health centers and clinics
Outpatient sleep disorder centers and clinics

Cross-References.

- Physician walk-in centers are classified in U.S. Industry 621111, Offices of Physicians (except Mental Health Specialists);
- Centers and clinics of health practitioners from the same industry primarily engaged in the independent practice of their profession are classified in Industry 62111, Offices of Physicians; Industry 621210, Offices of Dentists; and Industry Group 6213, Offices of Other Health Practitioners;
- Family planning centers are classified in Industry 621410, Family Planning Centers;
- Outpatient mental health and substance abuse centers are classified in Industry 621420, Outpatient Mental Health and Substance Abuse Centers;
- HMO medical centers are classified in U.S. Industry 621491, HMO Medical Centers;
- Dialysis centers are classified in U.S. Industry 621492, Kidney Dialysis Centers; and
- Freestanding ambulatory surgical and emergency centers are classified in U.S. Industry 621493, Freestanding Ambulatory Surgical and Emergency Centers.

6215 Medical and Diagnostic Laboratories[T]

62151 Medical and Diagnostic Laboratories[T]

This industry comprises establishments known as medical and diagnostic laboratories primarily engaged in providing analytic or diagnostic services, including body fluid analysis and diagnostic imaging, generally to the medical profession or to the patient on referral from a health practitioner.

T—Canadian, Mexican, and United States industries are comparable.

Illustrative Examples:

Dental or medical X-ray laboratories
Medical pathology laboratories
Diagnostic imaging centers

Medical testing laboratories
Medical forensic laboratories

Cross-References.

Establishments, such as dental, optical, and orthopedic laboratories, primarily engaged in providing the following activities to the medical profession, respectively: making dentures, artificial teeth, and orthodontic appliances to prescription; grinding lenses to prescription; and making orthopedic or prosthetic appliances to prescription are classified in Industry 33911, Medical Equipment and Supplies Manufacturing.

621511 Medical Laboratories

This U.S. industry comprises establishments known as medical laboratories primarily engaged in providing analytic or diagnostic services, including body fluid analysis, generally to the medical profession or to the patient on referral from a health practitioner.

Illustrative Examples:

Blood analysis laboratories
Medical pathology laboratories
Medical bacteriological laboratories

Medical testing laboratories
Medical forensic laboratories

Cross-References.

- Establishments known as dental laboratories primarily engaged in making dentures, artificial teeth, and orthodontic appliances to prescription are classified in U.S. Industry 339116, Dental Laboratories;
- Establishments known as optical laboratories primarily engaged in grinding lenses to prescription are classified in U.S. Industry 339115, Ophthalmic Goods Manufacturing; and
- Establishments known as orthopedic laboratories primarily engaged in making orthopedic or prosthetic appliances to prescription are classified in U.S. Industry 339113, Surgical Appliance and Supplies Manufacturing.

621512 Diagnostic Imaging Centers

This U.S. industry comprises establishments known as diagnostic imaging centers primarily engaged in producing images of the patient generally on referral from a health practitioner.

Illustrative Examples:

Computer tomography (CT-scan) centers
Medical radiological laboratories
Dental or medical X-ray laboratories

Ultrasound imaging centers
Magnetic resonance imaging (MRI) centers

6216   Home Health Care Services[T]

62161   Home Health Care Services[T]
See industry description for 621610.

621610 Home Health Care Services

This industry comprises establishments primarily engaged in providing skilled nursing services in the home, along with a range of the following: personal care services; homemaker and companion services; physical therapy;

T—Canadian, Mexican, and United States industries are comparable.

medical social services; medications; medical equipment and supplies; counseling; 24-hour home care; occupation and vocational therapy; dietary and nutritional services; speech therapy; audiology; and high-tech care, such as intravenous therapy.

Illustrative Examples:

Home health care agencies	Home infusion therapy services
Visiting nurse associations	In-home hospice care services

Cross-References.

- In-home health services provided by establishments of health practitioners and others primarily engaged in the independent practice of their profession are classified in Industry 62111, Offices of Physicians; Industry 621210, Offices of Dentists; Industry Group 6213, Offices of Other Health Practitioners; and U.S. Industry 621999, All Other Miscellaneous Ambulatory Health Care Services; and
- Establishments primarily engaged in renting or leasing products for home health care are classified in U.S. Industry 532283, Home Health Equipment Rental.

6219   Other Ambulatory Health Care Services[T]

This industry group comprises establishments primarily engaged in providing ambulatory health care services (except offices of physicians, dentists, and other health practitioners; outpatient care centers; medical laboratories and diagnostic imaging centers; and home health care providers).

62191   Ambulance Services[T]
See industry description for 621910.

621910 Ambulance Services

This industry comprises establishments primarily engaged in providing transportation of patients by ground or air, along with medical care. These services are often provided during a medical emergency but are not restricted to emergencies. The vehicles are equipped with lifesaving equipment operated by medically trained personnel.

Cross-References.

Establishments primarily engaged in providing transportation of the disabled or elderly (without medical care) are classified in U.S. Industry 485991, Special Needs Transportation.

62199   All Other Ambulatory Health Care Services[T]

This industry comprises establishments primarily engaged in providing ambulatory health care services (except offices of physicians, dentists, and other health practitioners; outpatient care centers; medical and diagnostic laboratories; home health care providers; and ambulances).

Illustrative Examples:

Blood donor stations	Health screening services (except by offices of health
Pacemaker monitoring services	practitioners)
Blood or body organ banks	Smoking cessation programs
Physical fitness evaluation services (except by offices	Hearing testing services (except by offices of
of health practitioners)	audiologists)

T—Canadian, Mexican, and United States industries are comparable.

Cross-References.

- Establishments primarily engaged in the independent practice of medicine are classified in Industry 62111, Offices of Physicians;
- Establishments primarily engaged in the independent practice of dentistry are classified in Industry 62121, Offices of Dentists;
- Establishments primarily engaged in the independent practice of health care (except offices of physicians and dentists) are classified in Industry Group 6213, Offices of Other Health Practitioners;
- Establishments primarily engaged in providing general or specialized outpatient care services are classified in Industry Group 6214, Outpatient Care Centers;
- Establishments primarily engaged in providing home health care services are classified in Industry 62161, Home Health Care Services;
- Establishments primarily engaged in transportation of patients by ground or air, along with medical care are classified in Industry 62191, Ambulance Services; and
- Establishments known as medical and diagnostic laboratories primarily engaged in providing analytic or diagnostic services are classified in Industry 62151, Medical and Diagnostic Laboratories.

621991 Blood and Organ Banks

This U.S. industry comprises establishments primarily engaged in collecting, storing, and distributing blood and blood products and storing and distributing body organs.

621999 All Other Miscellaneous Ambulatory Health Care Services

This U.S. industry comprises establishments primarily engaged in providing ambulatory health care services (except offices of physicians, dentists, and other health practitioners; outpatient care centers; medical and diagnostic laboratories; home health care providers; ambulances; and blood and organ banks).

Illustrative Examples:

Health screening services (except by offices of health practitioners)

Physical fitness evaluation services (except by offices of health practitioners)

Hearing testing services (except by offices of audiologists)

Smoking cessation programs

Pacemaker monitoring services

Cross-References.

- Establishments primarily engaged in the independent practice of medicine are classified in Industry 62111, Offices of Physicians;
- Establishments primarily engaged in the independent practice of dentistry are classified in Industry 621210, Offices of Dentists;
- Establishments primarily engaged in the independent practice of health care (except offices of physicians and dentists) are classified in Industry Group 6213, Offices of Other Health Practitioners;
- Establishments primarily engaged in providing general or specialized outpatient care services are classified in Industry Group 6214, Outpatient Care Centers;
- Establishments primarily engaged in providing home health care services are classified in Industry 621610, Home Health Care Services;
- Establishments primarily engaged in the transportation of patients by ground or air, along with medical care are classified in Industry 621910, Ambulance Services;
- Establishments known as medical and diagnostic laboratories primarily engaged in providing analytic or diagnostic services are classified in Industry 62151, Medical and Diagnostic Laboratories; and
- Blood and organ banks are classified in U.S. Industry 621991, Blood and Organ Banks.

T—Canadian, Mexican, and United States industries are comparable.

622   Hospitals[T]

Industries in the Hospitals subsector provide medical, diagnostic, and treatment services that include physician, nursing, and other health services to inpatients and the specialized accommodation services required by inpatients. Hospitals may also provide outpatient services as a secondary activity. Establishments in the Hospitals subsector provide inpatient health services, many of which can only be provided using the specialized facilities and equipment that form a significant and integral part of the production process.

6221   General Medical and Surgical Hospitals[T]

62211   General Medical and Surgical Hospitals[T]
See industry description for 622110.

622110   General Medical and Surgical Hospitals

This industry comprises establishments known and licensed as general medical and surgical hospitals primarily engaged in providing diagnostic and medical treatment (both surgical and nonsurgical) to inpatients with any of a wide variety of medical conditions. These establishments maintain inpatient beds and provide patients with food services that meet their nutritional requirements. These hospitals have an organized staff of physicians and other medical staff to provide patient care services. These establishments usually provide other services, such as outpatient services, anatomical pathology services, diagnostic X-ray services, clinical laboratory services, operating room services for a variety of procedures, and pharmacy services.

6222   Psychiatric and Substance Abuse Hospitals[T]

62221   Psychiatric and Substance Abuse Hospitals[T]
See industry description for 622210.

622210   Psychiatric and Substance Abuse Hospitals

This industry comprises establishments known and licensed as psychiatric and substance abuse hospitals primarily engaged in providing diagnostic, medical treatment, and monitoring services for inpatients who suffer from mental illness or substance abuse disorders. The treatment often requires an extended stay in the hospital. These establishments maintain inpatient beds and provide patients with food services that meet their nutritional requirements. They have an organized staff of physicians and other medical staff to provide patient care services. Psychiatric, psychological, and social work services are available at the facility. These hospitals usually provide other services, such as outpatient services, clinical laboratory services, diagnostic X-ray services, and electroencephalograph services.

Cross-References.

- Establishments primarily engaged in providing treatment of mental health and substance abuse illnesses on an exclusively outpatient basis are classified in Industry 621420, Outpatient Mental Health and Substance Abuse Centers;
- Establishments referred to as hospitals but primarily engaged in providing inpatient treatment of mental health and substance abuse illnesses with the emphasis on counseling rather than medical treatment are classified in Industry 623220, Residential Mental Health and Substance Abuse Facilities; and
- Establishments referred to as hospitals but primarily engaged in providing residential care for persons diagnosed with intellectual and developmental disabilities are classified in Industry 623210, Residential Intellectual and Developmental Disability Facilities.

6223   Specialty (except Psychiatric and Substance Abuse) Hospitals[T]

62231   Specialty (except Psychiatric and Substance Abuse) Hospitals[T]
See industry description for 622310.

T—Canadian, Mexican, and United States industries are comparable.

622310 Specialty (except Psychiatric and Substance Abuse) Hospitals

This industry comprises establishments known and licensed as specialty hospitals primarily engaged in providing diagnostic and medical treatment to inpatients with a specific type of disease or medical condition (except psychiatric or substance abuse). Hospitals providing long-term care for the chronically ill and hospitals providing rehabilitation, restorative, and adjustive services to physically challenged or disabled people are included in this industry. These establishments maintain inpatient beds and provide patients with food services that meet their nutritional requirements. They have an organized staff of physicians and other medical staff to provide patient care services. These hospitals may provide other services, such as outpatient services, diagnostic X-ray services, clinical laboratory services, operating room services, physical therapy services, educational and vocational services, and psychological and social work services.

Cross-References.

- Establishments known and licensed as hospitals primarily engaged in providing diagnostic and therapeutic inpatient services for a variety of medical conditions, both surgical and nonsurgical, are classified in Industry 622110, General Medical and Surgical Hospitals;
- Establishments known and licensed as hospitals primarily engaged in providing diagnostic and treatment services for inpatients with psychiatric or substance abuse illnesses are classified in Industry 622210, Psychiatric and Substance Abuse Hospitals;
- Establishments referred to as hospitals but primarily engaged in providing inpatient nursing and rehabilitative services to persons requiring convalescence are classified in Industry 623110, Nursing Care Facilities (Skilled Nursing Facilities);
- Establishments referred to as hospitals but primarily engaged in providing residential care of persons diagnosed with intellectual and developmental disabilities are classified in Industry 623210, Residential Intellectual and Developmental Disability Facilities; and
- Establishments referred to as hospitals but primarily engaged in providing inpatient treatment for mental health and substance abuse illnesses with the emphasis on counseling rather than medical treatment are classified in Industry 623220, Residential Mental Health and Substance Abuse Facilities.

623   Nursing and Residential Care Facilities[T]

Industries in the Nursing and Residential Care Facilities subsector provide residential care combined with either nursing, supervisory, or other types of care as required by the residents. In this subsector, the facilities are a significant part of the production process, and the care provided is a mix of health and social services with the health services being largely some level of nursing services.

6231   Nursing Care Facilities (Skilled Nursing Facilities)[T]

62311   Nursing Care Facilities (Skilled Nursing Facilities)[T]
See industry description for 623110.

623110 Nursing Care Facilities (Skilled Nursing Facilities)

This industry comprises establishments primarily engaged in providing inpatient nursing and rehabilitative services. The care is generally provided for an extended period of time to individuals requiring nursing care. These establishments have a permanent core staff of registered or licensed practical nurses who, along with other staff, provide nursing and continuous personal care services.

Illustrative Examples:

Convalescent homes or convalescent
hospitals (except psychiatric)
Nursing homes
Rest homes with nursing care

Assisted living facilities for the elderly with nursing
care
Inpatient care hospices

T—Canadian, Mexican, and United States industries are comparable.

Cross-References.

- Assisted living facilities with on-site nursing care facilities are classified in U.S. Industry 623311, Continuing Care Retirement Communities; and
- Psychiatric convalescent homes are classified in Industry 623220, Residential Mental Health and Substance Abuse Facilities.

6232 Residential Intellectual and Developmental Disability, Mental Health, and Substance Abuse Facilities[T]

This industry group comprises establishments primarily engaged in providing residential care (but not licensed hospital care) to people with intellectual and developmental disabilities, mental illness, or substance abuse problems.

62321 Residential Intellectual and Developmental Disability Facilities[T]
See industry description for 623210.

623210 Residential Intellectual and Developmental Disability Facilities

This industry comprises establishments (e.g., group homes, hospitals, intermediate care facilities) primarily engaged in providing residential care services for persons diagnosed with intellectual and developmental disabilities. These facilities may provide some health care, though the focus is room, board, protective supervision, and counseling.

Cross-References.

- Establishments primarily engaged in providing inpatient treatment of mental health and substance abuse illnesses with an emphasis on counseling rather than medical treatment are classified in Industry 623220, Residential Mental Health and Substance Abuse Facilities;
- Establishments primarily engaged in providing treatment of mental health and substance abuse illnesses on an exclusively outpatient basis are classified in Industry 621420, Outpatient Mental Health and Substance Abuse Centers; and
- Establishments known and licensed as hospitals primarily engaged in providing inpatient treatment of mental health and substance abuse illnesses with an emphasis on medical treatment and monitoring are classified in Industry 622210, Psychiatric and Substance Abuse Hospitals.

62322 Residential Mental Health and Substance Abuse Facilities[T]
See industry description for 623220.

623220 Residential Mental Health and Substance Abuse Facilities

This industry comprises establishments primarily engaged in providing residential care and treatment for patients with mental health and substance abuse illnesses. These establishments provide room, board, supervision, and counseling services. Although medical services may be available at these establishments, they are incidental to the counseling, mental rehabilitation, and support services offered. These establishments generally provide a wide range of social services in addition to counseling.

Illustrative Examples:

Alcoholism or drug addiction rehabilitation facilities (except licensed hospitals)
Psychiatric convalescent homes or hospitals

Mental health halfway houses
Residential group homes for the emotionally disturbed

T—Canadian, Mexican, and United States industries are comparable.

Cross-References.

- Establishments primarily engaged in providing treatment of mental health and substance abuse illnesses on an exclusively outpatient basis are classified in Industry 621420, Outpatient Mental Health and Substance Abuse Centers;
- Establishments primarily engaged in providing residential care for persons diagnosed with intellectual and developmental disabilities are classified in Industry 623210, Residential Intellectual and Developmental Disability Facilities; and
- Establishments known and licensed as hospitals primarily engaged in providing inpatient treatment of mental health and substance abuse illnesses with an emphasis on medical treatment and monitoring are classified in Industry 622210, Psychiatric and Substance Abuse Hospitals.

6233   Continuing Care Retirement Communities and Assisted Living Facilities for the Elderly[T]

62331   Continuing Care Retirement Communities and Assisted Living Facilities for the Elderly[T]

This industry comprises establishments primarily engaged in providing residential and personal care services for (1) the elderly and other persons who are unable to fully care for themselves and/or (2) the elderly and other persons who do not desire to live independently. The care typically includes room, board, supervision, and assistance in daily living, such as housekeeping services. In some instances these establishments provide skilled nursing care for residents in separate on-site facilities.

Illustrative Examples:

Assisted living facilities
Assisted living facilities for the elderly without
nursing care

Continuing care retirement communities
Rest homes without nursing care

Cross-References.

- Establishments primarily engaged in providing inpatient nursing and rehabilitative services are classified in Industry 62311, Nursing Care Facilities (Skilled Nursing Facilities); and
- Apartment or condominium complexes where people live independently in rented housing units are classified in Industry 53111, Lessors of Residential Buildings and Dwellings.

623311   Continuing Care Retirement Communities

This U.S. industry comprises establishments primarily engaged in providing a range of residential and personal care services with on-site nursing care facilities for (1) the elderly and other persons who are unable to fully care for themselves and/or (2) the elderly and other persons who do not desire to live independently. Individuals live in a variety of residential settings with meals, housekeeping, social, leisure, and other services available to assist residents in daily living. Assisted living facilities with on-site nursing care facilities are included in this industry.

Cross-References.

- Establishments primarily engaged in providing inpatient nursing and rehabilitative services are classified in Industry 623110, Nursing Care Facilities (Skilled Nursing Facilities);
- Assisted living facilities without on-site nursing care facilities are classified in U.S. Industry 623312, Assisted Living Facilities for the Elderly; and
- Apartment or condominium complexes where people live independently in rented housing units are classified in Industry 531110, Lessors of Residential Buildings and Dwellings.

T—Canadian, Mexican, and United States industries are comparable.

623312 Assisted Living Facilities for the Elderly

This U.S. industry comprises establishments primarily engaged in providing residential and personal care services (i.e., without on-site nursing care facilities) for (1) the elderly or other persons who are unable to fully care for themselves and/or (2) the elderly or other persons who do not desire to live independently. The care typically includes room, board, supervision, and assistance in daily living, such as housekeeping services.

Illustrative Examples:

Assisted living facilities without on-site nursing care facilities
Rest homes without nursing care

Assisted living facilities for the elderly without nursing care

Cross-References.

- Assisted living facilities with on-site nursing care facilities are classified in U.S. Industry 623311, Continuing Care Retirement Communities;
- Assisted living facilities for the elderly with nursing care or rest homes with nursing care are classified in Industry 623110, Nursing Care Facilities (Skilled Nursing Facilities); and
- Apartment or condominium complexes where people live independently in rented or owned housing units are classified in Industry 531110, Lessors of Residential Buildings and Dwellings.

6239 Other Residential Care Facilities[T]

62399 Other Residential Care Facilities[T]
See industry description for 623990.

623990 Other Residential Care Facilities

This industry comprises establishments primarily engaged in providing residential care (except residential intellectual and developmental disability facilities, residential mental health and substance abuse facilities, continuing care retirement communities, and assisted living facilities for the elderly). These establishments also provide supervision and personal care services.

Illustrative Examples:

Boot or disciplinary camps (except correctional) for delinquent youth
Group homes for the hearing or visually impaired
Child group foster homes
Halfway group homes for delinquents or ex-offenders

Delinquent youth halfway group homes
Homes for unwed mothers
Group homes for the disabled without nursing care
Orphanages

Cross-References.

- Residential intellectual and developmental disability facilities are classified in Industry 623210, Residential Intellectual and Developmental Disability Facilities;
- Continuing care retirement communities are classified in U.S. Industry 623311, Continuing Care Retirement Communities;
- Residential mental health and substance abuse facilities are classified in Industry 623220, Residential Mental Health and Substance Abuse Facilities;
- Assisted living facilities for the elderly without nursing care are classified in U.S. Industry 623312, Assisted Living Facilities for the Elderly;
- Establishments primarily engaged in providing inpatient nursing and rehabilitative services are classified in Industry 623110, Nursing Care Facilities (Skilled Nursing Facilities);

T—Canadian, Mexican, and United States industries are comparable.

- Establishments primarily engaged in providing temporary shelter are classified in U.S. Industry 624221, Temporary Shelters; and
- Correctional camps are classified in Industry 922140, Correctional Institutions.

624   Social Assistance[T]

Industries in the Social Assistance subsector provide a wide variety of social assistance services directly to their clients. These services do not include residential or accommodation services, except on a short-stay basis.

6241   Individual and Family Services[T]

This industry group comprises establishments primarily engaged in providing nonresidential social assistance to children and youth, the elderly, persons with disabilities, and all other individuals and families.

62411   Child and Youth Services[T]
See industry description for 624110.

624110 Child and Youth Services

This industry comprises establishments primarily engaged in providing nonresidential social assistance services for children and youth. These establishments provide for the welfare of children in such areas as adoption and foster care, drug prevention, life skills training, and positive social development.

Illustrative Examples:

Adoption agencies
Youth centers (except recreational only)
Child guidance organizations

Youth self-help organizations
Foster care placement services

Cross-References.

- Youth recreational centers are classified in Industry 713940, Fitness and Recreational Sports Centers;
- Youth recreational sports teams and leagues are classified in Industry 713990, All Other Amusement and Recreation Industries;
- Scouting organizations are classified in Industry 813410, Civic and Social Organizations; and
- Establishments primarily engaged in providing day care services for children are classified in Industry 624410, Child Day Care Services.

62412   Services for the Elderly and Persons with Disabilities[T]
See industry description for 624120.

624120 Services for the Elderly and Persons with Disabilities

This industry comprises establishments primarily engaged in providing nonresidential social assistance services to improve the quality of life for the elderly, persons diagnosed with intellectual and developmental disabilities, or persons with disabilities. These establishments provide for the welfare of these individuals in such areas as day care, non-medical home care or homemaker services, social activities, group support, and companionship.

Cross-References.   Establishments primarily engaged in--

- Providing job training for persons diagnosed with intellectual and developmental disabilities or persons with disabilities--are classified in Industry 624310, Vocational Rehabilitation Services;
- Providing residential care for the elderly, persons diagnosed with intellectual and developmental disabilities, or persons with disabilities--are classified in Subsector 623, Nursing and Residential Care Facilities; and

---

T—Canadian, Mexican, and United States industries are comparable.

- Providing in-home health care services--are classified in Subsector 621, Ambulatory Health Care Services.

62419   Other Individual and Family Services[T]
See industry description for 624190.

624190 Other Individual and Family Services

This industry comprises establishments primarily engaged in providing nonresidential individual and family social assistance services (except those specifically directed toward children, the elderly, persons diagnosed with intellectual and developmental disabilities, or persons with disabilities).

Illustrative Examples:

Community action services agencies
Marriage counseling services (except by offices of mental health practitioners)
Crisis intervention centers
Multi-purpose social services centers
Family social services agencies
Family welfare services

Self-help organizations (except for disabled persons, the elderly, persons diagnosed with intellectual and developmental disabilities)
Suicide crisis centers
Hotline centers
Telephone counseling services

Cross-References.   Establishments primarily engaged in--

- Providing clinical psychological and psychiatric social counseling services--are classified in Industry 621330, Offices of Mental Health Practitioners (except Physicians);
- Providing child and youth social assistance services (except day care)--are classified in Industry 624110, Child and Youth Services;
- Providing child day care services--are classified in Industry 624410, Child Day Care Services;
- Providing social assistance services for the elderly, persons diagnosed with intellectual and developmental disabilities, and persons with disabilities--are classified in Industry 624120, Services for the Elderly and Persons with Disabilities;
- Community action advocacy--are classified in U.S. Industry 813319, Other Social Advocacy Organizations; and
- Providing in-home health care services--are classified in Subsector 621, Ambulatory Health Care Services.

6242   Community Food and Housing, and Emergency and Other Relief Services[T]

This industry group comprises establishments primarily engaged in one of the following: (1) collecting, preparing, and delivering food for the needy; (2) providing short-term emergency shelter, temporary residential shelter, transitional housing, volunteer construction or repair of low-cost housing, and/or repair of homes for individuals or families in need; or (3) providing food, shelter, clothing, medical relief, resettlement, and counseling to victims of domestic or international disasters or conflicts (e.g., wars).

62421   Community Food Services[T]
See industry description for 624210.

624210 Community Food Services

This industry comprises establishments primarily engaged in the collection, preparation, and delivery of food for the needy. Establishments in this industry may also distribute clothing and blankets to the poor. These establishments may prepare and deliver meals to persons who by reason of age, disability, or illness are unable to prepare meals for themselves; collect and distribute salvageable or donated food; or prepare and provide meals at fixed or mobile locations. Food banks, meal delivery programs, and soup kitchens are included in this industry.

T—Canadian, Mexican, and United States industries are comparable.

62422   Community Housing Services[T]

This industry comprises establishments primarily engaged in providing one or more of the following community housing services: (1) short-term emergency shelter for victims of domestic violence, sexual assault, or child abuse; (2) temporary residential shelter for the homeless, runaway youths, and patients and families caught in medical crises; (3) transitional housing for low-income individuals and families; (4) volunteer construction or repair of low-cost housing, in partnership with the homeowner who may assist in construction or repair work; and (5) repair of homes for elderly or disabled homeowners. These establishments may operate their own shelter, they may subsidize housing using existing homes, apartments, hotels, or motels, or they may require a low-cost mortgage or work (sweat) equity.

Cross-References.

Central offices of government housing programs are classified in Industry 92511, Administration of Housing Programs.

624221 Temporary Shelters

This U.S. industry comprises establishments primarily engaged in providing (1) short-term emergency shelter for victims of domestic violence, sexual assault, or child abuse and/or (2) temporary residential shelter for homeless individuals or families, runaway youth, and patients and families caught in medical crises. These establishments may operate their own shelters or may subsidize housing using existing homes, apartments, hotels, or motels.

Cross-References.

Establishments primarily engaged in providing emergency shelter for victims of domestic or international disasters or conflicts are classified in Industry 624230, Emergency and Other Relief Services.

624229 Other Community Housing Services

This U.S. industry comprises establishments primarily engaged in providing one or more of the following community housing services: (1) transitional housing to low-income individuals and families; (2) volunteer construction or repair of low-cost housing, in partnership with the homeowner who may assist in the construction or repair work; and (3) the repair of homes for elderly or disabled homeowners. These establishments may subsidize housing using existing homes, apartments, hotels, or motels or may require a low-cost mortgage or sweat equity. These establishments may also provide low-income families with furniture and household supplies.

Cross-References.

Central offices of government housing programs are classified in Industry 925110, Administration of Housing Programs.

62423   Emergency and Other Relief Services[T]
See industry description for 624230.

624230 Emergency and Other Relief Services

This industry comprises establishments primarily engaged in providing food, shelter, clothing, medical relief, resettlement, and counseling to victims of domestic or international disasters or conflicts (e.g., wars).

6243   Vocational Rehabilitation Services[T]

62431   Vocational Rehabilitation Services[T]
See industry description for 624310.

T—Canadian, Mexican, and United States industries are comparable.

census.gov/naics

624310 Vocational Rehabilitation Services

This industry comprises (1) establishments primarily engaged in providing vocational rehabilitation or habilitation services, such as job counseling, job training, and work experience, to unemployed and underemployed persons, persons with disabilities, and persons who have a job market disadvantage because of lack of education, job skill, or experience and (2) establishments primarily engaged in providing training and employment to persons with disabilities. Vocational rehabilitation job training facilities (except schools) and sheltered workshops (i.e., work experience centers) are included in this industry.

Cross-References.

- Schools (except high schools) primarily engaged in providing vocational training are classified in Industry 61151, Technical and Trade Schools;
- Vocational high schools are classified in Industry 611110, Elementary and Secondary Schools; and
- Establishments primarily engaged in providing career and vocational counseling (except rehabilitative) are classified in Industry 611710, Educational Support Services.

6244   Child Day Care Services[T]

62441   Child Day Care Services[T]
See industry description for 624410.

624410 Child Day Care Services

This industry comprises establishments primarily engaged in providing day care of infants or children. These establishments generally care for preschool children, but may care for older children when they are not in school and may also offer pre-kindergarten and/or kindergarten educational programs.

Illustrative Examples:

Child day care babysitting services
Nursery schools

Child or infant day care centers
Preschool centers

Cross-References.

Establishments primarily engaged in offering kindergarten educational programs are classified in Industry 611110, Elementary and Secondary Schools.

T—Canadian, Mexican, and United States industries are comparable.

Sector 71--Arts, Entertainment, and Recreation[T]

The Sector as a Whole

The Arts, Entertainment, and Recreation sector includes a wide range of establishments that operate facilities or provide services to meet varied cultural, entertainment, and recreational interests of their patrons. This sector comprises (1) establishments that are involved in producing, promoting, or participating in live performances, events, or exhibits intended for public viewing; (2) establishments that preserve and exhibit objects and sites of historical, cultural, or educational interest; and (3) establishments that operate facilities or provide services that enable patrons to participate in recreational activities or pursue amusement, hobby, and leisure-time interests.

Some establishments that provide cultural, entertainment, or recreational facilities and services are classified in other sectors. Excluded from this sector are: (1) establishments that provide both accommodations and recreational facilities, such as hunting and fishing camps and resort and casino hotels are classified in Subsector 721, Accommodation; (2) restaurants and night clubs that provide live entertainment in addition to the sale of food and beverages are classified in Subsector 722, Food Services and Drinking Places; (3) motion picture theaters, libraries and archives, and publishers of newspapers, magazines, books, periodicals, and computer software are classified in Sector 51, Information; and (4) establishments using transportation equipment to provide recreational and entertainment services, such as those operating sightseeing buses, dinner cruises, or helicopter rides, are classified in Subsector 487, Scenic and Sightseeing Transportation.

711 Performing Arts, Spectator Sports, and Related Industries[T]

Industries in the Performing Arts, Spectator Sports, and Related Industries subsector group establishments that produce or organize and promote live presentations involving the performances of actors and actresses, singers, dancers, musical groups and artists, athletes, and other entertainers, including independent (i.e., freelance) entertainers and the establishments that manage their careers. The classification recognizes four basic processes: (1) producing (i.e., presenting) events; (2) organizing, managing, and/or promoting events; (3) managing and representing entertainers; and (4) providing the artistic, creative and technical skills necessary to the production of these live events. Also, this subsector contains four industries for performing arts companies. Each is defined on the basis of the particular skills of the entertainers involved in the presentations.

The industry structure for this subsector makes a clear distinction between performing arts companies and performing artists (i.e., independent or freelance). Although not unique to arts and entertainment, freelancing is a particularly important phenomenon in this Performing Arts, Spectator Sports, and Related Industries subsector. Distinguishing this activity from the production activity is a meaningful process differentiation. This approach, however, is difficult to implement in the case of musical groups (i.e., companies) and artists, especially pop groups. These establishments tend to be more loosely organized and it can be difficult to distinguish companies from freelancers. For this reason, NAICS includes one industry that covers both musical groups and musical artists.

This subsector contains two industries for Industry Group 7113, Promoters of Performing Arts, Sports, and Similar Events, one for those that operate facilities and another for those that do not. This is because there are significant differences in cost structures between those promoters that manage and provide the staff to operate facilities and those that do not. In addition to promoters without facilities, other industries in this subsector include establishments that may operate without permanent facilities. These types of establishments include performing arts companies; musical groups and artists; spectator sports; and independent (i.e., freelance) artists, writers, and performers.

Excluded from this subsector are nightclubs. Some nightclubs promote live entertainment on a regular basis and it can be argued that they could be classified in Industry Group 7113, Promoters of Performing Arts, Sports, and Similar Events. However, since most of these establishments function as any other drinking place when they do not promote entertainment and because most of their revenue is derived from sale of food and beverages, they are classified in Subsector 722, Food Services and Drinking Places.

7111 Performing Arts Companies[T]

This industry group comprises establishments primarily engaged in producing live presentations involving the performances of actors and actresses, singers, dancers, musical groups and artists, and other performing artists.

T—Canadian, Mexican, and United States industries are comparable.

71111   Theater Companies and Dinner Theaters[T]
See industry description for 711110.

711110 Theater Companies and Dinner Theaters

This industry comprises (1) companies, groups, or theaters primarily engaged in producing the following live theatrical presentations: musicals; operas; plays; and comedy, improvisational, mime, and puppet shows and (2) establishments, commonly known as dinner theaters, engaged in producing live theatrical productions and in providing food and beverages for consumption on the premises. Theater groups or companies may or may not operate their own theater or other facility for staging their shows.

Illustrative Examples:

Comedy troupes   Theatrical stock or repertory companies
Opera companies   Musical theater companies
Live theatrical productions (except dance)

Cross-References.

- Establishments, such as nightclubs, primarily engaged in providing food and beverages for consumption on the premises and that also present live nontheatrical entertainment are classified in Subsector 722, Food Services and Drinking Places;
- Establishments primarily engaged in organizing, managing, and/or promoting performing arts productions without producing their own shows are classified in Industry Group 7113, Promoters of Performing Arts, Sports, and Similar Events;
- Companies, groups, or theaters primarily engaged in producing all types of live theatrical dance presentations are classified in Industry 711120, Dance Companies;
- Freelance producers and performing artists (except musicians and vocalists) primarily engaged in theatrical activities independent of a company or group are classified in Industry 711510, Independent Artists, Writers, and Performers; and
- Musicians and vocalists are classified in Industry 711130, Musical Groups and Artists.

71112   Dance Companies[T]
See industry description for 711120.

711120 Dance Companies

This industry comprises companies, groups, or theaters primarily engaged in producing all types of live theatrical dance (e.g., ballet, contemporary dance, folk dance) presentations. Dance companies or groups may or may not operate their own theater or other facility for staging their shows.

Cross-References.

- Establishments, such as exotic dance clubs, primarily engaged in providing food and beverages for consumption on the premises and that also present live dance entertainment are classified in Subsector 722, Food Services and Drinking Places;
- Establishments primarily engaged in organizing, promoting, and/or managing dance productions without producing their own shows are classified in Industry Group 7113, Promoters of Performing Arts, Sports, and Similar Events; and
- Freelance producers and dancers primarily engaged in theatrical activities independent of a company or group are classified in Industry 711510, Independent Artists, Writers, and Performers.

71113   Musical Groups and Artists[T]
See industry description for 711130.

T—Canadian, Mexican, and United States industries are comparable.

census.gov/naics

711130 Musical Groups and Artists

This industry comprises (1) groups primarily engaged in producing live musical entertainment (except theatrical musical or opera productions) and (2) independent (i.e., freelance) artists primarily engaged in providing live musical entertainment. Musical groups and artists may perform in front of a live audience or in a studio, and may or may not operate their own facilities for staging their shows.

Illustrative Examples:

Bands
Musical groups (except theatrical musical groups)
Drum and bugle corps (i.e., drill teams)

Orchestras
Independent musicians or vocalists

Cross-References.

- Establishments primarily engaged in organizing, promoting, and/or managing concerts and other musical performances without producing their own shows are classified in Industry Group 7113, Promoters of Performing Arts, Sports, and Similar Events;
- Companies, groups, or theaters primarily engaged in producing theatrical musicals and opera productions are classified in Industry 711110, Theater Companies and Dinner Theaters; and
- Freelance producers (except musical groups and artists) primarily engaged in musical activities independent of a company or group are classified in Industry 711510, Independent Artists, Writers, and Performers.

71119 Other Performing Arts Companies[T]
See industry description for 711190.

711190 Other Performing Arts Companies

This industry comprises companies or groups (except theater companies, dance companies, and musical groups and artists) primarily engaged in producing live theatrical presentations.

Illustrative Examples:

Carnival traveling shows
Ice skating companies

Circuses
Magic shows

Cross-References.

- Establishments, such as nightclubs, primarily engaged in providing food and beverages for consumption on the premises and that also present live nontheatrical entertainment are classified in Subsector 722, Food Services and Drinking Places;
- Establishments primarily engaged in organizing, promoting, and/or managing ice skating shows, circuses, and other live performing arts presentations without producing their own shows are classified in Industry Group 7113, Promoters of Performing Arts, Sports, and Similar Events;
- Theater companies and groups (except dance) or dinner theaters engaged in producing musicals; plays; operas; and comedy, improvisational, mime, and puppet shows are classified in Industry 711110, Theater Companies and Dinner Theaters;
- Dance companies or groups are classified in Industry 711120, Dance Companies;
- Freelance producers and performing artists (except musicians and vocalists) are classified in Industry 711510, Independent Artists, Writers, and Performers; and
- Musical groups and independent musicians and vocalists are classified in Industry 711130, Musical Groups and Artists.

T—Canadian, Mexican, and United States industries are comparable.

7112   Spectator Sports[T]

71121   Spectator Sports[T]

This industry comprises (1) sports teams or clubs primarily participating in live sporting events before a paying audience; (2) establishments primarily engaged in operating racetracks; (3) independent athletes engaged in participating in live sporting or racing events before a paying audience; (4) owners of racing participants, such as cars, dogs, and horses, primarily engaged in entering them in racing events or other spectator sports events; and (5) establishments, such as sports trainers, primarily engaged in providing specialized services to support participants in sports events or competitions. The sports teams and clubs included in this industry may or may not operate their own arena, stadium, or other facility for presenting their games or other spectator sports events.

Cross-References.

- Establishments primarily engaged in promoting sporting events without participating in sporting events are classified in Industry Group 7113, Promoters of Performing Arts, Sports, and Similar Events;
- Establishments, such as youth league baseball teams, primarily engaged in participating in sporting events for recreational purposes without playing before a paying audience are classified in Industry 71399, All Other Amusement and Recreation Industries;
- Amateur, semiprofessional, or professional athletic associations or leagues are classified in Industry 81399, Other Similar Organizations (except Business, Professional, Labor, and Political Organizations);
- Establishments primarily engaged in representing or managing the careers of sports figures are classified in Industry 71141, Agents and Managers for Artists, Athletes, Entertainers, and Other Public Figures;
- Independent athletes engaged in providing sports instruction without participating in sporting events before a paying audience are classified in Industry 61162, Sports and Recreation Instruction;
- Independent athletes exclusively engaged in endorsing products or making speeches are classified in Industry 71151, Independent Artists, Writers, and Performers; and
- Establishments primarily engaged in raising horses, mules, donkeys, and other equines are classified in Industry 11292, Horses and Other Equine Production.

711211   Sports Teams and Clubs

This U.S. industry comprises professional or semiprofessional sports teams or clubs primarily engaged in participating in live sporting events, such as baseball, basketball, football, hockey, soccer, and jai alai games, before a paying audience. These establishments may or may not operate their own arena, stadium, or other facility for presenting these events.

Cross-References.

- Establishments primarily engaged in promoting sporting events without participating in sporting events are classified in Industry Group 7113, Promoters of Performing Arts, Sports, and Similar Events;
- Establishments, such as youth league baseball teams, primarily engaged in participating in sporting events for recreational purposes without playing before a paying audience are classified in Industry 713990, All Other Amusement and Recreation Industries; and
- Amateur, semiprofessional, or professional athletic associations or leagues are classified in Industry 813990, Other Similar Organizations (except Business, Professional, Labor, and Political Organizations).

711212   Racetracks

This U.S. industry comprises establishments primarily engaged in operating racetracks. These establishments may also present and/or promote the events, such as auto, dog, and horse races, held in these facilities.

T—Canadian, Mexican, and United States industries are comparable.

Cross-References.

- Owners of racing participants, such as cars, dogs, and horses, primarily engaged in entering them in racing events; trainers of racing participants; and independent athletes, such as jockeys and race car drivers, primarily engaged in participating in racing events are classified in U.S. Industry 711219, Other Spectator Sports; and
- Establishments primarily engaged in operating stand-alone casinos are classified in Industry 713210, Casinos (except Casino Hotels).

711219 Other Spectator Sports

This U.S. industry comprises (1) independent athletes, such as professional or semiprofessional golfers, boxers, and race car drivers, primarily engaged in participating in live sporting or racing events before a paying audience; (2) owners of racing participants, such as cars, dogs, and horses, primarily engaged in entering them in racing events or other spectator events; and (3) establishments, such as sports trainers, primarily engaged in providing specialized services required to support participants in sports events or competitions.

Cross-References.

- Establishments primarily engaged in operating racetracks are classified in U.S. Industry 711212, Racetracks;
- Establishments primarily engaged in representing or managing the careers of sports figures are classified in Industry 711410, Agents and Managers for Artists, Athletes, Entertainers, and Other Public Figures;
- Independent athletes engaged in providing sports instruction without participating in sporting events before a paying audience are classified in Industry 611620, Sports and Recreation Instruction;
- Independent athletes exclusively engaged in endorsing products or making speeches are classified in Industry 711510, Independent Artists, Writers, and Performers; and
- Establishments primarily engaged in raising horses, mules, donkeys, and other equines are classified in Industry 112920, Horses and Other Equine Production.

7113 Promoters of Performing Arts, Sports, and Similar Events[T]

This industry group comprises establishments primarily engaged in organizing, promoting, and/or managing live performing arts productions, sports events, and similar events, held in facilities that they manage and operate or in facilities that are managed and operated by others.

71131 Promoters of Performing Arts, Sports, and Similar Events with Facilities[T]
See industry description for 711310.

711310 Promoters of Performing Arts, Sports, and Similar Events with Facilities

This industry comprises establishments primarily engaged in (1) organizing, promoting, and/or managing live performing arts productions, sports events, and similar events, such as state fairs, county fairs, agricultural fairs, concerts, and festivals, held in facilities that they manage and operate and/or (2) managing and providing the staff to operate arenas, stadiums, theaters, or other related facilities for rent to other promoters.

Cross-References.   Establishments primarily engaged in--

- Producing live performances (but may also promote the performances and/or operate the facilities where the performances take place)--are classified in Industry Group 7111, Performing Arts Companies;
- Operating racetracks (but may also promote the events held in these facilities)--are classified in U.S. Industry 711212, Racetracks;
- Presenting sporting events (but may also promote the sporting events and/or operate the stadiums or arenas where the sporting events take place)--are classified in U.S. Industry 711211, Sports Teams and Clubs;

T—Canadian, Mexican, and United States industries are comparable.

- Organizing, promoting, and/or managing conventions, conferences, and trade shows (but may also operate the facilities where these events take place)--are classified in Industry 561920, Convention and Trade Show Organizers;
- Organizing, promoting, and/or managing performing arts productions, sports events, and similar events in facilities managed and operated by others--are classified in Industry 711320, Promoters of Performing Arts, Sports, and Similar Events without Facilities; and
- Leasing stadiums, arenas, theaters, and other related facilities to others without operating the facilities--are classified in Industry 531120, Lessors of Nonresidential Buildings (except Miniwarehouses).

71132   Promoters of Performing Arts, Sports, and Similar Events without Facilities[T]
See industry description for 711320.

711320 Promoters of Performing Arts, Sports, and Similar Events without Facilities

This industry comprises promoters primarily engaged in organizing, promoting, and/or managing live performing arts productions, sports events, and similar events, such as state fairs, county fairs, agricultural fairs, concerts, and festivals, in facilities that are managed and operated by others. Theatrical (except motion picture) booking agencies are included in this industry.

Cross-References.   Establishments primarily engaged in--

- Booking motion pictures or videos--are classified in U.S. Industry 512199, Other Motion Picture and Video Industries;
- Producing live performances (but may also promote the performances)--are classified in Industry Group 7111, Performing Arts Companies;
- Operating racetracks (but may also promote the events held in these facilities)--are classified in U.S. Industry 711212, Racetracks;
- Presenting sporting events (but may also promote the sporting events)--are classified in U.S. Industry 711211, Sports Teams and Clubs;
- Organizing, promoting, and/or managing conventions, conferences, and trade shows (but may also operate the facilities where these events take place)--are classified in Industry 561920, Convention and Trade Show Organizers;
- Organizing, promoting, and/or managing performing arts, sports, and similar events in facilities they manage or operate--are classified in Industry 711310, Promoters of Performing Arts, Sports, and Similar Events with Facilities; and
- Operating amateur, semiprofessional, or professional athletic associations or leagues--are classified in Industry 813990, Other Similar Organizations (except Business, Professional, Labor, and Political Organizations).

7114   Agents and Managers for Artists, Athletes, Entertainers, and Other Public Figures[T]

71141   Agents and Managers for Artists, Athletes, Entertainers, and Other Public Figures[T]
See industry description for 711410.

711410 Agents and Managers for Artists, Athletes, Entertainers, and Other Public Figures

This industry comprises establishments of agents and managers primarily engaged in representing and/or managing creative and performing artists, sports figures, entertainers, and other public figures. The representation and management includes activities, such as representing clients in contract negotiations; managing or organizing clients' financial affairs; and generally promoting the careers of their clients.

Illustrative Examples:

Celebrities' agents or managers   Sports figures' agents or managers

---

T—Canadian, Mexican, and United States industries are comparable.

Literary agents   Modeling agents
Talent agents

Cross-References.

- Establishments primarily engaged in supplying models to clients are classified in Industry 561320, Temporary Help Services; and
- Establishments known as model registries primarily engaged in recruiting and placing models for clients are classified in U.S. Industry 561311, Employment Placement Agencies.

7115   Independent Artists, Writers, and Performers^T

71151   Independent Artists, Writers, and Performers^T
See industry description for 711510.

711510 Independent Artists, Writers, and Performers

This industry comprises independent (i.e., freelance) individuals primarily engaged in performing in artistic productions, in creating artistic and cultural works or productions, or in providing technical expertise necessary for these productions. This industry also includes athletes and other celebrities exclusively engaged in endorsing products and making speeches or public appearances for which they receive a fee.

Illustrative Examples:

Independent actors or actresses   Independent cartoonists
Independent producers   Independent theatrical costume designers
Independent art restorers   Independent dancers
Independent recording technicians   Independent theatrical lighting technicians
Independent artists (except musical, commercial, or   Independent journalists
medical)   Independent technical writers
Independent speakers

Cross-References.

- Freelance musicians and vocalists are classified in Industry 711130, Musical Groups and Artists;
- Independent commercial artists and graphic designers are classified in Industry 541430, Graphic Design Services; and
- Artisans and craftspersons are classified in Sector 31-33, Manufacturing.

712   Museums, Historical Sites, and Similar Institutions^T

Industries in the Museums, Historical Sites, and Similar Institutions subsector engage in the preservation and exhibition of objects, sites, and natural wonders of historical, cultural, and/or educational value.

7121   Museums, Historical Sites, and Similar Institutions^T

71211   Museums^T
See industry description for 712110.

712110 Museums

This industry comprises establishments primarily engaged in the preservation and exhibition of objects of historical, cultural, and/or educational value.

T—Canadian, Mexican, and United States industries are comparable.

Illustrative Examples:

Art galleries (except retail)

Planetariums

Art museums

Science or technology museums

Halls of fame

Wax museums

Cross-References.

Commercial art galleries primarily engaged in selling art objects are classified in Industry 453920, Art Dealers.

71212   Historical Sites[T]
        See industry description for 712120.

712120 Historical Sites

  This industry comprises establishments primarily engaged in the preservation and exhibition of sites, buildings, forts, or communities that describe events or persons of particular historical interest. Archeological sites, battlefields, historical ships, and pioneer villages are included in this industry.

71213   Zoos and Botanical Gardens[T]
        See industry description for 712130.

712130 Zoos and Botanical Gardens

  This industry comprises establishments primarily engaged in the preservation and exhibition of live plant and animal life displays.

Illustrative Examples:

Aquariums

Wild animal parks

Arboreta

Zoological gardens

Aviaries

71219   Nature Parks and Other Similar Institutions[T]
        See industry description for 712190.

712190 Nature Parks and Other Similar Institutions

  This industry comprises establishments primarily engaged in the preservation and exhibition of natural areas or settings.

Illustrative Examples:

Bird or wildlife sanctuaries

Natural wonder tourist attractions (e.g., caverns, waterfalls)

Conservation areas

Nature centers or preserves

National parks

Cross-References.

  Establishments primarily engaged in operating commercial hunting or fishing preserves (e.g., game farms) are classified in Industry 114210, Hunting and Trapping.

T—Canadian, Mexican, and United States industries are comparable.

713   Amusement, Gambling, and Recreation Industries[T]

Industries in the Amusement, Gambling, and Recreation Industries subsector (1) operate facilities where patrons can primarily engage in sports, recreation, amusement, or gambling activities and/or (2) provide other amusement and recreation services, such as supplying and servicing amusement devices in places of business operated by others; operating sports teams, clubs, or leagues engaged in playing games for recreational purposes; and guiding tours without using transportation equipment.

This subsector does not cover all establishments providing recreational services. Other sectors of NAICS also provide recreational services. Providers of recreational services are often engaged in processes classified in other sectors of NAICS. For example, operators of resorts and hunting and fishing camps provide both accommodation and recreational facilities and services. These establishments are classified in Subsector 721, Accommodation, partly to reflect the significant costs associated with the provision of accommodation services and partly to ensure consistency with international standards. Likewise, establishments using transportation equipment to provide recreational and entertainment services, such as those operating sightseeing buses, dinner cruises, or helicopter rides, are classified in Sector 48-49, Transportation and Warehousing.

The industry groups in this subsector highlight particular types of activities: amusement parks and arcades, gambling industries, and other amusement and recreation industries. The groups, however, are not all-inclusive of the activity. The Gambling Industries industry group does not provide for full coverage of gambling activities. For example, casino hotels are classified in Subsector 721, Accommodation; and horse and dog racing tracks are classified in Industry Group 7112, Spectator Sports.

7131   Amusement Parks and Arcades[T]

This industry group comprises establishments primarily engaged in operating amusement parks and amusement arcades and parlors.

71311   Amusement and Theme Parks[T]
See industry description for 713110.

713110 Amusement and Theme Parks

This industry comprises establishments, known as amusement or theme parks, primarily engaged in operating a variety of attractions, such as mechanical rides, water rides, games, shows, theme exhibits, refreshment stands, and picnic grounds. These establishments may lease space to others on a concession basis.

Cross-References.   Establishments primarily engaged in--

- Operating mechanical or water rides on a concession basis in amusement parks, fairs, and carnivals or operating a single attraction, such as a waterslide--are classified in Industry 713990, All Other Amusement and Recreation Industries;
- Operating refreshment stands on a concession basis--are classified in Industry 72251, Restaurants and Other Eating Places;
- Supplying and servicing coin-operated amusement (except gambling) devices in places of business operated by others--are classified in Industry 713990, All Other Amusement and Recreation Industries;
- Supplying and servicing coin-operated gambling devices (e.g., slot machines or video gambling terminals) in places of business operated by others--are classified in Industry 713290, Other Gambling Industries; and
- Organizing, promoting, and/or managing events, such as carnivals and fairs, with or without facilities--are classified in Industry Group 7113, Promoters of Performing Arts, Sports, and Similar Events.

71312   Amusement Arcades[T]
See industry description for 713120.

T—Canadian, Mexican, and United States industries are comparable.

713120 Amusement Arcades

This industry comprises establishments primarily engaged in operating amusement (except gambling, billiard, or pool) arcades and parlors.

Cross-References.   Establishments primarily engaged in--

- Supplying and servicing coin-operated amusement (except gambling) devices in places of business operated by others or in operating billiard or pool parlors--are classified in Industry 713990, All Other Amusement and Recreation Industries;
- Operating bingo, off-track betting, or slot machine parlors or in supplying and servicing coin-operated gambling devices (e.g., slot machines or video gambling terminals) in places of business operated by others--are classified in Industry 713290, Other Gambling Industries;
- Operating casinos (except casino hotels)--are classified in Industry 713210, Casinos (except Casino Hotels); and
- Operating casino hotels--are classified in Industry 721120, Casino Hotels.

7132   Gambling Industries[T]

This industry group comprises establishments (except casino hotels) primarily engaged in operating gambling facilities, such as casinos, bingo halls, and video gaming terminals, or in the provision of gambling services, such as lotteries and off-track betting. Casino hotels are classified in Industry 72112, Casino Hotels.

71321   Casinos (except Casino Hotels)[T]
See industry description for 713210.

713210 Casinos (except Casino Hotels)

This industry comprises establishments primarily engaged in operating gambling facilities that offer table wagering games along with other gambling activities, such as slot machines and sports betting. These establishments often provide food and beverage services. Included in this industry are floating casinos (i.e., gambling cruises, riverboat casinos).

Cross-References.   Establishments primarily engaged in--

- Operating bingo, off-track betting, or slot machine parlors or in supplying and servicing coin-operated gambling devices, such as slot machines and video gaming terminals, in places of business operated by others--are classified in Industry 713290, Other Gambling Industries; and
- Operating casino hotels--are classified in Industry 721120, Casino Hotels.

71329   Other Gambling Industries[T]
See industry description for 713290.

713290 Other Gambling Industries

This industry comprises establishments primarily engaged in operating gambling facilities (except casinos or casino hotels) or providing gambling services.

Illustrative Examples:

Bingo, off-track betting, or slot machine parlors	Bookmakers
Coin-operated gambling device concession operators (i.e., supplying and servicing in others' facilities)	Lottery ticket sales agents (except retail stores)
	Card rooms (e.g., poker rooms)

T—Canadian, Mexican, and United States industries are comparable.

Cross-References.   Establishments primarily engaged in--

- Operating casinos--are classified in Industry 713210, Casinos (except Casino Hotels);
- Operating casino hotels--are classified in Industry 721120, Casino Hotels;
- Operating facilities with coin-operated amusement (except gambling) devices--are classified in Industry 713120, Amusement Arcades;
- Supplying and servicing coin-operated amusement (except gambling) devices in places of business operated by others--are classified in Industry 713990, All Other Amusement and Recreation Industries; and
- Operating racetracks or presenting live racing or sporting events--are classified in Industry 71121, Spectator Sports.

7139   Other Amusement and Recreation Industries[T]

This industry group comprises establishments primarily engaged in operating golf courses and country clubs; skiing facilities; marinas; fitness and recreational sports centers; bowling centers; and providing other amusement and recreation services.

71391   Golf Courses and Country Clubs[T]
See industry description for 713910.

713910 Golf Courses and Country Clubs

This industry comprises (1) establishments primarily engaged in operating golf courses (except miniature) and (2) establishments primarily engaged in operating golf courses, along with dining facilities and other recreational facilities that are known as country clubs. These establishments often provide food and beverage services, equipment rental services, and golf instruction services.

Cross-References.   Establishments primarily engaged in--

- Operating driving ranges and miniature golf courses--are classified in Industry 713990, All Other Amusement and Recreation Industries; and
- Operating resorts where golf facilities are combined with accommodations--are classified in Industry Group 7211, Traveler Accommodation.

71392   Skiing Facilities[T]
See industry description for 713920.

713920 Skiing Facilities

This industry comprises establishments engaged in (1) operating downhill, cross country, or related skiing areas and/or (2) operating equipment, such as ski lifts and tows. These establishments often provide food and beverage services, equipment rental services, and ski instruction services. Four season resorts without accommodations are included in this industry.

Cross-References.

Establishments primarily engaged in operating resorts where skiing facilities are combined with accommodations are classified in Industry Group 7211, Traveler Accommodation.

71393   Marinas[T]
See industry description for 713930.

T—Canadian, Mexican, and United States industries are comparable.

713930 Marinas

This industry comprises establishments, commonly known as marinas, engaged in operating docking and/or storage facilities for pleasure craft owners, with or without one or more related activities, such as retailing fuel and marine supplies; and repairing, maintaining, or renting pleasure boats.

Cross-References.   Establishments primarily engaged in--

- Building ships--are classified in U.S. Industry 336611, Ship Building and Repairing;
- Building boats--are classified in U.S. Industry 336612, Boat Building;
- Renting pleasure boats--are classified in U.S. Industry 532284, Recreational Goods Rental;
- Repairing pleasure boats--are classified in Industry 811490, Other Personal and Household Goods Repair and Maintenance;
- Retailing marine supplies--are classified in U.S. Industry 441222, Boat Dealers; and
- Retailing fuel for boats--are classified in Industry 447190, Other Gasoline Stations.

71394   Fitness and Recreational Sports Centers[T]
See industry description for 713940.

713940 Fitness and Recreational Sports Centers

This industry comprises establishments primarily engaged in operating fitness and recreational sports facilities featuring exercise and other active physical fitness conditioning or recreational sports activities, such as swimming, skating, or racquet sports.

Illustrative Examples:

Aerobic dance or exercise centers
Ice or roller skating rinks
Gymnasiums

Physical fitness centers
Handball, racquetball, or tennis club facilities
Swimming or wave pools

Cross-References.

- Establishments primarily engaged in providing non-medical services to assist clients in attaining or maintaining a desired weight are classified in U.S. Industry 812191, Diet and Weight Reducing Centers;
- Establishments primarily engaged in providing personal fitness training services are classified in Industry 812990, All Other Personal Services;
- Establishments primarily engaged in operating health resorts and spas where recreational facilities are combined with accommodations are classified in Industry 721110, Hotels (except Casino Hotels) and Motels; and
- Recreational sports clubs (i.e., sports teams) not operating sports facilities are classified in Industry 713990, All Other Amusement and Recreation Industries.

71395   Bowling Centers[T]
See industry description for 713950.

713950 Bowling Centers

This industry comprises establishments engaged in operating bowling centers. These establishments often provide food and beverage services.

71399   All Other Amusement and Recreation Industries[T]
See industry description for 713990.

T—Canadian, Mexican, and United States industries are comparable.

713990 All Other Amusement and Recreation Industries

This industry comprises establishments (except amusement parks and arcades; gambling industries; golf courses and country clubs; skiing facilities; marinas; fitness and recreational sports centers; and bowling centers) primarily engaged in providing recreational and amusement services.

Illustrative Examples:

Amusement ride or coin-operated nongambling amusement device concession operators (i.e., supplying and servicing in others' facilities)
Miniature golf courses
Archery or shooting ranges
Recreational day camps (except instructional)
Billiard or pool parlors

Recreational or youth sports teams
Boating clubs (without marinas)
Recreational sports clubs (i.e., sports teams) not operating sports facilities
Dance halls
Riding stables

Cross-References.

- Establishments primarily engaged in operating amusement parks and arcades are classified in Industry Group 7131, Amusement Parks and Arcades;
- Establishments primarily engaged in operating gambling facilities (except casino hotels) or providing gambling services are classified in Industry Group 7132, Gambling Industries;
- Establishments primarily engaged in operating casino hotels are classified in Industry 721120, Casino Hotels;
- Establishments primarily engaged in operating golf courses (except miniature) and country clubs are classified in Industry 713910, Golf Courses and Country Clubs;
- Establishments primarily engaged in operating skiing facilities without hotel accommodation are classified in Industry 713920, Skiing Facilities;
- Establishments primarily engaged in operating resorts where recreational facilities are combined with lodging are classified in Industry Group 7211, Traveler Accommodation;
- Establishments primarily engaged in operating marinas are classified in Industry 713930, Marinas;
- Establishments primarily engaged in operating fitness and recreational sports centers are classified in Industry 713940, Fitness and Recreational Sports Centers;
- Establishments primarily engaged in operating bowling centers are classified in Industry 713950, Bowling Centers;
- Establishments primarily engaged in operating instructional camps, such as sports camps, fine arts camps, and computer camps, are classified in Sector 61, Educational Services, based on the nature of instruction;
- Independent athletes engaged in participating in sporting events before a paying audience are classified in U.S. Industry 711219, Other Spectator Sports;
- Independent athletes engaged in providing sports instruction without participating in sporting events before a paying audience are classified in Industry 611620, Sports and Recreation Instruction;
- Independent athletes exclusively engaged in endorsing products or making speeches are classified in Industry 711510, Independent Artists, Writers, and Performers;
- Establishments primarily engaged in providing scenic and sightseeing transportation are classified in Subsector 487, Scenic and Sightseeing Transportation;
- Aviation clubs primarily engaged in providing specialty air and flying services are classified in U.S. Industry 481219, Other Nonscheduled Air Transportation;
- Aviation clubs primarily engaged in advocating social and political causes are classified in U.S. Industry 813319, Other Social Advocacy Organizations; and
- Amateur, semiprofessional, or professional athletic associations or leagues are classified in Industry 813990, Other Similar Organizations (except Business, Professional, Labor, and Political Organizations).

T—Canadian, Mexican, and United States industries are comparable.

Sector 72--Accommodation and Food Services[T]

The Sector as a Whole

The Accommodation and Food Services sector comprises establishments providing customers with lodging and/or preparing meals, snacks, and beverages for immediate consumption. The sector includes both accommodation and food services establishments because the two activities are often combined at the same establishment.

Excluded from this sector are civic and social organizations; amusement and recreation parks; theaters; and other recreation or entertainment facilities providing food and beverage services.

721   Accommodation[T]

Industries in the Accommodation subsector provide lodging or short-term accommodations for travelers, vacationers, and others. There is a wide range of establishments in these industries. Some provide lodging only, while others provide meals, laundry services, and recreational facilities, as well as lodging. Lodging establishments are classified in this subsector even if the provision of complementary services generates more revenue. The types of complementary services provided vary from establishment to establishment.

The subsector is organized into three groups: (1) traveler accommodation, (2) recreational accommodation, and (3) rooming and boarding houses, dormitories, and workers' camps. The Traveler Accommodation industry group includes establishments that primarily provide traditional types of lodging services. This group includes hotels, motels, and bed-and-breakfast inns. In addition to lodging, these establishments may provide a range of other services to their guests. The RV (Recreational Vehicle) Parks and Recreational Camps industry group includes establishments that operate lodging facilities primarily designed to accommodate outdoor enthusiasts. Included are travel trailer campsites, recreational vehicle parks, and outdoor adventure retreats. The Rooming and Boarding Houses, Dormitories, and Workers' Camps industry group includes establishments providing temporary or longer-term accommodations, that for the period of occupancy, may serve as a principal residence. Board (i.e., meals) may be provided but is not essential.

Establishments that manage short-stay accommodation establishments (e.g., hotels and motels) on a contractual basis are classified in this subsector if they both manage the operation and provide the operating staff. Such establishments are classified based on the type of facility managed and operated.

7211   Traveler Accommodation[T]

This industry group comprises establishments primarily engaged in providing short-term lodging in facilities, such as hotels, motels, casino hotels, and bed-and-breakfast inns. In addition to lodging, these establishments may provide a range of other services to their guests.

72111   Hotels (except Casino Hotels) and Motels[T]
See industry description for 721110.

721110 Hotels (except Casino Hotels) and Motels

This industry comprises establishments primarily engaged in providing short-term lodging in facilities known as hotels, motor hotels, resort hotels, and motels. The establishments in this industry may offer food and beverage services, recreational services, conference rooms, convention services, laundry services, parking, and other services.

Cross-References.   Establishments primarily engaged in--

- Providing short-term lodging with a casino on the premises--are classified in Industry 721120, Casino Hotels; and
- Providing short-term lodging in facilities known as bed-and-breakfast inns, youth hostels, housekeeping cabins and cottages, and tourist homes--are classified in Industry 72119, Other Traveler Accommodation.

T—Canadian, Mexican, and United States industries are comparable.

72112 Casino Hotels[T]

See industry description for 721120.

721120 Casino Hotels

This industry comprises establishments primarily engaged in providing short-term lodging in hotel facilities with a casino on the premises. The casino on premises includes table wagering games and may include other gambling activities, such as slot machines and sports betting. These establishments generally offer a range of services and amenities, such as food and beverage services, entertainment, valet parking, swimming pools, and conference and convention facilities.

Cross-References.   Establishments primarily engaged in--

- Providing short-term lodging in facilities known as hotels and motels that provide limited gambling activities, such as slot machines, without a casino on the premises--are classified in Industry 721110, Hotels (except Casino Hotels) and Motels; and
- Operating stand-alone casinos--are classified in Industry 713210, Casinos (except Casino Hotels).

72119 Other Traveler Accommodation[T]

This industry comprises establishments primarily engaged in providing short-term lodging (except hotels, motels, and casino hotels).

Illustrative Examples:

Bed-and-breakfast inns   Youth hostels
Tourist homes   Housekeeping cabins and cottages
Guest houses

Cross-References.   Establishments primarily engaged in--

- Providing short-term lodging in facilities known as hotels without a casino on the premises--are classified in Industry 72111, Hotels (except Casino Hotels) and Motels; and
- Providing short-term lodging in facilities known as hotels with a casino on the premises--are classified in Industry 72112, Casino Hotels.

721191 Bed-and-Breakfast Inns

This U.S. industry comprises establishments primarily engaged in providing short-term lodging in facilities known as bed-and-breakfast inns. These establishments provide short-term lodging in private homes or small buildings converted for this purpose. Bed-and-breakfast inns are characterized by a highly personalized service and inclusion of a full breakfast in the room rate.

721199 All Other Traveler Accommodation

This U.S. industry comprises establishments primarily engaged in providing short-term lodging (except hotels, motels, casino hotels, and bed-and-breakfast inns).

Illustrative Examples:

Guest houses   Housekeeping cabins and cottages
Tourist homes   Youth hostels

T—Canadian, Mexican, and United States industries are comparable.

Cross-References.   Establishments primarily engaged in--

- Providing short-term lodging in facilities known as hotels without a casino on the premises--are classified in Industry 721110, Hotels (except Casino Hotels) and Motels;
- Providing short-term lodging in facilities known as hotels with a casino on the premises--are classified in Industry 721120, Casino Hotels; and
- Providing short-term lodging in establishments known as bed-and-breakfast inns--are classified in U.S. Industry 721191, Bed-and-Breakfast Inns.

7212   RV (Recreational Vehicle) Parks and Recreational Camps[T]

72121   RV (Recreational Vehicle) Parks and Recreational Camps[T]

This industry comprises establishments primarily engaged in operating recreational vehicle parks and campgrounds and recreational and vacation camps. These establishments cater to outdoor enthusiasts and are characterized by the type of accommodation and by the nature and the range of recreational facilities and activities provided to their clients.

Illustrative Examples:

Campgrounds	Outdoor adventure retreats
Fishing and hunting camps	Vacation camps (except instructional, day)
Travel trailer campsites	Recreational vehicle parks

Cross-References.   Establishments primarily engaged in--

- Operating recreational facilities without accommodations--are classified in Subsector 713, Amusement, Gambling, and Recreation Industries;
- Operating instructional camps, such as sports camps, fine arts camps, and computer camps--are classified in Sector 61, Educational Services, based on the nature of instruction;
- Operating children's day camps (except instructional)--are classified in Industry 71399, All Other Amusement and Recreation Industries; and
- Acting as lessors of residential mobile home sites (i.e., trailer parks)--are classified in Industry 53119, Lessors of Other Real Estate Property.

721211 RV (Recreational Vehicle) Parks and Campgrounds

This U.S. industry comprises establishments primarily engaged in operating sites to accommodate campers and their equipment, including tents, tent trailers, travel trailers, and RVs (recreational vehicles). These establishments may provide access to facilities, such as washrooms, laundry rooms, recreation halls, playgrounds, stores, and snack bars.

Cross-References.   Establishments primarily engaged in--

- Operating recreational facilities without accommodations--are classified in Subsector 713, Amusement, Gambling, and Recreation Industries; and
- Acting as lessors of residential mobile home sites (i.e., trailer parks)--are classified in Industry 531190, Lessors of Other Real Estate Property.

721214 Recreational and Vacation Camps (except Campgrounds)

This U.S. industry comprises establishments primarily engaged in operating overnight recreational camps, such as children's camps, family vacation camps, hunting and fishing camps, and outdoor adventure retreats, that offer trail riding, white water rafting, hiking, and similar activities. These establishments provide accommodation facilities,

---

T—Canadian, Mexican, and United States industries are comparable.

such as cabins and fixed campsites, and other amenities, such as food services, recreational facilities and equipment, and organized recreational activities.

Illustrative Examples:

Fishing camps with accommodation facilities
Dude ranches
Vacation camps (except campgrounds, day,
instructional)

Hunting camps with accommodation facilities
Wilderness camps
Outdoor adventure retreats with accommodation
facilities

Cross-References.   Establishments primarily engaged in--

- Operating instructional camps, such as sports camps, fine arts camps, and computer camps--are classified in Sector 61, Educational Services, based on the nature of instruction; and
- Operating children's day camps (except instructional)--are classified in Industry 713990, All Other Amusement and Recreation Industries.

7213   Rooming and Boarding Houses, Dormitories, and Workers' Camps[T]

72131   Rooming and Boarding Houses, Dormitories, and Workers' Camps[T]
See industry description for 721310.

721310 Rooming and Boarding Houses, Dormitories, and Workers' Camps

This industry comprises establishments primarily engaged in operating rooming and boarding houses and similar facilities, such as fraternity houses, sorority houses, off campus dormitories, residential clubs, and workers' camps. These establishments provide temporary or longer-term accommodations, which, for the period of occupancy, may serve as a principal residence. These establishments also may provide complementary services, such as housekeeping, meals, and laundry services.

Illustrative Examples:

Dormitories (off campus)
Sorority houses
Fraternity houses

Workers' camps
Rooming houses

722   Food Services and Drinking Places[T]

Industries in the Food Services and Drinking Places subsector prepare meals, snacks, and beverages to customer order for immediate on-premises and off-premises consumption. There is a wide range of establishments in these industries. Some provide food and drink only, while others provide various combinations of seating space, waiter/waitress services, and incidental amenities, such as limited entertainment. The industries in the subsector are grouped based on the type and level of services provided. The industry groups are Special Food Services, such as food service contractors, caterers, and mobile food services; Drinking Places (Alcoholic Beverages); and Restaurants and Other Eating Places.
Food and beverage services at hotels and motels, amusement parks, theaters, casinos, country clubs, similar recreational facilities, and civic and social organizations are included in this subsector only if these services are provided by a separate establishment primarily engaged in providing food and beverage services.
Excluded from this subsector are establishments operating dinner cruises. These establishments are classified in Subsector 487, Scenic and Sightseeing Transportation, because they utilize transportation equipment to provide scenic recreational entertainment.

T—Canadian, Mexican, and United States industries are comparable.

7223   Special Food Services[T]

This industry group comprises establishments primarily engaged in providing food services at one or more of the following locations: (1) the customer's location; (2) a location designated by the customer; or (3) from motorized vehicles or nonmotorized carts.

72231   Food Service Contractors[T]
See industry description for 722310.

722310   Food Service Contractors

This industry comprises establishments primarily engaged in providing food services at institutional, governmental, commercial, or industrial locations of others based on contractual arrangements with these types of organizations for a specified period of time. The establishments of this industry provide food services for the convenience of the contracting organization or the contracting organization's customers. The contractual arrangement of these establishments with contracting organizations may vary by type of facility operated (e.g., cafeteria, restaurant, fast-food eating place), revenue sharing, cost structure, and personnel provided. Management staff is always provided by food service contractors.

Illustrative Examples:

Airline food service contractors
Food concession contractors (e.g., at sporting, entertainment, convention facilities)

Cafeteria food service contractors (e.g., at schools, hospitals, government offices)

Cross-References.   Establishments primarily engaged in--

- Providing food services on a single-event basis--are classified in Industry 722320, Caterers; and
- Supplying and servicing food vending machines--are classified in Industry 454210, Vending Machine Operators.

72232   Caterers[T]
See industry description for 722320.

722320   Caterers

This industry comprises establishments primarily engaged in providing single event-based food services. These establishments generally have equipment and vehicles to transport meals and snacks to events and/or prepare food at an off-premise site. Banquet halls with catering staff are included in this industry. Examples of events catered by establishments in this industry are graduation parties, wedding receptions, business or retirement luncheons, and trade shows.

Cross-References.   Establishments primarily engaged in--

- Preparing and serving meals and snacks for immediate consumption from motorized vehicles or nonmotorized carts--are classified in Industry 722330, Mobile Food Services;
- Providing food services at institutional, governmental, commercial, or industrial locations of others (e.g., airline contractors, industrial caterers) based on contractual arrangements for a specified period of time--are classified in Industry 722310, Food Service Contractors; and
- Renting out facilities without providing catering staff--are classified in Industry 531120, Lessors of Nonresidential Buildings (except Miniwarehouses).

72233   Mobile Food Services[T]
See industry description for 722330.

T—Canadian, Mexican, and United States industries are comparable.

722330 Mobile Food Services

   This industry comprises establishments primarily engaged in preparing and serving meals and snacks for immediate consumption from motorized vehicles or nonmotorized carts. The establishment is the central location from which the caterer route is serviced, not each vehicle or cart. Included in this industry are establishments primarily engaged in providing food services from vehicles, such as hot dog carts and ice cream trucks.

Illustrative Examples:

Ice cream truck vendors   Mobile refreshment stands
Mobile food concession stands   Mobile food carts
Mobile canteens   Mobile snack stands

Cross-References.   Establishments primarily engaged in--

   •   Selling a specialty snack (e.g., ice cream, frozen yogurt, cookies, popcorn) or nonalcoholic beverages, except from mobile vehicles, for consumption on or near the premises--are classified in U.S. Industry 722515, Snack and Nonalcoholic Beverage Bars;
   •   Selling unprepared foods, such as vegetables, nuts, or fruit, from carts--are classified in Industry 454390, Other Direct Selling Establishments;
   •   Providing food services or selling food specialties, such as hamburgers, hot dogs, chicken, pizza, or specialty cuisines, except from mobile vehicles--are classified based on the type of food service provided to patrons; and
   •   Operating as street vendors (except food)--are classified in Industry 454390, Other Direct Selling Establishments.

7224   Drinking Places (Alcoholic Beverages)^T

72241   Drinking Places (Alcoholic Beverages)^T
          See industry description for 722410.

722410 Drinking Places (Alcoholic Beverages)

   This industry comprises establishments known as bars, taverns, nightclubs, or drinking places primarily engaged in preparing and serving alcoholic beverages for immediate consumption. These establishments may also provide limited food services.

Cross-References.   Establishments primarily engaged in--

   •   Preparing and serving alcoholic beverages (i.e., not known as bars or taverns) and providing food services to patrons--are classified in Industry 72251, Restaurants and Other Eating Places;
   •   Operating a civic or social association with a bar for the association members--are classified in Industry 813410, Civic and Social Organizations;
   •   Retailing packaged alcoholic beverages not for immediate consumption on the premises--are classified in Industry 445310, Beer, Wine, and Liquor Stores; and
   •   Operating discotheques or dance clubs without selling alcoholic beverages--are classified in Industry 713990, All Other Amusement and Recreation Industries.

7225   Restaurants and Other Eating Places^T

72251   Restaurants and Other Eating Places^T

   This industry comprises establishments primarily engaged in one of the following: (1) providing food services to patrons who order and are served while seated (i.e., waiter/waitress service) and pay after eating; (2) providing food services to patrons who generally order or select items (e.g., at a counter, in a buffet line) and pay before eating; or

---

T—Canadian, Mexican, and United States industries are comparable.

(3) preparing and/or serving a specialty snack (e.g., ice cream, frozen yogurt, cookies) and/or nonalcoholic beverages (e.g., coffee, juices, sodas) for consumption on or near the premises.

Cross-References.   Establishments primarily engaged in--

- Preparing and serving alcoholic beverages and known as bars, taverns, or nightclubs--are classified in Industry 72241, Drinking Places (Alcoholic Beverages);
- Preparing and serving snacks and nonalcoholic beverages from mobile vehicles--are classified in Industry 72233, Mobile Food Services;
- Presenting live theatrical productions and providing food and beverages for consumption on the premises-- are classified in Industry 71111, Theater Companies and Dinner Theaters;
- Retailing confectionery goods and nuts not packaged for immediate consumption--are classified in Industry 44529, Other Specialty Food Stores; and
- Retailing baked goods (e.g., pretzels, doughnuts, cookies, and bagels) not baked on the premises and not for immediate consumption--are classified in Industry 44529, Other Specialty Food Stores.

722511 Full-Service Restaurants

This U.S. industry comprises establishments primarily engaged in providing food services to patrons who order and are served while seated (i.e., waiter/waitress service) and pay after eating. These establishments may provide this type of food service to patrons in combination with selling alcoholic beverages, providing carryout services, or presenting live nontheatrical entertainment.

Cross-References.   Establishments primarily engaged in--

- Providing food services where patrons generally order or select items and pay before eating, other than mobile food services, cafeterias, grill buffets, buffets, and snack and nonalcoholic beverage bars--are classified in U.S. Industry 722513, Limited-Service Restaurants;
- Preparing and serving meals for immediate consumption using cafeteria-style or buffet serving equipment, known as cafeterias, grill buffets, or buffets--are classified in U.S. Industry 722514, Cafeterias, Grill Buffets, and Buffets;
- Selling a specialty snack (e.g., ice cream, frozen yogurt, cookies, popcorn) or nonalcoholic beverage, except from mobile vehicles, for consumption on or near the premises--are classified in U.S. Industry 722515, Snack and Nonalcoholic Beverage Bars;
- Preparing and serving alcoholic beverages and known as bars, taverns, or nightclubs--are classified in Industry 722410, Drinking Places (Alcoholic Beverages); and
- Presenting live theatrical productions and providing food and beverages for consumption on the premises-- are classified in Industry 711110, Theater Companies and Dinner Theaters.

722513 Limited-Service Restaurants

This U.S. industry comprises establishments primarily engaged in providing food services (except snack and nonalcoholic beverage bars) where patrons generally order or select items and pay before eating. Food and drink may be consumed on premises, taken out, or delivered to the customer's location. Some establishments in this industry may provide these food services in combination with selling alcoholic beverages.

Illustrative Examples:

Delicatessen restaurants
Pizza delivery shops
Family restaurants, limited-service
Takeout eating places

Fast-food restaurants
Fast casual restaurants
Takeout sandwich shops
Limited-service pizza parlors

T—Canadian, Mexican, and United States industries are comparable.

Cross-References.   Establishments primarily engaged in--

- Preparing and serving meals for immediate consumption using cafeteria-style serving equipment, known as cafeterias--are classified in U.S. Industry 722514, Cafeterias, Grill Buffets, and Buffets;
- Providing food services to patrons who order and are served while seated and pay after eating--are classified in U.S. Industry 722511, Full-Service Restaurants;
- Selling a specialty snack (e.g., ice cream, frozen yogurt, candy, cookies) or nonalcoholic beverages, except from mobile vehicles, for consumption on or near the premises--are classified in U.S. Industry 722515, Snack and Nonalcoholic Beverage Bars;
- Retailing confectionery goods and nuts not packaged for immediate consumption--are classified in U.S. Industry 445292, Confectionery and Nut Stores;
- Retailing baked goods (e.g., pretzels, doughnuts, cookies, and bagels) not baked on the premises and not for immediate consumption--are classified in U.S. Industry 445291, Baked Goods Stores; and
- Preparing and serving alcoholic beverages, known as bars, taverns, or nightclubs--are classified in Industry 722410, Drinking Places (Alcoholic Beverages).

722514 Cafeterias, Grill Buffets, and Buffets

This U.S. industry comprises establishments, known as cafeterias, grill buffets, or buffets, primarily engaged in preparing and serving meals for immediate consumption using cafeteria-style or buffet serving equipment, such as steam tables, refrigerated areas, display grills, and self-service nonalcoholic beverage dispensing equipment. Patrons select from food and drink items on display in a continuous cafeteria line or from buffet stations.

Cross-References.   Establishments primarily engaged in--

- Providing food services to patrons who order and are served while seated and pay after eating--are classified in U.S. Industry 722511, Full-Service Restaurants;
- Providing food services where patrons generally order or select items and pay before eating, other than mobile food services, cafeterias, grill buffets, buffets, and snack and nonalcoholic beverage bars--are classified in U.S. Industry 722513, Limited-Service Restaurants; and
- Selling a specialty snack (e.g., ice cream, frozen yogurt, cookies, popcorn) or nonalcoholic beverage, except from mobile vehicles, for consumption on or near the premises--are classified in U.S. Industry 722515, Snack and Nonalcoholic Beverage Bars.

722515 Snack and Nonalcoholic Beverage Bars

This U.S. industry comprises establishments primarily engaged in (1) preparing and/or serving a specialty snack, such as ice cream, frozen yogurt, cookies, or popcorn, or (2) serving nonalcoholic beverages, such as coffee, juices, or sodas for consumption on or near the premises. These establishments may carry and sell a combination of snack, nonalcoholic beverage, and other related products (e.g., coffee beans, mugs, coffee makers) but generally promote and sell a unique snack or nonalcoholic beverage.

Illustrative Examples:

Beverage bars
Carryout service doughnut shops with on-premises baking
Carryout service bagel shops with on-premises baking
Coffee shops, on-premises brewing

Carryout service pretzel shops with on-premises baking
Carryout service cookie shops with on-premises baking
Ice cream parlors

Cross-References.   Establishments primarily engaged in--

- Selling one or more of the following food specialties (except from mobile vehicles): hamburgers, hot dogs, pizza, chicken, specialty cuisines--are classified based on the type of food service provided to patrons;

T—Canadian, Mexican, and United States industries are comparable.

- Preparing and serving snacks and nonalcoholic beverages from mobile vehicles--are classified in Industry 722330, Mobile Food Services;
- Retailing confectionery goods and nuts not packaged for immediate consumption--are classified in U.S. Industry 445292, Confectionery and Nut Stores; and
- Retailing baked goods (e.g., pretzels, doughnuts, cookies, and bagels) not baked on the premises and not for immediate consumption--are classified in U.S. Industry 445291, Baked Goods Stores.

T—Canadian, Mexican, and United States industries are comparable.

Sector 81--Other Services (except Public Administration)[T]

The Sector as a Whole

The Other Services (except Public Administration) sector comprises establishments engaged in providing services not specifically provided for elsewhere in the classification system. Establishments in this sector are primarily engaged in activities such as equipment and machinery repairing, promoting or administering religious activities, grantmaking, advocacy, and providing drycleaning and laundry services, personal care services, death care services, pet care services, photofinishing services, temporary parking services, and dating services.

Private households that engage in employing workers on or about the premises in activities primarily concerned with the operation of the household are included in this sector.

Excluded from this sector are establishments primarily engaged in retailing new equipment and also performing repairs and general maintenance on equipment. These establishments are classified in Sector 44-45, Retail Trade.

811   Repair and Maintenance[T]

Industries in the Repair and Maintenance subsector restore machinery, equipment, and other products to working order. These establishments also typically provide general or routine maintenance (i.e., servicing) on such products to ensure they work efficiently and to prevent breakdown and unnecessary repairs.

The NAICS structure for this subsector brings together most types of repair and maintenance establishments and categorizes them based on production processes (i.e., on the type of repair and maintenance activity performed, and the necessary skills, expertise, and processes that are found in different repair and maintenance establishments). This NAICS classification does not delineate between repair services provided to businesses versus those that serve households. Although some industries primarily serve either businesses or households, separation by class of customer is limited by the fact that many establishments serve both. Establishments repairing computers and consumer electronics products are two examples of such overlap.

The Repair and Maintenance subsector does not include all establishments that do repair and maintenance. For example, a substantial amount of repair is done by establishments that also manufacture machinery, equipment, and other goods. These establishments are included in the Manufacturing sector in NAICS. In addition, repair of transportation equipment is often provided by or based at transportation facilities, such as airports and seaports, and these activities are included in the Transportation and Warehousing sector. A particularly unique situation exists with repair of buildings. Plumbing, electrical installation and repair, painting and decorating, and other construction-related establishments are often involved in performing installation or other work on new construction as well as providing repair services on existing structures. While some specialize in repair, it is difficult to distinguish between the two types and all are included in the Construction sector.

Excluded from this subsector are establishments primarily engaged in rebuilding or remanufacturing machinery and equipment. These are classified in Sector 31-33, Manufacturing. Also excluded are retail establishments that provide after-sale services and repair. These are classified in Sector 44-45, Retail Trade.

8111   Automotive Repair and Maintenance[T]

This industry group comprises establishments involved in providing repair and maintenance services for automotive vehicles, such as passenger cars, trucks, and vans, and all trailers. Establishments in this industry group employ mechanics with specialized technical skills to diagnose and repair the mechanical and electrical systems for automotive vehicles, repair automotive interiors, and paint or repair automotive exteriors.

81111   Automotive Mechanical and Electrical Repair and Maintenance[T]

This industry comprises establishments primarily engaged in providing mechanical or electrical repair and maintenance services for automotive vehicles, such as passenger cars, trucks, and vans, and all trailers. These establishments may specialize in a single service or may provide a wide range of these services.

T—Canadian, Mexican, and United States industries are comparable.

Cross-References. Establishments primarily engaged in--

- Retailing automotive vehicles and automotive parts and accessories and also providing automotive vehicle repair services--are classified in Subsector 441, Motor Vehicle and Parts Dealers;
- Retailing motor fuels and also providing automotive vehicle repair services--are classified in Industry Group 4471, Gasoline Stations;
- Changing motor oil and lubricating the chassis of automotive vehicles--are classified in Industry 81119, Other Automotive Repair and Maintenance;
- Providing automotive vehicle air-conditioning repair--are classified in Industry 81119, Other Automotive Repair and Maintenance; and
- Motorcycle repair and maintenance services--are classified in Industry 81149, Other Personal and Household Goods Repair and Maintenance.

811111 General Automotive Repair

  This U.S. industry comprises establishments primarily engaged in providing (1) a wide range of mechanical and electrical repair and maintenance services for automotive vehicles, such as passenger cars, trucks, and vans, and all trailers or (2) engine repair and replacement.

Illustrative Examples:

Automobile repair garages (except gasoline service stations)

General automotive repair shops
Automotive engine repair and replacement shops

Cross-References. Establishments primarily engaged in--

- Retailing new automotive parts and accessories and also providing automotive vehicle repair services--are classified in Industry 441310, Automotive Parts and Accessories Stores;
- Changing motor oil and lubricating the chassis of automotive vehicles--are classified in U.S. Industry 811191, Automotive Oil Change and Lubrication Shops;
- Replacing and repairing automotive vehicle exhaust systems--are classified in U.S. Industry 811112, Automotive Exhaust System Repair;
- Replacing and repairing automotive vehicle transmissions--are classified in U.S. Industry 811113, Automotive Transmission Repair;
- Retailing motor fuels and also providing automotive vehicle repair services--are classified in Industry Group 4471, Gasoline Stations;
- Retailing automobiles and light trucks for highway use and also providing automotive vehicle repair services--are classified in Industry Group 4411, Automobile Dealers; and
- Motorcycle repair and maintenance services--are classified in Industry 811490, Other Personal and Household Goods Repair and Maintenance.

811112 Automotive Exhaust System Repair

  This U.S. industry comprises establishments primarily engaged in replacing or repairing exhaust systems of automotive vehicles, such as passenger cars, trucks, and vans.

Illustrative Examples:

Automotive exhaust system replacement and repair shops

Automotive muffler replacement and repair shops

Cross-References.

  Establishments primarily engaged in motorcycle repair and maintenance services are classified in Industry 811490, Other Personal and Household Goods Repair and Maintenance.

T—Canadian, Mexican, and United States industries are comparable.

census.gov/naics

811113 Automotive Transmission Repair

This U.S. industry comprises establishments primarily engaged in replacing or repairing transmissions of automotive vehicles, such as passenger cars, trucks, and vans.

Cross-References.

Establishments primarily engaged in motorcycle repair and maintenance services are classified in Industry 811490, Other Personal and Household Goods Repair and Maintenance.

811118 Other Automotive Mechanical and Electrical Repair and Maintenance

This U.S. industry comprises establishments primarily engaged in providing specialized mechanical or electrical repair and maintenance services (except engine repair and replacement, exhaust systems repair, and transmission repair) for automotive vehicles, such as passenger cars, trucks, and vans, and all trailers.

Illustrative Examples:

Automotive brake repair shops
Automotive radiator repair shops

Automotive electrical repair shops
Automotive tune-up shops

Cross-References.   Establishments primarily engaged in--

- Providing a wide range of mechanical and electrical automotive vehicle repair or specializing in engine repair or replacement--are classified in U.S. Industry 811111, General Automotive Repair;
- Replacing and repairing automotive vehicle exhaust systems--are classified in U.S. Industry 811112, Automotive Exhaust System Repair;
- Replacing and repairing automotive vehicle transmissions--are classified in U.S. Industry 811113, Automotive Transmission Repair;
- Providing automotive vehicle air-conditioning repair--are classified in U.S. Industry 811198, All Other Automotive Repair and Maintenance; and
- Motorcycle repair and maintenance services--are classified in Industry 811490, Other Personal and Household Goods Repair and Maintenance.

81112 Automotive Body, Paint, Interior, and Glass Repair[T]

This industry comprises establishments primarily engaged in providing one or more of the following: (1) repairing or customizing automotive vehicles, such as passenger cars, trucks, and vans, and all trailer bodies and interiors; (2) painting automotive vehicle and trailer bodies; (3) replacing, repairing, and/or tinting automotive vehicle glass; and (4) customizing automobile, truck, and van interiors for the physically disabled or other customers with special requirements.

Illustrative Examples:

Automotive body shops
Automotive paint shops

Automotive glass shops
Automotive windshield repair shops

Cross-References.   Establishments primarily engaged in--

- Manufacturing automotive vehicles and trailers or customizing these vehicles on an assembly line basis--are classified in Subsector 336, Transportation Equipment Manufacturing; and
- Motorcycle repair and maintenance services--are classified in Industry 81149, Other Personal and Household Goods Repair and Maintenance.

T—Canadian, Mexican, and United States industries are comparable.

811121 Automotive Body, Paint, and Interior Repair and Maintenance

This U.S. industry comprises establishments primarily engaged in repairing or customizing automotive vehicles, such as passenger cars, trucks, and vans, and all trailer bodies and interiors; and/or painting automotive vehicles and trailer bodies.

Illustrative Examples:

Automotive body shops
Automotive body conversion services

Automotive upholstery shops
Automotive paint shops

Cross-References.   Establishments primarily engaged in--

- Automotive glass replacement, repair and/or tinting--are classified in U.S. Industry 811122, Automotive Glass Replacement Shops;
- Manufacturing automotive vehicles and trailers or customizing these vehicles on an assembly line basis-- are classified in Subsector 336, Transportation Equipment Manufacturing; and
- Motorcycle repair and maintenance services--are classified in Industry 811490, Other Personal and Household Goods Repair and Maintenance.

811122 Automotive Glass Replacement Shops

This U.S. industry comprises establishments primarily engaged in replacing, repairing, and/or tinting automotive vehicle glass, such as passenger car, truck, and van glass.

Cross-References.

Establishments primarily engaged in motorcycle repair and maintenance services are classified in Industry 811490, Other Personal and Household Goods Repair and Maintenance.

81119   Other Automotive Repair and Maintenance[T]

This industry comprises establishments primarily engaged in providing automotive repair and maintenance services (except mechanical and electrical repair and maintenance; transmission repair; and body, paint, interior, and glass repair) for automotive vehicles, such as passenger cars, trucks, and vans, and all trailers.

Illustrative Examples:

Automotive air-conditioning repair shops
Automotive tire repair (except retreading) shops
Automotive oil change and lubrication shops

Car washes
Automotive rustproofing and undercoating shops

Cross-References.   Establishments primarily engaged in--

- Tire retreading or recapping--are classified in Industry 32621, Tire Manufacturing;
- Automotive vehicle mechanical and electrical repair and maintenance--are classified in Industry 81111, Automotive Mechanical and Electrical Repair and Maintenance;
- Automotive body, paint, interior, and glass repair--are classified in Industry 81112, Automotive Body, Paint, Interior, and Glass Repair; and
- Motorcycle repair and maintenance services--are classified in Industry 81149, Other Personal and Household Goods Repair and Maintenance.

T—Canadian, Mexican, and United States industries are comparable.

811191　Automotive Oil Change and Lubrication Shops

This U.S. industry comprises establishments primarily engaged in changing motor oil and lubricating the chassis of automotive vehicles, such as passenger cars, trucks, and vans.

Cross-References.

Establishments primarily engaged in motorcycle repair and maintenance services are classified in Industry 811490, Other Personal and Household Goods Repair and Maintenance.

811192　Car Washes

This U.S. industry comprises establishments primarily engaged in cleaning, washing, and/or waxing automotive vehicles, such as passenger cars, trucks, and vans, and trailers.

Illustrative Examples:

Automotive detail shops
Mobile car and truck washes

Car washes

811198　All Other Automotive Repair and Maintenance

This U.S. industry comprises establishments primarily engaged in providing automotive repair and maintenance services (except mechanical and electrical repair and maintenance; body, paint, interior, and glass repair; motor oil change and lubrication; and car washing) for automotive vehicles, such as passenger cars, trucks, and vans, and all trailers.

Illustrative Examples:

Automotive air-conditioning repair shops
Automotive tire repair (except retreading) shops

Automotive rustproofing and undercoating shops

Cross-References.　　　Establishments primarily engaged in--

- Tire retreading or recapping--are classified in U.S. Industry 326212, Tire Retreading;
- Providing a range of mechanical and electrical automotive vehicle repair or specializing in engine repair or replacement--are classified in U.S. Industry 811111, General Automotive Repair;
- Replacing and repairing automotive vehicle exhaust systems--are classified in U.S. Industry 811112, Automotive Exhaust System Repair;
- Replacing and repairing automotive vehicle transmissions--are classified in U.S. Industry 811113, Automotive Transmission Repair;
- Repairing or customizing automotive vehicle bodies and interiors--are classified in U.S. Industry 811121, Automotive Body, Paint, and Interior Repair and Maintenance;
- Replacing, repairing, and/or tinting automotive glass--are classified in U.S. Industry 811122, Automotive Glass Replacement Shops;
- Changing motor oil and lubricating the chassis of automotive vehicles--are classified in U.S. Industry 811191, Automotive Oil Change and Lubrication Shops;
- Cleaning, washing, and/or waxing automotive vehicles and trailers--are classified in U.S. Industry 811192, Car Washes;
- Motorcycle repair and maintenance services--are classified in Industry 811490, Other Personal and Household Goods Repair and Maintenance; and
- Retailing and installing automotive audio equipment--are classified in Industry 441310, Automotive Parts and Accessories Stores.

T—Canadian, Mexican, and United States industries are comparable.

8112   Electronic and Precision Equipment Repair and Maintenance[T]

81121   Electronic and Precision Equipment Repair and Maintenance[T]

This industry comprises establishments primarily engaged in repairing and maintaining one or more of the following: (1) consumer electronic equipment; (2) computers; (3) office machines; (4) communication equipment; and (5) other electronic and precision equipment and instruments, without retailing these products as new. Establishments in this industry repair items, such as microscopes, radar and sonar equipment, televisions, stereos, video recorders, computers, fax machines, photocopying machines, two-way radios and other communications equipment, scientific instruments, and medical equipment.

Cross-References.   Establishments primarily engaged in--

- Installing and monitoring home security systems--are classified in Industry 56162, Security Systems Services;
- Retailing new radios, televisions, and other consumer electronics and also providing repair services--are classified in Industry 44314, Electronics and Appliance Stores;
- Retailing new computers and computer peripherals and also providing repair services--are classified in Industry 44314, Electronics and Appliance Stores;
- Retailing new cellular telephones and communication service plans, and also providing repair services--are classified in Industry 51731, Wired and Wireless Telecommunications Carriers;
- Rewinding armatures and rebuilding electric motors on a factory basis--are classified in Industry 33531, Electrical Equipment Manufacturing; and
- Factory rebuilding or overhauling of electronic and precision equipment--are classified in the Manufacturing sector by type of equipment.

811211 Consumer Electronics Repair and Maintenance

This U.S. industry comprises establishments primarily engaged in repairing and maintaining consumer electronics, such as televisions, stereos, speakers, video recorders, CD and DVD players, radios, and cameras, without retailing new consumer electronics.

Cross-References.   Establishments primarily engaged in--

- Repairing computers and peripheral equipment--are classified in U.S. Industry 811212, Computer and Office Machine Repair and Maintenance;
- Installing and monitoring home security systems--are classified in U.S. Industry 561621, Security Systems Services (except Locksmiths);
- Retailing new radios, televisions, and other consumer electronics and also providing repair services--are classified in U.S. Industry 443142, Electronics Stores; and
- Repairing telephones, fax machines, and two-way radios--are classified in U.S. Industry 811213, Communication Equipment Repair and Maintenance.

811212 Computer and Office Machine Repair and Maintenance

This U.S. industry comprises establishments primarily engaged in repairing and maintaining computers and office machines without retailing new computers and office machines, such as photocopying machines; computer terminals, storage devices, and printers; and CD-ROM drives.

Cross-References.   Establishments primarily engaged in--

- Retailing new computers and computer peripherals and also providing repair services--are classified in U.S. Industry 443142, Electronics Stores; and
- Repairing and servicing fax machines--are classified in U.S. Industry 811213, Communication Equipment Repair and Maintenance.

T—Canadian, Mexican, and United States industries are comparable.

811213 Communication Equipment Repair and Maintenance

This U.S. industry comprises establishments primarily engaged in repairing and maintaining communication equipment without retailing new communication equipment, such as telephones, fax machines, communications transmission equipment, and two-way radios.

Cross-References. Establishments primarily engaged in--

- Retailing new cellular telephones and communication service plans, and also providing repair services--are classified in U.S. Industry 517312, Wireless Telecommunications Carriers (except Satellite); and
- Repairing stereo and other consumer electronic equipment--are classified in U.S. Industry 811211, Consumer Electronics Repair and Maintenance.

811219 Other Electronic and Precision Equipment Repair and Maintenance

This U.S. industry comprises establishments primarily engaged in repairing and maintaining (without retailing) electronic and precision equipment (except consumer electronics, computers and office machines, and communications equipment). Establishments in this industry repair and maintain equipment, such as medical diagnostic imaging equipment, measuring and surveying instruments, laboratory instruments, and radar and sonar equipment.

Cross-References. Establishments primarily engaged in--

- Rewinding armatures and rebuilding electric motors on a factory basis--are classified in U.S. Industry 335312, Motor and Generator Manufacturing;
- Repairing stereo and other consumer electronic equipment--are classified in U.S. Industry 811211, Consumer Electronics Repair and Maintenance;
- Repairing computers and office machines--are classified in U.S. Industry 811212, Computer and Office Machine Repair and Maintenance;
- Repairing communication equipment--are classified in U.S. Industry 811213, Communication Equipment Repair and Maintenance; and
- Factory rebuilding or overhauling of electronic and precision equipment--are classified in the Manufacturing sector by type of equipment.

8113 Commercial and Industrial Machinery and Equipment (except Automotive and Electronic) Repair and Maintenance[T]

81131 Commercial and Industrial Machinery and Equipment (except Automotive and Electronic) Repair and Maintenance[T]
See industry description for 811310.

811310 Commercial and Industrial Machinery and Equipment (except Automotive and Electronic) Repair and Maintenance

This industry comprises establishments primarily engaged in the repair and maintenance of commercial and industrial machinery and equipment. Establishments in this industry either sharpen/install commercial and industrial machinery blades and saws or provide welding (e.g., automotive, general) repair services; or repair agricultural and other heavy and industrial machinery and equipment (e.g., forklifts and other material handling equipment, machine tools, commercial refrigeration equipment, construction equipment, and mining machinery).

Cross-References. Establishments primarily engaged in--

- Automotive repair (except welding) and maintenance--are classified in Industry Group 8111, Automotive Repair and Maintenance;

T—Canadian, Mexican, and United States industries are comparable.

- Repairing and maintaining electronic and precision equipment--are classified in Industry 81121, Electronic and Precision Equipment Repair and Maintenance;
- Oil well rig building, repairing, and dismantling, on a contract basis--are classified in U.S. Industry 213112, Support Activities for Oil and Gas Operations;
- Oil and gas pipeline and related structures construction and repair--are classified in Industry 237120, Oil and Gas Pipeline and Related Structures Construction;
- Repairing and servicing aircraft--are classified in Industry 488190, Other Support Activities for Air Transportation;
- Converting, rebuilding, and overhauling aircraft--are classified in Industry 33641, Aerospace Product and Parts Manufacturing;
- Repairing and servicing railroad cars and engines--are classified in Industry 488210, Support Activities for Rail Transportation;
- Rebuilding or remanufacturing railroad engines and cars--are classified in Industry 336510, Railroad Rolling Stock Manufacturing;
- Repairing and overhauling ships at floating drydocks--are classified in Industry 488390, Other Support Activities for Water Transportation;
- Repairing and overhauling ships at shipyards--are classified in U.S. Industry 336611, Ship Building and Repairing;
- Rewinding armatures or rebuilding electric motors on a factory basis--are classified in U.S. Industry 335312, Motor and Generator Manufacturing; and
- Repairing and maintaining home and garden equipment (e.g., sharpening or installing blades and saws)--are classified in U.S. Industry 811411, Home and Garden Equipment Repair and Maintenance.

8114   Personal and Household Goods Repair and Maintenance[T]

This industry group comprises establishments primarily engaged in home and garden equipment and appliance repair and maintenance; reupholstery and furniture repair; footwear and leather goods repair; and other personal and household goods repair and maintenance.

81141   Home and Garden Equipment and Appliance Repair and Maintenance[T]

This industry comprises establishments primarily engaged in repairing and servicing home and garden equipment and/or household-type appliances without retailing new equipment or appliances. Establishments in this industry repair and maintain items, such as lawnmowers, edgers, snowblowers, leaf blowers, washing machines, clothes dryers, and refrigerators.

Cross-References.   Establishments primarily engaged in--

- Retailing outdoor power equipment and also providing repair services--are classified in Industry 44421, Outdoor Power Equipment Stores;
- Retailing an array of new appliances and also providing repair services--are classified in Industry 44314, Electronics and Appliance Stores;
- Repairing, servicing, or installing central heating and air-conditioning equipment--are classified in Industry 23822, Plumbing, Heating, and Air-Conditioning Contractors; and
- Repairing commercial refrigeration equipment--are classified in Industry 81131, Commercial and Industrial Machinery and Equipment (except Automotive and Electronic) Repair and Maintenance.

811411   Home and Garden Equipment Repair and Maintenance

This U.S. industry comprises establishments primarily engaged in repairing and servicing home and garden equipment without retailing new home and garden equipment, such as lawnmowers, handheld power tools, edgers, snowblowers, leaf blowers, and trimmers.

T—Canadian, Mexican, and United States industries are comparable.

Cross-References.

Establishments primarily engaged in retailing new outdoor power equipment and also providing repair services are classified in Industry 444210, Outdoor Power Equipment Stores.

811412 Appliance Repair and Maintenance

This U.S. industry comprises establishments primarily engaged in repairing and servicing household appliances without retailing new appliances, such as refrigerators, stoves, washing machines, clothes dryers, and room air-conditioners.

Cross-References.   Establishments primarily engaged in--

- Installing central heating and air-conditioning equipment--are classified in Industry 238220, Plumbing, Heating, and Air-Conditioning Contractors;
- Repairing commercial refrigeration equipment--are classified in Industry 811310, Commercial and Industrial Machinery and Equipment (except Automotive and Electronic) Repair and Maintenance; and
- Retailing an array of new appliances and also providing repair services--are classified in U.S. Industry 443141, Household Appliance Stores.

81142   Reupholstery and Furniture Repair[T]
See industry description for 811420.

811420 Reupholstery and Furniture Repair

This industry comprises establishments primarily engaged in one or more of the following: (1) reupholstering furniture; (2) refinishing furniture; (3) repairing furniture; and (4) repairing and restoring furniture.

Cross-References.   Establishments primarily engaged in--

- Automotive vehicle and trailer upholstery repair--are classified in U.S. Industry 811121, Automotive Body, Paint, and Interior Repair and Maintenance; and
- The restoration of museum pieces--are classified in Industry 711510, Independent Artists, Writers, and Performers.

81143   Footwear and Leather Goods Repair[T]
See industry description for 811430.

811430 Footwear and Leather Goods Repair

This industry comprises establishments primarily engaged in repairing footwear and/or repairing other leather or leather-like goods without retailing new footwear and leather or leather-like goods, such as handbags and briefcases.

Cross-References.   Establishments primarily engaged in--

- Retailing new luggage and leather goods and also providing repair services--are classified in Industry 448320, Luggage and Leather Goods Stores;
- Shining shoes--are classified in Industry 812990, All Other Personal Services; and
- Repairing leather clothing--are classified in Industry 811490, Other Personal and Household Goods Repair and Maintenance.

81149   Other Personal and Household Goods Repair and Maintenance[T]
See industry description for 811490.

T—Canadian, Mexican, and United States industries are comparable.

811490 Other Personal and Household Goods Repair and Maintenance

This industry comprises establishments primarily engaged in repairing and servicing personal or household-type goods without retailing new personal or household-type goods (except home and garden equipment, appliances, furniture, and footwear and leather goods). Establishments in this industry repair items, such as garments; watches; jewelry; musical instruments; bicycles and motorcycles; and motorboats, canoes, sailboats, and other recreational boats.

Cross-References.   Establishments primarily engaged in--

- Repairing home and garden equipment--are classified in U.S. Industry 811411, Home and Garden Equipment Repair and Maintenance;
- Repairing appliances--are classified in U.S. Industry 811412, Appliance Repair and Maintenance;
- Reupholstering and repairing furniture--are classified in Industry 811420, Reupholstery and Furniture Repair;
- Repairing footwear and leather goods--are classified in Industry 811430, Footwear and Leather Goods Repair;
- Operating marinas and providing a range of other services including boat cleaning and repair--are classified in Industry 713930, Marinas; and
- Drycleaning garments--are classified in Industry Group 8123, Drycleaning and Laundry Services.

812   Personal and Laundry Services[T]

Industries in the Personal and Laundry Services subsector group establishments that provide personal and laundry services to individuals, households, and businesses. Services performed include: personal care services; death care services; laundry and drycleaning services; and a wide range of other personal services, such as pet care (except veterinary) services, photofinishing services, temporary parking services, and dating services.

The Personal and Laundry Services subsector is by no means all-inclusive of the services that could be termed personal services (i.e., those provided to individuals rather than businesses). There are many other subsectors, as well as sectors, that provide services to persons. Establishments providing legal, accounting, tax preparation, architectural, portrait photography, and similar professional services are classified in Sector 54, Professional, Scientific, and Technical Services; those providing job placement, travel arrangement, home security, interior and exterior house cleaning, exterminating, lawn and garden care, and similar support services are classified in Sector 56, Administrative and Support and Waste Management and Remediation Services; those providing health and social services are classified in Sector 62, Health Care and Social Assistance; those providing amusement and recreation services are classified in Sector 71, Arts, Entertainment, and Recreation; those providing educational instruction are classified in Sector 61, Educational Services; those providing repair services are classified in Subsector 811, Repair and Maintenance; and those providing spiritual, civic, and advocacy services are classified in Subsector 813, Religious, Grantmaking, Civic, Professional, and Similar Organizations.

8121   Personal Care Services

This industry group comprises establishments, such as barber and beauty shops, that provide appearance care services to individual consumers.

81211 Hair, Nail, and Skin Care Services

This industry comprises establishments primarily engaged in one or more of the following: (1) providing hair care services; (2) providing nail care services; and (3) providing facials or applying makeup (except permanent makeup).

Illustrative Examples:

Barber shops
Hair stylist shops
Beauty salons

Nail salons
Cosmetology salons

T—Canadian, Mexican, and United States industries are comparable.

Cross-References.   Establishments primarily engaged in--

- Offering training in barbering, hair styling, or the cosmetic arts--are classified in Industry 61151, Technical and Trade Schools;
- Providing massage, electrolysis (i.e., hair removal), permanent makeup, or tanning services--are classified in Industry 81219, Other Personal Care Services; and
- Providing medical skin care services (e.g., cosmetic surgery, dermatology)--are classified in Sector 62, Health Care and Social Assistance.

812111 Barber Shops

This U.S. industry comprises establishments known as barber shops or men's hair stylist shops primarily engaged in cutting, trimming, and styling men's and boys' hair; and/or shaving and trimming men's beards.

Cross-References.   Establishments primarily engaged in--

- Offering training in barbering--are classified in U.S. Industry 611511, Cosmetology and Barber Schools; and
- Providing hair care services (except establishments known as barber shops or men's hair stylists)--are classified in U.S. Industry 812112, Beauty Salons.

812112 Beauty Salons

This U.S. industry comprises establishments (except those known as barber shops or men's hair stylist shops) primarily engaged in one or more of the following: (1) cutting, trimming, shampooing, coloring, waving, or styling hair; (2) providing facials; and (3) applying makeup (except permanent makeup).

Illustrative Examples:

Beauty parlors or shops
Facial salons or shops
Combined beauty and barber shops

Hairdressing salons or shops
Cosmetology salons or shops
Unisex or women's hair stylist shops

Cross-References.   Establishments primarily engaged in--

- Cutting, trimming, and styling men's and boys' hair (known as barber shops or men's hair stylist shops)--are classified in U.S. Industry 812111, Barber Shops;
- Offering training in hair styling or the cosmetic arts--are classified in U.S. Industry 611511, Cosmetology and Barber Schools;
- Providing nail care services--are classified in U.S. Industry 812113, Nail Salons;
- Providing massage, electrolysis (i.e., hair removal), permanent makeup, or tanning services--are classified in U.S. Industry 812199, Other Personal Care Services; and
- Providing medical skin care services (e.g., cosmetic surgery, dermatology)--are classified in Sector 62, Health Care and Social Assistance.

812113 Nail Salons

This U.S. industry comprises establishments primarily engaged in providing nail care services, such as manicures, pedicures, and nail extensions.

81219 Other Personal Care Services

This industry comprises establishments primarily engaged in providing personal care services (except hair, nail, facial, or nonpermanent makeup services).

T—Canadian, Mexican, and United States industries are comparable.

Illustrative Examples:

Day spas
Depilatory or electrolysis (i.e., hair removal) salons
Permanent makeup salons
Ear piercing services
Steam or turkish baths
Tanning salons

Hair replacement (except by offices of physicians) or weaving services
Massage parlors
Tattoo parlors
Non-medical diet and weight reducing centers

Cross-References.   Establishments primarily engaged in--

- Providing hair, nail, facial, or nonpermanent makeup services--are classified in Industry 81211, Hair, Nail, and Skin Care Services;
- Operating physical fitness facilities--are classified in Industry 71394, Fitness and Recreational Sports Centers;
- Providing personal fitness training services--are classified in Industry 81299, All Other Personal Services;
- Operating health resorts and spas that provide lodging--are classified in Industry 72111, Hotels (except Casino Hotels) and Motels; and
- Providing medical or surgical hair replacement or weight reduction services--are classified in Sector 62, Health Care and Social Assistance.

812191 Diet and Weight Reducing Centers

This U.S. industry comprises establishments primarily engaged in providing non-medical services to assist clients in attaining or maintaining a desired weight. The sale of weight reduction products, such as food supplements, may be an integral component of the program. These services typically include individual or group counseling, menu and exercise planning, and weight and body measurement monitoring.

Cross-References.   Establishments primarily engaged in--

- Operating physical fitness facilities--are classified in Industry 713940, Fitness and Recreational Sports Centers;
- Providing personal fitness training services--are classified in Industry 812990, All Other Personal Services;
- Operating health resorts and spas that provide lodging--are classified in Industry 721110, Hotels (except Casino Hotels) and Motels; and
- Providing medical or surgical weight reduction--are classified in Sector 62, Health Care and Social Assistance.

812199 Other Personal Care Services

This U.S. industry comprises establishments primarily engaged in providing personal care services (except hair, nail, facial, nonpermanent makeup, or non-medical diet and weight reducing services).

Illustrative Examples:

Day spas
Depilatory or electrolysis (i.e., hair removal) salons
Saunas
Ear piercing services
Steam or turkish baths
Tanning salons

Hair replacement (except by offices of physicians) or weaving services
Massage parlors
Tattoo parlors
Permanent makeup salons

T—Canadian, Mexican, and United States industries are comparable.

Cross-References.   Establishments primarily engaged in--

- Cutting, trimming, and styling men's and boys' hair (known as barber shops or men's hair stylist shops)--are classified in U.S. Industry 812111, Barber Shops;
- Providing hair, facial, or nonpermanent makeup services (except establishments known as barber shops or men's hair stylist shops)--are classified in U.S. Industry 812112, Beauty Salons;
- Nail care services--are classified in U.S. Industry 812113, Nail Salons;
- Providing non-medical diet and weight reducing services--are classified in U.S. Industry 812191, Diet and Weight Reducing Centers;
- Operating health resorts and spas that provide lodging--are classified in Industry 721110, Hotels (except Casino Hotels) and Motels; and
- Providing medical or surgical hair replacement or weight reduction services--are classified in Sector 62, Health Care and Social Assistance.

8122   Death Care Services

This industry group comprises establishments primarily engaged in preparing the dead for burial or interment, conducting funerals, operating sites or structures reserved for the interment of human or animals remains, and/or cremating the dead.

81221   Funeral Homes and Funeral Services
See industry description for 812210.

812210 Funeral Homes and Funeral Services

This industry comprises establishments primarily engaged in preparing the dead for burial or interment and conducting funerals (i.e., providing facilities for wakes, arranging transportation for the dead, selling caskets and related merchandise). Funeral homes combined with crematories are included in this industry.

Cross-References.

Establishments (except funeral homes) primarily engaged in cremating the dead are classified in Industry 812220, Cemeteries and Crematories.

81222   Cemeteries and Crematories
See industry description for 812220.

812220 Cemeteries and Crematories

This industry comprises establishments primarily engaged in operating sites or structures reserved for the interment of human or animal remains and/or cremating the dead.

Illustrative Examples:

Cemetery associations (i.e., operators of cemeteries)   Pet cemeteries
Memorial gardens (i.e., burial places)   Mausoleums
Crematories (except combined with funeral homes)

Cross-References.

Crematories combined with funeral homes are classified in Industry 812210, Funeral Homes and Funeral Services.

T—Canadian, Mexican, and United States industries are comparable.

8123   Drycleaning and Laundry Services

This industry group comprises establishments primarily engaged in operating coin-operated or similar self-service laundries and drycleaners; providing drycleaning and laundry services (except coin-operated); and supplying, on a rental or contract basis, laundered items (e.g., uniforms, gowns, shop towels, etc.). Included in this industry group are establishments primarily engaged in supplying and servicing coin-operated laundry and drycleaning equipment in places of business operated by others, such as apartments and dormitories.

81231   Coin-Operated Laundries and Drycleaners
           See industry description for 812310.

812310 Coin-Operated Laundries and Drycleaners

This industry comprises establishments primarily engaged in (1) operating facilities with coin-operated or similar self-service laundry and drycleaning equipment for customer use on the premises and/or (2) supplying and servicing coin-operated or similar self-service laundry and drycleaning equipment for customer use in places of business operated by others, such as apartments and dormitories.

81232   Drycleaning and Laundry Services (except Coin-Operated)
           See industry description for 812320.

812320 Drycleaning and Laundry Services (except Coin-Operated)

This industry comprises establishments primarily engaged in one or more of the following: (1) providing drycleaning services (except coin-operated); (2) providing laundering services (except linen and uniform supply or coin-operated); (3) providing drop-off and pick-up sites for laundries and/or drycleaners; and (4) providing specialty cleaning services for specific types of garments and other textile items (except carpets and upholstery), such as fur, leather, or suede garments; wedding gowns; hats; draperies; and pillows. These establishments may provide all, a combination of, or none of the cleaning services on the premises.

Cross-References.   Establishments primarily engaged in--

- Supplying laundered linens and uniforms on a rental or contract basis--are classified in Industry 81233, Linen and Uniform Supply;
- Operating coin-operated or similar self-service laundry or drycleaning facilities--are classified in Industry 812310, Coin-Operated Laundries and Drycleaners; and
- Cleaning used carpets and upholstery--are classified in Industry 561740, Carpet and Upholstery Cleaning Services.

81233   Linen and Uniform Supply

This industry comprises establishments primarily engaged in supplying, on a rental or contract basis, laundered items, such as uniforms, gowns and coats, table linens, bed linens, towels, clean room apparel, and treated mops or shop towels.

812331 Linen Supply

This U.S. industry comprises establishments primarily engaged in supplying, on a rental or contract basis, laundered items, such as table and bed linens; towels; diapers; and uniforms, gowns, or coats of the type used by doctors, nurses, barbers, beauticians, and waitresses.

Cross-References.

Establishments primarily engaged in supplying, on a rental or contract basis, laundered industrial work uniforms and related work clothing are classified in U.S. Industry 812332, Industrial Launderers.

T—Canadian, Mexican, and United States industries are comparable.

812332 Industrial Launderers

This U.S. industry comprises establishments primarily engaged in supplying, on a rental or contract basis, laundered industrial work uniforms and related work clothing, such as protective apparel (flame and heat resistant) and clean room apparel; dust control items, such as treated mops, rugs, mats, dust tool covers, cloths, and shop or wiping towels.

Cross-References.

Establishments primarily engaged in supplying, on a rental or contract basis, laundered uniforms, gowns or coats of the type used by doctors, nurses, barbers, beauticians, and waitresses are classified in U.S. Industry 812331, Linen Supply.

8129   Other Personal Services

This industry group comprises establishments primarily engaged in providing personal services (except personal care services, death care services, or drycleaning and laundry services).

81291   Pet Care (except Veterinary) Services
See industry description for 812910.

812910 Pet Care (except Veterinary) Services

This industry comprises establishments primarily engaged in providing pet care services (except veterinary), such as boarding, grooming, sitting, and training pets.

Cross-References.   Establishments primarily engaged in--

- Practicing veterinary medicine--are classified in Industry 541940, Veterinary Services;
- Boarding horses--are classified in Industry 115210, Support Activities for Animal Production; and
- Transporting pets--are classified in U.S. Industry 485991, Special Needs Transportation.

81292   Photofinishing

This industry comprises establishments primarily engaged in developing film and/or making photographic slides, prints, and enlargements.

Cross-References.

Establishments primarily engaged in processing motion picture film for the motion picture and television industries are classified in Industry 51219, Postproduction Services and Other Motion Picture and Video Industries.

812921 Photofinishing Laboratories (except One-Hour)

This U.S. industry comprises establishments (except those known as "one-hour" photofinishing labs) primarily engaged in developing film and/or making photographic slides, prints, and enlargements.

Cross-References.

- Establishments primarily engaged in processing motion picture film for the motion picture and television industries are classified in U.S. Industry 512199, Other Motion Picture and Video Industries; and
- Establishments known as "one-hour" photofinishing labs are classified in U.S. Industry 812922, One-Hour Photofinishing.

T—Canadian, Mexican, and United States industries are comparable.

812922 One-Hour Photofinishing

This U.S. industry comprises establishments known as "one-hour" photofinishing labs primarily engaged in developing film and/or making photographic slides, prints, and enlargements on a short turnaround or while-you-wait basis.

Cross-References.

Photofinishing laboratories (except those known as "one-hour" photofinishing labs) are classified in U.S. Industry 812921, Photofinishing Laboratories (except One-Hour).

81293   Parking Lots and Garages
    See industry description for 812930.

812930 Parking Lots and Garages

This industry comprises establishments primarily engaged in providing parking space for motor vehicles, usually on an hourly, daily, or monthly basis and/or valet parking services.

Cross-References.

Establishments primarily engaged in providing extended or dead storage of motor vehicles are classified in Industry 493190, Other Warehousing and Storage.

81299   All Other Personal Services
    See industry description for 812990.

812990 All Other Personal Services

This industry comprises establishments primarily engaged in providing personal services (except personal care services, death care services, drycleaning and laundry services, pet care services, photofinishing services, or parking space and/or valet parking services).

Illustrative Examples:

Bail bonding or bondsperson services
Shoeshine services
Coin-operated personal services machine (e.g., blood pressure, locker, photographic, scale, shoeshine) concession operators

Social escort services
Consumer buying services
Wedding planning services
Dating services
Personal fitness training services

Cross-References.   Establishments primarily engaged in--

- Providing personal care services--are classified in Industry Group 8121, Personal Care Services;
- Providing death care services--are classified in Industry Group 8122, Death Care Services;
- Providing drycleaning and laundry services--are classified in Industry Group 8123, Drycleaning and Laundry Services;
- Providing pet care (except veterinary) services--are classified in Industry 812910, Pet Care (except Veterinary) Services;
- Practicing veterinary medicine--are classified in Industry 541940, Veterinary Services;
- Providing photofinishing services--are classified in Industry 81292, Photofinishing; and
- Providing parking space for motor vehicles and/or valet parking services--are classified in Industry 812930, Parking Lots and Garages.

T—Canadian, Mexican, and United States industries are comparable.

813   Religious, Grantmaking, Civic, Professional, and Similar Organizations[T]

Industries in the Religious, Grantmaking, Civic, Professional, and Similar Organizations subsector group establishments that organize and promote religious activities; support various causes through grantmaking; advocate various social and political causes; and promote and defend the interests of their members.

The industry groups within the subsector are defined in terms of their activities, such as establishments that provide funding for specific causes or for a variety of charitable causes; establishments that advocate and actively promote causes and beliefs for the public good; and establishments that have an active membership structure to promote causes and represent the interests of their members. Establishments in this subsector may publish newsletters, books, and periodicals for distribution to their members.

8131   Religious Organizations

81311   Religious Organizations
See industry description for 813110.

813110   Religious Organizations

This industry comprises (1) establishments primarily engaged in operating religious organizations, such as churches, religious temples, and monasteries, and/or (2) establishments primarily engaged in administering an organized religion or promoting religious activities.

Illustrative Examples:

Churches
Shrines, religious
Monasteries (except schools)

Synagogues
Mosques, religious
Temples, religious

Cross-References.

- Schools, colleges, or universities operated by religious organizations are classified in Sector 61, Educational Services;
- Radio and television stations operated by religious organizations are classified in Subsector 515, Broadcasting (except Internet);
- Publishing houses operated by religious organizations are classified in Subsector 511, Publishing Industries (except Internet);
- Establishments operated by religious organizations primarily engaged in health and social assistance for individuals are classified in Sector 62, Health Care and Social Assistance; and
- Used merchandise stores operated by religious organizations are classified in Industry 453310, Used Merchandise Stores.

8132   Grantmaking and Giving Services

81321   Grantmaking and Giving Services

This industry comprises (1) establishments known as grantmaking foundations or charitable trusts and (2) establishments primarily engaged in raising funds for a wide range of social welfare activities, such as health, educational, scientific, and cultural activities.

Cross-References.   Establishments primarily engaged in--

- Providing trust management services for others--are classified in Industry 52392, Portfolio Management;
- Organizing and conducting fundraising campaigns on a contract or fee basis--are classified in Industry 56149, Other Business Support Services;
- Providing telemarketing services for others--are classified in Industry 56142, Telephone Call Centers;

T—Canadian, Mexican, and United States industries are comparable.

- Raising funds for political purposes--are classified in Industry 81394, Political Organizations;
- Advocating social causes or issues--are classified in Industry 81331, Social Advocacy Organizations; and
- Conducting health research--are classified in Industry 54171, Research and Development in the Physical, Engineering, and Life Sciences.

813211 Grantmaking Foundations

This U.S. industry comprises establishments known as grantmaking foundations or charitable trusts. Establishments in this industry award grants from trust funds based on a competitive selection process or the preferences of the foundation managers and grantors; or fund a single entity, such as a museum or university.

Illustrative Examples:

Community foundations
Philanthropic trusts
Corporate foundations, awarding grants

Scholarship trusts
Grantmaking foundations

Cross-References.

Establishments primarily engaged in providing trust management services for others are classified in Industry 523920, Portfolio Management.

813212 Voluntary Health Organizations

This U.S. industry comprises establishments primarily engaged in raising funds for health related research, such as disease (e.g., heart, cancer, diabetes) prevention, health education, and patient services.

Illustrative Examples:

Disease awareness fundraising organizations
Health research fundraising organizations
Voluntary health organizations

Disease research (e.g., heart, cancer) fundraising organizations

Cross-References.

- Establishments primarily engaged in raising funds for a wide range of social welfare activities, such as educational, scientific, cultural, or health, are classified in U.S. Industry 813219, Other Grantmaking and Giving Services;
- Establishments primarily engaged in organizing and conducting fundraising campaigns on a contract or fee basis are classified in U.S. Industry 561499, All Other Business Support Services;
- Establishments primarily engaged in providing telemarketing services for others are classified in U.S. Industry 561422, Telemarketing Bureaus and Other Contact Centers;
- Establishments known as grantmaking foundations or charitable trusts are classified in U.S. Industry 813211, Grantmaking Foundations; and
- Establishments primarily engaged in conducting health research are classified in Industry 54171, Research and Development in the Physical, Engineering, and Life Sciences.

813219 Other Grantmaking and Giving Services

This U.S. industry comprises establishments (except voluntary health organizations) primarily engaged in raising funds for a wide range of social welfare activities, such as educational, scientific, cultural, and health.

T—Canadian, Mexican, and United States industries are comparable.

Illustrative Examples:

Community chests
United fund councils

Federated charities
United funds for colleges

Cross-References.

- Establishments primarily engaged in raising funds for health related research are classified in U.S. Industry 813212, Voluntary Health Organizations;
- Establishments known as grantmaking foundations or charitable trusts are classified in U.S. Industry 813211, Grantmaking Foundations;
- Establishments primarily engaged in organizing and conducting fundraising campaigns on a contract or fee basis are classified in U.S. Industry 561499, All Other Business Support Services;
- Establishments primarily engaged in providing telemarketing services for others are classified in U.S. Industry 561422, Telemarketing Bureaus and Other Contact Centers;
- Establishments primarily engaged in raising funds for political purposes are classified in Industry 813940, Political Organizations; and
- Establishments primarily engaged in advocating social causes or issues are classified in Industry 81331, Social Advocacy Organizations.

8133   Social Advocacy Organizations

81331   Social Advocacy Organizations

This industry comprises establishments primarily engaged in promoting a particular cause or working for the realization of a specific social or political goal to benefit a broad or specific constituency. These organizations may solicit contributions and offer memberships to support these goals.

Illustrative Examples:

Community action advocacy organizations
Firearms advocacy organizations
Conservation advocacy organizations

Human rights advocacy organizations
Environmental advocacy organizations
Wildlife preservation organizations

Cross-References.

- Establishments primarily engaged in promoting the civic and social interests of their members are classified in Industry 81341, Civic and Social Organizations;
- Establishments primarily engaged in promoting the interests of organized labor and union employees are classified in Industry 81393, Labor Unions and Similar Labor Organizations;
- Establishments primarily engaged in providing legal services for social advocacy organizations are classified in Industry Group 5411, Legal Services;
- Establishments primarily engaged in providing community action services, such as community action services agencies, are classified in Industry 62419, Other Individual and Family Services; and
- Government establishments primarily engaged in administering, overseeing, and managing governmental ecological restoration programs are classified in Industry 92411, Administration of Air and Water Resource and Solid Waste Management Programs.

813311 Human Rights Organizations

This U.S. industry comprises establishments primarily engaged in promoting causes associated with human rights either for a broad or specific constituency. Establishments in this industry address issues, such as protecting and promoting the broad constitutional rights and civil liberties of individuals and those suffering from neglect, abuse, or exploitation; promoting the interests of specific groups, such as children, women, senior citizens, or persons with

---

T—Canadian, Mexican, and United States industries are comparable.

disabilities; improving relations between racial, ethnic, and cultural groups; and promoting voter education and registration. These organizations may solicit contributions and offer memberships to support these causes.

Illustrative Examples:

Civil liberties organizations
Senior citizens' advocacy organizations

Human rights advocacy organizations
Veterans' rights organizations

Cross-References.　　　Establishments primarily engaged in--

- Promoting the interests of organized labor and union employees--are classified in Industry 813930, Labor Unions and Similar Labor Organizations; and
- Providing legal services for human rights organizations--are classified in Industry Group 5411, Legal Services.

813312 Environment, Conservation and Wildlife Organizations

This U.S. industry comprises establishments primarily engaged in promoting the preservation and protection of the environment and wildlife. Establishments in this industry address issues, such as clean air and water; global warming; conserving and developing natural resources, including land, plant, water, and energy resources; and protecting and preserving wildlife and endangered species. These organizations may solicit contributions and offer memberships to support these causes.

Illustrative Examples:

Animal rights organizations
Natural resource preservation organizations
Conservation advocacy organizations

Wildlife preservation organizations
Humane societies

Cross-References.

- Establishments primarily engaged in providing legal services for environment, conservation, and wildlife organizations are classified in Industry Group 5411, Legal Services; and
- Government establishments primarily engaged in administering, overseeing, and managing governmental ecological restoration programs are classified in Industry 924110, Administration of Air and Water Resource and Solid Waste Management Programs.

813319 Other Social Advocacy Organizations

This U.S. industry comprises establishments primarily engaged in social advocacy (except human rights and environmental protection, conservation, and wildlife preservation). Establishments in this industry address issues, such as peace and international understanding; community action (excluding civic organizations); or advancing social causes, such as firearms safety, drunk driving prevention, or drug abuse awareness. These organizations may solicit contributions and offer memberships to support these causes.

Illustrative Examples:

Community action advocacy organizations
Substance abuse prevention advocacy organizations
Firearms advocacy organizations

Taxpayers' advocacy organizations
Peace advocacy organizations

Cross-References.　　　Establishments primarily engaged in--

- Advocating human rights issues--are classified in U.S. Industry 813311, Human Rights Organizations;

T—Canadian, Mexican, and United States industries are comparable.

- Promoting the preservation and protection of the environment and wildlife--are classified in U.S. Industry 813312, Environment, Conservation and Wildlife Organizations;
- Promoting the civic and social interests of their members--are classified in Industry 813410, Civic and Social Organizations;
- Providing legal services for social advocacy organizations--are classified in Industry Group 5411, Legal Services; and
- Providing community action services, such as community action service agencies--are classified in Industry 624190, Other Individual and Family Services.

8134   Civic and Social Organizations

81341   Civic and Social Organizations
See industry description for 813410.

813410 Civic and Social Organizations

This industry comprises establishments primarily engaged in promoting the civic and social interests of their members. Establishments in this industry may operate bars and restaurants for their members.

Illustrative Examples:

Alumni associations	Scouting organizations
Granges	Ethnic associations
Automobile clubs (except travel)	Social clubs
Parent-teacher associations	Fraternal lodges
Booster clubs	Veterans' membership organizations

Cross-References.

- Establishments of insurance offices operated by fraternal benefit organizations are classified in Subsector 524, Insurance Carriers and Related Activities;
- Establishments primarily engaged in operating residential fraternity and sorority houses are classified in Industry 721310, Rooming and Boarding Houses, Dormitories, and Workers' Camps; and
- Establishments primarily engaged in providing travel arrangements and reservation services, such as automobile travel clubs or motor travel clubs, are classified in U.S. Industry 561599, All Other Travel Arrangement and Reservation Services.

8139   Business, Professional, Labor, Political, and Similar Organizations

This industry group comprises establishments primarily engaged in promoting the interests of their members (except religious organizations, social advocacy organizations, and civic and social organizations). Examples of establishments in this industry are business associations, professional organizations, labor unions, and political organizations.

81391   Business Associations
See industry description for 813910.

813910 Business Associations

This industry comprises establishments primarily engaged in promoting the business interests of their members. These establishments may conduct research on new products and services; develop market statistics; sponsor quality and certification standards; lobby public officials; or publish newsletters, books, or periodicals for distribution to their members.

T—Canadian, Mexican, and United States industries are comparable.

Illustrative Examples:

Agricultural organizations (except youth farming organizations, farm granges)
Real estate boards

Chambers of commerce
Trade associations
Manufacturers' associations

Cross-References.

- Establishments owned by their members but organized to perform a specific business function, such as common marketing of crops, joint advertising, or buying cooperatives, are classified according to their primary activity;
- Establishments primarily engaged in promoting the professional interests of their members and the profession as a whole are classified in Industry 813920, Professional Organizations;
- Establishments primarily engaged in promoting the interests of organized labor and union employees, such as trade unions, are classified in Industry 813930, Labor Unions and Similar Labor Organizations; and
- Establishments primarily engaged in lobbying public officials (i.e., lobbyists) are classified in Industry 541820, Public Relations Agencies.

81392   Professional Organizations
See industry description for 813920.

813920   Professional Organizations

This industry comprises establishments primarily engaged in promoting the professional interests of their members and the profession as a whole. These establishments may conduct research; develop statistics; sponsor quality and certification standards; lobby public officials; or publish newsletters, books, or periodicals for distribution to their members.

Illustrative Examples:

Bar associations
Learned societies
Dentists' associations
Peer review boards

Engineers' associations
Professional standards review boards
Health professionals' associations
Scientists' associations

Cross-References.   Establishments primarily engaged in--

- Promoting the business interests of their members--are classified in Industry 813910, Business Associations; and
- Lobbying public officials (i.e., lobbyists)--are classified in Industry 541820, Public Relations Agencies.

81393   Labor Unions and Similar Labor Organizations
See industry description for 813930.

813930   Labor Unions and Similar Labor Organizations

This industry comprises establishments primarily engaged in promoting the interests of organized labor and union employees.

81394   Political Organizations
See industry description for 813940.

813940 Political Organizations

This industry comprises establishments primarily engaged in promoting the interests of national, state, or local political parties or candidates. Included are political groups organized to raise funds for a political party or individual candidates.

Illustrative Examples:

Campaign organizations, political
Political organizations or clubs
Political action committees (PACs)

Political parties
Political campaign organizations

Cross-References.   Establishments primarily engaged in--

- Organizing and conducting fundraising campaigns on a contract or fee basis--are classified in U.S. Industry 561499, All Other Business Support Services; and
- Providing telemarketing services for others--are classified in U.S. Industry 561422, Telemarketing Bureaus and Other Contact Centers.

81399   Other Similar Organizations (except Business, Professional, Labor, and Political Organizations)
See industry description for 813990.

813990 Other Similar Organizations (except Business, Professional, Labor, and Political Organizations)

This industry comprises establishments (except religious organizations, social advocacy organizations, civic and social organizations, business associations, professional organizations, labor unions, and political organizations) primarily engaged in promoting the interests of their members.

Illustrative Examples:

Athletic associations and leagues, regulatory
Property owners' associations
Condominium and homeowners' associations

Tenants' associations (except advocacy)
Cooperative owners' associations

Cross-References.   Establishments primarily engaged in--

- Operating religious organizations, such as churches, religious temples, and monasteries--are classified in Industry 813110, Religious Organizations;
- Raising funds for a wide range of social welfare activities and establishments known as grantmaking foundations or charitable trusts--are classified in Industry 81321, Grantmaking and Giving Services;
- Advocating social causes or issues--are classified in Industry 81331, Social Advocacy Organizations;
- Promoting the civic and social interests of their members--are classified in Industry 813410, Civic and Social Organizations;
- Promoting the business interests of their members--are classified in Industry 813910, Business Associations;
- Promoting the professional interests of their members and the profession as a whole--are classified in Industry 813920, Professional Organizations;
- Promoting the interests of organized labor and union employees--are classified in Industry 813930, Labor Unions and Similar Labor Organizations;
- Promoting the interests of national, state, or local political parties or candidates--are classified in Industry 813940, Political Organizations; and
- Providing recreational and amusement services, such as recreational or youth sports league teams--are classified in Industry 713990, All Other Amusement and Recreation Industries.

T—Canadian, Mexican, and United States industries are comparable.

814   Private Households^T

Industries in the Private Households subsector include private households that engage in employing workers on or about the premises in activities primarily concerned with the operation of the household. These private households may employ individuals, such as cooks, maids, butlers, and outside workers, such as gardeners, caretakers, and other maintenance workers.

8141   Private Households^T

81411   Private Households^T
See industry description for 814110.

814110 Private Households

This industry comprises private households primarily engaged in employing workers on or about the premises in activities primarily concerned with the operation of the household. These private households may employ individuals, such as cooks, maids, nannies, butlers, and outside workers, such as gardeners, caretakers, and other maintenance workers.

T—Canadian, Mexican, and United States industries are comparable.

Sector 92--Public Administration[T]

The Sector as a Whole

The Public Administration sector consists of establishments of federal, state, and local government agencies that administer, oversee, and manage public programs and have executive, legislative, or judicial authority over other institutions within a given area. These agencies also set policy, create laws, adjudicate civil and criminal legal cases, and provide for public safety and for national defense. In general, government establishments in the Public Administration sector oversee governmental programs and activities that are not performed by private establishments. Establishments in this sector typically are engaged in the organization and financing of the production of public goods and services, most of which are provided for free or at prices that are not economically significant.

Government establishments also engage in a wide range of productive activities covering not only public goods and services but also individual goods and services similar to those produced in sectors typically identified with private-sector establishments. In general, ownership is not a criterion for classification in NAICS. Therefore, government establishments engaged in the production of private-sector-like goods and services should be classified in the same industry as private-sector establishments engaged in similar activities.

As a practical matter, it is difficult to identify separate establishment detail for many government agencies. To the extent that separate establishment records are available, the administration of governmental programs is classified in Sector 92, Public Administration, while the operation of governmental programs is classified elsewhere in NAICS based on the activities performed. For example, the governmental administrative authority for an airport is classified in Industry 92612, Regulation and Administration of Transportation Programs, while operating the airport is classified in Industry 48811, Airport Operations. When separate records for multi-establishment companies are not available to distinguish between the administration of a governmental program and the operation of it, the establishment is classified in Sector 92, Public Administration.

Examples of government-provided goods and services that are classified in sectors other than Public Administration include: schools, classified in Sector 61, Educational Services; hospitals, classified in Subsector 622, Hospitals; establishments operating transportation facilities, classified in Sector 48-49, Transportation and Warehousing; the operation of utilities, classified in Sector 22, Utilities; and the Government Printing Office, classified in Subsector 323, Printing and Related Support Activities.

921 Executive, Legislative, and Other General Government Support

The Executive, Legislative, and Other General Government Support subsector groups offices of government executives, legislative bodies, public finance, and general government support.

9211 Executive, Legislative, and Other General Government Support

92111 Executive Offices
See industry description for 921110.

921110 Executive Offices

This industry comprises government establishments serving as offices of chief executives and their advisory committees and commissions. This industry includes offices of the president, governors, and mayors, in addition to executive advisory commissions.

92112 Legislative Bodies
See industry description for 921120.

T—Canadian, Mexican, and United States industries are comparable.

921120 Legislative Bodies

This industry comprises government establishments serving as legislative bodies and their advisory committees and commissions. Included in this industry are legislative bodies, such as Congress, state legislatures, and advisory and study legislative commissions.

92113 Public Finance Activities
See industry description for 921130.

921130 Public Finance Activities

This industry comprises government establishments primarily engaged in public finance, taxation, and monetary policy. Included are financial administration activities, such as monetary policy; tax administration and collection; custody and disbursement of funds; debt and investment administration; auditing activities; and government employee retirement trust fund administration.

Cross-References.   Establishments primarily engaged in--

- Administering income maintenance programs--are classified in Industry 923130, Administration of Human Resource Programs (except Education, Public Health, and Veterans' Affairs Programs);
- Regulating insurance and banking institutions--are classified in Industry 926150, Regulation, Licensing, and Inspection of Miscellaneous Commercial Sectors; and
- Performing central banking functions, such as issuing currency and acting as the fiscal agent for the central government--are classified in Industry 521110, Monetary Authorities-Central Bank.

92114 Executive and Legislative Offices, Combined
See industry description for 921140.

921140 Executive and Legislative Offices, Combined

This industry comprises government establishments serving as councils and boards of commissioners or supervisors and such bodies where the chief executive (e.g., county executive or city mayor) is a member of the legislative body (e.g., county or city council) itself.

Cross-References.   Establishments primarily engaged in--

- Serving as offices of chief executives--are classified in Industry 921110, Executive Offices; and
- Serving as legislative bodies--are classified in Industry 921120, Legislative Bodies.

92115 American Indian and Alaska Native Tribal Governments
See industry description for 921150.

921150 American Indian and Alaska Native Tribal Governments

This industry comprises American Indian and Alaska Native governing bodies. Establishments in this industry perform legislative, judicial, and administrative functions for their American Indian and Alaska Native lands. Included in this industry are American Indian and Alaska Native councils, courts, and law enforcement bodies.

Cross-References.

- Establishments primarily engaged in providing funding for American Indian and Alaska Native tribal programs through commercial activities, such as gaming, are classified in the industry of the commercial activity; and
- Government establishments providing public administration of American Indian and Alaska Native affairs are classified in Industry 921190, Other General Government Support.

T--Canadian, Mexican, and United States industries are comparable.

92119   Other General Government Support
See industry description for 921190.

921190 Other General Government Support

This industry comprises government establishments primarily engaged in providing general support for government. Such support services include personnel services, election boards, and other general government support establishments that are not classified elsewhere in public administration.

Illustrative Examples:

Civil rights commissions
Personnel offices, government
Civil service commissions

Supply agencies, government
General services departments, government

Cross-References.

- Government establishments primarily engaged in serving as offices of chief executives and their advisory committees and commissions are classified in Industry 921110, Executive Offices;
- Government establishments primarily engaged in serving as legislative bodies and their advisory committees and commissions are classified in Industry 921120, Legislative Bodies;
- Government establishments primarily engaged in providing administration of public finance, tax collection, and monetary policy programs are classified in Industry 921130, Public Finance Activities;
- Government establishments primarily engaged in serving as combined executive and legislative offices are classified in Industry 921140, Executive and Legislative Offices, Combined; and
- Establishments primarily engaged in serving as American Indian or Alaska Native tribal leadership are classified in Industry 921150, American Indian and Alaska Native Tribal Governments.

922   Justice, Public Order, and Safety Activities

The Justice, Public Order, and Safety Activities subsector groups government establishments engaged in the administration of justice, public order, and safety programs.

9221   Justice, Public Order, and Safety Activities

92211   Courts
See industry description for 922110.

922110 Courts

This industry comprises civilian courts of law (except American Indian and Alaska Native tribal courts). Included in this industry are civilian courts, courts of law, and sheriffs' offices conducting court functions only.

Cross-References.

- Government establishments primarily engaged in operating military courts are classified in Industry 928110, National Security; and
- Establishments primarily engaged in operating American Indian or Alaska Native tribal courts are classified in Industry 921150, American Indian and Alaska Native Tribal Governments.

92212   Police Protection
See industry description for 922120.

T—Canadian, Mexican, and United States industries are comparable.

922120   Police Protection

This industry comprises government establishments primarily engaged in criminal and civil law enforcement, police, traffic safety, and other activities related to the enforcement of the law and preservation of order. Combined police and fire departments are included in this industry.

Cross-References.

- Government establishments primarily engaged in prosecution are classified in Industry 922130, Legal Counsel and Prosecution;
- Government establishments primarily engaged in collection of law enforcement statistics are classified in Industry 922190, Other Justice, Public Order, and Safety Activities;
- Government establishments primarily engaged in providing police service for the military or National Guard are classified in Industry 928110, National Security;
- Government establishments primarily engaged in providing police service for tribal governments are classified in Industry 921150, American Indian and Alaska Native Tribal Governments;
- Government establishments primarily engaged in enforcing immigration laws are classified in Industry 928120, International Affairs;
- Sheriffs' offices conducting court functions only are classified in Industry 922110, Courts; and
- Private establishments primarily engaged in providing security and investigation services are classified in Industry 56161, Investigation, Guard, and Armored Car Services.

92213   Legal Counsel and Prosecution
See industry description for 922130.

922130   Legal Counsel and Prosecution

This industry comprises government establishments primarily engaged in providing legal counsel or prosecution services for the government.

Illustrative Examples:

Attorney generals' offices   District attorneys' offices
Public defenders' offices   Public prosecutors' offices

Cross-References.

Government establishments primarily engaged in collecting criminal justice statistics are classified in Industry 922190, Other Justice, Public Order, and Safety Activities.

92214   Correctional Institutions
See industry description for 922140.

922140   Correctional Institutions

This industry comprises government establishments primarily engaged in managing and operating correctional institutions. The facility is generally designed for the confinement, correction, and rehabilitation of adult and/or juvenile offenders sentenced by a court.

Illustrative Examples:

Correctional institutions, public administration   Prisons, public administration
Penitentiaries, public administration   Jails, public administration
Detention centers, public administration

T—Canadian, Mexican, and United States industries are comparable.

Cross-References.

- Government establishments primarily engaged in operating halfway houses for ex-criminal offenders and delinquent youths are classified in Industry 623990, Other Residential Care Facilities; and
- Establishments primarily engaged in managing or operating correctional facilities owned by others are classified in Industry 561210, Facilities Support Services.

92215   Parole Offices and Probation Offices
See industry description for 922150.

922150   Parole Offices and Probation Offices

This industry comprises government establishments primarily engaged in judicially administering probation offices, parole offices and boards, and pardon boards.

Cross-References.

- Private establishments primarily engaged in providing parole or probation services are classified in Industry 624190, Other Individual and Family Services; and
- Government establishments primarily engaged in providing probation, parole, and pardon activities as an integral part of a central administrative corrections' office are classified in Industry 922140, Correctional Institutions.

92216   Fire Protection
See industry description for 922160.

922160   Fire Protection

This industry comprises government establishments primarily engaged in firefighting and other related fire protection activities. Government establishments providing combined fire protection and ambulance or rescue services are classified in this industry.

Cross-References.   Establishments primarily engaged in--

- Forest firefighting--are classified in Industry 115310, Support Activities for Forestry;
- Providing combined police and fire protection services--are classified in Industry 922120, Police Protection;
- Providing firefighting services as a commercial activity--are classified in Industry 561990, All Other Support Services; and
- Providing ambulance services without fire protection service--are classified in Industry 621910, Ambulance Services.

92219   Other Justice, Public Order, and Safety Activities
See industry description for 922190.

922190   Other Justice, Public Order, and Safety Activities

This industry comprises government establishments primarily engaged in public order and safety (except courts, police protection, legal counsel and prosecution, correctional institutions, parole offices, probation offices, pardon boards, and fire protection). These establishments include the general administration of public order and safety programs. Government establishments responsible for the collection of statistics on public safety are included in this industry.

T—Canadian, Mexican, and United States industries are comparable.

Illustrative Examples:

Consumer product safety commissions, public
administration
Emergency planning and management offices,
government

Disaster preparedness and management offices,
government
Public safety bureaus and statistics centers,
government

Cross-References.   Government establishments primarily engaged in--

- Serving as civilian courts of law (except American Indian and Alaska Native tribal courts)--are classified in Industry 922110, Courts;
- Criminal and civil law enforcement, police, traffic safety, and similar activities related to the enforcement of law--are classified in Industry 922120, Police Protection;
- Providing legal counsel to or prosecution services for their governments--are classified in Industry 922130, Legal Counsel and Prosecution;
- The confinement, correction, and rehabilitation of adult and juvenile offenders sentenced by a court--are classified in Industry 922140, Correctional Institutions;
- Judicially administering probation offices, parole offices and boards, and pardon boards--are classified in Industry 922150, Parole Offices and Probation Offices; and
- Firefighting and other related fire protection activities--are classified in Industry 922160, Fire Protection.

923   Administration of Human Resource Programs

The Administration of Human Resource Programs subsector groups government establishments primarily engaged in the administration of human resource programs.

9231   Administration of Human Resource Programs

92311   Administration of Education Programs
See industry description for 923110.

923110   Administration of Education Programs

This industry comprises government establishments primarily engaged in the central coordination, planning, supervision, and administration of funds, policies, intergovernmental activities, statistical reports and data collection, and centralized programs for educational administration. Government scholarship programs are included in this industry.

Illustrative Examples:

Education offices, nonoperating, public
administration
State education departments

Education statistics centers, government
University regents or boards, government

Cross-References.

Schools and local school boards are classified in Subsector 611, Educational Services.

92312   Administration of Public Health Programs
See industry description for 923120.

923120   Administration of Public Health Programs

This industry comprises government establishments primarily engaged in the planning, administration, and coordination of public health programs and services, including environmental health activities, mental health,

---

T—Canadian, Mexican, and United States industries are comparable.

categorical health programs, health statistics, and immunization services. Government establishments primarily engaged in conducting public health-related inspections are included in this industry.

Illustrative Examples:

Communicable disease program administration, public administration
Mental health program administration, public administration

Coroners' offices, public administration
Public health program administration, nonoperating, public administration
Health program administration, public administration

Cross-References.   Government establishments primarily engaged in--

- Operating hospitals (i.e., government or military)--are classified in Subsector 622, Hospitals;
- Providing health care in a clinical setting (i.e., military or government clinics)--are classified in Subsector 621, Ambulatory Health Care Services; and
- Inspecting food, plants, animals, and other agriculture products--are classified in Industry 926140, Regulation of Agricultural Marketing and Commodities.

92313   Administration of Human Resource Programs (except Education, Public Health, and Veterans' Affairs Programs)
See industry description for 923130.

923130 Administration of Human Resource Programs (except Education, Public Health, and Veterans' Affairs Programs)

  This industry comprises government establishments primarily engaged in the planning, administration, and coordination of programs for public assistance, social work, and welfare activities. The administration of Social Security, disability insurance, Medicare, unemployment insurance, and workers' compensation programs are included in this industry.

Cross-References.   Government establishments primarily engaged in--

- Administering veterans' programs--are classified in Industry 923140, Administration of Veterans' Affairs;
- Operating state employment job service offices--are classified in U.S. Industry 561311, Employment Placement Agencies; and
- Operating programs for public assistance, social work, and welfare--are classified in Subsector 624, Social Assistance.

92314   Administration of Veterans' Affairs
See industry description for 923140.

923140 Administration of Veterans' Affairs

  This industry comprises government establishments primarily engaged in the administration of programs of assistance, training, counseling, and other services to veterans and their dependents, heirs, or survivors. Included in this industry are Veterans' Affairs offices that maintain liaison and coordinate activities with other service organizations and governmental agencies.

Cross-References.

- Government establishments operating veterans' hospitals are classified in Subsector 622, Hospitals;
- Establishments providing veterans' insurance are classified in Subsector 524, Insurance Carriers and Related Activities; and
- Establishments operating civic and social organizations for veterans are classified in Industry 813410, Civic and Social Organizations.

T—Canadian, Mexican, and United States industries are comparable.

924   Administration of Environmental Quality Programs

The Administration of Environmental Quality Programs subsector groups government establishments primarily engaged in the administration of environmental quality.

9241   Administration of Environmental Quality Programs

92411   Administration of Air and Water Resource and Solid Waste Management Programs
See industry description for 924110.

924110 Administration of Air and Water Resource and Solid Waste Management Programs

This industry comprises government establishments primarily engaged in one or more of the following: (1) the administration, regulation, and enforcement of air and water resource programs; (2) the administration and regulation of solid waste management programs; (3) the administration and regulation of water and air pollution control and prevention programs; (4) the administration and regulation of flood control programs; (5) the administration and regulation of drainage development and water resource consumption programs; (6) the administration and regulation of toxic waste removal and cleanup programs; and (7) coordination of these activities at intergovernmental levels.

Illustrative Examples:

Environmental protection program administration, public administration

Waste management program (except sanitation districts) administration, public administration

Pollution control program administration, public administration

Water control and quality program administration, public administration

Cross-References.   Government establishments primarily engaged in--

- Operating water and irrigation systems--are classified in Industry 221310, Water Supply and Irrigation Systems;
- Administering sanitation districts--are classified in Industry 926130, Regulation and Administration of Communications, Electric, Gas, and Other Utilities;
- Operating sewage treatment facilities--are classified in Industry 221320, Sewage Treatment Facilities; and
- Providing waste collection, treatment, disposal, and/or remediation--are classified in Subsector 562, Waste Management and Remediation Services.

92412   Administration of Conservation Programs
See industry description for 924120.

924120 Administration of Conservation Programs

This industry comprises government establishments primarily engaged in the administration, regulation, supervision, and control of land use, including recreational areas; conservation and preservation of natural resources; erosion control; geological survey program administration; weather forecasting program administration; and the administration and protection of publicly and privately owned forest lands. Government establishments responsible for planning, management, regulation, and conservation of game, fish, and wildlife populations, including wildlife management areas and field stations; and other administrative matters relating to the protection of fish, game, and wildlife are included in this industry.

Cross-References.   Government establishments primarily engaged in--

- Operating parks--are classified in Industry 712190, Nature Parks and Other Similar Institutions;
- Operating forest property--are classified in Subsector 113, Forestry and Logging;

T—Canadian, Mexican, and United States industries are comparable.

- Geophysical surveying and/or mapping--are classified in Industry 541360, Geophysical Surveying and Mapping Services;
- Surveying and/or mapping (except geophysical)--are classified in Industry 541370, Surveying and Mapping (except Geophysical) Services;
- Weather forecasting--are classified in Industry 541990, All Other Professional, Scientific, and Technical Services;
- Operating fish and game preserves--are classified in Industry 712130, Zoos and Botanical Gardens; and
- Serving as urban planning commissions--are classified in Industry 925120, Administration of Urban Planning and Community and Rural Development.

925   Administration of Housing Programs, Urban Planning, and Community Development

The Administration of Housing Programs, Urban Planning, and Community Development subsector groups government establishments primarily engaged in the administration of housing, urban planning, and community development.

9251   Administration of Housing Programs, Urban Planning, and Community Development

92511   Administration of Housing Programs
See industry description for 925110.

925110 Administration of Housing Programs

This industry comprises government establishments primarily engaged in the administration and planning of housing programs.

Cross-References.   Government establishments primarily engaged in--

- Operating government rental housing--are classified in Subsector 531, Real Estate;
- Conducting building inspections and enforcing building codes and standards--are classified in Industry 926150, Regulation, Licensing, and Inspection of Miscellaneous Commercial Sectors; and
- Buying, pooling, and repackaging mortgages or home loans for sale to others on the secondary market--are classified in U.S. Industry 522294, Secondary Market Financing.

92512   Administration of Urban Planning and Community and Rural Development
See industry description for 925120.

925120 Administration of Urban Planning and Community and Rural Development

This industry comprises government establishments primarily engaged in the administration and planning of the development of urban and rural areas. Included in this industry are government zoning boards and commissions.

Illustrative Examples:

Land redevelopment agencies, government
Regional planning and development program administration, public administration

Urban planning commissions, government
Zoning boards and commissions, public administration

926   Administration of Economic Programs

This subsector comprises government establishments primarily engaged in the administration of economic programs.

T—Canadian, Mexican, and United States industries are comparable.

9261   Administration of Economic Programs

92611   Administration of General Economic Programs
See industry description for 926110.

926110 Administration of General Economic Programs

   This industry comprises government establishments primarily engaged in the administration, promotion, and development of economic resources, including business, industry, and tourism. Included in this industry are government establishments responsible for the development of general statistical data and analyses and promotion of the general economic well-being of the governed area.

Illustrative Examples:

Consumer protection offices, public administration
Small business development agencies, public administration
Economic development agencies, government

Trade commissions, government
General economics statistical agencies, public administration

92612   Regulation and Administration of Transportation Programs
See industry description for 926120.

926120 Regulation and Administration of Transportation Programs

   This industry comprises government establishments primarily engaged in the administration, regulation, licensing, planning, inspection, and investigation of transportation services and facilities. Included in this industry are government establishments responsible for motor vehicle and operator licensing, the Coast Guard (except the Coast Guard Academy), and parking authorities.

Cross-References.   Government establishments primarily engaged in--

- Operating airports, railroads, depots, ports, toll roads and bridges, and other transportation facilities and systems--are classified in Sector 48-49, Transportation and Warehousing;
- Operating parking lots and parking garages--are classified in Industry 812930, Parking Lots and Garages;
- Operating automobile safety inspection and emission testing facilities--are classified in Industry Group 8111, Automotive Repair and Maintenance;
- Building and/or maintaining roads and highways--are classified in Industry 237310, Highway, Street, and Bridge Construction;
- Providing air traffic control services--are classified in U.S. Industry 488111, Air Traffic Control; and
- Operating weigh stations--are classified in Industry 488490, Other Support Activities for Road Transportation.

92613   Regulation and Administration of Communications, Electric, Gas, and Other Utilities
See industry description for 926130.

926130 Regulation and Administration of Communications, Electric, Gas, and Other Utilities

   This industry comprises government establishments primarily engaged in the administration, regulation, licensing, and inspection of utilities, such as communications, electric power (including fossil, nuclear, solar, water, and wind), gas and water supply, and sewerage.

Cross-References.

   Government establishments primarily engaged in operating utilities are classified in Subsector 221, Utilities.

T—Canadian, Mexican, and United States industries are comparable.

92614   Regulation of Agricultural Marketing and Commodities
See industry description for 926140.

926140   Regulation of Agricultural Marketing and Commodities

This industry comprises government establishments primarily engaged in the planning, administration, and coordination of agricultural programs for production, marketing, and utilization, including educational and promotional activities. Included in this industry are government establishments responsible for regulating and controlling the grading and inspection of food, plants, animals, and other agricultural products.

Cross-References.   Government establishments primarily engaged in--

- Administering programs for developing economic data about agriculture and trade in agricultural products--are classified in Industry 926110, Administration of General Economic Programs;
- Administering programs for the conservation of natural resources--are classified in Industry Group 9241, Administration of Environmental Quality Programs; and
- Administering food stamp programs--are classified in Industry 923130, Administration of Human Resource Programs (except Education, Public Health, and Veterans' Affairs Programs).

92615   Regulation, Licensing, and Inspection of Miscellaneous Commercial Sectors
See industry description for 926150.

926150   Regulation, Licensing, and Inspection of Miscellaneous Commercial Sectors

This industry comprises government establishments primarily engaged in the regulation, licensing, and inspection of commercial sectors, such as retail trade, professional occupations, manufacturing, mining, construction, and services. Included in this industry are government establishments maintaining physical standards, regulating hazardous conditions not elsewhere classified, and enforcing alcoholic beverage control regulations.

Illustrative Examples:

Alcoholic beverage control boards, public administration
Labor management negotiations boards, government
Banking regulatory agencies, public administration
Licensing and permit issuance for business operations, government

Building inspections, government
Licensing and permit issuance for professional occupations, government
Insurance commissions, government
Securities regulation commissions, public administration

Cross-References.   Government establishments primarily engaged in--

- Regulating, administering, and inspecting transportation services and facilities--are classified in Industry 926120, Regulation and Administration of Transportation Programs; and
- Regulating, administering, and inspecting communications, electric, gas, and other utilities--are classified in Industry 926130, Regulation and Administration of Communications, Electric, Gas, and Other Utilities.

927   Space Research and Technology

This subsector comprises government establishments that conduct space research.

9271   Space Research and Technology

92711   Space Research and Technology
See industry description for 927110.

T—Canadian, Mexican, and United States industries are comparable.

927110 Space Research and Technology

This industry comprises government establishments primarily engaged in the administration and operations of space flights, space research, and space exploration. Included in this industry are government establishments operating space flight centers.

Cross-References.

- Private establishments primarily engaged in providing space freight transportation are classified in U.S. Industry 481212, Nonscheduled Chartered Freight Air Transportation;
- Government establishments primarily engaged in manufacturing aerospace vehicles and parts are classified in Industry 33641, Aerospace Product and Parts Manufacturing; and
- Government establishments primarily engaged in manufacturing space satellites are classified in Industry 334220, Radio and Television Broadcasting and Wireless Communications Equipment Manufacturing.

928 National Security and International Affairs

This subsector comprises government establishments primarily engaged in national security and international affairs.

9281 National Security and International Affairs

92811 National Security
See industry description for 928110.

928110 National Security

This industry comprises government establishments of the Armed Forces, including the National Guard, primarily engaged in national security and related activities.

Illustrative Examples:

Air Force	Marine Corps
Military police	National Guard
Army	Military courts
Military training schools (except military service academies)	Navy

Cross-References.   Government establishments primarily engaged in--

- Operating college level military service academies--are classified in Industry 611310, Colleges, Universities, and Professional Schools; and
- Regulating and administering water transportation, such as the U.S. Coast Guard and the Merchant Marine--are classified in Industry 926120, Regulation and Administration of Transportation Programs.

92812 International Affairs
See industry description for 928120.

928120 International Affairs

This industry comprises establishments of U.S. and foreign governments primarily engaged in international affairs and programs relating to other nations and peoples.

T—Canadian, Mexican, and United States industries are comparable.

census.gov/naics

Cross-References.

- Private-sector trade associations and councils are classified in Industry 813910, Business Associations; and
- Government establishments administering international trade, such as trade commissions and councils, are classified in Industry 926110, Administration of General Economic Programs.

T—Canadian, Mexican, and United States industries are comparable.

Part II
List of Short Titles

List of Short Titles

Standard Short Titles for 2017 NAICS United States are shown below. They have been created for the use of those who find that space limitations preclude the use of the full title for the dissemination of data classified to NAICS. The adoption of these titles is recommended in all cases when the full title cannot be used.

The standard short titles are limited to 45 spaces. If the official full title falls within 45 spaces, it remains unchanged.

Note: For definitions of abbreviations and acronyms see page 639.

Code	Short title	Code	Short title
11	**AGRICULTURE, FORESTRY, FISHING AND HUNTING**	111920	Cotton farming
		11193	Sugarcane farming
		111930	Sugarcane farming
111	**Crop production**	11194	Hay farming
		111940	Hay farming
1111	Oilseed and grain farming	11199	All other crop farming
11111	Soybean farming	111991	Sugar beet farming
111110	Soybean farming	111992	Peanut farming
11112	Oilseed, except soybean, farming	111998	All other miscellaneous crop farming
111120	Oilseed, except soybean, farming		
11113	Dry pea and bean farming	**112**	**Animal production and aquaculture**
111130	Dry pea and bean farming		
11114	Wheat farming	1121	Cattle ranching and farming
111140	Wheat farming	11211	Beef cattle ranching, farming, and feedlots
11115	Corn farming		
111150	Corn farming	112111	Beef cattle ranching and farming
11116	Rice farming	112112	Cattle feedlots
111160	Rice farming	11212	Dairy cattle and milk production
11119	Other grain farming	112120	Dairy cattle and milk production
111191	Oilseed and grain combination farming	11213	Dual-purpose cattle ranching and farming
111199	All other grain farming		
1112	Vegetable and melon farming	112130	Dual-purpose cattle ranching and farming
11121	Vegetable and melon farming		
111211	Potato farming	1122	Hog and pig farming
111219	Other vegetable and melon farming	11221	Hog and pig farming
1113	Fruit and tree nut farming	112210	Hog and pig farming
11131	Orange groves	1123	Poultry and egg production
111310	Orange groves	11231	Chicken egg production
11132	Citrus, except orange, groves	112310	Chicken egg production
111320	Citrus, except orange, groves	11232	Broilers and meat type chicken production
11133	Noncitrus fruit and tree nut farming		
111331	Apple orchards	112320	Broilers and meat type chicken production
111332	Grape vineyards		
111333	Strawberry farming	11233	Turkey production
111334	Berry, except strawberry, farming	112330	Turkey production
111335	Tree nut farming	11234	Poultry hatcheries
111336	Fruit and tree nut combination farming	112340	Poultry hatcheries
111339	Other noncitrus fruit farming	11239	Other poultry production
1114	Greenhouse and nursery production	112390	Other poultry production
11141	Food crops grown under cover	1124	Sheep and goat farming
111411	Mushroom production	11241	Sheep farming
111419	Other food crops grown under cover	112410	Sheep farming
11142	Nursery and floriculture production	11242	Goat farming
111421	Nursery and tree production	112420	Goat farming
111422	Floriculture production	1125	Aquaculture
1119	Other crop farming	11251	Aquaculture
11191	Tobacco farming	112511	Finfish farming and fish hatcheries
111910	Tobacco farming	112512	Shellfish farming
11192	Cotton farming	112519	Other aquaculture

Note: For definitions of abbreviations and acronyms see page 639.

1129	Other animal production
11291	Apiculture
112910	Apiculture
11292	Horses and other equine production
112920	Horses and other equine production
11293	Fur-bearing animal and rabbit production
112930	Fur-bearing animal and rabbit production
11299	All other animal production
112990	All other animal production

113 Forestry and logging

1131	Timber tract operations
11311	Timber tract operations
113110	Timber tract operations
1132	Forest nursery and gathering forest products
11321	Forest nursery and gathering forest products
113210	Forest nursery and gathering forest products
1133	Logging
11331	Logging
113310	Logging

114 Fishing, hunting and trapping

1141	Fishing
11411	Fishing
114111	Finfish fishing
114112	Shellfish fishing
114119	Other marine fishing
1142	Hunting and trapping
11421	Hunting and trapping
114210	Hunting and trapping

115 Agriculture and forestry support activities

1151	Support activities for crop production
11511	Support activities for crop production
115111	Cotton ginning
115112	Soil preparation, planting, and cultivating
115113	Crop harvesting, primarily by machine
115114	Other postharvest crop activities
115115	Farm labor contractors and crew leaders
115116	Farm management services

1152	Support activities for animal production
11521	Support activities for animal production
115210	Support activities for animal production
1153	Support activities for forestry
11531	Support activities for forestry
115310	Support activities for forestry

21 MINING, QUARRYING, AND OIL AND GAS EXTRACTION

211 Oil and gas extraction

2111	Oil and gas extraction
21112	Crude petroleum extraction
211120	Crude petroleum extraction
21113	Natural gas extraction
211130	Natural gas extraction

212 Mining, except oil and gas

2121	Coal mining
21211	Coal mining
212111	Bituminous coal and lignite surface mining
212112	Bituminous coal underground mining
212113	Anthracite mining
2122	Metal ore mining
21221	Iron ore mining
212210	Iron ore mining
21222	Gold ore and silver ore mining
212221	Gold ore mining
212222	Silver ore mining
21223	Copper, nickel, lead, and zinc mining
212230	Copper, nickel, lead, and zinc mining
21229	Other metal ore mining
212291	Uranium-radium-vanadium ore mining
212299	All other metal ore mining
2123	Nonmetallic mineral mining and quarrying
21231	Stone mining and quarrying
212311	Dimension stone mining and quarrying
212312	Crushed and broken limestone mining
212313	Crushed and broken granite mining
212319	Other crushed and broken stone mining
21232	Sand, gravel, clay, and refractory mining
212321	Construction sand and gravel mining
212322	Industrial sand mining

Note: For definitions of abbreviations and acronyms see page 639.

212324	Kaolin and ball clay mining
212325	Clay, ceramic, and refractory minerals mining
21239	Other nonmetallic mineral mining
212391	Potash, soda, and borate mineral mining
212392	Phosphate rock mining
212393	Other chemical and fertilizer mineral mining
212399	All other nonmetallic mineral mining

213   Support activities for mining

2131	Support activities for mining
21311	Support activities for mining
213111	Drilling oil and gas wells
213112	Support activities for oil and gas operations
213113	Support activities for coal mining
213114	Support activities for metal mining
213115	Support activities for nonmetallic minerals

22   UTILITIES

221   Utilities

2211	Power generation and supply
22111	Electric power generation
221111	Hydroelectric power generation
221112	Fossil fuel electric power generation
221113	Nuclear electric power generation
221114	Solar electric power generation
221115	Wind electric power generation
221116	Geothermal electric power generation
221117	Biomass electric power generation
221118	Other electric power generation
22112	Electric power transmission and distribution
221121	Electric bulk power transmission and control
221122	Electric power distribution
2212	Natural gas distribution
22121	Natural gas distribution
221210	Natural gas distribution
2213	Water, sewage and other systems
22131	Water supply and irrigation systems
221310	Water supply and irrigation systems
22132	Sewage treatment facilities
221320	Sewage treatment facilities
22133	Steam and air-conditioning supply

221330	Steam and air-conditioning supply

23   CONSTRUCTION

236   Construction of buildings

2361	Residential building construction
23611	Residential building construction
236115	New single-family general contractors
236116	New multifamily general contractors
236117	New housing for-sale builders
236118	Residential remodelers
2362	Nonresidential building construction
23621	Industrial building construction
236210	Industrial building construction
23622	Commercial building construction
236220	Commercial building construction

237   Heavy and civil engineering construction

2371	Utility system construction
23711	Water and sewer system construction
237110	Water and sewer system construction
23712	Oil and gas pipeline construction
237120	Oil and gas pipeline construction
23713	Power and communication system construction
237130	Power and communication system construction
2372	Land subdivision
23721	Land subdivision
237210	Land subdivision
2373	Highway, street, and bridge construction
23731	Highway, street, and bridge construction
237310	Highway, street, and bridge construction
2379	Other heavy construction
23799	Other heavy construction
237990	Other heavy construction

238   Specialty trade contractors

2381	Building foundation and exterior contractors
23811	Poured concrete structure contractors
238110	Poured concrete structure contractors
23812	Steel and precast concrete contractors
238120	Steel and precast concrete contractors

Note: For definitions of abbreviations and acronyms see page 639.

census.gov/naics

23813	Framing contractors
238130	Framing contractors
23814	Masonry contractors
238140	Masonry contractors
23815	Glass and glazing contractors
238150	Glass and glazing contractors
23816	Roofing contractors
238160	Roofing contractors
23817	Siding contractors
238170	Siding contractors
23819	Other building exterior contractors
238190	Other building exterior contractors
2382	Building equipment contractors
23821	Electrical and wiring contractors
238210	Electrical and wiring contractors
23822	Plumbing and HVAC contractors
238220	Plumbing and HVAC contractors
23829	Other building equipment contractors
238290	Other building equipment contractors
2383	Building finishing contractors
23831	Drywall and insulation contractors
238310	Drywall and insulation contractors
23832	Painting and wall covering contractors
238320	Painting and wall covering contractors
23833	Flooring contractors
238330	Flooring contractors
23834	Tile and terrazzo contractors
238340	Tile and terrazzo contractors
23835	Finish carpentry contractors
238350	Finish carpentry contractors
23839	Other building finishing contractors
238390	Other building finishing contractors
2389	Other specialty trade contractors
23891	Site preparation contractors
238910	Site preparation contractors
23899	All other specialty trade contractors
238990	All other specialty trade contractors

31-33   MANUFACTURING

311   Food manufacturing

3111	Animal food manufacturing
31111	Animal food manufacturing
311111	Dog and cat food manufacturing
311119	Other animal food manufacturing
3112	Grain and oilseed milling
31121	Flour milling and malt manufacturing
311211	Flour milling
311212	Rice milling
311213	Malt manufacturing

31122	Starch and vegetable oil manufacturing
311221	Wet corn milling
311224	Soybean and other oilseed processing
311225	Fats and oils refining and blending
31123	Breakfast cereal manufacturing
311230	Breakfast cereal manufacturing
3113	Sugar and confectionery product manufacturing
31131	Sugar manufacturing
311313	Beet sugar manufacturing
311314	Cane sugar manufacturing
31134	Nonchocolate confectionery manufacturing
311340	Nonchocolate confectionery manufacturing
31135	Chocolate and confectionery manufacturing
311351	Chocolate and confectionery mfg. from cacao
311352	Confectionery mfg. from purchased chocolate
3114	Fruit and vegetable preserving and specialty
31141	Frozen food manufacturing
311411	Frozen fruit and vegetable manufacturing
311412	Frozen specialty food manufacturing
31142	Fruit and vegetable canning and drying
311421	Fruit and vegetable canning
311422	Specialty canning
311423	Dried and dehydrated food manufacturing
3115	Dairy product manufacturing
31151	Dairy product, except frozen, manufacturing
311511	Fluid milk manufacturing
311512	Creamery butter manufacturing
311513	Cheese manufacturing
311514	Dry, condensed, and evaporated dairy products
31152	Ice cream and frozen dessert manufacturing
311520	Ice cream and frozen dessert manufacturing
3116	Animal slaughtering and processing
31161	Animal slaughtering and processing
311611	Animal, except poultry, slaughtering
311612	Meat processed from carcasses
311613	Rendering and meat byproduct processing
311615	Poultry processing

Note: For definitions of abbreviations and acronyms see page 639.

3117	Seafood product preparation and packaging
31171	Seafood product preparation and packaging
311710	Seafood product preparation and packaging
3118	Bakeries and tortilla manufacturing
31181	Bread and bakery product manufacturing
311811	Retail bakeries
311812	Commercial bakeries
311813	Frozen cakes and other pastries manufacturing
31182	Cookie, cracker, and pasta manufacturing
311821	Cookie and cracker manufacturing
311824	Pasta, dough and mixes from purchased flour
31183	Tortilla manufacturing
311830	Tortilla manufacturing
3119	Other food manufacturing
31191	Snack food manufacturing
311911	Roasted nuts and peanut butter manufacturing
311919	Other snack food manufacturing
31192	Coffee and tea manufacturing
311920	Coffee and tea manufacturing
31193	Flavoring syrup and concentrate manufacturing
311930	Flavoring syrup and concentrate manufacturing
31194	Seasoning and dressing manufacturing
311941	Mayonnaise, dressing, and sauce manufacturing
311942	Spice and extract manufacturing
31199	All other food manufacturing
311991	Perishable prepared food manufacturing
311999	All other miscellaneous food manufacturing

312	**Beverage and tobacco product manufacturing**
3121	Beverage manufacturing
31211	Soft drink and ice manufacturing
312111	Soft drink manufacturing
312112	Bottled water manufacturing
312113	Ice manufacturing
31212	Breweries
312120	Breweries

31213	Wineries
312130	Wineries
31214	Distilleries
312140	Distilleries
3122	Tobacco manufacturing
31223	Tobacco manufacturing
312230	Tobacco manufacturing

313	**Textile mills**
3131	Fiber, yarn, and thread mills
31311	Fiber, yarn, and thread mills
313110	Fiber, yarn, and thread mills
3132	Fabric mills
31321	Broadwoven fabric mills
313210	Broadwoven fabric mills
31322	Narrow fabric mills and schiffli embroidery
313220	Narrow fabric mills and schiffli embroidery
31323	Nonwoven fabric mills
313230	Nonwoven fabric mills
31324	Knit fabric mills
313240	Knit fabric mills
3133	Textile and fabric finishing mills
31331	Textile and fabric finishing mills
313310	Textile and fabric finishing mills
31332	Fabric coating mills
313320	Fabric coating mills

314	**Textile product mills**
3141	Textile furnishings mills
31411	Carpet and rug mills
314110	Carpet and rug mills
31412	Curtain and linen mills
314120	Curtain and linen mills
3149	Other textile product mills
31491	Textile bag and canvas mills
314910	Textile bag and canvas mills
31499	All other textile product mills
314994	Rope, twine, tire cord and tire fabric mills
314999	All other miscellaneous textile product mills

315	**Apparel manufacturing**
3151	Apparel knitting mills
31511	Hosiery and sock mills
315110	Hosiery and sock mills

Note: For definitions of abbreviations and acronyms see page 639.

31519	Other apparel knitting mills
315190	Other apparel knitting mills
3152	Cut and sew apparel manufacturing
31521	Cut and sew apparel contractors
315210	Cut and sew apparel contractors
31522	Men's and boys' cut and sew apparel mfg
315220	Men's and boys' cut and sew apparel mfg
31524	Women's, girls', infants' cut-sew apparel mfg
315240	Women's, girls', infants' cut-sew apparel mfg
31528	Other cut and sew apparel manufacturing
315280	Other cut and sew apparel manufacturing
3159	Accessories and other apparel manufacturing
31599	Accessories and other apparel manufacturing
315990	Accessories and other apparel manufacturing

316   **Leather and allied product manufacturing**

3161	Leather and hide tanning and finishing
31611	Leather and hide tanning and finishing
316110	Leather and hide tanning and finishing
3162	Footwear manufacturing
31621	Footwear manufacturing
316210	Footwear manufacturing
3169	Other leather product manufacturing
31699	Other leather product manufacturing
316992	Women's handbag and purse manufacturing
316998	All other leather and allied good mfg.

321   **Wood product manufacturing**

3211	Sawmills and wood preservation
32111	Sawmills and wood preservation
321113	Sawmills
321114	Wood preservation
3212	Plywood and engineered wood product mfg.
32121	Plywood and engineered wood product mfg.
321211	Hardwood veneer and plywood manufacturing

321212	Softwood veneer and plywood manufacturing
321213	Engineered wood member manufacturing
321214	Truss manufacturing
321219	Reconstituted wood product manufacturing
3219	Other wood product manufacturing
32191	Millwork
321911	Wood window and door manufacturing
321912	Cut stock, resawing lumber, and planing
321918	Other millwork, including flooring
32192	Wood container and pallet manufacturing
321920	Wood container and pallet manufacturing
32199	All other wood product manufacturing
321991	Manufactured home, mobile home, manufacturing
321992	Prefabricated wood building manufacturing
321999	Miscellaneous wood product manufacturing

322   **Paper manufacturing**

3221	Pulp, paper, and paperboard mills
32211	Pulp mills
322110	Pulp mills
32212	Paper mills
322121	Paper, except newsprint, mills
322122	Newsprint mills
32213	Paperboard mills
322130	Paperboard mills
3222	Converted paper product manufacturing
32221	Paperboard container manufacturing
322211	Corrugated and solid fiber box manufacturing
322212	Folding paperboard box manufacturing
322219	Other paperboard container manufacturing
32222	Paper bag and coated and treated paper mfg.
322220	Paper bag and coated and treated paper mfg.
32223	Stationery product manufacturing
322230	Stationery product manufacturing
32229	Other converted paper product manufacturing

Note: For definitions of abbreviations and acronyms see page 639.

322291	Sanitary paper product manufacturing
322299	All other converted paper product mfg.

323   Printing and related support activities

3231	Printing and related support activities
32311	Printing
323111	Commercial printing, except screen and books
323113	Commercial screen printing
323117	Books printing
32312	Support activities for printing
323120	Support activities for printing

324   Petroleum and coal products manufacturing

3241	Petroleum and coal products manufacturing
32411	Petroleum refineries
324110	Petroleum refineries
32412	Asphalt paving and roofing materials mfg.
324121	Asphalt paving mixture and block mfg.
324122	Asphalt shingle and coating materials mfg.
32419	Other petroleum and coal products mfg.
324191	Petroleum lubricating oil and grease mfg.
324199	All other petroleum and coal products mfg.

325   Chemical manufacturing

3251	Basic chemical manufacturing
32511	Petrochemical manufacturing
325110	Petrochemical manufacturing
32512	Industrial gas manufacturing
325120	Industrial gas manufacturing
32513	Synthetic dye and pigment manufacturing
325130	Synthetic dye and pigment manufacturing
32518	Other basic inorganic chemical manufacturing
325180	Other basic inorganic chemical manufacturing
32519	Other basic organic chemical manufacturing

325193	Ethyl alcohol manufacturing
325194	Cyclic crude, intermediate, wood chemical mfg
325199	All other basic organic chemical mfg.
3252	Resin, rubber, and artificial fibers mfg.
32521	Resin and synthetic rubber manufacturing
325211	Plastics material and resin manufacturing
325212	Synthetic rubber manufacturing
32522	Artificial fibers and filaments manufacturing
325220	Artificial fibers and filaments manufacturing
3253	Agricultural chemical manufacturing
32531	Fertilizer manufacturing
325311	Nitrogenous fertilizer manufacturing
325312	Phosphatic fertilizer manufacturing
325314	Fertilizer, mixing only, manufacturing
32532	Pesticide and other ag. chemical mfg.
325320	Pesticide and other ag. chemical mfg.
3254	Pharmaceutical and medicine manufacturing
32541	Pharmaceutical and medicine manufacturing
325411	Medicinal and botanical manufacturing
325412	Pharmaceutical preparation manufacturing
325413	In-vitro diagnostic substance manufacturing
325414	Other biological product manufacturing
3255	Paint, coating, and adhesive manufacturing
32551	Paint and coating manufacturing
325510	Paint and coating manufacturing
32552	Adhesive manufacturing
325520	Adhesive manufacturing
3256	Soap, cleaning compound, and toiletry mfg.
32561	Soap and cleaning compound manufacturing
325611	Soap and other detergent manufacturing
325612	Polish and other sanitation good mfg.
325613	Surface active agent manufacturing
32562	Toilet preparation manufacturing
325620	Toilet preparation manufacturing
3259	Other chemical product and preparation mfg.
32591	Printing ink manufacturing

Note: For definitions of abbreviations and acronyms see page 639.

325910	Printing ink manufacturing	32622	Rubber and plastics hose and belting mfg.
32592	Explosives manufacturing		
325920	Explosives manufacturing	326220	Rubber and plastics hose and belting mfg.
32599	All other chemical preparation manufacturing	32629	Other rubber product manufacturing
325991	Custom compounding of purchased resins	326291	Rubber product mfg. for mechanical use
325992	Photographic film and chemical manufacturing	326299	All other rubber product manufacturing
325998	Other miscellaneous chemical product mfg.	**327**	**Nonmetallic mineral product manufacturing**
326	**Plastics and rubber products manufacturing**	3271	Clay product and refractory manufacturing
		32711	Pottery, ceramics, and plumbing fixture mfg.
3261	Plastics product manufacturing		
32611	Plastics packaging materials, film and sheet	327110	Pottery, ceramics, and plumbing fixture mfg.
326111	Plastics bag and pouch manufacturing	32712	Clay building material and refractories mfg.
326112	Plastics packaging film and sheet mfg.		
326113	Nonpackaging plastics film and sheet mfg.	327120	Clay building material and refractories mfg.
32612	Plastics pipe, fittings, and profile shapes	3272	Glass and glass product manufacturing
		32721	Glass and glass product manufacturing
326121	Unlaminated plastics profile shape mfg.	327211	Flat glass manufacturing
		327212	Other pressed and blown glass and glassware
326122	Plastics pipe and pipe fitting manufacturing		
		327213	Glass container manufacturing
32613	Laminated plastics plate, sheet, and shapes	327215	Glass product mfg. made of purchased glass
326130	Laminated plastics plate, sheet, and shapes	3273	Cement and concrete product manufacturing
32614	Polystyrene foam product manufacturing	32731	Cement manufacturing
		327310	Cement manufacturing
326140	Polystyrene foam product manufacturing	32732	Ready-mix concrete manufacturing
		327320	Ready-mix concrete manufacturing
32615	Urethane and other foam product manufacturing	32733	Concrete pipe, brick, and block manufacturing
326150	Urethane and other foam product manufacturing	327331	Concrete block and brick manufacturing
32616	Plastics bottle manufacturing	327332	Concrete pipe manufacturing
326160	Plastics bottle manufacturing	32739	Other concrete product manufacturing
32619	Other plastics product manufacturing	327390	Other concrete product manufacturing
326191	Plastics plumbing fixture manufacturing	3274	Lime and gypsum product manufacturing
326199	All other plastics product manufacturing	32741	Lime manufacturing
		327410	Lime manufacturing
3262	Rubber product manufacturing	32742	Gypsum product manufacturing
32621	Tire manufacturing	327420	Gypsum product manufacturing
326211	Tire manufacturing, except retreading	3279	Other nonmetallic mineral products
326212	Tire retreading	32791	Abrasive product manufacturing

Note: For definitions of abbreviations and acronyms see page 639.

327910	Abrasive product manufacturing
32799	All other nonmetallic mineral products mfg.
327991	Cut stone and stone product manufacturing
327992	Ground or treated minerals and earths mfg.
327993	Mineral wool manufacturing
327999	Miscellaneous nonmetallic mineral products

331   Primary metal manufacturing

3311	Iron and steel mills and ferroalloy mfg.
33111	Iron and steel mills and ferroalloy mfg.
331110	Iron and steel mills and ferroalloy mfg.
3312	Steel product mfg. from purchased steel
33121	Iron, steel pipe and tube from purchase steel
331210	Iron, steel pipe and tube from purchase steel
33122	Rolling and drawing of purchased steel
331221	Rolled steel shape manufacturing
331222	Steel wire drawing
3313	Alumina and aluminum production
33131	Alumina and aluminum production
331313	Alumina refining, primary aluminum production
331314	Secondary smelting and alloying of aluminum
331315	Aluminum sheet, plate, and foil manufacturing
331318	Other aluminum rolling, drawing and extruding
3314	Other nonferrous metal production
33141	Other nonferrous metal production
331410	Other nonferrous metal production
33142	Rolled, drawn, extruded, and alloyed copper
331420	Rolled, drawn, extruded, and alloyed copper
33149	Nonferrous metal, except Cu and Al, shaping
331491	Nonferrous metal, except Cu and Al, shaping
331492	Secondary processing of other nonferrous
3315	Foundries
33151	Ferrous metal foundries
331511	Iron foundries

331512	Steel investment foundries
331513	Steel foundries, except investment
33152	Nonferrous metal foundries
331523	Nonferrous metal die-casting foundries
331524	Aluminum foundries, except die-casting
331529	Other nonferrous foundries, exc. die-casting

332   Fabricated metal product manufacturing

3321	Forging and stamping
33211	Forging and stamping
332111	Iron and steel forging
332112	Nonferrous forging
332114	Custom roll forming
332117	Powder metallurgy part manufacturing
332119	Other metal stamping, except automotive
3322	Cutlery and handtool manufacturing
33221	Cutlery and handtool manufacturing
332215	Metal cookware, cutlery and flatware mfg.
332216	Saw blade and handtool manufacturing
3323	Architectural and structural metals mfg.
33231	Plate work and fabricated structural products
332311	Prefabricated metal buildings and components
332312	Fabricated structural metal manufacturing
332313	Plate work manufacturing
33232	Ornamental and architectural metal products
332321	Metal window and door manufacturing
332322	Sheet metal work manufacturing
332323	Ornamental and architectural metal work mfg.
3324	Boiler, tank, and shipping container mfg.
33241	Power boiler and heat exchanger manufacturing
332410	Power boiler and heat exchanger manufacturing
33242	Metal tank, heavy gauge, manufacturing
332420	Metal tank, heavy gauge, manufacturing

Note: For definitions of abbreviations and acronyms see page 639.

33243	Metal can, box, and other container mfg.	3331	Ag., construction, and mining machinery mfg.
332431	Metal can manufacturing	33311	Agricultural implement manufacturing
332439	Other metal container manufacturing	333111	Farm machinery and equipment manufacturing
3325	Hardware manufacturing		
33251	Hardware manufacturing	333112	Lawn and garden equipment manufacturing
332510	Hardware manufacturing		
3326	Spring and wire product manufacturing	33312	Construction machinery manufacturing
33261	Spring and wire product manufacturing	333120	Construction machinery manufacturing
332613	Spring manufacturing	33313	Mining and oil and gas field machinery mfg.
332618	Other fabricated wire product manufacturing		
3327	Machine shops and threaded product mfg.	333131	Mining machinery and equipment manufacturing
33271	Machine shops	333132	Oil and gas field machinery and equipment
332710	Machine shops		
33272	Turned product and screw, nut, and bolt mfg.	3332	Industrial machinery manufacturing
		33324	Industrial machinery manufacturing
332721	Precision turned product manufacturing	333241	Food product machinery manufacturing
332722	Bolt, nut, screw, rivet, and washer mfg.	333242	Semiconductor machinery manufacturing
3328	Coating, engraving, and heat treating metals	333243	Sawmill, woodworking, and paper machinery mfg
33281	Coating, engraving, and heat treating metals	333244	Printing machinery and equipment mfg.
332811	Metal heat treating	333249	Other industrial machinery manufacturing
332812	Metal coating and nonprecious engraving	3333	Commercial and service industry machinery
332813	Electroplating, anodizing, and coloring metal	33331	Commercial and service industry machinery
3329	Other fabricated metal product manufacturing	333314	Optical instrument and lens manufacturing
33291	Metal valve manufacturing		
332911	Industrial valve manufacturing	333316	Photographic and photocopying equipment mfg.
332912	Fluid power valve and hose fitting mfg.		
332913	Plumbing fixture fitting and trim mfg.	333318	Other commercial and service machinery mfg.
332919	Other metal valve and pipe fitting mfg.		
33299	All other fabricated metal product mfg.	3334	HVAC and commercial refrigeration equipment
332991	Ball and roller bearing manufacturing	33341	HVAC and commercial refrigeration equipment
332992	Small arms ammunition manufacturing		
332993	Ammunition, except small arms, manufacturing	333413	Fan, blower, air purification equipment mfg.
332994	Small arms and ordnance manufacturing	333414	Heating equipment, except warm air furnaces
332996	Fabricated pipe and pipe fitting mfg.	333415	AC, refrigeration, and forced air heating
332999	Miscellaneous fabricated metal product mfg.	3335	Metalworking machinery manufacturing
333	**Machinery manufacturing**	33351	Metalworking machinery manufacturing

Note: For definitions of abbreviations and acronyms see page 639.

333511	Industrial mold manufacturing	3341	Computer and peripheral equipment mfg.
333514	Special tool, die, jig, and fixture mfg.		
333515	Cutting tool and machine tool accessory mfg.	33411	Computer and peripheral equipment mfg.
333517	Machine tool manufacturing	334111	Electronic computer manufacturing
333519	Other metalworking machinery manufacturing	334112	Computer storage device manufacturing
3336	Turbine and power transmission equipment mfg.	334118	Other computer peripheral equipment mfg.
33361	Turbine and power transmission equipment mfg.	3342	Communications equipment manufacturing
333611	Turbine and turbine generator set units mfg.	33421	Telephone apparatus manufacturing
333612	Speed changer, drive, and gear manufacturing	334210	Telephone apparatus manufacturing
		33422	Broadcast and wireless communications equip.
333613	Mechanical power transmission equipment mfg.	334220	Broadcast and wireless communications equip.
333618	Other engine equipment manufacturing	33429	Other communications equipment manufacturing
3339	Other general purpose machinery manufacturing	334290	Other communications equipment manufacturing
33391	Pump and compressor manufacturing	3343	Audio and video equipment manufacturing
333912	Air and gas compressor manufacturing	33431	Audio and video equipment manufacturing
333914	Measuring, dispensing, and pumping equip. mfg	334310	Audio and video equipment manufacturing
33392	Material handling equipment manufacturing	3344	Semiconductor and electronic component mfg.
333921	Elevator and moving stairway manufacturing	33441	Semiconductor and electronic component mfg.
333922	Conveyor and conveying equipment mfg.	334412	Bare printed circuit board manufacturing
333923	Overhead cranes, hoists, and monorail systems	334413	Semiconductors and related device mfg.
333924	Industrial truck, trailer, and stacker mfg.	334416	Capacitor, resistor, and inductor mfg.
33399	All other general purpose machinery mfg.	334417	Electronic connector manufacturing
333991	Power-driven handtool manufacturing	334418	Printed circuit assembly manufacturing
333992	Welding and soldering equipment manufacturing	334419	Other electronic component manufacturing
333993	Packaging machinery manufacturing	3345	Electronic instrument manufacturing
333994	Industrial process furnace and oven mfg.	33451	Electronic instrument manufacturing
333995	Fluid power cylinder and actuator mfg.	334510	Electromedical apparatus manufacturing
333996	Fluid power pump and motor manufacturing	334511	Search, detection, and navigation instruments
333997	Scale and balance manufacturing	334512	Automatic environmental control manufacturing
333999	Miscellaneous general purpose machinery mfg.	334513	Industrial process variable instruments
		334514	Totalizing fluid meters and counting devices

334   Computer and electronic product manufacturing

Note: For definitions of abbreviations and acronyms see page 639.

census.gov/naics

334515	Electricity and signal testing instruments
334516	Analytical laboratory instrument mfg.
334517	Irradiation apparatus manufacturing
334519	Other measuring and controlling device mfg.
3346	Magnetic media manufacturing and reproducing
33461	Magnetic media manufacturing and reproducing
334613	Blank magnetic and optical media mfg
334614	Software and prerecorded media reproducing

335 Electrical equipment and appliance mfg.

3351	Electric lighting equipment manufacturing
33511	Electric lamp bulb and part manufacturing
335110	Electric lamp bulb and part manufacturing
33512	Lighting fixture manufacturing
335121	Residential electric lighting fixture mfg.
335122	Nonresidential electric lighting fixture mfg.
335129	Other lighting equipment manufacturing
3352	Household appliance manufacturing
33521	Small electrical appliance manufacturing
335210	Small electrical appliance manufacturing
33522	Major household appliance manufacturing
335220	Major household appliance manufacturing
3353	Electrical equipment manufacturing
33531	Electrical equipment manufacturing
335311	Electric power and specialty transformer mfg.
335312	Motor and generator manufacturing
335313	Switchgear and switchboard apparatus mfg.
335314	Relay and industrial control manufacturing
3359	Other electrical equipment and component mfg.
33591	Battery manufacturing

335911	Storage battery manufacturing
335912	Primary battery manufacturing
33592	Communication and energy wire and cable mfg.
335921	Fiber optic cable manufacturing
335929	Other communication and energy wire mfg.
33593	Wiring device manufacturing
335931	Current-carrying wiring device manufacturing
335932	Noncurrent-carrying wiring device mfg.
33599	Other electrical equipment and component mfg.
335991	Carbon and graphite product manufacturing
335999	Miscellaneous electrical equipment mfg.

336 Transportation equipment manufacturing

3361	Motor vehicle manufacturing
33611	Automobile and light truck manufacturing
336111	Automobile manufacturing
336112	Light truck and utility vehicle manufacturing
33612	Heavy duty truck manufacturing
336120	Heavy duty truck manufacturing
3362	Motor vehicle body and trailer manufacturing
33621	Motor vehicle body and trailer manufacturing
336211	Motor vehicle body manufacturing
336212	Truck trailer manufacturing
336213	Motor home manufacturing
336214	Travel trailer and camper manufacturing
3363	Motor vehicle parts manufacturing
33631	Motor vehicle gasoline engine and parts mfg.
336310	Motor vehicle gasoline engine and parts mfg.
33632	Motor vehicle electric equipment mfg.
336320	Motor vehicle electric equipment mfg.
33633	Motor vehicle steering and suspension parts
336330	Motor vehicle steering and suspension parts

Note: For definitions of abbreviations and acronyms see page 639.

33634	Motor vehicle brake system manufacturing	3371	Household and institutional furniture mfg.
336340	Motor vehicle brake system manufacturing	33711	Wood kitchen cabinet and countertop mfg.
33635	Motor vehicle power train components mfg.	337110	Wood kitchen cabinet and countertop mfg.
336350	Motor vehicle power train components mfg.	33712	Other household and institutional furniture
33636	Motor vehicle seating and interior trim mfg.	337121	Upholstered household furniture manufacturing
336360	Motor vehicle seating and interior trim mfg.	337122	Nonupholstered wood household furniture mfg.
33637	Motor vehicle metal stamping	337124	Metal household furniture manufacturing
336370	Motor vehicle metal stamping	337125	Household furniture, exc. wood or metal, mfg.
33639	Other motor vehicle parts manufacturing	337127	Institutional furniture manufacturing
336390	Other motor vehicle parts manufacturing	3372	Office furniture and fixtures manufacturing
3364	Aerospace product and parts manufacturing	33721	Office furniture and fixtures manufacturing
33641	Aerospace product and parts manufacturing	337211	Wood office furniture manufacturing
336411	Aircraft manufacturing	337212	Custom architectural woodwork and millwork
336412	Aircraft engine and engine parts mfg.	337214	Office furniture, except wood, manufacturing
336413	Other aircraft parts and equipment	337215	Showcases, partitions, shelving, and lockers
336414	Guided missile and space vehicle mfg.	3379	Other furniture related product manufacturing
336415	Space vehicle propulsion units and parts mfg.	33791	Mattress manufacturing
336419	Other guided missile and space vehicle parts	337910	Mattress manufacturing
3365	Railroad rolling stock manufacturing	33792	Blind and shade manufacturing
33651	Railroad rolling stock manufacturing	337920	Blind and shade manufacturing
336510	Railroad rolling stock manufacturing		
3366	Ship and boat building	**339**	**Miscellaneous manufacturing**
33661	Ship and boat building		
336611	Ship building and repairing	3391	Medical equipment and supplies manufacturing
336612	Boat building	33911	Medical equipment and supplies manufacturing
3369	Other transportation equipment manufacturing	339112	Surgical and medical instrument manufacturing
33699	Other transportation equipment manufacturing	339113	Surgical appliance and supplies manufacturing
336991	Motorcycle, bicycle, and parts manufacturing	339114	Dental equipment and supplies manufacturing
336992	Military armored vehicles and tank parts mfg.	339115	Ophthalmic goods manufacturing
336999	All other transportation equipment mfg.	339116	Dental laboratories
		3399	Other miscellaneous manufacturing
337	**Furniture and related product manufacturing**	33991	Jewelry and silverware manufacturing

Note: For definitions of abbreviations and acronyms see page 639.

339910	Jewelry and silverware manufacturing	423310	Lumber and wood merchant wholesalers
33992	Sporting and athletic goods manufacturing	42332	Masonry material merchant wholesalers
339920	Sporting and athletic goods manufacturing	423320	Masonry material merchant wholesalers
33993	Doll, toy, and game manufacturing	42333	Roofing and siding merchant wholesalers
339930	Doll, toy, and game manufacturing	423330	Roofing and siding merchant wholesalers
33994	Office supplies, except paper, manufacturing	42339	Other const. material merchant wholesalers
339940	Office supplies, except paper, manufacturing	423390	Other const. material merchant wholesalers
33995	Sign manufacturing	4234	Commercial equip. merchant wholesalers
339950	Sign manufacturing		
33999	All other miscellaneous manufacturing	42341	Photographic equip. merchant wholesalers
339991	Gasket, packing, and sealing device mfg.	423410	Photographic equip. merchant wholesalers
339992	Musical instrument manufacturing	42342	Office equipment merchant wholesalers
339993	Fastener, button, needle, and pin mfg.	423420	Office equipment merchant wholesalers
339994	Broom, brush, and mop manufacturing		
339995	Burial casket manufacturing	42343	Computer and software merchant wholesalers
339999	All other miscellaneous manufacturing	423430	Computer and software merchant wholesalers

42   WHOLESALE TRADE

423   Merchant wholesalers, durable goods

4231	Motor vehicle and parts merchant wholesalers	42344	Other commercial equip. merchant wholesalers
42311	Motor vehicle merchant wholesalers	423440	Other commercial equip. merchant wholesalers
423110	Motor vehicle merchant wholesalers	42345	Medical equipment merchant wholesalers
42312	New motor vehicle parts merchant wholesalers	423450	Medical equipment merchant wholesalers
423120	New motor vehicle parts merchant wholesalers	42346	Ophthalmic goods merchant wholesalers
42313	Tire and tube merchant wholesalers	423460	Ophthalmic goods merchant wholesalers
423130	Tire and tube merchant wholesalers	42349	Other professional equip. merchant wholesaler
42314	Used motor vehicle parts merchant wholesalers	423490	Other professional equip. merchant wholesaler
423140	Used motor vehicle parts merchant wholesalers	4235	Metal and mineral merchant wholesalers
4232	Furniture and furnishing merchant wholesalers	42351	Metal merchant wholesalers
42321	Furniture merchant wholesalers	423510	Metal merchant wholesalers
423210	Furniture merchant wholesalers	42352	Coal and other mineral merchant wholesalers
42322	Home furnishing merchant wholesalers		
423220	Home furnishing merchant wholesalers		
4233	Lumber and const. supply merchant wholesalers		
42331	Lumber and wood merchant wholesalers		

Note: For definitions of abbreviations and acronyms see page 639.

423520	Coal and other mineral merchant wholesalers
4236	Appliance and electric goods merchant whls.
42361	Elec. equip. and wiring merchant wholesalers
423610	Elec. equip. and wiring merchant wholesalers
42362	Appliance and electronics merchant whls.
423620	Appliance and electronics merchant whls.
42369	Other electronic parts merchant wholesalers
423690	Other electronic parts merchant wholesalers
4237	Hardware and plumbing merchant wholesalers
42371	Hardware merchant wholesalers
423710	Hardware merchant wholesalers
42372	Plumbing equip. merchant wholesalers
423720	Plumbing equip. merchant wholesalers
42373	HVAC equip. merchant wholesalers
423730	HVAC equip. merchant wholesalers
42374	Refrigeration equip. merchant wholesalers
423740	Refrigeration equip. merchant wholesalers
4238	Machinery and supply merchant wholesalers
42381	Construction equipment merchant wholesalers
423810	Construction equipment merchant wholesalers
42382	Farm and garden equip. merchant wholesalers
423820	Farm and garden equip. merchant wholesalers
42383	Industrial machinery merchant wholesalers
423830	Industrial machinery merchant wholesalers
42384	Industrial supplies merchant wholesalers
423840	Industrial supplies merchant wholesalers
42385	Service estab. equip. merchant wholesalers
423850	Service estab. equip. merchant wholesalers
42386	Transport. goods merchant wholesalers

423860	Transport. goods merchant wholesalers
4239	Misc. durable goods merchant wholesalers
42391	Sporting goods merchant wholesalers
423910	Sporting goods merchant wholesalers
42392	Toy and hobby goods merchant wholesalers
423920	Toy and hobby goods merchant wholesalers
42393	Recyclable material merchant wholesalers
423930	Recyclable material merchant wholesalers
42394	Jewelry merchant wholesalers
423940	Jewelry merchant wholesalers
42399	Other durable goods merchant wholesalers
423990	Other durable goods merchant wholesalers

424	**Merchant wholesalers, nondurable goods**
4241	Paper and paper product merchant wholesalers
42411	Printing and writing paper merch. whls.
424110	Printing and writing paper merch. whls.
42412	Office supplies merchant wholesalers
424120	Office supplies merchant wholesalers
42413	Industrial paper merchant wholesalers
424130	Industrial paper merchant wholesalers
4242	Druggists' goods merchant wholesalers
42421	Druggists' goods merchant wholesalers
424210	Druggists' goods merchant wholesalers
4243	Apparel and piece goods merchant wholesalers
42431	Piece goods merchant wholesalers
424310	Piece goods merchant wholesalers
42432	Men's and boys' clothing merchant wholesalers
424320	Men's and boys' clothing merchant wholesalers
42433	Women's and children's clothing merch. whls.
424330	Women's and children's clothing merch. whls.
42434	Footwear merchant wholesalers
424340	Footwear merchant wholesalers

Note: For definitions of abbreviations and acronyms see page 639.

census.gov/naics

4244	Grocery and related product wholesalers
42441	General line grocery merchant wholesalers
424410	General line grocery merchant wholesalers
42442	Packaged frozen food merchant wholesalers
424420	Packaged frozen food merchant wholesalers
42443	Dairy product merchant wholesalers
424430	Dairy product merchant wholesalers
42444	Poultry product merchant wholesalers
424440	Poultry product merchant wholesalers
42445	Confectionery merchant wholesalers
424450	Confectionery merchant wholesalers
42446	Fish and seafood merchant wholesalers
424460	Fish and seafood merchant wholesalers
42447	Meat and meat product merchant wholesalers
424470	Meat and meat product merchant wholesalers
42448	Fruit and vegetable merchant wholesalers
424480	Fruit and vegetable merchant wholesalers
42449	Other grocery product merchant wholesalers
424490	Other grocery product merchant wholesalers
4245	Farm product raw material merch. whls.
42451	Grain and field bean merchant wholesalers
424510	Grain and field bean merchant wholesalers
42452	Livestock merchant wholesalers
424520	Livestock merchant wholesalers
42459	Other farm product raw material merch. whls.
424590	Other farm product raw material merch. whls.
4246	Chemical merchant wholesalers
42461	Plastics materials merchant wholesalers
424610	Plastics materials merchant wholesalers
42469	Other chemicals merchant wholesalers
424690	Other chemicals merchant wholesalers
4247	Petroleum merchant wholesalers
42471	Petroleum bulk stations and terminals
424710	Petroleum bulk stations and terminals
42472	Other petroleum merchant wholesalers
424720	Other petroleum merchant wholesalers
4248	Alcoholic beverage merchant wholesalers
42481	Beer and ale merchant wholesalers
424810	Beer and ale merchant wholesalers
42482	Wine and spirit merchant wholesalers
424820	Wine and spirit merchant wholesalers
4249	Misc. nondurable goods merchant wholesalers
42491	Farm supplies merchant wholesalers
424910	Farm supplies merchant wholesalers
42492	Book and periodical merchant wholesalers
424920	Book and periodical merchant wholesalers
42493	Nursery and florist merchant wholesalers
424930	Nursery and florist merchant wholesalers
42494	Tobacco and tobacco product merch. whls.
424940	Tobacco and tobacco product merch. whls.
42495	Paint and supplies merchant wholesalers
424950	Paint and supplies merchant wholesalers
42499	Other nondurable goods merchant wholesalers
424990	Other nondurable goods merchant wholesalers
425	**Electronic markets and agents and brokers**
4251	Electronic markets and agents and brokers
42511	Business to business electronic markets
425110	Business to business electronic markets
42512	Wholesale trade agents and brokers
425120	Wholesale trade agents and brokers
44-45	**RETAIL TRADE**
441	**Motor vehicle and parts dealers**
4411	Automobile dealers
44111	New car dealers
441110	New car dealers

Note: For definitions of abbreviations and acronyms see page 639.

44112	Used car dealers
441120	Used car dealers
4412	Other motor vehicle dealers
44121	Recreational vehicle dealers
441210	Recreational vehicle dealers
44122	Motorcycle, boat, and other vehicle dealers
441222	Boat dealers
441228	Motorcycle, ATV, and other vehicle dealers
4413	Auto parts, accessories, and tire stores
44131	Automotive parts and accessories stores
441310	Automotive parts and accessories stores
44132	Tire dealers
441320	Tire dealers

442 Furniture and home furnishings stores

4421	Furniture stores
44211	Furniture stores
442110	Furniture stores
4422	Home furnishings stores
44221	Floor covering stores
442210	Floor covering stores
44229	Other home furnishings stores
442291	Window treatment stores
442299	All other home furnishings stores

443 Electronics and appliance stores

4431	Electronics and appliance stores
44314	Electronics and appliance stores
443141	Household appliance stores
443142	Electronics stores

444 Building material and garden supply stores

4441	Building material and supplies dealers
44411	Home centers
444110	Home centers
44412	Paint and wallpaper stores
444120	Paint and wallpaper stores
44413	Hardware stores
444130	Hardware stores
44419	Other building material dealers
444190	Other building material dealers

4442	Lawn and garden equipment and supplies stores
44421	Outdoor power equipment stores
444210	Outdoor power equipment stores
44422	Nursery, garden, and farm supply stores
444220	Nursery, garden, and farm supply stores

445 Food and beverage stores

4451	Grocery stores
44511	Supermarkets and other grocery stores
445110	Supermarkets and other grocery stores
44512	Convenience stores
445120	Convenience stores
4452	Specialty food stores
44521	Meat markets
445210	Meat markets
44522	Fish and seafood markets
445220	Fish and seafood markets
44523	Fruit and vegetable markets
445230	Fruit and vegetable markets
44529	Other specialty food stores
445291	Baked goods stores
445292	Confectionery and nut stores
445299	All other specialty food stores
4453	Beer, wine, and liquor stores
44531	Beer, wine, and liquor stores
445310	Beer, wine, and liquor stores

446 Health and personal care stores

4461	Health and personal care stores
44611	Pharmacies and drug stores
446110	Pharmacies and drug stores
44612	Cosmetic and beauty supply stores
446120	Cosmetic and beauty supply stores
44613	Optical goods stores
446130	Optical goods stores
44619	Other health and personal care stores
446191	Food, health, supplement stores
446199	All other health and personal care stores

447 Gasoline stations

4471	Gasoline stations
44711	Gasoline stations with convenience stores

Note: For definitions of abbreviations and acronyms see page 639.

census.gov/naics

447110	Gasoline stations with convenience stores		**452**	**General merchandise stores**
44719	Other gasoline stations		4522	Department stores
447190	Other gasoline stations		45221	Department stores
			452210	Department stores
448	**Clothing and clothing accessories stores**		4523	Other general merchandise stores
			45231	Other general merchandise stores
			452311	Warehouse clubs and supercenters
4481	Clothing stores		452319	All other general merchandise stores
44811	Men's clothing stores			
448110	Men's clothing stores		**453**	**Miscellaneous store retailers**
44812	Women's clothing stores			
448120	Women's clothing stores		4531	Florists
44813	Children's and infants' clothing stores		45311	Florists
448130	Children's and infants' clothing stores		453110	Florists
44814	Family clothing stores		4532	Office supplies, stationery, and gift stores
448140	Family clothing stores			
44815	Clothing accessories stores		45321	Office supplies and stationery stores
448150	Clothing accessories stores		453210	Office supplies and stationery stores
44819	Other clothing stores		45322	Gift, novelty, and souvenir stores
448190	Other clothing stores		453220	Gift, novelty, and souvenir stores
4482	Shoe stores		4533	Used merchandise stores
44821	Shoe stores		45331	Used merchandise stores
448210	Shoe stores		453310	Used merchandise stores
4483	Jewelry, luggage, and leather goods stores		4539	Other miscellaneous store retailers
			45391	Pet and pet supplies stores
44831	Jewelry stores		453910	Pet and pet supplies stores
448310	Jewelry stores		45392	Art dealers
44832	Luggage and leather goods stores		453920	Art dealers
448320	Luggage and leather goods stores		45393	Manufactured, mobile, home dealers
			453930	Manufactured, mobile, home dealers
451	**Sports, hobby, music instrument, book stores**		45399	All other miscellaneous store retailers
			453991	Tobacco stores
			453998	Store retailers not specified elsewhere
4511	Sporting goods and musical instrument stores			
			454	**Nonstore retailers**
45111	Sporting goods stores			
451110	Sporting goods stores		4541	Electronic shopping and mail-order houses
45112	Hobby, toy, and game stores			
451120	Hobby, toy, and game stores		45411	Electronic shopping and mail-order houses
45113	Sewing, needlework, and piece goods stores			
			454110	Electronic shopping and mail-order houses
451130	Sewing, needlework, and piece goods stores			
			4542	Vending machine operators
45114	Musical instrument and supplies stores		45421	Vending machine operators
451140	Musical instrument and supplies stores		454210	Vending machine operators
4512	Book stores and news dealers		4543	Direct selling establishments
45121	Book stores and news dealers		45431	Fuel dealers
451211	Book stores		454310	Fuel dealers
451212	News dealers and newsstands		45439	Other direct selling establishments
			454390	Other direct selling establishments

Note: For definitions of abbreviations and acronyms see page 639.

48-49   TRANSPORTATION AND WAREHOUSING

481   Air transportation

4811	Scheduled air transportation
48111	Scheduled air transportation
481111	Scheduled passenger air transportation
481112	Scheduled freight air transportation
4812	Nonscheduled air transportation
48121	Nonscheduled air transportation
481211	Nonscheduled air passenger chartering
481212	Nonscheduled air freight chartering
481219	Other nonscheduled air transportation

482   Rail transportation

4821	Rail transportation
48211	Rail transportation
482111	Line-haul railroads
482112	Short line railroads

483   Water transportation

4831	Sea, coastal, and Great Lakes transportation
48311	Sea, coastal, and Great Lakes transportation
483111	Deep sea freight transportation
483112	Deep sea passenger transportation
483113	Coastal and Great Lakes freight transport.
483114	Coastal and Great Lakes passenger transport.
4832	Inland water transportation
48321	Inland water transportation
483211	Inland water freight transportation
483212	Inland water passenger transportation

484   Truck transportation

4841	General freight trucking
48411	General freight trucking, local
484110	General freight trucking, local
48412	General freight trucking, long-distance
484121	General freight trucking, long-distance TL
484122	General freight trucking, long-distance LTL
4842	Specialized freight trucking

48421	Used household and office goods moving
484210	Used household and office goods moving
48422	Other specialized trucking, local
484220	Other specialized trucking, local
48423	Other specialized trucking, long-distance
484230	Other specialized trucking, long-distance

485   Transit and ground passenger transportation

4851	Urban transit systems
48511	Urban transit systems
485111	Mixed mode transit systems
485112	Commuter rail systems
485113	Bus and other motor vehicle transit systems
485119	Other urban transit systems
4852	Interurban and rural bus transportation
48521	Interurban and rural bus transportation
485210	Interurban and rural bus transportation
4853	Taxi and limousine service
48531	Taxi service
485310	Taxi service
48532	Limousine service
485320	Limousine service
4854	School and employee bus transportation
48541	School and employee bus transportation
485410	School and employee bus transportation
4855	Charter bus industry
48551	Charter bus industry
485510	Charter bus industry
4859	Other ground passenger transportation
48599	Other ground passenger transportation
485991	Special needs transportation
485999	All other ground passenger transportation

486   Pipeline transportation

4861	Pipeline transportation of crude oil
48611	Pipeline transportation of crude oil
486110	Pipeline transportation of crude oil
4862	Pipeline transportation of natural gas

Note: For definitions of abbreviations and acronyms see page 639.

48621	Pipeline transportation of natural gas		48833	Navigational services to shipping
486210	Pipeline transportation of natural gas		488330	Navigational services to shipping
4869	Other pipeline transportation		48839	Other support activities for water transport.
48691	Refined petroleum product pipeline transport.		488390	Other support activities for water transport.
486910	Refined petroleum product pipeline transport.		4884	Support activities for road transportation
48699	All other pipeline transportation		48841	Motor vehicle towing
486990	All other pipeline transportation		488410	Motor vehicle towing
			48849	Other support activities for road transport.

487 Scenic and sightseeing transportation

			488490	Other support activities for road transport.
4871	Scenic and sightseeing transportation, land		4885	Freight transportation arrangement
48711	Scenic and sightseeing transportation, land		48851	Freight transportation arrangement
			488510	Freight transportation arrangement
487110	Scenic and sightseeing transportation, land		4889	Other support activities for transportation
4872	Scenic and sightseeing transportation, water		48899	Other support activities for transportation
48721	Scenic and sightseeing transportation, water		488991	Packing and crating
487210	Scenic and sightseeing transportation, water		488999	All other support activities for transport.
4879	Scenic and sightseeing transportation, other			

491 Postal service

48799	Scenic and sightseeing transportation, other		4911	Postal service
487990	Scenic and sightseeing transportation, other		49111	Postal service
			491110	Postal service

492 Couriers and messengers

488 Support activities for transportation

			4921	Couriers and express delivery services
4881	Support activities for air transportation		49211	Couriers and express delivery services
48811	Airport operations		492110	Couriers and express delivery services
488111	Air traffic control		4922	Local messengers and local delivery
488119	Other airport operations		49221	Local messengers and local delivery
48819	Other support activities for air transport.		492210	Local messengers and local delivery
488190	Other support activities for air transport.			

493 Warehousing and storage

4882	Support activities for rail transportation		4931	Warehousing and storage
48821	Support activities for rail transportation		49311	General warehousing and storage
488210	Support activities for rail transportation		493110	General warehousing and storage
4883	Support activities for water transportation		49312	Refrigerated warehousing and storage
			493120	Refrigerated warehousing and storage
48831	Port and harbor operations		49313	Farm product warehousing and storage
488310	Port and harbor operations		493130	Farm product warehousing and storage
48832	Marine cargo handling		49319	Other warehousing and storage
488320	Marine cargo handling		493190	Other warehousing and storage

Note: For definitions of abbreviations and acronyms see page 639.

51 INFORMATION

511 Publishing industries, except Internet

5111	Newspaper, book, and directory publishers
51111	Newspaper publishers
511110	Newspaper publishers
51112	Periodical publishers
511120	Periodical publishers
51113	Book publishers
511130	Book publishers
51114	Directory and mailing list publishers
511140	Directory and mailing list publishers
51119	Other publishers
511191	Greeting card publishers
511199	All other publishers
5112	Software publishers
51121	Software publishers
511210	Software publishers

512 Motion picture and sound recording industries

5121	Motion picture and video industries
51211	Motion picture and video production
512110	Motion picture and video production
51212	Motion picture and video distribution
512120	Motion picture and video distribution
51213	Motion picture and video exhibition
512131	Motion picture theaters, except drive-ins
512132	Drive-in motion picture theaters
51219	Postproduction and other related industries
512191	Teleproduction and postproduction services
512199	Other motion picture and video industries
5122	Sound recording industries
51223	Music publishers
512230	Music publishers
51224	Sound recording studios
512240	Sound recording studios
51225	Record production and distribution
512250	Record production and distribution
51229	Other sound recording industries
512290	Other sound recording industries

515 Broadcasting, except Internet

5151	Radio and television broadcasting
51511	Radio broadcasting
515111	Radio networks
515112	Radio stations
51512	Television broadcasting
515120	Television broadcasting
5152	Cable and other subscription programming
51521	Cable and other subscription programming
515210	Cable and other subscription programming

517 Telecommunications

5173	Wired and wireless carriers
51731	Wired and wireless carriers
517311	Wired telecommunications carriers
517312	Wireless telecommunications carriers
5174	Satellite telecommunications
51741	Satellite telecommunications
517410	Satellite telecommunications
5179	Other telecommunications
51791	Other telecommunications
517911	Telecommunications resellers
517919	All other telecommunications

518 Data processing, hosting and related services

5182	Data processing, hosting and related services
51821	Data processing, hosting and related services
518210	Data processing, hosting and related services

519 Other information services

5191	Other information services
51911	News syndicates
519110	News syndicates
51912	Libraries and archives
519120	Libraries and archives
51913	Internet publishing and web search portals
519130	Internet publishing and web search portals
51919	All other information services
519190	All other information services

Note: For definitions of abbreviations and acronyms see page 639.

52   FINANCE AND INSURANCE

521   Monetary authorities-central bank

5211	Monetary authorities-central bank
52111	Monetary authorities-central bank
521110	Monetary authorities-central bank

522   Credit intermediation and related activities

5221	Depository credit intermediation
52211	Commercial banking
522110	Commercial banking
52212	Savings institutions
522120	Savings institutions
52213	Credit unions
522130	Credit unions
52219	Other depository credit intermediation
522190	Other depository credit intermediation
5222	Nondepository credit intermediation
52221	Credit card issuing
522210	Credit card issuing
52222	Sales financing
522220	Sales financing
52229	Other nondepository credit intermediation
522291	Consumer lending
522292	Real estate credit
522293	International trade financing
522294	Secondary market financing
522298	All other nondepository credit intermediation
5223	Activities related to credit intermediation
52231	Mortgage and nonmortgage loan brokers
522310	Mortgage and nonmortgage loan brokers
52232	Financial transaction processing and clearing
522320	Financial transaction processing and clearing
52239	Other credit intermediation activities
522390	Other credit intermediation activities

523   Securities, commodity contracts, investments

5231	Securities and commodity contracts brokerage
52311	Investment banking and securities dealing
523110	Investment banking and securities dealing
52312	Securities brokerage
523120	Securities brokerage
52313	Commodity contracts dealing
523130	Commodity contracts dealing
52314	Commodity contracts brokerage
523140	Commodity contracts brokerage
5232	Securities and commodity exchanges
52321	Securities and commodity exchanges
523210	Securities and commodity exchanges
5239	Other financial investment activities
52391	Miscellaneous intermediation
523910	Miscellaneous intermediation
52392	Portfolio management
523920	Portfolio management
52393	Investment advice
523930	Investment advice
52399	All other financial investment activities
523991	Trust, fiduciary, and custody activities
523999	Miscellaneous financial investment activities

524   Insurance carriers and related activities

5241	Insurance carriers
52411	Direct life and health insurance carriers
524113	Direct life insurance carriers
524114	Direct health and medical insurance carriers
52412	Direct insurers, except life and health
524126	Direct property and casualty insurers
524127	Direct title insurance carriers
524128	Other direct insurance carriers
52413	Reinsurance carriers
524130	Reinsurance carriers
5242	Insurance agencies and brokerages
52421	Insurance agencies and brokerages
524210	Insurance agencies and brokerages
52429	Other insurance related activities
524291	Claims adjusting
524292	Third party administration of insurance funds
524298	All other insurance related activities

525   Funds, trusts, and other financial vehicles

Note: For definitions of abbreviations and acronyms see page 639.

5251	Insurance and employee benefit funds
52511	Pension funds
525110	Pension funds
52512	Health and welfare funds
525120	Health and welfare funds
52519	Other insurance funds
525190	Other insurance funds
5259	Other investment pools and funds
52591	Open-end investment funds
525910	Open-end investment funds
52592	Trusts, estates, and agency accounts
525920	Trusts, estates, and agency accounts
52599	Other financial vehicles
525990	Other financial vehicles

53   REAL ESTATE AND RENTAL AND LEASING

531   Real estate

5311	Lessors of real estate
53111	Lessors of residential buildings
531110	Lessors of residential buildings
53112	Lessors of nonresidential buildings
531120	Lessors of nonresidential buildings
53113	Miniwarehouse and self-storage unit operators
531130	Miniwarehouse and self-storage unit operators
53119	Lessors of other real estate property
531190	Lessors of other real estate property
5312	Offices of real estate agents and brokers
53121	Offices of real estate agents and brokers
531210	Offices of real estate agents and brokers
5313	Activities related to real estate
53131	Real estate property managers
531311	Residential property managers
531312	Nonresidential property managers
53132	Offices of real estate appraisers
531320	Offices of real estate appraisers
53139	Other activities related to real estate
531390	Other activities related to real estate

532   Rental and leasing services

5321	Automotive equipment rental and leasing
53211	Passenger car rental and leasing
532111	Passenger car rental
532112	Passenger car leasing
53212	Truck, trailer, and RV rental and leasing
532120	Truck, trailer, and RV rental and leasing
5322	Consumer goods rental
53221	Consumer electronics and appliances rental
532210	Consumer electronics and appliances rental
53228	Other consumer goods rental
532281	Formal wear and costume rental
532282	Video tape and disc rental
532283	Home health equipment rental
532284	Recreational goods rental
532289	All other consumer goods rental
5323	General rental centers
53231	General rental centers
532310	General rental centers
5324	Machinery and equipment rental and leasing
53241	Heavy machinery rental and leasing
532411	Transportation equipment rental and leasing
532412	Other heavy machinery rental and leasing
53242	Office equipment rental and leasing
532420	Office equipment rental and leasing
53249	Other machinery rental and leasing
532490	Other machinery rental and leasing

533   Lessors of nonfinancial intangible assets

5331	Lessors of nonfinancial intangible assets
53311	Lessors of nonfinancial intangible assets
533110	Lessors of nonfinancial intangible assets

54   PROFESSIONAL AND TECHNICAL SERVICES

541   Professional and technical services

5411	Legal services
54111	Offices of lawyers
541110	Offices of lawyers
54112	Offices of notaries

Note: For definitions of abbreviations and acronyms see page 639.

541120	Offices of notaries
54119	Other legal services
541191	Title abstract and settlement offices
541199	All other legal services
5412	Accounting and bookkeeping services
54121	Accounting and bookkeeping services
541211	Offices of certified public accountants
541213	Tax preparation services
541214	Payroll services
541219	Other accounting services
5413	Architectural and engineering services
54131	Architectural services
541310	Architectural services
54132	Landscape architectural services
541320	Landscape architectural services
54133	Engineering services
541330	Engineering services
54134	Drafting services
541340	Drafting services
54135	Building inspection services
541350	Building inspection services
54136	Geophysical surveying and mapping services
541360	Geophysical surveying and mapping services
54137	Other surveying and mapping services
541370	Other surveying and mapping services
54138	Testing laboratories
541380	Testing laboratories
5414	Specialized design services
54141	Interior design services
541410	Interior design services
54142	Industrial design services
541420	Industrial design services
54143	Graphic design services
541430	Graphic design services
54149	Other specialized design services
541490	Other specialized design services
5415	Computer systems design and related services
54151	Computer systems design and related services
541511	Custom computer programming services
541512	Computer systems design services
541513	Computer facilities management services
541519	Other computer related services
5416	Management and technical consulting services
54161	Management consulting services

541611	Administrative management consulting services
541612	Human resources consulting services
541613	Marketing consulting services
541614	Process and logistics consulting services
541618	Other management consulting services
54162	Environmental consulting services
541620	Environmental consulting services
54169	Other technical consulting services
541690	Other technical consulting services
5417	Scientific research and development services
54171	Physical, engineering and biological research
541713	Research and development in nanotechnology
541714	Research and development in biotechnology
541715	Other physical and biological research
54172	Social science and humanities research
541720	Social science and humanities research
5418	Advertising, PR, and related services
54181	Advertising agencies
541810	Advertising agencies
54182	Public relations agencies
541820	Public relations agencies
54183	Media buying agencies
541830	Media buying agencies
54184	Media representatives
541840	Media representatives
54185	Outdoor advertising
541850	Outdoor advertising
54186	Direct mail advertising
541860	Direct mail advertising
54187	Advertising material distribution services
541870	Advertising material distribution services
54189	Other services related to advertising
541890	Other services related to advertising
5419	Other professional and technical services
54191	Marketing research and public opinion polling
541910	Marketing research and public opinion polling
54192	Photographic services
541921	Photography studios, portrait
541922	Commercial photography
54193	Translation and interpretation services

Note: For definitions of abbreviations and acronyms see page 639.

541930	Translation and interpretation services
54194	Veterinary services
541940	Veterinary services
54199	All other professional and technical services
541990	All other professional and technical services

55 MANAGEMENT OF COMPANIES AND ENTERPRISES

551 Management of companies and enterprises

5511	Management of companies and enterprises
55111	Management of companies and enterprises
551111	Offices of bank holding companies
551112	Offices of other holding companies
551114	Managing offices

56 ADMINISTRATIVE AND WASTE SERVICES

561 Administrative and support services

5611	Office administrative services
56111	Office administrative services
561110	Office administrative services
5612	Facilities support services
56121	Facilities support services
561210	Facilities support services
5613	Employment services
56131	Employment placement and executive search
561311	Employment placement agencies
561312	Executive search services
56132	Temporary help services
561320	Temporary help services
56133	Professional employer organizations
561330	Professional employer organizations
5614	Business support services
56141	Document preparation services
561410	Document preparation services
56142	Telephone call centers
561421	Telephone answering services
561422	Telemarketing and other contact centers
56143	Business service centers
561431	Private mail centers

561439	Other business service centers
56144	Collection agencies
561440	Collection agencies
56145	Credit bureaus
561450	Credit bureaus
56149	Other business support services
561491	Repossession services
561492	Court reporting and stenotype services
561499	All other business support services
5615	Travel arrangement and reservation services
56151	Travel agencies
561510	Travel agencies
56152	Tour operators
561520	Tour operators
56159	Other travel arrangement services
561591	Convention and visitors bureaus
561599	All other travel arrangement services
5616	Investigation and security services
56161	Security and armored car services
561611	Investigation services
561612	Security guards and patrol services
561613	Armored car services
56162	Security systems services
561621	Security systems services, except locksmiths
561622	Locksmiths
5617	Services to buildings and dwellings
56171	Exterminating and pest control services
561710	Exterminating and pest control services
56172	Janitorial services
561720	Janitorial services
56173	Landscaping services
561730	Landscaping services
56174	Carpet and upholstery cleaning services
561740	Carpet and upholstery cleaning services
56179	Other services to buildings and dwellings
561790	Other services to buildings and dwellings
5619	Other support services
56191	Packaging and labeling services
561910	Packaging and labeling services
56192	Convention and trade show organizers
561920	Convention and trade show organizers
56199	All other support services
561990	All other support services

Note: For definitions of abbreviations and acronyms see page 639.

562	**Waste management and remediation services**
5621	Waste collection
56211	Waste collection
562111	Solid waste collection
562112	Hazardous waste collection
562119	Other waste collection
5622	Waste treatment and disposal
56221	Waste treatment and disposal
562211	Hazardous waste treatment and disposal
562212	Solid waste landfill
562213	Solid waste combustors and incinerators
562219	Other nonhazardous waste disposal
5629	Remediation and other waste services
56291	Remediation services
562910	Remediation services
56292	Materials recovery facilities
562920	Materials recovery facilities
56299	All other waste management services
562991	Septic tank and related services
562998	Miscellaneous waste management services

61 EDUCATIONAL SERVICES

611 Educational services

6111	Elementary and secondary schools
61111	Elementary and secondary schools
611110	Elementary and secondary schools
6112	Junior colleges
61121	Junior colleges
611210	Junior colleges
6113	Colleges and universities
61131	Colleges and universities
611310	Colleges and universities
6114	Business, computer and management training
61141	Business and secretarial schools
611410	Business and secretarial schools
61142	Computer training
611420	Computer training
61143	Management training
611430	Management training
6115	Technical and trade schools
61151	Technical and trade schools
611511	Cosmetology and barber schools
611512	Flight training

611513	Apprenticeship training
611519	Other technical and trade schools
6116	Other schools and instruction
61161	Fine arts schools
611610	Fine arts schools
61162	Sports and recreation instruction
611620	Sports and recreation instruction
61163	Language schools
611630	Language schools
61169	All other schools and instruction
611691	Exam preparation and tutoring
611692	Automobile driving schools
611699	Miscellaneous schools and instruction
6117	Educational support services
61171	Educational support services
611710	Educational support services

62 HEALTH CARE AND SOCIAL ASSISTANCE

621 Ambulatory health care services

6211	Offices of physicians
62111	Offices of physicians
621111	Offices of physicians, except mental health
621112	Offices of mental health physicians
6212	Offices of dentists
62121	Offices of dentists
621210	Offices of dentists
6213	Offices of other health practitioners
62131	Offices of chiropractors
621310	Offices of chiropractors
62132	Offices of optometrists
621320	Offices of optometrists
62133	Offices of mental health practitioners
621330	Offices of mental health practitioners
62134	Offices of specialty therapists
621340	Offices of specialty therapists
62139	Offices of all other health practitioners
621391	Offices of podiatrists
621399	Offices of miscellaneous health practitioners
6214	Outpatient care centers
62141	Family planning centers
621410	Family planning centers
62142	Outpatient mental health centers
621420	Outpatient mental health centers
62149	Other outpatient care centers
621491	HMO medical centers
621492	Kidney dialysis centers

Note: For definitions of abbreviations and acronyms see page 639.

621493	Freestanding emergency medical centers
621498	All other outpatient care centers
6215	Medical and diagnostic laboratories
62151	Medical and diagnostic laboratories
621511	Medical laboratories
621512	Diagnostic imaging centers
6216	Home health care services
62161	Home health care services
621610	Home health care services
6219	Other ambulatory health care services
62191	Ambulance services
621910	Ambulance services
62199	All other ambulatory health care services
621991	Blood and organ banks
621999	Miscellaneous ambulatory health care services

622   Hospitals

6221	General medical and surgical hospitals
62211	General medical and surgical hospitals
622110	General medical and surgical hospitals
6222	Psychiatric and substance abuse hospitals
62221	Psychiatric and substance abuse hospitals
622210	Psychiatric and substance abuse hospitals
6223	Other hospitals
62231	Other hospitals
622310	Other hospitals

623   Nursing and residential care facilities

6231	Nursing care facilities, skilled nursing
62311	Nursing care facilities, skilled nursing
623110	Nursing care facilities, skilled nursing
6232	Residential mental health facilities
62321	Residential developmental disability homes
623210	Residential developmental disability homes
62322	Residential mental and substance abuse care
623220	Residential mental and substance abuse care
6233	Continuing care, assisted living facilities

62331	Continuing care, assisted living facilities
623311	Continuing care retirement communities
623312	Assisted living facilities for the elderly
6239	Other residential care facilities
62399	Other residential care facilities
623990	Other residential care facilities

624   Social assistance

6241	Individual and family services
62411	Child and youth services
624110	Child and youth services
62412	Services for the elderly and disabled
624120	Services for the elderly and disabled
62419	Other individual and family services
624190	Other individual and family services
6242	Emergency and other relief services
62421	Community food services
624210	Community food services
62422	Community housing services
624221	Temporary shelters
624229	Other community housing services
62423	Emergency and other relief services
624230	Emergency and other relief services
6243	Vocational rehabilitation services
62431	Vocational rehabilitation services
624310	Vocational rehabilitation services
6244	Child day care services
62441	Child day care services
624410	Child day care services

71   ARTS, ENTERTAINMENT, AND RECREATION

711   Performing arts and spectator sports

7111	Performing arts companies
71111	Theater companies and dinner theaters
711110	Theater companies and dinner theaters
71112	Dance companies
711120	Dance companies
71113	Musical groups and artists
711130	Musical groups and artists
71119	Other performing arts companies
711190	Other performing arts companies
7112	Spectator sports
71121	Spectator sports
711211	Sports teams and clubs
711212	Racetracks

Note: For definitions of abbreviations and acronyms see page 639.

711219	Other spectator sports
7113	Promoters of performing arts and sports
71131	Promoters with facilities
711310	Promoters with facilities
71132	Promoters without facilities
711320	Promoters without facilities
7114	Agents and managers for public figures
71141	Agents and managers for public figures
711410	Agents and managers for public figures
7115	Independent artists, writers, and performers
71151	Independent artists, writers, and performers
711510	Independent artists, writers, and performers

712   **Museums, historical sites, zoos, and parks**

7121	Museums, historical sites, zoos, and parks
71211	Museums
712110	Museums
71212	Historical sites
712120	Historical sites
71213	Zoos and botanical gardens
712130	Zoos and botanical gardens
71219	Nature parks and other similar institutions
712190	Nature parks and other similar institutions

713   **Amusements, gambling, and recreation**

7131	Amusement parks and arcades
71311	Amusement and theme parks
713110	Amusement and theme parks
71312	Amusement arcades
713120	Amusement arcades
7132	Gambling industries
71321	Casinos, except casino hotels
713210	Casinos, except casino hotels
71329	Other gambling industries
713290	Other gambling industries
7139	Other amusement and recreation industries
71391	Golf courses and country clubs
713910	Golf courses and country clubs
71392	Skiing facilities

713920	Skiing facilities
71393	Marinas
713930	Marinas
71394	Fitness and recreational sports centers
713940	Fitness and recreational sports centers
71395	Bowling centers
713950	Bowling centers
71399	All other amusement and recreation industries
713990	All other amusement and recreation industries

72   **ACCOMMODATION AND FOOD SERVICES**

721   **Accommodation**

7211	Traveler accommodation
72111	Hotels and motels, except casino hotels
721110	Hotels and motels, except casino hotels
72112	Casino hotels
721120	Casino hotels
72119	Other traveler accommodation
721191	Bed-and-breakfast inns
721199	All other traveler accommodation
7212	RV parks and recreational camps
72121	RV parks and recreational camps
721211	RV parks and campgrounds
721214	Recreational and vacation camps
7213	Rooming and boarding houses and dorms
72131	Rooming and boarding houses and dorms
721310	Rooming and boarding houses and dorms

722   **Food services and drinking places**

7223	Special food services
72231	Food service contractors
722310	Food service contractors
72232	Caterers
722320	Caterers
72233	Mobile food services
722330	Mobile food services
7224	Drinking places, alcoholic beverages
72241	Drinking places, alcoholic beverages
722410	Drinking places, alcoholic beverages
7225	Restaurants and other eating places
72251	Restaurants and other eating places
722511	Full-service restaurants

Note: For definitions of abbreviations and acronyms see page 639.

722513	Limited-service restaurants
722514	Cafeterias, grill buffets, and buffets
722515	Snack and nonalcoholic beverage bars

81   OTHER SERVICES, EXCEPT PUBLIC ADMINISTRATION

811   Repair and maintenance

8111	Automotive repair and maintenance
81111	Automotive mechanical and electrical repair
811111	General automotive repair
811112	Automotive exhaust system repair
811113	Automotive transmission repair
811118	Other automotive mechanical and elec. repair
81112	Automotive body, interior, and glass repair
811121	Automotive body and interior repair
811122	Automotive glass replacement shops
81119	Other automotive repair and maintenance
811191	Automotive oil change and lubrication shops
811192	Car washes
811198	All other automotive repair and maintenance
8112	Electronic equipment repair and maintenance
81121	Electronic equipment repair and maintenance
811211	Consumer electronics repair and maintenance
811212	Computer and office machine repair
811213	Communication equipment repair
811219	Other electronic equipment repair
8113	Commercial machinery repair and maintenance
81131	Commercial machinery repair and maintenance
811310	Commercial machinery repair and maintenance
8114	Household goods repair and maintenance
81141	Home and garden equip. and appliance repair
811411	Home and garden equipment repair
811412	Appliance repair and maintenance
81142	Reupholstery and furniture repair
811420	Reupholstery and furniture repair

81143	Footwear and leather goods repair
811430	Footwear and leather goods repair
81149	Other household goods repair and maintenance
811490	Other household goods repair and maintenance

812   Personal and laundry services

8121	Personal care services
81211	Hair, nail, and skin care services
812111	Barber shops
812112	Beauty salons
812113	Nail salons
81219	Other personal care services
812191	Diet and weight reducing centers
812199	Other personal care services
8122	Death care services
81221	Funeral homes and funeral services
812210	Funeral homes and funeral services
81222	Cemeteries and crematories
812220	Cemeteries and crematories
8123	Drycleaning and laundry services
81231	Coin-operated laundries and drycleaners
812310	Coin-operated laundries and drycleaners
81232	Drycleaning and laundry services
812320	Drycleaning and laundry services
81233	Linen and uniform supply
812331	Linen supply
812332	Industrial launderers
8129	Other personal services
81291	Pet care, except veterinary, services
812910	Pet care, except veterinary, services
81292	Photofinishing
812921	Photofinishing laboratories, except one-hour
812922	One-hour photofinishing
81293	Parking lots and garages
812930	Parking lots and garages
81299	All other personal services
812990	All other personal services

813   Membership associations and organizations

8131	Religious organizations
81311	Religious organizations
813110	Religious organizations
8132	Grantmaking and giving services

Note: For definitions of abbreviations and acronyms see page 639.

census.gov/naics

81321	Grantmaking and giving services		921150	Tribal governments
813211	Grantmaking foundations		92119	Other general government support
813212	Voluntary health organizations		921190	Other general government support
813219	Other grantmaking and giving services			
8133	Social advocacy organizations		**922**	**Justice, public order, and safety activities**
81331	Social advocacy organizations			
813311	Human rights organizations		9221	Justice, public order, and safety activities
813312	Environment and conservation organizations		92211	Courts
813319	Other social advocacy organizations		922110	Courts
8134	Civic and social organizations		92212	Police protection
81341	Civic and social organizations		922120	Police protection
813410	Civic and social organizations		92213	Legal counsel and prosecution
8139	Professional and similar organizations		922130	Legal counsel and prosecution
81391	Business associations		92214	Correctional institutions
813910	Business associations		922140	Correctional institutions
81392	Professional organizations		92215	Parole offices and probation offices
813920	Professional organizations		922150	Parole offices and probation offices
81393	Labor unions and similar labor organizations		92216	Fire protection
813930	Labor unions and similar labor organizations		922160	Fire protection
81394	Political organizations		92219	Other justice and safety activities
813940	Political organizations		922190	Other justice and safety activities
81399	Other similar organizations			
813990	Other similar organizations		**923**	**Administration of human resource programs**
814	**Private households**		9231	Administration of human resource programs
8141	Private households		92311	Administration of education programs
81411	Private households		923110	Administration of education programs
814110	Private households		92312	Administration of public health programs
92	**PUBLIC ADMINISTRATION**		923120	Administration of public health programs
921	**Executive, legislative and general government**		92313	Other human resource programs administration
			923130	Other human resource programs administration
9211	Executive, legislative and general government		92314	Administration of veterans' affairs
92111	Executive offices		923140	Administration of veterans' affairs
921110	Executive offices			
92112	Legislative bodies		**924**	**Administration of environmental programs**
921120	Legislative bodies			
92113	Public finance activities		9241	Administration of environmental programs
921130	Public finance activities			
92114	Executive and legislative offices, combined		92411	Air, water, and waste program administration
921140	Executive and legislative offices, combined		924110	Air, water, and waste program administration
92115	Tribal governments			

Note: For definitions of abbreviations and acronyms see page 639.

92412	Administration of conservation programs
924120	Administration of conservation programs

925   Community and housing program administration

9251	Community and housing program administration
92511	Administration of housing programs
925110	Administration of housing programs
92512	Urban and rural development administration
925120	Urban and rural development administration

926   Administration of economic programs

9261	Administration of economic programs
92611	Administration of general economic programs
926110	Administration of general economic programs
92612	Transportation program administration
926120	Transportation program administration

92613	Utility regulation and administration
926130	Utility regulation and administration
92614	Agricultural market and commodity regulation
926140	Agricultural market and commodity regulation
92615	Licensing and regulating commercial sectors
926150	Licensing and regulating commercial sectors

927   Space research and technology

9271	Space research and technology
92711	Space research and technology
927110	Space research and technology

928   National security and international affairs

9281	National security and international affairs
92811	National security
928110	National security
92812	International affairs
928120	International affairs

Note: For definitions of abbreviations and acronyms see page 639.

census.gov/naics

Abbreviations and Acronyms Used in Short Titles

Abbreviation/Acronym	Word
AC	air-conditioning
ag.	agriculture
Al	aluminum
ATV	all-terrain vehicle
const.	construction
Cu	copper
elec.	electrical
equip.	equipment
estab.	establishment
exc.	except
HMO	health maintenance organization
HVAC	heating, ventilation, and air-conditioning
LTL	less than truckload
merch.	merchant
mfg. or mfg	manufacturing
misc.	miscellaneous
PR	public relations
RV	recreational vehicle
TL	truckload
transport.	transportation
whls.	wholesalers

Part III

Appendixes

Appendixes A and B map the changes for 2017 NAICS to the 2012 NAICS in 2017 NAICS sequence (Appendix A) and 2012 NAICS sequence (Appendix B). The tables do not provide a comprehensive guide to all economic activities, but rather provide a map for the largest and most important changes from 2012 to 2017.

A full concordance for 2012 NAICS to 2017 NAICS is available on the Census Bureau's Web site at census.gov/naics.

Appendix A

2017 NAICS U.S. Matched to 2012 NAICS U.S.

2017 NAICS Code	2017 NAICS U.S. Description	Status Code	2012 NAICS Code	2012 NAICS U.S. Description
21112	Crude Petroleum Extraction			
211120	Crude Petroleum Extraction	N	*211111	Crude Petroleum and Natural Gas Extraction - *crude petroleum extraction*
21113	Natural Gas Extraction			
211130	Natural Gas Extraction	N	*211111	Crude Petroleum and Natural Gas Extraction - *natural gas extraction*
			211112	Natural Gas Liquid Extraction
212230	Copper, Nickel, Lead, and Zinc Mining	N	212231	Lead Ore and Zinc Ore Mining
			212234	Copper Ore and Nickel Ore Mining
333914	Measuring, Dispensing, and Other Pumping Equipment Manufacturing	N	333911	Pump and Pumping Equipment Manufacturing
			333913	Measuring and Dispensing Pump Manufacturing
33522	Major Household Appliance Manufacturing			
335220	Major Household Appliance Manufacturing	N	335221	Household Cooking Appliance Manufacturing
			335222	Household Refrigerator and Home Freezer Manufacturing
			335224	Household Laundry Equipment Manufacturing
			335228	Other Major Household Appliance Manufacturing

*—Part of 2012 NAICS United States industry; N—New NAICS industry for 2017

2017 NAICS Code	2017 NAICS U.S. Description	Status Code	2012 NAICS Code	2012 NAICS U.S. Description
4522	Department Stores			
45221	Department Stores			
452210	Department Stores	N	452111	Department Stores (except Discount Department Stores)
			*452112	Discount Department Stores - *insignificant perishable grocery sales*
4523	General Merchandise Stores, including Warehouse Clubs and Supercenters			
45231	General Merchandise Stores, including Warehouse Clubs and Supercenters			
452311	Warehouse Clubs and Supercenters	N	452910	Warehouse Clubs and Supercenters
			*452112	Discount Department Stores - *significant perishable grocery sales*
452319	All Other General Merchandise Stores	N	452990	All Other General Merchandise Stores
454110	Electronic Shopping and Mail-Order Houses	N	454111	Electronic Shopping
			454112	Electronic Auctions
			454113	Mail-Order Houses
51225	Record Production and Distribution			
512250	Record Production and Distribution	N	512210	Record Production
			512220	Integrated Record Production/Distribution
5173	Wired and Wireless Telecommunications Carriers			
51731	Wired and Wireless Telecommunications Carriers			
517311	Wired Telecommunications Carriers	N	517110	Wired Telecommunications Carriers

*—Part of 2012 NAICS United States industry; N—New NAICS industry for 2017

2017 NAICS Code	2017 NAICS U.S. Description	Status Code	2012 NAICS Code	2012 NAICS U.S. Description
517312	Wireless Telecommunications Carriers (except Satellite)	N	517210	Wireless Telecommunications Carriers (except Satellite)
53228	Other Consumer Goods Rental			
532281	Formal Wear and Costume Rental	N	532220	Formal Wear and Costume Rental
532282	Video Tape and Disc Rental	N	532230	Video Tape and Disc Rental
532283	Home Health Equipment Rental	N	532291	Home Health Equipment Rental
532284	Recreational Goods Rental	N	532292	Recreational Goods Rental
532289	All Other Consumer Goods Rental	N	532299	All Other Consumer Goods Rental
541713	Research and Development in Nanotechnology	N	*541711	Research and Development in Biotechnology - *nanobiotechnologies research and experimental development laboratories*
			*541712	Research and Development in the Physical, Engineering, and Life Sciences (except Biotechnology) - *nanotechnology research and experimental development laboratories*
541714	Research and Development in Biotechnology (except Nanobiotechnology)	N	*541711	Research and Development in Biotechnology - *except nanobiotechnologies research and experimental development laboratories*
541715	Research and Development in the Physical, Engineering, and Life Sciences (except Nanotechnology and Biotechnology)	N	*541712	Research and Development in the Physical, Engineering, and Life Sciences (except Biotechnology) - *except nanotechnology research and experimental development laboratories*

---

*—Part of 2012 NAICS United States industry; N—New NAICS industry for 2017

Appendix B

2012 NAICS U.S. Matched to
2017 NAICS U.S.

2012 NAICS Code	2012 NAICS U.S. Description	Status Code	2017 NAICS Code	2017 NAICS U.S. Description
211111	Crude Petroleum and Natural Gas Extraction			
	crude petroleum extraction		211120	Crude Petroleum Extraction
	natural gas extraction	pt.	211130	Natural Gas Extraction
211112	Natural Gas Liquid Extraction	pt.	211130	Natural Gas Extraction
212231	Lead Ore and Zinc Ore Mining	pt.	212230	Copper, Nickel, Lead, and Zinc Mining
212234	Copper Ore and Nickel Ore Mining	pt.	212230	Copper, Nickel, Lead, and Zinc Mining
333911	Pump and Pumping Equipment Manufacturing	pt.	333914	Measuring, Dispensing, and Other Pumping Equipment Manufacturing
333913	Measuring and Dispensing Pump Manufacturing	pt.	333914	Measuring, Dispensing, and Other Pumping Equipment Manufacturing
335221	Household Cooking Appliance Manufacturing	pt.	335220	Major Household Appliance Manufacturing
335222	Household Refrigerator and Home Freezer Manufacturing	pt.	335220	Major Household Appliance Manufacturing
335224	Household Laundry Equipment Manufacturing	pt.	335220	Major Household Appliance Manufacturing
335228	Other Major Household Appliance Manufacturing	pt.	335220	Major Household Appliance Manufacturing
452111	Department Stores (except Discount Department Stores)	pt.	452210	Department Stores

pt.—Part of 2017 NAICS United States industry

2012 NAICS Code	2012 NAICS U.S. Description	Status Code	2017 NAICS Code	2017 NAICS U.S. Description
452112	Discount Department Stores			
	insignificant perishable grocery sales	pt.	452210	Department Stores
	significant perishable grocery sales	pt.	452311	Warehouse Clubs and Supercenters
452910	Warehouse Clubs and Supercenters	pt.	452311	Warehouse Clubs and Supercenters
452990	All Other General Merchandise Stores		452319	All Other General Merchandise Stores
454111	Electronic Shopping	pt.	454110	Electronic Shopping and Mail-Order Houses
454112	Electronic Auctions	pt.	454110	Electronic Shopping and Mail-Order Houses
454113	Mail-Order Houses	pt.	454110	Electronic Shopping and Mail-Order Houses
512210	Record Production	pt.	512250	Record Production and Distribution
512220	Integrated Record Production/Distribution	pt.	512250	Record Production and Distribution
517110	Wired Telecommunications Carriers		517311	Wired Telecommunications Carriers
517210	Wireless Telecommunications Carriers (except Satellite)		517312	Wireless Telecommunications Carriers (except Satellite)
532220	Formal Wear and Costume Rental		532281	Formal Wear and Costume Rental
532230	Video Tape and Disc Rental		532282	Video Tape and Disc Rental
532291	Home Health Equipment Rental		532283	Home Health Equipment Rental
532292	Recreational Goods Rental		532284	Recreational Goods Rental
532299	All Other Consumer Goods Rental		532289	All Other Consumer Goods Rental

pt.—Part of 2017 NAICS United States industry

2012 NAICS Code	2012 NAICS U.S. Description	Status Code	2017 NAICS Code	2017 NAICS U.S. Description
541711	Research and Development in Biotechnology			
	nanobiotechnologies research and experimental development laboratories	pt.	541713	Research and Development in Nanotechnology
	except nanobiotechnologies research and experimental development laboratories		541714	Research and Development in Biotechnology (except Nanobiotechnology)
541712	Research and Development in the Physical, Engineering, and Life Sciences (except Biotechnology)			
	nanotechnology research and experimental development laboratories	pt.	541713	Research and Development in Nanotechnology
	except nanotechnology research and experimental development laboratories		541715	Research and Development in the Physical, Engineering, and Life Sciences (except Nanotechnology and Biotechnology)

pt.—Part of 2017 NAICS United States industry

Part IV

Alphabetic Index

Alphabetic Index

311611   Abattoirs

621410   Abortion clinics

334519   Abrasion testing machines manufacturing

339114   Abrasive points, wheels, and disks, dental, manufacturing

327910   Abrasive products manufacturing

212322   Abrasive sand quarrying and/or beneficiating

212399   Abrasive stones (e.g., emery, grindstones, hones, pumice) mining and/or beneficiating

423840   Abrasives merchant wholesalers

212399   Abrasives, natural, mining and/or beneficiating

322121   Absorbent paper stock manufacturing

332420   Absorbers, gas, heavy gauge metal, manufacturing

334513   Absorption analyzers, industrial process type (e.g., infrared), manufacturing

237310   Abutment construction

611691   Academic tutoring services

611310   Academies, college or university

611110   Academies, elementary or secondary

611210   Academies, junior college

611310   Academies, military service (college)

611620   Academies, riding instruction

334511   Acceleration indicators and systems components, aerospace type, manufacturing

325199   Accelerators (i.e., basic synthetic chemical) manufacturing

334519   Accelerometers (except aerospace type) manufacturing

238330   Access flooring installation

424320   Accessories, clothing, men's and boy's, merchant wholesalers

813319   Accident prevention associations

524130   Accidental and health reinsurance carriers

524113   Accidental death and dismemberment insurance carriers, direct

524113   Accidental death and dismemberment insurance underwriting, direct

339992   Accordions and parts manufacturing

561440   Account collection services

541219   Accountants' (except CPAs) offices

541219   Accountants' (except CPAs) private practices

541211   Accountants' (i.e., CPAs) offices, certified public

541211   Accountants' (i.e., CPAs) private practices, certified public

813920   Accountants' associations

541211   Accounting (i.e., CPAs) services, certified public

423420   Accounting machines merchant wholesalers

541219   Accounting services (except CPAs)

332420   Accumulators, industrial pressure vessels, heavy gauge metal, manufacturing

325211   Acetal resins manufacturing

325199   Acetaldehyde manufacturing

325220   Acetate fibers and filaments manufacturing

325194   Acetate of lime, natural, made by distillation of wood

313110   Acetate spun yarns made from purchased fiber

325199   Acetates, not specified elsewhere by process, manufacturing

325199   Acetic acid manufacturing

325199   Acetic anhydride manufacturing

325199   Acetin manufacturing

325194   Acetone, natural, manufacturing

325199   Acetone, synthetic, manufacturing

332420   Acetylene cylinders, heavy gauge metal, manufacturing

325120   Acetylene manufacturing

325411   Acetylsalicylic acid manufacturing

325130   Acid dyes, synthetic organic, manufacturing

325199   Acid esters, not specified elsewhere by process, manufacturing

324110   Acid oils made in petroleum refineries

236210   Acid plant construction

562211   Acid waste disposal facilities

562211   Acid waste treatment facilities

334513   Acidity (i.e., pH) instruments, industrial process type, manufacturing

334516   Acidity (i.e., pH) measuring equipment, laboratory analysis-type, manufacturing

213112	Acidizing oil and gas field wells on a contract basis
311511	Acidophilus milk manufacturing
424690	Acids merchant wholesalers
325199	Acids, organic, not specified elsewhere by process, manufacturing
111219	Acorn squash farming, field, bedding plant and seed production
238310	Acoustical ceiling tile and panel installation
541330	Acoustical engineering consulting services
238310	Acoustical foam (i.e., sound barrier) installation
332323	Acoustical suspension systems, metal, manufacturing
541330	Acoustical system engineering design services
541380	Acoustics testing laboratories or services
325199	Acrolein manufacturing
325212	Acrylate rubber manufacturing
325212	Acrylate-butadiene rubber manufacturing
313110	Acrylic and modacrylic filament yarn throwing, twisting, texturizing, or winding purchased yarn
325220	Acrylic fibers and filaments manufacturing
326113	Acrylic film and unlaminated sheet (except packaging) manufacturing
325211	Acrylic resins manufacturing
325212	Acrylic rubber manufacturing
313110	Acrylic spun yarns made from purchased fiber
325220	Acrylonitrile fibers and filaments manufacturing
325199	Acrylonitrile manufacturing
325211	Acrylonitrile-butadiene-styrene (ABS) resins manufacturing
334519	Actinometers, meteorological, manufacturing
339930	Action figures manufacturing
325998	Activated carbon or charcoal manufacturing
624120	Activity centers for disabled persons, the elderly, and persons diagnosed with intellectual and developmental disabilities
711510	Actors, independent
711510	Actresses, independent
541612	Actuarial consulting services (except insurance actuarial services)
524298	Actuarial services, insurance
333995	Actuators, fluid power, manufacturing
423830	Actuators, fluid power, merchant wholesalers
611519	Acupuncture training
621399	Acupuncturists' (except MDs or DOs) offices (e.g., centers, clinics)
621111	Acupuncturists' (MDs or DOs) offices (e.g., centers, clinics)
325110	Acyclic hydrocarbons (e.g., butene, ethylene, propene) (except acetylene) made from refined petroleum or liquid hydrocarbons
332993	Adapters, bombcluster, manufacturing
333318	Adding machines manufacturing
236118	Addition, alteration and renovation (i.e., construction), multifamily building
236118	Addition, alteration and renovation (i.e., construction), residential building
236118	Addition, alteration and renovation of single-family dwellings
236220	Addition, alteration and renovation, commercial and institutional building
236220	Addition, alteration and renovation, commercial warehouse
236220	Addition, alteration and renovation, for-sale builders, commercial and institutional building
236220	Addition, alteration and renovation, for-sale builders, commercial warehouse
236220	Addition, alteration and renovation, for-sale builders, hotel and motel
236210	Addition, alteration and renovation, for-sale builders, industrial building (except warehouses)
236220	Addition, alteration and renovation, for-sale builders, industrial warehouse
236220	Addition, alteration and renovation, general contractors, commercial and institutional building
236220	Addition, alteration and renovation, general contractors, commercial warehouse
236220	Addition, alteration and renovation, general contractors, hotel and motel
236210	Addition, alteration and renovation, general contractors, industrial building (except warehouses)
236220	Addition, alteration and renovation, general contractors, industrial warehouse
236220	Addition, alteration and renovation, hotel and motel
236210	Addition, alteration and renovation, industrial building (except warehouses)
236220	Addition, alteration and renovation, industrial warehouse
236118	Addition, alteration and renovation, multifamily building, for-sale builders

236118 Addition, alteration and renovation, multifamily building, general contractors

236118 Addition, alteration and renovation, residential building, for-sale builders

236118 Addition, alteration and renovation, residential building, general contractors

236118 Addition, alteration and renovation, single-family housing, for-sale builders

236118 Addition, alteration and renovation, single-family housing, general contractors

333249 Additive manufacturing machinery manufacturing

325998 Additive preparations for gasoline (e.g., antiknock preparations, detergents, gum inhibitors) manufacturing

561499 Address bar coding services

511140 Address list publishers (except exclusive Internet publishing)

511140 Address list publishers and printing combined

323111 Address lists commercial printing (except screen) without publishing

323113 Address lists screen printing without publishing

423420 Addressing machines merchant wholesalers

322220 Adhesive tape (except medical) made from purchased materials

339113 Adhesive tape, medical, manufacturing

325520 Adhesives (except asphalt, dental, gypsum base) manufacturing

424690 Adhesives and sealants merchant wholesalers

325199 Adipic acid esters or amines manufacturing

325199 Adipic acid manufacturing

325199 Adiponitrile manufacturing

561440 Adjustment agencies (except insurance)

236220 Administration building construction

922110 Administrative courts

541611 Administrative management consulting services

561110 Administrative management services

523991 Administrators of private estates

327120 Adobe bricks manufacturing

624110 Adoption agencies

624110 Adoption services, child

325411 Adrenal derivatives, uncompounded, manufacturing

325412 Adrenal medicinal preparations manufacturing

624120 Adult day care centers

611691 Adult literacy instruction

327110 Advanced and technical ceramic products manufacturing

621399 Advanced practicing registered nurses' (APRNs) offices (e.g., centers, clinics)

541810 Advertising agencies

541810 Advertising agency consulting services

541870 Advertising material (e.g., coupons, flyers, samples) direct distribution services

541860 Advertising material preparation services for mailing or other direct distribution

323111 Advertising materials (e.g., coupons, flyers) commercial printing (except screen) without publishing

541840 Advertising media representatives (i.e., independent of media owners)

511120 Advertising periodical publishers (except exclusive Internet publishing)

511120 Advertising periodical publishers and printing combined

519130 Advertising periodical publishers, exclusively on Internet

515112 Advertising sales offices of independent and public radio broadcast stations

541850 Advertising services, indoor or outdoor display

541890 Advertising specialty (e.g., keychain, magnet, pen) distribution services

541850 Advertising, aerial

921110 Advisory commissions, executive government

921120 Advisory commissions, legislative

487990 Aerial cable car, scenic and sightseeing, operation

333316 Aerial cameras manufacturing

115112 Aerial crop dusting or spraying (i.e., using specialized or dedicated aircraft)

115310 Aerial forest mulching or seeding

541360 Aerial geophysical surveying services

238910 Aerial or picker truck, construction, rental with operator

541370 Aerial surveying (except geophysical) services

487990 Aerial tramway, scenic and sightseeing, operation

333923 Aerial work platforms manufacturing

713940 Aerobic dance and exercise centers

611620 Aerobic dance and exercise instruction

423860 Aeronautical equipment and supplies merchant wholesalers

334511	Aeronautical systems and instruments manufacturing
334511	Aeronautical systems and instruments overhauling, conversion, or rebuilding
325998	Aerosol can filling on a job-order or contract basis
332431	Aerosol cans, light gauge metal, manufacturing
325998	Aerosol packaging services
332919	Aerosol valves manufacturing
423860	Aerospace equipment and supplies merchant wholesalers
541715	Aerospace research and development (except prototype production)
332410	Aftercoolers (i.e., heat exchangers) manufacturing
423120	Aftermarket parts, automotive, merchant wholesalers
325620	After-shave preparations manufacturing
325414	Agar culture media manufacturing
325411	Agar-agar manufacturing
212399	Agate mining and/or beneficiating
111998	Agave farming
522293	Agencies of foreign banks (i.e., trade financing)
524210	Agencies, insurance
522310	Agencies, loan
531210	Agencies, real estate
531390	Agencies, real estate escrow
425120	Agents and brokers, durable goods, wholesale trade
425120	Agents and brokers, nondurable goods, wholesale trade
531390	Agents' offices, real estate escrow
711410	Agents, artists'
711410	Agents, authors'
711410	Agents, celebrities'
711410	Agents, entertainers'
812320	Agents, laundry and drycleaning
711410	Agents, modeling
711410	Agents, public figures'
531210	Agents, real estate
488510	Agents, shipping
711410	Agents, sports figures'
711410	Agents, talent
711410	Agents, theatrical talent
212210	Agglomerates, iron ore, beneficiating
333120	Aggregate spreaders manufacturing
325414	Aggressins (except in-vitro) manufacturing
551112	Agreement corporation (except international trade financing)
522293	Agreement corporations (i.e., international trade financing)
524126	Agricultural (i.e., crop, livestock) insurance carriers, direct
424910	Agricultural chemicals merchant wholesalers
541690	Agricultural consulting services
926140	Agricultural cooperative extension program administration
522298	Agricultural credit institutions, making loans or extending credit (except real estate, sales financing)
711320	Agricultural fair managers without facilities
711320	Agricultural fair organizers without facilities
711320	Agricultural fair promoters without facilities
332216	Agricultural handtools (e.g., hay forks, hoes, rakes, spades), nonpowered, manufacturing
423820	Agricultural implements merchant wholesalers
522298	Agricultural lending (except real estate, sales financing)
327410	Agricultural lime manufacturing
424910	Agricultural limestone merchant wholesalers
212312	Agricultural limestone mining and/or beneficiating
423820	Agricultural machinery and equipment merchant wholesalers
532490	Agricultural machinery and equipment rental or leasing
811310	Agricultural machinery and equipment repair and maintenance services
511120	Agricultural magazine and periodical publishers (except exclusive Internet publishing)
511120	Agricultural magazine and periodical publishers and printing combined
519130	Agricultural magazine and periodical publishers, exclusively on Internet
323111	Agricultural magazines and periodicals commercial printing (except screen) without publishing
323113	Agricultural magazines and periodicals screen printing without publishing
926140	Agricultural marketing services government

813910	Agricultural organizations (except youth farming organizations, farm granges)
926140	Agricultural pest and weed regulation, government
484220	Agricultural products trucking, local
531190	Agricultural property rental or leasing
926140	Agriculture fair boards administration
115115	Agriculture production or harvesting crews
541715	Agriculture research and development laboratories or services (except biotechnology and nanotechnology research and development)
541690	Agrology consulting services
541690	Agronomy consulting services
624110	Aid to families with dependent children (AFDC)
621910	Air ambulance services
336390	Air bag assemblies manufacturing
336390	Air bag initiators manufacturing
336612	Air boat building
336340	Air brake systems and parts, automotive, truck, and bus, manufacturing
481212	Air cargo carriers (except air couriers), nonscheduled
481112	Air cargo carriers (except air couriers), scheduled
332439	Air cargo containers, light gauge metal, manufacturing
335313	Air circuit breakers manufacturing
481111	Air commuter carriers, scheduled
333912	Air compressors (except air-conditioning, refrigeration) manufacturing
423830	Air compressors (except air-conditioning, refrigeration) merchant wholesalers
492110	Air courier services (except establishments operating under a universal service obligation)
332322	Air cowls, sheet metal (except stampings), manufacturing
336390	Air filters, automotive, truck, and bus, manufacturing
334512	Air flow controllers (except valves), air-conditioning and refrigeration, manufacturing
928110	Air Force
325612	Air fresheners manufacturing
313230	Air laid nonwoven fabrics manufacturing
481211	Air passenger carriers, nonscheduled
481111	Air passenger carriers, scheduled
423730	Air pollution control equipment and

	supplies merchant wholesalers
335210	Air purification equipment, portable, manufacturing
333413	Air purification equipment, stationary, manufacturing
332420	Air receiver tanks, heavy gauge metal, manufacturing
333413	Air scrubbing systems manufacturing
711310	Air show managers with facilities
711320	Air show managers without facilities
711310	Air show organizers with facilities
711320	Air show organizers without facilities
711310	Air show promoters with facilities
711320	Air show promoters without facilities
238220	Air system balancing and testing
481211	Air taxi services
334511	Air traffic control radar systems and equipment manufacturing
611519	Air traffic control schools
488111	Air traffic control services (except military)
928110	Air traffic control, military
238220	Air vent installation
333413	Air washers (i.e., air scrubbers) manufacturing
487210	Airboat (i.e., swamp buggy) operation
334511	Airborne navigational systems manufacturing
334220	Airborne radio communications equipment manufacturing
532210	Air-conditioner rental
811412	Air-conditioner, window, repair and maintenance services
336390	Air-conditioners, motor vehicle, manufacturing
423620	Air-conditioners, room, merchant wholesalers
333415	Air-conditioners, unit (e.g., motor home, travel trailer, window), manufacturing
333415	Air-conditioning and warm air heating combination units manufacturing
333415	Air-conditioning compressors (except motor vehicle) manufacturing
333415	Air-conditioning condensers and condensing units manufacturing
333415	Air-conditioning equipment (except motor vehicle) manufacturing
423730	Air-conditioning equipment (except room units) merchant wholesalers

221330	Air-conditioning supply
238220	Air-conditioning system (except window) installation
331491	Aircraft and automotive wire and cable (except aluminum, copper) made from purchased nonferrous metals (except aluminum, copper) in wire drawing plants
331420	Aircraft and automotive wire or cable made from purchased copper in wire drawing plants
332994	Aircraft artillery manufacturing
336413	Aircraft assemblies, subassemblies, and parts (except engines) manufacturing
336413	Aircraft auxiliary parts (e.g., crop dusting, external fuel tanks, inflight refueling equipment) manufacturing
336413	Aircraft brakes manufacturing
333999	Aircraft carrier catapults manufacturing
481219	Aircraft charter services (i.e., general purpose aircraft used for a variety of specialty air and flying services)
481211	Aircraft charter services, passenger
336413	Aircraft control surface assemblies manufacturing
336411	Aircraft conversions (i.e., major modifications to system)
441228	Aircraft dealers
336412	Aircraft engine and engine parts (except carburetors, pistons, piston rings, valves) manufacturing
333924	Aircraft engine cradles manufacturing
334519	Aircraft engine instruments manufacturing
336412	Aircraft engine overhauling
336412	Aircraft engine rebuilding
423860	Aircraft engines and parts merchant wholesalers
423860	Aircraft equipment and supplies merchant wholesalers
488190	Aircraft ferrying services
334511	Aircraft flight instruments (except engine instruments) manufacturing
336413	Aircraft fuselage wing tail and similar assemblies manufacturing
488119	Aircraft hangar rental
332510	Aircraft hardware, metal, manufacturing
488190	Aircraft inspection services
926120	Aircraft inspection, government
561720	Aircraft janitorial services
336320	Aircraft lighting fixtures manufacturing
333924	Aircraft loading hoists manufacturing
488190	Aircraft maintenance and repair services (except factory conversion, factory overhaul, factory rebuilding)
336411	Aircraft manufacturing
423860	Aircraft merchant wholesalers
336411	Aircraft overhauling
488119	Aircraft parking service
336413	Aircraft propellers and parts manufacturing
336411	Aircraft rebuilding (i.e., restoration to original design specifications)
532411	Aircraft rental or leasing without operator
336360	Aircraft seats manufacturing
488190	Aircraft testing services
314999	Aircraft tie-down strap assemblies (except leather) manufacturing
326211	Aircraft tire manufacturing
336412	Aircraft turbines manufacturing
811420	Aircraft upholstery repair
336413	Aircraft wheels manufacturing
333413	Aircurtains manufacturing
336413	Airframe assemblies (except for guided missiles) manufacturing
336419	Airframe assemblies for guided missiles manufacturing
334511	Airframe equipment instruments manufacturing
722310	Airline food services contractors
561599	Airline reservation services
561599	Airline ticket offices
332313	Airlocks, fabricated metal plate work, manufacturing
481112	Airmail carriers, scheduled
532411	Airplane rental or leasing without operator
488119	Airport baggage handling services
236220	Airport building construction
488119	Airport cargo handling services
531190	Airport leasing, not operating airport, rental or leasing
335311	Airport lighting transformers manufacturing
485999	Airport limousine services (i.e., shuttle)
488119	Airport operators (e.g., civil, international, national)
488190	Airport passenger screening security services
237310	Airport runway construction
238210	Airport runway lighting contractors

237310 Airport runway line painting (e.g., striping)

488119 Airport runway maintenance services

485999 Airport shuttle services

236220 Airport terminal construction

488119 Airports, civil, operation and maintenance

334511 Airspeed instruments (aeronautical) manufacturing

212399 Alabaster mining and/or beneficiating

423610 Alarm apparatus, electric, merchant wholesalers

334519 Alarm clocks manufacturing

238210 Alarm system (e.g., fire, burglar), electric, installation only

334290 Alarm system central monitoring equipment manufacturing

561621 Alarm system monitoring services

334290 Alarm systems and equipment manufacturing

561621 Alarm systems sales combined with installation, repair, or monitoring services

323111 Albums (e.g., photo, scrap) and refills manufacturing

424120 Albums, photo, merchant wholesalers

424690 Alcohol, industrial, merchant wholesalers

922120 Alcohol, tobacco, and firearms control

926150 Alcoholic beverage control boards

492210 Alcoholic beverage delivery service

722410 Alcoholic beverage drinking places

312140 Alcoholic beverages (except brandy) distilling

424810 Alcoholic beverages (except distilled spirits, wine) merchant wholesalers

312130 Alcoholic beverages, brandy, distilling

424820 Alcoholic beverages, wine, and distilled spirits merchant wholesalers

624190 Alcoholism and drug addiction self-help organizations

624190 Alcoholism counseling (except medical treatment), nonresidential

623220 Alcoholism rehabilitation facilities (except licensed hospitals), residential

622210 Alcoholism rehabilitation hospitals

624190 Alcoholism self-help organizations

621420 Alcoholism treatment centers and clinics (except hospitals), outpatient

325199 Aldehydes manufacturing

312120 Ale brewing

424810 Ale merchant wholesalers

111940 Alfalfa hay farming

311119 Alfalfa meal, dehydrated, manufacturing

424910 Alfalfa merchant wholesalers

311119 Alfalfa prepared as feed for animals

111998 Alfalfa seed farming

111419 Alfalfa sprout farming, grown under cover

311119 Alfalfa, cubed, manufacturing

112519 Algae farming

325199 Alginates (e.g., calcium, potassium, sodium) manufacturing

325199 Alginic acid manufacturing

334519 Alidades, surveying, manufacturing

333318 Alignment equipment, motor vehicle, manufacturing

325110 Aliphatic (e.g., hydrocarbons) (except acetylene) made from refined petroleum or liquid hydrocarbons

324110 Aliphatic chemicals (i.e., acyclic) made in petroleum refineries

325180 Alkalies manufacturing

424690 Alkalies merchant wholesalers

335912 Alkaline cell primary batteries manufacturing

335911 Alkaline cell storage batteries (i.e., nickel-cadmium, nickel-iron, silver oxide-zinc) manufacturing

335912 Alkaline manganese primary batteries manufacturing

325211 Alkyd resins manufacturing

324110 Alkylates made in petroleum refineries

325414 Allergenic extracts (except diagnostic substances) manufacturing

325414 Allergens manufacturing

621111 Allergists' offices (e.g., centers, clinics)

112519 Alligator production, farm raising

331513 Alloy steel castings (except investment), unfinished, manufacturing

331314 Alloying purchased aluminum metals

331420 Alloying purchased copper

331420 Alloying purchased copper metals

331492 Alloying purchased nonferrous metals (except aluminum, copper)

441228 All-terrain vehicle (ATV) dealers

423110 All-terrain vehicles (ATVs) merchant wholesalers

336999 All-terrain vehicles (ATVs), wheeled or tracked, manufacturing

325211 Allyl resins manufacturing

323120 Almanac binding without printing

511130 Almanac publishers (except exclusive Internet publishing)

511130 Almanac publishers and printing combined

519130 Almanac publishers, exclusively on Internet

323117 Almanacs printing and binding without publishing

323117 Almanacs printing without publishing

111335 Almond farming

115114 Almond hulling and shelling

311999 Almond pastes manufacturing

111998 Aloe farming

112990 Alpaca production

721110 Alpine skiing facilities with accommodations (i.e., ski resorts)

713920 Alpine skiing facilities without accommodations

237130 Alternative energy (e.g., geothermal, ocean wave, solar, wind) structure construction

454310 Alternative fuels, direct selling

334515 Alternator and generator testers manufacturing

336320 Alternators and generators for internal combustion engines manufacturing

334511 Altimeters, aeronautical, manufacturing

212391 Alum, natural, mining and/or beneficiating

327120 Alumina fused refractories manufacturing

327110 Alumina porcelain insulators manufacturing

331313 Alumina refining

327120 Aluminous refractory cement manufacturing

331313 Aluminum alloys made from bauxite or alumina producing primary aluminum and manufacturing

331314 Aluminum alloys made from scrap or dross

423510 Aluminum and aluminum alloy primary forms merchant wholesalers

331318 Aluminum bar made by extruding purchased aluminum

331318 Aluminum bar made in integrated secondary smelting and extruding mills

331314 Aluminum billet made from purchased aluminum

331314 Aluminum billet made in integrated secondary smelting and rolling mills

332431 Aluminum cans, light gauge metal, manufacturing

331524 Aluminum castings (except die-castings), unfinished, manufacturing

325180 Aluminum chloride manufacturing

332812 Aluminum coating of metal products for the trade

325180 Aluminum compounds, not specified elsewhere by process, manufacturing

331523 Aluminum die-casting foundries

331523 Aluminum die-castings, unfinished, manufacturing

238350 Aluminum door and window, residential-type, installation

331314 Aluminum extrusion ingot (i.e., billet), secondary

331314 Aluminum flakes made from purchased aluminum

331315 Aluminum foil made by flat rolling purchased aluminum

331315 Aluminum foil made in integrated secondary smelting and flat rolling mills

423510 Aluminum foil, plate, sheet, coil, and roll products merchant wholesalers

332112 Aluminum forgings made from purchased metals, unfinished

331524 Aluminum foundries (except die-casting)

332999 Aluminum freezer foil not made in rolling mills

325180 Aluminum hydroxide (i.e., alumina trihydrate) manufacturing

331313 Aluminum ingot and other primary aluminum production shapes made from bauxite or alumina

331314 Aluminum ingot made from purchased aluminum

331314 Aluminum ingot, secondary smelting of aluminum and manufacturing

331314 Aluminum ingot, secondary, manufacturing

332999 Aluminum ladders manufacturing

327910 Aluminum oxide (fused) abrasives manufacturing

331313 Aluminum oxide refining

331318 Aluminum pipe made by extruding purchased aluminum

331318 Aluminum pipe made in integrated secondary smelting and extruding mills

236210 Aluminum plant construction

331315 Aluminum plate made by continuous casting purchased aluminum

331315 Aluminum plate made by flat rolling purchased aluminum

331315 Aluminum plate made in integrated secondary smelting and continuous casting mills

331315 Aluminum plate made in integrated secondary smelting and flat rolling mills

331313 Aluminum producing from alumina

331314 Aluminum recovering from scrap and making ingot and billet (except by rolling)

331318 Aluminum rod made by extruding purchased aluminum

331318 Aluminum rod made in integrated secondary smelting and extruding mills

331313 Aluminum shapes (e.g., bar, ingot, rod, sheet) made by producing primary aluminum and manufacturing

331315 Aluminum sheet made by flat rolling purchased aluminum

331315 Aluminum sheet made in integrated secondary smelting and flat rolling mills

238170 Aluminum siding installation

331314 Aluminum smelting, secondary, and making ingot and billet (except by rolling)

325180 Aluminum sulfate manufacturing

331318 Aluminum tube blooms made by extruding purchased aluminum

331318 Aluminum tube blooms made in integrated secondary smelting and extruding mills

331318 Aluminum tube made by drawing or extruding purchased aluminum

331318 Aluminum tube made in integrated secondary smelting and drawing plants

331318 Aluminum tube made in integrated secondary smelting and extruding mills

331315 Aluminum welded tube made by flat rolling purchased aluminum

331315 Aluminum welded tube made in integrated secondary smelting and flat rolling mills

813410 Alumni associations

813410 Alumni clubs

325180 Alums (e.g., aluminum ammonium sulfate, aluminum potassium sulfate) manufacturing

212393 Alunite mining and/or beneficiating

515112 AM radio stations

333131 Amalgamators (i.e., metallurgical and mining machinery) manufacturing

339114 Amalgams, dental, manufacturing

111998 Amaranth farming

713990 Amateur sports teams, recreational

325920 Amatols manufacturing

212393 Amblygonite mining and/or beneficiating

922160 Ambulance and fire service combined

336211 Ambulance bodies manufacturing

423110 Ambulance merchant wholesalers

621910 Ambulance services, air or ground

336211 Ambulances assembling on purchased chassis

621493 Ambulatory surgical centers and clinics, freestanding

921150 American Indian or Alaska Native tribal councils

921150 American Indian or Alaska Native tribal courts

921150 American Indian or Alaska Native, tribal chief's or chairman's office

212399 Amethyst mining and/or beneficiating

334516 Amino acid analyzers, laboratory-type, manufacturing

325211 Amino resins manufacturing

325211 Amino-aldehyde resins manufacturing

325194 Aminoanthraquinone manufacturing

325194 Aminoazobenzene manufacturing

325194 Aminoazotoluene manufacturing

325194 Aminophenol manufacturing

424690 Ammonia (except fertilizer material) merchant wholesalers

325311 Ammonia, anhydrous and aqueous, manufacturing

424910 Ammonia, fertilizer material, merchant wholesalers

325612 Ammonia, household-type, manufacturing

325180 Ammonium chloride manufacturing

325180 Ammonium compounds, not specified elsewhere by process, manufacturing

325180 Ammonium hydroxide manufacturing

325180 Ammonium molybdate manufacturing

325311 Ammonium nitrate manufacturing

325180 Ammonium perchlorate manufacturing

325312 Ammonium phosphates manufacturing

236210 Ammonium plant construction

325311 Ammonium sulfate manufacturing

325180 Ammonium thiosulfate manufacturing

423990 Ammunition (except sporting) merchant wholesalers

332993 Ammunition (i.e., more than 30 mm., more than 1.18 inch) manufacturing

332439 Ammunition boxes, light gauge metal, manufacturing

321920 Ammunition boxes, wood, manufacturing

332994 Ammunition carts manufacturing

332993 Ammunition loading and assembling plants

332992	Ammunition, small arms (i.e., 30 mm. or less, 1.18 inch or less), manufacturing
423910	Ammunition, sporting, merchant wholesalers
334515	Ampere-hour meters manufacturing
325411	Amphetamines, uncompounded, manufacturing
334310	Amplifiers (e.g., auto, home, musical instrument, public address) manufacturing
334220	Amplifiers (e.g., RF power and IF), broadcast and studio equipment, manufacturing
423690	Amplifiers, audio (except household-type), merchant wholesalers
335999	Amplifiers, magnetic, pulse, and maser, manufacturing
713120	Amusement arcades
713990	Amusement device (except gambling) concession operators (i.e., supplying and servicing in others' facilities)
713120	Amusement device (except gambling) parlors, coin-operated
713120	Amusement devices (except gambling) operated in own facilities
236220	Amusement facility construction
531120	Amusement facility rental or leasing
339999	Amusement machines, coin-operated, manufacturing
423850	Amusement park equipment merchant wholesalers
713110	Amusement parks (e.g., theme, water)
713990	Amusement ride concession operators (i.e., supplying and servicing in others' facilities)
325199	Amyl acetate manufacturing
325412	Analgesic preparations manufacturing
334111	Analog computers manufacturing
423490	Analytical instruments (e.g., chromatographic, photometers, spectrographs) merchant wholesalers
334515	Analyzers for testing electrical characteristics manufacturing
334513	Analyzers, industrial process control type, manufacturing
237990	Anchored earth retention contractors
114111	Anchovy fishing
212325	Andalusite mining and/or beneficiating
332999	Andirons manufacturing
339112	Anesthesia apparatus manufacturing
621111	Anesthesiologists' offices (e.g., centers, clinics)
325412	Anesthetic preparations manufacturing

325411	Anesthetics, uncompounded, manufacturing
325412	Angiourographic diagnostic preparations manufacturing
332999	Angle irons, metal, manufacturing
333515	Angle rings (i.e., a machine tool accessory) manufacturing
332911	Angle valves, industrial-type, manufacturing
334511	Angle-of-attack instrumentation manufacturing
334511	Angle-of-yaw instrumentation manufacturing
112420	Angora goat farming
325311	Anhydrous ammonia manufacturing
311512	Anhydrous butterfat manufacturing
325220	Anidex fibers and filaments manufacturing
325194	Aniline manufacturing
112519	Animal aquaculture (except finfish, shellfish)
325180	Animal black manufacturing
813910	Animal breeders' associations
812220	Animal cemeteries
712130	Animal exhibits, live
311611	Animal fats (except poultry and small game) produced in slaughtering plants
311613	Animal fats rendering
311119	Animal feed mills (except dog and cat) manufacturing
311111	Animal feed mills, dog and cat, manufacturing
424910	Animal feeds (except pet food) merchant wholesalers
311119	Animal feeds, prepared (except dog and cat), manufacturing
311111	Animal feeds, prepared, dog and cat, manufacturing
313110	Animal fiber yarn twisting or winding of purchased yarn
812910	Animal grooming services
424590	Animal hair, wool, or mohair merchant wholesalers
541940	Animal hospitals
311613	Animal oil rendering
926140	Animal quarantine service, government
813312	Animal rights organizations
712130	Animal safari parks
115210	Animal semen banks
236220	Animal shelter and clinic construction

812910	Animal shelters
114210	Animal trapping, commercial
332999	Animal traps, metal (except wire), manufacturing
813312	Animal welfare associations or leagues
336999	Animal-drawn vehicles and parts manufacturing
711510	Animated cartoon artists, independent
512120	Animated cartoon distribution
512110	Animated cartoon production
512110	Animated cartoon production and distribution
325998	Anise oil manufacturing
315110	Anklets, sheer hosiery or socks, knitting or knitting and finishing
325194	Annatto extract manufacturing
332811	Annealing metals and metal products for the trade
332420	Annealing vats, heavy gauge metal, manufacturing
711510	Announcers, independent radio and television
524113	Annuities underwriting
332991	Annular ball bearings manufacturing
334513	Annunciators, relay and solid-state types, industrial display, manufacturing
333249	Anodizing equipment manufacturing
332813	Anodizing metals and metal products for the trade
561421	Answering services, telephone
325320	Ant poisons manufacturing
325412	Antacid preparations manufacturing
238290	Antenna, household-type, installation
423690	Antennas merchant wholesalers
334220	Antennas, satellite, manufacturing
334220	Antennas, transmitting and receiving, manufacturing
325412	Anthelmintic preparations manufacturing
325194	Anthracene manufacturing
212113	Anthracite beneficiating (e.g., crushing, screening, washing, cleaning, sizing)
213113	Anthracite mine tunneling on a contract basis
212113	Anthracite mining and/or beneficiating
213113	Anthracite mining services (except site preparation and related construction contractor activities) on a contract basis
325130	Anthraquinone dyes manufacturing

332994	Antiaircraft artillery manufacturing
325412	Antibacterial preparations manufacturing
325412	Antibiotic preparations manufacturing
424210	Antibiotics merchant wholesalers
325411	Antibiotics, uncompounded, manufacturing
325411	Anticholinergics, uncompounded, manufacturing
325411	Anticonvulsants, uncompounded, manufacturing
325412	Antidepressant preparations manufacturing
325411	Antidepressants, uncompounded, manufacturing
424690	Antifreeze merchant wholesalers
325998	Antifreeze preparations manufacturing
325414	Antigens manufacturing
325412	Antihistamine preparations manufacturing
325130	Antimony based pigments manufacturing
212299	Antimony concentrates mining and/or beneficiating
212299	Antimony ores mining and/or beneficiating
325180	Antimony oxide (except pigments) manufacturing
331410	Antimony refining, primary
325412	Antineoplastic preparations manufacturing
325620	Antiperspirants, personal, manufacturing
813319	Antipoverty advocacy organizations
325412	Antipyretic preparations manufacturing
811121	Antique and classic automotive restoration
441120	Antique auto dealers
424920	Antique book merchant wholesalers
453310	Antique dealers (except motor vehicles)
423210	Antique furniture merchant wholesalers
811420	Antique furniture repair and restoration shops
423220	Antique home furnishings merchant wholesalers
423220	Antique houseware merchant wholesalers
423940	Antique jewelry merchant wholesalers
453310	Antique shops
332913	Antiscald bath and shower valves, plumbing, manufacturing
325998	Antiscaling compounds manufacturing
325412	Antiseptic preparations manufacturing
424210	Antiseptics merchant wholesalers
325414	Antiserums manufacturing
325412	Antispasmodic preparations manufacturing

332994	Antisubmarine projectors manufacturing
332994	Antitank rocket launchers manufacturing
325414	Antitoxins manufacturing
325414	Antivenoms manufacturing
236116	Apartment building construction general contractors
236117	Apartment building for-sale builders
531110	Apartment building rental or leasing
531110	Apartment hotel rental or leasing
531311	Apartment managers' offices
531110	Apartment rental or leasing
212392	Apatite mining and/or beneficiating
212325	Aplite mining and/or beneficiating
446110	Apothecaries
331491	Apparatus wire and cord (except aluminum, copper) made from purchased nonferrous metals (except aluminum, copper) in wire drawing plants
331420	Apparatus wire or cord made from purchased copper in wire drawing plants
331318	Apparatus wire or cord made in aluminum wire drawing plants
448150	Apparel accessory stores
315210	Apparel cut and sew contractors
314999	Apparel fillings (e.g., cotton mill waste, kapok) manufacturing
315990	Apparel findings and trimmings cut and sewn from purchased fabric (except apparel contractors)
561910	Apparel folding and packaging services
812320	Apparel pressing services
448130	Apparel stores, children's and infants' clothing
448110	Apparel stores, men's and boys' clothing
453310	Apparel stores, used clothing
448120	Apparel stores, women's and girls' clothing
315210	Apparel trimmings and findings cut and sew apparel contractors
424310	Apparel trimmings merchant wholesalers
313220	Apparel webbings manufacturing
315280	Apparel, fur (except apparel contractors), manufacturing
315210	Apparel, fur, cut and sew apparel contractors
111331	Apple orchards
312130	Applejack distilling
334512	Appliance controls manufacturing
335999	Appliance cords made from purchased insulated wire
423710	Appliance hardware merchant wholesalers
332510	Appliance hardware, metal, manufacturing
334512	Appliance regulators (except switches) manufacturing
532210	Appliance rental
443141	Appliance stores, household-type
453310	Appliance stores, household-type, used
334519	Appliance timers manufacturing
811412	Appliance, household-type, repair and maintenance services without retailing new appliances
423620	Appliances, household-type (except water heaters, heating stoves (i.e., noncooking)), gas and electric, merchant wholesalers
423450	Appliances, surgical, merchant wholesalers
518210	Application hosting
511210	Applications development and publishing, except on a custom basis
541511	Applications software programming services, custom computer
511210	Applications software, computer, packaged
321999	Applicators, wood, manufacturing
315210	Appliqueing on apparel
314999	Appliqueing on textile products (except apparel)
323111	Appointment books and refills manufacturing
541990	Appraisal (except real estate) services
531320	Appraisal services, real estate
531320	Appraisers' offices, real estate
611513	Apprenticeship training programs
111339	Apricot farming
812331	Apron supply services
316998	Aprons for textile machinery, leather, manufacturing
316998	Aprons, leather (e.g., blacksmith's, welder's), manufacturing
315990	Aprons, waterproof (e.g., plastics, rubberized fabric), rubberizing fabric and manufacturing aprons
315210	Aprons, waterproof (including rubberized fabric, plastics), cut and sew apparel contractors
315990	Aprons, waterproof (including rubberized fabric, plastics), cut and sewn from purchased fabric (except apparel contractors)
315210	Aprons, work (except leather), cut and sew apparel contractors

315220	Aprons, work (except leather, waterproof), men's and boys', cut and sewn from purchased fabric (except apparel contractors)
315240	Aprons, work (except waterproof, leather), women's and girls', cut and sewn from purchased fabric (except apparel contractors)
332999	Aquarium accessories, metal, manufacturing
424990	Aquarium fish and supplies merchant wholesalers
712130	Aquariums
327215	Aquariums made from purchased glass
237110	Aqueduct construction
541990	Arbitration and conciliation services (except by attorney, paralegal)
333517	Arbor presses, metalworking, manufacturing
712130	Arboreta
712130	Arboretums
561730	Arborist services
333515	Arbors (i.e., a machine tool accessory) manufacturing
334510	Arc lamp units, electrotherapeutic (except infrared, ultraviolet), manufacturing
335129	Arc lighting fixtures (except electrotherapeutic), electric, manufacturing
713120	Arcades, amusement
339113	Arch supports, orthopedic, manufacturing
541720	Archeological research and development services
712120	Archeological sites (i.e., public display)
339920	Archery equipment manufacturing
423910	Archery equipment merchant wholesalers
713990	Archery ranges
321213	Arches, glue laminated or pre-engineered wood, manufacturing
541310	Architects' (except landscape) offices
541310	Architects' (except landscape) private practices
813920	Architects' associations
423490	Architects' equipment and supplies merchant wholesalers
541320	Architects' offices, landscape
541320	Architects' private practices, landscape
541310	Architectural (except landscape) consultants' offices
541310	Architectural (except landscape) design services

541310	Architectural (except landscape) services
327331	Architectural block, concrete (e.g., fluted, ground face, screen, slump, split), manufacturing
325510	Architectural coatings (i.e., paint) manufacturing
332323	Architectural metalwork manufacturing
423390	Architectural metalwork merchant wholesalers
453310	Architectural salvage dealers
327110	Architectural sculptures, clay, manufacturing
327991	Architectural sculptures, stone, manufacturing
541320	Architectural services, landscape
453998	Architectural supply stores
327120	Architectural terra cotta manufacturing
327390	Architectural wall panels, precast concrete, manufacturing
337212	Architectural woodwork and fixtures (i.e., custom designed interiors) manufacturing
519120	Archives
316210	Arctics, plastics or plastics soled fabric upper, manufacturing
316210	Arctics, rubber or rubber soled fabric, manufacturing
333992	Arc-welding equipment manufacturing
335311	Arc-welding transformers, separate solid-state, manufacturing
335129	Area and sports luminaries (e.g., stadium lighting fixtures), electric, manufacturing
236220	Arena construction
711310	Arena operators
531120	Arena, no promotion of events, rental or leasing
212311	Argillite mining or quarrying
325120	Argon manufacturing
315210	Arm bands cut and sew apparel contractors
315990	Arm bands, elastic, cut and sewn from purchased fabric (except apparel contractors)
335314	Armature relays manufacturing
335312	Armature rewinding on a factory basis
811310	Armature rewinding services (except on an assembly line or factory basis)
335312	Armatures, industrial, manufacturing
928110	Armed forces
332993	Arming and fusing devices, missile, manufacturing
331110	Armor plate made in iron and steel mills

331420	Armored cable made from purchased copper in wire drawing plants
331420	Armored cable, copper, made in integrated secondary smelting and drawing plants
561613	Armored car services
336992	Armored military vehicles (except tanks) and parts manufacturing
236220	Armory construction
928110	Army
424690	Aromatic chemicals merchant wholesalers
325110	Aromatic petrochemicals made from refined petroleum or liquid hydrocarbons
113210	Aromatic wood gathering
488999	Arrangement of car pools and vanpools
335931	Arrestors and coils, lighting, manufacturing
325320	Arsenate insecticides manufacturing
325180	Arsenates (except insecticides) manufacturing
325130	Arsenic based pigments manufacturing
325180	Arsenic compounds, not specified elsewhere by process, manufacturing
212393	Arsenic mineral mining and/or beneficiating
325320	Arsenite insecticides manufacturing
325180	Arsenites (except insecticides) manufacturing
611610	Art (except commercial or graphic) instruction
453920	Art auctions
453920	Art dealers
712110	Art galleries (except retail)
453920	Art galleries retailing art
327420	Art goods (e.g., gypsum, plaster of paris) manufacturing
424990	Art goods merchant wholesalers
712110	Art museums
314999	Art needlework contractors on apparel
314999	Art needlework on clothing for the trade
511199	Art print (except exclusive Internet publishing) publishers
511199	Art print publishers and printing combined
323111	Art prints commercial printing (except screen) without publishing
323113	Art prints screen printing without publishing
511199	Art publishers (except exclusive Internet publishing)
519130	Art publishers, exclusively on Internet
711510	Art restorers, independent
611610	Art schools (except academic), fine
611519	Art schools, commercial or graphic
541430	Art services, commercial
541430	Art services, graphic
541430	Art studios, commercial
453998	Art supply stores
621340	Art therapists' offices (e.g., centers, clinics)
237110	Artesian well construction
111219	Artichoke farming, field, bedding plant and seed production
311421	Artichokes, canned, manufacturing
424990	Artificial Christmas trees merchant wholesalers
339999	Artificial flower arrangements assembled from purchased components
424930	Artificial flowers and plants merchant wholesalers
334511	Artificial horizon instrumentation manufacturing
115210	Artificial insemination services for livestock
115210	Artificial insemination services for pets
339113	Artificial limbs manufacturing
423450	Artificial limbs merchant wholesalers
238990	Artificial turf installation
312111	Artificially carbonated waters manufacturing
332993	Artillery ammunition (i.e., more than 30 mm., more than 1.18 inch) manufacturing
711510	Artists (except commercial, musical), independent
711510	Artists (i.e., painters), independent
711410	Artists' agents or managers
339940	Artist's paint manufacturing
339940	Artist's supplies (except paper) manufacturing
424990	Artists' supplies merchant wholesalers
541430	Artists, independent commercial
541430	Artists, independent graphic
541430	Artists, independent medical
926110	Arts and cultural program administration, government
711310	Arts event managers with facilities
711320	Arts event managers without facilities
711310	Arts event organizers with facilities
711320	Arts event organizers without facilities

711310   Arts event promoters with facilities

711320   Arts event promoters without facilities

711310   Arts festival managers with facilities

711320   Arts festival managers without facilities

711310   Arts festival organizers with facilities

711320   Arts festival organizers without facilities

711310   Arts festival promoters with facilities

711320   Arts festival promoters without facilities

562910   Asbestos abatement services

212399   Asbestos mining and/or beneficiating

327999   Asbestos products (except brake shoes and clutches) manufacturing

562910   Asbestos removal contractors

325411   Ascorbic acid (i.e., vitamin C), uncompounded, manufacturing

315210   Ascots cut and sew apparel contractors

315990   Ascots, men's and boys', cut and sewn from purchased fabric (except apparel contractors)

562111   Ash collection services

562111   Ash hauling, local

484220   Ash, garbage, recyclable material, refuse, rubbish, trash, or waste hauling (except collection or disposal)

212399   Ash, volcanic, mining and/or beneficiating

327215   Ashtrays made from purchased glass

327212   Ashtrays, glass, made in glass making plants

327110   Ashtrays, pottery, manufacturing

111219   Asparagus farming, field, bedding plant and seed production

324110   Asphalt and asphaltic materials made in petroleum refineries

423320   Asphalt and concrete mixtures merchant wholesalers

424710   Asphalt binder bulk stations and terminals, merchant wholesalers

424720   Asphalt binder merchant wholesalers (except bulk stations, terminals)

238990   Asphalt coating and sealing, residential and commercial parking lot and driveway

327999   Asphalt concrete crushing and grinding (except at construction site)

423330   Asphalt felts and coatings merchant wholesalers

238330   Asphalt flooring, installation only

322121   Asphalt paper made in paper mills

237310   Asphalt paving (i.e., highway, road, street, public sidewalk)

324121   Asphalt paving blocks made from purchased asphaltic materials

324121   Asphalt paving mixtures made from purchased asphaltic materials

324110   Asphalt paving mixtures made in petroleum refineries

324121   Asphalt road compounds made from purchased asphaltic materials

212399   Asphalt rock mining and/or beneficiating

238160   Asphalt roof shingle installation

324122   Asphalt roofing cements made from purchased asphaltic materials

324122   Asphalt roofing coatings made from purchased asphaltic materials

333120   Asphalt roofing construction machinery manufacturing

423330   Asphalt roofing shingles merchant wholesalers

324122   Asphalt saturated boards made from purchased asphaltic materials

324122   Asphalt saturated mats and felts made from purchased asphaltic materials and paper

324122   Asphalt shingles made from purchased asphaltic materials

424710   Asphalt, liquid, bulk stations and terminals, merchant wholesalers

424720   Asphalt, liquid, merchant wholesalers (except bulk stations, terminals)

212399   Asphalt, native, mining and/or beneficiating

238990   Asphalting, residential and commercial driveway and parking area

541380   Assaying services

336213   Assembly line conversions of purchased vans and minivans

336310   Assembly line rebuilding of automotive and truck gasoline engines

336350   Assembly line rebuilding of automotive, truck, and bus transmissions

333519   Assembly machines manufacturing

236210   Assembly plant construction

336120   Assembly plants, heavy trucks, and buses on chassis of own manufacture

336112   Assembly plants, light trucks on chassis of own manufacture

336112   Assembly plants, minivans on chassis of own manufacture

336111   Assembly plants, passenger car, on chassis of own manufacture

336112   Assembly plants, sport utility vehicles on chassis of own manufacture

921130   Assessor's offices, tax

325613	Assistants, textile and leather finishing, manufacturing
623311	Assisted living facilities with on-site nursing facilities
623312	Assisted living facilities without on-site nursing care facilities
813311	Associations for retired persons, advocacy
522120	Associations, savings and loan
325412	Astringent preparations manufacturing
812990	Astrology services
711219	Athletes, amateur, independent
711219	Athletes, independent (i.e., participating in live sports events)
813990	Athletic associations, regulatory
315220	Athletic clothing (except team athletic uniforms), men's, boys' and unisex (i.e., sized without regard to gender), cut and sewn from purchased fabric (except apparel contractors)
315240	Athletic clothing (except team athletic uniforms), women's and girls', cut and sewn from purchased fabric (except apparel contractors)
315210	Athletic clothing cut and sew apparel contractors
315190	Athletic clothing made in apparel knitting mills
713940	Athletic club facilities, physical fitness
713990	Athletic clubs (i.e., sports teams) not operating sports facilities, recreational
236220	Athletic court, indoor, construction
451110	Athletic equipment and supply stores (including uniforms)
237990	Athletic field (except stadium) construction
424340	Athletic footwear merchant wholesalers
339920	Athletic goods (except ammunition, clothing, footwear, small arms) manufacturing
423910	Athletic goods (except apparel, footwear, nonspecialty) merchant wholesalers
813990	Athletic leagues (i.e., regulating bodies)
448210	Athletic shoe (except bowling, golf, spiked) stores
316210	Athletic shoes manufacturing
316210	Athletic shoes, plastics or plastics soled fabric upper, manufacturing
316210	Athletic shoes, rubber or rubber soled fabric upper, manufacturing
315110	Athletic socks knitting or knitting and finishing
423910	Athletic uniforms merchant wholesalers

315210	Athletic uniforms, team, cut and sew apparel contractors
315280	Athletic uniforms, team, cut and sewn from purchased fabric (except apparel contractors)
511130	Atlas publishers (except exclusive Internet publishing)
511130	Atlas publishers and printing combined
519130	Atlas publishers, exclusively on Internet
323111	Atlases commercial printing (except screen) without publishing
424920	Atlases merchant wholesalers
323113	Atlases screen printing without publishing
238290	ATMs (automatic teller machines) installation
334118	ATMs (automatic teller machines) manufacturing
335999	Atom smashers (i.e., particle accelerators) manufacturing
334516	Atomic force microscopes manufacturing
339999	Atomizers (e.g., perfumes) manufacturing
325411	Atropine and derivatives manufacturing
316998	Attache cases, all materials, manufacturing
333112	Attachments, powered lawn and garden equipment, manufacturing
333413	Attic fans manufacturing
238310	Attic space insulating
922130	Attorney generals' offices
541110	Attorneys' offices
541110	Attorneys' private practices
453998	Auction houses (general merchandise)
424520	Auction markets, livestock (except horses, mules), merchant wholesalers
424590	Auction markets, tobacco, horses, mules, merchant wholesalers
561990	Auctioneers, independent
531210	Auctioning real estate for others (i.e., agents, brokers)
454110	Auctions, Internet retail
454110	Audio and video content downloading retail sales sites
423990	Audio and video tapes and disks, prerecorded, merchant wholesalers
321999	Audio cabinets (i.e., housings), wood, manufacturing
238210	Audio equipment installation (except automotive) contractors
443142	Audio equipment stores (except automotive)
423620	Audio equipment, household-type, merchant wholesalers

512290	Audio recording of meetings or conferences
512240	Audio recording postproduction services
512240	Audio recording restoration services
532490	Audio visual equipment rental or leasing
334515	Audiofrequency oscillators manufacturing
334510	Audiological equipment, electromedical, manufacturing
621340	Audiologists' offices (e.g., centers, clinics)
334515	Audiometers (except medical) manufacturing
334613	Audiotape, blank, manufacturing
423690	Audiotapes, blank, merchant wholesalers
541211	Auditing accountants' (i.e., CPAs) offices
541211	Auditing accountants' (i.e., CPAs) private practices
541211	Auditing services (i.e., CPA services), accounts
236220	Auditorium construction
531120	Auditorium rental or leasing
541211	Auditors' (i.e., CPAs) offices, accounts
541211	Auditors' (i.e., CPAs) private practices, accounts
921190	Auditor's offices, government
213113	Auger coal mining services (except site preparation and related construction contractor activities) on a contract basis
333120	Augers (except mining-type) manufacturing
333131	Augers, mining-type, manufacturing
332216	Augers, nonpowered, manufacturing
711410	Authors' agents or managers
711510	Authors, independent
423120	Auto body shop supplies merchant wholesalers
721110	Auto courts, lodging
441310	Auto supply stores
339114	Autoclaves, dental, manufacturing
332420	Autoclaves, industrial-type, heavy gauge metal, manufacturing
339113	Autoclaves, laboratory-type (except dental), manufacturing
336411	Autogiros manufacturing
238290	Automated and revolving door installation
334510	Automated blood and body fluid analyzers (except laboratory) manufacturing
522320	Automated clearinghouses, bank or check (except central bank)
518210	Automated data processing services
522320	Automated Teller Machine (ATM) or Automated Loan Machine (ALM) network operation
332911	Automatic (i.e., controlling-type, regulating) valves, industrial-type, manufacturing
423690	Automatic call distributors merchant wholesalers
334516	Automatic chemical analyzers, laboratory-type, manufacturing
238290	Automatic gate (e.g., garage, parking lot) installation
812310	Automatic laundries, coin-operated
454210	Automatic merchandising machine operators
333517	Automatic screw machines, metal cutting type, manufacturing
334118	Automatic teller machines (ATM) manufacturing
423420	Automatic teller machines (ATM) merchant wholesalers
336350	Automatic transmissions, automotive, truck, and bus, manufacturing
423120	Automobile accessories (except tires, tubes) merchant wholesalers
334220	Automobile antennas manufacturing
423110	Automobile auction merchant wholesalers
425120	Automobile auctions, wholesale
336211	Automobile bodies, passenger car, manufacturing
484220	Automobile carrier trucking, local
484230	Automobile carrier trucking, long-distance
813410	Automobile clubs (except road and travel services)
561599	Automobile clubs, road and travel services
721110	Automobile courts, lodging
493190	Automobile dead storage
441110	Automobile dealers, new only or new and used
441120	Automobile dealers, used only
611692	Automobile driving schools
522220	Automobile finance leasing companies
522220	Automobile financing
423120	Automobile glass merchant wholesalers
332510	Automobile hardware, metal, manufacturing
541420	Automobile industrial design services
524126	Automobile insurance carriers, direct

532112	Automobile leasing
333921	Automobile lifts (i.e., garage-type, service station) manufacturing
423110	Automobile merchant wholesalers
812930	Automobile parking garages or lots
441310	Automobile parts dealers
325612	Automobile polishes and cleaners manufacturing
541380	Automobile proving and testing grounds
711212	Automobile racetracks
611620	Automobile racing schools
711219	Automobile racing teams
334310	Automobile radio receivers manufacturing
532111	Automobile rental
485320	Automobile rental with driver (except shuttle service, taxis)
561491	Automobile repossession services
336360	Automobile seat covers manufacturing
336360	Automobile seat frames, metal, manufacturing
423120	Automobile service station equipment merchant wholesalers
561920	Automobile show managers
561920	Automobile show organizers
561920	Automobile show promoters
332618	Automobile skid chains made from purchased wire
335911	Automobile storage batteries manufacturing
332613	Automobile suspension springs, heavy gauge metal, manufacturing
336212	Automobile transporter trailers, multi-car, manufacturing
336214	Automobile transporter trailers, single car, manufacturing
336360	Automobile trimmings, textile, manufacturing
333923	Automobile wrecker (i.e., tow truck) hoists manufacturing
336211	Automobile wrecker truck bodies manufacturing
336211	Automobile wreckers assembling on purchased chassis
336111	Automobiles assembling on chassis of own manufacture
339930	Automobiles, children's, manufacturing
423730	Automotive air-conditioners merchant wholesalers
811198	Automotive air-conditioning repair shops

334515	Automotive ammeters and voltmeters manufacturing
441310	Automotive audio equipment stores
811121	Automotive body shops
811118	Automotive brake repair shops
423120	Automotive brakes merchant wholesalers
424690	Automotive chemicals (except lubricating greases, lubrication oils) merchant wholesalers
811192	Automotive detail shops
811192	Automotive detailing services (i.e., cleaning, polishing)
334515	Automotive electrical engine diagnostic equipment manufacturing
811118	Automotive electrical repair shops
335931	Automotive electrical switches manufacturing
334519	Automotive emissions testing equipment manufacturing
811198	Automotive emissions testing services
811111	Automotive engine repair and replacement shops
811112	Automotive exhaust system repair and replacement shops
424310	Automotive fabrics merchant wholesalers
811111	Automotive fleet repair and maintenance services
811118	Automotive front end alignment shops
811122	Automotive glass shops
336320	Automotive harness and ignition sets manufacturing
335110	Automotive light bulbs manufacturing
336320	Automotive lighting fixtures manufacturing
332710	Automotive machine shops
336390	Automotive mirrors, framed, manufacturing
811191	Automotive oil change and lubrication shops
331318	Automotive or aircraft wire and cable made in aluminum wire drawing plants
811121	Automotive paint shops
424950	Automotive paints merchant wholesalers
441310	Automotive parts and supply stores
441310	Automotive parts dealers, used
423120	Automotive parts, new, merchant wholesalers
423140	Automotive parts, used, merchant wholesalers

811118 Automotive radiator repair shops

423620 Automotive radios merchant wholesalers

811111 Automotive repair and replacement shops, general

811198 Automotive rustproofing and undercoating shops

811198 Automotive safety inspection services

423120 Automotive stampings merchant wholesalers

334290 Automotive theft alarm systems manufacturing

441320 Automotive tire dealers

811198 Automotive tire repair (except retreading) shops

811113 Automotive transmission repair shops

811118 Automotive tune-up shops

811121 Automotive upholstery shops

811192 Automotive washing and polishing

336330 Automotive, truck and bus steering assemblies and parts manufacturing

336330 Automotive, truck and bus suspension assemblies and parts (except springs) manufacturing

339992 Autophones (organs with perforated music rolls) manufacturing

335311 Autotransformers for switchboards (except telephone switchboards) manufacturing

335311 Autotransformers manufacturing

237990 Avalanche, rockslide, mudslide, or roadside protection construction

712130 Aviaries

112990 Aviaries (i.e., raising birds for sale)

813319 Aviation advocacy organizations

481219 Aviation clubs providing a variety of air transportation activities to the general public

488119 Aviation clubs, primarily providing flying field services to the general public

713990 Aviation clubs, recreational

324110 Aviation fuels manufacturing

611512 Aviation schools

111339 Avocado farming

332216 Awls manufacturing

238190 Awning installation

423390 Awnings (except canvas) merchant wholesalers

314910 Awnings and canopies, outdoor, made from purchased fabrics

424990 Awnings, canvas, merchant wholesalers

326199 Awnings, rigid plastics or fiberglass, manufacturing

332322 Awnings, sheet metal (except stampings), manufacturing

332216 Axes manufacturing

336350 Axle bearings, automotive, truck, and bus, manufacturing

331110 Axles, rolled or forged, made in iron and steel mills

111421 Azalea farming

325920 Azides explosive materials manufacturing

325130 Azine dyes manufacturing

325130 Azo dyes manufacturing

325194 Azobenzene manufacturing

424330 Baby and infant car seats merchant wholesalers

424330 Baby and infant high chairs merchant wholesalers

424330 Baby bottles merchant wholesalers

424330 Baby clothing merchant wholesalers

448130 Baby clothing shops

311422 Baby foods (including meats) canning

424490 Baby foods, canned, merchant wholesalers

311514 Baby formula, fresh, processed, and bottled, manufacturing

423210 Baby furniture merchant wholesalers

325620 Baby powder and baby oil manufacturing

333997 Baby scales manufacturing

812990 Baby shoe bronzing services

561311 Babysitting bureaus (i.e., registries)

624410 Babysitting services in provider's own home, child day care

624410 Babysitting services, child day care

238910 Backfilling, construction

332913 Backflow preventers, plumbing, manufacturing

561611 Background check services

112111 Backgrounding, cattle

238910 Backhoe rental with operator

333120 Backhoes manufacturing

424990 Backpacks, textile, merchant wholesalers

311612 Bacon, slab and sliced, made from purchased carcasses

311611 Bacon, slab and sliced, produced in slaughtering plants

325414 Bacterial vaccines manufacturing

325414 Bacterins (i.e., bacterial vaccines) manufacturing

621511	Bacteriological laboratories, diagnostic
621511	Bacteriological laboratories, medical
424210	Bacteriological medicines merchant wholesalers
541715	Bacteriological research and development laboratories or services (except biotechnology and nanotechnology research and development)
314999	Badges, fabric, manufacturing
332999	Badges, metal, manufacturing
326199	Badges, plastics, manufacturing
339920	Badminton equipment manufacturing
332313	Baffles, fabricated metal plate work, manufacturing
316110	Bag leather manufacturing
332993	Bag loading plants, ammunition, manufacturing
333993	Bag opening, filling, and closing machines manufacturing
722511	Bagel shops, full service
722515	Bagel shops, on premise baking and carryout service
311812	Bagels made in commercial bakeries
322220	Bags (except plastics only) made by laminating or coating combinations of purchased plastics, foil and paper
316998	Bags (i.e., luggage), all materials, manufacturing
313240	Bags and bagging fabrics made in warp or weft knitting mills
316998	Bags, athletic, manufacturing
322220	Bags, coated paper, made from purchased paper
322220	Bags, foil, made from purchased foil
339920	Bags, golf, manufacturing
313110	Bags, hemp, made from purchased fiber
322220	Bags, multiwall, made from purchased uncoated paper
424130	Bags, paper and disposable plastics, merchant wholesalers
322220	Bags, paper, uncoated, made from purchased paper
326111	Bags, plastics film, single wall or multiwall, manufacturing
314910	Bags, plastics, made from purchased woven plastics
339920	Bags, punching, manufacturing
423930	Bags, reclaimed, merchant wholesalers
314910	Bags, rubberized fabric, manufacturing
314999	Bags, sleeping, manufacturing
314910	Bags, textile, made from purchased woven or knitted materials
424990	Bags, textile, merchant wholesalers
322220	Bags, uncoated paper, made from purchased paper
812990	Bail bonding services
423390	Bailey bridges merchant wholesalers
339920	Bait, artificial, fishing, manufacturing
423910	Bait, artificial, merchant wholesalers
424990	Bait, live, merchant wholesalers
112511	Baitfish production, farm raising
311422	Baked beans canning
311813	Baked goods (except bread, bread-type rolls), frozen, manufacturing
445291	Baked goods stores, retailing only (except immediate consumption)
445210	Baked ham stores
311811	Bakeries with baking from flour on the premises, retailing not for immediate consumption
315210	Bakers' service apparel, washable, cut and sew apparel contractors
315220	Bakers' service apparel, washable, men's and boys', cut and sewn from purchased fabric (except apparel contractors)
315240	Bakers' service apparel, washable, women's and girls', cut and sewn from purchased fabric (except apparel contractors)
722515	Bakery cafes, on premise baking and selling for immediate consumption
333241	Bakery machinery and equipment manufacturing
423830	Bakery machinery and equipment merchant wholesalers
333241	Bakery ovens manufacturing
424490	Bakery products (except frozen) merchant wholesalers
311821	Bakery products, dry (e.g., biscuits, cookies, crackers), manufacturing
311812	Bakery products, fresh (i.e., bread, cakes, doughnuts, pastries), made in commercial bakeries
424420	Bakery products, frozen, merchant wholesalers
311351	Baking chocolate made from cacao beans
311352	Baking chocolate made from purchased chocolate
311999	Baking powder manufacturing
423440	Balances and scales (except laboratory) merchant wholesalers
423490	Balances and scales, laboratory (except dental, medical), merchant wholesalers

333997	Balances, including laboratory-type, manufacturing
333318	Balancing equipment, motor vehicle, manufacturing
423120	Balancing equipment, motor vehicle, merchant wholesalers
423830	Balancing machines (except automotive) merchant wholesalers
332323	Balcony railings, metal, manufacturing
238190	Balcony, metal, installation
238120	Balcony, precast concrete, installation
333111	Bale throwers manufacturing
332618	Bale ties made from purchased wire
333111	Balers, farm-type (e.g., cotton, hay, straw), manufacturing
333999	Baling machinery (e.g., paper, scrap metal) manufacturing
332991	Ball bearings manufacturing
212324	Ball clay mining and/or beneficiating
333613	Ball joints (except aircraft, motor vehicle) manufacturing
339940	Ball point pens manufacturing
332911	Ball valves, industrial-type, manufacturing
335311	Ballasts (i.e., transformers) manufacturing
711120	Ballet companies
711510	Ballet dancers, independent
711120	Ballet productions, live theatrical
611610	Ballet schools (except academic)
316210	Ballet slippers manufacturing
453220	Balloon shops
812990	Balloon-o-gram services
326199	Balloons, plastics, manufacturing
326299	Balloons, rubber, manufacturing
713990	Ballrooms
339920	Balls, baseball, basketball, football, golf, tennis, pool, and bowling, manufacturing
339930	Balls, rubber (except athletic equipment), manufacturing
331110	Balls, steel, made in iron and steel mills
113210	Balsam needles gathering
111339	Banana farming
115114	Banana ripening
315210	Band uniforms cut and sew apparel contractors
315280	Band uniforms cut and sewn from purchased fabric (except apparel contractors)
424210	Bandages (except surgical) merchant wholesalers
339113	Bandages and dressings, surgical and orthopedic, manufacturing
315210	Bandeaux cut and sew apparel contractors
315240	Bandeaux, women's and girls', cut and sewn from purchased fabric (except apparel contractors)
711130	Bands
711130	Bands, dance
711130	Bands, musical
333243	Bandsaws, woodworking-type, manufacturing
339992	Banjos and parts manufacturing
334511	Bank and turn indicators and components (aeronautical instruments) manufacturing
236220	Bank building construction
531120	Bank building rental or leasing
332999	Bank chests, metal, manufacturing
522320	Bank clearinghouse associations
524128	Bank deposit insurance carriers, direct
423420	Bank equipment merchant wholesalers
332323	Bank fixtures, ornamental metal, manufacturing
551111	Bank holding companies (except managing)
523991	Bank trust offices
813910	Bankers' associations
926150	Banking regulatory agencies
611519	Banking schools (training in banking)
521110	Banking, central
523110	Banking, investment
525920	Bankruptcy estates
522110	Banks, commercial
522210	Banks, credit card
521110	Banks, Federal Reserve
522190	Banks, industrial (i.e., known as), depository
522298	Banks, industrial (i.e., known as), nondepository
522190	Banks, private (i.e., unincorporated)
522120	Banks, savings
522293	Banks, trade (i.e., international trade financing)
314999	Banners made from purchased fabrics (except banner printing)
332323	Bannisters, metal, manufacturing

531120	Banquet hall rental or leasing
722320	Banquet halls with catering staff
327991	Baptismal fonts, cut stone, manufacturing
813920	Bar associations
561499	Bar code imprinting services
423440	Bar equipment merchant wholesalers
331318	Bar made by extruding purchased aluminum
331318	Bar made by rolling purchased aluminum
333519	Bar mill machinery, metalworking, manufacturing
325611	Bar soaps manufacturing
331318	Bar, aluminum, made in integrated secondary smelting and extruding mills
331318	Bar, aluminum, made in integrated secondary smelting and rolling mills
331420	Bar, copper and copper alloy, made from purchased copper or in integrated secondary smelting and rolling, drawing or extruding plants
331491	Bar, nonferrous metals (except aluminum, copper), made from purchased metals in wire drawing plants or in integrated secondary smelting and rolling, drawing, or extruding plants
311421	Barbecue sauce manufacturing
335220	Barbecues, grills, and braziers manufacturing
331222	Barbed and twisted wire made in wire drawing plants
332618	Barbed wire made from purchased wire
611511	Barber colleges
236220	Barber shop construction
423850	Barber shop equipment and supplies merchant wholesalers
812111	Barber shops
332215	Barber's scissors, manufacturing
315210	Barbers' service apparel, washable, cut and sew apparel contractors
315220	Barbers' service apparel, washable, men's and boys', cut and sewn from purchased fabric (except apparel contractors)
325412	Barbiturate preparations manufacturing
325411	Barbiturates, uncompounded, manufacturing
325411	Barbituric acid manufacturing
336611	Barge building
532411	Barge rental or leasing without crew
332312	Barge sections, prefabricated metal, manufacturing
483211	Barge transportation, canal (freight)
483113	Barge transportation, coastal or Great Lakes (including St. Lawrence Seaway)
212393	Barite mining and/or beneficiating
327992	Barite processing beyond beneficiation
325180	Barium compounds, not specified elsewhere by process, manufacturing
325180	Barium hydroxide manufacturing
325412	Barium in-vivo diagnostic substances manufacturing
212393	Barium ores mining and/or beneficiating
327992	Barium processing beyond beneficiation
113210	Bark gathering
111199	Barley farming, field and seed production
311119	Barley feed, chopped, crushed or ground, manufacturing
311211	Barley flour manufacturing
311213	Barley, malt, manufacturing
332323	Barn stanchions and standards manufacturing
334519	Barographs manufacturing
334519	Barometers manufacturing
423490	Barometers merchant wholesalers
332410	Barometric condensers manufacturing
236220	Barrack construction
321920	Barrel heading and staves manufacturing
332994	Barrels, gun, manufacturing
332439	Barrels, light gauge metal, manufacturing
423840	Barrels, new and reconditioned, merchant wholesalers
321920	Barrels, wood, coopered, manufacturing
332999	Barricades, metal, manufacturing
541110	Barristers' offices
541110	Barristers' private practices
722410	Bars (i.e., drinking places), alcoholic beverage
331410	Bars made in primary copper smelting and refining mills
331110	Bars, concrete reinforcing (rebar) made in steel mills
331221	Bars, concrete reinforcing (rebar), made from purchased steel in steel rolling mills
332312	Bars, concrete reinforcing, manufacturing
331110	Bars, iron, made in iron and steel mills
423510	Bars, metal (except precious), merchant wholesalers
331221	Bars, steel, made from purchased steel in cold rolling mills

331110	Bars, steel, made in iron and steel mills
611519	Bartending schools
561990	Bartering services
325130	Barytes based pigments manufacturing
212393	Barytes mining and/or beneficiating
212319	Basalt crushed and broken stone mining and/or beneficiating
212311	Basalt mining or quarrying
561210	Base facilities operation support services
315210	Baseball caps (except plastics) cut and sew apparel contractors
315990	Baseball caps cut and sewn from purchased fabric (except apparel contractors)
711211	Baseball clubs, professional or semiprofessional
713990	Baseball clubs, recreational
339920	Baseball equipment and supplies (except footwear, uniforms) manufacturing
423910	Baseball equipment and supplies merchant wholesalers
611620	Baseball instruction, camps, or schools
711211	Baseball teams, professional or semiprofessional
315210	Baseball uniforms cut and sew apparel contractors
315280	Baseball uniforms cut and sewn from purchased fabric (except apparel contractors)
423730	Baseboard heaters, electric, non-portable, merchant wholesalers
333414	Baseboard heating equipment manufacturing
321918	Baseboards, floor, wood, manufacturing
332321	Baseboards, metal, manufacturing
711211	Basketball clubs, professional or semiprofessional
713990	Basketball clubs, recreational
339920	Basketball equipment and supplies (except footwear, uniforms) manufacturing
611620	Basketball instruction, camps, or schools
711211	Basketball teams, professional or semiprofessional
315210	Basketball uniforms cut and sew apparel contractors
315280	Basketball uniforms cut and sewn from purchased fabric (except apparel contractors)
424990	Baskets merchant wholesalers
331222	Baskets, iron or steel, made in wire drawing plants
332618	Baskets, metal, made from purchased wire
321920	Baskets, wood (e.g., round stave, veneer), manufacturing
337125	Bassinets, reed and rattan, manufacturing
339992	Bassoons manufacturing
212299	Bastnaesite mining and/or beneficiating
335210	Bath fans with integral lighting fixture, residential, manufacturing
335210	Bath fans, residential, manufacturing
314110	Bath mats and bath sets made in carpet mills
326299	Bath mats, rubber, manufacturing
325620	Bath salts manufacturing
442299	Bath shops
713990	Bathing beaches
315990	Bathing caps, rubber, manufacturing
315210	Bathing suits cut and sew apparel contractors
315190	Bathing suits made in apparel knitting mills
315220	Bathing suits, men's and boys', cut and sewn from purchased fabric (except apparel contractors)
315240	Bathing suits, women's, girls', and infants', cut and sewn from purchased fabric (except apparel contractors)
315210	Bathrobes cut and sew apparel contractors
315190	Bathrobes made in apparel knitting mills
315220	Bathrobes, men's and boys', cut and sewn from purchased fabric (except apparel contractors)
315240	Bathrobes, women's, girls', and infants', cut and sewn from purchased fabric (except apparel contractors)
423220	Bathroom accessories merchant wholesalers
327110	Bathroom accessories, vitreous china and earthenware, manufacturing
326199	Bathroom and toilet accessories, plastics, manufacturing
332999	Bathroom fixtures, metal, manufacturing
238220	Bathroom plumbing fixture and sanitary ware installation
333997	Bathroom scales manufacturing
337110	Bathroom vanities (except freestanding), stock or custom wood, manufacturing
812199	Baths, steam or turkish
238390	Bathtub refinishing, on-site
423720	Bathtubs merchant wholesalers
332999	Bathtubs, metal, manufacturing
326191	Bathtubs, plastics, manufacturing

611620	Baton instruction
624221	Battered women's shelters
423610	Batteries (except automotive) merchant wholesalers
441310	Batteries, automotive, dealers
423120	Batteries, automotive, merchant wholesalers
453998	Batteries, except automotive, dealers
335912	Batteries, primary, dry or wet, manufacturing
335911	Batteries, rechargeable, manufacturing
335911	Batteries, storage, manufacturing
311824	Batters, prepared, made from purchased flour
311211	Batters, prepared, made in flour mills
335999	Battery chargers, solid-state, manufacturing
334515	Battery testers, electrical, manufacturing
712120	Battlefields
314999	Batts and batting (except nonwoven fabrics) manufacturing
327120	Bauxite brick manufacturing
423520	Bauxite merchant wholesalers
212299	Bauxite mining and/or beneficiating
325998	Bay oil manufacturing
454390	Bazaars (i.e., temporary stands)
332994	BB guns manufacturing
332992	BB shot manufacturing
532284	Beach chair rental
713990	Beach clubs, recreational
562998	Beach maintenance and cleaning services
316210	Beach sandals, plastics or plastics soled fabric upper, manufacturing
316210	Beach sandals, rubber or rubber soled fabric upper, manufacturing
532284	Beach umbrella rental
339999	Beach umbrellas manufacturing
713990	Beaches, bathing
315210	Beachwear cut and sew apparel contractors
315190	Beachwear made in apparel knitting mills
315220	Beachwear, men's and boys', cut and sewn from purchased fabric (except apparel contractors)
315240	Beachwear, women's, girls', and infants', cut and sewn from purchased fabric (except apparel contractors)
333517	Beader machines, metalworking, manufacturing
314999	Beading on textile products (except apparel) for the trade
333249	Beaming machinery for yarn manufacturing
313110	Beaming yarn
321113	Beams, wood, made from logs or bolts
111219	Bean (except dry) farming, field and seed production
115114	Bean cleaning
111130	Bean farming, dry, field and seed production
111419	Bean sprout farming, grown under cover
311422	Beans, baked, canning
424490	Beans, dry edible, merchant wholesalers
424510	Beans, dry inedible, merchant wholesalers
423510	Bearing piles, metal, merchant wholesalers
332216	Bearing pullers, handtools, manufacturing
336310	Bearings (e.g., camshaft, crankshaft, connecting rod), automotive and truck gasoline engine, manufacturing
423840	Bearings merchant wholesalers
332991	Bearings, ball and roller, manufacturing
333613	Bearings, plain (except internal combustion engine), manufacturing
812112	Beautician services
333318	Beauty and barber shop equipment (except chairs) manufacturing
812112	Beauty and barber shops, combined
711310	Beauty pageant managers with facilities
711320	Beauty pageant managers without facilities
711310	Beauty pageant organizers with facilities
711320	Beauty pageant organizers without facilities
711310	Beauty pageant promoters with facilities
711320	Beauty pageant promoters without facilities
423850	Beauty parlor equipment and supplies merchant wholesalers
812112	Beauty parlors
424210	Beauty preparations merchant wholesalers
236220	Beauty salon construction
812112	Beauty salons
611511	Beauty schools
812112	Beauty shops
424210	Beauty supplies merchant wholesalers
446120	Beauty supply stores
721191	Bed and breakfast inns

337122	Bed frames, wood household-type, manufacturing
812331	Bed linen supply services
442110	Bed stores, retail
335210	Bedcoverings, electric, manufacturing
111422	Bedding plant growing (except vegetable and melon bedding plants)
424930	Bedding plants merchant wholesalers
315210	Bedjackets cut and sew apparel contractors
315240	Bedjackets, women's and girls', cut and sewn from purchased fabric (except apparel contractors)
337122	Bedroom furniture (except upholstered), wood household-type, manufacturing
423210	Beds (except hospital) merchant wholesalers
337122	Beds (except hospital), wood household-type, manufacturing
337124	Beds (including cabinet and folding), metal household-type (except hospital), manufacturing
339113	Beds, hospital, manufacturing
423450	Beds, hospital, merchant wholesalers
337910	Beds, sleep-system ensembles (i.e., flotation, adjustable), manufacturing
337122	Beds, wood dormitory-type, manufacturing
337122	Beds, wood hotel-type, manufacturing
314120	Bedspreads and bed sets made from purchased fabrics
313240	Bedspreads and bed sets made in lace mills
313240	Bedspreads and bed sets made in warp or weft knitting mills
112910	Bee pollen collection
112910	Bee production (i.e., apiculture)
311611	Beef carcasses, half carcasses, primal and sub-primal cuts, produced in slaughtering plants
112112	Beef cattle feedlots (except stockyards for transportation)
112111	Beef cattle ranching or farming
311611	Beef produced in slaughtering plants
311612	Beef stew made from purchased carcasses
311612	Beef, primal and sub-primal cuts, made from purchased carcasses
424910	Beekeeping supplies merchant wholesalers
517312	Beeper (i.e., radio pager) communication carriers
327213	Beer bottles, glass, manufacturing
312120	Beer brewing
332431	Beer cans, light gauge metal, manufacturing
333415	Beer cooling and dispensing equipment manufacturing
332439	Beer kegs, light gauge metal, manufacturing
453998	Beer making supply stores
424810	Beer merchant wholesalers
445310	Beer stores, packaged
424590	Bees merchant wholesalers
325612	Beeswax polishes and waxes manufacturing
112910	Beeswax production
111219	Beet farming (except sugar beets), field, bedding plant and seed production
311313	Beet pulp, dried, manufacturing
311313	Beet sugar refining
541720	Behavioral research and development services
325412	Belladonna preparations manufacturing
332999	Bellows, hand, manufacturing
333999	Bellows, industrial-type, manufacturing
339992	Bells (musical instruments) manufacturing
335999	Bells, electric, manufacturing
424310	Belt and buckle assembly kits merchant wholesalers
333922	Belt conveyor systems manufacturing
316998	Belt laces, leather, manufacturing
316110	Belting butts, curried or rough, manufacturing
313220	Belting fabrics, narrow woven
316998	Belting for machinery, leather, manufacturing
316110	Belting leather, manufacturing
314999	Belting made from purchased fabrics
423840	Belting, industrial, merchant wholesalers
326220	Belting, rubber (e.g., conveyor, elevator, transmission), manufacturing
482112	Beltline railroads
315210	Belts, apparel (e.g., fabric, leather, vinyl), cut and sew apparel contractors
315990	Belts, apparel (e.g., fabric, leather, vinyl), cut and sewn from purchased fabric (except apparel contractors)
332618	Belts, conveyor, made from purchased wire
332618	Belts, drying, made from purchased wire
316998	Belts, leather safety, manufacturing
332994	Belts, machine gun, manufacturing

315210	Belts, money, any material, cut and sew apparel contractors
315990	Belts, money, any material, cut and sewn from purchased fabric (except apparel contractors)
337127	Benches, park-type (except concrete, stone), manufacturing
337127	Benches, public building-type, manufacturing
337127	Benches, work, manufacturing
333517	Bending and forming machines, metalworking, manufacturing
332996	Bends, pipe, made from purchased metal pipe
541612	Benefit consulting services
111998	Bentgrass seed farming
212325	Bentonite mining and/or beneficiating
321999	Bentwood (steam bent) products (except furniture) manufacturing
325194	Benzaldehyde manufacturing
325320	Benzene hexachloride (BHC) insecticides manufacturing
325110	Benzene made from refined petroleum or liquid hydrocarbons
324110	Benzene made in petroleum refineries
325194	Benzoic acid manufacturing
311421	Berries, canned, manufacturing
424480	Berries, fresh, merchant wholesalers
115113	Berries, machine harvesting
111334	Berry (except strawberry) farming
321920	Berry crates, wood, wirebound, manufacturing
321920	Berry cups, veneer and splint, manufacturing
333111	Berry harvesting machines manufacturing
212299	Beryl mining and/or beneficiating
327110	Beryllia porcelain insulators manufacturing
331529	Beryllium castings (except die-castings), unfinished manufacturing
212299	Beryllium concentrates beneficiating
331523	Beryllium die-castings, unfinished, manufacturing
212299	Beryllium ores mining and/or beneficiating
325180	Beryllium oxide manufacturing
331410	Beryllium refining, primary
334517	Beta-ray irradiation equipment manufacturing
335999	Betatrons manufacturing
813910	Better business bureaus
713290	Betting information services
722515	Beverage (e.g., coffee, juice, soft drink) bars, nonalcoholic, fixed location
311930	Beverage bases manufacturing
424490	Beverage bases merchant wholesalers
423830	Beverage bottling machinery merchant wholesalers
424490	Beverage concentrates merchant wholesalers
327213	Beverage containers, glass, manufacturing
423740	Beverage coolers, mechanical, merchant wholesalers
311930	Beverage flavorings (except coffee based) manufacturing
423830	Beverage processing machinery merchant wholesalers
722330	Beverage stands, nonalcoholic, mobile
311930	Beverage syrups (except coffee based) manufacturing
424810	Beverages, alcoholic (except distilled spirits, wine), merchant wholesalers
312120	Beverages, beer, ale, and malt liquors, manufacturing
311514	Beverages, dietary, dairy and nondairy based
312111	Beverages, fruit and vegetable drinks, cocktails, and ades, manufacturing
311421	Beverages, fruit and vegetable juice, manufacturing
312140	Beverages, liquors (except brandies), manufacturing
311511	Beverages, milk based (except dietary), manufacturing
312112	Beverages, naturally carbonated bottled water, manufacturing
312111	Beverages, soft drink (including artificially carbonated waters), manufacturing
424820	Beverages, wine and distilled spirits, merchant wholesalers
312130	Beverages, wines and brandies, manufacturing
314999	Bias bindings made from purchased fabrics
313220	Bias bindings, woven, manufacturing
611699	Bible schools (except degree granting)
813110	Bible societies
315210	Bibs and aprons, waterproof (e.g., plastics, rubber, similar materials), cut and sew apparel contractors
315990	Bibs and aprons, waterproof (e.g., plastics, rubber, similar materials), cut and sewn from purchased fabric (except apparel contractors)

315990 Bibs and aprons, waterproof (e.g., plastics, rubber, similar materials), rubberizing fabric and manufacturing bibs and aprons

451110 Bicycle (except motorized) shops

453310 Bicycle (except motorized) shops, used

492210 Bicycle courier

333912 Bicycle pumps manufacturing

532284 Bicycle rental

811490 Bicycle repair and maintenance shops without retailing new bicycles

441228 Bicycle shops, motorized

423910 Bicycle tires and tubes merchant wholesalers

423110 Bicycle, motorized, merchant wholesalers

423910 Bicycles (except motorized) merchant wholesalers

336991 Bicycles and parts manufacturing

327110 Bidets, vitreous china, manufacturing

561440 Bill collection services

541850 Billboard display advertising services

238990 Billboard erection

339950 Billboards manufacturing

423990 Billboards merchant wholesalers

333519 Billet mill machinery, metalworking, manufacturing

423510 Billets, metal, merchant wholesalers

331110 Billets, steel, made in iron and steel mills

316998 Billfolds, all materials, manufacturing

339920 Billiard equipment and supplies manufacturing

423910 Billiard equipment and supplies merchant wholesalers

713990 Billiard parlors

713990 Billiard rooms

541219 Billing services

322130 Binder's board manufacturing

424120 Binders, looseleaf, merchant wholesalers

333244 Bindery machinery manufacturing

314999 Binding carpets and rugs for the trade

333318 Binding equipment (i.e., plastics or tape binding), office-type, manufacturing

424310 Binding, textile, merchant wholesalers

314999 Bindings, bias, made from purchased fabrics

313220 Bindings, narrow woven, manufacturing

713290 Bingo halls

713290 Bingo parlors

316998 Binocular cases manufacturing

453998 Binocular stores

333314 Binoculars manufacturing

423460 Binoculars merchant wholesalers

332313 Bins, fabricated metal plate work, manufacturing

332439 Bins, light gauge metal, manufacturing

423390 Bins, storage, merchant wholesalers

324110 Biodiesel fuels made in petroleum refineries

324199 Biodiesel fuels not made in petroleum refineries and blended with purchased refined petroleum

325199 Biodiesel fuels not made in petroleum refineries and not blended with petroleum

621498 Biofeedback centers and clinics, outpatient

562910 Biohazard cleanup services

339113 Biohazard protective clothing and accessories manufacturing

541380 Biological (except medical, veterinary) testing laboratories or services

541690 Biological consulting services

621511 Biological laboratories, diagnostic

424210 Biologicals and allied products merchant wholesalers

541715 Biology research and development laboratories or services (except biotechnology and nanotechnology research and development)

221117 Biomass electric power generation

334118 Biometrics system input devices (e.g., retinal scan, iris pattern recognition, hand geometry) manufacturing

541714 Biotechnology research and development laboratories or services (except nanobiotechnology research and development)

541714 Biotechnology research and development laboratories or services in agriculture (except nanobiotechnology research and development)

541714 Biotechnology research and development laboratories or services in bacteriology (except nanobiotechnology research and development)

541714 Biotechnology research and development laboratories or services in biology (except nanobiotechnology research and development)

541714 Biotechnology research and development laboratories or services in botany (except nanobiotechnology research and development)

541714	Biotechnology research and development laboratories or services in chemical sciences (except nanobiotechnology research and development)
541714	Biotechnology research and development laboratories or services in entomology (except nanobiotechnology research and development)
541714	Biotechnology research and development laboratories or services in environmental science (except nanobiotechnology research and development)
541714	Biotechnology research and development laboratories or services in food science (except nanobiotechnology research and development)
541714	Biotechnology research and development laboratories or services in genetics (except nanobiotechnology research and development)
541714	Biotechnology research and development laboratories or services in health sciences (except nanobiotechnology research and development)
541714	Biotechnology research and development laboratories or services in industrial research (except nanobiotechnology research and development)
541714	Biotechnology research and development laboratories or services in the medical sciences (except nanobiotechnology research and development)
541714	Biotechnology research and development laboratories or services in the physical sciences (except nanobiotechnology research and development)
541714	Biotechnology research and development laboratories or services in the veterinary sciences (except nanobiotechnology research and development)
423690	Bipolar transistors merchant wholesalers
311119	Bird feed, prepared, manufacturing
112990	Bird production (e.g., canaries, love birds, parakeets, parrots)
561710	Bird proofing services
712190	Bird sanctuaries
621410	Birth control clinics
326299	Birth control devices (i.e., diaphragms, prophylactics) manufacturing
325412	Birth control pills manufacturing
311812	Biscuits, bread-type, made in commercial bakeries
331410	Bismuth refining, primary

112990	Bison production
333515	Bits and knives for metalworking lathes, planers, and shapers manufacturing
333515	Bits, drill, metalworking, manufacturing
332216	Bits, edge tool, woodworking, manufacturing
333120	Bits, rock drill, construction and surface mining-type, manufacturing
333132	Bits, rock drill, oil and gas field-type, manufacturing
333131	Bits, rock drill, underground mining-type, manufacturing
212111	Bituminous coal and lignite surface mine site development for own account
212111	Bituminous coal cleaning plants
212111	Bituminous coal crushing
213113	Bituminous coal mining services (except site preparation and related construction contractor activities) on a contract basis
212111	Bituminous coal or lignite beneficiating (e.g., cleaning, crushing, screening, washing)
213113	Bituminous coal or lignite surface mine site development (except site preparation and related construction contractor activities) on a contract basis
212111	Bituminous coal screening plants
212111	Bituminous coal stripping (except on a contract, fee, or other basis)
213113	Bituminous coal stripping service on a contract basis
212111	Bituminous coal surface mining and/or beneficiating
212112	Bituminous coal underground mine site development for own account
212112	Bituminous coal underground mining or mining and beneficiating
212111	Bituminous coal washeries
212319	Bituminous limestone mining and/or beneficiating
213113	Bituminous or lignite auger mining service on a contract basis
212319	Bituminous sandstone mining and/or beneficiating
325130	Black pigments (except carbon black, bone black, lamp black) manufacturing
423510	Black plate merchant wholesalers
111334	Blackberry farming
423490	Blackboards merchant wholesalers
339940	Blackboards, framed, manufacturing
327991	Blackboards, unframed, slate, manufacturing

331110	Blackplate made in iron and steel mills
316998	Blacksmith's aprons, leather, manufacturing
311314	Blackstrap molasses manufacturing
238990	Blacktop work, residential and commercial driveway and parking area
811310	Blade sharpening, commercial and industrial machinery and equipment
423710	Blades (e.g., knife, saw) merchant wholesalers
333120	Blades for graders, scrapers, bulldozers, and snowplows manufacturing
332215	Blades, knife and razor, manufacturing
424210	Blades, razor, merchant wholesalers
332216	Blades, saw, all types, manufacturing
325130	Blanc fixe (i.e., barium sulfate, precipitated) manufacturing
332992	Blank cartridges (i.e., 30 mm. or less, 1.18 inch or less) manufacturing
423690	Blank CDs and DVDs merchant wholesalers
423690	Blank diskettes merchant wholesalers
334613	Blank tapes, audio and video, manufacturing
423690	Blank tapes, audio and video, merchant wholesalers
323111	Blankbooks and refills manufacturing
424120	Blankbooks merchant wholesalers
314910	Blanket bags manufacturing
314120	Blankets (except electric) made from purchased fabrics or felts
423220	Blankets (except electric) merchant wholesalers
313210	Blankets and bedspreads made in broadwoven fabric mills
335210	Blankets, electric, manufacturing
423620	Blankets, electric, merchant wholesalers
313230	Blankets, nonwoven fabric, manufacturing
327212	Blanks for electric light bulbs, glass, made in glass making plants
333515	Blanks, cutting tool, manufacturing
327215	Blanks, ophthalmic lens and optical glass, made from purchased glass
327212	Blanks, ophthalmic lens and optical glass, made in glass making plants
423830	Blanks, tips, and inserts merchant wholesalers
321912	Blanks, wood (e.g., bowling pins, handles, textile machinery accessories), manufacturing

311411	Blast freezing on a contract basis
236210	Blast furnace construction
327992	Blast furnace slag processing
331110	Blast furnaces
238910	Blast hole drilling (except mining)
212322	Blast sand quarrying and/or beneficiating
325920	Blasting accessories (e.g., caps, fuses, ignitors, squibbs) manufacturing
325920	Blasting powders manufacturing
213113	Blasting services, coal mining, on a contract basis
213114	Blasting services, metal mining, on a contract basis
213115	Blasting services, nonmetallic minerals mining (except fuels) on a contract basis
238910	Blasting, building demolition
238910	Blasting, construction site
238390	Bleacher installation
337127	Bleacher seating manufacturing
424690	Bleaches merchant wholesalers
325612	Bleaches, formulated for household use, manufacturing
325180	Bleaching agents, inorganic, manufacturing
325199	Bleaching agents, organic, manufacturing
212325	Bleaching clay mining and/or beneficiating
333249	Bleaching machinery for textiles manufacturing
313310	Bleaching textile products, apparel, and fabrics
212230	Blende (zinc) mining and/or beneficiating
311211	Blended flour made in flour mills
335210	Blenders, household-type electric, manufacturing
325620	Blending and compounding perfume bases
311119	Blending animal feed
312130	Blending brandy
312140	Blending distilled beverages (except brandy)
312130	Blending wines
336411	Blimps (i.e., aircraft) manufacturing
337920	Blinds (e.g., mini, venetian, vertical), all materials, manufacturing
423220	Blinds and shades, window, merchant wholesalers
331410	Blister copper manufacturing
561910	Blister packaging services
333923	Block and tackle manufacturing

312113	Block ice manufacturing
324121	Blocks, asphalt paving, made from purchased asphaltic materials
327331	Blocks, concrete and cinder, manufacturing
327120	Blocks, fire clay, manufacturing
327212	Blocks, glass, made in glass making plants
321999	Blocks, tackle, wood, manufacturing
321999	Blocks, tailors' pressing wood, manufacturing
621511	Blood analysis laboratories
334516	Blood bank process equipment manufacturing
621991	Blood banks
325413	Blood derivative in-vitro diagnostic substances manufacturing
325414	Blood derivatives manufacturing
424210	Blood derivatives merchant wholesalers
621991	Blood donor stations
325414	Blood fractions manufacturing
325413	Blood glucose test kits manufacturing
424210	Blood plasma merchant wholesalers
339112	Blood pressure apparatus manufacturing
621999	Blood pressure screening facilities
621999	Blood pressure screening services
812990	Blood pressure testing machine concession operators, coin-operated
339113	Blood testing apparatus, laboratory-type, manufacturing
339112	Blood transfusion equipment manufacturing
333519	Blooming and slabbing mill machinery, metalworking, manufacturing
423510	Blooms, metal, merchant wholesalers
331110	Blooms, steel, made in iron and steel mills
315210	Blouses cut and sew apparel contractors
315190	Blouses made in apparel knitting mills
315240	Blouses, women's, girls', and infants', cut and sewn from purchased fabric (except apparel contractors)
335210	Blow dryers, household-type electric, manufacturing
333249	Blow molding machinery for plastics manufacturing
332216	Blow torches manufacturing
333413	Blower filter units manufacturing
238220	Blower or fan, cooling and dry heating, installation

333111	Blowers, forage, manufacturing
423830	Blowers, industrial, merchant wholesalers
333112	Blowers, leaf, manufacturing
423820	Blowers, snow and leaf, merchant wholesalers
238310	Blown-in insulation (e.g., cellulose, vermiculite) installation
221210	Blue gas, carbureted, distribution
111334	Blueberry farming
114111	Bluefish fishing
111998	Bluegrass-Kentucky seed farming
541340	Blueprint drafting services
333316	Blueprint equipment manufacturing
423420	Blueprinting equipment merchant wholesalers
561439	Blueprinting services
212311	Bluestone mining or quarrying
325620	Blushes, face, manufacturing
423920	Board games merchant wholesalers
921130	Board of Governors, Federal Reserve
321219	Board, bagasse, manufacturing
327420	Board, gypsum, manufacturing
321219	Board, particle, manufacturing
115210	Boarding horses (except racehorses)
721310	Boarding houses
611110	Boarding schools, elementary or secondary
812910	Boarding services, pet
921120	Boards of supervisors, county and local
813910	Boards of trade
324122	Boards, asphalt saturated, made from purchased asphaltic materials
321999	Boards, bulletin, wood and cork, manufacturing
321999	Boards, wood (e.g., clip, ironing, meat, pastry), manufacturing
321113	Boards, wood, made from logs or bolts
321912	Boards, wood, resawing purchased lumber
336320	Boat and ship lighting fixtures manufacturing
441222	Boat dealers, new and used
541330	Boat engineering design services
484220	Boat hauling, truck, local
484230	Boat hauling, truck, long-distance
238990	Boat lift installation
333923	Boat lifts manufacturing
532411	Boat rental (except pleasure) without crew

532411	Boat rental or leasing, commercial
532284	Boat rental, pleasure
332312	Boat sections, prefabricated metal, manufacturing
423910	Boat supplies, pleasure, merchant wholesalers
441222	Boat trailer dealers
336212	Boat transporter trailers, multi-unit, manufacturing
336214	Boat transporter trailers, single-unit, manufacturing
336612	Boat yards (i.e., boat manufacturing facilities)
487210	Boat, fishing charter, operation
811490	Boat, pleasure, repair and maintenance services without retailing new boats
713930	Boating clubs with marinas
713990	Boating clubs without marinas
423860	Boats (except pleasure) merchant wholesalers
336612	Boats (i.e., suitable or intended for personal use) manufacturing
336612	Boats, inflatable plastics (except toy-type), manufacturing
423910	Boats, pleasure (e.g., canoes, motorboats, sailboats), merchant wholesalers
321912	Bobbin blocks and blanks, wood, manufacturing
322219	Bobbins, fiber, made from purchased paperboard
333249	Bobbins, textile machinery, manufacturing
339920	Bobsleds manufacturing
812320	Bobtailers, laundry and drycleaning
713990	Boccie ball courts
423110	Bodies, motor vehicle, merchant wholesalers
713940	Body building studios, physical fitness
811121	Body conversion services, automotive
561612	Body guard services
811121	Body shops, automotive
315210	Body stockings cut and sew apparel contractors
315190	Body stockings made in apparel knitting mills
315240	Body stockings, women's and girls', cut and sewn from purchased fabric (except apparel contractors)
332994	Bofors guns manufacturing
238290	Boiler and pipe insulation installation
332410	Boiler casings manufacturing
238220	Boiler chipping, cleaning and scaling
334513	Boiler controls, industrial, power, and marine-type, manufacturing
332919	Boiler couplings and drains, plumbing and heating-type, manufacturing
238290	Boiler covering installation
332911	Boiler gauge cocks, industrial-type, manufacturing
331210	Boiler tubes, wrought, made from purchased iron
238220	Boiler, heating, installation
423720	Boilers (e.g., heating, hot water, power, steam) merchant wholesalers
333414	Boilers, heating, manufacturing
332410	Boilers, power, manufacturing
311612	Bologna made from purchased carcasses
332722	Bolts, metal, manufacturing
326199	Bolts, nuts, and rivets, plastics, manufacturing
423710	Bolts, nuts, rivets, screws, and other fasteners merchant wholesalers
333924	Bomb lifts manufacturing
332993	Bomb loading and assembling plants
332993	Bombcluster adapters manufacturing
332993	Bombs manufacturing
523120	Bond brokerages
523110	Bond dealing (i.e., acting as a principal in dealing securities to investors)
322230	Bond paper made from purchased paper
322121	Bond paper made in paper mills
493190	Bonded warehousing (except farm products, general merchandise, refrigerated)
493130	Bonded warehousing, farm products (except refrigerated)
493110	Bonded warehousing, general merchandise
493120	Bonded warehousing, refrigerated
313230	Bonded-fiber fabrics manufacturing
332812	Bonderizing metal and metal products for the trade
524126	Bonding, fidelity or surety insurance, direct
812990	Bondsperson services
325180	Bone black manufacturing
327110	Bone china manufacturing
339112	Bone drills manufacturing
311119	Bone meal prepared as feed for animals and fowls
339999	Bone novelties manufacturing

339112	Bone plates and screws manufacturing
339112	Bone rongeurs manufacturing
311613	Bones, fat, rendering
511130	Book (e.g., hardback, paperback, audio) publishers (except exclusive Internet publishing)
454110	Book clubs, not publishing, mail-order
813410	Book discussion clubs
332999	Book ends, metal, manufacturing
322220	Book paper made by coating purchased paper
322220	Book paper, coated, made from purchased paper
322121	Book paper, coated, made in paper mills
511130	Book publishers and printing combined
519130	Book publishers, exclusively on Internet
511130	Book publishers, university press (except exclusive Internet publishing)
451211	Book stores
453310	Book stores, used
316110	Bookbinder's leather manufacturing
333244	Bookbinding machines manufacturing
323120	Bookbinding shops
323120	Bookbinding without printing
337125	Bookcases (except wood and metal), household-type, manufacturing
337214	Bookcases (except wood), office-type, manufacturing
337124	Bookcases, metal household-type, manufacturing
337122	Bookcases, wood household-type, manufacturing
337211	Bookcases, wood office-type, manufacturing
713290	Bookies
561599	Booking (e.g., airline, car rental, hotel, restaurant) services
512199	Booking agencies, motion picture
512199	Booking agencies, motion picture or video productions
711320	Booking agencies, theatrical (except motion picture)
541219	Bookkeepers' offices
541219	Bookkeepers' private practices
423420	Bookkeeping machines merchant wholesalers
541219	Bookkeeping services
713290	Bookmakers
519120	Bookmobiles
424920	Books merchant wholesalers
323117	Books printing and binding without publishing
323117	Books printing without publishing
424120	Books, sales or receipt, merchant wholesalers
323111	Books, sales, manifold, printing
339920	Boomerangs manufacturing
813410	Booster clubs
486990	Booster pumping station (except natural gas, petroleum)
486110	Booster pumping station, crude oil transportation
486210	Booster pumping station, natural gas transportation
486910	Booster pumping station, refined petroleum products transportation
424330	Booster seats merchant wholesalers
332993	Boosters and bursters, artillery, manufacturing
335311	Boosters, feeder voltage (i.e., electrical transformers), manufacturing
423850	Boot and shoe cut stock and findings merchant wholesalers
316998	Boot and shoe cut stock and findings, leather, manufacturing
321999	Boot and shoe lasts, all materials, manufacturing
623990	Boot camps for delinquent youth
333249	Boot making and repairing machinery manufacturing
811430	Boot repair shops without retailing new boots
812990	Bootblack parlors
424340	Boots (e.g., hiking, western, work) merchant wholesalers
316210	Boots, dress and casual, children's and infants', manufacturing
316210	Boots, dress and casual, men's, manufacturing
316210	Boots, dress and casual, women's, manufacturing
316210	Boots, hiking, children's and infants', manufacturing
316210	Boots, hiking, men's, manufacturing
316210	Boots, hiking, women's, manufacturing
316210	Boots, plastics or plastics soled fabric upper, manufacturing
316210	Boots, rubber or rubber soled fabric upper, manufacturing

212391	Borate, natural, mining and/or beneficiating
325180	Borax (i.e., sodium borate) manufacturing
212391	Borax, crude, ground or pulverized, mining and/or beneficiating
325320	Bordeaux mixture insecticides manufacturing
325180	Boric acid manufacturing
333517	Boring machines, metalworking, manufacturing
213114	Boring test holes for metal mining on a contract basis
213115	Boring test holes for nonmetallic minerals mining (except fuels) on a contract basis
333517	Boring, drilling, and milling machine combinations, metalworking, manufacturing
238910	Boring, for building construction
212391	Boron compounds prepared at beneficiating plants
325180	Boron compounds, not specified elsewhere by process, manufacturing
212391	Boron mineral mining and/or beneficiating
325180	Borosilicate manufacturing
424210	Botanical drugs and herbs merchant wholesalers
325412	Botanical extract preparations (except in-vitro diagnostics) manufacturing
712130	Botanical gardens
325320	Botanical insecticides manufacturing
424210	Botanicals merchant wholesalers
541715	Botany research and development laboratories or services (except biotechnology and nanotechnology research and development)
326199	Bottle caps and lids, plastics, manufacturing
332119	Bottle caps and tops, metal, stamping
321999	Bottle corks manufacturing
321999	Bottle covers, willow, rattan, and reed, manufacturing
561990	Bottle exchanges
335210	Bottle warmers, household-type electric, manufacturing
333993	Bottle washers, packaging machinery, manufacturing
454310	Bottled gas dealers, direct selling
424490	Bottled water (except water treating) merchant wholesalers
454390	Bottled water providers, direct selling
423840	Bottles (except waste) merchant wholesalers
327213	Bottles (i.e., bottling, canning, packaging), glass, manufacturing
326160	Bottles, plastics, manufacturing
332439	Bottles, vacuum, light gauge metal, manufacturing
423930	Bottles, waste, merchant wholesalers
333993	Bottling machinery (e.g., capping, filling, labeling, sterilizing, washing) manufacturing
423830	Bottling machinery and equipment merchant wholesalers
335121	Boudoir lamp fixtures manufacturing
311422	Bouillon canning
311423	Bouillon made in dehydration plants
212319	Boulder crushed and broken mining and/or beneficiating
324199	Boulets (i.e., fuel bricks) made from refined petroleum
561611	Bounty hunting services
424590	Bovine semen merchant wholesalers
315210	Bow ties cut and sew apparel contractors
315990	Bow ties, men's and boys', cut and sewn from purchased fabric (except apparel contractors)
238290	Bowling alley equipment installation
713950	Bowling alleys
337127	Bowling center furniture manufacturing
713950	Bowling centers
423910	Bowling equipment and supplies merchant wholesalers
451110	Bowling equipment and supply stores
611620	Bowling instruction
713990	Bowling leagues or teams, recreational
321912	Bowling pin blanks manufacturing
339920	Bowling pin machines, automatic, manufacturing
326199	Bowls and bowl covers, plastics, manufacturing
321999	Bowls, wood, turned and shaped, manufacturing
314999	Bows made from purchased fabrics
339920	Bows, archery, manufacturing
316998	Bows, shoe, leather, manufacturing
321920	Box cleats, wood, manufacturing
311991	Box lunches (for sale off premises) manufacturing

321920	Box shook manufacturing
423840	Box shooks merchant wholesalers
337215	Box spring frames manufacturing
423210	Box springs merchant wholesalers
337910	Box springs, assembled, made from purchased spring
316998	Box toes (i.e., shoe cut stock), leather, manufacturing
311612	Boxed beef made from purchased carcasses
311611	Boxed beef produced in slaughtering plants
311612	Boxed meat produced from purchased carcasses
311611	Boxed meats produced in slaughtering plants
711219	Boxers, independent professional
423840	Boxes and crates, industrial (except disposable plastics, paperboard, waste), merchant wholesalers
423610	Boxes and fittings, electrical, merchant wholesalers
321920	Boxes, cigar, wood or part wood, manufacturing
322211	Boxes, corrugated and solid fiber, made from purchased paper or paperboard
335932	Boxes, electrical wiring (e.g., junction, outlet, switch), manufacturing
322212	Boxes, folding (except corrugated), made from purchased paperboard
316998	Boxes, hat (except paper or paperboard), manufacturing
321920	Boxes, jewelry, wood or part wood, manufacturing
316998	Boxes, leather, manufacturing
332439	Boxes, light gauge metal, manufacturing
424130	Boxes, paperboard and disposable plastics, merchant wholesalers
322219	Boxes, sanitary food (except folding), made from purchased paper or paperboard
322219	Boxes, setup (i.e., not shipped flat), made from purchased paperboard
322211	Boxes, shipping, laminated paper and paperboard, made from purchased paperboard
336211	Boxes, truck (e.g., cargo, dump, utility, van), assembled on purchased chassis
423930	Boxes, waste, merchant wholesalers
321920	Boxes, wood, manufacturing
321920	Boxes, wood, plain or fabric covered, nailed or lock corner, manufacturing
711211	Boxing clubs, professional or semiprofessional
713990	Boxing clubs, recreational
339920	Boxing equipment manufacturing
711310	Boxing event managers with facilities
711320	Boxing event managers without facilities
711310	Boxing event organizers with facilities
711320	Boxing event organizers without facilities
711310	Boxing event promoters with facilities
711320	Boxing event promoters without facilities
813410	Boy guiding organizations
623990	Boys' and girls' residential facilities (e.g., homes, ranches, villages)
721214	Boys' camps (except day, instructional)
611620	Boys' camps, sports instruction
611620	Boys' camps, sports instructor
713990	Boys' day camps (except instructional)
315110	Boys' socks manufacturing
111334	Boysenberry farming
339910	Bracelets, precious metal, manufacturing
115112	Bracing of orchard trees and vines
332510	Brackets (i.e., builder's hardware-type), metal, manufacturing
332618	Brackets made from purchased wire
321918	Brackets, wood, manufacturing
423710	Brads merchant wholesalers
331222	Brads, iron or steel, wire or cut, made in wire drawing plants
332618	Brads, metal, made from purchased wire
333249	Braiding machinery for textiles manufacturing
313220	Braiding narrow fabrics
336340	Brake and brake parts, automotive, truck, and bus, manufacturing
336340	Brake caliper assemblies, automotive, truck, and bus, manufacturing
336340	Brake cylinders, master and wheel, automotive, truck, and bus, manufacturing
336340	Brake discs (rotor), automotive, truck, and bus, manufacturing
336340	Brake drums, automotive, truck, and bus, manufacturing
325998	Brake fluid, synthetic, manufacturing
324191	Brake fluids, petroleum, made from refined petroleum
336340	Brake hose assemblies manufacturing
336340	Brake linings, automotive, truck, and bus, manufacturing

336340 Brake pads and shoes, automotive, truck, and bus, manufacturing

811118 Brake repair shops, automotive

333318 Brake service equipment (except mechanic's handtools), motor vehicle, manufacturing

336340 Brake shoes and pads, asbestos, manufacturing

335314 Brakes and clutches, electromagnetic, manufacturing

336510 Brakes and parts for railroad rolling stock manufacturing

335314 Brakes, electromagnetic, manufacturing

333517 Brakes, press, metalworking, manufacturing

311212 Bran and other residues of milling rice

522110 Branches of foreign banks

521110 Branches, Federal Reserve Bank

533110 Brand name licensing

115210 Branding

339940 Branding irons (i.e., marking irons) manufacturing

424820 Brandy and brandy spirits merchant wholesalers

312130 Brandy distilling

315210 Bra-slips cut and sew apparel contractors

315240 Bra-slips, women's and girls', cut and sewn from purchased fabric (except apparel contractors)

331523 Brass die-castings, unfinished, manufacturing

331529 Brass foundries (except die-casting)

423720 Brass goods, plumbers', merchant wholesalers

325612 Brass polishes manufacturing

331420 Brass products, rolling, drawing, or extruding, made from purchased copper or in integrated secondary smelting and rolling, drawing or extruding plants

315210 Brassieres cut and sew apparel contractors

315240 Brassieres cut and sewn from purchased fabric (except apparel contractors)

332323 Brasswork, ornamental, manufacturing

335220 Braziers, barbecue, manufacturing

111335 Brazil nut farming

325194 Brazilwood extract manufacturing

332811 Brazing (i.e., hardening) metals and metal products for the trade

311824 Bread and bread-type roll mixes made from purchased flour

311812 Bread and bread-type rolls made in commercial bakeries

311999 Bread crumbs not made in bakeries

335210 Bread machines, household-type electric, manufacturing

333241 Bread slicing machinery manufacturing

333993 Bread wrapping machines manufacturing

424490 Bread, packaged (except frozen), merchant wholesalers

212113 Breakers, anthracite mining and/or beneficiating

333131 Breakers, coal, manufacturing

332919 Breakers, vacuum, plumbing, manufacturing

311340 Breakfast bars, nonchocolate covered, manufacturing

311230 Breakfast cereals manufacturing

424490 Breakfast cereals merchant wholesalers

237990 Breakwater construction

332313 Breechings, fabricated metal plate work, manufacturing

112990 Breeding of pets (e.g., birds, cats, dogs)

115210 Breeding, animal, services

312120 Breweries

311211 Brewers' and distillers' flakes and grits, corn, manufacturing

311213 Brewers' malt manufacturing

325194 Brewers' pitch made by distillation of wood

311212 Brewers' rice manufacturing

424490 Brewers' yeast merchant wholesalers

333241 Brewery machinery manufacturing

238990 Brick driveway contractors

238990 Brick paver (e.g., driveways, patios, sidewalks) installation

238140 Brick veneer, installation

238140 Bricklaying contractors

423320 Bricks (except refractory) merchant wholesalers

327120 Bricks (i.e., common, face, glazed, hollow, vitrified), clay, manufacturing

327120 Bricks, adobe, manufacturing

327120 Bricks, clay refractory, manufacturing

327331 Bricks, concrete, manufacturing

327215 Bricks, glass, made from purchased glass

327212 Bricks, glass, made in glass making plants

327120 Bricks, nonclay refractory, manufacturing

315210 Bridal dresses or gowns cut and sew apparel contractors

315240	Bridal dresses or gowns, custom made
315240	Bridal dresses or gowns, women's and girls', cut and sewn from purchased fabric (except apparel contractors)
448190	Bridal gown shops (except custom)
532281	Bridal wear rental
333999	Bridge and gate lifting machinery manufacturing
611699	Bridge and other card game instruction
321114	Bridge and trestle parts, wood, treating
237310	Bridge approach construction
713990	Bridge clubs, recreational
237310	Bridge construction
237310	Bridge decking construction
238320	Bridge painting
332312	Bridge sections, prefabricated metal, manufacturing
488490	Bridge, tunnel, and highway operations
339116	Bridges, custom made in dental laboratories
334515	Bridges, electrical (e.g., Kelvin, megohm, vacuum tube, Wheatstone), manufacturing
316110	Bridle leather manufacturing
237990	Bridle path construction
423990	Briefcases merchant wholesalers
316998	Briefcases, all materials, manufacturing
315210	Briefs cut and sew apparel contractors
315190	Briefs, underwear, made in apparel knitting mills
315220	Briefs, underwear, men's and boys', cut and sewn from purchased fabric (except apparel contractors)
315240	Briefs, underwear, women's, girls', and infants', cut and sewn from purchased fabric (except apparel contractors)
212393	Brimstone mining and/or beneficiating
311421	Brining of fruits and vegetables
212210	Briquets, iron, mining and/or beneficiating
324199	Briquettes, petroleum, made from refined petroleum
424590	Bristles merchant wholesalers
322130	Bristols board stock manufacturing
322121	Bristols paper stock manufacturing
333515	Broaches (i.e., a machine tool accessory) manufacturing
423830	Broaches (i.e., a machine tool accessory) merchant wholesalers
333517	Broaching machines, metalworking, manufacturing

334220	Broadcast equipment (including studio), for radio and television, manufacturing
811213	Broadcast equipment repair and maintenance services
541910	Broadcast media rating services
423690	Broadcasting equipment merchant wholesalers
519130	Broadcasting exclusively on Internet, audio
519130	Broadcasting exclusively on Internet, video
515111	Broadcasting networks, radio
515120	Broadcasting networks, television
611519	Broadcasting schools
236220	Broadcasting station construction
515112	Broadcasting stations (except exclusively on Internet), radio
515120	Broadcasting stations, television
515112	Broadcasting studio, radio station
711110	Broadway theaters
313210	Broadwoven fabrics (except rugs, tire fabrics) weaving
313310	Broadwoven fabrics finishing
313210	Brocades weaving
111219	Broccoli farming, field, bedding plant and seed production
424920	Brochures merchant wholesalers
112320	Broiler chicken production
523140	Brokerages, commodity contracts
524210	Brokerages, insurance
522310	Brokerages, loan
522310	Brokerages, mortgage
531210	Brokerages, real estate
523120	Brokerages, securities
524210	Brokers' offices, insurance
522310	Brokers' offices, loan
522310	Brokers' offices, mortgage
531210	Brokers' offices, real estate
325180	Bromine manufacturing
325199	Bromochloromethane manufacturing
339112	Bronchoscopes (except electromedical) manufacturing
334510	Bronchoscopes, electromedical, manufacturing
331523	Bronze die-castings, unfinished, manufacturing
331529	Bronze foundries (except die-casting)
325910	Bronze printing inks manufacturing

331420	Bronze products, rolling, drawing, or extruding, made from purchased copper or in integrated secondary smelting and rolling, drawing or extruding plants
111199	Broomcorn farming
424590	Broomcorn merchant wholesalers
423850	Brooms (except household-type) merchant wholesalers
423220	Brooms and brushes, household-type, merchant wholesalers
339994	Brooms, hand and machine, manufacturing
311422	Broth (except seafood) canning
311313	Brown beet sugar refining
212111	Brown coal mining and/or beneficiating
212210	Brown ore mining and/or beneficiating
311313	Brown sugar made from beet sugar
311314	Brown sugar manufacturing
325411	Brucine manufacturing
212325	Brucite mining and/or beneficiating
335991	Brush blocks, carbon or molded graphite, manufacturing
321912	Brush blocks, wood, turned and shaped
562119	Brush collection services
562119	Brush hauling, local
562119	Brush removal services
335991	Brushes and brush stock contacts, electric, carbon and graphite, manufacturing
339940	Brushes, artists', manufacturing
424990	Brushes, artists', merchant wholesalers
339994	Brushes, household-type and industrial, manufacturing
423840	Brushes, industrial, merchant wholesalers
339994	Brushes, paint (except artists'), manufacturing
326299	Brushes, rubber, manufacturing
333517	Brushing machines, metalworking, manufacturing
335991	Brushplates, carbon or graphite, manufacturing
111219	Brussel sprout farming, field, bedding plant and seed production
325620	Bubble bath preparations manufacturing
326199	Bubble packaging materials, plastics, manufacturing
333120	Bucket and scarifier teeth manufacturing
333922	Buckets, elevator or conveyor, manufacturing
333120	Buckets, excavating (e.g., clamshell, concrete, drag scraper, dragline, shovel), manufacturing
321920	Buckets, wood, coopered, manufacturing
339993	Buckles and buckle parts (including shoe) manufacturing
111199	Buckwheat farming
311211	Buckwheat flour manufacturing
921130	Budget agencies, government
112990	Buffalo production
722514	Buffet eating places
337122	Buffets (furniture), wood, manufacturing
333517	Buffing and polishing machines, metalworking, manufacturing
327910	Buffing and polishing wheels, abrasive and nonabrasive, manufacturing
325612	Buffing compounds manufacturing
333991	Buffing machines, handheld power-driven, manufacturing
332813	Buffing metals and metal products for the trade
316110	Buffings, russet, manufacturing
332510	Builder's hardware, metal, manufacturing
541310	Building architectural design services
238210	Building automation system installation contractors
423320	Building blocks (e.g., cinder, concrete) merchant wholesalers
423310	Building board (e.g., fiber, flake, particle) merchant wholesalers
561720	Building cleaning services, interior
561720	Building cleaning services, janitorial
238910	Building demolition
541690	Building envelope consulting services
561790	Building exterior cleaning services (except sandblasting, window cleaning)
238310	Building fireproofing contractors
238390	Building fixture and fitting (except mechanical equipment) installation
238130	Building framing (except structural steel)
561790	Building gas systems conversion (e.g., from manufactured to natural gas) services
541350	Building inspection bureaus
541350	Building inspection services
926150	Building inspections, government
238310	Building insulation contractors
237210	Building lot subdividing
326199	Building materials (e.g., fascia, panels, siding, soffit), plastics, manufacturing
444190	Building materials supply dealers

423390	Building materials, fiberglass (except insulation, roofing, siding), merchant wholesalers
213112	Building oil and gas well foundations on a contract basis
326199	Building panels, corrugated and flat, plastics, manufacturing
423390	Building paper merchant wholesalers
322121	Building paper stock manufacturing
334512	Building services monitoring controls, automatic, manufacturing
925110	Building standards agencies, government
423320	Building stone merchant wholesalers
327120	Building tile, clay, manufacturing
531110	Building, apartment, rental or leasing
213112	Building, erecting, repairing, and dismantling oil and gas field rigs and derricks on a contract basis
531120	Building, nonresidential (except miniwarehouse), rental or leasing
236118	Building, residential, addition, alteration and renovation
531110	Building, residential, rental or leasing
321991	Buildings, mobile, commercial use, manufacturing
332311	Buildings, prefabricated metal, manufacturing
423390	Buildings, prefabricated nonwood, merchant wholesalers
423310	Buildings, prefabricated wood, merchant wholesalers
321992	Buildings, prefabricated, wood, manufacturing
238350	Built-in wood cabinets constructed on site
327999	Built-up mica manufacturing
335110	Bulbs, electric light, complete, manufacturing
311211	Bulgur (flour) manufacturing
424710	Bulk gasoline stations, merchant wholesalers
484220	Bulk liquids trucking, local
484230	Bulk liquids trucking, long-distance
484110	Bulk mail truck transportation, contract, local
484121	Bulk mail truck transportation, contract, long-distance (TL)
493190	Bulk petroleum storage
424710	Bulk stations, petroleum, merchant wholesalers
332420	Bulk storage tanks, heavy gauge metal, manufacturing

237990	Bulkhead wall or embarkment construction
115210	Bull testing stations
532412	Bulldozer rental or leasing without operator
238910	Bulldozer rental with operator
333120	Bulldozers manufacturing
332992	Bullet jackets and cores (i.e., 30 mm. or less, 1.18 inch or less) manufacturing
321999	Bulletin boards, wood and cork, manufacturing
339113	Bulletproof vests manufacturing
423990	Bulletproof vests merchant wholesalers
212221	Bullion, gold, produced at the mine
212222	Bullion, silver, produced at the mine
336390	Bumpers and bumperettes assembled, automotive, truck, and bus, manufacturing
333318	Bundling machinery (e.g., box strapping, mail, newspaper) manufacturing
321999	Bungs, wood, manufacturing
236220	Bunkhouse construction
339113	Bunsen burners manufacturing
315210	Buntings cut and sew apparel contractors
315240	Buntings, infants', cut and sewn from purchased fabric (except apparel contractors)
334513	Buoyancy instruments, industrial process-type, manufacturing
321999	Buoys, cork, manufacturing
332313	Buoys, fabricated plate work metal, manufacturing
561621	Burglar alarm monitoring services
561621	Burglar alarm sales combined with installation, repair, or monitoring services
238210	Burglar alarm system, electric, installation only
334290	Burglar alarm systems and equipment manufacturing
524126	Burglary and theft insurance carriers, direct
339995	Burial caskets and cases manufacturing
423850	Burial caskets merchant wholesalers
315210	Burial garments cut and sew apparel contractors
315280	Burial garments cut and sewn from purchased fabric (except apparel contractors)
524128	Burial insurance carriers, direct
339995	Burial vaults (except concrete, stone) manufacturing

327390	Burial vaults, concrete and precast terrazzo, manufacturing
327991	Burial vaults, stone, manufacturing
424990	Burlap merchant wholesalers
711110	Burlesque companies
212325	Burley mining and/or beneficiating
313310	Burling and mending fabrics
335311	Burner ignition transformers manufacturing
423720	Burners, fuel oil and distillate oil, merchant wholesalers
333414	Burners, heating, manufacturing
423830	Burners, industrial, merchant wholesalers
332811	Burning metals and metal products for the trade
333517	Burnishing machines, metalworking, manufacturing
321999	Burnt wood articles manufacturing
314999	Burnt-out laces manufacturing
112920	Burro production
212399	Burrstones, natural, mining and/or beneficiating
335313	Bus bar structures, switchgear-type, manufacturing
335931	Bus bars, electrical conductors (except switchgear-type), manufacturing
336211	Bus bodies assembling on purchased chassis
336211	Bus bodies manufacturing
541850	Bus card advertising services
485510	Bus charter services (except scenic, sightseeing)
541850	Bus display advertising services
611519	Bus driver training
485210	Bus line operation, intercity
485113	Bus line, local (except mixed mode)
423110	Bus merchant wholesalers
485410	Bus operation, school and employee
532120	Bus rental or leasing
485113	Bus services, urban and suburban (except mixed mode)
236220	Bus shelter construction
236220	Bus terminal construction
488490	Bus terminal operation, independent
561599	Bus ticket offices
485113	Bus transit systems (except mixed mode)
423610	Busbars and trolley ducts merchant wholesalers
336120	Buses (except trackless trolley) assembling on chassis of own manufacture
487110	Buses, scenic and sightseeing operation
336510	Buses, trackless trolley, manufacturing
333613	Bushings, plain (except internal combustion engine), manufacturing
326199	Bushings, plastics, manufacturing
321999	Bushings, wood, manufacturing
813910	Business associations
541990	Business brokers (except real estate brokers)
611410	Business colleges or schools not offering academic degrees
611310	Business colleges or schools offering baccalaureate or graduate degrees
323111	Business directories commercial printing (except screen) without publishing
323113	Business directories screen printing without publishing
511140	Business directory publishers (except exclusive Internet publishing)
511140	Business directory publishers and printing combined
519130	Business directory publishers, exclusively on Internet
323113	Business forms (except manifold) screen printing without publishing
323111	Business forms commercial printing (except screen) without publishing
323111	Business forms, manifold, printing
423420	Business machines and equipment (except computers) merchant wholesalers
541611	Business management consulting services
561110	Business management services
541720	Business research and development services
611410	Business schools not offering academic degrees
561439	Business service centers (except private mail centers)
561439	Business service centers (except private mail centers) providing range of office support services (except printing)
541611	Business start-up consulting services
425110	Business to business electronic markets, durable goods, wholesale trade
425110	Business to business electronic markets, nondurable goods, wholesale trade
454110	Business to Consumer retail sales Internet sites
325211	Butadiene copolymers containing less than 50 percent butadiene manufacturing

325212	Butadiene copolymers containing more than 50 percent butadiene manufacturing
325199	Butadiene made from alcohol
325110	Butadiene made from refined petroleum or liquid hydrocarbons
325212	Butadiene rubber (i.e., polybutadiene) manufacturing
424720	Butane gas merchant wholesalers (except bulk stations, terminals)
325110	Butane made from refined petroleum or liquid hydrocarbons
211130	Butane, natural, mining
445210	Butcher shops
332215	Butcher's knives manufacturing
311512	Butter manufacturing
424430	Butter merchant wholesalers
333241	Butter processing machinery manufacturing
424490	Butter substitutes merchant wholesalers
311512	Butter, creamery and whey, manufacturing
332911	Butterfly valves, industrial-type, manufacturing
311511	Buttermilk manufacturing
424430	Buttermilk merchant wholesalers
111219	Butternut squash farming, field, bedding plant and seed production
335912	Button cells, primary batteries, manufacturing
333249	Buttonhole and eyelet machinery manufacturing
315210	Buttonhole making apparel contractors
315210	Buttonhole making, fur goods, cut and sew apparel contractors
315210	Buttonholing and button covering apparel contractors
339993	Buttons (except precious metal, precious stones, semiprecious stones) manufacturing
424310	Buttons merchant wholesalers
339910	Buttons, precious metal, precious stones, semiprecious stones, manufacturing
325199	Butyl acetate manufacturing
325212	Butyl rubber manufacturing
324110	Butylene (i.e., butene) made in petroleum refineries
325110	Butylene made from refined petroleum or liquid hydrocarbons
531210	Buyers' agents, real estate, offices
531210	Buying agencies, real estate
531210	Buying real estate for others (i.e., agents, brokers)
485310	Cab (i.e., taxi) services
336112	Cab and chassis, light trucks and vans, manufacturing
111219	Cabbage farming, field, bedding plant and seed production
236115	Cabin construction general contractors
336612	Cabin cruiser building
334511	Cabin environment indicators, transmitters, and sensors manufacturing
236117	Cabin for-sale builders
423710	Cabinet hardware and fittings merchant wholesalers
332510	Cabinet hardware, metal, manufacturing
444190	Cabinet stores, kitchen (except custom), to be installed
238350	Cabinet work performed at the construction site
238350	Cabinetry work performed at the construction site
337214	Cabinets (except wood), office-type, freestanding, manufacturing
321999	Cabinets (i.e., housings), wood (e.g., sewing machines, stereo, television), manufacturing
337110	Cabinets, kitchen (except freestanding), stock or custom wood, manufacturing
423310	Cabinets, kitchen, built-in, merchant wholesalers
423210	Cabinets, kitchen, freestanding, merchant wholesalers
337124	Cabinets, metal (i.e., bathroom, kitchen) (except freestanding), manufacturing
337124	Cabinets, metal household-type, freestanding, manufacturing
337124	Cabinets, metal, radio and television, manufacturing
238350	Cabinets, wood built-in, constructed on site
337122	Cabinets, wood household-type, freestanding, manufacturing
337211	Cabinets, wood office-type, freestanding, manufacturing
721199	Cabins, housekeeping
515210	Cable broadcasting networks
485119	Cable car systems (except mixed mode), commuter
487110	Cable car, land, scenic and sightseeing operation
334220	Cable decoders manufacturing
237130	Cable laying (e.g., cable television, electricity, marine, telephone), including underground

517311	Cable program distribution operators
238990	Cable splicing (except electrical or fiber optic)
238210	Cable splicing, electrical or fiber optic
517311	Cable television distribution services
238210	Cable television hookup contractors
515210	Cable television networks
334220	Cable television transmission and receiving equipment manufacturing
517311	Cable TV providers (except networks)
331420	Cable, copper (e.g., armored, bare, insulated), made from purchased copper in wire drawing plants
331420	Cable, copper (e.g., armored, bare, insulated), made in integrated secondary smelting and wire drawing plants
331222	Cable, iron or steel, insulated or armored, made in wire drawing plants
335929	Cable, nonferrous, insulated, or armored, made from purchased nonferrous wire
332618	Cable, noninsulated wire, made from purchased wire
423510	Cable, wire (except insulated), merchant wholesalers
333111	Cabs for agricultural machinery manufacturing
333120	Cabs for construction machinery manufacturing
333924	Cabs for industrial trucks manufacturing
111339	Cactus fruit farming
541512	CAD (computer-aided design) systems integration design services
541370	Cadastral surveying services
339920	Caddy carts manufacturing
331410	Cadmium refining, primary
541512	CAE (computer-aided engineering) systems integration design services
722513	Cafes, limited-service
337215	Cafeteria fixtures manufacturing
722310	Cafeteria food services contractors (e.g., government office cafeterias, hospital cafeterias, school cafeterias)
337127	Cafeteria furniture manufacturing
337127	Cafeteria tables and benches manufacturing
722514	Cafeterias
325411	Caffeine and derivatives (i.e., basic chemicals) manufacturing
315210	Caftans cut and sew apparel contractors
315220	Caftans, men's and boys', cut and sewn from purchased fabric (except apparel contractors)
315240	Caftans, women's, girls', and infants', cut and sewn from purchased fabric (except apparel contractors)
332618	Cages made from purchased wire
238910	Caisson (i.e., drilled building foundations) construction
237990	Caisson (i.e., marine or pneumatic structures) construction
332420	Caissons, underwater work, heavy gauge metal, manufacturing
453998	Cake decorating supply stores
311999	Cake frosting manufacturing
311942	Cake frosting mixes manufacturing
311824	Cake mixes made from purchased flour
311340	Cake ornaments, confectionery, manufacturing
311813	Cake, frozen, manufacturing
311812	Cakes, baking (except frozen), made in commercial bakeries
212230	Calamine mining and/or beneficiating
212221	Calaverite mining and/or beneficiating
212312	Calcareous tufa crushed and broken stone mining and/or beneficiating
212311	Calcareous tufa mining or quarrying
325510	Calcimines manufacturing
424950	Calcimines merchant wholesalers
212392	Calcined phosphate rock mining and/or beneficiating
324199	Calcining petroleum coke from refined petroleum
212399	Calcite mining and/or beneficiating
325180	Calcium carbide, chloride, and hypochlorite manufacturing
325199	Calcium citrate manufacturing
327410	Calcium hydroxide (i.e., hydrated lime) manufacturing
325180	Calcium hypochlorite manufacturing
325180	Calcium inorganic compounds, not specified elsewhere by process, manufacturing
325199	Calcium organic compounds, not specified elsewhere by process, manufacturing
325199	Calcium oxalate manufacturing
327410	Calcium oxide (i.e., quicklime) manufacturing
423420	Calculators and calculating machines merchant wholesalers
333318	Calculators manufacturing
511199	Calendar publishers (except exclusive Internet publishing)

511199	Calendar publishers and printing combined
519130	Calendar publishers, exclusively on Internet
453998	Calendar shops
323111	Calendars commercial printing (except screen) without publishing
323113	Calendars screen printing without publishing
333249	Calendering machinery for plastics manufacturing
333249	Calendering machinery for textiles manufacturing
313310	Calendering textile products, apparel, and fabrics
112111	Calf (e.g., feeder, stocker, veal) production
315110	Calf high sheer hosiery knitting or knitting and finishing
541380	Calibration and certification testing laboratories or services
332216	Calipers and dividers, machinists' precision tools, manufacturing
336340	Calipers, brake, automotive, truck, and bus, manufacturing
339992	Calliopes (steam organs) manufacturing
541512	CAM (computer-aided manufacturing) systems integration design services
532210	Camcorder rental
423410	Camcorders (except household-type) merchant wholesalers
334310	Camcorders manufacturing
326211	Camelback (i.e., retreading material) manufacturing
333249	Camelback (i.e., retreading materials) machinery manufacturing
316998	Camera carrying bags, all materials, manufacturing
423410	Camera equipment and supplies, photographic, merchant wholesalers
333314	Camera lenses manufacturing
811211	Camera repair shops without retailing new cameras
443142	Camera shops, photographic
711510	Cameramen, independent (freelance)
333316	Cameras (except television, video) manufacturing
334220	Cameras, television, manufacturing
423410	Cameras, television, merchant wholesalers
423410	Cameras, video (except household-type), merchant wholesalers
315210	Camisoles cut and sew apparel contractors
315240	Camisoles, women's and girls', cut and sewn from purchased fabric (except apparel contractors)

337124	Camp furniture, metal, manufacturing
337125	Camp furniture, reed and rattan, manufacturing
337122	Camp furniture, wood, manufacturing
813940	Campaign organizations, political
441210	Camper dealers, recreational
441210	Camper parts and accessories stores
532120	Camper rental
336214	Camper units, slide-in, for pick-up trucks, manufacturing
721211	Campgrounds
325194	Camphor, natural, manufacturing
325199	Camphor, synthetic, manufacturing
423910	Camping equipment and supplies merchant wholesalers
423110	Camping trailer merchant wholesalers
336214	Camping trailers and chassis manufacturing
721214	Camps (except day, instructional)
713990	Camps (except instructional), day
623990	Camps, boot or disciplinary (except correctional), for delinquent youth
611620	Camps, sports instruction
721211	Campsites
333515	Cams (i.e., a machine tool accessory) manufacturing
333517	Can forming machines, metalworking, manufacturing
332618	Can keys made from purchased wire
332431	Can lids and ends, light gauge metal, manufacturing
332216	Can openers (except electric) manufacturing
335210	Can openers, household-type electric, manufacturing
483211	Canal barge transportation (freight)
237990	Canal construction
488310	Canal maintenance services (except dredging)
488310	Canal operation
483212	Canal passenger transportation
221310	Canal, irrigation
333318	Canceling machinery, postal office-type, manufacturing
923120	Cancer detection program administration
622310	Cancer hospitals
311340	Candied fruits and fruit peel manufacturing
713950	Candle pin bowling alleys

713950 Candle pin bowling centers
453998 Candle shops
339999 Candles manufacturing
424990 Candles merchant wholesalers
311351 Candy bars, chocolate (including chocolate covered), made from cacao beans
311340 Candy bars, nonchocolate, manufacturing
424450 Candy merchant wholesalers
311352 Candy stores, chocolate, candy made on premises not for immediate consumption
311340 Candy stores, nonchocolate, candy made on premises, not for immediate consumption
445292 Candy stores, packaged, retailing only
311351 Candy, chocolate, made from cacao beans
111930 Cane farming, sugar, field production
311314 Cane sugar manufacturing
424490 Cane sugar, refined, merchant wholesalers
311314 Cane syrup manufacturing
339999 Canes (except orthopedic) manufacturing
332993 Canisters, ammunition, manufacturing
424490 Canned foods (e.g., fish, meat, seafood, soups) merchant wholesalers
311611 Canned meats (except poultry) produced in slaughtering plants
311911 Canned nuts manufacturing
236210 Cannery construction
311710 Cannery, seafood
311421 Canning fruits and vegetables
311421 Canning jams and jellies
333993 Canning machinery manufacturing
311615 Canning poultry (except baby and pet food)
311422 Canning soups (except seafood)
423840 Canning supplies merchant wholesalers
311710 Canning, fish, crustacea, and mollusks
332994 Cannons manufacturing
339112 Cannulae manufacturing
532284 Canoe rental
713990 Canoeing, recreational
311225 Canola (rapeseed) oil, cake and meal, made from purchased oils
311224 Canola (rapeseed) oil, cake and meal, made in crushing mills
111120 Canola farming, field and seed production
332322 Canopies, sheet metal (except stampings), manufacturing

332431 Cans, aluminum, light gauge metal, manufacturing
332431 Cans, light gauge metal, manufacturing
332431 Cans, steel, light gauge metal, manufacturing
111219 Cantaloupe farming, field, bedding plant and seed production
722515 Canteens, fixed location
722330 Canteens, mobile
321912 Cants, resawed (lumber), manufacturing
314910 Canvas bags manufacturing
339940 Canvas board, artist's, manufacturing
314910 Canvas products made from purchased canvas or canvas substitutes
424990 Canvas products merchant wholesalers
316210 Canvas shoes, plastics soled fabric upper, manufacturing
316210 Canvas shoes, rubber soled fabric upper, manufacturing
339940 Canvas, artist's, prepared on frames, manufacturing
313210 Canvases weaving
454390 Canvassers (door-to-door), headquarters for retail sale of merchandise, direct selling
423610 Capacitors (except electronic) merchant wholesalers
335999 Capacitors (except electronic), fixed and variable, manufacturing
334416 Capacitors, electronic, fixed and variable, manufacturing
423690 Capacitors, electronic, merchant wholesalers
315240 Capes (except fur, waterproof), women's and girls', cut and sewn from purchased fabric (except apparel contractors)
315210 Capes cut and sew apparel contractors
315280 Capes, fur (except apparel contractors), manufacturing
315280 Capes, waterproof (e.g., plastics, rubber, similar materials), cut and sewn from purchased fabric (except apparel contractors)
237110 Capping of water wells
333993 Capping, sealing, and lidding packaging machinery manufacturing
325199 Caprolactam manufacturing
315990 Caps (except fur, leather) cut and sewn from purchased fabric (except apparel contractors)
315210 Caps (i.e., apparel accessory) cut and sew apparel contractors

315990	Caps (i.e., apparel accessory) cut and sewn from purchased fabric (except fur, leather, apparel contractors)
315210	Caps and gowns, academic, cut and sew apparel contractors
315280	Caps and gowns, academic, cut and sewn from purchased fabric (except apparel contractors)
335931	Caps and plugs, attachment, electric, manufacturing
332119	Caps and tops, bottle, metal, stamping
336214	Caps for pick-up trucks manufacturing
325998	Caps for toy pistols manufacturing
315190	Caps made in apparel knitting mills
325920	Caps, blasting and detonating, manufacturing
332993	Caps, bomb, manufacturing
315280	Caps, fur (except apparel contractors), manufacturing
316998	Caps, heel and toe, leather, manufacturing
315280	Caps, leather (except apparel contractors), manufacturing
315210	Caps, textiles, straw, fur-felt, and wool-felt, cut and sew apparel contractors
315990	Caps, textiles, straw, fur-felt, and wool-felt, cut and sewn from purchased fabric (except apparel contractors)
325998	Capsules, gelatin, empty, manufacturing
334290	Car alarm manufacturing
336211	Car bodies, kit, manufacturing
811192	Car detailers
532112	Car leasing
483212	Car lighters (i.e., ferries), inland waters (except on Great Lakes system)
485999	Car pool operation
488999	Car pools, arrangement of
532111	Car rental
532111	Car rental agencies
561599	Car rental reservation services
811111	Car repair shops, general
332999	Car seals, metal, manufacturing
337125	Car seats, infant (except metal), manufacturing
334310	Car stereos manufacturing
522298	Car title lending
423850	Car wash equipment and supplies merchant wholesalers
811192	Car washes
333318	Car washing machinery manufacturing
331110	Car wheels, rolled steel, made in iron and steel mills
325180	Carbides (e.g., boron, calcium, silicon, tungsten) manufacturing
332994	Carbines manufacturing
325199	Carbinol manufacturing
325211	Carbohydrate plastics manufacturing
423510	Carbon and alloy steel primary forms merchant wholesalers
334510	Carbon arc lamp units, electrotherapeutic (except infrared and ultraviolet), manufacturing
325180	Carbon black manufacturing
424690	Carbon black merchant wholesalers
327120	Carbon brick manufacturing
325120	Carbon dioxide manufacturing
325180	Carbon disulfide manufacturing
335991	Carbon electrodes and contacts, electric, manufacturing
325180	Carbon inorganic compounds manufacturing
334290	Carbon monoxide detectors manufacturing
423690	Carbon monoxide detectors, electronic, merchant wholesalers
325199	Carbon organic compounds, not specified elsewhere by process, manufacturing
339940	Carbon paper manufacturing
335991	Carbon specialties for aerospace use (except gaskets) manufacturing
335991	Carbon specialties for electrical use manufacturing
335991	Carbon specialties for mechanical use (except gaskets) manufacturing
325199	Carbon tetrachloride manufacturing
325998	Carbon, activated, manufacturing
424490	Carbonated beverages merchant wholesalers
312111	Carbonated soda manufacturing
312111	Carbonated soft drinks manufacturing
325180	Carbonic acid manufacturing
333249	Carbonizing equipment for processing wool manufacturing
313310	Carbonizing textile fibers
335991	Carbons, electric, manufacturing
335991	Carbons, lighting, manufacturing
325998	Carburetor cleaners manufacturing
336310	Carburetors, all types, manufacturing
316998	Card cases (except metal) manufacturing

339910	Card cases, precious metal, manufacturing
423920	Card games merchant wholesalers
713290	Card rooms (e.g., poker rooms)
453220	Card shops, greeting
337122	Card table sets (furniture), wood, manufacturing
337124	Card table sets, metal, manufacturing
424130	Cardboard products merchant wholesalers
322130	Cardboard stock manufacturing
322220	Cardboard, laminated or surface coated, made from purchased paperboard
313230	Carded nonwoven fabrics manufacturing
313110	Carded yarn manufacturing
325412	Cardiac preparations manufacturing
333249	Carding machinery for textiles manufacturing
313310	Carding textile fibers
334510	Cardiodynameter manufacturing
334510	Cardiographs manufacturing
621111	Cardiologists' offices (e.g., centers, clinics)
334510	Cardiophone, electric, manufacturing
334510	Cardioscope manufacturing
334510	Cardiotachometer manufacturing
323111	Cards (e.g., business, greeting, playing, postcards, trading) commercial printing (except screen) without publishing
323113	Cards (e.g., business, greeting, playing, postcards, trading) screen printing without publishing
322299	Cards, die-cut (except office supply) made from purchased paper or paperboard
322230	Cards, die-cut office supply (e.g., index, library, time recording), made from purchased paper or paperboard
424120	Cards, greeting, merchant wholesalers
******	Cards, publishing -- see specific product
611710	Career and vocational counseling services (except rehabilitative)
481112	Cargo carriers, air, scheduled
488390	Cargo checkers, marine
811310	Cargo container repair and maintenance services
488330	Cargo salvaging, marine
336611	Cargo ship building
488390	Cargo surveyors, marine
488490	Cargo surveyors, truck transportation
423110	Cargo van merchant wholesalers

333318	Carnival and amusement park rides manufacturing
333318	Carnival and amusement park shooting gallery machinery manufacturing
423850	Carnival equipment merchant wholesalers
713990	Carnival ride concession operators (i.e., supplying and servicing in others' facilities)
711190	Carnival traveling shows
212291	Carnotite mining and/or beneficiating
333922	Carousel conveyors (e.g., luggage) manufacturing
333318	Carousels (i.e., merry-go-rounds) manufacturing
238350	Carpenters (except framing)
611513	Carpenters' apprenticeship training
332216	Carpenter's handtools, nonelectric, manufacturing
423710	Carpenters' tools merchant wholesalers
532490	Carpentry equipment rental or leasing
238350	Carpentry work (except framing)
238130	Carpentry, framing
333318	Carpet and floor cleaning equipment, electric commercial-type, manufacturing
335210	Carpet and floor cleaning equipment, household-type electric, manufacturing
532490	Carpet and rug cleaning equipment rental or leasing
313110	Carpet and rug yarn spinning
532289	Carpet and rug, residential, rental
423850	Carpet cleaning equipment and supplies merchant wholesalers
561740	Carpet cleaning on customers' premises
561740	Carpet cleaning plants
561740	Carpet cleaning services
314999	Carpet cutting and binding
313210	Carpet linings (except felt) weaving
423220	Carpet merchant wholesalers
313230	Carpet paddings, nonwoven, manufacturing
442210	Carpet stores
333318	Carpet sweepers, mechanical, manufacturing
238330	Carpet, installation only
314110	Carpets and rugs made from textile materials
321999	Carpets, cork, manufacturing
332311	Carports, prefabricated metal, manufacturing
487110	Carriage, horse-drawn, operation

339930	Carriages, baby, manufacturing
339930	Carriages, doll, manufacturing
334210	Carrier equipment (i.e., analog, digital), telephone, manufacturing
111219	Carrot farming, field, bedding plant and seed production
311991	Carrots, cut, peeled or sliced fresh, manufacturing
722513	Carryout restaurants
336111	Cars, electric, for highway use, assembling on chassis of own manufacture
333131	Cars, mining, manufacturing
541370	Cartographic surveying services
333993	Carton filling machinery manufacturing
423840	Cartons (except paper and paperboard) merchant wholesalers
322299	Cartons, egg, molded pulp manufacturing
322212	Cartons, folding (except milk), made from purchased paperboard
322219	Cartons, milk, made from purchased paper or paperboard
424130	Cartons, paper and paperboard, merchant wholesalers
711510	Cartoonists, independent
333991	Cartridge (i.e., powder) handheld power-driven tools manufacturing
332992	Cartridge cases for ammunition (i.e., 30 mm. or less, 1.18 inch or less) manufacturing
331420	Cartridge cups, discs, and sheets, copper and copper alloy, made from purchased copper or in integrated secondary smelting and rolling, drawing or extruding plants
424120	Cartridge toner merchant wholesalers
332992	Cartridges (i.e., 30 mm. or less, 1.18 inch or less) manufacturing
339920	Carts, caddy, manufacturing
423860	Carts, golf, motorized passenger merchant wholesalers
333924	Carts, grocery, made from purchased wire
333112	Carts, lawn and garden-type, manufacturing
332215	Carving sets manufacturing
111219	Casaba melon farming, field, bedding plant and seed production
316110	Case leather manufacturing
325220	Casein fibers and filaments manufacturing
325211	Casein plastics manufacturing
311514	Casein, dry and wet, manufacturing
332321	Casements, metal, manufacturing
316998	Cases, jewelry (except metal), manufacturing
339910	Cases, jewelry, metal, manufacturing
316998	Cases, luggage, manufacturing
316998	Cases, musical instrument, manufacturing
321920	Cases, shipping, wood, wirebound, manufacturing
321920	Cases, wood packing, nailed or lock corner, manufacturing
321920	Cases, wood shipping, nailed or lock corner, manufacturing
332439	Cash boxes, light gauge metal, manufacturing
532420	Cash register rental or leasing
333318	Cash registers (except point of sales terminals) manufacturing
423420	Cash registers merchant wholesalers
111335	Cashew farming
211130	Casing-head butane and propane production
326121	Casings, sausage, nonrigid plastics, manufacturing
332313	Casings, scroll, fabricated metal plate work, manufacturing
332322	Casings, sheet metal (except stampings), manufacturing
236220	Casino construction
721120	Casino hotels
423910	Casino supplies merchant wholesalers
713210	Casinos (except casino hotels)
332510	Casket hardware, metal, manufacturing
339995	Caskets, burial, manufacturing
423850	Caskets, burial, merchant wholesalers
321920	Casks, wood, coopered, manufacturing
111219	Cassava farming, field and seed production
335210	Casseroles, household-type electric, manufacturing
334614	Cassette tapes, prerecorded audio, mass reproducing
532282	Cassette, prerecorded video, rental
423990	Cassettes, prerecorded audio and video, merchant wholesalers
331511	Cast iron brake shoes, railroad, manufacturing
331511	Cast iron pipe and pipe fittings manufacturing
423510	Cast iron pipe merchant wholesalers
331511	Cast iron railroad car wheels manufacturing

331513 Cast steel railroad car wheels, unfinished, manufacturing

327390 Cast stone, concrete (except structural), manufacturing

327120 Castable refractories, clay, manufacturing

327120 Castable refractories, nonclay, manufacturing

332510 Casters, furniture, metal manufacturing

332510 Casters, industrial, metal, manufacturing

561311 Casting agencies (i.e., motion picture, theatrical, video)

561311 Casting agencies, motion picture or video

561311 Casting agencies, theatrical

561311 Casting bureaus (e.g., motion picture, theatrical, video)

561311 Casting bureaus, motion picture or video

561311 Casting bureaus, theatrical

331529 Castings (except die-castings), nonferrous metals (except aluminum), unfinished, manufacturing

331524 Castings (except die-castings), unfinished, aluminum, manufacturing

331511 Castings, compacted graphite iron, unfinished, manufacturing

331511 Castings, malleable iron, unfinished, manufacturing

423510 Castings, metal, merchant wholesalers

331513 Castings, steel (except investment), unfinished, manufacturing

331511 Castings, unfinished iron (e.g., ductile, gray, malleable, semisteel), manufacturing

311224 Castor oil and pomace made in crushing mills

316210 Casual shoes, children's and infants', manufacturing

316210 Casual shoes, men's, manufacturing

316210 Casual shoes, women's, manufacturing

524126 Casualty insurance carriers, direct

621512 CAT (computerized axial tomography) scanner centers

311111 Cat food manufacturing

325998 Cat litter manufacturing

112990 Cat production

511199 Catalog (i.e., mail-order, store merchandise) publishers (except exclusive Internet publishing)

511199 Catalog (i.e., mail-order, store merchandise) publishers and printing combined

454110 Catalog (i.e., order-taking) offices of mail-order houses

511140 Catalog of collections publishers (except exclusive Internet publishing)

511140 Catalog of collections publishers and printing combined

519130 Catalog of collections publishers, exclusively on Internet

452319 Catalog showrooms, general merchandise (except catalog mail-order)

323111 Catalogs commercial printing (except screen) without publishing

323111 Catalogs of collections commercial printing (except screen) without publishing

323113 Catalogs of collections screen printing without publishing

323113 Catalogs screen printing without publishing

336390 Catalytic converters, engine exhaust, automotive, truck, and bus, manufacturing

332994 Catapult guns manufacturing

562998 Catch basin cleaning services

722320 Caterers

722320 Catering services, social

112511 Catfish production, farm raising

325412 Cathartic preparations manufacturing

339112 Catheters manufacturing

334419 Cathode ray tubes (CRT) manufacturing

335999 Cathodic protection equipment manufacturing

238190 Cathodic protection, installation

212399 Catlinite mining and/or beneficiating

424990 Cats merchant wholesalers

311421 Catsup manufacturing

112111 Cattle conditioning operations

112111 Cattle farming or ranching

333111 Cattle feeding and watering equipment manufacturing

112112 Cattle feedlots (except stockyards for transportation)

311119 Cattle feeds, supplements, concentrates, and premixes, manufacturing

424520 Cattle merchant wholesalers

115210 Cattle spraying

111219 Cauliflower farming, field, bedding plant and seed production

238390 Caulking (i.e., waterproofing) contractors

325520 Caulking compounds (except gypsum base) manufacturing

332216 Caulking guns, nonpowered, manufacturing

424690	Caulking materials merchant wholesalers
524291	Cause-of-loss investigators, insurance
237310	Causeway construction
325180	Caustic potash manufacturing
325180	Caustic soda (i.e., sodium hydroxide) manufacturing
424690	Caustic soda merchant wholesalers
712190	Caverns (i.e., natural wonder tourist attractions)
334220	CB (citizens' band) radios manufacturing
332216	C-clamps manufacturing
334112	CD-ROM drives manufacturing
334614	CD-ROM, software, mass reproducing
337122	Cedar chests manufacturing
325998	Cedar oil manufacturing
238130	Ceiling beam, wood, installation
444190	Ceiling fan stores
335210	Ceiling fans with integral lighting fixture, residential, manufacturing
335210	Ceiling fans, residential, manufacturing
335122	Ceiling lighting fixtures, commercial, industrial, and institutional, manufacturing
335121	Ceiling lighting fixtures, residential, manufacturing
321912	Ceiling lumber, dressed, resawing purchased lumber
321113	Ceiling lumber, made from logs or bolts
238310	Ceiling tile installation
423390	Ceiling tile merchant wholesalers
238390	Ceiling, metal, installation
334519	Ceilometers manufacturing
711410	Celebrities' agents or managers
711510	Celebrity spokespersons, independent
111219	Celery farming, field, bedding plant and seed production
212393	Celestite mining and/or beneficiating
325220	Cellophane film or sheet manufacturing
424120	Cellophane tape merchant wholesalers
339992	Cellos and parts manufacturing
237130	Cellular phone tower construction
443142	Cellular telephone accessories stores
517312	Cellular telephone communication carriers
517312	Cellular telephone services
517312	Cellular telephone stores, primarily selling cellular phone service plans
334220	Cellular telephones manufacturing

423690	Cellular telephones merchant wholesalers
325199	Cellulose acetate (except resins) manufacturing
325211	Cellulose acetate resins manufacturing
424610	Cellulose film merchant wholesalers
325211	Cellulose nitrate resins manufacturing
325211	Cellulose propionate resins manufacturing
325211	Cellulose resins manufacturing
325211	Cellulose xanthate (viscose) manufacturing
238310	Cellulosic fiber insulation installation
325220	Cellulosic fibers and filaments manufacturing
325220	Cellulosic filament yarn manufacturing
326113	Cellulosic plastics film and unlaminated sheet (except packaging) manufacturing
325220	Cellulosic staple fibers manufacturing
327310	Cement (e.g., hydraulic, masonry, portland, pozzolana) manufacturing
238140	Cement block laying
327310	Cement clinker manufacturing
333249	Cement kilns manufacturing
423320	Cement merchant wholesalers
236210	Cement plant construction
212312	Cement rock crushed and broken stone mining and/or beneficiating
327120	Cement, clay refractory, manufacturing
327420	Cement, Keene's (i.e., tiling plaster), manufacturing
325520	Cement, rubber, manufacturing
213112	Cementing oil and gas well casings on a contract basis
423830	Cement-making machinery merchant wholesalers
324122	Cements, asphalt roofing, made from purchased asphaltic materials
339114	Cements, dental, manufacturing
812220	Cemeteries
812220	Cemetery associations (i.e., operators)
812220	Cemetery management services
453998	Cemetery memorial dealers (e.g., headstones, markers, vaults)
561730	Cemetery plot care services
812220	Cemetery subdividers
333517	Centering machines, metalworking, manufacturing
519120	Centers for documentation (i.e., archives)
624120	Centers, senior citizens'

238220	Central air-conditioning equipment installation
521110	Central bank, monetary authorities
238220	Central cooling equipment and piping installation
238220	Central heating equipment and piping installation
423730	Central heating equipment, warm air, merchant wholesalers
325412	Central nervous system stimulant preparations manufacturing
334210	Central office and switching equipment, telephone, manufacturing
522320	Central reserve financial institutions (except central bank)
333318	Central vacuuming systems, commercial-type, manufacturing
335210	Central vacuuming systems, household-type, manufacturing
551114	Centralized administrative offices
327320	Central-mixed concrete manufacturing
333914	Centrifugal pumps manufacturing
333999	Centrifuges, industrial and laboratory-type, manufacturing
325411	Cephalosporin, uncompounded, manufacturing
423330	Ceramic and clay roofing materials merchant wholesalers
325130	Ceramic colors manufacturing
423320	Ceramic construction materials (except refractory and ceramic roofing tile) merchant wholesalers
327999	Ceramic fiber manufacturing
333994	Ceramic kilns and furnaces manufacturing
238340	Ceramic tile installation
444190	Ceramic tile stores
327120	Ceramic tiles, floor and wall, manufacturing
423220	Ceramic wall (except structural) and floor tile merchant wholesalers
611610	Ceramics instruction
311211	Cereal grain flour manufacturing
311211	Cereal grain germ manufacturing
424490	Cereal products merchant wholesalers
212299	Cerium concentrates mining and/or beneficiating
212299	Cerium ores mining and/or beneficiating
325180	Cerium salts manufacturing
523120	Certificate of deposit (CD) brokers' offices
923110	Certification of schools and teachers

541211	Certified accountants' offices
523930	Certified financial planners, customized, fees paid by client
541211	Certified public accountants' (CPAs) offices
621399	Certified registered nurse anesthetists' (CRNAs) offices (e.g., centers, clinics)
212230	Cerussite mining and/or beneficiating
339113	Cervical collars manufacturing
325180	Cesium and cesium compounds, not specified elsewhere by process, manufacturing
562991	Cesspool cleaning services
238910	Cesspool construction
325199	Cetyl alcohol manufacturing
335210	Chafing dishes, household-type electric, manufacturing
332999	Chain fittings manufacturing
333923	Chain hoists manufacturing
332323	Chain ladders, metal, manufacturing
238990	Chain link fence installation
332618	Chain link fencing and fence gates made from purchased wire
331222	Chain link fencing, iron or steel, made in wire drawing plants
332618	Chain made from purchased wire
332216	Chain saw blades manufacturing
333991	Chain saws, handheld power-driven, manufacturing
332618	Chain, welded, made from purchased wire
339910	Chains or necklace, precious metal, manufacturing
333613	Chains, power transmission, manufacturing
334519	Chains, surveyor's, manufacturing
423830	Chainsaws merchant wholesalers
337121	Chair and couch springs, assembled, manufacturing
337215	Chair glides manufacturing
337215	Chair seats for furniture manufacturing
337122	Chairs (except upholstered), wood household-type, manufacturing
337214	Chairs (except wood), office-type, manufacturing
337127	Chairs, barber, beauty shop (i.e., hydraulic), manufacturing
337125	Chairs, cane, wood household-type, manufacturing
339114	Chairs, dentist's, manufacturing

423850	Chairs, hydraulic, beauty and barber shop, merchant wholesalers
337124	Chairs, metal household-type (except upholstered), manufacturing
337127	Chairs, portable folding, auditorium-type, manufacturing
337127	Chairs, stacking, auditorium-type, manufacturing
337121	Chairs, upholstered household-type (except dining room, kitchen), manufacturing
337211	Chairs, wood office-type, manufacturing
212230	Chalcocite mining and/or beneficiating
212230	Chalcopyrite mining and/or beneficiating
339940	Chalk (e.g., artist's, blackboard, carpenter's, marking, tailor's), manufacturing
212312	Chalk crushed and broken stone mining and/or beneficiating
212312	Chalk, ground or otherwise treated, mining and/or beneficiating
339940	Chalkboards, framed, manufacturing
711130	Chamber musical groups
711130	Chamber orchestras
813910	Chambers of commerce
313210	Chambrays weaving
333517	Chamfering machines, metalworking, manufacturing
316110	Chamois leather manufacturing
424990	Chamois, leather, merchant wholesalers
312130	Champagne method sparkling wine, manufacturing
335122	Chandeliers, commercial, industrial, and institutional electric, manufacturing
335121	Chandeliers, residential, manufacturing
333318	Change making machines manufacturing
325180	Channel black manufacturing
237990	Channel construction
332323	Channels, furring metal, manufacturing
325194	Charcoal (except activated) manufacturing
325194	Charcoal briquettes, wood, manufacturing
424990	Charcoal merchant wholesalers
325998	Charcoal, activated, manufacturing
522210	Charge card issuing
423410	Charged coupled devices (CCD) merchant wholesalers
813211	Charitable trusts, awarding grants
611699	Charm schools
481212	Charter air freight services
481211	Charter air passenger services
485510	Charter bus services (except scenic, sightseeing)
487210	Charter fishing boat operation
611110	Charter schools
333515	Chasers (i.e., a machine tool accessory) manufacturing
212399	Chasers mining and/or beneficiating
332812	Chasing metals and metal products (except printing plates) for the trade
336111	Chassis, automobile, manufacturing
336120	Chassis, heavy truck, with or without cabs, manufacturing
336112	Chassis, light truck and utility, manufacturing
423110	Chassis, motor vehicle, merchant wholesalers
561311	Chauffeur registries
611519	Chauffeur training
315210	Chauffeurs' hats and caps cut and sew apparel contractors
315990	Chauffeurs' hats and caps cut and sewn from purchased fabric (except apparel contractors)
522390	Check cashing services
521110	Check clearing activities of the central bank
522320	Check clearing services (except central banks)
522320	Check clearinghouse services (except central banks)
423420	Check handling machines merchant wholesalers
812990	Check room services
522320	Check validation services
332911	Check valves, industrial-type, manufacturing
333318	Check writing machines manufacturing
316998	Checkbook covers (except metal) manufacturing
339910	Checkbook covers, precious metal, manufacturing
323111	Checkbooks and refills printing
339930	Checkers and checkerboards manufacturing
611620	Cheerleading instruction, camps, or schools
311513	Cheese (except cottage cheese) manufacturing
311513	Cheese analogs manufacturing
311941	Cheese based salad dressing manufacturing

424450	Cheese confections (e.g., curls, puffs) merchant wholesalers
311919	Cheese curls and puffs manufacturing
424430	Cheese merchant wholesalers
333241	Cheese processing machinery manufacturing
311513	Cheese products, imitation or substitute, manufacturing
311513	Cheese spreads manufacturing
311511	Cheese, cottage, manufacturing
311513	Cheese, imitation or substitute, manufacturing
311513	Cheese, natural (except cottage cheese), manufacturing
313210	Cheesecloths weaving
236210	Chemical (except petrochemical process-type) plant construction
424690	Chemical additives (e.g., concrete, food, fuel, oil) merchant wholesalers
423490	Chemical and technical pottery products merchant wholesalers
541690	Chemical consulting services
541330	Chemical engineering services
313310	Chemical finishing (e.g., fire, mildew, water resistance) fabrics
424690	Chemical gases merchant wholesalers
423830	Chemical industries machinery and equipment merchant wholesalers
333249	Chemical kilns manufacturing
332710	Chemical milling job shops
333517	Chemical milling machines, metalworking, manufacturing
333249	Chemical processing machinery and equipment manufacturing
541715	Chemical research and development laboratories or services (except biotechnology and nanotechnology research and development)
327110	Chemical stoneware (i.e., pottery products) manufacturing
326191	Chemical toilets, plastics, manufacturing
115112	Chemical treatment of soil for crops
213112	Chemically treating oil and gas wells (e.g., acidizing, bailing, swabbing) on a contract basis
424690	Chemicals (except agriculture) (e.g., automotive, household, industrial, photographic) merchant wholesalers
424910	Chemicals, agricultural, merchant wholesalers
315210	Chemises cut and sew apparel contractors
315190	Chemises made in apparel knitting mills
315240	Chemises, women's and girls', cut and sewn from purchased fabric (except apparel contractors)
111339	Cherry farming
113210	Cherry gum, gathering
339930	Chessmen and chessboards manufacturing
325194	Chestnut extract manufacturing
113210	Chestnut gum, gathering
321920	Chests for tools, wood, manufacturing
332999	Chests, fire or burglary resistive, metal, manufacturing
332999	Chests, money, metal, manufacturing
332999	Chests, safe deposit, metal, manufacturing
311340	Chewing gum base manufacturing
333241	Chewing gum machinery manufacturing
311340	Chewing gum manufacturing
424450	Chewing gum merchant wholesalers
312230	Chewing tobacco manufacturing
424940	Chewing tobacco merchant wholesalers
424440	Chicken and chicken products (except canned and packaged frozen) merchant wholesalers
333111	Chicken brooders manufacturing
321920	Chicken coops (i.e., crates), wood, wirebound for shipping poultry, manufacturing
321992	Chicken coops, prefabricated, wood, manufacturing
112310	Chicken egg production
112310	Chicken eggs (table, hatching) production
333111	Chicken feeders manufacturing
311119	Chicken feeds, prepared, manufacturing
112340	Chicken hatcheries
332618	Chicken netting made from purchased wire
112320	Chicken production (except egg laying)
311615	Chickens, processing, fresh, frozen, canned, or cooked (except baby and pet food)
311615	Chickens, slaughtering and dressing
424590	Chicks, live, merchant wholesalers
111998	Chicory farming
624410	Child day care centers
624410	Child day care services
624410	Child day care services in provider's own home
624410	Child day care, before or after school, separate from schools

623990	Child group foster homes
624110	Child guidance agencies
624110	Child welfare services
621410	Childbirth preparation classes
721214	Children's camps (except day, instructional)
424330	Children's clothing merchant wholesalers
511199	Children's coloring book publishers (except exclusive Internet publishing)
519130	Children's coloring book publishers, exclusively on Internet
622110	Children's hospitals, general
622210	Children's hospitals, psychiatric or substance abuse
622310	Children's hospitals, specialty (except psychiatric, substance abuse)
448210	Children's shoe stores
316210	Children's shoes (except orthopedic extension) manufacturing
315110	Children's socks manufacturing
423920	Children's vehicles (except bicycles) merchant wholesalers
623990	Children's villages
311422	Chili con carne canning
311942	Chili pepper or powder manufacturing
311421	Chili sauce manufacturing
238220	Chilled water system installation
339992	Chimes and parts (musical instruments) manufacturing
335999	Chimes, electric, manufacturing
327390	Chimney caps, concrete, manufacturing
561790	Chimney cleaning services
238220	Chimney liner installation
561790	Chimney sweep (i.e., cleaning) services
238140	Chimney, brick, block or stone, contractors
238110	Chimney, concrete, construction
212324	China clay mining and/or beneficiating
337122	China closets, wood, manufacturing
327110	China cooking ware manufacturing
811490	China repair services
327110	China tableware, vitreous, manufacturing
442299	Chinaware stores
423440	Chinaware, commercial, merchant wholesalers
423220	Chinaware, household-type, merchant wholesalers
112930	Chinchilla production
311422	Chinese foods canning
311999	Chinese noodles, fried, manufacturing
111219	Chinese pea farming, bedding plant and seed production
313210	Chintzes weaving
333249	Chip placement machinery manufacturing
322130	Chipboard (i.e., paperboard) stock manufacturing
321219	Chipboard (i.e., particle core, wood chip face) manufacturing
322220	Chipboard, laminated or surface coated, made from purchased paperboard
321113	Chipper mills (except portable)
333112	Chippers (i.e., shredders), lawn and garden-type, manufacturing
333120	Chippers, portable, commercial (e.g., brush, limb, log), manufacturing
333243	Chippers, stationary (e.g., log), manufacturing
424450	Chips (e.g., corn, potato) merchant wholesalers
621310	Chiropractors' offices (e.g., centers, clinics)
332216	Chisels manufacturing
333991	Chisels, handheld power-driven, manufacturing
111219	Chive farming, field, bedding plant and seed production
325199	Chloral manufacturing
325320	Chlordane insecticides manufacturing
325180	Chloride of lime manufacturing
325212	Chlorinated rubber, synthetic, manufacturing
325180	Chlorine compounds, not specified elsewhere by process, manufacturing
325180	Chlorine dioxide manufacturing
325180	Chlorine manufacturing
424690	Chlorine merchant wholesalers
325199	Chloroacetic acid manufacturing
325194	Chlorobenzene manufacturing
325120	Chlorodifluoromethane manufacturing
325120	Chlorofluorocarbon gases manufacturing
325199	Chloroform manufacturing
325194	Chloronaphthalene manufacturing
325194	Chlorophenol manufacturing
325199	Chloropicrin manufacturing
325212	Chloroprene rubber manufacturing
325212	Chlorosulfonated polyethylenes manufacturing

325180	Chlorosulfonic acid manufacturing
325194	Chlorotoluene manufacturing
311352	Chocolate (coating, instant, liquor, syrups) made from purchased chocolate
311351	Chocolate (e.g., coatings, instant, liquor, syrups) made from cacao beans
424490	Chocolate (except candy) merchant wholesalers
311351	Chocolate bars made from cocoa beans
424450	Chocolate candy merchant wholesalers
311352	Chocolate coatings and syrups made from purchased chocolate
424490	Chocolate coatings merchant wholesalers
311352	Chocolate covered candy bars made from purchased chocolate
311352	Chocolate covered granola bars made from purchased chocolate
311511	Chocolate drink (milk based) manufacturing
311511	Chocolate milk manufacturing
333241	Chocolate processing machinery manufacturing
424490	Chocolate syrups (except fountain) merchant wholesalers
311351	Chocolate, confectionery, made from cacao beans
711130	Choirs
334416	Chokes for electronic circuitry manufacturing
325414	Cholera serums manufacturing
325320	Cholinesterase inhibitors used as insecticides manufacturing
311412	Chop suey, frozen, manufacturing
115113	Chopping and silo filling
711510	Choreographers, independent
311412	Chow mein, frozen, manufacturing
311710	Chowders, seafood, manufacturing
621399	Christian Science practitioners' offices (e.g., centers, clinics)
424990	Christmas ornaments merchant wholesalers
453220	Christmas stores
333132	Christmas tree assemblies, oil and gas field-type, manufacturing
111421	Christmas tree growing
335129	Christmas tree lighting sets, electric, manufacturing
339999	Christmas tree ornaments (except electric, glass) manufacturing
327215	Christmas tree ornaments made from purchased glass
327212	Christmas tree ornaments, glass, made in glass making plants
424990	Christmas trees (e.g., artificial, cut) merchant wholesalers
339999	Christmas trees, artificial, manufacturing
454390	Christmas trees, cut, direct selling
334516	Chromatographic instruments, laboratory-type, manufacturing
334513	Chromatographs, industrial process-type, manufacturing
325130	Chrome pigments (e.g., chrome green, chrome orange, chrome yellow) manufacturing
332813	Chrome plating metals and metal products for the trade
325180	Chromic acid manufacturing
212299	Chromite mining and/or beneficiating
325180	Chromium compounds, not specified elsewhere by process, manufacturing
212299	Chromium concentrates beneficiating
212299	Chromium ore mining and/or beneficiating
325180	Chromium oxide manufacturing
331410	Chromium refining, primary
325180	Chromium salts manufacturing
622310	Chronic disease hospitals
334519	Chronographs manufacturing
334519	Chronometers manufacturing
334516	Chronoscopes manufacturing
333517	Chucking machines, automatic, metalworking, manufacturing
333515	Chucks (i.e., a machine tool accessory) manufacturing
112390	Chukar partridge production
238290	Church bell and tower clock installation
337127	Church furniture (except concrete, stone) manufacturing
423490	Church supplies (except plated ware, silverware) merchant wholesalers
813110	Churches
332313	Chutes, fabricated metal plate work, manufacturing
333241	Cider presses manufacturing
311941	Cider vinegar manufacturing
312130	Cider, alcoholic, manufacturing
311941	Cider, nonalcoholic, manufacturing
326199	Cigar and cigarette holders, plastics, manufacturing
321920	Cigar boxes, wood and part wood, manufacturing

316998	Cigar cases (except metal) manufacturing
339910	Cigar cases, precious metal, manufacturing
312230	Cigar manufacturing
453991	Cigar stores
316998	Cigarette cases (except metal) manufacturing
339910	Cigarette cases, precious metal, manufacturing
339999	Cigarette holders manufacturing
339999	Cigarette lighter flints manufacturing
339999	Cigarette lighters (except precious metal) manufacturing
424990	Cigarette lighters merchant wholesalers
333249	Cigarette making machinery manufacturing
322299	Cigarette paper made from purchased paper
322121	Cigarette paper made in paper mills
322299	Cigarette paper, book, made from purchased paper
453991	Cigarette stands, permanent
454390	Cigarette stands, temporary
325220	Cigarette tow, cellulosic fiber, manufacturing
333318	Cigarette vending machines manufacturing
312230	Cigarettes manufacturing
424940	Cigarettes merchant wholesalers
424940	Cigars merchant wholesalers
325411	Cinchona and derivatives (i.e., basic chemicals) manufacturing
327331	Cinder (clinker) block, concrete, manufacturing
238140	Cinder block installation
236220	Cinema construction
512131	Cinemas
711510	Cinematographers, independent
212299	Cinnabar mining and/or beneficiating
333249	Circuit board making machinery manufacturing
423690	Circuit boards merchant wholesalers
334412	Circuit boards, printed, bare, manufacturing
423610	Circuit breakers merchant wholesalers
335313	Circuit breakers, air, manufacturing
335313	Circuit breakers, power, manufacturing
922110	Circuit courts
334515	Circuit testers manufacturing
423690	Circuits, integrated, merchant wholesalers

313240	Circular (i.e., weft) fabrics knitting
541870	Circular direct distribution services
333249	Circular knitting machinery manufacturing
333991	Circular saws, handheld power-driven, manufacturing
333243	Circular saws, woodworking-type, stationary, manufacturing
519120	Circulating libraries
711190	Circus companies
711190	Circuses
443142	Citizens' band (CB) radio stores
334220	Citizens' band (CB) radios manufacturing
423690	Citizens' band (CB) radios merchant wholesalers
325199	Citral manufacturing
325199	Citrates, not specified elsewhere by process, manufacturing
325199	Citric acid manufacturing
325998	Citronella oil manufacturing
325199	Citronellal manufacturing
115112	Citrus grove cultivation services
111320	Citrus groves (except orange)
311119	Citrus pulp, cattle feed, manufacturing
311411	Citrus pulp, frozen, manufacturing
921120	City and town councils
921110	City and town managers' offices
485113	City bus services (except mixed mode)
922110	City or county courts
541320	City planning services
813410	Civic associations
236220	Civic center construction
541330	Civil engineering services
813311	Civil liberties organizations
921190	Civil rights commissions
921190	Civil service commissions
524291	Claims adjusting, insurance
524292	Claims processing services, insurance, third party
114112	Clam digging
112512	Clam production, farm raising
333515	Clamps (i.e., a machine tool accessory) manufacturing
339112	Clamps, surgical, manufacturing
339992	Clarinets and parts manufacturing
316998	Clasps, shoe (leather), manufacturing

813410 Classic car clubs

711120 Classical dance companies

711130 Classical musical artists, independent

711130 Classical musical groups

212325 Clay (except kaolin, ball) mining and/or beneficiating

327110 Clay and ceramic statuary manufacturing

212325 Clay bleaching

423320 Clay construction materials (except refractory and clay roofing tile) merchant wholesalers

327120 Clay refractories (e.g., mortar, brick, tile, block) manufacturing

212324 Clay, ball, mining and/or beneficiating

212325 Clay, ceramic and refractory minerals, mining and/or beneficiating

212325 Clay, fire, mining and/or beneficiating

339940 Clay, modeling, manufacturing

212324 Clay, natural, mining and/or beneficiating

333249 Clayworking and tempering machinery manufacturing

812332 Clean room apparel supply services

236210 Clean room construction

339113 Clean room suits and accessories manufacturing

812320 Cleaners, drycleaning and laundry service (except coin-operated)

335210 Cleaners, household-type electric vacuum, manufacturing

561790 Cleaning (e.g., power sweeping, washing) driveways and parking lots

332813 Cleaning and descaling metals and metal products for the trade

812320 Cleaning and dyeing plants (except rug cleaning plants)

311212 Cleaning and polishing rice

561790 Cleaning building exteriors (except sandblasting, window cleaning)

238990 Cleaning building interiors during and immediately after construction

561740 Cleaning carpets

424690 Cleaning compounds and preparations merchant wholesalers

335999 Cleaning equipment, ultrasonic (except dental, medical), manufacturing

561720 Cleaning homes

333131 Cleaning machinery, mining-type, manufacturing

238990 Cleaning new building interiors immediately after construction

561720 Cleaning offices

213112 Cleaning oil and gas field lease tanks on a contract basis

213112 Cleaning out (e.g., bailing out, steam cleaning, swabbing) wells on a contract basis

212113 Cleaning plants, anthracite coal

212111 Cleaning plants, bituminous coal

561740 Cleaning plants, carpet and rug

115210 Cleaning poultry houses

561740 Cleaning rugs

561740 Cleaning services, carpet and rug

561720 Cleaning shopping centers

561790 Cleaning swimming pools

213112 Cleaning wells on a contract basis

213112 Cleaning, repairing, and dismantling oil and gas field lease tanks on a contract basis

321918 Clear and finger joint wood moldings manufacturing

522320 Clearinghouses, bank or check

523999 Clearinghouses, commodity exchange or securities exchange

316210 Cleated athletic shoes manufacturing

332215 Cleavers manufacturing

611410 Clerical schools

315210 Clerical vestments cut and sew apparel contractors

315280 Clerical vestments cut and sewn from purchased fabric (except apparel contractors)

315190 Clerical vestments made in apparel knitting mills

316210 Climbing shoes, plastics or plastics soled fabric upper, manufacturing

316210 Climbing shoes, rubber or rubber soled fabric upper, manufacturing

236220 Clinic construction

621399 Clinical nurse specialists' (CNSs) offices (e.g., centers, clinics)

621111 Clinical pathologists' offices (e.g., centers, clinics)

621399 Clinical pharmacists' offices (e.g., centers, clinics)

621330 Clinical psychologists' offices (e.g., centers, clinics)

****** Clinics, medical -- see type

621498 Clinics/centers of health practitioners from more than one industry practicing within the same establishment

621498	Clinics/centers of health practitioners with multi-industry degrees
321999	Clipboards, wood, manufacturing
332216	Clippers for animal use, nonelectric, manufacturing
332215	Clippers, fingernail and toenail, manufacturing
519190	Clipping services, news
332994	Clips, gun, manufacturing
334519	Clock materials and parts (except crystals) manufacturing
334519	Clock or watch springs, precision, made from purchased wire
334310	Clock radios manufacturing
811490	Clock repair shops without retailing new clocks
448310	Clock shops
334519	Clocks assembling
334519	Clocks assembling from purchased components
423940	Clocks merchant wholesalers
541714	Cloning research and experimental development laboratories
561492	Closed captioning services, real-time (i.e., simultaneous)
512191	Closed captioning services, taped material
517311	Closed-circuit television (CCTV) services
334220	Closed-circuit television equipment manufacturing
525990	Closed-end investment funds
423220	Closet accessories merchant wholesalers
453998	Closet organizer stores
238390	Closet organizer system installation
423840	Closures, industrial, merchant wholesalers
332119	Closures, metal, stamping
424130	Closures, paper and disposable plastics, merchant wholesalers
327910	Cloth (e.g., aluminum oxide, garnet, emery, silicon carbide) coated manufacturing
561990	Cloth cutting, bolting, or winding for the trade
333249	Cloth spreading machinery manufacturing
321999	Cloth winding reels, wood, manufacturing
332618	Cloth, woven wire, made from purchased wire
334512	Clothes dryer controls, including dryness controls, manufacturing
811412	Clothes dryer, household-type, repair and maintenance services without retailing new clothes dryers
321999	Clothes dryers (clothes horses), wood, manufacturing
423850	Clothes dryers (except household-type) merchant wholesalers
423620	Clothes dryers merchant wholesalers
424990	Clothes hangers merchant wholesalers
326199	Clothes hangers, plastics, manufacturing
321999	Clothes poles, wood, manufacturing
326199	Clothespins, plastics, manufacturing
321999	Clothespins, wood, manufacturing
448150	Clothing accessories stores
424330	Clothing accessories, women's, children's, and infants', merchant wholesalers
541490	Clothing design services
532281	Clothing rental (except industrial launderer, linen supply)
811490	Clothing repair shops, alterations only
448130	Clothing stores, children's and infants'
448140	Clothing stores, family
448110	Clothing stores, men's and boys'
453310	Clothing stores, used
448120	Clothing stores, women's and girls'
339930	Clothing, doll, manufacturing
315280	Clothing, fur (except apparel contractors), manufacturing
315210	Clothing, fur, cut and sew apparel contractors
315280	Clothing, leather or sheep-lined (except apparel contractors), manufacturing
315210	Clothing, leather or sheep-lined, cut and sew apparel contractors
424320	Clothing, men's and boys', merchant wholesalers
315210	Clothing, water resistant, cut and sew apparel contractors
315220	Clothing, water resistant, men's and boys', cut and sewn from purchased fabric (except apparel contractors)
315240	Clothing, water resistant, women's, girls', and infants', cut and sewn from purchased fabric (except apparel contractors)
315210	Clothing, waterproof, cut and sew apparel contractors
315280	Clothing, waterproof, cut and sewn from purchased fabric (except apparel contractors)
315210	Clothing, water-repellent, cut and sew apparel contractors

315220 Clothing, water-repellent, men's and boys', cut and sewn from purchased fabric (except apparel contractors)

315240 Clothing, water-repellent, women's, girls', and infants', cut and sewn from purchased fabric (except apparel contractors)

424330 Clothing, women's, children's, and infants', merchant wholesalers

339994 Cloths (except chemically treated), dusting and polishing, manufacturing

325612 Cloths, dusting and polishing, chemically treated, manufacturing

325998 Clove oil manufacturing

111940 Clover hay farming

111998 Clover seed farming

721310 Clubs, residential

339920 Clubs, sporting goods (e.g., golf, Indian), manufacturing

336350 Clutches and clutch discs, asbestos, manufacturing

525990 CMOs (collateralized mortgage obligations)

325413 Coagulation in-vitro diagnostic substances manufacturing

325412 Coagulation in-vivo diagnostic substances manufacturing

333922 Coal and ore conveyors manufacturing

212113 Coal beneficiating plants, anthracite

212111 Coal beneficiating plants, bituminous or lignite (surface or underground)

333131 Coal breakers, cutters, and pulverizers manufacturing

332322 Coal chutes, sheet metal (except stampings), manufacturing

454310 Coal dealers, direct selling

423520 Coal dust merchant wholesalers

211130 Coal gasification at mine site

484220 Coal hauling, truck, local

211130 Coal liquefaction at mine site

423520 Coal merchant wholesalers

213113 Coal mining services (except site preparation and related construction contractor activities)

213113 Coal mining support services (tunneling, blasting, training, overburden removal)(except site preparation and related construction contractor activities)

486990 Coal pipeline transportation

211130 Coal pyrolysis

424690 Coal tar distillates and resins merchant wholesalers

325194 Coal tar distillates manufacturing

324121 Coal tar paving materials made from purchased coal tar

423320 Coal tar paving materials merchant wholesalers

424690 Coal tar products, primary and intermediate, merchant wholesalers

325211 Coal tar resins manufacturing

212113 Coal, anthracite, mining and/or beneficiating

212111 Coal, bituminous, beneficiating

212112 Coal, bituminous, underground mining or mining and beneficiating

212111 Coal, brown, mining and/or beneficiating

926120 Coast Guard (except academy)

483113 Coastal freight transportation to and from domestic ports

483114 Coastal passenger transportation to and from domestic ports

483113 Coastal shipping of freight to and from domestic ports

812331 Coat (e.g., barber's, beautician's, doctor's, nurse's) supply services

332618 Coat hangers made from purchased wire

315280 Coat linings, fur (except apparel contractors), manufacturing

315210 Coat linings, fur, cut and sew apparel contractors

448190 Coat stores

315990 Coat trimmings fabric cut and sewn from purchased fabric (except apparel contractors)

315210 Coat trimmings, fabric, cut and sew apparel contractors

322220 Coated board made from purchased paperboard

322130 Coated board made in paperboard mills

324122 Coating compounds, tar, made from purchased asphaltic materials

238390 Coating concrete structures with plastics

332812 Coating metals and metal products for the trade

332812 Coating of metal and metal products with plastics for the trade

335110 Coating purchased light bulbs

322220 Coating purchased papers for nonpackaging applications (except photosensitive paper)

322220 Coating purchased papers for packaging applications

311351 Coatings, chocolate, made from cacao beans

315210	Coats (e.g., tailored, fur, artificial leather, leather, sheep-lined), cut and sew apparel contractors
315220	Coats (except fur, leather, waterproof), men's and boys', cut and sewn from purchased fabric (except apparel contractors)
315240	Coats (except fur, leather, waterproof), women's, girls', and infants', cut and sewn from purchased fabric (except apparel contractors)
315280	Coats (including tailored), leather or sheep-lined (except apparel contractors), manufacturing
315280	Coats, artificial leather, cut and sewn from purchased fabric (except apparel contractors)
315280	Coats, fur (except apparel contractors), manufacturing
315280	Coats, leather (except apparel contractors), manufacturing
424320	Coats, men's and boys', merchant wholesalers
315220	Coats, nontailored service apparel (e.g., laboratory, mechanics', medical), men's and boys', cut and sewn from purchased fabric (except apparel contractors)
315210	Coats, nontailored service apparel (e.g., laboratory, medical, mechanics'), cut and sew apparel contractors
315240	Coats, nontailored service apparel (e.g., laboratory, medical, mechanics'), women's and girls', cut and sewn from purchased fabric (except apparel contractors)
315220	Coats, tailored (except fur, leather), men's and boys', cut and sewn from purchased fabric (except apparel contractors)
315240	Coats, tailored (except fur, leather), women's and girls', cut and sewn from purchased fabric
315280	Coats, waterproof (e.g., plastics, rubberized fabric, similar materials), cut and sewn from purchased fabric (except apparel contractors)
315280	Coats, waterproof (e.g., plastics, rubberized fabric, similar materials), rubberizing fabric and manufacturing coats
315210	Coats, waterproof (i.e., plastics, rubberized fabric, similar materials), cut and sew apparel contractors
424330	Coats, women's, children's, and infants', merchant wholesalers
331318	Coaxial cable made in aluminum wire drawing plants
423610	Coaxial cable merchant wholesalers
331420	Coaxial cable, copper, made from purchased copper in wire drawing plants
331491	Coaxial cable, nonferrous metals (except aluminum, copper), made from purchased nonferrous metals (except aluminum, copper) in wire drawing plants
335929	Coaxial cable, nonferrous, made from purchased nonferrous wire
334417	Coaxial connectors manufacturing
339991	Coaxial mechanical face seals manufacturing
325180	Cobalt 60 (i.e., radioactive cobalt) manufacturing
325180	Cobalt chloride manufacturing
325180	Cobalt compounds, not specified elsewhere by process, manufacturing
212299	Cobalt concentrates beneficiating
212299	Cobalt ores mining and/or beneficiating
331410	Cobalt refining, primary
325180	Cobalt sulfate manufacturing
325411	Cocaine and derivatives (i.e., basic chemicals) manufacturing
332913	Cocks, drain, plumbing, manufacturing
722410	Cocktail lounges
311999	Cocktail mixes, dry, manufacturing
424820	Cocktails, alcoholic, premixed, merchant wholesalers
311351	Cocoa (e.g., instant, mix, mixed with other ingredients, powder drink, powdered) made from cacao beans
424590	Cocoa beans merchant wholesalers
311351	Cocoa butter made from cocoa beans
311352	Cocoa, powdered drink, prepared, made from purchased chocolate
311352	Cocoa, powdered, made from purchased chocolate
311352	Cocoa, powdered, mixed with other ingredients, made from purchased chocolate
311225	Coconut oil made from purchased oils
311224	Coconut oil made in crushing mills
111339	Coconut tree farming
311999	Coconut, desiccated and shredded, manufacturing
114111	Cod catching
114111	Cod fishing
311710	Cod liver oil extraction, crude, processing
325411	Cod liver oil, medicinal, uncompounded, manufacturing

325411	Codeine and derivatives (i.e., basic chemicals) manufacturing
333993	Coding, dating, and imprinting packaging machinery manufacturing
561330	Co-employment staffing services
445299	Coffee and tea (i.e., packaged) stores
722330	Coffee carts, mobile
311920	Coffee concentrates (i.e., instant coffee) manufacturing
311920	Coffee extracts manufacturing
111339	Coffee farming
322299	Coffee filters made from purchased paper
311920	Coffee flavoring and syrups (i.e., made from coffee) manufacturing
333318	Coffee makers and urns, commercial-type, manufacturing
423440	Coffee makers, commercial, merchant wholesalers
335210	Coffee makers, household-type electric, manufacturing
423620	Coffee makers, household-type, merchant wholesalers
424490	Coffee merchant wholesalers
311920	Coffee roasting
333241	Coffee roasting and grinding machinery (i.e., food manufacturing-type) manufacturing
722515	Coffee shops, on premise brewing
311920	Coffee substitute manufacturing
337122	Coffee tables, wood, manufacturing
311920	Coffee, blended, manufacturing
312111	Coffee, iced, manufacturing
311920	Coffee, instant and freeze-dried, manufacturing
454390	Coffee-break supplies providers, direct selling
237990	Cofferdam construction
423850	Coffins merchant wholesalers
487110	Cog railway, scenic and sightseeing, operation
237130	Co-generation plant construction
541720	Cognitive research and development services
811310	Coil rewinding (except on an assembly line or factory basis)
333519	Coil winding and cutting machinery, metalworking, manufacturing
423830	Coil winding machines, spring, merchant wholesalers

332613	Coiled springs (except clock, watch), light gauge, made from purchased wire or strip, manufacturing
332613	Coiled springs, heavy gauge metal, manufacturing
335312	Coils for motors and generators manufacturing
423690	Coils, electronic, merchant wholesalers
336320	Coils, ignition, internal combustion engines, manufacturing
332996	Coils, pipe, made from purchased metal pipe
333318	Coin counting machinery manufacturing
561990	Coin pick-up services, parking meter
316998	Coin purses (except metal) manufacturing
339910	Coin purses, precious metal, manufacturing
423420	Coin sorting machines merchant wholesalers
333318	Coin wrapping machines manufacturing
339999	Coin-operated amusement machines (except jukebox) manufacturing
812310	Coin-operated drycleaners and laundries
713290	Coin-operated gambling device concession operators (i.e., supplying and servicing in others' facilities)
339999	Coin-operated gambling devices manufacturing
423990	Coin-operated game machines merchant wholesalers
334310	Coin-operated jukebox manufacturing
812310	Coin-operated laundry and drycleaning routes (i.e., concession operators)
423440	Coin-operated merchandising machine merchant wholesalers
713990	Coin-operated nongambling amusement device concession operators (i.e., supplying and servicing in others' facilities)
812990	Coin-operated personal service machine (e.g., blood pressure, locker, photographic, scale, shoeshine) concession operators
423440	Coin-operated phonographs and vending machines merchant wholesalers
333318	Coin-operated vending machines manufacturing
423940	Coins merchant wholesalers
423520	Coke merchant wholesalers
221210	Coke oven gas distribution
324199	Coke oven products (e.g., coke, gases, tars) made in coke oven establishments
331110	Coke oven products made in iron and steel mills

324110	Coke, petroleum, made in petroleum refineries
335110	Cold cathode fluorescent lamp tubes manufacturing
332111	Cold forgings made from purchased iron or steel, unfinished
332112	Cold forgings made from purchased nonferrous metals, unfinished
325412	Cold remedies manufacturing
333519	Cold rolling mill machinery, metalworking, manufacturing
331221	Cold rolling steel shapes (e.g., bar, plate, rod, sheet, strip) made from purchased steel
493120	Cold storage locker services
423740	Cold storage machinery merchant wholesalers
236220	Cold storage plant construction
493120	Cold storage warehousing
332811	Cold treating metals for the trade
311991	Cole slaw, fresh, manufacturing
212391	Colemanite mining and/or beneficiating
311612	Collagen sausage casings made from purchased hides
332439	Collapsible tubes (e.g., toothpaste, glue), light gauge metal, manufacturing
315210	Collar and cuff sets cut and sew apparel contractors
315190	Collar and cuff sets made in apparel knitting mills
315240	Collar and cuff sets, women's and girls', cut and sewn from purchased fabric (except apparel contractors)
316110	Collar leather, manufacturing
111219	Collard farming, field, bedding plant and seed production
333515	Collars (i.e., a machine tool accessory) manufacturing
316998	Collars and collar pads (i.e., harness) manufacturing
316998	Collars, dog, manufacturing
333613	Collars, shaft for power transmission equipment, manufacturing
522294	Collateralized mortgage obligation (CMO) issuing, private
525990	Collateralized mortgage obligations (CMOs)
333244	Collating machinery for printing and bookbinding manufacturing
333318	Collating machinery, office-type, manufacturing
453220	Collectible gift shops (e.g., crystal, pewter, porcelain)
812320	Collecting and distributing agents, laundry and drycleaning
561440	Collection agencies
561440	Collection agencies, accounts
221320	Collection, treatment, and disposal of waste through a sewer system
813930	Collective bargaining units
335312	Collector rings for motors and generators manufacturing
453998	Collectors' items (e.g., autograph, card, coin, stamp) shops (except used rare items)
454110	Collectors' items, mail-order houses
611691	College board preparation centers
611691	College entrance exam preparation instruction
611710	College selection services
611310	Colleges (except junior colleges)
611511	Colleges, barber and beauty
611210	Colleges, community
611210	Colleges, junior
611310	Colleges, universities, and professional schools
333515	Collets (i.e., a machine tool accessory) manufacturing
325620	Colognes manufacturing
424210	Colognes merchant wholesalers
334510	Colonscopes, electromedical, manufacturing
812199	Color consulting services (i.e., personal care services)
325130	Color pigments, inorganic (except bone black, carbon black, lamp black), manufacturing
325130	Color pigments, organic (except animal black, bone black), manufacturing
323120	Color separation services, for the printing trade
334516	Colorimeters, laboratory-type, manufacturing
423920	Coloring books merchant wholesalers
316110	Coloring leather
332813	Coloring metals and metal products (except coating) for the trade
339113	Colostomy appliances manufacturing
812220	Columbariums
212299	Columbite mining and/or beneficiating
212299	Columbium ores mining and/or beneficiating
327420	Columns, architectural or ornamental plaster work, manufacturing

332420	Columns, fractionating, heavy gauge metal, manufacturing
321918	Columns, porch, wood, manufacturing
316998	Comb cases (except metal) manufacturing
339910	Comb cases, precious metal, manufacturing
334512	Combination limit and fan controls manufacturing
112990	Combination livestock farming (except dairy, poultry)
334512	Combination oil and hydronic controls manufacturing
333111	Combines (i.e., harvester-threshers) manufacturing
423820	Combines merchant wholesalers
313310	Combing and converting top
333249	Combing machinery for textiles manufacturing
313310	Combing textile fibers
115113	Combining, agricultural
332999	Combs, metal, manufacturing
326199	Combs, plastics, manufacturing
326299	Combs, rubber, manufacturing
334513	Combustion control instruments (except commercial, household furnace-type) manufacturing
541330	Combustion engineering consulting services
562211	Combustors, hazardous waste
562213	Combustors, nonhazardous solid waste
711510	Comedians, independent
711110	Comedy troupes
812990	Comfort station operation
314120	Comforters made from purchased fabrics
511120	Comic book publishers (except exclusive Internet publishing)
511120	Comic book publishers and printing combined (except exclusive Internet publishing)
519130	Comic book publishers, exclusively on Internet
451212	Comic book stores
323111	Comic books commercial printing (except screen) without publishing
323113	Comic books screen printing without publishing
811310	Commercial and industrial machinery repair and maintenance services
522220	Commercial and inventory financing (except international trade financing)
541430	Commercial art services

541430	Commercial artists, independent
311812	Commercial bakeries
522110	Commercial banking
522110	Commercial banks
236220	Commercial building construction
236220	Commercial building construction for-sale builders
236220	Commercial building construction general contractors
531120	Commercial building rental or leasing
561450	Commercial credit reporting bureaus
323111	Commercial digital printing (except books)
323111	Commercial engraving printing (except books)
423830	Commercial fishing equipment and supplies (except boats, ships) merchant wholesalers
323111	Commercial flexographic printing (except books)
238220	Commercial freezer installation
811310	Commercial gaming machine repair and maintenance services
323111	Commercial gravure printing (except books)
541430	Commercial illustration services
541430	Commercial illustrators, independent
238290	Commercial kitchen food preparation equipment (e.g., mixers, ovens, stoves) installation
323111	Commercial letterpress printing (except books)
335122	Commercial lighting fixtures, electric, manufacturing
323111	Commercial lithographic (offset) printing (except books)
523120	Commercial note brokers' offices
523110	Commercial paper dealing (i.e., acting as a principal in dealing securities to investors)
541922	Commercial photography services
323111	Commercial printing (except screen, books)
531312	Commercial property managing
323111	Commercial quick printing (except books)
531210	Commercial real estate agencies
531210	Commercial real estate agents' offices
531312	Commercial real estate property managers' offices
811310	Commercial refrigeration equipment repair and maintenance services

238220	Commercial refrigeration system installation
323113	Commercial screen printing (except books, manifold business forms, grey goods)
424120	Commercial stationery supplies merchant wholesalers
334519	Commercial timing mechanisms manufacturing
512110	Commercials, television, production
238290	Commercial-type door installation
445110	Commissaries, primarily groceries
523140	Commodity contract pool operators
523130	Commodity contract trading companies
523140	Commodity contracts brokerages
523140	Commodity contracts brokers' offices
523130	Commodity contracts dealing (i.e., acting as a principal in dealing commodities to investors)
523210	Commodity contracts exchanges
523140	Commodity contracts floor brokers
523130	Commodity contracts floor traders (i.e., acting as a principal in dealing commodities to investors)
523130	Commodity contracts floor trading (i.e., acting as a principal in dealing commodities to investors)
523140	Commodity contracts options brokerages
523130	Commodity contracts options dealing (i.e., acting as a principal in dealing commodities to investors)
523130	Commodity contracts traders (i.e., acting as a principal in dealing commodities to investors)
522298	Commodity Credit Corporation
523140	Commodity futures brokerages
541990	Commodity inspection services
212325	Common clay mining and/or beneficiating
212321	Common sand quarrying and/or beneficiating
212325	Common shale mining and/or beneficiating
923120	Communicable disease program administration
237130	Communication antenna construction
541430	Communication design services, visual
238210	Communication equipment installation
811213	Communication equipment repair and maintenance services
237130	Communication tower construction
926130	Communications commissions
423690	Communications equipment merchant wholesalers
334220	Communications equipment, mobile and microwave, manufacturing
334210	Communications headgear, telephone, manufacturing
926130	Communications licensing commissions and agencies
334515	Communications signal testing and evaluation equipment manufacturing
335929	Communications wire and cable, nonferrous, made from purchased nonferrous wire
331318	Communications wire or cable made in aluminum wire drawing plants
331420	Communications wire or cable, copper, made from purchased copper in wire drawing plants
331491	Communications wire or cable, nonferrous metals (except aluminum, copper), made from purchased nonferrous metals (except aluminum, copper) in wire drawing plants
311812	Communion wafer manufacturing
813319	Community action advocacy organizations
624190	Community action service agencies
624120	Community centers (except recreational only), adult
624110	Community centers (except recreational only), youth
813219	Community chests
611210	Community colleges
611210	Community colleges offering a wide variety of academic and technical training
925120	Community development agencies, government
813211	Community foundations
621498	Community health centers and clinics, outpatient
624190	Community health education services (except health care services)
923120	Community health programs administration
624210	Community meals, social services
712110	Community museums
924120	Community recreation programs, government
923130	Community social service program administration
711110	Community theaters
335312	Commutators, electric motor, manufacturing

481111	Commuter air carriers, scheduled
485113	Commuter bus operation (except mixed mode)
485112	Commuter rail systems (except mixed mode)
485111	Commuter transit systems, mixed mode (e.g., bus, commuter rail, subway combination)
334310	Compact disc players (e.g., automotive, household-type) manufacturing
423620	Compact disc players merchant wholesalers
423990	Compact discs (CDs), prerecorded, merchant wholesalers
334614	Compact discs (i.e., CD-ROM), software, mass reproducing
334614	Compact discs, prerecorded audio, mass reproducing
334613	Compact discs, recordable or rewritable, blank, manufacturing
335110	Compact fluorescent light bulbs manufacturing
423830	Compactors, trash, industrial, merchant wholesalers
339910	Compacts, precious metal, manufacturing
316998	Compacts, solid leather, manufacturing
112990	Companion animals production (e.g., cats, dogs, parakeets, parrots)
624120	Companion services for disabled persons, the elderly, and persons diagnosed with intellectual and developmental disabilities
333314	Comparators, optical, manufacturing
334511	Compasses, gyroscopic and magnetic (except portable), manufacturing
334519	Compasses, portable magnetic-type, manufacturing
541612	Compensation consulting services
541612	Compensation planning services
525190	Compensation, workers, insurance funds
311119	Complete feed, livestock, manufacturing
711510	Composers, independent
322219	Composite cans (i.e., foil-fiber and other combinations) manufacturing
562219	Compost dumps
325314	Compost manufacturing
325120	Compressed and liquefied industrial gas manufacturing
332911	Compressed gas cylinder valves manufacturing
424690	Compressed gases (except LP gas) merchant wholesalers
424710	Compressed liquefied petroleum gas (LPG) bulk stations and terminals, merchant wholesalers
321219	Compression modified wood manufacturing
333249	Compression molding machinery for plastics manufacturing
339991	Compression packings manufacturing
532490	Compressor, air and gas, rental or leasing
237120	Compressor, metering and pumping station, gas and oil pipeline, construction
423830	Compressors (except air-conditioning, refrigeration) merchant wholesalers
333912	Compressors, air and gas, general purpose-type, manufacturing
423730	Compressors, air-conditioning, merchant wholesalers
336390	Compressors, motor vehicle air-conditioning, manufacturing
423740	Compressors, refrigeration, merchant wholesalers
238210	Computer and network cable installation
541715	Computer and related hardware research and development laboratories or services (except nanotechnology research and development)
423430	Computer boards, loaded, merchant wholesalers
423690	Computer boards, unloaded, merchant wholesalers
334419	Computer cable sets (e.g., monitor, printer) manufacturing
423690	Computer chips merchant wholesalers
423430	Computer data storage devices merchant wholesalers
518210	Computer data storage services
541519	Computer disaster recovery services
813410	Computer enthusiasts clubs
811212	Computer equipment repair and maintenance services without retailing new computers
443142	Computer equipment stores
238330	Computer flooring installation
323111	Computer forms (manifold or continuous) printing
337124	Computer furniture, metal household-type, manufacturing
337122	Computer furniture, wood household-type, manufacturing
541512	Computer hardware consulting services or consultants

518210	Computer input preparation services
334118	Computer input/output equipment manufacturing
611420	Computer operator training
424120	Computer paper supplies merchant wholesalers
322230	Computer paper, die-cut, made from purchased paper
423430	Computer peripheral equipment merchant wholesalers
532420	Computer peripheral equipment rental or leasing
811212	Computer peripheral equipment repair and maintenance, without retailing new computer peripheral equipment
325992	Computer printer toner cartridges manufacturing
423430	Computer printers merchant wholesalers
541511	Computer program or software development, custom
611420	Computer programming schools
541511	Computer programming services, custom
532420	Computer rental or leasing
811212	Computer repair and maintenance services, without retailing new computers
611519	Computer repair training
334111	Computer servers manufacturing
541511	Computer software analysis and design services, custom
541512	Computer software consulting services or consultants
541511	Computer software programming services, custom
511210	Computer software publishers, packaged
511210	Computer software publishing and reproduction
541511	Computer software support services, custom
334613	Computer software tapes and disks, blank, rigid and floppy, manufacturing
611420	Computer software training
454110	Computer software, mail-order houses
423430	Computer software, packaged, merchant wholesalers
443142	Computer stores
541513	Computer systems facilities (i.e., clients' facilities) management and operation services
541512	Computer systems integration analysis and design services
541512	Computer systems integration design

	consulting services
541512	Computer systems integrator services
334118	Computer terminals manufacturing
423430	Computer terminals merchant wholesalers
518210	Computer time leasing
518210	Computer time rental
518210	Computer time sharing services
621512	Computer tomography (CT-SCAN) centers
611420	Computer training (except repair)
532282	Computer video game rental
541340	Computer-aided design drafting (CADD) services
541512	Computer-aided design (CAD) systems integration design services
541512	Computer-aided engineering (CAE) systems integration design services
541512	Computer-aided manufacturing (CAM) systems integration design services
334517	Computerized axial tomography (CT/CAT) scanners manufacturing
334512	Computerized environmental control systems for buildings manufacturing
334111	Computers manufacturing
423430	Computers merchant wholesalers
325411	Concentrated medicinal chemicals, uncompounded, manufacturing
311930	Concentrates, drink (except frozen fruit juice), manufacturing
311930	Concentrates, flavoring (except coffee based), manufacturing
424450	Concentrates, fountain (except soft drink), merchant wholesalers
311411	Concentrates, frozen fruit juice, manufacturing
423520	Concentrates, metallic, merchant wholesalers
333131	Concentration machinery, mining-type, manufacturing
711130	Concert artists, independent
711320	Concert booking agencies
711310	Concert hall operators
531120	Concert hall, no promotion of events, rental or leasing
711310	Concert managers with facilities
711320	Concert managers without facilities
711310	Concert organizers with facilities
711320	Concert organizers without facilities
711310	Concert promoters with facilities

711320	Concert promoters without facilities
561599	Concert ticket offices
713990	Concession operators, amusement device (except gambling) and ride
722330	Concession snack stands, mobile
812990	Concierge services
926150	Conciliation and mediation services, government
325998	Concrete additive preparations (e.g., curing, hardening) manufacturing
424690	Concrete additives merchant wholesalers
327320	Concrete batch plants (including temporary)
238140	Concrete block laying
238910	Concrete breaking and cutting for demolition
423320	Concrete building products merchant wholesalers
238390	Concrete coating, glazing or sealing
327999	Concrete crushing and grinding (except at construction site)
238110	Concrete finishing
333120	Concrete finishing machinery manufacturing
238110	Concrete floor surfacing
238190	Concrete form contractors
332322	Concrete forms, sheet metal (except stampings), manufacturing
327390	Concrete furniture (e.g., benches, tables) manufacturing
333120	Concrete gunning equipment manufacturing
333120	Concrete mixing machinery, portable, manufacturing
423320	Concrete mixtures merchant wholesalers
238990	Concrete patio construction
237310	Concrete paving (i.e., highway, road, street, public sidewalk)
238990	Concrete paving, residential and commercial driveway and parking area
238110	Concrete pouring
423810	Concrete processing equipment merchant wholesalers
238120	Concrete product (e.g., structural precast, structural prestressed) installation
333249	Concrete products forming machinery manufacturing
327390	Concrete products, precast (except block, brick and pipe), manufacturing
238110	Concrete pumping (i.e., placement)
238120	Concrete reinforcement placement

332312	Concrete reinforcing bar (rebar) assemblies, fabrication
331110	Concrete reinforcing bar (rebar) made in iron and steel mills
331221	Concrete reinforcing bar (rebar), made from purchased steel in cold rolling mills
331221	Concrete reinforcing bar (rebar), made from purchased steel in steel rolling mills
423510	Concrete reinforcing bars merchant wholesalers
332618	Concrete reinforcing mesh made from purchased wire
238110	Concrete repair
238110	Concrete resurfacing
238990	Concrete sawing and drilling (except demolition)
327390	Concrete tanks manufacturing
327999	Concrete, dry mixture, manufacturing
211130	Condensate, cycle, natural gas production
333241	Condensed and evaporated milk machinery manufacturing
311514	Condensed milk manufacturing
311514	Condensed, evaporated or powdered whey, manufacturing
332410	Condenser boxes, metal, manufacturing
335999	Condensers (except electronic), fixed and variable, manufacturing
334416	Condensers, electronic, manufacturing
423690	Condensers, electronic, merchant wholesalers
332410	Condensers, steam, manufacturing
335312	Condensers, synchronous, electric, manufacturing
423830	Condensing units (except air-conditioning, refrigeration) merchant wholesalers
423730	Condensing units, air-conditioning, merchant wholesalers
423740	Condensing units, refrigeration, merchant wholesalers
326299	Condom manufacturing
813990	Condominium corporations
236117	Condominium for-sale builders
531312	Condominium managers' offices, commercial
531311	Condominium managers' offices, residential
813990	Condominium owners' associations
561599	Condominium time-share exchange services
236116	Condominium, multifamily, construction general contractors

236115	Condominium, single-family, construction general contractors
335931	Conductor connectors, solderless connectors, sleeves, or soldering lugs, manufacturing
711510	Conductors, independent
423320	Conduit and pipe, concrete, merchant wholesalers
423610	Conduit, electric wire and cable, merchant wholesalers
327120	Conduit, vitrified clay, manufacturing
331210	Conduit, welded and lock joint, made from purchased iron or steel
335932	Conduits and fittings, electrical, manufacturing
423610	Conduits and raceways, electrical, merchant wholesalers
327332	Conduits, concrete, manufacturing
322219	Cones (e.g., winding yarn, string, ribbon, cloth), fiber, made from purchased paperboard
311821	Cones, ice cream, manufacturing
327110	Cones, pyrometric, earthenware, manufacturing
311313	Confectioner's beet sugar manufacturing
311314	Confectioner's powdered sugar manufacturing
311351	Confectionery chocolate made from cacao beans
333241	Confectionery machinery manufacturing
424450	Confectionery merchant wholesalers
722515	Confectionery snack shops, made on premises with carryout services
445292	Confectionery stores, packaged, retailing only
311340	Confectionery, nonchocolate, manufacturing
531120	Conference center, no promotion of events, rental or leasing
322299	Confetti made from purchased paper
921120	Congress of the United States
336310	Connecting rods, automotive and truck gasoline engine, manufacturing
335931	Connectors and terminals for electrical devices manufacturing
335931	Connectors, electric cord, manufacturing
423610	Connectors, electrical, merchant wholesalers
334417	Connectors, electronic (e.g., coaxial, cylindrical, printed circuit, rack and panel), manufacturing
423690	Connectors, electronic, merchant wholesalers
335313	Connectors, power, manufacturing
335931	Connectors, solderless (wiring devices), manufacturing
335931	Connectors, twist on wire (i.e., nuts), manufacturing
813312	Conservation advocacy organizations
924120	Conservation and reclamation agencies
712190	Conservation areas
611310	Conservatories of music (colleges or universities)
712130	Conservatories, botanical
711510	Conservators (i.e., art, artifact restorers), independent
611610	Conservatory of music (except academic)
453310	Consignment shops, used merchandise
336350	Constant velocity joints, automotive, truck, and bus, manufacturing
813940	Constituencies' associations, political party
325520	Construction adhesives (except asphalt, gypsum base) manufacturing
813910	Construction associations
238990	Construction elevator (i.e., temporary use during construction) erection and dismantling
541330	Construction engineering services
238910	Construction equipment (except crane) rental with operator
541990	Construction estimation services
532412	Construction form rental
522292	Construction lending
423810	Construction machinery and equipment merchant wholesalers
532412	Construction machinery and equipment rental or leasing without operator
811310	Construction machinery and equipment repair and maintenance services
333120	Construction machinery manufacturing
236220	Construction management, commercial and institutional building
237990	Construction management, dam
237310	Construction management, highway, road, street and bridge
236210	Construction management, industrial building (except warehouses)
237990	Construction management, marine structure
237990	Construction management, mass transit

236116 Construction management, multifamily building
237120 Construction management, oil and gas pipeline
237120 Construction management, oil refinery and petrochemical complex
237990 Construction management, outdoor recreation facility
237130 Construction management, power and communication transmission line
236118 Construction management, residential remodeling
236115 Construction management, single-family building
237990 Construction management, tunnel
237110 Construction management, water and sewage treatment plant
237110 Construction management, water and sewer line
423610 Construction materials, electrical, merchant wholesalers
322230 Construction paper, school and art, made from purchased paper
322121 Construction paper, school and art, made in paper mills
212321 Construction sand and gravel beneficiating (e.g., grinding, screening, washing)
212321 Construction sand or gravel dredging
541370 Construction surveying services
333120 Construction-type tractors and attachments manufacturing
928120 Consulates
****** Consultants -- see specific activity
813920 Consultants' associations
531390 Consultants', real estate (except appraisers), offices
541330 Consulting engineers' offices
541330 Consulting engineers' private practices
812990 Consumer buying services
541990 Consumer credit counseling services
561450 Consumer credit reporting bureaus
423620 Consumer electronics merchant wholesalers
532210 Consumer electronics rental
811211 Consumer electronics repair and maintenance services without retailing new consumer electronics
522291 Consumer finance companies (i.e., unsecured cash loans)
522291 Consumer lending
922190 Consumer product safety commissions

926110 Consumer protection offices
443142 Consumer-type electronic stores (e.g., televisions, computers, cameras)
334514 Consumption meters (e.g., gas, water) manufacturing
524128 Contact lens insurance, direct
339115 Contact lenses manufacturing
423460 Contact lenses merchant wholesalers
335931 Contacts, electrical (except carbon and graphite), manufacturing
335991 Contacts, electrical, carbon and graphite, manufacturing
322130 Container board stock manufacturing
336611 Container ship building
484110 Container trucking services, local
484121 Container trucking services, long-distance (TL)
327213 Containers for packaging, bottling, and canning, glass, manufacturing
332439 Containers, air cargo, light gauge metal, manufacturing
332999 Containers, foil (except bags), manufacturing
423220 Containers, household (except paper and disposable plastics), merchant wholesalers
423840 Containers, industrial, merchant wholesalers
332439 Containers, light gauge metal (except cans), manufacturing
424130 Containers, paper and disposable plastics, merchant wholesalers
321920 Containers, wood, manufacturing
712110 Contemporary art museums
711120 Contemporary dance companies
623311 Continuing care retirement communities
611430 Continuing education seminars or conferences
325412 Contraceptive preparations manufacturing
213112 Contract services (except site preparation and related construction contractor activities) for oil and gas fields
561320 Contract staffing services
****** Contractors -- see specific activity
813910 Contractors' associations
315210 Contractors, cut and sew apparel
325412 Contrast media in-vivo diagnostic substances (e.g., iodine, barium) manufacturing
335314 Control circuit devices, magnet and solid-state, manufacturing

335314	Control circuit relays, industrial, manufacturing
335314	Control equipment, electric, manufacturing
335313	Control panels, electric power distribution, manufacturing
238210	Control system (e.g., environmental, humidity, temperature) installation
335311	Control transformers manufacturing
332912	Control valves, fluid power, manufacturing
332911	Control valves, industrial-type, manufacturing
921130	Controllers' and comptrollers' offices, government
334513	Controllers for process variables (e.g., electric, electronic, mechanical, pneumatic operation) manufacturing
334290	Controlling equipment, street light, manufacturing
335314	Controls and control accessories, industrial, manufacturing
335314	Controls for adjustable speed drives manufacturing
334514	Controls, revolution and timing instruments, manufacturing
623110	Convalescent homes or convalescent hospitals (except psychiatric)
623220	Convalescent homes or hospitals for psychiatric patients
446199	Convalescent supply stores
335220	Convection ovens (including portable), household-type, manufacturing
423720	Convectors merchant wholesalers
445120	Convenience food stores
447110	Convenience food with gasoline stations
335931	Convenience outlets, electric, manufacturing
561591	Convention and visitors bureaus
561591	Convention bureaus
531120	Convention center, no promotion of events, rental or leasing
561920	Convention decorators
561920	Convention managers
561920	Convention or trade show event planners
561920	Convention organizers
561920	Convention promoters
561920	Convention services
813110	Convents (except schools)
424130	Converted paper (except stationery and office supplies) merchant wholesalers
316110	Converters, leather
335312	Converters, phase and rotary, electrical equipment, manufacturing
313310	Converters, piece goods
337121	Convertible sofas (except futons) manufacturing
336390	Convertible tops for automotive, truck, and bus, manufacturing
313310	Converting textiles
423830	Conveying equipment (except farm) merchant wholesalers
423820	Conveying equipment, farm, merchant wholesalers
326220	Conveyor belts, rubber, manufacturing
238290	Conveyor system installation
333922	Conveyors and conveying equipment manufacturing
311612	Cooked meats made from purchased carcasses
311824	Cookie dough made from purchased flour
722515	Cookie shops, on premise baking and carryout service
311821	Cookies manufacturing
424490	Cookies merchant wholesalers
311821	Cookies, filled, manufacturing
311225	Cooking and baking oil sprays made from purchased oils
335210	Cooking appliances (except convection, microwave ovens), household-type electric portable, manufacturing
311351	Cooking chocolate made from cacao beans
333318	Cooking equipment (i.e., fryers, microwave ovens, ovens, ranges), commercial-type, manufacturing
423440	Cooking equipment, commercial, merchant wholesalers
423620	Cooking equipment, gas and electric, household-type, merchant wholesalers
424490	Cooking oils merchant wholesalers
611519	Cooking schools
331511	Cooking utensils, cast iron, manufacturing
332215	Cooking utensils, fabricated metal, manufacturing
327212	Cooking utensils, glass and glass ceramic, made in glass making plants
423220	Cooking utensils, household-type, merchant wholesalers
327110	Cooking ware (e.g., stoneware, coarse earthenware, pottery), manufacturing
327215	Cooking ware made from purchased glass

327212	Cooking ware made in glass making plants
327110	Cooking ware, china, manufacturing
327110	Cooking ware, fine earthenware, manufacturing
332215	Cookware, fabricated metal, manufacturing
221330	Cooled air distribution
326199	Coolers or ice chests, plastics (except foam), manufacturing
326140	Coolers or ice chests, polystyrene foam, manufacturing
423740	Coolers, mechanical, merchant wholesalers
333415	Coolers, refrigeration, manufacturing
333415	Coolers, water, manufacturing
423730	Cooling equipment and supplies merchant wholesalers
238220	Cooling tower installation
333415	Cooling towers manufacturing
321920	Cooperage manufacturing
321920	Cooperage stock (e.g., heading, hoops, staves) manufacturing
423840	Cooperage stock merchant wholesalers
321920	Cooperage stock mills
236117	Cooperative apartment for-sale builders
531311	Cooperative apartment managers' offices
236116	Cooperative apartment, construction general contractors
812331	Cooperative hospital laundries (i.e., linen supply services)
524113	Cooperative life insurance organizations
813990	Cooperative owners' associations
321920	Coopered tubs manufacturing
332216	Coordinate and contour measuring machines, machinists' precision tools, manufacturing
532420	Copier rental or leasing
327120	Coping, wall, clay, manufacturing
327390	Copings, concrete, manufacturing
331529	Copper alloy castings (except die-castings), unfinished, manufacturing
331420	Copper alloys (e.g., brass, bronze) made from purchased metal or scrap
331410	Copper alloys made in primary copper smelting and refining mills
423510	Copper and copper alloy primary forms merchant wholesalers
331420	Copper and copper-based shapes (e.g., cake, ingot, slag, wire bar) made from purchased metal or scrap
325130	Copper base pigments manufacturing
212230	Copper beneficiating plants
325180	Copper chloride manufacturing
325612	Copper cleaners manufacturing
325180	Copper compounds, not specified elsewhere by process, manufacturing
331410	Copper concentrate refining
331523	Copper die-casting foundries
331523	Copper die-castings, unfinished, manufacturing
331420	Copper foil made from purchased metal or scrap
332999	Copper foil not made in rolling mills
332112	Copper forgings made from purchased metals, unfinished
331529	Copper foundries (except die-casting)
325180	Copper iodide manufacturing
212230	Copper ore concentrates recovery
212230	Copper ore mine site development for own account
212230	Copper ores mining and/or beneficiating
331420	Copper powder, flakes, and paste made from purchased copper
331420	Copper products made by drawing purchased copper
331420	Copper products made by rolling, drawing, or extruding purchased copper
331420	Copper products made in integrated secondary smelting and extruding mills
331420	Copper products made in integrated secondary smelting mills and drawing plants
238160	Copper roofing installation
331420	Copper secondary smelting and alloying
331420	Copper secondary smelting and refining from purchased metal or scrap
331410	Copper shapes (e.g., bar, billet, ingot, plate, sheet) made in primary copper smelting and refining mills
331410	Copper smelting and refining, primary
325180	Copper sulfate manufacturing
212230	Copper-water precipitates
561439	Copy centers (except combined with printing services)
561439	Copy shops (except combined with printing services)
423420	Copying machines merchant wholesalers
314994	Cord (except wire) manufacturing
335931	Cord connectors, electric, manufacturing

314994	Cord for reinforcing rubber tires, industrial belting, and fuel cells manufacturing
331420	Cord sets, flexible, made from purchased copper in wire drawing plants
331318	Cord sets, flexible, made in aluminum wire drawing plants
331491	Cord sets, flexible, nonferrous metals (except aluminum, copper), made from purchased nonferrous metals (except aluminum, copper) in wire drawing plants
314994	Cordage (except wire) manufacturing
333249	Cordage and rope (except wire) making machines manufacturing
423840	Cordage merchant wholesalers
325920	Cordite explosive materials manufacturing
334210	Cordless telephones (except cellular) manufacturing
313220	Cords and braids, narrow woven, manufacturing
313210	Corduroys weaving
333994	Core baking and mold drying ovens manufacturing
213112	Core cutting in oil and gas wells, on a contract basis
238910	Core drilling and test boring for construction
213112	Core drilling, exploration services, oil and gas field
333131	Core drills, underground mining-type, manufacturing
322219	Cores (i.e., all-fiber, nonfiber ends of any material), fiber, made from purchased paperboard
332992	Cores, bullet (i.e., 30 mm. or less, 1.18 inch or less), manufacturing
332999	Cores, sand foundry, manufacturing
423840	Cork merchant wholesalers
321999	Cork products (except gaskets) manufacturing
321999	Corks, bottle, manufacturing
111421	Corms farming
311230	Corn breakfast foods manufacturing
311919	Corn chips and related corn snacks manufacturing
424450	Corn chips and related corn snacks merchant wholesalers
311340	Corn confections manufacturing
321992	Corn cribs, prefabricated, wood, manufacturing
311221	Corn dextrin manufacturing
115114	Corn drying
111150	Corn farming (except sweet corn), field and seed production
311211	Corn flour manufacturing
311221	Corn gluten feed manufacturing
311221	Corn gluten meal manufacturing
333111	Corn heads for combines manufacturing
311211	Corn meal made in flour mills
424490	Corn milling products (except pet and livestock feeds) merchant wholesalers
311221	Corn oil cake and meal manufacturing
311225	Corn oil made from purchased oils
311221	Corn oil mills
311221	Corn oil, crude and refined, made by wet milling corn
333111	Corn pickers and shellers manufacturing
335210	Corn poppers, household-type electric, manufacturing
333241	Corn popping machinery (i.e., food manufacturing-type) manufacturing
333318	Corn popping machines, commercial-type, manufacturing
339113	Corn remover and bunion pad manufacturing
115114	Corn shelling
311221	Corn starch manufacturing
311221	Corn sweeteners (e.g., dextrose, fructose, glucose) made by wet milling corn
311999	Corn syrups made from purchased sweeteners
311213	Corn, malt, manufacturing
424510	Corn, raw (except seed corn), merchant wholesalers
339112	Corneal microscopes manufacturing
311612	Corned meats made from purchases carcasses
316998	Corners, luggage, leather, manufacturing
339992	Cornets and parts manufacturing
332322	Cornices, sheet metal (except stampings), manufacturing
321918	Cornices, wood, manufacturing
112320	Cornish hen production
424490	Cornmeal, edible, merchant wholesalers
212325	Cornwall stone mining and/or beneficiating
923120	Coroners' offices
522130	Corporate credit unions
813211	Corporate foundations, awarding grants
541430	Corporate identification (i.e., logo) design services

541110 Corporate law offices

551114 Corporate offices

721310 Corporate rooming and boarding houses

115210 Corralling, drovers

332323 Corrals, metal, manufacturing

325998 Correction fluids (i.e., typewriter) manufacturing

922140 Correctional boot camps

561210 Correctional facilities, privately operated

561210 Correctional facility operation on a contract or fee basis

922140 Correctional institutions

237120 Corrosion protection, underground pipeline and oil storage tank

322211 Corrugated and solid fiber boxes made from purchased paper or paperboard

322211 Corrugated and solid fiberboard pads made from purchased paper or paperboard

238160 Corrugated metal roofing installation

322211 Corrugated paper made from purchased paper or paperboard

424130 Corrugated paper merchant wholesalers

331221 Corrugating iron or steel in cold rolling mills made from purchased iron or steel

315210 Corselets cut and sew apparel contractors

315240 Corselets, women's and girls', cut and sewn from purchased fabric (except apparel contractors)

315210 Corsets and allied garments (except surgical) cut and sew apparel contractors

315240 Corsets and allied garments (except surgical), women's and girls', cut and sewn from purchased fabric (except apparel contractors)

339113 Corsets, surgical, manufacturing

325411 Cortisone, uncompounded, manufacturing

212399 Corundum mining and/or beneficiating

611511 Cosmetic art schools (e.g., makeup, skin care)

316998 Cosmetic bags (except metal) manufacturing

339910 Cosmetic bags, precious metal, manufacturing

325620 Cosmetic creams, lotions, and oils manufacturing

561910 Cosmetic kit assembling and packaging services

424210 Cosmetics merchant wholesalers

446120 Cosmetics stores

812112 Cosmetology salons or shops

611511 Cosmetology schools

541490 Costume design services (except independent theatrical costume designers)

711510 Costume designers, independent theatrical

339910 Costume jewelry manufacturing

423940 Costume jewelry merchant wholesalers

448150 Costume jewelry stores

532281 Costume rental

448190 Costume stores (including theatrical)

315210 Costumes (e.g., lodge, masquerade, theatrical) cut and sew apparel contractors

315280 Costumes (e.g., lodge, masquerade, theatrical) cut and sewn from purchased fabric (except apparel contractors)

424320 Costumes, clothing, men's and boys', merchant wholesalers

424330 Costumes, women's, children's, and infants', merchant wholesalers

337121 Cot springs, assembled, manufacturing

337124 Cots, metal household-type, manufacturing

337122 Cots, wood household-type, manufacturing

311511 Cottage cheese manufacturing

236115 Cottage construction general contractors

236117 Cottage for-sale builders

531110 Cottage rental or leasing

721199 Cottages, housekeeping

332722 Cotter pins, metal, manufacturing

424990 Cotton (except raw) merchant wholesalers

339113 Cotton and cotton balls, absorbent, manufacturing

333111 Cotton balers and presses manufacturing

314999 Cotton battings (except nonwoven batting) manufacturing

313110 Cotton cordage spun yarns made from purchased fiber

313210 Cotton fabrics, broadwoven, weaving

313220 Cotton fabrics, narrow woven weaving

111920 Cotton farming, field and seed production

322121 Cotton fiber paper stock manufacturing

115111 Cotton ginning

333111 Cotton ginning machinery manufacturing

333111 Cotton picker and stripper harvesting machinery manufacturing

313110 Cotton spun yarns made from purchased fiber

313110 Cotton thread manufacturing

339113 Cotton tipped applicators manufacturing

115113	Cotton, machine harvesting
424590	Cotton, raw, merchant wholesalers
111920	Cottonseed farming
311225	Cottonseed oil made from purchased oils
311224	Cottonseed oil, cake and meal, made in crushing mills
337121	Couch springs, assembled, manufacturing
337121	Couches, upholstered, manufacturing
311340	Cough drops (except medicated) manufacturing
325412	Cough drops, medicated, manufacturing
325412	Cough medicines manufacturing
334513	Coulometric analyzers, industrial process-type, manufacturing
334516	Coulometric analyzers, laboratory-type, manufacturing
325199	Coumarin manufacturing
325211	Coumarone-indene resins manufacturing
926110	Councils of Economic Advisers
624190	Counseling services (except by psychiatrists, psychoanalysts, or psychotherapists)
621410	Counseling services, family planning
541110	Counselors' at law offices
541110	Counselors' at law private practices
334519	Count rate meters, nuclear radiation, manufacturing
334514	Counter type registers manufacturing
337215	Counter units (except refrigerated) manufacturing
333515	Counterbores (i.e., a machine tool accessory), metalworking, manufacturing
332216	Counterbores and countersinking bits, woodworking, manufacturing
334511	Countermeasure sets (e.g., active countermeasures, jamming equipment) manufacturing
334514	Counters (e.g., electrical, electronic, mechanical), totalizing, manufacturing
316998	Counters (i.e., shoe cut stock), leather, manufacturing
333415	Counters and display cases, refrigerated, manufacturing
334514	Counters, revolution, manufacturing
333515	Countersinks (i.e., a machine tool accessory) manufacturing
238390	Countertop and cabinet, metal (except residential-type), installation
238350	Countertop, residential-type, installation
423310	Countertops (except granite) merchant wholesalers
337215	Countertops (except kitchen and bathroom), wood or plastics laminated on wood, manufacturing
337110	Countertops (i.e., kitchen, bathroom), wood or plastics laminated on wood, manufacturing
326199	Countertops, plastics, manufacturing
327991	Countertops, stone, manufacturing
337110	Countertops, wood, manufacturing
334514	Counting devices manufacturing
713910	Country clubs
711130	Country musical artists, independent
711130	Country musical groups
921120	County commissioners
925120	County development agencies
921110	County supervisors' and executives' offices
923110	County supervisors of education (except school boards)
332919	Couplings, hose, metal (except fluid power), manufacturing
333613	Couplings, mechanical power transmission, manufacturing
332996	Couplings, pipe, made from purchased metal pipe
541870	Coupon direct distribution services
561990	Coupon processing services
561990	Coupon redemption services (i.e., clearinghouse)
492110	Courier services (i.e., intercity network) (except establishments operating under a universal service obligation)
611410	Court reporting schools
561492	Court reporting services
922110	Courts of law, civilian (except American Indian or Alaska Native)
921150	Courts, American Indian or Alaska Native
922110	Courts, civilian (except American Indian or Alaska Native)
928110	Courts, military
922110	Courts, small claims
315210	Coveralls, work, cut and sew apparel contractors
315220	Coveralls, work, men's and boys', cut and sewn from purchased fabric (except apparel contractors)
315240	Coveralls, work, women's and girls', cut and sewn from purchased fabric (except apparel contractors)

314910	Covers (e.g., boat, swimming pool, truck) made from purchased fabrics
332313	Covers, annealing, fabricated metal plate work, manufacturing
321999	Covers, bottle and demijohn, willow, rattan, and reed, manufacturing
332313	Covers, floating, fabricated metal plate work, manufacturing
332322	Cowls, sheet metal (except stampings), manufacturing
111219	Cowpea (except dry) farming, field and seed production
111130	Cowpea farming, dry, field and seed production
541211	CPAs' (certified public accountants) offices
611699	CPR (cardiopulmonary resuscitation) training and certification
332618	Crab traps made from purchased wire
114112	Crabbing
333241	Cracker making machinery manufacturing
311821	Crackers (e.g., graham, soda) manufacturing
424490	Crackers merchant wholesalers
333519	Cradle assembly machinery (i.e., wire making equipment) manufacturing
337122	Cradles, wood, manufacturing
453220	Craft (except craft supply) stores
339930	Craft and hobby kits and sets manufacturing
561920	Craft fair managers
561920	Craft fair organizers
561920	Craft fair promoters
423920	Craft kits merchant wholesalers
451120	Craft supply stores (except needlecraft)
611513	Craft union apprenticeship training programs
111334	Cranberry farming
335314	Crane and hoist controls, including metal mill, manufacturing
532412	Crane rental or leasing without operator
238990	Crane rental with operator
423810	Cranes (except industrial) merchant wholesalers
333120	Cranes, construction-type, manufacturing
333924	Cranes, industrial truck, manufacturing
423830	Cranes, industrial, merchant wholesalers
423810	Cranes, mining, merchant wholesalers
333923	Cranes, overhead traveling, manufacturing
325998	Crankcase additive preparations manufacturing
336310	Crankshaft assemblies, automotive and truck gasoline engine, manufacturing
333517	Crankshaft grinding machines metal cutting type, manufacturing
321920	Crates (e.g., berry, butter, fruit, vegetable) made of wood, wirebound, manufacturing
424130	Crates, paperboard and disposable plastics, merchant wholesalers
488991	Crating goods for shipping
112512	Crawfish production, farm raising
238910	Crawler tractor rental with operator
114112	Crayfish fishing
339940	Crayons manufacturing
311511	Cream manufacturing
424430	Cream merchant wholesalers
325199	Cream of tartar manufacturing
333111	Cream separators, farm-type, manufacturing
333241	Cream separators, industrial, manufacturing
424430	Cream stations merchant wholesalers
311514	Cream, dried and powdered, manufacturing
311512	Creamery butter manufacturing
424430	Creamery products (except canned) merchant wholesalers
424490	Creamery products, canned, merchant wholesalers
313310	Crease resistant finishing of fabrics
561450	Credit agencies
323111	Credit and identification card imprinting, embossing, and encoding
326199	Credit and identification card stock, plastics, manufacturing
524126	Credit and other financial responsibility insurance carriers, direct
561440	Credit arrears collection services
561450	Credit bureaus
522210	Credit card banks
522210	Credit card issuing
812990	Credit card notification services (i.e., lost or stolen card reporting)
522320	Credit card processing services
561450	Credit clearinghouses
561450	Credit investigation services
524113	Credit life insurance carriers, direct
561450	Credit rating services

541990	Credit repair (i.e., counseling) services, consumer
561450	Credit reporting bureaus
522130	Credit unions
333999	Cremating ovens manufacturing
812220	Crematories (except combined with funeral homes)
111219	Crenshaw melon farming, field, bedding plant and seed production
325194	Creosote made by distillation of coal tar
325194	Creosote made by distillation of wood tar
321114	Creosoting of wood
322299	Crepe paper made from purchased paper
325211	Cresol resins manufacturing
325211	Cresol-furfural resins manufacturing
325194	Cresols made by distillation of coal tar
325194	Cresylic acids made from refined petroleum or natural gas
115115	Crew leaders, farm labor
315110	Crew socks knitting or knitting and finishing
237990	Cribbing (i.e., shore protection), construction
337124	Cribs (i.e., baby beds), metal, manufacturing
337122	Cribs (i.e., baby beds), wood, manufacturing
112990	Cricket production
562910	Crime scene cleanup services
922120	Criminal investigation offices, government
922190	Criminal justice statistics centers, government
541110	Criminal law offices
111998	Crimson cloves seed farming
624190	Crisis intervention centers
114111	Croaker fishing
313110	Crochet spun yarns (e.g., cotton, manmade fiber, silk, wool) made from purchased fiber
314999	Crochet ware made from purchased materials
335210	Crock pots, household-type electric, manufacturing
327110	Crockery manufacturing
311812	Croissants, baking, made in commercial bakeries
115114	Crop cleaning
333111	Crop driers manufacturing
115112	Crop dusting
524126	Crop insurance carrier, direct
423820	Crop preparation machinery (e.g., cleaning, conditioning, drying) merchant wholesalers
115112	Crop spraying
316998	Crops, riding, manufacturing
339920	Croquet sets manufacturing
713920	Cross country skiing facilities without accommodations
332911	Cross valves, industrial-type, manufacturing
321114	Crossties, treating
311812	Croutons and bread crumbs made in commercial bakeries
423840	Crowns and closures, metal, merchant wholesalers
332119	Crowns, metal (e.g., bottle, can), stamping
334419	CRT (cathode ray tube) manufacturing
327120	Crucibles, fire clay, manufacturing
327120	Crucibles, graphite, magnesite, chrome, silica, or other nonclay materials, manufacturing
311221	Crude corn oil manufacturing
424720	Crude oil merchant wholesalers (except bulk stations, terminals)
486110	Crude oil pipeline transportation
324110	Crude oil refining
424710	Crude oil terminals, merchant wholesalers
211120	Crude petroleum from oil sand
211120	Crude petroleum from oil shale
211120	Crude petroleum lease condensate production
211120	Crude petroleum production
324110	Crude petroleum refineries
424990	Crude rubber merchant wholesalers
336320	Cruise control mechanisms, electronic, automotive, truck, and bus, manufacturing
483114	Cruise lines (i.e., deep sea passenger transportation to and from domestic ports, including Puerto Rico)
483112	Cruise lines (i.e., deep sea passenger transportation to or from foreign ports)
561599	Cruise reservation services
561599	Cruise ship ticket offices
713210	Cruises, gambling
115310	Cruising timber
311812	Crullers (except frozen) made in commercial bakeries

311813	Crullers, frozen, made in a commercial bakery
423320	Crushed stone merchant wholesalers
333120	Crushing machinery, portable, manufacturing
333131	Crushing machinery, stationary, manufacturing
212111	Crushing plants, bituminous coal
423810	Crushing, pulverizing, and screening machinery, construction and mining, merchant wholesalers
423830	Crushing, pulverizing, and screening machinery, industrial, merchant wholesalers
333120	Crushing, pulverizing, and screening machinery, portable, manufacturing
112512	Crustacean production, farm raising
339113	Crutches and walkers manufacturing
423450	Crutches merchant wholesalers
532283	Crutches, invalid, rental
423830	Cryogenic cooling devices merchant wholesalers
332420	Cryogenic tanks, heavy gauge metal, manufacturing
332811	Cryogenic treating metals for the trade
212399	Cryolite mining and/or beneficiating
311340	Crystallized fruits and fruit peel manufacturing
334419	Crystals and crystal assemblies, electronic, manufacturing
334517	CT/CAT (computerized axial tomography) scanners manufacturing
621512	CT-SCAN (computer tomography) centers
335313	Cubicles (i.e., electric switchboard equipment) manufacturing
111219	Cucumber farming (except under cover), field, bedding plant and seed production
111419	Cucumber farming, grown under cover
339993	Cuff links (except precious) manufacturing
339910	Cuff links, precious metal, manufacturing
332999	Cuffs, leg, iron, manufacturing
611519	Culinary arts schools
112310	Cull hen production
212113	Culm bank recovery, anthracite (except on a contract basis)
213113	Culm bank recovery, anthracite, on a contract basis
212111	Culm bank recovery, bituminous coal or lignite (except on a contract basis)
213113	Culm bank recovery, coal, on a contract basis
315210	Culottes cut and sew apparel contractors
315240	Culottes, women's and girls', cut and sewn from purchased fabric (except apparel contractors)
111422	Cultivated florist greens growing
423820	Cultivating machinery and equipment merchant wholesalers
115112	Cultivation services
333111	Cultivators, farm-type, manufacturing
333112	Cultivators, powered, lawn and garden-type, manufacturing
926110	Cultural and arts development support program administration
325414	Culture media manufacturing
326191	Cultured marble plumbing fixtures manufacturing
326199	Cultured marble products (except plumbing fixtures) manufacturing
112512	Cultured pearl production, farm raising
326199	Cultured stone products (except plumbing fixtures) manufacturing
238910	Culvert or bridge removal
327332	Culvert pipe, concrete, manufacturing
238990	Culvert, concrete, residential and commercial paved area
332313	Culverts, fabricated metal plate work, manufacturing
237310	Culverts, highway, road and street, construction
332322	Culverts, sheet metal (except stampings), manufacturing
325110	Cumene made from refined petroleum or liquid hydrocarbons
324110	Cumene made in petroleum refineries
315210	Cummerbunds cut and sew apparel contractors
315990	Cummerbunds cut and sewn from purchased fabric (except apparel contractors)
332313	Cupolas, fabricated metal plate work, manufacturing
212230	Cuprite mining and/or beneficiating
423440	Cups, commercial (except paper and disposable plastics), merchant wholesalers
322299	Cups, molded pulp, manufacturing
424130	Cups, paper and disposable plastics, merchant wholesalers
423220	Cups, plastics (except disposable), merchant wholesalers

326199	Cups, plastics (except foam), manufacturing
326140	Cups, polystyrene foam, manufacturing
238990	Curb and gutter construction, residential and commercial driveway and parking area, concrete
327991	Curbing, granite and stone, manufacturing
237310	Curbs and street gutters, highway, road and street, construction
311513	Curds, cheese, made in a cheese plant, manufacturing
424460	Cured fish merchant wholesalers
311611	Cured hides and skins produced in slaughtering plants
311612	Cured meats (e.g., brined, dried, and salted) made from purchased carcasses
333111	Curers, tobacco, manufacturing
311710	Curing fish and seafood
453220	Curio shops
424990	Curios merchant wholesalers
326299	Curlers, hair, rubber, manufacturing
713990	Curling facilities
423620	Curling irons, electric, merchant wholesalers
335210	Curling irons, household-type electric, manufacturing
111334	Currant farming
333318	Currency counting machinery manufacturing
423420	Currency handling machines merchant wholesalers
335311	Current limiting reactors, electrical, manufacturing
334515	Current measuring equipment manufacturing
335931	Current taps, attachment plug and screw shell types, manufacturing
423610	Current-carrying wiring devices merchant wholesalers
316110	Currying furs
316110	Currying leather
442291	Curtain and drapery stores, packaged
812320	Curtain cleaning services
337920	Curtain or drapery fixtures (e.g., poles, rods, rollers) manufacturing
337920	Curtain rods and fittings manufacturing
321999	Curtain stretchers, wood, manufacturing
238150	Curtain wall, glass, installation
238190	Curtain wall, metal, installation

332323	Curtain wall, metal, manufacturing
238120	Curtain wall, precast concrete, installation
313210	Curtains and draperies made in broadwoven fabric mills
314120	Curtains and draperies, window, made from purchased fabrics
313240	Curtains made in lace mills
313240	Curtains made in warp or weft knitting mills
423220	Curtains merchant wholesalers
337121	Cushion springs, assembled, manufacturing
314120	Cushions (except carpet, springs) made from purchased fabrics
326150	Cushions, carpet and rug, urethane and other foam plastics (except polystrene), manufacturing
311520	Custard, frozen, manufacturing
561720	Custodial services
337212	Custom architectural millwork and fixtures, manufacturing on a job shop basis
236116	Custom builders (except for-sale), multifamily buildings
236115	Custom builders (except for-sale), single-family home
236117	Custom builders, for-sale builders, multifamily buildings
236117	Custom builders, for-sale builders, single-family home
325991	Custom compounding (i.e., blending and mixing) of purchased plastics resins
337212	Custom design interiors (i.e., coordinated furniture, architectural woodwork, fixtures), manufacturing
311119	Custom milling of animal feed
442299	Custom picture frame shops
333517	Custom roll forming machines, metalworking, manufacturing
332114	Custom roll forming metal products
321113	Custom sawmills
311611	Custom slaughtering
315220	Custom tailors, men's and boys' dress shirts, cut and sewn from purchased fabric
315220	Custom tailors, men's and boys' suits, cut and sewn from purchased fabric
315240	Custom tailors, women's and girls' dresses cut and sewn from purchased fabric (except apparel contractors)
561422	Customer service call centers
541613	Customer service management consulting services

488510	Customs brokers
921130	Customs bureaus
541614	Customs consulting services
327215	Cut and engraved glassware made from purchased glass
315210	Cut and sew apparel contractors
111422	Cut flower growing
111422	Cut rose growing
316998	Cut stock for boots and shoes manufacturing
321912	Cut stock manufacturing
327991	Cut stone bases (e.g., desk sets pedestals, lamps, plaques and similar small particles) manufacturing
327991	Cut stone products (e.g., blocks, statuary) manufacturing
811490	Cutlery (e.g., knives, scissors) sharpening, household-type
423710	Cutlery merchant wholesalers
332215	Cutlery, nonprecious and precious plated metal, manufacturing
339910	Cutlery, precious metal (except precious plated), manufacturing
333517	Cut-off machines, metalworking, manufacturing
335931	Cutouts, switch and fuse, manufacturing
333131	Cutters, coal, manufacturing
332216	Cutters, glass, manufacturing
333515	Cutters, metal milling, manufacturing
113310	Cutting and transporting timber
213112	Cutting cores in oil and gas wells on a contract basis
332216	Cutting dies (e.g., paper, leather, textile) manufacturing
332216	Cutting dies (except metal cutting) manufacturing
333514	Cutting dies, metalworking, manufacturing
315210	Cutting fabric owned by others for apparel
339114	Cutting instruments, dental, manufacturing
333517	Cutting machines, metalworking, manufacturing
238910	Cutting new rights of way
316110	Cutting of leather
424470	Cutting of purchased carcasses (except boxed meat cut on an assembly line basis) merchant wholesalers
324191	Cutting oils made from refined petroleum
325998	Cutting oils, synthetic, manufacturing
113310	Cutting timber
327215	Cutting, engraving, etching, painting or polishing purchased glass
111422	Cuttings farming
325180	Cyanides manufacturing
212325	Cyanite mining and/or beneficiating
211130	Cycle condensate production
325110	Cyclic aromatic hydrocarbons made from refined petroleum or liquid hydrocarbons
324110	Cyclic aromatic hydrocarbons made in petroleum refineries
424690	Cyclic crudes and intermediates merchant wholesalers
325194	Cyclic crudes made by distillation of coal tar
325194	Cyclic intermediates made from refined petroleum or natural gas (except aromatic petrochemicals)
325212	Cyclo rubber, synthetic, manufacturing
325194	Cyclohexane manufacturing
332313	Cyclones, industrial, fabricated metal plate work, manufacturing
325194	Cyclopentane made from refined petroleum or natural gas
325194	Cyclopropane made from refined petroleum or natural gas
325412	Cyclopropane medicinal preparations manufacturing
325194	Cycloterpenes manufacturing
335999	Cyclotrons manufacturing
333517	Cylinder boring machines metal cutting type, manufacturing
336310	Cylinder heads, automotive and truck gasoline engine, manufacturing
327332	Cylinder pipe, prestressed concrete, manufacturing
332618	Cylinder wire cloth made from purchased wire
332994	Cylinders and clips, gun, manufacturing
333995	Cylinders, fluid power, manufacturing
336340	Cylinders, master brake (new and rebuilt), manufacturing
332420	Cylinders, pressure, heavy gauge metal, manufacturing
334417	Cylindrical connectors, electronic, manufacturing
332991	Cylindrical roller bearings manufacturing
339992	Cymbals and parts manufacturing
339112	Cystoscopes (except electromedical) manufacturing

334510	Cystoscopes, electromedical, manufacturing
325413	Cytology and histology in-vitro diagnostic substances manufacturing
621511	Cytology health laboratories
112120	Dairy cattle farming
311119	Dairy cattle feeds, supplements, concentrates, and premixes, manufacturing
424430	Dairy depots merchant wholesalers
311514	Dairy food canning
112420	Dairy goat farming
112111	Dairy heifer replacement production
541690	Dairy herd consulting services
115210	Dairy herd improvement associations
333241	Dairy product plant machinery and equipment
445299	Dairy product stores
424430	Dairy products (except canned, dried) merchant wholesalers
424490	Dairy products, dried or canned, merchant wholesalers
424430	Dairy products, frozen, merchant wholesalers
112410	Dairy sheep farming
237990	Dam construction
332312	Dam gates, metal plate, manufacturing
334512	Damper operators (e.g., electric, pneumatic, thermostatic) manufacturing
332322	Dampers, sheet metal (except stampings), manufacturing
238390	Dampproofing contractors
711130	Dance bands
713940	Dance centers, aerobic
711120	Dance companies
711310	Dance festival managers with facilities
711320	Dance festival managers without facilities
711310	Dance festival organizers with facilities
711320	Dance festival organizers without facilities
711310	Dance festival promoters with facilities
711320	Dance festival promoters without facilities
531120	Dance hall rental or leasing
713990	Dance halls
611610	Dance instruction
711120	Dance productions, live theatrical
611610	Dance schools
611610	Dance studios
711120	Dance theaters

621340	Dance therapists' offices (e.g., centers, clinics)
711120	Dance troupes
711510	Dancers, independent
313110	Darning thread (e.g., cotton, manmade fibers, silk, wool) manufacturing
332994	Dart guns manufacturing
339930	Darts and dart games manufacturing
518210	Data capture imaging services
334210	Data communications equipment (e.g., bridges, gateways, routers) manufacturing
518210	Data entry services
423430	Data keying equipment merchant wholesalers
334513	Data loggers, industrial process-type, manufacturing
518210	Data processing computer services
541513	Data processing facilities (i.e., clients' facilities) management and operation services
423430	Data processing machines, computer, merchant wholesalers
518210	Data processing services (except payroll services, financial transaction processing services)
323111	Databases commercial printing (except screen) without publishing
323113	Databases screen printing without publishing
111339	Date farming
339940	Date stamps, hand operated, manufacturing
311423	Dates, dried, made in dehydration plants
311340	Dates, sugared and stuffed, manufacturing
334519	Dating devices and machines (except rubber stamps) manufacturing
812990	Dating services
333923	Davits manufacturing
******	Day camps, instructional -- see type of instruction
624120	Day care centers for disabled persons, the elderly, and persons diagnosed with intellectual and developmental disabilities
624120	Day care centers, adult
624410	Day care centers, child or infant
624410	Day care services, child or infant
812199	Day spas
621310	DCs' (doctors of chiropractic) offices (e.g., centers, clinics)
621210	DDSs' (doctors of dental surgery) offices (e.g., centers, clinics)

325320 DDT (dichlorodiphenyltrichloroethane) insecticides manufacturing

922120 DEA (Drug Enforcement Administration)

332510 Dead bolts, metal, manufacturing

****** Dealers -- see type

562119 Debris removal services

561440 Debt collection services

333517 Deburring machines, metalworking, manufacturing

334515 Decade boxes (i.e., capacitance, inductance, resistance) manufacturing

325199 Decahydronaphthalene manufacturing

327110 Decalcomania on china and glass for the trade

339999 Decalcomania work (except on china, glass)

111339 Deciduous tree fruit (except apples, citrus) farming

238190 Deck and grate (except roof), metal, installation

238350 Deck construction, residential-type

327215 Decorated glassware made from purchased glass

327110 Decorating china (e.g., encrusting gold, silver, other metal on china) for the trade

541410 Decorating consulting services, interior

335129 Decorative area lighting fixtures (except residential) manufacturing

335121 Decorative area lighting fixtures, residential, manufacturing

712110 Decorative art museums

238150 Decorative glass and mirror installation

327212 Decorative glassware made in glass making plants

335110 Decorative lamp bulbs manufacturing

238190 Decorative steel and wrought iron work installation

314999 Decorative stitching contractors on apparel

314999 Decorative stitching on textile articles and apparel

321918 Decorative wood moldings (e.g., base, chair rail, crown, shoe) manufacturing

115114 Decorticating flax

483113 Deep sea freight transportation to or from domestic ports (including Puerto Rico)

483111 Deep sea freight transportation to or from foreign ports

483114 Deep sea passenger transportation to and from domestic ports (including Puerto Rico)

483112 Deep sea passenger transportation to or from foreign ports

333318 Deep-fat fryers, commercial-type, manufacturing

335210 Deep-fat fryers, household-type electric, manufacturing

112990 Deer production

334510 Defibrillators manufacturing

325312 Defluorinated phosphates manufacturing

325998 Defoamers and antifoaming agents manufacturing

325320 Defoliants manufacturing

325998 Degreasing preparations for machinery parts manufacturing

325612 Degreasing preparations, household-type, manufacturing

333415 Dehumidifiers (except portable electric) manufacturing

335210 Dehumidifiers, portable electric, manufacturing

311514 Dehydrated milk manufacturing

311423 Dehydrating fruits and vegetables

311423 Dehydrating potato products (e.g., flakes, granules)

325998 Deicing preparations manufacturing

322110 Deinking plants

322110 Deinking recovered paper

424470 Deli meats merchant wholesalers

722513 Delicatessen restaurants

333997 Delicatessen scales manufacturing

445210 Delicatessens (except grocery store, restaurants)

445110 Delicatessens primarily retailing a range of grocery items and meats

561440 Delinquent account collection services

623990 Delinquent youth halfway group homes

115114 Delinting cottonseed

332618 Delivery cases made from purchased wire

492210 Delivery service (except as part of intercity courier network, U.S. Postal Service)

334515 Demand meters, electric, manufacturing

541720 Demographic research and development services

238910 Demolition contractor

238910 Demolition, building and structure

541890 Demonstration services, merchandise

336212 Demountable cargo containers manufacturing

325193	Denatured alcohol manufacturing
313210	Denims weaving
321219	Densified wood manufacturing
333316	Densitometers (except laboratory analytical) manufacturing
334516	Densitometers, laboratory analytical, manufacturing
334513	Density and specific gravity instruments, industrial process-type, manufacturing
339114	Dental alloys for amalgams manufacturing
424210	Dental care preparations merchant wholesalers
339114	Dental chairs manufacturing
423450	Dental chairs merchant wholesalers
339114	Dental equipment and instruments manufacturing
423450	Dental equipment and supplies merchant wholesalers
811219	Dental equipment repair and maintenance services
325620	Dental floss manufacturing
339114	Dental glues and cements manufacturing
339114	Dental hand instruments (e.g., forceps) manufacturing
611519	Dental hygienist schools
621399	Dental hygienists' offices (e.g., centers, clinics)
339114	Dental impression materials manufacturing
339114	Dental instrument delivery systems manufacturing
524114	Dental insurance carriers, direct
339116	Dental laboratories
339114	Dental laboratory equipment manufacturing
541715	Dental research and development laboratories or services
611310	Dental schools
621210	Dental surgeons' offices (e.g., centers, clinics)
611519	Dental technician schools
339114	Dental wax manufacturing
621512	Dental X-ray laboratories
325611	Dentifrices manufacturing
424210	Dentifrices merchant wholesalers
813920	Dentists' associations
621210	Dentists' offices (e.g., centers, clinics)
423450	Dentists' professional supplies merchant wholesalers
325620	Denture adhesives manufacturing

325620	Denture cleaners, effervescent, manufacturing
339114	Denture materials manufacturing
339116	Dentures, custom made in dental laboratories
621399	Denturists' offices (e.g., centers, clinics)
561720	Deodorant servicing of rest rooms
325612	Deodorants (except personal) manufacturing
424690	Deodorants (except personal) merchant wholesalers
325620	Deodorants, personal, manufacturing
424210	Deodorants, personal, merchant wholesalers
238290	Deodorization (i.e., air filtration) system installation
561720	Deodorizing services
452210	Department stores
812199	Depilatory (i.e., hair removal) salons
325620	Depilatory preparations manufacturing
332813	Depolishing metals and metal products for the trade
523999	Deposit brokers
524128	Deposit or share insurance carriers, direct
561492	Deposition services
522110	Depository trust companies
339113	Depressors, tongue, manufacturing
332994	Depth charge projectors manufacturing
332993	Depth charges manufacturing
424210	Dermatological medicines merchant wholesalers
325412	Dermatological preparations manufacturing
621111	Dermatologists' offices (e.g., centers, clinics)
213112	Derrick building, repairing, and dismantling at oil and gas fields on a contract basis
333132	Derricks, oil and gas field-type, manufacturing
325998	Desalination kits manufacturing
327992	Desiccants, activated clay, manufacturing
424120	Desk accessories, office, merchant wholesalers
335210	Desk fans, electric, manufacturing
335122	Desk lamps, commercial, electric, manufacturing
335121	Desk lamps, residential, electric, manufacturing
316998	Desk sets, leather, manufacturing

337214 Desks (except wood), office-type, manufacturing

337122 Desks, wood household-type, manufacturing

337211 Desks, wood office-type, manufacturing

561410 Desktop publishing services (i.e., document preparation services)

424490 Dessert powders merchant wholesalers

424430 Desserts, dairy, merchant wholesalers

311520 Desserts, frozen (except bakery), manufacturing

311813 Desserts, frozen bakery, manufacturing

811192 Detailing services (i.e., cleaning and polishing), automotive

115112 Detasseling corn

561611 Detective agencies

334519 Detectors, scintillation, manufacturing

922140 Detention centers

325611 Detergents (e.g., dishwashing, industrial, laundry) manufacturing

424690 Detergents merchant wholesalers

331492 Detinning scrap (e.g., cans)

325920 Detonating caps, cord, fuses, and primers manufacturing

325920 Detonators (except ammunition) manufacturing

424690 Detonators (except ammunition) merchant wholesalers

332993 Detonators, ammunition (i.e., more than 30 mm., more than 1.18 inch), manufacturing

621420 Detoxification centers and clinics (except hospitals), outpatient

622210 Detoxification hospitals

325180 Deuterium oxide (i.e., heavy water) manufacturing

325992 Developers, prepared photographic, manufacturing

336411 Developing and producing prototypes for aircraft

336412 Developing and producing prototypes for aircraft engines and engine parts

336413 Developing and producing prototypes for aircraft parts (except engines) and auxiliary equipment

336414 Developing and producing prototypes for complete guided missiles and space vehicles

336419 Developing and producing prototypes for guided missile and space vehicle components

336415 Developing and producing prototypes for guided missile and space vehicle engines

423410 Developing apparatus, photographic, merchant wholesalers

333316 Developing equipment, film, manufacturing

926110 Development assistance program administration

813311 Developmentally disabled advocacy organizations

238910 Dewatering contractors

111334 Dewberry farming

325520 Dextrin glues manufacturing

311221 Dextrin made by wet milling corn

212319 Diabase crushed and broken stone mining and/or beneficiating

212311 Diabase mining or quarrying

325412 Diagnostic biological preparations (except in-vitro) manufacturing

811198 Diagnostic centers without repair, automotive

334510 Diagnostic equipment, electromedical, manufacturing

423450 Diagnostic equipment, medical, merchant wholesalers

334510 Diagnostic equipment, MRI (magnetic resonance imaging), manufacturing

621512 Diagnostic imaging centers (medical)

811219 Diagnostic imaging equipment repair and maintenance services

424210 Diagnostic reagents merchant wholesalers

325413 Diagnostic substances, in-vitro, manufacturing

424210 Diagnostics, in-vitro and in-vivo, merchant wholesalers

332216 Dial indicators, machinists' precision tools, manufacturing

517919 Dial-up Internet service providers, using client-supplied telecommunications connections

621492 Dialysis centers and clinics

334510 Dialysis equipment, electromedical, manufacturing

325312 Diammonium phosphates manufacturing

332618 Diamond cloths made from purchased wire

339910 Diamond cutting and polishing

333514 Diamond dies, metalworking, manufacturing

327910 Diamond dressing wheels manufacturing

423940 Diamonds (except industrial) merchant wholesalers

423840	Diamonds, industrial, merchant wholesalers
212399	Diamonds, industrial, mining and/or beneficiating
315240	Diaper covers, infants', cut and sewn from purchased fabric (except apparel contractors)
315210	Diaper covers, water resistant and waterproof, cut and sew apparel contractors
812331	Diaper supply services
314999	Diapers (except disposable) made from purchased fabrics
424330	Diapers (except paper) merchant wholesalers
322291	Diapers, disposable, made from purchased paper or textile fiber
322121	Diapers, disposable, made in paper mills
424130	Diapers, paper, merchant wholesalers
326299	Diaphragms (i.e., birth control device), rubber, manufacturing
323111	Diaries manufacturing
511199	Diary and time scheduler publishers (except exclusive Internet publishing)
519130	Diary and time scheduler publishers, exclusively on Internet
212325	Diaspore mining and/or beneficiating
334510	Diathermy apparatus, electromedical, manufacturing
334510	Diathermy units manufacturing
212399	Diatomaceous earth mining and/or beneficitating
327992	Diatomaceous earth processing beyond beneficiation
212399	Diatomite mining and/or beneficiating
325992	Diazo (i.e., whiteprint) paper and cloth, sensitized, manufacturing
325120	Dichlorodifluoromethane manufacturing
325180	Dichromates manufacturing
315210	Dickeys cut and sew apparel contractors
315240	Dickeys, women's and girls', cut and sewn from purchased fabric (except apparel contractors)
333318	Dictating machines manufacturing
423420	Dictating machines merchant wholesalers
561410	Dictation services
611699	Diction schools
323117	Dictionaries printing and binding without publishing
323117	Dictionaries printing without publishing
323120	Dictionary binding without printing

511130	Dictionary publishers (except exclusive Internet publishing)
511130	Dictionary publishers and printing combined
519130	Dictionary publishers, exclusively on Internet
325211	Dicyandiamine resins manufacturing
333514	Die sets for metal stamping presses manufacturing
333517	Die sinking machines, metalworking, manufacturing
333511	Die-casting dies manufacturing
333517	Die-casting machines, metalworking, manufacturing
331523	Die-castings, aluminum, unfinished, manufacturing
331523	Die-castings, nonferrous metals, unfinished, manufacturing
322299	Die-cut paper products (except for office use) made from purchased paper or paperboard
322230	Die-cut paper products for office use made from purchased paper or paperboard
333994	Dielectric industrial heating equipment manufacturing
333514	Dies and die holders for metal cutting and forming (except threading) manufacturing
333515	Dies and taps (i.e., a machine tool accessory) manufacturing
332216	Dies, cutting (except metal cutting), manufacturing
333514	Dies, metalworking (except threading), manufacturing
423830	Dies, metalworking, merchant wholesalers
333514	Dies, plastics forming, manufacturing
332216	Dies, steel rule (except metal cutting), manufacturing
333514	Dies, steel rule, metal cutting, manufacturing
333618	Diesel and semidiesel engines manufacturing
811111	Diesel engine repair shops, automotive
423830	Diesel engines and parts, industrial, merchant wholesalers
424710	Diesel fuel bulk stations and terminals, merchant wholesalers
424720	Diesel fuel merchant wholesalers (except bulk stations, terminals)
324110	Diesel fuels made in petroleum refineries
812191	Diet centers, non-medical
812191	Diet workshops

311514   Dietary drinks, dairy and nondairy based, manufacturing

424210   Dietary supplements merchant wholesalers

325412   Dietary supplements, compounded, manufacturing

325411   Dietary supplements, uncompounded, manufacturing

325194   Diethylcyclohexane manufacturing

325199   Diethylene glycol manufacturing

813920   Dietitians' associations

621399   Dietitians' offices (e.g., centers, clinics)

336350   Differential and rear axle assemblies, automotive, truck, and bus, manufacturing

334513   Differential pressure instruments, industrial process-type, manufacturing

334516   Differential thermal analysis instruments, laboratory-type, manufacturing

332420   Digesters, industrial-type, heavy gauge metal, manufacturing

325412   Digestive system preparations manufacturing

238910   Digging foundations

333316   Digital cameras manufacturing

334111   Digital computers manufacturing

334513   Digital displays of process variables manufacturing

334515   Digital panel meters, electricity measuring, manufacturing

323111   Digital printing (e.g., billboards, other large format graphic materials, high resolution) (except books)

333244   Digital printing presses manufacturing

334515   Digital test equipment (e.g., electronic and electrical circuits and equipment testing) manufacturing

423620   Digital video disc (DVD) players merchant wholesalers

334310   Digital video disc players manufacturing

423990   Digital video discs (DVDs), prerecorded, merchant wholesalers

325412   Digitalis medicinal preparations manufacturing

423430   Digitizer and light pen tables merchant wholesalers

325411   Digitoxin, uncompounded, manufacturing

325211   Diisocyanate resins manufacturing

237990   Dike and other flood control structure construction

111219   Dill farming, field and seed production

321113   Dimension lumber, hardwood, made from logs or bolts

321912   Dimension lumber, hardwood, resawing purchased lumber

321113   Dimension lumber, made from logs or bolts

321912   Dimension lumber, resawing purchased lumber

321113   Dimension lumber, softwood, made from logs or bolts

321912   Dimension lumber, softwood, resawing purchased lumber

321912   Dimension stock, hardwood, manufacturing

321912   Dimension stock, softwood, manufacturing

321912   Dimension stock, wood, manufacturing

327991   Dimension stone dressing and manufacturing

327991   Dimension stone for buildings manufacturing

212311   Dimension stone mining or quarrying

325199   Dimethyl divinyl acetylene (di-isopropenyl acetylene) manufacturing

325199   Dimethylhydrazine manufacturing

335931   Dimmer switches, outlet box mounting-type, manufacturing

722511   Diners, full service

722513   Diners, limited-service

337124   Dinette sets, metal household-type, manufacturing

336612   Dinghies manufacturing

337124   Dining room chairs (including upholstered), metal, manufacturing

337125   Dining room chairs (including upholstered), plastics manufacturing

337122   Dining room chairs (including upholstered), wood, manufacturing

337124   Dining room furniture, metal household-type, manufacturing

337122   Dining room furniture, wood household-type, manufacturing

487210   Dinner cruises

711110   Dinner theaters

311412   Dinners, frozen (except seafood-based), manufacturing

311710   Dinners, frozen seafood, manufacturing

424420   Dinners, frozen, merchant wholesalers

326199   Dinnerware, plastics (except polystyrene foam), manufacturing

326140   Dinnerware, polystyrene foam, manufacturing

334515   Diode and transistor testers manufacturing

423690	Diodes merchant wholesalers
334413	Diodes, solid-state (e.g., germanium, silicon), manufacturing
212313	Diorite crushed and broken stone mining and/or beneficiating
212311	Diorite mining or quarrying
325194	Diphenylamine manufacturing
928120	Diplomatic services
311941	Dips (except cheese and sour cream based) manufacturing
325320	Dips (i.e., pesticides), cattle and sheep, manufacturing
311513	Dips, cheese based, manufacturing
311511	Dips, sour cream based, manufacturing
334112	Direct access storage devices manufacturing
517311	Direct broadcast satellite (DBS) services
325130	Direct dyes manufacturing
541860	Direct mail advertising services
541860	Direct mail or other direct distribution advertising campaign services
454110	Direct mailers (i.e., selling own merchandise)
331110	Direct reduction of iron ore
454390	Direct selling of merchandise (door-to-door)
213111	Directional drilling of oil and gas wells on a contract basis
812210	Director services, funeral
323111	Directories commercial printing (except screen) without publishing
323113	Directories screen printing without publishing
711510	Directors (i.e., film, motion picture, music, theatrical), independent
711510	Directors, independent motion picture
711510	Directors, independent music
511140	Directory and mailing list publishers (except exclusive Internet publishing)
511140	Directory and mailing list publishers and printing combined
511140	Directory publishers (except exclusive Internet publishing)
511140	Directory publishers and printing combined
519130	Directory publishers, exclusively on Internet
541870	Directory, telephone, distribution on a contract basis
517311	Direct-to-home satellite system (DTH) services
238910	Dirt moving for construction
524113	Disability insurance carriers, direct
524113	Disability insurance underwriting, direct
624120	Disability support groups
623990	Disabled group homes without nursing care
922190	Disaster preparedness and management offices, government
624230	Disaster relief services
711510	Disc jockeys, independent
623990	Disciplinary camps for delinquent youth
713990	Discotheques (except those serving alcoholic beverages)
722410	Discotheques, alcoholic beverage
812990	Discount buying services, including medical cards and similar negotiated discount plans for individuals
511199	Discount coupon book publishers (except exclusive Internet publishing)
511199	Discount coupon book publishers and printing combined
519130	Discount coupon book publishers, exclusively on Internet
323111	Discount coupon books commercial printing (except screen) without publishing
323113	Discount coupon books screen printing without publishing
813212	Disease awareness fundraising organizations
115112	Disease control for crops
813212	Disease research (e.g., cancer, heart) fundraising organizations
541940	Disease testing services, veterinary
313240	Dishcloths made in warp or weft knitting mills
423440	Dishes, commercial (except paper and disposable plastics), merchant wholesalers
423220	Dishes, household-type (except disposable plastics, paper), merchant wholesalers
424130	Dishes, paper and disposable plastics, merchant wholesalers
327110	Dishes, pottery, manufacturing
339930	Dishes, toy, manufacturing
321999	Dishes, wood, manufacturing
325611	Dishwasher detergents manufacturing
811412	Dishwasher, household-type, repair and maintenance services without retailing new dishwashers
335220	Dishwashers, household-type, manufacturing

423620 Dishwashers, household-type, merchant wholesalers

423440 Dishwashing equipment, commercial-type, merchant wholesalers

333318 Dishwashing machines, commercial-type, manufacturing

335220 Dishwashing machines, household-type, manufacturing

424690 Disinfectants (except agricultural) merchant wholesalers

325612 Disinfectants, household-type and industrial, manufacturing

561720 Disinfecting services

518210 Disk and diskette conversion services

518210 Disk and diskette recertification services

332613 Disk and ring springs, heavy gauge metal, manufacturing

334112 Disk drives, computer, manufacturing

423430 Disk drives, computer, merchant wholesalers

423430 Diskettes, blank computer, merchant wholesalers

334613 Diskettes, blank, manufacturing

423690 Diskettes, blank, merchant wholesalers

238910 Dismantling engineering structures (e.g., oil storage tank)

238290 Dismantling large-scale machinery and equipment

213112 Dismantling of oil well rigs on a contract basis

333914 Dispensing and measuring pumps (e.g., gasoline, lubricants) manufacturing

325130 Disperse dyes manufacturing

325510 Dispersions, pigment, manufacturing

541850 Display advertising services

423440 Display cases (except refrigerated) merchant wholesalers

337215 Display cases and fixtures (except refrigerated) manufacturing

333415 Display cases, refrigerated, manufacturing

423740 Display cases, refrigerated, merchant wholesalers

334513 Display instruments, industrial process control-type, manufacturing

541890 Display lettering services

339950 Displays (e.g., counter, floor, point-of-purchase) manufacturing

335912 Disposable flashlight batteries manufacturing

424130 Disposable plastics products (e.g., boxes, cups, cutlery, dishes, sanitary food containers) merchant wholesalers

334511 Distance measuring equipment (DME), aeronautical, manufacturing

325194 Distillates, wood, manufacturing

333994 Distillation ovens, charcoal and coke, manufacturing

424820 Distilled alcoholic beverages merchant wholesalers

325998 Distilled water manufacturing

312140 Distilleries

311213 Distiller's malt manufacturing

423830 Distillery machinery merchant wholesalers

312140 Distilling alcoholic beverages (except brandy)

312130 Distilling brandy

333249 Distilling equipment (except beverage), including laboratory-type, manufacturing

333241 Distilling equipment, beverage, manufacturing

312140 Distilling potable liquor (except brandy)

334515 Distortion meters and analyzers manufacturing

335313 Distribution boards, electric, manufacturing

335313 Distribution cutouts manufacturing

423610 Distribution equipment, electrical, merchant wholesalers

237120 Distribution line, gas and oil, construction

237110 Distribution line, sewer and water, construction

221330 Distribution of cooled air

221122 Distribution of electric power

221330 Distribution of heated air

221210 Distribution of manufactured gas

221210 Distribution of natural gas

221330 Distribution of steam heat

335311 Distribution transformers, electric, manufacturing

336320 Distributor cap and rotor for internal combustion engines manufacturing

813910 Distributors' associations

336320 Distributors for internal combustion engines manufacturing

551114 District and regional offices

922130 District attorneys' offices

333120 Ditchers and trenchers, self-propelled, manufacturing

325412 Diuretic preparations manufacturing

332216 Dividers, machinists' precision tools, manufacturing

451110 Diving equipment stores

561990	Diving services on a contract or fee basis
621210	DMDs' (doctors of dental medicine) offices (e.g., centers, clinics)
541714	DNA technologies (e.g., microarrays) research and experimental development laboratories
621511	DNA testing laboratories
531120	Dock and associated building rental or leasing
237990	Dock construction
488330	Docking and undocking marine vessel services
488310	Docking facility operations
621310	Doctors of chiropractic (DCs) offices (e.g., centers, clinics)
621210	Doctors of dental medicine (DMDs) offices (e.g., centers, clinics)
621210	Doctors of dental surgery (DDSs) offices (e.g., centers, clinics)
621320	Doctors of optometry (ODs) offices (e.g., centers, clinics)
621112	Doctors of osteopathy (DOs), mental health, offices (e.g., centers, clinics)
621111	Doctors of osteopathy (DOs, except mental health) offices (e.g., centers, clinics)
621391	Doctors of podiatry (DPs) offices (e.g., centers, clinics)
621330	Doctors of psychology offices (e.g., centers, clinics)
561439	Document copying services (except combined with printing services)
561439	Document duplicating services (except combined with printing services)
561410	Document preparation services
561990	Document shredding services
493190	Document storage and warehousing
561410	Document transcription services
325110	Dodecene made from refined petroleum or liquid hydrocarbons
311111	Dog and cat food (e.g., canned, dry, frozen, semimoist), manufacturing
311111	Dog food manufacturing
316998	Dog furnishings (e.g., collars, harnesses, leashes, muzzles) manufacturing
711219	Dog owners, race (i.e., racing dogs)
812910	Dog pounds
112990	Dog production
711212	Dog racetracks
711219	Dog racing kennels
424990	Dogs merchant wholesalers
322299	Doilies, paper, made from purchased paper
339930	Doll carriages and carts manufacturing
339930	Doll clothing manufacturing
452319	Dollar stores
333924	Dollies manufacturing
423920	Dolls merchant wholesalers
339930	Dolls, doll parts, and doll clothing (except wigs) manufacturing
212312	Dolomite crushed and broken stone mining and/or beneficiating
212311	Dolomite mining or quarrying
327410	Dolomite, dead-burned, manufacturing
327410	Dolomitic lime manufacturing
212319	Dolomitic marble crushed and broken stone mining and/or beneficiating
212311	Dolomitic marble mining or quarrying
114111	Dolphin fishing
112920	Donkey production
332321	Door and jamb assemblies, metal, manufacturing
238350	Door and window frame construction
238350	Door and window, prefabricated, installation
332321	Door frames and sash, metal, manufacturing
321911	Door frames and sash, wood and covered wood, manufacturing
332322	Door hoods, sheet metal (except stampings), manufacturing
321911	Door jambs, wood, manufacturing
332510	Door locks, metal, manufacturing
332510	Door opening and closing devices (except electrical), metal, manufacturing
335999	Door opening and closing devices, electrical, manufacturing
321918	Door shutters, wood, manufacturing
444190	Door stores
321918	Door trim, wood molding, manufacturing
321911	Door units, prehung, wood and covered wood, manufacturing
238290	Door, commercial- or industrial-type, installation
238350	Door, folding, installation
314110	Doormats, all materials (except entirely of rubber or plastics), manufacturing
326199	Doormats, plastics, manufacturing
326299	Doormats, rubber, manufacturing
423310	Doors and door frames merchant wholesalers

326199 Doors and door frames, plastics, manufacturing

321911 Doors, combination screen-storm, wood, manufacturing

332321 Doors, metal, manufacturing

332999 Doors, safe and vault, metal, manufacturing

327215 Doors, unframed glass, made from purchased glass

321911 Doors, wood and covered wood, manufacturing

541870 Door-to-door distribution of advertising materials (e.g., coupons, flyers, samples)

454390 Door-to-door retailing of merchandise, direct selling

325510 Dopes, paint, and lacquer manufacturing

336612 Dories building

721310 Dormitories, off campus

236220 Dormitory construction

621112 DOs' (doctors of osteopathy), mental health, offices (e.g., centers, clinics)

621111 DOs' (doctors of osteopathy, except mental health) offices (e.g., centers, clinics)

334519 Dosimetry devices manufacturing

333241 Dough mixing machinery (i.e., food manufacturing-type) manufacturing

722511 Doughnut shops, full service

722515 Doughnut shops, on premise baking and carryout service

311812 Doughnuts (except frozen) made in commercial bakeries

311813 Doughnuts, frozen, manufacturing

424420 Doughs, frozen, merchant wholesalers

311211 Doughs, prepared, made in flour mills

311824 Doughs, refrigerated or frozen, made from purchased flour

812990 Doula services (providing coaching and support during childbirth)

333243 Dovetailing machines, woodworking-type, manufacturing

332722 Dowel pins, metal, manufacturing

321999 Dowels, wood, manufacturing

315210 Down-filled clothing cut and sew apparel contractors

315220 Down-filled clothing, men's and boys', cut and sewn from purchased fabric (except apparel contractors)

315240 Down-filled clothing, women's, girls', and infants', cut and sewn from purchased fabric (except apparel contractors)

713920 Downhill skiing facilities without accommodations

238170 Downspout, gutter, and gutter guard installation

332322 Downspouts, sheet metal (except stampings), manufacturing

621391 DPs' (doctors of podiatry) offices (e.g., centers, clinics)

334513 Draft gauges, industrial process-type, manufacturing

334519 Drafting instruments manufacturing

423490 Drafting instruments merchant wholesalers

339940 Drafting materials (except instruments and tables) manufacturing

541340 Drafting services

337127 Drafting tables and boards manufacturing

423490 Drafting tables merchant wholesalers

541340 Draftsmen's offices

711212 Drag strips

333120 Draglines, crawler, manufacturing

423860 Draglines, ship, merchant wholesalers

325194 Dragon's blood manufacturing

333111 Drags, farm-type equipment, manufacturing

333120 Drags, road construction and road maintenance equipment, manufacturing

212399 Dragstones mining and/or beneficiating

561790 Drain cleaning services

332913 Drain cocks, plumbing, manufacturing

325612 Drain pipe cleaners manufacturing

332999 Drain plugs, magnetic, metal, manufacturing

327120 Drain tile, clay, manufacturing

238220 Drain, waste and vent system installation

237990 Drainage canal and ditch construction

237990 Drainage project construction

238910 Drainage system (e.g., cesspool, septic tank) installation

337110 Drainboards, wood or plastics laminated on wood, manufacturing

213113 Draining or pumping coal mines on a contract basis

213114 Draining or pumping of metal mines on a contract basis

213115 Draining or pumping of nonmetallic mineral mines (except fuels) on a contract basis

611610 Drama schools (except academic)

314120 Draperies made from purchased fabrics or sheet goods

423220	Draperies merchant wholesalers
812320	Drapery cleaning services
238390	Drapery fixture (e.g., hardware, rods, tracks) installation
423710	Drapery hardware merchant wholesalers
424310	Drapery material merchant wholesalers
339113	Drapes, surgical, disposable, manufacturing
333519	Draw bench machines manufacturing
315210	Drawers cut and sew apparel contractors
315190	Drawers, apparel, made in apparel knitting mills
315220	Drawers, men's and boys', cut and sewn from purchased fabric (except apparel contractors)
315240	Drawers, women's and girls', cut and sewn from purchased fabric (except apparel contractors)
325998	Drawing inks manufacturing
331222	Drawing iron or steel wire from purchased iron or steel
331222	Drawing iron or steel wire from purchased iron or steel and fabricating wire products
333249	Drawing machinery for textiles manufacturing
337127	Drawing tables and boards, artist's, manufacturing
332216	Drawknives manufacturing
336611	Dredge building
423810	Dredges (except ships') merchant wholesalers
423860	Dredges, ship, merchant wholesalers
237990	Dredging (e.g., canal, channel, ditch, waterway)
333120	Dredging machinery manufacturing
315210	Dress and semidress gloves cut and sew apparel contractors
315990	Dress and semidress gloves cut and sewn from purchased fabric (except apparel contractors)
315190	Dress and semidress gloves made in apparel knitting mills
316210	Dress shoes, children's and infants', manufacturing
316210	Dress shoes, men's, manufacturing
316210	Dress shoes, women's, manufacturing
448190	Dress shops
532281	Dress suit rental
315210	Dress trimmings cut and sew apparel contractors

315990	Dress trimmings cut and sewn from purchased fabric (except apparel contractors)
424990	Dressed furs and skins merchant wholesalers
337124	Dressers, metal, manufacturing
337122	Dressers, wood, manufacturing
315210	Dresses cut and sew apparel contractors
315190	Dresses made in apparel knitting mills
424330	Dresses merchant wholesalers
315190	Dresses, hand-knit, manufacturing
315240	Dresses, women's, girls', and infants', cut and sewn from purchased fabric (except apparel contractors)
316110	Dressing (i.e., bleaching, blending, currying, scraping, tanning) furs
315210	Dressing gowns cut and sew apparel contractors
315240	Dressing gowns, women's and girls', cut and sewn from purchased fabric (except apparel contractors)
316110	Dressing hides
311615	Dressing small game
337124	Dressing tables, metal, manufacturing
337122	Dressing tables, wood, manufacturing
423450	Dressings, medical, merchant wholesalers
339113	Dressings, surgical, manufacturing
424490	Dried foods (e.g., fruits, milk, vegetables) merchant wholesalers
311612	Dried meats made from purchased carcasses
212392	Dried phosphate rock mining and/or beneficiating
325510	Driers, paint and varnish, manufacturing
325992	Driers, photographic chemical, manufacturing
333316	Driers, photographic, manufacturing
334511	Driftmeters, aeronautical, manufacturing
333515	Drill bits, metalworking, manufacturing
332216	Drill bits, woodworking, manufacturing
333517	Drill presses, metalworking, manufacturing
333243	Drill presses, woodworking-type, manufacturing
332999	Drill stands, metal, manufacturing
238910	Drilled pier (i.e., for building foundations) contractors
238910	Drilled shaft (i.e., drilled building foundations) construction

336611	Drilling and production platforms, floating, oil and gas, building
213111	Drilling directional oil and gas field wells on a contract basis
333132	Drilling equipment, oil and gas field-type, manufacturing
333131	Drilling equipment, underground mining-type, manufacturing
213111	Drilling for gas on a contract basis
213111	Drilling for oil on a contract basis
213111	Drilling gas and oil field wells on a contract basis
333517	Drilling machines, metalworking, manufacturing
325998	Drilling mud compounds, conditioners, and additives (except bentonites) manufacturing
424690	Drilling muds merchant wholesalers
213111	Drilling oil and gas field service wells on a contract basis
339910	Drilling pearls
213112	Drilling rat holes and mouse holes at oil and gas fields on a contract basis
333132	Drilling rigs, oil and gas field-type, manufacturing
213113	Drilling services for coal mining on a contract basis
213114	Drilling services for metal mining on a contract basis
213115	Drilling services for nonmetallic mineral (except fuels) mining on a contract basis
213112	Drilling shot holes at oil and gas fields on a contract basis
213112	Drilling site preparation at oil and gas fields on a contract basis
213111	Drilling water intake wells, oil and gas field on a contract basis
237110	Drilling water wells (except water intake wells in oil and gas fields)
313210	Drills weaving
333131	Drills, core, underground mining-type, manufacturing
339114	Drills, dental, manufacturing
333991	Drills, handheld power-driven (except heavy construction and mining-type), manufacturing
332216	Drills, handheld, nonelectric, manufacturing
333131	Drills, rock, underground mining-type, manufacturing
213112	Drill-stem testing in oil, gas, dry, and service well drilling on a contract basis
311999	Drink powder mixes (except chocolate, coffee, milk based, tea) manufacturing
311351	Drink powdered mixes, cocoa, made from cacao
311352	Drink powdered mixes, cocoa, made from purchased cocoa
311511	Drink, chocolate milk, manufacturing
238220	Drinking fountain installation
332999	Drinking fountains (except mechanically refrigerated), metal, manufacturing
326191	Drinking fountains (except mechanically refrigerated), plastics, manufacturing
423720	Drinking fountains (except refrigerated) merchant wholesalers
333415	Drinking fountains, refrigerated, manufacturing
423740	Drinking fountains, refrigerated, merchant wholesalers
327110	Drinking fountains, vitreous china, non-refrigerated, manufacturing
722410	Drinking places (i.e., bars, lounges, taverns), alcoholic
312111	Drinks, fruit (except juice), manufacturing
333613	Drive chains, bicycle and motorcycle, manufacturing
811118	Drive shaft repair shops, automotive
336350	Drive shafts and half shafts, automotive, truck, and bus, manufacturing
512132	Drive-in motion picture theaters
237990	Drive-in movie facility construction
722513	Drive-in restaurants
611692	Driver education
611692	Driver training schools (except bus, heavy equipment, truck)
711219	Drivers, harness or race car
423840	Drives and gears merchant wholesalers
333612	Drives, high-speed industrial (except hydrostatic), manufacturing
561790	Driveway cleaning (e.g., power sweeping, washing) services
238990	Driveway paving or sealing
713990	Driving ranges, golf
488490	Driving services (e.g., automobile, truck delivery)
238310	Drop ceiling installation
332111	Drop forgings made from purchased iron or steel, unfinished
333517	Drop hammers, metal forging and shaping, manufacturing
812320	Drop-off and pick-up sites for laundries and drycleaners

813319	Drug abuse prevention advocacy organizations
623220	Drug addiction rehabilitation facilities (except licensed hospitals), residential
622210	Drug addiction rehabilitation hospitals
624190	Drug addiction self-help organizations
621420	Drug addiction treatment centers and clinics (except hospitals), outpatient
922120	Drug enforcement agencies and offices
424210	Drug proprietaries merchant wholesalers
446110	Drug stores
424210	Druggists' sundries merchant wholesalers
424210	Drugs merchant wholesalers
711130	Drum and bugle corps (i.e., drill teams)
333924	Drum cradles manufacturing
339992	Drums (musical instruments), parts, and accessories manufacturing
332439	Drums, light gauge metal, manufacturing
423840	Drums, new and reconditioned, merchant wholesalers
326199	Drums, plastics (i.e., containers), manufacturing
321920	Drums, plywood, manufacturing
321920	Drums, shipping, wood, wirebound, manufacturing
813319	Drunk driving prevention advocacy organizations
311422	Dry beans canning
424510	Dry beans, inedible, merchant wholesalers
484230	Dry bulk carrier, truck, long-distance
484220	Dry bulk trucking (except garbage collection, garbage hauling), local
335912	Dry cell primary batteries, single and multiple cell, manufacturing
335912	Dry cells, primary (e.g., AAA, AA, C, D, 9V), manufacturing
238220	Dry heating equipment installation
325120	Dry ice (i.e., solid carbon dioxide) manufacturing
424690	Dry ice merchant wholesalers
311514	Dry milk manufacturing
333241	Dry milk processing machinery manufacturing
311514	Dry milk products and mixture manufacturing
311514	Dry milk products for animal feed manufacturing
327999	Dry mix concrete manufacturing
311824	Dry mixes made from purchased flour
311824	Dry pasta manufacturing
311824	Dry pasta packaged with other ingredients made in dry pasta plants
335210	Dry shavers (i.e., electric razors) manufacturing
238910	Dry well construction
812320	Drycleaner drop-off and pick-up sites
812320	Drycleaners (except coin-operated)
335220	Drycleaning and laundry machines, household-type, manufacturing
333318	Drycleaning equipment and machinery manufacturing
423850	Drycleaning equipment and supplies merchant wholesalers
812310	Drycleaning machine routes (i.e., concession operators), coin-operated or similar self-service
236220	Drycleaning plant construction
812320	Drycleaning plants (except rug cleaning plants)
325612	Drycleaning preparations manufacturing
812320	Drycleaning services (except coin-operated)
812310	Drycleaning services, coin-operated or similar self-service
424690	Drycleaning solvents and chemicals merchant wholesalers
336611	Drydock, floating, building
488390	Drydocks, floating (i.e., routine repair and maintenance of ships)
532210	Dryer, clothes, rental
335220	Dryers, clothes, household-type, gas and electric, manufacturing
423620	Dryers, clothes, merchant wholesalers
423620	Dryers, hair, merchant wholesalers
335220	Dryers, household-type laundry, manufacturing
339113	Dryers, laboratory-type, manufacturing
333318	Dryers, laundry (except household-type), manufacturing
311710	Drying fish and seafood
333249	Drying kilns, lumber, manufacturing
333249	Drying machinery for textiles manufacturing
423310	Drywall board merchant wholesalers
238310	Drywall contractors
238310	Drywall finishing (e.g., sanding, spackling, stippling, taping, texturing)
238310	Drywall hanging
238310	Drywall installation

423320	Drywall supplies merchant wholesalers
713950	Duck pin bowling alleys
713950	Duck pin bowling centers
112390	Duck production
313210	Ducks weaving
311615	Ducks, processing, fresh, frozen, canned, or cooked
311615	Ducks, slaughtering and dressing
561790	Duct cleaning services
238290	Duct insulation installation
322220	Duct tape made from purchased materials
238220	Duct work (e.g., cooling, dust collection, exhaust, heating, ventilation) installation
331511	Ductile iron castings, unfinished, manufacturing
331511	Ductile iron foundries
332313	Ducting, fabricated metal plate work, manufacturing
335313	Ducts for electrical switchboard apparatus manufacturing
332322	Ducts, sheet metal, manufacturing
721214	Dude ranches
339920	Dumbbells manufacturing
238290	Dumbwaiter installation
333921	Dumbwaiters manufacturing
212325	Dumortierite mining and/or beneficiating
336212	Dump trailers manufacturing
532120	Dump truck rental or leasing without operator
484220	Dump trucking (e.g., gravel, sand, top-soil)
562119	Dump trucking of rubble or brush with collection or disposal
333131	Dumpers, mining car, manufacturing
562219	Dumps, compost
562212	Dumps, nonhazardous solid waste (e.g., trash)
336211	Dump-truck lifting mechanisms manufacturing
315210	Dungarees cut and sew apparel contractors
315220	Dungarees, men's and boys', cut and sewn from purchased fabric (except apparel contractors)
315240	Dungarees, women's, girls', and infants', cut and sewn from purchased fabric (except apparel contractors)
423860	Dunnage, marine supplies, merchant wholesalers
236116	Duplex (i.e., one unit above the other), construction general contractors
236115	Duplex (i.e., side-by-side) construction general contractors
236117	Duplex for-sale builders
531110	Duplex houses (i.e., single-family) rental or leasing
335931	Duplex receptacles, electrical, manufacturing
325910	Duplicating inks manufacturing
532420	Duplicating machine (e.g., copier) rental or leasing
333517	Duplicating machines (e.g., key cutting), metalworking, manufacturing
425120	Durable goods agents and brokers, wholesale trade
425110	Durable goods business to business electronic markets, wholesale trade
311211	Durum flour manufacturing
333413	Dust and fume collecting equipment manufacturing
314999	Dust cloths made from purchased fabrics
238220	Dust collecting and bag house equipment installation
423730	Dust collection equipment merchant wholesalers
812332	Dust control textile item (e.g., cloths, mats, mops, rugs, shop towels) supply services
315210	Dusters (i.e., apparel) cut and sew apparel contractors
315240	Dusters (i.e., apparel), women's and girls', cut and sewn from purchased fabric (except apparel contractors)
333111	Dusters, farm-type, manufacturing
115112	Dusting crops
445310	Duty free liquor shops
334112	DVD (digital video disc) drives, computer peripheral equipment, manufacturing
334310	DVD (digital video disc) players manufacturing
531110	Dwelling rental or leasing
332311	Dwellings, prefabricated metal, manufacturing
325998	Dye preparations, clothing, household-type, manufacturing
316110	Dyeing furs
313310	Dyeing gloves, woven or knit, for the trade
316110	Dyeing leather
333249	Dyeing machinery for textiles manufacturing
423830	Dyeing machinery, textile, merchant wholesalers
313310	Dyeing textile products and fabrics

424690	Dyes, industrial, merchant wholesalers
325130	Dyes, inorganic, manufacturing
325194	Dyes, natural, manufacturing
325130	Dyes, synthetic organic, manufacturing
424690	Dyestuffs merchant wholesalers
325920	Dynamite manufacturing
424690	Dynamite merchant wholesalers
334519	Dynamometers manufacturing
335312	Dynamos, electric (except automotive), manufacturing
335312	Dynamotors manufacturing
812199	Ear piercing services
237990	Earth retention system construction
334220	Earth station communications equipment manufacturing
517919	Earth stations (except satellite telecommunication carriers)
517410	Earth stations for satellite communication carriers
212399	Earth, diatomaceous, mining and/or beneficiating
212325	Earth, fuller's (e.g., all natural bleaching clays), mining and/or beneficiating
327110	Earthenware table and kitchen articles, coarse, manufacturing
327110	Earthenware, commercial and household, semivitreous, manufacturing
237990	Earth-filled dam construction
532412	Earthmoving equipment rental or leasing without operator
311119	Earthworm food and bedding manufacturing
112990	Earthworm hatcheries
339940	Easels, artists', manufacturing
424130	Eating utensils, disposable plastics, merchant wholesalers
332322	Eaves, sheet metal (except stampings), manufacturing
238170	Eavestrough installation
423330	Eavestroughing merchant wholesalers
327110	Ecclesiastical statuary, clay, manufacturing
327420	Ecclesiastical statuary, gypsum, manufacturing
327999	Ecclesiastical statuary, paper mache, manufacturing
327991	Ecclesiastical statuary, stone, manufacturing
332999	Ecclesiastical ware, precious plated metal, manufacturing
541620	Ecological restoration consulting services
541690	Economic consulting services
926110	Economic development agencies, government
928120	Economic development assistance (i.e., international), government
541720	Economic research and development services
332410	Economizers (i.e., power boiler accessory) manufacturing
522298	Edge Act corporations (except international trade financing)
522293	Edge Act corporations (i.e., international trade financing)
332216	Edge tools, woodworking (e.g., augers, bits, countersinks), manufacturing
333316	Editing equipment, motion picture (e.g., rewinders, splicers, titlers, viewers), manufacturing
561410	Editing services
923110	Education offices, nonoperating
923110	Education program administration
923110	Education statistics centers, government
236220	Educational building construction
611710	Educational consultants
611710	Educational curriculum development services
611710	Educational guidance counseling services
611710	Educational support services
611710	Educational testing evaluation services
611710	Educational testing services
813211	Educational trusts, awarding grants
813920	Educators' associations
114111	Eel fishing
325412	Effervescent salts manufacturing
541614	Efficiency management (i.e., efficiency expert) consulting services
424130	Egg cartons, paper and disposable plastics, merchant wholesalers
321920	Egg cases, wood, manufacturing
335210	Egg cookers, household-type electric, manufacturing
112340	Egg hatcheries, poultry
311824	Egg noodles, dry, manufacturing
311991	Egg noodles, fresh, manufacturing
112310	Egg production, chicken
112330	Egg production, turkey
311999	Egg substitutes manufacturing

312140	Eggnog, alcoholic, manufacturing
311514	Eggnog, canned, nonalcoholic, manufacturing
311511	Eggnog, fresh, nonalcoholic, manufacturing
311511	Eggnog, nonalcoholic (except canned), manufacturing
111219	Eggplant farming (except under cover), field, bedding plant and seed production
111419	Eggplant farming, grown under cover
424440	Eggs merchant wholesalers
112310	Eggs, chicken (table, hatching) production
311999	Eggs, processed, manufacturing
334515	Elapsed time meters, electronic, manufacturing
313210	Elastic fabrics, more than 12 inches in width, weaving
313220	Elastic fabrics, narrow woven, manufacturing
339113	Elastic hosiery, orthopedic, manufacturing
325220	Elastomeric fibers and filaments manufacturing
325211	Elastomers (except synthetic rubber) manufacturing
325212	Elastomers, synthetic rubber, manufacturing
332322	Elbows for conductor pipe, hot air ducts, and stovepipe, sheet metal (except stampings), manufacturing
332919	Elbows, pipe, metal (except made from purchased pipe), manufacturing
921190	Election boards
334512	Electric air cleaner controls, automatic, manufacturing
334513	Electric and electronic controllers, industrial process-type, manufacturing
336111	Electric automobiles for highway use manufacturing
335999	Electric bells manufacturing
335210	Electric blankets manufacturing
423620	Electric blankets merchant wholesalers
335210	Electric comfort heating equipment, portable, manufacturing
238210	Electric contracting
335999	Electric fence chargers manufacturing
335311	Electric furnace transformers manufacturing
334512	Electric heat proportioning controls, modulating controls, manufacturing

335110	Electric lamp bulb parts (except glass blanks) manufacturing
335110	Electric lamps (i.e., light bulbs) manufacturing
237130	Electric light and power plant (except hydroelectric) construction
335110	Electric light bulbs, complete, manufacturing
423610	Electric light fixtures merchant wholesalers
811310	Electric motor repair and maintenance services, commercial or industrial
423610	Electric motors, wiring supplies, and lighting fixtures merchant wholesalers
339992	Electric musical instruments manufacturing
333618	Electric outboard motors manufacturing
221122	Electric power brokers
221121	Electric power control
238210	Electric power control panel and outlet installation
221122	Electric power distribution systems
221117	Electric power generation, biomass
221112	Electric power generation, fossil fuel (e.g., coal, oil, gas)
221116	Electric power generation, geothermal
221111	Electric power generation, hydroelectric
221113	Electric power generation, nuclear
221114	Electric power generation, solar
221118	Electric power generation, tidal
221115	Electric power generation, wind
237130	Electric power transmission line and tower construction
221121	Electric power transmission systems
423610	Electric prime movers merchant wholesalers
334512	Electric space heater controls, automatic, manufacturing
335210	Electric space heaters, portable, manufacturing
333415	Electric warm air (i.e., forced air) furnaces manufacturing
423610	Electrical apparatus merchant wholesalers
238210	Electrical contractors
336320	Electrical control chips (modules), motor vehicle, manufacturing
541330	Electrical engineering services
238210	Electrical equipment and appliance installation
811310	Electrical generating and transmission equipment repair and maintenance services
541360	Electrical geophysical surveying services

336320	Electrical ignition cable sets for internal combustion engines manufacturing
327110	Electrical insulators, ceramic, manufacturing
811219	Electrical measuring instrument repair and maintenance services
335932	Electrical metallic tube (EMTs) manufacturing
561990	Electrical meter reading services, contract
334515	Electrical network analyzers manufacturing
334515	Electrical power measuring equipment manufacturing
811118	Electrical repair shops, automotive
339950	Electrical signs manufacturing
423440	Electrical signs merchant wholesalers
327110	Electrical supplies, ceramic, manufacturing
444190	Electrical supply stores
541380	Electrical testing laboratories or services
238210	Electrical wiring contractors
238210	Electrical work
238210	Electrical, electrical wiring, and low voltage electrical work
335210	Electrically heated bed coverings manufacturing
238210	Electrician
611513	Electricians' apprenticeship training
334515	Electricity and electrical signal measuring instruments manufacturing
334515	Electricity and electrical signal testing equipment manufacturing
237130	Electricity generating plant (except hydroelectric) construction
237990	Electricity generating plant, hydroelectric, construction
334510	Electrocardiographs manufacturing
335999	Electrochemical generators (i.e., fuel cells) manufacturing
333517	Electrochemical milling machines, metalworking, manufacturing
333517	Electrode discharge metal cutting machines manufacturing
333992	Electrode holders, welding, manufacturing
335991	Electrodes for thermal and electrolytic uses, carbon and graphite, manufacturing
334513	Electrodes used in industrial process measurement manufacturing
335110	Electrodes, cold cathode fluorescent lamp, manufacturing
333992	Electrodes, welding, manufacturing
334510	Electroencephalographs manufacturing
334510	Electrogastrograph manufacturing
332912	Electrohydraulic servo valves, fluid power, manufacturing
812199	Electrolysis (i.e., hair removal) salons
325412	Electrolyte in-vivo diagnostic substances manufacturing
334513	Electrolytic conductivity instruments, industrial process-type, manufacturing
334516	Electrolytic conductivity instruments, laboratory-type, manufacturing
333517	Electrolytic metal cutting machines manufacturing
334513	Electromagnetic flowmeters manufacturing
541360	Electromagnetic geophysical surveying services
334514	Electromechanical counters manufacturing
334510	Electromedical diagnostic equipment manufacturing
334510	Electromedical equipment manufacturing
423450	Electromedical equipment merchant wholesalers
334510	Electromedical therapy equipment manufacturing
331110	Electrometallurgical ferroalloy manufacturing
331110	Electrometallurgical steel manufacturing
334510	Electromyographs manufacturing
333992	Electron beam welding equipment manufacturing
335999	Electron linear accelerators manufacturing
334516	Electron microprobes, laboratory-type, manufacturing
334516	Electron microscopes manufacturing
334516	Electron paramagnetic spin-type apparatus manufacturing
333249	Electron tube machinery manufacturing
334419	Electron tube parts (e.g., bases, getters, guns) (except glass blanks) manufacturing
327215	Electron tube parts, glass blanks, made from purchased glass
327212	Electron tube parts, glass blanks, made in glass making plants
334515	Electron tube test equipment manufacturing
334419	Electron tubes manufacturing
333517	Electron-discharge metal cutting machines manufacturing

423690	Electronic aircraft instruments merchant wholesalers
454110	Electronic auctions, retail
453998	Electronic cigarette stores
325998	Electronic cigarette vapor refills manufacturing
339999	Electronic cigarettes manufacturing
424940	Electronic cigarettes merchant wholesalers
541990	Electronic communication content verification services
423690	Electronic communications equipment merchant wholesalers
238210	Electronic containment fencing for pets, installation
238210	Electronic control installation and service
238210	Electronic control system installation
518210	Electronic data processing services
511140	Electronic directory publishers (except exclusive Internet publishing)
519130	Electronic directory publishers, exclusively on Internet
611519	Electronic equipment repair training
522320	Electronic financial payment services
522320	Electronic funds transfer services
713120	Electronic game arcades
423920	Electronic games merchant wholesalers
334511	Electronic guidance systems and equipment manufacturing
541870	Electronic marketing services
425110	Electronic markets, durable goods, business to business, wholesale trade
425110	Electronic markets, nondurable goods, business to business, wholesale trade
443142	Electronic part and component stores
423690	Electronic parts (e.g., condensers, connectors, switches) merchant wholesalers
323120	Electronic prepress services for the printing trade
541715	Electronic research and development laboratories or services (except nanotechnology research and development)
423690	Electronic sound equipment (except household-type and automotive) merchant wholesalers
334515	Electronic test equipment for testing electrical characteristics manufacturing
541380	Electronic testing laboratories or services
334514	Electronic totalizing counters manufacturing
339930	Electronic toys and games manufacturing
423690	Electronic tubes (e.g., industrial, receiving, transmitting) merchant wholesalers
423930	Electronics parts, recyclable, merchant wholesalers
334516	Electrophoresis instruments manufacturing
333249	Electroplating machinery and equipment manufacturing
332813	Electroplating metals and formed products for the trade
238320	Electrostatic painting, on-site, contractors
335999	Electrostatic particle accelerators manufacturing
333413	Electrostatic precipitation equipment manufacturing
334510	Electrotherapeutic apparatus manufacturing
335110	Electrotherapeutic lamp bulbs for ultraviolet and infrared radiation manufacturing
334510	Electrotherapy units manufacturing
323120	Electrotype plate preparation services
333244	Electrotyping machinery manufacturing
334516	Elemental analyzers manufacturing
611110	Elementary and secondary schools
611110	Elementary schools
237310	Elevated highway construction
332323	Elevator guide rails, metal, manufacturing
238290	Elevator installation
423830	Elevators merchant wholesalers
333922	Elevators, farm, manufacturing
333921	Elevators, passenger and freight, manufacturing
112990	Elk production
325998	Embalming fluids manufacturing
812210	Embalming services
237990	Embankment construction
928120	Embassies
316110	Embossing leather
323120	Embossing plate preparation services
339940	Embossing stamps manufacturing
313310	Embossing textile products and fabrics
313220	Embroideries, Schiffli machine, manufacturing
314999	Embroidering contractors on apparel
314999	Embroidering on textile products or apparel for the trade
339930	Embroidery kits manufacturing

333249	Embroidery machinery manufacturing
424310	Embroidery products merchant wholesalers
313110	Embroidery spun yarns (e.g., cotton, manmade fiber, silk, wool) made from purchased fiber
313110	Embroidery thread (e.g., cotton, manmade fibers, silk, wool) manufacturing
335122	Emergency lighting (i.e., battery backup) manufacturing
621493	Emergency medical centers and clinics, freestanding
621910	Emergency medical transportation services, air or ground
922190	Emergency planning and management offices, government
453998	Emergency preparedness supply stores
624230	Emergency relief services
488410	Emergency road services (i.e., tow service)
624221	Emergency shelters (except for victims of domestic or international disasters or conflicts)
624230	Emergency shelters for victims of domestic or international disasters or conflicts
561421	Emergency telephone dispatch (i.e., contractor) services
212399	Emery mining and/or beneficiating
811198	Emissions testing without repair, automotive
541612	Employee assessment consulting services
541612	Employee benefit consulting services
525110	Employee benefit pension plans
525120	Employee benefit plans (except pension)
524292	Employee benefit plans, third party administrative processing services
485410	Employee bus services
541612	Employee compensation consulting services
621999	Employee drug testing services
561330	Employee leasing services
813930	Employees' associations for improvement of wages and working conditions
561311	Employment agencies
561311	Employment agencies, motion picture or video
561311	Employment agencies, radio or television
561311	Employment agencies, theatrical
561311	Employment placement agencies or services
561311	Employment referral agencies or services
561311	Employment registries

335932	EMTs (electrical metallic tube) manufacturing
112390	Emu production
325613	Emulsifiers (i.e., surface active agents) manufacturing
325510	Enamel paints manufacturing
212322	Enamel sand quarrying and/or beneficiating
332215	Enameled metal cutting utensils
332812	Enameling metals and metal products for the trade
333994	Enameling ovens manufacturing
424950	Enamels merchant wholesalers
339114	Enamels, dental, manufacturing
323120	Encyclopedia binding without printing
511130	Encyclopedia publishers (except exclusive Internet publishing)
511130	Encyclopedia publishers and printing combined
519130	Encyclopedia publishers, exclusively on Internet
323117	Encyclopedias printing and binding without publishing
323117	Encyclopedias printing without publishing
337124	End tables, metal, manufacturing
337122	End tables, wood, manufacturing
111219	Endive farming (except under cover), field, bedding plant and seed production
111419	Endive farming, grown under cover
325411	Endocrine products, uncompounded, manufacturing
424210	Endocrine substances merchant wholesalers
621210	Endodontists' offices (e.g., centers, clinics)
334510	Endoscopic equipment, electromedical (e.g., bronchoscopes, colonoscopes, cystoscopes), manufacturing
325320	Endrin insecticides manufacturing
624229	Energy assistance programs
541690	Energy consulting services
334512	Energy cutoff controls, residential and commercial types, manufacturing
926110	Energy development and conservation agencies, nonoperating
926130	Energy development and conservation programs, government
541350	Energy efficiency inspection services
334515	Energy measuring equipment, electrical, manufacturing

926110 Energy program administration

331318 Energy wire or cable made in aluminum wire drawing plants

331420 Energy wire or cable, copper, made from purchased copper in wire drawing plants

331491 Energy wire or cable, nonferrous metals (except aluminum, copper), made from purchased nonferrous metals (except aluminum, copper) in wire drawing plants

924110 Enforcement of environmental and pollution control regulations

336310 Engine block assemblies, automotive and truck gasoline, manufacturing

325998 Engine degreasers manufacturing

336310 Engine intake and exhaust valves manufacturing

811310 Engine repair (except automotive, small engine)

811111 Engine repair and replacement shops, automotive

811411 Engine repair, small

325998 Engine starting fluids manufacturing

423120 Engine testing equipment, motor vehicle, merchant wholesalers

541330 Engineering consulting services

541330 Engineering design services

541715 Engineering research and development laboratories or services (except nanotechnology research and development)

541330 Engineering services

238320 Engineering structure (e.g., oil storage tank, water tower) painting

813920 Engineers' associations

423490 Engineers' equipment and supplies merchant wholesalers

541330 Engineers' offices

541330 Engineers' private practices

336412 Engines and engine parts, aircraft (except carburetors, pistons, piston rings, valves), manufacturing

336310 Engines and parts (except diesel), automotive and truck, manufacturing

423860 Engines and parts, aircraft, merchant wholesalers

423120 Engines and parts, automotive, new, merchant wholesalers

423860 Engines and turbines, marine, merchant wholesalers

333618 Engines, diesel and semidiesel, manufacturing

333618 Engines, diesel locomotive, manufacturing

423830 Engines, internal combustion (except

aircraft, automotive), merchant wholesalers

333618 Engines, internal combustion (except aircraft, nondiesel automotive), manufacturing

333618 Engines, natural gas, manufacturing

111219 English pea farming (except under cover), field, bedding plant and seed production

111419 English pea farming, grown under cover

332216 Engraver's handtools, nonpowered, manufacturing

339910 Engraving and etching precious metal flatware

339910 Engraving and etching precious metal jewelry

339910 Engraving and/or etching costume jewelry

423830 Engraving machinery merchant wholesalers

332812 Engraving metals and metal products (except printing plates) for the trade

323120 Engraving printing plate, for the printing trade

333316 Enlargers, photographic, manufacturing

315210 Ensemble dresses cut and sew apparel contractors

315190 Ensemble dresses made in apparel knitting mills

315240 Ensemble dresses, women's and girls', cut and sewn from purchased fabric (except apparel contractors)

711130 Ensembles, musical

926110 Enterprise development program administration

711410 Entertainers' agents or managers

711510 Entertainers, independent

519130 Entertainment sites, Internet

541715 Entomological research and development laboratories or services (except biotechnology and nanotechnology research and development)

115112 Entomological service, agricultural

541690 Entomology consulting services

333243 Envelope making machinery manufacturing

424110 Envelope paper, bulk, merchant wholesalers

333318 Envelope stuffing, sealing, and addressing machinery manufacturing

322230 Envelopes (i.e., mailing, stationery) made from any material

424120 Envelopes merchant wholesalers

813312 Environmental advocacy organizations

541620	Environmental consulting services
238210	Environmental control system installation
423830	Environmental controlling instruments and equipment merchant wholesalers
541330	Environmental engineering services
923120	Environmental health program administration
924110	Environmental protection program administration
541620	Environmental reclamation planning services
562910	Environmental remediation services
541715	Environmental research and development laboratories or services (except biotechnology and nanotechnology research and development)
541380	Environmental testing laboratories or services
325413	Enzyme and isoenzyme in-vitro diagnostic substances manufacturing
325199	Enzyme proteins (i.e., basic synthetic chemicals) (except pharmaceutical use) manufacturing
325411	Enzyme proteins (i.e., basic synthetic chemicals), pharmaceutical use, manufacturing
325130	Eosin dyes manufacturing
325411	Ephedrine and derivatives (i.e., basic chemicals) manufacturing
325211	Epichlorohydrin bisphenol manufacturing
325211	Epichlorohydrin diphenol manufacturing
325212	Epichlorohydrin elastomers manufacturing
325520	Epoxy adhesives manufacturing
238190	Epoxy application contractors
325510	Epoxy coatings made from purchased resins
325211	Epoxy resins manufacturing
923130	Equal employment opportunity offices
621340	Equestrian physical therapists' offices (e.g., centers, clinics)
115210	Equine boarding
522220	Equipment finance leasing
238910	Equipment rental (except crane), construction, with operator
531130	Equity real estate investment trusts (REITs), primarily leasing miniwarehouses and self-storage units
531120	Equity real estate investment trusts (REITs), primarily leasing nonresidential buildings (except miniwarehouses)

531190	Equity real estate investment trusts (REITs), primarily leasing real estate (except residential buildings and dwellings, nonresidential buildings, miniwarehouses, and self-storage units)
531110	Equity real estate investment trusts (REITs), primarily leasing residential buildings and dwellings
326299	Erasers, rubber or rubber and abrasive combined, manufacturing
238120	Erecting structural steel
238190	Erection and dismantling, poured concrete form
325411	Ergot alkaloids (i.e., basic chemicals) manufacturing
541330	Erosion control engineering services
238290	Escalator installation
333921	Escalators manufacturing
423830	Escalators merchant wholesalers
111219	Escarole farming (except under cover), field, bedding plant and seed production
111419	Escarole farming, grown under cover
812990	Escort services, social
523991	Escrow agencies (except real estate)
531390	Escrow agencies, real estate
325998	Essential oils manufacturing
424690	Essential oils merchant wholesalers
325199	Essential oils, synthetic, manufacturing
541990	Estate assessment (i.e., appraisal) services
541110	Estate law offices
325211	Ester gum manufacturing
325199	Esters, not specified elsewhere by process, manufacturing
812112	Esthetician (i.e., skin care) services
115310	Estimating timber
454110	E-tailers
333242	Etching equipment, semiconductor, manufacturing
332812	Etching metals and metal products (except printing plates) for the trade
325110	Ethane made from refined petroleum or liquid hydrocarbons
211130	Ethane recovered from oil and gas field gases
325193	Ethanol, nonpotable, manufacturing
813410	Ethnic associations
711510	Ethnic dancers, independent
711320	Ethnic festival managers without facilities

711320 Ethnic festival organizers without facilities

711310 Ethnic festival promoters with facilities

711320 Ethnic festival promoters without facilities

325194 Ethyl acetate, natural, manufacturing

325199 Ethyl acetate, synthetic, manufacturing

424820 Ethyl alcohol merchant wholesalers

325193 Ethyl alcohol, nonpotable, manufacturing

312140 Ethyl alcohol, potable, manufacturing

325199 Ethyl butyrate manufacturing

325199 Ethyl cellulose (except resins) manufacturing

325199 Ethyl chloride manufacturing

325199 Ethyl ether manufacturing

325199 Ethyl formate manufacturing

325199 Ethyl nitrite manufacturing

325199 Ethyl perhydrophenanthrene manufacturing

325110 Ethylbenzene made from refined petroleum or liquid hydrocarbons

325211 Ethylcellulose plastics manufacturing

325199 Ethylene glycol ether manufacturing

325199 Ethylene glycol manufacturing

325110 Ethylene made from refined petroleum or liquid hydrocarbons

324110 Ethylene made in petroleum refineries

325199 Ethylene oxide manufacturing

325212 Ethylene-propylene rubber manufacturing

325212 Ethylene-propylene-nonconjugated diene (EPDM) rubber manufacturing

325211 Ethylene-vinyl acetate resins manufacturing

325998 Eucalyptus oil manufacturing

311514 Evaporated milk manufacturing

334519 Evaporation meters manufacturing

333415 Evaporative condensers (i.e., heat transfer equipment) manufacturing

561920 Event and meeting planning services

611691 Exam preparation services

423810 Excavating machinery and equipment merchant wholesalers

213112 Excavating mud pits, slush pits, and cellars at oil and gas fields on a contract basis

238910 Excavating, earthmoving or land clearing, mining (except overburden removal at open pit mine sites or quarries)

238910 Excavating, earthmoving, or land clearing contractors

238910 Excavation contractors

333120 Excavators (e.g., power shovels) manufacturing

321999 Excelsior (e.g., pads, wrappers) manufacturing

423840 Excelsior (e.g., pads, wrappers) merchant wholesalers

523999 Exchange clearinghouses, commodities or securities

332410 Exchangers, heat, manufacturing

523210 Exchanges, commodity contracts

523210 Exchanges, securities

335312 Exciter assemblies, motor and generator, manufacturing

531210 Exclusive buyers' agencies

531210 Exclusive buyers' agents, offices of

487210 Excursion boat operation

921140 Executive and legislative office combinations

561110 Executive management services

921110 Executive offices, federal, state, and local (e.g., governor, mayor, president)

561312 Executive placement consulting services

561312 Executive placement services

561312 Executive search consulting services

561312 Executive search services

531120 Executive suites (i.e., full service office space provision)

811490 Exercise and athletic equipment repair and maintenance services without retailing new exercise and athletic equipment

713940 Exercise centers

532284 Exercise equipment rental

451110 Exercise equipment stores

339920 Exercise machines manufacturing

621340 Exercise physiologists' offices (e.g., centers, clinics)

336390 Exhaust and tail pipes, automotive, truck, and bus, manufacturing

333413 Exhaust fans, industrial and commercial-type, manufacturing

238220 Exhaust system (e.g., kitchens, industrial work areas) installation

811112 Exhaust system repair and replacement shops, automotive

336390 Exhaust systems and parts, automotive, truck, and bus, manufacturing

531120 Exhibition hall, no promotion of events, rental or leasing

624190 Ex-offender rehabilitation agencies

624190 Ex-offender self-help organizations

316110	Exotic leathers manufacturing
332312	Expansion joints, metal, manufacturing
541715	Experimental farms
213113	Exploration services for coal (except geophysical surveying and mapping) on a contract basis
213114	Exploration services for metal (except geophysical surveying and mapping) on a contract basis
213115	Exploration services for nonmetallic minerals (except geophysical surveying and mapping) on a contract basis
213112	Exploration services for oil and gas (except geophysical surveying and mapping) on a contract basis
424690	Explosives (except ammunition, fireworks) merchant wholesalers
325920	Explosives manufacturing
522293	Export trading companies (i.e., international trade financing)
522293	Export-Import banks
333316	Exposure meters, photographic, manufacturing
492110	Express delivery services (except establishments operating under a universal service obligation)
622310	Extended care hospitals (except mental, substance abuse)
335999	Extension cords made from purchased insulated wire
321999	Extension ladders, wood, manufacturing
321999	Extension planks, wood, manufacturing
238310	Exterior insulation finish system installation
321918	Exterior wood shutters manufacturing
325320	Exterminating chemical products (e.g., fungicides, insecticides, pesticides) manufacturing
561710	Exterminating services
423990	Extinguishers, fire, merchant wholesalers
333120	Extractors, piling, manufacturing
311920	Extracts, essences and preparations, coffee, manufacturing
311920	Extracts, essences and preparations, tea, manufacturing
311942	Extracts, food (except coffee, meat), manufacturing
311942	Extracts, malt, manufacturing
325194	Extracts, natural dyeing and tanning, manufacturing
326291	Extruded, molded or lathe-cut rubber goods manufacturing

333249	Extruding machinery for plastics and rubber manufacturing
333249	Extruding machinery for yarn manufacturing
333517	Extruding machines, metalworking, manufacturing
331318	Extrusion billet made by rolling purchased aluminum
331318	Extrusion billet, aluminum, made in integrated secondary smelting and rolling mills
333514	Extrusion dies for use with all materials manufacturing
331318	Extrusion ingot made by rolling purchased aluminum
331318	Extrusion ingot, aluminum, made in integrated secondary smelting and rolling mills
331313	Extrusion ingot, primary aluminum, manufacturing
325412	Eye and ear preparations manufacturing
621991	Eye banks
339112	Eye examining instruments and apparatus manufacturing
325620	Eye makeup (e.g., eye shadow, eyebrow pencil, mascara) manufacturing
622310	Eye, ear, nose, and throat hospitals
316998	Eyeglass cases, all materials, manufacturing
339115	Eyeglass frames (i.e., fronts and temples), ophthalmic, manufacturing
423460	Eyeglasses merchant wholesalers
315210	Eyelet making contractors on apparel
339993	Eyelets, metal, manufacturing
339115	Eyes, glass and plastics, manufacturing
313310	Fabric finishing
313310	Fabric mercerizing
451130	Fabric shops
325612	Fabric softeners manufacturing
424690	Fabric softeners merchant wholesalers
238310	Fabric wall system, noise insulating, installation
332312	Fabricated bar joists manufacturing
332996	Fabricated pipe and pipe fittings made from purchased pipe
332313	Fabricated plate work manufacturing
314994	Fabricated rope products (e.g., nets, slings) made in cordage or twine mills
332312	Fabricated structural metal manufacturing
321213	Fabricated structural wood members (except trusses) manufacturing

238390	Fabrication, metal cabinet or countertop, on site
313210	Fabrics (except rug, tire fabrics), broadwoven, weaving
314994	Fabrics for reinforcing rubber tires, industrial belting, and fuel cells manufacturing
313240	Fabrics, knit, made in warp or weft knit fabric mills
313240	Fabrics, lace, made in lace mills
313220	Fabrics, narrow woven, weaving
313230	Fabrics, nonwoven, manufacturing
424310	Fabrics, textile (except burlap, felt), merchant wholesalers
332618	Fabrics, woven wire, made from purchased wire
325620	Face creams (e.g., cleansing, moisturizing) manufacturing
335932	Face plates (i.e., outlet or switch covers) manufacturing
525990	Face-amount certificate funds
812112	Facial salons
424130	Facial tissue merchant wholesalers
322291	Facial tissues made from purchased paper
322121	Facial tissues made in paper mills
561210	Facilities (except computer operation) support services
541513	Facilities (i.e., clients' facilities) management and operation services, computer systems or data processing
541513	Facilities (i.e., clients' facilities) support services, computer systems or data processing
333517	Facing machines, metalworking, manufacturing
334210	Facsimile equipment, stand-alone, manufacturing
532420	Facsimile machine rental or leasing
811213	Facsimile machine repair and maintenance services
423690	Facsimile machines merchant wholesalers
325992	Facsimile toner cartridges manufacturing
522298	Factoring accounts receivable
236210	Factory construction
711310	Fair managers with facilities, agricultural
711320	Fair managers without facilities, agricultural
711310	Fair organizers with facilities, agricultural
711320	Fair organizers without facilities, agricultural
711310	Fair promoters with facilities

711310	Fair promoters with facilities, agricultural
711320	Fair promoters without facilities
711320	Fair promoters without facilities, agricultural
238190	Falsework construction
448140	Family clothing stores
621210	Family dentists' offices (e.g., centers, clinics)
713120	Family fun centers
541110	Family law offices
621111	Family physicians' offices (e.g., centers, clinics)
621410	Family planning centers
621410	Family planning counseling services
722511	Family restaurants, full service
722513	Family restaurants, limited-service
624190	Family social service agencies
624190	Family welfare services
326220	Fan belts, rubber or plastics, manufacturing
813410	Fan clubs
334512	Fan controls, temperature responsive, manufacturing
316110	Fancy leathers manufacturing
335210	Fans (except attic), household-type electric, manufacturing
336320	Fans, electric cooling, automotive, truck, and bus, manufacturing
335210	Fans, household-type kitchen, manufacturing
423620	Fans, household-type, merchant wholesalers
333413	Fans, industrial and commercial-type, manufacturing
423830	Fans, industrial, merchant wholesalers
423850	Fare boxes, public transit vehicle, merchant wholesalers
334514	Fare collection equipment manufacturing
311211	Farina (except breakfast food) made in flour mills
311230	Farina, breakfast cereal, manufacturing
236220	Farm building construction
332311	Farm buildings, prefabricated metal, manufacturing
321992	Farm buildings, prefabricated wood, manufacturing
237990	Farm drainage tile installation
532490	Farm equipment rental or leasing
813410	Farm granges

115115	Farm labor contractors
423820	Farm machinery and equipment merchant wholesalers
811310	Farm machinery and equipment repair and maintenance services
115116	Farm management services
522292	Farm mortgage lending
493130	Farm product warehousing and storage (except refrigerated)
493120	Farm product warehousing and storage, refrigerated
484220	Farm products hauling, local
484230	Farm products trucking, long-distance
332420	Farm storage tanks, heavy gauge metal, manufacturing
424910	Farm supplies merchant wholesalers
444220	Farm supply stores
532490	Farm tractor rental or leasing
333111	Farm tractors and attachments manufacturing
333111	Farm wagons manufacturing
813910	Farmers' associations
813910	Farmers' unions
******	Farming -- see type
531190	Farmland rental or leasing
333922	Farm-type conveyors manufacturing
115210	Farriers
112210	Farrow-to-finish operations
238170	Fascia and soffit installation
423330	Fascia, building (except wood), merchant wholesalers
541490	Fashion design services
541490	Fashion designer services
722513	Fast casual restaurants
423710	Fasteners (e.g., bolts, nuts, rivets, screws) merchant wholesalers
339993	Fasteners (e.g., glove, hook and eye, slide, snap) manufacturing
424310	Fasteners, clothing, merchant wholesalers
423610	Fastening devices, electrical, merchant wholesalers
722513	Fast-food restaurants
334511	Fathometers manufacturing
334519	Fatigue testing machines, industrial, mechanical, manufacturing
311611	Fats, animal (except poultry, small game), produced in slaughtering plants
311613	Fats, animal, rendering

112112	Fattening cattle
325199	Fatty acid esters and amines manufacturing
325199	Fatty acids (e.g., margaric, oleic, stearic) manufacturing
325199	Fatty alcohols manufacturing
327110	Faucet handles, vitreous china and earthenware, manufacturing
332913	Faucets, plumbing, manufacturing
532420	Fax machine rental or leasing
811213	Fax machine repair and maintenance services
339999	Feather dusters manufacturing
315210	Feather-filled clothing cut and sew apparel contractors
315240	Feather-filled clothing, jackets, and vests, women's, girls', and infants', cut and sewn from purchased fabric (except apparel contractors)
315220	Feather-filled clothing, men's and boys', cut and sewn from purchased fabric (except apparel contractors)
424590	Feathers merchant wholesalers
339999	Feathers, preparing (i.e., for use in apparel and textile products)
519110	Feature syndicates (i.e., advice columns, comic, news)
522294	Federal Agricultural Mortgage Corporation
926120	Federal Aviation Administration (except air traffic control)
922120	Federal Bureau of Investigation (FBI)
926130	Federal Communications Commission (FCC)
522130	Federal credit unions
522298	Federal Home Loan Banks (FHLB)
522294	Federal Home Loan Mortgage Corporation (FHLMC)
522294	Federal Intermediate Credit Bank
522292	Federal Land Banks
522294	Federal National Mortgage Association (FNMA)
922120	Federal police services
521110	Federal Reserve Banks or Branches
921130	Federal Reserve Board of Governors
522120	Federal savings and loan associations (S&L)
522120	Federal savings banks
813219	Federated charities
813930	Federation of workers, labor organizations
813930	Federations of labor

424910	Feed additives merchant wholesalers
316998	Feed bags for horses manufacturing
314910	Feed bags made from purchased woven or knitted materials
311119	Feed concentrates, animal, manufacturing
311514	Feed grade dry milk products manufacturing
311119	Feed premixes, animal, manufacturing
333111	Feed processing equipment, farm-type, manufacturing
444220	Feed stores (except pet)
453910	Feed stores, pet
311119	Feed supplements, animal (except cat, dog), manufacturing
311111	Feed supplements, dog and cat, manufacturing
112112	Feed yards (except stockyards for transportation), cattle
112111	Feeder calf production
112210	Feeder pig farming
335311	Feeder voltage regulators and boosters (i.e., electrical transformers) manufacturing
423820	Feeders, animal, merchant wholesalers
333131	Feeders, mineral beneficiating-type, manufacturing
112112	Feedlots (except stockyards for transportation), cattle
112210	Feedlots (except stockyards for transportation), hog
112410	Feedlots (except stockyards for transportation), lamb
424910	Feeds (except pet) merchant wholesalers
311111	Feeds, prepared for dog and cat, manufacturing
311119	Feeds, prepared, for animals (except cat, dog) manufacturing
311119	Feeds, specialty (e.g., guinea pig, mice, mink), manufacturing
212325	Feldspar mining and/or beneficiating
327992	Feldspar processing beyond beneficiation
424990	Felt merchant wholesalers
339940	Felt tip markers manufacturing
322121	Felts, asphalt, made in paper mills
313210	Felts, broadwoven, weaving
313230	Felts, nonwoven, manufacturing
331222	Fence gates, posts, and fittings, iron or steel, made in wire drawing plants
238990	Fence installation (except electronic containment fencing for pets)
331110	Fence posts, iron or steel, made in iron and steel mills
332323	Fences and gates (except wire), metal, manufacturing
423390	Fencing (except wood) merchant wholesalers
332618	Fencing and fence gates made from purchased wire
423390	Fencing and fencing accessories, wire, merchant wholesalers
238990	Fencing contractors (except electronic containment fencing for pets)
444190	Fencing dealers
339920	Fencing equipment (sporting goods) manufacturing
321999	Fencing, prefabricated sections, wood, manufacturing
321999	Fencing, wood (except rough pickets, poles, and rails), manufacturing
423310	Fencing, wood, merchant wholesalers
212299	Ferberite ores and concentrates mining and/or beneficiating
333249	Fermentation equipment, chemical, manufacturing
332420	Fermentation tanks, heavy gauge metal, manufacturing
424810	Fermented malt beverages merchant wholesalers
325180	Ferric chloride manufacturing
325180	Ferric oxide manufacturing
325130	Ferric oxide pigments manufacturing
333318	Ferris wheels manufacturing
212299	Ferroalloy ores (except vanadium) (e.g., chromium, columbium, molybdenum, tungsten) mining and/or beneficiating
331110	Ferroalloys manufacturing
423510	Ferroalloys merchant wholesalers
331110	Ferrochromium manufacturing
325180	Ferrocyanides manufacturing
331110	Ferromanganese manufacturing
331110	Ferromolybdenum manufacturing
331110	Ferrophosphorus manufacturing
331110	Ferrosilicon manufacturing
331110	Ferrotitanium manufacturing
331110	Ferrotungsten manufacturing
332111	Ferrous forgings made from purchased iron or steel, unfinished
331221	Ferrous metal powder, paste, and flake made from purchased iron or steel

423510	Ferrous metals merchant wholesalers
331110	Ferrovanadium manufacturing
483114	Ferry passenger transportation, Great Lakes (including St. Lawrence Seaway)
336611	Ferryboat building
621410	Fertility clinics
424910	Fertilizer and fertilizer materials merchant wholesalers
115112	Fertilizer application for crops
212393	Fertilizer minerals, natural, mining and/or beneficiating
325314	Fertilizers, mixed, made in plants not manufacturing fertilizer materials
325311	Fertilizers, mixed, made in plants producing nitrogenous fertilizer materials
325312	Fertilizers, mixed, made in plants producing phosphatic fertilizer materials
325311	Fertilizers, natural organic (except compost), manufacturing
325311	Fertilizers, of animal waste origin, manufacturing
325311	Fertilizers, of sewage origin, manufacturing
561730	Fertilizing lawns
333111	Fertilizing machinery, farm-type, manufacturing
111998	Fescue seed farming
711310	Festival managers with facilities
711320	Festival managers without facilities
711310	Festival of arts managers with facilities
711320	Festival of arts managers without facilities
711310	Festival of arts organizers with facilities
711320	Festival of arts organizers without facilities
711310	Festival of arts promoters with facilities
711320	Festival of arts promoters without facilities
711310	Festival organizers with facilities
711320	Festival organizers without facilities
711310	Festival promoters with facilities
711320	Festival promoters without facilities
325412	Fever remedy preparations manufacturing
522294	FHLMC (Federal Home Loan Mortgage Corporation)
322219	Fiber cans and drums (i.e., all-fiber, nonfiber ends of any material) made from purchased paperboard
424130	Fiber cans and drums merchant wholesalers
322219	Fiber drums made from purchased paperboard
337125	Fiber furniture (except upholstered), household-type, manufacturing
238210	Fiber optic cable (except transmission lines) installation
335921	Fiber optic cable made from purchased fiber optic strand
237130	Fiber optic cable transmission line construction
334417	Fiber optic connectors manufacturing
322219	Fiber spools, reels, blocks made from purchased paperboard
322219	Fiber tubes made from purchased paperboard
314999	Fiber, textile recovery from textile mill waste and rags
321219	Fiberboard manufacturing
423310	Fiberboard merchant wholesalers
423390	Fiberglass building materials (except insulation, roofing, siding) merchant wholesalers
424310	Fiberglass fabrics merchant wholesalers
313210	Fiberglass fabrics weaving
327993	Fiberglass insulation products manufacturing
313220	Fiberglasses, narrow woven, weaving
325220	Fibers and filaments, cellulosic, manufacturing and texturizing
325220	Fibers and filaments, noncellulosic, manufacturing and texturizing
335991	Fibers, carbon and graphite, manufacturing
327212	Fibers, glass, textile, made in glass making plants
424690	Fibers, manmade, merchant wholesalers
424590	Fibers, vegetable, merchant wholesalers
511130	Fiction book publishers (except exclusive Internet publishing)
511130	Fiction book publishers and printing combined
519130	Fiction book publishers, exclusively on Internet
323120	Fiction bookbinding without printing
323117	Fiction books printing and binding without publishing
323117	Fiction books printing without publishing
524126	Fidelity insurance carriers, direct
531390	Fiduciaries', real estate, offices
523991	Fiduciary agencies (except real estate)
332994	Field artillery manufacturing
315210	Field jackets, military, cut and sew apparel contractors

315220	Field jackets, military, men's and boys', cut and sewn from purchased fabric (except apparel contractors)
111421	Field nurseries (i.e., growing of flowers and shrubbery)
238140	Field stone (i.e., masonry) installation
334515	Field strength and intensity measuring equipment, electrical, manufacturing
336211	Fifth-wheel assemblies manufacturing
111339	Fig farming
711219	Figure skaters, independent
335110	Filaments for electric lamp bulbs manufacturing
111335	Filbert farming
115114	Filbert hulling and shelling
424120	File cards and folders merchant wholesalers
322230	File folders (e.g., accordion, expanding, hanging, manila) made from purchased paper and paperboard
333515	Files (i.e., a machine tool accessory) manufacturing
332216	Files, handheld, manufacturing
337214	Filing cabinets (except wood), office-type, manufacturing
337211	Filing cabinets, wood, office-type, manufacturing
333517	Filing machines, metalworking, manufacturing
212399	Fill dirt pits mining and/or beneficiating
424120	Filler paper, looseleaf, merchant wholesalers
325510	Fillers, wood (e.g., dry, liquid, paste), manufacturing
314999	Filling (except nonwoven textile), upholstery, manufacturing
311999	Fillings, cake or pie (except fruits, meat, vegetables), manufacturing
711510	Film actors, independent
519120	Film archives
541380	Film badge testing (i.e., radiation testing) laboratories or services
812921	Film developing and printing (except motion picture, one-hour)
812922	Film developing and printing, one-hour
333316	Film developing equipment manufacturing
423410	Film developing equipment merchant wholesalers
512120	Film distribution agencies
512120	Film distribution, motion picture and video
512131	Film festivals exhibitors
423410	Film finishing equipment merchant wholesalers
512120	Film libraries, commercial distribution
512199	Film libraries, motion picture or video, stock footage
512191	Film or tape closed captioning
512191	Film or video transfer services
512199	Film processing laboratories, motion picture
711510	Film producers, independent
512199	Film restoration services
512110	Film studios producing films
423410	Film, camera, merchant wholesalers
423410	Film, photographic, merchant wholesalers
326113	Film, plastics (except packaging), manufacturing
326112	Film, plastics, packaging, manufacturing
325992	Film, sensitized (e.g., camera, motion picture, X-ray), manufacturing
512110	Films, motion picture production
512110	Films, motion picture production and distribution
424130	Filter papers merchant wholesalers
327110	Filtering media, pottery, manufacturing
336390	Filters (e.g., air, engine oil, fuel) automotive, truck, and bus, manufacturing
333413	Filters, air-conditioner, manufacturing
334419	Filters, electronic component-type, manufacturing
333413	Filters, furnace, manufacturing
333999	Filters, industrial and general purpose-type (except internal combustion engine, warm air furnace), manufacturing
322299	Filters, paper, made from purchased paper
221310	Filtration plant, water
212322	Filtration sand quarrying and/or beneficiating
332993	Fin assemblies, mortar, manufacturing
332993	Fin assemblies, torpedo and bomb, manufacturing
522291	Finance companies (i.e., unsecured cash loans)
523140	Financial futures brokerages
551112	Financial holding companies
523930	Financial investment advice services, customized, fees paid by client

511120	Financial magazine and periodical publishers (except exclusive Internet publishing)
511120	Financial magazine and periodical publishers and printing combined
519130	Financial magazine and periodical publishers, exclusively on Internet
323111	Financial magazines and periodicals commercial printing (except screen) without publishing
323113	Financial magazines and periodicals screen printing without publishing
541611	Financial management consulting (except investment advice) services
523930	Financial planning services, customized, fees paid by client
522320	Financial transactions processing (except central bank)
521110	Financial transactions processing of the central bank
522220	Financing, sales
522294	Financing, secondary market
316998	Findings, boot and shoe, manufacturing
339910	Findings, jeweler's, manufacturing
315210	Findings, suit and coat (e.g., coat fronts, pockets), cut and sew apparel contractors
315990	Findings, suit and coat (e.g., coat fronts, pockets), cut and sewn from purchased fabric (except apparel contractors)
712110	Fine arts museums
611610	Fine arts schools (except academic)
722511	Fine dining restaurants, full service
424110	Fine paper, bulk, merchant wholesalers
114111	Finfish fishing (e.g., flounder, salmon, trout)
112511	Finfish production, farm raising
112511	Finfish, hatcheries
321213	Finger joint lumber manufacturing
561611	Fingerprint services
238350	Finish carpentry
314110	Finishing (e.g., dyeing) rugs and carpets
325613	Finishing agents, textile and leather, manufacturing
238310	Finishing drywall contractors
316110	Finishing hides and skins on a contract basis
316110	Finishing leather
333249	Finishing machinery for textile manufacturing
611110	Finishing schools, secondary

561621	Fire alarm monitoring services
561621	Fire alarm sales combined with installation, repair, or monitoring services
238210	Fire alarm system, electric, installation only
236220	Fire and flood restoration of commercial and institutional buildings
236118	Fire and flood restoration, multifamily building, general contractors
236118	Fire and flood restoration, single-family housing, general contractors
922160	Fire and rescue service
212325	Fire clay mining and/or beneficiating
922160	Fire departments (e.g., government, volunteer (except private))
334290	Fire detection and alarm systems manufacturing
334519	Fire detector systems, nonelectric, manufacturing
332321	Fire doors, metal, manufacturing
238190	Fire escape installation
332323	Fire escapes, metal, manufacturing
325998	Fire extinguisher chemical preparations manufacturing
238220	Fire extinguisher installation
238220	Fire extinguisher installation and repair
424690	Fire extinguisher preparations merchant wholesalers
811310	Fire extinguisher repair and maintenance, without installation
423990	Fire extinguisher sales combined with rental and/or service, merchant wholesalers
541990	Fire extinguisher testing and/or inspection, without sales, service, or installation
423990	Fire extinguishers merchant wholesalers
339999	Fire extinguishers, portable, manufacturing
611519	Fire fighter training schools
314999	Fire hose, textile, made from purchased materials
237110	Fire hydrant installation
332911	Fire hydrant valves manufacturing
423840	Fire hydrants merchant wholesalers
332911	Fire hydrants, complete, manufacturing
524126	Fire insurance carriers, direct
541380	Fire insurance underwriters' laboratories
524291	Fire investigators
922160	Fire marshals' offices
922160	Fire prevention offices, government

115310	Fire prevention, forest
325998	Fire retardant chemical preparations manufacturing
238220	Fire sprinkler system installation
236220	Fire station construction
423990	Firearms (except sporting) merchant wholesalers
813319	Firearms advocacy organizations
611699	Firearms training
332994	Firearms, small, manufacturing
423910	Firearms, sporting, merchant wholesalers
336611	Fireboat building
327120	Firebrick, clay refractories, manufacturing
315210	Firefighters' dress uniforms cut and sew apparel contractors
315220	Firefighters' dress uniforms, men's, cut and sewn from purchased fabric (except apparel contractors)
315240	Firefighters' dress uniforms, women's, cut and sewn from purchased fabric (except apparel contractors)
922160	Firefighting (except forest), government and volunteer (except private)
423850	Firefighting equipment and supplies merchant wholesalers
922160	Firefighting services (except forest and private)
561990	Firefighting services as a commercial activity
339113	Firefighting suits and accessories manufacturing
115310	Firefighting, forest
332999	Fireplace fixtures and equipment manufacturing
333414	Fireplace inserts (i.e., heat directing) manufacturing
423320	Fireplace linings merchant wholesalers
335129	Fireplace logs, electric, manufacturing
238140	Fireplace, masonry, installation
238220	Fireplace, natural gas, installation
423720	Fireplaces, gas, merchant wholesalers
423220	Fireplaces, prefabricated (except gas), merchant wholesalers
423720	Fireplaces, prefabricated gas, merchant wholesalers
238310	Fireproof flooring installation
238310	Fireproofing buildings
238310	Firestop contractors
321999	Firewood and fuel wood containing fuel binder manufacturing
454310	Firewood dealers, direct selling
423990	Firewood merchant wholesalers
713990	Fireworks display services
325998	Fireworks manufacturing
423920	Fireworks merchant wholesalers
453998	Fireworks shops (i.e., permanent location)
327110	Firing china for the trade
321920	Firkins and kits, wood, coopered, manufacturing
611699	First-aid instruction
424210	First-aid kits (except industrial) merchant wholesalers
423450	First-aid kits, industrial, merchant wholesalers
424210	First-aid supplies merchant wholesalers
339113	First-aid, snake bite, or burn kits manufacturing
424460	Fish (except canned, packaged frozen) merchant wholesalers
924120	Fish and game agencies
311710	Fish and marine animal oils processing
924120	Fish and wildlife conservation program administration
311710	Fish egg bait canning
112511	Fish farms, finfish
112512	Fish farms, shellfish
334511	Fish finders (i.e., sonar) manufacturing
311119	Fish food for feeding fish manufacturing
311710	Fish freezing (e.g., blocks, fillets, ready-to-serve products)
325411	Fish liver oils, medicinal, uncompounded, manufacturing
311710	Fish manufacturing
445220	Fish markets
311710	Fish meal processing
236210	Fish processing plant construction
332216	Fish wire (i.e., electrical wiring tool) manufacturing
424490	Fish, canned, merchant wholesalers
311710	Fish, curing, drying, pickling, salting, and smoking
424420	Fish, packaged frozen, merchant wholesalers
424460	Fish, salted or preserved (except canned), merchant wholesalers
424990	Fish, tropical, merchant wholesalers
541715	Fisheries research and development laboratories or services
114111	Fisheries, finfish

114112	Fisheries, shellfish
487210	Fishing boat charter operation
336611	Fishing boat, commercial, building
721214	Fishing camps with accommodation facilities
713990	Fishing clubs, recreational
423910	Fishing equipment and supplies (except commercial) merchant wholesalers
213112	Fishing for tools at oil and gas fields on a contract basis
713990	Fishing guide services
332215	Fishing knives manufacturing
314999	Fishing nets made from purchased materials
713990	Fishing piers
114210	Fishing preserves
451110	Fishing supply stores (e.g., bait)
339920	Fishing tackle and equipment (except lines, nets, seines) manufacturing
713940	Fitness centers
423910	Fitness equipment and supplies merchant wholesalers
713940	Fitness salons
713940	Fitness spas without accommodations
326122	Fittings and unions, rigid plastics pipe, manufacturing
423720	Fittings and valves, plumbers', merchant wholesalers
423610	Fittings, electrical, merchant wholesalers
423840	Fittings, industrial, merchant wholesalers
326122	Fittings, rigid plastics pipe, manufacturing
331511	Fittings, soil and pressure pipe, cast iron, manufacturing
713950	Five pin bowling centers
445299	Fix-and-freeze meal stores
488119	Fixed base operators
722515	Fixed location refreshment stands
325992	Fixers, prepared photographic, manufacturing
337920	Fixtures (e.g., poles, rods, rollers), curtain and drapery, manufacturing
423610	Fixtures, electric lighting, merchant wholesalers
423740	Fixtures, refrigerated, merchant wholesalers
423440	Fixtures, store (except refrigerated), merchant wholesalers
337215	Fixtures, store display, manufacturing
453998	Flag and banner shops
561990	Flagging (i.e., traffic control) services
238990	Flagpole installation
332323	Flagpoles, metal, manufacturing
321999	Flagpoles, wood, manufacturing
314999	Flags, textile (e.g., banners, bunting, emblems, pennants), made from purchased fabrics
212311	Flagstone mining or quarrying
327991	Flagstones cutting
321219	Flakeboard manufacturing
331221	Flakes made from purchased iron or steel
331314	Flakes, aluminum, made from purchased aluminum
331110	Flakes, iron or steel, made in iron and steel mills
334516	Flame photometers manufacturing
812332	Flame resistant clothing supply services
334512	Flame safety controls for furnaces and boilers manufacturing
332994	Flame throwers manufacturing
333517	Flange facing machines, metalworking, manufacturing
332991	Flange units, ball or roller bearing, manufacturing
332919	Flanges and flange unions, pipe, metal, manufacturing
315210	Flannel shirts cut and sew apparel contractors
315220	Flannel shirts, men's and boys', cut and sewn from purchased fabric (except apparel contractors)
315240	Flannel shirts, women's, girls', and infants', cut and sewn from purchased fabric (except apparel contractors)
313210	Flannels, broadwoven, weaving
325998	Flares manufacturing
333316	Flash apparatus, photographic, manufacturing
335110	Flash bulbs, photographic, manufacturing
238170	Flashing contractors
335912	Flashlight batteries, disposable, manufacturing
335110	Flashlight bulb manufacturing
335129	Flashlights manufacturing
423610	Flashlights merchant wholesalers
313240	Flat (i.e., warp) fabrics knitting
331221	Flat bright steel strip made in cold rolling mills made from purchased steel
327211	Flat glass (e.g., float, plate) manufacturing

423390	Flat glass merchant wholesalers
334118	Flat panel displays (i.e., complete units), computer peripheral equipment, manufacturing
332613	Flat springs (except clock, watch), light gauge, made from purchased wire or strip, manufacturing
332613	Flat springs, heavy gauge metal, manufacturing
336212	Flatbed trailers, commercial, manufacturing
484220	Flatbed trucking, local
484230	Flatbed trucking, long-distance
331110	Flats, iron or steel, made in iron and steel mills
321920	Flats, wood, greenhouse, manufacturing
423220	Flatware (except plated, precious) merchant wholesalers
332215	Flatware, nonprecious and precious plated metal, manufacturing
423940	Flatware, precious and plated, merchant wholesalers
311942	Flavor extracts (except coffee) manufacturing
311511	Flavored milk drinks manufacturing
312111	Flavored water manufacturing
311930	Flavoring concentrates (except coffee based) manufacturing
424490	Flavoring extracts (except for fountain use) merchant wholesalers
325199	Flavoring materials (i.e., basic synthetic chemicals such as coumarin) manufacturing
311930	Flavoring pastes, powders, and syrups for soft drink manufacturing
313110	Flax spun yarns made from purchased fiber
111120	Flaxseed farming, field and seed production
311225	Flaxseed oil made from purchased oils
311224	Flaxseed oil made in crushing mills
531190	Flea market space (except under roof) rental or leasing
531120	Flea market space, under roof, rental or leasing
454390	Flea markets, temporary location, direct selling
453310	Flea markets, used merchandise, permanent
325320	Flea powders or sprays manufacturing
532112	Fleet leasing, passenger vehicle
316110	Fleshers, leather (i.e., flesh side of split leather), manufacturing
334112	Flexible (i.e., floppy) magnetic disk drives manufacturing
332999	Flexible metal hose and tubing manufacturing
322220	Flexible packaging sheet materials made by coating or laminating purchased paper
322220	Flexible packaging sheet materials made by laminating purchased foil
326112	Flexible packaging, plastics film, manufacturing
334412	Flexible wiring boards, bare, manufacturing
325910	Flexographic inks manufacturing
323120	Flexographic plate preparation services
323111	Flexographic printing (except books, grey goods)
333244	Flexographic printing presses manufacturing
339920	Flies, artificial fishing, manufacturing
334511	Flight and navigation sensors, transmitters, and displays manufacturing
611519	Flight attendant schools
334511	Flight recorders (i.e., black boxes) manufacturing
333318	Flight simulation machinery manufacturing
611512	Flight simulation training
611512	Flight training schools
212325	Flint clay mining and/or beneficiating
327992	Flint processing beyond beneficiation
339999	Flints, lighter, manufacturing
321113	Flitches (i.e., veneer stock) made in sawmills
334512	Float controls, residential and commercial types, manufacturing
561990	Float decorating services
541490	Float design services
327120	Floaters, glasshouse, clay, manufacturing
713210	Floating casinos (i.e., gambling cruises, riverboat casinos)
332313	Floating covers, fabricated metal plate work, manufacturing
311710	Floating factory ships, seafood processing
332812	Flocking metals and metal products for the trade
237990	Flood control project construction
332312	Flood gates, metal plate, manufacturing
335129	Floodlights (i.e., lighting fixtures) manufacturing
237990	Floodway canal and ditch construction

321918	Floor baseboards, wood, manufacturing
442210	Floor covering stores (except wood or ceramic tile only)
444190	Floor covering stores, wood or ceramic tile only
423220	Floor coverings merchant wholesalers
326199	Floor coverings, linoleum, manufacturing
326199	Floor coverings, resilient, manufacturing
326199	Floor coverings, rubber, manufacturing
326199	Floor coverings, vinyl, manufacturing
332312	Floor jacks, metal, manufacturing
335121	Floor lamps (i.e., lighting fixtures), residential, manufacturing
238330	Floor laying, scraping, finishing and refinishing
423850	Floor maintenance equipment merchant wholesalers
326299	Floor mats (e.g., bath, door), rubber, manufacturing
325612	Floor polishes and waxes manufacturing
332312	Floor posts, adjustable metal, manufacturing
532490	Floor sanding machine rental or leasing
333318	Floor sanding, washing, and polishing machines, commercial-type, manufacturing
335210	Floor scrubbing and shampooing machines, household-type electric, manufacturing
335210	Floor standing fans, household-type electric, manufacturing
238330	Floor tile and sheets, installation only
327120	Floor tile, ceramic, manufacturing
321214	Floor trusses, wood, manufacturing
335210	Floor waxers and polishers, household-type electric, manufacturing
532490	Floor waxing equipment rental or leasing
332323	Flooring, open steel (i.e., grating), manufacturing
332322	Flooring, sheet metal (except stampings), manufacturing
321114	Flooring, wood block, treating
321918	Flooring, wood, manufacturing
423310	Flooring, wood, merchant wholesalers
334112	Floppy disk drives manufacturing
561422	Floral wire services (i.e., telemarketing services)
453110	Florists
327110	Florists' articles, red earthenware, manufacturing
424930	Florist's supplies merchant wholesalers
333131	Flotation machinery, mining-type, manufacturing
114111	Flounder fishing
314910	Flour bags made from purchased woven or knitted materials
424490	Flour merchant wholesalers
333241	Flour milling machinery manufacturing
311230	Flour mills, breakfast cereal, manufacturing
311211	Flour mills, cereals grains (except breakfast cereals, rice)
311211	Flour mixes made in flour mills
311824	Flour, blended or self-rising, made from purchased flour
311211	Flour, blended, prepared, or self-rising (except rice), made in flour mills
311213	Flour, malt, manufacturing
311212	Flour, rice, manufacturing
321999	Flour, wood, manufacturing
335314	Flow actuated electrical switches manufacturing
334513	Flow instruments, industrial process-type, manufacturing
327420	Flower boxes, plaster of paris, manufacturing
111421	Flower bulb growing
424910	Flower bulbs merchant wholesalers
111422	Flower growing
327110	Flower pots, red earthenware, manufacturing
111422	Flower seed production
453998	Flower shops, artificial or dried
453110	Flower shops, fresh
561920	Flower show managers
561920	Flower show organizers
561920	Flower show promoters
424930	Flowers merchant wholesalers
339999	Flowers, artificial (except glass, plastics), manufacturing
327120	Flue lining, clay, manufacturing
423320	Flue pipe and linings merchant wholesalers
332322	Flues, stove and furnace, sheet metal (except stampings), manufacturing
423830	Fluid meters, industrial, merchant wholesalers
332439	Fluid milk shipping containers, light gauge metal, manufacturing
311511	Fluid milk substitutes processing

333995	Fluid power actuators manufacturing
332912	Fluid power aircraft subassemblies manufacturing
333995	Fluid power cylinders manufacturing
332912	Fluid power hose assemblies manufacturing
333996	Fluid power motors manufacturing
333996	Fluid power pumps manufacturing
423830	Fluid power transmission equipment merchant wholesalers
332912	Fluid power valves and hose fittings manufacturing
334513	Fluidic devices, circuits, and systems for process control, manufacturing
332313	Flumes, fabricated metal plate work, manufacturing
332322	Flumes, sheet metal (except stampings), manufacturing
325180	Fluoboric acid manufacturing
335311	Fluorescent ballasts (i.e., transformers) manufacturing
325130	Fluorescent dyes manufacturing
335110	Fluorescent lamp electrodes, cold cathode, manufacturing
335110	Fluorescent lamp tubes, electric, manufacturing
335122	Fluorescent lighting fixtures, commercial, institutional, and industrial electric, manufacturing
335121	Fluorescent lighting fixtures, residential, manufacturing
335311	Fluorescent lighting transformers manufacturing
325120	Fluorinated hydrocarbon gases manufacturing
325180	Fluorine manufacturing
212393	Fluorite mining and/or beneficiating
325212	Fluoro rubbers manufacturing
325212	Fluorocarbon derivative rubbers manufacturing
325220	Fluorocarbon fibers and filaments manufacturing
325120	Fluorocarbon gases manufacturing
325211	Fluorohydrocarbon resins manufacturing
325211	Fluoro-polymer resins manufacturing
334517	Fluoroscopes manufacturing
334517	Fluoroscopic X-ray apparatus and tubes manufacturing
212393	Fluorspar mining and/or beneficiating

332999	Flush tanks, metal, manufacturing
332913	Flush valves, plumbing, manufacturing
332911	Flushing hydrant manufacturing
339992	Flutes and parts manufacturing
325998	Fluxes (e.g., brazing, galvanizing, soldering, welding) manufacturing
325320	Fly sprays manufacturing
339999	Fly swatters manufacturing
541870	Flyer direct distribution (except direct mail) services
713990	Flying clubs, recreational
488119	Flying field operators
611512	Flying instruction
335129	Flytraps, electrical, manufacturing
336310	Flywheels and ring gears, automotive and truck gasoline engine, manufacturing
515112	FM radio stations
522294	FNMA (Federal National Mortgage Association)
238310	Foam insulation installation
424130	Foam plastic trays merchant wholesalers
326150	Foam plastics products (except polystrene) manufacturing
326140	Foam polystyrene products manufacturing
424990	Foam rubber merchant wholesalers
424610	Foam, plastics, resins and shapes, merchant wholesalers
322220	Foil bags made from purchased foil
332999	Foil containers (except bags) manufacturing
332999	Foil not made in rolling mills
322220	Foil sheet, laminating purchased foil sheets for packaging applications
331315	Foil, aluminum, made by flat rolling purchased aluminum
331315	Foil, aluminum, made in integrated secondary smelting and flat rolling mills
331420	Foil, copper, made from purchased metal or scrap
331491	Foil, gold, made by rolling purchased metals or scrap
331491	Foil, nickel, made by rolling purchased metals or scrap
331491	Foil, silver, made by rolling purchased metals or scrap
424120	Folders, file, merchant wholesalers
561910	Folding and packaging services, textile and apparel

322130	Folding boxboard stock manufacturing
322212	Folding boxes (except corrugated) made from purchased paperboard
322212	Folding paper and paperboard containers (except corrugated) made from purchased paperboard
111422	Foliage growing
711120	Folk dance companies
711510	Folk dancers, independent
423430	Font cartridges merchant wholesalers
445110	Food (i.e., groceries) stores
446191	Food (i.e., health) supplement stores
336999	Food (vendor) carts on wheels manufacturing
424690	Food additives, chemical, merchant wholesalers
624210	Food banks
722330	Food carts, mobile
333241	Food choppers, grinders, mixers, and slicers (i.e., food manufacturing-type) manufacturing
311942	Food coloring, natural, manufacturing
325130	Food coloring, synthetic, manufacturing
722310	Food concession contractors (e.g., convention facilities, entertainment facilities, sporting facilities)
722330	Food concession stands, mobile
322299	Food containers made from molded pulp
326140	Food containers, polystyrene foam, manufacturing
322219	Food containers, sanitary (except folding), made from purchased paper or paperboard
322212	Food containers, sanitary, folding, made from purchased paperboard
333241	Food dehydrating equipment (except household-type) manufacturing
923130	Food distribution program administration, government
311942	Food extracts (except coffee, meat) manufacturing
926140	Food inspection agencies
811310	Food machinery repair and maintenance services
335210	Food mixers, household-type electric, manufacturing
333993	Food packaging machinery manufacturing
327213	Food packaging, glass, manufacturing
624210	Food pantries
423830	Food processing machinery and equipment merchant wholesalers

236210	Food processing plant construction
333241	Food product machinery manufacturing
541715	Food research and development laboratories or services (except biotechnology and nanotechnology research and development)
722310	Food service contractors, airline
722310	Food service contractors, cafeteria
722310	Food service contractors, concession operators (e.g., convention facilities, entertainment facilities, sporting facilities)
722310	Food service contractors, industrial
722310	Food service contractors, institutional
423440	Food service equipment (except refrigerated), commercial, merchant wholesalers
923120	Food service health inspections
326111	Food storage bags, plastics film, single wall or multiwall, manufacturing
541380	Food testing laboratories or services
322299	Food trays, molded pulp, manufacturing
333318	Food warming equipment, commercial-type, manufacturing
335220	Food waste disposal units, household-type, manufacturing
424410	Food, general-line, merchant wholesalers
311991	Food, prepared, perishable, packaged for individual resale
424420	Foods, prepared, packaged frozen, merchant wholesalers
339113	Foot appliances, orthopedic, manufacturing
621391	Foot specialists' (podiatry) offices (e.g., centers, clinics)
711211	Football clubs, professional or semiprofessional
713990	Football clubs, recreational
339920	Football equipment and supplies (except footwear, uniforms) manufacturing
423910	Football equipment and supplies merchant wholesalers
611620	Football instruction, camps, or schools
711211	Football teams, professional or semiprofessional
316210	Footholds, plastics or plastics soled fabric upper, manufacturing
316210	Footholds, rubber or rubber soled fabric upper, manufacturing
315110	Footies, sheer, knitting or knitting and finishing
238110	Footing and foundation concrete contractors

451110	Footwear (e.g., bowling, golf, spiked), specialty sports, stores
333249	Footwear making or repairing machinery manufacturing
424340	Footwear merchant wholesalers
326199	Footwear parts (e.g., heels, soles), plastics, manufacturing
326299	Footwear parts (e.g., heels, soles, soling strips), rubber, manufacturing
316210	Footwear, athletic, manufacturing
316210	Footwear, children's (except orthopedic extension), manufacturing
316210	Footwear, children's, leather or vinyl upper with rubber or plastics soles, manufacturing
316210	Footwear, men's (except orthopedic extension), manufacturing
316210	Footwear, men's leather or vinyl upper with rubber or plastics soles, manufacturing
316210	Footwear, plastics or plastics soled fabric uppers, manufacturing
316210	Footwear, women's (except orthopedic extension), manufacturing
316210	Footwear, women's leather or vinyl upper with rubber or plastics soles, manufacturing
339112	Forceps, surgical, manufacturing
523140	Foreign currency exchange brokering services
523130	Foreign currency exchange dealing (i.e., acting as a principal in dealing commodities to investors)
523130	Foreign currency exchange services (i.e., selling to the public)
928120	Foreign economic and social development services, government
928120	Foreign government service
611630	Foreign language schools
928120	Foreign missions
541380	Forensic (except medical) laboratories or services
621511	Forensic laboratories, medical
621111	Forensic pathologists' offices
531190	Forest land rental or leasing
115310	Forest management plans preparation
113210	Forest nurseries for reforestation, growing trees
423990	Forest products (except lumber) merchant wholesalers
484230	Forest products trucking, long-distance
115310	Forest thinning
423810	Forestry machinery and equipment merchant wholesalers
532412	Forestry machinery and equipment rental or leasing
811310	Forestry machinery and equipment repair and maintenance services
541715	Forestry research and development laboratories or services
115310	Forestry services
333517	Forging machinery and hammers manufacturing
332111	Forgings made from purchased iron or steel, unfinished
331110	Forgings, iron or steel, made in iron and steel mills
423510	Forgings, metal, merchant wholesalers
811310	Forklift repair and maintenance services
423830	Forklift trucks (except log) merchant wholesalers
333924	Forklifts manufacturing
332216	Forks, handtools (e.g., garden, hay, manure), manufacturing
332215	Forks, table, nonprecious and precious plated metal, manufacturing
331222	Form ties made in wire drawing plants
315210	Formal jackets cut and sew apparel contractors
315220	Formal jackets, men's and boys', cut and sewn from purchased fabric (except apparel contractors)
532281	Formal wear rental
325199	Formaldehyde manufacturing
325199	Formalin manufacturing
325199	Formic acid manufacturing
238190	Forming contractor
333517	Forming machines (except drawing), metalworking, manufacturing
327110	Forms for dipped rubber products, pottery, manufacturing
238190	Forms for poured concrete, erecting and dismantling
423420	Forms handling machines merchant wholesalers
332322	Forms, concrete, sheet metal (except stampings), manufacturing
321999	Forms, display, boot and shoe, all materials, manufacturing
424120	Forms, paper (e.g., business, office, sales), merchant wholesalers
236220	For-sale builders (i.e., building on own land, for sale), commercial and institutional building

236210	For-sale builders (i.e., building on own land, for sale), industrial building (except warehouses)
236117	For-sale builders (i.e., building on own land, for sale), residential
236117	For-sale builders (i.e., building on own land, for sale), single-family housing
312130	Fortified wines manufacturing
812990	Fortune-telling services
624110	Foster care placement agencies
624110	Foster home placement services
238140	Foundation (e.g., brick, block, stone), building, contractors
238390	Foundation dampproofing (including installing rigid foam insulation)
238910	Foundation digging (i.e., excavation)
238910	Foundation drilling contractors
315210	Foundation garments cut and sew apparel contractors
315240	Foundation garments, women's and girls', cut and sewn from purchased fabric (except apparel contractors)
238110	Foundation, building, poured concrete, contractors
238130	Foundation, building, wood, contractors
325620	Foundations (i.e., makeup) manufacturing
331529	Foundries (except die-casting), nonferrous metals (except aluminum)
331524	Foundries, aluminum (except die-casting)
331523	Foundries, die-casting, aluminum
331523	Foundries, die-casting, nonferrous metals
331511	Foundries, iron (i.e., ductile, gray, malleable, semisteel)
331513	Foundries, steel (except investment)
331512	Foundries, steel investment
333511	Foundry casting molds manufacturing
236210	Foundry construction
325998	Foundry core oil, wash, and wax manufacturing
332999	Foundry cores manufacturing
423830	Foundry machinery and equipment merchant wholesalers
811310	Foundry machinery and equipment repair and maintenance services
332999	Foundry pattern making
423510	Foundry products merchant wholesalers
212322	Foundry sand quarrying and/or beneficiating
424450	Fountain fruits and syrups (except soft drink) merchant wholesalers
335129	Fountain lighting fixtures manufacturing
339940	Fountain pens manufacturing
424450	Fountain syrups (except soft drink) merchant wholesalers
332999	Fountains (except drinking), metal, manufacturing
332999	Fountains, drinking (except mechanically refrigerated), metal, manufacturing
423720	Fountains, drinking (except refrigerated), merchant wholesalers
423740	Fountains, drinking, refrigerated, merchant wholesalers
327420	Fountains, plaster of paris, manufacturing
333415	Fountains, refrigerated drinking, manufacturing
713920	Four season ski resorts without accommodations
333243	Fourdrinier machinery manufacturing
332618	Fourdrinier wire cloth made from purchased wire
112930	Fox production
335312	Fractional horsepower electric motors manufacturing
333249	Fractionating equipment, chemical, manufacturing
211130	Fractionating natural gas liquids
333318	Frame and body alignment equipment, motor vehicle, manufacturing
332999	Frames and handles, handbag and luggage, metal, manufacturing
423220	Frames and pictures merchant wholesalers
339940	Frames for artist's canvases (i.e., stretchers) manufacturing
333249	Frames for textile making machinery manufacturing
332321	Frames, door and window, metal, manufacturing
321911	Frames, door and window, wood, manufacturing
332999	Frames, metal, lamp shade, manufacturing
332999	Frames, metal, umbrella and parasol, manufacturing
339999	Frames, mirror and picture, all materials, manufacturing
423460	Frames, ophthalmic, merchant wholesalers
238130	Framework, house, contractors
238130	Framing contractors
533110	Franchise agreements, leasing, selling or licensing, without providing other services

813410 Fraternal associations or lodges, social or civic
524113 Fraternal life insurance organizations
813410 Fraternal lodges
813410 Fraternal organizations
813410 Fraternities (except residential)
721310 Fraternity houses
621493 Freestanding ambulatory surgical centers and clinics
621498 Freestanding birth centers, outpatient
621493 Freestanding emergency medical centers and clinics
311423 Freeze-dried, food processing, fruits and vegetables
811310 Freezer, commercial, repair and maintenance services
335220 Freezers, chest and upright household-type, manufacturing
423740 Freezers, commercial-type, merchant wholesalers
423620 Freezers, household-type, merchant wholesalers
333415 Freezing equipment, industrial and commercial-type, manufacturing
311710 Freezing fish (e.g., blocks, fillets, ready-to-serve products)
488210 Freight car cleaning services
481112 Freight carriers (except air couriers), air, scheduled
481212 Freight charter services, air
488510 Freight forwarding
482111 Freight railways, line-haul
482112 Freight railways, short-line or beltline
541614 Freight rate auditor services
541614 Freight rate consulting services
483113 Freight shipping on the Great Lakes system (including St. Lawrence Seaway)
541614 Freight traffic consulting services
481212 Freight transportation, air, charter services
481212 Freight transportation, air, nonscheduled
483113 Freight transportation, deep sea, to and from domestic ports
483111 Freight transportation, deep sea, to or from foreign ports
483211 Freight transportation, inland waters (except on Great Lakes system)
311411 French fries, frozen, pre-cooked, manufacturing
311412 French toast, frozen, manufacturing

335312 Frequency converters (i.e., electric generators) manufacturing
334515 Frequency meters (e.g., electrical, electronic, mechanical) manufacturing
334515 Frequency synthesizers manufacturing
238310 Fresco (i.e., decorative plaster finishing) contractors
424460 Fresh fish merchant wholesalers
424480 Fresh fruits, vegetables, and berries merchant wholesalers
424470 Fresh meats merchant wholesalers
424440 Fresh poultry merchant wholesalers
424460 Fresh seafood merchant wholesalers
339992 Fretted instruments and parts manufacturing
313220 Fringes weaving
325510 Frit manufacturing
114119 Frog fishing
112519 Frog production, farm raising
331110 Frogs, iron or steel, made in iron and steel mills
811118 Front end alignment shops, automotive
423820 Frost protection machinery merchant wholesalers
311999 Frosting, prepared, manufacturing
311411 Frozen ades, drinks and cocktail mixes, manufacturing
311812 Frozen bread and bread-type rolls, made in commercial bakeries
311813 Frozen cake manufacturing
311411 Frozen citrus pulp manufacturing
311520 Frozen custard manufacturing
722515 Frozen custard stands, fixed location
311520 Frozen desserts (except bakery) manufacturing
311412 Frozen dinners (except seafood-based) manufacturing
311824 Frozen doughs made from purchased flour
424460 Frozen fish (except packaged) merchant wholesalers
454390 Frozen food and freezer meal plan providers, direct selling
326111 Frozen food bags, plastics film, single wall or multiwall, manufacturing
311412 Frozen food entrees (except seafood-based), packaged, manufacturing
424420 Frozen foods, packaged (except dairy products), merchant wholesalers
311411 Frozen fruit and vegetable processing

311411	Frozen fruits, fruit juices, and vegetables, manufacturing
311612	Frozen meat pies (i.e., tourtires) made from purchased carcasses
445210	Frozen meat stores
424470	Frozen meats (except packaged) merchant wholesalers
311412	Frozen pizza manufacturing
311412	Frozen pot pies manufacturing
424440	Frozen poultry (except packaged) merchant wholesalers
311412	Frozen rice dishes manufacturing
424460	Frozen seafood (except packaged) merchant wholesalers
311412	Frozen side dishes manufacturing
311412	Frozen soups (except seafood) manufacturing
311412	Frozen waffles manufacturing
424430	Frozen yogurt merchant wholesalers
111336	Fruit and tree nut combination farming
445230	Fruit and vegetable stands, permanent
311423	Fruit and vegetables, dehydrating, manufacturing
453220	Fruit basket or fruit bouquet stores (except exclusively by Internet)
321920	Fruit baskets, veneer and splint, manufacturing
311421	Fruit brining
311421	Fruit butters manufacturing
424450	Fruit concentrates, fountain, merchant wholesalers
321920	Fruit crates, wood, wirebound, manufacturing
312111	Fruit drinks (except juice), manufacturing
311942	Fruit extracts manufacturing
111419	Fruit farming, grown under cover
311211	Fruit flour, meal, and powders, manufacturing
333111	Fruit harvesting machines manufacturing
311421	Fruit juice canning
311411	Fruit juice concentrates, frozen, manufacturing
311421	Fruit juices, fresh, manufacturing
445230	Fruit markets
311340	Fruit peel products (e.g., candied, crystallized, glace, glazed) manufacturing
311421	Fruit pickling
311421	Fruit pie fillings, canning
311520	Fruit pops, frozen, manufacturing

115114	Fruit precooling
115114	Fruit sorting, grading, and packing
445230	Fruit stands, permanent
454390	Fruit stands, temporary
111421	Fruit stock (e.g., plants, seedlings, trees) growing
311930	Fruit syrups, flavoring, manufacturing
311991	Fruit, cut or peeled, fresh, manufacturing
115113	Fruit, machine harvesting
115114	Fruit, sun drying
115114	Fruit, vacuum cooling
311340	Fruits (e.g., candied, crystallized, glazed) manufacturing
326199	Fruits and vegetables, artificial, plastics, manufacturing
311423	Fruits dehydrating (except sun drying)
311421	Fruits pickling
339999	Fruits, artificial (except glass, plastics), manufacturing
327215	Fruits, artificial, made from purchased glass
327212	Fruits, artificial, made in glass making plants
311421	Fruits, canned, manufacturing
424490	Fruits, canned, merchant wholesalers
424480	Fruits, fresh, merchant wholesalers
311411	Fruits, frozen, manufacturing
424420	Fruits, frozen, merchant wholesalers
112320	Fryer chicken production
335210	Fryers, household-type electric, manufacturing
311351	Fudge, chocolate, made from cacao beans
311352	Fudge, chocolate, made from purchased chocolate
311340	Fudge, nonchocolate, manufacturing
424690	Fuel additives merchant wholesalers
326299	Fuel bladders, rubber, manufacturing
324199	Fuel briquettes or boulets made from refined petroleum
335999	Fuel cells, electrochemical generators, manufacturing
334413	Fuel cells, solid-state, manufacturing
334519	Fuel densitometers, aircraft engine, manufacturing
336310	Fuel injection systems and parts, automotive and truck gasoline engine, manufacturing

334519	Fuel mixture indicators, aircraft engine, manufacturing
454310	Fuel oil (i.e., heating) dealers, direct selling
424710	Fuel oil bulk stations and terminals, merchant wholesalers
238220	Fuel oil burner installation
424720	Fuel oil merchant wholesalers (except bulk stations, terminals)
424720	Fuel oil truck jobbers
324110	Fuel oils manufacturing
325180	Fuel propellants, solid inorganic, not specified elsewhere by process, manufacturing
325199	Fuel propellants, solid organic, not specified elsewhere by process, manufacturing
336320	Fuel pumps, electric, automotive, truck, and bus, manufacturing
336310	Fuel pumps, mechanical, automotive and truck gasoline engine, manufacturing
334519	Fuel system instruments, aircraft, manufacturing
334519	Fuel totalizers, aircraft engine, manufacturing
424720	Fuel, aircraft, merchant wholesalers (except bulk stations, terminals)
423520	Fuel, coal and coke, merchant wholesalers
424720	Fueling aircraft (except on contract basis), merchant wholesalers
488190	Fueling aircraft on a contract or fee basis
324110	Fuels, jet, manufacturing
531120	Full service office space provision
722511	Full service restaurants
423520	Fuller's earth merchant wholesalers
212325	Fuller's earth mining and/or beneficiating
327992	Fuller's earth processing beyond beneficiating
332313	Fumigating chambers, fabricated metal plate work, manufacturing
115114	Fumigating grain
561710	Fumigating services (except crop fumigating)
334515	Function generators manufacturing
561499	Fundraising campaign organization services on a contract or fee basis
334118	Funds transfer devices manufacturing
525110	Funds, employee benefit pension
525120	Funds, health and welfare
525990	Funds, mutual, closed-end

525910	Funds, mutual, open-ended
525110	Funds, pension
525190	Funds, self-insurance (except employee benefit funds)
812210	Funeral director services
423850	Funeral home supplies merchant wholesalers
812210	Funeral homes
812210	Funeral homes combined with crematories
524128	Funeral insurance carriers, direct
812210	Funeral parlors
325320	Fungicides manufacturing
424910	Fungicides, agricultural, merchant wholesalers
315280	Fur accessories and trimmings (except apparel contractors) manufacturing
315210	Fur accessories and trimmings cut and sew apparel contractors
315280	Fur apparel (e.g., capes, coats, hats, jackets, neckpieces) (except apparel contractors) manufacturing
315210	Fur apparel (e.g., capes, coats, hats, jackets, neckpieces) cut and sew apparel contractors
448190	Fur apparel stores
315280	Fur clothing (except apparel contractors) manufacturing
315210	Fur clothing cut and sew apparel contractors
424330	Fur clothing merchant wholesalers
423930	Fur cuttings and scraps merchant wholesalers
541490	Fur design services
315210	Fur finishers, liners, and buttonhole makers cut and sew apparel contractors
812320	Fur garment cleaning services
811490	Fur garment repair shops without retailing new fur garments
315280	Fur plates and trimmings (except apparel contractors) manufacturing
315210	Fur plates and trimmings cut and sew apparel contractors
532281	Fur rental
493120	Fur storage warehousing for the trade
316110	Fur stripping
112930	Fur-bearing animal production
236210	Furnace (i.e., industrial plant structure) construction
325180	Furnace black manufacturing

332322	Furnace casings, sheet metal (except stampings), manufacturing
238220	Furnace conversion (i.e., from one fuel to another)
333413	Furnace filters manufacturing
332322	Furnace flues, sheet metal (except stampings), manufacturing
238220	Furnace humidifier installation
238220	Furnace installation
238220	Furnace, forced air, installation
333414	Furnaces (except forced air), heating, manufacturing
423720	Furnaces (except forced air), heating, merchant wholesalers
333994	Furnaces and ovens for drying and redrying, industrial process-type, manufacturing
333994	Furnaces and ovens, semiconductor wafer, manufacturing
339114	Furnaces, dental laboratory, manufacturing
333414	Furnaces, floor and wall, manufacturing
333994	Furnaces, industrial and laboratory-type (except dental), manufacturing
423830	Furnaces, industrial process, merchant wholesalers
333415	Furnaces, warm air (i.e., forced air), manufacturing
423730	Furnaces, warm air (i.e., forced air), merchant wholesalers
424320	Furnishings (except shoes), men's and boys', merchant wholesalers
424330	Furnishings (except shoes), women's, girls', and infants', merchant wholesalers
448150	Furnishings stores, men's and boys'
448150	Furnishings stores, women's and girls'
423210	Furniture (except drafting tables, hospital beds, medical furniture) merchant wholesalers
337124	Furniture (except upholstered), metal household-type, manufacturing
337214	Furniture (except wood), office-type, padded, upholstered, or plain, manufacturing
337125	Furniture (except wood, metal, upholstered) indoor and outdoor household-type, manufacturing
532289	Furniture (i.e., residential) rental centers
442110	Furniture and appliance stores (i.e., primarily retailing furniture)
561740	Furniture cleaning on customers' premises
561740	Furniture cleaning services
423220	Furniture coverings and protectors
	merchant wholesalers
541420	Furniture design services
321912	Furniture dimension stock, hardwood, unfinished, manufacturing
321912	Furniture dimension stock, softwood, unfinished, manufacturing
321912	Furniture dimension stock, unfinished wood, manufacturing
337215	Furniture frames and parts, metal, manufacturing
337215	Furniture frames, wood, manufacturing
332510	Furniture hardware, metal, manufacturing
321999	Furniture inlays manufacturing
484210	Furniture moving, used
423210	Furniture parts merchant wholesalers
337215	Furniture parts, finished metal, manufacturing
337215	Furniture parts, finished plastics, manufacturing
337215	Furniture parts, finished wood, manufacturing
325612	Furniture polishes and waxes manufacturing
811420	Furniture refinishing shops
811420	Furniture repair shops
811420	Furniture reupholstering shops
332613	Furniture springs, light gauge, unassembled, made from purchased wire or strip
321912	Furniture squares, unfinished hardwood, manufacturing
442110	Furniture stores (e.g., household, office, outdoor)
453310	Furniture stores, used
327215	Furniture tops, glass (e.g., beveled, cut, polished), made from purchased glass
314999	Furniture trimmings made from purchased fabrics
327991	Furniture, cut stone (i.e., benches, tables, church), manufacturing
337127	Furniture, factory-type (e.g., cabinets, stools, tool stands, work benches), manufacturing
532283	Furniture, home health, rental
339113	Furniture, hospital, specialized (e.g., hospital beds, operating room furniture), manufacturing
337121	Furniture, household-type, upholstered on frames of any material, manufacturing
532490	Furniture, institutional (i.e. public building), rental or leasing

337127	Furniture, institutional, manufacturing
337127	Furniture, laboratory-type (e.g., benches, cabinets, stools, tables), manufacturing
532420	Furniture, office, rental or leasing
337211	Furniture, office-type, padded, upholstered, or plain wood, manufacturing
337124	Furniture, outdoor metal household-type (e.g., beach, garden, lawn, porch), manufacturing
337122	Furniture, outdoor wood household-type (e.g., beach, garden, lawn, porch), manufacturing
337127	Furniture, public building (e.g., church, library, school, theater), manufacturing
532289	Furniture, residential, rental or leasing
337127	Furniture, restaurant-type, manufacturing
337122	Furniture, unassembled or knock-down wood household-type, manufacturing
337122	Furniture, unfinished wood household-type, manufacturing
337122	Furniture, wood household-type, not upholstered (except TV and radio housings, and sewing machine cabinets), manufacturing
448190	Furriers
423850	Furriers equipment and supplies merchant wholesalers
332323	Furring channels, sheet metal, manufacturing
316110	Furs, dressed (e.g., bleached, curried, dyed, scraped, tanned), manufacturing
424990	Furs, dressed, merchant wholesalers
424590	Furs, raw, merchant wholesalers
335313	Fuse clips and blocks, electric, manufacturing
335931	Fuse cutouts manufacturing
335313	Fuse mountings, electric power, manufacturing
332993	Fuses ammunition (i.e., more than 30 mm., more than 1.18 inch) manufacturing
423610	Fuses, electric, merchant wholesalers
335313	Fuses, electrical, manufacturing
325194	Fustic wood extract manufacturing
337122	Futon frames manufacturing
337121	Futons with frames manufacturing
523140	Futures commodity contracts brokerages
523140	Futures commodity contracts brokers' offices
523130	Futures commodity contracts dealing (i.e., acting as a principal in dealing commodities to investors)
523210	Futures commodity contracts exchanges
212319	Gabbro crushed and broken stone mining and/or beneficiating
212311	Gabbro mining or quarrying
237990	Gabion construction
316210	Gaiters, plastics or plastics soled fabric upper, manufacturing
316210	Gaiters, rubber or rubber soled fabric upper, manufacturing
212230	Galena mining and/or beneficiating
712110	Galleries, art (except retail)
453920	Galleries, art, retail
713990	Galleries, shooting
316210	Galoshes, plastics or plastics soled fabric upper, manufacturing
316210	Galoshes, rubber, or rubber soled fabric upper, manufacturing
423510	Galvanized iron and steel products merchant wholesalers
238160	Galvanized iron roofing installation
333519	Galvanizing machinery manufacturing
331110	Galvanizing metals and metal formed products made in iron and steel mills
332812	Galvanizing metals and metal products for the trade
334515	Galvanometers (except geophysical) manufacturing
334519	Galvanometers, geophysical, manufacturing
325194	Gambier extract manufacturing
921130	Gambling control boards, nonoperating
713290	Gambling control boards, operating gambling activities
713210	Gambling cruises
713290	Gambling device arcades or parlors, coin-operated
713290	Gambling device concession operators (i.e., supplying and servicing in others' facilities), coin-operated
924120	Game and inland fish agencies
334614	Game cartridge software, mass reproducing
114210	Game preserves, commercial
114210	Game propagation
114210	Game retreats
713120	Game rooms (except gambling)
423430	Game software merchant wholesalers
924120	Game wardens
423920	Games (except coin-operated) merchant wholesalers

339930	Games (except coin-operated), children's and adult, manufacturing
339999	Games, coin-operated, manufacturing
423990	Games, coin-operated, merchant wholesalers
334614	Games, computer software, mass reproducing
511210	Games, computer software, publishing
423920	Gaming consoles merchant wholesalers
334517	Gamma-ray irradiation equipment manufacturing
212319	Ganister crushed and broken stone mining and/or beneficiating
236220	Garage and service station, commercial, construction
444190	Garage door dealers
335999	Garage door openers manufacturing
238290	Garage door, commercial- or industrial-type, installation
238350	Garage door, residential-type, installation
332321	Garage doors, metal, manufacturing
321911	Garage doors, wood, manufacturing
812930	Garages, automobile parking
811198	Garages, do-it-yourself automotive repair
811111	Garages, general automotive repair (except gasoline service stations)
332311	Garages, prefabricated metal, manufacturing
321992	Garages, prefabricated wood, manufacturing
332439	Garbage cans, light gauge metal, manufacturing
562111	Garbage collection services
562213	Garbage disposal combustors or incinerators
562212	Garbage disposal landfills
236210	Garbage disposal plant construction
333318	Garbage disposal units, commercial-type, manufacturing
423440	Garbage disposal units, commercial-type, merchant wholesalers
335220	Garbage disposal units, household-type, manufacturing
423620	Garbage disposal units, household-type, merchant wholesalers
562212	Garbage dumps
562111	Garbage hauling, local
333994	Garbage incinerators (except precast concrete) manufacturing
327390	Garbage incinerators, precast concrete, manufacturing
562111	Garbage pick-up services
336211	Garbage truck bodies manufacturing
336120	Garbage trucks assembling on chassis of own manufacture
336211	Garbage trucks assembling on purchased chassis
111130	Garbanzo farming, dry, field and seed production
236116	Garden apartment construction general contractors
236117	Garden apartment for-sale builders
444220	Garden centers
813410	Garden clubs
811411	Garden equipment repair and maintenance services without retailing new garden equipment
327390	Garden furniture, precast concrete, manufacturing
327991	Garden furniture, stone, manufacturing
337122	Garden furniture, wood, manufacturing
326220	Garden hose, rubber or plastics, manufacturing
423820	Garden machinery and equipment merchant wholesalers
333112	Garden machinery and equipment, powered, manufacturing
561730	Garden maintenance services
541320	Garden planning services
327110	Garden pottery manufacturing
444210	Garden power equipment stores
424910	Garden supplies (e.g., fertilizers, pesticides) merchant wholesalers
811411	Garden tool sharpening and repair services
532490	Garden tractor rental or leasing
339999	Garden umbrellas manufacturing
712130	Gardens, zoological or botanical
111219	Garlic farming (except under cover), field, bedding plant and seed production
111419	Garlic farming, grown under cover
811490	Garment alteration and/or repair shops without retailing new garments
812320	Garment cleaning (e.g., fur, leather, suede) services
321999	Garment hangers, wood, manufacturing
316110	Garment leather manufacturing
314910	Garment storage bags manufacturing
315280	Garments, leather or sheep-lined (except apparel contractors), manufacturing
315210	Garments, leather or sheep-lined, cut and sew apparel contractors

313320	Garments, oiling (i.e., waterproofing)
212399	Garnet mining and/or beneficiating
333249	Garnetting machinery for textiles manufacturing
314999	Garnetting of textile waste and rags
315210	Garter belts cut and sew apparel contractors
315240	Garter belts cut and sewn from purchased fabric (except apparel contractors)
315210	Garters cut and sew apparel contractors
315240	Garters, women's and girls', cut and sewn from purchased fabric (except apparel contractors)
334513	Gas analyzers, industrial process-type, manufacturing
334516	Gas analyzers, laboratory-type, manufacturing
334513	Gas and liquid analysis instruments, industrial process-type, manufacturing
334512	Gas burner automatic controls (except valves) manufacturing
333414	Gas burners, heating, manufacturing
334513	Gas chromatographic instruments, industrial process-type, manufacturing
334516	Gas chromatographic instruments, laboratory-type, manufacturing
423830	Gas detecting equipment and supplies (except household-type) merchant wholesalers
211130	Gas field development for own account
211130	Gas field exploration for own account
333414	Gas fireplaces manufacturing
423720	Gas fireplaces merchant wholesalers
238220	Gas fitting contractor
334513	Gas flow instrumentation, industrial process-type, manufacturing
333999	Gas generating machinery, general purpose-type, manufacturing
423720	Gas hot water heaters merchant wholesalers
334519	Gas leak detectors manufacturing
523999	Gas lease brokers' offices
335129	Gas lighting fixtures manufacturing
423990	Gas lighting fixtures merchant wholesalers
238220	Gas line installation, individual hookup, contractors
333249	Gas liquefying machinery manufacturing
237120	Gas main construction
339113	Gas masks manufacturing
561990	Gas meter reading services, contract
333318	Gas ranges, commercial-type, manufacturing
335220	Gas ranges, household-type, manufacturing
333999	Gas separating machinery manufacturing
333414	Gas space heaters manufacturing
332420	Gas storage tanks, heavy gauge metal, manufacturing
336390	Gas tanks assembled, automotive, truck, and bus, manufacturing
333611	Gas turbine generator set units manufacturing
333611	Gas turbines (except aircraft) manufacturing
336412	Gas turbines, aircraft, manufacturing
332911	Gas valves, industrial-type, manufacturing
333992	Gas welding equipment manufacturing
333992	Gas welding rods, coated or cored, manufacturing
213111	Gas well drilling on a contract basis
333132	Gas well machinery and equipment manufacturing
213112	Gas well rig building, repairing, and dismantling on a contract basis
213112	Gas, compressing natural, in the field on a contract basis
221210	Gas, manufactured, distribution
221210	Gas, mixed natural and manufactured, distribution
211130	Gas, natural liquefied petroleum, extraction
221210	Gas, natural, distribution
211130	Gas, natural, extraction
211130	Gas, natural, liquids, extraction
486210	Gas, natural, pipeline operation
211130	Gas, residue, extraction
424690	Gases, compressed and liquefied (except liquefied petroleum gas), merchant wholesalers
325120	Gases, industrial (i.e., compressed, liquefied, solid), manufacturing
211130	Gases, petroleum, liquefied, extraction
339991	Gasket, packing, and sealing devices manufacturing
339991	Gaskets manufacturing
423840	Gaskets merchant wholesalers
334514	Gasmeters, consumption registering, manufacturing
334514	Gasmeters, large capacity, domestic and industrial, manufacturing

424710	Gasohol bulk stations and terminals, merchant wholesalers
424720	Gasohol merchant wholesalers (except bulk stations, terminals)
333414	Gas-oil burners, combination, manufacturing
424710	Gasoline bulk stations and terminals, merchant wholesalers
334514	Gasoline dispensing meters (except pumps) manufacturing
336412	Gasoline engine parts (except carburetors, pistons, piston rings, valves), aircraft, manufacturing
336310	Gasoline engine parts, mechanical, automotive and truck, manufacturing
333618	Gasoline engines (except aircraft, automotive, truck) manufacturing
336310	Gasoline engines for hybrid automotive vehicles manufacturing
336412	Gasoline engines, aircraft, manufacturing
336310	Gasoline engines, automotive and truck, manufacturing
324110	Gasoline made in petroleum refineries
423120	Gasoline marketing equipment merchant wholesalers
333914	Gasoline measuring and dispensing pumps manufacturing
423120	Gasoline measuring and dispensing pumps merchant wholesalers
424720	Gasoline merchant wholesalers (except bulk stations, terminals)
486910	Gasoline pipeline transportation
238290	Gasoline pump, service station, installation
423120	Gasoline service station equipment merchant wholesalers
447110	Gasoline stations with convenience stores
447190	Gasoline stations without convenience stores
447110	Gasoline with convenience stores
211130	Gasoline, natural, production
313310	Gassing yarn (i.e., singeing)
621111	Gastroenterologists' offices (e.g., centers, clinics)
339112	Gastroscopes (except electromedical) manufacturing
334510	Gastroscopes, electromedical, manufacturing
333999	Gate and bridge lifting machinery manufacturing
423390	Gate and fence hardware merchant wholesalers
332911	Gate valves, industrial-type, manufacturing

332323	Gates, holding, sheet metal, manufacturing
332323	Gates, metal (except wire), manufacturing
237120	Gathering line, gas and oil field, construction
113210	Gathering of forest products (e.g., barks, gums, needles, seeds)
113210	Gathering, extracting, and selling tree seeds
332216	Gauge blocks, machinists' precision tools, manufacturing
334514	Gauges (e.g., oil pressure, water temperature, speedometer, tachometer), motor vehicle, manufacturing
334513	Gauges (i.e., analog, digital), industrial process-type, manufacturing
334514	Gauges for computing pressure-temperature corrections manufacturing
333314	Gauges, machinist's precision tool, optical, manufacturing
332216	Gauges, machinists' precision tools (except optical), manufacturing
424210	Gauze merchant wholesalers
339113	Gauze, surgical, made from purchased fabric
313210	Gauzes, surgical, made in broadwoven fabric mills
321999	Gavels, wood, manufacturing
333517	Gear cutting and finishing machines, metalworking, manufacturing
332216	Gear pullers, handtools, manufacturing
333517	Gear rolling machines, metalworking, manufacturing
333612	Gearmotors (i.e., power transmission equipment) manufacturing
336350	Gears (e.g., crown, pinion, spider), automotive, truck, and bus, manufacturing
423840	Gears merchant wholesalers
333612	Gears, power transmission (except aircraft, motor vehicle), manufacturing
112390	Geese production
311615	Geese, processing, fresh, frozen, canned, or cooked
311615	Geese, slaughtering and dressing
334519	Geiger counters manufacturing
325998	Gelatin (except dessert preparations) manufacturing
325998	Gelatin capsules, empty, manufacturing
311999	Gelatin dessert preparations manufacturing
311999	Gelatin for cooking manufacturing
424490	Gelatin, edible, merchant wholesalers

424690	Gelatin, inedible, merchant wholesalers
212399	Gem stone (e.g., amethyst, garnet, agate, ruby, sapphire, jade) mining and/or beneficiating
333249	Gem stone processing machinery manufacturing
448310	Gem stone shops, precious and semi-precious
423940	Gem stones merchant wholesalers
325414	Gene therapy preparations manufacturing
812990	Genealogical investigation services
921190	General accounting offices, government
811111	General automotive repair shops
112990	General combination animal farming
111998	General combination crop farming (except fruit and nut combinations, oilseed and grain, vegetable)
926110	General economics statistical agencies
484110	General freight trucking, local
484122	General freight trucking, long-distance, less-than-truckload (LTL)
484121	General freight trucking, long-distance, truckload (TL)
541611	General management consulting services
622110	General medical and surgical hospitals
423990	General merchandise, durable goods, merchant wholesalers
424990	General merchandise, nondurable goods, merchant wholesalers
921190	General public administration
423830	General purpose industrial machinery and equipment merchant wholesalers
532310	General rental centers
921190	General services departments, government
452319	General stores
493110	General warehousing and storage
424210	General-line drugs merchant wholesalers
424410	General-line groceries merchant wholesalers
423840	General-line industrial supplies merchant wholesalers
423930	General-line scrap merchant wholesalers
336320	Generating apparatus and parts for internal combustion engines manufacturing
335312	Generating apparatus and parts, electrical (except internal combustion engine and welding), manufacturing
333992	Generating apparatus and parts, welding, electrical, manufacturing
335313	Generator control and metering panels,

	switchgear-type, manufacturing
532490	Generator rental or leasing
335312	Generator sets, prime mover (except turbine generator sets), manufacturing
333611	Generator sets, turbine (e.g., gas, hydraulic, steam), manufacturing
335311	Generator voltage regulators, electric induction and step-type (except engine electrical equipment), manufacturing
335312	Generators and sets, electric (except internal combustion engine, welding, turbine generator sets), manufacturing
335312	Generators for gas-electric and oil-electric vehicles, manufacturing
336320	Generators for internal combustion engines manufacturing
335312	Generators for storage battery chargers (except internal combustion engine and aircraft) manufacturing
423610	Generators, electrical (except motor vehicle), merchant wholesalers
423120	Generators, motor vehicle electrical, new, merchant wholesalers
423140	Generators, motor vehicle electrical, used, merchant wholesalers
332994	Generators, smoke, manufacturing
334517	Generators, X-ray, manufacturing
621511	Genetic testing laboratories
541715	Genetics research and development laboratories or services (except biotechnology and nanotechnology research and development)
541690	Geochemical consulting services
321992	Geodesic domes, prefabricated, wood, manufacturing
541370	Geodetic surveying services
541370	Geographic information system (GIS) base mapping services
541330	Geological engineering services
213112	Geological exploration (except surveying) for oil and gas on a contract basis
541715	Geological research and development laboratories or services (except nanotechnology research and development)
924120	Geological research program administration
541360	Geological surveying services
541330	Geophysical engineering services
213112	Geophysical exploration (except surveying) for oil and gas on a contract basis
334519	Geophysical instruments manufacturing

541360	Geophysical mapping services
541360	Geophysical surveying services
541370	Geospatial mapping services
541380	Geotechnical testing laboratories or services
237110	Geothermal drilling
221116	Geothermal electric power generation
221330	Geothermal steam production
325199	Geraniol manufacturing
331492	Germanium recovering from scrap and/or alloying purchased metals
331410	Germanium refining, primary
335931	GFCI (ground fault circuit interrupters) manufacturing
711510	Ghost writers, independent
453220	Gift shops
453220	Gift stands, permanent location
322220	Gift wrap made from purchased materials
424120	Gift wrapping paper merchant wholesalers
561910	Gift wrapping services
212399	Gilsonite mining and/or beneficiating
111219	Gingerroot farming (except under cover), field, bedding plant and seed production
111419	Gingerroot farming, grown under cover
115111	Ginning cotton
111219	Ginseng farming (except under cover), field, bedding plant and seed production
111419	Ginseng farming, grown under cover
113210	Ginseng gathering
327390	Girders and beams, prestressed concrete, manufacturing
327390	Girders, prestressed concrete, manufacturing
315190	Girdles and other foundation garments made in apparel knitting mills
315210	Girdles cut and sew apparel contractors
315240	Girdles, women's and girls', cut and sewn from purchased fabric (except apparel contractors)
813410	Girl guiding organizations
721214	Girls' camps (except day, instructional)
611620	Girls' camps, sports instruction
713990	Girls' day camps (except instructional)
315110	Girls' hosiery, sheer, full-length and knee-length, knitting or knitting and finishing
315110	Girls' socks manufacturing
325411	Glandular derivatives, uncompounded, manufacturing

325412	Glandular medicinal preparations manufacturing
325612	Glass and tile cleaning preparations manufacturing
327215	Glass blanks for electric light bulbs made from purchased glass
327212	Glass blanks for electric light bulbs made in glass making plants
238140	Glass block laying
334290	Glass breakage detection and signaling devices
313210	Glass broadwoven fabrics weaving
238150	Glass cladding (i.e., curtain wall), installation
238150	Glass coating and tinting (except automotive) contractors
313220	Glass fabrics, narrow woven weaving
238310	Glass fiber insulation installation
327212	Glass fiber, optical, made in glass making plants
327212	Glass fiber, textile type, made in glass making plants
327212	Glass fiber, unsheathed, made in glass making plants
238150	Glass installation (except automotive) contractors
811122	Glass installation, automotive repair
327212	Glass making and blowing by hand
333249	Glass making machinery (e.g., blowing, forming, molding) manufacturing
327213	Glass packaging containers manufacturing
238150	Glass partitions, installation
327215	Glass products (except packaging containers) made from purchased glass
327212	Glass products (except packaging containers) made in a glass making plants
212322	Glass sand quarrying and/or beneficiating
423930	Glass scrap merchant wholesalers
811122	Glass shops, automotive
444190	Glass stores
811122	Glass tinting, automotive
238140	Glass unit (i.e., glass block) masonry
811122	Glass work, automotive
327215	Glass, automotive, made from purchased glass
327212	Glass, automotive, made in glass making plants
423120	Glass, automotive, merchant wholesalers
423390	Glass, block and brick, merchant wholesalers

327211 Glass, plate, made in glass making plants

423390 Glass, plate, merchant wholesalers

333314 Glasses, field or opera, manufacturing

423460 Glasses, optical, merchant wholesalers

327120 Glasshouse refractories manufacturing

322299 Glassine wrapping paper made from purchased paper

322121 Glassine wrapping paper made in paper mills

327215 Glassware for industrial, scientific, and technical use made from purchased glass

327212 Glassware for industrial, scientific, and technical use made in glass making plants

327215 Glassware for lighting fixtures made from purchased glass

327212 Glassware for lighting fixtures made in glass making plants

442299 Glassware stores

327215 Glassware, art decorative and novelty, made from purchased glass

327212 Glassware, art, decorative, and novelty made in glass making plants

327215 Glassware, cutting and engraving, made from purchased glass

423220 Glassware, household-type, merchant wholesalers

423450 Glassware, medical, merchant wholesalers

325180 Glauber's salt manufacturing

212391 Glauber's salt mining and/or beneficiating

325510 Glaziers' putty manufacturing

238150 Glazing contractors

315280 Glazing furs

332812 Glazing metals and metal products for the trade

334511 Glide slope instrumentation manufacturing

487990 Glider excursions

336411 Gliders (i.e., aircraft) manufacturing

334220 Global positioning system (GPS) equipment manufacturing

511130 Globe cover publishers

511130 Globe cover publishers and printing combined

323111 Globe covers and maps commercial printing (except screen) without publishing

323113 Globe covers and maps screen printing without publishing

332911 Globe valves, industrial-type, manufacturing

339999 Globes, geographical, manufacturing

316110 Glove leather manufacturing

315990 Glove linings (except fur) manufacturing

315280 Glove linings, fur (except apparel contractors), manufacturing

315210 Glove linings, fur, cut and sew apparel contractors

315210 Gloves and mittens (except athletic), leather, fabric, fur, or combinations, cut and sew apparel contractors

315990 Gloves and mittens (except athletic), leather, fabric, fur, or combinations, cut and sewn from purchased fabric (except apparel contractors)

315210 Gloves and mittens, woven or knit, cut and sew apparel contractors

315990 Gloves and mittens, woven or knit, cut and sewn from purchased fabric (except apparel contractors), manufacturing

315190 Gloves, knit, made in apparel knitting mills

315990 Gloves, leather (except athletic, cut and sewn apparel contractors), manufacturing

424320 Gloves, men's and boys', merchant wholesalers

326199 Gloves, plastics, manufacturing

339113 Gloves, rubber (e.g., electrician's, examination, household-type, surgeon's), manufacturing

339920 Gloves, sport and athletic (e.g., baseball, boxing, racketball, handball), manufacturing

424330 Gloves, women's, children's, and infants', merchant wholesalers

335110 Glow lamp bulbs manufacturing

339114 Glue, dental, manufacturing

325520 Glues (except dental) manufacturing

424690 Glues merchant wholesalers

311221 Gluten feed, flour, and meal, made by wet milling corn

311221 Gluten manufacturing

325611 Glycerin (i.e., glycerol), natural, manufacturing

325199 Glycerin (i.e., glycerol), synthetic, manufacturing

325411 Glycosides, uncompounded, manufacturing

212313 Gneiss crushed and broken stone mining and/or beneficiating

212311 Gneiss mining or quarrying

522294 GNMA (Government National Mortgage Association)

112420 Goat farming (e.g., meat, milk, mohair production)

424520	Goats merchant wholesalers
713990	Gocart raceways (i.e., amusement rides)
713990	Gocart tracks (i.e., amusement rides)
336999	Gocarts (except children's) manufacturing
423910	Gocarts merchant wholesalers
339930	Gocarts, children's, manufacturing
339115	Goggles (e.g., industrial, safety, sun, underwater) manufacturing
331491	Gold and gold alloy bar, sheet, strip, and tubing made from purchased metals or scrap
332813	Gold and silver plating metals and metal products for the trade
332999	Gold beating (i.e., foil, leaf)
331410	Gold bullion or dore bar produced at primary metal refineries
332999	Gold foil and leaf not made in rolling mills
331491	Gold foil made by rolling purchased metals or scrap
212221	Gold lode mining and/or beneficiating
212221	Gold ore mine site development for own account
212221	Gold ore mining and/or beneficiating plants
212221	Gold ores, concentrates, bullion, and/or precipitates mining and/or beneficiating
212221	Gold placer mining and/or beneficiating
325910	Gold printing inks manufacturing
331492	Gold recovering from scrap and/or alloying purchased metals
331410	Gold refining, primary
331491	Gold rolling and drawing purchased metals or scrap
323120	Gold stamping books for the trade
813410	Golden age clubs
112511	Goldfish production, farm raising
713910	Golf and country clubs
441228	Golf cart dealers, powered
532284	Golf cart rental
423910	Golf carts (except motorized passenger) merchant wholesalers
336999	Golf carts and similar motorized passenger carriers manufacturing
423860	Golf carts, motorized passenger, merchant wholesalers
336999	Golf carts, powered, manufacturing
237990	Golf course construction
541320	Golf course design services
713910	Golf courses (except miniature, pitch-n-putt)
713990	Golf courses, miniature
713990	Golf courses, pitch-n-putt
713990	Golf driving ranges
423910	Golf equipment and supplies merchant wholesalers
611620	Golf instruction, camps, or schools
713990	Golf practice ranges
451110	Golf pro shops
316210	Golf shoes, men's cleated, manufacturing
316210	Golf shoes, women's cleated, manufacturing
711219	Golfers, independent professional (i.e., participating in sports events)
339920	Golfing equipment (e.g., bags, balls, caddy carts, clubs, tees) manufacturing
335999	Gongs, electric, manufacturing
111334	Gooseberry farming
332216	Gouges, woodworking, manufacturing
445299	Gourmet food stores
561210	Government base facilities operation support services
522294	Government National Mortgage Association (GNMA)
522294	Government-sponsored enterprises providing secondary market financing
336310	Governors for automotive gasoline engines manufacturing
921110	Governors' offices
333618	Governors, diesel engine, manufacturing
333618	Governors, gasoline engine (except automotive), manufacturing
333611	Governors, steam, manufacturing
812331	Gown (e.g., doctors, nurses, hospital, beauticians) supply services
532281	Gown rental
315210	Gowns (e.g., academic, choir, clerical) cut and sew apparel contractors
315280	Gowns (e.g., academic, choir, clerical) cut and sewn from purchased fabric (except apparel contractors)
315210	Gowns, formal, cut and sew apparel contractors
315240	Gowns, formal, women's and girls', cut and sewn from purchased fabric (except apparel contractors)
315210	Gowns, hospital, surgical and patient, cut and sew apparel contractors
315280	Gowns, hospital, surgical and patient, cut and sewn from purchased fabric (except apparel contractors)

315210	Gowns, wedding, cut and sew apparel contractors
315240	Gowns, wedding, women's and girls', cut and sewn from purchased fabric (except apparel contractors)
334220	GPS (global positioning system) equipment manufacturing
333120	Grader attachments manufacturing
333120	Graders, road, manufacturing
238910	Grading construction sites
333241	Grading, cleaning, and sorting machinery (i.e., food manufacturing-type) manufacturing
333111	Grading, cleaning, and sorting machinery, farm-type, manufacturing
237310	Grading, highway, road, street and airport runway
334512	Gradual switches, pneumatic, manufacturing
532281	Graduation cap and gown rental
315210	Graduation caps and gowns cut and sew apparel contractors
315280	Graduation caps and gowns cut and sewn from purchased fabric (except apparel contractors)
311211	Graham flour manufacturing
311821	Graham wafers manufacturing
212399	Grahamite mining and/or beneficiating
312140	Grain alcohol, beverage, manufacturing
325193	Grain alcohol, nonpotable, manufacturing
236220	Grain bin construction
115114	Grain cleaning
333111	Grain drills manufacturing
115114	Grain drying
236220	Grain elevator construction
424510	Grain elevators merchant wholesalers
493130	Grain elevators, storage only
115114	Grain fumigation
115114	Grain grinding (except custom grinding for animal feed)
311119	Grain grinding, custom, for animal feed
484220	Grain hauling, local
484230	Grain hauling, long-distance
488210	Grain leveling and trimming in railroad cars
321999	Grain measures, wood, turned and shaped, manufacturing
424510	Grain merchant wholesalers

333241	Grain milling machinery manufacturing
311211	Grain mills (except animal feed, breakfast cereal, rice)
311119	Grain mills, animal feed
311230	Grain mills, breakfast cereal
311212	Grain mills, rice
333111	Grain stackers manufacturing
311230	Grain, breakfast cereal, manufacturing
312120	Grain, brewers' spent, manufacturing
115113	Grain, machine harvesting
327910	Grains, abrasive, natural and artificial, manufacturing
813410	Granges
212313	Granite beneficiating plants (e.g., grinding or pulverizing)
212313	Granite crushed and broken stone mining and/or beneficiating
212311	Granite mining or quarrying
238140	Granite, exterior, contractors
238340	Granite, interior, installation
311351	Granola bars and clusters, chocolate, made from cacao beans
311352	Granola bars and clusters, chocolate, made from purchased chocolate
311340	Granola bars and clusters, nonchocolate, manufacturing
311230	Granola, cereal (except bars and clusters), manufacturing
813211	Grantmaking foundations
311313	Granulated beet sugar manufacturing
311314	Granulated cane sugar manufacturing
333249	Granulator and pelletizer machinery for plastics manufacturing
212319	Granules, slate, mining and/or beneficiating
312130	Grape farming and making wine
111332	Grape farming without making wine
111320	Grapefruit groves
325998	Grapefruit oil manufacturing
311423	Grapes, artificially drying
541430	Graphic art and related design services
541430	Graphic artists, independent
325992	Graphic arts plates, sensitized, manufacturing
611519	Graphic arts schools
541430	Graphic design services
334515	Graphic recording meters, electric, manufacturing

335991	Graphite electrodes and contacts, electric, manufacturing
212399	Graphite mining and/or beneficiating
335991	Graphite specialties for aerospace use (except gaskets) manufacturing
335991	Graphite specialties for electrical use manufacturing
335991	Graphite specialties for mechanical use (except gaskets) manufacturing
327992	Graphite, natural (e.g., ground, pulverized, refined, blended), manufacturing
111940	Grass hay farming
333111	Grass mowing equipment (except lawn and garden) manufacturing
332216	Grass mowing equipment, nonpowered lawn and garden, manufacturing
333112	Grass mowing equipment, powered lawn and garden, manufacturing
111998	Grass seed farming
332323	Gratings (i.e., open steel flooring) manufacturing
333314	Gratings, diffraction, manufacturing
238910	Grave excavation contractors
484220	Gravel hauling, local
484230	Gravel hauling, long-distance
212321	Gravel quarrying and/or beneficiating
423320	Gravel, construction, merchant wholesalers
541360	Gravity geophysical surveying services
325910	Gravure inks manufacturing
323120	Gravure plate and cylinder preparation services
323111	Gravure printing (except books, grey goods)
333244	Gravure printing presses manufacturing
311422	Gravy canning
311942	Gravy mixes, dry, manufacturing
331511	Gray iron foundries
531190	Grazing land rental or leasing
311613	Grease rendering
339991	Grease seals manufacturing
562998	Grease trap cleaning
311225	Grease, inedible, animal and vegetable, refining and blending purchased oils
424990	Greases, inedible animal and vegetable, merchant wholesalers
324191	Greases, petroleum lubricating, made from refined petroleum
325998	Greases, synthetic lubricating, manufacturing
483113	Great Lakes freight transportation (including St. Lawrence Seaway)
483114	Great Lakes passenger transportation (including St. Lawrence Seaway)
111219	Green bean farming, field and seed production
111219	Green cowpea farming, field and seed production
111219	Green lima bean farming, field and seed production
111219	Green pea farming, field and seed production
332311	Greenhouses, prefabricated metal, manufacturing
212399	Greensand mining and/or beneficiating
212311	Greenstone mining or quarrying
511191	Greeting card publishers (except exclusive Internet publishing)
511191	Greeting card publishers and printing combined
519130	Greeting card publishers, exclusively on Internet
453220	Greeting card shops
323111	Greeting cards (e.g., birthday, holiday, sympathy) commercial printing (except screen) without publishing
323113	Greeting cards (e.g., birthday, holiday, sympathy) screen printing without publishing
424120	Greeting cards merchant wholesalers
332994	Grenade launchers manufacturing
332993	Grenades, hand or projectile, manufacturing
711212	Greyhound dog racetracks
335210	Griddles and grills, household-type portable electric, manufacturing
332618	Grilles and grillwork made from purchased wire
332323	Grills and grillwork, sheet metal, manufacturing
332323	Grillwork, ornamental metal, manufacturing
333991	Grinders, handheld power-driven, manufacturing
325411	Grinding and milling botanicals (i.e., for medicinal or dietary supplement use)
423510	Grinding balls merchant wholesalers
327910	Grinding balls, ceramic, manufacturing

333517	Grinding machines, metalworking, manufacturing
324191	Grinding oils, petroleum, made from refined petroleum
212399	Grinding pebbles mining and/or beneficiating
212322	Grinding sand quarrying and/or beneficiating
311942	Grinding spices
327910	Grinding wheels manufacturing
212399	Grindstones mining and/or beneficiating
326299	Grips and handles, rubber, manufacturing
311211	Grits and flakes, corn brewer's, manufacturing
212319	Grits crushed and broken stone mining and/or beneficiating
424410	Groceries, general-line, merchant wholesalers
322220	Grocers' bags and sacks made from purchased uncoated paper
326111	Grocery bags, plastics film, single wall or multiwall, manufacturing
333924	Grocery carts made from purchased wire
492210	Grocery delivery services (i.e., independent service from grocery store)
445110	Grocery stores
423840	Grommets merchant wholesalers
326299	Grommets, rubber, manufacturing
812910	Grooming services, animal
335931	Ground clamps (i.e., electric wiring devices) manufacturing
335931	Ground fault circuit interrupters (GFCI) manufacturing
335312	Ground Power Units (GPU) manufacturing
238910	Ground thawing for construction site digging
322122	Groundwood paper products (e.g., publication and printing paper, tablet stock, wallpaper base) made in newsprint mills
424110	Groundwood paper, bulk, merchant wholesalers
322121	Groundwood paper, coated, laminated, or treated in paper mills
322220	Groundwood paper, coated, made from purchased paper
322121	Groundwood paper, coated, made in paper mills
322122	Groundwood paper, newsprint, made in paper mills
322110	Groundwood pulp manufacturing
624410	Group day care centers, child or infant
623990	Group foster homes for children
623110	Group homes for the disabled with nursing care
623990	Group homes for the disabled without nursing care
623990	Group homes for the hearing impaired
623990	Group homes for the visually impaired
623210	Group homes, intellectual and developmental disability
621491	Group hospitalization plans providing health care services
524114	Group hospitalization plans without providing health care services
114111	Grouper fishing
238110	Grouting (i.e., reinforcing with concrete)
335122	Grow light fixtures (except residential) manufacturing
335121	Grow light fixtures, residential, electric, manufacturing
813910	Growers' associations
212393	Guano mining and/or beneficiating
111998	Guar farming
524127	Guaranteeing titles
561612	Guard dog services
812910	Guard dog training services
561612	Guard services
237310	Guardrail construction
332322	Guardrails, highway, sheet metal (except stampings), manufacturing
332323	Guards, bannisters, and railings, sheet metal, manufacturing
332618	Guards, wire, made from purchased wire
111339	Guava farming
721199	Guest houses
721214	Guest ranches with accommodation facilities
812910	Guide dog training services
713990	Guide services (i.e., fishing, hunting, tourist)
713990	Guide services, fishing
713990	Guide services, hunting
713990	Guide services, tourist
511130	Guide, street map, publishers (except exclusive Internet publishing)
511130	Guide, street map, publishers and printing combined
519130	Guide, street map, publishers, exclusively on Internet

336415	Guided missile and space vehicle engine manufacturing
541715	Guided missile and space vehicle engine research and development
336414	Guided missile and space vehicle manufacturing
336419	Guided missile and space vehicle parts (except engines) manufacturing
541715	Guided missile and space vehicle parts (except engines) research and development
423860	Guided missiles and space vehicles merchant wholesalers
336414	Guided missiles, complete, assembling
323111	Guides, street map, commercial printing (except screen) without publishing
323113	Guides, street map, screen printing without publishing
339992	Guitars and parts, electric and nonelectric, manufacturing
113210	Gum (i.e., forest product) gathering
325194	Gum and wood chemicals manufacturing
424690	Gum and wood chemicals merchant wholesalers
311340	Gum, chewing, manufacturing
424450	Gum, chewing, merchant wholesalers
322220	Gummed paper products (e.g., labels, sheets, tapes) made from purchased paper
424130	Gummed tapes (except cellophane) merchant wholesalers
424120	Gummed tapes, cellophane, merchant wholesalers
332994	Gun barrels manufacturing
332994	Gun cleaning kits manufacturing
325612	Gun cleaning preparations
713990	Gun clubs, recreational
813319	Gun control organizations
332111	Gun forgings made from purchased iron or steel, unfinished
331110	Gun forgings made in iron and steel mills
332994	Gun magazines manufacturing
811490	Gun repair and maintenance shops without retailing new guns
451110	Gun shops
333314	Gun sighting and fire control equipment and instruments, optical, manufacturing
333314	Gun sights, optical, manufacturing
332613	Gun springs, light gauge, made from purchased wire or strip, manufacturing
321912	Gun stock blanks manufacturing
332510	Gun trigger locks, metal, manufacturing
332994	Gun turrets manufacturing
238110	Gunite contractors
334413	Gunn effect devices manufacturing
238110	Gunning shotcrete
325920	Gunpowder manufacturing
423990	Guns (except sporting) merchant wholesalers
332994	Guns manufacturing
332994	Guns, BB and pellet, manufacturing
332216	Guns, caulking, nonpowered, manufacturing
423910	Guns, sporting equipment, merchant wholesalers
811490	Gunsmith shops without retailing new guns
238170	Gutter and downspout contractors
561790	Gutter cleaning services
423330	Gutters and down spouts (except wood) merchant wholesalers
332114	Gutters and down spouts sheet metal, custom roll formed, manufacturing
326199	Gutters and down spouts, plastics, manufacturing
238170	Gutters, seamless roof, formed and installed on site
332322	Gutters, sheet metal (except custom roll formed), manufacturing
339920	Gymnasium and playground equipment, manufacturing
423910	Gymnasium equipment merchant wholesalers
713940	Gymnasiums
611620	Gymnastics instruction, camps, or schools
713940	Gyms, physical fitness
339113	Gynecological supplies and appliances manufacturing
621111	Gynecologists' offices (e.g., centers, clinics)
212399	Gypsite mining and/or beneficiating
238310	Gypsum board installation
327420	Gypsum building products manufacturing
423390	Gypsum building products merchant wholesalers
212399	Gypsum mining and/or beneficiating
327420	Gypsum products (e.g., block, board, plaster, lath, rock, tile) manufacturing
327420	Gypsum statuary manufacturing
334511	Gyrocompasses manufacturing
334511	Gyrogimbals manufacturing
334511	Gyroscopes manufacturing

624310	Habilitation job counseling and training, vocational
114111	Haddock fishing
212299	Hafnium mining and/or beneficiating
424310	Hair accessories merchant wholesalers
326299	Hair care products (e.g., combs, curlers), rubber, manufacturing
424210	Hair care products merchant wholesalers
333111	Hair clippers for animal use, electric, manufacturing
332216	Hair clippers for animal use, nonelectric, manufacturing
335210	Hair clippers for human use, electric, manufacturing
332215	Hair clippers for human use, nonelectric, manufacturing
325620	Hair coloring preparations manufacturing
335210	Hair curlers, household-type electric, manufacturing
332999	Hair curlers, metal, manufacturing
333318	Hair dryers, beauty parlor-type, manufacturing
335210	Hair dryers, electric (except equipment designed for beauty parlor use), manufacturing
423620	Hair dryers, personal, merchant wholesalers
339999	Hair nets made from purchased netting
325620	Hair preparations (e.g., conditioners, dyes, rinses, shampoos) manufacturing
424210	Hair preparations (except professional) merchant wholesalers
423850	Hair preparations, professional, merchant wholesalers
812199	Hair removal (i.e., depilatory, electrolysis, laser, waxing) services
812199	Hair replacement services (except by offices of physicians)
325620	Hair sprays manufacturing
812112	Hair stylist salons or shops, unisex or women's
812111	Hair stylist services, men's
812112	Hair stylist services, unisex or women's
812111	Hair stylist shops, men's
812199	Hair weaving services
339994	Hairbrushes manufacturing
424990	Hairbrushes merchant wholesalers
812112	Hairdresser services
812112	Hairdressing salons or shops, unisex or women's
339999	Hairpieces (e.g., toupees, wigs, wiglets) manufacturing
424990	Hairpieces (e.g., toupees, wigs, wiglets) merchant wholesalers
339993	Hairpins (except rubber) manufacturing
326299	Hairpins, rubber, manufacturing
332613	Hairsprings (except clock, watch), light gauge, made from purchased wire or strip, manufacturing
114111	Hake fishing
623990	Halfway group homes for delinquents and ex-offenders
623220	Halfway houses for patients with mental health illnesses
623220	Halfway houses, substance abuse (e.g., alcoholism, drug addiction)
114111	Halibut fishing
531120	Hall and banquet room, nonresidential, rental or leasing
334413	Hall effect devices manufacturing
531120	Hall, nonresidential, rental or leasing
712110	Halls of fame
335110	Halogen light bulbs manufacturing
325194	Halogenated aromatic hydrocarbon derivatives manufacturing
325199	Halogenated hydrocarbon derivatives (except aromatic) manufacturing
311340	Halvah manufacturing
332111	Hammer forgings made from purchased iron or steel, unfinished
332112	Hammer forgings made from purchased nonferrous metals, unfinished
333120	Hammer mill machinery (i.e., rock and ore crushing machines), portable, manufacturing
333131	Hammer mill machinery (i.e., rock and ore crushing machines), stationary, manufacturing
332216	Hammers, handtools, manufacturing
339992	Hammers, piano, manufacturing
321999	Hammers, wood, meat, manufacturing
314999	Hammocks, fabric, manufacturing
337124	Hammocks, metal framed, manufacturing
337122	Hammocks, wood framed, manufacturing
326199	Hampers, laundry, plastics, manufacturing
337125	Hampers, laundry, reed, wicker, rattan, manufacturing
332322	Hampers, laundry, sheet metal (except stampings), manufacturing
311611	Hams (except poultry) produced in slaughtering plants

311612	Hams, canned, made from purchased carcasses
311615	Hams, poultry, manufacturing
311612	Hams, preserved (except poultry), made from purchased carcasses
327215	Hand blowing purchased glass
313240	Hand knitting lace or warp fabric products
812320	Hand laundries
325620	Hand lotions manufacturing
339940	Hand operated stamps (e.g., canceling, postmark, shoe, textile marking) manufacturing
325611	Hand soaps (e.g., hard, liquid, soft) manufacturing
334519	Hand stamps (e.g., date, time), timing mechanism operated, manufacturing
333924	Hand trucks manufacturing
313220	Hand weaving fabric, 12 inches or less (30cm)
313210	Hand weaving fabrics, more than 12 inches (30 cm) in width
316110	Handbag leather manufacturing
448150	Handbag stores
316998	Handbags (except metal), men's, manufacturing
424330	Handbags merchant wholesalers
339910	Handbags, precious metal, manufacturing
316992	Handbags, women's, all materials (except precious metal), manufacturing
713940	Handball club facilities
541870	Handbill direct distribution services
332999	Handcuffs manufacturing
332216	Handheld edge tools (except scissors-type), nonelectric, manufacturing
485991	Handicapped passenger transportation services
611110	Handicapped, schools for, elementary or secondary
611610	Handicrafts instruction
315210	Handkerchiefs (except paper) cut and sew apparel contractors
315990	Handkerchiefs (except paper) cut and sewn from purchased fabric
322291	Handkerchiefs, paper, made from purchased paper
321912	Handle blanks, wood, manufacturing
321912	Handle stock, sawed or planed, manufacturing
321999	Handles (e.g., broom, mop, handtool), wood, manufacturing

424990	Handles (e.g., broom, mop, paint) merchant wholesalers
326199	Handles (e.g., brush, tool, umbrella), plastics, manufacturing
316998	Handles (e.g., luggage, whip), leather, manufacturing
332999	Handles (e.g., parasol, umbrella), metal, manufacturing
327110	Handles, faucet, vitreous china and earthenware, manufacturing
541420	Handtool industrial design services
332216	Handtool metal blades (e.g., putty knives, scrapers, screw drivers) manufacturing
423710	Handtools (except motor vehicle mechanics', machinists' precision) merchant wholesalers
332216	Handtools, machinists' precision, manufacturing
423830	Handtools, machinists' precision, merchant wholesalers
332216	Handtools, motor vehicle mechanics', manufacturing
423120	Handtools, motor vehicle mechanics', merchant wholesalers
333991	Handtools, power-driven, manufacturing
444130	Handtools, power-driven, repair and maintenance services retailing new power-driven handtools
811411	Handtools, power-driven, repair and maintenance services without retailing new power-driven handtools
541990	Handwriting analysis services
541990	Handwriting expert services
236220	Handyman construction service, commercial and institutional building
236118	Handyman construction service, residential building
336411	Hang gliders manufacturing
236220	Hangar construction
332321	Hangar doors, metal, manufacturing
488119	Hangar rental, aircraft
321999	Hangers, wooden, garment, manufacturing
111422	Hanging basket plant growing
423610	Hanging devices, electrical, merchant wholesalers
237990	Harbor construction
488310	Harbor maintenance services (except dredging)
488310	Harbor operation
487210	Harbor sightseeing tours
488330	Harbor tugboat services

213112	Hard banding oil and gas field service on a contract basis
311340	Hard candies manufacturing
424820	Hard cider merchant wholesalers
212113	Hard coal (i.e., anthracite) surface mining
212113	Hard coal (i.e., anthracite) underground mining
334112	Hard disk drives manufacturing
334613	Hard drive media manufacturing
313210	Hard fiber fabrics, broadwoven, weaving
313110	Hard fiber spun yarns made from purchased fiber
313110	Hard fiber thread manufacturing
313220	Hard fiber, narrow woven, weaving
339113	Hard hats manufacturing
321219	Hardboard manufacturing
332811	Hardening (i.e., heat treating) metals and metal products for the trade
334519	Hardness testing equipment manufacturing
423710	Hardware (except motor vehicle) merchant wholesalers
332618	Hardware cloth, woven wire, made from purchased wire
444130	Hardware stores
423120	Hardware, motor vehicle, merchant wholesalers
326199	Hardware, plastics, manufacturing
335932	Hardware, transmission pole and line, manufacturing
423610	Hardware, transmission pole and line, merchant wholesalers
321912	Hardwood dimension lumber and stock, resawing purchased lumber
325194	Hardwood distillates manufacturing
444190	Hardwood flooring dealers
238330	Hardwood flooring, installation only
321211	Hardwood plywood composites manufacturing
321211	Hardwood veneer or plywood manufacturing
339992	Harmonicas manufacturing
334419	Harness assemblies for electronic use manufacturing
711219	Harness drivers
424910	Harness equipment merchant wholesalers
316110	Harness leather manufacturing
332999	Harness parts, metal, manufacturing
711212	Harness racetracks
316998	Harnesses and harness parts, leather, manufacturing
316998	Harnesses, dog, manufacturing
339992	Harps and parts manufacturing
339992	Harpsichords manufacturing
333111	Harrows (e.g., disc, spring, tine) manufacturing
315990	Harvest hats, straw, manufacturing
113210	Harvesting berries or nuts from native and non-cultivated plants
333111	Harvesting machinery and equipment, agriculture, manufacturing
423820	Harvesting machinery and equipment, agriculture, merchant wholesalers
335210	Hassock fans, electric, manufacturing
424310	Hat and cap materials merchant wholesalers
448150	Hat and cap stores
339999	Hat blocks manufacturing
315210	Hat bodies (e.g., fur-felt, straw, wool-felt) cut and sew apparel contractors
315990	Hat bodies (e.g., fur-felt, straw, wool-felt) cut and sewn from purchased fabric (except apparel contractors)
812320	Hat cleaning services
315210	Hat findings cut and sew apparel contractors
315990	Hat findings cut and sewn from purchased fabric (except apparel contractors)
315210	Hat linings and trimmings cut and sew apparel contractors
315990	Hat linings and trimmings cut and sewn from purchased fabric (except apparel contractors)
112511	Hatcheries, finfish
112340	Hatcheries, poultry
112512	Hatcheries, shellfish
236220	Hatchery construction
332216	Hatchets manufacturing
315210	Hats (e.g., cloth, fur, fur-felt, leather, straw, wool-felt) cut and sew apparel contractors
315990	Hats (except fur, knitting mill products, leather) cut and sewn from purchased fabric (except apparel contractors)
424320	Hats and caps, men's and boys', merchant wholesalers
424330	Hats and caps, women's, girls', and infants', merchant wholesalers
322299	Hats made from purchased paper
315190	Hats made in apparel knitting mills

315990	Hats, cloth, cut and sewn from purchased fabric (except apparel contractors)
315280	Hats, fur (except apparel contractors), manufacturing
315990	Hats, fur-felt, straw, and wool-felt, cut and sewn from purchased fabric (except apparel contractors)
315280	Hats, leather (except apparel contractors), manufacturing
315210	Hats, trimmed, cut and sew apparel contractors
315990	Hats, trimmed, cut and sewn from purchased fabric (except apparel contractors)
333111	Hay balers and presses manufacturing
111940	Hay farming (e.g., alfalfa hay, clover hay, grass hay)
424910	Hay merchant wholesalers
115113	Hay mowing, raking, baling, and chopping
111998	Hay seed farming
311119	Hay, cubed, manufacturing
333111	Haying machines manufacturing
423820	Haying machines merchant wholesalers
562910	Hazardous material storage tank removal and disposal services
562112	Hazardous waste collection services
562211	Hazardous waste disposal facilities
562211	Hazardous waste disposal facilities combined with collection and/or local hauling of hazardous waste
562211	Hazardous waste material disposal facilities
562211	Hazardous waste material treatment facilities
562211	Hazardous waste treatment facilities
562211	Hazardous waste treatment facilities combined with collection and/or local hauling of hazardous waste
111335	Hazelnut farming
334613	Head cleaners for magnetic tape equipment, manufacturing
551114	Head offices
311212	Head rice manufacturing
624410	Head start programs, separate from schools
315210	Headbands cut and sew apparel contractors
315990	Headbands, women's and girls', cut and sewn from purchased fabric (except apparel contractors)
337122	Headboards, wood, manufacturing
321920	Heading, barrel (i.e., cooperage stock), wood, manufacturing
551114	Headquarters offices
334419	Heads (e.g., recording, read/write) manufacturing
334511	Heads-up display (HUD) systems, aeronautical, manufacturing
236220	Health and athletic club construction
525120	Health and welfare funds
713940	Health club facilities, physical fitness
424490	Health foods (except fresh fruits, vegetables) merchant wholesalers
424480	Health foods, fresh fruits and vegetables, merchant wholesalers
524114	Health insurance carriers, direct
335110	Health lamp bulbs, infrared and ultraviolet radiation, manufacturing
621491	Health maintenance organization (HMO) medical centers and clinics
923120	Health planning and development agencies, government
813920	Health professionals' associations
926150	Health professions licensure agencies
923120	Health program administration
541715	Health research and development laboratories or services (except biotechnology and nanotechnology research and development)
813212	Health research fundraising organizations
621999	Health screening services (except by offices of health practitioners)
621111	Health screening services in physicians' offices
721110	Health spas (i.e., physical fitness facilities) with accommodations
713940	Health spas without accommodations, physical fitness
923120	Health statistics centers, government
713940	Health studios, physical fitness
446199	Hearing aid stores
423450	Hearing aids merchant wholesalers
334510	Hearing aids, electronic, manufacturing
621999	Hearing testing services (except by offices of audiologists)
621340	Hearing testing services by offices of audiologists
336211	Hearse bodies manufacturing
485320	Hearse rental with driver
532111	Hearse rental without driver
336111	Hearses assembling on chassis of own manufacture

336211	Hearses assembling on purchased chassis
334510	Heart-lung machine manufacturing
423830	Heat exchange equipment, industrial, merchant wholesalers
332410	Heat exchangers manufacturing
238220	Heat pump installation
333415	Heat pumps manufacturing
423730	Heat pumps merchant wholesalers
325992	Heat sensitized (i.e., thermal) paper made from purchased paper
335991	Heat shields, carbon or graphite, manufacturing
332811	Heat treating metals and metal products for the trade
333994	Heat treating ovens, industrial process-type, manufacturing
221330	Heat, steam, distribution
221330	Heated air distribution
335210	Heaters, portable electric space, manufacturing
423620	Heaters, portable electric, merchant wholesalers
333414	Heaters, space (except portable electric), manufacturing
333414	Heaters, swimming pool, manufacturing
335210	Heaters, tape, manufacturing
333415	Heating and air-conditioning combination units manufacturing
238220	Heating and cooling duct work installation
334512	Heating and cooling system controls, residential and commercial, manufacturing
238220	Heating and ventilation system component (e.g., air registers, diffusers, filters, grilles, sound attenuators) installation
238220	Heating boiler installation
423720	Heating boilers, steam and hot water, merchant wholesalers
238220	Heating contractors
541330	Heating engineering consulting services
238220	Heating equipment installation
333414	Heating equipment, hot water (except hot water heaters), manufacturing
423720	Heating equipment, hot water, merchant wholesalers
423730	Heating equipment, warm air (i.e. forced air), merchant wholesalers
333415	Heating equipment, warm air (i.e., forced air), manufacturing
424710	Heating oil bulk stations and terminals, merchant wholesalers
454310	Heating oil dealers, direct selling
324110	Heating oils made in petroleum refineries
335210	Heating pads, electric, manufacturing
334512	Heating regulators manufacturing
221330	Heating steam (suppliers of heat) providers
335210	Heating units for electric appliances manufacturing
333414	Heating units, baseboard, manufacturing
238220	Heating, ventilation and air-conditioning (HVAC) contractors
532412	Heavy construction equipment rental without operator
611519	Heavy equipment operation schools
611519	Heavy equipment repair training
811310	Heavy machinery and equipment repair and maintenance services
423130	Heavy truck tires and tubes merchant wholesalers
336120	Heavy trucks assembling on chassis of own manufacture
336211	Heavy trucks assembling on purchased chassis
325180	Heavy water (i.e., deuterium oxide) manufacturing
332216	Hedge shears and trimmers, nonelectric, manufacturing
333112	Hedge trimmers, powered, manufacturing
316998	Heel caps, leather or metal, manufacturing
316998	Heel lifts, leather, manufacturing
321999	Heels, boot and shoe, finished wood, manufacturing
316998	Heels, boot and shoe, leather, manufacturing
332613	Helical springs, hot wound heavy gauge metal, manufacturing
332613	Helical springs, light gauge, made from purchased wire or strip, manufacturing
481212	Helicopter carriers, freight, nonscheduled
481112	Helicopter freight carriers, scheduled
481211	Helicopter passenger carriers (except scenic, sightseeing), nonscheduled
481111	Helicopter passenger carriers, scheduled
487990	Helicopter ride, scenic and sightseeing, operation
336411	Helicopters manufacturing
325120	Helium manufacturing
325120	Helium recovery from natural gas

339113	Helmets (except athletic), safety (e.g., motorized vehicle crash helmets, space helmets), manufacturing
339920	Helmets, athletic (except motorized vehicle crash helmets), manufacturing
561320	Help supply services
212210	Hematite mining and/or beneficiating
334516	Hematology instruments manufacturing
325413	Hematology in-vitro diagnostic substances manufacturing
325412	Hematology in-vivo diagnostic substances manufacturing
325414	Hematology products (except diagnostic substances) manufacturing
325194	Hemlock extract manufacturing
113210	Hemlock gum gathering
621492	Hemodialysis centers and clinics
313110	Hemp bags made from purchased fiber
313110	Hemp ropes made from purchased fiber
313110	Hemp spun yarns made from purchased fiber
315210	Hemstitching apparel contractors on apparel
325110	Heptanes made from refined petroleum or liquid hydrocarbons
325110	Heptenes made from refined petroleum or liquid hydrocarbons
111419	Herb farming, grown under cover
111998	Herb farming, open field
111421	Herbaceous perennial growing
446191	Herbal supplement stores
424210	Herbal supplements merchant wholesalers
325412	Herbal supplements, compounded, manufacturing
325411	Herbal supplements, uncompounded, manufacturing
621399	Herbalists' offices (e.g., centers, clinics)
712110	Herbariums
325320	Herbicides manufacturing
424910	Herbicides merchant wholesalers
711310	Heritage festival managers with facilities
711320	Heritage festival managers without facilities
711310	Heritage festival organizers with facilities
711320	Heritage festival organizers without facilities
711310	Heritage festival promoters with facilities
711320	Heritage festival promoters without facilities

712120	Heritage villages
238150	Hermetically sealed window unit, commercial-type, installation
238350	Hermetically sealed window unit, residential-type, installation
114111	Herring fishing
325199	Heterocyclic chemicals, not specified elsewhere by process, manufacturing
325199	Hexadecanol manufacturing
325199	Hexamethylenediamine manufacturing
325199	Hexamethylenetetramine manufacturing
325199	Hexanol manufacturing
311221	HFCS (high fructose corn syrup) manufacturing
311611	Hides and skins produced in slaughtering plants
316110	Hides and skins, finishing on a contract basis
424590	Hides merchant wholesalers
316110	Hides, tanning, currying, dressing, and finishing
337122	High chairs, wood, children's, manufacturing
311221	High fructose corn syrup (HFCS) manufacturing
335110	High intensity lamp bulbs manufacturing
331110	High percentage nonferrous alloying elements (i.e., ferroalloys) manufacturing
611691	High school equivalency (e.g., GED) exam instruction
611110	High schools
611110	High schools offering both academic and technical courses
611110	High schools offering both academic and vocational courses
236116	High-rise apartment construction general contractors
236117	High-rise apartment for-sale builders
332312	Highway bridge sections, prefabricated metal, manufacturing
237310	Highway construction
332322	Highway guardrails, sheet metal (except stampings), manufacturing
333120	Highway line marking machinery manufacturing
237310	Highway line painting
922120	Highway patrols, police
336120	Highway tractors assembled on chassis of own manufacture
336211	Highway tractors assembling on purchased chassis

238210	Highway, street and bridge lighting and electrical signal installation
423710	Hinges merchant wholesalers
332510	Hinges, metal, manufacturing
541720	Historic and cultural preservation research and development services
813410	Historical clubs
712120	Historical forts
712110	Historical museums
712120	Historical ships
712120	Historical sites
336390	Hitches, trailer, automotive, truck, and bus, manufacturing
325413	HIV test kits manufacturing
621491	HMO (health maintenance organization) medical centers and clinics
423920	Hobby craft kits merchant wholesalers
451120	Hobby shops
339930	Hobbyhorses manufacturing
423920	Hobbyists' supplies merchant wholesalers
333515	Hobs (i.e., metal gear cutting tool) manufacturing
711211	Hockey clubs, professional or semiprofessional
713990	Hockey clubs, recreational
339920	Hockey equipment (except apparel) manufacturing
423910	Hockey equipment and supplies merchant wholesalers
611620	Hockey instruction, camps, or schools
339920	Hockey skates manufacturing
711211	Hockey teams, professional or semiprofessional
713990	Hockey teams, recreational
115112	Hoeing
332216	Hoes, garden and mason's handtools, manufacturing
112210	Hog and pig (including breeding, farrowing, nursery, and finishing activities) farming
333111	Hog feeding and watering equipment manufacturing
112210	Hog feedlots (except stockyards for transportation)
424520	Hogs merchant wholesalers
321920	Hogsheads, coopered wood, manufacturing
238290	Hoisting and placement of large-scale apparatus
333923	Hoists (except aircraft loading) manufacturing

423830	Hoists (except automotive) merchant wholesalers
333924	Hoists, aircraft loading, manufacturing
423120	Hoists, automotive, merchant wholesalers
551112	Holding companies (except bank, managing)
551114	Holding companies that manage
551111	Holding companies, bank (except managing)
333318	Holepunchers (except hand operated), office-type, manufacturing
339940	Holepunchers, hand operated, manufacturing
423220	Hollowware (except precious metal) merchant wholesalers
339910	Hollowware, precious metal, manufacturing
423940	Hollowware, precious metal, merchant wholesalers
332999	Hollowware, precious plated metal, manufacturing
316998	Holsters, leather, manufacturing
452319	Home and auto supply stores
532310	Home and garden equipment rental centers
238210	Home automation system installation
236116	Home builders (except for-sale), multifamily
236115	Home builders (except for-sale), single-family
236117	Home builders, for-sale
332119	Home canning lids and rings, metal stamping
621610	Home care of elderly, medical
624120	Home care of elderly, non-medical
444110	Home centers, building materials
624229	Home construction organizations, work (sweat) equity
454390	Home delivery newspaper routes, direct selling
337124	Home entertainment centers, metal, manufacturing
337122	Home entertainment centers, wood, manufacturing
522292	Home equity credit lending
423220	Home furnishings merchant wholesalers
442299	Home furnishings stores
621610	Home health agencies
611519	Home health aid schools

621610	Home health care agencies
423450	Home health care supplies merchant wholesalers
532283	Home health furniture and equipment rental
236118	Home improvement (e.g., adding on, remodeling, renovating)
236118	Home improvement (e.g., adding on, remodeling, renovating), multifamily building, for-sale builders
236118	Home improvement (e.g., adding on, remodeling, renovating), multifamily building, general contractors
236118	Home improvement (e.g., adding on, remodeling, renovating), single-family housing, for-sale builders
236118	Home improvement (e.g., adding on, remodeling, renovating), single-family housing, general contractors
444110	Home improvement centers
621610	Home infusion therapy services
541350	Home inspection services
621610	Home nursing services (except private practices)
621399	Home nursing services, private practice
236118	Home renovation
453998	Home security equipment stores
561920	Home show managers
561920	Home show organizers
561920	Home show promoters
334310	Home stereo systems manufacturing
334310	Home tape recorders and players (e.g., cartridge, cassette, reel) manufacturing
334310	Home theater audio and video equipment manufacturing
238210	Home theater installation
333517	Home workshop metal cutting machine tools (except handtools, welding equipment) manufacturing
624221	Homeless shelters
624120	Homemaker's service for elderly or disabled persons, non-medical
621399	Homeopaths' offices (e.g., centers, clinics)
813990	Homeowners' associations
813990	Homeowners' associations, condominium
524126	Homeowners' insurance carriers, direct
524128	Homeowners' warranty insurance carriers, direct
623990	Homes for children with health care incidental
623220	Homes for emotionally disturbed adults or children
623110	Homes for the aged with nursing care
623312	Homes for the aged without nursing care
623110	Homes for the elderly with nursing care
623312	Homes for the elderly without nursing care
623990	Homes for unwed mothers
623210	Homes with or without health care, intellectual and developmental disability
623220	Homes, psychiatric convalescent
311211	Hominy grits (except breakfast food), manufacturing
311230	Hominy grits, prepared as cereal breakfast food, manufacturing
311421	Hominy, canned, manufacturing
333241	Homogenizing machinery, food, manufacturing
311511	Homogenizing milk
212399	Hones mining and/or beneficiating
112910	Honey bee production
424490	Honey merchant wholesalers
311999	Honey processing
111219	Honeydew melon farming, field, bedding plant and seed production
333517	Honing and lapping machines, metal cutting type, manufacturing
333515	Honing heads (i.e., a machine tool accessory) manufacturing
922140	Honor camps, correctional
332313	Hoods, industrial, fabricated metal plate work, manufacturing
332322	Hoods, range (except household-type), sheet metal (except stampings), manufacturing
335210	Hoods, range, household-type, manufacturing
115210	Hoof trimming
339993	Hook and eye fasteners (i.e., sewing accessories) manufacturing
332722	Hook and eye latches, metal, manufacturing
313220	Hook and loop fastener fabric manufacturing
713990	Hookah lounges (except primarily selling food and beverages)
332722	Hooks (i.e., general purpose fasteners), metal, manufacturing
339920	Hooks, fishing, manufacturing

332216	Hooks, handtools (e.g., baling, bush, grass, husking), manufacturing
332722	Hooks, metal screw, manufacturing
331110	Hoops made in iron and steel mills
331110	Hoops, galvanized, made in iron and steel mills
332999	Hoops, metal (except wire), fabricated from purchased metal
321920	Hoops, sawed or split wood for tight or slack cooperage, manufacturing
311942	Hop extract manufacturing
424490	Hop extract merchant wholesalers
111998	Hop farming
333515	Hopper feed devices (i.e., a machine tool accessory) manufacturing
332313	Hoppers, fabricated metal plate work, manufacturing
332439	Hoppers, light gauge metal, manufacturing
424590	Hops merchant wholesalers
334511	Horizon situation instrumentation manufacturing
237990	Horizontal drilling (e.g., underground cable, pipeline, sewer installation)
325413	Hormone in-vitro diagnostic substances manufacturing
325412	Hormone preparations (except in-vitro diagnostics) manufacturing
325411	Hormones and derivatives, uncompounded, manufacturing
112920	Horse (including thoroughbreds) production
332999	Horse bits manufacturing
316998	Horse boots and muzzles manufacturing
711212	Horse racetracks
711219	Horse racing stables
713990	Horse rental services, recreational saddle
711310	Horse show managers with facilities
711320	Horse show managers without facilities
711310	Horse show organizers with facilities
711320	Horse show organizers without facilities
711310	Horse show promoters with facilities
711320	Horse show promoters without facilities
711190	Horse shows
441228	Horse trailer dealers
336214	Horse trailers (except fifth-wheel-type) manufacturing
336212	Horse trailers, fifth-wheel-type, manufacturing
713990	Horseback riding, recreational
487110	Horse-drawn carriage operation
311611	Horsemeat produced in slaughtering plants
311111	Horsemeat, processing, for dog and cat food
311421	Horseradish (except sauce) canning
311941	Horseradish, prepared sauce, manufacturing
115210	Horses (except racehorses), boarding
424590	Horses merchant wholesalers
115210	Horses, training (except racehorses)
331222	Horseshoe nails, iron or steel, made in wire drawing plants
115210	Horseshoeing
332111	Horseshoes, ferrous forged, made from purchased iron or steel
541690	Horticultural consulting services
424910	Horticultural products merchant wholesalers
332912	Hose assemblies for fluid power systems manufacturing
332722	Hose clamps, metal, manufacturing
332912	Hose couplings and fittings, fluid power, manufacturing
332919	Hose couplings, metal (except fluid power), manufacturing
313220	Hose fabrics, tubular, weaving
332999	Hose, flexible metal, manufacturing
423840	Hose, industrial, merchant wholesalers
326220	Hoses, reinforced, rubber or plastics, manufacturing
326220	Hoses, rubberized fabric, manufacturing
333249	Hosiery machines manufacturing
448190	Hosiery stores
424320	Hosiery, men's and boys', merchant wholesalers
339113	Hosiery, orthopedic support, manufacturing
315110	Hosiery, sheer, women's, misses', and girls' full-length and knee-length, knitting or knitting and finishing
424330	Hosiery, women's and girls', merchant wholesalers
424330	Hosiery, women's, children's, and infants', merchant wholesalers
315110	Hosiery, women's, girls', and infants', manufacturing
621610	Hospice care services, in-home
623110	Hospices, inpatient care
813920	Hospital administrators' associations

524114	Hospital and medical service plans, direct, without providing health care services
813910	Hospital associations
532283	Hospital bed rental and leasing (i.e., home use)
339113	Hospital beds manufacturing
423450	Hospital beds merchant wholesalers
236220	Hospital construction
423450	Hospital equipment and supplies merchant wholesalers
532283	Hospital equipment rental (i.e. home use)
532283	Hospital furniture and equipment rental (i.e. home use)
423450	Hospital furniture merchant wholesalers
339113	Hospital furniture, specialized (e.g., hospital beds, operating room furniture)
423450	Hospital gowns merchant wholesalers
926150	Hospital licensure agencies
611519	Hospital management schools (except academic)
611310	Hospital management schools offering baccalaureate or graduate degrees
315210	Hospital service apparel, washable, cut and sew apparel contractors
315220	Hospital service apparel, washable, men's and boys', cut and sewn from purchased fabric (except apparel contractors)
315240	Hospital service apparel, washable, women's and girls', cut and sewn from purchased fabric (except apparel contractors)
611519	Hospitality management schools (except academic)
611310	Hospitality management schools offering baccalaureate or graduate degrees
524114	Hospitalization insurance carriers, direct, without providing health care services
******	Hospitals -- see type
622210	Hospitals for alcoholics
622210	Hospitals, addiction
541940	Hospitals, animal
622110	Hospitals, general medical and surgical
622110	Hospitals, general pediatric
623210	Hospitals, intellectual and developmental disability
622210	Hospitals, mental (except intellectual and developmental disability)
622210	Hospitals, psychiatric (except convalescent)
623220	Hospitals, psychiatric convalescent

622210	Hospitals, psychiatric pediatric
622310	Hospitals, specialty (except psychiatric, substance abuse)
622210	Hospitals, substance abuse
721199	Hostels
487990	Hot air balloon ride, scenic and sightseeing, operation
333318	Hot beverage vending machines manufacturing
332812	Hot dip galvanizing metals and metal products for the trade
311612	Hot dogs (except poultry) made from purchased carcasses
311611	Hot dogs (except poultry) produced in slaughtering plants
311615	Hot dogs, poultry, manufacturing
332111	Hot forgings made from purchased iron or steel, unfinished
332112	Hot forgings made from purchased nonferrous metals, unfinished
213112	Hot oil treating of oil field tanks on a contract basis
213112	Hot shot service on a contract basis
333519	Hot strip mill machinery, metalworking, manufacturing
453998	Hot tub stores
423910	Hot tubs merchant wholesalers
321920	Hot tubs, coopered, manufacturing
326191	Hot tubs, plastics or fiberglass, manufacturing
326299	Hot water bottles, rubber, manufacturing
335220	Hot water heaters (including nonelectric), household-type, manufacturing
238220	Hot water heating system installation
238220	Hot water tank installation
531120	Hotel building rental or leasing, not operating hotel
236220	Hotel construction
423440	Hotel equipment and supplies (except furniture) merchant wholesalers
423210	Hotel furniture merchant wholesalers
561110	Hotel management services (except complete operation of client's business)
721110	Hotel management services (i.e., providing management and operating staff to run hotel)
561599	Hotel reservation services
327110	Hotel tableware and kitchen articles, vitreous china, manufacturing

721110	Hotels (except casino hotels)
721110	Hotels (except casino hotels) with golf courses, tennis courts, and/or other health spa facilities (i.e., resorts)
721120	Hotels, casino
721110	Hotels, membership
721120	Hotels, resort, with casinos
721110	Hotels, resort, without casinos
721120	Hotels, seasonal, with casinos
721110	Hotels, seasonal, without casinos
624190	Hotline centers
333318	Hotplates, commercial-type, manufacturing
335210	Hotplates, household-type electric, manufacturing
331110	Hot-rolling iron or steel products in iron and steel mills
333519	Hot-rolling mill machinery, metalworking, manufacturing
331221	Hot-rolling purchased steel
238910	House demolishing
238130	House framing
238990	House moving (i.e., raising from one site, moving, and placing on a new foundation)
238320	House painting
111422	House plant growing
238910	House razing
812990	House sitting services
316210	House slippers manufacturing
316210	House slippers, plastics or plastics soled fabric upper, manufacturing
316210	House slippers, rubber or rubber soled fabric upper, manufacturing
423330	House wrapping insulation materials merchant wholesalers
532284	Houseboat rental
315210	Housecoats cut and sew apparel contractors
315190	Housecoats made in apparel knitting mills
315240	Housecoats, women's, girls', and infants', cut and sewn from purchased fabric (except apparel contractors)
315210	Housedresses cut and sew apparel contractors
315240	Housedresses, women's and girls', cut and sewn from purchased fabric (except apparel contractors)
238220	Household oil storage tank installation
814110	Households, private, employing (e.g., cooks, maids, chauffeurs, gardeners)
814110	Households, private, employing domestic personnel
443141	Household-type appliance stores
423620	Household-type appliances (except water heaters, heating stoves (i.e., noncooking)), gas and electric, merchant wholesalers
327110	Household-type earthenware, semivitreous, manufacturing
423210	Household-type furniture merchant wholesalers
337121	Household-type furniture, upholstered, manufacturing
337122	Household-type furniture, wood, not upholstered (except TV and radio housings and sewing machine cabinets), manufacturing
325320	Household-type insecticides manufacturing
423620	Household-type laundry equipment (e.g., dryers, washers) merchant wholesalers
327110	Household-type tableware and kitchen articles, vitreous china, manufacturing
334519	Household-type timing mechanisms manufacturing
321999	Household-type woodenware manufacturing
721199	Housekeeping cabins
721199	Housekeeping cottages
561720	Housekeeping services (i.e., cleaning services)
922140	Houses of correction
531110	Houses rental or leasing
332311	Houses, prefabricated metal, manufacturing
321991	Houses, prefabricated mobile homes, manufacturing
321992	Houses, prefabricated, wood (except mobile homes), manufacturing
454390	House-to-house direct selling
423220	Housewares (except electric) merchant wholesalers
442299	Housewares stores
423620	Housewares, gas and electric, merchant wholesalers
624229	Housing assistance agencies
531110	Housing authorities owning and operating residential buildings
925110	Housing authorities, nonoperating
236117	Housing construction, for-sale builder
236117	Housing construction, merchant builder
922120	Housing police, government
925110	Housing programs, planning and development, government

624229	Housing repair organizations, volunteer
236116	Housing, multifamily, construction general contractors
236115	Housing, single-family, construction general contractors
336612	Hovercraft building
487210	Hovercraft sightseeing operation
332994	Howitzers manufacturing
321999	Hubs, wood, manufacturing
111334	Huckleberry farming
113210	Huckleberry greens, gathering of
334511	HUD (heads-up display) systems, aeronautical, manufacturing
212299	Huebnerite mining and/or beneficiating
115114	Hulling and shelling of nuts
333111	Hulling machinery, farm-type, manufacturing
621991	Human egg or ova banks
621991	Human embryo storage services
712110	Human history museums
541612	Human resource consulting services
813311	Human rights advocacy organizations
921190	Human rights commissions, government
813312	Humane societies
541720	Humanities research and development services
423730	Humidifiers and dehumidifiers (except portable) merchant wholesalers
423620	Humidifiers and dehumidifiers, portable, merchant wholesalers
335210	Humidifiers, portable electric, manufacturing
333415	Humidifying equipment (except portable) manufacturing
334512	Humidistats (e.g., duct, skeleton, wall) manufacturing
238210	Humidity control system installation
334512	Humidity controls, air-conditioning-type, manufacturing
334519	Humidity instruments (except industrial process and air-conditioning type) manufacturing
334513	Humidity instruments, industrial process-type, manufacturing
212399	Humus, peat, mining and/or beneficiating
112390	Hungarian partridge production
721214	Hunting camps with accommodation facilities
713990	Hunting clubs, recreational
315210	Hunting coats and vests cut and sew apparel contractors
315220	Hunting coats and vests, men's and boys', cut and sewn from purchased fabric (except apparel contractors)
423910	Hunting equipment and supplies merchant wholesalers
713990	Hunting guide services
332215	Hunting knives manufacturing
114210	Hunting preserves
813319	Hunting, fishing, and sport shooting advocacy organizations
238220	HVAC (heating, ventilation and air-conditioning) contractors
423730	HVAC equipment merchant wholesalers
334111	Hybrid computers manufacturing
334413	Hybrid integrated circuits manufacturing
112511	Hybrid striped bass production
237110	Hydrant and flushing hydrant installation
327410	Hydrated lime (i.e., calcium hydroxide) manufacturing
332912	Hydraulic aircraft subassemblies manufacturing
333995	Hydraulic cylinders, fluid power, manufacturing
811310	Hydraulic equipment repair and maintenance services
324110	Hydraulic fluids made in petroleum refineries
324191	Hydraulic fluids, petroleum, made from refined petroleum
325998	Hydraulic fluids, synthetic, manufacturing
213112	Hydraulic fracturing wells on a contract basis
332912	Hydraulic hose fittings, fluid power, manufacturing
326220	Hydraulic hoses (without fitting), rubber or plastics, manufacturing
423830	Hydraulic power transmission equipment merchant wholesalers
423830	Hydraulic pumps and parts merchant wholesalers
333996	Hydraulic pumps, fluid power, manufacturing
336340	Hydraulic slave cylinders, automotive, truck, and bus clutch, manufacturing
333611	Hydraulic turbine generator set units manufacturing
333611	Hydraulic turbines manufacturing
332912	Hydraulic valves, fluid power, manufacturing

325180	Hydrazine manufacturing
325180	Hydrochloric acid manufacturing
325180	Hydrocyanic acid manufacturing
238910	Hydrodemolition (i.e., demolition with pressurized water) contractors
237990	Hydroelectric generating facility construction
221111	Hydroelectric power generation
325180	Hydrofluoric acid manufacturing
325180	Hydrofluosilicic acid manufacturing
336611	Hydrofoil vessel building and repairing in shipyard
325120	Hydrogen manufacturing
325180	Hydrogen peroxide manufacturing
325180	Hydrogen sulfide manufacturing
311225	Hydrogenating purchased oil
541370	Hydrographic mapping services
323111	Hydrographic printing
541370	Hydrographic surveying services
541690	Hydrology consulting services
334519	Hydrometers (except industrial process-type) manufacturing
334513	Hydrometers, industrial process-type, manufacturing
334512	Hydronic circulator control, automatic, manufacturing
423720	Hydronic heating equipment and supplies merchant wholesalers
333414	Hydronic heating equipment manufacturing
238220	Hydronic heating system installation
334512	Hydronic limit control manufacturing
334512	Hydronic limit, pressure, and temperature controls, manufacturing
334511	Hydrophones manufacturing
111419	Hydroponic crop farming
325194	Hydroquinone manufacturing
561730	Hydroseeding services (e.g., decorative, erosion control purposes)
333996	Hydrostatic drives manufacturing
541380	Hydrostatic testing laboratories or services
333996	Hydrostatic transmissions manufacturing
325180	Hydrosulfites manufacturing
339113	Hydrotherapy equipment manufacturing
424210	Hygiene products, oral, merchant wholesalers
334519	Hygrometers (except industrial process-type) manufacturing

334513	Hygrometers, industrial process-type, manufacturing
334519	Hygrothermographs manufacturing
621399	Hypnotherapists' offices (e.g., centers, clinics)
325411	Hypnotic drugs, uncompounded, manufacturing
325180	Hypochlorites manufacturing
339112	Hypodermic needles and syringes manufacturing
325180	Hypophosphites manufacturing
312113	Ice (except dry ice) manufacturing
424990	Ice (except dry ice) merchant wholesalers
238170	Ice apron, roof, installation
334512	Ice bank controls manufacturing
335220	Ice boxes, household-type, manufacturing
326199	Ice buckets, plastics (except foam), manufacturing
326140	Ice buckets, polystyrene foam, manufacturing
326150	Ice buckets, urethane or other plastics foam (except polystyrene), manufacturing
332439	Ice chests or coolers, light gauge metal, manufacturing
326199	Ice chests or coolers, plastics (except plastics foam), manufacturing
326140	Ice chests or coolers, polystyrene foam, manufacturing
326150	Ice chests or coolers, urethane or other plastics foam (except polystyrene) manufacturing
445299	Ice cream (i.e., packaged) stores
424430	Ice cream and ices merchant wholesalers
311821	Ice cream cones manufacturing
424490	Ice cream cones merchant wholesalers
333241	Ice cream making machinery manufacturing
311520	Ice cream manufacturing
424430	Ice cream merchant wholesalers
311514	Ice cream mix manufacturing
722515	Ice cream parlors
311520	Ice cream specialties manufacturing
722330	Ice cream truck vendors
333318	Ice cream vending machines manufacturing
335210	Ice crushers, household-type electric, manufacturing
333999	Ice crushers, industrial and commercial-type, manufacturing

711211	Ice hockey clubs, professional or semiprofessional
713990	Ice hockey clubs, recreational
334512	Ice maker controls manufacturing
333415	Ice making machinery manufacturing
423740	Ice making machines merchant wholesalers
311520	Ice milk manufacturing
424430	Ice milk merchant wholesalers
311514	Ice milk mix manufacturing
311520	Ice milk specialties manufacturing
237990	Ice rink (except indoor) construction
236220	Ice rink, indoor, construction
339920	Ice skates manufacturing
711190	Ice skating companies
713940	Ice skating rinks
711190	Ice skating shows
312130	Ice wine
325120	Ice, dry, manufacturing
424690	Ice, dry, merchant wholesalers
312111	Iced coffee manufacturing
312111	Iced tea manufacturing
212399	Iceland spar (i.e., optical grade calcite), mining and/or beneficiating
311520	Ices, flavored sherbets, manufacturing
332999	Identification plates, metal, manufacturing
423410	Identity recorders merchant wholesalers
812990	Identity theft protection services
332993	Igniters, ammunition tracer (i.e., more than 30 mm., more than 1.18 inch), manufacturing
811118	Ignition and battery repair shops, automotive
334512	Ignition controls for gas appliances and furnaces, automatic, manufacturing
336320	Ignition points and condensers for internal combustion engines manufacturing
334515	Ignition testing instruments manufacturing
336320	Ignition wiring harness for internal combustion engines manufacturing
321213	I-joists, wood, fabricating
335122	Illuminated indoor lighting fixtures (e.g., directional, exit) manufacturing
541430	Illustrators, independent commercial
212299	Ilmenite ores mining and/or beneficiating
327420	Images, small gypsum, manufacturing
327999	Images, small papier-mache, manufacturing
323120	Imagesetting services, prepress
312230	Imitation tobacco cigarettes, manufacturing
335210	Immersion heaters, household-type electric, manufacturing
624230	Immigrant resettlement services
928120	Immigration services
923120	Immunization program administration
621111	Immunologists' offices (e.g., centers, clinics)
334516	Immunology instruments, laboratory, manufacturing
333991	Impact wrenches, handheld power-driven, manufacturing
334515	Impedance measuring equipment manufacturing
334514	Impeller and counter driven flow meters manufacturing
339113	Implants, surgical, manufacturing
213112	Impounding and storing salt water in connection with petroleum production
221310	Impounding reservoirs, irrigation
339114	Impression material, dental, manufacturing
711110	Improvisational theaters
334512	In-built thermostats, filled system and bimetal types, manufacturing
335110	Incandescent filament lamp bulbs, complete, manufacturing
325998	Incense manufacturing
334512	Incinerator control systems, residential and commercial-type, manufacturing
236210	Incinerator, mass-burn type, construction
236210	Incinerator, municipal waste disposal, construction
333994	Incinerators (except precast concrete) manufacturing
238290	Incinerators, building equipment type, installation
562211	Incinerators, hazardous waste, operating
562213	Incinerators, nonhazardous solid waste
327390	Incinerators, precast concrete, manufacturing
541213	Income tax compilation services
541213	Income tax return preparation services
333318	Incoming mail handling equipment (e.g., opening, scanning, sorting) manufacturing
339113	Incubators, infant, manufacturing
339113	Incubators, laboratory-type, manufacturing
333111	Incubators, poultry, manufacturing
325998	Indelible inks manufacturing

488190 Independent pilot, air (except owner-operators)

711510 Independent technical writers

488490 Independent truck driver (except owner-operators)

333515 Indexing, rotary tables (i.e., a machine tool accessory) manufacturing

325998 India inks manufacturing

921190 Indian affairs programs, government

334515 Indicating instruments, electric, manufacturing

334519 Indicator testers, turntable, manufacturing

334513 Indicators, industrial process control-type, manufacturing

325180 Indium chloride manufacturing

624190 Individual and family social services, multi-purpose

523910 Individuals investing in financial contracts on own account

541850 Indoor display advertising services

713120 Indoor play areas

236220 Indoor swimming pool construction

333994 Induction heating equipment, industrial process-type, manufacturing

334416 Inductors, electronic component-type (e.g., chokes, coils, transformers), manufacturing

813910 Industrial associations

522190 Industrial banks (i.e., known as), depository

522298 Industrial banks (i.e., known as), nondepository

314994 Industrial belting reinforcement, cord and fabric, manufacturing

236210 Industrial building (except warehouses) construction

236210 Industrial building (except warehouses) construction, for-sale builders

236210 Industrial building (except warehouses) construction, general contractors

531120 Industrial building rental or leasing

722310 Industrial caterers (i.e., providing food services on a contractual arrangement (except single-event basis))

424690 Industrial chemicals merchant wholesalers

423840 Industrial containers merchant wholesalers

335314 Industrial controls (e.g., pushbutton, selector, and pilot switches) manufacturing

423610 Industrial controls, electrical, merchant wholesalers

541420 Industrial design consulting services

533110 Industrial design licensing

541420 Industrial design services

926110 Industrial development program administration

423840 Industrial diamonds merchant wholesalers

541330 Industrial engineering services

811310 Industrial equipment and machinery repair and maintenance services

315210 Industrial garments cut and sew apparel contractors

315220 Industrial garments, men's and boys', cut and sewn from purchased fabric (except apparel contractors)

315240 Industrial garments, women's and girls', cut and sewn from purchased fabric (except apparel contractors)

325120 Industrial gases manufacturing

424690 Industrial gases merchant wholesalers

327212 Industrial glassware and glass products, pressed or blown, made in glass making plants

327215 Industrial glassware made from purchased glass

813930 Industrial labor unions

541320 Industrial land use planning services

812332 Industrial launderers

423840 Industrial leather products merchant wholesalers

335122 Industrial lighting fixtures, electric, manufacturing

522298 Industrial loan companies, nondepository

336510 Industrial locomotives and parts manufacturing

423830 Industrial machinery and equipment (except electrical) merchant wholesalers

561110 Industrial management services

335122 Industrial mercury lighting fixtures, electric, manufacturing

333511 Industrial molds (except steel ingot) manufacturing

331511 Industrial molds, steel ingot, manufacturing

332999 Industrial pattern manufacturing

423840 Industrial pottery products merchant wholesalers

334513 Industrial process control instruments manufacturing

238220 Industrial process piping installation

325510 Industrial product finishes and coatings (i.e., paint) manufacturing

541715 Industrial research and development laboratories or services (except biotechnology and nanotechnology research and development)

423450	Industrial safety devices (e.g., eye shields, face shields, first-aid kits) merchant wholesalers
325998	Industrial salt manufacturing
424690	Industrial salts merchant wholesalers
212322	Industrial sand beneficiating (e.g., screening, washing)
212322	Industrial sand sandpits and dredging
333997	Industrial scales manufacturing
423840	Industrial supplies (except disposable plastics, paper) merchant wholesalers
424130	Industrial supplies, disposable plastics, paper, merchant wholesalers
541380	Industrial testing laboratories or services
621340	Industrial therapists' offices (e.g., centers, clinics)
811310	Industrial truck (e.g., forklifts) repair and maintenance services
532490	Industrial truck rental or leasing
333924	Industrial trucks and tractors manufacturing
423830	Industrial trucks, tractors, or trailers merchant wholesalers
812332	Industrial uniform supply services
423930	Industrial wastes to be reclaimed merchant wholesalers
311611	Inedible products (e.g., hides, skins, pulled wool, wool grease) produced in slaughtering plants
334511	Inertial navigation systems, aeronautical, manufacturing
311422	Infant and junior food canning
311230	Infant cereals, dry, manufacturing
624410	Infant day care centers
624410	Infant day care services
339113	Infant incubators manufacturing
315240	Infants' apparel cut and sewn from purchased fabric (except apparel contractors)
424330	Infants' clothing merchant wholesalers
315210	Infants' cut and sew apparel contractors
311514	Infant's formulas manufacturing
316210	Infant's shoes manufacturing
315240	Infants' water resistant outerwear cut and sewn from purchased fabric (except apparel contractors)
336612	Inflatable plastic boats, heavy-duty, manufacturing
336612	Inflatable rubber boats, heavy-duty, manufacturing
541512	Information management computer systems integration design services
334516	Infrared analytical instruments, laboratory-type, manufacturing
334511	Infrared homing systems, aeronautical, manufacturing
334513	Infrared instruments, industrial process-type, manufacturing
335110	Infrared lamp bulbs manufacturing
335129	Infrared lamp fixtures manufacturing
333994	Infrared ovens, industrial, manufacturing
334413	Infrared sensors, solid-state, manufacturing
621498	Infusion therapy centers and clinics, outpatient
331318	Ingot made by rolling purchased aluminum
331110	Ingot made in iron and steel mills
331318	Ingot, aluminum, made in integrated secondary smelting and rolling mills
331492	Ingot, nonferrous metals (except aluminum, copper), secondary smelting and refining
331313	Ingot, primary aluminum, manufacturing
331410	Ingot, primary, nonferrous metals (except aluminum), manufacturing
423510	Ingots (except precious) merchant wholesalers
423940	Ingots, precious, merchant wholesalers
621399	Inhalation therapists' offices (e.g., centers, clinics)
339112	Inhalation therapy equipment manufacturing
339112	Inhalators, surgical and medical, manufacturing
325998	Inhibitors (e.g., corrosion, oxidation, polymerization) manufacturing
454390	In-home sales of merchandise, direct selling
333249	Injection molding machinery for plastics manufacturing
325612	Ink eradicators manufacturing
424120	Ink, writing, merchant wholesalers
339940	Inked ribbons manufacturing
424120	Inked ribbons merchant wholesalers
325910	Inkjet cartridges manufacturing
325910	Inkjet inks manufacturing
424120	Inks, pastes, and solvents, office, merchant wholesalers
325910	Inks, printing, manufacturing
423840	Inks, printing, merchant wholesalers

325998	Inks, writing, manufacturing
316998	Inner soles, leather, manufacturing
326211	Inner tubes manufacturing
337910	Innerspring cushions manufacturing
721191	Inns, bed and breakfast
424690	Inorganic chemicals merchant wholesalers
325130	Inorganic pigments (except bone black, carbon black, lamp black) manufacturing
334118	Input/output equipment, computer, manufacturing
423620	Insect control devices, electric, merchant wholesalers
115112	Insect control for crops
335129	Insect lamps, electric, manufacturing
332618	Insect screening made from purchased wire
424690	Insecticides (except lawn and agricultural) merchant wholesalers
325320	Insecticides manufacturing
424910	Insecticides, agricultural, merchant wholesalers
333515	Inserts, cutting tool, manufacturing
541350	Inspection bureaus, building
926150	Inspection for labor standards
488490	Inspection or weighing services, truck transportation
488190	Inspection services, aircraft
541350	Inspection services, building or home
238210	Installation of photovoltaic panels
213112	Installing production equipment at the oil or gas field on a contract basis
522220	Installment sales financing
311920	Instant coffee manufacturing
311230	Instant hot cereals manufacturing
323111	Instant printing (i.e., quick printing) (except books)
311920	Instant tea manufacturing
236220	Institutional building construction
236220	Institutional building construction for-sale builders
236220	Institutional building construction general contractors
337127	Institutional furniture manufacturing
335122	Institutional lighting fixtures, electric, manufacturing
454110	Institutional pharmacies, off-site, exclusively on Internet
454110	Institutional pharmacies, off-site, mail-order
446110	Institutional pharmacies, on-site
522120	Institutions, savings
******	Instruction -- see type of training
512110	Instructional video production
336320	Instrument control panels (i.e., assembling purchased gauges), automotive, truck, and bus, manufacturing
334511	Instrument landing system instrumentation, airborne or airport, manufacturing
333314	Instrument lenses manufacturing
334514	Instrument panels, assembling gauges made in the same establishment
334515	Instrument shunts manufacturing
332613	Instrument springs, precision (except clock, watch), light gauge, made from purchased wire or strip, manufacturing
335311	Instrument transformers (except complete instruments) for metering or protective relaying use manufacturing
334519	Instrumentation for reactor controls, auxiliary, manufacturing
423830	Instruments (except electrical) (e.g., controlling, indicating, recording) merchant wholesalers
334513	Instruments for industrial process control manufacturing
334515	Instruments for measuring electrical quantities manufacturing
334511	Instruments, aeronautical, manufacturing
423450	Instruments, dental and medical, merchant wholesalers
334515	Instruments, electric (i.e., testing electrical characteristics), manufacturing
423610	Instruments, electric measuring, merchant wholesalers
339112	Instruments, mechanical microsurgical, manufacturing
339992	Instruments, musical, manufacturing
423990	Instruments, musical, merchant wholesalers
423490	Instruments, professional and scientific, merchant wholesalers
331420	Insulated wire or cable made from purchased copper in wire drawing plants
331318	Insulated wire or cable made in aluminum wire drawing plants
423610	Insulated wire or cable merchant wholesalers
331420	Insulated wire or cable, copper, made in integrated secondary smelting and wire drawing plants
322299	Insulating batts, fills, or blankets made from purchased paper

327993	Insulating batts, fills, or blankets, fiberglass, manufacturing
327120	Insulating firebrick and shapes, clay, manufacturing
327215	Insulating glass, sealed units, made from purchased glass
327211	Insulating glass, sealed units, made in glass making plants
321999	Insulating materials, cork, manufacturing
325998	Insulating oils manufacturing
335929	Insulating purchased nonferrous wire
326150	Insulation and cushioning, foam plastics (except polystrene), manufacturing
326140	Insulation and cushioning, polystyrene foam plastics, manufacturing
321219	Insulation board, cellular fiber or hard pressed wood, manufacturing
238310	Insulation contractors
423330	Insulation materials (except wood) merchant wholesalers
238290	Insulation, boiler, duct and pipe, installation
335932	Insulators, electrical (except glass, porcelain), manufacturing
327110	Insulators, electrical porcelain, manufacturing
327215	Insulators, electrical, glass, made from purchased glass
327212	Insulators, electrical, glass, made in glass making plants
423610	Insulators, electrical, merchant wholesalers
325412	Insulin preparations manufacturing
325411	Insulin, uncompounded, manufacturing
524298	Insurance actuarial services
524298	Insurance advisory services
524210	Insurance agencies
524210	Insurance brokerages
531120	Insurance building rental or leasing
524113	Insurance carriers, disability, direct
524126	Insurance carriers, fidelity, direct
524114	Insurance carriers, health, direct
524113	Insurance carriers, life, direct
524126	Insurance carriers, property and casualty, direct
524126	Insurance carriers, surety, direct
524127	Insurance carriers, title, direct
524291	Insurance claims adjusting
524291	Insurance claims investigation services
524292	Insurance claims processing services, third party
926150	Insurance commissions, government
524298	Insurance coverage consulting services
524298	Insurance exchanges
524292	Insurance fund, third party administrative services (except claims adjusting only)
551112	Insurance holding companies
524298	Insurance investigation services (except claims investigation)
524298	Insurance loss prevention services
524292	Insurance plan administrative services (except claims adjusting only), third party
522220	Insurance premium financing
524298	Insurance rate making services
524298	Insurance reporting services
524291	Insurance settlement offices
524298	Insurance underwriters laboratories and standards services
524113	Insurance underwriting, disability, direct
524114	Insurance underwriting, health and medical, direct
524113	Insurance underwriting, life, direct
524126	Insurance underwriting, property and casualty, direct
524127	Insurance underwriting, title, direct
813910	Insurers' associations
323111	Intaglio printing (except books)
335312	Integral horsepower electric motors manufacturing
423690	Integrated circuits merchant wholesalers
334413	Integrated microcircuits manufacturing
512250	Integrated record companies (i.e., releasing, promoting, distributing)
512250	Integrated record production and distribution
334515	Integrated-circuit testers manufacturing
334515	Integrating electricity meters manufacturing
334514	Integrating meters, nonelectric, manufacturing
623210	Intellectual and developmental disability facilities (e.g., homes, hospitals, intermediate care facilities), residential
623210	Intellectual and developmental disability homes
623210	Intellectual and developmental disability hospitals
623210	Intellectual and developmental disability intermediate care facilities

813311 Intellectually and developmentally disabled advocacy groups
712110 Interactive museums
485210 Intercity bus line operation
483113 Intercoastal freight transportation to and from domestic ports
483114 Intercoastal transportation of passengers to and from domestic ports
334290 Intercom systems and equipment manufacturing
238210 Intercommunication (intercom) system installation
332410 Intercooler shells manufacturing
333314 Interferometers manufacturing
541410 Interior decorating consultant services
541410 Interior decorating consulting services
541410 Interior design consulting services
541410 Interior design services
541410 Interior designer services
561730 Interior landscaping services
811121 Interior repair shops, automotive
238990 Interlocking brick and block installation
623210 Intermediate care facilities, intellectual and developmental disability
334515 Internal combustion engine analyzers (i.e., testing electrical characteristics) manufacturing
333618 Internal combustion engines (except aircraft, nondiesel automotive, nondiesel truck) manufacturing
423830 Internal combustion engines (except aircraft, nondiesel automotive, nondiesel truck) merchant wholesalers
333618 Internal combustion engines for hybrid drive systems (except automotive) manufacturing
336412 Internal combustion engines, aircraft, manufacturing
336310 Internal combustion engines, automotive and truck gasoline, manufacturing
921130 Internal Revenue Service
928120 International Monetary Fund
522293 International trade financing
454110 Internet auctions, retail
519130 Internet book publishers
519130 Internet broadcasting
561439 Internet cafes (i.e., not serving food and beverages)
519130 Internet comic book publishing

519130 Internet entertainment sites
561311 Internet job listing services
519130 Internet magazine publishing
519130 Internet news publishers
519130 Internet newsletter publishing
519130 Internet newspaper publishing
519130 Internet periodical publishers
519130 Internet radio stations
561311 Internet resume listing services
454110 Internet retail sales sites
519130 Internet search portals
519130 Internet search Web sites
517919 Internet service providers, using client-supplied telecommunications (e.g., dial-up ISPs)
517311 Internet service providers, using own operated wired telecommunications infrastructure (e.g., cable, DSL)
519130 Internet sports sites
519130 Internet video broadcast sites
621111 Internists' offices (e.g., centers, clinics)
541940 Internists' offices, veterinary
541930 Interpretation services, language
712190 Interpretive centers, nature
711120 Interpretive dance companies
711510 Interpretive dancers, independent
485210 Interstate bus line operation
485210 Interurban bus line operation
339113 Intra ocular lenses manufacturing
483211 Intracoastal transportation of freight
483212 Intracoastal transportation of passengers
339113 Intrauterine devices manufacturing
325412 Intravenous (IV) solution preparations manufacturing
812990 Introduction services, social
532283 Invalid equipment rental (i.e., home use)
561990 Inventory computing services
541614 Inventory planning and control management consulting services
561990 Inventory taking services
311314 Invert sugar manufacturing
335312 Inverters, rotating electrical, manufacturing
335999 Inverters, solid-state, manufacturing
561611 Investigation services (except credit), private

561450	Investigation services, credit
561611	Investigators, private
523930	Investment advice consulting services, customized, fees paid by client
523930	Investment advice counseling services, customized, fees paid by client
523930	Investment advisory services, customized, fees paid by client
523110	Investment banking
331524	Investment castings, aluminum, unfinished, manufacturing
331529	Investment castings, nonferrous metal (except aluminum), unfinished, manufacturing
331512	Investment castings, steel, unfinished, manufacturing
523910	Investment clubs
525990	Investment funds, closed-end
525910	Investment funds, open-ended
523920	Investment management
325413	In-vitro diagnostic substances manufacturing
325412	In-vivo diagnostic substances manufacturing
325180	Iodides manufacturing
325412	Iodinated in-vivo diagnostic substances manufacturing
325180	Iodine, crude or resublimed, manufacturing
334519	Ion chambers manufacturing
325211	Ion exchange resins manufacturing
325211	Ionomer resins manufacturing
325199	Ionone manufacturing
331491	Iridium bar, rod, sheet, strip and tubing made from purchased metals or scrap
212299	Iridium mining and/or beneficiating
331492	Iridium recovering from scrap and/or alloying purchased metals
331410	Iridium refining, primary
423390	Iron and steel architectural shapes merchant wholesalers
325130	Iron based pigments manufacturing
331511	Iron castings, unfinished, manufacturing
325180	Iron compounds, not specified elsewhere by process, manufacturing
332111	Iron forgings made from purchased iron, unfinished
331511	Iron foundries
339113	Iron lungs manufacturing
212210	Iron ore (e.g., hematite, magnetite, siderite, taconite) mining and/or beneficiating
212210	Iron ore agglomerates mining and/or beneficiating
212210	Iron ore beneficiating plants (e.g., agglomeration, sintering)
212210	Iron ore mine site development for own account
331110	Iron ore recovery from open hearth slag
212210	Iron ore, blocked, mining and/or beneficiating
331110	Iron sinter made in iron and steel mills
325180	Iron sulphate manufacturing
238120	Iron work, structural, contractors
331110	Iron, pig, manufacturing
335220	Ironers and mangles, household-type (except portable irons), manufacturing
423220	Ironing boards merchant wholesalers
332999	Ironing boards, metal, manufacturing
321999	Ironing boards, wood, manufacturing
335210	Irons, household-type electric, manufacturing
423620	Irons, household-type, electric, merchant wholesalers
334517	Irradiation apparatus and tubes (e.g., industrial, medical diagnostic, medical therapeutic, research, scientific), manufacturing
334517	Irradiation equipment manufacturing
115114	Irradiation of fruits and vegetables
926130	Irrigation districts, nonoperating
423820	Irrigation equipment merchant wholesalers
333111	Irrigation equipment, agriculture, manufacturing
327332	Irrigation pipe, concrete, manufacturing
332322	Irrigation pipe, sheet metal (except stampings), manufacturing
237110	Irrigation project construction (except lawn)
221310	Irrigation system operation
325110	Isobutane made from refined petroleum or liquid hydrocarbons
211130	Isobutane recovered from oil and gas field gases
325110	Isobutene made from refined petroleum or liquid hydrocarbons
325211	Isobutylene polymer resins manufacturing
325212	Isobutylene-isoprene rubber manufacturing
325212	Isocyanate rubber manufacturing
325194	Isocyanates manufacturing
335311	Isolation transformers manufacturing

211130 Isopentane recovered from oil and gas field gases

325110 Isoprene made from refined petroleum or liquid hydrocarbons

325199 Isopropyl alcohol manufacturing

522210 Issuing, credit card

311422 Italian foods canning

339112 IV apparatus manufacturing

333120 Jack hammers manufacturing

315220 Jackets (except fur, leather, sheep-lined), men's and boys', cut and sewn from purchased fabric (except apparel contractors)

315240 Jackets (except fur, leather, sheep-lined), women's, girls', and infants', cut and sewn from purchased fabric (except apparel contractors)

315210 Jackets cut and sew apparel contractors

315190 Jackets made in apparel knitting mills

332992 Jackets, bullet (i.e., 30 mm. or less, 1.18 inch or less), manufacturing

315280 Jackets, fur (except apparel contractors), manufacturing

315210 Jackets, fur, cut and sew apparel contractors

332313 Jackets, industrial, fabricated metal plate work, manufacturing

315280 Jackets, leather (except welders') or sheep-lined (except apparel contractors), manufacturing

315210 Jackets, leather (except welders') or sheep-lined, cut and sew apparel contractors

315210 Jackets, service apparel (e.g., laboratory, medical), cut and sew apparel contractors

315220 Jackets, service apparel (e.g., laboratory, medical), men's and boys', cut and sewn from purchased fabric (except apparel contractors)

315240 Jackets, service apparel (e.g., laboratory, medical), women's and girls', cut and sewn from purchased fabric (except apparel contractors)

315210 Jackets, ski, cut and sew apparel contractors

315220 Jackets, ski, men's and boys', cut and sewn from purchased fabric (except apparel contractors)

315240 Jackets, ski, women's, girls', and infants', cut and sewn from purchased fabric (except apparel contractors)

315220 Jackets, tailored (except fur, leather, sheep-lined), men's and boys', cut and sewn from

purchased fabric (except apparel contractors)

316998 Jackets, welder's, leather, manufacturing

332216 Jacks (except hydraulic, pneumatic) manufacturing

333999 Jacks, hydraulic and pneumatic, manufacturing

333249 Jacquard card cutting machinery manufacturing

313210 Jacquard woven fabrics weaving

212399 Jade mining and/or beneficiating

611620 Jai alai instruction, camps, or schools

711211 Jai alai teams, professional or semiprofessional

236220 Jail construction

561210 Jail operation on a contract or fee basis

922140 Jails (except private operation of)

561210 Jails, privately operated

332321 Jalousies, metal, manufacturing

424690 Janitorial chemicals merchant wholesalers

423850 Janitorial equipment and supplies merchant wholesalers

453998 Janitorial equipment and supplies stores

561720 Janitorial services

561720 Janitorial services, aircraft

332812 Japanning metals and metal products for the trade

316110 Japanning of leather

333994 Japanning ovens manufacturing

327213 Jars for packaging, bottling, and canning, glass, manufacturing

326199 Jars, plastics, manufacturing

711120 Jazz dance companies

711510 Jazz dancers, independent

711130 Jazz musical artists, independent

711130 Jazz musical groups

315210 Jean-cut casual slacks cut and sew apparel contractors

315220 Jean-cut casual slacks, men's and boys', cut and sewn from purchased fabric (except apparel contractors)

315240 Jean-cut casual slacks, women's and girls', cut and sewn from purchased fabric (except apparel contractors)

315210 Jeans cut and sew apparel contractors

315240 Jeans, women's, girls', and infants', cut and sewn from purchased fabric (except apparel contractors)

311421	Jellies and jams manufacturing
424490	Jellies and jams merchant wholesalers
311340	Jelly candies manufacturing
315210	Jerseys cut and sew apparel contractors
315190	Jerseys made in apparel knitting mills
315220	Jerseys, men's and boys', cut and sewn from purchased fabric (except apparel contractors)
315240	Jerseys, women's and girls', cut and sewn from purchased fabric (except apparel contractors)
424710	Jet fuel bulk stations and terminals, merchant wholesalers
454310	Jet fuel bulk stations, selling for consumption
324110	Jet fuels manufacturing
336412	Jet propulsion and internal combustion engines and parts, aircraft, manufacturing
332993	Jet propulsion projectiles (except guided missiles) manufacturing
423910	Jet skis merchant wholesalers
237990	Jetty construction
339910	Jewel settings and mountings, precious metal, manufacturing
339910	Jeweler's findings and materials manufacturing
423940	Jewelers' findings merchant wholesalers
332216	Jeweler's handtools, nonelectric, manufacturing
424990	Jewelry boxes merchant wholesalers
541490	Jewelry design services
423940	Jewelry merchant wholesalers
811490	Jewelry repair shops without retailing new jewelry
448150	Jewelry stores, costume
448310	Jewelry stores, precious
339910	Jewelry, costume, manufacturing
339910	Jewelry, natural or cultured pearls, manufacturing
339910	Jewelry, precious metal, manufacturing
333514	Jigs (e.g., checking, gauging, inspection) manufacturing
333514	Jigs and fixtures for use with machine tools manufacturing
423830	Jigs merchant wholesalers
333991	Jigsaws, handheld power-driven, manufacturing
333243	Jigsaws, woodworking-type, stationary, manufacturing
624310	Job counseling, vocational rehabilitation or habilitation
323111	Job printing (except screen, books)
323111	Job printing, engraving (except books)
323111	Job printing, flexographic (except books)
323111	Job printing, gravure (except books)
323111	Job printing, letterpress (except books)
323111	Job printing, lithographic (except books)
323111	Job printing, offset (except books)
323113	Job printing, screen
336370	Job stampings, automotive, metal, manufacturing
624310	Job training, vocational rehabilitation or habilitation
711219	Jockeys, horse racing
339920	Jogging machines, manufacturing
315210	Jogging suits cut and sew apparel contractors
315190	Jogging suits made in apparel knitting mills
315220	Jogging suits, men's and boys', cut and sewn from purchased fabric (except apparel contractors)
315240	Jogging suits, women's, girls', and infants', cut and sewn from purchased fabric (except apparel contractors)
325520	Joint compounds (except gypsum base) manufacturing
327420	Joint compounds, gypsum based, manufacturing
333243	Jointers, woodworking-type, manufacturing
333613	Joints, swivel (except aircraft, motor vehicle), manufacturing
333613	Joints, universal (except aircraft, motor vehicle), manufacturing
336413	Joints, universal, aircraft, manufacturing
336350	Joints, universal, automotive, truck, and bus, manufacturing
332312	Joists, fabricated bar, manufacturing
332322	Joists, sheet metal (except stampings), manufacturing
111998	Jojoba farming
711510	Journalists, independent (freelance)
334118	Joystick devices manufacturing
611620	Judo instruction, camps, or schools
326150	Jugs, vacuum, foam plastics (except polystyrene), manufacturing
332439	Jugs, vacuum, light gauge metal, manufacturing

326140	Jugs, vacuum, polystyrene foam plastics, manufacturing
333241	Juice extractors (i.e., food manufacturing-type) manufacturing
335210	Juice extractors, household-type electric, manufacturing
311520	Juice pops, frozen, manufacturing
424490	Juices, canned or fresh, merchant wholesalers
424420	Juices, frozen, merchant wholesalers
311411	Juices, fruit or vegetable concentrates, frozen, manufacturing
311421	Juices, fruit or vegetable, canned manufacturing
311421	Juices, fruit or vegetable, fresh, manufacturing
311411	Juices, fruit or vegetable, frozen, manufacturing
713990	Jukebox concession operators (i.e., supplying and servicing in others' facilities)
334310	Jukeboxes manufacturing
315210	Jumpsuits cut and sew apparel contractors
315240	Jumpsuits, women's and girls', cut and sewn from purchased fabric (except apparel contractors)
335932	Junction boxes, electrical wiring, manufacturing
813910	Junior chambers of commerce
611210	Junior colleges
611210	Junior colleges offering a wide variety of academic and technical training
611110	Junior high schools
423140	Junk yards, auto, merchant wholesalers
541199	Jury consulting services
313210	Jute bags made in broadwoven mills
424310	Jute piece goods (except burlap) merchant wholesalers
337124	Juvenile furniture (except upholstered), metal manufacturing
337122	Juvenile furniture (except upholstered), wood, manufacturing
337125	Juvenile furniture, rattan and reed, manufacturing
337121	Juvenile furniture, upholstered, manufacturing
623990	Juvenile halfway group homes
511120	Juvenile magazine and periodical publishers (except exclusive Internet publishing)
511120	Juvenile magazine and periodical publishers and printing combined
519130	Juvenile magazine and periodical publishers, exclusively on Internet
323111	Juvenile magazines and periodicals commercial printing (except screen) without publishing
323113	Juvenile magazines and periodicals screen printing without publishing
111219	Kale farming, field, bedding plant and seed production
212324	Kaolin mining and/or beneficiating
327992	Kaolin, processing beyond beneficiation
611620	Karate instruction, camps or schools
713990	Kayaking, recreational
327420	Keene's cement manufacturing
321920	Kegs, wood, coopered, manufacturing
311119	Kelp meal and pellets, animal feed manufacturing
334515	Kelvin bridges (i.e., electrical measuring instruments) manufacturing
111998	Kenaf farming
112990	Kennels, breeding and raising stock for sale
711219	Kennels, dog racing
812910	Kennels, pet boarding
212391	Kernite mining and/or beneficiating
211120	Kerogen processing
424710	Kerosene bulk stations and terminals, merchant wholesalers
324110	Kerosene manufacturing
424720	Kerosene merchant wholesalers (except bulk stations, terminals)
333414	Kerosene space heaters manufacturing
311421	Ketchup manufacturing
325199	Ketone compounds, not specified elsewhere by process, manufacturing
332420	Kettles, heavy gauge metal, manufacturing
332510	Key blanks, metal, manufacturing
316998	Key cases (except metal) manufacturing
339910	Key cases, precious metal, manufacturing
333517	Key cutting machines, metal cutting type, manufacturing
811490	Key duplicating shops
332618	Key rings made from purchased wire
334118	Keyboards, computer peripheral equipment, manufacturing
423430	Keyboards, computer, merchant wholesalers
339992	Keyboards, piano or organ, manufacturing

336320 Keyless entry systems, automotive, truck, and bus, manufacturing

423710 Keys and locks merchant wholesalers

334210 Keysets, telephone, manufacturing

621492 Kidney dialysis centers and clinics

236210 Kiln construction

321999 Kiln drying lumber

327120 Kiln furniture, clay, manufacturing

333994 Kilns (except cement, chemical, wood) manufacturing

333249 Kilns (i.e., cement, chemical, wood) manufacturing

423830 Kilns, industrial, merchant wholesalers

611110 Kindergartens

611110 Kindergartens, combined with preschools

334519 Kinematic test and measuring equipment manufacturing

561910 Kit assembling and packaging services

336211 Kit car bodies manufacturing

423440 Kitchen appliances, commercial (except refrigerated), merchant wholesalers

423620 Kitchen appliances, household-type, gas and electric, merchant wholesalers

327110 Kitchen articles, coarse earthenware, manufacturing

444190 Kitchen cabinet (except custom) stores

337110 Kitchen cabinets (except freestanding), stock or custom wood, manufacturing

238350 Kitchen cabinets and counters, constructed on site

423310 Kitchen cabinets, built-in, merchant wholesalers

337122 Kitchen chairs (e.g., upholstered), wood, manufacturing

337124 Kitchen chairs (including upholstered), metal, manufacturing

337125 Kitchen chairs (including upholstered), plastics manufacturing

332215 Kitchen cutlery, nonprecious and precious plated metal, manufacturing

325612 Kitchen degreasing and cleaning preparations manufacturing

337124 Kitchen furniture, household-type, metal, manufacturing

337124 Kitchen furniture, metal household-type, manufacturing

337122 Kitchen furniture, wood household-type, manufacturing

238220 Kitchen sink and hardware installation

423440 Kitchen utensils, commercial, merchant wholesalers

332215 Kitchen utensils, fabricated metal (e.g., colanders, garlic presses, ice cream scoops, spatulas), manufacturing

423220 Kitchen utensils, household-type, merchant wholesalers

326199 Kitchen utensils, plastics, manufacturing

442299 Kitchenware stores

327110 Kitchenware, commercial and household-type, vitreous china, manufacturing

327110 Kitchenware, semivitreous earthenware, manufacturing

321999 Kitchenware, wood, manufacturing

339930 Kites manufacturing

111339 Kiwi fruit farming

334419 Klystron tubes manufacturing

423690 Klystron tubes merchant wholesalers

314910 Knapsacks (e.g., backpacks, book bags) manufacturing

314910 Knapsacks, made from purchased woven or knitted materials

315210 Knickers cut and sew apparel contractors

315220 Knickers, men's and boys', cut and sewn from purchased fabric (except apparel contractors)

315240 Knickers, women's, girls', and infants', cut and sewn from purchased fabric (except apparel contractors)

337122 Knickknack shelves, wood, manufacturing

332215 Knife blades manufacturing

332215 Knife blanks manufacturing

335313 Knife switches, electric power switchgear-type, manufacturing

311812 Knishes (except frozen) made in commercial bakeries

311813 Knishes, frozen, manufacturing

315210 Knit gloves cut and sew apparel contractors

315990 Knit gloves cut and sewn from purchased fabric (except apparel contractors)

315190 Knit gloves made in apparel knitting mills

313110 Knitting and crocheting thread manufacturing

313240 Knitting and finishing lace

313240 Knitting and finishing warp or weft fabric

313240 Knitting lace

333249 Knitting machinery manufacturing

313110 Knitting spun yarns (e.g., cotton, manmade fiber, silk, wool) made from purchased fiber

313240 Knitting warp or weft fabric

332215	Knives (e.g., hunting, pocket, table nonprecious, table precious plated) manufacturing
423710	Knives (except disposable plastics) merchant wholesalers
333515	Knives and bits for metalworking lathes, planers, and shapers manufacturing
332216	Knives and bits for woodworking lathes, planers, and shapers manufacturing
424130	Knives, disposable plastics, merchant wholesalers
335210	Knives, household-type electric carving, manufacturing
339112	Knives, surgical, manufacturing
339992	Knobs, organ, manufacturing
321999	Knobs, wood, manufacturing
333249	Knot tying machinery for textiles manufacturing
333517	Knurling machines, metalworking, manufacturing
322130	Kraft linerboard manufacturing
322121	Kraft paper stock manufacturing
212325	Kyanite mining and/or beneficiating
339940	Label making equipment, handheld, manufacturing
333993	Labeling (i.e., packaging) machinery manufacturing
423420	Labeling machines merchant wholesalers
561910	Labeling services
313220	Labels weaving
323111	Labels, commercial printing (except screen), on a job-order basis
424310	Labels, textile, merchant wholesalers
561320	Labor (except farm) contractors (i.e., personnel suppliers)
561320	Labor (except farm) pools
115115	Labor contractors, farm
813930	Labor federations
561330	Labor leasing services
926150	Labor management negotiations boards, government
541612	Labor relations consulting services
926110	Labor statistics agencies
813930	Labor unions (except apprenticeship programs)
******	Laboratories -- see specific type
621512	Laboratories, dental X-ray
621511	Laboratories, medical (except radiological, X-ray)
621512	Laboratories, medical radiological or X-ray
334516	Laboratory analytical instruments (except optical) manufacturing
333314	Laboratory analytical optical instruments (e.g., microscopes) manufacturing
311119	Laboratory animal feed manufacturing
112990	Laboratory animal production (e.g., guinea pigs, mice, rats)
315210	Laboratory coats cut and sew apparel contractors
315220	Laboratory coats, men's and boys', cut and sewn from purchased fabric (except apparel contractors)
315240	Laboratory coats, women's and girls', cut and sewn from purchased fabric (except apparel contractors)
236220	Laboratory construction
423490	Laboratory equipment (except dental, medical, ophthalmic) merchant wholesalers
423450	Laboratory equipment, dental and medical, merchant wholesalers
238390	Laboratory furniture and equipment installation
327215	Laboratory glassware (e.g., beakers, test tubes, vials) made from purchased glass
327212	Laboratory glassware (e.g., beakers, test tubes, vials) made in glass making plants
811219	Laboratory instrument repair and maintenance services
512199	Laboratory services, motion picture
334515	Laboratory standards testing instruments (e.g., capacitance, electrical resistance, inductance) manufacturing
541380	Laboratory testing (except medical, veterinary) services
621511	Laboratory testing services, medical (except radiological, X-ray)
621512	Laboratory testing services, medical radiological or X-ray
541940	Laboratory testing services, veterinary
339113	Laboratory-type evaporation apparatus manufacturing
333415	Laboratory-type freezers manufacturing
337127	Laboratory-type furniture (e.g., benches, cabinets, stools, tables) (except dental) manufacturing
339113	Laboratory-type sample preparation apparatus manufacturing
333249	Lace and net making machinery manufacturing
316110	Lace leather manufacturing

313240	Lace manufacturing
313240	Lace products (except apparel) made in lace mills
314999	Lace, burnt-out, manufacturing
316998	Laces (e.g., shoe), leather, manufacturing
313220	Laces (e.g., shoe), textile, manufacturing
332812	Lacquering metals and metal products for the trade
333994	Lacquering ovens manufacturing
325510	Lacquers manufacturing
424950	Lacquers merchant wholesalers
325199	Lactic acid manufacturing
311514	Lactose manufacturing
332999	Ladder jacks, metal, manufacturing
321999	Ladder jacks, wood, manufacturing
321912	Ladder rounds or rungs, hardwood, manufacturing
423830	Ladders merchant wholesalers
321999	Ladders, extension, wood, manufacturing
326199	Ladders, fiberglass, manufacturing
332323	Ladders, metal chain, manufacturing
332323	Ladders, permanently installed, metal, manufacturing
332999	Ladders, portable metal, manufacturing
332313	Ladle bails, fabricated metal plate work, manufacturing
332313	Ladles, fabricated metal plate work, manufacturing
312120	Lager brewing
237110	Lagoon, sewage treatment construction
483211	Lake freight transportation (except on Great Lakes system)
483113	Lake freight transportation, Great Lakes (including St. Lawrence Seaway)
562998	Lake maintenance and cleaning services
483212	Lake passenger transportation (except on Great Lakes system)
483114	Lake passenger transportation, Great Lakes (including St. Lawrence Seaway)
325130	Lakes (i.e., organic pigments) manufacturing
311611	Lamb carcasses, half carcasses, primal and sub-primal cuts, produced in slaughtering plants
112410	Lamb feedlots (except stockyards for transportation)
311612	Lamb, primal and sub-primal cuts, made from purchased carcasses
327215	Laminated glass made from purchased glass
327211	Laminated glass made in glass making plants
326130	Laminated plastics plate, rod, and sheet, manufacturing
321213	Laminated structural wood members (except trusses) manufacturing
321213	Laminated veneer lumber (LVL) manufacturing
423310	Laminates, wood, merchant wholesalers
322220	Laminating foil for flexible packaging applications
332813	Laminating metals and metal formed products without fabricating
322220	Laminating purchased foil sheets for nonpackaging applications
322220	Laminating purchased paperboard
322220	Laminating purchased papers for nonpackaging applications
322220	Laminating purchased papers for packaging applications
313320	Laminating purchased textiles
335311	Lamp ballasts manufacturing
327110	Lamp bases, pottery, manufacturing
325180	Lamp black manufacturing
335110	Lamp bulb parts (except glass blanks), electric, manufacturing
335110	Lamp bulbs and tubes, electric (i.e., fluorescent, incandescent filament, vapor), manufacturing
335110	Lamp bulbs and tubes, health, infrared and ultraviolet radiation, manufacturing
332618	Lamp frames, wire, made from purchased wire
335931	Lamp holders manufacturing
332999	Lamp shade frames, metal, manufacturing
335121	Lamp shades (except glass, plastics), residential, manufacturing
327215	Lamp shades made from purchased glass
327212	Lamp shades made in glass making plants
326199	Lamp shades, plastics, manufacturing
442299	Lamp shops, electric
335931	Lamp sockets and receptacles (i.e., electric wiring devices) manufacturing
423220	Lamps (i.e., lighting fixtures) merchant wholesalers
335122	Lamps (i.e., lighting fixtures), commercial, industrial, and institutional, manufacturing

335121 Lamps (i.e., lighting fixtures), residential, electric, manufacturing

335129 Lamps, insect, electric fixture, manufacturing

334517 Lamps, X-ray, manufacturing

237210 Land (except cemeteries) subdividers

237210 Land acquisition, assembling and subdividing

238910 Land clearing

237210 Land developers (i.e., subdividing and installing infrastructure)

237990 Land drainage contractors

238910 Land leveling contractors

924120 Land management program administration

423820 Land preparation machinery, agricultural, merchant wholesalers

333120 Land preparation machinery, construction, manufacturing

423810 Land preparation machinery, construction, merchant wholesalers

925120 Land redevelopment agencies, government

531190 Land rental or leasing

237210 Land subdividing and utility installation (e.g., electric, sewer and water)

541370 Land surveying services

335312 Land transportation motors and generators manufacturing

541320 Land use design services

541320 Land use planning services

562212 Landfills

332312 Landing mats, aircraft, metal, manufacturing

531390 Landman services

541320 Landscape architects' offices

541320 Landscape architects' private practices

541320 Landscape architectural services

561730 Landscape care and maintenance services

541320 Landscape consulting services

561730 Landscape contractors (except construction)

541320 Landscape design services

561730 Landscape installation services

541320 Landscape planning services

561730 Landscaping services (except planning)

541930 Language interpretation services

541720 Language research and development services

611630 Language schools

541930 Language services (e.g., interpretation, sign, translation)

541930 Language translation services

335129 Lanterns (e.g., carbide, electric, gas, gasoline, kerosene) manufacturing

423840 Lapidary equipment, industrial, merchant wholesalers

339910 Lapidary work manufacturing

334111 Laptop computers manufacturing

311613 Lard made from purchased fat

424470 Lard merchant wholesalers

311611 Lard produced in slaughtering plants

333517 Laser boring, drilling, and cutting machines, metalworking, manufacturing

334413 Laser diodes manufacturing

532282 Laser disc, video, rental

334614 Laser disks, prerecorded video, mass reproducing

334510 Laser equipment, electromedical, manufacturing

621493 Laser surgery centers, freestanding

334510 Laser systems and equipment, medical, manufacturing

333992 Laser welding equipment manufacturing

316998 Lashes (i.e., whips) manufacturing

321999 Last sole patterns, all materials, manufacturing

212325 Laterite mining and/or beneficiating

326299 Latex foam rubber manufacturing

326299 Latex foam rubber products manufacturing

325510 Latex paint (i.e., water based) manufacturing

325212 Latex rubber, synthetic, manufacturing

332323 Lath, expanded metal, manufacturing

321219 Lath, fiber, manufacturing

327420 Lath, gypsum, manufacturing

321912 Lath, wood, manufacturing

333517 Lathes, metalworking, manufacturing

333243 Lathes, woodworking-type, manufacturing

238310 Lathing contractors

321912 Lathmills, wood

316110 Latigo leather manufacturing

812332 Laundered mat and rug supply services

812332 Launderers, industrial

812310 Launderettes

812320	Laundries (except coin-operated, linen supply, uniform supply)
812310	Laundries, coin-operated or similar self-service
812331	Laundries, linen and uniform supply
812310	Laundromats
812320	Laundry and drycleaning agents
314910	Laundry bags made from purchased woven or knitted materials
325612	Laundry bluing manufacturing
812320	Laundry drop-off and pick-up sites
335220	Laundry equipment (e.g., dryers, washers), household-type, manufacturing
333318	Laundry extractors manufacturing
332439	Laundry hampers, light gauge metal, manufacturing
337125	Laundry hampers, rattan, reed, wicker or willow, manufacturing
812310	Laundry machine routes (i.e., concession operators), coin-operated or similar self-service
333318	Laundry machinery and equipment (except household-type) manufacturing
423620	Laundry machinery and equipment, household-type (e.g., dryers, washers), merchant wholesalers
423850	Laundry machinery, equipment, and supplies, commercial, merchant wholesalers
314999	Laundry nets made from purchased materials
333318	Laundry pressing machines (except household-type) manufacturing
812320	Laundry services (except coin-operated, linen supply, uniform supply)
812310	Laundry services, coin-operated or similar self-service
812332	Laundry services, industrial
812331	Laundry services, linen supply
325611	Laundry soap, chips, and powder manufacturing
424690	Laundry soap, chips, and powder, merchant wholesalers
332999	Laundry tubs, metal, manufacturing
326191	Laundry tubs, plastics, manufacturing
325199	Lauric acid esters and amines manufacturing
332999	Lavatories, metal, manufacturing
327110	Lavatories, vitreous china, manufacturing
423720	Lavatory fixtures merchant wholesalers

423850	Law enforcement equipment (except safety) merchant wholesalers
922190	Law enforcement statistics centers, government
541110	Law firms
541110	Law offices
541110	Law practices
611310	Law schools
333112	Lawn and garden equipment manufacturing
811411	Lawn and garden equipment repair and maintenance services without retailing new lawn and garden equipment
713990	Lawn bowling clubs
561730	Lawn care services (e.g., fertilizing, mowing, seeding, spraying)
424910	Lawn care supplies (e.g., chemicals, fertilizers, pesticides) merchant wholesalers
332216	Lawn edgers, nonpowered, manufacturing
333112	Lawn edgers, powered, manufacturing
561730	Lawn fertilizing services
337125	Lawn furniture (except concrete, metal, stone, wood) manufacturing
337124	Lawn furniture, metal, manufacturing
337122	Lawn furniture, wood, manufacturing
332919	Lawn hose nozzles and lawn sprinklers manufacturing
423820	Lawn maintenance machinery and equipment merchant wholesalers
561730	Lawn maintenance services
561730	Lawn mowing services
561730	Lawn mulching services
444210	Lawn power equipment stores
561730	Lawn seeding services
561730	Lawn spraying services
238220	Lawn sprinkler system installation
444220	Lawn supply stores
562219	Lawn waste disposal facilities
532490	Lawnmower rental or leasing
811411	Lawnmower repair and maintenance shops without retailing new lawnmowers
333112	Lawnmowers (except agricultural-type), powered, manufacturing
423820	Lawnmowers merchant wholesalers
333111	Lawnmowers, agricultural-type, powered, manufacturing
332216	Lawnmowers, nonpowered, manufacturing

541110 Lawyers' offices
541110 Lawyers' private practices
325412 Laxative preparations manufacturing
112310 Layer-type chicken production
334419 LCD (liquid crystal display) unit screens manufacturing
212291 Leaching of uranium, radium, or vanadium ores
335911 Lead acid storage batteries manufacturing
331491 Lead and lead alloy bar, pipe, plate, rod, sheet, strip, and tubing made from purchased metals or scrap
325130 Lead based pigments manufacturing
331529 Lead castings (except die-castings), unfinished, manufacturing
331523 Lead die-castings, unfinished, manufacturing
332999 Lead foil not made in rolling mills
238390 Lead lining walls for X-ray room contractors
212230 Lead ore mine site development for own account
212230 Lead ore mining and/or beneficiating
325180 Lead oxides (except pigments) manufacturing
562910 Lead paint abatement services
562910 Lead paint removal contractors
325130 Lead pigments manufacturing
423510 Lead primary forms merchant wholesalers
331492 Lead recovering from scrap and/or alloying purchased metals
331491 Lead rolling, drawing, or extruding purchased metals or scrap
325180 Lead silicate manufacturing
331410 Lead smelting and refining, primary
327992 Lead, black (i.e., natural graphite), ground, refined, or blended, manufacturing
335110 Lead-in wires, electric lamp, made from purchased wire
212230 Lead-zinc ore mining and/or beneficiating
333112 Leaf blowers manufacturing
332216 Leaf skimmers and rakes, nonpowered swimming pool, manufacturing
332613 Leaf springs, heavy gauge metal, manufacturing
424590 Leaf tobacco merchant wholesalers
332999 Leaf, metal, manufacturing
334519 Leak detectors, water, manufacturing
813920 Learned societies

611691 Learning centers offering remedial courses
541720 Learning disabilities research and development services
213112 Lease tank cleaning and repairing on a contract basis
316998 Leashes, dog, manufacturing
****** Leasing -- see type of property or article being leased
522220 Leasing in combination with sales financing
315280 Leather apparel (e.g., capes, coats, hats, jackets) (except apparel contractors) manufacturing
315210 Leather apparel (e.g., capes, coats, hats, jackets) cut and sew apparel contractors
316998 Leather belting manufacturing
315280 Leather clothing (except apparel contractors) manufacturing
315210 Leather clothing cut and sew apparel contractors
448190 Leather coat stores
316110 Leather coloring, cutting, embossing, and japanning
316110 Leather converters
424990 Leather cut stock (except boot, shoe) merchant wholesalers
316998 Leather cut stock for shoe and boot manufacturing
424340 Leather cut stock for shoe and boot merchant wholesalers
316210 Leather footwear manufacturing
316210 Leather footwear, men's, manufacturing
316210 Leather footwear, slippers, manufacturing
316210 Leather footwear, women's, manufacturing
812320 Leather garment cleaning services
315210 Leather gloves or mittens (except athletic) cut and sew apparel contractors
315990 Leather gloves or mittens (except athletic, cut and sewn apparel contractors) manufacturing
339920 Leather gloves, athletic, manufacturing
424990 Leather goods (except belting, footwear, handbags, gloves, luggage) merchant wholesalers
811430 Leather goods repair shops without retailing new leather goods
448320 Leather goods stores
316998 Leather goods, small personal (e.g., coin purses, eyeglass cases, key cases), manufacturing
316992 Leather handbags and purses manufacturing

316210	Leather house slippers manufacturing
316998	Leather luggage manufacturing
316110	Leather tanning, currying, and finishing
316210	Leather upper athletic footwear manufacturing
316998	Leather welting manufacturing
333249	Leather working machinery manufacturing
313320	Leather, artificial, made from purchased fabric
322220	Leatherboard (i.e., paperboard based) made from purchased paperboard
322130	Leatherboard (i.e., paperboard based) made in paperboard mills
311225	Lecithin made from purchased oils
311224	Lecithin, cottonseed, made in crushing mills
311224	Lecithin, soybean, made in crushing mills
711410	Lecture bureaus
711510	Lecturers, independent
334413	LED (light emitting diode) manufacturing
111219	Leek farming, field, bedding plant and seed production
541110	Legal aid services
922130	Legal counsel offices, government
315210	Leggings cut and sew apparel contractors
315110	Leggings knitting or knitting and finishing
316998	Leggings, welder's, leather, manufacturing
315240	Leggings, women's, girls', and infants', cut and sewn from purchased fabric (except apparel contractors)
921140	Legislative and executive office combinations
921120	Legislative assemblies
921120	Legislative bodies (e.g., federal, local, and state)
921120	Legislative commissions
111320	Lemon groves
325998	Lemon oil manufacturing
519120	Lending libraries
423460	Lens blanks, ophthalmic, merchant wholesalers
327215	Lens blanks, optical and ophthalmic, made from purchased glass
327212	Lens blanks, optical and ophthalmic, made in glass making plants
326199	Lens blanks, plastics ophthalmic or optical, manufacturing
333314	Lens coating (except ophthalmic)
339115	Lens coating, ophthalmic
333314	Lens grinding (except ophthalmic)
339115	Lens grinding, ophthalmic (except in retail stores)
446130	Lens grinding, ophthalmic, in retail stores
333316	Lens hoods, camera, manufacturing
333314	Lens mounting (except ophthalmic)
339115	Lens mounts, ophthalmic, manufacturing
333314	Lens polishing (except ophthalmic)
339115	Lens polishing, ophthalmic
333314	Lenses (except ophthalmic) manufacturing
339115	Lenses, ophthalmic, manufacturing
423460	Lenses, optical, merchant wholesalers
111130	Lentil farming, dry, field and seed production
315210	Leotards cut and sew apparel contractors
315190	Leotards made in apparel knitting mills
315240	Leotards, women's and girls', cut and sewn from purchased fabric (except apparel contractors)
212393	Lepidolite mining and/or beneficiating
622310	Leprosy hospitals
******	Lessors -- see specific type of asset or property being rented or leased
531130	Lessors of miniwarehouses
531120	Lessors of nonresidential buildings (except miniwarehouses)
531110	Lessors of residential buildings and dwellings
531130	Lessors of self-storage units
423420	Letter and envelope handling machines merchant wholesalers
333318	Letter folding, stuffing, and sealing machinery manufacturing
333515	Letter pins (e.g., gauging, measuring) manufacturing
561410	Letter writing services
325910	Letterpress inks manufacturing
323120	Letterpress plate preparation services
333244	Letterpress printing presses manufacturing
339950	Letters for signs manufacturing
322230	Letters, die-cut, made from purchased cardboard
111219	Lettuce farming, field, bedding plant and seed production
237990	Levee construction
334513	Level and bulk measuring instruments, industrial process-type, manufacturing

334519 Level gauges, radiation-type, manufacturing

334519 Levels and tapes, surveying, manufacturing

332216 Levels, carpenter's, manufacturing

524126 Liability insurance carriers, direct

519120 Libraries (except motion picture stock footage, motion picture commercial distribution)

512199 Libraries, motion picture stock footage film

512199 Libraries, video tape, stock footage

236220 Library construction

561990 License issuing services (except government), motor vehicle

621399 Licensed practical nurses' (LPNs) offices (e.g., centers, clinics)

926130 Licensing and inspecting of utilities

926150 Licensing and permit issuance for business operations, government

926150 Licensing and permit issuance for professional occupations, government

926120 Licensing of transportation equipment, facilities, and services

311340 Licorice candy manufacturing

332431 Lids and ends, can, light gauge metal, manufacturing

332119 Lids, jar, metal, stamping

561611 Lie detection services

334519 Lie detectors manufacturing

611699 Life guard training

524210 Life insurance agencies

524113 Life insurance carriers, direct

339113 Life preservers manufacturing

336612 Life rafts, inflatable, manufacturing

524130 Life reinsurance carriers

541715 Life sciences research and development laboratories or services (except biotechnology and nanotechnology research and development)

423830 Lift trucks, industrial, merchant wholesalers

316998 Lifts, heel, leather, manufacturing

333249 Light bulb and tube (i.e., electric lamp) machinery manufacturing

335110 Light bulbs manufacturing

423610 Light bulbs merchant wholesalers

335110 Light bulbs, sealed beam automotive, manufacturing

334413 Light emitting diodes (LED) manufacturing

333316 Light meters, photographic, manufacturing

336510 Light rail cars and equipment manufacturing

237990 Light rail system construction

485119 Light rail systems (except mixed mode), commuter

334511 Light reconnaissance and surveillance systems and equipment manufacturing

334512 Light responsive appliance controls manufacturing

441110 Light utility truck dealers, new only or new and used

441120 Light utility truck dealers, used only

336112 Light utility trucks assembling on chassis of own manufacture

325998 Lighter fluids (e.g., charcoal, cigarette) manufacturing

483211 Lighterage (i.e., freight transportation except vessel supply services)

339999 Lighters, cigar and cigarette (except motor vehicle, precious metal), manufacturing

339910 Lighters, cigar and cigarette, clad with precious metal, manufacturing

424990 Lighters, cigar and cigarette, merchant wholesalers

488310 Lighthouse operation

335991 Lighting carbons manufacturing

541490 Lighting design services

423990 Lighting equipment, gas, merchant wholesalers

444190 Lighting fixture stores

335129 Lighting fixtures, airport (e.g., approach, ramp, runway, taxi), manufacturing

335122 Lighting fixtures, commercial electric, manufacturing

423610 Lighting fixtures, electric, merchant wholesalers

335122 Lighting fixtures, industrial electric, manufacturing

335122 Lighting fixtures, institutional electric, manufacturing

335129 Lighting fixtures, nonelectric (e.g., propane, kerosene, carbide), manufacturing

335121 Lighting fixtures, residential electric, manufacturing

561790 Lighting maintenance services (e.g., bulb and fuse replacement and cleaning)

238210 Lighting system installation

711510 Lighting technicians, theatrical, independent

335311 Lighting transformers manufacturing

335311	Lighting transformers, street and airport, manufacturing
335931	Lightning arrestors and coils manufacturing
423610	Lightning arrestors merchant wholesalers
238290	Lightning protection equipment (e.g., lightning rod) installation
335931	Lightning protection equipment manufacturing
238290	Lightning rod and conductor installation
325211	Lignin plastics manufacturing
213113	Lignite mining services (except site preparation and related construction contractor activities) on a contract basis
212111	Lignite surface mining and/or beneficiating
111130	Lima bean farming, dry, field and seed production
339113	Limbs, artificial, manufacturing
423320	Lime (except agricultural) merchant wholesalers
111320	Lime groves
325998	Lime oil manufacturing
327410	Lime production
212312	Lime rock, ground, mining and/or beneficiating
424910	Lime, agricultural, merchant wholesalers
212312	Limestone (except bituminous) crushed and broken stone mining and/or beneficiating
212312	Limestone beneficiating plants (e.g., grinding or pulverizing)
212311	Limestone mining or quarrying
212319	Limestone, bituminous, mining and/or beneficiating
325320	Lime-sulfur fungicides manufacturing
334512	Limit controls (e.g., air-conditioning, appliance, heating) manufacturing
511199	Limited editions art print publishers (except exclusive Internet publishing)
452319	Limited price variety stores
212210	Limonite mining and/or beneficiating
532111	Limousine rental without driver
485320	Limousine services (except shuttle services)
485320	Limousines for hire with driver (except taxis)
325320	Lindane pesticides manufacturing
334512	Line or limit control for electric heat manufacturing

561730	Line slash (i.e., rights of way) maintenance services
238910	Line slashing or cutting (except maintenance)
335311	Line voltage regulators (i.e., electric transformers) manufacturing
335999	Linear accelerators manufacturing
332991	Linear ball bearings manufacturing
334514	Linear counters manufacturing
325220	Linear esters fibers and filaments manufacturing
332991	Linear roller bearings manufacturing
442299	Linen stores
812331	Linen supply services
423220	Linens (e.g., bath, bed, table) merchant wholesalers
314120	Linens made from purchased materials
327120	Liner brick and plates, vitrified clay, manufacturing
332313	Liners, industrial, fabricated metal plate work, manufacturing
114111	Lingcod fishing
315210	Lingerie cut and sew apparel contractors
424330	Lingerie merchant wholesalers
448190	Lingerie stores
315240	Lingerie, women's and girls', cut and sewn from purchased fabric (except apparel contractors)
316110	Lining leather manufacturing
316998	Linings, boot and shoe, leather, manufacturing
314999	Linings, casket, manufacturing
315210	Linings, hat, cut and sew apparel contractors
315990	Linings, hat, men's, cut and sewn from purchased fabric (except apparel contractors)
314999	Linings, luggage, manufacturing
332999	Linings, metal safe and vault, manufacturing
332994	Links, ammunition, manufacturing
325199	Linoleic acid esters and amines manufacturing
326199	Linoleum floor coverings manufacturing
238330	Linoleum, installation only
333244	Linotype machines manufacturing
311225	Linseed oil made from purchased oils
311224	Linseed oil, cake and meal, made in crushing mills

327390 Lintels, concrete, manufacturing

325412 Lip balms manufacturing

325620 Lipsticks manufacturing

424690 Liquefied gases (except LP) merchant wholesalers

488999 Liquefied natural gas (LNG) plants

424710 Liquefied petroleum gas (LPG) bulk stations and terminals, merchant wholesalers

332420 Liquefied petroleum gas (LPG) cylinders manufacturing

454310 Liquefied petroleum gas (LPG) dealers, direct selling

221210 Liquefied petroleum gas (LPG) distribution through mains

324110 Liquefied petroleum gas (LPG) made in refineries

424720 Liquefied petroleum gas (LPG) merchant wholesalers (except bulk stations, terminals)

211130 Liquefied petroleum gases (LPG), natural

325120 Liquid air manufacturing

334513 Liquid analysis instruments, industrial process-type, manufacturing

311313 Liquid beet syrup manufacturing

334516 Liquid chromatographic instruments, laboratory-type, manufacturing

334513 Liquid concentration instruments, industrial process-type, manufacturing

423690 Liquid crystal displays merchant wholesalers

334514 Liquid flow meters manufacturing

211130 Liquid hydrocarbons recovered from oil and gas field gases

334512 Liquid level controls, residential and commercial heating-type, manufacturing

334513 Liquid level instruments, industrial process-type, manufacturing

332420 Liquid oxygen tanks manufacturing

311313 Liquid sugar made from beet sugar

311314 Liquid sugar manufacturing

211130 Liquids, natural gas (e.g., ethane, isobutane, natural gasoline, propane) recovered from oil and gas field gases

445310 Liquor stores, package

311351 Liquor, chocolate, made from cacao beans

311352 Liquor, chocolate, made from purchased chocolate

424820 Liquors merchant wholesalers

312130 Liquors, brandy, distilling and blending

424820 Liquors, distilled, merchant wholesalers

312140 Liquors, distilling and blending (except brandy)

339940 List finders and roledex address files manufacturing

531390 Listing services, real estate

711410 Literary agents

325130 Litharge manufacturing

335912 Lithium batteries, primary, manufacturing

335911 Lithium batteries, storage, manufacturing

325180 Lithium compounds, not specified elsewhere by process, manufacturing

212393 Lithium mineral mining and/or beneficiating

325910 Lithographic inks manufacturing

323120 Lithographic plate preparation services

323111 Lithographic printing (except books, grey goods)

333244 Lithographic printing presses manufacturing

325130 Lithopone manufacturing

334510 Lithotripters manufacturing

711310 Live arts center operators

424990 Live bait merchant wholesalers

711310 Live theater operators

332994 Livens projectors (i.e., ordnance) manufacturing

424520 Livestock (except horses, mules, and feedlots) merchant wholesalers

541690 Livestock breeding consulting services

115210 Livestock breeding services (except consulting)

424910 Livestock feeds merchant wholesalers

311119 Livestock feeds, supplements, concentrates and premixes, manufacturing

541940 Livestock inspecting and testing services, veterinary

115210 Livestock spraying

484220 Livestock trucking, local

484230 Livestock trucking, long-distance

541940 Livestock veterinary services

337124 Living room furniture (except upholstered), metal, manufacturing

337122 Living room furniture (except upholstered), wood, manufacturing

337121 Living room furniture, upholstered, manufacturing

112990 Llama production

334418 Loaded computer boards manufacturing

423430	Loaded computer boards merchant wholesalers
423810	Loaders merchant wholesalers
333120	Loaders, shovel, manufacturing
332993	Loading and assembling bombs
488490	Loading and unloading at truck terminals
488320	Loading and unloading services at ports and harbors
488210	Loading and unloading services at rail terminals
333131	Loading machines, underground mining, manufacturing
334418	Loading printed circuit boards
522310	Loan brokerages
522310	Loan brokers' or agents' offices (i.e., independent)
522291	Loan companies (i.e., consumer, personal, small, student)
522292	Loan correspondents (i.e., lending funds with real estate as collateral)
522390	Loan servicing
541820	Lobbying services
541820	Lobbyists' offices
114112	Lobster fishing
334210	Local area network (LAN) communications equipment (e.g., bridges, gateways, routers) manufacturing
541512	Local area network (LAN) computer systems integration design services
611420	Local area network (LAN) management training
485113	Local bus services (except mixed mode)
561421	Local call centers
492210	Local letter and parcel delivery services (except as part of intercity courier network, U.S. Postal Service)
492110	Local letter and parcel delivery services as part of intercity courier network
485112	Local passenger rail systems (except mixed mode)
813940	Local political organizations
517311	Local telephone carriers, wired
485111	Local transit systems, mixed mode (e.g., bus, commuter rail, subway combinations)
561990	Locating underground utility lines prior to digging
237990	Lock and waterway construction
561622	Lock rekeying services
332722	Lock washers, metal, manufacturing
454390	Locker meat provisioners, direct selling

337215	Lockers (except refrigerated) manufacturing
423440	Lockers (except refrigerated) merchant wholesalers
812990	Lockers, coin-operated, rental
333415	Lockers, refrigerated, manufacturing
423740	Lockers, refrigerated, merchant wholesalers
332510	Locks (except coin-operated, time locks), metal, manufacturing
333318	Locks, coin-operated, manufacturing
423710	Locks, security, merchant wholesalers
423850	Locksmith equipment and supplies merchant wholesalers
561622	Locksmith services
561622	Locksmith services with or without sales of locking devices, safes, and security vaults
561622	Locksmith shops
488210	Locomotive and rail car repair (except factory conversion, factory overhaul, factory rebuilding)
336320	Locomotive and railroad car light fixtures manufacturing
333923	Locomotive cranes manufacturing
333618	Locomotive diesel engines manufacturing
336510	Locomotives manufacturing
423860	Locomotives merchant wholesalers
336510	Locomotives rebuilding
212221	Lode gold mining and/or beneficiating
321992	Log cabins, prefabricated wood, manufacturing
333120	Log debarking machinery, portable, manufacturing
333243	Log debarking machinery, stationary, manufacturing
113310	Log harvesting
484220	Log hauling, local
484230	Log hauling, long-distance
236115	Log home construction general contractors
236117	Log home for-sale builders
333120	Log splitters, portable, manufacturing
333243	Log splitters, stationary, manufacturing
111334	Loganberry farming
113310	Logging
236220	Logging camp construction
541330	Logging engineering services
423810	Logging equipment merchant wholesalers

532412 Logging equipment rental or leasing without operator

482112 Logging railroads

237310 Logging road construction

336212 Logging trailers manufacturing

213112 Logging wells on a contract basis

334515 Logic circuit testers manufacturing

541614 Logistics and integrated supply chain management consulting services

541614 Logistics management consulting services

423990 Logs merchant wholesalers

333414 Logs, gas fireplace, manufacturing

325194 Logwood extract manufacturing

517911 Long-distance telecommunication resellers (except satellite)

517311 Long-distance telephone carriers, wired

517410 Long-distance telephone satellite communication carriers

488320 Longshoremen services

333249 Loom bobbins manufacturing

333249 Loom reeds manufacturing

333249 Looms for textiles manufacturing

333249 Loopers for textiles manufacturing

323111 Looseleaf binders and devices manufacturing

424120 Looseleaf binders merchant wholesalers

322230 Looseleaf fillers and paper made from purchased paper

322121 Looseleaf fillers and paper made in paper mills

524291 Loss control consultants

325620 Lotions (e.g., body, face, hand) manufacturing

713290 Lottery control boards (i.e., operating lotteries)

921130 Lottery control boards, nonoperating

713290 Lottery corporations

713290 Lottery ticket sales agents (except retail stores)

334118 Lottery ticket sales terminals manufacturing

713290 Lottery ticket vendors (except retail stores)

334310 Loudspeakers manufacturing

722410 Lounges, cocktail

315210 Lounging robes and dressing gowns cut and sew apparel contractors

315190 Lounging robes and dressing gowns made in apparel knitting mills

315220 Lounging robes and dressing gowns, men's and boys', cut and sewn from purchased fabric (except apparel contractors)

315240 Lounging robes and dressing gowns, women's, girls', and infants', cut and sewn from purchased fabric (except apparel contractors)

333314 Loupes (e.g., jewelers) manufacturing

321911 Louver windows and doors, made from purchased glass with wood frame

332321 Louver windows, metal, manufacturing

332322 Louvers, sheet metal (except stampings), manufacturing

236117 Low income housing construction for-sale builders

236116 Low income housing, multifamily, construction general contractors

236115 Low income housing, single-family, construction general contractors

238160 Low slope roofing installation

238210 Low voltage electrical work

335121 Low voltage lighting equipment, residential, electric, manufacturing

236116 Low-rise apartment construction general contractors

236117 Low-rise apartment for-sale builders

311340 Lozenges, nonmedicated, candy, manufacturing

621399 LPNs' (licensed practical nurses) offices (e.g., centers, clinics)

484122 LTL (less-than-truckload) long-distance freight trucking

424710 Lubricating oils and greases bulk stations and terminals, merchant wholesalers

324110 Lubricating oils and greases made in petroleum refineries

424720 Lubricating oils and greases merchant wholesalers (except bulk stations, terminals)

324191 Lubricating oils and greases, petroleum, made from refined petroleum

325998 Lubricating oils and greases, synthetic, manufacturing

811191 Lubrication shops, automotive

336510 Lubrication systems, locomotive (except pumps), manufacturing

332510 Luggage hardware, metal, manufacturing

314999 Luggage linings manufacturing

423990 Luggage merchant wholesalers

336390 Luggage racks, car top, automotive, truck, and bus, manufacturing

811430	Luggage repair shops without retailing new luggage
448320	Luggage stores
316998	Luggage, all materials, manufacturing
335931	Lugs and connectors, electrical, manufacturing
423610	Lugs and connectors, electrical, merchant wholesalers
423310	Lumber (e.g., dressed, finished, rough) merchant wholesalers
321113	Lumber (i.e., rough, dressed) made from logs or bolts
561990	Lumber grading services
444190	Lumber retailing yards
493190	Lumber storage terminals
321113	Lumber, hardwood dimension, made from logs or bolts
321912	Lumber, hardwood dimension, resawing purchased lumber
321999	Lumber, kiln drying
321213	Lumber, parallel strand, manufacturing
321113	Lumber, softwood dimension, made from logs or bolts
321912	Lumber, softwood dimension, resawing purchased lumber
335122	Luminous panel ceilings, electric, manufacturing
335311	Luminous tube transformers manufacturing
332439	Lunch boxes, light gauge metal, manufacturing
722330	Lunch wagons
311612	Luncheon meat (except poultry) made from purchased carcasses
311611	Luncheon meat (except poultry) produced in slaughtering plants
311615	Luncheon meat, poultry, manufacturing
337127	Lunchroom tables and chairs manufacturing
532111	Luxury automobile rental without driver
485320	Luxury automobiles for hire with driver (except taxis)
321213	LVL (laminated veneer lumber) manufacturing
325612	Lye, household-type, manufacturing
111335	Macadamia farming
424490	Macaroni merchant wholesalers
311824	Macaroni, dry, manufacturing
311991	Macaroni, fresh, manufacturing
311412	Macaroni, frozen, manufacturing

332216	Machetes manufacturing
332999	Machine bases, metal, manufacturing
332322	Machine guards, sheet metal (except stampings), manufacturing
332994	Machine gun belts manufacturing
332994	Machine guns manufacturing
332722	Machine keys, metal, manufacturing
332216	Machine knives (except metal cutting) manufacturing
333515	Machine knives, metal cutting, manufacturing
238290	Machine rigging
332710	Machine shops
333515	Machine tool attachments and accessories manufacturing
335311	Machine tool transformers manufacturing
423830	Machine tools and accessories merchant wholesalers
811310	Machine tools repair and maintenance services
333517	Machine tools, metal cutting, manufacturing
333517	Machine tools, metal forming, manufacturing
238290	Machinery and equipment, large-scale, installation
522220	Machinery finance leasing
238910	Machinery, construction (except cranes), rental with operator
423420	Machines, office, merchant wholesalers
332216	Machinists' precision measuring tools (except optical) manufacturing
423830	Machinists' precision measuring tools merchant wholesalers
334511	Machmeters manufacturing
114111	Mackerel fishing
315210	Mackinaws cut and sew apparel contractors
315220	Mackinaws, men's and boys', cut and sewn from purchased fabric (except apparel contractors)
315240	Mackinaws, women's, girls', and infants', cut and sewn from purchased fabric (except apparel contractors)
541840	Magazine advertising representatives (i.e., independent of media owners)
511120	Magazine publishers (except exclusive Internet publishing)
511120	Magazine publishers and printing combined
519130	Magazine publishers, exclusively on Internet

337122 Magazine racks, wood, manufacturing

451212 Magazine stands (i.e., permanent)

323111 Magazines and periodicals commercial printing (except screen) without publishing

323113 Magazines and periodicals screen printing without publishing

424920 Magazines merchant wholesalers

711190 Magic shows

451120 Magic supply stores

711510 Magicians, independent

327120 Magnesia refractory cement manufacturing

325411 Magnesia, medicinal, uncompounded, manufacturing

212325 Magnesite mining and/or beneficiating

327992 Magnesite, crude (e.g., calcined, dead-burned, ground), manufacturing

331491 Magnesium and magnesium alloy bar, rod, shape, sheet, strip, and tubing made from purchased metals or scrap

325180 Magnesium carbonate manufacturing

331529 Magnesium castings (except die-castings), unfinished, manufacturing

325180 Magnesium chloride manufacturing

325180 Magnesium compounds, not specified elsewhere by process, manufacturing

331523 Magnesium die-castings, unfinished, manufacturing

331491 Magnesium foil made by rolling purchased metals or scrap

332999 Magnesium foil not made in rolling mills

423520 Magnesium ores merchant wholesalers

331492 Magnesium recovering from scrap and/or alloying purchased metals

331410 Magnesium refining, primary

331491 Magnesium rolling, drawing, or extruding purchased metals or scrap

331420 Magnet wire, insulated, made from purchased copper in wire drawing plants

331318 Magnet wire, insulated, made in aluminum wire drawing plants

331491 Magnet wire, nonferrous metals (except aluminum, copper), made from purchased nonferrous metals (except aluminum, copper) in wire drawing plants

334613 Magnetic and optical media, blank, manufacturing

423690 Magnetic bubble memories merchant wholesalers

334514 Magnetic counters manufacturing

334513 Magnetic flow meters, industrial process-type, manufacturing

333517 Magnetic forming machines, metalworking, manufacturing

541360 Magnetic geophysical surveying services

334118 Magnetic ink recognition devices, computer peripheral equipment, manufacturing

334613 Magnetic recording media for tapes, cassettes, and disks, manufacturing

621512 Magnetic resonance imaging (MRI) centers

334510 Magnetic resonance imaging (MRI) medical diagnostic equipment manufacturing

334516 Magnetic resonance imaging (MRI) type apparatus (except medical diagnostic) manufacturing

334613 Magnetic tapes, cassettes and disks, blank, manufacturing

423690 Magnetic tapes, cassettes, and disks, blank, merchant wholesalers

334112 Magnetic/optical combination storage units for computers manufacturing

334519 Magnetometers manufacturing

334419 Magnetron tubes manufacturing

327110 Magnets, permanent, ceramic or ferrite, manufacturing

332999 Magnets, permanent, metallic, manufacturing

339115 Magnifiers, corrective vision-type, manufacturing

333314 Magnifying glasses (except corrective vision-type) manufacturing

423460 Magnifying glasses merchant wholesalers

333314 Magnifying instruments, optical, manufacturing

114111 Mahimahi fishing

561311 Maid registries

561720 Maid services (i.e., cleaning services)

238990 Mail box units, outdoor, multiple box-type, erection

337215 Mail carrier cases and tables, wood, manufacturing

332322 Mail chutes, sheet metal (except stampings), manufacturing

561499 Mail consolidation services

333318 Mail handling machinery, post office-type, manufacturing

561499 Mail presorting services

561431 Mailbox rental centers, private

561431	Mailbox rental services combined with one or more other office support services, private
423990	Mailboxes merchant wholesalers
332439	Mailboxes, light gauge metal, manufacturing
322219	Mailing cases and tubes, paper fiber (i.e., all-fiber, nonfiber ends of any material), made from purchased paperboard
532420	Mailing equipment rental or leasing
511140	Mailing list publishers (except exclusive Internet publishing)
423420	Mailing machines merchant wholesalers
454110	Mail-order houses
334111	Mainframe computers manufacturing
488190	Maintenance and repair services, aircraft (except factory conversion, factory overhaul, factory rebuilding)
561730	Maintenance of plants and shrubs in buildings
488210	Maintenance of rights of way and structures, railway
488119	Maintenance services, runway
488310	Maintenance services, waterfront terminal (except dredging)
711211	Major league baseball clubs
812112	Makeup (except permanent) salons
325620	Makeup (i.e., cosmetics) manufacturing
812199	Makeup salons, permanent
523110	Making markets for securities
337125	Malacca furniture (except upholstered), household-type, manufacturing
325320	Malathion insecticides manufacturing
325194	Maleic anhydride manufacturing
531120	Mall property operation (i.e., not operating contained businesses) rental or leasing
331511	Malleable iron foundries
332216	Mallets (e.g., rubber, wood) manufacturing
321999	Mallets, wood, manufacturing
325199	Malonic dinitrile manufacturing
524126	Malpractice insurance carriers, direct
311942	Malt extract and syrups manufacturing
424490	Malt extract merchant wholesalers
311213	Malt flour manufacturing
312120	Malt liquor brewing
424810	Malt liquor merchant wholesalers
311213	Malt manufacturing
424490	Malt merchant wholesalers

333241	Malt milling machinery manufacturing
311213	Malt sprouts manufacturing
311514	Malted milk manufacturing
311213	Malting (germinating and drying grains)
311221	Maltodextrins manufacturing
621512	Mammogram (i.e., breast imaging) centers
711410	Management agencies for artists, entertainers, and other public figures
611430	Management development training
525910	Management investment offices, open-ended
561110	Management services (except complete operation of client's business)
115116	Management services, farm
711310	Managers of agricultural fairs with facilities
711320	Managers of agricultural fairs without facilities
711310	Managers of arts events with facilities
711320	Managers of arts events without facilities
711310	Managers of festivals with facilities
711320	Managers of festivals without facilities
711310	Managers of live performing arts productions (e.g., concerts) with facilities
711320	Managers of live performing arts productions (e.g., concerts) without facilities
711310	Managers of sports events with facilities
711320	Managers of sports events without facilities
531312	Managers' offices, commercial condominium
531312	Managers' offices, commercial real estate
531312	Managers' offices, nonresidential real estate
531311	Managers' offices, residential condominium
531311	Managers' offices, residential real estate
711410	Managers, authors'
711410	Managers, celebrities'
561920	Managers, convention
711410	Managers, entertainers'
711410	Managers, public figures'
711410	Managers, sports figures'
561920	Managers, trade fair or show
531312	Managing commercial condominiums
531312	Managing commercial real estate
531311	Managing cooperative apartments
523920	Managing investment funds

523920	Managing mutual funds
561110	Managing offices of dentists
561110	Managing offices of physicians and surgeons
561110	Managing offices of professionals (e.g., dentists, physicians, surgeons)
523920	Managing personal investment trusts
531311	Managing residential condominiums
531311	Managing residential real estate
523920	Managing trusts
111320	Mandarin groves
339992	Mandolins manufacturing
333515	Mandrels (i.e., a machine tool accessory) manufacturing
212299	Manganese concentrates beneficiating
325180	Manganese dioxide manufacturing
331110	Manganese metal ferroalloys manufacturing
212299	Manganese ores mining and/or beneficiating
212210	Manganiferous ores valued for iron content, mining and/or beneficiating
212299	Manganiferousares ores (not valued for iron content) mining and/or beneficiating
212299	Manganite mining and/or beneficiating
111339	Mango farming
325194	Mangrove extract manufacturing
331511	Manhole covers, cast iron, manufacturing
237120	Manhole, oil and gas, construction
812113	Manicure and pedicure salons
611511	Manicure and pedicure schools
325620	Manicure preparations manufacturing
812113	Manicurist services
423850	Manicurists supplies merchant wholesalers
424120	Manifold business forms merchant wholesalers
323111	Manifold business forms printing
336310	Manifolds (i.e., intake and exhaust), automotive and truck gasoline engine, manufacturing
332996	Manifolds, pipe, made from purchased metal pipe
322230	Manila folders, die-cut, made from purchased paper or paperboard
327999	Manmade and engineered proppants (e.g., resin-coated sand, ceramic materials) manufacturing
325220	Manmade cellulosic fibers manufacturing
313220	Manmade fabric, narrow woven, weaving
313210	Manmade fabrics, broadwoven, weaving
313110	Manmade fiber thread manufacturing
424690	Manmade fibers merchant wholesalers
325220	Manmade noncellulosic fibers and filaments manufacturing
313110	Manmade staple spun yarns made from purchased fiber
541890	Mannequin decorating services
339999	Mannequins manufacturing
423440	Mannequins merchant wholesalers
325920	Mannitol hexanitrate explosive materials manufacturing
334513	Manometers, industrial process-type, manufacturing
561320	Manpower pools
238340	Mantel, marble or stone, installation
621399	Manual-arts therapists' offices (e.g., centers, clinics)
423390	Manufactured (i.e., mobile) homes merchant wholesalers
321991	Manufactured (mobile) buildings for commercial use (e.g., banks, offices) manufacturing
321991	Manufactured (mobile) classrooms manufacturing
453930	Manufactured (mobile) home dealers
531190	Manufactured (mobile) home parks
238990	Manufactured (mobile) home set up and tie-down work
531190	Manufactured (mobile) home sites rental or leasing
321991	Manufactured (mobile) homes manufacturing
221210	Manufactured gas distribution
813910	Manufacturers' associations
236210	Manufacturing building construction
531120	Manufacturing building rental or leasing
532490	Manufacturing machinery and equipment rental or leasing
423830	Manufacturing machinery and equipment, industrial, merchant wholesalers
541614	Manufacturing management consulting services
541614	Manufacturing operations improvement consulting services
511130	Map publishers (except exclusive Internet publishing)

511130	Map publishers and printing combined
519130	Map publishers, exclusively on Internet
111998	Maple sap concentrating (i.e., producing pure maple syrup in the field)
111998	Maple sap gathering
111998	Maple syrup (i.e., maple sap reducing)
424490	Maple syrup merchant wholesalers
311999	Maple syrup mixing into other products
541370	Mapping (except geophysical) services
541360	Mapping services, geophysical
424920	Maps (except globe, school, wall) merchant wholesalers
323111	Maps commercial printing (except screen) without publishing
323113	Maps screen printing without publishing
212319	Marble crushed and broken stone mining and/or beneficiating
212311	Marble mining or quarrying
238140	Marble, granite and slate, exterior, contractors
238340	Marble, granite, and slate, interior installation contractors
339930	Marbles manufacturing
212393	Marcasite mining and/or beneficiating
325199	Margaric acid manufacturing
311221	Margarine and other corn oils made by wet milling corn
424490	Margarine merchant wholesalers
311225	Margarine-butter blend made from purchased fats and oils
311225	Margarines (including imitation) made from purchased fats and oils
424590	Marijuana merchant wholesalers
453998	Marijuana stores, medical or recreational
111998	Marijuana, grown in an open field
111419	Marijuana, grown under cover
713930	Marinas
335314	Marine and navy auxiliary controls, manufacturing
713930	Marine basins, operation of
488390	Marine cargo checkers and surveyors
488320	Marine cargo handling services
237990	Marine construction
928110	Marine Corps
541330	Marine engineering services
333618	Marine engines manufacturing
541990	Marine forecasting services

332510	Marine hardware, metal, manufacturing
332999	Marine horns, compressed air or steam, metal, manufacturing
524126	Marine insurance carriers, direct
712110	Marine museums
611519	Marine navigational schools
325510	Marine paints manufacturing
332410	Marine power boilers manufacturing
334220	Marine radio communications equipment manufacturing
524130	Marine reinsurance carriers
488330	Marine salvaging services
447190	Marine service stations
488510	Marine shipping agency
335911	Marine storage batteries manufacturing
423860	Marine supplies (except pleasure) merchant wholesalers
423910	Marine supplies, pleasure, merchant wholesalers
441222	Marine supply dealers
541990	Marine surveyor (i.e., ship appraiser) services
488330	Marine vessel traffic reporting services
339999	Marionettes (i.e., puppets) manufacturing
541330	Maritime technology engineering services
339940	Marker boards (i.e., whiteboards) manufacturing
523110	Market making for securities
541910	Marketing analysis services
541613	Marketing consulting services
541613	Marketing management consulting services
541910	Marketing research services
339940	Marking devices manufacturing
424120	Marking devices merchant wholesalers
333519	Marking machines, metal, manufacturing
212312	Marl crushed and broken stone mining and/or beneficiating
311421	Marmalade manufacturing
424490	Marmalade merchant wholesalers
321999	Marquetry, wood, manufacturing
624190	Marriage counseling services (except by offices of mental health practitioners)
922120	Marshals' offices
311340	Marshmallow creme manufacturing
311340	Marshmallows manufacturing
611620	Martial arts instruction, camps, or schools

311340 Marzipan (i.e., candy) manufacturing

335999 Maser (i.e., microwave amplification by stimulated emission of radiation) amplifiers manufacturing

321999 Mashers, potato, wood, manufacturing

322220 Masking tape made from purchased paper

444190 Masonry (e.g., block, brick, stone) dealers

238140 Masonry contractors

238140 Masonry pointing, cleaning or caulking

332216 Mason's handtools manufacturing

423320 Mason's materials merchant wholesalers

334516 Mass spectrometers manufacturing

334516 Mass spectroscopy instrumentation manufacturing

423850 Massage equipment merchant wholesalers

335210 Massage machines, electric (except designed for beauty and barber shop use), manufacturing

812199 Massage parlors

611519 Massage therapist instruction

621399 Massage therapists' offices (e.g., centers, clinics)

512250 Master recording leasing and licensing

424690 Mastics (except construction) merchant wholesalers

423390 Mastics, construction, merchant wholesalers

321999 Masts, wood, manufacturing

812332 Mat and rug supply services

325998 Matches and match books manufacturing

424990 Matches and match books merchant wholesalers

238290 Material handling equipment installation

811310 Material handling equipment repair and maintenance services

423830 Material handling machinery and equipment merchant wholesalers

532490 Material handling machinery and equipment rental or leasing

541614 Materials management consulting services

562920 Materials recovery facilities (MRF)

236210 Materials recovery facility construction

923120 Maternity and child health program administration

315210 Maternity bras and corsets cut and sew apparel contractors

315240 Maternity bras and corsets, women's and girls', cut and sewn from purchased fabric (except apparel contractors)

622310 Maternity hospitals

448120 Maternity shops

541715 Mathematics research and development laboratories or services

332618 Mats and matting made from purchased wire

332216 Mattocks (i.e., handtools) manufacturing

326299 Mattress protectors, rubber, manufacturing

332613 Mattress springs and spring units, light gauge, made from purchased wire or strip

442110 Mattress stores (including waterbeds)

337910 Mattresses (i.e., box spring, innerspring, noninnerspring) manufacturing

337910 Mattresses made from felt, foam rubber, urethane and similar materials

423210 Mattresses merchant wholesalers

326199 Mattresses, air, plastics, manufacturing

326299 Mattresses, air, rubber, manufacturing

311812 Matzo baking made in commercial bakeries

332216 Mauls, metal, manufacturing

321999 Mauls, wood, manufacturing

236220 Mausoleum (i.e., building) construction

812220 Mausoleums

311941 Mayonnaise manufacturing

921110 Mayor's offices

321219 MDF (medium density fiberboard) manufacturing

621112 MDs' (medical doctors), mental health, offices (e.g., centers, clinics)

621111 MDs' (medical doctors, except mental health) offices (e.g., centers, clinics)

624210 Meal delivery programs

311119 Meal, alfalfa, manufacturing

311119 Meal, bone, prepared as feed for animals and fowls, manufacturing

311211 Meal, corn, for human consumption made in flour mills

423830 Measuring and testing equipment (except electric measuring and automotive) merchant wholesalers

333515 Measuring attachments (e.g., sine bars) for machine tool manufacturing

334515 Measuring equipment for electronic and electrical circuits and equipment manufacturing

811219 Measuring instrument repair and maintenance services

334515 Measuring instruments and meters, electric, manufacturing

334513	Measuring instruments, industrial process control-type, manufacturing
332216	Measuring tools, machinist's (except optical), manufacturing
334514	Measuring wheels manufacturing
311613	Meat and bone meal and tankage, produced in rendering plant
333241	Meat and poultry processing and preparation machinery
311612	Meat canning (except baby, pet food, poultry), made from purchased carcasses
311611	Meat canning (except poultry) produced in slaughtering plants
311422	Meat canning, baby food, manufacturing
311111	Meat canning, dog and cat, pet food, made from purchased carcasses
311615	Meat canning, poultry (except baby and pet food), manufacturing
311612	Meat extracts made from purchased carcasses
333241	Meat grinders, food-type, manufacturing
445210	Meat markets
311615	Meat products (e.g., hot dogs, luncheon meats, sausages) made from a combination of poultry and other meats
311612	Meat products canning (except baby, pet food, poultry) made from purchased carcasses
311111	Meat products, dog and cat, pet food, canning, made from purchased carcasses
311612	Meats (except poultry), cured or smoked, made from purchased carcasses
424470	Meats and meat products (except canned, packaged frozen) merchant wholesalers
311611	Meats fresh, chilled or frozen (except poultry and small game), produced in slaughtering plants
424490	Meats, canned, merchant wholesalers
424470	Meats, cured or smoked, merchant wholesalers
311611	Meats, cured or smoked, produced in slaughtering plants
311612	Meats, fresh or chilled (except poultry and small game), frozen, made from purchased carcasses
424470	Meats, fresh, merchant wholesalers
424470	Meats, frozen (except packaged), merchant wholesalers
424420	Meats, packaged frozen, merchant wholesalers
238220	Mechanical contractors
541330	Mechanical engineering services
238290	Mechanical equipment insulation
313310	Mechanical finishing of fabrics
316110	Mechanical leather manufacturing
334513	Mechanical measuring instruments, industrial process-type, manufacturing
339940	Mechanical pencil refills manufacturing
339940	Mechanical pencils manufacturing
811310	Mechanical power transmission equipment repair and maintenance services
423840	Mechanical power transmission supplies (e.g., gears, pulleys, sprockets) merchant wholesalers
326291	Mechanical rubber goods (i.e., extruded, lathe-cut, molded) manufacturing
423840	Mechanical rubber goods merchant wholesalers
541380	Mechanical testing laboratories or services
611513	Mechanic's apprenticeship training
333924	Mechanic's creepers manufacturing
325611	Mechanic's hand soaps and pastes manufacturing
332216	Mechanic's handtools, nonpowered, manufacturing
611519	Mechanic's schools (except apprenticeship)
423120	Mechanic's tools merchant wholesalers
333318	Mechanisms for coin-operated machines manufacturing
334519	Mechanisms, clockwork operated device, manufacturing
423940	Medallions merchant wholesalers
541840	Media advertising representatives (i.e., independent of media owners)
541830	Media buying agencies
541830	Media buying services
541840	Media representatives (i.e., independent of media owners)
518210	Media streaming services
926150	Mediation and conciliation services, government
541990	Mediation product services (except by lawyer, attorney, paralegal offices, family and social services)
624190	Mediation, social service, family, agencies
811219	Medical and surgical equipment repair and maintenance services
541430	Medical art services
541430	Medical artists, independent
923130	Medical assistance programs administration, government

813920   Medical associations

531120   Medical building rental or leasing

621999   Medical care management services

621999   Medical case management services

334510   Medical cleaning equipment, ultrasonic, manufacturing

541219   Medical coding services combined with accounting services (except CPA services)

524298   Medical cost evaluation services

621112   Medical doctors' (MDs), mental health, offices (e.g., centers, clinics)

621111   Medical doctors' (MDs, except mental health) offices (e.g., centers, clinics)

532490   Medical equipment (except home health furniture and equipment) rental or leasing

446199   Medical equipment and supplies stores

423450   Medical equipment merchant wholesalers

423450   Medical furniture merchant wholesalers

424690   Medical gases merchant wholesalers

327215   Medical glassware made from purchased glass

327212   Medical glassware made in glass making plants

423450   Medical glassware merchant wholesalers

541430   Medical illustration services

541430   Medical illustrators, independent

423450   Medical instruments merchant wholesalers

524114   Medical insurance carriers, direct

511120   Medical journal and periodical publishers (except exclusive Internet publishing)

511120   Medical journal and periodical publishers and printing combined

519130   Medical journal and periodical publishers, exclusively on Internet

621511   Medical laboratories (except radiological, X-ray)

621512   Medical laboratories, radiological or X-ray

541611   Medical office management consulting services or consultants

561110   Medical office management services

621511   Medical pathology laboratories

541922   Medical photography services

334517   Medical radiation therapy equipment manufacturing

621512   Medical radiological laboratories

524130   Medical reinsurance carriers

541715   Medical research and development laboratories or services (except biotechnology and nanotechnology research and development)

611310   Medical schools

315210   Medical service apparel cut and sew apparel contractors

315220   Medical service apparel, men's and boys', cut and sewn from purchased fabric (except apparel contractors)

315240   Medical service apparel, women's and girls', cut and sewn from purchased fabric (except apparel contractors)

524114   Medical service plans without providing health care services

424210   Medical sundries, rubber, merchant wholesalers

423450   Medical supplies (except household first-aid kits and non-surgical bandages) merchant wholesalers

611519   Medical technician schools

339112   Medical thermometers manufacturing

334510   Medical ultrasound equipment manufacturing

562211   Medical waste treatment facilities, hazardous

621512   Medical X-ray laboratories

923130   Medicare and Medicaid administration

325411   Medicinal chemicals, uncompounded, manufacturing

325411   Medicinal gelatins manufacturing

337110   Medicine cabinets (except freestanding), wood household-type, manufacturing

337124   Medicine cabinets, metal household-type, manufacturing

321219   Medium density fiberboard (MDF) manufacturing

212399   Meerschaum mining and/or beneficiating

531120   Meeting hall and room rental or leasing

325211   Melamine resins manufacturing

111219   Melon farming (e.g., cantaloupe, casaba, honeydew, watermelon), field, bedding plant and seed production

111419   Melon farming, grown under cover

313230   Melt blown nonwoven fabrics manufacturing

315210   Melton jackets cut and sew apparel contractors

315220   Melton jackets, men's and boys', cut and sewn from purchased fabric (except apparel contractors)

315240   Melton jackets, women's, girls', and infants', cut and sewn from purchased fabric (except apparel contractors)

813410   Membership associations, civic or social

721110   Membership hotels

812220	Memorial gardens (i.e., burial places)
334418	Memory boards manufacturing
423430	Memory boards merchant wholesalers
712130	Menageries
114111	Menhaden fishing
424320	Men's and boys' clothing merchant wholesalers
424320	Men's and boys' furnishings (except shoes) merchant wholesalers
315110	Men's socks knitting or knitting and finishing
622210	Mental (except intellectual and developmental disability) hospitals
621420	Mental health centers and clinics (except hospitals), outpatient
623220	Mental health facilities, residential
623220	Mental health halfway houses
622210	Mental health hospitals
621112	Mental health physicians' offices (e.g., centers, clinics)
923120	Mental health program administration
561450	Mercantile credit reporting bureaus
333249	Mercerizing machinery manufacturing
313310	Mercerizing textile products and fabrics
326111	Merchandise bags, plastics film, single wall or multiwall, manufacturing
423440	Merchandising machines, coin-operated, merchant wholesalers
236117	Merchant builders (i.e., building on own land, for sale), residential
926120	Merchant Marine (except academy)
813910	Merchants' associations
335912	Mercuric oxide batteries manufacturing
212299	Mercury (quicksilver) mining and/or beneficiating
335999	Mercury arc rectifiers (i.e., electrical apparatus) manufacturing
325180	Mercury chloride manufacturing
325180	Mercury compounds, not specified elsewhere by process, manufacturing
325920	Mercury fulminate explosive materials manufacturing
335110	Mercury halide lamp bulbs manufacturing
212299	Mercury ores mining and/or beneficiating
325180	Mercury oxide manufacturing
332618	Mesh made from purchased wire
331420	Mesh, wire, made from purchased copper in wire drawing plants

331318	Mesh, wire, made in aluminum wire drawing plants
331110	Mesh, wire, made in iron and steel mills
331222	Mesh, wire, made in wire drawing mills
331491	Mesh, wire, nonferrous metals (except aluminum, copper), made from purchased nonferrous metals (except aluminum, copper) in wire drawing plants
561421	Message services, telephone answering
492210	Messenger service
325412	Metabolite in-vivo diagnostic substances manufacturing
423390	Metal buildings merchant wholesalers
332431	Metal cans, light gauge metal, manufacturing
333249	Metal casting machinery and equipment manufacturing
333517	Metal cutting machine tools manufacturing
332216	Metal cutting saw blades manufacturing
424690	Metal cyanides merchant wholesalers
333517	Metal deposit forming machines manufacturing
334519	Metal detectors manufacturing
339113	Metal fabric and mesh safety gloves manufacturing
332999	Metal foil containers (except bags) manufacturing
333517	Metal forming machine tools manufacturing
337121	Metal framed furniture, household-type, upholstered, manufacturing
238190	Metal furring contractors
339940	Metal hand stamps manufacturing
333994	Metal melting furnaces, industrial, manufacturing
213114	Metal mining support services (shaft sinking, tunneling, blasting) (except site preparation and related construction contractor activities)
336370	Metal motor vehicle body parts stamping
423520	Metal ores merchant wholesalers
334413	Metal oxide silicon (MOS) devices manufacturing
423510	Metal pipe merchant wholesalers
325612	Metal polishes (i.e., tarnish removers) manufacturing
331314	Metal powder and flake made from purchased aluminum
331420	Metal powder and flake made from purchased copper

331221	Metal powder and flake made from purchased iron or steel
331492	Metal powder and flake nonferrous (except aluminum, copper) made from purchased metal
236210	Metal processing plant construction
423510	Metal products (e.g., bars, ingots, plates, rods, shapes, sheets) merchant wholesalers
423930	Metal scrap and waste merchant wholesalers
238170	Metal siding installation
332119	Metal stampings (except automotive, cans, coins), unfinished, manufacturing
335991	Metal-graphite products manufacturing
423520	Metallic concentrates merchant wholesalers
325130	Metallic pigments, inorganic, manufacturing
325199	Metallic soap manufacturing
313320	Metallizing purchased textiles
541380	Metallurgical testing laboratories or services
423510	Metals sales offices
423510	Metals service centers
423510	Metals, ferrous and nonferrous, merchant wholesalers
423940	Metals, precious, merchant wholesalers
424690	Metalworking compounds merchant wholesalers
333517	Metalworking lathes manufacturing
423830	Metalworking machinery and equipment merchant wholesalers
532490	Metalworking machinery and equipment rental or leasing
423830	Metalworking tools (drills, taps, dies, grinding wheels) merchant wholesalers
334519	Meteorologic tracking systems manufacturing
811219	Meteorological instrument repair and maintenance services
334519	Meteorological instruments manufacturing
541990	Meteorological services
561990	Meter reading services, contract
334514	Metering devices (except electrical and industrial process control) manufacturing
335313	Metering panels, electric, manufacturing
334514	Meters (except electrical and industrial process control) manufacturing
423830	Meters (except electrical, parking) merchant wholesalers
334515	Meters, electrical (i.e., graphic recording, panelboard, pocket, portable), manufacturing
423610	Meters, electrical, merchant wholesalers
334513	Meters, industrial process control-type, manufacturing
334514	Meters, parking, manufacturing
423850	Meters, parking, merchant wholesalers
334515	Meters, power factor and phase angle, manufacturing
325320	Methoxychlor insecticides manufacturing
325194	Methyl acetone manufacturing
325211	Methyl acrylate resins manufacturing
325199	Methyl alcohol (i.e., methanol), synthetic, manufacturing
325194	Methyl alcohol (methanol), natural, manufacturing
325211	Methyl cellulose resins manufacturing
325199	Methyl chloride manufacturing
325211	Methyl methacrylate resins manufacturing
325199	Methyl perhydrofluorine manufacturing
325199	Methyl salicylate manufacturing
325130	Methyl violet toners manufacturing
325199	Methylamine manufacturing
325199	Methylene chloride manufacturing
311422	Mexican foods canning
311412	Mexican foods, frozen, manufacturing
212399	Mica mining and/or beneficiating
327992	Mica processing beyond beneficiation
327999	Mica products manufacturing
212319	Mica schist crushed and broken stone mining and/or beneficiating
212311	Mica schist mining or quarrying
311119	Micro and macro premixes, livestock, manufacturing
334516	Microbiology instruments manufacturing
325413	Microbiology, virology, and serology in-vitro diagnostic substances manufacturing
334111	Microcomputers manufacturing
334413	Microcontroller chip manufacturing
333316	Microfiche equipment (e.g., cameras, projectors, readers) manufacturing
518210	Microfiche recording and imaging services
333316	Microfilm equipment (e.g., cameras, projectors, readers) manufacturing
423420	Microfilm equipment and supplies merchant wholesalers

518210	Microfilm recording and imaging services
212299	Microlite mining and/or beneficiating
333242	Micro-lithography equipment, semiconductor, manufacturing
332216	Micrometers, machinist's precision tools, manufacturing
334310	Microphones (except broadcast and studio equipment) manufacturing
334220	Microphones, broadcast and studio equipment, manufacturing
334516	Microprobes (e.g., electron, ion, laser, X-ray) manufacturing
334413	Microprocessor chip manufacturing
423430	Microprocessors merchant wholesalers
333314	Microscopes (except electron, proton) manufacturing
334516	Microscopes, electron and proton, manufacturing
237990	Microtunneling contractors
334220	Microwave communications equipment manufacturing
334419	Microwave components manufacturing
811412	Microwave oven, household-type, repair and maintenance services, without retailing new microwave ovens
335220	Microwave ovens (including portable), household-type, manufacturing
423440	Microwave ovens, commercial, merchant wholesalers
333318	Microwave ovens, commercial-type, manufacturing
423620	Microwave ovens, household-type, merchant wholesalers
237130	Microwave relay tower construction
517911	Microwave telecommunication resellers
334515	Microwave test equipment manufacturing
326199	Microwaveware, plastics, manufacturing
315210	Middies cut and sew apparel contractors
315240	Middies, women's, girls', and infants', cut and sewn from purchased fabric (except apparel contractors)
611110	Middle schools
621399	Midwives' offices (e.g., clinics)
721310	Migrant workers' camps
611310	Military academies, college level
611110	Military academies, elementary or secondary
561210	Military base support services
928110	Military bases and camps
315210	Military dress uniforms cut and sew apparel contractors
315220	Military dress uniforms, men's and boys', cut and sewn from purchased fabric (except apparel contractors)
315240	Military dress uniforms, tailored, women's and girls', cut and sewn from purchased fabric (except apparel contractors)
611512	Military flight instruction training
332999	Military insignia, metal, manufacturing
314999	Military insignia, textile, manufacturing
712110	Military museums
928110	Military police
928110	Military reserve armories and bases
611310	Military service academies (college)
928110	Military training schools (except academies)
423860	Military vehicles (except trucks) merchant wholesalers
311511	Milk based drinks (except dietary) manufacturing
311514	Milk based drinks, dietary, manufacturing
322130	Milk carton board made in paperboard mills
322220	Milk carton board stock made from purchased paperboard
322219	Milk cartons made from purchased paper or paperboard
311511	Milk drink, chocolate, manufacturing
484220	Milk hauling, local
311511	Milk pasteurizing
311511	Milk processing (e.g., bottling, homogenizing, pasteurizing, vitaminizing) manufacturing
333241	Milk processing (except farm-type) machinery manufacturing
112120	Milk production, dairy cattle
311511	Milk substitutes manufacturing
115210	Milk testing for butterfat and milk solids
311511	Milk, acidophilus, manufacturing
424490	Milk, canned or dried, merchant wholesalers
311514	Milk, concentrated, condensed, dried, evaporated, and powdered, manufacturing
311511	Milk, fluid (except canned), manufacturing
424430	Milk, fluid (except canned), merchant wholesalers
311514	Milk, malted, manufacturing
311514	Milk, powdered, manufacturing
311514	Milk, ultra high temperature, manufacturing

112120	Milking dairy cattle
112420	Milking dairy goat
112410	Milking dairy sheep
423820	Milking machinery and equipment merchant wholesalers
333111	Milking machines manufacturing
311514	Milkshake mixes manufacturing
314999	Mill menders, contract, woven fabrics
316998	Mill strapping for textile mills, leather, manufacturing
423840	Mill supplies merchant wholesalers
315210	Millinery cut and sew apparel contractors
315990	Millinery cut and sewn from purchased fabric (except apparel contractors)
424330	Millinery merchant wholesalers
424310	Millinery supplies merchant wholesalers
315210	Millinery trimmings cut and sew apparel contractors
315990	Millinery trimmings cut and sewn from purchased fabric (except apparel contractors)
333517	Milling machines, metalworking, manufacturing
311212	Milling rice
212399	Millstones mining and/or beneficiating
238350	Millwork installation
423310	Millwork merchant wholesalers
337212	Millwork, custom architectural, manufacturing
321114	Millwork, treating
238290	Millwrights
111199	Milo farming, field and seed production
711110	Mime theaters
333922	Mine conveyors manufacturing
213114	Mine development (except site preparation and related construction contractor activities) for metal mining on a contract basis
213115	Mine development for nonmetallic minerals mining (except fuels) on a contract basis
236210	Mine loading and discharging station construction
321114	Mine props, treating
562910	Mine reclamation services, integrated (e.g., demolition, hazardous material removal, soil remediation, revegetation)
213113	Mine shaft sinking services for coal mining on a contract basis

213114	Mine shaft sinking services for metal mining on a contract basis
213115	Mine shaft sinking services for nonmetallic minerals (except fuels) on a contract basis
238910	Mine site preparation and related construction activities, construction contractors
321114	Mine ties, wood, treated, manufacturing
213113	Mine tunneling services for coal mining on a contract basis
213114	Mine tunneling services for metal mining on a contract basis
213115	Mine tunneling services for nonmetallic minerals (except fuels) on a contract basis
325130	Mineral colors and pigments manufacturing
311119	Mineral feed supplements (except cat, dog) manufacturing
212393	Mineral pigments, natural, mining and/or beneficiating
333131	Mineral processing and beneficiating machinery manufacturing
523910	Mineral royalties or leases dealing (i.e., acting as a principal in dealing royalties or leases to investors)
311119	Mineral supplements, animal (except cat, dog), manufacturing
424910	Mineral supplements, animal, merchant wholesalers
238310	Mineral wool insulation installation
327993	Mineral wool insulation materials manufacturing
327993	Mineral wool products (e.g., board, insulation, tile) manufacturing
423520	Minerals (except construction materials, petroleum) merchant wholesalers
335129	Miner's lamps manufacturing
332993	Mines, ammunition, manufacturing
713990	Miniature golf courses
337920	Miniblinds manufacturing
334111	Minicomputers manufacturing
331110	Mini-mills, steel
926150	Minimum wage program administration
******	Mining -- see type
813910	Mining associations
333131	Mining cars manufacturing
423810	Mining cranes merchant wholesalers
541330	Mining engineering services
336510	Mining locomotives and parts manufacturing

423810	Mining machinery and equipment (except petroleum) merchant wholesalers
532412	Mining machinery and equipment rental or leasing
811310	Mining machinery and equipment repair and maintenance services
423830	Mining machinery and equipment, petroleum, merchant wholesalers
531190	Mining property leasing
813110	Ministries, religious
423110	Minivan merchant wholesalers
336112	Minivans assembling on chassis of own manufacture
531130	Miniwarehouse rental or leasing
112930	Mink production
112511	Minnow production, farm raising
711211	Minor league baseball clubs
111998	Mint farming
238150	Mirror installation
423220	Mirrors (except automotive) merchant wholesalers
423120	Mirrors, automotive, merchant wholesalers
327215	Mirrors, framed (except automotive) or unframed, made from purchased glass
333314	Mirrors, optical, manufacturing
237990	Missile facility construction
332993	Missile warheads manufacturing
561611	Missing person tracing services
813110	Missions, religious organization
332216	Miter boxes manufacturing
315210	Mittens (e.g., leather, woven or knit) cut and sew apparel contractors
315990	Mittens cut and sewn from purchased fabric (except apparel contractors)
315190	Mittens, knit, made in apparel knitting mills
315990	Mittens, leather (except apparel contractors), manufacturing
315990	Mittens, woven or knit, cut and sewn from purchased fabric (except apparel contractors)
311230	Mix grain breakfast manufacturing
311514	Mix, ice cream, manufacturing
312140	Mixed drinks, alcoholic, manufacturing
111940	Mixed hay farming
485111	Mixed mode transit systems (e.g., bus, commuter rail, subway combinations)
333120	Mixers, concrete, portable, manufacturing
423810	Mixers, construction and mining, merchant wholesalers
424490	Mixes (e.g., cake, dessert, pie) merchant wholesalers
311211	Mixes, flour (e.g., biscuit, cake, doughnut, pancake) made in flour mills
311824	Mixes, flour (e.g., biscuit, cake, doughnut, pancake), made from purchased flour
325314	Mixing purchased fertilizer materials
531190	Mobile (manufactured) home parks
531110	Mobile (manufactured) home rental or leasing, on-site
531190	Mobile (manufactured) home sites rental or leasing
811111	Mobile automotive and truck repair services
621512	Mobile breast imaging centers
811192	Mobile car and truck washes
334220	Mobile communications equipment manufacturing
311119	Mobile feed mill
722330	Mobile food stands
453930	Mobile home dealers, manufactured
532120	Mobile home rental, off-site
484220	Mobile home towing services, local
484230	Mobile home towing services, long-distance
321991	Mobile homes manufacturing
712110	Mobile museums
532490	Mobile office building rental or leasing, off-site
531120	Mobile office building rental or leasing, on-site
517312	Mobile phone stores, primarily selling mobile phone service plans
624210	Mobile soup kitchens
333924	Mobile straddle carriers manufacturing
517312	Mobile telephone communication carriers (except satellite)
621512	Mobile X-ray facilities (medical)
316210	Moccasins manufacturing
325220	Modacrylic fibers and filaments manufacturing
313110	Modacrylic spun yarns made from purchased fiber
339930	Model kits manufacturing
423920	Model kits merchant wholesalers
339930	Model railroad manufacturing
561311	Model registries

561320	Model supply services
711410	Modeling agents
339940	Modeling clay manufacturing
611519	Modeling schools
711410	Models' agents or managers
339999	Models, anatomical, manufacturing
711510	Models, independent
339930	Models, toy and hobby (e.g., airplane, boat, ship), manufacturing
423690	Modems merchant wholesalers
334210	Modems, carrier equipment, manufacturing
711120	Modern dance companies
532490	Modular building rental or leasing, off-site
238390	Modular furniture system attachment and installation
337214	Modular furniture systems (except wood frame), office-type, manufacturing
337211	Modular furniture systems, wood frame office-type, manufacturing
236117	Modular housing, residential, assembled on site by for-sale builders
236115	Modular single-family housing assembled on site by general contractors
334519	Modules for clocks and watches manufacturing
112420	Mohair farming
313110	Mohair yarn twisting or winding of purchased yarn
424590	Mohair, raw, merchant wholesalers
334516	Moisture analyzers, laboratory-type, manufacturing
334513	Moisture meters, industrial process-type, manufacturing
311313	Molasses made from sugar beets
311314	Molasses manufacturing
424490	Molasses merchant wholesalers
311314	Molasses, blackstrap, manufacturing
562910	Mold remediation services
339991	Molded packings and seals manufacturing
322299	Molded pulp products (e.g., egg cartons, food containers, food trays) manufacturing
423310	Molding (e.g., sheet metal, wood) merchant wholesalers
332321	Molding and trim (except motor vehicle), metal, manufacturing
238350	Molding or trim, wood or plastic, installation
212322	Molding sand quarrying and/or beneficiating

336370	Moldings and trim, motor vehicle, stamping
321918	Moldings, clear and finger joint wood, manufacturing
321918	Moldings, wood and covered wood, manufacturing
333511	Molds (except steel ingot), industrial, manufacturing
331511	Molds for casting steel ingots manufacturing
333511	Molds for forming materials (e.g., glass, plastics, rubber) manufacturing
333511	Molds for metal casting (except steel ingot) manufacturing
333511	Molds for plastics and rubber working machinery manufacturing
331511	Molds, steel ingot, industrial, manufacturing
112512	Mollusk production, farm raising
212299	Molybdenite mining and/or beneficiating
331491	Molybdenum and molybdenum alloy bar, plate, pipe, rod, sheet, tubing, and wire made from purchased metals or scrap
212299	Molybdenum ores mining and/or beneficiating
331491	Molybdenum rolling, drawing, or extruding purchased metals or scrap
331110	Molybdenum silicon ferroalloys manufacturing
212299	Molybdite mining and/or beneficiating
813110	Monasteries (except schools)
212299	Monazite mining and/or beneficiating
521110	Monetary authorities, central bank
332999	Money chests, metal, manufacturing
525990	Money market mutual funds, closed-end
525910	Money market mutual funds, open-ended
522390	Money order issuance services
522390	Money transmission services
423430	Monitor screen projection devices merchant wholesalers
334118	Monitors, computer peripheral equipment, manufacturing
423430	Monitors, computer, merchant wholesalers
325120	Monochlorodifluoromethane manufacturing
334516	Monochrometers, laboratory-type, manufacturing
334413	Monolithic integrated circuits (solid-state) manufacturing

325199	Monomethylparaminophenol sulfate manufacturing
237990	Monorail construction
333923	Monorail systems (except passenger-type) manufacturing
485119	Monorail transit systems (except mixed mode), commuter
487110	Monorail, scenic and sightseeing, operation
325199	Monosodium glutamate manufacturing
611110	Montessori schools, elementary or secondary
236220	Monument (i.e., building) construction
453998	Monument (i.e., burial marker) dealers
423990	Monuments and grave markers merchant wholesalers
327991	Monuments and tombstone, cut stone (except finishing or lettering to order only), manufacturing
333318	Mop wringers manufacturing
441228	Moped dealers
423110	Moped merchant wholesalers
532284	Moped rental
336991	Mopeds and parts manufacturing
339994	Mops, floor and dust, manufacturing
423220	Mops, household, merchant wholesalers
423850	Mops, industrial, merchant wholesalers
325130	Mordant dyes manufacturing
325613	Mordants manufacturing
325411	Morphine and derivatives (i.e., basic chemicals) manufacturing
522190	Morris Plans (i.e., known as), depository
522298	Morris Plans (i.e., known as), nondepository
333120	Mortar mixers, portable, manufacturing
332993	Mortar shells manufacturing
327120	Mortar, nonclay refractory, manufacturing
332994	Mortars manufacturing
327120	Mortars, clay refractory, manufacturing
522292	Mortgage banking (i.e., nondepository mortgage lending)
522310	Mortgage brokerages
522310	Mortgage brokers' or agents' offices (i.e., independent)
522292	Mortgage companies
523910	Mortgage dealers, buying and selling
524126	Mortgage guaranty insurance carriers, direct
525990	Mortgage real estate investment trusts (REITs)
525990	Mortgage-backed securities
812210	Mortician services
333243	Mortisers, woodworking-type, manufacturing
812210	Mortuaries
334413	MOS (metal oxide silicon) devices manufacturing
327120	Mosaic tile, ceramic, manufacturing
238340	Mosaic work
813110	Mosques, religious
926130	Mosquito eradication districts
561710	Mosquito eradication services
113210	Moss gathering
531120	Motel building rental or leasing, not operating motel
236220	Motel construction
561110	Motel management services (except complete operation of client's business)
721110	Motels
325320	Moth repellents manufacturing
423430	Motherboards, loaded, merchant wholesalers
334290	Motion alarms (e.g., swimming pool, perimeter) manufacturing
334290	Motion detectors, security system, manufacturing
512110	Motion picture and video production
512110	Motion picture and video production and distribution
512191	Motion picture animation, postproduction
512199	Motion picture booking agencies
333316	Motion picture cameras manufacturing
423410	Motion picture cameras, equipment, and supplies merchant wholesalers
541690	Motion picture consulting services
711510	Motion picture directors, independent
512120	Motion picture distribution exclusive of production
532490	Motion picture equipment rental or leasing
512131	Motion picture exhibition
512131	Motion picture exhibitors for airlines
512131	Motion picture exhibitors, itinerant
512120	Motion picture film distributors
512199	Motion picture film laboratories
512120	Motion picture film libraries
519120	Motion picture film libraries, archives

512199   Motion picture film libraries, stock footage

325992   Motion picture film manufacturing

512199   Motion picture film reproduction for theatrical distribution

512199   Motion picture laboratories

512191   Motion picture or video editing services

512191   Motion picture or video postproduction services

512191   Motion picture or video titling

711510   Motion picture producers, independent

512110   Motion picture production

512110   Motion picture production and distribution

512191   Motion picture production special effects, postproduction

333316   Motion picture projectors manufacturing

512110   Motion picture studios, producing motion pictures

512132   Motion picture theaters, drive-in

512131   Motion picture theaters, indoor

532281   Motion picture wardrobe and costume rental

711510   Motivational speakers, independent

926120   Motor carrier licensing and inspection offices

485210   Motor coach operation, interurban and rural

335314   Motor control accessories (including overload relays) manufacturing

335314   Motor control centers, manufacturing

335314   Motor controls, electric, manufacturing

423610   Motor controls, electric, merchant wholesalers

721110   Motor courts

484110   Motor freight carrier, general, local

484122   Motor freight carrier, general, long-distance, less-than-truckload (LTL)

484121   Motor freight carrier, general, long-distance, truckload (TL)

484210   Motor freight carrier, used household goods

335312   Motor generator sets (except automotive, turbine generator sets) manufacturing

333611   Motor generator sets, turbo generators, manufacturing

441210   Motor home dealers

423110   Motor home merchant wholesalers

532120   Motor home rental, off-site

336213   Motor homes, self-contained, assembling on purchased chassis

336120   Motor homes, self-contained, mounted on heavy truck chassis of own manufacture

336112   Motor homes, self-contained, mounted on light duty truck chassis of own manufacture

721110   Motor hotels without casinos

721110   Motor inns

721110   Motor lodges

324191   Motor oils, petroleum, made from refined petroleum

325998   Motor oils, synthetic, manufacturing

811310   Motor repair and maintenance services, commercial or industrial

441228   Motor scooters dealers

336991   Motor scooters manufacturing

335314   Motor starters, contractors, and controllers, industrial, manufacturing

561599   Motor travel clubs

333997   Motor truck scales manufacturing

236210   Motor vehicle assembly plant construction

326220   Motor vehicle belts, rubber or plastics, manufacturing

238290   Motor vehicle garage and service station mechanical equipment (e.g., gasoline pumps, hoists) installation

332510   Motor vehicle hardware, metal, manufacturing

326220   Motor vehicle hoses, rubber or plastics, manufacturing

334514   Motor vehicle instruments (e.g., fuel level gauges, oil pressure, speedometers, tachometers, water temperature) manufacturing

423120   Motor vehicle instruments, electric, merchant wholesalers

336360   Motor vehicle interior systems (e.g., headliners, panels, seats, trims) manufacturing

561990   Motor vehicle license issuing services, private franchise

926120   Motor vehicle licensing offices, government

423110   Motor vehicle merchant wholesalers

336370   Motor vehicle metal bumper stampings

336370   Motor vehicle metal parts stamping

336370   Motor vehicle metal stampings (e.g., body parts, fenders, hub caps, tops, trim) manufacturing

326199   Motor vehicle moldings and extrusions, plastics, manufacturing

325510   Motor vehicle paints manufacturing

423120	Motor vehicle parts and accessories, new, merchant wholesalers
423140	Motor vehicle parts, used, merchant wholesalers
336360	Motor vehicle seats manufacturing
336360	Motor vehicle seats, metal framed, manufacturing
423130	Motor vehicle tire and tube merchant wholesalers
326211	Motor vehicle tires manufacturing
488410	Motor vehicle towing services
336360	Motor vehicle trimmings manufacturing
441228	Motorbike dealers
811490	Motorboat (i.e., inboard and outboard) repair and maintenance services
336612	Motorboat, inboard or outboard, building
441228	Motorcycle dealers
611692	Motorcycle driving schools
423110	Motorcycle merchant wholesalers
441228	Motorcycle parts and accessories dealers
423120	Motorcycle parts, new, merchant wholesalers
711212	Motorcycle racetracks
711219	Motorcycle racing teams
532284	Motorcycle rental
811490	Motorcycle repair shops without retailing new motorcycles
336991	Motorcycles and parts manufacturing
423860	Motorized passenger golf carts merchant wholesalers
335312	Motors, electric (except engine starting motors, gearmotors, outboard), manufacturing
423610	Motors, electric, merchant wholesalers
333996	Motors, fluid power, manufacturing
333612	Motors, gear, manufacturing
333618	Motors, outboard, manufacturing
423910	Motors, outboard, merchant wholesalers
336320	Motors, starter, for internal combustion engines, manufacturing
713990	Mountain hiking, recreational
561910	Mounting merchandise on cards
334118	Mouse devices, computer peripheral equipment, manufacturing
213112	Mouse hole and rat hole drilling at oil and gas fields on a contract basis
339992	Mouthpieces for musical instruments manufacturing
325620	Mouthwashes (except medicinal) manufacturing
325412	Mouthwashes, medicated, manufacturing
334519	Movements, watch or clock, manufacturing
423620	Movie apparatus, home, merchant wholesalers
512110	Movie production and distribution
512131	Movie theaters (except drive-in)
512132	Movie theaters, drive-in
238290	Moving sidewalk installation
561730	Mowing services (e.g., highway, lawn, road strip)
562920	MRF (materials recovery facilities)
621512	MRI (magnetic resonance imaging) centers
334510	MRI (magnetic resonance imaging) medical diagnostic equipment manufacturing
325520	Mucilage adhesives manufacturing
213112	Mud service for oil field drilling on a contract basis
238110	Mud-jacking contractors
811112	Muffler repair and replacement shops
336390	Mufflers and resonators, automotive, truck, and buses manufacturing
315210	Mufflers cut and sew apparel contractors
315990	Mufflers cut and sewn from purchased fabric (except apparel contractors)
315190	Mufflers made in apparel knitting mills
423120	Mufflers, exhaust, merchant wholesalers
424910	Mulch merchant wholesalers
333112	Mulchers, lawn and garden-type, manufacturing
112920	Mule production
424590	Mules merchant wholesalers
114111	Mullet fishing
517311	Multichannel multipoint distribution services (MMDS)
712110	Multidisciplinary museums
236116	Multifamily building construction general contractors
236117	Multifamily building for-sale builders
334515	Multimeters manufacturing
334210	Multiplex equipment, telephone, manufacturing
624190	Multiservice centers, neighborhood
212391	Muriate of potash, mining
325412	Muscle relaxant preparations manufacturing
212399	Muscovite mining and/or beneficiating

561990	Museum cataloging services
236220	Museum construction
712110	Museums
111411	Mushroom farming
111411	Mushroom spawn farming
311421	Mushrooms canning
519120	Music archives
711510	Music arrangers, independent
512230	Music book (i.e., bound sheet music) publishers
512230	Music book (i.e., bound sheet music) publishers and printing combined
323117	Music books printing or printing and binding without publishing
339999	Music boxes manufacturing
512230	Music copyright authorizing use
512230	Music copyright buying and licensing
711510	Music directors, independent
711310	Music festival managers with facilities
711320	Music festival managers without facilities
711310	Music festival organizers with facilities
711320	Music festival organizers without facilities
711310	Music festival promoters with facilities
711320	Music festival promoters without facilities
611610	Music instruction (e.g., guitar, piano)
515112	Music program distribution (except exclusively on Internet), radio
517311	Music program distribution, cable or satellite
512290	Music program distribution, prerecorded
512230	Music publishers
339992	Music rolls, perforated, manufacturing
611610	Music schools (except academic)
443142	Music stores (e.g., cassette, compact disc, record, tape)
453310	Music stores (e.g., cassette, instrument, record, tape), used
451140	Music stores (i.e., instrument)
621340	Music therapists' offices (e.g., centers, clinics)
512110	Music video production
512110	Music video production and distribution
323111	Music, sheet, commercial printing (except screen) without publishing
424990	Music, sheet, merchant wholesalers
512230	Music, sheet, publishers and printing combined
323113	Music, sheet, screen printing without publishing
711130	Musical artists, independent
711130	Musical groups (except musical theater groups)
339992	Musical instrument accessories (e.g., mouthpieces, reeds, stands, traps) manufacturing
423990	Musical instrument accessories and supplies merchant wholesalers
316998	Musical instrument cases, all materials, manufacturing
532289	Musical instrument rental
811490	Musical instrument repair shops without retailing new musical instruments
451140	Musical instrument stores
339992	Musical instruments (except toy) manufacturing
423990	Musical instruments merchant wholesalers
339930	Musical instruments, toy, manufacturing
711130	Musical productions (except musical theater productions), live
512250	Musical recording, releasing, promoting, and distributing
423990	Musical recordings (e.g., compact discs, records, tapes) merchant wholesalers
711110	Musical theater companies or groups
711110	Musical theater productions, live
711130	Musicians, independent
111219	Muskmelon farming, field, bedding plant and seed production
114112	Mussel fishing
112512	Mussel production, farm raising
111120	Mustard seed farming, field and seed production
311941	Mustard, prepared, manufacturing
523120	Mutual fund agencies (i.e., brokerages)
523120	Mutual fund agents' (i.e., brokers') offices
523920	Mutual fund managing
525990	Mutual funds, closed-end
525910	Mutual funds, open-ended
522120	Mutual savings banks
621511	Mycology health laboratories
325194	Myrobalans extract manufacturing
333991	Nail guns, handheld power-driven, manufacturing
333517	Nail heading machines manufacturing
325620	Nail polish remover manufacturing
325620	Nail polishes manufacturing

812113	Nail salons
333991	Nailers and staplers, handheld power-driven, manufacturing
423510	Nails merchant wholesalers
331318	Nails, aluminum, made in wire drawing plants
332618	Nails, brads, and staples made from purchased wire
331222	Nails, iron or steel, made in wire drawing plants
331491	Nails, nonferrous metals (except aluminum, copper), made from purchased nonferrous metals (except aluminum, copper) in wire drawing plants
332999	Name plate blanks, metal, manufacturing
541713	Nanobiotechnologies research and experimental development laboratories
334513	Nanofluidic measurement and control devices manufacturing
333242	Nanoindentation equipment, semiconductor, manufacturing
334516	Nanomanipulator equipment manufacturing
334516	Nanosensor instruments manufacturing
541713	Nanotechnology research and development laboratories or services, all fields of science
325998	Napalm manufacturing
325194	Naphtha made by distillation of coal tar
324110	Naphtha made in petroleum refineries
325194	Naphtha, solvent, made by distillation of coal tar
325194	Naphthalene made from refined petroleum or natural gas
325194	Naphthalenesulfonic acid manufacturing
325199	Naphthenic acid soaps manufacturing
325194	Naphthenic acids made from refined petroleum or natural gas
324110	Naphthenic acids made in petroleum refineries
325194	Naphthol sulfonic acids manufacturing
325194	Naphthol, alpha and beta, manufacturing
423220	Napkins (except paper) merchant wholesalers
314120	Napkins made from purchased fabrics
424130	Napkins, paper, merchant wholesalers
322291	Napkins, table, made from purchased paper
322121	Napkins, table, made in paper mills
333249	Napping machinery for textiles manufacturing
313310	Napping textile products and fabrics
313220	Narrow fabrics weaving
927110	National Aeronautics and Space Administration
522110	National commercial banks
522298	National Credit Union Administration (NCUA)
928110	National Guard
712190	National parks
926120	National Transportation Safety Board
311422	Nationality specialty foods canning
311412	Nationality specialty foods, frozen, manufacturing
212399	Native asphalt mining and/or beneficiating
327310	Natural (i.e., calcined earth) cement manufacturing
212399	Natural abrasives (e.g., emery, grindstones, hones, pumice) (except sand) mining and/or beneficiating
313110	Natural fiber (i.e., hemp, linen, ramie) thread manufacturing
313210	Natural fiber fabrics (i.e., jute, linen, hemp, ramie), broadwoven, weaving
313220	Natural fiber fabrics (i.e., jute, linen, hemp, ramie), narrow woven, weaving
313110	Natural fiber spun yarns (i.e., hemp, jute, ramie, flax) made from purchased fiber
221210	Natural gas brokers
423690	Natural gas detectors, electronic, merchant wholesalers
221210	Natural gas distribution systems
221210	Natural gas distribution with transmission
333618	Natural gas engines manufacturing
211130	Natural gas liquid lease condensate production
211130	Natural gas liquids (e.g., ethane, isobutane, natural gasoline, propane) recovered from oil and gas field gases
486910	Natural gas liquids pipeline transportation
221210	Natural gas marketers
237120	Natural gas pipeline construction
486210	Natural gas pipeline transportation
238220	Natural gas piping installation
237120	Natural gas processing plant construction
211130	Natural gas production
486210	Natural gas transmission (i.e., processing plants to local distribution systems)
211130	Natural gas, offshore production

211130 Natural gasoline recovered from oil and gas field gases
712110 Natural history museums
325199 Natural nonfood coloring manufacturing
813312 Natural resource preservation organizations
712110 Natural science museums
712190 Natural wonder tourist attractions (e.g., caverns, waterfalls)
312112 Naturally carbonated water, purifying and bottling
712190 Nature centers
712190 Nature parks
712190 Nature preserves
712190 Nature reserves
621399 Naturopaths' offices (e.g., centers, clinics)
334511 Nautical systems and instruments manufacturing
332994 Naval artillery manufacturing
336611 Naval ship building
325194 Naval stores, gum or wood, manufacturing
811219 Navigational instruments (e.g., radar, sonar) repair and maintenance services
423860 Navigational instruments (except electronic) merchant wholesalers
334511 Navigational instruments manufacturing
423690 Navigational instruments, electronic (e.g., radar, sonar), merchant wholesalers
928110 Navy
312120 Near beer brewing
311613 Neatsfoot oil rendering
315280 Neckpieces, fur (except apparel contractors), manufacturing
315210 Neckpieces, fur, cut and sew apparel contractors
315210 Neckties cut and sew apparel contractors
315990 Neckties cut and sewn from purchased fabric (except apparel contractors)
315190 Neckties made in apparel knitting mills
424320 Neckties, men's and boys', merchant wholesalers
315210 Neckwear cut and sew apparel contractors
315990 Neckwear cut and sewn from purchased fabric (except apparel contractors)
315190 Neckwear made in a apparel knitting mills
448150 Neckwear stores
111339 Nectarine farming
332991 Needle roller bearings manufacturing
451130 Needlecraft sewing supply stores

339993 Needles (except hypodermic, phonograph, styli) manufacturing
333249 Needles for knitting machinery manufacturing
339112 Needles, hypodermic and suture, manufacturing
334419 Needles, phonograph and styli, manufacturing
424310 Needles, sewing, merchant wholesalers
314999 Needlework art contractors on apparel
315210 Negligees cut and sew apparel contractors
315190 Negligees made in apparel knitting mills
315240 Negligees, women's and girls', cut and sewn from purchased fabric (except apparel contractors)
813319 Neighborhood development advocacy organizations
325120 Neon manufacturing
339950 Neon signs manufacturing
325212 Neoprene manufacturing
212325 Nepheline syenite mining and/or beneficiating
334516 Nephelometers (except meteorological) manufacturing
334519 Nephoscopes manufacturing
621111 Nephrologists' offices (e.g., centers, clinics)
333249 Net and lace making machinery manufacturing
424310 Net goods merchant wholesalers
313210 Nets and nettings, more than 12 inches in width, weaving
313240 Netting made in warp or weft knitting mills
313240 Netting made on a lace or net machine
326199 Netting, plastics, manufacturing
332618 Netting, woven, made from purchased wire
515111 Network broadcasting service, radio
515111 Network radio broadcasting
541512 Network systems integration design services, computer
515120 Network television broadcasting
515210 Networks, cable television
622310 Neurological hospitals
621111 Neurologists' offices (e.g., centers, clinics)
621111 Neuropathologists' offices (e.g., centers, clinics)
312140 Neutral spirit, beverages (except fruit), manufacturing

424820	Neutral spirits merchant wholesalers
334516	Neutron activation analysis instruments manufacturing
441110	New car dealers
541613	New product development consulting services
321918	Newel posts, wood, manufacturing
519190	News clipping services
711510	News correspondents, independent (freelance)
451212	News dealers
519110	News picture gathering and distributing services
519110	News reporting services
519110	News service syndicates
519110	News ticker services
511120	Newsletter publishers (except exclusive Internet publishing)
511120	Newsletter publishers and printing combined (except Internet)
519130	Newsletter publishers, exclusively on Internet
323111	Newsletters commercial printing (except screen) without publishing
323113	Newsletters screen printing without publishing
541840	Newspaper advertising representatives (i.e., independent of media owners)
424920	Newspaper agencies merchant wholesalers
511110	Newspaper branch offices
711510	Newspaper columnists, independent (freelance)
519110	Newspaper feature syndicates
333244	Newspaper inserting equipment manufacturing
511110	Newspaper publishers (except exclusive Internet publishing)
511110	Newspaper publishers and printing combined
519130	Newspaper publishing, exclusively on Internet
323111	Newspapers commercial printing (except screen) without publishing
424920	Newspapers merchant wholesalers
323113	Newspapers screen printing without publishing
424110	Newsprint merchant wholesalers
322122	Newsprint mills
322122	Newsprint paper, manufacturing

451212	Newsstands (i.e., permanent)
339940	Nibs (i.e., pen points) manufacturing
331523	Nickel alloy die-castings, unfinished, manufacturing
325180	Nickel ammonium sulfate manufacturing
331491	Nickel and nickel alloy pipe, plate, sheet, strip, and tubing made from purchased metals or scrap
423510	Nickel and nickel alloy primary forms merchant wholesalers
325180	Nickel carbonate manufacturing
331529	Nickel castings (except die-castings), unfinished, manufacturing
325180	Nickel compounds, not specified elsewhere by process, manufacturing
212230	Nickel concentrates recovery
331523	Nickel die-castings, unfinished, manufacturing
332999	Nickel foil not made in rolling mills
212230	Nickel ore beneficiating plants
212230	Nickel ore mine site development for own account
212230	Nickel ores mining and/or beneficiating
331492	Nickel recovering from scrap and/or alloying purchased metals
331410	Nickel refining, primary
331491	Nickel rolling, drawing, or extruding purchased metals or scrap
325180	Nickel sulfate manufacturing
335911	Nickel-cadmium storage batteries manufacturing
325411	Nicotine and derivatives (i.e., basic chemicals) manufacturing
325320	Nicotine insecticides manufacturing
337122	Night stands, wood, manufacturing
333314	Night vision optical devices manufacturing
713990	Nightclubs without alcoholic beverages
722410	Nightclubs, alcoholic beverage
315210	Nightgowns cut and sew apparel contractors
315190	Nightgowns made in apparel knitting mills
315220	Nightgowns, men's and boys', cut and sewn from purchased fabric (except apparel contractors)
315240	Nightgowns, women's, girls', and infants', cut and sewn from purchased fabric (except apparel contractors)
315210	Nightshirts cut and sew apparel contractors
315190	Nightshirts made in apparel knitting mills

315220 Nightshirts, men's and boys', cut and sewn from purchased fabric (except apparel contractors)

315240 Nightshirts, women's, girls', and infants', cut and sewn from purchased fabric (except contractors)

315210 Nightwear cut and sew apparel contractors

315190 Nightwear made in apparel knitting mills

315220 Nightwear, men's and boys', cut and sewn from purchased fabric (except apparel contractors)

424320 Nightwear, men's and boys', merchant wholesalers

424330 Nightwear, women's, children's, and infants', merchant wholesalers

315240 Nightwear, women's, girls', and infants', cut and sewn from purchased fabric (except apparel contractors)

331410 Niobium refining, primary

326299 Nipples and teething rings, rubber, manufacturing

332996 Nipples, metal, made from purchased pipe

325194 Nitrated hydrocarbon derivatives manufacturing

325311 Nitric acid manufacturing

325212 Nitrile rubber manufacturing

325212 Nitrile-butadiene rubber manufacturing

325212 Nitrile-chloroprene rubbers manufacturing

325194 Nitroaniline manufacturing

325194 Nitrobenzene manufacturing

325211 Nitrocellulose (i.e., pyroxylin) resins manufacturing

325920 Nitrocellulose explosive materials manufacturing

325220 Nitrocellulose fibers manufacturing

325120 Nitrogen manufacturing

325311 Nitrogenous fertilizer materials manufacturing

325314 Nitrogenous fertilizers made by mixing purchased materials

325920 Nitroglycerin explosive materials manufacturing

325194 Nitrophenol manufacturing

325194 Nitrosated hydrocarbon derivatives manufacturing

325130 Nitroso dyes manufacturing

325920 Nitrostarch explosive materials manufacturing

325199 Nitrous ether manufacturing

325120 Nitrous oxide manufacturing

325411 N-methylpiperazine manufacturing

924110 NOAA (National Oceanic and Atmospheric Administration)

339113 Noise protectors, personal, manufacturing

312120 Nonalcoholic beer brewing

312130 Nonalcoholic wines manufacturing

551112 Nonbank holding companies (except managing)

325220 Noncellulosic fibers and filaments manufacturing

325220 Noncellulosic filament yarn manufacturing

325220 Noncellulosic staple fibers and filaments manufacturing

111339 Noncitrus fruit farming

327120 Nonclay refractories (e.g., block, brick, mortar, tile) manufacturing

311514 Nondairy creamers, dry, manufacturing

311511 Nondairy creamers, liquid, manufacturing

541380 Nondestructive testing laboratories or services

425120 Nondurable goods agents and brokers, wholesale trade

425110 Nondurable goods business to business electronic markets, wholesale trade

325110 Nonene made from refined petroleum or liquid hydrocarbons

311514 Nonfat dry milk manufacturing

331492 Nonferrous alloys (except aluminum, copper) made from purchased nonferrous metals

331492 Nonferrous alloys (except aluminum, copper) made in integrated secondary smelting and alloying plants

331523 Nonferrous die-casting foundries

331410 Nonferrous metal (except aluminum) shapes made in primary nonferrous metal smelting and refining mills

331491 Nonferrous metal shapes (except aluminum, copper) made by rolling, drawing, or extruding purchased nonferrous metal

331491 Nonferrous metal shapes (except aluminum, copper) made in integrated secondary smelting and extruding mills

331491 Nonferrous metal shapes (except aluminum, copper) made in integrated secondary smelting and rolling mills

331491 Nonferrous metal shapes (except aluminum, copper) made in integrated secondary smelting mills and wire drawing plants

331529	Nonferrous metals (except aluminum) foundries (except die-casting)
331410	Nonferrous metals (except aluminum) made in primary nonferrous metal smelting and refining mills
331410	Nonferrous metals (except aluminum) smelting and refining, primary
331529	Nonferrous metals (except aluminum) unfinished castings (except die-castings) manufacturing
331492	Nonferrous metals (except aluminum, copper) secondary smelting and refining
423510	Nonferrous metals (except precious) merchant wholesalers
331491	Nonferrous wire (except aluminum, copper) made from purchased nonferrous metals (except aluminum, copper) in wire drawing plants
331491	Nonferrous wire (except aluminum, copper) made in integrated secondary smelting mills and wire drawing plants
511130	Nonfiction book publishers (except exclusive Internet publishing)
511130	Nonfiction book publishers and printing combined
519130	Nonfiction book publishers, exclusively on Internet
323120	Nonfiction bookbinding without printing
323117	Nonfiction books printing and binding without publishing
323117	Nonfiction books printing without publishing
562219	Nonhazardous waste treatment and disposal facilities (except combustors, incinerators, landfills, sewer systems, sewage treatment facilities)
423510	Noninsulated wire merchant wholesalers
423520	Nonmetallic minerals (except precious and semiprecious stones and minerals used in construction, such as sand and gravel)
213115	Nonmetallic minerals mining support services (e.g., blasting, shaft sinking, tunneling) (except site preparation and related construction contractor activities) on a contract basis
423520	Nonmetallic ores merchant wholesalers
325412	Nonprescription drug preparations manufacturing
424210	Nonprescription drugs merchant wholesalers
531120	Nonresidential building (except miniwarehouse) rental or leasing
531312	Nonresidential property managing
481212	Nonscheduled air freight transportation
481211	Nonscheduled air passenger transportation
332215	Nonstick metal cooking utensils
337122	Nonupholstered, household-type, custom wood furniture, manufacturing
313230	Nonwoven fabric tapes manufacturing
313230	Nonwoven fabrics manufacturing
313230	Nonwoven felts manufacturing
311999	Noodle mixes made from purchased dry ingredients
311423	Noodle mixes made in dehydration plants
311824	Noodle mixes made in dry pasta plants
311824	Noodles, dry, manufacturing
311991	Noodles, fresh, manufacturing
311999	Noodles, fried, manufacturing
339113	Nose and ear plugs manufacturing
541199	Notary public services
541199	Notary publics' private practices
334111	Notebook computers manufacturing
322230	Notebooks (including mechanically bound by wire, or plastics) made from purchased paper
424120	Notebooks merchant wholesalers
424310	Notions merchant wholesalers
332999	Novelties and specialties, nonprecious metal and precious plated, manufacturing
424990	Novelties merchant wholesalers
316998	Novelties, leather (e.g., cigarette lighter covers, key fobs), manufacturing
339999	Novelties, not specified elsewhere, manufacturing
339910	Novelties, precious metal (except precious plated), manufacturing
321999	Novelties, wood fiber, manufacturing
453220	Novelty shops
314999	Novelty stitching contractors on apparel
326199	Nozzles, aerosol spray, plastics, manufacturing
332919	Nozzles, firefighting, manufacturing
332919	Nozzles, lawn hose, manufacturing
325212	N-type rubber manufacturing
332911	Nuclear application valves manufacturing
332410	Nuclear control drive mechanisms manufacturing
541690	Nuclear energy consulting services
926130	Nuclear energy inspection and regulation offices

325180 Nuclear fuel scrap reprocessing

325180 Nuclear fuels, inorganic, manufacturing

334519 Nuclear instrument modules manufacturing

334517 Nuclear irradiation equipment manufacturing

325412 Nuclear medicine (e.g., radioactive isotopes) preparations manufacturing

237130 Nuclear power plant construction

332410 Nuclear reactor steam supply systems manufacturing

332410 Nuclear reactors control rod drive mechanisms manufacturing

332410 Nuclear reactors manufacturing

332313 Nuclear shielding, fabricated metal plate work, manufacturing

332420 Nuclear waste casks, heavy gauge metal, manufacturing

237990 Nuclear waste disposal site construction

541714 Nucleic acid chemistry research and experimental development laboratories

721214 Nudist camps with accommodation facilities

713990 Nudist camps without accommodations

335314 Numerical controls, manufacturing

333517 Numerically controlled metal cutting machine tools manufacturing

812990 Numerology services

423940 Numismatic goods merchant wholesalers

621610 Nurse associations, visiting

621399 Nurse practitioners' offices (e.g., centers, clinics)

561311 Nurse registries

113210 Nurseries for reforestation growing trees

444220 Nurseries, retail, stock primarily grown off premises

444220 Nursery and garden centers without tree production

337122 Nursery furniture (except upholstered), wood, manufacturing

337124 Nursery furniture, metal, manufacturing

624410 Nursery schools

424930 Nursery stock (except plant bulbs, seeds) merchant wholesalers

111421 Nursery stock growing

111421 Nursery with tree production (except for reforestation)

611519 Nurse's aides schools

813920 Nurses' associations

621399 Nurses', licensed practical or registered, offices (e.g., centers, clinics)

621610 Nursing agencies, primarily providing home nursing services

621399 Nursing call centers

623110 Nursing homes

611519 Nursing schools (except academic)

445292 Nut (i.e., packaged) stores

115114 Nut hulling and shelling

331221 Nut rods, iron or steel, made in cold rolling mills

331110 Nut rods, iron or steel, made in iron and steel mills

333111 Nut shellers, farm-type, manufacturing

446191 Nutrition (i.e., food supplement) stores

621399 Nutritionists' offices (e.g., centers, clinics)

424450 Nuts (e.g., canned, roasted, salted) merchant wholesalers

311351 Nuts, chocolate covered, made from cacao beans

311352 Nuts, chocolate covered, made from purchased chocolate

311340 Nuts, covered (except chocolate covered), manufacturing

311911 Nuts, kernels and seeds, roasting and processing

115113 Nuts, machine harvesting

332722 Nuts, metal, manufacturing

311911 Nuts, salted, roasted, cooked, canned, manufacturing

424590 Nuts, unprocessed or shelled only, merchant wholesalers

325220 Nylon fibers and filaments manufacturing

424690 Nylon fibers merchant wholesalers

315110 Nylon hosiery, sheer, women's, misses', and girls' full-length and knee-length, knitting or knitting and finishing

325211 Nylon resins manufacturing

424610 Nylon resins merchant wholesalers

313110 Nylon spun yarns made from purchased fiber

313110 Nylon thread manufacturing

313110 Nylon yarn twisting or winding of purchased yarn

315110 Nylons, sheer, women's, misses', and girls' full-length and knee-length, knitting or knitting and finishing

325194 Oak extract manufacturing

321999 Oars, wood, manufacturing

111199 Oat farming, field and seed production

311211	Oat flour manufacturing
311230	Oatmeal (i.e., cereal breakfast food) manufacturing
311230	Oats, breakfast cereal, manufacturing
311230	Oats, rolled (i.e., cereal breakfast food), manufacturing
812910	Obedience training services, pet
339992	Oboes manufacturing
713990	Observation towers
712110	Observatories (except research institutions)
541715	Observatories, research institutions
622310	Obstetrical hospital
621111	Obstetricians' offices (e.g., centers, clinics)
339992	Ocarinas manufacturing
926150	Occupational safety and health administration
926150	Occupational safety and health standards agencies
813920	Occupational therapists' associations
621340	Occupational therapists' offices (e.g., centers, clinics)
541715	Oceanographic research and development laboratories or services
212393	Ocher mining and/or beneficiating
325130	Ocher pigments manufacturing
339992	Octophones manufacturing
114112	Octopus fishing
621399	Ocularists' offices (e.g., centers, clinics)
621320	ODs' (doctors of optometry) offices (e.g., centers, clinics)
332994	Oerlikon guns manufacturing
721310	Off campus dormitories
624190	Offender self-help organizations
336999	Off-highway tracked vehicles (except construction, armored military) manufacturing
333120	Off-highway trucks manufacturing
561110	Office administration services
541512	Office automation computer systems integration design services
236220	Office building construction
531120	Office building rental or leasing
561720	Office cleaning services
423420	Office equipment merchant wholesalers
337214	Office furniture (except wood), padded, upholstered, or plain (except wood), manufacturing
423210	Office furniture merchant wholesalers
532420	Office furniture rental or leasing
442110	Office furniture stores
238390	Office furniture, modular system, installation
337211	Office furniture, padded, upholstered, or plain wood, manufacturing
561320	Office help supply services
811212	Office machine repair and maintenance services (except communication equipment)
532420	Office machinery and equipment rental or leasing
423420	Office machines merchant wholesalers
561110	Office management services
322121	Office paper (e.g., computer printer, photocopy, plain paper) made in paper mills
322230	Office paper (e.g., computer printer, photocopy, plain paper), cut sheet, made from purchased paper
424120	Office supplies (except furniture, machines) merchant wholesalers
322230	Office supplies, die-cut paper, made from purchased paper or paperboard
561320	Office supply pools
453210	Office supply stores
551111	Offices of bank holding companies
441228	Off-road all-terrain vehicles (ATVs), wheeled or tracked, dealers
336999	Off-road all-terrain vehicles (ATVs), wheeled or tracked, manufacturing
325910	Offset inks manufacturing
323120	Offset plate preparation services
323111	Offset printing (except books, grey goods)
333244	Offset printing presses manufacturing
211120	Offshore crude petroleum production
211130	Offshore natural gas production
713290	Off-track betting parlors
334515	Ohmmeters manufacturing
324110	Oil (i.e., petroleum) refineries
325998	Oil additive preparations manufacturing
324110	Oil additives made in petroleum refineries
424690	Oil additives merchant wholesalers
237120	Oil and gas field distribution line construction
484220	Oil and gas field equipment trucking, local
484230	Oil and gas field equipment trucking, long-distance

811310	Oil and gas field machinery and equipment repair and maintenance services
213112	Oil and gas field services (except contract drilling, site preparation and related construction contractor activities) on a contract basis
333132	Oil and gas field-type drilling machinery and equipment (except offshore floating platforms) manufacturing
336611	Oil and gas offshore floating platforms manufacturing
213111	Oil and gas well drilling services (redrilling, spudding, tailing) on a contract basis
238220	Oil burner installation
333414	Oil burners, heating, manufacturing
423720	Oil burners, heating, merchant wholesalers
811191	Oil change and lubrication shops, automotive
424690	Oil drilling muds merchant wholesalers
211120	Oil field development for own account
423830	Oil field equipment merchant wholesalers
213112	Oil field exploration (except surveying) on a contract basis
211120	Oil field exploration for own account
532412	Oil field machinery and equipment rental or leasing
237310	Oil field road construction
423120	Oil filters, automotive, merchant wholesalers
336390	Oil filters, automotive, truck, and bus, manufacturing
424590	Oil kernels merchant wholesalers
523999	Oil lease brokers' offices
211130	Oil line drip, natural gas liquid
333914	Oil measuring and dispensing pumps manufacturing
424590	Oil nuts merchant wholesalers
237120	Oil pipeline construction
237120	Oil refinery construction
533110	Oil royalty companies
523910	Oil royalty dealing (i.e., acting as a principal in dealing royalties to investors)
533110	Oil royalty leasing
533110	Oil royalty traders (except for own account)
213112	Oil sampling services on a contract basis
339991	Oil seals manufacturing
211120	Oil shale mining and/or beneficiating
562910	Oil spill cleanup services
332420	Oil storage tanks, heavy gauge metal, manufacturing
333318	Oil water separators manufacturing
333914	Oil well and oil field pumps manufacturing
532412	Oil well drilling machinery and equipment rental or leasing
213111	Oil well drilling on a contract basis
213112	Oil well logging on a contract basis
423830	Oil well machinery and equipment merchant wholesalers
213112	Oil well rig building, repairing, and dismantling, on a contract basis
423830	Oil well supply houses merchant wholesalers
311613	Oil, animal, rendering
311221	Oil, corn crude and refined, made by wet milling corn
311225	Oil, olive, made from purchased oils
424710	Oil, petroleum, bulk stations and terminals, merchant wholesalers
424720	Oil, petroleum, merchant wholesalers (except bulk stations, terminals)
311225	Oil, vegetable stearin, made from purchased oils
423930	Oil, waste, merchant wholesalers
324199	Oil-based additives made from refined petroleum
313320	Oilcloth manufacturing
313320	Oiling of purchased textiles and apparel
325998	Oils (e.g., cutting, lubricating), synthetic, manufacturing
325194	Oils made by distillation of coal tar
424490	Oils, cooking and salad, merchant wholesalers
324110	Oils, fuel, manufacturing
424990	Oils, inedible, animal or vegetable, merchant wholesalers
324191	Oils, lubricating petroleum, made from refined petroleum
325998	Oils, lubricating, synthetic, manufacturing
324191	Oils, petroleum lubricating, re-refining used
325613	Oils, soluble (i.e., textile finishing assistants), manufacturing
325411	Oils, vegetable and animal, medicinal, uncompounded, manufacturing
325194	Oils, wood, made by distillation of wood
111191	Oilseed and grain combination farming, field and seed production
424990	Oilseed cake and meal merchant wholesalers

333241	Oilseed crushing and extracting machinery manufacturing
111120	Oilseed farming (except soybean), field and seed production
424590	Oilseeds merchant wholesalers
212399	Oilstones mining and/or beneficiating
111219	Okra farming, field, bedding plant and seed production
623312	Old age homes without nursing care
923130	Old age survivors and disability programs
623312	Old soldiers' homes without nursing care
325220	Olefin fibers and filaments manufacturing
325110	Olefins made from refined petroleum or liquid hydrocarbons
325199	Oleic acid (i.e., red oil) manufacturing
325199	Oleic acid esters manufacturing
325180	Oleum (i.e., fuming sulfuric acid) manufacturing
111339	Olive farming
311225	Olive oil made from purchased oils
311224	Olive oil made in crushing mills
311421	Olives brined
311423	Olives, dried, made in dehydration plants
212325	Olivine, non-gem, mining and/or beneficiating
334511	Omnibearing instrumentation manufacturing
621111	Oncologists' offices (e.g., centers, clinics)
812922	One-hour photofinishing services
111219	Onion farming, field, bedding plant and seed production
311421	Onions pickled
517919	On-line access service providers, using client-supplied telecommunications (e.g., dial-up ISPs)
517311	On-line access service providers, using own operated wired telecommunications infrastructure
561422	On-line customer service centers
212319	Onyx marble crushed and broken stone mining and/or beneficiating
212311	Onyx marble mining or quarrying
512132	Open air motion picture theaters
711110	Opera companies
315210	Opera hats cut and sew apparel contractors
315990	Opera hats cut and sewn from purchased fabric (except apparel contractors)
711130	Opera singers, independent

927110	Operating and launching government satellites
213112	Operating condensate gasoline field gathering lines on a contract basis
211120	Operating crude petroleum field gathering lines, except on a contract basis
211130	Operating natural gas liquid field gathering lines, except on a contract basis
339113	Operating room tables manufacturing
511210	Operating systems software, computer, packaged
541614	Operations research consulting services
325411	Ophthalmic agents, uncompounded, manufacturing
423460	Ophthalmic goods (except cameras) merchant wholesalers
339112	Ophthalmic instruments and apparatus (except laser surgical) manufacturing
621111	Ophthalmologists' offices (e.g., centers, clinics)
339112	Ophthalmometers and ophthalmoscopes manufacturing
541910	Opinion research services
325411	Opium and opium derivatives (i.e., basic chemicals) manufacturing
333314	Optical alignment and display instruments (except photographic) manufacturing
334112	Optical disk drives manufacturing
423460	Optical goods (except cameras) merchant wholesalers
446130	Optical goods stores (except offices of optometrists)
212399	Optical grade calcite mining and/or beneficiating
333314	Optical gun sighting and fire control equipment and instruments manufacturing
811219	Optical instrument repair and maintenance services (e.g., microscopes, telescopes)
333249	Optical lens making and grinding machinery manufacturing
334118	Optical readers and scanners manufacturing
518210	Optical scanning services
333314	Optical test and inspection equipment manufacturing
334413	Optoelectronic devices manufacturing
339112	Optometers manufacturing
423460	Optometric equipment and supplies merchant wholesalers
813920	Optometrists' associations

621320 Optometrists' offices (e.g., centers, clinics)

621210 Oral and maxillofacial surgeons' offices (e.g., centers, clinics)

325412 Oral contraceptive preparations manufacturing

621210 Oral pathologists' offices (e.g., centers, clinics)

111310 Orange groves

325998 Orange oil manufacturing

115112 Orchard cultivation services (e.g., bracing, planting, pruning, removal, spraying, surgery)

111998 Orchard grass seed farming

711510 Orchestra conductors, independent

711130 Orchestras

561422 Order-taking for clients over the Internet

454110 Order-taking offices of mail-order houses

423990 Ordnance and accessories merchant wholesalers

236210 Ore and metal refinery construction

423520 Ore concentrates merchant wholesalers

333131 Ore crushing, washing, screening, and loading machinery manufacturing

423520 Ores (e.g., gold, iron, lead, silver, zinc) merchant wholesalers

621991 Organ banks, body

621991 Organ donor centers, body

424690 Organic chemicals merchant wholesalers

325220 Organic noncellulosic fibers and filaments manufacturing

325130 Organic pigments, dyes, lakes, and toners manufacturing

541612 Organization development consulting services

928120 Organization for Economic Cooperation and Development

928120 Organization of American States

326199 Organizers for closets, drawers, and shelves, plastics, manufacturing

711310 Organizers of agricultural fairs with facilities

711320 Organizers of agricultural fairs without facilities

711310 Organizers of arts events with facilities

711320 Organizers of arts events without facilities

711310 Organizers of festivals with facilities

711320 Organizers of festivals without facilities

711310 Organizers of live performing arts productions (e.g., concerts) with facilities

711320 Organizers of live performing arts productions (e.g., concerts) without facilities

711310 Organizers of sports events with facilities

711320 Organizers of sports events without facilities

325199 Organo-inorganic compound manufacturing

325320 Organo-phosphate based insecticides manufacturing

321219 Oriented strandboard (OSB) manufacturing

327420 Ornamental and architectural plaster work (e.g., columns, mantels, molding) manufacturing

327390 Ornamental and statuary precast concrete products manufacturing

112511 Ornamental fish production, farm raising

423390 Ornamental ironwork merchant wholesalers

238190 Ornamental metal work installation

332323 Ornamental metalwork manufacturing

111422 Ornamental plant growing

424930 Ornamental plants and flowers merchant wholesalers

561730 Ornamental tree and shrub services

321918 Ornamental woodwork (e.g., cornices, mantels) manufacturing

339999 Ornaments, Christmas tree (except electric, glass), manufacturing

335129 Ornaments, Christmas tree, electric, manufacturing

327212 Ornaments, Christmas tree, glass, made in glass making plants

327215 Ornaments, Christmas tree, made from purchased glass

623990 Orphanages

325998 Orris oil manufacturing

325194 Orthodichlorobenzene manufacturing

339116 Orthodontic appliance, custom made in dental laboratories

339114 Orthodontic appliances manufacturing

621210 Orthodontists' offices (e.g., centers, clinics)

339113 Orthopedic canes manufacturing

339113 Orthopedic device manufacturing and sale in retail environment

339113 Orthopedic devices manufacturing

423450 Orthopedic equipment and supplies merchant wholesalers

339113 Orthopedic extension shoes manufacturing

339113 Orthopedic hosiery, elastic, manufacturing

622310 Orthopedic hospitals

621111	Orthopedic physicians' offices (e.g., centers, clinics)
327420	Orthopedic plaster, gypsum, manufacturing
316210	Orthopedic shoes (except extension shoes), children's, manufacturing
316210	Orthopedic shoes (except extension shoes), men's, manufacturing
316210	Orthopedic shoes (except extension shoes), women's, manufacturing
448210	Orthopedic shoes stores
621111	Orthopedic surgeons' offices (e.g., centers, clinics)
621399	Orthotists' offices (e.g., centers, clinics)
321219	OSB (oriented strandboard) manufacturing
334515	Oscillators (e.g., instrument type audiofrequency and radiofrequency) manufacturing
334515	Oscilloscopes manufacturing
212299	Osmium mining and/or beneficiating
334516	Osmometers manufacturing
325998	Ossein manufacturing
622110	Osteopathic hospitals
621111	Osteopathic physicians' (except mental health) offices (e.g., centers, clinics)
112390	Ostrich production
621111	Otolaryngologists' offices (e.g., centers, clinics)
334510	Otoscopes, electromedical, manufacturing
337121	Ottomans, upholstered, manufacturing
441222	Outboard motor dealers
811490	Outboard motor repair shops
333618	Outboard motors manufacturing
423910	Outboard motors merchant wholesalers
713990	Outdoor adventure operations (e.g., white water rafting) without accommodations
721214	Outdoor adventure retreats with accommodation facilities
541850	Outdoor display advertising services
423210	Outdoor furniture merchant wholesalers
423620	Outdoor grills merchant wholesalers
237990	Outdoor recreation facility construction
451110	Outdoor sporting equipment stores
315190	Outerwear handknitted for the trade
424320	Outerwear, men's and boys', merchant wholesalers
424330	Outerwear, women's, children's, and infants', merchant wholesalers

713990	Outfitters (i.e., providing trips and equipment)
335932	Outlet boxes, electrical wiring, manufacturing
335931	Outlets (i.e., receptacles), electrical, manufacturing
335931	Outlets, convenience, electrical, manufacturing
541850	Out-of-home media (i.e., display) advertising services
621420	Outpatient mental health centers and clinics (except hospitals)
621420	Outpatient treatment centers and clinics (except hospitals) for substance abuse (i.e., alcoholism, drug addiction)
621420	Outpatient treatment centers and clinics for alcoholism
621420	Outpatient treatment centers and clinics for drug addiction
561320	Outplacement consulting services
561320	Outplacement services
325612	Oven cleaners manufacturing
334512	Oven temperature controls, nonindustrial, manufacturing
811412	Oven, household-type, repair and maintenance services without retailing new ovens
236210	Oven, industrial plant, construction
333241	Ovens, bakery, manufacturing
333318	Ovens, commercial-type, manufacturing
423440	Ovens, commercial-type, merchant wholesalers
335220	Ovens, freestanding household-type, manufacturing
423620	Ovens, gas and electric, household-type, merchant wholesalers
333994	Ovens, industrial process and laboratory-type, manufacturing
423830	Ovens, industrial, merchant wholesalers
335210	Ovens, portable household-type (except microwave and convection ovens), manufacturing
335220	Ovens, portable household-type convection and microwave, manufacturing
327215	Ovenware made from purchased glass
327212	Ovenware, glass, made in glass making plants
315210	Overall jackets, work, cut and sew apparel contractors
315220	Overall jackets, work, men's and boys', cut and sewn from purchased fabric (except apparel contractors)

315210 Overalls, work, cut and sew apparel contractors

315220 Overalls, work, men's and boys', cut and sewn from purchased fabric (except apparel contractors)

213113 Overburden removal for coal mining on a contract basis

213114 Overburden removal for metal mining on a contract basis

213115 Overburden removal for nonmetallic minerals mining (except fuels) on a contract basis

315210 Overcoats cut and sew apparel contractors

315220 Overcoats, men's and boys', cut and sewn from purchased fabric (except apparel contractors)

315240 Overcoats, women's and girls', cut and sewn from purchased fabric (except apparel contractors)

333922 Overhead conveyors manufacturing

238290 Overhead door, commercial- or industrial-type, installation

238350 Overhead door, residential-type, installation

333316 Overhead projectors (except computer peripheral) manufacturing

334118 Overhead projectors, computer peripheral-type, manufacturing

333923 Overhead traveling cranes manufacturing

237310 Overpass construction

316210 Overshoes, plastics or plastics soled fabric upper, manufacturing

316210 Overshoes, rubber, or rubber soled fabric, manufacturing

325199 Oxalates (e.g., ammonium oxalate, ethyl oxalate, sodium oxalate) manufacturing

325199 Oxalic acid manufacturing

532283 Oxygen equipment rental (i.e., home use)

325120 Oxygen manufacturing

339112 Oxygen tents manufacturing

114112 Oyster dredging

112512 Oyster production, farm raising

212399 Ozokerite mining and/or beneficiating

333318 Ozone machines for water purification manufacturing

621999 Pacemaker monitoring services

334510 Pacemakers manufacturing

326299 Pacifiers, rubber, manufacturing

713990 Pack trains (i.e., trail riding), recreational

445310 Package stores (i.e., liquor)

511210 Packaged computer software publishers

424440 Packaged poultry (except canned and frozen) merchant wholesalers

326112 Packaging film, plastics, single-web or multiweb, manufacturing

115114 Packaging fresh or farm-dried fruits and vegetables

541420 Packaging industrial design services

333993 Packaging machinery manufacturing

423840 Packaging materials merchant wholesalers

561910 Packaging services (except packing and crating for transportation)

326150 Packaging, foam plastics (except polystyrene), manufacturing

326199 Packaging, plastics (e.g., blister, bubble), manufacturing

325998 Packer's fluids manufacturing

488991 Packing and preparing goods for shipping

321920 Packing cases, wood, nailed or lock corner, manufacturing

321920 Packing crates, wood, manufacturing

115114 Packing fruits and vegetables

423830 Packing machinery and equipment merchant wholesalers

423840 Packing materials merchant wholesalers

813940 PACs (Political Action Committees)

316210 Pacs, plastics or plastics soled fabric upper, manufacturing

316210 Pacs, rubber or rubber soled fabric upper, manufacturing

322230 Padded envelopes manufacturing

314999 Padding and wadding (except nonwoven fabric) manufacturing

423850 Padding, upholstery filling, merchant wholesalers

424310 Paddings, apparel, merchant wholesalers

321999 Paddles, wood, manufacturing

332510 Padlocks, metal, manufacturing

314120 Pads and protectors (e.g., ironing board, mattress, table), textile, made from purchased fabrics or felts

313230 Pads and wadding, nonwoven, manufacturing

322211 Pads, corrugated and solid fiberboard, made from purchased paper or paperboard

322230 Pads, desk, made from purchased paper

321999 Pads, excelsior, wood, manufacturing

322291 Pads, incontinent and bed, manufacturing

332999	Pads, soap impregnated scouring, manufacturing
321999	Pads, table, rattan, reed, and willow, manufacturing
334220	Pagers manufacturing
517312	Paging services (except satellite)
321920	Pails, coopered wood, manufacturing
326199	Pails, plastics, manufacturing
321920	Pails, plywood, manufacturing
321920	Pails, wood, manufacturing
621498	Pain therapy centers and clinics, outpatient
325510	Paint and varnish removers manufacturing
238320	Paint and wallpaper stripping
333994	Paint baking and drying ovens manufacturing
424950	Paint removers merchant wholesalers
339994	Paint rollers manufacturing
424950	Paint rollers merchant wholesalers
811121	Paint shops, automotive
333991	Paint spray guns, handheld pneumatic, manufacturing
333912	Paint sprayers (i.e., compressor and spray gun unit) manufacturing
332999	Paint sticks, metal, manufacturing
326199	Paint sticks, plastics, manufacturing
321999	Paint sticks, wood, manufacturing
444120	Paint stores
325510	Paint thinner and reducer preparations manufacturing
424950	Paint thinners merchant wholesalers
713990	Paintball, laser tag, and similar fields and arenas
325510	Paintbrush cleaners manufacturing
339994	Paintbrushes manufacturing
424950	Paintbrushes merchant wholesalers
711510	Painters (i.e., artists), independent
424950	Painter's supplies (except artists', turpentine) merchant wholesalers
238320	Painting (except roof) contractors
238320	Painting and wallpapering
611610	Painting instruction
237310	Painting lines on highways, streets and bridges
332812	Painting metals and metal products for the trade
711510	Painting restorers, independent
237310	Painting traffic lanes or parking lots
238160	Painting, spraying, or coating, roof
325510	Paints (except artist's) manufacturing
424950	Paints (except artists') merchant wholesalers
339940	Paints, artist's, manufacturing
424990	Paints, artist's, merchant wholesalers
325510	Paints, emulsion (i.e., latex paint), manufacturing
325510	Paints, oil and alkyd vehicle, manufacturing
315210	Pajamas cut and sew apparel contractors
315190	Pajamas made in apparel knitting mills
315220	Pajamas, men's and boys', cut and sewn from purchased fabric (except apparel contractors)
315240	Pajamas, women's, girls', and infants', cut and sewn from purchased fabric (except apparel contractors)
339940	Palettes, artist's, manufacturing
212299	Palladium mining and/or beneficiating
321920	Pallet containers, wood or wood and metal combination, manufacturing
333924	Pallet movers manufacturing
333924	Pallet or skid jacks manufacturing
332999	Pallet parts, metal, manufacturing
321920	Pallet parts, wood, manufacturing
532490	Pallet rental or leasing
423830	Pallets and skids merchant wholesalers
322211	Pallets, corrugated and solid fiber, made from purchased paper or paperboard
332999	Pallets, metal, manufacturing
321920	Pallets, wood or wood and metal combination, manufacturing
812990	Palm reading services
325199	Palmitic acid esters and amines manufacturing
311225	Palm-kernel oil made from purchased oils
311224	Palm-kernel oil, cake, and meal made in crushing mills
323120	Pamphlet binding without printing
511130	Pamphlet publishers (except exclusive Internet publishing)
511130	Pamphlet publishers and printing combined
519130	Pamphlet publishers, exclusively on Internet
424920	Pamphlets merchant wholesalers
323117	Pamphlets printing and binding without publishing

323117 Pamphlets printing without publishing

315210 Panama hats cut and sew apparel contractors

315990 Panama hats cut and sewn from purchased fabric (except apparel contractors)

311824 Pancake mixes made from purchased flour

311999 Pancake syrups (except pure maple) manufacturing

311412 Pancakes, frozen, manufacturing

238310 Panel or rigid board insulation installation

321918 Panel work, wood millwork, manufacturing

238390 Panel, metal, installation

334513 Panelboard indicators, recorders, and controllers, receiver industrial process-type, manufacturing

335313 Panelboards, electric power distribution, manufacturing

423610 Panelboards, electric power distribution, merchant wholesalers

238350 Paneling installation

423310 Paneling merchant wholesalers

236117 Panelized housing, residential, assembled on site by for-sale builders

236117 Panelized multifamily housing assembled on site by for-sale builders

236116 Panelized multifamily housing assembled on site by general contractors

236115 Panelized single-family housing assembled on site by general contractors

335313 Panels, generator control and metering, manufacturing

321211 Panels, hardwood plywood, manufacturing

332311 Panels, prefabricated metal building, manufacturing

321992 Panels, prefabricated wood building, manufacturing

321212 Panels, softwood plywood, manufacturing

423440 Pans, commercial, merchant wholesalers

315210 Panties cut and sew apparel contractors

315190 Panties made in apparel knitting mills

315240 Panties, women's, girls', and infants', cut and sewn from purchased fabric (except apparel contractors)

315210 Pants (e.g., athletic, dress, leather, sweat, waterproof outerwear, work) cut and sew apparel contractors

315220 Pants (e.g., athletic, dress, sweat, work), men's and boys', cut and sewn from purchased fabric (except apparel contractors)

315210 Pants outfits cut and sew apparel contractors

315240 Pants outfits, women's and girls', cut and sewn from purchased fabric (except apparel contractors)

315190 Pants, athletic, made in apparel knitting mills

315240 Pants, athletic, women's, girls', and infants', cut and sewn from purchased fabric (except apparel contractors)

315280 Pants, leather (except apparel contractors), manufacturing

315190 Pants, outerwear, made in apparel knitting mills

315280 Pants, rubber and rubberized fabric, made in the same establishment as the basic material

315240 Pants, sweat, women's, girls', and infants', cut and sewn from purchased fabric (except apparel contractors)

315280 Pants, vulcanized rubber, manufacturing

315280 Pants, waterproof outerwear, cut and sewn from purchased fabric (except apparel contractors)

315240 Pants, women's, girls', and infants', cut and sewn from purchased fabric (except apparel contractors)

315210 Pantsuits cut and sew apparel contractors

315240 Pantsuits, women's, girls', and infants', cut and sewn from purchased fabric (except apparel contractors)

315210 Panty girdles cut and sew apparel contractors

315240 Panty girdles, women's and girls', cut and sewn from purchased fabric (except apparel contractors)

315110 Panty hose, women's and girls', knitting or knitting and finishing

111339 Papaya farming

327910 Paper (e.g., aluminum oxide, emery, garnet, silicon carbide), abrasive-coated, made from purchased paper

424110 Paper (e.g., fine, printing, writing), bulk, merchant wholesalers

322121 Paper (except newsprint, uncoated groundwood) manufacturing

322121 Paper (except newsprint, uncoated groundwood) products made in paper mills

322121 Paper (except newsprint, uncoated groundwood), coated, laminated or treated, made in paper mills

424130 Paper (except office supplies, printing paper, stationery, writing paper) merchant wholesalers

333243	Paper and paperboard coating and finishing machinery manufacturing
333243	Paper and paperboard converting machinery manufacturing
333243	Paper and paperboard corrugating machinery manufacturing
333243	Paper and paperboard cutting and folding machinery manufacturing
333243	Paper and paperboard die-cutting and stamping machinery manufacturing
423830	Paper and pulp industries manufacturing machinery merchant wholesalers
333243	Paper bag making machinery manufacturing
424130	Paper bags merchant wholesalers
322220	Paper bags, coated, made from purchased paper
322220	Paper bags, uncoated, made from purchased paper
212324	Paper clay mining and/or beneficiating
332618	Paper clips made from purchased wire
331222	Paper clips, iron or steel, made in wire drawing plants
322219	Paper cups made from purchased paper or paperboard
339940	Paper cutters, office-type, manufacturing
322299	Paper dishes (e.g., cups, plates) made from molded pulp
322219	Paper dishes (e.g., cups, plates) made from purchased paper or paperboard
315210	Paper dresses cut and sew apparel contractors
315240	Paper dresses, women's and girls', cut and sewn from purchased fabric (except apparel contractors)
313220	Paper fabric, narrow woven, weaving
313210	Paper fabrics, broadwoven, weaving
332618	Paper machine wire cloth made from purchased wire
333243	Paper making machinery manufacturing
811310	Paper making machinery repair and maintenance services
322121	Paper mills (except newsprint, uncoated groundwood paper mills)
322122	Paper mills, newsprint
322122	Paper mills, uncoated groundwood
322291	Paper napkins and tablecloths made from purchased paper
322299	Paper novelties made from purchased paper
236210	Paper or pulp mill construction
322219	Paper plates made from purchased paper or paperboard
322299	Paper products (except office supply), die-cut, made from purchased paper or paperboard
322230	Paper products, die-cut office supply, made from purchased paper or paperboard
332992	Paper shells (i.e., 30 mm. or less, 1.18 inch or less) manufacturing
423420	Paper shredders merchant wholesalers
322121	Paper stock for conversion into paper products (e.g., bag and sack stock, envelope stock, tissue stock, wallpaper stock) manufacturing
322291	Paper towels made from purchased paper
322121	Paper towels made in paper mills
424130	Paper towels merchant wholesalers
313110	Paper yarn manufacturing
322121	Paper, asphalt, made in paper mills
423390	Paper, building, merchant wholesalers
339940	Paper, carbon, manufacturing
322211	Paper, corrugated, made from purchased paper or paperboard
523110	Paper, dealing of commercial (i.e., acting as principal in dealing securities to investors)
322122	Paper, newsprint and uncoated groundwood, manufacturing
424120	Paper, office (e.g., carbon, computer, copier, typewriter), merchant wholesalers
325992	Paper, photographic sensitized, manufacturing
423930	Paper, scrap, merchant wholesalers
339940	Paper, stencil, manufacturing
322130	Paperboard (e.g., can/drum stock, container board, corrugating medium, folding carton stock, linerboard, tube) manufacturing
424130	Paperboard and paperboard products (except office supplies) merchant wholesalers
333243	Paperboard box making machinery manufacturing
322130	Paperboard coating, laminating, or treating in paperboard mills
333243	Paperboard making machinery manufacturing
322130	Paperboard mills
322130	Paperboard products (e.g., containers) made in paperboard mills

322220 Paperboard, pasted, lined, laminated, or surface coated, made from purchased paperboard

238320 Paperhanging and removal contractors

238320 Paperhanging or removal contractors

327999 Papier-mache statuary and related art goods (e.g., urns, vases) manufacturing

713990 Para sailing, recreational

314999 Parachutes manufacturing

213112 Paraffin services, oil and gas field, on a contract basis

324110 Paraffin waxes made in petroleum refineries

325110 Paraffins made from refined petroleum or liquid hydrocarbons

541199 Paralegal services

321213 Parallel strand lumber manufacturing

621399 Paramedics' offices (e.g., centers, clinics)

325130 Pararosaniline dyes manufacturing

621511 Parasitology health laboratories

339999 Parasols manufacturing

325320 Parathion insecticides manufacturing

485991 Paratransit transportation services

561431 Parcel mailing services combined with one or more other office support services, private

561431 Parcel mailing services, private

561910 Parcel packing services

333997 Parcel post scales manufacturing

316110 Parchment leather manufacturing

922150 Pardon boards and offices

624190 Parenting support services

813410 Parent-teachers' associations

325320 Paris green insecticides manufacturing

237990 Park and recreational open space improvement construction

922120 Park police

332812 Parkerizing metals and metal products for the trade

236220 Parking garage construction

812930 Parking garages, automobile

561790 Parking lot cleaning (e.g., power sweeping, washing) services

237310 Parking lot marking and line painting

238990 Parking lot paving and sealing

812930 Parking lots, automobile

334514 Parking meters manufacturing

561612 Parking security services

488119 Parking services, aircraft

812930 Parking services, valet

713110 Parks (e.g., theme, water), amusement

924120 Parks and recreation commission, government

712190 Parks, national

712190 Parks, nature

712130 Parks, wild animal

237310 Parkway construction

611310 Parochial schools, college level

611110 Parochial schools, elementary or secondary

624190 Parole offices, privately operated

922150 Parole offices, publicly administered

238330 Parquet flooring installation

321918 Parquet flooring, hardwood, manufacturing

321918 Parquetry, hardwood, manufacturing

111219 Parsley farming, field, bedding plant and seed production

111219 Parsnip farming, field, bedding plant and seed production

335999 Particle accelerators, high-voltage, manufacturing

334516 Particle beam excitation instruments, laboratory-type, manufacturing

334516 Particle size analyzers manufacturing

321219 Particleboard manufacturing

423310 Particleboard merchant wholesalers

238390 Partition (e.g., office, washroom), metal, installation

238390 Partition, moveable and/or demountable, installation

337215 Partitions for floor attachment, prefabricated, manufacturing

423440 Partitions merchant wholesalers

322211 Partitions, corrugated and solid fiber, made from purchased paper or paperboard

337215 Partitions, freestanding, prefabricated, manufacturing

332323 Partitions, ornamental metal, manufacturing

112390 Partridge production

441310 Parts and accessories dealers, automotive

423120 Parts, new, motor vehicle, merchant wholesalers

423140 Parts, used, motor vehicle, merchant wholesalers

532289 Party (i.e., banquet) equipment rental

453220	Party goods (e.g., paper supplies, decorations, novelties) stores
454390	Party plan merchandisers, direct selling
812990	Party planning services
532289	Party rental supply centers
481211	Passenger air transportation, nonscheduled
481111	Passenger air transportation, scheduled
333922	Passenger baggage belt loaders (except industrial truck) manufacturing
532112	Passenger car leasing
532111	Passenger car rental
481211	Passenger carriers, air, nonscheduled
481111	Passenger carriers, air, scheduled
485320	Passenger limousine rental with driver (except shuttle service, taxi)
482111	Passenger railways, line-haul
336611	Passenger ship building
483114	Passenger transportation, coastal or Great Lakes (including St. Lawrence Seaway)
483114	Passenger transportation, deep sea, to and from domestic ports (including Puerto Rico)
483112	Passenger transportation, deep sea, to or from foreign ports
483212	Passenger transportation, inland waters (except on Great Lakes system)
532112	Passenger van leasing
532111	Passenger van rental
532111	Passenger van rental agencies
485320	Passenger van rental with driver (except shuttle service, taxi)
532112	Passenger vehicle fleet leasing
111339	Passion fruit farming
928120	Passport issuing services
541921	Passport photography services
311422	Pasta based products canning
333241	Pasta making machinery (i.e., food manufacturing-type) manufacturing
311999	Pasta mixes made from purchased dry ingredients
311824	Pasta, dry, manufacturing
311991	Pasta, fresh, manufacturing
331314	Paste made from purchased aluminum
331420	Paste made from purchased copper
331221	Paste made from purchased iron or steel
331110	Paste, iron or steel, made in iron and steel mills
331492	Paste, nonferrous metals (except aluminum, copper), made from purchased metal
325520	Pastes, adhesive, manufacturing
311421	Pastes, fruit and vegetable, canning
333241	Pasteurizing equipment, food, manufacturing
311511	Pasteurizing milk
311612	Pastrami made from purchased carcasses
311812	Pastries (e.g., Danish, French), fresh, made in commercial bakeries
311813	Pastries (e.g., Danish, French), frozen, manufacturing
311824	Pastries, uncooked, manufacturing
321999	Pastry boards, wood, manufacturing
541199	Patent agent services (i.e., patent filing and searching services)
541110	Patent attorneys' offices
541110	Patent attorneys' private practices
541990	Patent broker services (i.e., patent marketing services)
533110	Patent buying and licensing
533110	Patent leasing
316110	Patent leather manufacturing
325412	Patent medicine preparations manufacturing
621511	Pathological analysis laboratories
621111	Pathologists' (except oral, speech, voice) offices (e.g., centers, clinics)
621111	Pathologists', forensic, offices (e.g., centers, clinics)
621111	Pathologists', neuropathological, offices (e.g., centers, clinics)
621210	Pathologists', oral, offices (e.g., centers, clinics)
621340	Pathologists', speech or voice, offices (e.g., centers, clinics)
621111	Pathologists', surgical, offices (e.g., centers, clinics)
621511	Pathology laboratories, medical
334510	Patient monitoring equipment (e.g., intensive care, coronary care unit) manufacturing
423450	Patient monitoring equipment merchant wholesalers
327331	Patio block, concrete, manufacturing
238990	Patio construction
336611	Patrol boat building
561612	Patrol services, security

541990	Patrolling (i.e., visual inspection) of electric transmission or gas lines
511199	Pattern and plan (e.g., clothing patterns) publishers (except exclusive Internet publishing)
511199	Pattern and plan (e.g., clothing patterns) publishers and printing combined
519130	Pattern and plan (e.g., clothing patterns) publishers, exclusively on Internet
332999	Patterns (except shoe), industrial, manufacturing
423830	Patterns (except shoe), industrial, merchant wholesalers
323111	Patterns and plans (e.g., clothing patterns) commercial printing (except blueprinting, screen) without publishing
323113	Patterns and plans (e.g., clothing patterns) screen printing without publishing
339999	Patterns, shoe, manufacturing
423850	Patterns, shoe, merchant wholesalers
237310	Pavement, highway, road, street, bridge or airport runway, construction
238990	Paver, brick (e.g., driveway, patio, sidewalk), installation
423810	Pavers merchant wholesalers
212399	Pavers mining and/or beneficiating
324121	Paving blocks and mixtures made from purchased asphaltic materials
327331	Paving blocks, concrete, manufacturing
327120	Paving brick, clay, manufacturing
333120	Paving machinery manufacturing
423320	Paving mixtures merchant wholesalers
238990	Paving, residential and commercial driveway and parking lot
522298	Pawnshops
812990	Pay telephone equipment concession operators
515210	Pay television networks
522390	Payday lending services
515210	Pay-per-view cable programming
541214	Payroll processing services
334210	PBX (private branch exchange) equipment manufacturing
111219	Pea (except dry) farming, field and seed production
111130	Pea farming, dry, field and seed production
813319	Peace advocacy organizations
928120	Peace Corps
111339	Peach farming
325130	Peacock blue lake manufacturing
311911	Peanut butter blended with jelly manufacturing
311911	Peanut butter manufacturing
311224	Peanut cake, meal, and oil made in crushing mills
333111	Peanut combines (i.e., diggers, packers, threshers) manufacturing
111992	Peanut farming
311225	Peanut oil made from purchased oils
333241	Peanut roasting machines (i.e., food manufacturing-type) manufacturing
115114	Peanut shelling
115113	Peanut, machine harvesting
424590	Peanuts, bulk, unprocessed, merchant wholesalers
111339	Pear farming
339910	Pearl drilling, peeling, or sawing
325130	Pearl essence pigment, synthetic, manufacturing
331511	Pearlitic castings, malleable iron, unfinished, manufacturing
423940	Pearls merchant wholesalers
339910	Pearls, costume, manufacturing
212399	Peat grinding
212399	Peat humus mining and/or beneficiating
212399	Peat mining and/or beneficiating
327999	Peat pots, molded pulp, manufacturing
212321	Pebbles (except grinding) mining and/or beneficiating
212399	Pebbles grinding
111335	Pecan farming
115114	Pecan hulling and shelling
311942	Pectin manufacturing
621111	Pediatricians' (except mental health) offices (e.g., centers, clinics)
621112	Pediatricians', mental health, offices (e.g., centers, clinics)
812113	Pedicure and manicure salons
812113	Pedicurist services
115210	Pedigree (i.e., livestock, pets, poultry) record services
812910	Pedigree record services, pet
334514	Pedometers manufacturing
621399	Pedorthics' offices (e.g., centers, clinics)
813920	Peer review boards
212325	Pegmatite, feldspar, mining and/or beneficiating

316998	Pegs, leather shoe, manufacturing
332994	Pellet guns manufacturing
333131	Pellet mills machinery, mining-type, manufacturing
332992	Pellets, air rifle and pistol, manufacturing
316110	Pelts bleaching, currying, dyeing, scraping, and tanning
424590	Pelts, raw, merchant wholesalers
339112	Pelvimeters manufacturing
339940	Pen refills and cartridges manufacturing
339940	Pencil leads manufacturing
339940	Pencil sharpeners manufacturing
321999	Pencil slats, wood, manufacturing
339940	Pencils manufacturing
424120	Pencils merchant wholesalers
335122	Pendant lamps (except residential), electric, manufacturing
335121	Pendant lamps fixtures, residential electric, manufacturing
325613	Penetrants manufacturing
325998	Penetrating fluids, synthetic, manufacturing
325412	Penicillin preparations manufacturing
325411	Penicillin, uncompounded, manufacturing
922140	Penitentiaries
236220	Penitentiary construction
212113	Pennsylvania anthracite mining and/or beneficiating
339940	Pens manufacturing
424120	Pens, writing, merchant wholesalers
523920	Pension fund managing
524292	Pension fund, third party administrative services
525110	Pension funds
525110	Pension plans (e.g., employee benefit, retirement)
332313	Penstocks, fabricated metal plate, manufacturing
325194	Pentachlorophenol manufacturing
325199	Pentaerythritol manufacturing
325110	Pentanes made from refined petroleum or liquid hydrocarbons
325110	Pentenes made from refined petroleum or liquid hydrocarbons
325920	Pentolite explosive materials manufacturing
561330	PEO (professional employer organizations)
111219	Pepper (e.g., bell, chili, green, hot, red, sweet) farming
311942	Pepper (i.e., spice) manufacturing
325998	Peppermint oil manufacturing
313210	Percales weaving
114111	Perch fishing
325180	Perchloric acid manufacturing
325199	Perchloroethylene manufacturing
335210	Percolators, household-type electric, manufacturing
332992	Percussion caps (i.e., 30 mm. or less, 1.18 inch or less), ammunition, manufacturing
339992	Percussion musical instruments manufacturing
423420	Perforating machines merchant wholesalers
213112	Perforating oil and gas well casings on a contract basis
533110	Performance rights, licensing of
711510	Performers (i.e., entertainers), independent
711510	Performing artists, independent
711310	Performing arts center operators
611610	Performing arts schools (except academic)
561599	Performing arts ticket offices
325199	Perfume materials (i.e., basic synthetic chemicals, such as terpineol) manufacturing
446120	Perfume stores
325620	Perfumes manufacturing
424210	Perfumes merchant wholesalers
511120	Periodical publishers (except exclusive Internet publishing)
511120	Periodical publishers and printing combined
519130	Periodical publishers, exclusively on Internet
323111	Periodicals commercial printing (except screen) without publishing
424920	Periodicals merchant wholesalers
323113	Periodicals screen printing without publishing
621210	Periodontists' offices (e.g., centers, clinics)
334418	Peripheral controller boards manufacturing
423430	Peripheral equipment, computer, merchant wholesalers
333314	Periscopes manufacturing
327992	Perlite aggregates manufacturing
212399	Perlite mining and/or beneficiating
327992	Perlite, expanded, manufacturing

331524	Permanent mold castings, aluminum, unfinished, manufacturing
331529	Permanent mold castings, nonferrous metal (except aluminum), unfinished, manufacturing
325620	Permanent wave preparations manufacturing
238130	Permanent wood foundation installation
325180	Peroxides, inorganic, manufacturing
325199	Peroxides, organic, manufacturing
325130	Persian orange lake manufacturing
111339	Persimmon farming
423620	Personal care appliances, electric, merchant wholesalers
812990	Personal chef services
334418	Personal computer modems manufacturing
334111	Personal computers manufacturing
522291	Personal credit institutions (i.e., unsecured cash loans)
611699	Personal development schools
525920	Personal estates (i.e., managing assets)
522291	Personal finance companies (i.e., unsecured cash loans)
611519	Personal fitness instructor training
812990	Personal fitness training services
339910	Personal goods, metal, manufacturing
551112	Personal holding companies
525920	Personal investment trusts
523991	Personal investments trust administration
523920	Personal investments trusts, managing
316998	Personal leather goods (e.g., coin purses, eyeglass cases, key cases), small, manufacturing
446199	Personal mobility scooter dealers
812990	Personal organizer services
561612	Personal protection services (except security systems services)
339113	Personal safety devices, not specified elsewhere, manufacturing
424130	Personal sanitary paper products merchant wholesalers
812990	Personal shopping services
525920	Personal trusts
441228	Personal watercraft dealers
336999	Personal watercraft manufacturing
532284	Personal watercraft rental
561320	Personnel (e.g., industrial, office) suppliers
813920	Personnel management associations
541612	Personnel management consulting services
921190	Personnel offices, government
325320	Pest (e.g., ant, rat, roach, rodent) control poison manufacturing
561710	Pest (e.g., termite) inspection services
561710	Pest control (except agricultural, forestry) services
926140	Pest control programs, agriculture, government
115112	Pest control services, agricultural
115310	Pest control services, forestry
424690	Pesticides (except agricultural) merchant wholesalers
325320	Pesticides manufacturing
424910	Pesticides, agricultural, merchant wholesalers
334510	PET (positron emission tomography) scanners manufacturing
812910	Pet boarding services
812220	Pet cemeteries
311119	Pet food (except cat, dog) manufacturing
424490	Pet food merchant wholesalers
311111	Pet food, dog and cat, manufacturing
812910	Pet grooming services
524128	Pet health insurance carriers, direct
541940	Pet hospitals
926150	Pet licensing
453910	Pet shops
812910	Pet sitting services
424990	Pet supplies (except pet food) merchant wholesalers
453910	Pet supply stores
812910	Pet training services
485991	Pet transportation services
324110	Petrochemical feedstocks made in petroleum refineries
237120	Petrochemical plant construction
324110	Petrochemicals made in petroleum refineries
424710	Petroleum and petroleum products bulk stations and terminals, merchant wholesalers
424720	Petroleum and petroleum products merchant wholesalers (except bulk stations, terminals)
425120	Petroleum brokers
324110	Petroleum coke made in petroleum refineries
424720	Petroleum coke merchant wholesalers

324110	Petroleum cracking and reforming
324110	Petroleum distillation
541330	Petroleum engineering services
211130	Petroleum gases, liquefied, recovering from oil and gas field gases
324199	Petroleum jelly made from refined petroleum
324110	Petroleum jelly made in petroleum refineries
324191	Petroleum lubricating oils made from refined petroleum
324110	Petroleum lubricating oils made in petroleum refineries
486110	Petroleum pipelines, crude
486910	Petroleum pipelines, refined
325211	Petroleum polymer resins manufacturing
423830	Petroleum production machinery and equipment merchant wholesalers
324110	Petroleum refineries
237120	Petroleum refinery construction
333249	Petroleum refining machinery manufacturing
332420	Petroleum storage tanks, heavy gauge metal, manufacturing
324199	Petroleum waxes made from refined petroleum
211120	Petroleum, crude, production (i.e., extraction)
424990	Pets merchant wholesalers
712130	Petting zoos
337127	Pews, church, manufacturing
339910	Pewter ware manufacturing
236210	Pharmaceutical manufacturing plant construction
325412	Pharmaceutical preparations (e.g., capsules, liniments, ointments, tablets) manufacturing
424210	Pharmaceuticals merchant wholesalers
446110	Pharmacies
813920	Pharmacists' associations
334515	Phase angle meters manufacturing
335312	Phase converters (i.e., electrical equipment) manufacturing
112390	Pheasant production
325194	Phenol manufacturing
325211	Phenol-formaldehyde resins manufacturing
325211	Phenol-furfural resins manufacturing
325211	Phenolic resins manufacturing

325211	Phenoxy resins manufacturing
813211	Philanthropic trusts, awarding grants
212399	Phlogopite mining and/or beneficiating
334510	Phonocardiographs manufacturing
334614	Phonograph records manufacturing
423990	Phonograph records merchant wholesalers
423440	Phonographs, coin-operated, merchant wholesalers
325199	Phosgene manufacturing
212392	Phosphate rock mining and/or beneficiating
424910	Phosphate rock, ground, merchant wholesalers
325312	Phosphatic fertilizer materials manufacturing
325314	Phosphatic fertilizers made by mixing purchased materials
325130	Phosphomolybdic acid lakes and toners manufacturing
325199	Phosphoric acid esters manufacturing
325312	Phosphoric acid manufacturing
325180	Phosphorus compounds, not specified elsewhere by process, manufacturing
325180	Phosphorus oxychloride manufacturing
325130	Phosphotungstic acid lakes and toners manufacturing
323111	Photo albums and refills manufacturing
424120	Photo albums merchant wholesalers
323120	Photocomposition services, for the printing trade
424120	Photocopy supplies merchant wholesalers
811212	Photocopying machine repair and maintenance services without retailing new photocopying machines
333316	Photocopying machines manufacturing
561439	Photocopying services (except combined with printing services)
325992	Photocopying toner cartridges manufacturing
334413	Photoelectric cells, solid-state (e.g., electronic eye), manufacturing
333244	Photoengraving machinery manufacturing
323120	Photoengraving plate preparation services
423410	Photofinishing equipment merchant wholesalers
812921	Photofinishing labs (except one-hour)
812922	Photofinishing labs, one-hour
812921	Photofinishing services (except one-hour)
812922	Photofinishing services, one-hour

335110 Photoflash and photoflood lamp bulbs and tubes manufacturing

333316 Photoflash equipment manufacturing

541370 Photogrammetric mapping services

322299 Photograph folders, mats, and mounts manufacturing

541922 Photographers specializing in aerial photography

711510 Photographers, independent artistic

325992 Photographic chemicals manufacturing

333316 Photographic equipment (except lenses) manufacturing

423410 Photographic equipment and supplies merchant wholesalers

532210 Photographic equipment rental

811211 Photographic equipment repair shops without retailing new photographic equipment

423410 Photographic film and plates merchant wholesalers

325992 Photographic film, cloth, paper, and plate, sensitized, manufacturing

333314 Photographic lenses manufacturing

812990 Photographic machine concession operators, coin-operated

443142 Photographic supply stores

326113 Photographic, micrographic, and X-ray plastics, sheet, and film (except sensitized), manufacturing

611610 Photography schools, art

611519 Photography schools, commercial

541922 Photography services, commercial

541921 Photography services, portrait (e.g., still, video)

541922 Photography studios, commercial

541921 Photography studios, portrait

711510 Photojournalists, independent (freelance)

327212 Photomask blanks, glass, made in glass making plants

325992 Photomasks manufacturing

334516 Photometers (except photographic exposure meters) manufacturing

334516 Photonexcitation analyzers manufacturing

334413 Photonic integrated circuits manufacturing

541715 Photonics research and development services (except nanotechnology research and development)

325992 Photosensitized paper manufacturing

323120 Phototypesetting services

334413 Photovoltaic cells manufacturing

334413 Photovoltaic devices, solid-state, manufacturing

335999 Photovoltaic panels made from purchased cells

325199 Phthalate acid manufacturing

325211 Phthalic alkyd resins manufacturing

325194 Phthalic anhydride manufacturing

325211 Phthalic anhydride resins manufacturing

325130 Phthalocyanine pigments manufacturing

541614 Physical distribution consulting services

713940 Physical fitness centers

621999 Physical fitness evaluation services (except by offices of health practitioners)

713940 Physical fitness facilities

713940 Physical fitness studios

334519 Physical properties testing and inspection equipment manufacturing

622310 Physical rehabilitation hospitals

541715 Physical science research and development laboratories or services (except biotechnology and nanotechnology research and development)

621340 Physical therapists' offices (e.g., centers, clinics)

621340 Physical therapy offices (e.g., centers, clinics)

621340 Physical-integration practitioners' offices (e.g., centers, clinics)

621111 Physicians' (except mental health) offices (e.g., centers, clinics)

621399 Physicians' assistants' offices (e.g., centers, clinics)

423450 Physicians' equipment and supplies merchant wholesalers

621112 Physicians', mental health, offices (e.g., centers, clinics)

541690 Physics consulting services

541715 Physics research and development laboratories or services (except nanotechnology research and development)

621340 Physiotherapists' offices (e.g., centers, clinics)

339112 Physiotherapy equipment (except electrotherapeutic) manufacturing

325411 Physostigmine and derivatives (i.e., basic chemicals) manufacturing

332510 Piano hardware, metal, manufacturing

339992 Piano parts and materials (except piano hardware) manufacturing

532289 Piano rental

451140 Piano stores

339992	Piccolos and parts manufacturing
333249	Picker machinery for textiles manufacturing
333249	Picker sticks for looms manufacturing
311710	Picking crab meat
333519	Picklers and pickling machinery, metalworking, manufacturing
311421	Pickles manufacturing
311421	Pickling fruits and vegetables
332813	Pickling metals and metal products for the trade
332216	Picks (i.e., handtools) manufacturing
812320	Pick-up and drop-off sites for drycleaners and laundries
336214	Pick-up canopies, caps, or covers manufacturing
336112	Pick-up trucks, light duty, assembling on chassis of own manufacture
713990	Picnic grounds
326199	Picnic jugs, plastics (except foam), manufacturing
325920	Picric acid explosive materials manufacturing
334511	Pictorial situation instrumentation manufacturing
442299	Picture frame shops, custom
311824	Pie crust shells, uncooked, made from purchased flour
424310	Piece goods (except burlap, felt) merchant wholesalers
451130	Piece goods stores
424990	Piece goods, burlap and felt, merchant wholesalers
237990	Pier construction
531120	Piers and associated building rental or leasing
713110	Piers, amusement
424420	Pies (e.g., fruit, meat, poultry), frozen, merchant wholesalers
311812	Pies, fresh, made in commercial bakeries
311813	Pies, frozen, manufacturing
334419	Piezoelectric crystals manufacturing
334419	Piezoelectric devices manufacturing
112210	Pig farming
331110	Pig iron manufacturing
423510	Pig iron merchant wholesalers
325130	Pigment, scarlet lake, manufacturing
325130	Pigments (except animal black, bone black), organic, manufacturing

325130	Pigments (except bone black, carbon black, lamp black), inorganic, manufacturing
212393	Pigments, natural, mineral, mining and/or beneficiating
424950	Pigments, paint, merchant wholesalers
311612	Pig's feet, cooked and pickled, made from purchased carcasses
114111	Pilchard fishing
238910	Pile driving, building foundation
237990	Pile driving, marine
313240	Pile fabrics made in warp or weft knitting mills
332313	Pile shells, fabricated metal plate, manufacturing
332322	Pile shells, sheet metal (except stampings), manufacturing
333120	Pile-driving equipment manufacturing
238910	Piling (i.e., bored, cast-in-place, drilled), building foundation, contractors
321114	Pilings, foundation and marine construction, treating
331110	Pilings, iron or steel plain sheet, made in iron and steel mills
423510	Pilings, metal, merchant wholesalers
321114	Pilings, round wood, cutting and treating
321114	Pilings, wood, treating
332991	Pillow blocks with ball or roller bearings manufacturing
812320	Pillow cleaning services
314120	Pillowcases, bed, made from purchased fabrics
314120	Pillows, bed, made from purchased materials
488490	Pilot car services (i.e., wide load warning services)
488330	Piloting services, water transportation
713120	Pinball arcades
713990	Pinball machine concession operators (i.e., supplying and servicing in others' facilities)
339999	Pinball machines, coin-operated, manufacturing
113210	Pine gum extracting
325194	Pine oil manufacturing
111339	Pineapple farming
325194	Pinene manufacturing
713990	Ping pong parlors
212325	Pinite mining and/or beneficiating
339993	Pins (except precious) manufacturing

339910	Pins and brooches, precious metal, manufacturing
712120	Pioneer villages
331210	Pipe (e.g., heavy riveted, lock joint, seamless, welded) made from purchased iron or steel
423720	Pipe and boiler coverings merchant wholesalers
332996	Pipe and pipe fittings made from purchased metal pipe
331511	Pipe and pipe fittings, cast iron, manufacturing
333519	Pipe and tube rolling mill machinery, metalworking, manufacturing
332323	Pipe bannisters, metal, manufacturing
326299	Pipe bits and stems, tobacco, hard rubber, manufacturing
339999	Pipe cleaners manufacturing
332996	Pipe couplings made from purchased metal pipe
331511	Pipe couplings, cast iron, manufacturing
238290	Pipe covering
333517	Pipe cutting and threading machines, metalworking, manufacturing
332996	Pipe fabricating (i.e., bending, cutting, threading) made from purchased metal pipe
238220	Pipe fitting contractors
423840	Pipe fittings and valves (except plumbing) merchant wholesalers
423720	Pipe fittings and valves, plumbers', merchant wholesalers
326122	Pipe fittings, rigid plastics, manufacturing
332323	Pipe guards, metal, manufacturing
332999	Pipe hangers and supports, metal, manufacturing
332996	Pipe headers made from purchased metal pipe
237120	Pipe lining (except thermal insulating) contractors
331318	Pipe made by extruding purchased aluminum
332323	Pipe railings, metal, manufacturing
325520	Pipe sealing compounds manufacturing
213112	Pipe testing services, oil and gas field, on a contract basis
424940	Pipe tobacco merchant wholesalers
312230	Pipe tobacco, prepared, manufacturing
331318	Pipe, aluminum, made in integrated secondary smelting and extruding mills
327332	Pipe, concrete, manufacturing
238290	Pipe, duct and boiler insulation
331420	Pipe, extruded and drawn, brass, bronze, and copper, made from purchased copper or in integrated secondary smelting and rolling, drawing or extruding plants
332313	Pipe, fabricated metal plate, manufacturing
331110	Pipe, iron or steel, made in iron and steel mills
423510	Pipe, metal, merchant wholesalers
331491	Pipe, nonferrous metals (except aluminum, copper), made from purchased metals or scrap
326122	Pipe, rigid plastics, manufacturing
332322	Pipe, sheet metal (except stampings), manufacturing
515112	Piped-in music services, radio transmitted
237990	Pipe-jacking contractors
237120	Pipeline construction on oil and gas field gathering lines to point of distribution on a contract basis
541990	Pipeline inspection (i.e., visual) services
423830	Pipeline machinery and equipment merchant wholesalers
237120	Pipeline rehabilitation contractors
488999	Pipeline terminal facilities, independently operated
486990	Pipeline transportation (except crude oil, natural gas, refined petroleum products)
486110	Pipeline transportation, crude oil
486910	Pipeline transportation, gasoline and other refined petroleum products
486210	Pipeline transportation, natural gas
237120	Pipeline wrapping contractors
237120	Pipeline, gas and oil, construction
339992	Pipes, organ, manufacturing
339999	Pipes, smoker's, manufacturing
212399	Pipestones mining and/or beneficiating
111335	Pistachio farming
332994	Pistols manufacturing
336310	Pistons and piston rings manufacturing
423120	Pistons and valves, automotive, merchant wholesalers
423840	Pistons and valves, industrial, merchant wholesalers
423830	Pistons, hydraulic and pneumatic, merchant wholesalers
325194	Pitch made by distillation of coal tar
324122	Pitch, roofing, made from purchased asphaltic materials
325194	Pitch, wood, manufacturing
212291	Pitchblende mining and/or beneficiating

334519	Pitometers manufacturing
325411	Pituitary gland derivatives, uncompounded, manufacturing
325412	Pituitary gland preparations manufacturing
722513	Pizza delivery shops
311824	Pizza doughs made from purchased flour
722511	Pizza parlors, full service
722513	Pizza parlors, limited-service
424490	Pizzas (except frozen) merchant wholesalers
311991	Pizzas, fresh, manufacturing
311412	Pizzas, frozen, manufacturing
424420	Pizzas, frozen, merchant wholesalers
722511	Pizzerias, full service
722513	Pizzerias, limited-service (e.g., takeout)
314120	Placemats, all materials, made from purchased materials
561311	Placement agencies or services, employment
621991	Placenta banks
212221	Placer gold mining and/or beneficiating
212222	Placer silver mining and/or beneficiating
813110	Places of worship
238120	Placing and tying reinforcing rod at a construction site
334417	Planar cable connectors manufacturing
333243	Planers woodworking-type, stationary, manufacturing
333120	Planers, bituminous, manufacturing
333991	Planers, handheld power-driven, manufacturing
333517	Planers, metalworking, manufacturing
332216	Planes, handheld, nonpowered, manufacturing
712110	Planetariums
321912	Planing mills (except millwork)
321918	Planing mills, millwork
321912	Planing purchased lumber
525120	Plans, health- and welfare-related employee benefit
522190	Plans, Morris (i.e., known as), depository
522298	Plans, Morris (i.e., known as), nondepository
525110	Plans, pension
561730	Plant and shrub maintenance in buildings
112519	Plant aquaculture
424910	Plant bulbs merchant wholesalers
424990	Plant food merchant wholesalers
325311	Plant foods, mixed, made in plants producing nitrogenous fertilizer materials
325312	Plant foods, mixed, made in plants producing phosphatic fertilizer materials
325320	Plant growth regulants manufacturing
561730	Plant maintenance services
111422	Plant, ornamental, growing
111422	Plant, potted flower and foliage, growing
111339	Plantain farming
115112	Planting crops
423820	Planting machinery and equipment, farm-type, merchant wholesalers
333111	Planting machines, farm-type, manufacturing
424930	Plants, potted, merchant wholesalers
621991	Plasma collection services
333517	Plasma jet spray metal forming machines manufacturing
333517	Plasma process metal cutting machines (except welding equipment) manufacturing
333992	Plasma welding equipment manufacturing
621991	Plasmapheresis centers
325414	Plasmas manufacturing
424210	Plasmas, blood, merchant wholesalers
327420	Plaster and plasterboard, gypsum, manufacturing
423320	Plaster merchant wholesalers
327420	Plaster of paris manufacturing
327420	Plaster of paris products (e.g., columns, statuary, urns) manufacturing
327420	Plaster, gypsum, manufacturing
238310	Plastering (i.e., ornamental, plain) contractors
212325	Plastic fire clay mining and/or beneficiating
621111	Plastic surgeons' offices (e.g., centers, clinics)
325510	Plastic wood fillers manufacturing
332813	Plastic, glass, or other media blasting services
325199	Plasticizers (i.e., basic synthetic chemicals) manufacturing
424610	Plasticizers merchant wholesalers
337125	Plastics (including fiberglass) furniture (except upholstered), household-type, manufacturing
326220	Plastics and rubber belts and hoses (without fittings) manufacturing

325211	Plastics and synthetic resins regenerating, precipitating, and coagulating
424130	Plastics bags merchant wholesalers
424610	Plastics basic shapes (e.g., film, rod, sheet, sheeting, tubing) merchant wholesalers
313320	Plastics coating of textiles and apparel
326113	Plastics film and unlaminated sheet (except packaging) manufacturing
424610	Plastics foam merchant wholesalers
423840	Plastics foam packing and packaging materials merchant wholesalers
424990	Plastics foam products (except disposable and packaging) merchant wholesalers
424130	Plastics foam products, disposable (except packaging, packing), merchant wholesalers
315210	Plastics gowns cut and sew apparel contractors
315280	Plastics gowns cut and sewn from purchased fabric (except apparel contractors)
423830	Plastics industries machinery, equipment, and supplies merchant wholesalers
337110	Plastics laminated over particleboard (e.g., fixture tops) manufacturing
424610	Plastics materials merchant wholesalers
315210	Plastics rainwear cut and sew apparel contractors
315280	Plastics rainwear cut and sewn from purchased fabric (except apparel contractors)
325991	Plastics resins compounding from recycled materials
424610	Plastics resins merchant wholesalers
325991	Plastics resins, custom compounding of purchased
423930	Plastics scrap merchant wholesalers
333249	Plastics working machinery manufacturing
325510	Plastisol coating compounds manufacturing
524126	Plate glass insurance carriers, direct
423390	Plate glass merchant wholesalers
333519	Plate rolling mill machinery, metalworking, manufacturing
332313	Plate work (e.g., bending, cutting, punching, shaping, welding), fabricated metal, manufacturing
331315	Plate, aluminum, made by continuous casting purchased aluminum
331315	Plate, aluminum, made by flat rolling purchased aluminum
331315	Plate, aluminum, made in integrated secondary smelting and continuous casting mills

331315	Plate, aluminum, made in integrated secondary smelting and flat rolling mills
331420	Plate, copper and copper alloy, made from purchased copper or in integrated secondary smelting and rolling, drawing or extruding plants
331110	Plate, iron or steel, made in iron and steel mills
326130	Plate, laminated plastics, manufacturing
331491	Plate, nonferrous metals (except aluminum, copper), made from purchased metals or scrap
332215	Plated metal cutlery manufacturing
423940	Plated metal cutlery or flatware merchant wholesalers
332215	Plated metal flatware manufacturing
332999	Plated ware (e.g., ecclesiastical ware, hollowware, toilet ware) manufacturing
335932	Plates (i.e., outlet or switch covers), face, manufacturing
322299	Plates, molded pulp, manufacturing
326140	Plates, polystyrene foam, manufacturing
332813	Plating metals and metal products for the trade
331491	Platinum and platinum alloy rolling, drawing, or extruding from purchased metals or scrap
331491	Platinum and platinum alloy sheet and tubing made from purchased metals or scrap
332999	Platinum foil and leaf not made in rolling mills
212299	Platinum mining and/or beneficiating
331492	Platinum recovering from scrap and/or alloying purchased metals
331410	Platinum refining, primary
237990	Playground construction
423910	Playground equipment and supplies merchant wholesalers
238990	Playground equipment installation
423920	Playing cards merchant wholesalers
337124	Playpens, children's metal, manufacturing
337122	Playpens, children's wood, manufacturing
315210	Playsuits cut and sew apparel contractors
315240	Playsuits, women's, girls', and infants', cut and sewn from purchased fabric (except apparel contractors)
711510	Playwrights, independent
811490	Pleasure boat maintenance services (e.g., cleaning, scaling, waxing)
532284	Pleasure boat rental

336612	Pleasure boats manufacturing
423910	Pleasure boats merchant wholesalers
315210	Pleating contractors on apparel
332216	Pliers, handtools, manufacturing
327331	Plinth blocks, precast terrazzo, manufacturing
334418	Plotter controller boards manufacturing
423430	Plotters merchant wholesalers
334118	Plotters, computer, manufacturing
115112	Plowing
333120	Plows, construction (e.g., excavating, grading), manufacturing
423820	Plows, farm, merchant wholesalers
333111	Plows, farm-type, manufacturing
111422	Plug (i.e., floriculture products) growing
332911	Plug valves, industrial-type, manufacturing
213112	Plugging and abandoning wells on a contract basis
335931	Plugs, electric cord, manufacturing
332999	Plugs, magnetic metal drain, manufacturing
321999	Plugs, wood, manufacturing
111339	Plum farming
238220	Plumbers
611513	Plumbers' apprenticeship training
423720	Plumbers' brass goods merchant wholesalers
332216	Plumbers' handtools, nonpowered, manufacturing
325520	Plumbers' putty manufacturing
423710	Plumbers' tools and equipment merchant wholesalers
238220	Plumbing and heating contractors
332919	Plumbing and heating inline valves (e.g., check, cutoffs, stop) manufacturing
423720	Plumbing and heating valves merchant wholesalers
238220	Plumbing contractors
423720	Plumbing equipment merchant wholesalers
532490	Plumbing equipment rental or leasing
332913	Plumbing fittings and couplings (e.g., compression fittings, metal elbows, metal unions) manufacturing
332913	Plumbing fixture fittings and trim, all materials, manufacturing
238220	Plumbing fixture installation
326191	Plumbing fixtures (e.g., shower stalls, toilets, urinals), plastics or fiberglass, manufacturing

423720	Plumbing fixtures merchant wholesalers
332999	Plumbing fixtures, metal, manufacturing
327110	Plumbing fixtures, vitreous china, manufacturing
423720	Plumbing supplies merchant wholesalers
444190	Plumbing supply stores
423310	Plywood merchant wholesalers
321211	Plywood, faced with nonwood materials, hardwood, manufacturing
321212	Plywood, faced with nonwood materials, softwood, manufacturing
321211	Plywood, hardwood faced, manufacturing
321211	Plywood, hardwood, manufacturing
321212	Plywood, softwood faced, manufacturing
321212	Plywood, softwood, manufacturing
332912	Pneumatic aircraft subassemblies manufacturing
334513	Pneumatic controllers, industrial process type, manufacturing
333995	Pneumatic cylinders, fluid power, manufacturing
326220	Pneumatic hose (without fittings), rubber or plastics, manufacturing
332912	Pneumatic hose fittings, fluid power, manufacturing
423830	Pneumatic pumps and parts merchant wholesalers
333996	Pneumatic pumps, fluid power, manufacturing
334512	Pneumatic relays, air-conditioning-type, manufacturing
238290	Pneumatic tube conveyor system installation
333922	Pneumatic tube conveyors manufacturing
332912	Pneumatic valves, fluid power, manufacturing
322230	Pocket folders made from purchased paper or paperboard
332215	Pocket knives manufacturing
339910	Pocketbooks, precious metal, men's or women's, manufacturing
315210	Pockets (e.g., coat, suit) cut and sew apparel contractors
621391	Podiatrists' offices (e.g., centers, clinics)
813410	Poetry clubs
711510	Poets, independent
334118	Point of sale terminals manufacturing
423420	Point of sale terminals merchant wholesalers

334118	Pointing devices, computer peripheral equipment, manufacturing
315280	Pointing furs
339114	Points, abrasive dental, manufacturing
334516	Polariscopes manufacturing
334516	Polarizers manufacturing
334516	Polarographic equipment manufacturing
238990	Pole (e.g., telephone) removal
237130	Pole line construction
423610	Pole line hardware merchant wholesalers
327390	Poles, concrete, manufacturing
423510	Poles, metal, merchant wholesalers
321114	Poles, round wood, cutting and treating
321113	Poles, wood, made from log or bolts
321114	Poles, wood, treating
922120	Police academies
922120	Police and fire departments, combined
315210	Police caps and hats (except protective head gear) cut and sew apparel contractors
315990	Police caps and hats (except protective head gear) cut and sewn from purchased fabric (except apparel contractors)
922120	Police departments (except American Indian or Alaska Native)
315220	Police dress uniforms, men's, cut and sewn from purchased fabric (except apparel contractors)
315240	Police dress uniforms, women's, cut and sewn from purchased fabric (except apparel contractors)
453998	Police supply stores
611519	Police training schools
315210	Police uniforms cut and sew apparel contractors
921150	Police, American Indian or Alaska Native tribal
311212	Polished rice manufacturing
333991	Polishers, handheld power-driven, manufacturing
325612	Polishes (e.g., automobile, furniture, metal, shoe) manufacturing
424690	Polishes (e.g., automobile, furniture, metal, shoe, stove) merchant wholesalers
333517	Polishing and buffing machines, metalworking, manufacturing
332813	Polishing metals and metal products for the trade
325612	Polishing preparations manufacturing
327910	Polishing wheels manufacturing

813940	Political action committees (PACs)
813940	Political campaign organizations
711510	Political cartoonists, independent
541820	Political consulting services
541910	Political opinion polling services
813940	Political organizations or clubs
813940	Political parties
115112	Pollinating
114111	Pollock fishing
423830	Pollution control equipment (except air) merchant wholesalers
423730	Pollution control equipment, air, merchant wholesalers
924110	Pollution control program administration
541380	Pollution testing (except automotive emissions testing) services
315210	Polo shirts cut and sew apparel contractors
315190	Polo shirts made in apparel knitting mills
315220	Polo shirts, men's and boys', cut and sewn from purchased fabric (except apparel contractors)
315240	Polo shirts, women's and girls', cut and sewn from purchased fabric (except apparel contractors)
325211	Polyacrylonitrile resins manufacturing
325211	Polyamide resins manufacturing
325211	Polycarbonate resins manufacturing
325220	Polyester fibers and filaments manufacturing
424690	Polyester fibers merchant wholesalers
313110	Polyester filament yarn throwing, twisting, texturizing, or winding of purchased yarn
326113	Polyester film and unlaminated sheet (except packaging) manufacturing
325211	Polyester resins manufacturing
424610	Polyester resins merchant wholesalers
313110	Polyester spun yarns made from purchased fiber
313110	Polyester thread manufacturing
326113	Polyethylene film and unlaminated sheet (except packaging) manufacturing
325211	Polyethylene resins manufacturing
325212	Polyethylene rubber manufacturing
325220	Polyethylene terephthalate (PET) fibers and filaments manufacturing
325211	Polyethylene terephthalate (PET) resins manufacturing
334519	Polygraph machines manufacturing

561611	Polygraph services
325211	Polyhexamethylenediamine adipamide resins manufacturing
325199	Polyhydric alcohol esters and amines manufacturing
325199	Polyhydric alcohols manufacturing
325211	Polyisobutylene resins manufacturing
325212	Polyisobutylene rubber manufacturing
325212	Polyisobutylene-isoprene rubber manufacturing
325211	Polymethacrylate resins manufacturing
325212	Polymethylene rubber manufacturing
325220	Polyolefin fibers and filaments manufacturing
313110	Polypropylene filament yarn throwing, twisting, texturizing, or winding of puchased yarn
326113	Polypropylene film and unlaminated sheet (except packaging) manufacturing
325211	Polypropylene resins manufacturing
313110	Polypropylene spun yarns made from purchased fiber
238310	Polystyrene board insulation installation
326140	Polystyrene foam packaging manufacturing
325211	Polystyrene resins manufacturing
325212	Polysulfide rubber manufacturing
325211	Polytetrafluoroethylene resins manufacturing
325510	Polyurethane coatings manufacturing
326150	Polyurethane foam products manufacturing
325211	Polyurethane resins manufacturing
325211	Polyvinyl alcohol resins manufacturing
325211	Polyvinyl chloride (PVC) resins manufacturing
325220	Polyvinyl ester fibers and filaments manufacturing
326113	Polyvinyl film and unlaminated sheet (except packaging) manufacturing
325211	Polyvinyl halide resins manufacturing
325211	Polyvinyl resins manufacturing
325220	Polyvinylidene chloride (i.e., saran) fibers and filaments manufacturing
111339	Pomegranate farming
315210	Ponchos and similar waterproof raincoats cut and sew apparel contractors
315280	Ponchos and similar waterproof raincoats cut and sewn from purchased fabric (except apparel contractors)
562998	Pond maintenance and cleaning services

112920	Pony production
423910	Pool (billiards) tables and supplies merchant wholesalers
423910	Pool (swimming) and equipment merchant wholesalers
713990	Pool halls
713990	Pool parlors
713990	Pool rooms
312111	Pop, soda, manufacturing
311919	Popcorn (except candy covered), popped, manufacturing
311999	Popcorn (except popped) manufacturing
311340	Popcorn balls manufacturing
111150	Popcorn farming, field and seed production
424450	Popcorn merchant wholesalers
335210	Popcorn poppers, household-type electric, manufacturing
311340	Popcorn, candy covered popped, manufacturing
313210	Poplins weaving
621391	Popopediatricians' offices (e.g., centers, clinics)
711130	Popular musical artists, independent
711130	Popular musical groups
532120	Popup camper rental
327110	Porcelain parts, electrical and electronic device, molded, manufacturing
327110	Porcelain, chemical, manufacturing
236118	Porch construction, residential-type
337122	Porch furniture (except upholstered), wood, manufacturing
337920	Porch shades, wood slat, manufacturing
337124	Porch swings, metal, manufacturing
321918	Porch work (e.g., columns, newels, rails, trellises), wood, manufacturing
114111	Porgy fishing
311422	Pork and beans canning
311611	Pork carcasses, half carcasses, and primal and sub-primal cuts produced in slaughtering plants
311919	Pork rinds manufacturing
311612	Pork, primal and sub-primal cuts, made from purchased carcasses
926120	Port authorities and districts, nonoperating
237990	Port facility construction
488310	Port facility operation
332311	Portable buildings, prefabricated metal, manufacturing

332999	Portable chemical toilets, metal, manufacturing
334111	Portable computers manufacturing
335210	Portable cooking appliances (except convection, microwave ovens), household-type electric, manufacturing
335210	Portable electric space heaters manufacturing
335210	Portable hair dryers, electric, manufacturing
335210	Portable humidifiers and dehumidifiers manufacturing
334290	Portable intrusion detection and signaling devices manufacturing
334310	Portable stereo systems manufacturing
334515	Portable test meters manufacturing
562991	Portable toilet pumping (i.e., cleaning) services
562991	Portable toilet renting and/or servicing
326191	Portable toilets, plastics, manufacturing
519130	Portals, web search
312120	Porter brewing
424810	Porter merchant wholesalers
812990	Porter services
523920	Portfolio fund managing
541921	Portrait photography services
541921	Portrait photography studios
334511	Position indicators (e.g., for landing gear, stabilizers), airframe equipment, manufacturing
336310	Positive crankcase ventilation (PCV) valves, engine, manufacturing
334514	Positive displacement meters manufacturing
621512	Positron emission tomography (PET) scanner centers
334510	Positron emission tomography (PET) scanners manufacturing
238130	Post framing contractors
332216	Post hole diggers, nonpowered, manufacturing
333120	Post hole diggers, powered, manufacturing
236220	Post office construction
333997	Post office-type scales manufacturing
333318	Postage meters manufacturing
423420	Postage meters merchant wholesalers
333318	Postage stamp vending machines manufacturing
491110	Postal delivery services, local, operated by U.S. Postal Service
491110	Postal delivery services, local, operated on a contract basis
337215	Postal service lock boxes manufacturing
491110	Postal services operated by U.S. Postal Service
491110	Postal stations operated by U.S. Postal Service
491110	Postal stations operated on a contract basis
511199	Postcard publishers (except exclusive Internet publishing)
511199	Postcard publishers and printing combined
519130	Postcard publishers, exclusively on Internet
323111	Postcards commercial printing (except screen) without publishing
424120	Postcards merchant wholesalers
323113	Postcards screen printing without publishing
511199	Poster publishers (except exclusive Internet publishing)
511199	Poster publishers and printing combined
519130	Poster publishers, exclusively on Internet
323111	Posters commercial printing (except screen) without publishing
323113	Posters screen printing without publishing
238990	Posthole digging
323120	Postpress services (e.g., beveling, bronzing, folding, gluing, edging, foil stamping, gilding) on printed materials
512191	Postproduction facilities, motion picture or video
327390	Posts, concrete, manufacturing
423510	Posts, metal, merchant wholesalers
321114	Posts, round wood, cutting and treating
321114	Posts, wood, treating
512191	Post-synchronization sound dubbing
311412	Pot pies, frozen, manufacturing
212391	Potash mining and/or beneficiating
325314	Potassic fertilizers made by mixing purchased materials
325180	Potassium aluminum sulfate manufacturing
325180	Potassium bichromate and chromate manufacturing
325199	Potassium bitartrate manufacturing
325180	Potassium bromide manufacturing
212391	Potassium bromide, natural, mining and/or beneficiating
325180	Potassium carbonate manufacturing
325180	Potassium chlorate manufacturing
325180	Potassium chloride manufacturing

212391	Potassium chloride mining and/or beneficiating
212391	Potassium compounds prepared at beneficiating plants
212391	Potassium compounds, natural, mining and/or beneficiating
325180	Potassium cyanide manufacturing
325180	Potassium hydroxide (i.e., caustic potash) manufacturing
325180	Potassium hypochlorate manufacturing
325180	Potassium inorganic compounds, not specified elsewhere by process, manufacturing
325180	Potassium iodide manufacturing
325180	Potassium nitrate manufacturing
325199	Potassium organic compounds, not specified elsewhere by process, manufacturing
325180	Potassium permanganate manufacturing
325180	Potassium salts manufacturing
212391	Potassium salts, natural, mining and/or beneficiating
325180	Potassium sulfate manufacturing
424450	Potato chips and related snacks merchant wholesalers
311919	Potato chips manufacturing
115114	Potato curing
333111	Potato diggers, harvesters, and planters manufacturing
111211	Potato farming, field and seed potato production
311211	Potato flour manufacturing
332215	Potato mashers manufacturing
311999	Potato mixes made from purchased dry ingredients
311423	Potato products (e.g., flakes, granules) dehydrating
311221	Potato starches manufacturing
311919	Potato sticks manufacturing
311991	Potatoes, peeled or cut, manufacturing
334515	Potentiometric instruments (except industrial process-type) manufacturing
334513	Potentiometric instruments (except X-Y recorders), industrial process-type, manufacturing
237310	Pothole filling, highway, road, street or bridge
339999	Potpourri manufacturing
332420	Pots (e.g., annealing, melting, smelting), heavy gauge metal, manufacturing
332215	Pots and pans, fabricated metal, manufacturing
327120	Pots, glasshouse, clay refractory, manufacturing
311612	Potted meats made from purchased carcasses
451120	Pottery (unfinished pottery to be painted by customer on premises) stores
327110	Pottery made and sold on site
327110	Pottery products manufacturing
424990	Pottery, novelty, merchant wholesalers
325314	Potting soil manufacturing
311615	Poultry (e.g., canned, cooked, fresh, frozen) manufacturing
311615	Poultry (e.g., canned, cooked, fresh, frozen) processing
424440	Poultry and poultry products (except canned, packaged frozen) merchant wholesalers
333111	Poultry brooders, feeders, and waterers manufacturing
311615	Poultry canning (except baby, pet food)
115210	Poultry catching services
445210	Poultry dealers
423820	Poultry equipment merchant wholesalers
311119	Poultry feeds, supplements, and concentrates manufacturing
112340	Poultry hatcheries
332618	Poultry netting made from purchased wire
424440	Poultry pies (except packaged frozen) merchant wholesalers
423830	Poultry processing machinery merchant wholesalers
311615	Poultry slaughtering, dressing, and packing
424490	Poultry, canned, merchant wholesalers
424440	Poultry, live and dressed, merchant wholesalers
424420	Poultry, packaged frozen, merchant wholesalers
333991	Powder actuated handheld power tools manufacturing
332812	Powder coating metals and metal products for the trade
325510	Powder coatings manufacturing
331314	Powder made from purchased aluminum
331420	Powder made from purchased copper
331221	Powder made from purchased iron or steel
333517	Powder metal forming presses manufacturing

332117 Powder metallurgy products manufactured on a job or order basis

314999 Powder puffs and mitts manufacturing

331110 Powder, iron or steel, made in iron and steel mills

331492 Powder, nonferrous metals (except aluminum, copper), made from purchased metal

311999 Powdered drink mixes (except chocolate, coffee, tea, milk based) manufacturing

311514 Powdered milk manufacturing

325620 Powders (e.g., baby, body, face, talcum, toilet) manufacturing

311999 Powders, baking, manufacturing

333912 Power (i.e., pressure) washer units manufacturing

441222 Power boat dealers

238290 Power boiler, installation only

332410 Power boilers manufacturing

335313 Power circuit breakers manufacturing

335313 Power connectors manufacturing

335999 Power converter units (i.e., AC to DC), static, manufacturing

444210 Power equipment stores, outdoor

334515 Power factor meters manufacturing

335313 Power fuses (i.e., 600 volts and over) manufacturing

238290 Power generating equipment installation

221117 Power generation, biomass

221112 Power generation, fossil fuel (e.g., coal, gas, oil), electric

221116 Power generation, geothermal

221111 Power generation, hydroelectric

562213 Power generation, nonhazardous solid waste combustor or incinerator electric

221113 Power generation, nuclear electric

221114 Power generation, solar electric

221118 Power generation, tidal electric

221115 Power generation, wind electric

335312 Power generators manufacturing

423710 Power handtools (e.g., drills, sanders, saws) merchant wholesalers

812320 Power laundries, family

541990 Power line inspection (i.e., visual) services

237130 Power line stringing

334515 Power measuring equipment, electrical, manufacturing

237130 Power plant (except hydroelectric) construction

423830 Power plant machinery (except electrical) merchant wholesalers

237990 Power plant, hydroelectric, construction

238910 Power shovel, construction, rental with operator

336330 Power steering hose assemblies manufacturing

336330 Power steering pumps manufacturing

335999 Power supplies, regulated and unregulated, manufacturing

335313 Power switchboards manufacturing

335313 Power switching equipment manufacturing

335311 Power transformers, electric, manufacturing

423610 Power transmission equipment, electrical, merchant wholesalers

423840 Power transmission supplies (e.g., gears, pulleys, sprockets), mechanical, merchant wholesalers

333318 Power washer cleaning equipment manufacturing

532490 Power washer rental or leasing

561790 Power washing building exteriors

336320 Power window and door lock systems, automotive, truck, and bus, manufacturing

238910 Power, communication and pipe line right of way clearance (except maintenance)

333991 Power-driven handtools manufacturing

212399 Pozzolana mining and/or beneficiating

621399 Practical nurses' offices (e.g., centers, clinics), licensed

315210 Prayer shawls cut and sew apparel contractors

315280 Prayer shawls cut and sewn from purchased fabric (except apparel contractors)

315190 Prayer shawls made in apparel knitting mills

327331 Precast concrete block and brick manufacturing

238120 Precast concrete panel, slab, or form installation

327332 Precast concrete pipe manufacturing

327390 Precast concrete products (except brick, block, pipe) manufacturing

423940 Precious and semiprecious stones merchant wholesalers

331491 Precious metal bar, rod, sheet, strip, and tubing made from purchased metals or scrap

423520 Precious metal ores merchant wholesalers

423940 Precious metals merchant wholesalers

331492	Precious metals recovering from scrap and/or alloying purchased metals
331410	Precious metals refining, primary
212399	Precious stones mining and/or beneficiating
811219	Precision equipment calibration
332216	Precision tools, machinist's (except optical), manufacturing
332721	Precision turned product manufacturing
488999	Precooling of fruits and vegetables in connection with transportation
236117	Precut housing, residential, assembled on site by for-sale builders
236116	Precut multifamily housing assembled on site by general contractors
236115	Precut single-family housing assembled on site by general contractors
334514	Predetermined counters manufacturing
444190	Prefabricated building dealers
423390	Prefabricated buildings (except wood) merchant wholesalers
332311	Prefabricated buildings, metal, manufacturing
326199	Prefabricated buildings, plastics, manufacturing
423310	Prefabricated buildings, wood, merchant wholesalers
236220	Prefabricated commercial building erection
321992	Prefabricated homes (except mobile homes), wood, manufacturing
332311	Prefabricated homes, metal, manufacturing
236210	Prefabricated industrial building (except warehouses) erection
236220	Prefabricated institutional building erection
238350	Prefabricated kitchen and bath cabinet, residential-type, installation
238350	Prefabricated sash and door installation
321992	Prefabricated wood buildings manufacturing
238130	Prefabricated wood frame component (e.g., trusses) installation
321211	Prefinished hardwood plywood manufacturing
321212	Prefinished softwood plywood manufacturing
621410	Pregnancy counseling centers
325413	Pregnancy test kits manufacturing
624410	Pre-kindergarten centers (except part of elementary school system)
236117	Premanufactured housing assembled on site by for-sale builders
236115	Premanufactured single-family housing assembled on site by general contractors
334614	Prepackaged software, mass reproducing
424990	Pre-paid calling card distribution, merchant wholesalers
517911	Pre-paid calling cards, telecommunications resellers
213112	Preparation of oil and gas field drilling sites (except site preparation and related construction contractor activities) on a contract basis
212113	Preparation plants, anthracite
611110	Preparatory schools, elementary or secondary
311824	Prepared flour mixes made from purchased flour
311211	Prepared flour mixes made in flour mills
424490	Prepared foods (except frozen) merchant wholesalers
424420	Prepared foods, frozen (except dairy products), merchant wholesalers
424430	Prepared foods, frozen dairy, merchant wholesalers
311991	Prepared meals, perishable, packaged for individual resale
311941	Prepared sauces (except gravy, tomato-based) manufacturing
237210	Preparing and subdividing land for sale
488991	Preparing goods for transportation (i.e., crating, packing)
323120	Prepress printing services (e.g., color separation, imagesetting, photocomposition, typesetting)
541350	Prepurchase home inspection services
423990	Prerecorded audio and video tapes and discs merchant wholesalers
512250	Prerecorded audio tapes and compact discs integrated manufacture, release, and distribution
334614	Prerecorded magnetic audio tapes and cassettes mass reproducing
454110	Prerecorded tape, compact disc, and record mail-order houses
624410	Preschool centers
424210	Prescription drugs merchant wholesalers
111421	Preseeded mat farming
311421	Preserves (e.g., imitation) canning
321114	Preserving purchased wood and wood products
313310	Preshrinking textile products and fabrics
921110	President's office, United States
325611	Presoaks manufacturing

333517	Press brakes, metalworking, manufacturing
519190	Press clipping services
332111	Press forgings made from purchased iron or steel, unfinished
332112	Press forgings made from purchased nonferrous metals, unfinished
424130	Pressed and molded pulp goods (e.g., egg cartons, shipping supplies) merchant wholesalers
313230	Pressed felts manufacturing
321999	Pressed logs of sawdust and other wood particles, nonpetroleum binder, manufacturing
333517	Presses (e.g., bending, punching, shearing, stamping), metal forming, manufacturing
333241	Presses (i.e., food manufacturing-type) manufacturing
333243	Presses for making composite woods (e.g., hardboard, medium density fiberboard (MDF), particleboard, plywood) manufacturing
333111	Presses, farm-type, manufacturing
333999	Presses, metal baling, manufacturing
333244	Presses, printing (except textile), manufacturing
321999	Pressing blocks, wood, tailor's, manufacturing
336350	Pressure and clutch plate assemblies, automotive, truck, and bus, manufacturing
334519	Pressure and vacuum indicators, aircraft engine, manufacturing
332911	Pressure control valves (except fluid power), industrial-type, manufacturing
332912	Pressure control valves, fluid power, manufacturing
334512	Pressure controllers, air-conditioning system-type, manufacturing
332215	Pressure cookers, household-type, manufacturing
334513	Pressure gauges (e.g., dial, digital), industrial process-type, manufacturing
334513	Pressure instruments, industrial process-type, manufacturing
327332	Pressure pipe, reinforced concrete, manufacturing
322220	Pressure sensitive paper and tape (except medical) made from purchased materials
334519	Pressure transducers manufacturing
321113	Pressure treated lumber made from logs or bolts and treated
321114	Pressure treated lumber made from purchased lumber
423850	Pressure washers merchant wholesalers
561790	Pressure washing (e.g., buildings, decks, fences)
334512	Pressurestats manufacturing
238120	Prestressed concrete beam, slab or other component installation
327331	Prestressed concrete blocks or bricks manufacturing
327332	Prestressed concrete pipes manufacturing
327390	Prestressed concrete products (except blocks, bricks, pipes) manufacturing
722515	Pretzel shops, on premise baking and carryout service
424490	Pretzels (except frozen) merchant wholesalers
311919	Pretzels (except soft) manufacturing
424420	Pretzels, frozen, merchant wholesalers
311812	Pretzels, soft, manufacturing
335129	Prewired poles, brackets, and accessories for electric lighting, manufacturing
926150	Price control agencies
111339	Prickly pear farming
331313	Primary aluminum production and manufacturing aluminum alloys
331313	Primary aluminum production and manufacturing aluminum shapes (e.g., bar, ingot, rod, sheet)
335912	Primary batteries manufacturing
334513	Primary elements for process flow measurement (i.e., orifice plates) manufacturing
334512	Primary oil burner controls (e.g., cadmium cells, stack controls) manufacturing
334513	Primary process temperature sensors manufacturing
331313	Primary refining of aluminum
331410	Primary refining of copper
331410	Primary refining of nonferrous metals (except aluminum)
611110	Primary schools
331313	Primary smelting of aluminum
331410	Primary smelting of copper
331410	Primary smelting of nonferrous metals (except aluminum)
335312	Prime mover generator sets (except turbine generator sets) manufacturing
332993	Primers (i.e., more than 30 mm., more than 1.18 inch), ammunition, manufacturing
325510	Primers, paint, manufacturing

323111	Print shops, digital (except printing books)
323111	Print shops, engraving (except printing books)
323111	Print shops, flexographic (except printing books)
323111	Print shops, gravure (except printing books)
323111	Print shops, letterpress (except printing books)
323111	Print shops, lithographic (offset) (except printing books)
323111	Print shops, quick (except printing books)
323113	Print shops, screen
334418	Printed circuit assemblies manufacturing
334418	Printed circuit boards loading
423690	Printed circuit boards merchant wholesalers
334412	Printed circuit boards, bare, manufacturing
334419	Printed circuit laminates manufacturing
333249	Printer machinery, 3D, manufacturing
334118	Printers, computer, manufacturing
423430	Printers, computer, merchant wholesalers
323117	Printing and binding books without publishing
323111	Printing apparel (except screen printing)
323117	Printing books without publishing
561990	Printing brokers
313310	Printing fabric grey goods
325910	Printing inks manufacturing
423840	Printing inks merchant wholesalers
333249	Printing machinery for textiles manufacturing
323111	Printing manifold business forms
424120	Printing paper (except bulk) merchant wholesalers
424110	Printing paper, bulk, merchant wholesalers
236210	Printing plant construction
333244	Printing plate engraving machinery manufacturing
323120	Printing plate preparation services
333244	Printing plates, blank (except photosentive), manufacturing
323120	Printing postpress services (e.g., beveling, bronzing, folding, gluing, edging, foil stamping) to printed products (e.g., books, cards, paper)
323120	Printing prepress services (e.g., color separation, imagesetting, photocomposition, typesetting)
333244	Printing press rollers manufacturing
333244	Printing presses (except textile) manufacturing
313310	Printing textile banners (except screen printing)
313310	Printing textile products (except screen and apparel printing)
811310	Printing trade machinery repair and maintenance services
423830	Printing trade machinery, equipment, and supplies merchant wholesalers
323111	Printing, digital (e.g., billboards, other large format graphical materials, high resolution) (except books, grey goods)
323111	Printing, engraving, on paper products
323111	Printing, flexographic (except books, grey goods)
323111	Printing, gravure (except books, grey goods)
323111	Printing, letterpress (except books, grey goods)
323111	Printing, lithographic (except books, grey goods)
323111	Printing, photo-offset (except books, grey goods)
323111	Printing, quick (except books, grey goods)
323113	Printing, screen (except books, manifold business forms, grey goods)
423410	Printmaking apparatus, photographic, merchant wholesalers
333314	Prisms, optical, manufacturing
337127	Prison bed manufacturing
236220	Prison construction
922140	Prison farms
922140	Prisons
522190	Private banks (i.e., unincorporated)
334210	Private branch exchange (PBX) equipment manufacturing
611310	Private colleges (except community or junior college)
561611	Private detective services
238210	Private driveway or parking area lighting contractors
523920	Private equity fund managing
525920	Private estates (i.e., administering on behalf of beneficiaries)
814110	Private households employing domestic personnel
814110	Private households with employees
561611	Private investigation services (except credit)

561431 Private mail centers

561431 Private mailbox rental centers

611110 Private schools, elementary or secondary

561990 Private volunteer firefighting

493190 Private warehousing and storage (except farm products, general merchandise, refrigerated)

493130 Private warehousing and storage, farm products (except refrigerated)

493110 Private warehousing and storage, general merchandise

493120 Private warehousing and storage, refrigerated

451110 Pro shops (e.g., golf, skiing, tennis)

624190 Probation offices, privately operated

922150 Probation offices, publicly administered

212391 Probertite mining and/or quarrying

334510 Probes, electric medical, manufacturing

339112 Probes, surgical, manufacturing

325411 Procaine and derivatives (i.e., basic chemicals) manufacturing

334513 Process control instruments, industrial, manufacturing

238220 Process piping installation

541199 Process server services

541199 Process serving services

311513 Processed cheeses manufacturing

424470 Processed meats (e.g., luncheon, sausage) merchant wholesalers

311612 Processed meats manufacturing

424440 Processed poultry (e.g., luncheon) merchant wholesalers

311615 Processed poultry manufacturing

423410 Processing and finishing equipment, photographic, merchant wholesalers

522320 Processing financial transactions

314999 Processing of textile mill waste and recovering fibers

621111 Proctologists' offices (e.g., centers, clinics)

424910 Produce containers merchant wholesalers

445230 Produce markets

445230 Produce stands, permanent

454390 Produce stands, temporary

424480 Produce, fresh, merchant wholesalers

813910 Producers' associations

711510 Producers, independent

512290 Producers, recorded radio shows (except independent producers)

561910 Product sterilization and packaging services

541380 Product testing laboratories or services

524128 Product warranty insurance carriers, direct

334514 Production counters manufacturing

541614 Production planning and control consulting services

541614 Productivity improvement consulting services

813920 Professional associations

711219 Professional athletes, independent (i.e., participating in sports events)

711211 Professional baseball clubs

511130 Professional book publishers (except exclusive Internet publishing)

511130 Professional book publishers and printing combined

519130 Professional book publishers, exclusively on Internet

323120 Professional bookbinding without printing

323117 Professional books printing and binding without publishing

323117 Professional books printing without publishing

611430 Professional development training

561330 Professional employer organizations (PEO)

423490 Professional equipment and supplies (except dental, medical, ophthalmic) merchant wholesalers

423460 Professional equipment and supplies, optical, merchant wholesalers

611691 Professional examination review instruction

711211 Professional football clubs

423490 Professional furniture (except dental, metal, ophthalmic, and school) merchant wholesalers

423490 Professional instruments merchant wholesalers

511120 Professional magazine and periodical publishers (except exclusive Internet publishing)

511120 Professional magazine and periodical publishers and printing combined

519130 Professional magazine and periodical publishers, exclusively on Internet

323111 Professional magazines and periodicals commercial printing (except screen) without publishing

323113 Professional magazines and periodicals screen printing without publishing

813920	Professional membership associations
531120	Professional office building rental or leasing
611310	Professional schools (e.g., business administration, dental, law, medical)
315210	Professional service apparel, washable, cut and sew apparel contractors
315220	Professional service apparel, washable, men's and boys', cut and sewn from purchased fabric (except apparel contractors)
315240	Professional service apparel, washable, women's and girls', cut and sewn from purchased fabric (except apparel contractors)
611620	Professional sports (e.g., golf, skiing, swimming, tennis) instructors (i.e., not participating in sporting events)
711211	Professional sports clubs
711310	Professional sports promoters with facilities
711320	Professional sports promoters without facilities
813920	Professional standards review boards
326130	Profile shapes (e.g., plate, rod, sheet), laminated plastics, manufacturing
326121	Profile shapes (e.g., rod, tube), nonrigid plastics, manufacturing
525990	Profit-sharing funds
512110	Program producing, television
334513	Programmers, process-type, manufacturing
511210	Programming language and compiler software publishers, packaged
541511	Programming services, custom computer
332993	Projectiles (except guided missile), jet propulsion, manufacturing
333316	Projection equipment (e.g., motion picture, slide), photographic, manufacturing
423410	Projection equipment (e.g., motion picture, slide), photographic, merchant wholesalers
333314	Projection lenses manufacturing
333316	Projection screens (i.e., motion picture, overhead, slide) manufacturing
334310	Projection television manufacturing
332994	Projectors (e.g., antisub, depth charge release, grenade, livens, rocket), ordnance, manufacturing
711310	Promoters of agricultural fairs with facilities
711320	Promoters of agricultural fairs without facilities
711310	Promoters of arts events with facilities

711320	Promoters of arts events without facilities
561920	Promoters of conventions with or without facilities
711310	Promoters of festivals with facilities
711320	Promoters of festivals without facilities
711310	Promoters of live performing arts productions (e.g., concerts) with facilities
711320	Promoters of live performing arts productions (e.g., concerts) without facilities
711310	Promoters of sports events with facilities
711320	Promoters of sports events without facilities
561920	Promoters of trade fairs or shows with or without facilities
561410	Proofreading services
111421	Propagation material farming
424710	Propane bulk stations and terminals, merchant wholesalers
324110	Propane gases made in petroleum refineries
424720	Propane merchant wholesalers (except bulk stations, terminals)
211130	Propane recovered from oil and gas field gases
333519	Propeller straightening presses manufacturing
334514	Propeller type meters with registers manufacturing
332999	Propellers, ship and boat, made from purchased metal
524126	Property and casualty insurance carriers, direct
524130	Property and casualty reinsurance carriers
524126	Property damage insurance carriers, direct
531312	Property managers' offices, commercial real estate
531312	Property managers' offices, nonresidential real estate
531311	Property managers' offices, residential real estate
531312	Property managing, commercial real estate
531312	Property managing, nonresidential real estate
531311	Property managing, residential real estate
813990	Property owners' associations
561612	Property protection services (except armored car, security systems)
921130	Property tax assessors' offices
326299	Prophylactics manufacturing
112910	Propolis production, bees

423860	Propulsion systems, marine, merchant wholesalers
336415	Propulsion units and parts, guided missile and space vehicle, manufacturing
325199	Propylcarbinol manufacturing
324110	Propylene (i.e., propene) made in petroleum refineries
325199	Propylene glycol manufacturing
325110	Propylene made from refined petroleum or liquid hydrocarbons
325211	Propylene resins manufacturing
213113	Prospect and test drilling services for coal mining on contract basis
213114	Prospect and test drilling services for metal mining on contract basis
213115	Prospect and test drilling services for nonmetallic mineral mining (except fuels) on a contract basis
339113	Prosthetic appliances and supplies manufacturing
423450	Prosthetic appliances and supplies merchant wholesalers
446199	Prosthetic stores
621399	Prosthetists' offices (e.g., centers, clinics)
621210	Prosthodontists' offices (e.g., centers, clinics)
561612	Protection services (except armored car, security systems), personal or property
812332	Protective apparel supply services
523999	Protective committees, security holders
316210	Protective footwear, plastics or plastics soled fabric upper, manufacturing
316210	Protective footwear, rubber or rubber soled fabric upper, manufacturing
561612	Protective guard services
339920	Protectors, sports (e.g., baseball, basketball, hockey), manufacturing
334516	Protein analyzers, laboratory-type, manufacturing
541714	Protein engineering research and experimental development laboratories
325220	Protein fibers and filaments manufacturing
325211	Protein plastics manufacturing
712190	Provincial parks
334511	Proximity warning (i.e., collision avoidance) equipment manufacturing
111339	Prune farming
332216	Pruners manufacturing
311423	Prunes, dried, made in dehydration plants
115112	Pruning of orchard trees and vines
561730	Pruning services, ornamental tree and shrub
325130	Prussian blue pigments manufacturing
332216	Pry (i.e., crow) bars manufacturing
212299	Psilomelane mining and/or beneficiating
621420	Psychiatric centers and clinics (except hospitals), outpatient
623220	Psychiatric convalescent homes or hospitals
622210	Psychiatric hospitals (except convalescent)
621112	Psychiatrists' offices (e.g., centers, clinics)
812990	Psychic services
621330	Psychoanalysts' (except MDs or DOs) offices (e.g., centers, clinics)
621112	Psychoanalysts' (MDs or DOs) offices (e.g., centers, clinics)
813920	Psychologists' associations
621330	Psychologists' offices (e.g., centers, clinics), clinical
541720	Psychology research and development services
621330	Psychotherapists' (except MDs or DOs) offices (e.g., centers, clinics)
621112	Psychotherapists' (MDs or DOs) offices (e.g., centers, clinics)
541211	Public accountants' (CPAs) offices, certified
541211	Public accountants' (CPAs) private practices, certified
541219	Public accountants' (except CPAs) offices
541219	Public accountants' (except CPAs) private practices
238210	Public address system installation
532490	Public address system rental or leasing
811213	Public address system repair and maintenance services
334310	Public address systems and equipment manufacturing
423690	Public address systems and equipment merchant wholesalers
423210	Public building furniture merchant wholesalers
922130	Public defenders' offices
711410	Public figures' agents or managers
923120	Public health program administration, nonoperating
541910	Public opinion polling services
541910	Public opinion research services
922150	Public parole offices
922150	Public probation offices

921190	Public property management services, government
922130	Public prosecutors' offices
541820	Public relations agencies
541820	Public relations consulting services
541820	Public relations services
813319	Public safety advocacy organizations
922190	Public safety bureaus and statistics centers, government
922190	Public safety statistics centers, government
611110	Public schools, elementary or secondary
926130	Public service (except transportation) commissions, nonoperating
813410	Public speaking improvement clubs
611699	Public speaking training
561492	Public stenography services
926120	Public transportation commissions, nonoperating
926130	Public utility (except transportation) commissions, nonoperating
813910	Public utility associations
551112	Public utility holding companies
236220	Public warehouse construction
493190	Public warehousing and storage (except farm products, general merchandise, refrigerated, self-storage)
493110	Public warehousing and storage (except self-storage), general merchandise
493130	Public warehousing and storage, farm products (except refrigerated)
493120	Public warehousing and storage, refrigerated
******	Publishers -- see specific type
511130	Publishers (except exclusive Internet publishing), book
511140	Publishers (except exclusive Internet publishing), directory
511191	Publishers (except exclusive Internet publishing), greeting card
511120	Publishers (except exclusive Internet publishing), magazine
511130	Publishers (except exclusive Internet publishing), map
511120	Publishers (except exclusive Internet publishing), periodical
511199	Publishers (except exclusive Internet publishing), racing form
541840	Publishers' advertising representatives (i.e., independent of media owners)
******	Publishers and printing combined -- see specific type of publisher
******	Publishers or publishing -- see specific type
511130	Publishers, book, combined with printing
511191	Publishers, greeting card, combined with printing
519130	Publishers, Internet greeting card
519130	Publishers, Internet map
519130	Publishers, Internet racing form
511120	Publishers, magazine, combined with printing
512230	Publishers, music
511110	Publishers, newspaper (except exclusive Internet publishing)
511110	Publishers, newspaper, combined with printing
511210	Publishers, packaged computer software
511120	Publishers, periodical, combined with printing
311520	Pudding pops, frozen, manufacturing
311999	Puddings, canned dessert, manufacturing
311999	Puddings, dessert, manufacturing
333923	Pulleys (except power transmission), metal, manufacturing
333613	Pulleys, power transmission, manufacturing
321999	Pulleys, wood, manufacturing
213112	Pulling oil and gas field casings, tubes, or rods on a contract basis
621111	Pulmonary specialists' offices (e.g., centers, clinics)
322122	Pulp and newsprint combined manufacturing
322121	Pulp and paper (except groundwood, newsprint) combined manufacturing
322130	Pulp and paperboard combined manufacturing
333243	Pulp making machinery manufacturing
322110	Pulp manufacturing (i.e., chemical, mechanical, or semichemical processes) without making paper
322110	Pulp manufacturing (made from bagasse, linters, rags, straw, wastepaper, or wood) without making paper
322122	Pulp mills and groundwood paper, uncoated and untreated, manufacturing
322110	Pulp mills not making paper or paperboard
322122	Pulp mills producing newsprint paper
322121	Pulp mills producing paper (except groundwood, newsprint)

322130 Pulp mills producing paperboard

322299 Pulp products, molded, manufacturing

333243 Pulp, paper, and paperboard molding machinery manufacturing

212399 Pulpstones, natural, mining and/or beneficiating

113310 Pulpwood logging camps

423990 Pulpwood merchant wholesalers

334515 Pulse (i.e., signal) generators manufacturing

334519 Pulse analyzers, nuclear monitoring, manufacturing

423830 Pulverizing machinery and equipment, industrial, merchant wholesalers

327992 Pumice (except abrasives) processing beyond beneficiation

327910 Pumice and pumicite abrasives manufacturing

212399 Pumice mining and/or beneficiating

212399 Pumicite mining and/or beneficiating

562991 Pumping (i.e., cleaning) cesspools and septic tanks

562991 Pumping (i.e., cleaning) portable toilets

213112 Pumping oil and gas wells on a contract basis

213113 Pumping or draining coal mines on a contract basis

213114 Pumping or draining metal mines on a contract basis

213115 Pumping or draining nonmetallic mineral mines (except fuel) on a contract basis

237120 Pumping station, gas and oil transmission, construction

237110 Pumping station, water and sewage system, construction

238220 Pumping system, water, installation

111219 Pumpkin farming, field and seed production

423120 Pumps (e.g., fuel, oil, power steering, water), automotive, merchant wholesalers

336310 Pumps (e.g., fuel, oil, water), mechanical, automotive and truck gasoline engine (except power steering), manufacturing

333914 Pumps (except fluid power), general purpose, manufacturing

316210 Pumps (i.e., dress shoes) manufacturing

423830 Pumps and pumping equipment, industrial-type, merchant wholesalers

333914 Pumps for railroad equipment lubrication systems manufacturing

333996 Pumps, fluid power, manufacturing

333914 Pumps, industrial and commercial-type, general purpose, manufacturing

333914 Pumps, measuring and dispensing (e.g., gasoline), manufacturing

333914 Pumps, oil field or well, manufacturing

333914 Pumps, sump or water, residential-type, manufacturing

313230 Punched felts manufacturing

332216 Punches (except paper), nonpowered handtool, manufacturing

333514 Punches for use with machine tools manufacturing

333517 Punching machines, metalworking, manufacturing

711110 Puppet theaters

339999 Puppets manufacturing

921190 Purchasing and supply agencies, government

522298 Purchasing of accounts receivable

332323 Purlins, metal, manufacturing

316998 Purses (except precious metal), men's, manufacturing

316992 Purses (except precious metal), women's, manufacturing

424330 Purses merchant wholesalers

339910 Purses, precious metal or clad with precious metal, manufacturing

333515 Pushers (i.e., a machine tool accessory) manufacturing

332216 Putty knives manufacturing

423920 Puzzles merchant wholesalers

326122 PVC pipe manufacturing

325320 Pyrethrin insecticides manufacturing

334519 Pyrheliometers manufacturing

212393 Pyrite concentrates mining and/or beneficiating

212393 Pyrite mining and/or beneficiating

325194 Pyroligneous acids manufacturing

212299 Pyrolusite mining and/or beneficiating

327110 Pyrometer tubes manufacturing

334513 Pyrometers, industrial process-type, manufacturing

327110 Pyrometric cones, earthenware, manufacturing

212399 Pyrophyllite mining and/or beneficiating

327992 Pyrophyllite processing beyond beneficiation

332994 Pyrotechnic pistols and projectors manufacturing

325998	Pyrotechnics (e.g., flares, flashlight bombs, signals) manufacturing
325211	Pyroxylin (i.e., nitrocellulose) resins manufacturing
212393	Pyrrhotite mining and/or beneficiating
112390	Quail production
611430	Quality assurance training
541990	Quantity surveyor services
327120	Quarry tiles, clay, manufacturing
333131	Quarrying machinery and equipment manufacturing
423810	Quarrying machinery and equipment merchant wholesalers
316998	Quarters (i.e., shoe cut stock), leather, manufacturing
212399	Quartz crystal, pure, mining and/or beneficiating
334419	Quartz crystals, electronic application, manufacturing
212319	Quartzite crushed and broken stone mining and/or beneficiating
212311	Quartzite dimension stone mining or quarrying
325194	Quebracho extracts manufacturing
112910	Queen bee production
325194	Quercitron extracts manufacturing
323111	Quick printing (except books)
327410	Quicklime (i.e., calcium oxide) manufacturing
811191	Quick-lube shops
212299	Quicksilver ores and metal mining and/or beneficiating
314999	Quilting of textiles
314120	Quilts made from purchased materials
111339	Quince farming
325411	Quinine and derivatives (i.e., basic chemicals) manufacturing
523999	Quotation services, securities
523999	Quotation services, stock
311119	Rabbit food manufacturing
112930	Rabbit production
311615	Rabbits processing (i.e., canned, cooked, fresh, frozen)
311615	Rabbits slaughtering and dressing
711219	Race car drivers
711219	Race car owners (i.e., racing cars)
336999	Race cars manufacturing
711219	Race dog owners (i.e., racing dogs)
711219	Racehorse owners (i.e., racing horses)
711219	Racehorse trainers
711219	Racehorse training
332991	Races, ball or roller bearings, manufacturing
511199	Racetrack program publishers (except Internet)
511199	Racetrack program publishers and printing combined
519130	Racetrack program publishers, exclusively on Internet
323111	Racetrack programs commercial printing (except screen) without publishing
323113	Racetrack programs screen printing without publishing
711212	Racetracks (e.g., automobile, dog, horse)
713990	Racetracks, slot car (i.e., amusement devices)
335932	Raceways manufacturing
713990	Raceways, gocart (i.e., amusement rides)
511199	Racing form publishers (except exclusive Internet publishing)
511199	Racing form publishers and printing combined
519130	Racing form publishers, exclusively on Internet
323111	Racing forms commercial printing (except screen) without publishing
323113	Racing forms screen printing without publishing
711219	Racing stables, horse
711219	Racing teams (e.g., automobile, motorcycle, snowmobile)
334417	Rack and panel connectors manufacturing
336330	Rack and pinion steering assemblies manufacturing
336390	Racks (e.g., bicycle, luggage, ski, tire), automotive, truck, and buses manufacturing
332313	Racks (e.g., trash), fabricated metal plate, manufacturing
332618	Racks, household-type, made from purchased wire
713940	Racquetball club facilities
811219	Radar and sonar equipment repair and maintenance services
334511	Radar detectors manufacturing
423690	Radar equipment merchant wholesalers
517919	Radar station operations
334511	Radar systems and equipment manufacturing

334515 Radar testing instruments, electric, manufacturing

334519 RADIAC (radioactivity detection, identification, and computation) equipment manufacturing

238220 Radiant floor heating equipment installation

334519 Radiation detection and monitoring instruments manufacturing

541380 Radiation dosimetry (i.e., radiation testing) laboratories or services

812332 Radiation protection garment supply services

339113 Radiation shielding aprons, gloves, and sheeting manufacturing

541380 Radiation testing laboratories or services

325998 Radiator additive preparations manufacturing

326220 Radiator and heater hoses, rubber or plastics, manufacturing

811118 Radiator repair shops, automotive

332322 Radiator shields and enclosures, sheet metal (except stampings), manufacturing

333414 Radiators (except motor vehicle, portable electric) manufacturing

336390 Radiators and cores manufacturing

423720 Radiators, heating, nonelectric, merchant wholesalers

423120 Radiators, motor vehicle, merchant wholesalers

335210 Radiators, portable electric, manufacturing

811211 Radio (except two-way radio) repair and maintenance services without retailing new radios

541840 Radio advertising representatives (i.e., independent of media owners)

236220 Radio and television broadcast studio construction

443142 Radio and television stores

332312 Radio and television tower sections, fabricated structural metal, manufacturing

488330 Radio beacon (i.e., ship navigation) services

515112 Radio broadcasting (except exclusively on Internet) stations (e.g., AM, FM, shortwave)

515111 Radio broadcasting network services

515111 Radio broadcasting networks

515111 Radio broadcasting syndicates

711510 Radio commentators, independent

541690 Radio consulting services

334419 Radio frequency identification (RFID) devices manufacturing

423690 Radio frequency identification (RFID) equipment merchant wholesalers

511120 Radio guide publishers (except exclusive Internet publishing)

511120 Radio guide publishers and printing combined

519130 Radio guide publishers, exclusively on Internet

323111 Radio guides commercial printing (except screen) without publishing

323113 Radio guides screen printing without publishing

334310 Radio headphones manufacturing

326199 Radio housings, plastics, manufacturing

334511 Radio magnetic instrumentation (RMI) manufacturing

517312 Radio paging services communications carriers

423690 Radio parts and accessories (e.g., transistors, tubes) merchant wholesalers

512290 Radio program recording production (except independent producers)

334310 Radio receiving sets manufacturing

811211 Radio repair, automotive, without retailing new

511120 Radio schedule publishers (except exclusive Internet publishing)

511120 Radio schedule publishers and printing combined

519130 Radio schedule publishers, exclusively on Internet

323111 Radio schedules commercial printing (except screen) without publishing

323113 Radio schedules screen printing without publishing

236220 Radio station construction

515112 Radio stations (except exclusively on Internet)

561410 Radio transcription services

334220 Radio transmitting antennas and ground equipment manufacturing

237130 Radio transmitting tower construction

325180 Radioactive elements manufacturing

541360 Radioactive geophysical surveying services

325412 Radioactive in-vivo diagnostic substances manufacturing

325180 Radioactive isotopes manufacturing

424210 Radioactive pharmaceutical isotopes merchant wholesalers

562112 Radioactive waste collecting and/or local hauling

562211	Radioactive waste collecting and/or local hauling in combination with disposal and/or treatment facilities
562211	Radioactive waste disposal facilities
484230	Radioactive waste hauling, long-distance
562211	Radioactive waste treatment facilities
334519	Radioactivity detection, identification, and computation (RADIAC) equipment manufacturing
334515	Radiofrequency measuring equipment manufacturing
334515	Radiofrequency oscillators manufacturing
541380	Radiographic testing laboratories or services
541380	Radiographing welded joints on pipes and fittings
541380	Radiography inspection services
621512	Radiological laboratories, medical
621512	Radiological laboratory services, medical
621111	Radiologists' offices (e.g., centers, clinics)
424210	Radiopharmaceuticals merchant wholesalers
423690	Radios (except household-type) merchant wholesalers
423620	Radios, household-type, merchant wholesalers
111219	Radish farming, field and seed production
325180	Radium chloride manufacturing
334517	Radium equipment manufacturing
325180	Radium luminous compounds manufacturing
212291	Radium ores mining and/or beneficiating
238990	Radon gas alleviation contractors
541380	Radon testing laboratories or services
326299	Rafts, swimming pool-type, rubber inflatable, manufacturing
423930	Rags merchant wholesalers
335931	Rail bonds, propulsion and signal circuit electric, manufacturing
331110	Rail joints and fastenings made in iron and steel mills
336510	Rail laying and tamping equipment manufacturing
485112	Rail transportation (except mixed mode), commuter
332323	Railings, metal, manufacturing
321918	Railings, wood stair, manufacturing
423310	Railings, wood, merchant wholesalers
926120	Railroad and warehouse commissions, nonoperating

333613	Railroad car journal bearings, plain, manufacturing
532411	Railroad car rental or leasing
336510	Railroad cars and car equipment manufacturing
423860	Railroad cars merchant wholesalers
336510	Railroad cars, self-propelled, manufacturing
237990	Railroad construction
331110	Railroad crossings, iron or steel, made in iron and steel mills
423860	Railroad equipment and supplies merchant wholesalers
551112	Railroad holding companies
336510	Railroad locomotives and parts (except diesel engines) manufacturing
339930	Railroad models, hobby and toy, manufacturing
923130	Railroad Retirement Board
531190	Railroad right of way leasing
336510	Railroad rolling stock manufacturing
336360	Railroad seating manufacturing
238210	Railroad signaling equipment installation
334290	Railroad signaling equipment manufacturing
488210	Railroad switching services
488210	Railroad terminals, independent operation
561599	Railroad ticket offices
321114	Railroad ties (i.e., bridge, cross, switch) treating
423990	Railroad ties, wood, merchant wholesalers
333997	Railroad track scales manufacturing
482111	Railroad transportation, line-haul
487110	Railroad transportation, scenic and sightseeing
482112	Railroad transportation, short-line or beltline
487110	Railroad, scenic and sightseeing, operation
482111	Railroads, line-haul
482112	Railroads, short-line or beltline
321999	Rails (except rough), wood fence, manufacturing
423510	Rails and accessories, metal, merchant wholesalers
331318	Rails made by rolling or drawing purchased aluminum
331110	Rails rerolled or renewed in iron and steel mills

331318 Rails, aluminum, made in integrated secondary smelting and drawing plants

331318 Rails, aluminum, made in integrated secondary smelting and rolling mills

331110 Rails, iron or steel, made in iron and steel mills

113310 Rails, rough wood, manufacturing

332312 Railway bridge sections, prefabricated metal, manufacturing

237990 Railway construction (e.g., interlocker, roadbed, signal, track)

335312 Railway motors and control equipment, electric, manufacturing

237990 Railway roadbed construction

236220 Railway station construction

485112 Railway systems (except mixed mode), commuter

488210 Railway terminals, independent operation

482111 Railway transportation, line-haul

487110 Railway transportation, scenic and sightseeing

482112 Railway transportation, short-line or beltline

334519 Rain gauges manufacturing

315210 Raincoats (e.g., water resistant, waterproof, water-repellent) cut and sew apparel contractors

313320 Raincoats waterproofing (i.e., oiling)

315280 Raincoats, rubber or rubberized fabric, manufacturing

315220 Raincoats, water resistant, men's and boys', cut and sewn from purchased fabric (except apparel contractors)

315240 Raincoats, water resistant, women's, girls', and infants', cut and sewn from purchased fabric (except apparel contractors)

315280 Raincoats, waterproof, cut and sewn from purchased fabric (except apparel contractors)

315220 Raincoats, water-repellent, men's and boys', cut and sewn from purchased fabric (except apparel contractors)

315240 Raincoats, water-repellent, women's, girls', and infants', cut and sewn from purchased fabric (except apparel contractors)

111332 Raisin farming

112990 Raising swans, peacocks, flamingos, or other adornment birds

311423 Raisins made in dehydration plants

333111 Rakes, hay, manufacturing

332216 Rakes, nonpowered handtool, manufacturing

313110 Ramie spun yarns made from purchased fiber

423690 Random access memory (RAM) chips merchant wholesalers

316998 Rands (i.e., shoe cut stock), leather, manufacturing

333316 Range finders, photographic, manufacturing

335210 Range hoods with integral lighting fixtures, household-type, manufacturing

335210 Range hoods, household-type, manufacturing

333318 Ranges, commercial-type, manufacturing

423620 Ranges, gas and electric, merchant wholesalers

335220 Ranges, household-type cooking, manufacturing

624190 Rape crisis centers

311225 Rapeseed (i.e., canola) oil made from purchased oils

311224 Rapeseed (i.e., canola) oil made in crushing mills

111120 Rapeseed farming, field and seed production

336510 Rapid transit cars and equipment manufacturing

325180 Rare earth compounds, not specified elsewhere by process, manufacturing

212299 Rare earth metal concentrates beneficiating

212299 Rare earth metal ores mining and/or beneficiating

325180 Rare earth salts manufacturing

453310 Rare manuscript stores

111334 Raspberry farming

332216 Rasps, handheld, manufacturing

332216 Ratchets, nonpowered, manufacturing

524298 Ratemaking services, insurance

334511 Rate-of-climb instrumentation manufacturing

213112 Rathole and mousehole drilling at oil and gas fields on a contract basis

112390 Ratite production

337125 Rattan furniture, household-type, manufacturing

321999 Rattan ware (except furniture) manufacturing

112990 Rattlesnake production

311313 Raw beet sugar manufacturing

424590 Raw farm products (except field beans, grains) merchant wholesalers

424430	Raw milk merchant wholesalers
316110	Rawhide manufacturing
114111	Ray fishing
325220	Rayon fibers and filaments manufacturing
313110	Rayon spun yarns made from purchased fiber
313110	Rayon thread manufacturing
313110	Rayon yarn throwing, twisting, texturizing, or winding purchased filament
331221	Razor blade strip steel made in cold rolling mills
332215	Razor blades manufacturing
424210	Razor blades merchant wholesalers
316998	Razor strops manufacturing
332215	Razors (except electric) manufacturing
424210	Razors (except electric) merchant wholesalers
335210	Razors, electric, manufacturing
423620	Razors, electric, merchant wholesalers
332313	Reactor containment vessels, fabricated metal plate, manufacturing
332410	Reactors, nuclear, manufacturing
333316	Readers, microfilm or microfiche, manufacturing
327320	Ready-mix concrete manufacturing and distributing
336211	Ready-mix concrete trucks assembling on purchased chassis
531190	Real estate (except building) rental or leasing
237210	Real estate (except cemeteries) subdividers
531210	Real estate agencies
531210	Real estate agents' offices
531320	Real estate appraisal services
531320	Real estate appraisers' offices
531390	Real estate asset management services (except property management)
813910	Real estate boards
531210	Real estate brokerages
531210	Real estate brokers' offices
531390	Real estate consultants' (except agents, appraisers) offices
522292	Real estate credit lending
531390	Real estate escrow agencies
531390	Real estate escrow agents' offices
531390	Real estate fiduciaries' offices
541110	Real estate law offices
531390	Real estate listing services
525990	Real estate mortgage investment conduits (REMICs)
522294	Real estate mortgage investment conduits (REMICs) issuing, private
531312	Real estate property managers' offices, commercial
531311	Real estate property managers' offices, residential
531130	Real estate rental or leasing of miniwarehouses and self-storage units
531120	Real estate rental or leasing of nonresidential building (except miniwarehouse)
531110	Real estate rental or leasing of residential building
611519	Real estate schools
524127	Real estate title insurance carriers, direct
237210	Real property (except cemeteries) subdivision
561492	Real-time (i.e., simultaneous) closed captioning of live television performances, meetings, conferences, and so forth
333515	Reamers (i.e., a machine tool accessory) manufacturing
333517	Reaming machines, metalworking, manufacturing
238120	Rebar contractors
323120	Rebinding books, magazines, or pamphlets
515112	Rebroadcast radio stations (except exclusively on Internet)
336310	Rebuilding automotive and truck gasoline engines
326212	Rebuilding tires
423130	Recapped tires merchant wholesalers
423830	Recapping machinery, tire, merchant wholesalers
326212	Recapping tires
424120	Receipt books merchant wholesalers
334220	Receiver-transmitter units (i.e., transceivers) manufacturing
335931	Receptacles (i.e., outlets), electrical, manufacturing
423610	Receptacles, electrical, merchant wholesalers
531120	Reception hall rental or leasing
335122	Recessed lighting housings and trim (except residential), electric, manufacturing
335121	Recessed lighting housings and trim, residential electric, manufacturing
335911	Rechargeable battery packs made from purchased battery cells and housings

335911	Rechargeable nickel-cadmium (NICAD) batteries manufacturing
314999	Reclaimed wool processing
326299	Reclaiming rubber from waste or scrap
337121	Recliners, upholstered, manufacturing
332994	Recoil mechanisms, gun, manufacturing
332994	Recoilless rifles manufacturing
541714	Recombinant DNA research and experimental development laboratories
423840	Reconditioned barrels and drums merchant wholesalers
213111	Reconditioning oil and gas field wells on a contract basis
811310	Reconditioning shipping barrels and drums
321219	Reconstituted wood panels manufacturing
321219	Reconstituted wood sheets and boards manufacturing
312230	Reconstituting tobacco
512250	Record producers (except independent)
711510	Record producers, independent
512250	Record production (except independent record producers) without duplication or distribution
512250	Record releasing, promoting, and distributing combined with mass duplication
443142	Record stores, new
453310	Record stores, used
423620	Recorders (e.g., tape, video), household-type, merchant wholesalers
334513	Recorders, industrial process control-type, manufacturing
334515	Recorders, oscillographic, manufacturing
512290	Recording books on tape or disc (except publishers)
512290	Recording seminars and conferences, audio
512240	Recording studios, sound, operating on a contract or fee basis
711510	Recording technicians, independent
541611	Records management consulting services
314999	Recovered fibers processing
331492	Recovering and refining of nonferrous metals (except aluminum, copper) from scrap
331492	Recovering silver from used photographic film or X-ray plates
237990	Recreation area, open space, construction
621340	Recreational (e.g., art, dance, music) therapists' offices (e.g., centers, clinics)

721214	Recreational camps with accommodation facilities (except campgrounds)
713990	Recreational camps without accommodations
713990	Recreational day camps (except instructional)
423910	Recreational equipment and supplies (except vehicles) merchant wholesalers
236220	Recreational facility building construction
532284	Recreational goods rental
924120	Recreational programs administration, government
713940	Recreational sports club facilities
713990	Recreational sports clubs (i.e., sports teams) not operating sports facilities
713990	Recreational sports teams and leagues
532120	Recreational trailer rental
441210	Recreational vehicle (RV) dealers
441210	Recreational vehicle (RV) parts and accessories stores
532120	Recreational vehicle (RV) rental or leasing
423110	Recreational vehicle merchant wholesalers
237990	Recreational vehicle park construction
721211	Recreational vehicle parks
335999	Rectifiers (except electronic component-type, semiconductor) manufacturing
334419	Rectifiers, electronic component-type (except semiconductor), manufacturing
423690	Rectifiers, electronic, merchant wholesalers
334413	Rectifiers, semiconductor, manufacturing
333249	Rectifying equipment, chemical, manufacturing
562111	Recyclable material collection services
562111	Recyclable material hauling, local
484230	Recyclable material hauling, long-distance
423930	Recyclable materials (e.g., glass, metal, paper) merchant wholesalers
562920	Recyclable materials recovery facilities
325612	Recycling drycleaning fluids
811212	Recycling inkjet cartridges
325998	Recycling services for degreasing solvents (e.g., engine, machinery) manufacturing
325199	Red oil (i.e., oleic acid) manufacturing
925120	Redevelopment land agencies, government
334516	Redox (i.e., oxidation-reduction potential) instruments manufacturing
333612	Reducers, speed, manufacturing

333612	Reduction gears and gear units (except aircraft power transmission equipment, automotive) manufacturing
337125	Reed furniture (except upholstered), household-type, manufacturing
212399	Reed peat mining and/or beneficiating
321999	Reed ware (except furniture) manufacturing
339992	Reeds, musical instrument, manufacturing
339920	Reels, fishing, manufacturing
332999	Reels, metal, manufacturing
326199	Reels, plastics, manufacturing
321999	Reels, plywood, manufacturing
321999	Reels, wood, manufacturing
711219	Referees and umpires
519120	Reference libraries
561311	Referral agencies or services, employment
624190	Referral services for personal and social problems
486910	Refined petroleum products pipeline transportation
324110	Refineries, petroleum
324110	Refinery gases made in petroleum refineries
423830	Refinery machinery and equipment merchant wholesalers
237120	Refinery, petroleum, construction
331313	Refining aluminum, primary
331314	Refining aluminum, secondary
331410	Refining copper, primary
331420	Refining copper, secondary
331410	Refining nonferrous metals and alloys (except aluminum), primary
331492	Refining nonferrous metals and alloys (except aluminum, copper), secondary
335129	Reflectors for lighting equipment, metal, manufacturing
333314	Reflectors, optical, manufacturing
326199	Reflectors, plastics, manufacturing
115310	Reforestation
922140	Reformatories
325991	Reformulating plastics resins from recycled plastics products
334513	Refractometers, industrial process-type, manufacturing
334516	Refractometers, laboratory-type, manufacturing
327120	Refractories (e.g., block, brick, mortar, tile), clay, manufacturing
327120	Refractories (e.g., block, brick, mortar, tile), nonclay, manufacturing
238140	Refractory brick contractors
327120	Refractory cement, nonclay, manufacturing
423840	Refractory materials (e.g., block, brick, mortar, tile) merchant wholesalers
212325	Refractory minerals mining and/or beneficiating
722515	Refreshment stands, fixed location
722330	Refreshment stands, mobile
423740	Refrigerated display cases merchant wholesalers
311824	Refrigerated doughs made from purchased flour
333415	Refrigerated lockers manufacturing
484220	Refrigerated products trucking, local
484230	Refrigerated products trucking, long-distance
493120	Refrigerated warehousing
333415	Refrigeration compressors manufacturing
334512	Refrigeration controls, residential and commercial-type, manufacturing
423740	Refrigeration equipment and supplies, commercial-type, merchant wholesalers
811310	Refrigeration equipment repair and maintenance services, industrial and commercial-type
333415	Refrigeration equipment, industrial and commercial-type, manufacturing
238220	Refrigeration system (e.g., commercial, industrial, scientific) installation
334512	Refrigeration thermostats manufacturing
423740	Refrigeration units, motor vehicle, merchant wholesalers
333415	Refrigeration units, truck-type, manufacturing
334512	Refrigeration/air-conditioning defrost controls manufacturing
532210	Refrigerator rental
811412	Refrigerator, household-type, repair and maintenance services without retailing new refrigerators
335220	Refrigerator/freezer combinations, household-type, manufacturing
335220	Refrigerators (e.g., absorption, mechanical), household-type, manufacturing
423740	Refrigerators (e.g., reach-in, walk-in), commercial-type, merchant wholesalers
423620	Refrigerators, household-type, merchant wholesalers

624230	Refugee settlement services
562212	Refuse collecting and operating solid waste landfills
562111	Refuse collection services
562213	Refuse disposal combustors or incinerators
562212	Refuse disposal landfills
236210	Refuse disposal plant (except sewage treatment) construction
562111	Refuse hauling, local
484230	Refuse hauling, long-distance
325220	Regenerated cellulosic fibers manufacturing
925120	Regional planning and development program administration
621399	Registered nurses' (RNs) offices (e.g., centers, clinics)
334514	Registers, linear tallying, manufacturing
332323	Registers, metal air, manufacturing
561311	Registries, employment
561311	Registries, teacher
335311	Regulating transformers, power system-type, manufacturing
926140	Regulation and inspection of agricultural products
926130	Regulation of utilities
335311	Regulators (i.e., electric transformers), feeder voltage, manufacturing
336320	Regulators, motor vehicle voltage for internal combustion engines manufacturing
335313	Regulators, power, manufacturing
423610	Regulators, voltage (except motor vehicle), merchant wholesalers
624190	Rehabilitation agencies for offenders
622310	Rehabilitation hospitals (except alcoholism, drug addiction)
622210	Rehabilitation hospitals, alcoholism and drug addiction
624310	Rehabilitation job counseling and training, vocational
922150	Rehabilitation services, correctional, government
423510	Reinforcement mesh and wire merchant wholesalers
332618	Reinforcing mesh, concrete, made from purchased wire
238120	Reinforcing rod, bar, mesh and cage installation
238120	Reinforcing steel contractors
524130	Reinsurance carriers
334515	Relays (except electrical, electronic), instrument, manufacturing
423610	Relays merchant wholesalers
335314	Relays, electrical and electronic, manufacturing
624230	Relief services, disaster
624230	Relief services, emergency
511130	Religious book publishers (except exclusive Internet publishing)
511130	Religious book publishers and printing combined
519130	Religious book publishers, exclusively on Internet
451211	Religious book stores
323120	Religious bookbinding without printing
323117	Religious books printing and binding without publishing
323117	Religious books printing without publishing
236220	Religious building (e.g., church, synagogue, mosque, temple) construction
337127	Religious furniture manufacturing
423210	Religious furniture merchant wholesalers
453998	Religious goods (except books) stores
511120	Religious magazine and periodical publishers (except exclusive Internet publishing)
511120	Religious magazine and periodical publishers and printing combined
519130	Religious magazine and periodical publishers, exclusively on Internet
323111	Religious magazines and periodicals commercial printing (except screen) without publishing
323113	Religious magazines and periodicals screen printing without publishing
813110	Religious organizations
423490	Religious supplies merchant wholesalers
311421	Relishes canning
562910	Remediation and cleanup of contaminated buildings, mine sites, soil, or ground water
562910	Remediation services, environmental
525990	REMICs (real estate mortgage investment conduits)
522294	REMICs (real estate mortgage investment conduits) issuing, private
424310	Remnants, piece goods, merchant wholesalers
236118	Remodeling and renovating for-sale builders
236118	Remodeling and renovating general contractors, multifamily building

236118	Remodeling and renovating general contractors, residential
236118	Remodeling and renovating general contractors, single-family housing
236118	Remodeling and renovating single-family housing
236118	Remodeling and renovating, residential building
334290	Remote control units (e.g., garage door, television) manufacturing
541360	Remote sensing geophysical surveying services
238910	Removal of dams, dikes, and other heavy and civil engineering constructions
213113	Removal of overburden for coal mining on a contract basis
213114	Removal of overburden for metal mining on a contract basis
213115	Removal of overburden for nonmetallic minerals mining (except fuels) on a contract basis
562920	Removal of recyclable materials from a waste stream
621492	Renal dialysis centers and clinics
311613	Rendering animals (carrion) for feed
311613	Rendering fats
311613	Rendering plants
424990	Rennets merchant wholesalers
926150	Rent control agencies
******	Rental -- see type of article or property being rented
532310	Rent-all centers
532490	Renting coin-operated amusement devices (except concession operators)
531210	Renting real estate for others (i.e., agents, brokers)
541611	Reorganizational consulting services
522294	Repackaging loans for sale to others (i.e., private conduits)
******	Repair -- see type of article being repaired
237310	Repair, highway, road, street, bridge or airport runway
323120	Repairing books
334210	Repeater and transceiver equipment, carrier line, manufacturing
711110	Repertory companies, theatrical
322230	Report covers made from purchased paper or paperboard
711510	Reporters, independent (freelance)
561491	Repossession services
512199	Reproduction of motion picture films for theatrical distribution
115210	Reproductive flushing services for animals
621410	Reproductive health services centers
561439	Reprographic services
712130	Reptile exhibits, live
324191	Re-refining used petroleum lubricating oils
321912	Resawing purchased lumber
621910	Rescue services, air
621910	Rescue services, medical
517410	Resellers, satellite telecommunication
517911	Resellers, telecommunication (except satellite)
325411	Reserpines (i.e., basic chemicals) manufacturing
561599	Reservation (e.g., airline, car rental, hotel, restaurant) services
522320	Reserve and liquidity services (except central bank)
237110	Reservoir construction
562998	Reservoir maintenance and cleaning services
721310	Residence clubs, organizational
531110	Residential building rental or leasing
561720	Residential cleaning services
721310	Residential clubs
236116	Residential construction, multifamily, general contractors
236115	Residential construction, single-family, general contractors
236117	Residential for-sale builders
623220	Residential group homes for the emotionally disturbed
531110	Residential hotel rental or leasing
531311	Residential property managing
531210	Residential real estate agencies
531210	Residential real estate agents' offices
531210	Residential real estate brokerages
531210	Residential real estate brokers' offices
531311	Residential real estate property managers' offices
531190	Residential trailer parks
211130	Residue gas production
326199	Resilient floor coverings (e.g., sheet, tile) manufacturing
238330	Resilient floor tile or sheet (e.g., linoleum, rubber, vinyl), installation only

325211	Resins, plastics (except custom compounding purchased resins), manufacturing
424610	Resins, plastics, merchant wholesalers
424690	Resins, synthetic rubber, merchant wholesalers
334515	Resistance measuring equipment manufacturing
334513	Resistance thermometers and bulbs, industrial process-type, manufacturing
333992	Resistance welding equipment manufacturing
334416	Resistors, electronic, manufacturing
423690	Resistors, electronic, merchant wholesalers
335312	Resolvers manufacturing
334516	Resonance instruments (i.e., laboratory-type) manufacturing
334419	Resonant reed devices, electronic, manufacturing
325194	Resorcinol manufacturing
721120	Resort hotels with casinos
721110	Resort hotels without casinos
531311	Resort or vacation property managers' offices
334510	Respiratory analysis equipment, electromedical, manufacturing
339113	Respiratory protection mask manufacturing
621399	Respiratory therapists' offices (e.g., centers, clinics)
623110	Rest homes with nursing care
623312	Rest homes without nursing care
561720	Rest room cleaning services
812990	Rest room operation
813910	Restaurant associations
236220	Restaurant construction
423440	Restaurant equipment (except furniture) merchant wholesalers
337127	Restaurant furniture (e.g., carts, chairs, foodwagons, tables) manufacturing
423210	Restaurant furniture merchant wholesalers
561720	Restaurant kitchen cleaning services
611519	Restaurant management schools (except academic)
492210	Restaurant meals delivery services (i.e., independent delivery services)
722513	Restaurants, carryout
722513	Restaurants, fast-food
722511	Restaurants, full service
811420	Restoration and repair of antique furniture
811121	Restoration shops, antique and classic automotive
339113	Restraints, patient, manufacturing
561410	Resume writing services
238330	Resurfacing hardwood flooring
237310	Resurfacing, highway, road, street, bridge or airport runway
******	Retail -- see type of dealer, shop, or store
333997	Retail scales (e.g., butcher, delicatessen, produce) manufacturing
813910	Retailers' associations
238110	Retaining wall (except anchored earth), poured concrete, construction
238140	Retaining wall, masonry (i.e., block, brick, stone), construction
237990	Retaining walls, anchored (e.g., with piles, soil nails, tieback anchors), construction
325998	Retarders (e.g., flameproofing agents, mildewproofing agents) manufacturing
339112	Retinoscopes (except electromedical) manufacturing
334510	Retinoscopes, electromedical, manufacturing
813410	Retirement associations, social
623311	Retirement communities, continuing care
623110	Retirement homes with nursing care
623312	Retirement homes without nursing care
531110	Retirement hotel rental or leasing
525110	Retirement pension plans
332420	Retorts, heavy gauge metal, manufacturing
339112	Retractors, medical, manufacturing
326211	Retreading materials, tire, manufacturing
326212	Retreading tires
813110	Retreat houses, religious
115114	Retting flax
811420	Reupholstery shops, furniture
522292	Reverse mortgage lending
237990	Revetment construction
332994	Revolvers manufacturing
238290	Revolving door installation
811310	Rewinding armatures (except on an assembly line or factory basis)
213111	Reworking oil and gas wells on a contract basis
331410	Rhenium refining, primary
335931	Rheostats (i.e., dimmer switches), current-carrying wiring device, manufacturing
334419	Rheostats, electronic, manufacturing

335314	Rheostats, industrial control, manufacturing
212299	Rhodium mining and/or beneficiating
212299	Rhodochrosite mining and/or beneficiating
111219	Rhubarb farming, field and seed production
111419	Rhubarb, grown under cover
339940	Ribbons (e.g., cash register, printer, typewriter), inked, manufacturing
314999	Ribbons made from purchased fabrics
313220	Ribbons made in narrow woven fabric mills
313230	Ribbons made in nonwoven fabric mills
339940	Ribbons, inked, manufacturing
424120	Ribbons, inked, merchant wholesalers
424310	Ribbons, textile, merchant wholesalers
111160	Rice (except wild rice) farming, field and seed production
311212	Rice bran, flour, and meals, manufacturing
311230	Rice breakfast foods manufacturing
311212	Rice cleaning and polishing
115114	Rice drying
311212	Rice flour manufacturing
311213	Rice malt manufacturing
311212	Rice meal manufacturing
311212	Rice milling
311999	Rice mixes (i.e., uncooked and packaged with other ingredients) made from purchased rice and dry ingredients
311423	Rice mixes (i.e., uncooked and packaged with other ingredients) made in dehydration plants
311212	Rice mixes (i.e., uncooked and packaged with other ingredients) made in rice mills
311221	Rice starches manufacturing
311212	Rice, brewer's, manufacturing
311212	Rice, brown, manufacturing
424490	Rice, polished, merchant wholesalers
424510	Rice, unpolished, merchant wholesalers
315210	Riding clothes cut and sew apparel contractors
315220	Riding clothes, men's and boys', cut and sewn from purchased fabric (except apparel contractors)
315240	Riding clothes, women's and girls', cut and sewn from purchased fabric (except apparel contractors)
713990	Riding clubs, recreational
316998	Riding crops manufacturing
611620	Riding instruction academies or schools
713990	Riding stables
713990	Rifle clubs, recreational
332994	Rifles (except toy) manufacturing
332994	Rifles, BB and pellet, manufacturing
332994	Rifles, pneumatic, manufacturing
332994	Rifles, recoilless, manufacturing
339930	Rifles, toy, manufacturing
333517	Rifling machines, metalworking, manufacturing
213112	Rig skidding, oil and gas field, on a contract basis
238290	Rigging large-scale equipment
238910	Right of way cutting (except maintenance)
336612	Rigid inflatable boats (RIBs) manufacturing
336390	Rims, automotive, truck, and bus wheel, manufacturing
336310	Rings, piston, manufacturing
713940	Rinks, ice or roller skating
212319	Riprap (except granite, limestone) preparation plants
212319	Riprap (except limestone and granite) mining or quarrying
237990	Riprap installation
212313	Riprap, granite, mining or quarrying
212313	Riprap, granite, preparation plants
212312	Riprap, limestone, mining or quarrying
212312	Riprap, limestone, preparation plants
483211	River freight transportation
483212	River passenger transportation
713990	River rafting, recreational
713210	Riverboat casinos
333991	Riveting guns, handheld power-driven, manufacturing
333517	Riveting machines, metalworking, manufacturing
332722	Rivets, metal, manufacturing
621399	RNs' (registered nurses) offices (e.g., centers, clinics)
325320	Roach poisons manufacturing
711110	Road companies, theatrical
237310	Road construction
423810	Road construction and maintenance machinery merchant wholesalers
238910	Road decommissioning

324199 Road oils made from refined petroleum

324110 Road oils made in petroleum refineries

311911 Roasted nuts and seeds manufacturing

112320 Roaster chicken production

335210 Roasters (i.e., cooking appliances), household-type electric, manufacturing

311920 Roasting coffee

333241 Roasting machinery manufacturing

315210 Robes, lounging, cut and sew apparel contractors

315190 Robes, lounging, made in apparel knitting mills

315220 Robes, lounging, men's and boys', cut and sewn from purchased fabric (except apparel contractors)

315240 Robes, lounging, women's, girls', and infants', cut and sewn from purchased fabric (except apparel contractors)

333120 Rock crushing machinery, portable, manufacturing

333131 Rock crushing machinery, stationary, manufacturing

333132 Rock drill bits, oil and gas field-type, manufacturing

333120 Rock drills, construction and surface mining-type, manufacturing

333131 Rock drills, underground mining-type, manufacturing

711130 Rock musical artists, independent

711130 Rock musical groups

237990 Rock removal, underwater

212393 Rock salt mining and/or beneficiating

336310 Rocker arms and parts, automotive and truck gasoline engine, manufacturing

337122 Rockers (except upholstered), wood, manufacturing

337121 Rockers, upholstered, manufacturing

332313 Rocket casings, fabricated metal work, manufacturing

336412 Rocket engines, aircraft, manufacturing

336415 Rocket engines, guided missile, manufacturing

332994 Rocket launchers manufacturing

336414 Rockets (guided missiles), space and military, complete, manufacturing

332993 Rockets, ammunition (except guided missiles, pyrotechnic), manufacturing

114111 Rockfish fishing

339930 Rocking horses manufacturing

331318 Rod made by extruding purchased aluminum

331318 Rod made by rolling purchased aluminum

333519 Rod rolling mill machinery, metalworking, manufacturing

331318 Rod, aluminum, made in integrated secondary smelting and extruding mills

331318 Rod, aluminum, made in integrated secondary smelting and rolling mills

331420 Rod, copper and copper alloy, made from purchased copper or in integrated secondary smelting and rolling, drawing or extruding plants

326130 Rod, laminated plastics, manufacturing

331491 Rod, nonferrous metals (except aluminum, copper), made from purchased metals or scrap

326121 Rod, nonrigid plastics, manufacturing

325320 Rodent poisons manufacturing

325320 Rodenticides manufacturing

711310 Rodeo managers with facilities

711320 Rodeo managers without facilities

711310 Rodeo organizers with facilities

711320 Rodeo organizers without facilities

711310 Rodeo promoters with facilities

711320 Rodeo promoters without facilities

339920 Rods and rod parts, fishing, manufacturing

326299 Rods, hard rubber, manufacturing

331110 Rods, iron or steel, made in iron and steel mills

423510 Rods, metal (except precious), merchant wholesalers

334519 Rods, surveyor's, manufacturing

238160 Roll roofing installation

332991 Roller bearings manufacturing

711211 Roller hockey clubs, professional or semiprofessional

316110 Roller leather manufacturing

339920 Roller skates manufacturing

713940 Roller skating rinks

333120 Rollers, road construction and maintenance machinery, manufacturing

321999 Rollers, wood, manufacturing

332321 Rolling doors for industrial buildings and warehouses, metal, manufacturing

333519 Rolling mill machinery and equipment, metalworking, manufacturing

423830 Rolling mill machinery merchant wholesalers

333519 Rolling mill roll machines, metalworking, manufacturing

331511	Rolling mill rolls, iron, manufacturing
331513	Rolling mill rolls, steel, manufacturing
321999	Rolling pins, wood, manufacturing
336510	Rolling stock, railroad, rebuilding
311812	Rolls and buns (including frozen) made in commercial bakeries
326299	Rolls and roll coverings, rubber (e.g., industrial, papermill, painters', steelmill) manufacturing
111219	Romaine lettuce farming, field and seed production
315210	Rompers cut and sew apparel contractors
315240	Rompers, infants', cut and sewn from purchased fabric (except apparel contractors)
541690	Roof consulting services
332322	Roof deck, sheet metal (except stampings), manufacturing
238310	Roof insulation contractor
238160	Roof membrane installation
238160	Roof painting, spraying, or coating
238130	Roof truss (wood) installation
321214	Roof trusses, wood, manufacturing
326299	Roofing (i.e., single ply rubber membrane) manufacturing
324122	Roofing cements, asphalt, made from purchased asphaltic materials
324122	Roofing coatings made from purchased asphaltic materials
238160	Roofing contractors
324122	Roofing felts made from purchased asphaltic materials
444190	Roofing material dealers
423330	Roofing materials (except wood) merchant wholesalers
423310	Roofing materials, wood, merchant wholesalers
327120	Roofing tile, clay, manufacturing
327390	Roofing tile, concrete, manufacturing
238160	Roofing, built-up tar and gravel, installation
332322	Roofing, sheet metal (except stampings), manufacturing
333415	Room air-conditioners manufacturing
423620	Room air-conditioners merchant wholesalers
337122	Room dividers, wood household-type, manufacturing
333414	Room heaters (except portable electric) manufacturing

335210	Room heaters, portable electric, manufacturing
334512	Room thermostats manufacturing
721310	Rooming and boarding houses
325320	Root removing chemicals manufacturing
311221	Root starches manufacturing
332999	Rope fittings manufacturing
332618	Rope, wire, made from purchased wire
314994	Ropes (except wire rope) manufacturing
423840	Ropes (except wire rope) merchant wholesalers
423510	Ropes, wire (except insulated), merchant wholesalers
339910	Rosaries and other small religious articles, precious metal, manufacturing
212291	Roscoelite (vanadium hydromica) mining and/or beneficiating
111421	Rose bush growing
325211	Rosins (i.e., modified resins) manufacturing
325194	Rosins made by distillation of pine gum or pine wood
424690	Rosins merchant wholesalers
333111	Rotary hoes manufacturing
333111	Rotary tillers, farm-type, manufacturing
334514	Rotary type meters, consumption registering, manufacturing
325320	Rotenone insecticides manufacturing
323111	Rotogravure printing (except books)
323120	Rotogravure printing plates and cylinders preparation services
335312	Rotor retainers and housings manufacturing
335312	Rotors (i.e., for motors) manufacturing
325620	Rouge, cosmetic, manufacturing
321920	Round stave baskets (e.g., fruit, vegetable) manufacturing
321912	Rounds or rungs, furniture, hardwood, manufacturing
331110	Rounds, tube, steel, made in iron and steel mills
423990	Roundwood merchant wholesalers
213112	Roustabout mining services, on a contract basis
333991	Routers, handheld power-driven, manufacturing
333249	Roving machinery for textiles manufacturing
236115	Row house (i.e., single-family type) construction general contractors

236117	Row house construction for-sale builders
532284	Rowboat rental
336612	Rowboats manufacturing
713990	Rowing clubs, recreational
112910	Royal jelly production, bees
326220	Rubber and plastics belts and hoses (without fittings) manufacturing
326299	Rubber bands manufacturing
325520	Rubber cements manufacturing
212324	Rubber clay mining and/or beneficiating
238290	Rubber door installation
326199	Rubber floor coverings manufacturing
326291	Rubber goods, mechanical (i.e., extruded, lathe-cut, molded), manufacturing
423840	Rubber goods, mechanical (i.e., extruded, lathe-cut, molded), merchant wholesalers
424210	Rubber goods, medical, merchant wholesalers
325998	Rubber processing preparations (e.g., accelerators, stabilizers) manufacturing
423930	Rubber scrap and scrap tires merchant wholesalers
339940	Rubber stamps manufacturing
424120	Rubber stamps merchant wholesalers
313220	Rubber thread and yarns, fabric covered, manufacturing
326299	Rubber tubing manufacturing
333249	Rubber working machinery manufacturing
424990	Rubber, crude, merchant wholesalers
325212	Rubber, synthetic, manufacturing
313320	Rubberizing purchased capes
313320	Rubberizing purchased cloaks
313320	Rubberizing purchased clothing
313320	Rubberizing purchased coats
313320	Rubberizing purchased textiles and apparel
212399	Rubbing stones mining and/or beneficiating
562111	Rubbish (i.e., nonhazardous solid waste) hauling, local
562111	Rubbish collection services
562213	Rubbish disposal combustors or incinerators
562212	Rubbish disposal landfills
484230	Rubbish hauling without collection or disposal, truck, long-distance
562119	Rubble hauling, local
562119	Rubble removal services
212399	Ruby mining and/or beneficiating

532289	Rug and carpet rental
561740	Rug cleaning plants
325612	Rug cleaning preparations manufacturing
561740	Rug cleaning services
442210	Rug stores
314110	Rugs and carpets made from textile materials
423220	Rugs merchant wholesalers
321999	Rulers and rules (except slide), wood, manufacturing
332216	Rulers, metal, manufacturing
326199	Rulers, plastics, manufacturing
334519	Rules, slide, manufacturing
624221	Runaway youth shelters
488119	Runway maintenance services
237310	Runway, airport, line painting (e.g., striping)
485210	Rural bus services
324191	Rust arresting petroleum compounds made from refined petroleum
325998	Rust preventive preparations manufacturing
325612	Rust removers manufacturing
238320	Rustproofing (except automotive)
332812	Rustproofing metals and metal products for the trade
811198	Rustproofing shops, automotive
111219	Rutabaga farming, field and seed production
212299	Ruthenium ore mining and/or beneficiating
212299	Rutile mining and/or beneficiating
721211	RV (recreational vehicle) parks
532120	RV (recreational vehicle) rental or leasing
441210	RV dealers
111199	Rye farming, field and seed production
311211	Rye flour manufacturing
311213	Rye malt manufacturing
111998	Ryegrass seed farming
114111	Sablefish fishing
325199	Saccharin manufacturing
325620	Sachet, scented, manufacturing
322220	Sacks, multiwall, made from purchased uncoated paper
424130	Sacks, paper, merchant wholesalers
713990	Saddle horse rental services, recreational
325612	Saddle soaps manufacturing

321999	Saddle trees, wood, manufacturing
316110	Saddlery leather manufacturing
424910	Saddlery merchant wholesalers
332999	Saddlery parts, metal, manufacturing
811430	Saddlery repair shops without retailing new saddlery
451110	Saddlery stores
316998	Saddles and parts, leather, manufacturing
332999	Safe deposit boxes and chests, metal, manufacturing
332999	Safe doors and linings, metal, manufacturing
332999	Safes, metal, manufacturing
423420	Safes, security, merchant wholesalers
332911	Safety (i.e., pop-off) valves, industrial-type, manufacturing
316998	Safety belts, leather, manufacturing
541690	Safety consulting services
423990	Safety deposit boxes merchant wholesalers
423990	Safety devices (e.g., eye shields, face shields) merchant wholesalers
325920	Safety fuses, blasting, manufacturing
327215	Safety glass (including motor vehicle) made from purchased glass
238990	Safety net system, erecting and dismantling at construction site
339993	Safety pins manufacturing
332215	Safety razor blades manufacturing
332215	Safety razors manufacturing
111120	Safflower farming, field and seed production
311225	Safflower oil made from purchased oils
311224	Safflower oil made in crushing mills
339920	Sailboards manufacturing
336612	Sailboat building, not done in shipyards
441222	Sailboat dealers
532284	Sailboat rental
713930	Sailing clubs with marinas
713990	Sailing clubs without marinas
336611	Sailing ships, commercial, manufacturing
314910	Sails made from purchased fabrics
312130	Sake manufacturing
325180	Sal soda (i.e., washing soda) manufacturing
311423	Salad dressing mixes, dry, made in dehydration plants
311942	Salad dressing mixes, dry, manufacturing
311941	Salad dressings manufacturing

424490	Salad dressings merchant wholesalers
424490	Salad oils merchant wholesalers
311991	Salads, fresh or refrigerated, manufacturing
424480	Salads, prepackaged, merchant wholesalers
424120	Sales books merchant wholesalers
323111	Sales books, manifold, printing
522220	Sales financing
541613	Sales management consulting services
325199	Salicylic acid (except medicinal) manufacturing
325411	Salicylic acid, medicinal, uncompounded, manufacturing
212391	Salines (except common salt) mining and/or beneficiating
114111	Salmon fishing
236220	Salon construction
311421	Salsa canning
325998	Salt (except table) manufacturing
311942	Salt substitute manufacturing
213112	Salt water disposal systems, oil and gas field, on a contract basis
212393	Salt, common, mining and/or beneficiating
212393	Salt, rock, mining and/or beneficiating
311942	Salt, table, manufacturing
424490	Salt, table, merchant wholesalers
311612	Salted meats made from purchased carcasses
311821	Saltines manufacturing
424210	Salts, bath, merchant wholesalers
424690	Salts, industrial, merchant wholesalers
423930	Salvage, scrap, merchant wholesalers
334516	Sample analysis instruments (except medical) manufacturing
316998	Sample cases, all materials, manufacturing
334519	Sample changers, nuclear radiation, manufacturing
541870	Sample direct distribution services
323120	Samples mounting
541910	Sampling services, statistical
423320	Sand (except industrial) merchant wholesalers
212321	Sand and gravel quarrying (i.e., construction grade) and/or beneficiating
331524	Sand castings, aluminum, unfinished, manufacturing
331529	Sand castings, nonferrous metals (except aluminum), unfinished, manufacturing
484220	Sand hauling, local

484230 Sand hauling, long-distance

333120 Sand mixers manufacturing

212322 Sand, blast, quarrying and/or beneficiating

212321 Sand, construction grade, quarrying and/or beneficiating

212322 Sand, industrial (e.g., engine, filtration, glass grinding, proppant), quarrying and/or beneficiating

423840 Sand, industrial, merchant wholesalers

316210 Sandals, children's, manufacturing

316210 Sandals, men's footwear, manufacturing

316210 Sandals, plastics or plastics soled fabric upper, manufacturing

316210 Sandals, rubber or rubber soled fabric upper, manufacturing

316210 Sandals, women's footwear, manufacturing

332813 Sandblasting metals and metal products for the trade

213112 Sandblasting pipelines on lease, oil and gas field on a contract basis

238990 Sandblasting, building exterior

333991 Sanders, handheld power-driven, manufacturing

333318 Sanding machines, floor, manufacturing

333243 Sanding machines, woodworking-type, stationary, manufacturing

333243 Sandpaper making machines manufacturing

327910 Sandpaper manufacturing

212319 Sandstone crushed and broken stone mining

212311 Sandstone mining or quarrying

722513 Sandwich shops, limited-service

311612 Sandwich spreads, meat, made from purchased carcasses

311941 Sandwich spreads, salad dressing based, manufacturing

335210 Sandwich toasters and grills, household-type electric, manufacturing

424490 Sandwiches merchant wholesalers

311991 Sandwiches, fresh (i.e., assembled and packaged for wholesale market), manufacturing

322212 Sanitary food container, folding, made from purchased paperboard

424130 Sanitary food containers (e.g., disposable plastics, paper, paperboard) merchant wholesalers

322219 Sanitary food containers (except folding) made from purchased paper or paperboard

562212 Sanitary landfills

322291 Sanitary napkins and tampons made from purchased paper or textile fiber

322121 Sanitary napkins and tampons made in paper mills

322121 Sanitary paper products (except newsprint, uncoated groundwood) made in paper mills

424130 Sanitary paper products merchant wholesalers

322121 Sanitary paper stock manufacturing

322291 Sanitary products made from purchased sanitary paper stock

322121 Sanitary products made in paper mills

237110 Sanitary sewer construction

332999 Sanitary ware (e.g., bathtubs, lavatories, sinks), metal, manufacturing

238220 Sanitary ware installation

423720 Sanitary ware, china or enameled iron, merchant wholesalers

541620 Sanitation consulting services

926130 Sanitation districts, nonoperating

924110 Sanitation engineering agencies, government

212399 Sapphire mining and/or beneficiating

325220 Saran (i.e., polyvinylidene chloride) fibers and filaments manufacturing

332613 Sash balance springs, light gauge, made from purchased wire or strip

332321 Sash, door and window, metal, manufacturing

321911 Sash, door and window, wood and covered wood, manufacturing

316998 Satchels, all materials, manufacturing

334220 Satellite antennas manufacturing

334220 Satellite communications equipment manufacturing

238290 Satellite dish, household-type, installation

517311 Satellite master antenna television service (SMATV)

515111 Satellite radio networks

237130 Satellite receiving station construction

517410 Satellite telecommunication carriers

517410 Satellite telecommunication resellers

517919 Satellite telemetry operations on a contract or fee basis

517311 Satellite television distribution systems

515210 Satellite television networks

517919 Satellite tracking stations

325130	Satin white pigments manufacturing
335311	Saturable transformers manufacturing
324122	Saturated felts made from purchased paper
322121	Saturated felts made in paper mills
311423	Sauce mixes, dry, made in dehydration plants
311942	Sauce mixes, dry, manufacturing
311941	Sauces (except tomato-based) manufacturing
311941	Sauces for meat (except tomato-based) manufacturing
311941	Sauces for seafood (except tomato-based) manufacturing
311941	Sauces for vegetable (except tomato-based) manufacturing
311421	Sauces, tomato-based, canning
311421	Sauerkraut manufacturing
335210	Sauna heaters, electric, manufacturing
321992	Sauna rooms, prefabricated, wood, manufacturing
812199	Saunas
311612	Sausage and similar cased products made from purchased carcasses
424490	Sausage casings merchant wholesalers
311612	Sausage casings, collagen, made from purchased hides
311611	Sausage casings, natural, produced in slaughtering plant
326121	Sausage casings, plastics, manufacturing
522120	Savings and loan associations (S&L)
551112	Savings and loan holding companies
524113	Savings bank life insurance carriers, direct
522120	Savings banks
522120	Savings institutions
332216	Saw blades, all types, manufacturing
811411	Saw repair and maintenance (except sawmills) without retailing new saws
321113	Sawdust and shavings (i.e., sawmill byproducts) manufacturing
424990	Sawdust merchant wholesalers
321999	Sawdust, regrinding
321113	Sawed lumber made in sawmills
321912	Sawed lumber, resawing purchased lumber
333517	Sawing machines, metalworking, manufacturing
333243	Sawmill equipment manufacturing
532490	Sawmill machinery rental or leasing
423830	Sawmill machinery, equipment, and supplies merchant wholesalers
321113	Sawmills
333243	Saws, bench and table, power-driven, woodworking-type, manufacturing
332216	Saws, hand, nonpowered, manufacturing
333991	Saws, handheld power-driven, manufacturing
423830	Saws, industrial, merchant wholesalers
339112	Saws, surgical, manufacturing
339992	Saxophones and parts manufacturing
238990	Scaffold erecting and dismantling
423810	Scaffolding merchant wholesalers
532490	Scaffolding rental or leasing
332323	Scaffolds, metal, manufacturing
334519	Scalers, nuclear radiation, manufacturing
333997	Scales, including laboratory-type, manufacturing
423490	Scales, laboratory (except dental and medical), merchant wholesalers
114112	Scallop fishing
812199	Scalp treating services
423430	Scanners, computer, merchant wholesalers
518210	Scanning services, optical
334516	Scanning tunneling microscopes manufacturing
333243	Scarfing machines, woodworking-type, manufacturing
333519	Scarfing units, rolling mill machinery, metalworking, manufacturing
333120	Scarifiers, road, manufacturing
325130	Scarlet 2 R lake manufacturing
315210	Scarves cut and sew apparel contractors
315990	Scarves cut and sewn from purchased fabric (except apparel contractors)
315190	Scarves made in apparel knitting mills
336350	Scattershield, engine, manufacturing
711510	Scenery designers, independent theatrical
532490	Scenery, theatrical, rental or leasing
487990	Scenic and sightseeing excursions, aerial
487110	Scenic and sightseeing excursions, land
487210	Scenic and sightseeing excursions, water
481112	Scheduled air freight carriers
481112	Scheduled air freight transportation
481111	Scheduled air passenger carriers
481111	Scheduled air passenger transportation

212299	Scheelite mining and/or beneficiating
313220	Schiffli machine embroideries manufacturing
333249	Schiffli machinery manufacturing
212319	Schist, mica, crushed and broken stone, mining and/or beneficiating
212311	Schist, mica, mining or quarrying
511120	Scholarly journal publishers (except exclusive Internet publishing)
511120	Scholarly journal publishers and printing combined
519130	Scholarly journal publishers, exclusively on Internet
323111	Scholarly journals commercial printing (except screen) without publishing
323113	Scholarly journals screen printing without publishing
813211	Scholarship trusts (i.e., grantmaking, charitable trust foundations)
511120	Scholastic magazine and periodical publishers (except exclusive Internet publishing)
511120	Scholastic magazine and periodical publishers and printing combined
519130	Scholastic magazine and periodical publishers, exclusively on Internet
323111	Scholastic magazines and periodicals commercial printing (except screen) without publishing
323113	Scholastic magazines and periodicals screen printing without publishing
611110	School boards, elementary and secondary
511130	School book publishers (except exclusive Internet publishing)
511130	School book publishers and printing combined
519130	School book publishers, exclusively on Internet
323117	School books printing and binding without publishing
323117	School books printing without publishing
236220	School building construction
611710	School bus attendant services
423110	School bus merchant wholesalers
532120	School bus rental or leasing
485410	School bus services
336211	School buses assembling on purchased chassis
611110	School districts, elementary or secondary
423490	School equipment and supplies (except books, furniture) merchant wholesalers
337127	School furniture manufacturing
423210	School furniture merchant wholesalers
541921	School photography (i.e., portrait photography) services
453210	School supply stores
511130	School textbook publishers (except exclusive Internet publishing)
511130	School textbook publishers and printing combined
519130	School textbook publishers, exclusively on Internet
323120	School textbooks binding without printing
448190	School uniform stores
611110	Schools for the handicapped, elementary or secondary
611110	Schools for the intellectually and developmentally disabled (except preschool, job training, vocational rehabilitation)
611110	Schools for the physically disabled, elementary or secondary
611512	Schools, aviation
611511	Schools, barber
611511	Schools, beauty
611410	Schools, business, not offering academic degrees
611310	Schools, correspondence, college level
611511	Schools, cosmetology
611610	Schools, drama (except academic)
611110	Schools, elementary
611210	Schools, junior college
611210	Schools, junior college vocational
611630	Schools, language
611310	Schools, medical
611310	Schools, music (colleges or universities)
611610	Schools, music (except academic)
611310	Schools, professional (colleges or universities)
611110	Schools, secondary
611620	Schools, sports instruction
712110	Science and technology museums
339930	Science kits (e.g., chemistry sets, microscopes, natural science sets) manufacturing
423920	Science kits and sets merchant wholesalers
327215	Scientific apparatus glassware made from purchased glass
813920	Scientific associations
327215	Scientific glassware made from purchased glass

327212	Scientific glassware, pressed or blown, made in glass making plants
423490	Scientific instruments merchant wholesalers
511120	Scientific journal and periodical publishers (except exclusive Internet publishing)
511120	Scientific journal and periodical publishers and printing combined
519130	Scientific journal and periodical publishers, exclusively on Internet
423490	Scientific laboratory equipment merchant wholesalers
334519	Scintillation detectors manufacturing
335210	Scissors, electric, manufacturing
332215	Scissors, nonelectric, manufacturing
332216	Scoops, metal (except kitchen-type), manufacturing
321999	Scoops, wood, manufacturing
339930	Scooters, children's, manufacturing
339950	Scoreboards manufacturing
212399	Scoria mining and/or beneficiating
313310	Scouring and combing textile fibers
325611	Scouring cleansers (e.g., pastes, powders) manufacturing
332999	Scouring pads, soap impregnated, manufacturing
813410	Scouting organizations
423930	Scrap materials (e.g., automotive, industrial) merchant wholesalers
323111	Scrapbooks and refills manufacturing
424120	Scrapbooks merchant wholesalers
333131	Scraper loaders, underground mining-type, manufacturing
333120	Scrapers, construction-type, manufacturing
332321	Screen doors, metal frame, manufacturing
323120	Screen for printing, preparation services
323113	Screen printing (except books, manifold business forms, grey goods)
323113	Screen printing apparel and textile products (e.g., caps, napkins, placemats, T-shirts, towels) (except grey goods)
313310	Screen printing fabric grey goods
323113	Screen printing textile banners
325910	Screen process inks manufacturing
333999	Screening and sifting machinery for general industrial use manufacturing
423830	Screening machinery and equipment, industrial, merchant wholesalers
333120	Screening machinery, portable, manufacturing
333131	Screening machinery, stationary, manufacturing
212399	Screening peat
212113	Screening plants, anthracite
212111	Screening plants, bituminous coal or lignite
326199	Screening, window, plastics, manufacturing
711510	Screenplay writers, independent
334419	Screens for liquid crystal display (LCD) manufacturing
332321	Screens, door and window, metal frame, manufacturing
321911	Screens, door and window, wood framed, manufacturing
333316	Screens, projection (i.e., motion picture, overhead, slide), manufacturing
423310	Screens, window and door, merchant wholesalers
333517	Screw and nut slotting machines, metalworking, manufacturing
333922	Screw conveyors manufacturing
332216	Screw drivers, nonelectric, manufacturing
332722	Screw eyes, metal, manufacturing
333519	Screwdowns and boxes machinery, metal, manufacturing
333991	Screwdrivers and nut drivers, handheld power-driven, manufacturing
333519	Screwdriving machines manufacturing
332216	Screwjacks manufacturing
332722	Screws, metal, manufacturing
711510	Script writers, independent
238220	Scrubber, air purification, installation
339920	Scuba diving equipment manufacturing
611620	Scuba instruction, camps, or schools
711510	Sculptors, independent
611610	Sculpture instruction
327420	Sculptures (e.g., gypsum, plaster of paris) manufacturing
327110	Sculptures, architectural, clay, manufacturing
332216	Scythes manufacturing
212399	Scythestones mining and/or beneficiating
114111	Sea bass fishing
114111	Sea herring fishing
713990	Sea kayaking, recreational
112519	Sea plant agriculture
114111	Sea trout fishing

114112	Sea urchin fishing
424460	Seafood (except canned, packaged frozen) merchant wholesalers
311710	Seafood and seafood products canning
311710	Seafood and seafood products curing
311710	Seafood and seafood products manufacturing
311710	Seafood dinners, frozen, manufacturing
445220	Seafood markets
424490	Seafood, canned, merchant wholesalers
424420	Seafoods, packaged frozen, merchant wholesalers
339940	Seal presses (e.g., notary), hand operated, manufacturing
424690	Sealants merchant wholesalers
335110	Sealed beam automotive light bulbs manufacturing
325520	Sealing compounds for pipe threads and joints manufacturing
423840	Seals merchant wholesalers
339991	Seals, grease or oil, manufacturing
333992	Seam welding equipment manufacturing
334511	Search and detection systems and instruments manufacturing
519130	Search portals, Internet
335129	Searchlights, electric and nonelectric, manufacturing
453220	Seasonal and holiday decoration stores
721110	Seasonal hotels without casinos
561730	Seasonal property maintenance services (i.e., snow plowing in winter, landscaping during other seasons)
311942	Seasoning salt manufacturing
336360	Seat belts, motor vehicle and aircraft, manufacturing
423120	Seat belts, motor vehicle, merchant wholesalers
423120	Seat covers, automotive, merchant wholesalers
321999	Seat covers, rattan, manufacturing
326150	Seat cushions, foam plastics (except polystyrene), manufacturing
316998	Seatbelts, leather, manufacturing
336360	Seats for public conveyances, manufacturing
336360	Seats, railroad, manufacturing
321999	Seats, toilet, wood, manufacturing
237990	Seawall, wave protection, construction
488310	Seaway operation
112519	Seaweed farming
114119	Seaweed gathering
311710	Seaweed processing (e.g., dulse)
325199	Sebacic acid esters manufacturing
325199	Sebacic acid manufacturing
611630	Second language instruction
522294	Secondary market financing (i.e., buying, pooling, repackaging loans for sale to others)
331492	Secondary refining of nonferrous metals (except aluminum, copper)
611110	Secondary schools offering both academic and technical courses
331492	Secondary smelting of nonferrous metals (except aluminum, copper)
453310	Secondhand merchandise stores
611410	Secretarial schools
561410	Secretarial services
332311	Sections for prefabricated metal buildings manufacturing
321992	Sections, prefabricated wood building, manufacturing
523120	Securities brokerages
523120	Securities brokers' offices
523991	Securities custodians
523110	Securities dealers (i.e., acting as a principal in dealing securities to investors)
523110	Securities dealing (i.e., acting as a principal in dealing securities to investors)
523110	Securities distributing (i.e., acting as a principal in dealing securities to investors)
523210	Securities exchanges
523120	Securities floor brokers
523110	Securities floor traders (i.e., acting as a principal in dealing securities to investors)
523110	Securities flotation companies
523999	Securities holders' protective services
523110	Securities originating (i.e., acting as a principal in dealing securities to investors)
926150	Securities regulation commissions
523910	Securities speculators for own account
523110	Securities trading (i.e., acting as a principal in dealing securities to investors)
523999	Securities transfer agencies
523110	Securities underwriting

561621	Security alarm systems sales combined with installation, repair, or monitoring services
238210	Security and fire system, installation only
541690	Security consulting services
561612	Security guard services
611519	Security guard training
561612	Security patrol services
423420	Security safes merchant wholesalers
561621	Security system monitoring services
423610	Security systems merchant wholesalers
325412	Sedative preparations manufacturing
212399	Sedge peat mining and/or beneficiating
237990	Sediment control system construction
333131	Sedimentary mineral machinery manufacturing
314910	Seed bags made from purchased woven or knitted materials
115112	Seed bed preparing
115114	Seed cleaning
322230	Seed packets made from purchased paper
115114	Seed processing, postharvest for propagation
541380	Seed testing laboratories or services
325320	Seed treatment preparations manufacturing
333111	Seeders, farm-type, manufacturing
333112	Seeders, lawn and garden-type, manufacturing
115112	Seeding crops
561730	Seeding lawns
424450	Seeds (e.g., canned, roasted, salted) merchant wholesalers
424910	Seeds (e.g., field, flower, garden) merchant wholesalers
311911	Seeds, snack (e.g., canned, cooked, roasted, salted) manufacturing
541360	Seismic geophysical surveying services
213112	Seismograph exploration (except surveying) for oil and gas on a contract basis
334519	Seismographs manufacturing
334519	Seismometers manufacturing
334519	Seismoscopes manufacturing
212399	Selenite mining and/or beneficiating
331491	Selenium bar, rod, sheet, strip, and tubing made from purchased metals or scrap
325180	Selenium compounds, not specified elsewhere by process, manufacturing
325180	Selenium dioxide manufacturing
331492	Selenium recovering from scrap and/or alloying purchased metals
331410	Selenium refining, primary
611699	Self defense (except martial arts) instruction
624190	Self-help organizations (except for disabled persons, the elderly, persons diagnosed with intellectual and developmental disabilities)
624120	Self-help organizations for disabled persons, the elderly, and persons diagnosed with intellectual and developmental disabilities
624110	Self-help organizations, youth
525190	Self-insurance funds (except employee benefit funds)
811192	Self-service car washes
812310	Self-service drycleaners and laundries
531130	Self-storage unit rental or leasing
531130	Self-storage warehousing
531210	Selling real estate for others (i.e., agents, brokers)
531210	Selling time-share condominiums for others (i.e., agents, brokers)
115210	Semen collection
424590	Semen, bovine, merchant wholesalers
212111	Semianthracite surface mining and/or beneficiating
212112	Semianthracite underground mining or mining and beneficiating
212111	Semibituminous coal surface mining and/or beneficiating
212112	Semibituminous coal underground mining or mining and beneficiating
333242	Semiconductor assembly and packaging machinery manufacturing
335999	Semiconductor battery chargers manufacturing
334413	Semiconductor circuit networks (i.e., solid-state integrated circuits) manufacturing
334413	Semiconductor devices manufacturing
423690	Semiconductor devices merchant wholesalers
334413	Semiconductor dice and wafers manufacturing
335999	Semiconductor high-voltage power supplies manufacturing
333242	Semiconductor making machinery manufacturing

334413	Semiconductor memory chips manufacturing
334515	Semiconductor test equipment manufacturing
333618	Semidiesel engines manufacturing
423510	Semi-finished metal products merchant wholesalers
611110	Seminaries, below university grade
611310	Seminaries, theological, offering baccalaureate or graduate degrees
212399	Semiprecious stones mining and/or beneficiating
711211	Semiprofessional baseball clubs
711211	Semiprofessional football clubs
711211	Semiprofessional sports clubs
331511	Semisteel foundries
532120	Semi-trailer rental or leasing
336212	Semi-trailers manufacturing
311211	Semolina flour manufacturing
624120	Senior citizens activity centers
813311	Senior citizens advocacy organizations
813410	Senior citizens' associations, social
624120	Senior citizens centers
623312	Senior citizens' homes without nursing care
485991	Senior citizens transportation services
561312	Senior executive search services
325992	Sensitized cloth or paper (e.g., blueprint, photographic) manufacturing
333316	Sensitometers, photographic, manufacturing
334510	Sentinel, cardiac, manufacturing
238910	Septic system contractors
238910	Septic tank and weeping tile installation
562991	Septic tank cleaning services
562991	Septic tank pumping (i.e., cleaning) services
423390	Septic tanks (except concrete) merchant wholesalers
423320	Septic tanks, concrete, merchant wholesalers
332420	Septic tanks, heavy gauge metal, manufacturing
326199	Septic tanks, plastics or fiberglass, manufacturing
334512	Sequencing controls for electric heating equipment manufacturing
335999	Series capacitors (except electronic) manufacturing
212319	Serpentine crushed and broken stone mining and/or beneficiating
212311	Serpentine mining or quarrying
325414	Serums (except diagnostic substances) manufacturing
315210	Service apparel, washable, cut and sew apparel contractors
315220	Service apparel, washable, men's and boys', cut and sewn from purchased fabric (except apparel contractors)
315240	Service apparel, washable, women's and girls', cut and sewn from purchased fabric (except apparel contractors)
423850	Service establishment equipment and supplies merchant wholesalers
813910	Service industries associations
237120	Service line, gas and oil, construction
811310	Service machinery and equipment repair and maintenance services
561720	Service station cleaning and degreasing services
236220	Service station construction
447190	Service stations, gasoline
213111	Service well drilling on a contract basis
213112	Servicing oil and gas wells on a contract basis
337124	Serving carts, metal household-type, manufacturing
337122	Serving carts, wood household-type, manufacturing
335312	Servomotors manufacturing
111120	Sesame farming, field and seed production
711510	Set designers, independent theatrical
541191	Settlement offices, real estate
525920	Settlement trust funds
322219	Setup (i.e., not shipped flat) boxes made from purchased paperboard
322130	Setup boxboard stock manufacturing
237110	Sewage collection and disposal line construction
237110	Sewage disposal plant construction
221320	Sewage disposal plants
333318	Sewage treatment equipment manufacturing
237110	Sewage treatment plant construction
221320	Sewage treatment plants or facilities
562998	Sewer cleaning and rodding services
562998	Sewer cleanout services
237110	Sewer construction

238220	Sewer hookup and connection, building
237110	Sewer main, pipe and connection, construction
327120	Sewer pipe and fittings, clay, manufacturing
331511	Sewer pipe, cast iron, manufacturing
423320	Sewer pipe, clay (except refractory), merchant wholesalers
327332	Sewer pipe, concrete, manufacturing
423510	Sewer pipe, metal, merchant wholesalers
221320	Sewer systems
424310	Sewing accessories merchant wholesalers
339999	Sewing and mending kits assembling
316998	Sewing cases (except metal) manufacturing
339910	Sewing cases, precious metal, manufacturing
315210	Sewing fabric owned by others for apparel
321999	Sewing machine cabinets, wood, manufacturing
443141	Sewing machine stores, household-type
811412	Sewing machine, household-type, repair shops without retailing new sewing machines
333249	Sewing machines (including household-type) manufacturing
423620	Sewing machines, household-type, merchant wholesalers
423830	Sewing machines, industrial, merchant wholesalers
451130	Sewing supply stores
313110	Sewing threads manufacturing
334511	Sextants (except surveying) manufacturing
334519	Sextants, surveying, manufacturing
337920	Shade pulls, window, manufacturing
335121	Shades, lamp (except glass, plastics), residential-type, manufacturing
337920	Shades, window (except outdoor canvas awnings), manufacturing
213113	Shaft sinking for coal mines on a contract basis
213114	Shaft sinking for metal mines on a contract basis
238160	Shake and shingle, roof, installation
321113	Shakes (i.e., hand split shingles) manufacturing
212325	Shale (except oil shale) mining and/or beneficiating
327992	Shale, expanded, manufacturing
211120	Shale, oil, mining and/or beneficiating

111219	Shallot farming, field and seed production
325620	Shampoos and conditioners, hair, manufacturing
316998	Shanks, shoe, leather, manufacturing
333243	Shapers, woodworking-type, manufacturing
114111	Shark fishing
339994	Shaving brushes manufacturing
333517	Shaving machines, metalworking, manufacturing
325620	Shaving preparations (e.g., creams, gels, lotions, powders) manufacturing
424210	Shaving preparations merchant wholesalers
333517	Shearing machines, metal forming, manufacturing
316110	Shearling (i.e., prepared sheepskin) manufacturing
333991	Shears and nibblers, handheld power-driven, manufacturing
332215	Shears, nonelectric, household-type (e.g., kitchen, barber, tailor) manufacturing
332216	Shears, nonelectric, tool-type (e.g., garden, pruners, tinsnip), manufacturing
333111	Shears, powered, for use on animals, manufacturing
322121	Sheathing paper (except newsprint, uncoated groundwood) made in paper mills
324122	Sheathing, asphalt saturated, made from refined petroleum
238130	Sheathing, wood, installation
333613	Sheaves, mechanical power transmission, manufacturing
332311	Sheds (e.g., garden, storage, utility), prefabricated metal, manufacturing
321992	Sheds (e.g., garden, storage, utility), prefabricated wood, manufacturing
115210	Sheep dipping and shearing
112410	Sheep farming (e.g., meat, milk, wool production)
424520	Sheep merchant wholesalers
333111	Sheep shears, powered, manufacturing
326140	Sheet (i.e., board), polystyrene foam insulation, manufacturing
423730	Sheet metal duct work (heating and air-conditioning) merchant wholesalers
238220	Sheet metal duct work installation
333517	Sheet metal forming machines manufacturing
238160	Sheet metal roofing installation

423330	Sheet metal roofing materials merchant wholesalers
332322	Sheet metal work (except stampings) manufacturing
611513	Sheet metal workers' apprenticeship training
323111	Sheet music commercial printing (except screen) without publishing
424990	Sheet music merchant wholesalers
512230	Sheet music publishers
512230	Sheet music publishers and printing combined
323113	Sheet music screen printing without publishing
451140	Sheet music stores
331110	Sheet pilings, plain, iron or steel, made in iron and steel mills
331315	Sheet, aluminum, made by flat rolling purchased aluminum
331315	Sheet, aluminum, made in integrated secondary smelting and flat rolling mills
331420	Sheet, copper and copper alloy, made from purchased copper or in integrated secondary smelting and rolling, drawing or extruding plants
326130	Sheet, laminated plastics (except flexible packaging), manufacturing
326113	Sheet, plastics, unlaminated (except packaging), manufacturing
326299	Sheeting, rubber, manufacturing
314120	Sheets and pillowcases made from purchased fabrics
313210	Sheets and pillowcases made in broadwoven fabric mills
331110	Sheets, steel, made in iron and steel mills
311119	Shell crushing and grinding for animal feed
311119	Shell crushing for feed
332993	Shell loading and assembly plants
212399	Shell mining and/or beneficiating
339999	Shell novelties
331110	Shell slugs, steel, made in iron and steel mills
325510	Shellac manufacturing
424950	Shellac merchant wholesalers
311710	Shellfish and shellfish products canning
311710	Shellfish and shellfish products manufacturing
311710	Shellfish curing
114112	Shellfish fishing (e.g., clam, crab, oyster, shrimp)
112512	Shellfish hatcheries
332993	Shells, artillery, manufacturing
332992	Shells, small arms (i.e., 30 mm. or less, 1.18 inch or less), manufacturing
624310	Sheltered workshops (i.e., work experience centers)
624221	Shelters (except for victims of domestic or international disasters or conflicts), emergency
624230	Shelters for victims of domestic or international disasters or conflicts, emergency
624221	Shelters, battered women's
624221	Shelters, homeless
624221	Shelters, runaway youth
624221	Shelters, temporary (e.g., battered women's, homeless, runaway youth)
337215	Shelving (except wire) manufacturing
423440	Shelving, commercial, merchant wholesalers
238390	Shelving, metal, constructed on site
332618	Shelving, wire, made from purchased wire
238350	Shelving, wood, constructed on site
332812	Sherardizing of metals and metal products for the trade
311520	Sherbets manufacturing
922120	Sheriffs' offices (except court functions only)
922110	Sheriffs' offices, court functions only
332999	Shims, metal, manufacturing
321113	Shingle mills, wood
423330	Shingles (except wood) merchant wholesalers
324122	Shingles made from purchased asphaltic materials
423310	Shingles, wood, merchant wholesalers
321113	Shingles, wood, sawed or hand split, manufacturing
331529	Ship and boat propellers, cast brass, bronze and copper (except die-casting), unfinished, manufacturing
424990	Ship chandler merchant wholesalers
483113	Ship chartering with crew, coastal or Great Lakes freight transportation (including St. Lawrence Seaway)
483114	Ship chartering with crew, coastal or Great Lakes passenger transportation (including St. Lawrence Seaway)
483111	Ship chartering with crew, deep sea freight transportation to or from foreign ports

483112	Ship chartering with crew, deep sea passenger transportation to or from foreign ports
483211	Ship chartering with crew, freight transportation, inland waters (except on Great Lakes system)
483212	Ship chartering with crew, passenger transportation, inland waters (except on Great Lakes system)
333923	Ship cranes and derricks manufacturing
561311	Ship crew employment agencies
561311	Ship crew registries
423930	Ship dismantling (except at floating drydocks and shipyards) merchant wholesalers
488390	Ship dismantling at floating drydock
336611	Ship dismantling at shipyards
337127	Ship furniture manufacturing
488320	Ship hold cleaning services
238350	Ship joinery contractors
238320	Ship painting contractors
532411	Ship rental or leasing without crew
336611	Ship repair done in a shipyard
336611	Ship scaling services done at a shipyard
488390	Ship scaling services not done at a shipyard
332312	Ship sections, prefabricated metal, manufacturing
331420	Shipboard cable made from purchased copper in wire drawing plants
331318	Shipboard cable made in aluminum wire drawing plants
488510	Shipping agents (freight forwarding)
314910	Shipping bags made from purchased woven or knitted materials
332439	Shipping barrels, drums, kegs, and pails, light gauge metal, manufacturing
321920	Shipping cases and drums, wood, wirebound, manufacturing
321920	Shipping cases, wood, nailed or lock corner, manufacturing
813910	Shipping companies' associations
423840	Shipping containers (except disposable plastics, paper) merchant wholesalers
322211	Shipping containers made from purchased paperboard
322211	Shipping containers, corrugated, made from purchased paper or paperboard
321920	Shipping crates, wood, manufacturing

483113	Shipping freight to and from domestic ports (i.e., coastal, deep sea (including Puerto Rico), Great Lakes system (including St. Lawrence Seaway))
483111	Shipping freight to or from foreign ports, deep sea
483211	Shipping freight, inland waters (except on Great Lakes system)
326150	Shipping pads and shaped cushioning, foam plastics (except polystyrene), manufacturing
326140	Shipping pads and shaped cushioning, polystyrene foam, manufacturing
423840	Shipping pails, metal, merchant wholesalers
323111	Shipping registers commercial printing (except screen) without publishing
323113	Shipping registers screen printing without publishing
424130	Shipping supplies, paper and disposable plastics, merchant wholesalers
336611	Ships (i.e., not suitable or intended for personal use) manufacturing
423860	Ships merchant wholesalers
517312	Ship-to-shore broadcasting communication carriers (except satellite)
336611	Shipyard (i.e., facility capable of building ships)
315210	Shirts, outerwear, cut and sew apparel contractors
315190	Shirts, outerwear, made in apparel knitting mills
315220	Shirts, outerwear, men's and boys', cut and sewn from purchased fabric (except apparel contractors)
315220	Shirts, outerwear, unisex (i.e., sized without regard to gender), cut and sewn from purchased fabric (except apparel contractors)
315240	Shirts, outerwear, women's, girls', and infants', cut and sewn from purchased fabric (except apparel contractors)
315210	Shirts, underwear, cut and sew apparel contractors
315190	Shirts, underwear, made in apparel knitting mills
315220	Shirts, underwear, men's and boys', cut and sewn from purchased fabric (except apparel contractors)
315240	Shirts, underwear, women's, girls', and infants', cut and sewn from purchased fabric (except apparel contractors)
111411	Shitake mushroom farming

336330	Shock absorbers, automotive, truck, and bus, manufacturing
448210	Shoe (except bowling, golf, spiked) stores
424340	Shoe accessories merchant wholesalers
326299	Shoe and boot parts (e.g., heels, soles, soling strips), rubber, manufacturing
322212	Shoe boxes, folding, made from purchased paperboard
322219	Shoe boxes, setup, made from purchased paperboard
541490	Shoe design services
321999	Shoe display forms, all materials, manufacturing
316998	Shoe kits (i.e., cases), all materials, manufacturing
333249	Shoe making and repairing machinery manufacturing
423830	Shoe manufacturing and repairing machinery merchant wholesalers
326199	Shoe parts (e.g., heels, soles), plastics, manufacturing
335210	Shoe polishers, household-type electric, manufacturing
325612	Shoe polishes and cleaners manufacturing
423850	Shoe repair materials merchant wholesalers
811430	Shoe repair shops without retailing new shoes
316998	Shoe soles, leather, manufacturing
448210	Shoe stores, orthopedic
451110	Shoe stores, specialty sports footwear (e.g., bowling, golf, spiked)
321999	Shoe stretchers manufacturing
321999	Shoe trees manufacturing
424340	Shoes merchant wholesalers
316210	Shoes, athletic, manufacturing
316210	Shoes, ballet, manufacturing
316210	Shoes, children's and infant's (except orthopedic extension), manufacturing
316210	Shoes, cleated or spiked, all materials, manufacturing
316210	Shoes, men's (except orthopedic extension), manufacturing
339113	Shoes, orthopedic extension, manufacturing
316210	Shoes, plastics or plastics soled fabric upper, manufacturing
316210	Shoes, rubber or rubber soled fabric upper, manufacturing
316210	Shoes, theatrical, manufacturing
316210	Shoes, women's (except orthopedic extension), manufacturing
316210	Shoes, wooden, manufacturing
812990	Shoeshine parlors
812990	Shoeshine services
321920	Shook, box, manufacturing
713990	Shooting clubs, recreational
713990	Shooting galleries
713990	Shooting ranges
423120	Shop equipment, service station, merchant wholesalers
424130	Shopping bags, paper and plastics, merchant wholesalers
531120	Shopping center (i.e., not operating contained businesses) rental or leasing
236220	Shopping center construction
236220	Shopping mall construction
812990	Shopping services, personal
******	Shops -- see type
238990	Shoring, construction
111421	Short rotation woody tree growing (i.e., growing and harvesting cycle ten years or less)
311225	Shortening made from purchased fats and oils
311224	Shortening made in crushing mills
424490	Shortening, vegetable, merchant wholesalers
482112	Short-line railroads
315210	Shorts, outerwear, cut and sew apparel contractors
315190	Shorts, outerwear, made in apparel knitting mills
315220	Shorts, outerwear, men's and boys', cut and sewn from purchased fabric (except apparel contractors)
315240	Shorts, outerwear, women's, girls', and infants', cut and sewn from purchased fabric (except apparel contractors)
315210	Shorts, underwear, cut and sew apparel contractors
315190	Shorts, underwear, made in apparel knitting mills
315220	Shorts, underwear, men's and boys', cut and sewn from purchased fabric (except apparel contractors)
522298	Short-term inventory credit lending
213112	Shot hole drilling, oil and gas field, on a contract basis
332811	Shot peening metal and metal products for the trade
332992	Shot, BB, manufacturing

332992	Shot, lead, manufacturing
332992	Shot, pellet, manufacturing
332992	Shot, steel, manufacturing
238110	Shotcrete contractors
332992	Shotgun shells manufacturing
332994	Shotguns manufacturing
333120	Shovel loaders manufacturing
332216	Shovels, handheld, manufacturing
333120	Shovels, power, manufacturing
423810	Shovels, power, merchant wholesalers
337215	Showcases (except refrigerated) manufacturing
423440	Showcases (except refrigerated) merchant wholesalers
333415	Showcases, refrigerated, manufacturing
423740	Showcases, refrigerated, merchant wholesalers
314120	Shower and bath curtains, all materials, made from purchased fabric or sheet goods
332913	Shower heads, plumbing, manufacturing
332999	Shower receptors, metal, manufacturing
332999	Shower rods, metal, manufacturing
316210	Shower sandals or slippers, rubber, manufacturing
332999	Shower stalls, metal, manufacturing
326191	Shower stalls, plastics or fiberglass, manufacturing
115210	Showing of cattle, hogs, sheep, goats, and poultry
333111	Shredders, farm-type, manufacturing
212399	Shredding peat mining and/or beneficiating
114112	Shrimp fishing
112512	Shrimp production, farm raising
813110	Shrines, religious
561910	Shrink wrapping services
313310	Shrinking textile products and fabrics
561730	Shrub services (e.g., bracing, planting, pruning, removal, spraying, surgery, trimming)
111421	Shrubbery farming
311710	Shucking and packing fresh shellfish
488490	Shunting of trailers in truck terminals
488210	Shunting trailers in rail terminals
334515	Shunts, instrument, manufacturing
238190	Shutter installation
332321	Shutters, door and window, metal, manufacturing
321918	Shutters, door and window, wood and covered wood, manufacturing
326199	Shutters, plastics, manufacturing
321918	Shutters, wood, manufacturing
485999	Shuttle services (except employee bus)
333249	Shuttles for textile weaving machinery manufacturing
446199	Sick room supply stores
332216	Sickles manufacturing
212210	Siderite mining and/or beneficiating
238990	Sidewalk construction, residential and commercial
237310	Sidewalk, public, construction
238170	Siding (e.g., vinyl, wood, aluminum) installation
423330	Siding (except wood) merchant wholesalers
238170	Siding contractors
444190	Siding dealers
324122	Siding made from purchased asphaltic materials
321113	Siding mills, wood
321113	Siding, dressed lumber, manufacturing
326199	Siding, plastics, manufacturing
332322	Siding, sheet metal (except stampings), manufacturing
423310	Siding, wood, merchant wholesalers
212393	Sienna mining and/or beneficiating
325130	Sienna pigment manufacturing
333241	Sieves and screening equipment (i.e., food manufacturing-type) manufacturing
333249	Sieves and screening equipment, chemical preparation-type, manufacturing
333999	Sieves and screening equipment, general purpose-type, manufacturing
333131	Sieves and screening equipment, mineral beneficiating, manufacturing
332618	Sieves, made from purchased wire, manufacturing
333241	Sifting machine (i.e., food manufacturing-type) manufacturing
333314	Sights, telescopic, manufacturing
487210	Sightseeing boat operation
487110	Sightseeing bus operation
487110	Sightseeing operation, human-drawn vehicle
238990	Sign (except on highways, streets, bridges and tunnels) erection

237310	Sign erection, highway, road, street, or bridge
611630	Sign language instruction
611630	Sign language schools
541930	Sign language services
541890	Sign lettering and painting services
238990	Sign, building, erection
331420	Signal and control cable made from purchased copper in wire drawing plants
331318	Signal and control cable made in aluminum wire drawing plants
334515	Signal generators and averagers manufacturing
423610	Signal systems and devices merchant wholesalers
335311	Signaling transformers, electric, manufacturing
334290	Signals (e.g., highway, pedestrian, railway, traffic) manufacturing
423990	Signs (except electrical) merchant wholesalers
339950	Signs and signboards (except paper, paperboard) manufacturing
423440	Signs, electrical, merchant wholesalers
325180	Silica gel manufacturing
212322	Silica mining and/or beneficiating
212322	Silica sand quarrying and/or beneficiating
325180	Silica, amorphous, manufacturing
325180	Silicofluorides manufacturing
331110	Silicomanganese ferroalloys manufacturing
327910	Silicon carbide abrasives manufacturing
334413	Silicon wafers, chemically doped, manufacturing
334413	Silicon wave guides manufacturing
327992	Silicon, ultra high purity, manufacturing
325199	Silicone (except resins) manufacturing
325211	Silicone resins manufacturing
325212	Silicone rubber manufacturing
313210	Silk fabrics, broadwoven, weaving
541430	Silk screen design services
333249	Silk screens for textile fabrics manufacturing
313110	Silk spun yarns made from purchased fiber
313110	Silk thread manufacturing
313110	Silk throwing, spooling, twisting, or winding of purchased yarn
424590	Silk, raw, merchant wholesalers
212325	Sillimanite mining and/or beneficiating
327390	Sills, concrete, manufacturing
236220	Silo construction
327390	Silos, prefabricated concrete, manufacturing
332311	Silos, prefabricated metal, manufacturing
423390	Silt fence and other fabrics (e.g., for erosion control) merchant wholesalers
331491	Silver and silver alloy bar, rod, sheet, strip, and tubing made from purchased metals or scrap
332999	Silver beating (i.e., foil, leaf)
325180	Silver bromide manufacturing
331410	Silver bullion or dore bar produced at primary metal refineries
325180	Silver chloride manufacturing
325180	Silver compounds, not specified elsewhere by process, manufacturing
332999	Silver foil and leaf not made in rolling mills
331491	Silver foil made by rolling purchased metals or scrap
325180	Silver nitrate manufacturing
212222	Silver ores mining and/or beneficiating
325612	Silver polishes manufacturing
331492	Silver recovering from scrap and/or alloying purchased metals
331492	Silver recovering from used photographic film or X-ray plates
331410	Silver refining, primary
331491	Silver rolling, drawing, or extruding purchased metals or scrap
532289	Silverware rental
423940	Silverware, precious and plated, merchant wholesalers
333515	Sine bars (i.e., a machine tool accessory) manufacturing
711130	Singers, independent
611610	Singing instruction
813410	Singing societies
812990	Singing telegram services
621512	Single photon emission computerized tomography (SPECT) centers
236115	Single-family attached housing construction general contractors
236115	Single-family detached housing construction general contractors
236115	Single-family homes built on land owned by others, general contractors of
236115	Single-family house construction by general contractors

531110	Single-family house rental or leasing
236117	Single-family housing built on own land for sale (i.e., for-sale builders)
236117	Single-family housing construction for-sale builders
213113	Sinking shafts for coal mining on a contract basis
213114	Sinking shafts for metal mining on a contract basis
423720	Sinks merchant wholesalers
332999	Sinks, metal, manufacturing
326191	Sinks, plastics, manufacturing
327110	Sinks, vitreous china, manufacturing
212210	Sintered iron ore produced at the mine
212392	Sintered phosphate rock mining and/or beneficiating
334290	Sirens (e.g., air raid, industrial, marine, vehicle) manufacturing
541611	Site location consulting services
541620	Site remediation consulting services
562910	Site remediation services
541611	Site selection consulting services
812990	Sitting services, house
812910	Sitting services, pet
313310	Sizing of fabrics
339920	Skateboards manufacturing
339920	Skates and parts, ice and roller, manufacturing
713990	Skeet shooting facilities
331110	Skelp, iron or steel, made in iron and steel mills
711510	Sketch artists, independent
321999	Skewers, wood, manufacturing
541320	Ski area design services
541320	Ski area planning services
532284	Ski equipment rental
713920	Ski lift and tow operators
721110	Ski lodges and resorts with accommodations
315210	Ski pants cut and sew apparel contractors
315190	Ski pants made in apparel knitting mills
315220	Ski pants, men's and boys', cut and sewn from purchased fabric (except apparel contractors)
315240	Ski pants, women's, girls', and infants', cut and sewn from purchased fabric (except apparel contractors)
713920	Ski resorts without accommodations
315210	Ski suits cut and sew apparel contractors
315190	Ski suits made in apparel knitting mills
315220	Ski suits, men's and boys', cut and sewn from purchased fabric (except apparel contractors)
315240	Ski suits, women's, girls', and infants', cut and sewn from purchased fabric (except apparel contractors)
237990	Ski tow construction
532490	Skid rental or leasing
213112	Skidding of rigs, oil and gas field, on a contract basis
321920	Skids and pallets, wood or wood and metal combination, manufacturing
423830	Skids merchant wholesalers
332999	Skids, metal, manufacturing
711219	Skiers, independent (i.e., participating in sports events)
423910	Skiing equipment and supplies merchant wholesalers
713920	Skiing facilities, cross country, without accommodations
713920	Skiing facilities, downhill, without accommodations
611620	Skiing instruction, camps, or schools
623110	Skilled nursing facilities
561910	Skin blister packaging services
424210	Skin care preparations merchant wholesalers
611620	Skin diving instruction, camps, or schools
339112	Skin grafting equipment manufacturing
424990	Skins, dressed, merchant wholesalers
424590	Skins, raw, merchant wholesalers
316110	Skins, tanning, currying and finishing
561611	Skip tracing services
316110	Skirting leather manufacturing
315210	Skirts cut and sew apparel contractors
315190	Skirts made in apparel knitting mills
315240	Skirts, tennis, women's and girls', cut and sewn from purchased fabric (except apparel contractors)
315240	Skirts, women's, girls', and infants', cut and sewn from purchased fabric (except apparel contractors)
339920	Skis and skiing equipment (except apparel) manufacturing
316110	Skivers, leather, manufacturing
611620	Sky diving instruction, camps, or schools
238160	Skylight installation